Civil Rights in Public Service

Promises of justice and equality made in the U.S. Constitution, numerous Amendments, and decisions of the Supreme Court are hallmarks of American civil rights. Yet the realities of inequality remain facts of modern life for too many Native Americans, African Americans, and Latino Americans, even though state-mandated racial segregation has been outlawed for years. Women still face a variety of forms of discrimination—some subtle and others more overt. There remain many laws that treat people differently because of sexual orientation. People with disabilities are supposed to be protected by a variety of statutes, but many of these policies remain unfulfilled promises. These are just some of the many challenges of civil rights that persist in a nation that proudly points to the words above the entrance to the U.S. Supreme Court that read "Equal Justice Under Law."

This text is for public service professionals—whether they are in government agencies, in nonprofit organizations that provide social services for government, or contractors who operate as state actors—who face a twofold challenge. First, they serve an increasingly diverse community with a range of complex challenges. Second, they work and manage within organizations that, fortunately, are themselves more diverse than ever before. For those who work and serve in such settings, civil rights is not an abstract academic study, but a critically important and very practical fact of daily life. Through an engaging exploration of edited court cases, legislation, and speeches, this text examines the civil rights law and policy pertaining to African Americans, Native Americans, Latinos/Latinas, gender, sexual orientation, and disabilities, to learn what civil rights require, but also to come to a more empathetic understanding of how different groups of people understand civil rights and the unique challenges they face. Each chapter further considers key public policy hurdles in the fight for civil rights as well as the implications for public service practice.

Phillip J. Cooper is Professor of Public Administration in the Mark O. Hatfield School of Government at Portland State University, USA.

Civil Rights in Public Service

Phillip J. Cooper

Routledge
Taylor & Francis Group

NEW YORK AND LONDON

First published 2017
by Routledge
711 Third Avenue, New York, NY 10017

and by Routledge
2 Park Square, Milton Park, Abingdon, Oxon OX14 4RN

Routledge is an imprint of the Taylor & Francis Group, an informa business

Library of Congress Cataloging in Publication Data
A catalog record for this book has been requested

ISBN: 978-1-138-85652-3 (hbk)
ISBN: 978-1-138-85653-0 (pbk)
ISBN: 978-1-315-71956-6 (ebk)

Typeset in Times New Roman
by Out of House Publishing

Printed and bound in Great Britain by
TJ International Ltd, Padstow, Cornwall

For Dr. Carol Locust, a strong, but sensitive teacher and advocate, guiding others in understanding the great heritage of Native American culture as well as contemporary challenges faced by tribal people. She helps those she serves and teaches to meet the needs of today's society, with mind, body, and spirit in harmony in her own life and with lessons for the rest of us.

Contents

Preface

It is now more than two hundred years since "We the people" declared that our common purpose in creating the Constitution was "to form a more perfect Union, establish Justice, insure domestic Tranquillity, provide for the common defence, promote the general Welfare, and secure the Blessings of Liberty to ourselves and our Posterity." It has been more than one hundred and fifty years since the Thirteenth, Fourteenth, and Fifteenth Amendments were added to the Constitution, following a devastating civil war when the union faced a fundamental threat to its continued existence, in part because we had not truly established justice or promoted the blessings of liberty for so many of our people, and particularly for those held in bondage or relegated to conditions of inequality, such that even many of those who were supposedly free were nevertheless unable to vote or participate fully in their own governance or enjoy the full protections of the legal rights of citizens. Thus, the Fourteenth Amendment declared that: "No State shall make or enforce any law which shall abridge the privileges or immunities of citizens of the United States; nor shall any State deprive any person of life, liberty, or property, without due process of law; nor deny to any person within its jurisdiction the equal protection of the laws." It is now more than fifty years since the Supreme Court declared "unanimously" that public programs operated in a manner separated by race, even if equal in terms of physical conditions, are "inherently unequal." Yet inequality in educational opportunities remains a reality of modern life for too many Native Americans, African Americans, and Latino Americans, even though state-mandated racial segregation has been outlawed for all those years. Women still face a variety of forms of discrimination—some subtle and others more overt. Despite the 2015 Supreme Court ruling holding that same-sex marriage is safeguarded by equal protection and due process of law, Congress has, session after session, refused to pass legislation that would make Title VII protections against discrimination, including discrimination on the grounds of sexual orientation and identity. People with disabilities are supposed to be protected by a variety of statutes like the Americans with Disabilities Act and the Individuals with Disabilities Education Act, but judicial interpretations of those statutes have raised a host of difficulties. These are just some of the many challenges of civil rights that remain in a nation that proudly points to the words above the entrance to the U.S. Supreme Court that read "EQUAL JUSTICE UNDER LAW."

For public service professionals, whatever their chosen field and whether they are in government agencies, in nonprofit organizations that provide social services for government, or contractors who operate as state actors, conducting a range of functions from the operation of corrections institutions to those who adjudicate social service claims on behalf of government, the challenges are twofold. First, they serve an increasingly diverse community with a range of complex challenges. Second, they work and manage within organizations that, fortunately, are themselves more diverse than ever before. For those who work and serve in such settings, civil rights is not an abstract academic study, but a critically important and practical fact of daily life. It is not the preserve of lawyers or law professors, but of each and every public service professional—and indeed of every American.

Unfortunately, many who anticipate a career in public service, in government or elsewhere, have never seriously engaged civil rights. For those who have studied the subject, it was usually in an undergraduate constitutional rights and liberties class in which civil rights was treated as half or less of a one-term course, taught along with civil liberties like those protected by the First Amendment and sometimes even issues related to constitutional criminal process issues such as search and seizure or fair trial rights. Some have been exposed to training courses on the job, but these are often extremely thin and limited attempts to explain the rules and policies of a particular agency or even more general efforts to encourage sensitivity to diversity issues. Although certainly better than no training at all—and with apologies to the fine people who present such training programs—they are not sufficient in the contemporary context to provide public service professionals with the range and depth of knowledge they require.

Even where public service professionals have taken civil rights-related courses, the courses and the texts these courses employed have focused primarily, indeed overwhelmingly, on the essential history of the effort to address discrimination against African Americans in the years from the enunciation by the U.S. Supreme Court of the so-called separate but equal doctrine in 1896 to the rejection of that line of cases in 1954, along with the battles to make the promise of the *Brown v. Board of Education* ruling a reality in the face of massive resistance and later more subtle roadblocks to equality. That is a critically important, indeed vital, part of the civil rights story in the United States, but it is not the whole story and too often even that part of the story is not adequately conveyed.

It becomes clear to those who study the challenges facing different groups of people in our society that they share many of the challenges that have faced African Americans in modern America, but that each group has encountered different problems, and may and often do see their challenges as different from one another. If public service professionals are to serve their diverse communities adequately, and function productively within their complex organizational communities as well, it is critically important to attempt to understand in depth the different ways in which different groups understand civil rights challenges and what the bases for those concerns may be. That tells us much about what employees bring to work with them and what those in the community carry with them when they come to our organizations for any of the services we provide or regulatory programs we operate.

This book grows out of many years of dissatisfaction with the limited traditional method of teaching civil rights law and policy, and with the texts that have not provided what is needed to address the more complex reality of civil rights that contemporary professionals engage on a daily basis. It begins with the traditional material that faces the terrible history of legalized slavery of African Americans, and the battle to end segregation and achieve equal protection of the law. However, it starts well before the 1896 *Plessy v. Ferguson* ruling. It then seeks to develop an understanding of the quite different and also terrible history of discrimination against Native Americans as well as the law that developed in that area. It turns next to a Latino perspective, which provides yet a third, and to some perhaps surprisingly different set of civil rights law and challenges.

Whatever their ethnocultural heritage, women have also faced a particular history of discrimination and the battle to end it. Civil rights law addressing gender-based discrimination is far more complex than is often understood. The text addresses this little understood set of challenges. Quite recently the U.S. Supreme Court and other courts at both the federal and state levels have begun to recognize protections related to sexual orientation and identity, but the challenges that people face in this area are only beginning to be understood. Finally, it comes as a particular surprise to many Americans that persons with disabilities have for so long enjoyed so little protection under the Constitution and have largely been dependent upon a series of relatively recent civil rights statutes for protection against discrimination. The text addresses this little understood set of challenges.

This book brings the student along on a journey through the law and policy in each of these areas, both to learn what civil rights requires, but also to come to a more empathetic understanding of how different groups of people understand civil rights and the special challenges they see. This journey relies principally upon a series of edited judicial opinions to achieve those goals, but other materials and new analyses as well.

For civil rights scholars, this book provides an analysis different in several respects from what has been done before. In the process of its analysis and in a consideration in the final chapter of the agenda of civil rights law and policy for the future, it presents challenges not only to policy and administration but also opportunities to reconsider how the literature frames, analyzes, and addresses the state of civil rights for everyone in this country and how to contemplate the work yet to be done.

Because of the different perspective taken in this book, the opinions have not been edited for traditional law school purposes, but to provide not only the law, but also the context, character, and development of the field, again with an effort to present a better sense of how one who walks in the shoes of a person in that group might see the challenges. The tone and attitudes conveyed in those materials matter. The materials presented here go beyond just the edited cases and seek to convey the reality that today civil rights law and policy is not merely a body of Supreme Court opinions interpreting the Constitution of the United States, but is also a fabric woven from constitutional law, legislative enactments, and administrative action.

Each chapter ends with a section on "Issues for Policy and Practice" that examines the key public policy challenges that are presented by the discussions in each chapter and also the implications for public service practice. These sections are written for both government professionals and nonprofit executives who are so intimately involved in the delivery of public services throughout contracts with federal, state, and local governments. The concluding chapter of the book considers the agenda for policy and practice going forward. This is key, since one of the important themes of the text is that civil rights is very much a work in progress and far from finished, not just with regard to issues receiving obvious attention such as same-sex marriage or continuing challenges to gender equality, but also across the range of problems identified in the text.

Acknowledgments

This book owes a great debt to people who never met the author, or did so only briefly, and had no idea they were teaching someone who would like to think he is a teacher and advocate of civil rights. I have learned about civil rights progress and the lack of it in many parts of this country and abroad, and from people of many backgrounds and experiences.

The volume also owes a great deal to the many students in my civil rights classes over the years. The students at the University of Vermont and at Portland State University have been particularly important, since they experienced the course using the approach taken in this volume and with many of the cases and materials presented here. They demonstrated in the clearest terms that they learned from this approach far better than through the use of other texts or approaches that I have tried or have seen others employ in the past.

I have also learned from judges and other policymakers and administrators whose experiences have provided perspective on so many aspects of civil rights law and policy.

Sadly, this work was also inspired by a history of injustice that is far from over. On completing this project, it was difficult to see how often it was necessary to say that efforts in the various areas of civil rights in the United States are, at best, works in progress. In other places, it is difficult even to use the word "progress."

I have appreciated the good wishes and support of my colleagues at the Hatfield School, Douglas Morgan and Craig Shinn.

Dr. Carol Locust was kind enough to read the chapters on Native American civil rights. Elizabeth Furse, former director of the Institute for Tribal Government in the Mark O. Hatfield School of Government at Portland State University, was also kind enough to read those parts of the manuscript.

In addition, John Rohr, for many years a distinguished faculty member at Virginia Polytechnic and State University, was a colleague who has departed physically but whose memory and influence remain with me. John was convinced, and convinced many others, of the importance of judicial opinions as journals that record the great debates and issues of American life, in addition to their specific legal importance. He knew of their power as teaching tools and foci for reflection on the state of society and its needs in the future.

Most of all, I am grateful to Dr. Claudia María Vargas. During an extremely challenging period, she took the time to read drafts of this manuscript and to comment on virtually every aspect of the project as I worked through it. She is also a wonderful and careful editor who knows how to relate content and style. More than anything, her passion for this field and the problems of civil rights in the community matches and indeed exceeds my own.

Apart from her professional contributions to the project, she is in this, as in everything, a wonderful partner. There are no words to thank her enough for all that she is and does.

1 Miles' Law and the Challenge of Civil Rights in the United States

In 1949 Rufus Miles, then a branch chief in the Bureau of the Budget, coined a saying that has since become a widely acknowledged principle of human behavior known as Miles' Law. "Where you stand depends on where you sit."[1] The point is not that people are narrowly self-interested in interpreting their life and its challenges, but that we cannot help but see the world with our own eyes, which function from a place and with a set of lenses that are shaped by our history and our current condition. Indeed, we can never completely put ourselves in someone else's place and see with his or her eyes. What we can do is to try to understand why they might see the world as they do and what biases we bring to that conversation. This challenge is sometimes referred to as the effort to bring empathy and respect to our understanding of and our relationship with others.

For public service professionals, who work with and for increasingly diverse communities and in organizations that are also complex and diverse, both empathy and respect are important characteristics of our efforts. We also work within a framework of law and public policy that provides a variety of civil rights protections for those who receive public services and those who are employed in public agencies as well as for the nonprofit or for-profit organizations that work with government to deliver public services. The term "constitutional rights and liberties" is often applied to this set of protections. Civil liberties refers to the protections for individual freedoms provided essentially by the Bill of Rights, such as freedom of speech and press, free exercise of religion, and the prohibition against the establishment of religion. Civil rights, by contrast, are, in American constitutional history, most often seen as protections from discrimination against individuals based on the fact that they are members of a particular group such as women, Native Americans, Latinos, and African Americans. Additionally, although it is true that civil rights protections flow from the Constitution, particularly the Thirteenth, Fourteenth, Fifteenth, and Nineteenth Amendments, even more protections are provided by legislative enactments. These include such important laws as the Civil Rights Act of 1964, Equal Opportunity Amendments of 1972, Civil Rights Act of 1991, Age Discrimination in Employment Act of 1967, Americans with Disabilities Act (ADA) of 1990, and many others.

However, as will be clear in the chapters that follow, different groups of people understand what civil rights protection means in very different ways. There are cross-cutting issues about discrimination, to be sure, but the particular kinds of problems and concerns vary, at least from the perspective of those most affected by them. For Native Americans, for example, issues of tribal sovereignty and control of lands and resources are very much civil rights matters. Many women see issues in employment or protections against harassment that differ from the kinds of issues that are commonly discussed with regard to race discrimination. Latinos often experience civil rights from a perspective that has some similarities with, but also differences from, African Americans. Thus, Miles' Law in civil rights reaches even to the very definition of just what civil rights are and what they mean for different groups with different historical experiences.

Civil Rights, Courts, and other Policymakers: The Dialogue Continues on the Unfinished Agenda

The chapters that follow explore that body of civil rights law and policy from the perspective of diverse groups of people and from the view of public service professionals who work with and serve those varied people. In particular, the chapters do so through an exploration of the opinions of courts, and mostly of the Supreme Court of the United States, on civil rights issues. As John Rohr explained, these judicial opinions provide not only a statement of what the law is on the subject and how it came to be that way, but also an ongoing structured conversation about some of the most important problems in American life. We learn both from the rulings and from the arguments that support them as well as from the concurring and dissenting opinions offered by other members of the Court that explain the debate among the justices.[2]

These opinions are structured and presented according to a particular form of logic known as legal reasoning and are expected to meet a set of standards that require support for the arguments from properly applied legal authorities, including judicial precedents. Some of the opinions are beautifully written and state noble principles that reaffirm what Americans think the Constitution and laws ought to do. In other cases, they are badly written and surprisingly, to many readers, anything but supportive of the conception of equality under the law to which many Americans would subscribe. Yet they are all part of the story that has produced the law and policy of civil rights that apply today and shape the discussion for the years ahead.

These judicial opinions are not ultimate statements of law that end debate. Indeed, those opinions often come in cases that flowed from a statute passed by the legislature or enforcement actions taken by an executive branch agency. Once the court has ruled on the case, the other branches in their turn will decide on next steps in something Louis Fisher has referred to as a constitutional dialogue.[3] Thus, when Congress passed and the president signed the ADA Amendments Act of 2008, the legislature stated plainly that the new statute was intended to reverse interpretations of the ADA by the U.S. Supreme Court and the Equal Employment Opportunity Commission that violated the purposes of that law.

> (b)   PURPOSES.—The purposes of this Act are—
>
> (1)   to carry out the ADA's objectives of providing "a clear and comprehensive national mandate for the elimination of discrimination" and "clear, strong, consistent, enforceable standards addressing discrimination" by reinstating a broad scope of protection to be available under the ADA;
>
> (2)   to reject the requirement enunciated by the Supreme Court in *Sutton v. United Air Lines, Inc.*, 527 U.S. 471 (1999) ... that whether an impairment substantially limits a major life activity is to be determined with reference to the ameliorative effects of mitigating measures;
>
> (3)   to reject the Supreme Court's reasoning in *Sutton v. United Air Lines, Inc.*, 527 U.S. 471 (1999) ... and to reinstate the reasoning of the Supreme Court in *School Board of Nassau County v. Arline*, 480 U.S. 273 (1987) which set forth a broad view of the third prong of the definition of handicap under the Rehabilitation Act of 1973;

(4)   to reject the standards enunciated by the Supreme Court in *Toyota Motor Manufacturing, Kentucky, Inc. v. Williams,* 534 U.S. 184 (2002), that the terms "substantially" and "major" in the definition of disability under the ADA "need to be interpreted strictly to create a demanding standard for qualifying as disabled," and that to be substantially limited in performing a major life activity under the ADA "an individual must have an impairment that prevents or severely restricts the individual from doing activities that are of central importance to most people's daily lives";

(5)   to convey congressional intent that the standard created by the Supreme Court in the case of *Toyota Motor Manufacturing, Kentucky, Inc. v. Williams,* 534 U.S. 184 (2002) for "substantially limits" ... has created an inappropriately high level of limitation necessary to obtain coverage under the ADA ...; and

(6)   to express Congress' expectation that the Equal Employment Opportunity Commission will revise that portion of its current regulations that defines the term "substantially limits" as "significantly restricted" to be consistent with this Act, including the amendments made by this Act.[4]

Of course, following the passage of that new legislation, it became the responsibility of the courts to interpret it in particular cases. In part because it is an ongoing discussion, the substance and logic of the judicial opinions, and not just their legal holdings (announcement of the rule on which the decision was made), are important.

Miles' Law in Civil Rights

These opinions are important as well because they have contributed to the successes and sometimes to the failures in the civil rights history of the United States. It is one thing to know that *Brown v. Board of Education*[5] declared segregated education to be a violation of the Constitution, but quite another to read the language of earlier rulings like *Dred Scott*[6] that not only pronounced discrimination to be lawful but also denigrated those who sought equal justice under law. It is informative to know that the courts began to work through some of the problems of gender discrimination in the early 1970s, but it is also a part of the discussion that the Supreme Court had blocked gender equality under the law at the very time that the Fourteenth Amendment, with its promise that no state could "deny to any person within its jurisdiction the equal protection of the laws," went into effect a century earlier. In so doing, the Court used language in its opinions that not only damaged the law but also contributed to a history of demeaning treatment of women.[7] There is no doubt that Native Americans have suffered a long history of discrimination—even to the point of efforts by the U.S. government to eliminate them—but quite another to read the actual language of the U.S. Supreme Court, pronouncing that the government has full authority over them by right of conquest, and to see themselves described by that Court as "domestic dependent nations" such that "Their relation to the United States resembles that of a ward to his guardian."[8] It is important to know the failures of our civil rights story as well as its successes.

As these observations about civil rights case law indicate, the story of civil rights, past or present, is different for various groups in the society who have been, and in too many cases still are, subjected to discrimination. While the story of African Americans' efforts to achieve equal protection of the laws, from the days of slavery to the end of lawful state-imposed segregation in *Brown v. Board of Education* and beyond, through massive resistance by the states and more subtle forms of discrimination to follow, is a critically important part of the civil rights story, there are other parts as well. Certainly Native Americans are justified in seeing

U.S. civil rights through their own eyes, from which perspective it is clear that there have been and continue to be a string of official pronouncements that do not meet the promise of full protection of equality of rights.[9] Many people have suffered cruel discrimination because of their sexual orientation or identity. They are only recently seeing some advances, but there are still no national protections against discrimination in employment in the civil rights statutes other Americans can access. Persons with disabilities continue to see opinions by justices of the Supreme Court that have been far from supportive and, in some cases, patently offensive.[10]

In some instances the problems and frustrations come from direct rulings or extremely blunt and sometimes even offensive language, while in others the difficulties arise from complex procedural rulings that seem to address arcane points of law that are of interest only to legal scholars and practicing attorneys. Thus, rulings that make it difficult for those alleging discrimination even to get their cases heard or to carry onerous burdens of proof can be as important in practical effect as others that are more direct and obvious rulings on the substance of civil rights protections.[11] Indeed, as will become clear, it is in part because of some of these kinds of rulings with regard to constitutional provisions and some statutes that those seeking to enforce their civil rights are increasingly relying on legislation rather than constitutional claims to make their cases.

As Miles would say, where civil rights law and policy stand depends upon where one sits in the diverse American community. By any measure, though, it is a work in progress, with many serious inadequacies yet to be resolved. In the chapters that follow the edited opinions will take the reader from the foundation points in the development of civil rights law for each of these groups to the rulings that operate presently. As the reader moves through this material, it is important to consider six important questions. First, how do different groups of people understand civil rights given their history and life experience? Second, how has the law developed to this point? Third, what is the current state of civil rights law with respect to each of the kinds of people and problems presented? Fourth, how does the quality and character of the constitutional dialogue, as Fisher puts it, affect an individual as he or she seeks to understand his or her ability to enjoy the equal protection of the laws? Fifth, what is the unfinished business of civil rights that needs to be addressed going forward? Finally, how can the answers to these five questions inform professional practice in public service to diverse communities and within diverse organizations?

Notes on Reading and Analyzing Judicial Opinions

Many public service professionals have never learned how to find or read judicial opinions or other legal authorities. This part of the chapter explains how to find, read, and analyze judicial opinions. The next section provides a brief primer on the process of legal reasoning. The next few pages walk through the steps required to read and analyze virtually any legal opinion issued by any court in the United States.[12] This process is sometimes referred to as briefing a case—a kind of systematic way to summarize an opinion. (This is different from another use of the term "briefing," which refers to the preparation of the full formal written arguments submitted to the Court by the parties in the case.)

1. Understand the Citation to the Opinion

This is the way we identify opinions and find them as well as the way we refer to them in other materials. The citation consists of two parts: the case title and the reference. Consider, for example:

DeShaney v. Winnebago County Department of Social Services, 489 U.S. 189 (1989).

The title of the case [*DeShaney v. Winnebago County Department of Social Services*] is underlined or italicized as a proper title. It is made up of the names of the parties in the case. Thus, this was a case brought on behalf of Joshua DeShaney against the Winnebago County Department of Social Services. The name that appears first is that of the person or organization bringing the suit. Of course, this case came up through the court system to the U.S. Supreme Court, so the first name is the name of the party who petitioned to have the case heard on appeal. Not surprisingly, that person is called the petitioner. Just as logically, we call the party answering that petition the respondent. (It may seem complicated at first blush, but it is actually quite logical.)

The reference in a citation [489 U.S. 189 (1989)] indicates where the cited opinion may be found. It begins with the volume number in which the item is found. The initials abbreviate the name of the publication in which the item is printed. The second number indicates the page on which the case begins. Finally, the date in parentheses tells the reader the year in which the opinion was published. *DeShaney*, then, may be found in volume 489 of the *United States Reports* (the official reporter for the U.S. Supreme Court), beginning on page 189, decided in 1989. There are two other commonly cited, commercially produced series of books that also publish the opinions of the Supreme Court [L.Ed.2d, which stands for Lawyer's Edition, Second Series; and S. Ct., which stands for Supreme Court Reporter]. Do not worry about all of this complexity; the language from the opinion is the same in all three. Just use the U.S. citation.

The citations for lower court opinions are slightly different, but the reason for this difference is also logical. Remember that there are three levels of federal courts: U.S. District Courts, the U.S. Courts of Appeals for the several circuits, and the U.S. Supreme Court (with a parallel structure in most states). Lower court rulings, such as the U.S. District Court for the District of Oregon or the U.S. Court of Appeals for the 9th Circuit (which covers the West Coast, Alaska, and Hawaii), are only binding within the area covered by those courts—their jurisdiction. So, in the reference part of the citation below, we include the volume number (20), the book in which the opinion appears (F. Supp. 2d, which stands for the *Federal Supplement, Second Series*, which reports the rulings of federal district courts), the page on which the opinion begins (675), and the date and the court that issued the opinion (District Court for the District of Vermont issued in 1998).

St. Johnsbury Academy v. D.H., 20 F. Supp. 2d 675 (DVT 1998).

This was an important case about the obligations of private schools as compared with the local school district with respect to student services under the Individuals with Disabilities Education Act (IDEA). St. Johnsbury Academy lost in the District Court and took an appeal to the next higher level, which is the U.S. Court of Appeals for the 2nd Circuit. The Academy won at that level and the opinion was reported at volume 240 of the *Federal Reporter, Third Series* [the Federal Reporter provides opinions of the U.S. Courts of Appeals], beginning on page 163, rendered by the U.S. Court of Appeals for the Second Circuit in 2001:

St. Johnsbury Academy v. D.H., 240 F.3d 163 (2nd Cir. 2001).

The next level above the U.S. Circuit Court of Appeals is the U.S. Supreme Court. The *St. Johnsbury* case did not go to that last step.

The same basic form for citations applies in court opinions, statutes, regulations, and even law review articles. Now let us turn back to how to think about the substance of an opinion.

2. Get the Facts

Read the report to find out the story of the case. What happened that brought about the case in the first place? What is often called the fact pattern consists of the who, what, when, where, and why of the case. Be specific in your understanding (and, if you are writing a brief, in your description of the facts). Think of it chronologically. What happened from the earliest event to the current status in the Court? That often reaches back to when a policy was created, such as by the passage of legislation or the adoption of administrative regulations. Do not begin a brief with "This case comes to the Supreme Court from the U.S. Circuit Court of Appeals." There were many things that happened to bring the case to its present point before it ever got anywhere near a court.

In the chapters to follow most of the edited cases have an introduction that comes before the opinion that announces that "Justice___ delivered the opinion of the Court." The introduction to the edited cases is not part of the opinion handed down by the Court, but is provided by the text author. Many of these opinions were extremely lengthy in their original form and contained pages of discussion just of the facts. In order to reduce them to a readable size, the text author provides some of the factual material in summary form in these introductions. Where the Court's discussion of the facts is particularly interesting or important, the edited version of the opinion may be slightly longer than normal in this book and may include some of the recitation of the facts from the opinion itself.

3. Clarify the Issues

What is the issue (or issues) the Court was asked to resolve? The issues should be phrased in the form of questions. The easiest method (and perfectly adequate) is to think of the issues as questions that can be answered with a simple "yes" or "no." Do not simply ask whether a particular statute or activity is "constitutional" or "legal." Consider which part of the Constitution or what law has allegedly been violated. For example, was the question about a violation of the due process clause of the Fourteenth Amendment, did it concern the IDEA, or did it perhaps present a claim about some other provision of law? There may be more than one question in a given case. Keep the issues as clear and as simple as you can make them. An issue statement, whether in public policy or in law, should be clear and complete enough that it can stand alone and still convey to the reader a clear sense of what it is about and why it matters.

Sometimes the judges will be kind and lay out the issues clearly right at the beginning of the opinion. Unfortunately, that is not always the case.

Here again, the opinions in the chapters to follow are often edited so as to eliminate a number of the issues that are not central to the purpose for which the case is presented in this text. Usually, these are procedural issues that are raised in an attempt to stop further consideration of the merits of the case (the substantive questions that were presented). Where those issues are key to the case or the development of civil rights law, they are included in the edited opinions.

4. What Was the Decision?

This section of a brief is nothing more than an answer to the question presented in the "issues" section. A simple "yes" or "no" answer is all that is needed.

There are two other ways of thinking about the Court's decision. One of these is to concentrate on what is termed the *holding* in the case, which means the legal principle announced by the Court that controlled the ruling in the case. The other commonly used term is the *disposition* of the case. That is, did the Court *affirm* the lower court ruling, *reverse* it, *remand* it (send it back for further proceedings), or *vacate* it (totally reject the case and the record supporting it to that point, requiring the parties to start over if they really want to proceed with the case)?

5. *What Was the Majority's Rationale?*

This is the section of the opinion of greatest long-term value for most of us, most of the time. It tells us not merely what the Court decided, but why it came to that conclusion in this case and what it is telling us about how the law will be going forward. The central feature of the rationale is the logic that took the Court from the issue to the legal premise where it began its reasoning (whether it is a part of the Constitution or a piece of legislation) to whatever statement of the law it reached and the application of that interpretation to the facts of the present case. Of course, a description of logic is not merely a listing of reasons, but an explanation as to the premise used by the Justice writing the opinion, and the reasoning by which he or she moved from premise to conclusion. Like most things in life, it takes a bit of practice to sort out what really matters and what does not amidst all of that language (referred to as *obiter dictum* or just *dicta*, which means language not essential to the holding or reasoning of the court). In seeking to understand the logic of the opinion, be open to the language the judge is using and the way it speaks of the people involved in the case. The tone and nature of some of these rulings find their way into a variety of aspects of our national conversation about equality before the law. That tone can alienate people or bring them together in ways far more real than might be immediately apparent.

6. *What Separate Opinions Were Filed by Members of the Court in the Case?*

The Supreme Court—or other courts with several members—decides cases by majority vote. The author of the majority opinion tries to attract as many other members of the Court to agree with his or her opinion as possible. However, some justices may agree with the conclusion reached by the Court, but disagree with the reasoning used by the majority to reach its conclusion. They may publish what is called a *concurring opinion*, explaining the basis for the disagreement. If there are justices who disagree with the Court's conclusion in the case, they may file *dissenting opinions*, explaining their criticisms of the majority opinion. It is useful to read them, particularly for the purposes that opinions are presented in this text, and to make a brief note about the basis for the disagreements.

There are two reasons for noting the separate opinions. First, they help us to better understand the debate within the Court by emphasizing where there was agreement and disagreement. This provides a sense about how the Court might rule in the future. The second reason is that, over time, dissents or concurrences may be turned into law by later cases. For example, when the Supreme Court upheld racial segregation in 1896, only Justice Harlan dissented from the *Plessy v. Ferguson* decision. However, his opinion was an important influence on many judges in the decades that followed and, in 1954, in *Brown v. Board of Education of Topeka*, *Plessy* was reversed and Harlan's view vindicated.

What follows is a sample of a simple brief in one important U.S. Supreme Court case.

Griswold v. Connecticut

381 U.S. 479 (1965)

FACTS: The Connecticut Planned Parenthood organization opened a family planning clinic at which contraceptives and information concerning birth control were provided. A Connecticut criminal statute prohibited the use of contraceptives or counseling someone to use them. The clinic provided birth control counseling to a married couple. The Director of Planned Parenthood was convicted and fined under the statute.

ISSUE: (1) Does the Constitution provide a right to privacy that is applied to the state through the due process clause of the Fourteenth Amendment?

(2) Does a statute that punishes the counseling of married couples to use contraceptives violate the right to privacy applied to the states through the due process clause of the Fourteenth Amendment?

DECISION: Yes.

RATIONALE: (Douglas) The Court has recognized a number of rights not specifically mentioned in the Constitution. These include the right to marry and raise children, the freedom of association and privacy in those associations, and a number of implied related rights under the freedoms of speech and press. The right to privacy is an implied right, based in freedom of association protected by the First Amendment and is also supported by the Third, Fourth, Fifth, Ninth, and Fourteenth Amendments. Decisions regarding the right to bear children are some of the most intensely private matters involving the family, the most basic unit of association. Government actions touching upon those decisions must serve compelling interests and the means chosen to enforce those ends may not "sweep unnecessarily broad." The Connecticut restrictions do not meet either part of this test.

CONCURRING: (Goldberg) The Ninth Amendment is the appropriate constitutional provision for protection of the right to privacy.

(Harlan) There is a right to privacy of the sort described by the Court, but it stems from the concept of liberty protected by the due process clause of the Fourteenth Amendment and not specific Bill of Rights guarantees.

(White) A law of this sort is not "reasonably necessary for the effectuation of a legitimate and substantial end."

DISSENTING: (Black) There is no specific constitutional language which supports a right to privacy and he is not willing to read either the Bill of Rights or the due process clause so broadly as to create one.

(Stewart) Though this is a "silly law," it is for the legislature to remove it from the books, not the Court.

Legal Reasoning: A Structured Logic Based in Legal Authority

In order to understand a judicial opinion and to see the rationale that takes the reader from the issues, through the premise, and to the holding in the case, one needs to understand the process known as legal reasoning. Consider two important caveats at the outset and then the three different types of reasoning that make up the larger term, legal reasoning.

The first caveat is that although politicians and lawyers repeat the mantra that judges should not make law, and should only interpret it, that statement is simply not possible in a common law-based legal system like that of the United States. The Constitution was intentionally written for the most part in broad language that was not intended to speak to each situation that might arise over the centuries and it was expected to endure. Therefore, the application of that law requires interpretation. An authoritative interpretation of the law by a court like the United States Supreme Court is a legal precedent. In that sense, judicial opinions do make law. Even a decision not to decide a case for procedural reasons, like a lack of standing to sue by the parties, can set precedent. Judge-made law is just as likely to be produced by conservatives as by liberals, although the substantive conclusions those jurists reach may be different. Political rhetoric to the contrary is just that—political rhetoric and not reality.

Second, and related to that first point, it is not helpful to approach the reading and interpretation of judicial opinions with ideological baggage and language like "judicial activism" or "judicial restraint." While there are certainly arguments that can be made about what these terms truly mean at their core, over time they have come to be little more than ideologically applied labels. Opinions that one likes are often labeled exemplars of judicial restraint and those that one dislikes are often simply termed activist decisions that exceed the proper boundaries of judicial behavior. Again, both ends of the political spectrum participate in these verbal broadsides.

This book will avoid both of these two unhelpful practices. The author asks the reader to do the same and to concentrate instead on a careful and thoughtful analysis of the opinions. Indeed, one of the points that is important to legal reasoning is that because there are some understood conventions as to how legal arguments are to be constructed, it is possible to read an opinion that reaches a conclusion with which the reader disagrees and yet consider that it is well written and well reasoned. By contrast, it is also possible to read opinions that came to the correct conclusion, in the reader's mind, and yet find that the opinion was badly crafted.[13] It is not acceptable for a judge, even a justice of the Supreme Court, simply to ignore the existing body of law. Precedents are to be used according to an accepted set of principles of usage. There are canons (principles) of statutory interpretation.

That said, there are two sets of considerations to keep in mind when reading an opinion. The first concerns the standard process of legal reasoning. The second concerns the structure of an opinion.

Legal Reasoning: Really Three Types of Logic Often Used in a Single Case

The United States operates from a written Constitution, a collection of federal and state statutes, and a set of administrative rules having the force of law. In that sense, it is what is termed a positive law system. However, the United States also borrowed portions of the British common law system, which relies on judicial interpretation and precedent as an important force in the development of the law. When we speak of legal reasoning in the United States, therefore, we refer to constitutional reasoning, statutory reasoning, and common law reasoning. Which types of reasoning are required depends upon the legal issue in the case.

Consider first a case that raises a constitutional issue. Since the Constitution is a written document that is the highest source of law in the land, judges begin with the language of the Constitution as the starting point. Unfortunately, as noted above, much of the Constitution is written in broad and quite general language. There are rare exceptions, and in those cases it is relatively easy to reach a decision. For example, when Congress passed legislation providing for the so-called line item veto, under which the president could veto portions of some spending legislation while signing the rest into law, the Supreme Court had little difficulty applying the language of the so-called presentment clause of Article I, Section 7 to strike down the statute.[14] The language is quite clear as to the process to be followed when a bill is adopted by Congress and goes to the president.

But since the language is rarely clear enough to resolve a constitutional question, the next step in legal reasoning is to establish the intent of the framers to the extent that information is available and provides a clear statement.[15] Again, the presentment clause interpretation was helped by the fact that the history of the constitutional convention was relatively clear about the desire to both provide enough power for an effective executive branch and chief executive, but also to place boundaries around the powers of the president, including the veto power, so that he or she would not become a home-grown version of the king against whom the colonies had rebelled. Often, however, there is considerable debate over just what the framers intended and, in any case, quite a number of them, led by James Madison, rejected the idea that the interpretations of the eighteenth century should be frozen into the Constitution to bind future generations whose circumstances were unknown and unknowable to the founders.

Third, judges turn to what is sometimes known as the judicial gloss that has been placed on the language of the document in the two centuries since its adoption. Another way of saying this is to refer to the precedents that have been handed down by the courts in their interpretation of constitutional provisions. Thus, when the Supreme Court decides an equal protection of the law case today, it draws on dozens of prior precedents interpreting just what the equal protection clause of the Fourteenth Amendment means. (The Court has also read the due process clause of the Fifth Amendment to incorporate the concept of equal protection of the law where the federal government is concerned.)[16] Every now and again, however, cases known as "cases of first impression" arise for which there is no clear precedent. And even where there are a good many precedents, new circumstances arise for which existing precedents are not a good fit.

Judges then determine whether there is a need to factor in the changed circumstances of society. Thus, when Justice Douglas authored the *Griswold v. Connecticut* opinion announcing a right to privacy,[17] there was broad criticism, but some years later even one of the most vocal of those critics announced, during confirmation hearings on his nomination to the Supreme Court, that he would not reverse the *Griswold* conclusion that there was a right to privacy.[18] More recently, the Court pointed to such a need for change in rendering its decision in *Lawrence v. Texas*, concerning a claim that the Constitution protects the rights of homosexuals.[19] The Court found that there was "an emerging awareness that liberty gives substantial protection to adult persons in deciding how to conduct their private lives in matters pertaining to sex."[20]

Needless to say, there are continuing debates among scholars, judges, political figures, and the public about one or more of these factors used in constitutional interpretation, but they remain the most common features of constitutional reasoning. That said, judges are mindful that a mistaken interpretation of the Constitution requires either that the Court later reverse itself to correct its error, which judges sometimes but rarely do, or that the Constitution be amended, which is an extremely difficult process.

Statutory interpretation, on the other hand, is quite different. Over time the language of legislation has become increasingly detailed. There is certainly more detailed and contemporary information than is presented in the Constitution. Judges are also aware that Congress can and often does change legislation to correct what it considers to be misinterpretations by the courts or to address problems in the legislation pointed out in judicial opinions. Therefore, the starting point for statutory interpretation is a strict application of the language of the legislation. Even here there can be difficulties, such as in the fact that some fields of activity change so rapidly that legislation can quickly become outdated or at least does not encompass new developments. Thus, although telecommunications legislation was passed in 1996, the courts soon found that there were problems arising on a day-to-day basis that Congress did not contemplate in that relatively modern statute because contemporary Internet technologies like social media did not exist at the time. Thus, the Court found itself dealing with a case that discussed the fact that many Americans carry so much information about so many facets of their lives on a smartphone that allowing a police officer to rummage through it without a warrant presents serious search and seizure issues under the Fourth Amendment.[21]

Courts often start their interpretation of statutes by granting a considerable degree of deference to the initial interpretation of legislation by the administrative agency charged with its enforcement.[22] The reason for this is simply that those agencies have traditionally been thought to have both expertise and experience in the subject matter and the law that applies to their work. So the Supreme Court deferred to the conclusion by the Equal Employment Opportunity Commission (EEOC) that sexual harassment is sex discrimination in violation of Title VII of the Civil Rights Act of 1964, and that became the foundation for later judicial rulings on the subject.[23] Of course, while the courts start from that deferential position, they may nevertheless conclude that the agency got it wrong. A clear example of this was the Supreme Court's ruling that the Environmental Protection Agency misinterpreted the Clean Air Act when it refused to issue rules governing vehicle emissions that contribute to global warming.[24]

Judges turn to what is called the judicial gloss placed on the language of the statute by previous judicial opinions. This is a complex task, since there may be many cases that address a single point of a statute and there may be conflicts among some courts. The effort to resolve such conflicts is one of the reasons that the U.S. Supreme Court frequently gives for agreeing to hear a particular case.

Finally, as is true of constitutional reasoning, courts will sometimes consider the need to adapt to changing conditions that have emerged since the legislation was adopted. That has been a common problem in laws dealing with telecommunications, finance, and a number of other rapidly developing fields where there are statutes that may not have kept pace with recent changes in practice in the field.

The third type of reasoning is common law reasoning. Common law reasoning developed in the context of cases where there was no legislation or constitutional provision that addressed a problem. The courts fashioned rules to fit the new situation based either on analogies to other existing law or because they simply had to create new rules where there seemed to be no clear guidance from existing bodies of law. That said, today common law reasoning is used not only in those types of cases, but also wherever there is an attempt to apply, challenge, or change existing judicial precedents. So, yes, the technique is used in statutory and constitutional reasoning as well.

Common law reasoning starts from the basic premise that equal justice under law requires that people in similar situations should be treated similarly. Thus, if a client takes a problem to an attorney, he or she will seek to determine whether there are existing precedents that apply to the situation. If so, the attorney will advise the client to press forward with a legal action if the law is in his or her favor, or perhaps to settle if it is clear that existing precedents mean the client is likely to lose.

All of this is based on a three-step process of discovery, synthesis, and analogy. The parties attempt to assist the judge in discovering what the correct legal authority (precedent) is for a given problem. Obviously, that means that the facts and the question of law in the case in question is comparable to the facts and law in the precedent. Once the controlling authority is discovered, it is time to synthesize that precedent to determine the rule and reasoning on which it was decided. Clearly, both sides in a case will seek to convince the judge that their analysis is correct. Finally, the judge uses a process of analogy to apply the rule of the precedent case to the new case. If the fit is a good one, then the rule of the precedent can be applied directly and the case is relatively easy. If the new case is close, but still somewhat different from the precedent, then the judge may have to modify the rule from the precedent in order to fit the new situation. If the circumstances in the new case are sufficiently novel, the judge may simply have to create a new rule if he or she concludes that the precedent simply will not fit the changed circumstance.

Consider the following example of the use of common law reasoning in a civil rights setting involving a constitutional issue. The Supreme Court had decided that policies that treated people differently on the basis of race were inherently suspect and should be judged according to something called strict judicial scrutiny. (The legal criteria for deciding a case is often termed a standard or a test.) That standard required that the burden of proof would be placed on the government to demonstrate that its actions were justified by a compelling state interest and that the means chosen to achieve that end were narrowly tailored.[25] The Court was then faced with the claim that the same standard should be applied to policies that treat people differently on the basis of their gender. A majority of the members of the Court was not willing to agree that gender was a suspect classification and therefore would not apply the same kind of strict judicial scrutiny that applied to race-based classifications.[26] However, Justice William Brennan was able to argue successfully that even if the strictest standard did not apply, some kind of elevated standard was necessary. He was therefore able to convince the Court to adopt what has sometimes been called a middle standard because it was not as stringent as the standard for race-based classifications but was more rigorous than the usual standard that is applied to ordinary government actions, known as the rational basis test.[27] From then on, gender-based classifications were judged according to that new standard.[28]

The Structure of a Legal Opinion: Not Always Observed in Practice

An understanding that judges use precedent is necessary but not sufficient to really explain how judicial opinions are constructed, and therefore how to read them. Actually the structure is relatively clear, and particularly so when the judge involved is a good craftsperson.

Judicial opinions usually have some kind of brief introduction followed by major sections marked by Roman numerals. If the judge is particularly good, he or she will state, in a very brief introduction of the legal issues presented by the case, the court's answers to those questions, the disposition of the case as a whole, and perhaps even something about the organization of the remainder of the opinion.

Roman numeral I usually marks the beginning of the section in which the court explains the facts of the case. Lower court opinions usually provide more detail concerning the facts since they make decisions on trial level or first level appeal questions. By the time a case gets to the U.S. Supreme Court, the discussion of facts in the opinion tends to be relatively limited. Even so, the author of the opinion will usually be careful to provide a discussion of the facts that are particularly relevant to the legal issues addressed by the court.

Roman numeral II often addresses any procedural or jurisdictional questions that the court finds it necessary to resolve before moving on to what is called the merits (substantive issues). There are often a number of procedural issues presented in a case, since the party that won in the lower courts will try diligently to find a reason to keep the case from moving on to the appellate levels.

Roman numeral III is often the first substantive issue in a case. There may be several. If there are questions about statutes and constitutional issues, the court will often take up the statutory question first. If the case can be resolved on those grounds, it is then unnecessary to take on the larger constitutional concerns.

The court then takes the other substantive issues in turn, addressing as many of them as the court considers necessary to resolve the case. That means that the court may not decide all of the issues that were presented by the parties in the case. Often, in fact, if the court concludes that a new legal standard should be applied, it will state that standard and send the case back down (*remand*) for further consideration in the lower courts according to that new standard.

Once the judge starts into each issue discussion, we look for the classic signs of an effective deductive logic. It is helpful if the judge starts by restating the issue clearly and completely. Then we look for the premise, a generalization that will be understood and accepted by both sides and supported by the authority raised by the issue. Thus, if the issue is about a constitutional provision, we expect a premise that starts from that part of the Constitution. If it concerns a statute, such as Title IX of the Education Amendments of 1972, we expect that the premise will be grounded in that law. If the issue concerns an administrative agency's application of a regulation, we would expect the premise to start there.

After the premise is established, we try to follow the judge's logic, moving from the premise down to the standard or rule that is to be applied in the kind of situation presented by the issue. For example, it might be the strict scrutiny standard discussed earlier in this section of the chapter. We then look to see how the judge applies that standard to the case before the court. We also look to see what precedents or other authorities the judge uses to support each of his or her points of argument, the choice of legal standard to be applied, and the way he or she applies that standard in the present case.

We then look to the concurring opinion or dissents, if any, to see what else they may tell us about the majority's argument.

Conclusion

The study of civil rights in public service concerns both the need to understand the diverse communities that public service professionals serve and also the increasingly diverse groups of people who work in government agencies or nonprofit service agencies who work on behalf of government. That requires not only an understanding of civil rights law and policy, but also the perspectives of the various groups who have suffered discrimination over the history of our nation.

We can learn the law and policy by studying the judicial opinions issued by the U.S. Supreme Court and some important lower court opinions that explain not only what the Constitution and civil rights statutes require, but also how those interpretations have been developed and applied over time in various types of situations. In order to do that, it is important to understand how to access, read, and analyze judicial opinions. While that may seem a daunting challenge at first, there are some relatively easy-to-apply techniques for doing so, as discussed in the chapter.

But there is more to learn from reading judicial opinions that trace the development of civil rights protections over time. There is also a story there about the way different groups of people, such as African Americans, Native Americans, Latinos, women, persons with disabilities, and gays and lesbians, have been treated and the language that has been used to characterize and discuss them over the decades of our nation's history. That narrative not only provides context for understanding the more specific civil rights issues, but also helps us to develop an understanding as to why they may see and experience civil rights as they do from their perspective. Since, as Miles' Law explains, where one stands often depends upon where one sits, that kind of empathy can be extremely helpful to all of us and particularly to those of us who seek to serve diverse communities.

I. Issues for Policy and Practice

A. How do existing public policies ensure that Americans understand the meaning of civil rights and what they protect? Do they? If not, are there potential policy options that could assist in that effort?

B. How does the education system prepare students to understand, respect, and support civil rights? Does it? Given the reduction in time and attention to social studies and what was termed civics in the K-12 system, what options are there to address this challenge?

C. Is there a clear and coherent national civil rights policy? If not, is there an organizing framework that allows public service professionals and community members to find and understand the policies?

D. Do we know how people within our organization understand civil rights on a day-to-day basis and their significance among colleagues?

E. How can a local government understand how the local community perceives civil rights needs and concerns?

II. Discussion Questions

This chapter poses six questions to consider throughout the reading of the book, through any course that one might be taking, and as a public service practitioner.

A. First, how do different groups of people understand civil rights given their history and life experience?

B. Second, how has the law developed to this point?

C. Third, what is the current state of civil rights law with respect to each of the kinds of people and problems presented?

D. Fourth, how does the quality and character of the constitutional dialogue, as Fisher puts it, affect an individual as he or she seeks to understand his or her ability to enjoy the equal protection of the laws?

E. Fifth, what is the unfinished business of civil rights that needs to be addressed going forward?

F. Finally, how can the answers to the other five questions inform professional practice in public service to diverse communities and within diverse organizations?

Notes

1 Rufus Miles, "The Origin and Meaning of Miles' Law," *Public Administration Review* 38 (Sep/Oct 1978): 399.

2 See generally, John Rohr, *Ethics for Bureaucrats*, 2nd edn. (New York: Marcel Dekker, 1989).

3 Louis Fisher, *Constitutional Dialogues* (Princeton: Princeton University Press, 1988). See also Fisher, *Constitutional Conflicts Between Congress and the President*, 4th edn., Revised. (Lawrence, KS: Kansas University Press, 1997); Fisher, *The Constitution Between Friends: Congress, the President and the Law* (New York: St. Martin's Press, 1978).

4 ADA Amendments Act of 2008, P.L. 110–325, 122 Stat. 3553 Section 2(b).

5 347 U.S. 483 (1954).

6 *Dred Scott v. Sandford*, 60 U.S. 393 (1857).

7 See *Bradwell v. State*, 83 U.S. 130 (1873); *Minor v. Happersett*, 88 U.S. 162 (1874).

8 *Cherokee Nation v. Georgia*, 30 U.S. 1, 33 (1831).

9 See e.g., *City of Sherrill v. Oneida Nation*, 544 U.S. 197 (2005).

10 See e.g., the opinion for the Court by Chief Justice Rehnquist in *Board of Trustees of the University of Alabama v. Garrett*, 531 U.S. 356 (2001) and Justice Scalia's dissenting opinion in *PGA Tour, Inc. v. Martin*, 532 U.S. 661 (2001).

11 See *Alexander v. Sandoval*, 532 U.S. 275 (2001) denying individuals the ability to bring cases as implied private rights of action under Title VI of the Civil Rights Act of 1964. See also *Schaffer v. Weast*, 546

U.S. 49 (2005), placing the burden on parents, rather than the schools, to prove that the individualized education plan met the requirement of a "free and appropriate public education in the least restrictive environment" under the provisions of the Individuals with Disabilities Education Act.

12 While many of the points are similar in other countries, some, like Canada, do not present a single unified opinion for the court but what are called seriatim opinions in which the individual justices each offer their reasoning. Opinions that are issued by countries that have a continental European heritage, like Spain or France, are also different since they work from a code law base rather than a common law system like that of the U.S.

13 This subject is treated at greater length in Phillip J. Cooper and Howard Ball, *The U.S. Supreme Court From the Inside Out* (Englewood Cliffs, NJ: Prentice-Hall, 1995), Ch.10.

14 *Clinton v. City of New York*, 524 U.S. 417 (1998).

15 Sources commonly used by the Supreme Court include Max Farrand, ed., *Records of the Federal Convention of 1787*, revised edn., 4 vols. (New Haven, CT: Yale University Press, 1966); Jonathan Elliott, *Debates in the Several States on the Adoption of the Federal Constitution as Recommended by the General Convention at Philadelphia in 1787*, 2nd edn. (New York: Burt Franklin, 1888); and Alexander Hamilton, James Madison, and John Jay, *The Federalist Papers* (New York: Mentor, 1961).

16 See *Bolling v. Sharpe*, 347 U.S. 497 (1954).

17 381 U.S. 479 (1965).

18 That critic was Robert Bork, who had attacked Justice Douglas' opinion in a widely cited law review article, "Neutral Principles and Some First Amendment Problems," *Indiana Law Journal* 47 (No.1 1971): 1–35.

19 539 U.S. 558 (2003).

20 Id., at 572.

21 *Riley v. California*, 134 S. Ct. 2473 (2014).

22 *Chevron U.S.A. v. Natural Resources Defense Council*, 467 U.S. 837 (1984); *Florida Prepaid Postsecondary Ed. Expense Bd. v. College Savings Bank*, 527 U.S. 627 (1999).

23 *Meritor Savings Bank v. Vinson*, 477 U.S. 57 (1986).

24 *Massachusetts v. EPA*, 127 S. Ct. 1438 (2007).

25 *San Antonio Independent School District v. Rodriguez*, 411 U.S. 1 (1973).

26 See *Frontiero v. Richardson*, 411 U.S. 677 (1973).

27 *Craig v. Boren*, 429 U.S. 190 (1976).

28 See e.g., *United States v. Virginia*, 518 U.S. 515 (1996).

References

Bork, Robert. "Neutral Principles and Some First Amendment Problems," *Indiana Law Journal* 47 (No.1 1971): 1–35.

Cooper, Phillip J. and Howard Ball. *The U.S. Supreme Court From the Inside Out*. Englewood Cliffs, NJ: Prentice-Hall, 1995.

Elliott, Jonathan. *Debates in the Several States on the Adoption of the Federal Constitution as Recommended by the General Convention at Philadelphia in 1787*, 2nd edn. New York: Burt Franklin, 1888.

Farrand, Max, ed. *Records of the Federal Convention of 1787*, revised edn., 4 vols. New Haven, CT: Yale University Press, 1966.

Fisher, Louis. *The Constitution Between Friends: Congress, the President and the Law*. New York: St. Martin's Press, 1978.

———. *Constitutional Conflicts Between Congress and the President*, 4th edn., revised. Lawrence, KS: University Press of Kansas, 1997.

———. *Constitutional Dialogues*. Princeton: Princeton University Press, 1988.

Hamilton, Alexander, James Madison, and John Jay. *The Federalist Papers*. New York: Mentor, 1961.

Miles, Rufus. "The Origin and Meaning of Miles' Law," *Public Administration Review* 38 (Sep/Oct 1978): 399–403.

Rohr, John. *Ethics for Bureaucrats*, 2nd edn. New York: Marcel Dekker, 1989.

2   From the Heritage of African American Slavery to Modern Civil Rights Protection

Justice Thurgood Marshall, the first African American to sit on the United States Supreme Court, had been chief counsel for the National Association for the Advancement of Colored People Legal Defense and Education Fund (NAACP LDF).[1] In that role, and following his mentor Charles Hamilton Houston, Marshall led the legal fight to end segregation, including his ultimately successful argument in *Brown v. Board of Education*.[2] He had also experienced the massive resistance by Southern states for many years after the Supreme Court rulings striking down official segregation. By the mid-1970s, many of those who had resisted began to object that the courts had been involved in these matters for too long.

This issue arose when the first major affirmative action case was discussed by Supreme Court justices in conference. Justice Marshall was outraged at the very idea that the legacy of segregation had been adequately addressed in America. He wrote a memorandum to the other justices which said in part:

> I repeat, for next to the last time: the decision in this case depends on whether you consider the action of the Regents as admitting certain students or as excluding certain other students. If you view the program as admitting qualified students who, because of this Nation's sorry history of racial discrimination, have academic records that prevent them from effectively competing for medical school, then this is affirmative action to remove the vestiges of slavery and state imposed segregation by "root and branch." If you view the program as excluding students, it is a program of "quotas" which violates the principle that the "constitution is color-blind."
>
> If only the principle of color-blindness had been accepted by the majority in *Plessy* in 1896, we would not be faced with this problem in 1978. We must remember, however, that this principle appeared only in the dissent. In the 60 years from *Plessy* to *Brown*, ours was a Nation where, by law, individuals could be given "special" treatment based on race. For us now to say that the principle of color-blindness prevents the University from giving "special" consideration to race when this Court, in 1896 licensed the states to continue to consider race, is to make a mockery of the principle of "equal protection under law."
>
> As a result of our last discussion on this case, I wish also to address the question of whether Negroes have "arrived." Just a few examples illustrate that Negroes most certainly have not. In our own Court, we have had only three Negro law clerks, and not so far have we had a Negro Officer of the Court. On a broader scale, this week's U.S. News and World Report has a story about "Who Runs America." They list some 83 persons—not one Negro, even as a would-be runner-up. And the economic disparity between the races is increasing ....

The dream of America as the melting pot has not been realized by Negroes—either the Negro did not get into the pot, or he did not get melted down. The statistics on unemployment and the other statistics quoted in the briefs of the Solicitor General and other amici document the vast gulf between White and Black America. That gulf was brought about by centuries of slavery and then by another century in which, with the approval of this Court, states were permitted to treat Negroes "specially."

This case is here now because of that sordid history ... We are not yet all equals, in large part because of the refusal of the Plessy Court to adopt the principle of color-blindness. It would be the cruelest irony for this Court to adopt the dissent in Plessy now and hold that the University must use color-blind admissions.[3]

He was not able to convince his colleagues and, what was worse, the plurality opinion rejecting his argument was written by Justice Lewis Powell.[4] It seemed to Marshall that Powell had gone out of his way to dismiss his admonition to his colleagues.[5] For Marshall, not only was Powell wrong and insensitive, he was a powerful reminder of the kind of urbane and sophisticated Southerner who had maintained and perpetuated the segregated society against which Marshall had fought his entire professional life.[6] Powell had been a member of the Richmond School Board and later of the Virginia Board of Education during the years of massive resistance. In his dissent to the Court's opinion, Marshall again tried to explain that there was more at stake than a narrow legal argument. There was a heritage of slavery and discrimination that remained unresolved and only partially addressed.

I do not agree that petitioner's admissions program violates the Constitution. For it must be remembered that, during most of the past 200 years, the Constitution as interpreted by this Court did not prohibit the most ingenious and pervasive forms of discrimination against the Negro. Now, when a State acts to remedy the effects of that legacy of discrimination, I cannot believe that this same Constitution stands as a barrier.

Three hundred and fifty years ago, the Negro was dragged to this country in chains to be sold into slavery. Uprooted from his homeland and thrust into bondage for forced labor, the slave was deprived of all legal rights. It was unlawful to teach him to read; he could be sold away from his family and friends at the whim of his master; and killing or maiming him was not a crime. The system of slavery brutalized and dehumanized both master and slave ....

The position of the Negro today in America is the tragic but inevitable consequence of centuries of unequal treatment. Measured by any benchmark of comfort or achievement, meaningful equality remains a distant dream for the Negro ....

It is more than a little ironic that, after several hundred years of class-based discrimination against Negroes, the Court is unwilling to hold that a class-based remedy for that discrimination is permissible .... It is unnecessary in 20th-century America to have individual Negroes demonstrate that they have been victims of racial discrimination; the racism of our society has been so pervasive that none, regardless of wealth or position, has managed to escape its impact. The experience of Negroes in America has been different in kind, not just in degree, from that of other ethnic groups. It is not merely the history of slavery alone but also that a whole people were marked as inferior by the law. And that mark has endured. The dream of America as the great melting pot has not been realized for the Negro; because of his skin color he never even made it into the pot.[7]

Nearly ten years later, when the nation was preparing to celebrate the bicentennial of the Constitution, Marshall once again tried to make clear the need to understand the true heritage of slavery and segregation. He gave a speech at the Annual Seminar of the San Francisco Patent and Trademark Law Association that caused considerable consternation among those who wanted to paint the bicentennial and the document it celebrated in glowing terms.[8] The fact that a justice of the United States Supreme Court was suggesting that the nation should use the occasion of the 200th anniversary to recognize the weaknesses of the Constitution, the efforts to address those deficiencies, and the work that remained to make real the values the nation was preparing to celebrate was startling to many and scandalous to some.

Marshall began by reminding his audience that when the framers began the Preamble to the Constitution by speaking of "We the people," they were not referring to everyone. Slaves were clearly not included, and women would not be fully included as voting citizens for more than one hundred thirty years after that. It took, he said, a civil war, the post-Civil War amendments, and a long-running battle in the courts for African Americans to begin to enjoy what white Americans had taken for granted. "Thus," he wrote:

> in this bicentennial year, we may not all participate in the festivities with flag-waving fervor. Some may more quietly commemorate the suffering, struggle, and sacrifice that has triumphed over much of what was wrong with the original document, and observe the anniversary with hopes not realized and promises not fulfilled. I plan to celebrate the bicentennial of the Constitution as a living document, including the Bill of Rights and the other amendments protecting individual freedoms and human rights.[9]

Justice Marshall worked diligently to make clear the importance not only of understanding the specific arguments over issues of civil rights law, but of placing those cases into the historical context of the United States. This chapter seeks to do both of those things. It will present the case law that evolved over time in cases of critical importance to African Americans and to civil rights more generally. Second, the cases are edited and presented in an effort to be clear about the relationship between the legal issues and the history that Marshall was convinced needed to be kept in mind.

The Heritage of Slavery and Racism

As Marshall explained, there is a need to come to grips with the heritage of slavery and racism along with the need to see the development of civil rights law. That requires first a recognition of the failure of the Constitution to attack slavery and its actual legalization of that practice for the first two decades of the new country's life. Second, it is important to read carefully not only the rulings but also the language of early judicial opinions that both supported slavery and demeaned African Americans. Third, it is important to consider the post-Civil War amendments that sought to address that sad heritage and deplorable judicial pronouncements.

Cracks in the Foundation: The Failure to Attack Slavery and its Legitimation in the Constitution

As Marshall said, there is no contradiction in recognizing the positive contributions of the Constitution, particularly as it has evolved over two hundred years, and simultaneously recognizing the serious damage that was done by the unwillingness or perhaps the perceived inability to address the problems of racism in the original document. Consider the problems that Marshall and other African Americans have recognized in the document, but that others have been unwilling to address.

Marshall started his criticism with the preamble, finding that "We the people" certainly did not include African Americans.[10] In defining those who were to be counted in the apportionment of representatives, Article I, §2, without using the term "slavery," made clear that each slave was to be counted only as "three-fifths" of a person.

Even worse than the humiliation of the three-fifths compromise was the fact that the Constitution legalized and even protected slavery. Article I, §9, cl. 1 provided that:

> The Migration or Importation of such Persons as any of the States now existing shall think proper to admit, shall not be prohibited by the Congress prior to the Year one thousand eight hundred and eight, but a Tax or duty may be imposed on such Importation, not exceeding ten dollars for each Person.

Slavery was to be protected for twenty years. Further, Article V provided for a process to amend the Constitution, but that same provision stated that "no Amendment which may be made prior to the Year One thousand eight hundred and eight shall in any Manner affect the first and fourth Clauses in the Ninth Section of the first Article." Even the extraordinary process of constitutional amendment during those twenty years could not stop it.

Just to make sure that the interests of slave owners were protected, Article IV, §2, cl. 3 added what was known as the fugitive slave clause, which provided that:

> No Person held to Service or Labour in one State, under the Laws thereof, escaping into another, shall, in Consequence of any Law or Regulation therein, be discharged from such Service or Labour, but shall be delivered up on Claim of the Party to whom such Service or Labour may be due.

Even after importation of slaves was outlawed, the slave trade continued until the Civil War.

Marshall knew that historians had argued that the Constitution was extremely progressive for its time and that the compromises made regarding slavery in the Constitution were essential for obtaining the agreement of Southern states. First, he said, the profits of slavery did not flow only to Southerners. "New Englanders engaged in the 'carrying trade' would profit from transporting slaves from Africa as well as goods produced in America by slave labor."[11] Second, "the effects of the framers' compromise have remained for generations. They arose from the contradiction between guaranteeing liberty and justice to all, and denying both to Negroes."[12] That legacy of injustice and exclusion would remain a bitter force in American life and public policy for generations.

Early Supreme Court Opinions Support Slavery and Send Terrible Messages to African Americans

One of the first policies that flowed from these flaws came when Congress implemented Article IV, §2 with the Fugitive Slave Act of 1793.[13] Some officials had tried to support escaped slaves by making it difficult for those who purported to own the slaves to take custody of them. Congress adopted the legislation to make it clearer how slave owners were to legally reclaim an escaped slave. Even so, states with strong abolitionist movements, like Pennsylvania, maintained state policies intended to make it difficult to take those then living in a free state back into slavery.

Prigg v. Pennsylvania

41 U.S. 539 (1842)

INTRODUCTION: In 1780 the state had enacted a law entitled "An act for the gradual abolition of slavery," which was amended in 1788. Pennsylvania's legislation placed burdens on those who wanted to assert that someone living in the state was a runaway slave so that he or she could be returned to another state, sometimes known as "personal liberty laws."[14] To counter these actions, Congress adopted the Fugitive Slave Act in 1793.

In 1826 Pennsylvania enacted a statute making it a felony to remove a person for the purposes of putting them into slavery.

In April 1837 Edward Prigg and an accomplice were tried for kidnapping a former slave, Margaret Morgan, and her children from Pennsylvania and delivering them in Maryland to the heir of her previous owner, one Margaret Ashmore. Morgan had been in Pennsylvania for some five years by that point. Prigg had previously been refused an order by a magistrate to enforce the federal fugitive slave law against Morgan under state statutes. Prigg was found guilty of kidnapping, but he challenged the state law in light of the Fugitive Slave Act and Article IV, §2 of the Constitution.
Justice Story wrote the opinion for the Court.

[Prigg has] contended that the statute of Pennsylvania is unconstitutional; first, because Congress has the exclusive power of legislation upon the subject-matter under the Constitution of the United States, and under the act of the 12th of February, 1793 ... which was passed in pursuance thereof; secondly, that if this power is not exclusive in Congress, still the concurrent power of the state legislatures is suspended by the actual exercise of the power by Congress; and thirdly, that if not suspended, still the statute of Pennsylvania ... is in direct collision with the act of Congress, and therefore is unconstitutional and void....

... [Art. IV, Section 2 of the Constitution provides:] "No person held to service or labour in one state under the laws thereof, escaping into another, shall in consequence of any law or regulation therein, be discharged from such service or labour; but shall be delivered up, on claim of the party to whom such service or labour may be due." The ... object of this clause was to secure to the citizens of the slaveholding states the complete right and title of ownership in their slaves, as property, in every state in the Union into which they might escape.... The full recognition of this right and title was indispensable to the security of this species of property in all the slaveholding states; and, indeed, was so vital to the preservation of their domestic interests and institutions, that it cannot be doubted that it constituted a fundamental article, without the adoption of which the Union could not have been formed. Its true design was to guard against the doctrines and principles prevalent in the non-slaveholding states, by preventing them from intermeddling with, or obstructing, or abolishing the rights of the owners of slaves.

[I]f the Constitution had not contained this clause, every non-slave-holding state in the Union would have been at liberty to have declared free all runaway slaves coming within its limits, and to have given them entire immunity and protection against the claims of their masters; a course which would have ... engendered perpetual strife between the different states. The clause was, therefore, of the last importance to the safety and security of the southern states.... The clause was accordingly adopted into the Constitution by the unanimous consent of the framers of it; a proof at once of its intrinsic and practical necessity....

The clause manifestly contemplates the existence of a positive, unqualified right on the part of the owner of the slave, which no state law or regulation can in any way qualify, regulate, control, or restrain. The slave is not to be discharged from service or labour, in consequence of any state law or regulation.... [T]he owner must, therefore, have the right to seize and repossess the slave, which the local laws of his own state confer upon him as property.... Upon this ground we have not the slightest hesitation in holding, that, under and in virtue of the Constitution, the owner of a slave is clothed with entire authority, in every state in the Union, to seize and recapture his slave, whenever he can do it without any breach of the peace, or any illegal violence....

But the clause of the Constitution does not stop here.... Many cases must arise in which, if the remedy of the owner were confined to the mere right of seizure and recaption, he would be utterly without any adequate redress. He may not be able to lay his hands upon the slave. He may not be able to enforce his rights against persons who either secrete or conceal, or withhold the slave. He may be restricted by local legislation as to the mode of proofs of his ownership; as to the Courts in which he shall sue, and as to the actions which he may bring; or the process he may use to compel the delivery of the slave. Nay, the local legislation may be utterly inadequate to furnish the appropriate redress, ... leaving the owner ... not that right which the Constitution designed to secure—a specific delivery and repossession of the slave, but a mere remedy in damages; and that perhaps against persons utterly insolvent or worthless....

And this leads us to the consideration of the other part of the clause, which implies at once a guaranty and duty. It says, "But he (the slave) shall be delivered up on claim of the party to whom such service or labour may be due.".... If, indeed, the Constitution guarantees the right, and if it requires the delivery upon the claim of the owner ... the natural inference certainly is, that the national government is clothed with the appropriate authority ... to enforce it....

Congress, then, may [give] effect to that right [and] prescribe the mode and extent in which it shall be applied.... [T]he act of the 12th of February, 1793 ... which ... provide[s], that when a person held to labour or service in any of the United States, shall escape into any other of the states or territories, the person to whom such labour or service may be due, his agent or attorney, is hereby empowered to seize or arrest such fugitive from labour, and take him or her before any judge of the Circuit or District Courts of the United States, residing or being within the state, or before any magistrate of a county, city, or town corporate, wherein such seizure or arrest shall be made; and upon proof to the satisfaction of such judge or magistrate ... that the person so seized or arrested, doth, under the laws of the state or territory from which he or she fled, owe service or labour to the person claiming him or her, it shall be the duty of such judge or magistrate, to give a certificate thereof of such claimant, his agent or attorney, which shall be sufficient warrant for removing the said fugitive from labour, to the state or territory from which he or she fled. The fourth section provides a penalty against any person who shall knowingly and willingly obstruct or hinder such claimant, his agent, or attorney, in so seizing or arresting such fugitive from labour, or rescue such fugitive from the claimant, or his agent, or attorney when so arrested, or who shall harbour or conceal such fugitive after notice that he is such; and it also saves to the person claiming such labour or service, his right of action for or on account of such injuries.

[T]his act may be truly said to cover the whole ground of the Constitution ... as to fugitive slaves.... If this be so, then it would seem ... that the legislation of Congress, if constitutional, must supersede all state legislation upon the same subject; and by necessary implication prohibit it. For if Congress have a constitutional power to regulate a particular subject, and they do actually regulate it in a given manner, ... it cannot be that the state legislatures have a right to interfere; and ... to prescribe additional regulations.... In such a case, the legislation of Congress, in what it does prescribe, manifestly indicates that it does not intend that there shall be any farther legislation to act upon the subject-matter....[15]

But it has been argued, that the act of Congress is unconstitutional, because it does not fall within the scope of any of the enumerated powers of legislation confided to that body.... [T]he argument [is] that although rights are exclusively secured by ... the national government, yet, unless the power to enforce these rights, or to execute these duties can be found among the express powers of legislation enumerated in the Constitution, they remain without any means of giving them effect by any act of Congress.... Such a limited construction of the Constitution has never yet been adopted as correct.... No one has ever supposed that Congress could, constitutionally, ... enact laws beyond the powers delegated to it by the Constitution; but it has, on various occasions, exercised powers which were necessary and proper as means to carry into effect rights expressly given, and duties expressly enjoined thereby....[16] We hold the act to be clearly constitutional in all its leading provisions....

The remaining question is, whether the power of legislation upon this subject is exclusive in the national government, or concurrent in the states.... In our opinion it is exclusive.... It is scarcely conceivable that the slaveholding states would have been satisfied with leaving to the legislation of the non-slaveholding states, a power of regulation ... which would ... amount to a power to destroy the rights of the owner.... On the other hand, construe the right of legislation as exclusive in Congress, and every evil, and every danger vanishes. The right and the duty are then co-extensive and uniform in remedy and operation throughout the whole Union. The owner has the same security, and the same remedial justice, and the same exemption from state regulation and control, through however many states he may pass with his fugitive slave in his possession....

[W]e are by no means to be understood in any manner whatsoever to doubt or to interfere with the police power belonging to the states.... We entertain no doubt whatsoever, that the states, in virtue of their general police power, possess full jurisdiction to arrest and restrain runaway slaves, and remove them from their borders, and otherwise to secure themselves against their depredations and evil example, as they certainly may do in cases of idlers, vagabonds, and paupers.... But such regulations can never be permitted to interfere with or to obstruct the just rights of the owner to reclaim his slave, derived from the Constitution of the United States; or with the remedies prescribed by Congress to aid and enforce the same.

Upon these grounds, we are of opinion that the act of Pennsylvania upon which this indictment is founded, is unconstitutional and void. It purports to punish as a public offence against that state, the very act of seizing and removing a slave by his master, which the Constitution of the United States was designed to justify and uphold.... [T]he judgment of the Supreme Court of Pennsylvania upon the special verdict found in the case, ought to have been that the said Edward Prigg was not guilty.[17]

Justice Taney wrote an opinion dissenting in part.

> I concur in the opinion pronounced by the Court, that the law of Pennsylvania ... is unconstitutional and void.... But ... [t]he opinion of the Court decides that the power to provide a remedy for this right is vested exclusively in Congress; and that all laws upon the subject passed by a state ... are null and void; even although they were intended, in good faith, to protect the owner in the exercise of his rights of property, and do not conflict in any degree with the act of Congress.... I dissent therefore, ... from that part of the opinion of the Court which denies the obligation and the right of the state authorities to protect the master, when he is endeavouring to seize a fugitive from his service, in pursuance of the right given to him by the Constitution of the United States.[18]

Justice McLean dissenting in part.

> ... The slave, as a sensible and human being, is subject to the local authority into whatsoever jurisdiction he may go. He is answerable under the laws for his acts, and he may claim their protection.... Being within the jurisdiction of a state, a slave bears a very different relation to it from that of mere property.

> ... The act of 1793 authorizes a forcible seizure of the slave by the master, not to take him out of the state, but to take him before some judicial officer within it. The act of Pennsylvania punishes a forcible removal of a coloured person out of the state. Now, here is no conflict between the law of the state and the law of Congress....

> It is very clear that no power to seize and forcibly remove the slave without claim is given by the act of Congress.... The slave is found in a state where every man, black or white, is presumed to be free; and this state, to preserve the peace of its citizens, and its soil and jurisdiction from acts of violence, has prohibited the forcible abduction of persons of colour. Does this law conflict with the Constitution? It clearly does not....

> It is a most important police regulation.... The offence consists in the abduction of a person of colour. The presumption of the state that the coloured person is free may be erroneous in fact; and if so, there can be no difficulty in proving it. But may not the assertion of the master be erroneous also; and if so, how is his act of force to be remedied? The coloured person is taken, and forcibly conveyed beyond the jurisdiction of the state. This force, not being authorized by the act of Congress nor by the Constitution, may be prohibited by the state.

The fight among the states over slavery continued on several fronts, including whether slavery would be permitted in states newly admitted to the United States. The Missouri Compromise of 1820 was an attempt to address this question.[19] Under its terms, Maine was admitted as a free state and Missouri as a slave state, but the territory acquired by the Louisiana purchase was to be free. The Supreme Court addressed the Missouri Compromise in a case that would forever mark a low point in American history because it not only contributed to the likelihood of a civil war as a result of its ruling with respect to the Compromise, but also because of the way that it characterized African Americans. The edited version is relatively lengthy because it is so important to understand not just the ruling in the case, but the message it sent to African Americans—a message, as Justice Marshall made clear, that could never be forgotten.

Dred Scott v. Sandford

60 U.S. 393 (1857)

INTRODUCTION: Illinois had been a free state ever since the passage of the Northwest Ordinance of 1787. The Missouri Compromise of 1820 established Missouri as a slave state, but the territories, later states, west of there that had been part of the Louisiana purchase would be free.

Dred Scott was a slave owned by Dr. Emerson, a U.S. Army surgeon. Emerson took Scott with him when he was reassigned from Missouri to Rock Island, Illinois. Some two years after that, Emerson took Scott with him when he was reassigned to Fort Snelling in what was then called Upper Louisiana, part of the territory acquired in the Louisiana Purchase. While there, Emerson acquired a slave named Harriet who married Dred Scott and had two children. In 1838 Emerson took all of them back to Missouri and eventually sold the family to Sandford, who was also an Army officer.

Scott and his family sued in Missouri courts for their freedom and alleged cruelty by Mrs. Emerson. In this first round of litigation, the state courts ruled that they were free, but that decision was later reversed by the Missouri Supreme Court in 1852. That represented a sharp departure from previous rulings in the state that had held that slaves in situations like Scott's were free.

Mrs. Emerson sold the Scotts to her brother, who was a resident of New York. Scott sued in federal court for their freedom, claiming that, because they had resided in Illinois, a free state, and in a part of the Louisiana Purchase territory that was designated as free under the Missouri Compromise of 1820, they were no longer slaves.

Chief Justice Taney wrote the opinion for the Court.

> There are two leading questions presented by the record: 1. Had the Circuit Court of the United States jurisdiction to hear and determine the case between these parties? And 2. If it had jurisdiction, is the judgment it has given erroneous or not?...
>
> The question is simply this: Can a negro, whose ancestors were imported into this country, and sold as slaves, become a member of the political community formed and brought into existence by the Constitution of the United States, and as such become entitled to all the rights, and privileges, and immunities, guaranteed by that instrument to the citizen? One of which rights is the privilege of suing in a court of the United States in the cases specified in the Constitution....
>
> The words "people of the United States" and "citizens" ... both describe the political body who, according to our republican institutions, form the sovereignty, and who hold the power and conduct the Government through their representatives. They are what we familiarly call the "sovereign people," and every citizen is one of this people, and a constituent member of this sovereignty. The question before us is, whether the class of persons described in [this case] compose a portion of this people, and are constituent members of this sovereignty? We think they are not, and that they are not included, and were not intended to be included, under the word "citizens" in the Constitution, and can therefore claim none of the rights and privileges which that instrument provides for and secures to citizens of the United States. On the contrary, they were at that time considered as a subordinate and inferior class of beings, who had been subjugated by the dominant race, and ... had no rights or privileges but such as those who held the power and the Government might choose to grant them....
>
> The question then arises, whether the provisions of the Constitution, in relation to the personal rights and privileges to which the citizen of a State should be

entitled, embraced the negro African race...? Does the Constitution of the United States act upon him whenever he shall be made free under the laws of a State, and raised there to the rank of a citizen, and immediately clothe him with all the privileges of a citizen in every other State, and in its own courts? The court think the affirmative of these propositions cannot be maintained. And if it cannot, the plaintiff ... could not be a citizen of the State of Missouri, within the meaning of the Constitution of the United States, and, consequently, was not entitled to sue in its courts.

[All persons] ... who were at the time of the adoption of the Constitution recognized as citizens in the several States, became also citizens of this new political body; but none other.... [T]he legislation and histories of the times, and the language used in the Declaration of Independence, show, that neither the class of persons who had been imported as slaves, nor their descendants, whether they had become free or not, were then acknowledged as a part of the people, nor intended to be included in the general words used in that memorable instrument.

They had for more than a century before been regarded as beings of an inferior order, and altogether unfit to associate with the white race, either in social or political relations; and so far inferior, that they had no rights which the white man was bound to respect; and that the negro might justly and lawfully be reduced to slavery for his benefit. He was bought and sold, and treated as an ordinary article of merchandise and traffic, whenever a profit could be made by it. This opinion was at that time fixed and universal in the civilized portion of the white race. It was regarded as an axiom in morals as well as in politics ... without doubting for a moment the correctness of this opinion.

And in no nation was this opinion more firmly fixed or more uniformly acted upon than by the English.... They not only seized them on the coast of Africa, and sold them or held them in slavery for their own use; but they took them as ordinary articles of merchandise to every country where they could make a profit on them, and were far more extensively engaged in this commerce than any other nation in the world.

The opinion thus entertained and acted upon in England was naturally impressed upon the colonies they founded on this side of the Atlantic. And, accordingly, a negro of the African race was regarded by them as an article of property, and held, and bought and sold as such, in every one of the thirteen colonies which united in the Declaration of Independence, and afterwards formed the Constitution of the United States....

The legislation of the different colonies furnishes positive and indisputable proof of this fact.... The province of Maryland [for example], in 1717, ... passed a law declaring "that if any free negro or mulatto intermarry with any white woman, or if any white man shall intermarry with any negro or mulatto woman, such negro or mulatto shall become a slave during life, excepting mulattoes born of white women, who, for such intermarriage, shall only become servants for seven years, to be disposed of as the justices of the county court, where such marriage so happens, shall think fit; to be applied by them towards the support of a public school within the said county. And any white man or white woman who shall intermarry as aforesaid, with any negro or mulatto, such white man or white woman shall become servants during the term of seven years, and shall be disposed of by the justices as aforesaid, and be applied to the uses aforesaid." [T]he other colonial law to which we refer was passed by Massachusetts in 1705 ... is entitled "An act for the better preventing of a spurious and mixed issue," &c.; and it provides, that "if any negro or mulatto shall presume to smite or strike any person of the English or other Christian nation, such negro or mulatto shall be severely whipped, at the discretion of the justices before whom the offender shall be convicted.".…

[T]hese laws … show, too plainly to be misunderstood, the degraded condition of this unhappy race. They were still in force when the Revolution began, and are a faithful index to the state of feeling towards the class of persons of whom they speak, and of the position they occupied throughout the thirteen colonies, in the eyes and thoughts of the men who framed the Declaration of Independence and established the State Constitutions and Governments. They show that a perpetual and impassable barrier was intended to be erected between the white race and the one which they had reduced to slavery, and governed as subjects with absolute and despotic power, and which they then looked upon as so far below them in the scale of created beings, that intermarriages between white persons and negroes or mulattoes were regarded as unnatural and immoral, and punished as crimes, not only in the parties, but in the person who joined them in marriage.… [N]o distinction … was made between the free negro or mulatto and the slave, but this stigma, of the deepest degradation, was fixed upon the whole race.…

Yet the men who framed this [Declaration of Independence] were great men.… They perfectly understood the meaning of the language they used, and how it would be understood by others; and they knew that it would not in any part of the civilized world be supposed to embrace the negro race, which, by common consent, had been excluded from civilized Governments and the family of nations, and doomed to slavery.… The unhappy black race were separated from the white … and were never thought of or spoken of except as property.…

This state of public opinion had undergone no change when the Constitution was adopted, as is equally evident from its provisions and language.… [T]here are two clauses in the Constitution which point directly and specifically to the negro race as a separate class of persons, and show clearly that they were not regarded as a portion of the people or citizens of the Government then formed. One of these clauses reserves to each of the thirteen States the right to import slaves until the year 1808, if it thinks proper.… And by the other provision the States pledge themselves to each other to maintain the right of property of the master, by delivering up to him any slave who may have escaped from his service, and be found within their respective territories.…

It is very true, that in that portion of the Union where the labor of the negro race was found to be unsuited to the climate and unprofitable to the master, but few slaves were held at the time of the Declaration of Independence; and when the Constitution was adopted, it had entirely worn out in one of them, and measures had been taken for its gradual abolition in several others. But this change had not been produced by any change of opinion in relation to this race … for some of the States, where it had ceased … were actively engaged in the slave trade, procuring cargoes on the coast of Africa, and transporting them for sale to those parts of the Union where their labor was found to be profitable, and suited to the climate and productions. And this traffic was openly carried on, and fortunes accumulated by it, without reproach from the people of the States where they resided.…

And we may here again refer, in support of this proposition, to the plain and unequivocal language of the laws of the several States.… The legislation of the States therefore shows … the inferior and subject condition of that race at the time the Constitution was adopted, and long afterwards.... It cannot be supposed that they intended to secure to them rights, and privileges, and rank, in the new political body throughout the Union, which every one of them denied within the limits of its own dominion....

The right of naturalization was ... granted to Congress to establish an [*sic*] uniform rule of naturalization is ... confined to persons born in a foreign country, under a foreign Government. It is not a power to raise to the rank of a citizen any one born in the United States, who, from birth or parentage, by the laws of the country, belongs to an inferior and subordinate class.... Congress might ... have authorized the naturalization of Indians, because they were aliens and foreigners. But, in their then untutored and savage state no one would have thought of admitting them as citizens in a civilized community.... Neither was it used with any reference to the African race imported into or born in this country; because Congress had no power to naturalize them....

Undoubtedly, a person may be a citizen, ... although he exercises no share of the political power, and is incapacitated from holding particular offices. Women and minors, who form a part of the political family, cannot vote; and when a property qualification is required to vote or hold a particular office, those who have not the necessary qualification cannot vote or hold the office, yet they are citizens.... [I]n some of the States of the Union foreigners not naturalized are allowed to vote. And the State may give the right to free negroes and mulattoes, but that does not make them citizens of the State, and still less of the United States....

The only two provisions [of the Constitution] which point to them and include them, treat them as property, and make it the duty of the Government to protect it.... The Government of the United States had no right to interfere for any other purpose but that of protecting the rights of the owner, leaving it altogether with the several States to deal with this race, whether emancipated or not, as each State may think justice, humanity, and the interests and safety of society, require....

Dred Scott was not a citizen of Missouri within the meaning of the Constitution of the United States, and not entitled as such to sue in its courts; and, consequently, that the Circuit Court had no jurisdiction of the case, and that the judgment on the plea in abatement is erroneous....

We proceed, therefore, to inquire whether the facts relied on by the plaintiff entitled him to his freedom.... [T]wo questions arise: 1. Was he, together with his family, free in Missouri by reason of the stay in the territory of the United States hereinbefore mentioned? And 2. If they were not, is Scott himself free by reason of his removal to Rock Island, in the State of Illinois, as stated in the above admissions?...

The [Missouri Compromise], upon which the plaintiff relies, declares that slavery and involuntary servitude, except as a punishment for crime, shall be forever prohibited in all that part of the territory ceded by France, under the name of Louisiana, which lies north of thirty-six degrees thirty minutes north latitude, and not included within the limits of Missouri. And the difficulty which meets us at the threshold of this part of the inquiry is, whether Congress was authorized to pass this law under any of the powers granted to it by the Constitution....

The counsel for the plaintiff has laid much stress upon that article in the Constitution which confers on Congress the power "to dispose of and make all needful rules and regulations respecting the territory or other property belonging to the United States;"[20] but, in the judgement of the court, that provision had no bearing on the present controversy, and the power there given, whatever it may be, is confined, and was intended to be confined, to ... the particular territory [ceded by Virginia], and cannot, by any just rule of interpretation, be extended to territory which the new Government might afterwards obtain from a foreign nation....

There is certainly no power given by the Constitution to the Federal Government to establish or maintain colonies bordering on the United States or at a distance, to be ruled and governed at its own pleasure; nor to enlarge its territorial limits in any way, except by the admission of new States.... The power to expand the territory of the United States by the admission of new States is plainly given.... [T]here is no express regulation in the Constitution defining the power which the General Government may exercise over the person or property of a citizen in a Territory thus acquired.... And when the Territory becomes a part of the United States, the Federal Government [takes over] with its powers over the citizen strictly defined, and limited by the Constitution.... [T]he Federal Government can exercise no power over his person or property, beyond what that instrument confers, nor lawfully deny any right which it has reserved....

These powers, and others, in relation to rights of person, which it is not necessary here to enumerate, are, in express and positive terms, denied to the General Government; and the rights of private property have been guarded with equal care. Thus the rights of property are united with the rights of person, and placed on the same ground by the fifth amendment to the Constitution, which provides that no person shall be deprived of life, liberty, and property, without due process of law. And an act of Congress which deprives a citizen of the United States of his liberty or property, merely because he came himself or brought his property into a particular Territory of the United States ... could hardly be dignified with the name of due process of law. And if the Constitution recognizes the right of property of the master in a slave, ... no tribunal, acting under the authority of the United States, whether it be legislative, executive, or judicial, has a right to draw such a distinction, or deny to it the benefit of the provisions and guarantees which have been provided for the protection of private property against the encroachments of the Government.

[T]he right of property in a slave is distinctly and expressly affirmed in the Constitution.... Upon these considerations, it is the opinion of the court that the act of Congress which prohibited a citizen from holding and owning property of this kind in the territory of the United States north of the line therein mentioned, is not warranted by the Constitution, and is therefore void; and that neither Dred Scott himself, nor any of his family, were made free by being carried into this territory....

But ... it is contended, on the part of the plaintiff, that he is made free by being taken to Rock Island, in the State of Illinois, ... and being so made free, he was not again reduced to a state of slavery by being brought back to Missouri.... [In] the case of *Strader et al. v. Graham* ... slaves had been taken from Kentucky to Ohio, with the consent of the owner, and afterwards brought back to Kentucky. And this court held that their status or condition, as free or slave, depended upon the laws of Kentucky, when they were brought back into that State.... As Scott was a slave when taken into the State of Illinois by his owner, and was there held as such, and brought back in that character, his status, as free or slave, depended on the laws of Missouri, and not of Illinois.

It has, however, been urged in the argument, that by the laws of Missouri he was free on his return.... [W]e are satisfied ... that Scott and his family upon their return were not free, but were, by the laws of Missouri, the property of the defendant; and that the Circuit Court of the United States had no jurisdiction [since] the plaintiff was a slave, and not a citizen....[21]

Justice McLean wrote a dissenting opinion.

There is no [basis in this case] which shows ... an inability in the plaintiff to sue in the Circuit Court. It does not allege that the plaintiff had his domicil in any other State, nor that he is not a free man in Missouri. He is averred to have had a negro ancestry, but this does not show that he is not a citizen of Missouri, within the meaning of the act of Congress authorizing him to sue in the Circuit Court. It has never been held necessary, to constitute a citizen within the act, that he should have the qualifications of an elector. Females and minors may sue in the Federal courts, and so may any individual who has a permanent domicil in the State under whose laws his rights are protected, and to which he owes allegiance.

Being born under our Constitution and laws, no naturalization is required, as one of foreign birth, to make him a citizen. The most general and appropriate definition of the term citizen is "a freeman." Being a freeman, and having his domicil in a State different from that of the defendant, he is a citizen within the act of Congress, and the courts of the Union are open to him....

In the argument, it was said that a colored citizen would not be an agreeable member of society. This is more a matter of taste than of law. Several of the States have admitted persons of color to the right of suffrage, and in this view have recognized them as citizens; and this has been done in the slave as well as the free States. On the question of citizenship, it must be admitted that we have not been very fastidious. Under the late treaty with Mexico, we have made citizens of all grades, combinations, and colors. The same was done in the admission of Louisiana and Florida. No one ever doubted, and no court ever held, that the people of these Territories did not become citizens under the treaty. They have exercised all the rights of citizens, without being naturalized under the acts of Congress....

We need not refer to the mercenary spirit which introduced the infamous traffic in slaves, to show the degradation of negro slavery in our country. This system was imposed upon our colonial settlements by the mother country, and it is due to truth to say that the commercial colonies and States were chiefly engaged in the traffic....

I prefer the lights of Madison, Hamilton, and Jay, as a means of construing the Constitution in all its bearings, rather than to look behind that period, into a traffic which is now declared to be piracy, and punished with death by Christian nations. I do not like to draw the sources of our domestic relations from so dark a ground. Our independence was a great epoch in the history of freedom; and while I admit the Government was not made especially for the colored race, yet many of them were citizens of the New England States, and exercised the rights of suffrage when the Constitution was adopted, and it was not doubted by any intelligent person that its tendencies would greatly ameliorate their condition.

Many of the States, on the adoption of the Constitution, or shortly afterward, took measures to abolish slavery within their respective jurisdictions; and it is a well-known fact that a belief was cherished by the leading men, South as well as North, that the institution of slavery would gradually decline, until it would become extinct. The increased value of slave labor, in the culture of cotton and sugar, prevented the realization of this expectation. Like all other communities and States, the South were influenced by ... their own interests.

But if we are to turn our attention to the dark ages of the world, why confine our view to colored slavery? On the same principles, white men were made slaves. All slavery has its origin in power, and is against right.

The power of Congress to establish Territorial Governments, and to prohibit the introduction of slavery therein, is the next point to be considered.... On the 13th of July, the Ordinance of 1787 was passed, "for the government of the United States territory northwest of the river Ohio," with but one dissenting vote. This instrument provided there should be organized in the territory not less than three nor more than five States, designating their boundaries. It was passed while the Federal Convention was in session, about two months before the Constitution was adopted by the Convention.... It provided for a temporary Government, as initiatory to the formation of State Governments. Slavery was prohibited in the territory.

Can any one suppose that the eminent men of the Federal Convention could have overlooked or neglected a matter so vitally important to the country, in the organization of temporary Governments for the vast territory northwest of the river Ohio? In the 3d section of the 4th article of the Constitution, they did make provision for the admission of new States, the sale of the public lands, and the temporary Government of the territory. Without a temporary Government, new States could not have been formed, nor could the public lands have been sold.

... The power to make all needful rules and regulations is a power to legislate.... But it is argued that ... the rules and regulations of Congress are limited to the disposition of lands and other property belonging to the United States. That this is not the true construction of the section appears from the fact that in the first line of the section "the power to dispose of the public lands" is given expressly, and, in addition, to make all needful rules and regulations....

Chief Justice Marshall, speaking for the court, said, in regard to the people of Florida, "they do not, however, participate in political power; they do not share in the Government till Florida shall become a State; in the mean time, Florida continues to be a Territory of the United States, governed by virtue of that clause in the Constitution which empowers Congress to make all needful rules and regulations respecting the territory...."

... If Congress should deem slaves or free colored persons injurious to the population of a free Territory ... they have the power to prohibit them from becoming settlers in it.... The prohibition of slavery north of thirty-six degrees thirty minutes, and of the State of Missouri, contained in the act admitting that State into the Union, was passed by a vote of 134, in the House of Representatives, to 42. Before Mr. Monroe signed the act, it was submitted by him to his Cabinet, and they held the restriction of slavery in a Territory to be within the constitutional powers of Congress. It would be singular, if in 1804 Congress had power to prohibit the introduction of slaves in Orleans Territory from any other part of the Union, under the penalty of freedom to the slave, if the same power, embodied in the Missouri compromise, could not be exercised in 1820.

... If Congress may establish a Territorial Government in the exercise of its discretion, it is a clear principle that a court cannot control that discretion. This being the case, I do not see on what ground the act is held to be void. It did not purport to forfeit property, or take it for public purposes. It only prohibited slavery; in doing which, it followed the ordinance of 1787....

In this case, a majority of the court have said that a slave may be taken by his master into a Territory of the United States, the same as a horse, or any other kind of property.... A slave is not a mere chattel. He bears the impress of his Maker, and is amenable to the laws of God and man; and he is destined to an endless existence.... Illinois has declared in the most solemn and impressive form that there shall be neither slavery nor involuntary servitude in that State, and that any slave brought into it, with a view of becoming a resident, shall be emancipated. And effect has been given to this provision of the Constitution by the decision of the Supreme Court of that State. With a full knowledge of these facts, a slave is brought from Missouri to Rock Island, in the State of Illinois, and is retained there as a slave for two years, and then taken to Fort Snelling, where slavery is prohibited by the Missouri compromise act, and there he is detained two years longer in a state of slavery. Harriet, his wife, was also kept at the same place four years as a slave....

[A] majority of my brethren have held that on their being returned to Missouri the status of slavery attached to them.... I can perceive no reason why the institutions of Illinois should not receive the same consideration as those of Missouri.... There is no evidence before us that Dred Scott and his family returned to Missouri voluntarily.... It would be a mockery of law and an outrage on his rights to coerce his return, and then claim that it was voluntary, and on that ground that his former status of slavery attached.... The Missouri court disregards the express provisions of an act of Congress and the Constitution of a sovereign State, both of which laws for twenty-eight years it had not only regarded, but carried into effect.... I think the judgment of the court below should be reversed.

Justice Curtis wrote a dissent.

... At the time of the ratification of the Articles of Confederation, all free native-born inhabitants of the States of New Hampshire, Massachusetts, New York, New Jersey, and North Carolina, though descended from African slaves, were not only citizens of those States, but such of them as had the other necessary qualifications possessed the franchise of electors, on equal terms with other citizens.... These colored persons were not only included in the body of "the people of the United States," by whom the Constitution was ordained and established, but in at least five of the States they had the power to act, and doubtless did act, by their suffrages, upon the question of its adoption. It would be strange, if we were to find in that instrument anything which deprived of their citizenship any part of the people of the United States who were among those by whom it was established.

I can find nothing in the Constitution which ... deprives of their citizenship any class of persons who were citizens of the United States at the time of its adoption, or who should be native-born citizens of any State after its adoption; nor any power enabling Congress to disfranchise persons born on the soil of any State, and entitled to citizenship of such State by its Constitution and laws....

I dissent, therefore, from that part of the opinion of the majority of the court, in which it is held that a person of African descent cannot be a citizen of the United States; and I regret I must go further, and dissent both from what I deem their assumption of authority to examine the constitutionality of the act of Congress commonly called the Missouri compromise act, and the grounds and conclusions announced in their opinion....

There was to be established by the Constitution a frame of government, under which the people of the United States and their posterity were to continue indefinitely. To take one of its provisions, the language of which is broad enough to extend throughout the existence of the Government, and embrace all territory belonging to the United States throughout all time ... and narrow it down to territory belonging to the United States when the Constitution was framed ... seems to me to be an interpretation as inconsistent with the nature and purposes of the instrument, as it is with its language, and I can have no hesitation in rejecting it....

But it is insisted, that whatever other powers Congress may have respecting the territory of the United States, the subject of negro slavery forms an exception. The Constitution declares that Congress shall have power to make "all needful rules and regulations" respecting the territory belonging to the United States. The assertion is, though the Constitution says all, it does not mean all—though it says all, without qualification, it means all except such as allow or prohibit slavery.... There is nothing in the context which qualifies the grant of power.... No other clause of the Constitution has been referred to at the bar, or has been seen by me, which imposes any restriction or makes any exception concerning the power of Congress to allow or prohibit slavery in the territory belonging to the United States....

For these reasons, I am of opinion that so much of the several acts of Congress as prohibited slavery and involuntary servitude within that part of the Territory of Wisconsin lying north of thirty-six degrees thirty minutes north latitude, and west of the river Mississippi, were constitutional and valid laws.

The Civil War Amendments: The Attempt to Establish Foundations for Equality

The *Dred Scott* ruling contributed to the growing likelihood of a bloody civil war. During that war, of course, Abraham Lincoln issued the Emancipation Proclamation, which provided: "That on the first day of January, in the year of our Lord one thousand eight hundred and sixty-three, all persons held as slaves within any State or designated part of a State, the people whereof shall then be in rebellion against the United States, shall be then, thenceforward, and forever free...."[22] Unfortunately, it purported to free those who were not then within the reach of federal authorities and did not free those slaves who were held in other states that were not then in conflict with the national government. That is not to suggest that the proclamation was not profoundly important in symbolic terms and had other effects, but it was a long way from a resolution of the issue of slavery. A more complete effort to achieve that goal came with the adoption of the Thirteenth, Fourteenth, and Fifteenth Amendments to the U.S. Constitution, often now referred to collectively as the Civil War Amendments.

The Thirteenth Amendment provided in its first section that: "Neither slavery nor involuntary servitude, except as a punishment for crime whereof the party shall have been duly convicted, shall exist within the United States, or any place subject to their jurisdiction." The second section added that: "Congress shall have power to enforce this article by appropriate legislation."

The Fifteenth Amendment was also brief, providing only that: "The right of citizens of the United States to vote shall not be denied or abridged by the United States or by any

State on account of race, color, or previous condition of servitude." Like the Thirteenth Amendment, this one also ensured that: "Congress shall have power to enforce this article by appropriate legislation."

The Fourteenth Amendment, by contrast, was far more complex and comprehensive. The first section contained a number of provisions that applied not just to former slaves but to all "persons."

> All persons born or naturalized in the United States and subject to the jurisdiction thereof, are citizens of the United States and of the State wherein they reside. No State shall make or enforce any law which shall abridge the privileges or immunities of citizens of the United States; nor shall any State deprive any person of life, liberty, or property, without due process of law; nor deny to any person within its jurisdiction the equal protection of the laws.

The discussion of citizenship at the beginning of the amendment was a direct rejection of the ruling in *Dred Scott*. The second was also to be a rejection of the statements in Taney's ruling that those with issues about their rights and liberties should look to their states for protection. The amendment repeated the language of Article IV that the privileges and immunities of American citizens were not to be abridged by the states. Finally, Section 1 provided for the now familiar due process and equal protection protections against state violations. Like the other two Civil War Amendments, it also provided in Section 5 that: "The Congress shall have power to enforce, by appropriate legislation, the provisions of this article."

The U.S. Supreme Court Limits the Ability of Congress to Redress Civil Rights Abuses

The post-Civil War reconstruction era was a tumultuous time, but it was clear that Congress was going to take action to implement the provisions of the Fourteenth Amendment. However, the Supreme Court promptly moved to limit the legislature's ability to ensure full rights for all Americans. It would also move in other ways to block the realization of full equality for African Americans, barriers that would last for decades.

Two cases in particular quickly limited protections that had seemed to be at hand following the adoption of the Fourteenth Amendment. The first of these was an initial challenge to the amendment that all but erased any meaningful application of its "privileges and immunities" clause. It was known as the *Slaughter-House Cases*, because it involved a set of challenges by slaughterhouses and meat processing businesses in New Orleans.

Slaughter-House Cases

83 U.S. 36 (1873)

INTRODUCTION: Louisiana enacted a law governing slaughterhouses and meat processing facilities in New Orleans as a regulatory policy to protect public health and safety. It created a monopoly under the control of a newly created corporation to be known as the Crescent City Live-Stock Landing Company. In the process, the law ordered the closing of all existing facilities in the city. New Orleans butchers challenged the law unsuccessfully in state courts. Their appeal to the U.S. Supreme Court on all the key provisions of the Thirteenth and Fourteenth Amendments marked the Court's first opinion interpreting those new additions to the Constitution.

Justice Miller wrote the opinion for the Court.

... This statute is denounced ... as creating a monopoly and conferring odious and exclusive privileges upon a small number of persons at the expense of the great body of the community of New Orleans [and] deprives ... the whole of the butchers of the city of the right to exercise their trade, the business...; and that the unrestricted exercise of the business of butchering is necessary to the daily subsistence of the population of the city....

The power here exercised by the legislature of Louisiana is ... one which has been ... always conceded to belong to the States.... This is called the police power.... [T]he authority of the legislature of Louisiana to pass the present statute is ample, unless some restraint in the exercise of that power be found in the constitution of that State or in the amendments to the Constitution of the United States....

The plaintiffs ... allege that the statute ... creates an involuntary servitude forbidden by the thirteenth article of amendment; That it abridges the privileges and immunities of citizens of the United States; That it denies to the plaintiffs the equal protection of the laws; and, That it deprives them of their property without due process of law; contrary to the provisions of the first section of the fourteenth article of amendment. This court is thus called upon for the first time to give construction to these articles.... [N]o one can fail to be impressed with the one pervading purpose found in them all...; we mean the freedom of the slave race, the security and firm establishment of that freedom, and the protection of the newly made freeman and citizen from the oppressions of those who had formerly exercised unlimited dominion over him....

The first section of the fourteenth article ... opens with a definition of citizenship— not only citizenship of the United States, but citizenship of the States.... [I]t had been held by this court, in the celebrated *Dred Scott* case ... that a man of African descent, whether a slave or not, was not and could not be a citizen of a State or of the United States.... To remove this difficulty primarily, and to establish a clear and comprehensive definition of citizenship which should declare what should constitute citizenship of the United States, and also citizenship of a State, the first clause of the first section was framed. "All persons born or naturalized in the United States, and subject to the jurisdiction thereof, are citizens of the United States and of the State wherein they reside."... [It] declares that persons may be citizens of the United States without regard to their citizenship of a particular State, and it overturns the *Dred Scott* decision....

[T]here is a citizenship of the United States, and a citizenship of a State, which are distinct from each other.... We think this distinction and its explicit recognition in this amendment of great weight in this argument, because the next paragraph of this same section ... speaks only of privileges and immunities of citizens of the United States, and does not speak of those of citizens of the several States.... Of the privileges and immunities of the citizen of the United States, and of the privileges and immunities of the citizen of the State, ... it is only the former which are placed by this clause under the protection of the Federal Constitution, and that the latter, whatever they may be, are not intended to have any additional protection by this paragraph of the amendment. [T]he latter must rest for their security and protection where they have heretofore rested.... [T]he entire domain of the privileges and immunities of citizens of the States, as above defined, lay within the constitutional and legislative power of the States, and without that of the Federal government....

Having shown that the privileges and immunities relied on in the argument are those which belong to citizens of the States as such, and that they are left to the State governments for security and protection ... we may hold ourselves excused from defining the privileges and immunities of citizens of the United States which no State can abridge, until some case involving those privileges may make it necessary to do so.

... Under the pressure of all the excited feeling growing out of the war, our statesmen have still believed that the existence of the States with powers for domestic and local government, including the regulation of civil rights—the rights of person and of property—was essential to the perfect working of our complex form of government, though they have thought proper to impose additional limitations on the States, and to confer additional power on that of the Nation.... The judgments of the Supreme Court of Louisiana in these cases are affirmed.

Justice Field wrote a dissenting opinion, joined by the Chief Justice and Justices Swayne and Bradley.

... The question presented is ... one of the gravest importance, not merely to the parties here, but to the whole country. It is ... whether the recent amendments to the Federal Constitution protect the citizens of the United States against the deprivation of their common rights by State legislation. In my judgment the fourteenth amendment does afford such protection, and was so intended by the Congress which framed and the States which adopted it....

The first clause of this amendment determines who are citizens of the United States.... It recognizes in express terms ... citizens of the United States, and it makes their citizenship dependent upon the place of their birth, or the fact of their adoption, and not upon the constitution or laws of any State or the condition of their ancestry. A citizen of a State is now only a citizen of the United States residing in that State. The fundamental rights, privileges, and immunities which belong to him as a free man and a free citizen, now belong to him as a citizen of the United States, and are not dependent upon his citizenship of any State.... They do not derive their existence from its legislation, and cannot be destroyed by its power.

The amendment ... assumes that there are ... privileges and immunities which belong of right to citizens as such, and ordains that they shall not be abridged by State legislation. If this inhibition has no reference to privileges and immunities of this character, but only refers, as held by the majority of the court in their opinion, to such privileges and immunities as were before its adoption specially designated in the Constitution or necessarily implied as belonging to citizens of the United States, it was a vain and idle enactment, which accomplished nothing....

What, then, are the privileges and immunities which are secured against abridgment by State legislation? In the first section of the Civil Rights Act Congress ... has there declared that they include the right "to make and enforce contracts, to sue, be parties and give evidence, to inherit, purchase, lease, sell, hold, and convey real and personal property, and to full and equal benefit of all laws and proceedings for the security of person and property." That act, it is true, was passed before the fourteenth amendment.... Accordingly, after its ratification, Congress re-enacted the act under the belief that whatever doubts may have previously existed of its validity, they were removed by the amendment.

The terms, privileges and immunities, are not new in the amendment; they were in the Constitution before the amendment was adopted. They are found in the second section of the fourth article.... The privileges and immunities designated [there] are those ... which of right belong to the citizens of all free governments, and they can be enjoyed under that clause by the citizens of each State in the several States upon the same terms and conditions as they are enjoyed by the citizens of the latter States.... It will not be pretended that under the fourth article of the Constitution any State could create a monopoly in any known trade or manufacture in favor of her own citizens, or any portion of them, which would exclude an equal participation in the trade or manufacture monopolized by citizens of other States....

The privileges and immunities of citizens of the United States, of every one of them, is secured against abridgment in any form by any State. The fourteenth amendment places them under the guardianship of the National authority.... This equality of right, with exemption from all disparaging and partial enactments, in the lawful pursuits of life, throughout the whole country, is the distinguishing privilege of citizens of the United States. To them, everywhere, all pursuits, all professions, all avocations are open without other restrictions than such as are imposed equally upon all others of the same age, sex, and condition.... The fourteenth amendment, in my judgment, makes it essential to the validity of the legislation of every State that this equality of right should be respected....[23]

Justice Swayne joined the dissents of Justices Field and Bradley but also wrote a separate dissent.

The thirteenth amendment..., the fourteenth..., and the fifteenth ... mark an important epoch in the constitutional history of the country. They trench directly upon the power of the States, and deeply affect those bodies.... Fairly construed these amendments may be said to rise to the dignity of a new Magna Charta....

The first section of the fourteenth amendment is alone involved in the consideration of these cases. No searching analysis is necessary to [illuminate] its meaning.... A citizen of a State is *ipso facto* a citizen of the United States.... "The privileges and immunities" of a citizen of the United States include, among other things, the fundamental rights of life, liberty, and property, and also the rights which pertain to him by reason of his membership of the Nation....

The construction adopted by the majority of my brethren is, in my judgment, much too narrow. It defeats ... the intent of those by whom the instrument was framed and of those by whom it was adopted.... By the Constitution, as it stood before the war, ample protection was given against oppression by the Union, but little was given against wrong and oppression by the States. That want was intended to be supplied by this amendment. Against the former this court has been called upon more than once to interpose.... But this arm of our jurisdiction is, in these cases, stricken down by the judgment just given. Nowhere, than in this court, ought the will of the nation, as thus expressed, to be more liberally construed or more cordially executed. This determination of the majority seems to me to lie far in the other direction. I earnestly hope that the consequences to follow may prove less serious and far-reaching than the minority fear they will be.

Another major opinion, known as the *Civil Rights Cases*, followed and blocked efforts by Congress to enact civil rights statutes expected to provide meaningful protection against discrimination in a variety of areas of American life. The constraints imposed by the Court in the *Civil Rights Cases* have never been reversed, and this precedent has continued to present limitations on civil rights efforts in the contemporary era, as Congress has sought to use the commerce power under Article I, §8 in order to enact civil rights legislation while avoiding the constraints of the 1883 *Civil Rights Cases.*

Civil Rights Cases
109 U.S. 3 (1883)

INTRODUCTION: This case consolidated several different actions, all of which were brought together to test the constitutional validity of the Civil Rights Act of 1875. The act provides in part:

> SEC. 1. That all persons within the jurisdiction of the United States shall be entitled to the full and equal enjoyment of the accommodations, advantages, facilities, and privileges of inns, public conveyances on land or water, theatres, and other places of public amusement; subject only to the conditions and limitations established by law, and applicable alike to citizens of every race and color, regardless of any previous condition of servitude.
>
> SEC. 2. That any person who shall violate the foregoing section by denying to any citizen, except for reasons by law applicable to citizens of every race and color, and regardless of any previous condition of servitude, the full enjoyment of any of the accommodations, advantages, facilities, or privileges in said section enumerated, or by aiding or inciting such denial, shall for every such offence forfeit and pay the sum of five hundred dollars to the person aggrieved thereby, to be recovered in an action of debt, with full costs; and shall also, for every such offence, be deemed guilty of a misdemeanor....

States asserted that these provisions represented an intrusion into the powers of the state, while defenders focused on the enforcement authority provided by the post-Civil War amendments.

Justice Bradley wrote the opinion for the Court.

> [I]t is the purpose of the law to declare that, in the enjoyment of the accommodations and privileges of inns, public conveyances, theatres, and other places of public amusement, no distinction shall be made between citizens of different race or color, or between those who have, and those who have not, been slaves. Its effect is to declare, that in all inns, public conveyances, and places of amusement, colored citizens, whether formerly slaves or not, and citizens of other races, shall have the same accommodations and privileges in all inns, public conveyances, and places of amusement as are enjoyed by white citizens; and vice versa. The second section makes it a penal offence in any person to deny to any citizen of any race or color, regardless of previous servitude, any of the accommodations or privileges mentioned in the first section.
>
> Has Congress constitutional power to make such a law? ... The power is sought, first, in the Fourteenth Amendment [which] declares that: "No State shall make or enforce any law which shall abridge the privileges or immunities of citizens of the United States; nor shall any State deprive any person of life, liberty, or property without due process of law; nor deny to any person within its jurisdiction the

equal protection of the laws." It is State action of a particular character that is prohibited. Individual invasion of individual rights is not the subject-matter of the amendment.... It nullifies and makes void all State legislation, and State action of every kind, which impairs the privileges and immunities of citizens of the United States, or which injures them in life, liberty or property without due process of law, or which denies to any of them the equal protection of the laws.... [T]he last section of the amendment invests Congress with power to enforce it by appropriate legislation.... To adopt appropriate legislation for correcting the effects of such prohibited State laws and State acts, and thus to render them effectually null, void, and innocuous.... It does not invest Congress with power to legislate upon subjects which are within the domain of State legislation; but to provide modes of relief against State legislation, or State action, of the kind referred to. It does not authorize Congress to create a code of municipal law for the regulation of private rights; but to provide modes of redress against the operation of State laws, and the action of State officers executive or judicial, when these are subversive of the fundamental rights specified in the amendment....

[U]ntil some State law has been passed, or some State action through its officers or agents has been taken, adverse to the rights of citizens sought to be protected by the Fourteenth Amendment, no legislation of the United States under said amendment, nor any proceeding under such legislation, can be called into activity.... Of course, legislation may, and should be, provided in advance to meet the exigency when it arises; but it should be adapted to the mischief and wrong which the amendment was intended to provide against; and that is, State laws, or State action of some kind, adverse to the rights of the citizen secured by the amendment.... In fine, the legislation which Congress is authorized to adopt in this behalf is not general legislation upon the rights of the citizen, but corrective legislation, that is, such as may be necessary and proper for counteracting such laws as the States may adopt or enforce ... or such acts and proceedings as the States may commit or take, and which, by the amendment, they are prohibited from committing or taking....

An inspection of [this] law shows that it makes no reference whatever to any supposed or apprehended violation of the Fourteenth Amendment on the part of the States.... It proceeds ... to declare that certain acts committed by individuals shall be deemed offences, and shall be prosecuted and punished by proceedings in the courts of the United States. It does not profess to be corrective of any constitutional wrong committed by the States.... In other words, it steps into the domain of local jurisprudence, and lays down rules for the conduct of individuals in society towards each other....

[C]ivil rights, such as are guaranteed by the Constitution against State aggression, cannot be impaired by the wrongful acts of individuals, unsupported by State authority.... The wrongful act of an individual, unsupported by any such authority, is simply a private wrong ... and may presumably be vindicated by resort to the laws of the State for redress.... Hence, in all those cases where the Constitution seeks to protect the rights of the citizen against discriminative and unjust laws of the State by prohibiting such laws, it is not individual offences, but abrogation and denial of rights, which it denounces, and for which it clothes the Congress with power to provide a remedy....

[T]he law in question cannot be sustained by any grant of legislative power made to Congress by the Fourteenth Amendment.... The law in question, without any reference to adverse State legislation on the subject, declares that all persons shall be entitled to equal accommodations and privileges of inns, public conveyances, and places of public amusement, and imposes a penalty upon any individual who shall deny to any citizen such equal accommodations and privileges. This is not corrective legislation.... What we have to decide is, whether such plenary power has been conferred upon Congress by the Fourteenth Amendment; and, in our judgment, it has not.

But the power of Congress ... is sought, in the second place, from the Thirteenth Amendment, which abolishes slavery.... The only question under the present head, therefore, is, whether the refusal to any persons of the accommodations of an inn, or a public conveyance, or a place of public amusement, by an individual, and without any sanction or support from any State law or regulation, does inflict upon such persons any manner of servitude, or form of slavery, as those terms are understood in this country? ... The Thirteenth Amendment has respect, not to distinctions of race, or class, or color, but to slavery....

Can the act of a mere individual, the owner of the inn, the public conveyance or place of amusement, refusing the accommodation, be justly regarded as imposing any badge of slavery or servitude upon the applicant...? [W]e are forced to the conclusion that such an act of refusal has nothing to do with slavery or involuntary servitude, and that if it is violative of any right of the party, his redress is to be sought under the laws of the State.... It would be running the slavery argument into the ground to make it apply to every act of discrimination which a person may see fit to make as to the guests he will entertain, or as to the people he will take into his coach or cab or car, or admit to his concert or theatre, or deal with in other matters of intercourse or business.... [No] authority for the passage of the law in question can be found in either the Thirteenth or Fourteenth Amendment of the Constitution....

Justice Harlan wrote a dissenting opinion.

The opinion in these cases proceeds, it seems to me, upon grounds entirely too narrow and artificial. I cannot resist the conclusion that the substance and spirit of the recent amendments of the Constitution have been sacrificed by a subtle and ingenious verbal criticism.... Constitutional provisions, adopted in the interest of liberty, and for the purpose of securing, through national legislation, if need be, rights inhering in a state of freedom, and belonging to American citizenship, have been so construed as to defeat the ends the people desired to accomplish.... [T]he court has departed from the familiar rule requiring, in the interpretation of constitutional provisions, that full effect be given to the intent with which they were adopted....

The Thirteenth Amendment, it is conceded, did something more than to prohibit slavery as an institution, resting upon distinctions of race, and upheld by positive law.... [I]t established and decreed universal civil freedom throughout the United States. But did the freedom thus established involve nothing more than exemption from actual slavery? ... Were the States against whose protest the institution was destroyed, to be left free ... to make or allow discriminations against that race, as such, in the enjoyment of those fundamental rights which by universal concession, inhere in a state of freedom? ...

That there are burdens and disabilities which constitute badges of slavery and servitude, and that the power to enforce by appropriate legislation the Thirteenth

Amendment may be exerted by legislation of a direct and primary character, for the eradication, not simply of the institution, but of its badges and incidents, are propositions which ought to be deemed indisputable. They lie at the foundation of the Civil Rights Act of 1866.... I hold that since slavery ... was the moving or principal cause of the adoption of that amendment, and since that institution rested wholly upon the inferiority, as a race, of those held in bondage, their freedom necessarily involved immunity from, and protection against, all discrimination against them, because of their race, in respect of such civil rights as belong to freemen of other races. Congress, therefore, under its express power to enforce that amendment, by appropriate legislation, may enact laws to protect that people against the deprivation, because of their race, of any civil rights granted to other freemen in the same State; and such legislation may be of a direct and primary character, operating upon States, their officers and agents, and, also, upon, at least, such individuals and corporations as exercise public functions and wield power and authority under the State. What has been said is sufficient to show that the power of Congress under the Thirteenth Amendment is not necessarily restricted to legislation against slavery as an institution upheld by positive law, but may be exerted to the extent, at least, of protecting the liberated race against discrimination, in respect of legal rights belonging to freemen, where such discrimination is based upon race....

Congress has not, in [addressing these places of public accommodation], entered the domain of State control and supervision. It does not ... assume to prescribe the general conditions and limitations under which inns, public conveyances, and places of public amusement, shall be conducted or managed. It simply declares, in effect, that since the nation has established universal freedom in this country, for all time, there shall be no discrimination, based merely upon race or color, in respect of the accommodations and advantages of public conveyances, inns, and places of public amusement.

I am of the opinion that such discrimination practised by corporations and individuals in the exercise of their public or quasi-public functions is a badge of servitude the imposition of which Congress may prevent under its power, by appropriate legislation, to enforce the Thirteenth Amendment; and, consequently, ... [the act] is not repugnant to the Constitution.

It remains now to consider these cases with reference to the power Congress has possessed since the adoption of the Fourteenth Amendment.... The theory of the opinion of the majority of the court ... is, that the general government cannot, in advance of hostile State laws or hostile State proceedings, actively interfere for the protection of any of the rights, privileges, and immunities secured by the Fourteenth Amendment.... The assumption that this amendment consists wholly of prohibitions upon State laws and State proceedings in hostility to its provisions, is unauthorized by its language. The first clause of the first section ... is of a distinctly affirmative character. In its application to the colored race, previously liberated, it created and granted, as well citizenship of the United States, as citizenship of the State in which they respectively resided. It introduced all of that race, whose ancestors had been imported and sold as slaves, at once, into the political community known as the "People of the United States." ...

The citizenship thus acquired, by that race ... may be protected, not alone by the judicial branch of the government, but by congressional legislation of a primary direct character; this, because the power of Congress is not restricted to the enforcement of prohibitions upon State laws or State action. It is, in terms distinct and positive, to enforce "the provisions of this article" of amendment; not simply those of a prohibitive character, but the provisions—all of the provisions—affirmative and prohibitive, of the amendment. It is, therefore, a grave misconception to suppose that the fifth section of the amendment has reference exclusively to express prohibitions upon State laws or State action....

This court has always given a broad and liberal construction to the Constitution, so as to enable Congress, by legislation, to enforce rights secured by that instrument. The legislation which Congress may enact, in execution of its power to enforce the provisions of this amendment, is such as may be appropriate to protect the right granted.... Under given circumstances, that which the court characterizes as corrective legislation might be deemed by Congress appropriate and entirely sufficient. Under other circumstances primary direct legislation may be required. But it is for Congress, not the judiciary, to say that legislation is appropriate—that is—best adapted to the end to be attained....

I insist that the national legislature may, without transcending the limits of the Constitution, do for human liberty and the fundamental rights of American citizenship, what it did, with the sanction of this court, for the protection of slavery and the rights of the masters of fugitive slaves. If fugitive slave laws, providing modes and prescribing penalties, whereby the master could seize and recover his fugitive slave, were legitimate exercises of an implied power to protect and enforce a right recognized by the Constitution, why shall the hands of Congress be tied, so that—under an express power, by appropriate legislation, to enforce a constitutional provision granting citizenship—it may not, by means of direct legislation, bring the whole power of this nation to bear upon States and their officers, and upon such individuals and corporations exercising public functions as assume to abridge, impair, or deny rights confessedly secured by the supreme law of the land? ...

My brethren say, that when a man has emerged from slavery, and by the aid of beneficent legislation has shaken off the inseparable concomitants of that state, there must be some stage in the progress of his elevation when he takes the rank of a mere citizen, and ceases to be the special favorite of the laws, and when his rights as a citizen, or a man, are to be protected in the ordinary modes by which other men's rights are protected. It is, I submit, scarcely just to say that the colored race has been the special favorite of the laws. The statute of 1875, now adjudged to be unconstitutional, is for the benefit of citizens of every race and color. What the nation, through Congress, has sought to accomplish in reference to that race, is—what had already been done in every State of the Union for the white race—to secure and protect rights belonging to them as freemen and citizens; nothing more.

Separate but Equal: The Start of a Half-Century Battle

The Supreme Court also erected a barrier to challenges to a variety of laws at the state level designed to ensure segregation in a wide range of fields of endeavor. These laws, collectively referred to as "Jim Crow" segregation, were in many important respects intended to twist the meaning of the equal protection of the laws so as to maintain inequality by pretending to create separate but supposedly equal facilities and services.[24] It was clear to any reasonable observer that while they were separate, they were most assuredly not equal. In any case, how could enforced segregation of the races ever be equal under the Constitution when it operated to demean and hold back African Americans? That was the core of the battle against the separate but equal doctrine that would continue until *Brown v. Board of Education* in 1954.

The origins of the separate but equal doctrine reach back well before the adoption of the Fourteenth Amendment and, indeed, before the Civil War. In fact, they grew out of a case decided by the supreme court of a Northern state, Massachusetts. For many Southerners there was a kind of cynical humor about the fact that the separate but equal doctrine arose in a Northern state. Of course, no such case could have arisen in a Southern state, since the African Americans were slaves and entitled to no rights to education comparable to those contested in the Massachusetts case.

Sarah C. Roberts v. City of Boston

59 Mass. (5 Cush. 198) 198 (1849)

INTRODUCTION: African American parents in Boston had petitioned the school board for the creation of schools for their children since they had been the victims of discrimination in the community. However, over time parents concluded that their children were being excluded from fine schools and kept in segregated and inadequate schools. In 1846 a group of African American parents petitioned the school authorities to eliminate segregated schools. The school committee not only refused, but concluded that: "the continuance of the separate schools for colored children, and the regular attendance of all such children upon the schools, is not only legal and just, but is best adapted to promote the education of that class of our population." Benjamin F. Roberts sued on behalf of his five year old daughter, Sarah C. Roberts, to challenge the segregated schools, claiming that she had been denied admission and would be forced to attend an all-black school further from her home when there was a excellent white school closer to their residence.

Chief Justice Shaw wrote the opinion for the Court.

> The plaintiff has commenced this action ... against the city of Boston, upon the statute of 1845, c. 214, which provides, that any child unlawfully excluded from public school instruction, in this commonwealth, shall recover damages therefor, in an action against the city or town, by which such public school instruction is supported. The question therefore is, whether, upon the facts agreed, the plaintiff has been unlawfully excluded from such instruction.... The plaintiff had access to a school, set apart for colored children, as well conducted in all respects, and as well fitted, in point of capacity and qualification of the instructors, to advance the education of children under seven years old, as the other primary schools; the objection is, that the schools thus open to the plaintiff are exclusively appropriated to colored children, and are at a greater distance from her home. Under these circumstances, the plaintiff [has not] been unlawfully excluded from public school instruction? ...
>
> The great principle, advanced by the ... plaintiff, is, that by the constitution and laws of Massachusetts, all persons without distinction of age or sex, birth or color, origin or condition, are equal before the law. This, as a broad general principle, such as ought to appear in a declaration of rights, is perfectly sound.... But, when this great principle comes to be applied to the actual and various conditions of persons in society, it will not warrant the assertion, that men and women are legally clothed with the same civil and political powers, and that children and adults are legally to have the same functions and be subject to the

same treatment; but only that the rights of all, as they are settled and regulated by law, are equally entitled to the paternal consideration and protection of the law, for their maintenance and security. What those rights are, to which individuals, in the infinite variety of circumstances by which they are surrounded in society, are entitled, must depend on laws adapted to their respective relations and conditions....

We must then resort to the law, to ascertain what are the rights of individuals, in regard to the schools.... The statute, after directing what length of time schools shall be kept in towns of different numbers of inhabitants and families, provides that the inhabitants shall annually choose, by ballot, a school committee, who shall have the general charge and superintendence of all the public schools in such towns.... The power of general superintendence vests a plenary authority in the committee to arrange, classify, and distribute pupils, in such a manner as they think best adapted to their general proficiency and welfare.... [W]hen this power is reasonably exercised, without being abused or perverted by colorable pretenses, the decision of the committee must be deemed conclusive. The committee, apparently upon great deliberation, have come to the conclusion, that the good of both classes of schools will be best promoted, by maintaining the separate primary schools for colored and for white children, and we can perceive no ground to doubt, that this is the honest result of their experience and judgment.

It is urged, that this maintenance of separate schools tends to deepen and perpetuate the odious distinction of caste, founded in a deep-rooted prejudice in public opinion. This prejudice, if it exists, is not created by law, and probably cannot be changed by law. Whether this distinction and prejudice, existing in the opinion and feelings of the community, would not be as effectually fostered by compelling colored and white children to associate together in the same schools, may well be doubted; at all events, it is a fair and proper question for the committee to consider and decide upon ... and we cannot say, that their decision upon it is not founded on just grounds of reason and experience, and in the result of a discriminating and honest judgment.

In 1896 the U.S. Supreme Court would refer to the argument from the *Roberts* case and use it to make "separate but equal" lawful under the U.S. Constitution in *Plessy v. Ferguson*.

Plessy v. Ferguson

163 U.S. 537 (1896)

INTRODUCTION: In 1890 Louisiana enacted a separate car act which required that railroad passengers be segregated into separate cars on the basis of race. The act made it a criminal violation for a person to refuse to sit in the segregated coach if asked. The separate car act was also referred to as an Act for the Comfort and Convenience of Passengers. A group decided to challenge the law and selected Homer Adolph Plessy to test its constitutionality. Plessy appeared to be white and was by his own account only one-eighth non-white. The group purchased a ticket for Mr. Plessy and then informed the railroad of his heritage.

Plessy refused to move from the whites only coach to the segregated coach when asked to do so. He was arrested and the ensuing legal action provided the basis for a challenge to the separate car law.

Justice Brown wrote the opinion for the Court.

The constitutionality of this act is attacked upon the ground that it conflicts both with the Thirteenth Amendment of the Constitution, abolishing slavery, and the Fourteenth Amendment, which prohibits certain restrictive legislation on the part of the States.

That it does not conflict with the Thirteenth Amendment, which abolished slavery and involuntary servitude, except as a punishment for crime, is too clear for argument. Slavery implies involuntary servitude—a state of bondage; the ownership of mankind as a chattel, or at least the control of the labor and services of one man for the benefit of another.... [I]n the *Civil Rights Cases*, ... [Justice Bradley wrote:] "It would be running the slavery argument into the ground to make it apply to every act of discrimination which a person may see fit to make as to the guests he will entertain, or as to the people he will take into his coach or cab or car, or admit to his concert or theatre, or deal with in other matters of intercourse or business." A statute which implies merely a legal distinction between the white and colored races—a distinction which is founded in the color of the two races, and which must always exist so long as white men are distinguished from the other race by color—has no tendency to destroy the legal equality of the two races, or reestablish a state of involuntary servitude....

By the Fourteenth Amendment ... the States are forbidden from making or enforcing any law which shall ... deny to any person within their jurisdiction the equal protection of the laws.... The object of the amendment was undoubtedly to enforce the absolute equality of the two races before the law, but in the nature of things it could not have been intended to abolish distinctions based upon color, or to enforce social, as distinguished from political equality, or a commingling of the two races upon terms unsatisfactory to either. Laws permitting, and even requiring, their separation in places where they are liable to be brought into contact do not necessarily imply the inferiority of either race to the other, and have been generally, if not universally, recognized as within the competency of the state legislatures in the exercise of their police power. The most common instance of this is connected with the establishment of separate schools for white and colored children, which has been held to be a valid exercise of the legislative power even by courts of States where the political rights of the colored race have been longest and most earnestly enforced.

[In] *Roberts v. City of Boston* the Supreme Judicial Court of Massachusetts held that the general school committee of Boston had power to make provision for the instruction of colored children in separate schools established exclusively for them, and to prohibit their attendance upon the other schools.... Similar laws have been enacted by Congress under its general power of legislation over the District of Columbia ... as well as by the legislatures of many of the States, and have been generally, if not uniformly, sustained by the courts....

Laws forbidding the intermarriage of the two races may be said in a technical sense to interfere with the freedom of contract, and yet have been universally recognized as within the police power of the State....

[E]very exercise of the police power must be reasonable, and extend only to such laws as are enacted in good faith for the promotion for the public good, and not for the annoyance or oppression of a particular class.... So far, then, as a conflict with the Fourteenth Amendment is concerned, the case reduces itself to the question whether the statute of Louisiana is a reasonable regulation, and with respect to this there must necessarily be a large discretion on the part of the legislature. In determining the question of reasonableness it is at liberty to act with reference to the established usages, customs and traditions of the people, and with a view to the promotion of their comfort, and the preservation of the public peace and good order. Gauged by this standard, we cannot say that a law which authorizes or even requires the separation of the two races in public conveyances is unreasonable, or more obnoxious to the Fourteenth Amendment than the acts of Congress requiring separate schools for colored children in the District of Columbia, the constitutionality of which does not seem to have been questioned, or the corresponding acts of state legislatures.

We consider the underlying fallacy of the plaintiff's argument to consist in the assumption that the enforced separation of the two races stamps the colored race with a badge of inferiority. If this be so, it is not by reason of anything found in the act, but solely because the colored race chooses to put that construction upon it.... If the two races are to meet upon terms of social equality, it must be the result of natural affinities, a mutual appreciation of each other's merits and a voluntary consent of individuals.... If one race be inferior to the other socially, the Constitution of the United States cannot put them upon the same plane. The judgment of the court below is, therefore, affirmed.

Justice Harlan wrote a dissenting opinion.

... In respect of civil rights, common to all citizens, the Constitution of the United States does not, I think, permit any public authority to know the race of those entitled to be protected in the enjoyment of such rights.... I deny that any legislative body or judicial tribunal may have regard to the race of citizens when the civil rights of those citizens are involved. Indeed, such legislation, as that here in question, is inconsistent not only with that equality of rights which pertains to citizenship, National and State, but with the personal liberty enjoyed by every one within the United States.

The Thirteenth Amendment does not permit the withholding or the deprivation of any right necessarily inhering in freedom. It not only struck down the institution of slavery as previously existing in the United States, but it prevents the imposition of any burdens or disabilities that constitute badges of slavery or servitude. It decreed universal civil freedom in this country.... [It] was followed by the Fourteenth Amendment, which added greatly to the dignity and glory of American citizenship, and to the security of personal liberty.... These two amendments, if enforced according to their true intent and meaning, will protect all the civil rights that pertain to freedom and citizenship. Finally, ... it was declared by the Fifteenth Amendment that "the right of citizens of the United States to vote shall not be denied or abridged by the United States or by any State on account of race, color or previous condition of servitude."

These notable additions to the fundamental law were welcomed by the friends of liberty throughout the world. They removed the race line from our governmental systems. They had, as this court has said, a common purpose, namely, to secure "to a race recently emancipated, a race that through many generations have been held in slavery, all the civil rights that the superior race enjoy." They declared, in legal effect, this court has further said, "that the law in the States shall be the same for the black as for the white; that all persons, whether colored or white, shall stand equal before the laws of the States, and, in regard to the colored race, for whose protection the amendment was primarily designed, that no discrimination shall be made against them by law because of their color."...

It was said in argument that the statute of Louisiana does not discriminate against either race, but prescribes a rule applicable alike to white and colored citizens. But this argument does not meet the difficulty. Everyone knows that the statute in question had its origin in the purpose, not so much to exclude white persons from railroad cars occupied by blacks, as to exclude colored people from coaches occupied by or assigned to white persons.... The thing to accomplish was, under the guise of giving equal accommodation for whites and blacks, to compel the latter to keep to themselves while traveling in railroad passenger coaches. No one would be so wanting in candor as to assert the contrary. The fundamental objection, therefore, to the statute is that it interferes with the personal freedom of citizens.... If a white man and a black man choose to occupy the same public conveyance on a public highway, it is their right to do so, and no government, proceeding alone on grounds of race, can prevent it without infringing the personal liberty of each.

It is one thing for railroad carriers to furnish, or to be required by law to furnish, equal accommodations.... It is quite another thing for government to forbid citizens of the white and black races from traveling in the same public conveyance, and to punish officers of railroad companies for permitting persons of the two races to occupy the same passenger coach. If a State can prescribe, as a rule of civil conduct, that whites and blacks shall not travel as passengers in the same railroad coach, why may it not so regulate the use of the streets of its cities and towns as to compel white citizens to keep on one side of a street and black citizens to keep on the other? ...

The white race deems itself to be the dominant race in this country.... But in view of the Constitution, in the eye of the law, there is in this country no superior, dominant, ruling class of citizens. There is no caste here. Our Constitution is color-blind, and neither knows nor tolerates classes among citizens. In respect of civil rights, all citizens are equal before the law. The humblest is the peer of the most powerful. The law regards man as man, and takes no account of his surroundings or of his color when his civil rights as guaranteed by the supreme law of the land are involved. It is, therefore, to be regretted that this high tribunal, the final expositor of the fundamental law of the land, has reached the conclusion that it is competent for a State to regulate the enjoyment by citizens of their civil rights solely upon the basis of race.

In my opinion, the judgment this day rendered will, in time, prove to be quite as pernicious as the decision made by this tribunal in the *Dred Scott* case.... The present decision, it may well be apprehended, will not only stimulate aggressions, more or less brutal and irritating, upon the admitted rights of colored citizens, but will encourage the belief that it is possible, by means of state enactments, to defeat the beneficent purposes which the people of the United States had in view when they adopted the recent amendments of the Constitution.... The destinies of the two races, in this country, are indissolubly linked together, and the interests of both require that the common government of all shall not permit the seeds of race hate to be planted under the sanction of law. What can more certainly arouse race hate, what more certainly create and perpetuate a feeling of distrust between these races, than state enactments, which, in fact, proceed on the ground that colored citizens are so inferior and degraded that they cannot be allowed to sit in public coaches occupied by white citizens? That, as all will admit, is the real meaning of such legislation as was enacted in Louisiana.

The sure guarantee of the peace and security of each race is the clear, distinct, unconditional recognition by our governments, National and State, of every right that inheres in civil freedom, and of the equality before the law of all citizens of the United States without regard to race.... The arbitrary separation of citizens, on the basis of race, while they are on a public highway, is a badge of servitude wholly inconsistent with the civil freedom and the equality before the law established by the Constitution. It cannot be justified upon any legal grounds....

The *Plessy* case was about segregation in transportation, but the Supreme Court later extended the *Plessy* doctrine to schools as well in *Cumming v. Richmond County Board of Education*[25] and *Gong Lum v. Rice*.[26]

Conclusion

Justice Marshall pressed Americans to concentrate on the need to work together toward a Constitution in daily life that would live up to the promise of the great rhetoric it presents, not only as it was issued originally, but with all of the important improvements made to it over its more 200 year history. That includes not only the document itself, but the interpretations and application of that law by the courts of the United States so that all Americans, including African Americans, can be confident that they truly enjoy the equal protection of the laws.

At the same time Marshall argued passionately that Americans need to understand what the failures of our Constitutional history have meant for the ways in which many African Americans understand their nation and place in it. To do that, it is necessary to pay attention to what our founding documents and our case law have said to and about African Americans as well as the way in which their experiences over time have been described by officials whose task it is to ensure equal protection of the laws. This chapter has provided some of the saddest of lessons about that history and meanest of rhetoric from the very justices whose responsibility it was to do equal justice to all.

Chapter 3 presents the long struggle forward from *Plessy* to *Brown v. Board of Education* and beyond. It is a story of struggle and endurance with many steps forward, but it is also a story that Justice Marshall was quick to say is far from successfully completed.

I. Issues for Policy and Practice

A. Given the limitations imposed by the Supreme Court's opinion in the *Civil Rights Cases*, what can Congress do, if anything, using the enforcement powers of Section 5 of the Fourteenth Amendment to address discriminatory behavior by anyone other than government?

B. What are the implications of a requirement that Congress use the power to regulate interstate commerce to get at discrimination by businesses or individuals?

C. On the one hand, there is a longstanding goal of ensuring that policies are "color blind," in the sense that they are not discriminatory. On the other, there is a need to ensure that resources can be targeted to get to those who need them, which often involves policies designed to assist African Americans, Latinos, Native Americans, women, or persons with disabilities. What policy design approaches are available to accomplish both goals?

II. Discussion Questions

A.   Justice Marshall pointed out that, although it is easy to point to the Southern states where slavery was officially sanctioned and so much a part of life as the problem for both slavery and ultimately racism in the United States, Northern states were fully engaged in the slave trade and profited greatly from it. Is this unwillingness to see that the whole country was implicated in the history of slavery part of the contemporary difficulty with coming to grips with racism?

B.   Contemporary slavery prosecutions (often presented as human trafficking cases) show once again that race and economics are tied together. Is there a willingness to address the demand for cheap products and services and a desire to assert class status that is supporting this modern version of the historic problem? If so, what can be done to address those tendencies?

C.   The ruling in the *Slaughter-House Cases* that effectively nullified the "privileges and immunities" clause of the Fourteenth Amendment has never been overturned. However, Article IV also contains a privileges and immunities clause, and that clause has actually been used to strike down some state and local action. (See *United Building & Construction Trades Council v. Camden*, 465 U.S. 208 (1984); *Hicklin v. Orbeck*, 437 U.S. 518 (1978).) What do you think are (or should be) the privileges and immunities of an American citizen protected by the Constitution?

D.   Justice Marshall wrote of Justice Powell's comments about getting beyond history and not focusing on race. How can we deal with the fact that some Americans take the attitude that historic discrimination has been outlawed and it is a new day, while for many African Americans, and persons of other ethnocultural or racial minorities for that matter, things have not changed in many important respects? In any case, they are quick to note, the historical trauma of a legacy of discrimination is still very real in people's lives. Are there steps that we can take to recognize that there have been some changes and yet there remains discrimination, and also the impact of a long history of unequal protection of law and policy?

E.   Most Americans have encountered references to the *Dred Scott* decision at some point in their education. Now you have read the language of that opinion and the way it describes African Americans, something few Americans have done. What are your reactions to it? What do you think are the reactions that African Americans are likely to have to it?

Notes

1 See Howard Ball, *A Defiant Life: Thurgood Marshall & the Persistence of Racism in America* (New York: Crown Publishers, 1998); Michael D. Davis and Hunter R. Clark, *Thurgood Marshall: Warrior at the Bar, Rebel on the Bench*, revised edn. (New York: Citadel Press, 1994).
2 See Richard Kluger, *Simple Justice* (New York: Vintage, 1977).
3 Thurgood Marshall, "Memorandum to the Conference," April 13, 1978, Brennan Papers, Box 465, pp. 1–3.
4 *Regents v. Bakke*, 438 U.S. 265 (1978).
5 See John C. Jeffries, Jr., *Justice Lewis F. Powell, Jr.* (New York: Charles Scribner's Sons, 1994), p. 688.
6 Discussed further in Phillip J. Cooper, *Battles on the Bench* (Lawrence, KS: University Press of Kansas, 1995), pp. 11–17.
7 *Regents v. Bakke*, 438 U.S., at pp. 387–401, Marshall, J., dissenting.
8 Thurgood Marshall, "The Constitution's Bicentennial: Commemorating the Wrong Document?" *Vanderbilt Law Review* 40 (No.6 1987): 1337–1342; Commentary: "Reflections on the Bicentennial of the United States Constitution," *Harvard Law Review* 101 (Nov. 1987): 1–5; "We the People: A Celebration of the Bicentennial of the United States Constitution," *Howard Law Journal* 30 (1987): 623–628.
9 Thurgood Marshall, "Commentary: Reflections on the Bicentennial of the United States Constitution," p. 5.

10 Id., at 2.

11 Id.

12 Id., at 3.

13 1 Stat. 302 (1793).

14 See Abraham L. Davis and Barbara Luck Graham, eds., *The Supreme Court, Race, and Civil Rights* (Thousand Oaks, CA: Sage Publications, 1995), p. 6.

15 NOTE: In contemporary case law, this concept is known as pre-emption and is justified under the supremacy clause of Article VI. Specifically, when Congress is said to have intended to occupy the whole field, leaving no room for the state legislatures to act, it is known as "field pre-emption." See *Arizona v. United States*, 132 S. Ct. 2492, 2501–02 (2012); *Crosby v. National Foreign Trade Council*, 530 U.S. 363, 372 (2000).

16 NOTE: The "necessary and proper" language is a reference is to Article I, §8, cl. 18 which provides that Congress shall have the power: "To make all Laws which shall be necessary and proper for carrying into Execution the foregoing Powers and all other Powers vested by this Constitution in the Government of the United States, or in any Department or Officer thereof."

17 NOTE: Justice Wayne wrote a concurring opinion omitted here.

18 NOTE: Justices Thompson and Daniel issued separate opinions similar to the argument advanced by Taney.

19 16 Stat. 545 (1820).

20 NOTE: He is referring here to Article IV, §3, cl. 2 of the Constitution.

21 NOTE: Justices Wayne, Nelson, Grier, Daniel, Campbell, and Carton issued concurring opinions that have been omitted here.

22 Abraham Lincoln, Emancipation Proclamation, January 1, 1863, http://avalon.law.yale.edu/19th_century/emancipa.asp, April 6, 2013.

23 NOTE: Justice Bradley also filed a dissenting opinion on grounds similar to Justice Field's opinion.

24 The term Jim Crow is commonly traced to a routine performed in the 1830s and 1840s by a popular white entertainer named Thomas Dartmouth Rice, who sang and danced in blackface, affecting a demeaning caricature of African Americans named Jim Crow. In that act he sang a song entitled "Jump Jim Crow." This term later was used to refer to a series of laws enacted in the South during the reconstruction era to ensure segregation and inequality among African Americans. See Ferris State University, "Jim Crow Museum: Origins of Jim Crow," www.ferris.edu/jimcrow/origins.htm, June 14, 2014.

25 175 U.S. 528 (1899).

26 275 U.S. 78 (1927).

References

Ball, Howard. *A Defiant Life: Thurgood Marshall & the Persistence of Racism in America.* New York: Crown Publishers, 1998.

Cooper, Phillip J. *Battles on the Bench.* Lawrence, KS: University Press of Kansas, 1995.

Davis, Abraham L. and Barbara Luck Graham, eds. *The Supreme Court, Race, and Civil Rights.* Thousand Oaks, CA: Sage Publications, 1995.

Davis, Michael D. and Hunter R. Clark. *Thurgood Marshall: Warrior at the Bar, Rebel on the Bench,* revised edn. New York: Citadel Press, 1994.

Jeffries, John C., Jr. *Justice Lewis F. Powell, Jr.* New York: Charles Scribner's Sons, 1994.

Kluger, Richard. *Simple Justice.* New York: Vintage, 1977.

Marshall, Thurgood. "The Constitution's Bicentennial: Commemorating the Wrong Document?" *Vanderbilt Law Review* 40 (No.6 1987): 1337–1342.

———. Commentary: "Reflections on the Bicentennial of the United States Constitution," *Harvard Law Review* 101 (Nov. 1987): 1–5.

———. "We the People: A Celebration of the Bicentennial of the United States Constitution—The Constitution: A Living Document," *Howard Law Journal* 30 (1987): 623–628.

3 From *Plessy* to *Brown*
Momentous Years in the Struggle

The effort to fight Jim Crow segregation and, ultimately, to obtain a firm ruling that separate but equal is inherently unequal was a fundamental part of the battle by African American civil rights leaders in the NAACP and the NAACP Legal Defense and Education Fund. Over time they were joined by many others in that effort. In order to get from the *Plessy* doctrine to *Brown v. Board of Education* and beyond, it was necessary to address several components of racism and also to develop legal standards to be applied in civil rights cases alleging discrimination under the equal protection clause of the Constitution. Indeed, it ultimately required a body of legislative enactments as well. An understanding of that process of civil rights development also requires some sensitivity to the political context in which that process unfolded.

This chapter begins with a treatment of the pieces of civil rights foundation-building that took place along the road from *Plessy* to *Brown*, the specific run-up to the *Brown* rulings, and the challenges in the decades that followed that important set of rulings. The judicial responses to those challenges and the changing political context have helped to shape the standards that apply today for determining whether there has been a civil rights violation based on race, and on other forms of classification as well.

Along the Way from *Plessy* to *Brown*

After the Court's ruling in *Plessy*, there were many challenges for African Americans, who had supposedly been declared free and equally protected citizens under the Constitution. The most obvious challenge was *Plessy*'s support for outright segregation by law. Although Charles Hamilton Houston, Walter White, Thurgood Marshall, and many other leaders intended to address that direct segregation, they realized there would be many particular battles that would have to be waged in order ultimately to prevail in that larger war. Some of these specifically involved African American lawyers and clients, while others concerned different groups, particularly those of Asian extraction.

Racism in Fact if Not on the Face of the Law

A history of discrimination directed at people of Chinese and Japanese ancestry in this country provided key rulings that played important roles in shaping not only their protections under the Constitution, but also contributed to the establishment of standards that were important in the fight led by NAACP LDF lawyers and others in the African American community, and later others such as Latinos. One of these cases, decided before *Plessy*, raised the very fundamental issue of laws that appeared fair on their face (as written), but that were administered in a discriminatory manner. It also provided a statement by the Supreme Court that the Fourteenth Amendment applied to all persons, and not just to citizens or a particular group.

Yick Wo v. Hopkins

118 U.S. 356 (1886)

INTRODUCTION: San Francisco enacted an ordinance that required owners of wooden laundries to obtain a special permit from the Board of Supervisors to operate their businesses based on a claim that special care was needed to prevent fire and safety hazards. However, although some eighty applicants who were not Chinese were granted such permits, the more than two hundred Chinese laundry owners who applied were denied permits with no clear indication of reasons for this denial. Many of the Chinese laundry operators involved were not U.S. citizens, but were legally in the U.S. and were specially protected by an 1880 treaty between the governments of China and the U.S. to ensure that Chinese in this country would receive the full protection of the laws. Yick Wo and Wo Lee were two of those who were convicted and jailed for violation of the ordinance.

Justice Matthews wrote the opinion for the Court.

> [T]he determination of the question whether the proceedings under these ordinances and in enforcement of them are in conflict with the Constitution and laws of the United States, necessarily involves the meaning of the ordinances.... We are consequently constrained, at the outset, to differ from the Supreme Court of California upon the real meaning of the ordinances in question. That court considered these ordinances as vesting in the board of supervisors a not unusual discretion in granting or withholding their assent to the use of wooden buildings as laundries, to be exercised in reference to the circumstances of each case, with a view to the protection of the public against the dangers of fire. [These ordinances confer] not a discretion to be exercised upon a consideration of the circumstances of each case, but a naked and arbitrary power to give or withhold consent, not only as to places, but as to persons. So that, if an applicant ... should, failing to obtain the requisite consent of the supervisors to the prosecution of his business, apply for redress by the judicial process ... it would be a sufficient answer for them to say that the law had conferred upon them authority to withhold their assent, without reason and without responsibility. The power given to them is ... purely arbitrary, and acknowledges neither guidance nor restraint....
>
> The ordinance drawn in question in the present case is of a very different character [from police power regulations previously upheld by this Court]. It does not prescribe a rule and conditions for the regulation of the use of property for laundry purposes, to which all similarly situated may conform. It allows without restriction the use for such purposes of buildings of brick or stone; but, as to wooden buildings, constituting nearly all those in previous use, it divides the owners or occupiers into two classes, not having respect to their personal character and qualifications for the business, nor the situation and nature and adaptation of the buildings themselves, but merely by an arbitrary line, on one side of which are those who are permitted to pursue their industry by the mere will and consent of the supervisors, and on the other those from whom that consent is withheld, at their mere will and pleasure....
>
> The Fourteenth Amendment to the Constitution is not confined to the protection of citizens. It says: "Nor shall any State deprive any person of life, liberty, or property without due process of law; nor deny to any person within its jurisdiction the equal protection of the laws." These provisions are universal in their application, to all persons within the territorial jurisdiction, without regard to any differences

of race, of color, or of nationality; and the equal protection of the laws is a pledge of the protection of equal laws.... The questions we have to consider and decide in these cases, therefore, are to be treated as involving the rights of every citizen of the United States equally with those of the strangers and aliens who now invoke the jurisdiction of the court....

When we consider the nature and the theory of our institutions of government, the principles upon which they are supposed to rest, and review the history of their development, we are constrained to conclude that they do not mean to leave room for the play and action of purely personal and arbitrary power. Sovereignty itself is, of course, not subject to law, for it is the author and source of law; but in our system, while sovereign powers are delegated to the agencies of government, sovereignty itself remains with the people, by whom and for whom all government exists and acts. And the law is the definition and limitation of power.... For, the very idea that one man may be compelled to hold his life, or the means of living, or any material right essential to the enjoyment of life, at the mere will of another, seems to be intolerable in any country where freedom prevails, as being the essence of slavery itself....

[These] cases present the ordinances in actual operation, and the facts shown establish an administration directed so exclusively against a particular class of persons as to warrant and require the conclusion, that, whatever may have been the intent of the ordinances as adopted, they are applied by the public authorities charged with their administration, and thus representing the State itself, with a mind so unequal and oppressive as to amount to a practical denial by the State of that equal protection of the laws which is secured to the petitioners, as to all other persons, by the broad and benign provisions of the Fourteenth Amendment to the Constitution of the United States. Though the law itself be fair on its face and impartial in appearance, yet, if it is applied and administered by public authority with an evil eye and an unequal hand, so as practically to make unjust and illegal discriminations between persons in similar circumstances, material to their rights, the denial of equal justice is still within the prohibition of the Constitution....

The present cases, as shown by the facts disclosed in the record, are within this class. It appears that both petitioners have complied with every requisite, deemed by the law or by the public officers charged with its administration, necessary for the protection of neighboring property from fire, or as a precaution against injury to the public health. No reason whatever, except the will of the supervisors, is assigned why they should not be permitted to carry on, in the accustomed manner, their harmless and useful occupation, on which they depend for a livelihood. And while this consent of the supervisors is withheld from them and from two hundred others who have also petitioned, all of whom happen to be Chinese subjects, eighty others, not Chinese subjects, are permitted to carry on the same business under similar conditions. The fact of this discrimination is admitted. No reason for it is shown, and the conclusion cannot be resisted, that no reason for it exists except hostility to the race and nationality to which the petitioners belong, and which in the eye of the law is not justified. The discrimination is, therefore, illegal, and the public administration which enforces it is a denial of the equal protection of the laws and a violation of the Fourteenth Amendment of the Constitution. The imprisonment of the petitioners is, therefore, illegal, and they must be discharged.

Viewed from a contemporary perspective, the *Yick Wo* opinion seems to state truisms well understood by anyone. However, it was and is an extremely important precedent-setting ruling that continues to be cited regularly in civil rights cases. It is a reminder that what so many Americans would view as fundamental constitutional norms have had to be established in cases brought by people who suffered from discrimination. And persons of Asian descent have indeed suffered a long and terrible history of discrimination in the United States.

Wartime Challenges: Upholding Government Action but Establishing the Concept of Strict Judicial Scrutiny

Another set of cases focused on Asian Americans came with the onset of World War II. These cases spoke not only to those victimized by the racism of the time, but established a principle fundamental to the battle against race discrimination. The principle is that race-based actions are inherently suspect and laws or practices that classify people on the basis of race call for rigorous scrutiny by the courts. They also offered warnings for the future that, unfortunately, have not been heeded.

As the *Yick Wo* case demonstrated, there had been a history of discrimination against Asians and Asian Americans in the United States, and particularly on the West Coast. When World War II broke out, the president issued Executive Order 9066[1] authorizing the exclusion of persons from areas under military control if national security required it. The order:

> authorize[d] and direct[ed] the Secretary of War, and the Military Commanders whom he may from time to time designate, whenever he or any designated Commander deems such action necessary or desirable, to prescribe military areas in such places and of such extent as he or the appropriate Military Commander may determine, from which any or all persons may be excluded, and with respect to which, the right of any person to enter, remain in, or leave shall be subject to whatever restrictions the Secretary of War or the appropriate Military Commander may impose in his discretion.

Congress adopted war powers legislation that retroactively approved the order and other actions taken by the president. It also made it a misdemeanor to disobey the orders of military authorities acting under presidential direction.[2]

General J.L. DeWitt issued proclamations designating large areas to be covered by Executive Order 9066 and ordered first a curfew on persons of Japanese ancestry, then the exclusion of those persons from the covered areas, and ultimately their removal to concentration camps that were euphemistically referred to as relocation centers. The curfew was upheld in June 1943 by the U.S. Supreme Court in *Hirabayashi v. United States*.[3] The next case to reach the court involved the removal orders.

Korematsu v. United States

323 U.S. 214 (1944)

INTRODUCTION: The facts, as the Court understood them at the time, are provided in the opinion. It would later become clear that those "facts" were anything but factual and that government officials had intentionally deceived the Court. (This will be explained later.)

Justice Black wrote the opinion for the Court.

> The petitioner, an American citizen of Japanese descent, was convicted in a federal district court for remaining in San Leandro, California, a "Military Area,"

contrary to Civilian Exclusion Order No. 34 of the Commanding General of the Western Command, U.S. Army, which directed that after May 9, 1942, all persons of Japanese ancestry should be excluded from that area. No question was raised as to petitioner's loyalty to the United States....

It should be noted, to begin with, that all legal restrictions which curtail the civil rights of a single racial group are immediately suspect. That is not to say that all such restrictions are unconstitutional. It is to say that courts must subject them to the most rigid scrutiny. Pressing public necessity may sometimes justify the existence of such restrictions; racial antagonism never can.

In the instant case prosecution of the petitioner was begun by information charging violation of an Act of Congress, of March 21, 1942, 56 Stat. 173, which provides that

"... whoever shall enter, remain in, leave, or commit any act in any military area or military zone prescribed, under the authority of an Executive order of the President, by the Secretary of War, or by any military commander designated by the Secretary of War [shall] ... be guilty of a misdemeanor [and] liable to a fine of not to exceed $5,000 or to imprisonment for not more than one year, or both, for each offense."

Exclusion Order No. 34, which the petitioner knowingly ... violated, was one of a number of military orders and proclamations, all of which were substantially based upon Executive Order No. 9066.... That order ... declared that "the successful prosecution of the war requires every possible protection against espionage and against sabotage to national-defense material, national-defense premises, and national-defense utilities...."

[A] curfew order, which like the exclusion order here was promulgated pursuant to Executive Order 9066, subjected all persons of Japanese ancestry in prescribed West Coast military areas to remain in their residences from 8 p.m. to 6 a.m.... In *Hirabayashi v. United States* ... [we] upheld the curfew order as an exercise of the power of the government to take steps necessary to prevent espionage and sabotage in an area threatened by Japanese attack.

In the light of ... *Hirabayashi* ..., we are unable to conclude that it was beyond the war power of Congress and the Executive to exclude those of Japanese ancestry from the West Coast war area at the time they did. True, exclusion from the area in which one's home is located is a far greater deprivation than constant confinement to the home from 8 p.m. to 6 a.m. Nothing short of apprehension by the proper military authorities of the gravest imminent danger to the public safety can constitutionally justify either. But exclusion from a threatened area, no less than curfew, has a definite and close relationship to the prevention of espionage and sabotage. The military authorities, charged with the primary responsibility of defending our shores, concluded that curfew provided inadequate protection and ordered exclusion. They did so ... in accordance with Congressional authority to the military to say who should, and who should not, remain in the threatened areas....

Here, as in *Hirabayashi* "... we cannot reject as unfounded the judgment of the military authorities and of Congress that there were disloyal members of that population, whose number and strength could not be precisely and quickly ascertained. We cannot say that the war-making branches of the Government did not have ground for believing that in a critical hour such persons could not readily be isolated and separately dealt with, and constituted a menace to the national defense and safety, which demanded that prompt and adequate measures be taken to guard against it."

Like curfew, exclusion of those of Japanese origin was deemed necessary because of the presence of an unascertained number of disloyal members of the group, most of whom we have no doubt were loyal to this country.... In the instant case, temporary exclusion of the entire group was rested by the military on the same ground. The judgment that exclusion of the whole group was for the same reason a military imperative answers the contention that the exclusion was in the nature of group punishment based on antagonism to those of Japanese origin. That there were members of the group who retained loyalties to Japan has been confirmed by investigations made subsequent to the exclusion. Approximately five thousand American citizens of Japanese ancestry refused to swear unqualified allegiance to the United States and to renounce allegiance to the Japanese Emperor, and several thousand evacuees requested repatriation to Japan.

We uphold the exclusion order.... In doing so, we are not unmindful of the hardships imposed by it upon a large group of American citizens.... But hardships are part of war, and war is an aggregation of hardships. All citizens alike, both in and out of uniform, feel the impact of war in greater or lesser measure. Citizenship has its responsibilities as well as its privileges, and in time of war the burden is always heavier. Compulsory exclusion of large groups of citizens from their homes, except under circumstances of direst emergency and peril, is inconsistent with our basic governmental institutions. But when under conditions of modern warfare our shores are threatened by hostile forces, the power to protect must be commensurate with the threatened danger.

Some of the members of the Court are of the view that evacuation and detention in an Assembly Center were inseparable.... It is said that we are dealing here with the case of imprisonment of a citizen in a concentration camp solely because of his ancestry, without evidence or inquiry concerning his loyalty and good disposition towards the United States. Our task would be simple, our duty clear, were this a case involving the imprisonment of a loyal citizen in a concentration camp because of racial prejudice. Regardless of the true nature of the assembly and relocation centers—and we deem it unjustifiable to call them concentration camps with all the ugly connotations that term implies—we are dealing specifically with nothing but an exclusion order. To cast this case into outlines of racial prejudice, without reference to the real military dangers which were presented, merely confuses the issue. Korematsu was not excluded from the Military Area because of hostility to him or his race. He was excluded because we are at war with the Japanese Empire, because the properly constituted military authorities feared an invasion of our West Coast and felt constrained to take proper security measures, because they decided that the military urgency of the situation demanded that all citizens of Japanese ancestry be segregated from the West Coast temporarily, and finally, because Congress, reposing its confidence in this time of war in our military leaders—as inevitably it must—determined that they should have the power to do just this.... We cannot—by availing ourselves of the calm perspective of hindsight—now say that at that time these actions were unjustified.

Justice Frankfurter issued a concurring opinion.

> ... [W]e have had recent occasion to quote approvingly the statement of former Chief Justice Hughes that the war power of the Government is "the power to wage war successfully." ... Therefore, the validity of action under the war power must be judged wholly in the context of war.... The respective spheres of action of military authorities and of judges are of course very different. But within their sphere, military authorities are no more outside the bounds of obedience to the Constitution than are judges within theirs.... If a military order such as that under review does not transcend the means appropriate for conducting war, such action by the military is as constitutional as would be any authorized action by the Interstate Commerce Commission within the limits of the constitutional power to regulate commerce.... To find that the Constitution does not forbid the military measures now complained of does not carry with it approval of that which Congress and the Executive did. That is their business, not ours.

Justice Murphy wrote a dissent.[4]

> This exclusion of "all persons of Japanese ancestry, both alien and non-alien," from the Pacific Coast area on a plea of military necessity in the absence of martial law ought not to be approved. Such exclusion goes over "the very brink of constitutional power" and falls into the ugly abyss of racism.
>
> In dealing with matters relating to the prosecution and progress of a war, we must accord great respect and consideration to the judgments of the military authorities who are on the scene and who have full knowledge of the military facts. The scope of their discretion must, as a matter of necessity and common sense, be wide. And their judgments ought not to be overruled lightly by those whose training and duties ill-equip them to deal intelligently with matters so vital to the physical security of the nation. At the same time, however, it is essential that there be definite limits to military discretion, especially where martial law has not been declared. Individuals must not be left impoverished of their constitutional rights on a plea of military necessity that has neither substance nor support....
>
> The judicial test of whether the Government, on a plea of military necessity, can validly deprive an individual of any of his constitutional rights is whether the deprivation is reasonably related to a public danger that is so "immediate, imminent, and impending" as not to admit of delay and not to permit the intervention of ordinary constitutional processes to alleviate the danger. *United States v. Russell.*... Civilian Exclusion Order No. 34, banishing from a prescribed area of the Pacific Coast "all persons of Japanese ancestry ... clearly does not meet that test. Being an obvious racial discrimination, the order deprives all those within its scope of the equal protection of the laws as guaranteed by the Fifth Amendment. It further deprives these individuals of their constitutional rights to live and work where they will, to establish a home where they choose and to move about freely. In excommunicating them without benefit of hearings, this order also deprives them of all their constitutional rights to procedural due process. Yet no reasonable relation to an "immediate, imminent, and impending" public danger is evident to support this racial restriction which is one of the most sweeping and complete deprivations of constitutional rights in the history of this nation in the absence of martial law.
>
> ... In adjudging the military action taken in light of the then apparent dangers, we must not erect too high or too meticulous standards; it is necessary only that the action have some reasonable relation to the removal of the dangers of invasion,

sabotage and espionage. But the exclusion, either temporarily or permanently, of all persons with Japanese blood in their veins has no such reasonable relation. And that relation is lacking because the exclusion order necessarily must rely for its reasonableness upon the assumption that all persons of Japanese ancestry may have a dangerous tendency to commit sabotage and espionage and to aid our Japanese enemy in other ways....

That this forced exclusion was the result in good measure of this erroneous assumption of racial guilt rather than bona fide military necessity is evidenced by the Commanding General's Final Report on the evacuation from the Pacific Coast area. In it he refers to all individuals of Japanese descent as "subversive," as belonging to "an enemy race" whose "racial strains are undiluted," and as constituting "over 112,000 potential enemies ... at large today" along the Pacific Coast. In support of this blanket condemnation of all persons of Japanese descent, however, no reliable evidence is cited to show that such individuals were generally disloyal, or had generally so conducted themselves in this area as to constitute a special menace to defense installations or war industries, or had otherwise by their behavior furnished reasonable ground for their exclusion as a group....

The main reasons relied upon by those responsible for the forced evacuation, therefore, do not prove a reasonable relation between the group characteristics of Japanese Americans and the dangers of invasion, sabotage and espionage. The reasons appear, instead, to be largely an accumulation of much of the misinformation, half-truths and insinuations that for years have been directed against Japanese Americans by people with racial and economic prejudices—the same people who have been among the foremost advocates of the evacuation. A military judgment based upon such racial and sociological considerations is not entitled to the great weight ordinarily given the judgments based upon strictly military considerations. Especially is this so when every charge relative to race, religion, culture, geographical location, and legal and economic status has been substantially discredited by independent studies made by experts in these matters.

... [T]o infer that examples of individual disloyalty prove group disloyalty and justify discriminatory action against the entire group is to deny that under our system of law individual guilt is the sole basis for deprivation of rights. Moreover, this inference, which is at the very heart of the evacuation orders, has been used in support of the abhorrent and despicable treatment of minority groups by the dictatorial tyrannies which this nation is now pledged to destroy. To give constitutional sanction to that inference in this case ... is to adopt one of the cruelest of the rationales used by our enemies to destroy the dignity of the individual and to encourage and open the door to discriminatory actions against other minority groups in the passions of tomorrow.

No adequate reason is given for the failure to treat these Japanese Americans on an individual basis by holding investigations and hearings to separate the loyal from the disloyal, as was done in the case of persons of German and Italian ancestry.... Moreover, there was no adequate proof that the Federal Bureau of Investigation and the military and naval intelligence services did not have the espionage and sabotage situation well in hand during this long period. Nor is there any denial of the fact that not one person of Japanese ancestry was accused or convicted of espionage or sabotage after Pearl Harbor while they were still free, a fact which is some evidence of the loyalty of the vast majority of these individuals and of the effectiveness of the established methods of combatting these evils. It seems incredible that under these circumstances it would have been impossible to hold loyalty hearings for the mere 112,000 persons involved—or at least for the 70,000 American citizens—especially when a large part of this number represented children and elderly men and women. Any inconvenience that may have accompanied an attempt to conform to procedural due process cannot be said to justify violations of constitutional rights of individuals.

I dissent, therefore, from this legalization of racism. Racial discrimination in any form and in any degree has no justifiable part whatever in our democratic way of life. It is unattractive in any setting but it is utterly revolting among a free people who have embraced the principles set forth in the Constitution of the United States. All residents of this nation are kin in some way by blood or culture to a foreign land. Yet they are primarily and necessarily a part of the new and distinct civilization of the United States. They must accordingly be treated at all times as the heirs of the American experiment and as entitled to all the rights and freedoms guaranteed by the Constitution.

Justice Jackson wrote a dissenting opinion.

Korematsu was born on our soil, of parents born in Japan. The Constitution makes him a citizen of the United States by nativity and a citizen of California by residence. No claim is made that he is not loyal to this country. There is no suggestion that apart from the matter involved here he is not law-abiding and well disposed. Korematsu, however, has been convicted of an act not commonly a crime. It consists merely of being present in the state whereof he is a citizen, near the place where he was born, and where all his life he has lived....

A citizen's presence in the locality, however, was made a crime only if his parents were of Japanese birth. Had Korematsu been one of four—the others being, say, a German alien enemy, an Italian alien enemy, and a citizen of American-born ancestors, convicted of treason but out on parole—only Korematsu's presence would have violated the order. The difference between their innocence and his crime would result, not from anything he did, said, or thought, different than they, but only in that he was born of different racial stock.

Now, if any fundamental assumption underlies our system, it is that guilt is personal and not inheritable. Even if all of one's antecedents had been convicted of treason, the Constitution forbids its penalties to be visited upon him, for it provides that "no attainder of treason shall work corruption of blood, or forfeiture except during the life of the person attainted." But here is an attempt to make an otherwise innocent act a crime merely because this prisoner is the son of parents as to whom he had no choice, and belongs to a race from which there is no way to resign....

When an area is so beset that it must be put under military control at all, the paramount consideration is that its measures be successful, rather than legal. The armed services must protect a society, not merely its Constitution.... Defense measures will not, and often should not, be held within the limits that bind civil authority in peace.... But if we cannot confine military expedients by the Constitution, neither would I distort the Constitution to approve all that the military may deem expedient. That is what the Court appears to be doing, whether consciously or not. I cannot say, from any evidence before me, that the orders of General DeWitt were not reasonably expedient military precautions, nor could I say that they were. But even if they were permissible military procedures, I deny that it follows that they are constitutional. If, as the Court holds, it does follow, then we may as well say that any military order will be constitutional and have done with it.

The limitation under which courts always will labor in examining the necessity for a military order are illustrated by this case.... So the Court, having no real evidence before it, has no choice but to accept General DeWitt's own unsworn, self-serving statement, untested by any cross-examination, that what he did was reasonable. And thus it will always be when courts try to look into the reasonableness of a military order....

A military order, however unconstitutional, is not apt to last longer than the military emergency.... But once a judicial opinion rationalizes such an order to show that it conforms to the Constitution, or rather rationalizes the Constitution to show that the Constitution sanctions such an order, the Court for all time has validated the principle of racial discrimination in criminal procedure and of transplanting American citizens. The principle then lies about like a loaded weapon ready for the hand of any authority that can bring forward a plausible claim of an urgent need.... A military commander may overstep the bounds of constitutionality, and it is an incident. But if we review and approve, that passing incident becomes the doctrine of the Constitution. There it has a generative power of its own, and all that it creates will be in its own image. Nothing better illustrates this danger than does the Court's opinion in this case....

My duties as a justice as I see them do not require me to make a military judgment as to whether General DeWitt's evacuation and detention program was a reasonable military necessity. I do not suggest that the courts should have attempted to interfere with the Army in carrying out its task. But I do not think they may be asked to execute a military expedient that has no place in law under the Constitution. I would reverse the judgment and discharge the prisoner.

The *Korematsu* ruling has never been directly overturned by the Supreme Court. In later years, it became clear that the government had not provided truthful information to the Supreme Court and had indeed withheld critical evidence that demonstrated that DeWitt's actions were not driven by a well-founded concern for national security but out of blatant racism.

The evidence of the misconduct surfaced more than three decades later. Ms. Aiko Herzig-Yoshinaga was a professional researcher working between June 1981 and June 1983 for the Commission on Wartime Relocation and Internment of Civilians that was investigating the events of the exclusion and imprisonment of people of Japanese ancestry in preparation for a national apology for those events. She later testified that it was not until the end of 1982 that she happened upon the only surviving original copy of the report prepared by General DeWitt that supported his curfew, exclusion and relocation proclamations, and was able to recognize that there were obvious discrepancies between it and the later official version. That led to the discovery that Defense Department officials had ordered the creation of a dramatically revised report and had tried to destroy all copies of DeWitt's original—but one remained. It was the revised report that was ultimately distributed and used in the litigation.

The Commission ultimately found from this and other evidence that there was no military necessity that warranted the exclusion and detention of ethnic Japanese. It found that: "broad historical causes which shaped these decisions [exclusion and detention] were race prejudice, war hysteria and a failure of political leadership." As a result, "a grave injustice was done to American citizens and resident aliens of Japanese ancestry who, without individual review or any probative evidence against them, were excluded, removed and detained by the United States during World War II."[5]

When this information surfaced, Hirabayashi and Korematsu returned to the federal district court, seeking a writ of *coram nobis* that would overturn their wartime misdemeanor convictions for violations of DeWitt's orders on grounds that the government's conduct had resulted in a manifest injustice in their cases. Sadly, the Department of Justice opposed the writ in 1984, even as it accepted the accuracy of the facts as presented by Korematsu and Hirabayashi.

Judge Patel for the Northern District of California granted a writ of *coram nobis* to correct the manifest injustice done by the conviction of Fred Korematsu based on the deliberate withholding and falsification of evidence. He found that not only was the report switched, but:

> The record is replete with protestations of various Justice Department officials that the government had the obligation to advise the courts of the contrary facts and opinions.... In fact, several Department of Justice officials pointed out to their superiors and others the 'wilful historical inaccuracies and intentional falsehoods' contained in the DeWitt Report.[6]

The judge also found that:

> Omitted from the reports presented to the courts was information possessed by the Federal Communications Commission, the Department of the Navy, and the Justice Department which directly contradicted General DeWitt's statements. Thus, the court had before it a selective record.[7]

The U.S. Court of Appeals for the Ninth Circuit ultimately ordered the *coram nobis* writ for Hirabayashi in the case he brought in the U.S. District Court in Washington. In so doing, the court pointed out with obvious disdain that the United States had argued:

> that on the basis of the record before it, the Supreme Court should have known both that General DeWitt was a racist, and that he made no military judgment of emergency. The government asks us to hold, therefore, that the Supreme Court probably would have reached the same erroneous result even if the government had not suppressed the evidence and had accurately represented to the Court the basis of General DeWitt's decision.

The Court pointed out that, at the time, the proof of the racism was withheld from the Supreme Court, although Hirabayashi certainly alleged that racism was at the heart of the problem. It was only decades later the Ninth Circuit panel noted, that "the information now in the public record constitutes objective and irrefutable proof of the racial bias that was the cornerstone of the internment orders."[8]

In the end, Judge Patel warned:

> *Korematsu* remains on the pages of our legal and political history. As a legal precedent it is now recognized as having very limited application. As historical precedent it stands as a constant caution that in times of war or declared military necessity our institutions must be vigilant in protecting constitutional guarantees. It stands as a caution that in times of distress the shield of military necessity and national security must not be used

to protect governmental actions from close scrutiny and accountability. It stands as a caution that in times of international hostility and antagonisms our institutions, legislative, executive and judicial, must be prepared to exercise their authority to protect all citizens from the petty fears and prejudices that are so easily aroused.[9]

Sadly, after the attack on the World Trade Center on September 11, 2001, that warning and the history of World War II-era discrimination were forgotten as the Justice Department rounded up Americans of Middle Eastern ancestry, or in some cases those who were thought to be committed adherents of Islam. Immigration laws were manipulated to support these detentions so as to hold persons against whom there was no evidence or even a charge of violations of national security law.[10] They were held in conditions that even the Inspector General of the Department of Justice found were extreme and unacceptable.[11] So-called no-fly lists were created by federal authorities with no due process before listing someone and, initially at least, no process for challenging one's inclusion on the list. The Bush administration created by military order a detention facility at Guantánamo Bay, Cuba to house persons the administration termed illegal combatants, produced a completely unacceptable process for determining whether they were illegal combatants, and attempted to use the offshore location as a device to avoid the availability of the writ of habeas corpus—all actions eventually struck down by the U.S. Supreme Court.[12] Still, the administration fought to hold persons against whom there was no serious claim of illegal combatant status.[13] While there was repeated argument that many individuals were not being held because of their ethnocultural heritage or religion, the record is obviously to the contrary. So extreme were some of the behaviors in the early months after the attacks that the U.S. Commission on Civil Rights magazine carried a cover photo of a young man, apparently of Middle Eastern extraction, with the crosshairs of a rifle scope superimposed over his face together with the words "Flying While Arab."[14]

As unlikely as it seems, there was one part of the Supreme Court's opinion in the *Korematsu* case that would be extremely important for years to come for civil rights advocates. Justice Black began his discussion of the legal argument in the case by warning that: "It should be noted, to begin with, that all legal restrictions which curtail the civil rights of a single racial group are immediately suspect."[15] This established the standard that when a government classifies on the basis of race, its actions do not enjoy the normal presumption of validity, but are immediately suspect and are therefore subject to strict judicial scrutiny. As such, the burden of proof shifts to the government to demonstrate a compelling interest. That judgment would be the foundation for arguments alleging racial discrimination from that day to the present.

Foundation Rulings in the Attack on Racial Discrimination

There were other important problems to be addressed along the way from *Plessy* to *Brown* and beyond that addressed important pieces of the problem of discrimination and how to judge cases in which it is alleged to exist. These were cases apart from the specific series of education cases brought as part of the strategy to take on *Plessy*.

One of the strategies that came into early use by those who sought to maintain a segregated society was to employ various mechanisms to maintain segregated housing. If successful, such efforts would, without stating such an intention directly, effectively ensure segregated schools, employment, and community facilities and programs. The most direct tactic for that purpose was zoning, a practice of local establishment of land use controls that was used, in part, to exclude immigrants, the poor, and those of disfavored religious and ethnic affiliations from upper class areas.[16] Alternatively, private citizens used racially restrictive covenants to be enforced by courts to maintain segregation. In order to challenge these restrictive covenants, it was critical to obtain a ruling from the Supreme Court that, although the agreements may be purely private matters, any attempt to use the courts to enforce them constituted state action prohibited by the equal protection clause.

The Supreme Court struck down racial zoning in 1917,[17] long before it announced in 1926 that the zoning authority was, as a general matter, a valid exercise of the police powers of the state under the Tenth Amendment in *Euclid v. Ambler Realty*.[18] The unanimous opinion in *Buchanan v. Warley*,[19] focused on the due process rights of the white seller in the case who was prohibited from concluding the sale because the purchaser was African American, but it also clearly was intended to apply to African American property owners as well.

But the effort to maintain segregated residential areas was not yet over. The focus turned to the use of racially restrictive covenants attached to property deeds to do indirectly what the zoning efforts had tried to accomplish directly.[20] The mechanism of enforcement would be first to keep the African American purchaser out of the property on grounds of a purchase in violation of the covenant and, second, to render the seller vulnerable to suits by each of the other neighbors who were signatories to the covenant. The claim was that this was a purely private matter and that there was no state action involved. The NAACP LDF, headed by Thurgood Marshall, would have none of that sophistry and fought the issue back to the Supreme Court. In the process, Marshall and his colleagues were able to establish the larger point that the use of the courts to enforce actions that would be illegal if taken by government was itself state action in violation of the Constitution.

Shelley v. Kraemer

334 U.S. 1 (1948)

INTRODUCTION: This opinion addresses two cases involving racially restrictive covenants that were included with the title on real estate. They contained provisions such as the following: "[T]he ... property is hereby restricted.... [N]o part of [the] property ... shall be ... occupied by any person not of the Caucasian race, it being intended hereby to restrict the use of said property ... against the occupancy as owners or tenants ... by people of the Negro or Mongolian Race." One of the cases came from St. Louis and involved the Shelley family, who purchased a piece of property in a community covered by the restrictive covenant noted above and only found out about the problem after they had concluded the purchase. Other property owners in the community sued to prevent the couple from possessing the property. The Supreme Court of Missouri upheld the agreement and rejected constitutional challenges to its enforcement. The other case originated in Michigan. The Michigan Supreme Court upheld a court order to an African American family to vacate the property in which they lived and that decision was appealed to the U.S. Supreme Court.

Chief Justice Vinson wrote the opinion for the Court.

> These cases present ... questions relating to the validity of court enforcement of private agreements ... which have as their purpose the exclusion of persons of designated race or color from the ownership or occupancy of real property.... [Petitioners contend] that judicial enforcement of the restrictive agreements in these cases has violated rights guaranteed to petitioners by the Fourteenth Amendment.... Specifically, petitioners urge that they have been denied the equal protection of the laws, deprived of property without due process of law, and have been denied privileges and immunities of citizens of the United States....[21]

I. [In] *Corrigan v. Buckley*, 271 U.S. 323 (1926) ... [t]his Court concluded that since the inhibitions of the constitutional provisions invoked apply only to governmental action, as contrasted to action of private individuals, there was no showing that the covenants, which were simply agreements between private property owners, were invalid. [The present cases] raise the question of the validity, not of the private agreements as such, but of the judicial enforcement of those agreements....

The restrictions of these agreements ... are directed toward a designated class of persons and seek to determine who may and who may not own or make use of the properties for residential purposes. The excluded class is defined wholly in terms of race or color....

It cannot be doubted that among the civil rights intended to be protected from discriminatory state action by the Fourteenth Amendment are the rights to acquire, enjoy, own and dispose of property.... This Court has given specific recognition to the same principle. *Buchanan v. Warley*.... It is likewise clear that restrictions on the right of occupancy of the sort sought to be created by the private agreements in these cases could not be squared with the requirements of the Fourteenth Amendment if imposed by state statute or local ordinance.... In [*Buchanan*] a unanimous Court declared unconstitutional the provisions of a city ordinance which denied to colored persons the right to occupy houses in blocks in which the greater number of houses were occupied by white persons, and imposed similar restrictions on white persons with respect to blocks in which the greater number of houses were occupied by colored persons. "The Fourteenth Amendment ... operate[s] to qualify and entitle a colored man to acquire property without state legislation discriminating against him solely because of color."

In *Harmon v. Tyler*, 273 U.S. 668 (1927), a unanimous court ... declared invalid an ordinance which forbade any Negro to establish a home on any property in a white community or any white person to establish a home in a Negro community, "except on the written consent of a majority of the persons of the opposite race inhabiting such community or portion of the City to be affected." ...

But the present cases, unlike those just discussed, do not involve action by state legislatures or city councils. Here the particular patterns of discrimination and the areas in which the restrictions are to operate, are determined, in the first instance, by the terms of agreements among private individuals. Participation of the State consists in the enforcement of the restrictions so defined. The crucial issue with which we are here confronted is whether this distinction removes these cases from the operation of the prohibitory provisions of the Fourteenth Amendment.

Since the decision of this Court in the *Civil Rights Cases*, ... the principle has become firmly embedded in our constitutional law that the action inhibited by the first section of the Fourteenth Amendment is only such action as may fairly be said to be that of the States. That Amendment erects no shield against merely private conduct, however discriminatory or wrongful....

We conclude, therefore, that the restrictive agreements standing alone cannot be regarded as violative of any rights guaranteed to petitioners by the Fourteenth Amendment. So long as the purposes of those agreements are effectuated by voluntary adherence to their terms, it would appear clear that there has been no action by the State and the provisions of the Amendment have not been violated.... But here there was more. These are cases in which the purposes of the agreements were secured only by judicial enforcement by state courts of the restrictive terms of the agreements....

II. That the action of state courts and judicial officers in their official capacities is to be regarded as action of the State within the meaning of the Fourteenth Amendment, is a proposition which has long been established by decisions of this Court.... In the *Civil Rights Cases* ... this Court pointed out that the Amendment makes void "State action of every kind" which is inconsistent with the guaranties therein contained, and extends to manifestations of "State authority in the shape of laws, customs, or judicial or executive proceedings." ...

One of the earliest applications of the prohibitions contained in the Fourteenth Amendment to action of state judicial officials occurred in cases in which Negroes had been excluded from jury service in criminal prosecutions by reason of their race or color. These cases demonstrate, also, the early recognition by this Court that state action in violation of the Amendment's provisions is equally repugnant to the constitutional commands whether directed by state statute or taken by a judicial official in the absence of statute. *Strauder v. West Virginia*, 100 U.S. 303 (1880).... [F]rom the time of the adoption of the Fourteenth Amendment until the present, it has been the consistent ruling of this Court that the action of the States to which the Amendment has reference includes action of state courts and state judicial officials....

III. [W]e are called upon to consider whether enforcement by state courts of the restrictive agreements in these cases may be deemed to be the acts of those States; and, if so, whether that action has denied these petitioners the equal protection of the laws which the Amendment was intended to insure. We have no doubt that there has been state action in these cases in the full and complete sense of the phrase.... It is clear that but for the active intervention of the state courts, supported by the full panoply of state power, petitioners would have been free to occupy the properties in question without restraint.

These are not cases ... in which the States have merely abstained from action, leaving private individuals free to impose such discriminations as they see fit. Rather, these are cases in which the States have made available to such individuals the full coercive power of government to deny to petitioners, on the grounds of race or color, the enjoyment of property rights in premises which petitioners are willing and financially able to acquire and which the grantors are willing to sell....

We hold that in granting judicial enforcement of the restrictive agreements in these cases, the States have denied petitioners the equal protection of the laws.... We have noted that freedom from discrimination by the States in the enjoyment of property rights was among the basic objectives sought to be effectuated by the framers of the Fourteenth Amendment. That such discrimination has occurred in these cases is clear. Because of the race or color of these petitioners they have been denied rights of ownership or occupancy enjoyed as a matter of course by other citizens of different race or color.... *Yick Wo v. Hopkins*....

Respondents urge, however, that since the state courts stand ready to enforce restrictive covenants excluding white persons from the ownership or occupancy of property covered by such agreements, enforcement of covenants excluding colored persons may not be deemed a denial of equal protection of the laws to the colored persons who are thereby affected.... The rights created by the first section of the Fourteenth Amendment are, by its terms, guaranteed to the individual. The rights established are personal rights. It is, therefore, no answer to these petitioners to say that the courts may also be induced to deny white persons rights of ownership and occupancy on grounds of race or color. Equal protection of the laws is not achieved through indiscriminate imposition of inequalities.

Nor do we find merit in the suggestion that property owners who are parties to these agreements are denied equal protection of the laws if denied access to the courts to enforce the terms of restrictive covenants.... The Constitution confers upon no individual the right to demand action by the State which results in the denial of equal protection of the laws to other individuals.

The Battle to Overturn *Plessy*

These cases were part of a long journey from *Plessy* to *Brown v. Board of Education*. While there were many active participants in the battle, the NAACP was a critically important leader. Its counsel, first Charles Hamilton Houston and then Thurgood Marshall, would be the lead officers in that fight.

The NAACP LDF Strategy and Tactics

The NAACP attorneys pursued a carefully selected set of cases as part of a strategy to end segregation. The NAACP effort became particularly focused and energized in 1934, when Charles Hamilton Houston became the NAACP chief counsel, and he was the mastermind behind the strategy. It is essential to take a moment to discuss Mr. Houston, who is probably the most important of the nation's least-known civil rights leaders. His intelligence, persistence, calm and careful preparation, and his teaching and mentorship of other civil rights attorneys were crucial to so much of what would happen in the civil rights movement for years to come.

Charles Houston was the son of caring parents, Mary and Charles Houston. His mother was a hairdresser, whose clients included those involved in governance in the nation's capital. His father was a lawyer in private practice. Charles won a partial scholarship to Amherst College and his parents worked tirelessly to support his education. After graduation he became a teacher at Howard University, but left that position to serve as one of the nation's first African American officers in World War I. Long before the Tuskegee airmen became famous for their brave and skillful performance in World War II, Houston experienced the kind of discrimination and disrespect that were visited upon so many African Americans who wanted to serve their country in the military. Upon his return home from France, Houston was on a train when a white man demanded that Houston and another black officer be moved to a different table. Houston did not move. After that, he concluded, "My battleground," he declared, is "in America, not France."[22]

Houston was admitted to Harvard Law School and became the first African American to become a member of the Harvard Law Review editorial board. After graduation and advanced legal studies, Houston returned to teach in the law school at Howard University, eventually rising to Vice Dean of the law school.

Houston made it clear to his students that they would have to be extremely capable technical lawyers even if their goals were broadly concerned with changing the society in which they lived and practiced. One of those students was Thurgood Marshall. Sadly, Houston had a coronary condition that led to his death at only 55 years of age, but that cadre of civil rights advocates whom he left behind would move his fight forward. Indeed, he took Thurgood Marshall with him to the NAACP and then positioned Marshall to take over as special counsel when he left. Even after he left his role of special counsel, Houston remained a counselor and mentor for Marshall and his colleagues as well as an advisor with respect to the path of litigation that Houston had staked out for them.

Houston designed the strategy for the attack on *Plessy* based upon his recognition of two critical realities. First, he knew that there was no way that the states would actually provide separate but equal educational facilities and programs for graduate and professional degree programs. They would not spend the money and had no intention of supporting the rise of African American professionals in their communities. Second, he knew that a direct attack on elementary and secondary school segregation would, in the near term at least, lead to a politically impossible reaction. The intense fear that such relationships over the students' developmental years might lead to interracial marriage, what segregationists termed miscegenation, is nearly unbelievable from today's perspective.[23] He thus laid out the approach that the NAACP attorneys would use. First, they would challenge the states to meet the requirements of the separate but equal doctrine from *Plessy*. Then they would take on *Plessy* directly. They tried the first part of this strategy in the Maryland courts in a case involving an African American student from Maryland who, although he had an excellent undergraduate record from Amherst College, Houston's alma mater, was denied admission to the University of Maryland School of Law because of his race. Marshall was also from Maryland and attended Howard University School of Law in part because the same segregation rules barred him from the University of Maryland. Here the state provided neither admission, nor an alternative segregated law school, an obvious violation of the separate but equal doctrine, which resulted in an order to the university to admit Mr. Murray.[24]

Houston and Marshall were then ready to take on the case of *Missouri ex rel. Gaines v. Canada*. In this case the state had a segregated law school, but provided support for African American students to attend law school in another state. However, the NAACP argument was that *Plessy* required the state to provide in the state a separate and equal law school if it wanted to maintain a segregated University of Missouri Law School.

Missouri ex rel. Gaines v. Canada

305 U.S. 337 (1938)

INTRODUCTION: Lloyd Gaines was an African American who graduated from Lincoln University, a segregated state institution in Missouri. He applied for, but was refused admission to the law school at the University of Missouri, even though it was later admitted at trial that he was qualified to be a student there. He was a citizen of Missouri, but he was advised that although he could not attend the University of Missouri School of Law, under a Missouri statute the state would pay for him to go to law school in any adjoining state. Missouri indicated that it would likely create a law program at Lincoln University if at some point there were sufficient demand and support for it, but no indication was provided as to whether or when such a program would actually be developed. Gaines challenged his exclusion, but the existing external scholarship program was upheld by the state supreme court.

Chief Justice Hughes wrote the opinion for the Court.

> ... In answering petitioner's contention that this discrimination constituted a denial of his constitutional right [to equal protection under the Fourteenth Amendment], the state court has fully recognized the obligation of the State to provide [N]egroes with advantages for higher education substantially equal to the advantages afforded to white students. The State has sought to fulfill that obligation by furnishing equal facilities in separate schools, a method the validity of which has been sustained by our decisions. *Plessy v. Ferguson....* [T]he fact remains that instruction in law for [N]egroes is not now afforded by the State, either at Lincoln University or elsewhere within the State, and that the State excludes [N]egroes from the advantages of the law school it has established at the University of Missouri....

... The basic consideration is not ... what sort of opportunities other States provide, or whether they are as good as those in Missouri, but as to what opportunities Missouri itself furnishes to white students and denies to [N]egroes solely upon the ground of color. The admissibility of laws separating the races in the enjoyment of privileges afforded by the State rests wholly upon the equality of the privileges which the laws give to the separated groups within the State. The question here is not of a duty of the State to supply legal training, or of the quality of the training which it does supply, but of its duty when it provides such training to furnish it to the residents of the State upon the basis of an equality of right. By the operation of the laws of Missouri a privilege has been created for white law students which is denied to [N]egroes by reason of their race. The white resident is afforded legal education within the State; the [N]egro resident having the same qualifications is refused it there and must go outside the State to obtain it. That is a denial of the equality of legal right to the enjoyment of the privilege which the State has set up, and the provision for the payment of tuition fees in another State does not remove the discrimination.

The equal protection of the laws is "a pledge of the protection of equal laws." *Yick Wo v. Hopkins*.... Manifestly, the obligation of the State to give the protection of equal laws can be performed only where its laws operate, that is, within its own jurisdiction. It is there that the equality of legal right must be maintained. That obligation is imposed by the Constitution upon the States ... each responsible for its own laws establishing the rights and duties of persons within its borders. It is an obligation the burden of which cannot be cast by one State upon another, and no State can be excused from performance by what another State may do or fail to do. That separate responsibility of each State within its own sphere is of the essence of statehood maintained under our dual system.... We find it impossible to conclude that what otherwise would be an unconstitutional discrimination, with respect to the legal right to the enjoyment of opportunities within the State, can be justified by requiring resort to opportunities elsewhere.... Nor can we regard the fact that there is but a limited demand in Missouri for the legal education of [N]egroes as excusing the discrimination in favor of whites....

Here, petitioner's right was a personal one. It was as an individual that he was entitled to the equal protection of the laws, and the State was bound to furnish him within its borders facilities for legal education substantially equal to those which the State there afforded for persons of the white race, whether or not other [N]egroes sought the same opportunity.

It is urged, however, that the provision for tuition outside the State is a temporary one—that it is intended to operate merely pending the establishment of a law department for [N]egroes at Lincoln University. While in that sense the discrimination may be termed temporary, it may nevertheless continue for an indefinite period by reason of the discretion given to the curators of Lincoln University and the alternative of arranging for tuition in other States, as permitted by the state law as construed by the state court, so long as the curators find it unnecessary and impracticable to provide facilities for the legal instruction of [N]egroes within the State. In that view, we cannot regard the discrimination as excused by what is called its temporary character.

The judgment of the Supreme Court of Missouri is reversed and the cause is remanded for further proceedings not inconsistent with this opinion.[25]

The *Gaines* case was the leading edge of a challenge that would make clear the lack of seriousness of the separate but equal doctrine. But as Houston and Marshall pursued their efforts to change America, other forces were reshaping the nation as well.

The Political Context: World War II and its Aftermath Brought Major Change

While there was an ongoing debate about when and even whether the United States should declare war against Hitler's Germany, it was clear to most observers that the nation was moving inexorably toward war long before December 7, 1941. The Roosevelt administration was actively supporting the British through the Lend/Lease program and other efforts that meant that war production industries were stimulated. Once the U.S. entered the war, it was also obvious that there was a need to build a large and complex military force. Civil rights leaders like A. Philip Randolph, head of the Brotherhood of Sleeping Car Porters, and Walter White, Executive Secretary of the NAACP, among others, saw this as an opportunity to press for civil rights policies that allowed all Americans to participate in this massive endeavor.

Franklin Delano Roosevelt was dealing with a divided nation moving toward war while still feeling the effects of the Great Depression, and he was trying to hold together support for Lend/Lease and other assistance programs for the allies. But civil rights leaders insisted that this was the time to stop discrimination in war-related industries and the military, so that the nation would be able to access all of its essential resources and create a sense of common endeavor. A. Philip Randolph and Walter White called upon the president to issue an executive order that would address those problems. When Roosevelt delayed action, Randolph threatened to mount a massive march on Washington in July of 1941. Roosevelt responded by issuing an order in June that created the Fair Employment Practices Committee and Randolph called off the march.[26]

Still, the U.S. conducted World War II with a segregated military and, although they served with distinction, many African American soldiers, sailors, and airmen suffered racist abuse at the hands of their fellow soldiers. Even so, those who had served abroad had come home convinced that there were other places in the world where they were not treated in such a discriminatory manner, but valued as people and as military men. No sooner did they get back, however, than stories began to emerge in the media of terrible attacks on those veterans. One of those who was greatly affected by these events was the man who would succeed Roosevelt in 1945, Harry Truman. While Truman was a not a person who appeared to be a likely champion of civil rights, he stepped forward in dramatic fashion.

In July 1946 Truman ordered the Attorney General to investigate violent attacks on returning African American war veterans in Aiken, South Carolina and Monroe, Georgia, to determine whether federal laws could be used to take action against the perpetrators. In December of that year, Truman created the President's Committee on Civil Rights. Truman was very much aware that the committee report would be highly controversial—and it was. The report entitled *To Secure These Rights* issued on October 29, 1947 found evidence of widespread race discrimination and particularly targeted problems with the military. In February 1948 Truman issued his now famous civil rights message. He said, in part:

> The Federal Government has a clear duty to see that Constitutional guarantees of individual liberties and of equal protection under the laws are not denied or abridged anywhere in our Union. That duty is shared by all three branches of the Government, but it can be fulfilled only if the Congress enacts modern, comprehensive civil rights laws,

adequate to the needs of the day, and demonstrating our continuing faith in the free way of life. I recommend, therefore, that the Congress enact legislation at this session directed toward the following specific objectives:

1. Establishing a permanent Commission on Civil Rights, a Joint Congressional Committee on Civil Rights, and a Civil Rights Division in the Department of Justice.
2. Strengthening existing civil rights statutes.
3. Providing Federal protection against lynching.
4. Protecting more adequately the right to vote.
5. Establishing a Fair Employment Practice Commission to prevent unfair discrimination in employment.
6. Prohibiting discrimination in interstate transportation facilities.
7. Providing home-rule and suffrage in Presidential elections for the residents of the District of Columbia.
8. Providing Statehood for Hawaii and Alaska and a greater measure of self-government for our island possessions.
9. Equalizing the opportunities for residents of the United States to become naturalized citizens.
10. Settling the evacuation claims of Japanese-Americans.

This speech and his support of a civil rights plank in the 1948 presidential platform of the Democratic Party led to a walkout by segregationists under the leadership of Strom Thurmond of South Carolina, who then headed up what came to be known as the Dixiecrat Party. This added to already fractured party relationships and increasing odds against Truman's reelection. Indeed, as November approached, virtually no one except Truman thought he could win. He was warned by friends in addition to the challenges launched by his adversaries. To one letter that suggested that his civil rights stand would cost him his political career, Truman replied that he was sending a copy of the commission report and said, "if you still have that antebellum, proslavery outlook, I'll be thoroughly disappointed in you." He continued:

The main difficulty with the South is that they are living eighty years behind the times and the sooner they come out of it the better it will be for the country and themselves. I am not asking for social equality, because no such thing exists, but I am asking for equality of opportunity for all human beings, and, as long as I stay here, I am going to continue that fight. When the mob gangs can take four people out and shoot them in the back, and everybody in the [surrounding] country is acquainted with who did the shooting and nothing is done about it, that country is in a pretty bad fix from the law enforcement standpoint.

When a mayor and a City Marshal can take a negro Sergeant off a bus in South Carolina, beat him up and put out one of his eyes, and nothing is done about it by the State Authorities, something is radically wrong with the system.

On the Louisiana and Arkansas Railway when coal burning locomotives were used, the Negro firemen were the thing because it was a back-breaking job and a dirty one. As soon as they turned to oil as a fuel it became customary for people to take shots at Negro firemen and a number were murdered because it was thought that this was now a white-collar job and should go to a white man. I can't approve of such goings on and I shall never approve of it, as long as I am here.... I am going to try to remedy it and if that ends up in my failure to be reelected, that failure will be in a good cause.[27]

In July 1948 Truman issued his now famous Executive Order 9981, ending segregation in the military.[28] Even so, it would take an ongoing effort by the president to force the military to comply, including investigations carried out on complaints of discrimination in the armed services in Korea by Thurgood Marshall. On the same day as his military order, Truman issued Executive Order 9980 on ending discrimination within the federal service.[29] Truman also brought an end to the support by the federal government for racially restrictive covenants in real estate transactions and mortgage practices and asked the Solicitor General to file briefs in support of the NAACP opposition to restrictive covenants before the Supreme Court.[30]

The Run-Up to Brown v. Board of Education: *Eroding the Foundations of* Plessy

Despite the fact that the forces of change were increasingly apparent, die-hard segregationists were not about to concede that the days of separate but equal were numbered. In fact, the Dixiecrats were vowing that those days would never end. Rhetoric notwithstanding, following the *Gaines* ruling it was clear to segregationist states that they would have to provide alternative segregated graduate and professional programs if they wanted to maintain the *Plessy* doctrine. In Oklahoma the strategy was to create an internal segregation within the graduate program, while in Texas the plan was to create an internal segregated law school, although this was clearly a sham. Both of these actions found their way to the Supreme Court.

McLaurin v. Oklahoma

339 U.S. 637 (1950)

INTRODUCTION: Mr. McLaurin held a Master's Degree and sought to enter the doctoral program in Education at the University of Oklahoma. At first he was refused admission on the basis of race, since educational institutions in Oklahoma were segregated by state law. However, a federal district court struck down McLaurin's rejection on the basis of the *Missouri ex rel. Gaines v. Canada* ruling and another related precedent.

Mr. McLaurin was thereafter admitted to the graduate program at the University of Oklahoma, but then promptly segregated within the program itself. For example, when attending class, as the Supreme Court explained it:

> he was required to sit apart at a designated desk in an anteroom adjoining the classroom; to sit at a designated desk on the mezzanine floor of the library, but not to use the desks in the regular reading room; and to sit at a designated table and to eat at a different time from the other students in the school cafeteria.

Once again McLaurin went to court, but this time the district court found no violation of equal protection.

Chief Justice Vinson wrote the opinion for the Court.

> In this case, we are faced with the question whether a state may, after admitting a student to graduate instruction in its state university, afford him different treatment from other students solely because of his race....

> It is said that the separations imposed by the State in this case are in form merely nominal. McLaurin uses the same classroom, library and cafeteria as students of other races; there is no indication that the seats to which he is assigned in these rooms have any disadvantage of location. He may wait in line in the

cafeteria and there stand and talk with his fellow students, but while he eats he must remain apart.

… [I]n administering the facilities it affords for professional and graduate study, [it] sets McLaurin apart from the other students. The result is that appellant is handicapped in his pursuit of effective graduate instruction. Such restrictions impair and inhibit his ability to study, to engage in discussions and exchange views with other students, and, in general, to learn his profession.

Our society grows increasingly complex, and our need for trained leaders increases correspondingly. Appellant … is attempting to obtain an advanced degree in education, to become, by definition, a leader and trainer of others. Those who will come under his guidance and influence must be directly affected by the education he receives. Their own education and development will necessarily suffer to the extent that his training is unequal to that of his classmates. State-imposed restrictions which produce such inequalities cannot be sustained.

It may be argued that appellant will be in no better position when these restrictions are removed, for he may still be set apart by his fellow students. This we think irrelevant. There is a vast difference—a Constitutional difference—between restrictions imposed by the state which prohibit the intellectual commingling of students, and the refusal of individuals to commingle where the state presents no such bar.… The removal of the state restrictions will not necessarily abate individual and group predilections, prejudices and choices. But at the very least, the state will not be depriving appellant of the opportunity to secure acceptance by his fellow students on his own merits.

We conclude that the conditions under which this appellant is required to receive his education deprive him of his personal and present right to the equal protection of the laws.… Appellant … must receive the same treatment at the hands of the state as students of other races. The judgment is reversed.

The fact that these rulings were unanimous decisions was not lost on those challenging segregation, and neither was the fact that the *McLaurin* opinion was authored by Chief Justice Vinson, hardly a person inclined to press for the demise of segregation. Those same messages were delivered by the Court when Texas tried to maintain its segregation policy by launching what could only be described as a sham law school for African Americans. However, this time the Court pushed even further toward ending *Plessy*.

Sweatt v. Painter

339 U.S. 629 (1950)

INTRODUCTION: Hemann Sweatt applied to the University of Texas School of Law, but was denied admission because of race. There was at that time no separate law school for African American students. He won a challenge in state court to the lack of a separate and equal law program as required by *Missouri ex rel. Gaines v. Canada*. The district court did not order Sweatt's admission and gave the state time to create a separate program.

Texas quickly created what was, by any reasonable estimate, a sham program designed to forestall integration of its law school. Sweatt pressed his claim for admission to the well-established and nationally known University of Texas School of Law. The state then went on to develop an actual, but very limited, law program for African American students.

Chief Justice Vinson wrote the opinion for the Court.

... The University of Texas Law School, from which petitioner was excluded, was staffed by a faculty of sixteen full-time and three part-time professors, some of whom are nationally recognized authorities in their field. Its student body numbered 850. The library contained over 65,000 volumes. Among the other facilities available to the students were a law review, moot court facilities, scholarship funds, and Order of the Coif affiliation. The school's alumni occupy the most distinguished positions in the private practice of the law and in the public life of the State. It may properly be considered one of the nation's ranking law schools.

The law school for Negroes which was to have opened in February, 1947, would have had no independent faculty or library. The teaching was to be carried on by four members of the University of Texas Law School faculty, who were to maintain their offices at the University of Texas while teaching at both institutions. Few of the 10,000 volumes ordered for the library had arrived; nor was there any full-time librarian. The school lacked accreditation.

Since the trial of this case, respondents report the opening of a law school at the Texas State University for Negroes. It is apparently on the road to full accreditation. It has a faculty of five full-time professors; a student body of 23; a library of some 16,500 volumes serviced by a full-time staff; a practice court and legal aid association; and one alumnus who has become a member of the Texas Bar.

[W]e cannot find substantial equality in the educational opportunities offered white and Negro law students by the State. In terms of number of the faculty, variety of courses and opportunity for specialization, size of the student body, scope of the library, availability of law review and similar activities, the University of Texas Law School is superior. What is more important, the University of Texas Law School possesses to a far greater degree those qualities which are incapable of objective measurement but which make for greatness in a law school. Such qualities, to name but a few, include reputation of the faculty, experience of the administration, position and influence of the alumni, standing in the community, traditions and prestige. It is difficult to believe that one who had a free choice between these law schools would consider the question close.

Moreover, although the law is a highly learned profession, we are well aware that it is an intensely practical one. The law school, the proving ground for legal learning and practice, cannot be effective in isolation from the individuals and institutions with which the law interacts. Few students and no one who has practiced law would choose to study in an academic vacuum, removed from the interplay of ideas and the exchange of views with which the law is concerned. The law school to which Texas is willing to admit petitioner excludes from its student body members of the racial groups which number 85% of the population of the State and include most of the lawyers, witnesses, jurors, judges and other officials with whom petitioner will inevitably be dealing when he becomes a member of the Texas Bar. With such a substantial and significant segment of society excluded, we cannot conclude that the education offered petitioner is substantially equal to that which he would receive if admitted to the University of Texas Law School.

It may be argued that excluding petitioner from that school is no different from excluding white students from the new law school. This contention overlooks realities. It is unlikely that a member of a group so decisively in the majority, attending a school with rich traditions and prestige which only a history of consistently maintained excellence could command, would claim that the opportunities afforded him for legal education were unequal to those held open to petitioner. That such a claim, if made, would be dishonored by the State, is no answer. "Equal protection of the laws is not achieved through indiscriminate imposition of inequalities." ...

This Court has stated unanimously that "The State must provide [legal education] for [petitioner] in conformity with the equal protection clause of the Fourteenth Amendment and provide it as soon as it does for applicants of any other group." ... [Accordingly], petitioner may claim his full constitutional right: legal education equivalent to that offered by the State to students of other races. Such education is not available to him in a separate law school as offered by the State. We cannot, therefore, agree with respondents that the doctrine of *Plessy* ... requires affirmance.... Nor need we reach petitioner's contention that *Plessy* ... should be reexamined.... We hold that the Equal Protection Clause of the Fourteenth Amendment requires that petitioner be admitted to the University of Texas Law School.... Reversed.

Brown v. Board of Education: Rejection of the *Plessy* Doctrine

The ruling in *Sweatt* relied on intangibles to suggest that even if the facilities and programs were equal, segregated programs would not likely withstand scrutiny. Indeed, the *Sweatt* ruling came very close to asserting directly that separate education could not be equal. It was that next step that Thurgood Marshall wanted the Court to take in what became known as *Brown v. Board of Education*. Marshall and his colleagues chose a set of five cases with which to attack *Plessy*, involving at least some situations, like the Topeka, Kansas case, where the segregated facilities were reasonably equal in order to press the Court to take on *Plessy* directly.[31]

Brown v. Board of Education of Topeka
347 U.S. 483 (1954)

INTRODUCTION: This is the first of two rulings in this set of cases. There were cases brought from the states of Kansas, South Carolina, Virginia, Delaware, and the District of Columbia. In each location suits were filed by families testing the segregation of the public schools. In each case the lower courts upheld the segregation on the basis of *Plessy*. However, the court in the Delaware case concluded that the schools failed the "equal" part of the separate but equal standard.

The National Association for the Advancement of Colored People, Legal Defense and Education Fund, led by Thurgood Marshall, moved the cases through the system with the hope of ensuring a clear challenge in the U.S. Supreme Court to the *Plessy* doctrine.

Chief Justice Warren wrote the opinion for the unanimous Court.

These cases come to us from the States of Kansas, South Carolina, Virginia, and Delaware.... In each of the cases, minors of the Negro race ... seek the aid of the courts in obtaining admission to the public schools of their community on a nonsegregated basis. In each instance, they had been denied admission to schools attended by white children under laws requiring or permitting segregation according to race. This segregation was alleged to deprive the plaintiffs of the equal protection of the laws under the Fourteenth Amendment. In each of the cases other than the Delaware case, a three-judge federal district court denied relief to the plaintiffs on the so-called "separate but equal" doctrine announced by this Court in *Plessy v. Ferguson*.... Under that doctrine, equality of treatment is accorded when the races are provided substantially equal facilities, even though these facilities be separate.... The plaintiffs contend that segregated public schools are not "equal" and cannot be made "equal," and that hence they are deprived of the equal protection of the laws.

Reargument was largely devoted to the circumstances surrounding the adoption of the Fourteenth Amendment in 1868.... At best, they are inconclusive. The most avid proponents of the post-War Amendments undoubtedly intended them to remove all legal distinctions among "all persons born or naturalized in the United States." Their opponents, just as certainly, ... wished them to have the most limited effect....

In the first cases in this Court construing the Fourteenth Amendment, decided shortly after its adoption, the Court interpreted it as proscribing all state-imposed discriminations against the Negro race. The doctrine of "separate but equal" did not make its appearance in this Court until 1896 in the case of *Plessy v. Ferguson*, ... involving not education but transportation. American courts have since labored with the doctrine for over half a century. In this Court, ... cases involving the "separate but equal" doctrine in the field of public education ... [have not questioned] the validity of the doctrine itself.... In more recent cases, all on the graduate school level, inequality was found in that specific benefits enjoyed by white students were denied to Negro students of the same educational qualifications.... In none of these cases was it necessary to re-examine *Plessy*....

In the instant cases, that question is directly presented. Here ... there are findings below that the Negro and white schools involved have been equalized, or are being equalized, with respect to buildings, curricula, qualifications and salaries of teachers, and other "tangible" factors. Our decision, therefore, cannot turn on merely a comparison of these tangible factors in the Negro and white schools involved.... We must look instead to the effect of segregation itself on public education.

In approaching this problem, we cannot turn the clock back to 1868 when the Amendment was adopted, or even to 1896 when *Plessy v. Ferguson* was written. We must consider public education in the light of its full development and its present place in American life throughout the Nation. Only in this way can it be determined if segregation in public schools deprives these plaintiffs of the equal protection of the laws.

Today, education is perhaps the most important function of state and local governments. Compulsory school attendance laws and the great expenditures for education both demonstrate our recognition of the importance of education to our democratic society. It is required in the performance of our most basic public responsibilities, even service in the armed forces. It is the very foundation of good citizenship. Today it is a principal instrument in awakening the child to cultural values, in preparing him for later professional training, and in helping him to adjust normally to his environment. In these days, it is doubtful that any child may reasonably be expected to succeed in life if he is denied the opportunity of an education. Such an opportunity, where the state has undertaken to provide it, is a right which must be made available to all on equal terms.

We come then to the question presented: Does segregation of children in public schools solely on the basis of race, even though the physical facilities and other "tangible" factors may be equal, deprive the children of the minority group of equal educational opportunities? We believe that it does.

In *Sweatt v. Painter* ... in finding that a segregated law school for Negroes could not provide them equal educational opportunities, this Court relied in large part on "those qualities which are incapable of objective measurement but which make for greatness in a law school." In *McLaurin v. Oklahoma State Regents,* ... the Court, in requiring that a Negro admitted to a white graduate school be treated like all other students, again resorted to intangible considerations: "... his ability to study, to engage in discussions and exchange views with other students, and, in general, to learn his profession." Such considerations apply with added force to children in grade and high schools. To separate them from others of similar age and qualifications solely because of their race generates a feeling of inferiority as to their status in the community that may affect their hearts and minds in a way unlikely ever to be undone. The effect of this separation on their educational opportunities was well stated by a finding in the Kansas case by a court which nevertheless felt compelled to rule against the Negro plaintiffs: "Segregation of white and colored children in public schools has a detrimental effect upon the colored children. The impact is greater when it has the sanction of the law; for the policy of separating the races is usually interpreted as denoting the inferiority of the negro group. A sense of inferiority affects the motivation of a child to learn. Segregation with the sanction of law, therefore, has a tendency to [retard] the educational and mental development of negro children and to deprive them of some of the benefits they would receive in a racial[ly] integrated school system."

Whatever may have been the extent of psychological knowledge at the time of *Plessy v. Ferguson*, this finding is amply supported by modern authority.[32] Any language in *Plessy v. Ferguson* contrary to this finding is rejected.

We conclude that in the field of public education the doctrine of "separate but equal" has no place. Separate educational facilities are inherently unequal. Therefore, we hold that the plaintiffs and others similarly situated for whom the actions have been brought are, by reason of the segregation complained of, deprived of the equal protection of the laws guaranteed by the Fourteenth Amendment....

Because these are class actions, because of the wide applicability of this decision, and because of the great variety of local conditions, the formulation of decrees in these cases presents problems of considerable complexity. On reargument, the consideration of appropriate relief was necessarily subordinated to the primary question—the constitutionality of segregation in public education. We have now announced that such segregation is a denial of the equal protection of the laws. In order that we may have the full assistance of the parties in formulating decrees, the cases will be restored to the docket, and the parties are requested to present further argument on [remedy]....

The D.C. school case that was part of the set of cases in the *Brown* litigation presented not only the manifold problems presented by a history of discrimination in the nation's capital but also the question of just how the equal protection principle applies, since the District of Columbia is not a state and therefore not addressed by the Fourteenth Amendment. Although the Fifth Amendment contains a due process clause, it does not have an equal protection provision.

Bolling v. Sharpe

347 U.S. 497 (1954)

Chief Justice Warren wrote the opinion for the Court.

... We have this day held that the Equal Protection Clause of the Fourteenth Amendment prohibits the states from maintaining racially segregated public schools. *Brown v. Bd. of Education*.... The Fifth Amendment, which is applicable in the District of Columbia, does not contain an equal protection clause as does the Fourteenth Amendment which applies only to the states. But the concepts of equal protection and due process, both stemming from our American ideal of fairness, are not mutually exclusive. The "equal protection of the laws" is a more explicit safeguard of prohibited unfairness than "due process of law," and, therefore, we do not imply that the two are always interchangeable phrases. But, as this Court has recognized, discrimination may be so unjustifiable as to be violative of due process.

Classifications based solely upon race must be scrutinized with particular care, since they are contrary to our traditions and hence constitutionally suspect. *Korematsu*.... [I]n *Buchanan v. Warley* ... the Court held that a statute which limited the right of a property owner to convey his property to a person of another race was, as an unreasonable discrimination, a denial of due process of law.

Although the Court has not assumed to define "liberty" with any great precision, that term is not confined to mere freedom from bodily restraint. Liberty under law extends to the full range of conduct which the individual is free to pursue, and it cannot be restricted except for a proper governmental objective. Segregation in public education is not reasonably related to any proper governmental objective, and thus it imposes on Negro children of the District of Columbia a burden that constitutes an arbitrary deprivation of their liberty in violation of the Due Process Clause.

In view of our decision that the Constitution prohibits the states from maintaining racially segregated public schools, it would be unthinkable that the same Constitution would impose a lesser duty on the Federal Government. We hold that racial segregation in the public schools of the District of Columbia is a denial of the due process of law guaranteed by the Fifth Amendment to the Constitution.

Brown v. Board of Education (II)

349 U.S. 294 (1955)

Chief Justice Warren wrote the opinion for the Court.

[In May 1954 we held that] all provisions of federal, state, or local law requiring or permitting such discrimination must yield to th[e] principle [that racial discrimination in public education is unconstitutional]. There remains for consideration the manner in which relief is to be accorded.

Because these cases arose under different local conditions and their disposition will involve a variety of local problems, we requested further argument on the question of relief. In view of the nationwide importance of the decision, we invited the Attorney General of the United States and the Attorneys General of all states requiring or permitting racial discrimination in public education to present their views on that question....

Full implementation of these constitutional principles may require solution of varied local school problems. School authorities have the primary responsibility for elucidating, assessing, and solving these problems; courts will have to consider whether the action of school authorities constitutes good faith implementation of the governing constitutional principles. Because of their proximity to local conditions and the possible need for further hearings, the courts which originally heard these cases can best perform this judicial appraisal. Accordingly, we believe it appropriate to remand the cases to those courts.

In fashioning and effectuating the decrees, the courts will be guided by equitable principles. Traditionally, equity has been characterized by a practical flexibility in shaping its remedies and by a facility for adjusting and reconciling public and private needs.... At stake is the personal interest of the plaintiffs in admission to public schools as soon as practicable on a nondiscriminatory basis. To effectuate this interest may call for elimination of a variety of obstacles in making the transition to school systems operated in accordance with the constitutional principles set forth in [*Brown I*]. Courts of equity may properly take into account the public interest in the elimination of such obstacles in a systematic and effective manner. But it should go without saying that the vitality of these constitutional principles cannot be allowed to yield simply because of disagreement with them.

While giving weight to these public and private considerations, the courts will require that the defendants make a prompt and reasonable start toward full compliance with our May 17, 1954, ruling. Once such a start has been made, the courts may find that additional time is necessary to carry out the ruling in an effective manner. The burden rests upon the defendants to establish that such time is necessary in the public interest and is consistent with good faith compliance at the earliest practicable date. To that end, the courts may consider problems related to administration, arising from the physical condition of the school plant, the school transportation system, personnel, revision of school districts and attendance areas into compact units to achieve a system of determining admission to the public schools on a nonracial basis, and revision of local laws and regulations which may be necessary in solving the foregoing problems. They will also consider the adequacy of any plans the defendants may propose to meet these problems and to effectuate a transition to a racially nondiscriminatory school system. During this period of transition, the courts will retain jurisdiction of these cases.

The judgments below, except that in the Delaware case, are accordingly reversed and the cases are remanded to the District Courts to take such proceedings and enter such orders and decrees consistent with this opinion as are necessary and proper to admit to public schools on a racially nondiscriminatory basis with all deliberate speed the parties to these cases.

Conclusion

It was indeed a long and arduous journey from *Plessy v. Ferguson* to *Brown v. Board of Education*. Along the way, the Supreme Court established a range of key principles of equal protection of the law that provided a foundation for the development of that concept in the years ahead and with respect to questions brought by various groups apart from race or ethnicity. Even as the Court delivered its upsetting opinion in the Japanese exclusion case, it established the principle that classifications based on race were presumptively invalid and would be examined through what the Court termed strict judicial scrutiny. The restrictive covenant opinion established that it was the fact that race was the basis for differential treatment that mattered, and that the Court would not tolerate the sophistry involved in the argument that these statutes applied to both whites and nonwhites and were therefore not discriminatory. The *Yick Wo* case established the fundamental point that the Fourteenth Amendment equal protection and due process clauses apply to all persons regardless of status, and that laws that appeared acceptable on their face could nevertheless fall if they were applied in a discriminatory manner.

These critical steps and more emerged during this period, but it would quickly become clear that the battle for equality and against racial discrimination was far from over. The Southern states would launch what came to be known as a campaign of massive resistance to the desegregation rulings of the Court that went on for decades. Then there was the task of dealing with racial discrimination in those states where there had never been a specific law mandating it, but where a host of discriminatory practices had ensured segregated communities and services. Beyond establishing the fundamental principles of equal protection applied to race, it would also be necessary to turn to a wide range of problem areas. Unfortunately, as the country moved forward with that work, the Supreme Court was about to make constitutional challenges to discrimination much harder to mount and maintain. Chapter 4 addresses these challenges.

I. Issues for Policy and Practice

A. Do civil rights policies make clear how to determine whether an otherwise neutral statute or regulation is being implemented in a discriminatory manner, as emphasized in the *Yick Wo* opinion? There are some areas in which considerable attention has been paid to that question, such as with respect to employment discrimination under Title VII of the Civil Rights Act of 1964, but to what extent is this true of other key civil rights statutes or regulations?

B. Given the contemporary tendencies to use homeland security concerns or immigration exceptions, do current policies and practices actually ensure that all "persons" within the jurisdiction of the states and of the United States actually receive due process and equal protection of the law? Are there any mechanisms to evaluate policies in practice to ensure that exceptions for reasons such as these do not swallow the rule?

C. The evidence is that the United States has not learned the lessons of *Korematsu* and *Hirabayashi* about which Judge Patel warned in the 1984 *coram nobis* ruling he issued. Events following the 9/11 attacks and in recent political debates clearly show that discriminatory practices against Arab Americans and Muslims have been rampant. What checks are in place to review policies adopted in or after periods of emergency to prevent or stop discrimination against ethnocultural groups? Has there been any serious review of national policies since 9/11 to determine the nature and scope of the problem from a public policy perspective?

D. The relationships among economic exclusion, employment discrimination, housing discrimination, and de facto school segregation have long been clear. Yet they remain problems today. Despite claims by administrations of both political parties to address the problems of cities, there is still no clear national urban policy. What are the key elements required for such a policy and how could it implemented?

II. Discussion Questions

A. The history of the United States and other countries shows that during and after periods of tension or emergencies there is a tendency to single out members of various ethnocultural groups for harsh treatment. That has certainly happened in the years since the 9/11 attacks. Given that we know about the danger of such reactions from history, what can we do to prevent these kinds of discriminatory attitudes and actions?

B. What steps have we taken to learn lessons from the abuses that are so obvious from the nation's history? Is there any serious attempt to do that? If not, what is the likelihood that similar discriminatory behavior will happen again?

C. Most public service practitioners would absolutely reject the thought that any of us would behave in a discriminatory manner, even in the tense times when others in society, including elected officials or candidates for office, clearly are stereotyping and discriminating. Do we have any personal or organizational mechanisms in place for taking a hard look at ourselves and our agencies to test that assumption?

D. The relationships among economic exclusion, employment discrimination, housing discrimination, and de facto school segregation have long been clear. Even some communities that regard themselves as progressive with respect to equality and inclusion actually present a very different reality. Is your community realistically assessing these conditions and addressing them? If not, why not? If so, how?

Notes

1   Executive Order No. 9066, 7 Fed. Reg. 1407 (1942). The president later issued Executive Order 9102 which created an agency called the War Relocation Authority with the authority to administer the "removal, relocation, maintenance and supervision of persons designated under Executive Order No. 9066." 7 Fed. Reg. 2165 (1942).

2   Act of Congress of March 21, 1942, 56 Stat. 173 (1942).

3   320 U.S. 81 (1943).

4   NOTE: Justice Roberts wrote a dissent, omitted here, that argued that Korematsu was caught between contradictory military orders.

5   Quoted in *Korematsu v. United States*, 584 F. Supp. 1406, 1417 (NDCA 1984).

6   Id., at 1418.

7   Id., at 1419.

8   *Hirabayashi v. United States*, 828 F.2d 591, 601 (9th Cir. 1987).

9   584 F. Supp., at 1420.

10 See David Cole, *Enemy Aliens: Double Standards and Constitutional Freedoms in the War on Terrorism* (New York: The New Press, 2003). (An abbreviated version was published as "Enemy Aliens," *Stanford Law Review* 54 (May 2002): 953–1004.) See also Heidi Kitrosser, "Secrecy in the Immigration Courts and Beyond: Considering the Right to Know in the Administrative State," *Harvard Civil Rights—Civil Liberties Law Review* 39 (Winter 2004): 95–168.

11 See U.S. Department of Justice, Office of the Inspector General, *The September 11 Detainees: A Review of the Treatment of Aliens Held on Immigration Charges in Connection with the Investigation of the September 11 Attacks* (Washington, D.C.: U.S. Department of Justice, 2003), 158–164, https://oig.justice.gov/special/0306/full.pdf, January 15, 2016.

12 *Boumediene v. Bush*, 128 S. Ct. 2229 (2008); *Rasul v. Bush*, 542 U.S. 466 (2004); *Hamdi v. Rumsfeld*, 542 U.S. 507 (2004).

13 See the case of seventeen Chinese Uighurs in Guantánamo Bay for more than seven years. See *In re Guantanamo Bay Detainee Litigation*, 581 F. Supp. 2d 33 (D.D.C. 2008); reversed and remanded *Kiyemba v. Obama*, 555 F.3d 1022 (D.C. Cir. 2009); vacated and remanded 559 U.S. 131 (2010); reinstated and modified 605 F.3d 1046 (D.C. Cir. 2010), cert. denied 131 S. Ct. 1631 (2011).

14 David Harris, "Flying While Arab: Lessons from the Racial Profiling Controversy," *Civil Rights Journal* 6 (Winter 2002):8–13.

15 *Korematsu v. United States*, 323 U.S., at 215.

16 This history is explained in Phillip J. Cooper, *Hard Judicial Choices: Federal District Judges and State and Local Officials* (New York: Oxford University Press, 1988), Ch.2. See also Michael Danielson, *The Politics of Exclusion* (New York: Columbia University Press, 1976).

17 *Buchanan v. Warley*, 245 U.S. 60 (1917).

18 272 U.S. 365 (1926).

19 245 U.S. 60 (1917).

20 The classic work on this subject is Clement Vose, *Caucasians Only: The Supreme Court, the NAACP, and the Restrictive Covenant Cases* (Berkeley, CA: University of California Press, 1959).

21 NOTE: Because the Court found a violation of the equal protection clause, it did not find a need to address the due process or privileges and immunities claims.

22 Douglas O. Linder, "Before Brown: Charles H. Houston and the Gaines Case," http://law2.umkc.edu/faculty/projects/ftrials/trialheroes/charleshoustonessayF.html, December 26, 2015.

23 It would not be until 1967 that the Supreme Court declared laws against interracial marriage to be unconstitutional discrimination in *Loving v. Virginia*, 388 U.S. 1 (1967).

24 *Pearson v. Murray*, 182 A. 590 (Md.App. 1936).

25 NOTE: The dissents by Justices McReynolds and Butler are omitted.

26 Ruth P. Morgan, *The President and Civil Rights* (New York: St. Martin's Press, 1970), pp. 13–14.

27 Harry S. Truman to Ernest W. Roberts, August 18, 1948, Harry S. Truman Library, www.trumanlibrary.org/military_deseg/subFlash/assets/rightsLetter.pdf, December 27, 2015.

28 Establishing the President's Committee on Equality of Treatment and Opportunity in the Armed Services, 13 Fed. Reg. 4313 (1948).

29 Regulations Governing Fair Employment Practices Within the Federal Establishment, 13 Fed. Reg. 4311 (1948).

30 See Harry S. Truman, Address in Harlem, New York, Upon Receiving the Franklin Roosevelt Award, October 11, 1952, Harry S. Truman Library, http://trumanlibrary.org/publicpapers/viewpapers.php?pid=2278, December 27, 2015.

31 See Richard Kluger, *Simple Justice* (New York: Vintage, 1977).

32 K. B. Clark, "Effect of Prejudice and Discrimination on Personality Development" (Midcentury White House Conference on Children and Youth, 1950); Witmer and Kotinsky, Personality in the Making (1952), c. VI; M. Deutscher and I. Chein, "The Psychological Effects of Enforced Segregation: A Survey of Social Science Opinion," 26 *Journal of Psychology* (1948): 259–287; I. Chein, "What are the Psychological Effects of Segregation Under Conditions of Equal Facilities?" 3 *International Journal of Opinion and Attitude Research* (1949): 229; T. Brameld, 'Educational Costs,' in *Discrimination and National Welfare*, R. M. MacIver, ed. (New York: Institute for Religious and Social Studies, 1949), pp. 44–48; E. F. Frazier, *The Negro in the United States* (New York: Macmillan, 1949), pp. 674–681. And see generally G. Myrdal, *An American Dilemma* (New Brunswick, NJ: Harper & Bros., 1944).

References

Cole, David. *Enemy Aliens: Double Standards and Constitutional Freedoms in the War on Terrorism.* New York: The New Press, 2003.

———. "Enemy Aliens," *Stanford Law Review* 54 (May 2002): 953–1004.

Cooper, Phillip J. *Hard Judicial Choices: Federal District Court Judges and State and Local Officials.* New York: Oxford University Press, 1988.

Danielson, Michael. *The Politics of Exclusion.* New York: Columbia University Press, 1976.

Harris, David. "Flying While Arab: Lessons from the Racial Profiling Controversy," *Civil Rights Journal* 6 (Winter 2002): 8–13.

Kitrosser, Heidi. "Secrecy in the Immigration Courts and Beyond: Considering the Right to Know in the Administrative State," *Harvard Civil Rights—Civil Liberties Law Review* 39 (Winter 2004): 95–168.

Kluger, Richard. *Simple Justice.* New York: Vintage, 1977.

Linder, Douglas O. "Before Brown: Charles H. Houston and the Gaines Case," http://law2.umkc.edu/faculty/projects/ftrials/trialheroes/charleshoustonessayF.html, December 26, 2015.

Morgan, Ruth P. *The President and Civil Rights.* New York: St. Martin's Press, 1970.

U.S. Department of Justice, Office of the Inspector General. *The September 11 Detainees: A Review of the Treatment of Aliens Held on Immigration Charges in Connection with the Investigation of the September 11 Attacks* (Washington D.C.: U.S. Department of Justice, 2003), 158–164, https://oig.justice.gov/special/0306/full.pdf, January 15, 2016.

Vose, Clement. *Caucasians Only: The Supreme Court, the NAACP, and the Restrictive Covenant Cases.* Berkeley, CA: University of California Press, 1959.

4   Beyond *Brown v. Board of Education*
Politics, Policy, and Problems

As Chapter 3 demonstrated, the battle against slavery and the segregation that followed the Civil War was long, hard, and frustrating. For those who thought that *Brown v. Board of Education* would end all that, there would be decades of bitter disappointment to follow. Given the outright resistance by segregationist states, the lack of support by some presidents, and the unwillingness by many outside the South to come to grips with the discrimination that was pervasive even if it had never been formally adopted as policy, the effort to develop a new body of civil rights law and policy that would address the complex contemporary situation would be an ongoing challenge. This chapter considers the resistance to civil rights progress, judicial, presidential, and legislative responses to it, the development of legal standards for constitutional claims of discrimination, and continuing debates over unresolved issues.

Civil Rights after *Brown*: A Large Agenda with Many Challenges

For many Americans, there is a tendency to think of the civil rights movement as something that began when Reverend Martin Luther King, Jr. took up the leadership of opposition to segregation in Montgomery, Alabama following the arrest of Ms. Rosa Parks, who refused to give up her seat on a city bus to a white man. But the fact is that much had happened before Dr. King took up his first pastorate at the Dexter Avenue Baptist Church in Montgomery in 1954. The bus boycott did not begin until the end of 1955, after the second *Brown v. Board of Education* ruling had been delivered, and ended in mid-1956 because the United States District Court for the Middle District of Alabama declared the discriminatory Birmingham bus policies in violation of the equal protection clause;[1] a decision that was affirmed only a month later by the U.S. Supreme Court.[2] Indeed, the Southern Christian Leadership Conference, which Dr. King was to lead in many key civil rights battles, was not even created until 1957. And in the interim, there was the dramatic clash over the desegregation of the Little Rock Central High School.[3] It was not until 1959 that Dr. King came to the Ebenezer Baptist Church in Atlanta to join his father as co-pastor, the ministry for which he is perhaps best remembered by many today.

Thus the battle for equality would be long and hard even after the *Brown* ruling. What followed was an era of resistance to legally mandated desegregation. On the other hand, it was also a period in which the courts were called upon to respond to this "massive resistance," and the president and congress faced the need for the creation of a modern body of civil rights law. The path forward after *Brown* was not the kind of step-by-step legal campaign that led from the Maryland law school case to *Brown*, but the battle produced a number of important rulings in a variety of critical areas that, along with the new body of statutes, provided the framework for the civil rights protection with which we live and work today.

The Onset of Massive Resistance: The Little Rock School Fight

It was clear from the time of the oral argument in the *Brown II* case that there was little likelihood that the Southern states would comply with the ruling, and that they would even resist openly and directly. By that point, the law had been clearly stated and the only question was the form of the remedy that the Supreme Court would order for the proven cases of discrimination that the Court had addressed in *Brown I.* At oral argument, Chief Justice Earl Warren attempted to pin down S. Emory Rogers, representing the segregationist states, for assurances that they would obey the law. At the end of a frustrating exchange, Warren said: "But you are not willing to say here that there would be an honest attempt to conform to this decree if we did leave it to the district court?" Rogers replied: "No, I am not. Let us get the word 'honest' out of there." Warren answered sharply: "No, leave it in." Rogers then immediately replied: "No, because I would have to tell you that right now we would not conform—we would not send our white children to the Negro schools."[4]

After the ruling, the justices and the nation looked to President Eisenhower to see if he would commit the nation to fulfill the promises of the *Brown* rulings. He did not. Eisenhower had exchanges with any number of key players, but was clearly not going to take forceful action. He also made it clear that he was troubled by the *Brown* decision, and that his concern for the reaction of those who resisted was less about civil rights than it was the idea that it was a legal statement and refusal to obey threatened the fundamentals of the government. To his boyhood friend, Navy Captain "Swede" Hazlett, he wrote: "I think that no other single event has so disturbed the domestic scene in many years as did the Supreme Court's decision of 1954 in the school segregation case."[5] It was revealing that after that statement he went on in the letter to say: "I suppose at the moment a problem of possibly even greater importance to us is the threat of inflation."[6] He said that because inflation was threatening to rise to four percent.[7] He wrote those words after dozens of members of Congress had published the so-called "Southern Manifesto," after states like Arkansas had amended the state constitution to mandate resistance to desegregation, and after legislation had been passed to implement those provisions. In fact, the nation was less than a month and a half away from a showdown in Little Rock, Arkansas, where African American children were scheduled to begin the implementation of school integration in the face of threatened resistance by the state.

The Southern Manifesto was read into the Congressional Record as signed by nineteen Senators and seventy-seven members of the House. It committed the signatories, in part, as follows:

> ... We decry the Supreme Court's encroachment on the rights reserved to the States and to the people, contrary to established law, and to the Constitution.
>
> We commend the motives of those States which have declared the intention to resist forced integration by any lawful means.
>
> We appeal to the States and people who are not directly affected by these decisions to consider the constitutional principles involved against the time when they too, on issues vital to them may be the victims of judicial encroachment....
>
> We pledge ourselves to use all lawful means to bring about a reversal of this decision which is contrary to the Constitution and to prevent the use of force in its implementation.[8]

Warren and others were convinced that Eisenhower's failure to make a forceful statement of his intentions to enforce the Court's ruling not only signaled his own lack of commitment to racial equality, but also encouraged the resistance that was rapidly developing in the states.[9]

Indeed, Justice William O. Douglas later charged that: "Ike's ominous silence on our 1954 decision gave courage to the racists who decided to resist the decision ward by ward, precinct by precinct, town by town, and county by county."[10]

Douglas was correct that one of the strategies adopted by the opponents of desegregation was to claim that the *Brown* ruling applied only to the five specific school districts involved and that any other action would require school district by school district rulings, which they intended to fight at every turn. That was one of the arguments that would be used by Governor Orville Faubus and the state of Arkansas to block mandated desegregation and to prevent the integration of Little Rock Central High School. Beyond that, they used thinly veiled threats to the personal safety of the African American children involved in an eleventh-hour attempt to force the federal courts to back down. That action gave rise to the only opinion in the history of the United States Supreme Court that was signed by all the members of the Court, taking personal as well as collective responsibility for the ruling.

Cooper v. Aaron

358 U.S. 1 (1958)

INTRODUCTION: This is the famous Little Rock, Arkansas school desegregation case. The opinion explains the facts. However, the important point here is that the Governor, Orville Faubus, had threatened that children might be at risk if the federal courts did not delay the requirements for desegregation.

The Court's opinion was authored by Chief Justice Warren and Justices Black, Frankfurter, Douglas, Burton, Clark, Harlan, Brennan, and Whittaker.

As this case reaches us it raises questions of the highest importance to the maintenance of our federal system of government. It necessarily involves a claim by the Governor and Legislature of a State that there is no duty on state officials to obey federal court orders resting on this Court's considered interpretation of the United States Constitution. Specifically it involves actions by the Governor and Legislature of Arkansas upon the premise that they are not bound by our holding in *Brown v. Board of Education*.... We are urged to uphold a suspension of the Little Rock School Board's plan to do away with segregated public schools in Little Rock until state laws and efforts to upset and nullify our holding in *Brown* have been further challenged and tested in the courts. We reject these contentions.

The case was argued before us on September 11, 1958. On the following day we unanimously affirmed the judgment of the Court of Appeals for the Eighth Circuit, ... which had reversed a judgment of the District Court for the Eastern District of Arkansas.... The District Court had granted the application of the petitioners, the Little Rock School Board and School Superintendent, to suspend for two and one-half years the operation of the School Board's court-approved desegregation program. In order that the School Board might know, without doubt, its duty in this regard before the opening of school, which had been set for the following Monday, September 15, 1958, we immediately issued the judgment, reserving the expression of our supporting views to a later date. This opinion of all of the members of the Court embodies those views.

... On May 17, 1954, this Court decided that enforced racial segregation in the public schools of a State is a denial of the equal protection of the laws enjoined by the Fourteenth Amendment. The Court postponed, pending further argument, formulation of a decree to effectuate this decision. That decree was rendered May 31, 1955. *Brown v. Board of Education [II]*.... In the formulation of that decree the Court recognized that good faith compliance with the principles declared in *Brown* might in some situations "call for elimination of a variety of obstacles in making the transition to school systems operated in accordance with the constitutional principles set forth in our May 17, 1954, decision." ... The Court went on to state: "Courts of equity may properly take into account the public interest in the elimination of such obstacles in a systematic and effective manner. But it should go without saying that the vitality of these constitutional principles cannot be allowed to yield simply because of disagreement with them."

... [T]he District Courts were directed to require "a prompt and reasonable start toward full compliance," and to take such action as was necessary to bring about the end of racial segregation in the public schools "with all deliberate speed." ... It was made plain that delay in any guise in order to deny the constitutional rights of Negro children could not be countenanced, and that only a prompt start, diligently and earnestly pursued, to eliminate racial segregation from the public schools could constitute good faith compliance....

... [The] Little Rock District School Board ... approved ... a [desegregation] plan on May 24, 1955, seven days before the second *Brown* opinion.... [D]esegregation at the high school level would commence in the fall of 1957, and ... complete desegregation of the school system would be accomplished by 1963....

[O]ther state authorities, in contrast, were actively pursuing a program designed to perpetuate in Arkansas the system of racial segregation which this Court had held violated the Fourteenth Amendment. First came, in November 1956, an amendment to the State Constitution flatly commanding the Arkansas General Assembly to oppose "in every Constitutional manner the Un-constitutional desegregation decisions of May 17, 1954 and May 31, 1955 of the United States Supreme Court," .... Pursuant to this state constitutional command, a law relieving school children from compulsory attendance at racially mixed schools ... and a law establishing a State Sovereignty Commission ... were enacted by the General Assembly in February 1957.

The School Board and the Superintendent of Schools nevertheless continued with preparations to carry out the first stage of the desegregation program. Nine Negro children were scheduled for admission in September 1957 to Central High School, which has more than two thousand students.

On September 2, 1957, the day before these Negro students were to enter Central High, the school authorities were met with drastic opposing action on the part of the Governor of Arkansas who dispatched units of the Arkansas National Guard to the Central High School grounds and placed the school "off limits" to colored students.... [T]he Governor's action had not been requested by the school authorities, and was entirely unheralded....

The ... Governor's action caused the School Board to request the Negro students on September 2 not to attend the high school "until the legal dilemma was solved." ... The [District Court] determined that this was not a reason for departing from the approved plan, and ordered the School Board and Superintendent to proceed with it.

On the morning of the next day, September 4, 1957, the Negro children attempted to enter the high school but, as the District Court later found, units of the Arkansas National Guard "acting pursuant to the Governor's order, stood shoulder to shoulder at the school grounds and thereby forcibly prevented the 9 Negro students ... from entering," as they continued to do every school day during the following three weeks....

... [The U.S. Attorney] and the Attorney General of the United States, at the District Court's request ... filed a petition on behalf of the United States, as amicus curiae, to enjoin the Governor of Arkansas and officers of the Arkansas National Guard from further attempts to prevent obedience to the court's order. After hearings on the petition, the District Court found that the School Board's plan had been obstructed by the Governor through the use of National Guard troops, and granted a preliminary injunction on September enjoining the Governor and the officers of the Guard from preventing the attendance of Negro children at Central High School, and from otherwise obstructing or interfering with the orders of the court in connection with the plan.... The National Guard was then withdrawn from the school.

The next school day was Monday, September 23, 1957. The Negro children entered the high school that morning under the protection of the Little Rock Police Department and members of the Arkansas State Police. But the officers caused the children to be removed from the school during the morning because they had difficulty controlling a large and demonstrating crowd which had gathered at the high school.... On September 25, however, the President of the United States dispatched federal troops to Central High School and admission of the Negro students to the school was thereby effected. Regular army troops continued at the high school until November 27, 1957. They were then replaced by federalized National Guardsmen who remained throughout the balance of the school year. Eight of the Negro students remained in attendance at the school throughout the school year.

We come now to the aspect of the proceedings presently before us. On February 20, 1958, the School Board and the Superintendent of Schools filed a petition in the District Court seeking a postponement of their program for desegregation. Their position in essence was that because of extreme public hostility, which they stated had been engendered largely by the official attitudes and actions of the Governor and the Legislature, the maintenance of a sound educational program at Central High School, with the Negro students in attendance, would be impossible....

... [The] District Court granted the [delay].... The Court of Appeals ... reversed ... [and] we unanimously affirmed ... in the per curiam[11] opinion.... We ... have accepted the findings of the District Court as to the conditions at Central High School during the 1957–1958 school year.... The significance of these findings, however, is to be considered in light of the fact, indisputably revealed by the record before us, that the conditions they depict are directly traceable to the actions of legislators and executive officials of the State of Arkansas, taken in their official capacities, which reflect their own determination to resist this Court's decision in the *Brown* case and which have brought about violent resistance to that decision in Arkansas.... The constitutional rights of respondents are not to be sacrificed or yielded to the violence and disorder which have followed upon the actions of the Governor and Legislature. As this Court said some 41 years ago in a unanimous opinion in a case involving another aspect of racial segregation: "It is urged that this proposed segregation will promote the public peace by preventing race conflicts. Desirable as this is, and important as is the preservation of the public peace, this aim cannot be accomplished by laws or ordinances which deny rights created or protected by the Federal Constitution." *Buchanan v. Warley*.... Thus law and order are not here to be preserved by depriving the Negro children of their constitutional rights.

The controlling legal principles are plain. The command of the Fourteenth Amendment is that no "State" shall deny to any person within its jurisdiction the equal protection of the laws.... In short, the constitutional rights of children not to be discriminated against in school admission on grounds of race or color declared by this Court in the *Brown* case can neither be nullified openly and directly by state legislators or state executive or judicial officers, nor nullified indirectly by them through evasive schemes for segregation whether attempted "ingeniously or ingenuously." ...

[W]e should answer the premise of the actions of the Governor and Legislature that they are not bound by our holding in the *Brown* case. It is necessary only to recall some basic constitutional propositions which are settled doctrine. Article VI of the Constitution makes the Constitution the "supreme Law of the Land." In 1803, Chief Justice Marshall, speaking for a unanimous Court ... declared in the notable case of *Marbury v. Madison*, ... that "It is emphatically the province and duty of the judicial department to say what the law is." This decision declared the basic principle that the federal judiciary is supreme in the exposition of the law of the Constitution, and that principle has ever since been respected by this Court and the Country as a permanent and indispensable feature of our constitutional system. It follows that the interpretation of the Fourteenth Amendment enunciated by this Court in the *Brown* case is the supreme law of the land, and Art. VI of the Constitution makes it of binding effect on the States "any Thing in the Constitution or Laws of any State to the Contrary notwithstanding." ...

No state legislator or executive or judicial officer can war against the Constitution without violating his undertaking to support it. Chief Justice Marshall spoke for a unanimous Court in saying that: "If the legislatures of the several states may, at will, annul the judgments of the courts of the United States, and destroy the rights acquired under those judgments, the constitution itself becomes a solemn mockery ...." *United States v. Peters*, 5 Cranch 115, 136 [1809].

... The Constitution created a government dedicated to equal justice under law. The Fourteenth Amendment embodied and emphasized that ideal. State support of segregated schools through any arrangement, management, funds, or property cannot be squared with the Amendment's command that no State shall deny to any person within its jurisdiction the equal protection of the laws.... Since the first *Brown* opinion three new Justices have come to the Court. They are at one with the Justices still on the Court who participated in that basic decision as to its correctness, and that decision is now unanimously reaffirmed. The principles announced in that decision and the obedience of the States to them, according to the command of the Constitution, are indispensable for the protection of the freedoms guaranteed by our fundamental charter for all of us. Our constitutional ideal of equal justice under law is thus made a living truth.

The Court would not abide the attempt to sidestep what was clearly a ruling intended to address all states and all school districts. Neither would it permit segregationist officials to use the cowardly tactic of threats on the lives and safety of African American children to interfere with the lawful orders of the federal court responsible for providing a remedy for segregation. In the end, Eisenhower was forced to federalize the Arkansas National Guard and to provide support from federal troops to ensure against further illegal action by state and local officials and white residents of the affected communities.

Going to the Core: The Rejection of Anti-Miscegenation Laws

There was no question that one of the key forces at the heart of resistance to school desegregation was the dreaded fear that it might encourage interracial relationships and later marriages. The incredible irony of this situation, of course, was the fact that it was well known that there was a long history of sexual liaisons between white slave owners and African American women that produced any number of children. However, the wrong look from an African American man toward a white woman was often used as an excuse to lynch the man. The visceral reaction against the recognition of interracial marriage kept the laws against such relationships alive long after civil rights rulings had struck down many historical barriers to progress.

Loving v. Virginia

388 U.S. 1 (1967)

INTRODUCTION: The facts of this case are provided in the excerpt from the Court's opinion below. What may be surprising to some here is the date of this case. Many readers come to this opinion with the idea that this type of statute would have been struck far earlier than this. Others think that this was a formal recognition of what American society had already decreed. Unfortunately, that was not the case. Official discrimination against interracial marriage was also a factor in encouraging housing discrimination against mixed-race couples. This was a significant problem in an era when Americans were becoming more mobile than ever and moving from state to state for jobs or military service. Note the application of due process in this case.

Chief Justice Warren wrote the opinion for the Court.

> This case presents a constitutional question never addressed by this Court: whether a statutory scheme adopted by the State of Virginia to prevent marriages between persons solely on the basis of racial classifications violates the Equal Protection and Due Process Clauses of the Fourteenth Amendment. [W]e conclude that these statutes cannot stand consistently with the Fourteenth Amendment.

> In June 1958, two residents of Virginia, Mildred Jeter, a Negro woman, and Richard Loving, a white man, were married in the District of Columbia pursuant to its laws. Shortly after their marriage, the Lovings returned to Virginia and established their marital abode in Caroline County. At the October Term, 1958, of the Circuit Court of Caroline County, a grand jury issued an indictment charging the Lovings with violating Virginia's ban on interracial marriages. On January 6, 1959, the Lovings pleaded guilty to the charge and were sentenced to one year in jail; however, the trial judge suspended the sentence for a period of 25 years on the condition that the Lovings leave the State and not return to Virginia together for 25 years. He stated in an opinion that: "Almighty God created the races white, black, yellow, malay and red, and he placed them on separate continents. And but for the interference with his arrangement there would be no cause for such marriages. The fact that he separated the races shows that he did not intend for the races to mix."

> After their convictions, the Lovings took up residence in the District of Columbia.... The Supreme Court of Appeals upheld the constitutionality of the anti-miscegenation statutes and ... the convictions. The Lovings appealed this decision.

The two statutes under which appellants were convicted and sentenced are part of a comprehensive statutory scheme aimed at prohibiting and punishing interracial marriages.... Virginia is now one of 16 States which prohibit and punish marriages on the basis of racial classifications. Penalties for miscegenation arose as an incident to slavery and have been common in Virginia since the colonial period. The present statutory scheme dates from the adoption of the Racial Integrity Act of 1924, passed during the period of extreme nativism which followed the end of the First World War.

I. In upholding the constitutionality of these provisions in the decision below, the Supreme Court of Appeals of Virginia [found] that the State's legitimate purposes were "to preserve the racial integrity of its citizens," and to prevent "the corruption of blood," "a mongrel breed of citizens," and "the obliteration of racial pride," obviously an endorsement of the doctrine of White Supremacy.... The court also reasoned that marriage has traditionally been subject to state regulation without federal intervention, and, consequently, the regulation of marriage should be left to exclusive state control by the Tenth Amendment.

While the state court is no doubt correct in asserting that marriage is a social relation subject to the State's police power, ... the State does not contend ... that its powers to regulate marriage are unlimited.... Instead, the State argues that..., because its miscegenation statutes punish equally both the white and the Negro participants in an interracial marriage, these statutes, despite their reliance on racial classifications, do not constitute an invidious discrimination based upon race. The second argument advanced by the State assumes the validity of its equal application theory. The argument is that, if the Equal Protection Clause does not outlaw miscegenation statutes because of their reliance on racial classifications, the question of constitutionality would thus become whether there was any rational basis for a State to treat interracial marriages differently from other marriages. On this question, the State argues, the scientific evidence is substantially in doubt and, consequently, this Court should defer to the wisdom of the state legislature in adopting its policy of discouraging interracial marriages.

Because we reject the notion that the mere "equal application" of a statute containing racial classifications is enough to remove the classifications from the Fourteenth Amendment's proscription of all invidious racial discriminations, we do not accept the State's contention that these statutes should be upheld if there is any possible basis for concluding that they serve a rational purpose.... [W]e deal with statutes containing racial classifications, and the fact of equal application does not immunize the statute from the very heavy burden of justification which the Fourteenth Amendment has traditionally required of state statutes drawn according to race....

The State finds support for its "equal application" theory in the decision of the Court in *Pace v. Alabama* ... (1883). In that case, the Court upheld a conviction under an Alabama statute forbidding adultery or fornication between a white person and a Negro which imposed a greater penalty than that of a statute proscribing similar conduct by members of the same race. The Court reasoned that the statute could not be said to discriminate against Negroes because the punishment for each participant in the offense was the same. However, as recently as the 1964 Term, in rejecting the reasoning of that case, we stated "*Pace* represents a limited view of the Equal Protection Clause which has not withstood analysis in the subsequent decisions of this Court." ... [T]he Equal Protection Clause requires the consideration of whether the classifications drawn by any statute constitute an arbitrary and invidious discrimination. The clear and central purpose of the Fourteenth Amendment was to eliminate all official state sources of invidious racial discrimination in the States....

There can be no question but that Virginia's miscegenation statutes rest solely upon distinctions drawn according to race. The statutes proscribe generally accepted conduct if engaged in by members of different races. Over the years, this Court has consistently repudiated "distinctions between citizens solely because of their ancestry" as being "odious to a free people whose institutions are founded upon the doctrine of equality." ... At the very least, the Equal Protection Clause demands that racial classifications ... be subjected to the "most rigid scrutiny," *Korematsu v. United States*....

There is patently no legitimate overriding purpose independent of invidious racial discrimination which justifies this classification. The fact that Virginia prohibits only interracial marriages involving white persons demonstrates that the racial classifications must stand on their own justification, as measures designed to maintain White Supremacy. We have consistently denied the constitutionality of measures which restrict the rights of citizens on account of race. There can be no doubt that restricting the freedom to marry solely because of racial classifications violates the central meaning of the Equal Protection Clause.

II. These statutes also deprive the Lovings of liberty without due process of law in violation of the Due Process Clause of the Fourteenth Amendment. The freedom to marry has long been recognized as one of the vital personal rights essential to the orderly pursuit of happiness by free men.

Marriage is one of the "basic civil rights of man," fundamental to our very existence and survival. *Skinner v. Oklahoma* .... To deny this fundamental freedom on so unsupportable a basis as the racial classifications embodied in these statutes, classifications so directly subversive of the principle of equality at the heart of the Fourteenth Amendment, is surely to deprive all the State's citizens of liberty without due process of law. The Fourteenth Amendment requires that the freedom of choice to marry not be restricted by invidious racial discriminations. Under our Constitution, the freedom to marry, or not marry, a person of another race resides with the individual and cannot be infringed by the State. These convictions must be reversed.[12]

The Rise of Contemporary Civil Rights Statutes

In the years after *Brown* it became obvious that the courts alone could not ensure that civil rights would be protected in communities around the nation on a day-to-day basis. The legal pronouncements were a necessary but not sufficient condition to change the society. Although there was a developing social movement to confront racism, more was needed. One of the essential ingredients would have to be federal civil rights legislation along with the means to enforce it.

Although the *Civil Rights Cases* had eliminated a very important piece of the civil rights legislation that was originally adopted following the Civil War, two other key pieces remained. One of these was the Civil Rights Act of 1871, also known as the Ku Klux Klan Act, intended to allow federal court action where state or local governments or officials refused to protect persons whose civil rights were threatened or actually violated. That statute is still a central piece of civil rights law in the nation and is commonly known simply by its U.S. Code designation, 42 U.S.C. §1983. It is probably the most commonly cited civil rights provision in federal law.

The other piece of legislation is the Civil Rights Act of 1866[13] and was designed to protect the right of all persons "to inherit, purchase, lease, sell, hold, and convey real and personal property." That piece of legislation turned out to be complex and difficult to enforce for a variety of reasons, including state and local resistance, a failure of federal commitment and even active discriminatory behavior, and complex judicial interpretations.

Congress started a new round of legislation with the passage of the Civil Rights Act of 1957. Although it is not well known today, it was considered a major step when it was passed, and elicited what still stands as the longest filibuster by a single senator in history. That was the ardent segregationist Strom Thurmond, who battled to block the legislation. Among the things that legislation launched was the U.S. Commission on Civil Rights with subpoena power to investigate violations of civil rights. Those investigations have, over the years, led to significant federal enforcement actions as well as adoption of new or amended legislation in a wide range of fields, from voting rights to police conduct issues.

Even so, it was clear that far more effective civil rights legislation was needed. Although President Kennedy provided an executive order on civil rights, E.O. 10925, and ultimately supported legislation that would evolve into the Civil Rights Act of 1964, he resisted calls for his administration to take an active leadership role in civil rights action. Circumstances forced his hand on several occasions and the tragic loss of life among civil rights workers created a momentum for change that demanded a response.

For example, in 1962 Mississippi Governor Ross Barnett vowed to block the admission of James Meredith to the University of Mississippi. Kennedy ultimately issued a proclamation, warning the governor and others to "cease and desist therefrom and to disperse and retire peaceably forthwith."[14] He then also promulgated an executive order that sent federal Marshals and U.S. military units to the campus to restore order and protect Mr. Meredith. In the end, Barnett was held in criminal contempt of court.[15]

There had been violent attacks on freedom riders in the South. Civil rights workers seeking to register African Americans to vote were arrested and jailed on trumped-up charges. Others were badly beaten and in other cases murdered. The nation watched on television as officials in Birmingham turned police dogs and fire hoses on peaceful demonstrators. The violence was turned against African Americans who were not active in the movement, including bombing of churches that took the lives of four children attending Sunday school in Alabama. Following that attack, on June 11, 1963 President Kennedy gave a televised address to the nation announcing his intention to ask Congress for a new and comprehensive civil rights act. He added:

> We face, therefore, a moral crisis as a country and a people.... A great change is at hand, and our task, our obligation, is to make that revolution, that change, peaceful and constructive for all. Those who do nothing are inviting shame, as well as violence. Those who act boldly are recognizing right, as well as reality....[16]

After President Kennedy was assassinated in November 1963, President Lyndon Baines Johnson immediately announced in his first address to a joint session of Congress his intention to make the civil rights bill a major priority.

> [N]o memorial oration or eulogy could more eloquently honor President Kennedy's memory than the earliest possible passage of the civil rights bill for which he fought so long. We have talked long enough in this country about equal rights. We have talked for

one hundred years or more. It is time now to write the next chapter, and to write it in the books of law...."[17]

He began his State of the Union Address in 1964 by challenging Congress: "Let this session of Congress be known as the session which did more for civil rights than the last hundred sessions combined."[18] On July 2 of that year Johnson signed the Civil Rights Act of 1964.[19] That law outlawed discrimination in public accommodation, in the use of federal funds, and in employment. It became a foundation law that would be amended and strengthened over time.

The passage of the Civil Rights Act did not end the violence or bring a rapid halt to segregation. In fact, it did not address a critically important part of the civil rights struggle, the right to vote. In June 1964 civil rights workers Michael Schwerner, Andrew Goodman, and James Chaney disappeared in Mississippi and were later found murdered and buried in an earthen dam. In 1965 the campaign for the right to vote came with plans for a march from Selma, Alabama to the capitol in Birmingham. In the run-up to the march and during it, Jimmie Lee Jackson, Reverend James Reeb, and Viola Lieuzo were killed. The first day of the trek, March 7, 1965, became known as "bloody Sunday," for when the marchers reached the Edmund Pettus bridge as they were leaving Selma, they were viciously set upon by Alabama state troopers. The events were captured on film and the nation saw raw racist brutality in action. A week after the Pettus Bridge violence, on March 15, President Lyndon Johnson gave his now famous speech demanding passage of the Voting Rights Act.[20]

> ... At times, history and fate meet at a single time in a single place to shape a turning point in man's unending search for freedom. So it was at Lexington and Concord. So it was a century ago at Appomattox. So it was last week in Selma, Alabama. There, long suffering men and women peacefully protested the denial of their rights as Americans. Many of them were brutally assaulted. One good man—a man of God—was killed....
>
> [T]he cries of pain and the hymns and protests of oppressed people have summoned into convocation all the majesty of this great government—the government of the greatest nation on earth. Our mission is at once the oldest and the most basic of this country—to right wrong, to do justice, to serve man.... Our lives have been marked with debate about great issues, issues of war and peace, issues of prosperity and depression.
>
> But rarely in any time does an issue lay bare the secret heart of America itself. Rarely are we met with a challenge, not to our growth or abundance, or our welfare or our security, but rather to the values and the purposes and the meaning of our beloved nation. The issue of equal rights for American Negroes is such an issue. And should we defeat every enemy, and should we double our wealth and conquer the stars, and still be unequal to this issue, then we will have failed as a people and as a nation. For, with a country as with a person, "what is a man profited if he shall gain the whole world, and lose his own soul?"
>
> There is no Negro problem. There is no Southern problem. There is no Northern problem. There is only an American problem.
>
> And we are met here tonight as Americans—not as Democrats or Republicans; we're met here as Americans to solve that problem. This was the first nation in the history of the world to be founded with a purpose. The great phrases of that purpose still sound in every American heart, North and South: "All men are created equal." "Government by consent of the governed." "Give me liberty or give me

death." And those are not just clever words, and those are not just empty theories. In their name Americans have fought and died for two centuries and tonight around the world they stand there as guardians of our liberty risking their lives. Those words are promised to every citizen that he shall share in the dignity of man. This dignity cannot be found in a man's possessions. It cannot be found in his power or in his position. It really rests on his right to be treated as a man equal in opportunity to all others. It says that he shall share in freedom. He shall choose his leaders, educate his children, provide for his family according to his ability and his merits as a human being.

To apply any other test, to deny a man his hopes because of his color or race or his religion or the place of his birth is not only to do injustice, it is to deny American and to dishonor the dead who gave their lives for American freedom. Our fathers believed that if this noble view of the rights of man was to flourish it must be rooted in democracy. This most basic right of all was the right to choose your own leaders. The history of this country in large measure is the history of expansion of the right to all of our people.

Many of the issues of civil rights are very complex and most difficult. But about this there can and should be no argument: every American citizen must have an equal right to vote. There is no reason which can excuse the denial of that right. There is no duty which weighs more heavily on us than the duty we have to insure that right. Yet the harsh fact is that in many places in this country men and women are kept from voting simply because they are Negroes.

Every device of which human ingenuity is capable, has been used to deny this right. The Negro citizen may go to register only to be told that the day is wrong, or the hour is late, or the official in charge is absent. And if he persists and, if he manages to present himself to the registrar, he may be disqualified because he did not spell out his middle name, or because he abbreviated a word on the application. And if he manages to fill out an application, he is given a test. The registrar is the sole judge of whether he passes this test. He may be asked to recite the entire Constitution, or explain the most complex provisions of state law. And even a college degree cannot be used to prove that he can read and write. For the fact is that the only way to pass these barriers is to show a white skin....

The Constitution says that no person shall be kept from voting because of his race or his color. We have all sworn an oath before God to support and to defend that Constitution. We must now act in obedience to that oath. Wednesday, I will send to Congress a law designed to eliminate illegal barriers to the right to vote.... This bill will strike down restrictions to voting in all elections, federal, state and local, which have been used to deny Negroes the right to vote.

... There is no Constitutional issue here. The command of the Constitution is plain. There is no moral issue. It is wrong—deadly wrong—to deny any of your fellow Americans the right to vote in this country.

There is no issue of state's rights or national rights. There is only the struggle for human rights. I have not the slightest doubt what will be your answer.... [T]here must be no delay, or no hesitation, or no compromise with our purpose. We cannot, we must not, refuse to protect the right of every American to vote in every election that he may desire to participate in.

And we ought not, and we cannot, and we must not wait another eight months before we get a bill. We have already waited 100 years and more and the time for waiting is gone…. But even if we pass this bill the battle will not be over. What happened in Selma is part of a far larger movement which reaches into every section and state of America. It is the effort of American Negroes to secure for themselves the full blessings of American life. Their cause must be our cause too. Because it's not just Negroes, but really it's all of us, who must overcome the crippling legacy of bigotry and injustice.

And we shall overcome.

… I know how difficult it is to reshape the attitudes and the structure of our society. But a century has passed … since the Negro was freed. And he is not fully free tonight. It was more than 100 years ago that Abraham Lincoln … signed the Emancipation Proclamation. But emancipation is a proclamation and not a fact. A century has passed … since equality was promised, and yet the Negro is not equal. A century has passed since the day of promise, and the promise is unkept. The time of justice has now come, and I tell you that I believe sincerely that no force can hold it back. It is right in the eyes of man and God that it should come, and when it does, I think that day will brighten the lives of every American….

And so I say to all of you here and to all in the nation tonight that those who appeal to you to hold on to the past do so at the cost of denying you your future. This great rich, restless country can offer opportunity and education and hope to all…. These are the enemies: poverty, ignorance, disease. They are our enemies, not our fellow man, not our neighbor.

And these enemies too—poverty, disease and ignorance—we shall overcome….

All Americans must have the privileges of citizenship, regardless of race, [but] to exercise these privileges takes much more than just legal rights. It requires a trained mind and a healthy body. It requires a decent home and the chance to find a job and the opportunity to escape from the clutches of poverty…. So we want to open the gates to opportunity. But we're also going to give all our people, black and white, the help that they need to walk through those gates. My first job after college was as a teacher in Cotulla, Texas, in a small Mexican-American school. Few of them could speak English and I couldn't speak much Spanish. My students were poor and they often came to class without breakfast and hungry. And they knew even in their youth the pain of prejudice. They never seemed to know why people disliked them, but they knew it was so because I saw it in their eyes.

I often walked home late in the afternoon after the classes were finished wishing there was more that I could do. But all I knew was to teach them the little that I knew, hoping that I might help them against the hardships that lay ahead. And somehow you never forget what poverty and hatred can do when you see its scars on the hopeful face of a young child.

I never thought then, in 1928, that I would be standing here in 1965. It never even occurred to me in my fondest dreams that I might have the chance to help the sons and daughters of those students, and to help people like them all over this country. But now I do have that chance. And I'll let you in on a secret—I mean to use it. And I hope that you will use it with me.[21]

The other major piece of civil rights legislation that African American civil rights leaders had sought was protection against housing discrimination. It came in the form of the Civil Rights Act of 1968, also known popularly as the Fair Housing Act.[22] It was, sadly, signed by President Johnson just a week after the assassination of Dr. Martin Luther King, Jr.

The Constitutional Challenge to the Civil Rights Act of 1964

It is difficult for many Americans to believe decades after the fact, but the effort to enact the Civil Rights Act of 1964 was a hard-fought battle in which, at times, the outcome was far from clear. And even after the law went into effect, there were challenges to the constitutional validity of the Act. Cases from Atlanta and Birmingham reached the Supreme Court.

Heart of Atlanta Motel v. United States

379 U.S. 241 (1964)

INTRODUCTION: This is one of the two cases brought to test the Article I authority of Congress to enact the Civil Rights Act of 1964. The fact that the decision of the Supreme Court in the *Civil Rights Cases* had never been overturned meant that Congress had to rely on the commerce power rather than simply the enforcement clause of the Fourteenth Amendment for the authority to support the new statute. The challengers focused on the claim that there was no commerce clause justification for the law.

Justice Clark wrote the opinion for the Court.

> This is a declaratory judgment action ... attacking the constitutionality of Title II of the Civil Rights Act of 1964... A three-judge court ... sustained the validity of the Act.... We affirm the judgment.

> [T]he Heart of Atlanta Motel ... has 216 rooms available to transient guests. The motel is located on Courtland Street, two blocks from downtown Peachtree Street. It is readily accessible to interstate highways 75 and 85 and state highways 23 and 41. Appellant solicits patronage from outside the State of Georgia through various national advertising media, including magazines of national circulation; it maintains over 50 billboards and highway signs within the State, soliciting patronage for the motel; it accepts convention trade from outside Georgia and approximately 75% of its registered guests are from out of State. Prior to passage of the Act the motel had followed a practice of refusing to rent rooms to Negroes, and it alleged that it intended to continue to do so. In an effort to perpetuate that policy this suit was filed....

> The appellees counter that the unavailability to Negroes of adequate accommodations interferes significantly with interstate travel, and that Congress, under the Commerce Clause, has power to remove such obstructions and restraints; that the Fifth Amendment does not forbid reasonable regulation and that consequential damage does not constitute a "taking" within the meaning of that amendment; that the Thirteenth Amendment claim fails because it is entirely frivolous to say that an amendment directed to the abolition of human bondage and the removal of widespread disabilities associated with slavery places discrimination in public accommodations beyond the reach of both federal and state law.

> Congress first evidenced its interest in civil rights legislation in the Civil Rights or Enforcement Act of April 9, 1866. There followed four Acts, with a fifth, the Civil Rights Act of March 1, 1875, culminating the series. In 1883 this Court struck down the public accommodations sections of the 1875 Act in the *Civil Rights Cases*.... No major legislation in this field had been enacted by Congress for 82 years when the Civil Rights Act of 1957 became law. It was followed by the Civil Rights Act of 1960. Three years later, on June 19, 1963, the late President

Kennedy called for civil rights legislation in a message to Congress to which he attached a proposed bill. Its stated purpose was "to promote the general welfare by eliminating discrimination based on race, color, religion, or national origin in ... public accommodations through the exercise by Congress of the powers conferred upon it ... to enforce the provisions of the fourteenth and fifteenth amendments, to regulate commerce among the several States, and to make laws necessary and proper to execute the powers conferred upon it by the Constitution." H. R. Doc. No. 124, 88th Cong., 1st Sess., at 14.... However, it was not until July 2, 1964, upon the recommendation of President Johnson, that the Civil Rights Act of 1964, here under attack, was finally passed.... The Act as finally adopted was most comprehensive, undertaking to prevent through peaceful and voluntary settlement discrimination in voting, as well as in places of accommodation and public facilities, federally secured programs and in employment....

It is admitted that the operation of the motel brings it within the provisions ... of the Act and that appellant refused to provide lodging for transient Negroes because of their race or color and that it intends to continue that policy unless restrained.

The sole question posed is, therefore, the constitutional [authority] of Congress to adopt the Civil Rights Act of 1964.... The legislative history of the Act indicates that Congress based the Act on §5 and the Equal Protection Clause of the Fourteenth Amendment as well as its power to regulate interstate commerce under Art. I, §8, cl. 3, of the Constitution.

The Senate Commerce Committee made it quite clear that the fundamental object of Title II was to vindicate "the deprivation of personal dignity that surely accompanies denials of equal access to public establishments." At the same time, however, it noted that such an objective has been and could be readily achieved "by congressional action based on the commerce power of the Constitution." ... Our study of the legislative record ... has brought us to the conclusion that Congress possessed ample power in this regard, and we have therefore not considered the other grounds relied upon....

In light of our ground for decision, it might be well at the outset to discuss the *Civil Rights Cases*.... We think that decision inapposite, and without precedential value in determining the constitutionality of the present Act.... [T]he applicability of Title II is carefully limited to enterprises having a direct and substantial relation to the interstate flow of goods and people, except where state action is involved....

While the Act as adopted carried no congressional findings, the record of its passage through each house is replete with evidence of the burdens that discrimination by race or color places upon interstate commerce.... This testimony includ the fact that our people have become increasingly mobile with millions of peo of all races traveling from State to State; that Negroes in particular have the subject of discrimination in transient accommodations, having to trave distances to secure the same; that often they have been unable to obtain modations and have had to call upon friends to put them up overnight; these conditions had become so acute as to require the listing of availabl for Negroes in a special guidebook which was itself "dramatic testim difficulties" Negroes encounter in travel.... We shall not burden this op further details since the voluminous testimony presents overwhelmi that discrimination by hotels and motels impedes interstate travel.

The ... determinative test of the exercise of power by the Congress under the Commerce Clause is simply whether the activity sought to be regulated is "commerce which concerns more States than one" and has a real and substantial relation to the national interest. Let us now turn to this facet of the problem.

That the "intercourse" of which the Chief Justice spoke included the movement of persons through more States than one was settled as early as 1849, in the *Passenger Cases*.... In framing Title II of this Act Congress was also dealing with what it considered a moral problem. But that fact does not detract from the overwhelming evidence of the disruptive effect that racial discrimination has had on commercial intercourse. It was this burden which empowered Congress to enact appropriate legislation, and, given this basis for the exercise of its power, Congress was not restricted by the fact that the particular obstruction to interstate commerce with which it was dealing was also deemed a moral and social wrong.

It is said that the operation of the motel here is of a purely local character. But, assuming this to be true, "if it is interstate commerce that feels the pinch, it does not matter how local the operation which applies the squeeze." Thus the power of Congress to promote interstate commerce also includes the power to regulate the local incidents thereof, including local activities in both the States of origin and destination, which might have a substantial and harmful effect upon that commerce. One need only examine the evidence which we have discussed above to see that Congress may—as it has—prohibit racial discrimination by motels serving travelers, however "local" their operations may appear.

... The commerce power invoked here by the Congress is a specific and plenary one authorized by the Constitution itself. The only questions are: (1) whether Congress had a rational basis for finding that racial discrimination by motels affected commerce, and (2) if it had such a basis, whether the means it selected to eliminate that evil are reasonable and appropriate. If they are, appellant has no "right" to select its guests as it sees fit, free from governmental regulation....

We, therefore, conclude that the action of the Congress in the adoption of the Act as applied here to a motel which concededly serves interstate travelers is within the power granted it by the Commerce Clause of the Constitution.... It may be argued that Congress could have pursued other methods to eliminate the obstructions it found in interstate commerce caused by racial discrimination. But [h]ow obstructions in commerce may be removed—what means are to be employed—is within the sound and exclusive discretion of the Congress. It is subject only to one caveat—that the means chosen by it must be reasonably adapted to the end permitted by the Constitution. We cannot say that its choice here was not so adapted. The Constitution requires no more.

Justice Black wrote a concurring opinion for this case and *Katzenbach v. McClung*.

... It requires no novel or strained interpretation of the Commerce Clause to sustain Title II as applied in either of these cases. At least since *Gibbons v. Ogden*, ... in 1824 ... it has been uniformly accepted that the power of Congress to regulate commerce among the States is plenary, "complete in itself, may be exercised to its utmost extent, and acknowledges no limitations, other than are prescribed in the constitution." ... Nor is "Commerce" as used in the Commerce Clause to be limited to a narrow, technical concept. It includes not only, as Congress has numerated in the Act, "travel, trade, traffic, commerce, transportation, or communication," but also all other unitary transactions and activities that take place in more States than one. That some parts or segments of such unitary transactions may take place only in one State cannot, of course, take from Congress its plenary power to regulate them in the national interest. The facilities and instrumentalities used to carry on this commerce, such as railroads, truck lines, ships, rivers, and even highways are also subject to congressional regulation, so far as is necessary to keep interstate traffic upon fair and equal terms....

Furthermore, it has long been held that the Necessary and Proper Clause, Art. I, §8, cl. 18, adds to the commerce power of Congress the power to regulate local instrumentalities operating within a single State if their activities burden the flow of commerce among the States.... [T]his Court has steadfastly followed, and indeed has emphasized time and time again, that Congress has ample power to protect interstate commerce from activities adversely and injuriously affecting it, which but for this adverse effect on interstate commerce would be beyond the power of Congress to regulate....

Congress in §201 declared that the racially discriminatory "operations" of a motel of more than five rooms for rent or hire do adversely affect interstate commerce if it "provides lodging to transient guests...," and that a restaurant's "operations" affect such commerce if (1) "it serves or offers to serve interstate travelers" or (2) "a substantial portion of the food which it serves ... has moved in [interstate] commerce." ... There can be no doubt that the operations of both the motel and the restaurant here fall squarely within the measure Congress chose to adopt in the Act and deemed adequate to show a constitutionally prohibitable adverse effect on commerce. The choice of policy is of course within the exclusive power of Congress; but whether particular operations affect interstate commerce sufficiently to come under the constitutional power of Congress to regulate them is ultimately a judicial rather than a legislative question, and can be settled finally only by this Court. I agree that as applied to this motel and this restaurant the Act is a valid exercise of congressional power, in the case of the motel because the record amply demonstrates that its practice of discrimination tended directly to interfere with interstate travel, and in the case of the restaurant because Congress had ample basis for concluding that a widespread practice of racial discrimination by restaurants buying as substantial a quantity of goods shipped from other States as this restaurant buys could distort or impede interstate trade....

The ... facts [in these cases] are more than enough ... to show that Congress acting within its discretion and judgment has power under the Commerce Clause and the Necessary and Proper Clause to bar racial discrimination in the Heart of Atlanta Motel and Ollie's Barbecue. I recognize that every remote, possible, speculative effect on commerce should not be accepted as an adequate constitutional ground to uproot and throw into the discard all our traditional distinctions between what is purely local, and therefore controlled by state laws, and what affects the national interest and is therefore subject to control by federal laws.... But in deciding the constitutional power of Congress in cases like the two before us we do not consider the effect on interstate commerce of only one isolated, individual, local event, without regard to the fact that this single local event when added to many others of a similar nature may impose a burden on interstate commerce by reducing its volume or distorting its flow.... There are approximately 20,000,000 Negroes in our country. Many of them are able to, and do, travel among the States in automobiles. Certainly it would seriously discourage such travel by them if, as evidence before the Congress indicated has been true in the past, they should in the future continue to be unable to find a decent place along their way in which to lodge or eat.... And the flow of interstate commerce may be impeded or distorted substantially if local sellers of interstate food are permitted to exclude all Negro consumers. Measuring, as this Court has so often held is required, by the aggregate effect of a great number of such acts of discrimination, I am of the opinion that Congress has constitutional power under the Commerce and Necessary and Proper Clauses to protect interstate commerce from the injuries bound to befall it from these discriminatory practices.

Justice Douglas wrote a concurring opinion that also applied to *Katzenbach v. McClung*.

Though I join the Court's opinions, I am somewhat reluctant ... to rest solely on the Commerce Clause. My reluctance is not due to any conviction that Congress lacks power to regulate commerce in the interests of human rights. It is rather my belief that the right of people to be free of state action that discriminates against them because of race, like the "right of persons to move freely from State to State" ..., "occupies a more protected position in our constitutional system than does the movement of cattle, fruit, steel and coal across state lines." Moreover, ... the result reached by the Court is for me much more obvious as a protective measure under the Fourteenth Amendment than under the Commerce Clause. For the former deals with the constitutional status of the individual not with the impact on commerce of local activities or vice versa.

Hence I would prefer to rest on the assertion of legislative power contained in §5 of the Fourteenth Amendment which states: "The Congress shall have power to enforce, by appropriate legislation, the provisions of this article"—a power which the Court concedes was exercised at least in part in this Act.

A decision based on the Fourteenth Amendment would have a more settling effect, making unnecessary litigation over whether a particular restaurant or inn is within the commerce definitions of the Act or whether a particular customer is an interstate traveler. Under my construction, the Act would apply to all customers in all the enumerated places of public accommodation. And that construction would put an end to all obstructionist strategies and finally close one door on a bitter chapter in American history.

I think the Court is correct in concluding that the Act is not founded on the Commerce Clause to the exclusion of the Enforcement Clause of the Fourteenth Amendment.... [W]hile I agree with the Court that Congress in fashioning the present Act used the Commerce Clause to regulate racial segregation, it also used (and properly so) some of its power under §5 of the Fourteenth Amendment.

I repeat what I said earlier, that our decision should be based on the Fourteenth Amendment, thereby putting an end to all obstructionist strategies and allowing every person—whatever his race, creed, or color—to patronize all places of public accommodation without discrimination whether he travels interstate or intrastate.

Justice Goldberg wrote a concurring opinion that also applied to *Katzenbach v. McClung*.

I join in the opinions and judgments of the Court, since I agree "that the action of the Congress in the adoption of the Act as applied here ... is within the power granted it by the Commerce Clause of the Constitution, as interpreted by this Court for 140 years." ...

The primary purpose of the Civil Rights Act of 1964, however, as the Court recognizes, and as I would underscore, is the vindication of human dignity and not

mere economics. The Senate Commerce Committee made this quite clear: "...
Discrimination is not simply dollars and cents, hamburgers and movies; it is the
humiliation, frustration, and embarrassment that a person must surely feel when
he is told that he is unacceptable as a member of the public because of his race
or color." ...

In my concurring opinion in *Bell v. Maryland*, ... however, I expressed my conviction that §1 of the Fourteenth Amendment guarantees to all Americans the
constitutional right "to be treated as equal members of the community with
respect to public accommodations," and that "Congress [has] authority under
§5 of the Fourteenth Amendment, or under the Commerce Clause, Art. I, §8,
to implement the rights protected by §1 of the Fourteenth Amendment. In the
give-and-take of the legislative process, Congress can fashion a law drawing the
guidelines necessary and appropriate to facilitate practical administration and to
distinguish between genuinely public and private accommodations." The challenged Act is just such a law and, in my view, Congress clearly had authority
under both §5 of the Fourteenth Amendment and the Commerce Clause to enact
the Civil Rights Act of 1964.

Katzenbach v. McClung

379 U.S. 294 (1964)

INTRODUCTION: This was the companion case to *Heart of Atlanta*. The three-judge
federal district court rejected the application of the Civil Rights Act of 1964 to Ollie's
Barbecue in Birmingham, Alabama.

Justice Clark wrote the opinion for the Court.

1 ... Ollie's Barbecue is a family-owned restaurant in Birmingham, Alabama, spe-
cializing in barbecued meats and homemade pies, with a seating capacity of 220
customers. It is located on a state highway 11 blocks from an interstate one and a
somewhat greater distance from railroad and bus stations. The restaurant caters
to a family and white-collar trade with a take-out service for Negroes. It employs
36 persons, two-thirds of whom are Negroes.

In the 12 months preceding the passage of the Act, the restaurant purchased
locally approximately $150,000 worth of food, $69,683 or 46% of which was meat
that it bought from a local supplier who had procured it from outside the State.
The District Court expressly found that a substantial portion of the food served
in the restaurant had moved in interstate commerce. The restaurant has refused to
serve Negroes in its dining accommodations since its original opening in 1927....
The court below concluded that if it were required to serve Negroes it would lose
a substantial amount of business....

[I]n *Heart of Atlanta Motel* ... we found [Title II] a valid exercise of the power
to regulate interstate commerce insofar as it requires hotels and motels to serve
transients without regard to their race or color. In this case we consider its application to restaurants which serve food a substantial portion of which has moved
in commerce....

Sections 201(b)(2) and (c) place any "restaurant ... principally engaged in selling
food for consumption on the premises" under the Act "if ... it serves or offers to
serve interstate travelers or a substantial portion of the food which it serves ... has
moved in commerce." Ollie's Barbecue admits that it is covered by these provisions
of the Act.... The sole question [is] whether Title II, as applied to a restaurant

annually receiving about $70,000 worth of food which has moved in commerce, is a valid exercise of the power of Congress....

As we noted in *Heart of Atlanta Motel* both Houses of Congress conducted prolonged hearings on the Act.... The record is replete with testimony of the burdens placed on interstate commerce by racial discrimination in restaurants. A comparison of per capita spending by Negroes in restaurants, theaters, and like establishments indicated less spending, after discounting income differences, in areas where discrimination is widely practiced.... This diminutive spending springing from a refusal to serve Negroes and their total loss as customers has, regardless of the absence of direct evidence, a close connection to interstate commerce. The ... Attorney General testified that this type of discrimination imposed "an artificial restriction on the market" and interfered with the flow of merchandise.... In addition, there were many references to discriminatory situations causing wide unrest and having a depressant effect on general business conditions in the respective communities....

Moreover there was an impressive array of testimony that discrimination in restaurants had a direct and highly restrictive effect upon interstate travel by Negroes. This resulted, it was said, because discriminatory practices prevent Negroes from buying prepared food served on the premises while on a trip, except in isolated and unkempt restaurants and under most unsatisfactory and often unpleasant conditions. This obviously discourages travel and obstructs interstate commerce for one can hardly travel without eating. Likewise, it was said, that discrimination deterred professional, as well as skilled, people from moving into areas where such practices occurred and thereby caused industry to be reluctant to establish there....

We believe that this testimony afforded ample basis for the conclusion that established restaurants in such areas sold less interstate goods because of the discrimination, that interstate travel was obstructed directly by it, that business in general suffered and that many new businesses refrained from establishing there as a result of it. Hence the District Court was in error in concluding that there was no connection between discrimination and the movement of interstate commerce. The court's conclusion ... flies in the face of stubborn fact.

It goes without saying that, viewed in isolation, the volume of food purchased by Ollie's Barbecue from sources supplied from out of state was insignificant when compared with the total foodstuffs moving in commerce. But, as our late Brother Jackson said for the Court in *Wickard v. Filburn*, 317 U.S. 111 (1942): "That appellee's own contribution to the demand for wheat may be trivial by itself is not enough to remove him from the scope of federal regulation where, as here, his contribution, taken together with that of many others similarly situated, is far from trivial." ...

[The commerce power and the necessary and proper clause], as we have pointed out in *Heart of Atlanta Motel*, "extends to those activities intrastate which so affect interstate commerce, or the exertion of the power of Congress over it, as to make regulation of them appropriate means to the attainment of a legitimate end, the effective execution of the granted power to regulate interstate commerce." ... Much is said about a restaurant business being local but "even if appellee's activity be local and though it may not be regarded as commerce, it may still, whatever its nature, be reached by Congress if it exerts a substantial economic effect on interstate commerce ...." *Wickard v. Filburn*.... This Court has held time and

again that this power extends to activities of retail establishments, including restaurants, which directly or indirectly burden or obstruct interstate commerce....

Congress has determined for itself that refusals of service to Negroes have imposed
burdens both upon the interstate flow of food and upon the movement of products generally.... [W]here we find that the legislators, in light of the facts and testimony before them, have a rational basis for finding a chosen regulatory scheme
necessary to the protection of commerce, our investigation is at an end. The only
remaining question—one answered in the affirmative by the court below—is
whether the particular restaurant either serves or offers to serve interstate travelers
or serves food a substantial portion of which has moved in interstate commerce.
The Civil Rights Act of 1964, as here applied, we find to be plainly appropriate in
the resolution of what the Congress found to be a national commercial problem
of the first magnitude. We find it in no violation of any express limitations of the
Constitution and we therefore declare it valid.... [R]eversed.[23]

More than 25 years after these two rulings on the use of the commerce clause as a support
for civil rights legislation, the Court revisited the subject. In 2000 the Court, in a sharply
divided ruling written by then Chief Justice William Rehnquist, struck down an important
provision of the Violence Against Women Act for failure to satisfy the requirements of the
commerce clause in *United States v. Morrison*.[24] With that ruling, it was clear that the criticisms issued by Justices Douglas and Goldberg of the *Civil Rights Cases* and the damage
from that opinion was still a fact as the nation entered the twenty-first century, and one that
would limit the nation's ability to address serious problems.

The Voting Rights Act Faced the First of Many Court Tests

The Voting Rights Act of 1965 also faced constitutional challenge after its passage and survived, but this would be the beginning of a long line of Supreme Court rulings on the nature
and limits of the Act over time. The first came in *South Carolina v. Katzenbach*.

South Carolina v. Katzenbach
383 U.S. 301 (1966)

INTRODUCTION: After lengthy investigations and legislative hearings, Congress
enacted the Voting Rights Act of 1965. The legislation provided broad protections for
voting rights throughout the nation, but included specific provisions for states or portions of states with histories of exclusionary practices, such as a requirement that new
voting procedures be submitted to federal authorities for pre-clearance. These steps
were intended to stop the ongoing practice of creating new barriers as soon as a court
outlawed an existing discriminatory practice.

South Carolina brought this case on original jurisdiction in the Supreme Court to
challenge the authority of Congress to enact the law. The Court invited all of the other
states to enter the case as amici and representatives of seven states were permitted to
participate in oral argument.

Chief Justice Warren wrote the opinion for the Court.

South Carolina has filed a bill of complaint, seeking a declaration that selected
provisions of the Voting Rights Act of 1965 violate the Federal Constitution....
The Voting Rights Act was designed by Congress to banish the blight of racial
discrimination in voting, which has infected the electoral process in parts of our

country for nearly a century. The Act creates stringent new remedies for voting discrimination where it persists on a pervasive scale, and in addition the statute strengthens existing remedies for pockets of voting discrimination elsewhere in the country. Congress assumed the power to prescribe these remedies from §2 of the Fifteenth Amendment, which authorizes the National Legislature to effectuate by "appropriate" measures the constitutional prohibition against racial discrimination in voting. We hold that the sections of the Act which are properly before us are an appropriate means for carrying out Congress' constitutional responsibilities and are consonant with all other provisions of the Constitution. We therefore deny South Carolina's request that enforcement of these sections of the Act be enjoined.

I. The constitutional propriety of the Voting Rights Act of 1965 must be judged with reference to the historical experience which it reflects. Before enacting the measure, Congress explored with great care the problem of racial discrimination in voting.... Two points emerge vividly from the voluminous legislative history.... First: Congress felt itself confronted by an insidious and pervasive evil which had been perpetuated in certain parts of our country through unremitting and ingenious defiance of the Constitution. Second: Congress concluded that the unsuccessful remedies which it had prescribed in the past would have to be replaced by sterner and more elaborate measures in order to satisfy the clear commands of the Fifteenth Amendment.

... [B]eginning in 1890, the States of Alabama, Georgia, Louisiana, Mississippi, North Carolina, South Carolina, and Virginia enacted tests still in use which were specifically designed to prevent Negroes from voting. Typically, they made the ability to read and write a registration qualification and also required completion of a registration form. These laws were based on the fact that as of 1890 in each of the named States, more than two-thirds of the adult Negroes were illiterate while less than one-quarter of the adult whites were unable to read or write. At the same time, alternate tests were prescribed in all of the named States to assure that white illiterates would not be deprived of the franchise. These included grandfather clauses, property qualifications, "good character" tests, and the requirement that registrants "understand" or "interpret" certain matters.

The course of subsequent Fifteenth Amendment litigation in this Court demonstrates the variety and persistence of these and similar institutions designed to deprive Negroes of the right to vote. Grandfather clauses were invalidated in *Guinn v. United States*.... Procedural hurdles were struck down in *Lane v. Wilson*.... The white primary was outlawed in *Smith v. Allwright*.... Racial gerrymandering was forbidden by *Gomillion v. Lightfoot*.... Finally, discriminatory application of voting tests was condemned in *Schnell v. Davis*....

According to the evidence in recent Justice Department voting suits, the latter stratagem is now the principal method used to bar Negroes from the polls. Discriminatory administration of voting qualifications has been found in all eight Alabama cases, in all nine Louisiana cases, and in all nine Mississippi cases which have gone to final judgment. Moreover, in almost all of these cases, the courts have held that the discrimination was pursuant to a widespread "pattern or practice." White applicants for registration have often been excused altogether from the literacy and understanding tests or have been given easy versions, have received extensive help from voting officials, and have been registered despite serious errors in their answers. Negroes, on the other hand, have typically been required to pass difficult versions of all the tests, without any outside assistance and without the slightest error. The good-morals requirement is so vague and subjective that it has constituted an open invitation to abuse at the hands of voting officials. Negroes obliged to obtain vouchers from registered voters have found it virtually impossible to comply in areas where almost no Negroes are on the rolls....

Despite the earnest efforts of the Justice Department and of many federal judges, [other] new laws have done little to cure the problem of voting discrimination. According to estimates by the Attorney General during hearings on the Act, registration of voting-age Negroes in Alabama rose only from 14.2% to 19.4% between 1958 and 1964; in Louisiana it barely inched ahead from 31.7% to 31.8% between 1956 and 1965; and in Mississippi it increased only from 4.4% to 6.4% between 1954 and 1964. In each instance, registration of voting-age whites ran roughly 50 percentage points or more ahead of Negro registration....

During the hearings and debates on the Act, Selma, Alabama, was repeatedly referred to as the pre-eminent example of the ineffectiveness of existing legislation. In Dallas County, of which Selma is the seat, there were four years of litigation by the Justice Department and two findings by the federal courts of widespread voting discrimination. Yet in those four years, Negro registration rose only from 156 to 383, although there are approximately 15,000 Negroes of voting age in the county. Any possibility that these figures were attributable to political apathy was dispelled by the protest demonstrations in Selma in the early months of 1965....

II. The Voting Rights Act of 1965 reflects Congress' firm intention to rid the country of racial discrimination in voting. The heart of the Act is a complex scheme of stringent remedies aimed at areas where voting discrimination has been most flagrant.... The remedial sections of the Act assailed by South Carolina automatically apply to any State, or to any separate political subdivision such as a county or parish, for which two findings have been made: (1) the Attorney General has determined that on November 1, 1964, it maintained a "test or device," and (2) the Director of the Census has determined that less than 50% of its voting-age residents were registered on November 1, 1964, or voted in the presidential election of November 1964.... South Carolina was brought within the coverage formula of the Act on August 7, 1965.... On the same day, coverage was also extended to Alabama, Alaska, Georgia, Louisiana, Mississippi, Virginia, 26 counties in North Carolina, and one county in Arizona. Two more counties in Arizona, one county in Hawaii, and one county in Idaho were added to the list.... In a State or political subdivision covered by §4(b) of the Act, no person may be denied the right to vote in any election because of his failure to comply with a "test or device." §4(a)....

In any political subdivision covered by §4(b) of the Act, the Civil Service Commission shall appoint voting examiners whenever the Attorney General certifies either of the following facts: (1) that he has received meritorious written complaints from at least 20 residents alleging that they have been disenfranchised under color of law because of their race, or (2) that the appointment of examiners is otherwise necessary to effectuate the guarantees of the Fifteenth Amendment....

III. Th[e] provisions of the Voting Rights Act of 1965 are challenged on the fundamental ground that they exceed the powers of Congress and encroach on an area reserved to the States by the Constitution.... The language and purpose of the Fifteenth Amendment, the prior decisions construing its several provisions, and the general doctrines of constitutional interpretation, all point to one fundamental principle. As against the reserved powers of the States, Congress may use any rational means to effectuate the constitutional prohibition of racial discrimination in voting....

Section 1 of the Fifteenth Amendment ... has always been treated as self-executing and has repeatedly been construed, without further legislative specification, to invalidate state voting qualifications or procedures which are discriminatory on their face or in practice.... The gist of the matter is that the Fifteenth Amendment supersedes contrary exertions of state power....

South Carolina contends that the cases cited above are precedents only for the authority of the judiciary to strike down state statutes and procedures.... On the contrary, §2 of the Fifteenth Amendment expressly declares that "Congress shall have power to enforce this article by appropriate legislation." By adding this authorization, the Framers indicated that Congress was to be chiefly responsible for implementing the rights created in §1.... Accordingly, in addition to the courts, Congress has full remedial powers to effectuate the constitutional prohibition against racial discrimination in voting....

We therefore reject South Carolina's argument that Congress may appropriately do no more than to forbid violations of the Fifteenth Amendment in general terms.... Congress is not circumscribed by any such artificial rules under §2 of the Fifteenth Amendment....

We here hold that the portions of the Voting Rights Act properly before us are a valid means for carrying out the commands of the Fifteenth Amendment. Hopefully, millions of non-white Americans will now be able to participate for the first time on an equal basis in the government under which they live. We may finally look forward to the day when truly "the right of citizens of the United States to vote shall not be denied or abridged by the United States or by any State on account of race, color, or previous condition of servitude."

Justice Black wrote an opinion concurring in part and dissenting in part.

I agree with substantially all of the Court's opinion sustaining the power of Congress under §2 of the Fifteenth Amendment to suspend state literacy tests and similar voting qualifications and to authorize the Attorney General to secure the appointment of federal examiners to register qualified voters in various sections of the country.... [I]t is enough for me that Congress by creating this formula has merely exercised its hitherto unquestioned and undisputed power to decide when, where, and upon what conditions its laws shall go into effect....

... I dissent from its holding that every part of §5 of the Act is constitutional.... Section 5, by providing that some of the States cannot pass state laws or adopt state constitutional amendments without first being compelled to beg federal authorities to approve their policies, so distorts our constitutional structure of government as to render any distinction drawn in the Constitution between state and federal power almost meaningless.... Certainly if all the provisions of our Constitution which limit the power of the Federal Government and reserve other power to the States are to mean anything, they mean at least that the States have power to pass laws and amend their constitutions without first sending their officials hundreds of miles away to beg federal authorities to approve them.... I cannot help but believe that the inevitable effect of any such law which forces any one of the States to entreat federal authorities in far-away places for approval of local laws before they can become effective is to create the impression that the State or

States treated in this way are little more than conquered provinces.... Of course I do not mean to cast any doubt whatever upon the indisputable power of the Federal Government to invalidate a state law once enacted and operative on the ground that it intrudes into the area of supreme federal power. But the Federal Government has heretofore always been content to exercise this power to protect federal supremacy by authorizing its agents to bring lawsuits against state officials once an operative state law has created an actual case and controversy.

The End of All Deliberate Speed

Even with all of the legislation and Supreme Court rulings, the resistance in the segregationist states endured. This continued and even intensified a decade after the *Brown* rulings and despite the efforts of civil rights leaders like Dr. King. The Court in *Brown II* had placed the burden to desegregate on the school districts and the states that operated them, and required the district courts, when necessary, to fashion decrees that would ensure that those districts accomplished the task "with all deliberate speed." That language was added at the suggestion of Justice Felix Frankfurter and became instantly problematic. The idea was that the task would be done as quickly as possible consistent with a reasonable understanding of the complexities involved in desegregating the schools. The recalcitrant states took that as a statement that would work very well with their intentions to resist desegregation to the maximum extent possible for as long as possible.

Virginia was one of the leaders in the massive resistance movement, and its leaders tried a variety of tactics along the way. One of these shut down public schools that were going to be desegregated, but supported whites-only academies. Justice Hugo L. Black wrote for the Court in *Griffin v. County School Bd. of Prince Edward County*, striking down the Virginia action and, in the process, announcing that "The time for mere 'deliberate speed' has run out, and that phrase can no longer justify denying these Prince Edward County school children their constitutional rights to an education equal to that afforded by the public schools in the other parts of Virginia."[25]

Unfortunately, the recalcitrant officials did not halt their resistance and continued to call upon reviewing courts to grant them more time under the "all deliberate speed" language rejected by the Court in *Griffin*. The Supreme Court communicated its frustration with state officials and lower courts in the continuing use of resistance tactics and the willingness of some courts to defer to those state and local officials in *Green v. County School Board*.

Green v. County School Board

391 U.S. 430 (1968)

Justice Brennan wrote the opinion for the Court.

> The question for decision is whether ... respondent School Board's adoption of a "freedom-of-choice" plan which allows a pupil to choose his own public school constitutes adequate compliance with the Board's responsibility "to achieve a system of determining admission to the public schools on a nonracial basis ...." (*Brown II*).
>
> The pattern of separate "white" and "Negro" schools in the New Kent County school system established under compulsion of state laws is precisely the pattern of segregation to which *Brown I* and *Brown II* were particularly addressed, and which *Brown I* declared unconstitutionally denied Negro school children equal protection of the laws. Racial identification of the system's schools was complete,

extending not just to the composition of student bodies at the two schools but to every facet of school operations—faculty, staff, transportation, extracurricular activities and facilities. In short, the State, acting through the local school board and school officials, organized and operated a dual system, part "white" and part "Negro."

It was such dual systems that 14 years ago *Brown I* held unconstitutional and a year later *Brown II* held must be abolished.... The transition to a unitary, nonracial system of public education was and is the ultimate end to be brought about; it was because of the "complexities arising from the transition to a system of public education freed of racial discrimination" that we provided for "all deliberate speed" in the implementation of the principles of *Brown I.* Thus we recognized the task would necessarily involve solution of "varied local school problems." ... Yet we emphasized that the constitutional rights of Negro children required school officials to bear the burden of establishing that additional time to carry out the ruling in an effective manner "is necessary in the public interest and is consistent with good faith compliance at the earliest practicable date." ...

It is against this background that 13 years after *Brown II* commanded the abolition of dual systems we must measure the effectiveness of respondent School Board's "freedom-of-choice" plan to achieve that end. The School Board contends that it has fully discharged its obligation by adopting a plan by which every student, regardless of race, may "freely" choose the school he will attend.... [W]hat is involved here is the question whether the Board has achieved the "racially nondiscriminatory school system" *Brown II* held must be effectuated in order to remedy the established unconstitutional deficiencies of its segregated system.... *Brown II* was a call for the dismantling of well-entrenched dual systems tempered by an awareness that complex and multifaceted problems would arise which would require time and flexibility for a successful resolution. School boards such as the respondent then operating state-compelled dual systems were nevertheless clearly charged with the affirmative duty to take whatever steps might be necessary to convert to a unitary system in which racial discrimination would be eliminated root and branch.

In determining whether respondent School Board met that command by adopting its "freedom-of-choice" plan, it is relevant that this first step did not come until some 11 years after *Brown I* was decided and 10 years after *Brown II* directed the making of a "prompt and reasonable start." This deliberate perpetuation of the unconstitutional dual system can only have compounded the harm of such a system. Such delays are no longer tolerable.... Moreover, a plan that at this late date fails to provide meaningful assurance of prompt and effective disestablishment of a dual system is also intolerable. "The time for mere 'deliberate speed' has run out." ... The burden on a school board today is to come forward with a plan that promises realistically to work, and promises realistically to work now....

The New Kent School Board's "freedom-of-choice" plan cannot be accepted as a sufficient step to "effectuate a transition" to a unitary system. In three years of operation not a single white child has chosen to attend Watkins school and although 115 Negro children enrolled in New Kent school in 1967 (up from 35 in 1965 and 111 in 1966) 85% of the Negro children in the system still attend the all-Negro Watkins school. In other words, the school system remains a dual system. Rather than further the dismantling of the dual system, the plan has operated simply to burden children and their parents with a responsibility which *Brown II* placed squarely on the School Board. The Board must be required to formulate a new plan and, in light of other courses which appear open to the Board, such as zoning, fashion steps which promise realistically to convert promptly to a system without a "white" school and a "Negro" school, but just schools.

In overturning the court of appeals in *Alexander v. Holmes County Board of Education*, the Court rejected resistance by Mississippi officials and once again insisted on action.

[T]he Court of Appeals should have denied all motions for additional time because continued operation of segregated schools under a standard of allowing "all deliberate speed" for desegregation is no longer constitutionally permissible. Under explicit holdings of this Court the obligation of every school district is to terminate dual school systems at once and to operate now and hereafter only unitary schools. *Griffin*...; *Green* ....[26]

The Court then found itself drawn further into the discussion of the fashioning of court decrees to remedy these continuing violations of equal protection of the law, which has gone on for decades ever since.

The Two-Tier Test for Equal Protection

Even after these cases that sought to implement *Brown*, there were even more complex questions in cases where, most often, those involved did not openly advocate racial discrimination, but practiced it nonetheless. It became necessary for the Court to develop much further its standards for determining just where and when violations of equal protection had occurred. The judicial opinions that follow trace that development over time, which is important not only in terms of providing the standard for judging allegations of racial discrimination, but also because it is the foundation for discussions of other types of discrimination addressed in later chapters. However, as will become clear, as it did so, and particularly starting in the 1970s, the Supreme Court made it much more difficult for those seeking to vindicate civil rights to bring a case on constitutional grounds in federal courts.

Strict Scrutiny, Rational Basis, and the Two-Tier Test for Equal Protection

The earlier discussion of the World War II era Japanese exclusion case *Korematsu v. United States* noted that one of its important results was a clear statement that classifications of people by government based on race are inherently suspect and call for strict judicial scrutiny. That is a much higher standard for government to meet than what is normally applied when anyone challenges a governmental action.

Usually, there is a presumption of regularity in which a court will assume that the government and its officials acted lawfully. Therefore, the burden is on the challenger and all the government need do in the typical case is to demonstrate that its actions were rationally related to some legitimate state interest (often referred to as the rational basis test). However, the Court, in what has become a particularly famous footnote to the decision in the 1938 case of *United States v. Carolene Products*, explained:

There may be narrower scope for the operation of the presumption of constitutionality when legislation appears on its face to be within a specific prohibition of the Constitution.... It is unnecessary to consider now ... whether similar considerations

enter into the review of statutes directed at particular religious, or national, or racial minorities: whether prejudice against discrete and insular minorities may be a special condition, which tends seriously to curtail the operation of those political processes ordinarily to be relied upon to protect minorities, and which may call for a correspondingly more searching inquiry.[27]

Korematsu explained that differential treatment on the basis of race is that kind of problem and calls for strict scrutiny. Similarly, differential treatment that affects fundamental rights requires that same level of scrutiny.

As the Burger Court (as the Court was known during the era of Chief Justice Warren Burger) took shape in the early 1970s, the Court presented its two-tier standard that remains the basic test for discrimination. The case in which the Court presented this standard did not directly allege discrimination on the basis of race, but unequal educational opportunity on the basis of wealth. It came in a challenge to a Texas school finance policy that resulted in dramatic disparities in the funds available to support urban children as compared to suburban children. Challengers alleged that the Court in *Brown* had held that equal educational opportunity was indeed a right that required the protection of strict judicial scrutiny. In that opinion, the Court had held:

> In these days, it is doubtful that any child may reasonably be expected to succeed in life if he is denied the opportunity of an education. Such an opportunity, where the state has undertaken to provide it, is a right which must be made available to all on equal terms.[28]

San Antonio Independent School District v. Rodriguez

411 U.S. 1 (1973)

INTRODUCTION: The facts of this case are explained in the opinion. This was one of a set of cases brought in a number of states, all of which challenged the property tax-based funding systems for public schools on equal protection grounds.

It is interesting to note that, after this ruling rejected the challenges under the equal protection clause of the U.S. Constitution, the litigants in the other cases from other states and, indeed, litigants in Texas took their cases back to the state courts under state law and most prevailed at that level.

Justice Powell wrote the opinion for the Court.

> This suit attacking the Texas system of financing public education was initiated by Mexican-American parents whose children attend the elementary and secondary schools in the Edgewood Independent School District, an urban school district in San Antonio, Texas. They brought a class action on behalf of school children throughout the State who are members of minority groups or who are poor and reside in school districts having a low property tax base.... In 1971 [the three-judge federal district court[29] found] the Texas school finance system unconstitutional under the Equal Protection Clause of the Fourteenth Amendment.... [W]e reverse....
>
> I. The first Texas State Constitution ... provided for the establishment of a system of free schools. Early in its history, Texas adopted a dual approach to the financing of its schools, relying on mutual participation by the local school districts and the State. As early as 1883 the state constitution was amended to provide for the

creation of local school districts empowered to levy ad valorem taxes with the consent of local taxpayers [to finance public schools]. Such local funds as were raised were supplemented by funds distributed to each district from the State's Permanent and Available School Funds....

Sizable differences in the value of assessable property between local school districts became increasingly evident as the State became more industrialized and as rural-to-urban population shifts became more pronounced.... These growing disparities in population and taxable property between districts were responsible in part for increasingly notable differences in levels of local expenditure for education....

Recognizing the need for increased state funding to help offset disparities in local spending..., the state legislature in the late 1940's enacted the Texas Minimum Foundation School Program.... First, it was ... to assure that the Foundation Program would have an equalizing influence on expenditure levels between school districts by placing the heaviest burden on the school districts most capable of paying. Second, the Program ... sought to establish a Local Fund Assignment that would force every school district to contribute to the education of its children but that would not by itself exhaust any district's resources....

... [T]he Edgewood Independent School District, has been compared throughout this litigation with the Alamo Heights Independent School District.... Edgewood is one of seven public school districts in the metropolitan area. Approximately 22,000 students are enrolled in its 25 elementary and secondary schools. The district is situated in the core-city sector of San Antonio in a residential neighborhood that has little commercial or industrial property. The residents are predominantly of Mexican-American descent: approximately 90% of the student population is Mexican-American and over 6% is Negro. The average assessed property value per pupil is $5,960—the lowest in the metropolitan area—and the median family income ($4,686) is also the lowest. At an equalized tax rate of $1.05 per $100 of assessed property—the highest in the metropolitan area—the district contributed $26 to the education of each child for the 1967–1968 school year above its Local Fund Assignment for the Minimum Foundation Program. The Foundation Program contributed $222 per pupil for a state-local total of $248. Federal funds added another $108 for a total of $356 per pupil.

Alamo Heights is the most affluent school district in San Antonio. Its six schools, housing approximately 5,000 students, are situated in a residential community quite unlike the Edgewood District. The school population is predominantly "Anglo," having only 18% Mexican-Americans and less than 1% Negroes. The assessed property value per pupil exceeds $49,000, and the median family income is $8,001. In 1967–1968 the local tax rate of $.85 per $100 of valuation yielded $333 per pupil [which when added to the $225 provided from the state's Minimum Foundation Program meant that] the district was able to supply $558 per student. Supplemented by a $36 per-pupil grant from federal sources, Alamo Heights spent $594 per pupil....

Despite these recent increases, substantial interdistrict disparities in school expenditures found by the District Court to prevail in San Antonio and in varying degrees throughout the State still exist. And it was these disparities, largely attributable to differences in the amounts of money collected through local property taxation, that led the District Court to conclude that Texas' dual system of public school financing violated the Equal Protection Clause.... Finding that wealth is a "suspect" classification and that education is a "fundamental" interest, the District Court held that the Texas system could be sustained only if the State could show that it was premised upon some compelling state interest.... [T]he court concluded that "[n]ot only are defendants unable to demonstrate compelling state interests ... they fail even to establish a reasonable basis for these classifications." ...

... If, as previous decisions have indicated, strict scrutiny means that the State's system is not entitled to the usual presumption of validity, that the State rather than the complainants must carry a "heavy burden of justification," that the State must demonstrate that its educational system has been structured with "precision," and is "tailored" narrowly to serve legitimate objectives and that it has selected the "less drastic means" for effectuating its objectives, the Texas financing system ... will not pass muster.... Apart from its concession that educational financing in Texas has "defects" and "imperfections," the State defends the system's rationality with vigor and disputes the District Court's finding that it lacks a "reasonable basis."

This, then, establishes the framework for our analysis. We must decide, first, whether the Texas system of financing public education operates to the disadvantage of some suspect class or impinges upon a fundamental right explicitly or implicitly protected by the Constitution, thereby requiring strict judicial scrutiny. If so, the judgment of the District Court should be affirmed. If not, the Texas scheme must still be examined to determine whether it rationally furthers some legitimate, articulated state purpose and therefore does not constitute an invidious discrimination in violation of the Equal Protection Clause of the Fourteenth Amendment.

II. ... We ... find neither the suspect-classification nor the fundamental-interest analysis persuasive.... The individuals, or groups of individuals, who constituted the class discriminated against in our prior cases shared two distinguishing characteristics: because of their impecunity they were completely unable to pay for some desired benefit, and as a consequence, they sustained an absolute deprivation of a meaningful opportunity to enjoy that benefit....

... Even a cursory examination, however, demonstrates that neither of the two distinguishing characteristics of wealth classifications can be found here. First, ... appellees have made no effort to demonstrate that it operates to the peculiar disadvantage of any class [of] ... persons whose incomes are beneath any designated poverty level....

Second, ... [the] lack of personal resources has not occasioned an absolute deprivation of the desired benefit. The argument here is not that the children in districts having relatively low assessable property values are receiving no public education; rather, it is that they are receiving a poorer quality education than that available to children in districts having more assessable wealth.... [A] sufficient answer to appellees' argument is that, at least where wealth is involved, the Equal Protection Clause does not require absolute equality or precisely equal advantages....

However described, it is clear that appellees' suit asks this Court to extend its most exacting scrutiny to review a system that allegedly discriminates against a large, diverse, and amorphous class, unified only by the common factor of residence in districts that happen to have less taxable wealth than other districts. The system of alleged discrimination and the class it defines have none of the traditional indicia of suspectness: the class is not saddled with such disabilities, or subjected to such a history of purposeful unequal treatment, or relegated to such a position of political powerlessness as to command extraordinary protection from the majoritarian political process.

We thus conclude that the Texas system does not operate to the peculiar disadvantage of any suspect class. But ... appellees ... also assert that the State's system impermissibly interferes with the exercise of a "fundamental" right and that accordingly the prior decisions of this Court require the application of the strict standard of judicial review.... It is this question—whether education is a fundamental right, in the sense that it is among the rights and liberties protected by the Constitution—which has so consumed the attention of courts and commentators in recent years.

In *Brown v. Board of Education [I]*, a unanimous Court recognized that ... "In these days, it is doubtful that any child may reasonably be expected to succeed in life if he is denied the opportunity of an education. Such an opportunity, where the state has undertaken to provide it, is a right which must be made available to all on equal terms." ... Nothing this Court holds today in any way detracts from our historic dedication to public education.... But the importance of a service performed by the State does not determine whether it must be regarded as fundamental for purposes of examination under the Equal Protection Clause.... [T]he key to discovering whether education is "fundamental" is not to be found in comparisons of the relative societal significance of education as opposed to subsistence or housing.... Rather, the answer lies in assessing whether there is a right to education explicitly or implicitly guaranteed by the Constitution....

Education, of course, is not among the rights afforded explicit protection under our Federal Constitution. Nor do we find any basis for saying it is implicitly so protected.... [T]his is not a case in which the challenged state action must be subjected to the searching judicial scrutiny reserved for laws that create suspect classifications or impinge upon constitutionally protected rights.... A century of Supreme Court adjudication under the Equal Protection Clause affirmatively supports the application of the traditional standard of review, which requires only that the State's system be shown to bear some rational relationship to legitimate state purposes....

III. ... The District Court found that the State had failed even "to establish a reasonable basis" for a system that results in different levels of per-pupil expenditure.... We disagree.... While assuring a basic education for every child in the State, [the Texas system] permits and encourages a large measure of participation in and control of each district's schools at the local level. In an era that has witnessed a consistent trend toward centralization of the functions of government, local sharing of responsibility for public education has survived.... In part, local control means ... the freedom to devote more money to the education of one's children. Equally important, however, is the opportunity it offers for participation in the decision making process that determines how those local tax dollars will be spent. Each locality is free to tailor local programs to local needs....

While it is no doubt true that reliance on local property taxation for school revenues provides less freedom of choice with respect to expenditures for some districts than for others, the existence of "some inequality" in the manner in which the State's rationale is achieved is not alone a sufficient basis for striking down the entire system.... [T]o the extent that the Texas system of school financing results in unequal expenditures between children who happen to reside in different districts, we cannot say that such disparities are the product of a system that is so irrational as to be invidiously discriminatory.... The Texas plan is not the result of hurried, ill-conceived legislation. It certainly is not the product of purposeful discrimination against any group or class.... The constitutional standard under the Equal Protection Clause is whether the challenged state action rationally furthers a legitimate state purpose or interest.... We hold that the Texas plan abundantly satisfies this standard.[30]

Justice White wrote a dissenting opinion joined by Justices Douglas and Brennan.

[T]his case would be quite different if it were true that the Texas system, while insuring minimum educational expenditures in every district through state funding, extended a meaningful option to all local districts to increase their per-pupil expenditures and so to improve their children's education to the extent that increased funding would achieve that goal.... The difficulty ... is that it provides a meaningful option to Alamo Heights and like school districts but almost none to Edgewood and those other districts with a low per-pupil real estate tax base. In these latter districts, no matter how desirous parents are of supporting their schools with greater revenues, it is impossible to do so through the use of the real estate property tax....

The Equal Protection Clause permits discriminations between classes but requires that the classification bear some rational relationship to a permissible object sought to be attained by the statute. It is not enough that the Texas system before us seeks to achieve the valid, rational purpose of maximizing local initiative; the means chosen by the State must also be rationally related to the end sought to be achieved....

Justice Marshall wrote a dissenting opinion joined by Justice Douglas.

The Court today decides, in effect, that a State may constitutionally vary the quality of education which it offers its children in accordance with the amount of taxable wealth located in the school districts within which they reside. The ... majority's holding can only be seen as a retreat from our historic commitment to equality of educational opportunity and as unsupportable acquiescence in a system which deprives children in their earliest years of the chance to reach their full potential as citizens. The Court does this despite the absence of any substantial justification for a scheme which arbitrarily channels educational resources in accordance with the fortuity of the amount of taxable wealth within each district.

In my judgment, the right of every American to an equal start in life ... is far too vital to permit state discrimination on grounds as tenuous as those presented by this record. Nor can I accept the notion that it is sufficient to remit these appellees to the vagaries of the political process which, contrary to the majority's suggestion, has proved singularly unsuited to the task of providing a remedy for this discrimination. I, for one, am unsatisfied with the hope of an ultimate "political" solution sometime in the indefinite future while, in the meantime, countless children unjustifiably receive inferior educations that "may affect their hearts and minds in a way unlikely ever to be undone." *Brown*.... I must therefore respectfully dissent.

I. ... When the Texas financing scheme is taken as a whole, I do not think it can be doubted that it produces a discriminatory impact on substantial numbers of the school-age children of the State of Texas.... Despite these facts, the majority continually emphasizes how much state aid has, in recent years, been given to property-poor Texas school districts. What the Court fails to emphasize is the cruel irony of how much more state aid is being given to property-rich Texas school districts on top of their already substantial local property tax revenues.... And it is these stark differences in the treatment of Texas school districts and school children inherent in the Texas financing scheme, not the absolute amount of state aid provided to any particular school district, that are the crux of this case....

The appellants ... contend ... that whatever the differences in per-pupil spending among Texas districts, there are no discriminatory consequences for the children of the disadvantaged districts.... [E]ven an unadorned restatement of this contention is sufficient to reveal its absurdity. That a child forced to attend an underfunded school with poorer physical facilities, less experienced teachers, larger classes, and a narrower range of courses than a school with substantially more funds—and thus with greater choice in educational planning—may nevertheless excel is to the credit of the child, not the State.... Discrimination in the opportunity to learn that is afforded a child must be our standard.

Hence, even before this Court recognized its duty to tear down the barriers of state-enforced racial segregation in public education, it acknowledged that inequality in the educational facilities provided to students may be discriminatory state action as contemplated by the Equal Protection Clause. As a basis for striking down state-enforced segregation of a law school, the Court in *Sweatt v. Painter*, stated "... It is difficult to believe that one who had a free choice between these ... schools would consider the question close." ... Likewise, it is difficult to believe that if the children of Texas had a free choice, they would choose to be educated in districts with fewer resources, and hence with more antiquated plants, less experienced teachers, and a less diversified curriculum. In fact, if financing variations are so insignificant to educational quality, it is difficult to understand why a number of our country's wealthiest school districts, which have no legal obligation to argue in support of the constitutionality of the Texas legislation, have nevertheless zealously pursued its cause before this Court.... In my view, then, it is inequality—not some notion of gross inadequacy—of educational opportunity that raises a question of denial of equal protection of the laws....

II. ... [I]n [this Court's] view, the Texas scheme must be tested by nothing more than that lenient standard of rationality which we have traditionally applied to discriminatory state action in the context of economic and commercial matters.... I cannot accept such an emasculation of the Equal Protection Clause in the context of this case.... The Court apparently seeks to establish today that equal protection cases fall into one of two neat categories which dictate the appropriate standard of review—strict scrutiny or mere rationality. But this Court's decisions in the field of equal protection defy such easy categorization....

I ... cannot accept the majority's labored efforts to demonstrate that fundamental interests, which call for strict scrutiny of the challenged classification, encompass only established rights which we are somehow bound to recognize from the text of the Constitution itself.... [I]t will not do to suggest that the "answer" to whether an interest is fundamental for purposes of equal protection analysis is always determined by whether that interest "is a right ... explicitly or implicitly guaranteed by the Constitution." ...

I would like to know where the Constitution guarantees the right to procreate, *Skinner v. Oklahoma*, ... or the right to vote in state elections, e.g., *Reynolds v. Sims*, ... or the right to an appeal from a criminal conviction, e.g., *Griffin v. Illinois*.... These are instances in which, due to the importance of the interests at stake, the Court has displayed a strong concern with the existence of discriminatory state treatment. But the Court has never said or indicated that these are interests which independently enjoy full-blown constitutional protection....

As this Court held in *Brown*, ... the opportunity of education, "where the state has undertaken to provide it, is a right which must be made available to all on equal terms." The ... relationship between education and the social and political interests enshrined within the Constitution, compel us to recognize the fundamentality of education and to scrutinize with appropriate care the bases for state discrimination affecting equality of educational opportunity in Texas' school districts—a conclusion which is only strengthened when we consider the character of the classification in this case....

I do not question that local control of public education ... constitutes a very substantial state interest.... But ... on this record, it is apparent that the State's purported concern with local control is offered primarily as an excuse rather than as a justification for inter-district inequality.... In my judgment, any substantial degree of scrutiny of the operation of the Texas financing scheme reveals that the State has selected means wholly inappropriate to secure its purported interest in assuring its school districts local fiscal control.... If, for the sake of local education control, this Court is to sustain inter-district discrimination in the educational opportunity afforded Texas school children, it should require that the State present something more than the mere sham now before us.

The *San Antonio* case had indicated that the way that a suspect class is to be identified is based on whether it is a "discrete and insular minority," that has traditionally faced discrimination, and is, for whatever reasons, not in a position to have a reasonable consideration of its problems through the majoritarian political process. At different times in modern history, in addition to race, suspect class status has also been found for illegitimate children and aliens. However, the Court has been unwilling to extend that designation to government actions that treat people differently on the basis of gender (see Chapter 10).

The Court would add additional requirements in later cases. Most notably, the Court found itself faced with a host of cases in which the governments and officials involved denied any intention to discriminate. The Court had not previously required proof of intent to discriminate, because those who engaged in such behavior had long since become sophisticated enough to cloak their actions in permissible rhetoric and policy provisions. Thus, the Court surprised the civil rights community when, in 1976, it required proof of both intent and effect of discrimination in order to receive any further consideration by whatever standard would be applicable to the group involved.

Washington v. Davis

426 U.S. 229 (1976)

INTRODUCTION: The District of Columbia had recruitment and promotion policies that required satisfactory completion of a written examination. The test that was in use at the time resulted in "a disproportionately high" failure rate for African American applicants. The test, known as Test 21, was a standard federal civil service examination and was a general test for reading and writing knowledge. Two African American officers sued, joined later by others, charging that the use of the test discriminated on the basis of race in violation of the due process clause of the Fifth Amendment and under the civil rights act 42 U.S.C. §1981.

The district court ruled against the challengers, but the court of appeals reversed on grounds that the disproportionate impact of the test was sufficient to support the discrimination charge and proof of intent was not required.

Justice White wrote the opinion for the Court.

> This case involves the validity of a qualifying test administered to applicants for positions as police officers in the District of Columbia Metropolitan Police Department.... We are in agreement with the District Court and hence reverse the judgment of the Court of Appeals....
>
> II. ... The central purpose of the Equal Protection Clause of the Fourteenth Amendment is the prevention of official conduct discriminating on the basis of race. It is also true that the Due Process Clause of the Fifth Amendment contains an equal protection component prohibiting the United States from invidiously discriminating between individuals or groups. *Bolling v. Sharpe*.... But our cases have not embraced the proposition that a law or other official act, without regard to whether it reflects a racially discriminatory purpose, is unconstitutional solely because it has a racially disproportionate impact.
>
> This is not to say that the necessary discriminatory racial purpose must be express or appear on the face of the statute, or that a law's disproportionate impact is irrelevant in cases involving Constitution-based claims of racial discrimination. A statute, otherwise neutral on its face, must not be applied so as invidiously to discriminate on the basis of race. *Yick Wo v. Hopkins*.... It is also clear from the cases dealing with racial discrimination in the selection of juries that the systematic exclusion of Negroes is itself such an "unequal application of the law ... as to show intentional discrimination." ...
>
> Necessarily, an invidious discriminatory purpose may often be inferred from the totality of the relevant facts, including the fact, if it is true, that the law bears more heavily on one race than another. It is also not infrequently true that the discriminatory impact ... may for all practical purposes demonstrate unconstitutionality because in various circumstances the discrimination is very difficult to explain on nonracial grounds. Nevertheless, we have not held that a law, neutral on its face and serving ends otherwise within the power of government to pursue, is invalid under the Equal Protection Clause simply because it may affect a greater proportion of one race than of another. Disproportionate impact is not irrelevant, but it is not the sole touchstone of an invidious racial discrimination forbidden by the Constitution. Standing alone, it does not trigger the rule ... that racial classifications are to be subjected to the strictest scrutiny and are justifiable only by the weightiest of considerations.
>
> There are some indications to the contrary in our cases. [See] *Palmer v. Thompson*, 403 U.S. 217 (1971); *Wright v. Council of City of Emporia*, 407 U.S. 451 (1972).... Both before and after [these cases], various Courts of Appeals have held ... that the substantially disproportionate racial impact of a statute or official practice standing alone and without regard to discriminatory purpose, suffices to prove racial discrimination violating the Equal Protection Clause absent some justification going substantially beyond what would be necessary to validate most other

legislative classifications.... [W]ith all due respect, to the extent that those cases rested on or expressed the view that proof of discriminatory racial purpose is unnecessary in making out an equal protection violation, we are in disagreement.

As an initial matter, we have difficulty understanding how a law establishing a racially neutral qualification for employment ... denies "any person ... equal protection of the laws" simply because a greater proportion of Negroes fail to qualify than members of other racial or ethnic groups.... Test 21, which is administered generally to prospective Government employees, concededly seeks to ascertain whether those who take it have acquired a particular level of verbal skill; and it is untenable that the Constitution prevents the Government from seeking modestly to upgrade the communicative abilities of its employees rather than to be satisfied with some lower level of competence, particularly where the job requires special ability to communicate orally and in writing....

Nor on the facts of the case before us would the disproportionate impact of Test 21 warrant the conclusion that it is a purposeful device to discriminate against Negroes and hence an infringement of the constitutional rights of respondents as well as other black applicants. As we have said, the test is neutral on its face and rationally may be said to serve a purpose the Government is constitutionally empowered to pursue. Even agreeing with the District Court that the differential racial effect of Test 21 called for further inquiry, we think the District Court correctly held that the affirmative efforts of the Metropolitan Police Department to recruit black officers, the changing racial composition of the recruit classes and of the force in general, and the relationship of the test to the training program negated any inference that the Department discriminated on the basis of race.... [T]he District Judge concluded that Test 21 was directly related to the requirements of the police training program and that a positive relationship between the test and training-course performance was sufficient to validate the former, wholly aside from its possible relationship to actual performance as a police officer....

Justice Stevens wrote a concurring opinion.

... Frequently the most probative evidence of intent will be objective evidence of what actually happened rather than evidence describing the subjective state of mind of the actor.... It is unrealistic ... to require the victim of alleged discrimination to uncover the actual subjective intent of the decisionmaker or, conversely, to invalidate otherwise legitimate action simply because an improper motive affected the deliberation of a participant in the decisional process....

My point in making this observation is to suggest that the line between discriminatory purpose and discriminatory impact is not nearly as bright, and perhaps not quite as critical, as the reader of the Court's opinion might assume. I agree, of course, that a constitutional issue does not arise every time some disproportionate impact is shown. On the other hand, when the disproportion is as dramatic as in ... *Yick Wo v. Hopkins*, ... it really does not matter whether the standard is phrased in terms of purpose or effect. Therefore, although I accept the statement of the general rule in the Court's opinion, I am not yet prepared to indicate how that standard should be applied in the many cases which have formulated the governing standard in different language.[31]

The Court was not done. It followed the *Davis* case in 1977 with another case in which it elaborated on the evidence to be used to prove intent to discriminate. The case had arisen in a Chicago suburb and the lower courts had ruled against the community of Arlington Heights without finding intent, given that no such proof had been required in the law prior to *Davis*. The Court normally remands a case when it announces a completely new legal standard so that the lower court can address the newly announced standard in the case, since no such findings were initially made. Here, however, the Supreme Court announced the new standard and rejected the case against the suburb without allowing the lower courts to apply the new standard.

Village of Arlington Heights v. Metropolitan Housing Development Corporation

429 U.S. 252 (1977)

INTRODUCTION: In an earlier case, the City of Chicago and the U.S. Department of Housing and Urban Development (HUD) had been found guilty of intentional discrimination in housing on the basis of race. They were ordered to remedy the situation in a variety of ways, including supporting scattered site, small-scale low- and moderate-income housing efforts in the greater metropolitan area. Although the city did not have jurisdiction beyond its borders, HUD did.

With support from a number of fair housing advocates, the Metropolitan Housing Development Corporation (MHDC) planned to build a small, carefully designed group of 190 townhouses on 15 acres of land in suburban Arlington Heights. This overwhelmingly white northwestern suburb was in an important area for those seeking employment, since it was located close to O'Hare Airport and the Centex Industrial Village, a large light industrial park with literally hundreds of companies with a host of different types of employment opportunities.

The land for new housing was part of a property on which was located a Catholic school and parish, situated within a residential area. The church sought to assist in making low- and moderate-income housing available in the community and worked with MHDC to construct the townhouses, called Lincoln Green, on a portion of its property, with funding support from HUD.

The Village of Arlington Heights refused MHDC's request to rezone for the project. The Village was sued on grounds that its refusal to rezone was discriminatory on the basis of race. The district court ruled in favor of the village, but the Seventh Circuit reversed.

Justice Powell wrote the opinion for the Court.

> Our decision last Term in *Washington v. Davis* made it clear that official action will not be held unconstitutional solely because it results in a racially disproportionate impact. "Disproportionate impact is not irrelevant, but it is not the sole touchstone of an invidious racial discrimination." ... Proof of racially discriminatory intent or purpose is required to show a violation of the Equal Protection Clause....
>
> *Davis* does not require a plaintiff to prove that the challenged action rested solely on racially discriminatory purposes. Rarely can it be said that a legislature or administrative body operating under a broad mandate made a decision motivated solely by a single concern, or even that a particular purpose was the "dominant" or "primary" one. In fact, it is because legislators and administrators are properly concerned with balancing numerous competing considerations that courts refrain from reviewing the merits of their decisions, absent a showing of arbitrariness or irrationality. But racial discrimination is not just another competing

consideration. When there is a proof that a discriminatory purpose has been a motivating factor in the decision, this judicial deference is no longer justified.

Determining whether invidious discriminatory purpose was a motivating factor demands a sensitive inquiry into such circumstantial and direct evidence of intent as may be available. The impact of the official action—whether it "bears more heavily on one race than another" ... may provide an important starting point. Sometimes a clear pattern, unexplainable on grounds other than race, emerges from the effect of the state action even when the governing legislation appears neutral on its face. *Yick Wo v. Hopkins*.... The evidentiary inquiry is then relatively easy. But such cases are rare. Absent a pattern as stark as that in ... *Yick Wo*, impact alone is not determinative, and the Court must look to other evidence.

The historical background of the decision is one evidentiary source, particularly if it reveals a series of official actions taken for invidious purposes. The specific sequence of events leading up to the challenged decision also may shed some light on the decisionmaker's purposes. For example, if the property involved here always had been zoned R-5 but suddenly was changed to R-3 when the town learned of MHDC's plans to erect integrated housing, we would have a far different case.

Departures from the normal procedural sequence also might afford evidence that improper purposes are playing a role. Substantive departures too may be relevant, particularly if the factors usually considered important by the decisionmaker strongly favor a decision contrary to the one reached.

The legislative or administrative history may be highly relevant, especially where there are contemporary statements by members of the decisionmaking body, minutes of its meetings, or reports. In some extraordinary instances the members might be called to the stand at trial to testify concerning the purpose of the official action, although even then such testimony frequently will be barred by privilege.

The foregoing summary identifies, without purporting to be exhaustive, subjects of proper inquiry in determining whether racially discriminatory intent existed. With these in mind, we now address the case before us.

This case was tried in the District Court and reviewed in the Court of Appeals before our decision in *Washington v. Davis*.... The respondents proceeded on the erroneous theory that the Village's refusal to rezone carried a racially discriminatory effect and was, without more, unconstitutional. But both courts below understood that at least part of their function was to examine the purpose underlying the decision.

[On this record,] the evidence does not warrant overturning the concurrent findings of both courts below. Respondents simply failed to carry their burden of proving that discriminatory purpose was a motivating factor in the Village's decision. This conclusion ends the constitutional inquiry. The Court of Appeals' further finding that the Village's decision carried a discriminatory "ultimate effect" is without independent constitutional significance.

Respondents' complaint also alleged that the refusal to rezone violated the Fair Housing Act, 42 U.S.C. §3601 et seq. They continue to urge here that a zoning decision made by a public body may, and that petitioners' action did, violate §3604 or §3617. The Court of Appeals, however, proceeding in a somewhat (unorthodox) fashion, did not decide the statutory question. We remand the case for further consideration of respondents' statutory claims. Reversed and remanded.

Justice Marshall wrote an opinion, concurring in part and dissenting in part joined by Justice Brennan.

> I concur in Parts I–III of the Court's opinion. However, I believe the proper result would be to remand this entire case to the Court of Appeals for further proceedings consistent with *Washington v. Davis* ... and today's opinion.

Justice White wrote a dissenting opinion.

> The Court reverses the judgment of the Court of Appeals ... by interpreting our decision in *Washington v. Davis* ... and applying it to this case, notwithstanding that the Court of Appeals rendered its decision in this case before *Washington v. Davis* was handed down, and thus did not have the benefit of our decision when it found a Fourteenth Amendment violation.
>
> The Court gives no reason for its failure to follow our usual practice in this situation of vacating the judgment below and remanding in order to permit the lower court to reconsider its ruling in light of our intervening decision. The Court's articulation of a legal standard nowhere mentioned in *Davis* indicates that it feels that the application of *Davis* to these facts calls for substantial analysis. If this is true, we would do better to allow the Court of Appeals to attempt that analysis in the first instance.... I would vacate the judgment of the Court of Appeals and remand the case for consideration of the statutory issue and, if necessary, for consideration of the constitutional issue in light of *Washington v. Davis*.

The evidence that it was extremely difficult to prove intent to discriminate was to come in a case from Memphis Tennessee in which Justice Marshall was beside himself with frustration at a Court that seemed to be prepared to ignore a great deal of evidence of intentional discrimination.[32] In an opinion by Justice Stevens, the Court's majority concluded that the petition by an all-white neighborhood to block off the residential street at the point where it crossed into a predominantly African American neighborhood was justified by the desire to reduce traffic, concern for safety, and a desire to reduce noise. There was, Stevens said, no evidence to prove intent to discriminate.

Justice Marshall's dissent in the case, joined by Justices Brennan and Blackmun, demonstrated that, to the contrary, there was a great deal of evidence that the city had actively supported a deliberate effort to wall off a white neighborhood from an adjacent black neighborhood. He scoffed at the claim that this was a matter of concern about traffic.

> The stated explanation for the closing is of a sort all too familiar: "protecting the safety and tranquility of a residential neighborhood" by preventing "undesirable traffic" from entering it. Too often in our Nation's history, statements such as these have been little more than code phrases for racial discrimination.... Because I do not believe that either the Constitution or federal law permits a city to carve out racial enclaves I dissent."[33]

He went on to say that if the Court had actually applied the standard it announced in *Arlington Heights*, it would be unable to reach any other conclusion. He quoted a white resident who testified against the closing to the City Council but died before the trial in the case.

Emmanuel Goldberger, a white citizen who opposed the closing of West Drive but who died before trial, explained in testimony before the City Council some of the reasons that he considered the closing racially motivated:

> Mr. Chairman, there's been enough said about the number of cars, or the speed of the cars going on West Drive. You know and I know that that isn't the issue ... But if you

want me to, I will spell it out for you. Mr. Chairman, the answer is sitting right here. The well-to-do white people living in Hein Park do not want black people or the few of us who refuse to run away living north of Jackson to drive on ... what they think is their street. I phoned a man—I phoned a man with whom I have been friendly for more than 65 years. His wife answered and would not let me speak to him. So as the rights and wrongs were discussed, she said to me[,] "Leo and I were surprised to see you sitting with that group of niggers." That[,] Mr. Chairman[,] is the issue here.[34]

Marshall, who had argued in *Brown* the psychological injury to segregated children, warned:

The psychological effect of this barrier is likely to be significant.... Dr. Marvin Feit, a professor of psychiatry at the University of Tennessee, predicted that the barrier between West Drive and Springdale St. will reinforce feelings about the city's "favoritism" toward whites and will "serve as a monument to racial hostility." ... As the District Court put it: "[You] are not going to be able to convince those black people out there that they didn't do it because they were black. They are helping a white neighborhood. Now, that is a problem that somebody is going to have to live with ...." I cannot subscribe to the majority's apparent view that the city's erection of this "monument to racial hostility" amounts to nothing more than a "slight inconvenience."[35]

Still, the Court found no intent.

The Court was not through adding to the requirements for proof of intent. In a case in which it was clear that a state legislature knew that the state's absolute life-time veterans preference would result in a severely disproportionate negative impact on women, for conditions over which the women had no control, the Court nevertheless insisted upon proof that: "Discriminatory purpose, however, implies more than intent as volition or intent as awareness of consequences.... It implies that the decisionmaker, in this case a state legislature, selected or reaffirmed a particular course of action at least in part 'because of,' not merely 'in spite of,' its adverse effects upon an identifiable group."[36] That level of proof is extraordinarily difficult to meet.

This set of opinions has meant that most of those who suffer such discrimination have been forced to use civil rights statutes to bring their cases rather than constitutional cases, since several of the statutes do not require proof of intent but can use patterns of discriminatory effects to maintain cases.

Finally, there are two areas of the ongoing debate over race that remain very much active areas of dispute. The first is the racism that has existed in the criminal justice system and the second is the ongoing argument over affirmative action.

Racism in Criminal Justice

The U.S. Commission on Civil Rights conducted investigations into police/community relations in the 1960s and 1970s based on widespread charges of use of excessive force, discrimination, and other abuses by police departments targeted at African Americans.[37] As is evident, this was decades before the cases from Ferguson, Missouri to Baltimore, and other cities in 2014–15. The commission and other investigations of the criminal justice system at the time identified a wide range of issues, including the tendency for African Americans to be more often challenged by the police, arrested, charged with more (and more serious) charges, convicted more often, and sentenced more harshly than whites. Some of these issues will be addressed in later chapters with respect to Latinos as well.

Two issues became particularly important judicial questions in the years to follow for African Americans and other ethnocultural groups. The first concerned the makeup of juries, which had long been far from representative of the community and particularly tended, in many parts of the country, to lack African American participation. The second set of concerns arose with respect to the application of the death penalty, in significant part because of the evidence of discrimination in the manner of charging, the biases in the trial system, and the sentencing process. The first of these issues produced an important ruling in a case coming from Kentucky in 1986.

Batson v. Kentucky

476 U.S. 79 (1986)

INTRODUCTION: An African American defendant was tried for burglary and possession of stolen property. The parties were permitted to dismiss potential jurors for cause and each side was permitted a number of peremptory challenges.[38] The prosecutor employed peremptory challenges to eliminate the four African Americans who were part of the venire.[39] The result was that the defendant was convicted by an all-white jury. While the defense objected to the prosecutor's actions, the state supreme court upheld the conviction.

Justice Powell wrote the opinion for the Court.

... More than a century ago, the Court decided that the State denies a black defendant equal protection of the laws when it puts him on trial before a jury from which members of his race have been purposefully excluded. *Strauder v. West Virginia*, 100 U.S. 303 (1880). That decision laid the foundation for the Court's unceasing efforts to eradicate racial discrimination in the procedures used to select the venire from which individual jurors are drawn. In *Strauder*, the Court explained that the central concern of the recently ratified Fourteenth Amendment was to put an end to governmental discrimination on account of race.... Exclusion of black citizens from service as jurors constitutes a primary example of the evil the Fourteenth Amendment was designed to cure.

In holding that racial discrimination in jury selection offends the Equal Protection Clause, the Court in *Strauder* recognized, however, that a defendant has no right to a "petit jury composed in whole or in part of persons of his own race."[40]... But the defendant does have the right to be tried by a jury whose members are selected pursuant to non-discriminatory criteria.... The Equal Protection Clause guarantees the defendant that the State will not exclude members of his race from the jury venire on account of race....

Racial discrimination in selection of jurors harms not only the accused whose life or liberty they are summoned to try.... As long ago as *Strauder*, ... the Court recognized that by denying a person participation in jury service on account of his race, the State unconstitutionally discriminated against the excluded juror.... The harm from discriminatory jury selection extends beyond that inflicted on the defendant and the excluded juror to touch the entire community. Selection procedures that purposefully exclude black persons from juries undermine public confidence in the fairness of our system of justice....

In *Strauder*, the Court invalidated a state statute that provided that only white men could serve as jurors[, but] the Constitution requires ... that we look beyond the face of the statute defining juror qualifications and also consider challenged selection practices.... Thus, the Court has found a denial of equal protection where the procedures implementing a neutral statute operated to exclude persons from the venire [as well as the petit jury] on racial grounds.... [T]he State may not draw up its jury lists pursuant to neutral procedures but then resort to discrimination at "other stages in the selection process." ...

Accordingly, ... the State's privilege to strike individual jurors through peremptory challenges, is subject to the commands of the Equal Protection Clause. Although a prosecutor ordinarily is entitled to exercise permitted peremptory challenges "for any reason at all," ... the Equal Protection Clause forbids the prosecutor to challenge potential jurors solely on account of their race or on the assumption that black jurors as a group will be unable impartially to consider the State's case against a black defendant.

III. ... As in any equal protection case, the "burden is, of course," on the defendant who alleges discriminatory selection of the venire "to prove the existence of purposeful discrimination." In deciding if the defendant has carried his burden of persuasion, a court must undertake "a sensitive inquiry into such circumstantial and direct evidence of intent as may be available." *Arlington Heights v. Metropolitan Housing Development Corp....* We have observed that under some circumstances proof of discriminatory impact "may for all practical purposes demonstrate unconstitutionality because in various circumstances the discrimination is very difficult to explain on nonracial grounds." ... For example, "total or seriously disproportionate exclusion of Negroes from jury venires," [indicates] intentional discrimination.

Moreover, since *Swain* [*v. Alabama*, 380 US 202 (1965)], we have recognized that a black defendant alleging that members of his race have been impermissibly excluded from the venire may make out a prima facie case of purposeful discrimination by showing that the totality of the relevant facts gives rise to an inference of discriminatory purpose. *Washington v. Davis....* Once the defendant makes the requisite showing, the burden shifts to the State to explain adequately the racial exclusion.... [T]he State must demonstrate that "permissible racially neutral selection criteria and procedures have produced the monochromatic result." ...

[In order] to establish [a prima facie] case, the defendant first must show that he is a member of a cognizable racial group ... and that the prosecutor has exercised peremptory challenges to remove from the venire members of the defendant's race. Second, the defendant is entitled to rely on the fact ... that peremptory challenges constitute a jury selection practice that permits "those to discriminate who are of a mind to discriminate." ... Finally, the defendant must show that these facts and any other relevant circumstances raise an inference that the prosecutor used that practice to exclude the veniremen from the petit jury on account of their race. This combination of factors in the empaneling of the petit jury, as in the selection of the venire, raises the necessary inference of purposeful discrimination.

In deciding whether the defendant has made the requisite showing, the trial court should consider all relevant circumstances. For example, a "pattern" of strikes against black jurors included in the particular venire might give rise to an inference of discrimination. Similarly, the prosecutor's questions and statements during voir dire examination and in exercising his challenges may support or refute an inference of discriminatory purpose....[41]

Once the defendant makes a prima facie showing, the burden shifts to the State to come forward with a neutral explanation for challenging black jurors....

[T]he ... prosecutor may not rebut the defendant's prima facie case of discrimination by stating merely that he challenged jurors of the defendant's race on the assumption ... that they would be partial to the defendant because of their shared race.... Just as the Equal Protection Clause forbids the States to exclude black persons from the venire on the assumption that blacks as a group are unqualified to serve as jurors, ... so it forbids the States to strike black veniremen on the assumption that they will be biased in a particular case simply because the defendant is black.... The prosecutor therefore must articulate a neutral explanation related to the particular case to be tried....

V. In this case, petitioner made a timely objection to the prosecutor's removal of all black persons on the venire. Because the trial court flatly rejected the objection without requiring the prosecutor to give an explanation for his action, we remand this case for further proceedings....

Justice Marshall wrote a concurring opinion.

I join Justice Powell's eloquent opinion for the Court, which takes a historic step toward eliminating the shameful practice of racial discrimination in the selection of juries. The Court's opinion cogently explains the pernicious nature of the racially discriminatory use of peremptory challenges.... I nonetheless write separately to express my views. The decision today will not end the racial discrimination that peremptories inject into the jury-selection process. That goal can be accomplished only by eliminating peremptory challenges entirely....

Misuse of the peremptory challenge to exclude black jurors has become both common and flagrant.... An instruction book used by the prosecutor's office in Dallas County, Texas, explicitly advised prosecutors that they conduct jury selection so as to eliminate "any member of a minority group." In 100 felony trials in Dallas County in 1983–1984, prosecutors peremptorily struck 405 out of 467 eligible black jurors; the chance of a qualified black sitting on a jury was 1 in 10, compared to 1 in 2 for a white....

I wholeheartedly concur in the Court's conclusion that use of the peremptory challenge to remove blacks from juries, on the basis of their race, violates the Equal Protection Clause. I would go further, however, in fashioning a remedy adequate to eliminate that discrimination. Merely allowing defendants the opportunity to challenge the racially discriminatory use of peremptory challenges in individual cases will not end the illegitimate use of the peremptory challenge.

Evidentiary analysis similar to that set out by the Court ... has been adopted as a matter of state law in States including Massachusetts and California. Cases from those jurisdictions illustrate the limitations of the approach.... Prosecutors are left free to discriminate against blacks in jury selection provided that they hold that discrimination to an "acceptable" level.

Second, when a defendant can establish a prima facie case, trial courts face the difficult burden of assessing prosecutors' motives. Any prosecutor can easily assert facially neutral reasons for striking a juror, and trial courts are ill equipped to second-guess those reasons....

Nor is outright prevarication by prosecutors the only danger here.... A prosecutor's own conscious or unconscious racism may lead him easily to the conclusion that a prospective black juror is "sullen," or "distant," a characterization that would not have come to his mind if a white juror had acted identically. A judge's

124   *Beyond* Brown v. Board of Education

own conscious or unconscious racism may lead him to accept such an explanation as well supported.... Even if all parties approach the Court's mandate with the best of conscious intentions, that mandate requires them to confront and overcome their own racism on all levels—a challenge I doubt all of them can meet....

I applaud the Court's holding that the racially discriminatory use of peremptory challenges violates the Equal Protection Clause, and I join the Court's opinion. However, only by banning peremptories entirely can such discrimination be ended.[42]

Chief Justice Burger wrote a dissent joined by Justice Rehnquist.

Today the Court sets aside the peremptory challenge, a procedure which has been part of the common law for many centuries and part of our jury system for nearly 200 years.... Instead of even considering the history or function of the peremptory challenge, the bulk of the Court's opinion is spent recounting the well-established principle that intentional exclusion of racial groups from jury venires is a violation of the Equal Protection Clause....

[T]he Court also invokes general equal protection principles in support of its holding. But peremptory challenges are often lodged, of necessity, for reasons "normally thought irrelevant to legal proceedings or official action, namely, the race, religion, nationality, occupation or affiliations of people summoned for jury duty." *Swain*.... [I]t is quite probable that every peremptory challenge could be objected to on the basis that, because it excluded a venireman who had some characteristic not shared by the remaining members of the venire, it constituted a "classification" subject to equal protection scrutiny....

Our system permits two types of challenges: challenges for cause and peremptory challenges. Challenges for cause obviously have to be explained; by definition, peremptory challenges do not.... A challenge either has to be explained or it does not. It is readily apparent, then, that to permit inquiry into the basis for a peremptory challenge would force "the peremptory challenge [to] collapse into the challenge for cause." ...

Justice Rehnquist wrote a dissent joined by Chief Justice Burger.

... I cannot subscribe to the Court's unprecedented use of the Equal Protection Clause to restrict the historic scope of the peremptory challenge, which has been described as "a necessary part of trial by jury." ... In my view, there is simply nothing "unequal" about the State's using its peremptory challenges to strike blacks from the jury in cases involving black defendants, so long as such challenges are also used to exclude whites in cases involving white defendants, Hispanics in cases involving Hispanic defendants, Asians in cases involving Asian defendants, and so on.... Such use of peremptories is at best based upon seat-of-the-pants instincts, which are undoubtedly crudely stereotypical and may in many cases be hopelessly mistaken. But as long as they are applied across-the-board to jurors of all races and nationalities, I do not see ... how their use violates the Equal Protection Clause.

... The use of group affiliations, such as age, race, or occupation, as a "proxy" for potential juror partiality, based on the assumption or belief that members of one group are more likely to favor defendants who belong to the same group, has long been accepted as a legitimate basis for the State's exercise of peremptory challenges.... I do not believe there is anything in the Equal Protection Clause, or any other constitutional provision, that justifies such a departure from ... *Swain*.

The question of racial discrimination in the administration of the death penalty came to the Supreme Court in a case that presented the issues in stark terms, largely because it came with what became known simply as the Baldus Study; research that demonstrated in dramatic terms that the process was both arbitrary and failed to provide equal justice to African Americans.

McCleskey v. Kemp

481 U.S. 279 (1987)

INTRODUCTION: McCleskey was convicted of killing a police officer during a robbery and sentenced to death under Georgia law, and the state supreme court affirmed. His attorneys moved the case to the federal courts, seeking a writ of habeas corpus.[43]

The defense marshaled statistical testimony that demonstrated dramatic differences in the application of the death penalty by race. The majority opinion did address the specific findings, but Justice Brennan's dissent notes that the Baldus Study found that:

> The capital sentencing rate for all white-victim cases was almost 11 times greater than the rate for black-victim cases.... Furthermore, blacks who kill whites are sentenced to death at nearly 22 times the rate of blacks who kill blacks, and more than 7 times the rate of whites who kill blacks.... In addition, prosecutors seek the death penalty for 70% of black defendants with white victims, but for only 15% of black defendants with black victims, and only 19% of white defendants with black victims.... Since our decision upholding the Georgia capital sentencing system in *Gregg*, the State has executed seven persons. All of the seven were convicted of killing whites, and six of the seven executed were black. Such execution figures are especially striking in light of the fact that, during the period encompassed by the Baldus study, only 9.2% of Georgia homicides involved black defendants and white victims, while 60.7% involved black victims.

On the basis of this evidence, the defense sought to show that the Georgia death penalty process violated the Eighth and Fourteenth Amendments.

Justice Powell wrote the opinion for the Court.

> This case presents the question whether a complex statistical study that indicates a risk that racial considerations enter into capital sentencing determinations proves that petitioner McCleskey's capital sentence is unconstitutional under the Eighth or Fourteenth Amendment.

> I. McCleskey['s] petition [claimed] that the Georgia capital sentencing process is administered in a racially discriminatory manner in violation of the Eighth and Fourteenth Amendments to the United States Constitution. In support of his claim, McCleskey proffered a statistical study performed by Professors David C. Baldus, Charles Pulaski, and George Woodworth (the Baldus study) that purports to show a disparity in the imposition of the death sentence in Georgia based on the race of the murder victim and, to a lesser extent, the race of the defendant. The Baldus study is actually two sophisticated statistical studies that examine over 2,000 murder cases that occurred in Georgia during the 1970's. The raw numbers collected by Professor Baldus indicate that defendants charged with killing white persons received the death penalty in 11% of the cases, but defendants charged with killing blacks received the death penalty in only 1% of the cases. The raw numbers also indicate a reverse racial disparity according to the race of the defendant: 4% of the black defendants received the death penalty, as opposed to 7% of the white defendants.

Baldus also divided the cases according to the combination of the race of the defendant and the race of the victim. He found that the death penalty was assessed in 22% of the cases involving black defendants and white victims; 8% of the cases involving white defendants and white victims; 1% of the cases involving black defendants and black victims; and 3% of the cases involving white defendants and black victims. Similarly, Baldus found that prosecutors sought the death penalty in 70% of the cases involving black defendants and white victims; 32% of the cases involving white defendants and white victims; 15% of the cases involving black defendants and black victims; and 19% of the cases involving white defendants and black victims.

Baldus subjected his data to an extensive analysis, taking account of 230 variables that could have explained the disparities on nonracial grounds. One of his models concludes that, even after taking account of 39 nonracial variables, defendants charged with killing white victims were 4.3 times as likely to receive a death sentence as defendants charged with killing blacks. According to this model, black defendants were 1.1 times as likely to receive a death sentence as other defendants. Thus, the Baldus study indicates that black defendants, such as McCleskey, who kill white victims have the greatest likelihood of receiving the death penalty.

The District Court ... held that the Baldus study "fail[ed] to contribute anything of value" to McCleskey's claim ... and [t]he Court of Appeals ... found the statistics "insufficient to demonstrate discriminatory intent or unconstitutional discrimination.... We affirm.

II. ... [A] defendant who alleges an equal protection violation has the burden of proving "the existence of purposeful discrimination." ... McCleskey ... offers no evidence specific to his own case that would support an inference that racial considerations played a part in his sentence. Instead, ... McCleskey argues that the Baldus study compels an inference that his sentence rests on purposeful discrimination. McCleskey's claim that these statistics are sufficient proof of discrimination, without regard to the facts of a particular case, would extend to all capital cases in Georgia, at least where the victim was white and the defendant is black.

The Court has accepted statistics as proof of intent to discriminate in certain limited contexts.... But the nature of the capital sentencing decision, and the relationship of the statistics to that decision, are fundamentally different from the corresponding elements in the venire-selection or (Civil Rights Act of 1964) Title VII cases. Most importantly, each particular decision to impose the death penalty is made by a petit jury selected from a properly constituted venire.... Thus, the application of an inference drawn from the general statistics to a specific decision in a trial and sentencing simply is not comparable to the application of an inference drawn from general statistics to a specific venire-selection or Title VII case....

McCleskey also suggests that the Baldus study proves that the State as a whole has acted with a discriminatory purpose. He appears to argue that the State has violated the Equal Protection Clause by adopting the capital punishment statute and allowing it to remain in force despite its allegedly discriminatory application. But "'discriminatory purpose' ... implies more than intent as volition or intent as awareness of consequences. It implies that the decisionmaker, in this case a state legislature, selected or reaffirmed a particular course of action at least in part

'because of,' not merely 'in spite of,' its adverse effects upon an identifiable group."
Personnel Administrator of Massachusetts v. Feeney.... For this claim to prevail,
McCleskey would have to prove that the Georgia Legislature enacted or maintained the death penalty statute because of an anticipated racially discriminatory
effect.... There was no [such] evidence.... Nor has McCleskey demonstrated that
the legislature maintains the capital punishment statute because of the racially
disproportionate impact.... [W]e will not infer a discriminatory purpose on the
part of the State of Georgia. Accordingly, we reject McCleskey's equal protection
claims.

III. McCleskey also argues that the Baldus study demonstrates that the Georgia
capital sentencing system violates the Eighth Amendment.... Two principal
decisions guide our resolution of McCleskey's Eighth Amendment claim. In
Furman v. Georgia, 408 U.S. 238 (1972), the Court concluded that the death
penalty was so irrationally imposed that any particular death sentence could be
presumed excessive.... In *Gregg* [*v. Georgia*, 428 U.S. 153 (1976)], the Court ...
concluded ... "that the infliction of death as a punishment for murder is not without justification and thus is not unconstitutionally severe." ... [Gregg also upheld
the] then new Georgia statute....

IV. ... [McCleskey] contends that the Georgia capital punishment system is
arbitrary and capricious in application, and therefore his sentence is excessive, because racial considerations may influence capital sentencing decisions
in Georgia.... Even Professor Baldus does not contend that his statistics prove
that race enters into any capital sentencing decisions or that race was a factor in
McCleskey's particular case. Statistics at most may show only a likelihood that a
particular factor entered into some decisions.... McCleskey asks us to accept the
likelihood allegedly shown by the Baldus study as the constitutional measure of
an unacceptable risk of racial prejudice influencing capital sentencing decisions.
This we decline to do....

At most, the Baldus study indicates a discrepancy that appears to correlate with
race. Apparent disparities in sentencing are an inevitable part of our criminal
justice system.... In light of the safeguards designed to minimize racial bias in the
process, the fundamental value of jury trial in our criminal justice system, and the
benefits that discretion provides to criminal defendants, we hold that the Baldus
study does not demonstrate a constitutionally significant risk of racial bias affecting the Georgia capital sentencing process.

... [I]f we accepted McCleskey's claim that racial bias has impermissibly tainted
the capital sentencing decision, we could soon be faced with similar claims as to
other types of penalty. Moreover, the claim that his sentence rests on the irrelevant
factor of race easily could be extended to apply to claims based on unexplained
discrepancies that correlate to membership in other minority groups, and even to
gender.... As these examples illustrate, there is no limiting principle to the type of
challenge brought by McCleskey....

Second, McCleskey's arguments are best presented to the legislative bodies....
Capital punishment is now the law in more than two-thirds of our States. It is the
ultimate duty of courts to determine on a case-by-case basis whether these laws
are applied consistently with the Constitution.... [T]he only question before us is
whether in his case the law of Georgia was properly applied. We agree with the
[lower courts] that this was carefully and correctly done in this case.

Justice Brennan wrote a dissent joined by Justice Marshall. Justices Blackmun and Stevens joined the opinion as well except for Part I.

I. Adhering to my view that the death penalty is in all circumstances cruel and unusual punishment forbidden by the Eighth and Fourteenth Amendments, I would vacate the decision below.... Even if I did not hold this position, however, I would reverse..., for petitioner McCleskey has clearly demonstrated that his death sentence was imposed in violation of the Eighth and Fourteenth Amendments.... McCleskey has also demonstrated precisely the type of risk of irrationality in sentencing that we have consistently condemned in our Eighth Amendment jurisprudence.

II. At some point in this case, Warren McCleskey doubtless asked his lawyer whether a jury was likely to sentence him to die. A candid reply to this question would have been disturbing. First, counsel would have to tell McCleskey that few of the details of the crime or of McCleskey's past criminal conduct were more important than the fact that his victim was white.... Furthermore, counsel would feel bound to tell McCleskey that defendants charged with killing white victims in Georgia are 4.3 times as likely to be sentenced to death as defendants charged with killing blacks.... In addition, frankness would compel the disclosure that it was more likely than not that the race of McCleskey's victim would determine whether he received a death sentence: 6 of every 11 defendants convicted of killing a white person would not have received the death penalty if their victims had been black, ... while, among defendants with aggravating and mitigating factors comparable to McCleskey's, 20 of every 34 would not have been sentenced to die if their victims had been black.... Finally, the assessment would not be complete without the information that cases involving black defendants and white victims are more likely to result in a death sentence than cases featuring any other racial combination of defendant and victim.... The story could be told in a variety of ways, but McCleskey could not fail to grasp its essential narrative line: there was a significant chance that race would play a prominent role in determining if he lived or died.

The Court today ... finds no fault in a system in which lawyers must tell their clients that race casts a large shadow on the capital sentencing process. The Court arrives at this conclusion by stating that the Baldus study cannot "prove that race enters into any capital sentencing decisions or that race was a factor in McCleskey's particular case." ... Since, according to Professor Baldus, we cannot say "to a moral certainty" that race influenced a decision, ... we can identify only "a likelihood that a particular factor entered into some decisions," and "a discrepancy that appears to correlate with race." ... This "likelihood" and "discrepancy," holds the Court, is insufficient to establish a constitutional violation.... The Court's evaluation of the significance of petitioner's evidence is fundamentally at odds with our consistent concern for rationality in capital sentencing, and the considerations that the majority invokes to discount that evidence cannot justify ignoring its force.

III. It is important to emphasize at the outset that the Court's observation that McCleskey cannot prove the influence of race on any particular sentencing decision is irrelevant in evaluating his Eighth Amendment claim. Since *Furman v. Georgia*, ... the Court has been concerned with the risk of the imposition of an arbitrary sentence, rather than the proven fact of one." ... This emphasis on risk acknowledges the difficulty of divining the jury's motivation in an individual case. In addition, it reflects the fact that concern for arbitrariness focuses on the rationality of the system as a whole, and that a system that features a significant probability that sentencing decisions are influenced by impermissible considerations cannot be regarded as rational....

As a result, our inquiry under the Eighth Amendment has not been directed to the validity of the individual sentences before us.... We have required instead that they establish that the system under which they were sentenced posed a significant risk of such an occurrence. McCleskey's claim does differ, however, in one respect from these earlier cases: it is the first to base a challenge not on speculation about how a system might operate, but on empirical documentation of how it does operate.... Nonetheless, [the Court] finds the probability of prejudice insufficient to create constitutional concern.... Close analysis of the Baldus study, however, ... reveals that the risk that race influenced McCleskey's sentence is intolerable by any imaginable standard....

The capital sentencing rate for all white-victim cases was almost 11 times greater than the rate for black-victim cases.... Furthermore, blacks who kill whites are sentenced to death at nearly 22 times the rate of blacks who kill blacks, and more than 7 times the rate of whites who kill blacks.... In addition, prosecutors seek the death penalty for 70% of black defendants with white victims, but for only 15% of black defendants with black victims, and only 19% of white defendants with black victims.... Since our decision upholding the Georgia capital sentencing system in *Gregg*, the State has executed seven persons. All of the seven were convicted of killing whites, and six of the seven executed were black. Such execution figures are especially striking in light of the fact that, during the period encompassed by the Baldus study, only 9.2% of Georgia homicides involved black defendants and white victims, while 60.7% involved black victims....

The statistical evidence in this case thus relentlessly documents the risk that McCleskey's sentence was influenced by racial considerations.... In determining whether this risk is acceptable, our judgment must be shaped by the awareness that "the risk of racial prejudice infecting a capital sentencing proceeding is especially serious in light of the complete finality of the death sentence." ... In light of the gravity of the interest at stake, petitioner's statistics on their face are a powerful demonstration of the type of risk that our Eighth Amendment jurisprudence has consistently condemned....

Georgia's legacy of a race-conscious criminal justice system, as well as this Court's own recognition of the persistent danger that racial attitudes may affect criminal proceedings, indicates that McCleskey's claim is not a fanciful product of mere statistical artifice.... This Court has invalidated portions of the Georgia capital sentencing system three times over the past 15 years.... [I]t would be unrealistic to ignore the influence of history in assessing the plausible implications of McCleskey's evidence.... The conclusions drawn from McCleskey's statistical evidence are therefore consistent with the lessons of social experience.

The majority thus misreads our Eighth Amendment jurisprudence in concluding that McCleskey has not demonstrated a degree of risk sufficient to raise constitutional concern.... Sentencing data, history, and experience all counsel that Georgia has provided insufficient assurance of the heightened rationality we have required in order to take a human life.... The challenge to the Georgia system is not speculative or theoretical; it is empirical.... [W]e must critique its performance in terms of its results." ...

V. ... Warren McCleskey's evidence confronts us with the subtle and persistent influence of the past.... Nonetheless, we ignore him at our peril, for we remain imprisoned by the past as long as we deny its influence in the present.[44]

Once again, Justice Lewis Powell was key. This time he not only authored the opinion but was also the critical fifth vote in a 5–4 majority. However, after his retirement from the bench, only five years after the death penalty case, he regretted that decision. When his biographer, Professor John C. Jeffries, Jr., asked him in an interview in the summer of 1991 whether he would change any of the many votes he had cast on the Court, he replied, "Yes, *McCleskey v. Kemp*."[45] As Jeffries pointed out, that change of position did not help McCleskey, who was executed in September 1991.

The Affirmative Action Cases

There was another issue, however, that has remained very much a live topic of debate. It is about whether affirmative action programs initiated in an effort to redress the effects of a history of discrimination are themselves to be considered discriminatory in violation of the equal protection clause of the Fourteenth Amendment. The Supreme Court has dramatically constrained affirmative action programs where race is a factor, but there are still uncertainties and the Court has before it another such case at the time of this writing.

There are two types of affirmative action. The first concerns judicial remedies issued in cases where a prior case of discrimination has been proven. In those cases, remedies that use race or gender are clearly permissible and have been for a very long time in keeping with the powers of the courts to issue equitable remedies, sometimes referred to as remedial decrees.[46] These may be imposed by a court, but frequently they are negotiated by the parties once a ruling that there has been discrimination is issued by a court. Those negotiated agreements are then entered as orders of the court and are sometimes referred to as consent decrees.[47]

The most intense debates, however, have concerned situations in which a federal, state, or local policy includes a voluntary affirmative action program, either to remedy what the policymakers see as a previous history of exclusion or discrimination or because of a desire to make public services and programs more diverse to match the diverse community they are expected to serve. These programs, in many cases, trace their heritage to 1960s efforts by the Johnson administration not only to end discrimination but also to do something about the pattern of unequal treatment, services, and opportunities that had resulted from decades of prior discrimination.

While Vice President, Lyndon Johnson had been appointed chair of the Committee on Equal Employment Opportunity that President Kennedy had created with his Executive Order 10925. It was an experience that convinced Johnson that the effects of generations of segregation and discrimination would not be addressed merely by laws that urged Americans not to continue to discriminate. The history of discrimination had shaped the conditions of inequality in society in profound ways that he concluded could only be addressed by direct and affirmative action. Johnson's call for affirmative action came in his June 4, 1965 commencement address at Howard University entitled "To Fulfill These Rights," committing the administration to a more affirmative and active approach to civil rights.[48]

You do not wipe away the scars of centuries by saying: Now you are free to go where you want, and do as you desire, and choose the leaders you please.

You do not take a person who, for years, has been hobbled by chains and liberate him, bring him up to the starting line of a race and then say, "you are free to compete with all the others," and still justly believe that you have been completely fair.

Thus it is not enough just to open the gates of opportunity. All our citizens must have the ability to walk through those gates.[49]

Johnson convened a conference that took its title from the commencement address and also assigned Vice President Hubert Humphrey to study barriers to equality in the federal government. Humphrey delivered his memorandum in September of 1965 and Johnson responded with several actions, two of which had particular importance. He issued Executive Orders 11246 and 11247.[50] Following Humphrey's recommendations, E.O. 11246 mandated civil rights compliance and equal opportunity responsibilities for all agencies of the executive branch. The term "affirmative action" is often traced to §202 of the executive order, which required that contractors "take affirmative action" on equal employment opportunity, but the fact is that the Johnson order took that language from the previous executive order that had been issued during the Kennedy administration. It was, however, clear that the Johnson administration had a much more literal and committed approach to that language than did its predecessor.

Ironically, the rules for federal contractors were actually put into operation with orders that the Department of Labor issued in 1969 that required affirmative action hiring by contractors working on federal buildings under construction in Philadelphia. By this time, affirmative action steps were actually taken under the Nixon administration, known simply as the "Philadelphia Plan." There were immediate charges by contractors and others that the Philadelphia Plan was itself discriminatory and in violation of Title VII of the Civil Rights Act of 1964, a position that was supported by the Comptroller General of the United States, but the Attorney General provided a formal opinion stating that it was lawful.[51] The challenge went to the U.S. Court of Appeals for the Third Circuit, which upheld the affirmative action requirements.[52]

The next major round in that fight, however, saw a ruling by the U.S. Supreme Court, in *Fullilove v. Klutznick*, that upheld a contract set-aside program created by Congress in the Public Works Employment Act of 1977, under which a portion of the funds available for the program were to be used to hire minority business enterprises as contractors.[53] Chief Justice Burger concluded: "Congress has necessary latitude to try new techniques such as the limited use of racial and ethnic criteria to accomplish remedial objectives."[54] He did not apply strict scrutiny in light of the remedial purpose of the policy.

State and local governments around the country had also established affirmative action programs in hiring and contracting, and in educational admissions programs. In some cases these programs were the result of a determination that there had been a history of exclusion that needed to be remedied. In other cases they were undertaken because the U.S. Justice Department made it clear to state and local officials that they were not in compliance with civil rights statutes and faced possible legal action if they did not remedy the problems.

Just one year before the contracting ruling, a far more divided Supreme Court had ruled in a case concerning an affirmative action admissions program at the University of California, Davis Medical School. It was a complex case with an equally complicated set of facts, but it was the first major affirmative action admissions case to make it to the Supreme Court. There was no majority opinion, but Justice Lewis Powell issued the plurality opinion in *Regents v. Bakke*.[55] Powell affirmed the California Supreme Court ruling that the particular program in place at U.C. Davis was in violation of Title VI of the Civil Rights Act of 1964 that prohibits discrimination in programs receiving federal funds and the equal protection clause of the Fourteenth Amendment. However, Powell wrote: "Ethnic diversity ... is only one element in a range of factors a university properly may consider in attaining the goal of a heterogeneous student body."[56]

Meanwhile, state and local governments copied their own version of the federal contract affirmative action program that had been upheld by a solid majority of the Court in *Fullilove*. One of these was the city of Richmond, Virginia, the city that had been the "cradle of the Confederacy" and had adamantly resisted desegregation. In *Richmond v. J. A. Croson, Co.*, 488 U.S. 469 (1989), the Supreme Court, in an opinion by Justice Sandra Day O'Connor, rejected Richmond's claims that it was doing what the Court had upheld in the *Fullilove* opinion. She asserted that state and local governments were very different from Congress in creating such a policy. "What appellant ignores is that Congress, unlike any State or political subdivision, has a specific constitutional mandate to enforce the dictates of the Fourteenth Amendment."[57] Since the state does not have that obligation, then it cannot use remedial authority in the way Congress can. Because of that difference, state and local governments that make any decision in which race is a factor must face strict judicial scrutiny and the city lacked a compelling interest required by that standard.

Justice Marshall, in a dissent joined by Justices Brennan and Blackmun, made it clear that O'Connor's effort to differentiate the *Richmond* case from *Fullilove* simply could not be taken seriously. He also rejected the idea that this distinction could be based on some kind of notion that Congress had an obligation to enforce the Fourteenth Amendment, including remedying the effects of past discrimination, but that state and local governments do not.

> Today, for the first time, a majority of this Court has adopted strict scrutiny as its standard of Equal Protection Clause review of race-conscious remedial measures.... This is an unwelcome development. A profound difference separates governmental actions that themselves are racist, and governmental actions that seek to remedy the effects of prior racism or to prevent neutral governmental activity from perpetuating the effects of such racism.[58]

Even if the Court did apply strict scrutiny, he argued, the record was clear that Richmond has such an interest given its history of exclusion of minority businesses from city contracting and the city's larger history of segregation.

Justice Blackmun added a separate dissent, in which he said:

> I never thought that I would live to see the day when the city of Richmond, Virginia, the cradle of the Old Confederacy, sought on its own, within a narrow confine, to lessen the stark impact of persistent discrimination. But Richmond, to its great credit, acted. Yet this Court, the supposed bastion of equality, strikes down Richmond's efforts as though discrimination had never existed or was not demonstrated in this particular litigation.[59]

Another federal government affirmative action came back to the Court soon after the *Richmond* case, this time concerning a program to promote diversity among broadcast license holders. Justice Brennan wrote for the Court upholding the Federal Communications Commission program, explaining that the *Richmond* ruling had emphasized that state and local governments stood in a very different position with respect to the creation of affirmative action programs than did the federal government. That said, the *Fullilove v. Klutznick* precedent was still the applicable precedent to cover federal programs and therefore upheld the F.C.C. program (*Metro Broadcasting, Inc. v. FCC*).[60]

However, the composition of the Court changed. Justices Brennan and Marshall were gone. Justices Rehnquist, Scalia, Thomas, and Kennedy opposed affirmative action programs. Justice Sandra Day O'Connor now held the key fifth vote in this, as in other areas of the Court's work. O'Connor in the 1997 *Adarand* case,[61] involving a contract affirmative action program applied in a case concerning the construction of highway guard rails, promptly repudiated the distinction she had drawn in the *Richmond* ruling between actions by the federal government and those by the state or local governments and reversed the *Metro Broadcasting* ruling.[62] Justice Stevens, in a dissent joined by Justice Ginsburg, correctly pointed out that the Court's ruling flew directly in the face of both the rulings on federal programs and the *Richmond* opinion written by none other than the same justice who wrote the majority ruling in the present case. "Instead of deciding this case in accordance with controlling precedent, the Court today delivers a disconcerting lecture about the evils of governmental racial classifications."[63] Justice Souter also issued a dissent, joined by Justices Ginsburg and Breyer, arguing, inter alia, that the *Fullilove* ruling clearly should have been the controlling precedent in this case.[64] Justice Ginsburg also issued her own dissent, joined by Breyer, which insisted:

> Bias both conscious and unconscious, reflecting traditional and unexamined habits of thought, keeps up barriers that must come down if equal opportunity and nondiscrimination are ever genuinely to become this country's law and practice. Given this history and its practical consequences, Congress surely can conclude that a carefully designed affirmative action program may help to realize, finally, the "equal protection of the laws" the Fourteenth Amendment has promised since 1868.[65]

Following the *Adarand* ruling, opponents of affirmative action mobilized in an attempt to find cases that could be moved to the Supreme Court in such a posture that the Court would be forced to rule directly on whether affirmative action was to be a prohibited practice under the equal protection clause of the Fourteenth Amendment and the due process clause of the Fifth Amendment where federal government programs were involved. The assumption was that there were four solid votes to reject affirmative action and that Justice O'Connor appeared poised to become the fifth vote. The cases that ultimately pushed that challenge came from the University of Michigan and concerned affirmative action admissions programs for the law school and for undergraduate admissions, two very different admissions programs. The cases produced two separate opinions, authored by two different justices of the Court. The facts of these cases are presented in the edited version of the opinion below.

Grutter v. Bollinger

539 U.S. 306 (2003)

INTRODUCTION: The University of Michigan's Law School developed a diversity admissions program that made race one factor out of a complex list of factors to be considered in its process. The result was that some minority applicants with higher grades and LSAT scores than non-minority applicants were not admitted while in other cases the reverse was true. It was clear that race alone would not get an applicant admitted. However, affirmative action opponents targeted this admissions program with the hope that Justice O'Connor would be pushed into casting the deciding vote to end affirmative action in general.

Justice O'Connor delivered the opinion of the Court.

In the landmark *Bakke* case, ... the only holding for the Court ... was that a "State has a substantial interest that legitimately may be served by a properly devised admissions program involving the competitive consideration of race and ethnic origin." ... Justice Powell approved the university's use of race to further only one interest: "the attainment of a diverse student body." ... [T]oday we endorse Justice Powell's view that student body diversity is a compelling state interest that can justify the use of race in university admissions....

We have held that [under the equal protection clause] all racial classifications imposed by government "must be analyzed by a reviewing court under strict scrutiny." ... This means that such classifications are constitutional only if they are narrowly tailored to further compelling governmental interests.... Strict scrutiny is not "strict in theory, but fatal in fact." *Adarand*.... Although all governmental uses of race are subject to strict scrutiny, not all are invalidated by it....

III. ... The Law School's educational judgment that such diversity is essential to its educational mission is one to which we defer.... Our scrutiny of the interest asserted by the Law School is no less strict for taking into account complex educational judgments in an area that lies primarily within the expertise of the university.... Our conclusion that the Law School has a compelling interest in a diverse student body is informed by our view that attaining a diverse student body is at the heart of the Law School's proper institutional mission, and that "good faith" on the part of a university is "presumed" absent "a showing to the contrary." ...

As part of its goal of "assembling a class that is both exceptionally academically qualified and broadly diverse," the Law School seeks to "enroll a 'critical mass' of minority students." ... These benefits are substantial. As the District Court emphasized, the Law School's admissions policy promotes "cross-racial understanding," helps to break down racial stereotypes, and "enables [students] to better understand persons of different races." ... [N]umerous studies show that student body diversity promotes learning outcomes, and "better prepares students for an increasingly diverse workforce and society, and better prepares them as professionals." ...

These benefits are not theoretical but real, as major American businesses have made clear that the skills needed in today's increasingly global marketplace can only be developed through exposure to widely diverse people, cultures, ideas, and viewpoints.... What is more, high-ranking retired officers and civilian leaders of the United States military assert that, "based on [their] decades of experience," a "highly qualified, racially diverse officer corps ... is essential to the military's ability to fulfill its principle[sic] mission to provide national security." ... We agree that "it requires only a small step from this analysis to conclude that our country's other most selective institutions must remain both diverse and selective." ...

Even in the limited circumstance when drawing racial distinctions is permissible to further a compelling state interest, "... the means chosen to accomplish the [government's] asserted purpose must be specifically and narrowly framed to accomplish that purpose." ... To be narrowly tailored, a race-conscious admissions program cannot use a quota system.... Instead, a university may consider race or ethnicity only as a "'plus' in a particular applicant's file," without "insulating the individual from comparison with all other candidates for the available seats." ... In other words, an admissions program must be "flexible enough to consider all pertinent elements of diversity in light of the particular qualifications of each applicant, and to place them on the same footing for consideration, although not necessarily according them the same weight." ...

We find that the Law School's admissions program bears the hallmarks of a narrowly tailored plan.... We are satisfied that the Law School's admissions program ... does not operate as a quota. Properly understood, a "quota" is a program in which a certain fixed number or proportion of opportunities are "reserved exclusively for certain minority groups." ... In contrast, "a permissible goal ... requires only a good-faith effort ... to come within a range demarcated by the goal itself," ... and permits consideration of race as a "plus" factor in any given case.... The Law School's goal of attaining a critical mass of underrepresented minority students does not transform its program into a quota....

When using race as a "plus" factor in university admissions, a university's admissions program must remain flexible enough to ensure that each applicant is evaluated as an individual and not in a way that makes an applicant's race or ethnicity the defining feature of his or her application. The importance of this individualized consideration in the context of a race-conscious admissions program is paramount....

Here, the Law School engages in a highly individualized, holistic review of each applicant's file, giving serious consideration to all the ways an applicant might contribute to a diverse educational environment. The Law School affords this individualized consideration to applicants of all races. There is no policy, either de jure or de facto, of automatic acceptance or rejection based on any single "soft" variable.... What is more, the Law School actually gives substantial weight to diversity factors besides race. The Law School frequently accepts nonminority applicants with grades and test scores lower than underrepresented minority applicants (and other nonminority applicants) who are rejected....

Petitioner and the United States argue that the Law School's plan is not narrowly tailored.... We disagree. Narrow tailoring does not require exhaustion of every conceivable race-neutral alternative.... Narrow tailoring does, however, require serious, good faith consideration of workable race-neutral alternatives that will achieve the diversity the university seeks.[66]

Chief Justice Rehnquist wrote a dissent joined by Justices Scalia, Kennedy, and Thomas.

... I do not believe ... that the University of Michigan Law School's ... means are narrowly tailored to the interest it asserts.... Stripped of its "critical mass" veil, the Law School's program is revealed as a naked effort to achieve racial balancing.... Although the Court recites the language of our strict scrutiny analysis, its application of that review is unprecedented in its deference....

I do not believe that the Constitution gives the Law School such free rein in the use of race. The Law School has offered no explanation for its actual admissions practices and, unexplained, we are bound to conclude that the Law School has managed its admissions program, not to achieve a "critical mass," but to extend offers of admission to members of selected minority groups in proportion to their statistical representation in the applicant pool. But this is precisely the type of racial balancing that the Court itself calls "patently unconstitutional."

Justice Kennedy wrote a dissent.

... There is no constitutional objection to the goal of considering race as one modest factor among many others to achieve diversity, but an educational institution must ensure, through sufficient procedures, that each applicant receives individual consideration and that race does not become a predominant factor in the admissions decisionmaking. The Law School failed to comply with this requirement, and by no means has it carried its burden to show otherwise by the test of strict scrutiny....

Were the courts to apply a searching standard to race-based admissions schemes, that would force educational institutions to seriously explore race-neutral alternatives. The Court, by contrast, is willing to be satisfied by the Law School's profession of its own good faith.... If universities are given the latitude to administer programs that are tantamount to quotas, they will have few incentives to make the existing minority admissions schemes transparent and protective of individual review. The unhappy consequence will be to perpetuate the hostilities that proper consideration of race is designed to avoid....

Justice Thomas wrote an opinion concurring in part and dissenting in part in which Justice Scalia joined Parts I–VII.[67]

... I believe blacks can achieve in every avenue of American life without the meddling of university administrators. Because I wish to see all students succeed whatever their color, I share, in some respect, the sympathies of those who sponsor the type of discrimination advanced by the University of Michigan Law School. The Constitution does not, however, tolerate institutional devotion to the status quo in admissions policies when such devotion ripens into racial discrimination. Nor does the Constitution countenance the unprecedented deference the Court gives to the Law School, an approach inconsistent with the very concept of "strict scrutiny."

No one would argue that a university could set up a lower general admission standard and then impose heightened requirements only on black applicants. Similarly, a university may not maintain a high admission standard and grant exemptions to favored races. The Law School, of its own choosing, and for its own purposes, maintains an exclusionary admissions system that it knows produces racially disproportionate results. Racial discrimination is not a permissible solution to the self-inflicted wounds of this elitist admissions policy....

I. ... A majority of the Court has validated only two circumstances where "pressing public necessity" or a "compelling state interest" can possibly justify racial discrimination by state actors. First, the lesson of *Korematsu* is that national security constitutes a "pressing public necessity," though the government's use of race to advance that objective must be narrowly tailored. Second, the Court has recognized as a compelling state interest a government's effort to remedy past discrimination for which it is responsible. *Richmond v. J. A. Croson Co....*

The Law School maintains that it wishes to obtain "educational benefits that flow from student body diversity." ... Attaining "diversity," whatever it means, is the mechanism by which the Law School obtains educational benefits, not an end of itself. The Law School, however, apparently believes that only a racially mixed student body can lead to the educational benefits it seeks. How, then, is the Law School's interest in these allegedly unique educational "benefits" not simply the forbidden interest in "racial balancing" ... that the majority expressly rejects?

The proffered interest that the majority vindicates today, then, is not simply "diversity." Instead the Court upholds the use of racial discrimination as a tool to advance the Law School's interest in offering a marginally superior education while maintaining an elite institution. Unless each constituent part of this state interest is of pressing public necessity, the Law School's use of race is unconstitutional. I find each of them to fall far short of this standard.

I believe what lies beneath the Court's decision today are the benighted notions that one can tell when racial discrimination benefits (rather than hurts) minority groups ... and that racial discrimination is necessary to remedy general societal ills. This Court's precedents supposedly settled both issues, but clearly the majority still cannot commit to the principle that racial classifications are per se harmful and that almost no amount of benefit in the eye of the beholder can justify such classifications.

The Grutter case was argued on the same day as another case from the University of Michigan, *Gratz v. Bollinger*.[68] This case challenged the school's undergraduate diversity admissions program. The advocates for that program had a difficult time in the oral argument, unable to respond to questions from the justices about whether any minority applicant who was even minimally qualified had ever been rejected. That led to the conclusion that the only factor that really mattered in that program was race and ultimately led to a ruling against the undergraduate admissions process written by Chief Justice Rehnquist.

After Justice O'Connor retired and with the addition to the Court of Chief Justice Roberts and Justice Alito, opponents of affirmative action programs saw the possibility that the Court might change direction, overturn the *Grutter* ruling, and reject affirmative action outright. With that, anti-affirmative action advocates found a case they hoped would force the Court to reject such programs once and for all in a challenge to the University of Texas admissions program.

The facts of the *Fisher v. University of Texas at Austin* case are lengthy and complex.[69] After the *Grutter* case, the U.S. Department of Justice worked with colleges and universities to ensure that their admissions programs complied with the Court's requirements. The University of Texas at Austin was one of these. Its process was constructed so that, although race could be one factor, there were many others, consistent with the *Grutter* ruling.

Ms. Fisher was denied admission to the University and went on to complete her undergraduate education elsewhere. She sued, claiming that the UT admissions program discriminated against her in violation of the Fourteenth Amendment. The university claimed that her record was such that she would not have been admitted in any case and, additionally, that the evidence that the reason was not race was that although 1 Latino and 4 African Americans were admitted whose scores were not as high as hers, 168 African Americans and Latinos whose Academic Index (AI) and Personal Achievement Index (PAI) were higher than hers were also not admitted.

Justice Kennedy had become the critical vote in the years after O'Connor's departure and he wrote the opinion. He would not flatly rule against affirmative action programs, nor would he overturn the *Grutter* decisions, the two primary goals of the challengers (even though they did not formally ask the Court to overrule *Grutter*). He applied strict judicial scrutiny and even tightened that approach. Assuming that the state's effort to have a diverse student body was a compelling state interest, it was still necessary for the university to show that the means chosen were narrowly tailored to achieve that end. In order to meet that requirement, Kennedy said: "The reviewing court must ultimately be satisfied that no workable race-neutral alternatives would produce the educational benefits of diversity."[70] The case was remanded for the lower courts to determine whether these requirements had been met.

After these decisions, it appeared that race-conscious affirmative action programs were all but dead. However, the Fifth Circuit ruled in the University of Texas case on remand that the program satisfied even the tighter requirements mandated by the Supreme Court in the *Fisher* case. That court found:

> We have hewed this line here, persuaded by UT Austin from this record of its necessary use of race in a holistic process and the want of workable alternatives that would not require even greater use of race, faithful to the content given to it by the Supreme Court. To reject the UT Austin plan is to confound developing principles of neutral affirmative action, looking away from *Bakke* and *Grutter*, leaving them in uniform but without command—due only a courtesy salute in passing.[71]

The Supreme Court affirmed that decision.

Conclusion

The civil rights law of race discrimination was far from resolved when the Court decided the *Brown v. Board of Education* rulings. First, there were the important rulings that followed in an effort to ensure that the command of *Brown* was implemented. There were also related problems and cases along the way that were very different from the school segregation rulings, like the effort to strike down laws against interracial marriage.

With all that was taking place in the courts, it became increasingly clear that a new body of civil rights statutes was required to address problems ranging from access to public accommodations to employment discrimination and discrimination by organizations that were receiving federal funds. There was also a need for a Voting Rights Act and a Fair Housing Act. Over time, there would be efforts to strengthen these statutes and the agencies that were expected to enforce them.

The civil rights statutes became all the more important as the Supreme Court issued a series of rulings that made it more and more difficult to bring cases alleging discrimination in violation of the equal protection clause of the Fourteenth Amendment or the due process clause of the Fifth Amendment where federal government actions were involved. The requirements for proof of intent in an era when the kind of direct and overt statements of intent to discriminate had largely vanished meant that the use of civil rights statutes that did not require such extensive requirements would be the focus of most civil rights cases.

While there has certainly been progress in civil rights law and practice since the Constitution was drafted, after the Civil War, and beyond *Brown*, much remains to be done. And even apart from the rulings themselves and the status of the law, it should be clear why African Americans, as exemplified in this chapter by the continuing battle waged by Justice Thurgood Marshall, may carry great frustration and anger at the history their forebears and they have endured, and in some respects continue to face today.

I. Issues for Policy and Practice

A. The evidence of racial discrimination in the criminal justice system is overwhelmingly clear. In this chapter the discussion of jury selection and of the death penalty shows that. Certainly the discussion in Chapters 8 and 9 shows that it is also true for Latinos. The tragedies in Ferguson, Missouri, New York City, Baltimore, Pasco Washington, and numerous other cities attest to the fact that it continues in the twenty-first century, notwithstanding efforts over time to address it. To what degree are the problems policy-related and to what extent are they matters of administration and management? What are the policy issues relevant to the different levels of government?

B. Are policies needed to assess on an ongoing basis discriminatory surveillance, stops, detentions, arrests, charges, jury selection, and sentencing? If so, what are the critical elements
of such a policy design?
C. To the extent that the problems are management issues, what are the options for taking a
serious step beyond the standard mechanisms that have been used to date that are needed
to move from rhetoric to serious change?
D. How can managers engage these issues in a manner that is constructive and non-threatening
while simultaneously ensuring that policies against discriminatory practices are taken
seriously?

II. Discussion Questions

A. It is now more than half a century since the Court decided *Brown v. Board of Education*.
At that time there was great hope that the ruling would not just result in changes in education, but that it would fundamentally change the approach to racial equality in the United
States. Has it? Is so, how? If not, why not?
B. The discussion of President Eisenhower's and later President Kennedy's approach to civil
rights indicates that top-level leadership matters, not only in policymaking but in implementation as well. What are the critical cues needed from leadership, whether at the top
of federal or state government or in an individual organization, needed to ensure that
everyone understands the commitment to ensuring civil rights? What cues suggest a lack of
commitment?
C. Many students are surprised that it was only in 1967 that the Supreme Court struck
down bans on interracial marriage. Although the laws are no longer in place, is there
really full acceptance of couples who appear to be of different racial backgrounds? The
appear-to-be language here, of course, is because the fact is that we are all so mixed, that
people often respond to appearance rather than fact when it comes to their attitudes and
actions toward others. Have you asked anyone in such a relationship about what they
have experienced? If not, you might be very surprised about what happens, not only in
the grocery store, but also if and when they enter a county or state office for business
purposes.
D. The evidence of discrimination in enforcement and criminal justice is overwhelming, from
basic traffic stops to the most serious criminal allegations and punishments. Since even
President Obama has had to acknowledge the need felt by African American families to
have what they refer to as "the talk" or "the conversation" with their children, and particularly their sons, about what they are likely to experience from law enforcement or the
courts, how can we ensure real change?
E. To what extent are these systemic or organizational problems and to what degree are they
reflections of fears and stereotypes prevalent in the society?
F. Notice in the *McCleskey* case that Justice Powell (citing the *Feeney* case discussed in
Chapter 10) would require that someone prove that the legislature acted not merely in spite
of but because of race. Is he confusing what is needed to prove discrimination in violation
with the equal protection clause of the Fourteenth Amendment with what is required to
show that a particular criminal penalty is administered in a manner that is cruel and unusual in violation of the Eighth Amendment?

Notes

1 *Browder v. Gayle*, 142 F. Supp. 707 (MDAL 1956).
2 *Gayle v. Browder*, 352 U.S. 903 (1956).
3 *Cooper v. Aaron*, 358 U.S. 1 (1958).
4 Quoted in Bernard Schwartz, *Super Chief* (New York: New York University Press, 1983), p. 114.

5 Dwight David Eisenhower to "Swede" Hazlett, July 22, 1957, Dwight D. Eisenhower Library, www.eisenhower.archives.gov/research/online_documents/civil_rights_brown_v_boe/1954_10_23_DDE_to_Hazlett.pdf, December 27, 2015, p. 4.

6 Id., at p. 7.

7 Id.

8 102 Congressional Record, 4459–4460 (March 12, 1956), 84th Congress 2nd Sess. Senator Strom Thurmond (R, SC) is credited with the leadership in the development of this document. See "Strom Thurmond Biography," Strom Thurmond Institute, Clemson University, http://sti.clemson.edu/about-us-mainmenu-27/biography-mainmenu-126, January 15, 2016.

9 Id., at 125, 175.

10 William O. Douglas, *The Court Years 1939–1975: The Autobiography of William O. Douglas* (New York: Random House, 1980), p. 120.

11 NOTE: This term literally means "for the court" and is used to indicate an opinion issued in the name of the court, as opposed to one that is signed by a specific justice as author. These are open brief opinions.

12 NOTE: Justice Stewart's brief concurring opinion is omitted here.

13 42 U.S.C. §1982.

14 Proclamation of September 30, 1962, 76 Stat. 1506.

15 See *United States v. Barnett*, 376 U.S. 681 (1964).

16 John F. Kennedy, Civil Rights Address, June 11, 1963, Miller Center, University of Virginia, http://millercenter.org/president/speeches/speech-3375, January 15, 2016.

17 President Lyndon B. Johnson, "Address Before a Joint Session of the Congress November 27, 1963," in *Public Papers of the Presidents of the United States: Lyndon B. Johnson, 1963–64.* Vol. I, pp. 8–10 (Washington, D.C.: Government Printing Office, 1965). Online at Miller Center, University of Virginia, http://millercenter.org/president/lbjohnson/speeches/speech-3381, January 15, 2016.

18 President Lyndon B. Johnson, "Annual Message to the Congress on the State of the Union, January 8, 1964," in *Public Papers of the Presidents of the United States: Lyndon B. Johnson, 1963–64.* Vol. I, pp. 112–118 (Washington, D.C.: Government Printing Office, 1965). Online at Miller Center, University of Virginia, http://millercenter.org/president/lbjohnson/speeches/speech-3382, January 15, 2016.

19 P.L. 88–352, 78 Stat. 241 (1964).

20 P.L. 89–110, 79 Stat. 437 (1965).

21 President Lyndon B. Johnson, "Special Message Before Congress: The American Promise," in *Public Papers of the Presidents of the United States: Lyndon B. Johnson, 1965.* Vol. I, pp. 281–287 (Washington, D. C.: Government Printing Office, 1966), www.lbjlibrary.org/lyndon-baines-johnson/speeches-films/president-johnsons-special-message-to-the-congress-the-american-promise, January 15, 2016.

22 P.L. 90–284, 82 Stat. 73 (1968).

23 NOTE: Black, Douglas, and Goldberg filed concurrences with the *Heart of Atlanta* case that apply to this case as well.

24 529 U.S. 598 (2000).

25 *Griffin v. County School Bd. of Prince Edward County*, 377 U.S. 218, 234 (1964).

26 396 U.S. 19 (1969).

27 304 U.S. 144, 152, n. 4 (1938).

28 *Brown v. Board of Education of Topeka (Brown I)*, 347 U.S. 483, 493 (1954).

29 NOTE: When this case was brought, many challenges to the constitutional validity of state laws were brought before three-judge federal district courts. This process permitted a direct appeal from that court (avoiding a separate trip through the U.S. Circuit Court of Appeals) to the U.S. Supreme Court in order to provide a full and rapid opportunity for states to have their case heard and resolved. Since then, the rules have been amended to limit the use of three-judge courts. Even so, one still encounters opinions by three-judge district panels.

30 NOTE: The concurring opinion of Justice Stewart and the dissenting opinions of Justices Brennan and Douglas are omitted.

31 NOTE: Justice Brennan wrote a dissenting opinion, omitted here, joined by Justice Marshall focusing on the statutory aspects of the case.

32 *Memphis v. Greene*, 451 U.S. 100 (1981).

33 Id., at p. 136, Marshall, J., dissenting.

34 Id., at p. 142, n. 7.

35 Id., at pp. 139–140.

36 *Personnel Administrator of Massachusetts v. Feeney*, 442 U.S. 256, 279 (1979).

37 See e.g., U.S. Civil Rights Commission, *Who Is Guarding the Guardians? A Report on Police Practices* (Washington, D.C.: U.S. Commission on Civil Rights, 1981).

38 Preemptory challenges permit the attorneys for each side to reject potential jurors without providing specific reasons.

39 The panel from which the jury is drawn.

40 NOTE: A petit jury is a trial court jury, as compared to a grand jury that hands down indictments.

41 NOTE: Voir dire is the questioning of potential jurors by attorneys to decide whether to include them on the jury or to remove them from the panel.

42 NOTE: The concurring opinions by Justices Stevens and O'Connor are omitted.

43 NOTE: This is a proceeding challenging the basis for custody of a person by the state.

44 NOTE: The dissenting opinions of Justice Blackmun and Stevens are omitted.

45 John C. Jeffries Jr., *Justice Lewis F. Powell, Jr.* (New York: Charles Scribner's Sons, 1994), p. 451. See also David Von Drehle, "Retired Justice Changes Stand on Death Penalty: Powell Is Said to Favor Ending Executions," *The Washington Post*, June 10, 1994, p. A-1.

46 *Swann v. Charlotte-Mecklenberg Bd. of Ed.*, 402 U.S. 1 (1971).

47 These remedial decrees are discussed in greater detail in Phillip J. Cooper, *Hard Judicial Choices: Federal District Judges and State and Local Officials* (New York: Oxford University Press, 1988).

48 *Public Papers of the Presidents of the United States: Lyndon B. Johnson, 1965.* Vol. II, pp. 635–640 (Washington, D.C.: Government Printing Office, 1966). See also Vaughn Davis Bornet, *The Presidency of Lyndon B. Johnson* (Lawrence, KS: Kansas University Press, 1983), pp. 53–54. See also Bruce J. Schulman, *Lyndon B. Johnson and American Liberalism* (Boston, MA: Bedford Books, 1995), pp. 106–117.

49 Lyndon B. Johnson, "To Fulfill These Rights," Commencement Address at Howard University, June 4, 1965, in *Public Papers of the Presidents of the United States, Lyndon B. Johnson, 1965*. Vol. II (Washington, D.C.: Government Printing Office, 1966), p. 636.

50 30 Fed. Reg. 12327 (1965). Along with that order, he also issued E.O. 11247, which charged the Attorney General with responsibility for enforcement of Title VI of the 1964 Act that prohibited discrimination in programs or agencies that received federal funds.

51 Legality of Revised Philadelphia Plan, 42 Op. Atty Gen. 405 (1969).

52 *Contractors Association of Eastern Pennsylvania v. Secretary of Labor*, 442 F.2d 159 (3rd Cir. 1971).

53 *Fullilove v. Klutznick*, 448 U.S. 448 (1980).

54 Id., at 490.

55 438 U.S. 265 (1978).

56 Id., at 314.

57 488 U.S., at 490.

58 Id., at 551–552.

59 Id., at 561, Blackmun, J., dissenting.

60 497 U.S. 547 (1990).

61 *Adarand Constructors v. Peña*, 515 U.S. 200 (1995).

62 Id., at 228.

63 Id., at 242, Stevens, J., dissenting.

64 Id., at 266–267.

65 Id., at 274, Ginsburg, J., dissenting.

66 NOTE: Justice Ginsburg's concurring opinion is omitted.

67 NOTE: Justice Scalia's opinion dissenting in part and concurring in part is omitted.

68 539 U.S. 244 (2003).

69 133 S. Ct. 2411 (2013).

70 Id., at 2420.

71 *Fisher v. University of Texas at Austin*, 758 F.3d 633, 660 (5th Cir. 2014).

References

Bornet, Vaughn Davis. *The Presidency of Lyndon B. Johnson*. Lawrence, KS: Kansas University Press, 1983.

Cooper, Phillip J. *Hard Judicial Choices: Federal District Court Judges and State and Local Officials*. New York: Oxford University Press, 1988.

Douglas, William O. *The Court Years 1939–1975: The Autobiography of William O. Douglas*. New York: Random House, 1980.

Jeffries, John C., Jr. *Justice Lewis F. Powell, Jr*. New York: Charles Scribner's Sons, 1994.

Johnson, President Lyndon B. "Address Before a Joint Session of the Congress November 27, 1963," in *Public Papers of the Presidents of the United States: Lyndon B. Johnson, 1963–64*. Vol. I, pp. 8–10. Washington, D.C.: Government Printing Office, 1965, http://millercenter.org/president/lbjohnson/speeches/speech-3381, January 15, 2016.

———. "Annual Message to the Congress on the State of the Union, January 8, 1964," in *Public Papers of the Presidents of the United States: Lyndon B. Johnson, 1963–64*. Vol. I, pp. 112–118. Washington, D.C.: Government Printing Office, 1965, http://millercenter.org/president/lbjohnson/speeches/speech-3382, January 15, 2016.

———. "To Fulfill These Rights," Commencement Address, Howard University, June 4, 1965, in *Public Papers of the Presidents of the United States: Lyndon B. Johnson, 1965*. Vol. II, pp. 635–640. Washington, D.C.: Government Printing Office, 1966.

———. "Special Message Before Congress: The American Promise," March 15, 1965, in *Public Papers of the Presidents of the United States: Lyndon B. Johnson, 1965*. Vol. I, pp. 281–287. Washington, D.C.: Government Printing Office, 1966, www.lbjlibrary.org/lyndon-baines-johnson/speeches-films/president-johnsons-special-message-to-the-congress-the-american-promise, January 15, 2016.

Kennedy, John F. Civil Rights Address, June 11, 1963, Miller Center, University of Virginia, http://millercenter.org/president/speeches/speech-3375, January 15, 2016.

Schulman, Bruce J. *Lyndon B. Johnson and American Liberalism*. Boston, MA: Bedford Books, 1995.

Schwartz, Bernard. *Super Chief*. New York: New York University Press, 1983.

U.S. Civil Rights Commission, *Who Is Guarding the Guardians? A Report on Police Practices* (Washington, D.C.: U.S. Commission on Civil Rights, 1981).

5   The Native American Perspective

Toward Civil Rights from Conquest, but a Long Way from that Goal

Although the long history of the movement for civil rights for African Americans harkens back to the era when slaves were brought to what became the United States, the story for Native Americans is very different. The Native American nations, of course, were free and living in sophisticated communities in the Americas long before the arrival of the colonists. Indeed, the emerging United States, both before and after the Constitution was adopted, entered into treaties with a number of those native governments as it would with any other sovereign nation. But the situation for Native Americans was about to change dramatically for the worse, including their stature as free and sovereign nations (at least as they had known that status before), their control over the lands wherein they resided, and even their freedom itself. Even now, centuries later, Native Americans are still waging an ongoing battle for civil rights.

Nearly a year after the Supreme Court delivered its first opinion in *Brown v. Board of Education*, it announced a ruling far less noticed—less noticed that is by most people other than Native Americans—in a case involving Tee-Hit-Ton Indians, part of the Tlingit Tribe living in Alaska.[1] The Tlingit had lived in the area that became Alaska long before the Russians took control of the area and later sold it to the United States.

The case arose when the U.S. Department of Agriculture sold timber on Tlingit land. The Tlingit brought a claim against the U.S. government on grounds that the sale was a taking of their property without just compensation in violation of the Fifth Amendment to the U.S. Constitution. A Tee-Hit-Ton chief explained at trial that the land in question was part of a large tract throughout which the Tee-Hit-Ton moved during the year as the seasons and related hunting, fishing, and plant harvesting dictated. More specifically, the land on which the timber was harvested was an area of their tribal land in which they lived during the winter because of its sheltered character, and the other areas were used for summer residence, which provided access to fishing in rivers and bays. After he had returned from a time at the Carlisle Indian School, in 1904, the Chief had used his knowledge of English to work with his relatives so that they could indicate on maps just what the boundaries of that territory were.

Justice Stanley Reed wrote for the Supreme Court majority, rejecting the Tee-Hit-Ton claim on grounds that the area in which the timber was harvested was not tribal land and the Tlingit therefore had no right to compensation. But perhaps as important from a Native American perspective was the way in which the Court explained that ruling. Reed insisted that whatever historical claims they thought they had, the U.S. government held complete title to Native American lands by "right of discovery and conquest" and that, unless the Congress had specifically recognized a native claim, the only thing the tribe had was what was termed "Indian title," which carried no ownership but merely the ability to live on the land that was granted by the government not as a matter of right, but as a mater of "grace." He wrote: "Every American schoolboy knows that the savage tribes of this continent were deprived of their ancestral ranges by force and that, even when the Indians ceded millions of acres by treaty in return for blankets, food and trinkets, it was not a sale but the conquerors' will that deprived them of their land."[2] Besides, said Reed, "No case in this Court has ever held that taking of Indian title or use by Congress required compensation."[3]

In other cases, the Court referred to Native American communities not as full sovereign governments to be accorded the respect of other sovereign governments but as "domestic dependent nations" that stand in relation to the United States government as wards to their guardians.[4]

Students of traditional approaches to civil rights find these assertions deplorable, but ask just why they are issues of civil rights. After all, none of the matters noted above present an equal protection claim under the Fourteenth or the Fifth Amendment. Neither specifically addresses questions of discrimination. From their perspective, however, Native Americans contend that there are several different types of civil rights violations involved in these examples and, in so doing, underscore the fact that civil rights look different to different groups who are affected by governmental actions.

They point out, for example, that many native peoples cannot separate their culture and civilization from the place in which it is located, not because of ownership in a contemporary sense, but because of critical ties to the land, the larger environment in which it is located, and its relationship to the Creator. They point out that even where title had been recognized, it was not historically treated with the kind of respect accorded by government to titles held by Western property owners, as the assertion by Justice Reed about a right to Fifth Amendment compensation for taking of that property would indicate. Beyond that, they point to a history of broken treaty obligations by the United States government. They also underscore the fact that Native Americans were the only group here to be subjected to a deliberate attempt at genocide, both by actual attack, but also by deliberate relocation to hostile environments with the expectation that the tribes and nations would not survive. They point to cultural genocide in the form of the use of Indian schools, like the Carlisle school mentioned in the *Tee-Hit-Ton* case, where native children were made to look, talk, and behave like white men in an effort, as it was said at the time, to kill the Indian within them and leave behind a white man.[5] They note other actions, like the General Allotment Act of 1887, that were not so obvious and direct, but that were, nevertheless, designed to break the tie of Native Americans to their land and to their tribal governments, effectively destroying them as a people.[6] Thus, for Native Americans, the battle for civil rights may look somewhat different, as it has traditionally focused on African Americans, but it has been a long struggle, and one that continues to this day, with many tragic setbacks along the way and far less progress than most Americans would imagine.

This chapter addresses that civil rights struggle with an effort to perceive it as much as possible from the perspective of native peoples and through the presentation of judicial rulings that address the issues that are important to civil rights for Native Americans and with other key policy documents. The picture that emerges is of a civil rights movement that is still very much a work in progress with a sad and frustrating history of barriers along the path.

Native American Foundation Understandings

It seems surprising that, although Native Americans have been so important throughout American history and were here long before most contemporary U.S. citizens think that history began, Americans know little about Native Americans. Most know even less about the range of challenges Native Americans have faced in the past and, in too many cases, still encounter today. It is therefore important to consider a few basic facts and concepts before engaging Native American civil rights issues. Each of the elements of this discussion carries within it the seeds of critical civil rights issues for Native Americans. At the outset, please note that this chapter will use the terms "Native Americans," "Indians," "native peoples," and "indigenous people," all of which are employed in the law, in various Native American documents, and in the literature. Different native people prefer the use of different terms, and all are used here with respect for the dignity of native peoples and with a recognition that there are different members of the Native American community who have strong views about one term of reference or another.

Native American Tribes and Nations: Political Definitions and Historic Realities

First, Native Americans reject the idea that they are members of a minority group.[7] They point out that they are members of sovereign nations whose right to self-governance is recognized in law. Native American nations or tribes existed long before Europeans arrived on the shores of what would become the United States.

The question arises as to who defines what tribes or nations are and how that is done. Like members of any community, the first answer is that one understands his or her identity from within the family and the community. Native Americans define what the tribe is and who its members are. However, over the history of the United States there have come to be two other definitions that are determined by the United States government, in one instance, and by the state governments, in the second case. There are at the time of this writing 566 federally recognized tribes, bands, communities, and Alaska native villages.[8] There are also state-recognized tribes that are not recognized by the federal government and therefore do not have the kinds of protections or access to services available to recognized tribes.

Then there are many tribes which have tried, and are still trying, to obtain federal recognition, ranging from the Abenaki of New England to the Chinook, whose home is where the Columbia River meets the Pacific Ocean.[9] Many tribes that have struggled without success for political and therefore legal recognition by the U.S. government have long histories and unique cultures. Many have played important roles in regional trade among native peoples and with the Europeans who called themselves settlers. The fact that these proud tribes and nations have had to struggle to have their existence recognized by the U.S. government is at the heart of a number of important civil rights issues. This chapter will return later to the discussion of recognition and the lack of it in Native American civil rights.

Who Is a Native American? A Question More Complex than it May Appear to Be

It may seem strange to many Americans, but, like the question of just what is a tribe, the issue of how one can demonstrate his or her *bona fides* as a Native American, or as the term is used in law and by many indigenous people in the U.S. an "Indian," turns out, because of historic, political, and legal factors, to be more complex than one might think. The most obvious definition—and one that is important for the purposes of federal government programs and law—is that an Indian is a person who is an enrolled member of a Native American tribe. The tribe or nation determines who will be enrolled. That definition is relatively clear for those who reside on Native American lands under a tribal government.

However, many Native Americans live throughout the nation, in part because they choose to do so and in part because over the history of the nation efforts were made to push Native Americans out of ancestral lands and communities. For these people, the typical manner of determining their identity as Native Americans has been the method for demonstrating that one is a descendent of a tribe or nation, the so-called "blood quantum" test, in which an Indian is defined as one who has at least 25 percent Native American ancestry. This test in law reaches back to the Indian Reorganization Act of 1934.[10] However, that is a complex matter because there has been so much intermarriage over time, that it can be challenging to prove one's *bona fides* by blood quantum. Indeed, a leading scholar of Native American politics has explained that, for a variety of reasons, there has historically been a far higher percentage of intermarriage for Native Americans than for the general population, leading to an inevitable loss of identity—if that identity is to be determined simply by blood quantum.[11]

Some of those who live away from reservation and trust lands, like many other Americans, do not have close ties to their cultural heritage, but others just as clearly do. They understand themselves as Native Americans and may maintain close connections not only to their own tribes, but also to other tribal peoples. Some of these people are enrolled tribal members, but others may not have that kind of connection, although they view themselves as Native Americans. On the other hand tribal people have in some very controversial cases rejected claims by some people to be Native Americans who are not enrolled members of tribes and whose *bona fides* have not been established by sovereign Indian tribes, or in some cases the people involved have been disenrolled from the tribe.[12]

The debate about just who really is Native American is not only complex, but also raises serious issues for Native Americans, who ask what most Americans would say if suddenly Canada or Mexico could make definitive determinations as to who was or was not a U.S. citizen. As one woman put it, "I feel as if I'm not a real Indian until I've got that BIA stamp of approval.... You're told all your life that you're Indian, but sometimes you want to be that kind of Indian that everybody else accepts as Indian."[13]

With that set of issues in mind, population figures have been difficult to determine. David E. Wilkins has written that the Native American population was estimated at some 7 million before the arrival of the Europeans, but had declined to only 250,000 by 1900.[14] The most current census figures at the time of this writing indicate that the population has risen to 2,870,645 with another 2,205,535 identifying themselves as a combination of Indian and one or more additional ethnocultural groups.[15] Of course, census figures are based upon self-identification rather than any independent criteria and are not determined by enrolled tribal membership.

The data indicate that, for many Native Americans, there have been serious challenges, and particularly so in reservation communities. The State of the Indian Nations[16] Report is issued annually by the National Congress of American Indians. The following excerpt from the 2003 report explained some of the challenges as the nation entered the twenty-first century, and did so in a manner designed to help non-native people understand the situation in realistic terms.

The State of Indian Nations Today: Mapping a Course for the Next Seven Generations

Tex Hall, President, National Congress of American Indians January 31, 2003.

[W]e have come to realize that many of our fellow citizens do not know enough about Native America today to separate fact from fiction, past from present, or reality from stereotype. Somewhere between the romanticized images of our history and these sensationalized images of our contemporary existence, the truth is waiting to be told, and only we as Indian Nations are able to clearly offer forth that truth. It is for this reason that we come before you today.

I want to raise three of the major issues that occupy our hearts and thoughts as tribal leaders today.... These three concerns are before us: our future survival as independent, self-governing peoples; our ability to move out of poverty and unemployment to meaningful development in our economies; and the well being and quality of life of American Indian and Alaska Native people in this nation for the next seven generations to come.

• **Tribes' survival depends on maintaining our unique relationship to this nation as independent, self governing peoples, and it is of utmost importance to tribes to secure fairness in these relationships.**

Sovereignty—One of the most important things to understand about American Indian tribes is the simple fact that tribes are governments—not non-profit organizations, not interest groups, not an ethnic minority. We are one of only three sovereigns listed in the U.S. Constitution, alongside the federal and state governments. We provide many of the same services to our people that state governments do: tribal fire departments, tribal police, tribal schools. We make governmental decisions to protect public safety, stimulate our economies, and ensure a bright future for our young people. Our tribal courts work to ensure that the rights of all are protected in our communities....

Trust Responsibility—When you consider that every acre of this country once was under care of the tribes and provided for our people, it is easy to understand what is called the "trust responsibility." When these lands were taken from tribes, the U.S. gave its solemn promise to protect the rights of tribes to govern themselves, and to provide for the health, education, and well being of tribes. That commitment, the "trust responsibility"—is *not* a hand-out, but a *contract*—and that contract has been broken time and again by the federal government. It is time for the U.S. to honor those promises.

In his time with us in this world, Martin Luther King Jr. wisely said, "In the End, we will remember not the words of our enemies, but the silence of our friends." The Indian wars are long over. We have many friends throughout this nation. We pray that our friends will not be silent as year after year this trust continues to be ignored and eroded. Mr. President, we know that your burdens are many, but we ask that among them, you defend the integrity and honor of this Nation, make good its word—affirm the U.S. treaty promises to tribes. Restore that trust for the sake of the future of Indian people—and for the sake of our nation's soul.

Trust Reform—Over the past year, one of the issues that has consumed us in Indian Country has been the ongoing effort to secure meaningful reform of the badly mismanaged trust accounts held by the federal government for individual Indian accountholders and tribes. The ... U.S. government appointed itself as our banker and resource manager many generations ago—and ever since, they've been losing track of our money. Today, the system is such a mess that independent estimates suggest that billions of dollars that belong to Individual Indian people and Indian tribes have been lost by the federal government....

Somehow, the federal government manages to get Social Security checks out monthly to millions of Americans, effectively calculating complex formulas based on age, days a recipient worked, disabilities, marital status, and any number of additional factors. It has managed this information for decades without fail. Mr. President, what failure of will has caused the system managing monies that belong to American Indians to be so much less efficient? ...

• **The second overarching concern we face in Indian Country today is the need to move out of a century of poverty and unemployment toward meaningful development in our economies.**

Economic Development—We have heard a great deal in recent months about the need for "economic stimulus." ... But we have been troubled to see that neither the Administration's plan nor congressional democrats' counter-proposal addresses the need that exists in Indian Country for sustainable, *comprehensive* economic development.

With more than a quarter of Indian people living in poverty, and unemployment rates on reservations more than double the population at large—13.6% on average, and over 80% in some communities—there is no group of people with a more urgent economic crisis than American Indians. Our infrastructure, roads and bridges, tele-communications connections, and access to training often cannot support our best economic plans. Traditional sources of capital such as lending, banking, and bonding are all but non-existent on reservations....

Infrastructure—While states spend an average of $4,000 to $5,000 per mile for road maintenance annually, the federal government spends only $500 per mile for roads in Indian Country. The disparity adds up to a massive barrier to economic development, with many tribes lacking any way to transport the employees, customers, and goods that fuel healthy economies.

Many Americans will find this hard to believe, but while the rest of the country is seeing the arrival of DSL and wireless communications systems, many tribal communities still wait for the arrival of basic telephone service! Nearly a quarter of rural Native American households—23.4 percent have no telephone service....

Tribal lands are grossly underserved by electricity services—14.2 percent—nearly a sixth—of Indian households have no access to electricity. This shocking shortfall is ten times greater than the 1.4 percent of American households that lack access to electricity nationwide. Tribal community residents are generally at the lowest income levels in the nation, but pay a much greater portion of their income for electricity than the rest of the nation. Tribes have a wealth of energy resources—oil, gas, coal, and hydropower—but the non-tribal utilities that own both the power plants and power lines generally use them to export revenues *away* from tribal communities.

A majority of tribal communities are also experiencing public water supply problems.... Forty percent of households on the Navajo Indian reservation have no water except what they themselves haul in. This process greatly increases the risk of waterborne disease. Thirty-three percent of tribal homes, fully one-third, lack adequate solid waste management systems. These statistics are a point of shame to this nation....

Gaming—Perhaps one of the most misunderstood elements of tribal economic development has been the success of a small handful of tribes in developing tribally sponsored gaming enterprises. Just as many states have developed lotteries to fund a range of government functions, tribal government sponsored gaming enterprises are *required by law* to support critical governmental functions such as law enforcement, education, and health care. These revenues have enabled tribes to build new schools where children previously attended classes in substandard trailers, and have brought jobs and the revenues to diversify suffering reservation economies....

Despite what sensationalized media reports suggest, only a very small handful of tribes have had extraordinary success in this arena.... The majority of tribal casinos that do exist are like my tribe's small venture in North Dakota. It is no Caesar's Palace, but our small casino provides precious jobs to our people, extraordinarily important to the local economy for our entire area.... But gaming is certainly no panacea for the majority of tribes, and for many, not even a viable option. We need other options for comprehensive and sustainable economic development in Indian Country....

Housing—... Home ownership has reached all time highs for most segments of the population, with more African Americans and Latinos owning their own homes than ever before. Indian Country has felt the same economic losses the nation as a whole has felt in recent years—but families in Indian Country have been largely unable to benefit from homeownership, that one bright spot in our economy. Homeownership is virtually impossible where there is little access to mortgage lending, and the complications of trust land transactions have hurt home buying in reservation communities.... Mr. President, 40 percent of the homes in our tribal communities are overcrowded and have serious physical deficiencies. The comparable national average for such unacceptable living conditions is 5.9 percent, almost seven times lower....

• **The third overarching concern for tribes today is ensuring the well being and quality of life of our people today and for the next seven generations.**

Health—American Indians and Alaska Natives have a life expectancy 5 years less than all other races in this country. Our mortality rates from diabetes are more than three times the national average.... In spite of this disproportionate health care need, today the per capita expenditure for American Indian and Alaska Native medical services is less than one-third of the average annual expenditure for individual Medicaid assistance, and is even less than our per capita health expenditure for federal prisoners.... A strong federal commitment to make good on old promises to provide resources for services, prevention programs, and health care facilities is badly needed to turn around the troubling health statistics in Indian Country. To this end, I call on Congress to pass the Indian Health Care Improvement Act reauthorization and fully fund its programs, actions that will significantly improve Indian health care delivery and increase tribal self-determination.

Education—As a former school superintendent, I recognize that economic stability in Indian Country depends on how well we prepare our young people for the future.... The Bureau of Indian Affairs schools, once a shameful tool of assimilationist federal policies, are now tribally operated in many cases, offering an important tool for tribes to revive and pass on the traditions, cultural values, and native languages those institutions once sought to destroy.

But many of these schools are in terrible disrepair. In my travels throughout Indian Country, I have seen schools with exposed asbestos, leaking roofs, lack of electricity or even telephone lines. I have spoken with school administrators near tears because their transportation budgets cannot begin to address the actual cost of keeping their buses running on the mud-rutted, under-maintained roads that are the norm in reservation communities, and they face no choice but to dig into their scant classroom dollars. These dollars are precious few—Bureau of Indian Affairs schools are allotted just over $3,000 for each student annually. That is less than half of what other public schools spend on average per student....

Tribes have prioritized education in their communities, and there are signs of improvement.... Still, About 50 percent of American Indian students never finish high school. 50 percent! In some parts of the country the dropout rate is 90 percent or more. This is by far the highest dropout rate of any population in the United States and it has absolutely got to stop. The percentage of American Indian high school graduates who do go on to college is 17%, compared to the national average of 62%.

We have to turn these statistics around—and fast. We have to create productive learning environments for our students, and draw upon culturally relevant curricula that can re-engage the minds of our youth....

Environmental Protection—Tribes are deeply concerned about the environmental health of this country, and of tribal lands in particular. At least 170 tribes are located within a 50-mile radius of 432 EPA highly toxic "Superfund" sites. Other tribes struggle with efforts to secure return and clean up of federal sites such as the Hanford Military Reservation, tribal lands taken and utilized for nuclear weapons research and development. The toxic substances at these sites detrimentally impact human health as well as cultural and ecological resources....

Conclusion—... 120 years ago, Chief Joseph reminded us, "Treat all men alike. Give them the same law. Give them all an even chance to live and grow. All men were made by the same Great Spirit Chief. They are all brothers. The earth is the mother of all people, and all people should have equal rights upon it." ...

We look forward to a bright future for the seven generations to come and beyond, with roots in the past, flourishing in the future, if only we can work together today. Masehgedataz—I thank you.

While there has been some progress in the years since then in some areas, many challenges remain. In the 2008 State of the Indian Nations address, entitled "Through the Eyes of Our Children: Hope for a Restored Native America," National Congress of American Indians President Joe A. Garcia began by noting progress and important success stories. Even so, he said:

But there are also tragic endings, such as two homeless sixth-graders on the Flathead reservation in Montana who died recently to alcohol-related causes, and the fact that the nation-wide Native youth suicide rate is three times the national rate. Looking at life in Indian Country through the eyes of a child, there is often more risk than opportunity.

Poverty, lack of jobs and preventative health care, inadequate juvenile rehabilitation, shortfalls in education—all these problems push too many young people into failure, robbing them of full and worthwhile lives....

- Native children face devastating poverty. According to the most recent census data nearly a third of Native children live below the federal poverty level. On reservations, it's over 44 percent, with half of those living in what is defined as "deep poverty."
- With fewer than half of Native young people graduating from high school, and more than 8 in 10 eighth-graders reading below grade level, we need better education programs that work for our communities.
- We need intervention programs for at-risk Indian youth, and improved law enforcement overall.
- Finally, inadequate health care, and a lack of information about healthy lifestyles, are stealing years—sometimes decades—from Indian lives. Life expectancy for the average American is 76 years, 20 years longer than the life expectancy for males on the Pine Ridge Indian Reservation, who have the shortest lifespan of all Americans.

Additionally, the data are often too incomplete to allow a full picture of the severity of some of the challenges. Even so, for example, the 2007 National Healthcare Disparities Report showed that 50% of the measures used to assess access to care were not improving for American Indians and Alaskan Natives and 65% of the measures of quality of care were not improving for those populations.[17] The 2013 report showed that: "Previous NHDRs [National Healthcare Disparities Reports] showed that AI/

ANs [American Indians/Alaskan Natives] had poorer quality of care and worse access to care than Whites for many measures tracked in the reports. Among all measures of health care quality and access that are tracked in the reports and support trends over time, AI/ANs had worse care than Whites in the most recent year for 40 measures. Most of these measures showed no significant change in disparities over time."[18]

As President Hill's speech indicated, many of the issues relate to the status of Native American lands and the ability of the tribes to govern given complex relationships with the federal and state governments. Indeed, the place to begin consideration of Native American civil rights is, for many Indians, with the issue of the loss of the lands and the attack on their sovereignty.

The Early Years: Sovereignty and the Attack on Native American Lands and Rights

Soon after the United States launched its new life under the Constitution, tensions began for Native Americans as private individuals, states, and the federal government began to take their lands, by force, coerced sale, or various other means, and to challenge their sovereignty. This behavior became so outrageous that President George Washington issued a presidential proclamation in 1790, ordering Americans to respect the rights of Cherokee, Choctaw, and Chickasaw under existing treaties and statutes. Unfortunately, the problems continued and Washington issued another proclamation in 1791, and still another at the end of 1792. In his December 1792 proclamation, he said:

> Whereas I have received authentic information that certain lawless and wicked persons of the western frontier in the State of Georgia did lately invade, burn, and destroy a town belonging to the Cherokee Nation, although in amity with the United States, and put to death several Indians of that nation; and
>
> Whereas such outrageous conduct not only violates the rights of humanity, but also endangers the public peace, and it highly becomes the honor and good faith of the United States to pursue all legal means for the punishment of those atrocious offenders:
>
> I have therefore thought fit to issue this my proclamation, hereby exhorting all the citizens of the United States and requiring all the officers thereof, according to their respective stations, to use their utmost endeavors to apprehend and bring those offenders to justice. And I do moreover offer a reward of $500 for each and every of the above-named persons who shall be so apprehended and brought to justice and shall be proved to have assumed or exercised any command or authority among the perpetrators of the crimes aforesaid at the time of committing the same.[19]

However, a series of Supreme Court opinions followed that were far different in tone. It is important to read and understand the language of early legal opinions; for just as African Americans can never forget the manner in which they were described and treated by the courts, so Native Americans endured characterizations and rulings that were not only adverse to their rights and interests, but also demeaning. Even where tribes prevailed, they found themselves treated as if they were little more than children whose interests were to be looked after by the federal government.

There were three extremely important rulings by the U.S. Supreme Court in the years before the Civil War that addressed the status of Native American tribes and the control of their lands. Two of these are known to some Americans, since they were followed by what came to be known as the "Trail of Tears," the tragic forced movement of the Cherokee and others from their tribal homelands to reservations in the southwestern United States. However, even before the challenges to the Cherokee in the American Southeast, the Court rendered a ruling on a case involving the Illinois and the Piankeshaw Indians in what later became the State of Illinois that made it clear that Native American lands would be at the mercy of the U.S. government. This opinion is not easy reading because of the complexity of the facts as well as the nature of the rhetoric, but it became a central feature in the development in the law.

Johnson v. McIntosh

21 U.S. 543 (1823)

INTRODUCTION: This case arose from decisions by tribes in what was then the Northwest Territory—later the State of Illinois—to sell some of their land. However, others had claimed the land based on decisions made by officials in Virginia and in the national government. The detailed facts of the case are presented in the opinion.

In the course of deciding who owned the land, the Supreme Court made clear its view of the authority of the U.S. government to control what Native Americans had every reason to believe was their land. In the process, the Court described Native Americans in terms difficult for the modern reader to take in and even more difficult for indigenous people to forget.

Chief Justice Marshall wrote the opinion for the Court.

> The plaintiffs in this cause claim the land ... under two grants, purporting to be made [in 1773 and 1775] by the chiefs of ... the Illinois and the Piankeshaw nations; and the question is, whether this title can be recognised in the Courts of the United States? ... The inquiry [centers on] the power of Indians to give ... title which can be sustained in the Courts....

> On the discovery of this immense continent, the great nations of Europe were eager to appropriate to themselves so much of it as they could respectively acquire.... The potentates of the old world found no difficulty in convincing themselves that they made ample compensation to the inhabitants of the new world, by bestowing on them civilization and Christianity, in exchange for unlimited independence. But ... it was necessary, in order to avoid conflicting settlements, and consequent war with each other, to establish a principle, which all should acknowledge as the law by which the right of acquisition ... should be regulated [among the colonizing powers]. This principle was, that discovery gave title to the government by whose subjects, or by whose authority it was made, against all other European governments.... The exclusion of all other Europeans, necessarily gave to the nation making the discovery the sole right of acquiring the soil from the natives, and establishing settlements upon it....

> The rights thus acquired being exclusive, no other power could interpose between them. In the establishment of these relations, the rights of the original inhabitants were, in no instance, entirely disregarded; but were necessarily, to a considerable extent, impaired. They were admitted to be the rightful occupants of the soil, with a legal as well as just claim to retain possession of it, and to use it according to their own discretion; but their rights to complete sovereignty ... were necessarily diminished, and their power to dispose of the soil at their own will ... was denied by the original fundamental principle, that discovery gave exclusive title to those who made it.

While the different nations of Europe respected the right of the natives, as occupants, they asserted the ultimate dominion to be in themselves; and claimed ... as a consequence of this ultimate dominion, a power to grant the soil, while yet in possession of the natives. These grants have been understood by all, to convey a title to the grantees, subject only to the Indian right of occupancy....

Spain did not rest her title solely on the grant of the Pope. Her discussions respecting boundary, with France, with Great Britain, and with the United States, all show that she placed it on the rights given by discovery. Portugal sustained her claim to the Brazils by the same title. France, also, founded her title to the vast territories she claimed in America on discovery.... Henry Hudson ... discovered the country from the Delaware to the Hudson ... and this country they claimed [for Holland]....

[In 1496 the British] monarch granted a commission to the Cabots, to discover countries then unknown to Christian people.... Cabot ... discovered the continent of North America.... To this discovery the English trace their title. [He] was empowered to take possession ... notwithstanding the occupancy of the natives, who were heathens....

By the charter of 1606, under which the first permanent English settlement on this continent was made, James I granted to Sir Thomas Gates and others, those territories in America lying on the seacoast, between the 34th and 45th degrees of north latitude.... In 1609, ... a new and more enlarged charter was given by the crown to the first colony "... in Virginia...." A new and more enlarged charter was granted to the Duke of Lenox and others, in 1620, who were denominated the Plymouth Company, conveying to them in absolute property.... Thus has our whole country been granted by the crown while in the occupation of the Indians. These grants purport to convey the soil as well as the right of dominion to the grantees.... The governments of New-England, New-York, New-Jersey, Pennsylvania, Maryland, and a part of Carolina, were thus created. In all of them, the soil, at the time the grants were made, was occupied by the Indians.... Thus, all the nations of Europe, who have acquired territory on this continent, have asserted in themselves, and have recognised in others, the exclusive right of the discoverer to appropriate the lands occupied by the Indians....

By the treaty which concluded the war of our revolution, ... the powers of government, and the right to soil, which had previously been in Great Britain, passed definitively to these States.... It has never been doubted, that either the United States, or the several States, had a clear title to all the lands within the boundary lines described in the treaty, subject only to the Indian right of occupancy, and that the exclusive power to extinguish that right, was vested in that government which might constitutionally exercise it.

Virginia, ... within whose chartered limits the land in controversy lay, passed an act, in the year 1779, declaring her "exclusive right of pre-emption from the Indians, of all the lands within the limits of her own chartered territory, and that no person or persons whatsoever, have, or ever had, a right to purchase any lands within the same, from any Indian nation, except only persons duly authorized to make such purchase; formerly for the use and benefit of the colony", and ... Virginia proceeded ... to open her land office, for the sale of [what is now] Kentucky, ... every acre of which was then claimed and possessed by Indians.

The States, having within their chartered limits different portions of territory covered by Indians, ceded that territory, generally, to the United States, on conditions.... The lands in controversy lay within the chartered limits of Virginia, and were ceded with the whole country northwest of the river Ohio[, territory] occupied by numerous and warlike tribes of Indians; but the exclusive right of the United States to extinguish their title, and to grant the soil, has never, we believe, been doubted....

Conquest gives a title which the Courts of the conqueror cannot deny, whatever the private and speculative opinions of individuals may be, respecting the original justice of the claim which has been successfully asserted. The British government, ... whose rights have passed to the United States, asserted a title to all the lands occupied by Indians, ... a limited sovereignty over them, and the exclusive right of extinguishing the title which occupancy gave to them.... It is not for the Courts of this country to question the validity of this title....

The title by conquest is acquired and maintained by force. The conqueror prescribes its limits. Humanity, however, acting on public opinion, has established, as a general rule, that the conquered shall not be wantonly oppressed.... Most usually, they are incorporated with the victorious nation, and become subjects or citizens of the government....[20] The new and old members of the society mingle with each other; the distinction between them is gradually lost, and they make one people. Where this incorporation is practicable, humanity demands, and a wise policy requires, that the rights of the conquered to property should remain unimpaired; that the new subjects should be governed as equitably as the old, and that confidence in their security should gradually banish the painful sense of being separated from their ancient connexions, and united by force to strangers....

But the tribes of Indians inhabiting this country were fierce savages, whose occupation was war, and whose subsistence was drawn chiefly from the forest. To leave them in possession of their country, was to leave the country a wilderness; to govern them as a distinct people was impossible, because they were as brave and as high spirited as they were fierce, and were ready to repel by arms every attempt on their independence.

What was the inevitable consequence of this state of things? The Europeans were under the necessity either of abandoning the country, and relinquishing their pompous claims to it, or of enforcing those claims by the sword, and by the adoption of principles adapted to the condition of a people with whom it was impossible to mix, and who could not be governed as a distinct society, or of remaining in their neighbourhood, and exposing themselves and their families to the perpetual hazard of being massacred.

Frequent and bloody wars, in which the whites were not always the aggressors, unavoidably ensued. European policy, numbers, and skill prevailed. As the white population advanced, that of the Indians necessarily receded. The country in the immediate neighbourhood of agriculturists became unfit for them. The game fled into thicker and more unbroken forests, and the Indians followed. The soil, to which the crown originally claimed title, being no longer occupied by its ancient inhabitants, was parcelled out according to the will of the sovereign power....

However extravagant the pretension of converting the discovery of an inhabited country into conquest may appear; if the principle has been asserted in the first instance, and afterwards sustained; if a country has been acquired and held under it; if the property of the great mass of the community originates in it, it becomes the law of the land, and cannot be questioned. So, too, with respect to the concomitant principle, that the Indian inhabitants are to be considered merely as occupants, ... but to be deemed incapable of transferring the absolute title to others. However this restriction may be opposed to natural right, and to the usages of civilized nations, yet, if it be indispensable to that system under which the country has been settled, and be adapted to the actual condition of the two people, it may, perhaps, be supported by reason, and ... cannot be rejected by Courts.... [P]laintiffs do not exhibit a title which can be sustained.... Affirmed.

Given the claim to control native lands by "right of discovery and conquest," which right is "acquired and maintained by force," it is no surprise that state governments and private individuals considered themselves free to take tribal lands for themselves, particularly when they discovered that there were gold and other resources to be had. Just such actions brought about two cases from Georgia, *Cherokee Nation v. Georgia* and *Worcester v. Georgia.*

These cases provide early discussions of the ongoing themes in Native American civil rights problems, which include: Who controls the land that is so vital to the identity and spirituality of the people? Who exercises sovereignty over that land and the people who live on it? Who controls the natural resources that are on land long recognized as the traditional home of native people? The first two of these questions are discussed in this chapter and the next. Natural resources are addressed more specifically in Chapter 7.

Cherokee Nation v. Georgia
30 U.S. 1 (1831)

INTRODUCTION: The Treaty of Hopewell of 1785 recognized the independence and sovereignty of the Cherokee as well as their lands and rights to security. A number of other treaties with the federal government followed over the years. By 1802 Congress legislated a land swap arrangement that would lead to a movement of Indians west to other lands. However, until these changes could be accomplished by peaceful agreements, the legislation also provided for protections for Native American rights from violations.

In 1830 the state of Georgia adopted two statutes that claimed Cherokee lands for the state and initiated steps to redistribute those lands to Georgia residents. One of these called for surveyors to "enter upon the Cherokee territory and lay it off into districts and sections, which are to be distributed by lottery among the people of Georgia...." The other provision was "an act to authorize the governor to take possession of the gold and silver and other mines lying and being in that section of the chartered limits of Georgia, commonly called the Cherokee country, and ... for punishing persons who may be found trespassing on the mines." That legislation claimed title to the mines for the state of Georgia and called upon the governor to take possession and station armed forces there. It also made it a crime for Cherokee people to work in the mines.

The Cherokee brought suit on original jurisdiction in the U.S. Supreme Court as a sovereign foreign nation against a state of the United States, seeking an injunction to block implementation of the 1830 Georgia legislation.[21]

Chief Justice Marshall wrote the opinion for the Court.

This bill is brought by the Cherokee nation, praying an injunction to restrain the state of Georgia from the execution of certain laws of that state, which, as is alleged, go directly to annihilate the Cherokees as a political society, and to seize, for the use of Georgia, the lands of the nation which have been assured to them by the United States in solemn treaties....

If courts were permitted to indulge their sympathies, a case better calculated to excite them can scarcely be imagined. A people once numerous, powerful, and truly independent, found by our ancestors in the quiet and uncontrolled possession of an ample domain, gradually sinking beneath our superior policy, our arts and our arms, have yielded their lands by successive treaties, each of which contains a solemn guarantee of the residue, until they retain no more of their formerly extensive territory than is deemed necessary to their comfortable subsistence. To preserve this remnant, the present application is made.

Before we can look into the merits of the case, a preliminary inquiry presents itself. Has this court jurisdiction of the cause? The third article of the constitution describes the extent of the judicial power [and enumerates the cases it can hear on original jurisdiction]. Is the Cherokee nation a foreign state in the sense in which that term is used in the constitution? ...

So much of the argument as was intended to prove the character of the Cherokees as a state, as a distinct political society, separated from others, capable of managing its own affairs and governing itself, has, in the opinion of a majority of the judges, been completely successful. They have been uniformly treated as a state from the settlement of our country. The numerous treaties made with them by the United States recognize them as a people capable of maintaining the relations of peace and war, of being responsible in their political character for any violation of their engagements, or for any aggression committed on the citizens of the United States by any individual of their community. Laws have been enacted in the spirit of these treaties. The acts of our government plainly recognize the Cherokee nation as a state, and the courts are bound by those acts.

A question of much more difficulty remains. Do the Cherokees constitute a foreign state in the sense of the constitution? The counsel have shown conclusively that they are not a state of the union, and have insisted that individually they are aliens, not owing allegiance to the United States. An aggregate of aliens composing a state must, they say, be a foreign state. Each individual being foreign, the whole must be foreign.

The condition of the Indians in relation to the United States is perhaps unlike that of any other two people in existence. In the general, nations not owing a common allegiance are foreign to each other.... But the relation of the Indians to the United States is marked by peculiar and cardinal distinctions which exist no where else.

The Indian territory is admitted to compose a part of the United States. In all our maps, geographical treatises, histories, and laws, it is so considered. In all our intercourse with foreign nations, in our commercial regulations, in any attempt at intercourse between Indians and foreign nations, they are considered as within the jurisdictional limits of the United States, subject to many of those restraints which are imposed upon our own citizens. They acknowledge themselves in their treaties to be under the protection of the United States; they admit that the United States shall have the sole and exclusive right of regulating the trade with them, and managing all their affairs as they think proper; and the Cherokees in particular were allowed by the treaty of Hopewell, which preceded the constitution, "to send a deputy of their choice, whenever they think fit, to congress." ...

Though the Indians are acknowledged to have an unquestionable, and, heretofore, unquestioned right to the lands they occupy, until that right shall be extinguished by a voluntary cession to our government; yet it may well be doubted whether those tribes which reside within the acknowledged boundaries of the United States can, with strict accuracy, be denominated foreign nations. They may, more correctly, perhaps, be denominated domestic dependent nations.... Their relation to the United States resembles that of a ward to his guardian.

They look to our government for protection; rely upon its kindness and its power; appeal to it for relief to their wants; and address the president as their great father. They and their country are considered by foreign nations, as well as by ourselves, as being so completely under the sovereignty and dominion of the United States, that any attempt to acquire their lands, or to form a political connexion with them, would be considered by all as an invasion of our territory, and an act of hostility.

These considerations go far to support the opinion that the framers of our constitution had not the Indian tribes in view when they opened the courts of the union to controversies between a state or the citizens thereof, and foreign states.... At the time the constitution was framed, the idea of appealing to an American court of justice for an assertion of right or a redress of wrong had perhaps never entered the mind of an Indian or of his tribe. Their appeal was to the tomahawk, or to the government. This was well understood by the statesmen who framed the constitution of the United States, and might furnish some reason for omitting to enumerate them among the parties who might sue in the courts of the union.... [T]he peculiar relations between the United States and the Indians occupying our territory are such that we should feel much difficulty in considering them as designated by the term foreign state, were there no other part of the constitution which might shed light on the meaning of these words. But ... considerable aid is furnished by that clause in the eighth section of the [first] article; which empowers congress to "regulate commerce with foreign nations, and among the several states, and with the Indian tribes." ... The objects to which the power of regulating commerce might be directed are divided into three distinct classes—foreign nations, the several states, and Indian tribes. When forming this article, the convention considered them as entirely distinct....

[A]fter mature deliberation, the majority is of opinion that an Indian tribe or nation within the United States is not a foreign state in the sense of the constitution, and cannot maintain an action in the courts of the United States. If it be true that the Cherokee nation have rights, this is not the tribunal in which those rights are to be asserted. If it be true that wrongs have been inflicted, and that still greater are to be apprehended, this is not the tribunal which can redress the past or prevent the future. The motion for an injunction is denied.[22]

Justice Thompson wrote a dissent joined by Justice Story.

... Every nation that governs itself, under what form soever, without any dependence on a foreign power, is a sovereign state. Its rights are naturally the same as those of any other state.... Testing the character and condition of the Cherokee Indians by these rules, it is not perceived how it is possible to escape the conclusion that they form a sovereign state. They have always been dealt with as such by the government of the United States; both before and since the adoption of the present constitution. They have been admitted and treated as a people governed solely and exclusively by their own laws, usages, and customs within their own territory, claiming and exercising exclusive dominion over the same; yielding up by treaty, from time to time, portions of their land, but still claiming absolute sovereignty and self government over what remained unsold. And this has been the light in which they have, until recently, been considered from the earliest settlement of the country by the white people....

That numerous tribes of Indians, and among others the Cherokee nation, occupied many parts of this country long before the discovery by Europeans is abundantly established by history; and it is not denied but that the Cherokee nation occupied the territory now claimed by them long before that period.... And if the Cherokees were then a foreign nation, when or how have they lost that character and ceased to be a distinct people, and become incorporated with any other community?

They have never been, by conquest, reduced to the situation of subjects to any conqueror, and thereby lost their separate national existence, and the rights of self government, and become subject to the laws of the conqueror. When ever wars have taken place, they have been followed by regular treaties of peace, containing stipulations on each side...; the Indian nation always preserving its distinct and separate national character....

In this view of their situation, there is as full and complete recognition of their sovereignty, as if they were the absolute owners of the soil.... [I]t is their political condition that constitutes their foreign character, and in that sense must the term foreign be understood as used in the constitution. It can have no relation to local, geographical, or territorial position. It cannot mean a country beyond sea. Mexico or Canada is certainly to be considered a foreign country in reference to the United States. It is the political relation in which one government or country stands to another, which constitutes it foreign to the other....

... [A] foreign state, judicially considered, consists in its being under a different jurisdiction or government, without any reference to its territorial position.... And if, as here decided, a separate and distinct jurisdiction or government is the test by which to decide whether a nation be foreign or not, I am unable to perceive any sound and substantial reason why the Cherokee nation should not be so considered. It is governed by its own laws, usages and customs: it has no connexion with any other government or jurisdiction, except by way of treaties entered into with like form and ceremony as with other foreign nations....

And what possible objection can lie to the right of the complainants to sustain an action? The treaties made with this nation purport to secure to it certain rights. These are not gratuitous obligations assumed on the part of the United States. They are obligations founded upon a consideration paid by the Indians by cession of part of their territory. And if they, as a nation, are competent to make a treaty or contract, it would seem to me to be a strange inconsistency to deny to them the right and the power to enforce such a contract. And where the right secured by such treaty forms a proper subject for judicial cognizance, I can perceive no reason why this court has not jurisdiction of the case. The constitution expressly gives to the court jurisdiction in all cases of law and equity arising under treaties made with the United States....

... All negotiations carried on with the Cherokees and other Indian nations have been by way of treaty with all the formality attending the making of treaties with any foreign power.... What is a treaty as understood in the law of nations? It is an agreement or contract between two or more nations or sovereigns, entered into by agents appointed for that purpose, and duly sanctioned by the supreme power of the respective parties. And where is the authority, either in the constitution or in the practice of the government, for making any distinction between treaties made with the Indian nations and any other foreign power? They relate to peace and war; the surrender of prisoners; the cession of territory; and the various subjects which are usually embraced in such contracts between sovereign nations....

... The injuries complained of are violations committed and threatened upon the property of the complainants, secured to them by the laws and treaties of the United States. Under the constitution, the judicial power of the United States extends expressly to all cases in law and equity, arising under the laws of the United States, and treaties made or which shall be made, under the authority of the same.... The question presented in the present case is, under the ordinary form of judicial proceedings, to obtain an injunction to prevent or stay a violation of the rights of property claimed and held by the complainants, under the treaties and laws of the United States, which, it is alleged, have been violated by the state of Georgia. Both the form, and the subject matter of the complaint, therefore, fall properly under judicial cognizance....

That the Cherokee nation of Indians have, by virtue of these treaties, an exclusive right of occupancy of the lands in question, and that the United States are bound under their guarantee, to protect the nation in the enjoyment of such occupancy, cannot, in my judgment, admit of a doubt: and that some of the laws of Georgia set out in the bill are in violation of, and in conflict with those treaties and the act of 1802, is to my mind equally clear....

Upon the whole, I am of opinion, 1. that the Cherokees compose a foreign state within the sense and meaning of the constitution, and constitute a competent party to maintain a suit against the state of Georgia. 2. That the bill presents a case for judicial consideration, arising under the laws of the United States, and treaties made under their authority with the Cherokee nation, and which laws and treaties have been, and are threatened to be still further violated by the laws of the state of Georgia referred to in this opinion. 3. That an injunction is a fit and proper writ to be issued, to prevent the further execution of such laws, and ought therefore to be awarded.

Worcester v. Georgia

31 U.S. 515 (1832)

INTRODUCTION: Samuel A. Worcester was a missionary from Vermont working in Cherokee territory in Georgia with the approval of the president, the American Board of Commissioners for Foreign Missions, and the Cherokee. These arrangements flowed from prior treaties and federal legislation. In addition to preaching, Worcester and a colleague were translating the Bible into Cherokee. However, they were arrested in July 1831, later convicted, and sentenced to four years in prison for violation of Georgia legislation adopted in 1830, prohibiting anyone from residing on the Cherokee lands without permission from the governor and without swearing a loyalty oath. Worcester challenged the Georgia statutes under which he was convicted.

Chief Justice Marshall wrote the opinion for the Court.

... The defendant is a state ... which has exercised the powers of government over a people who deny its jurisdiction, and are under the protection of the United States. The plaintiff is a citizen of the state of Vermont, condemned to hard labour for four years in the penitentiary of Georgia under colour of an act which he alleges to be repugnant to the constitution, laws, and treaties of the United States....

The first step in the performance of this duty is the inquiry whether the record is properly before the court.... The plea avers that the residence, charged in the indictment, was under the authority of the president of the United States, and with the permission and approval of the Cherokee nation. That the treaties, subsisting between the United States and the Cherokees, acknowledge their right as a sovereign nation to govern themselves and all persons who have settled within their territory, free from any right of legislative interference by the several states composing the United States of America. That the act under which the prosecution was instituted is repugnant to the said treaties, and is, therefore, unconstitutional and void. That the said act is, also, unconstitutional because it interferes with, and attempts to regulate and control, the intercourse with the Cherokee nation, which belongs, exclusively, to congress; and, because, also, it is repugnant to the statute of the United States, entitled "an act to regulate trade and intercourse with the Indian tribes, and to preserve peace on the frontiers." ...

It is, then, we think, too clear for controversy that the act of congress, by which this court is constituted, has given it the power, and of course imposed on it the duty, of exercising jurisdiction in this case.... We must inquire and decide whether the act of the legislature of Georgia, under which the plaintiff in error has been prosecuted and condemned, be consistent with, or repugnant to, the constitution, laws and treaties of the United States.

It has been said at the bar that the acts of the legislature of Georgia seize on the whole Cherokee country, parcel it out among the neighbouring counties of the state, extend her code over the whole country, abolish its institutions and its laws, and annihilate its political existence. If this be the general effect of the system, let us inquire into the effect of the particular statute and section on which the indictment is founded....

The extra-territorial power of every legislature being limited in its action, to its own citizens or subjects, the very passage of this act is an assertion of jurisdiction over the Cherokee nation, and of the rights and powers consequent on jurisdiction. The first step, then, in the inquiry, which the constitution and laws impose on this court, is an examination of the rightfulness of this claim.

America, separated from Europe by a wide ocean, was inhabited by a distinct people, divided into separate nations, independent of each other and of the rest of the world, having institutions of their own, and governing themselves by their own laws. It is difficult to comprehend the proposition that the inhabitants of either quarter of the globe could have rightful original claims of dominion over the inhabitants of the other, or over the lands they occupied; or that the discovery of either by the other should give the discoverer rights in the country discovered, which annulled the pre-existing rights of its ancient possessors.

After lying concealed for a series of ages, the enterprise of Europe, guided by nautical science, conducted some of her adventurous sons into this western world. They found it in possession of a people who had made small progress in agriculture or manufactures, and whose general employment was war, hunting, and fishing....

The great maritime powers of Europe discovered and visited different parts of this continent at nearly the same time. The object was too immense for any one of them to grasp the whole; and the claimants were too powerful to submit to the exclusive or unreasonable pretensions of any single potentate. To avoid bloody conflicts, which might terminate disastrously to all, it was necessary for the nations of Europe to establish some principle which ... should decide their respective rights as between themselves.... This principle, acknowledged by all Europeans ... gave to the nation making the discovery, as its inevitable consequence, the sole right of acquiring the soil and of making settlements on it.... It regulated the right given by discovery among the European discoverers, but could not affect the rights of those already in possession, either as aboriginal occupants, or as occupants by virtue of a discovery made before the memory of man. It gave the exclusive right to purchase, but did not found that right on a denial of the right of the possessor to sell....

Soon after Great Britain determined on planting colonies in America, the king granted charters to companies of his subjects who associated for the purpose of carrying the views of the crown into effect, and of enriching themselves. The first of these charters was made before possession was taken of any part of the country. They purport, generally, to convey the soil, from the Atlantic to the South Sea. This soil was occupied by numerous and warlike nations, equally willing and able to defend their possessions. The extravagant and absurd idea that the feeble settlements made on the sea coast, or the companies under whom they were made, acquired legitimate power by them to govern the people, or occupy the lands from sea to sea, did not enter the mind of any man. They were well understood to convey the title which, according to the common law of European sovereigns respecting America, they might rightfully convey, and no more. This was the exclusive right of purchasing such lands as the natives were willing to sell. The crown could not be understood to grant what the crown did not affect to claim; nor was it so understood.

The charter to Georgia professes to be granted for the charitable purpose of enabling poor subjects to gain a comfortable subsistence by cultivating lands in the American provinces, "at present waste and desolate." ... The charters contain passages showing one of their objects to be the civilization of the Indians, and their conversion to Christianity—objects to be accomplished by conciliatory conduct and good example, not by extermination.

Fierce and warlike in their character, the [Indians] might be formidable enemies, or effective friends. Instead of rousing their resentments by asserting claims to their lands, or to dominion over their persons, their alliance was sought by flattering professions, and purchased by rich presents. The English, the French, and the Spaniards were equally competitors for their friendship and their aid. Not well acquainted with the exact meaning of words, nor supposing it to be material whether they were called the subjects or the children of their father in Europe; lavish in professions of duty and affection, in return for the rich presents they received; so long as their actual independence was untouched, and their right to self government acknowledged, they were willing to profess dependence on the power which furnished supplies of which they were in absolute need, and restrained dangerous intruders from entering their country: and this was probably the sense in which the term was understood by them.

Certain it is that our history furnishes no example, from the first settlement of our country, of any attempt on the part of the crown to interfere with the internal affairs of the Indians, farther than to keep out the agents of foreign powers, who, as traders or otherwise, might seduce them into foreign alliances. The king purchased their lands when they were willing to sell, at a price they were willing to take, but never coerced a surrender of them. He also purchased their alliance and dependence by subsidies, but never intruded into the interior of their affairs, or interfered with their self government, so far as respected themselves only....

The first treaty was made with the Delawares, in September 1778. The language of equality in which it is drawn, evinces the temper with which the negotiation was undertaken, and the opinion which then prevailed in the United States.... This treaty, in its language, and in its provisions, is formed, as near as may be, on the model of treaties between the crowned heads of Europe....

After [the Revolution], the United States [concluded the treaty of Hopewell with the Cherokee]. The treaty is introduced with the declaration that "the commissioners plenipotentiary of the United States give peace to all the Cherokees, and receive them into the favour and protection of the United States of America, on the following conditions." ... The first and second articles stipulate for the mutual restoration of prisoners, and are of course equal. The third article acknowledges the Cherokees to be under the protection of the United States of America, and of no other power....

The fourth article draws the boundary between the Indians and the citizens of the United States. But, in describing this boundary, the term "allotted" and the term "hunting ground" are used. Is it reasonable to suppose that the Indians, who could not write, and most probably could not read, who certainly were not critical judges of our language, should distinguish the word "allotted" from the words "marked out." The actual subject of contract was the dividing line between the two nations, and their attention may very well be supposed to have been confined to that subject....[23]

The fifth article withdraws the protection of the United States from any citizen who has settled, or shall settle, on the lands allotted to the Indians for their hunting grounds, and stipulates that, if he shall not remove within six months, the Indians may punish him....

The ninth article is in these words: "for the benefit and comfort of the Indians, and for the prevention of injuries or oppressions on the part of the citizens or Indians, the United States, in congress assembled, shall have the sole and exclusive right of regulating the trade with the Indians, and managing all their affairs, as they think proper." To construe the expression "managing all their affairs" into a surrender of self-government would be, we think, a perversion of their necessary meaning, and a departure from the construction which has been uniformly put on them....

To accommodate the differences still existing between the state of Georgia and the Cherokee nation, the treaty of Holston was negotiated in July 1791.... This treaty, thus explicitly recognizing the national character of the Cherokees and their right of self government; thus guarantying their lands; assuming the duty of protection, and of course pledging the faith of the United States for that protection; has been frequently renewed, and is now in full force....

From the commencement of our government, congress has passed acts to regulate trade and intercourse with the Indians, which treat them as nations, respect their rights, and manifest a firm purpose to afford that protection which treaties stipulate. All these acts, and especially that of 1802, which is still in force, manifestly consider the several Indian nations as distinct political communities, having territorial boundaries within which their authority is exclusive, and having a right to all the lands within those boundaries, which is not only acknowledged, but guarantied by the United States....

The treaties and laws of the United States contemplate the Indian territory as completely separated from that of the states, and provide that all intercourse with them shall be carried on exclusively by the government of the union.... The Indian nations had always been considered as distinct, independent political communities, retaining their original natural rights, as the undisputed possessors of the soil, from time immemorial.... The very term "nation," so generally applied to them, means "a people distinct from others." The constitution, by declaring treaties already made, as well as those to be made, to be the supreme law of the land, has adopted and sanctioned the previous treaties with the Indian nations, and consequently admits their rank among those powers who are capable of making treaties. The words "treaty" and "nation" are words of our own language, selected in our diplomatic and legislative proceedings by ourselves, having each a definite and well understood meaning. We have applied them to Indians, as we have applied them to the other nations of the earth. They are applied to all in the same sense.

The Cherokee nation, then, is a distinct community occupying its own territory, with boundaries accurately described, in which the laws of Georgia can have no force, and which the citizens of Georgia have no right to enter, but with the assent of the Cherokees themselves, or in conformity with treaties and with the acts of congress. The whole intercourse between the United States and this nation is, by our constitution and laws, vested in the government of the United States.

The act of the state of Georgia, under which the plaintiff in error was prosecuted, is consequently void, and the judgment a nullity.... [T]he acts of Georgia are repugnant to the constitution, laws, and treaties of the United States. They interfere forcibly with the relations established between the United States and the Cherokee nation, the regulation of which, according to the settled principles of our constitution, are committed exclusively to the government of the union.

They are in direct hostility with treaties, repeated in a succession of years, which mark out the boundary that separates the Cherokee country from Georgia; guaranty to them all the land within their boundary; solemnly pledge the faith of the United States to restrain their citizens from trespassing on it; and recognize the pre-existing power of the nation to govern itself.

They are in equal hostility with the acts of congress for regulating this intercourse, and giving effect to the treaties.

The forcible seizure and abduction of the plaintiff in error, who was residing in the nation with its permission, and by authority of the president of the United States, is also a violation of the acts which authorise the chief magistrate to exercise this authority....

[T]he judgment of the [Georgia court] was pronounced ... under colour of a law ... repugnant to the constitution, treaties, and laws of the United States, and [is] reversed.[24]

Sadly, as history records, the national government did not respect the rights of the Cherokee or other tribes, as Marshall explained them in this opinion, or honor the obligations of the United States toward them that he described. Indeed, they were pushed out of their lands and driven westward in the infamous "Trail of Tears."[25]

As the tribes were pushed westward, they encountered state governments that sought to control or tax them. Of course, as the Supreme Court had long before made clear, the power to tax can be the power to control or even to destroy.[26] For Native Americans, states are a subordinate unit of the national sovereign and tribal relationships are sovereign government-to-sovereign government. The Supreme Court was asked to address this situation in the *Kansas Indians* case.

The Kansas Indians

72 U.S. 737 (1867)

INTRODUCTION: The facts of this case are presented in the opinion. It is one opinion that addresses three related cases involving three nations. In reading this opinion for the Court, notice not only the legal argument, but also the language used to describe Indians and their nations. Also notice what it tells the reader about how repeated promises were made to protect the native lands guaranteed by the treaty "forever" or "in perpetuity" and then, in no time at all, the federal government decided that there needed to be new treaties taking more native land. On the other hand, notice the reference to Justice Marshall's *Worcester v. Georgia* opinion that "The language used in treaties with the Indians shall never be construed to their prejudice, if words be made use of which are susceptible of a more extended meaning than their plain import as connected with the tenor of their treaty."[27]

Justice Davis wrote the opinion for the Court.

In the Case of the Shawnees

The sole question presented by this record is, whether the lands belonging to the united tribe of Shawnee Indians, residing in Kansas, are taxable [by the state]? ... The solution of it depends on the construction of treaties, the relations of the general government to the Indian tribes, and the laws of Congress....

In 1825 the Shawnee tribe was divided—part being in Missouri and part in Ohio. The Missouri Shawnees were in possession of valuable lands [then] ceded them, by treaty, to the United States, and, in consideration of the cession, received for their use, and those of the same nation in Ohio, who chose to join them, a tract of country in Kansas.... In pursuance of the favorite policy of the government to persuade all the Indian tribes east of the Mississippi to migrate and settle on territory ... west of that river, in 1831, a convention was concluded with the Ohio Shawnees—they being willing to remove West.... In exchange for valuable lands and improvements in Ohio, they obtained [for themselves] and their heirs forever, so long as they shall exist as a nation ... land, to be located under the direction of the President of the United States, within the tract granted in 1825 to the Missouri Shawnees.... In obedience to the obligations of this treaty, they [moved], but were soon met by the advancing tide of civilization.

In view of the rapid increase of population in the Kansas country, and the small number of Shawnees ... it was deemed advisable to lessen their territorial limits. Accordingly another treaty was concluded with them [in] 1854. By this treaty the united Shawnee nation ceded to the United States all the large domain granted to them by the treaty of 1825. In consideration for this cession, two hundred thousand acres of these same lands were receded to them, and they also obtained annuities and other property. [The treaty] did not contemplate that the Indians should enjoy the whole tract, as the quantity for each individual was limited to two hundred acres. The unselected lands were to be sold by the government, and the proceeds appropriated to the uses of the Indians....

This treaty was silent about the guarantees of the treaty of 1831; but the Shawnees expressly acknowledged their dependence on the government of the United States, as formerly they had done, and invoked its protection and care.... [In 1861] Kansas was admitted into the Union; but the rights of the Indians, the powers of Congress over them, their lands, and property, and the stipulations of treaties, were fully preserved, and in the same words, both in the organic act and the act for the admission of Kansas.

The Ohio Shawnees, when they ceded their lands in Ohio, did it in pursuance of an act of Congress of May 28, 1830, which assured them the country to which they were [relocated] should be secured and guaranteed to them and their heirs forever.... It is plain to be seen that the covenants with the Shawnees in the treaty of 1861 that they should not be subject to the laws of organized States or Territories, nor their lands included within their boundaries, unless with their own consent, signified to the President, must have materially influenced their decision to part with their Ohio possessions and join their brethren in Kansas. They, therefore, removed under the assured protection of the government, to enjoy, as they expected, in perpetuity, free from encroachment, a home adapted to their habits and customs. But these expectations were not to be realized, for the spirit of American enterprise in a few years reached their country, and the same white population that pressed upon them in Ohio and Missouri followed them there.

The present and future wants of this population created the necessity for the treaty of 1854.... It is insisted [by the State], as the guarantees of the treaty of 1831 are not, in express words, reaffirmed in the treaty of 1854, they are, therefore, abrogated, and that the division of the Indian territory into separate estates so changes the status of the Indians that the property of those who hold in severalty is liable to State taxation....

But, it is not necessary to import the guarantees of the treaty of 1831 into that of 1854 in order to save the property of the entire tribe from State taxation.... If the tribal organization of the Shawnees is preserved intact, and recognized by the political department of the government as existing, then they are a "people distinct from others," capable of making treaties, separated from the jurisdiction of Kansas, and to be governed exclusively by the government of the Union. If under the control of Congress, from necessity there can be no divided authority. If they have outlived many things, they have not outlived the protection afforded by the Constitution, treaties, and laws of Congress. It may be that they cannot exist much longer as a distinct people in the presence of the civilization of Kansas, "but until they are clothed with the rights and bound to all the duties of citizens," they enjoy the privilege of total immunity from State taxation.... The treaty of 1854 left the Shawnee people a united tribe, with a declaration of their dependence on the National government for protection and the vindication of their rights. Ever since this their tribal organization has remained as it was before. They have elective chiefs and an elective council, meeting at stated periods, keeping a record of their proceedings, with powers regulated by custom, by which they punish offences, adjust differences, and exercise a general oversight over the affairs of the nation. This people have their own customs and laws by which they are governed. Because some of those customs have been abandoned, owing to the proximity of their white neighbors, may be an evidence of the superior influence of our race, but does not tend to prove that their tribal organization is not preserved....

[T]he action of the political department of the government settles, beyond controversy, that the Shawnees are as yet a distinct people, with a perfect tribal organization. Within a very recent period their head men negotiated a treaty with the United States, which, for some reason not explained in the record, was either not sent to the Senate, or, if sent, not ratified, and they are under the charge of an agent who constantly resides with them. While the general government has a superintending care over their interests, and continues to treat with them as a nation, the State of Kansas is estopped from denying their title to it.... As long as the United States recognizes their national character they are under the protection of treaties and the laws of Congress, and their property is withdrawn from the operation of State laws....

In the Case of the Weas

The opinion just rendered in the case of ... the united tribe of Shawnee Indians, controls the decision of this case.... This tribe being weak in numbers, united with three other tribes, equally weak, and ceded to the United States large possessions obtained under former treaties, reserving for each individual only one hundred and sixty acres of land, and ten sections for the common property of the united tribes, with one section in addition for the American Indian Mission Association. The reservation of the limited quantity for each individual was not to be in a compact body. Individuals and heads of families had the right of selection, as in the Shawnee treaty, and the lands were to be patented, with restrictions upon alienation, as the President or Congress should prescribe. The unselected lands were to be sold, and the proceeds paid over to the Indians. This policy produced, as in the case of the Shawnees, a mixed occupancy of the original Indian territory, and, in consequence, the same difficulties.... The basis of the treaty, doubtless, was that the separation of estates and interests would so weaken the tribal organization as to effect its voluntary abandonment and, as a natural result, the incorporation of the Indians with the great body of the people.

But this result, desirable as it may be, has not yet been accomplished with the Wea tribe, and, therefore, their lands cannot be taxed. It is conceded that the tribal organization is kept up and maintained in the county of Miami, where they live and where the annuities are paid to them, under the supervision of the Indian agent of the tribe. And it is further conceded that the chiefs and head men of the tribe represent it and transact its business, receive funds from the United States for tribal purposes and disburse it, and that an agent for the tribe resides in the county, where he transacts the business of the United States with the tribe through their chiefs and head men. These concessions place the Wea Indians in the same category with the Shawnees....

In the Case of the Miamis

The principle of the foregoing cases of the Shawnee and Wea tribes of Indians is also decisive of this controversy.... It is sufficient to state that they are a nation of people, recognized as such by the general government in the making of treaties with them and the relations always maintained towards them, and cannot, therefore, be taxed by the authorities of Kansas. Their tribal organization is fully preserved, and they are under the supervision of an agent who resides in the county where their lands are situated.... There is, however, one provision in the Miami treaty ... which, of itself, preserves the Miami lands from taxation. This particular provision exempts the lands from "levy, sale, execution, and forfeiture." ... [E]nlarged rules of construction are adopted in reference to Indian treaties. In speaking of these rules, Chief Justice Marshall says: "The language used in treaties with the Indians shall never be construed to their prejudice, if words be made use of which are susceptible of a more extended meaning than their plain import as connected with the tenor of their treaty."[28]... The object of the treaty was to hedge the lands around with guards and restrictions, so as to preserve them for the permanent homes of the Indians. In order to accomplish this object, they must be relieved from every species of levy, sale, and forfeiture—from a levy and sale for taxes, as well as the ordinary judicial levy and sale.

The judgment of the Supreme Court of Kansas in all three cases was reversed ... and remanded.

Dark Times and an Uncertain Future: Exclusion and Even Genocidal Actions

If the early rulings suggested that the federal government was going to protect Native American rights against attacks by states or private individuals, the actions taken by the U.S. government in the years that followed, including the period after the Civil War, demonstrated otherwise. Indeed, the federal government took a series of actions that were designed to eliminate the tribes, Indian identity, and even to destroy Native Americans as a people. Although most Americans would recoil at the use of the term genocide for actions taken by their government, that is indeed what was attempted, and it is understood in that way today by many Native Americans.[29] These efforts were encouraged by the movement of settlers into the ancestral home of many Native Americans following the passage of the Homestead Act of 1862.[30] There were three major prongs in the attack, including (1) unprovoked and brutal assaults that killed men, women, and children; (2) the use of residential Indian Schools to "kill the Indian and leave the man;" and (3) the Dawes Act process aimed at breaking up the tribal lands and eliminating the fundamental connection between individual Native Americans, the tribes, and the land that was central to their communities and identity.

Direct and Indirect Military Campaigns against Native Americans

From the beginning of the Trail of Tears, the nation saw case after case in which tribes were forcibly removed from their ancestral homelands and driven to reservations in parts of the country that were undesirable to white settlers and foreign to the Native Americans moved into them. Too often, these were hostile new environments in which even those who knew the area and had the necessary tools and knowledge would have struggled to survive. Historian Dee Brown presented the story of the so-called "Long Walk of the Navajos" in which, under orders from General James Carleton, Navajo crops and livestock were taken or destroyed and the Navajo driven off their lands to the Bosque Redondo reservation. Kit Carson, although one who had been a friend to many Native Americans, had been one of the key officers in this rout of the Navajo. Brown explained that while the Navajo could forgive him many things, they were outraged by his act of environmental warfare. "The Navahoes could forgive the Rope Thrower for fighting them as a soldier, for making prisoners of them, even for destroying their food supplies, but the one act they never forgive him for was cutting down their beloved peach trees."[31] Brown explained that even the new superintendent at the Bosque Redondo reservation recognized the cruelty of forcing the Navajo into such a hostile environment.

The superintendent examined the soil on the reservation and pronounced it unfit for cultivation of grain because of the presence of alkali. "The water is black and brackish, scarcely bearable to the taste, and said by the Indians to be unhealthy, because one-fourth of their population have been swept off by disease…. Would any sensible man select a spot for a reservation for 8,000 Indians where the water is scarcely bearable, where the soil is poor and cold, and where the muskite [mesquite] roots 12 miles distant are the only wood for the Indians to use?"[32] Carson defenders argued that he was willing to participate in this activity as the only way to save the Navajo from extinction, but the argument rang hollow. The situation was made worse by the fact that the Navajo were forced into a reservation with their enemies, the Mescalero Apaches.[33]

In other cases there were savage attacks against Native American communities, perhaps the best known of which is the massacre at Wounded Knee.[34] Another was the Sand Creek massacre in Colorado territory, where some 200, mostly women, children, and older persons, of the Cheyenne and Arapaho tribes were killed by troops under the command of Colonel John M. Chivington.[35] In some instances the attacks were against the environment in which the tribes then lived. Game and crops were deliberately destroyed by U.S. forces. While there is continuing debate over whether the infamous line supposedly originated by General Philip Sheridan that "the only good Indian is a dead Indian" was actually said by him or was directly stated as U.S. policy, the manifold attacks on native peoples demonstrate that it was the policy in fact, if not in terms, for many American officials—and Native Americans knew it, then and now.[36]

In some cases the forced relocations of tribes began initially as treaties later violated by the U.S. government or agreements that Native Americans entered into in good faith, but that were complex and written in another language from their own. So obvious were the violations that then President Rutherford B. Hayes addressed them in his inaugural address.

> [T]he Indians are certainly entitled to our sympathy and to a conscientious respect on our part for their claims upon our sense of justice. They were the aboriginal occupants of the land we now possess. They have been driven from place to place. The purchase money paid to them in some cases for what they called their own has still left them poor. In many instances, when they had settled down upon land assigned to them by compact and begun to support themselves by their own labor, they were rudely jostled off and thrust into the wilderness again. Many, if not most, of our Indian wars have had their origin in broken promises and acts of injustice upon our part, and the advance of the Indians in civilization has been slow because the treatment they received did not permit it to be faster and more general. We can not expect them to improve and to follow our guidance unless we keep faith with them in respecting the rights they possess, and unless, instead of depriving them of their opportunities, we lend them a helping hand.[37]

That same address, however, made reference to two approaches to Indian affairs that proved not to aid the tribes, but to destroy them. He spoke of:

> the establishment and maintenance of schools to bring them under the control of civilized influences. I see no reason why Indians who can give satisfactory proof of having by their own labor supported their families for a number of years, and who are willing

to detach themselves from their tribal relations, should not be admitted to the benefit of the homestead act and the privileges of citizenship, and I recommend the passage of a law to that effect.

The call for "civilizing" education was later manifest in the infamous Indian boarding school that sought to destroy Native American culture and remake Indian children "in the White Man's Image."[38] The second element, the provision of land for those willing to "detach themselves from tribal relations," would some ten years later become the Dawes Act.

The Dawes Act: A More Subtle but Very Effective Attack

The Dawes Act, more formally entitled "An Act to Provide for the Allotment of Lands in Severalty to Indians on the Various Reservations," was also known as the General Allotment Act.[39] This policy not only had—and was expected to have—a dramatic impact on Native American lands, resulting in a loss of more than 90,000,000 acres over time, but it was also an attack on the foundations of tribal life, culture, and governance, the effects of which continue to the present day, not only in fact, but also in law.

In order to understand why and how the Dawes Act was so devastating, it is necessary to understand a number of key features of Native American life before addressing the content of the Act itself. First, one of the foundation principles that many very different tribal communities have in common is a belief in the integration of mind, body, and spirit.[40] That spirituality is for many firmly grounded in the relationship of the Native American to the physical environment in which his or her tribe lives. Indeed, basic precepts of many indigenous religions are grounded in a place, not in a person or an event.

> [A]ll indigenous people have a special relationship with their land, which they see as being imbued with a spirituality and sacredness not generally comprehensible by others. The land for them is more than just a habitat of a political boundary; it is the basis of their social organization, economic system and cultural identification."[41]

The relocation of tribal communities, therefore, often dealt a serious blow to the sense of wholeness and connection with one's spiritual foundations in the ancestral homeland. Relocation or loss of that homeland also meant serious challenges to what in contemporary Western terms would be called the integrity of one's social fabric and one's economic well-being. At least, though, if the tribe had a reservation with reasonable resources and respect for its social, economic, political, and legal integrity and sovereignty, there was a chance, however difficult and with awareness of the spiritual damage of displacement, to build on inherent strengths of Native American cultures and rebuild tribal society, even if it had been reshaped by traumatic events. Thus, the integrity of reservations mattered mightily, even if they were an inadequate substitute for the tribal native home.

There is one other foundation point that is important here, which is that Native American conceptions of land were very different from the Western ideas of private property law inherited from England and later modified in what became the United States. The idea of an individual's land title in "fee simple absolute," as the Western term explained, was not familiar to most Native American cultures. Their view of their relationship to the land was not as fixed, as unlimited, or as individualistic as the Western idea. That is true not only for Native Americans, but for many indigenous peoples around the world.[42] For many native peoples, they are of the land and not owners of the land; and certainly not in the contemporary Western sense of ownership. That said, tribal lands were and are important, particularly since tribes or nations are to be sovereign within that territory according to the cases discussed to this point. It should also be noted that the U.S. government signaled its intentions to end traditional recognition of sovereignty of tribes and nations when it appended provisions to an appropriations act that provided: "Hereinafter no Indian nation or tribe within the territory of the United States shall be acknowledged or recognized as an independent nation, tribe, or power with whom the United States may contract by treaty."[43]

It was clear at the time that the ability to break up tribal lands was not only the key to obtaining property coveted by whites who had moved west in large numbers, taking advantage of the Homestead Act, and business owners seeking mineral wealth and other resources, but also a way to break down and even perhaps to eliminate tribes and tribal governments as viable political, economic, and social entities. The technique was to divide up the tribal lands and individualize portions of them while making other portions available for sale to non-Indians. Thus, the Dawes Act provided in part as follows:

An Act to Provide for the Allotment of Lands in Severalty to Indians on the Various Reservations (General Allotment Act or Dawes Act)[44]

Be it enacted by the Senate and House of Representatives of the United States of America in Congress assembled, That in all cases where any tribe or band of Indians has been, or shall hereafter be, located upon any reservation created for their use, either by treaty stipulation or by virtue of an act of Congress or executive order setting apart the same for their use, the President of the United States be, and he hereby is, authorized, whenever in his opinion any reservation or any part thereof of such Indians is advantageous for agricultural and grazing purposes, to cause said reservation, or any part thereof, to be surveyed, or resurveyed if necessary, and to allot the lands in said reservation in severalty to any Indian located thereon in quantities as follows:

To each head of a family, one-quarter of a section;
To each single person over eighteen years of age, one-eighth of a section;
To each orphan child under eighteen years of age, one-eighth of a section; and
To each other single person under eighteen years now living, or who may be born prior to the date of the order of the President directing an allotment of the lands embraced in any reservation, one-sixteenth of a section....

SEC. 5. That upon the approval of the allotments provided for in this act by the Secretary of the Interior, he shall cause patents to issue therefor in the name of the allottees, which patents shall be of the legal effect, and declare that the United States does and will hold the land thus allotted, for the period of twenty-five years, in trust for the sole use and benefit of the Indian to whom such allotment shall have been made, or, in case of his decease, of his heirs according to the laws of the State or Territory where such land is located, and that at the expiration of said period the United States will convey the same by patent to said Indian, or his heirs as aforesaid, in fee, discharged of said trust and free of all charge or incumbrance whatsoever: Provided, That the President of the United States may in any case in his discretion extend the period ....

SEC. 10. That nothing in this act contained shall be so construed to affect the right and power of Congress to grant the right of way through any lands granted to an Indian, or a tribe of Indians, for railroads or other highways, or telegraph lines, for the public use, or condemn such lands to public uses, upon making just compensation....

Of course, Native Americans who received allotments were not able to sell the land for 25 years, but it was clear that many would do so over time. The land that was not allotted was supposed to be managed in trust for the members of the tribes whose reservation lands were involved. Sadly, as was so often the case over American history, what was promised was often not delivered. The lands were often sold and managed in a way that could hardly be described as a trust relationship for the benefit of Native Americans. The funds involved were supposed to be available, but more than a century later it became clear that the U.S. government really did not know what the total amounts of money were or which Native Americans were entitled to what proceeds from this trust fund, later termed Indian money. The result of that was a lawsuit that ran for nearly two decades and that will be discussed in more detail later in the chapter.[45]

As will also become clear later in the chapter, even after the control and management of reservation lands were restored to the tribes and nations, the effects of the Dawes Act would continue to plague the basic concept of Native American sovereignty. The problem came from the fact that there were, over time, many sales of reservation land to persons who were not Native Americans, much less members of that tribe. The Dawes Act became a part of a process known as defeasance in which the definition of the sovereignty was undermined.[46] Hence, the Supreme Court would later conclude that tribal sovereignty could not be exercised over non-Indian property on reservation lands in the same manner as for tribal members and tribal-owned lands, leading to a responsibility to govern without the sovereign authority to do so.[47]

The Indian Schools: The Attempt to Kill the Indian and Leave the Person

During the same period, many who considered themselves reformers with the best interests of Native Americans at heart decided that Indians would either have to be assimilated into white culture or they would surely be destroyed. Of course, from a Native American perspective, either way it meant the end of their cultures and their ways of life. And the most effective way that could be accomplished, according to Richard Henry Pratt, first Superintendent of the Carlisle Indian boarding school, was to take Indian children away from the reservation and educate them in the white man's ways. Or, as Pratt put it, to "Kill the Indian in him and save the man."[48]

Students were taken far from their native communities into boarding schools in white communities. Their hair was cut short like the white man's, their native dress was removed and replaced with school uniforms, and they were forced to speak English and punished for speaking in their native tongue. Even their Indian names were taken, to be replaced with common names from the white community. The discipline was stern and the conditions often hard. When they returned home, some of the young graduates found that their families did not even recognize them and some even discovered that they had lost their language and were unable to communicate with family members who, not being English speakers, could also not communicate with their children.

The schools also aimed to convert the students to Christianity and drive from them their native faith and its practices. The schools sought to make them rugged individualists as compared to their traditions which most often valued the tribe's needs more highly than individual gain.

They were also trained for what was considered good citizenship. One of the problems with that training was that, at the time and for many years thereafter, Native Americans were not accorded the full rights of citizenship, including such basic characteristics as the right to vote. That was true notwithstanding the adoption of the Fourteenth and Fifteenth Amendments. It was even true for those who had chosen the path of assimilation or who lived away from the reservation. The case of *Elk v. Wilkins* made that point clear.

Elk v. Wilkins

112 U.S. 94 (1884)

INTRODUCTION: John Elk lived in Omaha, Nebraska. He had cut all ties to his Indian nation. He attempted to register to vote in city elections in 1860. However, the local registrar, Charles Wilkins, refused to register him on grounds that he was an Indian and not a citizen of the United States. Elk argued that he was a citizen within the meaning of the Fourteenth Amendment and he had satisfied all of the existing residency requirements that the state, county, and city demanded of any other voter. Elk came to the polling place on election day, but Wilkins, who was one of the officials at the polls, declared that he was not eligible to vote since he was not a citizen and not registered. Elk contended that his right to vote was violated.

While reading this opinion, think back about the earlier cases that concluded that Native American tribes were not foreign nations. If they are domestic, dependent nations, and not subject to naturalization processes, what did that mean for the individual Native American?

Justice Gray wrote the opinion for the Court.

> [Elk] relies on the [first section of the Fourteenth Amendment] by which "all persons born or naturalized in the United States, and subject to the jurisdiction thereof, are citizens of the United States and of the State wherein they reside;"; and on the [Fifteenth Amendment], which provides that "the right of citizens of the United States to vote shall not be denied or abridged by the United States or by any State on account of race, color, or previous condition of servitude." ...

> The decision ... depends upon the question whether the legal conclusion, that under ... the Fourteenth Amendment of the Constitution the plaintiff is a citizen of the United States, is supported by the facts alleged in the petition.... The plaintiff is an Indian, and was born in the United States, and has severed his tribal relation to the Indian tribes, and fully and completely surrendered himself to the jurisdiction of the United States, and still continues to be subject to the jurisdiction of the United States, and is a bona fide resident of the State of Nebraska and city of Omaha....

> Though the plaintiff alleges that he "had fully and completely surrendered himself to the jurisdiction of the United States," he does not allege that the United States accepted his surrender, or that he has ever been naturalized, or taxed, or in any way recognized or treated as a citizen, by the State or by the United States. Nor is it contended by his counsel that there is any statute or treaty that makes him a citizen.

> The question then is, whether an Indian, born a member of one of the Indian tribes within the United States, is, merely by reason of his birth within the United States, and of his afterwards voluntarily separating himself from his tribe and taking up his residency among white citizens, a citizen of the United States, within the meaning of the first section of the Fourteenth Amendment of the Constitution.

> Under the Constitution..., "Indians not taxed" were excluded from the persons according to whose numbers representatives and direct taxes were apportioned among the several States; and Congress had and exercised the power to regulate commerce with the Indian tribes, and the members thereof, whether within or without the boundaries of one of the States of the Union. The Indian tribes, being within the territorial limits of the United States, were not, strictly speaking,

foreign States; but they were alien nations, distinct political communities, with whom the United States might and habitually did deal ... either through treaties made by the President and Senate, or through acts of Congress in the ordinary forms of legislation. The members of those tribes owed immediate allegiance to their several tribes, and were not part of the people of the United States. They were in a dependent condition, a state of pupilage, resembling that of a ward to his guardian. Indians and their property, exempt from taxation by treaty or statute of the United States, could not be taxed by any State. General acts of Congress did not apply to Indians, unless so expressed as to clearly manifest an intention to include them....

The alien and dependent condition of the members of the Indian tribes could not be put off at their own will.... They were never deemed citizens of the United States, except under explicit provisions of treaty of statute to that effect, either declaring a certain tribe ... to be citizens, or authorizing individuals of particular tribes to become citizens on application to a court of the United States for naturalization....

The main object of the opening sentence of the Fourteenth Amendment was to settle the question ... and to put it beyond doubt that all persons, white or black, and whether formerly slaves or not, born or naturalized in the United States, and owing no allegiance to any alien power, should be citizens of the United States and of the State in which they reside....

This section contemplates two sources of citizenship, and two sources only: birth and naturalization.... Indians born within the territorial limits of the United States, members of, and owing immediate allegiance to, one of the Indian tribes ... although in a geographical sense born in the United States, are no more "born in the United States and subject to the jurisdiction thereof," within the meaning of the first section of the Fourteenth Amendment, than the children of subjects of any foreign government born within the domain of that government, or the children born within the United States of ambassadors or other public ministers of foreign nations.... Such Indians, then, not being citizens by birth, can only become citizens ... by being "naturalized in the United States," by or under some treaty or statute....

While the Amendment was pending before the legislatures of the several States, treaties containing provisions for the naturalization of members of Indian tribes as citizens of the United States were made ... with the Delawares, ... various tribes in Kansas, ... the Pottawatomies, and ... with the Sioux.... Since the ratification of the Fourteenth Amendment, Congress has passed several acts for naturalizing Indians of certain tribes, which would have been superfluous if they were, or might become without any action of the government, citizens of the United States....

The national legislation has tended ... towards the education and civilization of the Indians, and fitting them to be citizens. But the question whether any Indian tribes, or any members thereof, have become so far advanced in civilization that they should be let out of the state of pupilage, and admitted to the privileges and responsibilities of citizenship, is a question to be decided by the nation whose wards they are and whose citizens they seek to become, and not by each Indian for himself.... The plaintiff, not being a citizen ... has been deprived of no right secured by the Fifteenth Amendment, and cannot maintain this action. Judgment affirmed.

Justice Harlan wrote a dissent joined by Justice Woods.

> [Elk] was born within the territorial limits of the United States.... More than a year ... prior to his application to be registered as a voter in the city of Omaha, he had severed all relations with his tribe, and ... fully and completely surrendered himself to the jurisdiction of the United States ... in his act of becoming ... a bona fide resident of the State of Nebraska. When he applied in 1880 to be registered as a voter, he possessed ... the qualifications of age and residence in State, county, and ward, required for electors by the Constitution and laws of that State. It is likewise conceded that he was entitled to be so registered, if ... he was a citizen of the United States....
>
> While denying that national citizenship, as conferred by [the Fourteenth] amendment, necessarily depends upon the inquiry whether the person claiming it is taxed in the State of his residence, ... we submit that the petition does sufficiently show that the plaintiff is taxed, that is, belongs to the class which, by the laws of Nebraska, are subject to taxation. By the Constitution and laws of Nebraska all real and personal property in that State are subject to assessment and taxation. Every person of full age and sound mind, being a resident thereof, is required to list all of his personal property for taxation.... Of these provisions upon the subject of taxation this court will take judicial notice.... The plaintiff has become so far incorporated with the mass of the people of Nebraska that, being ... a citizen and resident thereof, he constitutes a part of her militia.... He may, being no longer a member of an Indian tribe, sue and be sued in her courts. And he is counted in every apportionment of representation in the legislature....
>
> At the adoption of the Constitution there were, in many of the States, Indians, not members of any tribe, who constituted a part of the people for whose benefit the State governments were established. This is apparent from that clause of article 1, section 3, which requires, in the apportionment of representatives and direct taxes among the several States..., the exclusion of "Indians not taxed." This implies that there were, at that time, in the United States, Indians who were taxed.... Indians not taxed were those who held tribal relations, and, therefore, were not subject to the authority of any State, and were subject only to the authority of the United States under the power conferred upon Congress in reference to Indian tribes....
>
> There is nothing in the history of the adoption of the Fourteenth Amendment which ... justifies the conclusion that only those Indians are included in its grant of national citizenship who were, at the time of their birth, subject to the complete jurisdiction of the United States.... Born, therefore, in the territory under the dominion, and within the jurisdictional limits of the United States, plaintiff has acquired, as was his undoubted right, a residence in one of the States, with her consent, and is subject to taxation and to all other burdens imposed by her upon residents of every race. If he did not acquire national citizenship on abandoning his tribe and becoming, by residence in one of the States, subject to the complete jurisdiction of the United States, then the Fourteenth Amendment has wholly failed to accomplish, in respect of the Indian race, what, we think, was intended by it; and there is still in this country a despised and rejected class of persons, with no nationality whatever, who, born in our territory, owing no allegiance to any foreign power, and subject, as residents of the States, to all the burdens of government, are yet not members of any political community nor entitled to any of the rights, privileges, or immunities of citizens of the United States.

Even as it was challenging the ability of tribes and nations to govern themselves, and without granting citizenship to the Native Americans affected by its action, the federal government was asserting expanded authority on Native Americans away from tribal lands as well. Here again what is most important about the ruling in the *United States v. Nice* case is the manner in which the Court explained congressional authority over Native Americans on or off reservations.

United States v. Nice

241 U.S. 591 (1916)

INTRODUCTION: The facts of this case are explained in the opinion below. Note the scope of the authority the Court found in Congress, not only for regulation on native lands but elsewhere, and not only for regulation of tribal activity as a whole but individual activity as well.

Justice Van Devanter wrote the opinion for the Court.

This is a prosecution for selling ... intoxicating liquors to an Indian in violation of the act of January 30, 1897.... According to the indictment, the sale was made August 9, 1914, in Tripp County, South Dakota; the Indian was a member of the Sioux tribe, a ward of the United States and under the charge of an Indian agent; and the United States was still holding in trust the title to land which had been allotted to him April 29, 1902.... [T]he indictment [was] dismissed on the ground that the statute is [as applied here] in excess of the power of Congress....

By the act of 1897 the sale of intoxicating liquor to "any Indian to whom allotment of land has been made while the title to the same shall be held in trust by the Government, or to any Indian a ward of the Government under charge of any Indian superintendent or agent, or any Indian, including mixed bloods, over whom the Government, through its departments, exercises guardianship," is denounced as a punishable offense. The allotment to this Indian was made from the tribal lands in the Rosebud Reservation, in South Dakota....

[T]he questions [are]...: What was the status of this Indian at the time the whiskey and other liquors are alleged to have been sold to him? And is it within the power of Congress to regulate or prohibit the sale of intoxicating liquor to Indians in his situation?

The power of Congress to regulate or prohibit traffic in intoxicating liquor with tribal Indians within a State, whether upon or off an Indian reservation, is well settled.... Its source is two-fold; first, the clause in the Constitution expressly investing Congress with authority "to regulate commerce ... with the Indian tribes", and, second, the dependent relation of such tribes to the United States. Of the first it was said in *United States v. Holliday*, "Commerce with the Indian tribes, means commerce with the individuals composing those tribes.... The locality of the traffic can have nothing to do with the power. The right to exercise it in reference to any Indian tribe, or any person who is a member of such tribe, is absolute, without reference to the locality of the traffic, or the locality of the tribe, or of a member of the tribe with whom it is carried on.... This power residing in Congress, that body is necessarily supreme in its exercise." And of the second it was said in *United States v. Kagama*: "These Indian tribes are the wards of the Nation. They are communities dependent on the United States.... From their very weakness and helplessness, so largely due to the course of dealing of the Federal Government with them and the treaties in which it has been promised, there arises the duty of protection, and with it the power." ...

Of course, when the Indians are prepared to exercise the privileges and bear the burdens of one *sui juris*,[49] the tribal relation may be dissolved and the national guardianship brought to an end, but it rests with Congress to determine when and how this shall be done, and whether the emancipation shall at first be complete or only partial.[50] Citizenship is not incompatible with tribal existence or continued guardianship, and so may be conferred without completely emancipating the Indians or placing them beyond the reach of congressional regulations adopted for their protection....

The ultimate question then is, whether §6 of the act of 1887 ... was intended to dissolve the tribal relation and terminate the national guardianship upon the making of the allotments and the issue of the trust patents, without waiting for the expiration of the trust period. According to a familiar rule, legislation affecting the Indians is to be construed in their interest and a purpose to make a radical departure is not lightly to be inferred. Upon examining the whole act, ... it seems certain that the dissolution of the tribal relation was in contemplation; but that this was not to occur when the allotments were completed and the trust patents issued is made very plain....

The Constitution invested Congress with power to regulate traffic in intoxicating liquors with the Indian tribes, meaning with the individuals composing them. That was a continuing power of which Congress could not divest itself. It could be exerted at any time and in various forms during the continuance of the tribal relation, and clearly there was no purpose to lay any obstacle in the way of enforcing the existing congressional regulations upon this subject or of adopting and enforcing new ones if deemed advisable....

As, therefore, these allottees remain tribal Indians and under national guardianship, the power of Congress to regulate or prohibit the sale of intoxicating liquor to them, as is done by the act of 1897, is not debatable. Judgment reversed.

Efforts to Address some of the Losses Suffered by Native Americans: The Trust Doctrine and Federal Policy Change

It was not until 1924 that Congress passed the Indian Citizenship Act, finally providing Native Americans with the right to vote.[51] It was a decade later that the Indian Reorganization Act sought to undo some of the damage done by the Dawes Act.[52]

John Collier had been a severe critic of Indian policy as carried out by the Hoover administration and before that led a successful campaign to defeat legislation proposed by New Mexico Senator Howard O. Bursum, at the instigation of Harding's Interior Secretary Albert B. Fall, that would have effectively destroyed the Pueblo peoples of the Southwest.[53] Collier was named Indian Commissioner by President Franklin Delano Roosevelt in 1933. He led an effort to develop a new law that would completely reorganize the way the federal government dealt with Native Americans and to correct some of the injustices and abuses that had become part of U.S. Indian policy.[54] This Act did not restore the land that had been lost to sale during the years of the Dawes Act, but it did address restoration of reservation governance and tribal control over remaining lands. However, it also left the Secretary of the Interior with a great deal of authority over natural resources on reservation land and a variety of other provisions that continued to be matters of controversy for years.

There was one other key concept that required clarification. The Trust Doctrine was intended to address the sense that although the federal government had often spoken of its obligations to Native Americans, owing to the fact that so much had been taken from tribal people and that their traditional ways of life had been so dramatically altered, the actions that followed did not evidence a clear commitment. This produced a call for clear and direct statement of the Trust Doctrine under which the United States accepts a special responsibility for the support of and assistance to Native Americans. The Supreme Court addressed that in *Seminole Nation v. United States.*

Seminole Nation v. United States

316 U.S. 286 (1942)

INTRODUCTION: Members of the Seminole Nation lost confidence in their leaders. The federal Indian agent was not making the payments due to individual Seminoles but to the leaders, as they demanded. Those frustrated by the leaders' behavior had considerable evidence that federal funds were either not being paid appropriately or were being used by corrupt officials, who were not carrying out their obligations to get the money to those who should have received it. That information was made available to federal authorities, but payments continued and the federal government did not address the charges. Indeed, two different U.S. Indian agents reported these problems to no effect. New Seminole leaders brought suit for the funds they claimed were not properly managed because the federal government failed in its fiduciary responsibilities to the people of the Seminole Nation.[55]

Justice Murphy wrote the opinion for the Court.

> This suit ... is now before us for the second time....[56] The Court of Claims [has] disallowed three items in their entirety, allowed one in full, and allowed the remaining two in part....
>
> I. We are of opinion that petitioner, the Seminole Nation, is entitled to no additional allowance on Items One, Three, and Four of its claim.
> II. With respect to Items Two and Five we are of opinion that the cause must be remanded to the Court of Claims for further material findings of fact.
>
> Item Two. This is a claim for $154,551.28 based on one of the provisions of Article VIII of the Treaty of 1856, namely, the Government's promise to establish a $500,000 trust fund ... the annual interest therefrom ... to be paid over to the members of the Seminole Nation per capita as an annuity. The findings of the Court of Claims show that, although Congress appropriated $25,000 annually for each of the fiscal years in controversy..., the Government fail[ed] to make direct per capita disbursements of a portion of the funds appropriated in 1867–1874, 1876, and 1879, the underpayments for those years totalling $92,051.28, and that one-half the appropriation in 1907 and the entire appropriation in 1908 and 1909 ($62,500 in all), instead of being paid directly to the individual Seminoles, was paid to the United States Indian Agent for the Seminole Nation....
>
> The Government contends that, since those payments were made at the request of the tribal council..., the tribe is not now entitled to receive payment a second time; and that, despite the fact that the Treaty of 1856 provided that the payments were to be made per capita for the benefit of each individual Indian, these payments at the request of the General Council discharged the treaty obligation, because the agreement was one between the United States and the Seminole Nation and not one between the United States and the individual members of the tribe.
>
> The argument for the Government, however sound it might otherwise be, fails to recognize the impact of certain equitable considerations and the effect of the fiduciary duty of the Government to its Indian wards....

It is a well established principle of equity that a third party who pays money to a fiduciary for the benefit of the beneficiary, with knowledge that the fiduciary intends to misappropriate the money or otherwise be false to his trust, is a participant in the breach of trust and liable therefor to the beneficiary.... The Seminole General Council, requesting the annuities originally intended for the benefit of the individual members of the tribe, stood in a fiduciary capacity to them. Consequently, the payments at the request of the Council did not discharge the treaty obligation if the Government, for this purpose the officials administering Indian affairs and disbursing Indian moneys, actually knew that the Council was defrauding the members of the Seminole Nation.

Furthermore, this Court has recognized the distinctive obligation of trust incumbent upon the Government in its dealings with these dependent and sometimes exploited people.... In carrying out its treaty obligations with the Indian tribes, the Government is something more than a mere contracting party. Under a humane and self imposed policy which has found expression in many acts of Congress and numerous decisions of this Court, it has charged itself with moral obligations of the highest responsibility and trust. Its conduct, as disclosed in the acts of those who represent it in dealings with the Indians, should therefore be judged by the most exacting fiduciary standards.[57] Payment of funds at the request of a tribal council which, to the knowledge of the Government officers charged with ... the disbursement of funds to satisfy treaty obligations, was composed of representatives faithless to their own people ... would be a clear breach of the Government's fiduciary obligation.[58] If those were the circumstances ... the Seminole Nation is entitled to recover that sum, minus such amounts as were actually expended for the benefit of the Nation by the Council.... [Reversed and remanded.][59]

Conclusion

Civil rights is a subject that has taken on a special perspective for Native Americans due to their long and devastating experience at the hands of Europeans who came to what is now the United States. Although leaders early in the history of the new nation recognized that Native American tribes and nations were sophisticated political communities and entered into a series of treaties with them, it quickly became clear that greed for the lands where native people lived and the resources on those lands would lead to an insatiable demand to take the lands and to displace the people who came to be described as Indians.

That historical experience included what could only be described as a genocide in which large numbers of Native Americans were killed outright and thousands more were literally driven across the continent far from their ancestral homelands to reservations in places that were foreign to their way of life and, in many cases, clearly inadequate to support a healthy community. Even then the pressure did not stop as those who described themselves as friends of the Native American people concluded that they could only survive if their culture was killed, leaving the man, but not the Indian. To this end, policies were enacted to divide up reservation land, to seek to make rugged individualists of people for whom tribal loyalties and cooperation had been central, to ship their children off to boarding schools at which they were to be pressed to lose their Native American language and identity, and even to use legal doctrines that significantly eroded the concept of tribal sovereignty.

Native Americans were regulated on and off the reservations by federal law and yet denied the right to vote, even if they did assimilate, as some chose to do. The Supreme Court recognized broad powers in the Congress under the so-called Indian Commerce Clause to reach virtually any aspect of Native American life, anywhere, and anytime.

It was not until 1924 that all Native Americans were given the right to vote and a decade later before any major effort was made to reform the policies under which the federal government dealt with tribes and Native American nations. The Supreme Court ultimately affirmed the so-called trust doctrine under which the United States accepted special responsibilities in its dealings with Native American people and tribes.

However, Native American civil rights were far from fully established and, in important respects, suffered a series of setbacks in the decades after *Brown v. Board of Education*, the point from which most Americans today mark a stream of civil rights improvement. It is to these later challenges that Chapter 6 turns.

I. Issues for Policy and Practice

A. It is well-established since as far back as the early nineteenth century, and certainly since the *Kansas Indians* opinion, that the relationship of tribal governments is a sovereign-to-sovereign relationship with the United States government and not with the states. However, given the nature of contemporary intergovernmental relations, tribal governments do sometimes engage formally with state agencies or local governments in intergovernmental agreements or other proceedings. Thus, the Confederated Tribes of the Warm Springs, the Confederated Tribes of the Umatilla, the Yakima, and the Nez Perce filed with the Oregon Department of State Lands opposing a permit by an energy company and the Port of Morrow to fill areas along the Columbia River to create a facility called the Coyote Island Terminal to offload coal from trains coming out of Wyoming and other areas to barges for transport down river intended for loading on ships that will take the coal abroad. The tribal governments asserted that there would be impacts on tribal fishing rights. The state agency denied the permit, but there is, at the time of this writing, an administrative appeals process in progress. The tribal governments have sought and received approval to participate as parties in that process. What policies are in place that explain the intergovernmental relationships among tribal governments, state agencies, and local governments? What issues have they raised in practice?

B. The trust doctrine, discussed in *Seminole Nation v. United States*, is a critically important foundation for the relationship of tribal people and their governments and the federal government. How is that concept protected in federal policy across the range of government agencies? In some cases, there is merely an obligation to consider and consult. Is that sufficient? What does it mean in practice?

C. Is there a basis in policy or administrative practice for ensuring that non-native people understand and respect the rights of Native Americans and tribal governments?

D. In terms of management of agencies or local governments, there are some programs that seek to train employees about civil rights, however limited those courses may be, but are the rights of Native Americans included in a meaningful way in those programs? Except for those states or local governments that have large tribal governments nearby, are those relationships even considered part of the concept of civil rights?

E. Do employees who are likely to deal with Native Americans, whether in areas near tribal lands or in cities far away from reservations, have any understanding of the real experience of Native Americans over the nation's history, as compared with the way the media often portray that experience? If so, what can management do to ensure their experience is integrated into the training of public service personnel?

II. Discussion Questions

A. What are contemporary Native Americans to make of the idea that their tribes or nations are considered by the U.S. Supreme Court to be domestic dependent nations that stand in relationship to the federal government as a ward does to his (or her) guardian? What does that language say about the status of Native Americans? What attitude does it convey?

B. If, as Chief Justice Marshall conceded, it was very likely that the Cherokee and other tribal governments did not understand the technical language of the treaties they signed, both because of the problem of English language translation and also because of the technical legal language of the Anglo-American body of property law, how can the Supreme Court confidently conclude that the tribes knowingly and willingly ceded their possessions or land or anything else in those treaties? And if the Court could not be sure they understood, were the lands and other resources taken in those treaties from the native peoples lawfully acquired?

C. Even if they did understand the terms of the treaty, is an agreement entered into under the circumstances the tribal governments faced a valid contract?

D. While reading the *Elk* opinion, think back about the earlier cases that concluded that Native American tribes were not foreign nations. If they are "domestic, dependent nations," and not subject to naturalization processes, where did that leave Elk and others in terms of their citizenship?

E. Native Americans did not become citizens until 1924. If you were Native American, and given this history as well as the status of your tribe or nation, how would you understand your own citizenship and your relationship to others in the community?

F. Would it make a difference if you lived on a reservation as compared to in other communities, like most Native Americans do?

G. *United States v. Nice* has never been overruled. Would its interpretation of the power of Congress under the so-called Indian Commerce Clause allow it to pass legislation today targeted at Native Americans living away from reservations in the nation's major cities?

H. As the cases in the chapter make clear, the U.S. government has frequently not honored the terms of its agreements with tribal governments and yet it has held those tribes or nations to the terms of agreements. If you were (or are) Native American and given the long history of broken promises by the U.S. government, how would you approach interactions with the federal government, the states, or local governments?

Notes

1 *Tee-Hit-Ton Indians v. United States*, 348 U.S. 272 (1955).
2 Id., at 289.
3 Id., at 281.
4 *Cherokee Nation v. Georgia*, 30 U.S. 1, 33 (1831).
5 See David Wallace Adams, *Education for Extinction: American Indians and the Boarding School Experience 1875–1928* (Lawrence, KS: Kansas University Press, 1995).
6 Indian General Allotment Act (Dawes Act), ch. 119, 24, Stat. 388 (1887).
7 David E. Wilkins, *American Indian Politics and the American Political System* (Lanham, MD: Rowman & Littlefield Publishers, Inc., 2002), p. 41.
8 79 Fed. Reg. 4748 (2014). See U.S. Department of the Interior, Bureau Of Indian Affairs, Tribal Directory, www.bia.gov/WhoWeAre/BIA/OIS/TribalGovernmentServices/TribalDirectory/, May 4, 2014.
9 Four bands of the Abenaki were recognized by the State of Vermont in 2011 and 2012, respectively, but federal recognition was formally denied in 2007 and the Abenaki remain unrecognized by the Bureau of Indian Affairs. See U.S. Department of the Interior, Bureau of Indian Affairs, "Summary Under the Criteria and Evidence for Final Determination against Federal Acknowledgement of the St. Francis/Sololi Band of the Abenakis of Vermont," June 22, 2007, http://ago.vermont.gov/assets/files/Civil/Final%20Determination%20-%20Abenaki.pdf, October 30, 2015.
10 P.L. 73–383, 48 Stat. 986 (1934).
11 Wilkins, *American Indian Politics*, p. 38.
12 See e.g., Gabriel S. Galanda and Ryan D. Dreveskracht, "Curing the Tribal Disenrollment Epidemic: In Search of a Remedy," *Arizona Law Review* 57 (No. 2 2015): 383–474; Greg Rubio, "Reclaiming

Indian Civil Rights: The Application of International Human Rights Law to Tribal Disenrollment Actions," *Oregon Review of International Law* 11 (No. 1 2009): 1–41.

13 Cynthia Hunt, Lumbee Indian, quoted in Keneisha M. Green, "Who's Who: Exploring the Discrepancy Between the Methods of Defining African Americans and Native Americans," *American Indian Law Review* 31 (No. 1 2006/2007): 93–110 at 94.

14 Wilkins, *American Indian Politics*, p. 34.

15 U.S. Census Bureau, 2010 Census CPH-T-6 American Indian and Alaska Native Tribes in the United States and Puerto Rico: 2010, www.census.gov/population/www/cen2010/cph-t/t-6tables/TABLE%20(1).xlsx, August 21, 2014.

16 National Congress of American Indians,"The State of the Indian Nations Today," January 31, 2003, www.ncai.org/resources/ncai-publications/2003_soin_speech.pdf, April 21, 2016.

17 U.S. Department of Health and Human Services, Agency for Healthcare Research and Quality, *National Healthcare Disparities Report 2007* (Rockville, MD: U.S. Dept. of Health and Human Services, 2008), p. 148, www.ahrq.gov/qual/nhdr07/nhdr07.pdf, October 31, 2015.

18 U.S. Department of Health and Human Services, Agency for Healthcare Research and Quality, *National Healthcare Disparities Report 2013* (Rockville, MD: U.S. Dept. of Health and Human Services, 2014), p. 253, www.ahrq.gov/sites/default/files/wysiwyg/research/findings/nhqrdr/nhdr13/2013nhdr.pdf, October 31, 2015.

19 George Washington, Proclamation of December 12, 1792, Originally published in Freneau's National Gazette of December 15, 1792, The Avalon Project, http://avalon.law.yale.edu/18th_century/gwproc07.asp.

20 NOTE: Of course, as the chapter explains later, it was not until 1924 that the United States recognized Native Americans as citizens.

21 NOTE: An injunction is a court order prohibiting illegal action or mandating action to enforce legal rights.

22 NOTE: The dissents of Justices Johnson and Baldwin are omitted.

23 NOTE: Marshall concedes that apart from the boundary question, the Native Americans might not have understood the language of the treaty. He wrote: "When, in fact, they are ceding lands to the United States, and describing the extent of their cession, it may very well be supposed that they might not understand the term employed, as indicating that, instead of granting, they were receiving lands." This is an early discussion of what was to be an ongoing problem of treaties that were likely not fully understood by Native Americans due both to translation difficulties but also to the use of technical legal knowledge familiar only to those trained in Anglo-American law.

24 NOTE: The separate opinions of Justices Baldwin and McLean are omitted.

25 See Cherokee Nation, "A Brief History of the Trail of Tears," www.cherokee.org/AboutTheNation/History/TrailofTears/ABriefHistoryoftheTrailofTears.aspx, November 1, 2015; Trail of Tears Association, "History of the Trail," http://nationaltota.org/history-trail, November 1, 2015.

26 *McCulloch v. Maryland*, 17 U.S. (4 Wheat.) 316, 431 (1819).

27 31 U.S. 515 (1832), at 543.

28 NOTE: The Court is quoting here from *Worcester v. Georgia*, 31 U.S. 515 (1832), at 581.

29 The term "genocide" is defined by the United Nations genocide convention treaty. "Article II: In the present Convention, genocide means any of the following acts committed with intent to destroy, in whole or in part, a national, ethnical, racial or religious group, as such:
    (a) Killing members of the group;
    (b) Causing serious bodily or mental harm to members of the group;
    (c) Deliberately inflicting on the group conditions of life calculated to bring about its physical destruction in whole or in part;
    (d) Imposing measures intended to prevent births within the group;
    (e) Forcibly transferring children of the group to another group."
Convention on the Prevention of the Crime of Genocide, Adopted by the General Assembly of the United Nations, 9 December 1948, 78 UNTS 278, 280 (1951).

30 12 Stat. 392 (1862).

31 Dee Brown, *Bury My Heart at Wounded Knee* (New York: Holt, Rinehart, Winston, 1970), p. 33.

32 Id.

33 Marc Simmons, *New Mexico: An Interpretive History* (Albuquerque, NM: University of New Mexico Press, 1988), pp. 151–152.

34 See generally Brown, *Bury My Heart at Wounded Knee.*

35 National Park Service, "Sand Creek Massacre," www.nps.gov/sand/historyculture/index.htm, October 23, 2014.

36 See Brown, *Bury My Heart at Wounded Knee*, Ch. 7.

37 Rutherford B. Hayes, First Annual Message, December 3, 1877, Online by Gerhard Peters and John T. Woolley, The American Presidency Project, www.presidency.ucsb.edu/ws/index.php?pid=29518, November 1, 2015.

38 "In the White Man's Image," became the title of an excellent documentary produced for the American Experience series by PBS. See also Adams, *Education for Extinction.*

39 24 Stat. 388 (1887).

40 See Carol Locust, "Wounding the Spirit: Discrimination and Traditional American Indian Belief Systems," *Harvard Educational Review* 58 (No. 3 1989): 315–330; "Walking in Two Worlds: Native Americans and the VR System," *American Rehabilitation* 22 (No. 2 1996): 2–12; "The Impact of Differing Belief Systems between Native Americans and their Rehabilitation Service Providers," *Rehabilitation Education* 9 (No. 2 1995): 205–215.

41 Colin Nicholas, "A Common Struggle: Regaining Control," in *Indigenous Peoples of Asia: Many People, One Struggle*, Colin Nicholas and Raajen Singh, eds. (Bangkok: Asia Indigenous Peoples Pact, 1996), p. 1.

42 See e.g. Judge Christopher G. Weeramantry, "Sustainable Development: An Ancient Concept Recently Revived," Speech, UNEP Judges Symposium on Law and Sustainable Development, Johannesburg, www.unep.org/delc/Portals/119/publications/Speeches/Weeramantry.pdf, November 1, 2015; Lloyd Burton, *Worship and Wilderness: Culture, Religion, and Law in Public Lands Management* (Madison, WI: University of Wisconsin Press, 2002).

43 Act of March 8, 1871, Ch. 120, 16 Stat. 566.

44 24 Stat. 388 (1887).

45 The *Cobell v. Kempthorne*, 532 F. Supp. 2d 37 (DCDC 2008) case will be discussed in detail in Chapter 7.

46 The Supreme Court has said as late as 1978 that: "The sovereignty that the Indian tribes retain is of a unique and limited character. It exists only at the sufferance of Congress and is subject to complete defeasance. But until Congress acts, the tribes retain their existing sovereign powers. In sum, Indian tribes still possess those aspects of sovereignty not withdrawn by treaty or statute, or by implication as a necessary result of their dependent status." *United States v. Wheeler*, 435 U.S. 313, 323 (1978).

47 See *Plains Commerce Bank v. Long Family Land & Cattle*, 554 U.S. 316 (2008), presented in detail in Chapter 6.

48 Quoted in Adams, *Education for Extinction*, p. 53.

49 NOTE: This term refers to a person who is independent and has all the options and rights of a citizen.

50 NOTE: Congress made Native Americans citizens in 1924 but it did not then or later limit its own authority with respect to individual native people in the manner described above.

51 43 Stat. 253 (1924).

52 48 Stat. 984 (1934).

53 See Simmons, *New Mexico*, pp. 171–176.

54 See Vine Deloria, *The Indian Reorganization Act* (Norman, OK: University of Oklahoma Press, 2002), p. vii.

55 NOTE: A fiduciary obligation is a relationship of special trust which imposes extraordinary responsibilities on the one who is the fiduciary.

56 NOTE: Their original suit was rejected for lack of jurisdiction by the U.S. Supreme Court, but Congress changed the statute and the suit was re-filed in the U.S. Court of Claims.

57 NOTE: Note here that the Court states flatly that the federal government under the trust doctrine has a fiduciary relationship such that its actions with respect to tribes and Native American people must be judged according to "the most exacting fiduciary standards." Compare this to the *United States v. Jicarilla Apache Nation*, 131 S. Ct. 2313 (2011) case presented in Chapter 7.

58 "As was well said by Chief Judge (later Mr. Justice) Cardozo in *Meinhard v. Salmon*, 249 N. Y. 458, 464, 164 N. E. 545, 546: 'Many forms of conduct permissible in a workaday world for those acting

at arm's length, are forbidden to those bound by fiduciary ties. A trustee is held to something stricter than the morals of the market place. Not honesty alone, but the punctilio of an honor the most sensitive, is then the standard of behavior. As to this there has developed a tradition that is unbending and inveterate.... Only thus has the level of conduct for fiduciaries been kept at a level higher than that trodden by the crowd.'"

59 Justice Jackson dissented [without opinion].

References

Adams, David Wallace. *Education for Extinction: American Indians and the Boarding School Experience 1875–1928*. Lawrence, KS: Kansas University Press, 1995.

Brown, Dee. *Bury My Heart at Wounded Knee.* New York: Holt, Rinehart, Winston, 1970.

Burton, Lloyd. *Worship and Wilderness: Culture, Religion, and Law in Public Lands Management*. Madison, WI: University of Wisconsin Press, 2002.

Deloria, Vine. *The Indian Reorganization Act*. Norman, OK: University of Oklahoma Press, 2002.

Galanda, Gabriel S. and Ryan D. Dreveskracht. "Curing the Tribal Disenrollment Epidemic: In Search of a Remedy," *Arizona Law Review* 57 (No. 2 2015): 383–474.

Green, Keneisha M. "Who's Who: Exploring the Discrepancy Between the Methods of Defining African Americans and Native Americans," *American Indian Law Review* 31 (No. 1 2006/2007): 93–110.

Hayes, Rutherford B. First Annual Message, December 3, 1877, Online by Gerhard Peters and John T. Woolley, The American Presidency Project, www.presidency.ucsb.edu/ws/index.php?pid=29518, November 1, 2015.

Locust, Carol. "The Impact of Differing Belief Systems between Native Americans and their Rehabilitation Service Providers," *Rehabilitation Education* 9 (No. 2 1995): 205–215.

———. "Walking in Two Worlds: Native Americans and the VR System," *American Rehabilitation* 22 (No. 2 1996): 2–12.

———. "Wounding the Spirit: Discrimination and Traditional American Indian Belief Systems," *Harvard Educational Review* 58 (No. 3 1989): 315–330.

National Congress of American Indians. "The State of the Indian Nations Today," January 31, 2003, www.ncai.org/resources/ncai-publications/2003_soin_speech.pdf, April 21, 2016.

———. "Through the Eyes of Our Children: Hope for a Restored Native America", January 31, 2008, www.ncai.org/resources/ncai-publications/2008_SOIN_Speech.pdf, April 21, 2016.

Nicholas, Colin. "A Common Struggle: Regaining Control," in *Indigenous Peoples of Asia: Many People, One Struggle*, Colin Nicholas and Raajen Singh, eds. (Bangkok: Asia Indigenous Peoples Pact, 1996).

Rubio, Greg. "Reclaiming Indian Civil Rights: The Application of International Human Rights Law to Tribal Disenrollment Actions," *Oregon Review of International Law* 11 (No. 1 2009): 1–41.

Simmons, Marc. *New Mexico: An Interpretive History*. Albuquerque, NM: University of New Mexico Press, 1988.

U.S. Department of Health and Human Services, Agency for Healthcare Research and Quality. *National Healthcare Disparities Report 2007*. Rockville, MD: U.S. Dept. of Health and Human Services, 2008, www.ahrq.gov/qual/nhdr07/nhdr07.pdf, November 21, 2008.

———. *National Healthcare Disparities Report 2013*. Rockville, MD: U.S. Dept. of Health and Human Services, 2014. www.ahrq.gov/sites/default/files/wysiwyg/research/findings/nhqrdr/nhdr13/2013nhdr.pdf, October 31, 2015.

U.S. Department of the Interior, Bureau of Indian Affairs. "Summary under the Criteria and Evidence for Final Determination against Federal Acknowledgement of the St. Francis/Sololi Band of the Abenakis of Vermont," June 22, 2007, http://ago.vermont.gov/assets/files/Civil/Final%20Determination%20-%20Abenaki.pdf, October 30, 2015.

Weeramantry, Christopher G. "Sustainable Development: An Ancient Concept Recently Revived," Speech, UNEP Judges Symposium on Law and Sustainable Development, www.unep.org/delc/Portals/119/publications/Speeches/Weeramantry.pdf, November 1, 2015.

Wilkins, David E. *American Indian Politics and the American Political System*. Lanham, MD: Rowman & Littlefield Publishers, 2002.

6   Continuing Challenges for Native Americans
Problems Persist Despite Civil Rights
Gains for Others

While most Americans were celebrating the Supreme Court's ruling in *Brown v. Board of Education*, the Court decided another case in a manner that highlighted the fact that Native Americans still faced humiliating discrimination. The same Supreme Court that had decided *Brown* appeared unwilling to confront the Native American needs for equality and dignity. This case, concerning a Native American military veteran, was but one of a number of rulings that have come during what many Americans would consider the modern era of civil rights policy. Yet it has been an era that has left Native Americans far short of serious civil rights progress in many important respects. This chapter considers these rulings in several different civil rights policy domains. The message that emerges is of an agenda far from accomplished.

Serious Challenges for Native Americans at a Moment of what Looked Like Civil Rights Progress

Sergeant First Class John Raymond Rice was killed in battle in Korea. Sergeant Rice was also a veteran of World War II. His decorations included the Bronze Star and the Purple Heart with Oak Leaf Cluster.[1] He was also a member of the Winnebago tribe whose Native American name translated to English was "Walking in the Blue Sky."[2] Sadly, Sergeant Rice would be the subject of conflict even as his body returned home and through a strange path to a final resting place. Indeed, there are hardly words to describe the indignity that his family and he suffered during that journey.

Rice had been born on the reservation and was sent away to the Indian boarding school at Genoa, Nebraska, although he returned home and finished high school there. Life on the reservation was hard for him and he left to enlist in the Army. He returned after the war, but later reenlisted for service in Korea where he was killed.

When Rice died at age 36, he left his wife, Evelyn Rice, and three children ages 4, 2, and 1. He was buried in a Catholic ceremony at a cemetery in Sioux City, Iowa, where his wife had purchased plots. However, during the ceremony someone from the cemetery saw that there were a number of Native Americans present and learned from the funeral director that Rice was Winnebago. After the ceremony, the cemetery workers removed his coffin from the grave and put it into a shed. Representatives of the cemetery went to the family home. They informed Mrs. Rice that only Caucasians could be buried in the cemetery and that she could either remove his body or sign a statement saying that he was not an Indian. Her daughter later remembered: " 'I hid under the kitchen table,' she said. 'They talked to my mother, and I remember her crying. I remember my grandmother being furious and my grandfather coming up to my mother and putting his arm around her.' "[3]

The next day President Harry Truman read of the incident and was outraged. This is the same president who had been fighting military officers to ensure that his order desegregating the military was implemented. His biographer, David McCulloch, tells what happened:

> Outraged, Truman picked up the phone. Within minutes, by telephone and telegram, it was arranged that Sergeant Rice would be buried in Arlington National Cemetery with full military honors and that an Air Force plane was on the way to bring his widow and three children to Washington. That, as President, was the least he could do.[4]

In a report on the fiftieth anniversary of his burial, Sioux City remembered and repudiated that terrible day in 1951. Mayor Martin Dougherty said: "There is nothing they could say then or that I can say now that will take away the memory of that day. His life tells us that the battle for freedom is not just fought across the ocean in some far away place."[5] However, the events in Iowa were not the end of the sad story. It continued in the Supreme Court of the United States.

Rice v. Sioux City Memorial Park Cemetery

349 U.S. 70 (1955)

INTRODUCTION: Sergeant Rice was a Winnebago whose wife, who was not a Native American, had purchased cemetery plots in the Sioux City Memorial Park Cemetery. After the grave-side services had been held, the cemetery refused to bury Mr. Rice in the plot because burial there was limited to "members of the Caucasian race." Mrs. Rice sued for breach of contract, but the cemetery defended, using the racial exclusion clause in its contract. She responded that the clause was void because it discriminated in violation of the Fourteenth Amendment. The state courts rejected her suit and the U.S. Supreme Court affirmed on a tie vote.[6]

Mrs. Rice's attorneys sought a rehearing in the Supreme Court and the Court granted certiorari.[7] While that second process was pending, Iowa enacted legislation prohibiting discrimination in cemeteries and authorizing suit, but specifically excluding pending cases, the only one of which was hers. (Justice Harlan, who had only recently joined the Court, did not participate in the rehearing.)

In reading the opinion, consider how its language, as well as its substance and conclusion, must have sounded to the Rice family. It is framed in technical language about whether the Court should decide the case, but the message is also plain that no justice would be done then or later for Sergeant Rice or his family, as the dissenters made clear.

Justice Frankfurter wrote the opinion for the Court.

> This is an action for damages brought by plaintiff ... to compensate her for mental suffering claimed to flow from defendant cemetery's refusal to bury her husband, a Winnebago Indian.... Plaintiff founded her action ... on breach of a contract ... of sale [for] the burial lot [which] provided that "burial privileges accrue only to members of the Caucasian race."

> Plaintiff asserted that this provision was void under both the Iowa and the United States Constitutions and that recognition of its validity would violate the Fourteenth Amendment.... The Iowa court ruled that the clause was not void but was unenforceable as a violation of the Constitutions and public policy of Iowa and the United States. Nevertheless, it held that the clause "may be relied upon as

a defense" and that "the action of a State or Federal court in permitting a defendant to stand upon the terms of its contract ... would not constitute state or federal
action" contrary to the Fifth and Fourteenth Amendments....

Only if a State deprives any person or denies him enforcement of a right guaranteed by the Fourteenth Amendment can its protection be invoked. Such a claim
involves the threshold problem whether ... what Iowa, through its courts, did
amounted to "state action." ... Were this hurdle cleared, the ultimate substantive
question, whether ... the action complained of was condemned by the Fourteenth
Amendment, would in turn present no easy constitutional problem.

The case was argued here and the stark fact is that the Court was evenly divided....
[A] petition was filed for a rehearing before a full Court. In our consideration of
this petition our attention has now been focused upon an Iowa statute enacted
since the commencement of this litigation.... This Iowa statute bars the ultimate
question presented in this case from again arising in that State. In light of this
fact ... we have considered anew whether this case is one in which "there are special and important reasons" for granting the writ of certiorari, as required by
Supreme Court Rule 19.... [C]ertiorari was granted, [but w]e were unmindful at
the time of Iowa's corrective legislation and of its implications....

As a result of this Act, in any other case arising under similar circumstances not
only would the statutory penalties be applicable, but also, under Iowa law, one in
petitioner's position would be entitled to recover damages in a civil action based
on a violation of the statute.... Had the statute been properly brought to our
attention..., the case would have assumed such an isolated significance that it
would hardly have been brought here in the first instance.... On the one hand, we
should hesitate to pass judgment on Iowa for unconstitutional action, were such
to be found, when it has already rectified any possible error.... [The] writ of certiorari is dismissed as improvidently granted.

Justice Black wrote a dissent joined by the Chief Justice and Justice Douglas.

We think that only very unusual circumstances can justify dismissal of cases on
the ground that certiorari was improvidently granted. Our objections to such dis-
missals are stronger when, as here, a case has already been argued and decided by
the Court. We do not agree that the circumstances relied on by the Court justify
this dismissal. We granted certiorari because serious questions were raised concerning a denial of the equal protection of the laws guaranteed by the Fourteenth
Amendment. Those questions remain undecided. The Court dismisses the case
because the Iowa Legislature has provided that every person in Iowa except one
who has already filed a suit can prosecute claims like this. Apparently this law
leaves everyone in Iowa free to vindicate this kind of right except the petitioner.
This raises a new question of denial of equal protection of the laws equally as
grave as those which prompted us to take this case originally. We cannot agree
that this dismissal is justified merely because this petitioner is the only one whose
rights may have been unconstitutionally denied.

What had happened in the Court at the time was that Justice Robert Jackson had died before the
conference that considered the first argument in the case. The Court tied 4–4, with Frankfurter
leading the justices who opposed overturning the Iowa court decision. Justice John Marshall
Harlan was newly appointed and did not participate when the case was reargued. Justice Clark
switched sides on the second consideration, providing Frankfurter with a 5–3 vote.

Justices Black and Douglas were outraged by the decision, particularly because Iowa had changed the statute, but excluded only Mrs. Rice from the new protections of the law. They could not understand how the Court could escape finding that action by itself to be a violation of the equal protection clause of the Fourteenth Amendment.

It would be reassuring to write off the tragic events of the *Rice* case to the times and to assume that surely nothing even remotely like that could happen in the contemporary context. It would be comforting, but it would be wrong. Although the circumstances were different, there is too much similarity in a far more recent event than will allow for any complacency with regard to attitudes toward Native Americans—even heroic ones.

The first American servicewoman to be killed in action in Iraq was Private First Class Lori Piestewa, a member of the Hopi tribe from Arizona. She died in an ambush outside Nasiriyah. In April 2003 Arizona Governor Janet Napolitano, addressing thousands gathered for a memorial service for Private Piestewa, promised to ask the legislature to name a mountain peak and a freeway in Phoenix in Piestewa's honor. Piestewa's parents and her two children were present for that event. In addition to honoring Piestawa, the governor's action would get rid of the names "squaw peak" and "squaw peak freeway," which had been a continuing offense to Native Americans. Hopi Tribal Chairman Wayne Taylor told reporters that "This would be a positive, healing way to end this long debate about what is a derogatory word for Native Americans."[8]

Almost immediately, the chairman of the Arizona State Board on Geographic and Historic Names, Tim J. Norton, denounced the governor's plan. First, he asserted that there was a mandatory five-year waiting period after the death of the person involved before any geographic site could be named in his or her honor. " 'Wholesale name changes are an atrocity,' Norton told the *Arizona Republic*... Even after the waiting period,' he added, 'I'm not sure that renaming something in Phoenix in honor of a woman who lived hundreds of miles away will meet our criteria.'"[9] Norton also indicated that he opposed the exercise of the board's authority to make exceptions to the waiting period because decisions to make such name changes should not be emotional matters.

Governor Napolitano told reporters that the board had the authority to make exceptions to the existing rules and ought to do so. " 'That's why they're called exceptions, and Lori Piestewa was an exception,' Napolitano said. 'To say he would never do it and it would be an "atrocity" ... indicated to me he was not prepared to carry out his duty.'"[10] Republican state legislators responded by criticizing the governor's actions, accusing her of "politicizing" Piestawa's death and of attempting to exercise improper influence over the board.[11]

To some, the argument about waiting periods rang hollow. Any limitations on whether an honoree had died or about waiting periods had not produced objections when Washington National Airport was renamed Reagan National Airport in 1998 while the former president was very much alive.[12]

Ultimately, one member of the state board resigned and Mr. Norton did not attend the meeting on April 17, 2003 at which the board voted 5–1 to approve the renaming of the peak and supported the name change for the highway.[13] The Arizona Department of Transportation later renamed the freeway.

Return for a moment to the time of *Brown v. Board of Education*. In this same period when the Court rejected Mrs. Rice's suit, the Court issued its opinion in the *Tee-Hit-Ton Indians* case described briefly at the beginning of Chapter 5. Like some of the other cases in the development of civil rights, the rhetoric and attitude displayed toward Native Americans in this opinion are as damaging as the conclusions the Court reached. In reading this opinion, it is useful to compare what is said here about control of land and the doctrine of discovery with the discussion in *Worcester v. Georgia*.

Tee-Hit-Ton Indians v. United States

348 U.S. 272 (1955)

INTRODUCTION: The facts of this case are provided in the opinion.
Justice Reed wrote the opinion for the Court.

This case rests upon a claim under the Fifth Amendment by petitioner, an identifiable group of American Indians ... residing in Alaska, for compensation for a taking by the United States of certain timber from Alaskan lands allegedly belonging to the group. The area claimed is said to contain over 350,000 acres of land and 150 square miles of water. The Tee-Hit-Tons, a clan of the Tlingit Tribe, brought this suit in the Court of Claims.... Payment, if it can be compelled, must be based upon a constitutional right of the Indians to recover....

The Alaskan area in which petitioner claims a compensable interest is located near and within the exterior lines of the Tongass National Forest. By Joint Resolution of August 8, 1947 ... the Secretary of Agriculture was authorized to contract for the sale of national forest timber located within this National Forest "notwithstanding any claim of possessory rights." ... The Secretary of Agriculture, ... pursuant to this authority contracted for sale to a private company of all merchantable timber in the area claimed by petitioner. This is the sale of timber which petitioner alleges constitutes a compensable taking by the United States of a portion of its proprietary interest in the land.

The problem presented is the nature of the petitioner's interest in the land, if any.... It is petitioner's contention that its tribal predecessors have continually claimed, occupied and used the land from time immemorial; that when Russia took Alaska, the Tlingits had a well-developed social order which included a concept of property ownership; that Russia while it possessed Alaska in no manner interfered with their claim to the land; that Congress has by subsequent acts confirmed and recognized petitioner's right to occupy the land permanently and therefore the sale of the timber off such lands constitutes a taking ... of its asserted rights in the area.

The Government denies that petitioner has any compensable interest. It asserts that the Tee-Hit-Tons' property interest, if any, is merely that of the right to the use of the land at the Government's will; that Congress has never recognized any legal interest of petitioner in the land and ... no compensation is due the petitioner for any taking by the United States.

I. Recognition.... Where the Congress by treaty or other agreement has declared that thereafter Indians were to hold the lands permanently, compensation must be paid for subsequent taking. The petitioner contends that Congress has sufficiently "recognized" its possessory rights in the land in question so as to make its interest compensable. Petitioner points specifically to two statutes to sustain this contention. The first is §8 of the Organic Act for Alaska of May 17, 1884.... The second is §27 of the Act of June 6, 1900, ... provid[ing] for a civil government for Alaska....

We have carefully examined these statutes and the pertinent legislative history and find nothing to indicate any intention by Congress to grant to the Indians any permanent rights in the lands of Alaska occupied by them by permission of Congress. Rather, it clearly appears that what was intended was merely to retain the status quo until further congressional or judicial action was taken. There is no particular form for congressional recognition of Indian right of permanent occupancy. It may be established in a variety of ways but there must be the definite intention by congressional action ... to accord legal rights, not merely permissive occupation....

This policy of Congress toward the Alaskan Indian lands was maintained and reflected ... in the Joint Resolution of 1947 under which the timber contracts were made.

II. Indian Title.... It is well settled that in all the States of the Union the tribes who inhabited the lands of the States held claim to such lands after the coming of the white man, under what is sometimes termed original Indian title or permission from the whites to occupy. That description means mere possession not specifically recognized as ownership by Congress. After conquest they were permitted to occupy portions of territory over which they had previously exercised "sovereignty," as we use that term. This is not a property right but amounts to a right of occupancy which the sovereign grants and protects against intrusion by third parties but which right of occupancy may be terminated and such lands fully disposed of by the sovereign itself without any legally enforceable obligation to compensate the Indians.

This position of the Indian has long been rationalized by the legal theory that discovery and conquest gave the conquerors sovereignty over and ownership of the lands thus obtained....

No case in this Court has ever held that taking of Indian title or use by Congress required compensation. The American people have compassion for the descendants of those Indians who were deprived of their homes and hunting grounds by the drive of civilization. They seek to have the Indians share the benefits of our society as citizens of this Nation. Generous provision has been willingly made to allow tribes to recover for wrongs, as a matter of grace, not because of legal liability....

The [Chief] learned the alleged boundaries of the Tee-Hit-Ton area from hunting and fishing with his uncle after his return from Carlisle Indian School about 1904. From the knowledge so obtained, he outlined in red on the map ... the territory claimed by the Tee-Hit-Tons.... On it he marked six places to show the Indians' use of the land: (1) his great uncle was buried here, (2) a town, (3) his uncle's house, (4) a town, (5) his mother's house, (6) smokehouse. He also pointed out the uses of this tract for fishing salmon and for hunting beaver, deer and mink....

In addition to this verbal testimony, exhibits were introduced by both sides as to the land use. These exhibits are secondary authorities but they bear out the general proposition that land claims among the Tlingits, and likewise of their smaller group, the Tee-Hit-Tons, was wholly tribal.... There was recognition of tribal rights to hunt and fish on certain general areas, with claims to that effect carved on totem poles. From all that was presented, the Court of Claims concluded, and we agree, that the Tee-Hit-Tons were in a hunting and fishing stage of civilization, with shelters fitted to their environment, and claims to rights to use identified territory for these activities as well as the gathering of wild products of the earth. We think this evidence introduced by both sides confirms the Court of Claims' conclusion that the petitioner's use of its lands was like the use of the nomadic tribes of the States [*sic*] Indians.

The line of cases adjudicating Indian rights on American soil leads to the conclusion that Indian occupancy, not specifically recognized as ownership by action authorized by Congress, may be extinguished by the Government without compensation. Every American schoolboy knows that the savage tribes of this continent were deprived of their ancestral ranges by force and that, even when the Indians ceded millions of acres by treaty in return for blankets, food and trinkets, it was not a sale but the conquerors' will that deprived them of their land....

In the light of the history of Indian relations in this Nation, no other course would meet the problem of the growth of the United States except to make congressional contributions for Indian lands rather than to subject the Government to an obligation to pay the value when taken with interest to the date of payment. Our conclusion does not uphold harshness as against tenderness toward the Indians, but it leaves with Congress, where it belongs, the policy of Indian gratuities for the termination of Indian occupancy of Government-owned land rather than making compensation for its value a rigid constitutional principle.... [A]ffirmed.

Justice Douglas wrote a dissent joined by the Chief Justice and Justice Frankfurter.

The first Organic Act for Alaska became a law on May 17, 1884.... It contained a provision ... which reads as follows: "the Indians or other persons in said district shall not be disturbed in the possession of any lands actually in their use or occupation or now claimed by them but the terms under which such persons may acquire title to such lands is reserved for future legislation by Congress: And provided further, That parties who have located mines or mineral privileges therein under the laws of the United States applicable to the public domain, or who have occupied and improved or exercised acts of ownership over such claims, shall not be disturbed therein, but shall be allowed to perfect their title to such claims by payment as aforesaid."

Section 12 provided for a report upon "the condition of the Indians residing in said Territory, what lands, if any, should be reserved for their use, what provision shall be made for their education[,] what rights by occupation of settlers should be recognized," etc....

The conclusion seems clear that Congress in the 1884 Act recognized the claims of these Indians to their Alaskan lands. What those lands were was not known. Where they were located, what were their metes and bounds, were also unknown.... But all agreed that the Indians were to keep them, wherever they lay. It must be remembered that the Congress was legislating about a Territory concerning which little was known. No report was available showing the nature and extent of any claims to the land. No Indian was present to point out his tribe's domain. Therefore, Congress did the humane thing of saving to the Indians all rights claimed; it let them keep what they had prior to the new Act. The future course of action was made clear—conflicting claims would be reconciled and the Indian lands would be put into reservations.

That purpose is wholly at war with the one now attributed to the Congress of reserving for some future day the question whether the Indians were to have any rights to the land.... The case should be remanded for those findings.... [T]he Court of Claims is empowered to entertain the complaint by reason of the recognition afforded the Indian rights by the Act of 1884.

If it appeared from these two cases that Native Americans were not seeing significant progress in civil rights by the 1950s, the right to vote and the Indian Reorganization Act (IRA) 1934 notwithstanding, the situation was, in some respects, even worse than it seemed. Recall the factors shaping the environment. The attitudes of the nineteenth century that determined that Indians needed to be assimilated and their unique culture destroyed did not disappear. Not only that, but the United States had been through a reactionary period with respect to race and ethnicity that began in the post-World War I period and intensified in the 1920s. There were two dynamics that continued for decades to plague the quest for civil rights for Native Americans. First, there was outright racism and a connection to the eugenics movement that continued to picture Native Americans in extremely negative ways. Second, there was a new set of policies aimed at ending tribal sovereignty, Native American culture and identity, and disbursing Indians from their tribal homelands, and even from the reservations to which they had been forced decades before.

While many Americans would prefer to regard the eugenics movement as a horror from Hitler's Germany, the fact is that the United States was home to a virulent eugenics movement that became particularly active in the 1920s (see Chapter 12). Sadly, the movement found support even in some of the nation's universities. Thus the Abenaki people of Vermont cannot forget that the Department of Zoology at the University of Vermont was home to some active adherents of the eugenics movement. Not only that, but their ideas found their way into policy with the passage of eugenics codes, like the statute adopted in the 1920s in Vermont that defined Abenaki families as unfit parents to raise children. Because the bands moved around the area at different times of the year to take advantage of the conditions and food supplies, they were labeled gypsies (another frequently and to this day victimized group in society) and the state decided that such people could not provide a nurturing home for children. Those children were subject to be removed by the state and placed for immediate adoption. These policies and the eugenics advocates who pressed for them are explained in Nancy L. Gallagher's *Breeding Better Vermonters*.[14]

At the national level, efforts were underway to effectively destroy tribes and nations and to disburse their members to cities around the nation even in the twentieth century. There were two policies in particular that implemented that goal. Congress adopted House Concurrent Resolution 108 in 1953, which effectively sought to end recognition of tribal governments and undo the trust relationship that had existed between the U.S. government and tribal peoples. Although it was couched in language that supposedly meant inclusion and an end to discrimination, the truth was far different.

House Concurrent Resolution 108[15]

Whereas it is the policy of Congress, as rapidly as possible, to make the Indians within the territorial limits of the United States subject to the same laws and entitled to the same privileges and responsibilities as are applicable to other citizens of the United States, to end their status as wards of the United States, and to grant them all of the rights and prerogatives pertaining to American citizenship; and

Whereas the Indians within the territorial limits of the United States should assume their full responsibilities as American citizens:

Now, therefore, be it Resolved by the House of Representatives (the Senate concurring),

That it is declared to be the sense of Congress that, at the earliest possible time, all of the Indian tribes and the individual members thereof located within the States of California, Florida, New York, and Texas, and all of the following named Indian tribes and individual members thereof, should be freed from Federal supervision and control and from all disabilities and limitations specially applicable to Indians: The

Flathead Tribe of Montana, the Klamath Tribe of Oregon, the Menominee Tribe of Wisconsin, the Potowatamie Tribe of Kansas and Nebraska, and those members of the Chippewa Tribe who are on the Turtle Mountain Reservation, North Dakota. It is further declared to be the sense of Congress that, upon the release of such tribes and individual members thereof from such disabilities and limitations, all offices of the Bureau of Indian Affairs in the States of California, Florida, New York, and Texas and all other offices of the Bureau of Indian Affairs whose primary purpose was to serve any Indian tribe or individual Indian freed from Federal supervision should be abolished. It is further declared to be the sense of Congress that the Secretary of the Interior should examine all existing legislation dealing with such Indians, and treaties between the Government of the United States and each such tribe, and report to Congress at the earliest practicable date, but not later than January 1, 1954, his recommendations for such legislation as, in his judgment, may be necessary to accomplish the purposes of this resolution.

This was the beginning of termination of recognition of tribal governments that extended to many tribes by the time the process was complete and continued until the 1970s. Also during this period, Congress indicated its intention in Public Law 83–280, adopted in August 1953, to convey criminal and civil legal jurisdiction over Native Americans to the states.[16]

In addition, the federal government launched what was called a voluntary relocation effort, in which it attempted to get Native Americans to leave reservations and move to the nation's major urban areas. In 1954 it was renamed the Employment Assistance Program. Field Offices were opened by the Bureau of Indian Affairs (BIA) in such cities as Chicago, Cleveland, Los Angeles, Oakland, Denver, and San Jose that were to provide assistance to those relocating.[17]

It was not until 1970 that the federal government confronted this set of policies directly. It comes as a surprise to some that it was none other than Richard Nixon who moved to overturn the de-recognition and dispersal policies. In 1970 he sent a special message to Congress calling for formal repeal of those policies.

President Richard Nixon
Special Message to the Congress on Indian Affairs

July 8, 1970

To the Congress of the United States:
The first Americans—the Indians—are the most deprived and most isolated minority group in our nation. On virtually every scale of measurement—employment, income, education, health—the condition of the Indian people ranks at the bottom.

This condition is the heritage of centuries of injustice. From the time of their first contact with European settlers, the American Indians have been oppressed and brutalized, deprived of their ancestral lands and denied the opportunity to control their own destiny. Even the Federal programs which are intended to meet their needs have frequently proven to be ineffective and demeaning.

But the story of the Indian in America is something more than the record of the white man's frequent aggression, broken agreements, intermittent remorse and prolonged failure. It is a record also of endurance, of survival, of adaptation and creativity in the face of overwhelming obstacles. It is a record of enormous contributions to this country—to its art and culture, to its strength and spirit, to its sense of history and its sense of purpose.

It is long past time that the Indian policies of the Federal government began to recognize and build upon the capacities and insights of the Indian people. Both as a matter of justice and as a matter of enlightened social policy, we must begin to act on the basis of what the Indians themselves have long been telling us. The time has come to break decisively with the past and to create the conditions for a new era in which the Indian future is determined by Indian acts and Indian decisions.

Self-Determination without Termination

The first and most basic question that must be answered with respect to Indian policy concerns the historic and legal relationship between the Federal government and Indian communities. In the past, this relationship has oscillated between two equally harsh and unacceptable extremes.

On the one hand, it has ... been the stated policy objective of both the Executive and Legislative branches of the Federal government eventually to terminate the trusteeship relationship between the Federal government and the Indian people. As recently as August of 1953, in House Concurrent Resolution 108, the Congress declared that termination was the long-range goal of its Indian policies. This would mean that Indian tribes would eventually lose any special standing they had under Federal law: the tax exempt status of their lands would be discontinued; Federal responsibility for their economic and social well-being would be repudiated; and the tribes themselves would be effectively dismantled. Tribal property would be divided among individual members who would then be assimilated into the society at large.

This policy of forced termination is wrong, in my judgment, for a number of reasons.

First, the premises on which it rests are wrong. Termination implies that the Federal government has taken on a trusteeship responsibility for Indian communities as an act of generosity toward a disadvantaged people and that it can therefore discontinue this responsibility on a unilateral basis whenever it sees fit. But the unique status of Indian tribes does not rest on any premise such as this. The special relationship between Indians and the Federal government is the result instead of solemn obligations which have been entered into by the United States Government. Down through the years, through written treaties and through formal and informal agreements, our government has made specific commitments to the Indian people. For their part, the Indians have often surrendered claims to vast tracts of land and have accepted life on government reservations. In exchange, the government has agreed to provide community services such as health, education and public safety, services which would presumably allow Indian communities to enjoy a standard of living comparable to that of other Americans.... To terminate this relationship would be no more appropriate than to terminate the citizenship rights of any other American.

The second reason for rejecting forced termination is that the practical results have been clearly harmful in the few instances in which termination actually has been tried. The removal of Federal trusteeship responsibility has produced considerable disorientation among the affected Indians and has left them unable to relate to a myriad of Federal, State and local assistance efforts. Their economic and social condition has often been worse after termination than it was before....

In short, the fear of one extreme policy, forced termination, has often worked to produce the opposite extreme: excessive dependence on the Federal government. In many cases this dependence is so great that the Indian community is almost entirely run by outsiders who are responsible and responsive to Federal officials in Washington, D.C., rather than to the communities they are supposed to be serving. This is the second of the two harsh approaches which have long plagued our Indian policies. Of the Department of the Interior's programs directly serving Indians, for example, only 1.5 percent are presently under Indian control. Only 2.4 percent of HEW's Indian health programs are run by Indians....

I believe that both of these policy extremes are wrong. Federal termination errs in one direction, Federal paternalism errs in the other.... Self-determination among the Indian people can and must be encouraged without the threat of eventual termination....

This, then, must be the goal of any new national policy toward the Indian people: to strengthen the Indian's sense of autonomy without threatening his sense of community. We must assure the Indian that he can assume control of his own life without being separated involuntarily from the tribal group. And we must make it clear that Indians can become independent of Federal control without being cut off from Federal concern and Federal support. My specific recommendations to the Congress are designed to carry out this policy.

1. Rejecting Termination

Because termination is morally and legally unacceptable, because it produces bad practical results, and because the mere threat of termination tends to discourage greater self-sufficiency among Indian groups, I am asking the Congress to pass a new Concurrent Resolution which would expressly renounce, repudiate and repeal the termination policy as expressed in House Concurrent Resolution 108 of the 83rd Congress. This resolution would explicitly affirm the integrity and right to continued existence of all Indian tribes and Alaska native governments, recognizing that cultural pluralism is a source of national strength. It would assure these groups that the United States Government would continue to carry out its treaty and trusteeship obligations to them as long as the groups themselves believed that such a policy was necessary or desirable. It would guarantee that whenever Indian groups decided to assume control or responsibility for government service programs, they could do so and still receive adequate Federal financial support. In short, such a resolution would reaffirm for the Legislative branch—as I hereby affirm for the Executive branch—that the historic relationship between the Federal government and the Indian communities cannot be abridged without the consent of the Indians.

2. The Right to Control and Operate Federal Programs

Even as we reject the goal of forced termination, so must we reject the suffocating pattern of paternalism.... In my judgment, it should be up to the Indian tribe to determine whether it is willing and able to assume administrative responsibility for a service program which is presently administered by a Federal agency. To this end, I am proposing legislation which would empower a tribe or a group of tribes or any other Indian community to take over the control or operation of Federally-funded and administered programs in the Department of the Interior and the Department of Health, Education and Welfare whenever the tribal council or comparable community governing group voted to do so....

3. Restoring the Sacred Lands near Blue Lake

No government policy toward Indians can be fully effective unless there is a relationship of trust and confidence between the Federal government and the Indian people.... [W]e can contribute significantly to such a relationship by responding to just grievances which are especially important to the Indian people.

One such grievance concerns the sacred Indian lands at and near Blue Lake in New Mexico.... In 1906, however, the United States Government appropriated these lands for the creation of a national forest ... "without compensation."

For 64 years, the Taos Pueblo has been trying to regain possession of this sacred lake and watershed area in order to preserve it in its natural condition and limit its non-Indian use.... I therefore take this opportunity wholeheartedly to endorse legislation which would restore 48,000 acres of sacred land to the Taos Pueblo people, with the statutory promise that they would be able to use these lands for traditional purposes and that except for such uses the lands would remain forever wild.

4. Indian Education

One of the saddest aspects of Indian life in the United States is the low quality of Indian education.... Consistent with our policy that the Indian community should have the right to take over the control and operation of federally funded programs, we believe every Indian community wishing to do so should be able to control its own Indian schools....

5. Economic Development Legislation

Economic deprivation is among the most serious of Indian problems. Unemployment among Indians is ten times the national average; the unemployment rate runs as high as 80 percent on some of the poorest reservations. Eighty percent of reservation Indians have an income which falls below the poverty line; the average annual income for such families is only $1,500.... [I]t is critically important that the Federal government support and encourage efforts which help Indians develop their own economic infrastructure. To that end, I am proposing the "Indian Financing Act of 1970."

This act would do two things:

1. It would broaden the existing Revolving Loan Fund, which loans money for Indian economic development projects. I am asking that the authorization for this fund be increased from approximately $25 million to $75 million.
2. It would provide additional incentives in the form of loan guarantees, loan insurance and interest subsidies to encourage private lenders to loan more money for Indian economic projects. An aggregate amount of $200 million would be authorized for loan guarantee and loan insurance purposes.

I also urge that legislation be enacted which would permit any tribe which chooses to do so to enter into leases of its land for up to 99 years. Indian people now own over 50 million acres of land that are held in trust by the Federal government.... Long-term leasing is preferable to selling such property since it enables tribes to preserve the trust ownership of their reservation homelands. But existing law limits the length of time for which many tribes can enter into such leases....

6. More Money for Indian Health

Despite significant improvements in the past decade and a half, the health of Indian people still lags 20 to 25 years behind that of the general population.... This Administration is determined that the health status of the first Americans will be improved. In order to initiate expanded efforts in this area, I will request the allocation of an additional $10 million for Indian health programs for the current fiscal year. This strengthened Federal effort will enable us to address ourselves more effectively to those health problems which are particularly important to the Indian community....

7. Helping Urban Indians

Our new census will probably show that a larger proportion of America's Indians are living off the reservation than ever before in our history. Some authorities even estimate that more Indians are living in cities and towns than are remaining on the reservation. Of those American Indians who are now dwelling in urban areas, approximately three-fourths are living in poverty.

The Bureau of Indian Affairs is organized to serve the 462,000 reservation Indians. The BIA's responsibility does not extend to Indians who have left the reservation, but this point is not always clearly understood....

In a joint effort, the Office of Economic Opportunity and the Department of Health, Education and Welfare will expand support to a total of seven urban Indian centers in major cities which will act as links between existing Federal, State and local service programs and the urban Indians. The Departments of Labor, Housing and Urban Development and Commerce have pledged to cooperate with such experimental urban centers and the Bureau of Indian Affairs has expressed its willingness to contract with these centers for the performance of relocation services which assist reservation Indians in their transition to urban employment....

8. Indian Trust Counsel Authority

The United States Government acts as a legal trustee for the land and water rights of American Indians. These rights are often of critical economic importance to the Indian people; frequently they are also the subject of extensive legal dispute. In many of these legal confrontations, the Federal government is faced with an inherent conflict of interest....

In order to correct this situation, I am calling on the Congress to establish an Indian Trust Counsel Authority to assure independent legal representation for the Indians' natural resource rights. This Authority would be governed by a three-man board of directors, appointed by the President with the advice and consent of the Senate. At least two of the board members would be Indian. The chief legal officer of the Authority would be designated as the Indian Trust Counsel.

The Indian Trust Counsel Authority would be independent of the Departments of the Interior and Justice and would be expressly empowered to bring suit in the name of the United States in its trustee capacity. The United States would waive its sovereign immunity from suit in connection with litigation involving the Authority.

9. Assistant Secretary for Indian and Territorial Affairs

To help guide the implementation of a new national policy concerning American Indians, I am recommending to the Congress the establishment of a new position in the Department of the Interior-Assistant Secretary for Indian and Territorial Affairs....

The Indians of America need Federal assistance—this much has long been clear. What has not always been clear, however, is that the Federal government needs Indian energies and Indian leadership if its assistance is to be effective in improving the conditions of Indian life. It is a new and balanced relationship between the United States government and the first Americans that is at the heart of our approach to Indian problems. And that is why we now approach these problems with new confidence that they will successfully be overcome.

Modern Battles for Recognition of the Proper Boundaries in Tribal and U.S. Government Relations

If anyone thought that Nixon's forceful announcement of change was the beginning of the end of the struggle, they would be wrong. Indeed, since then the battle for self-determination and protection of tribal and individual rights has continued. For one thing, it took until the beginning of 1975 to enact the Indian Self-Determination and Educational Assistance

Act,[18] which provided the foundation for a number of the policy changes Nixon advocated. Beyond that, there would be continuing clashes over governance, sovereignty, and identity; issues of tribal justice; the effort to obtain the long-promised trust funds due to Native Americans; and the challenge of civil rights and Native American spirituality.

Who Governs? The Effort to Ensure Native American Self-Determination

One of the problems that President Nixon emphasized was the need to end the history of federal governance of Native American issues and concerns by those who were not Native Americans. This was not a new concern. Indeed the effort to change that situation reached back at least to the days of the Indian Reorganization Act. However, by the 1970s there was a growing backlash against affirmative efforts to include those who had historically been excluded from public positions and programs. Bureau of Indian Affairs hiring practices provided one of the targets of that backlash. The Supreme Court opinion that follows is important not only for what it said about the specific policy, but because of its discussion of the governance issue.

Morton v. Mancari

417 U.S. 535 (1974)

INTRODUCTION: The Indian Reorganization Act of 1934 mandated an employment preference in the Bureau of Indian Affairs to Indians. The BIA Commissioner later added a preference in promotions. Non-Indian employees charged that this policy violated the due process clause of the Fifth Amendment and Title VII of the Civil Rights Act of 1964 as amended by the Equal Employment Opportunity Act of 1972. A New Mexico federal district court found that the 1972 Act eliminated the preference by implication if not directly.

Justice Blackmun wrote the opinion for the unanimous Court.

> The federal policy of according some hiring preference to Indians in the Indian service dates at least as far back as 1834. Since that time, Congress repeatedly has enacted various preferences of the general type here at issue. The purpose of these preferences, as variously expressed in the legislative history, has been to give Indians a greater participation in their own self-government; to further the Government's trust obligation toward the Indian tribes; and to reduce the negative effect of having non-Indians administer matters that affect Indian tribal life....

> The preference directly at issue here was enacted as an important part of the sweeping Indian Reorganization Act of 1934. The overriding purpose of that particular Act was to establish machinery whereby Indian tribes would be able to assume a greater degree of self-government.... Congress was seeking to modify the then-existing situation whereby the primarily non-Indian-staffed BIA had plenary control ... over the lives and destinies of the federally recognized Indian tribes.... The solution ultimately adopted was to strengthen tribal government while continuing the active role of the BIA, with the understanding that the Bureau would be more responsive to the interests of the people it was created to serve....

> One of the primary means by which self-government would be fostered and the Bureau made more responsive was to increase the participation of tribal Indians in the BIA operations. In order to achieve this end, it was recognized that some kind of preference and exemption from otherwise prevailing civil service requirements was necessary....

Congress was well aware that the proposed preference would result in employment disadvantages within the BIA for non-Indians. Not only was this displacement unavoidable if room were to be made for Indians, but it was explicitly determined that gradual replacement of non-Indians with Indians within the Bureau was a desirable feature of the entire program for self-government. Since 1934, the BIA has implemented the preference with a fair degree of success. The percentage of Indians employed in the Bureau rose from 34% in 1934 to 57% in 1972. This reversed the former downward trend, and was due, clearly, to the presence of the 1934 Act. The Commissioner's extension of the preference in 1972 to promotions within the BIA was designed to bring more Indians into positions of responsibility and, in that regard, appears to be a logical extension of the congressional intent....

III. It is against this background that we encounter the first issue in the present case: whether the Indian preference was repealed by the Equal Employment Opportunity Act of 1972. Title VII of the Civil Rights Act of 1964 ... was the first major piece of federal legislation prohibiting discrimination in private employment on the basis of "race, color, religion, sex, or national origin." ... (a) Significantly, §§701(b) and 703(I) of that Act explicitly exempted from its coverage the preferential employment of Indians by Indian tribes or by industries located on or near Indian reservations.... This exemption reveals a clear congressional recognition, within the framework of Title VII, of the unique legal status of tribal and reservation-based activities....

... [T]he District Court held, that since the 1972 Act proscribed racial discrimination in Government employment, the Act necessarily, albeit *sub silentio*,[19] repealed the provision of the 1934 Act that called for the preference in the BIA of one racial group, Indians, over non-Indians.

We disagree. For several reasons we conclude that Congress did not intend to repeal the Indian preference and that the District Court erred in holding that it was repealed. First: There are ... affirmative provisions in the 1964 Act excluding coverage of tribal employment and of preferential treatment by a business or enterprise on or near a reservation.... These 1964 exemptions as to private employment indicate Congress' recognition of the longstanding federal policy of providing a unique legal status to Indians in matters concerning tribal or "on or near" reservation employment. The exemptions reveal a clear congressional sentiment that an Indian preference in the narrow context of tribal or reservation-related employment did not constitute racial discrimination of the type otherwise proscribed....

Second: Three months after Congress passed the 1972 amendments, it enacted two new Indian preference laws. These were part of the Education Amendments of 1972.... The new laws explicitly require that Indians be given preference in Government programs for training teachers of Indian children....

Third: Indian preferences, for many years, have been treated as exceptions to Executive Orders forbidding Government employment discrimination. The 1972 extension of the Civil Rights Act to Government employment is in large part merely a codification of prior anti-discrimination Executive Orders that had proved ineffective because of inadequate enforcement machinery....

Fourth: Appellees encounter head-on the " 'cardinal rule ... that repeals by implication are not favored.' ... The intention of the legislature to repeal 'must be clear and manifest.' " In light of the factors indicating no repeal, we simply cannot conclude that Congress consciously abandoned its policy of furthering Indian self-government when it passed the 1972 amendments.

We therefore hold that the District Court erred in ruling that the Indian preference was repealed by the 1972 Act.

IV. We still must decide whether, as the appellees contend, the preference constitutes invidious racial discrimination in violation of the Due Process Clause of the Fifth Amendment.... Resolution of the instant issue turns on the unique legal status of Indian tribes under federal law and upon the plenary power of Congress, based on a history of treaties and the assumption of a "guardian-ward" status, to legislate on behalf of federally recognized Indian tribes. The plenary power of Congress to deal with the special problems of Indians is drawn both explicitly and implicitly from the Constitution itself. Article I, §8, cl. 3, provides Congress with the power to "regulate Commerce ... with the Indian Tribes," and thus, to this extent, singles Indians out as a proper subject for separate legislation. Article II, §2, cl. 2, gives the President the power, by and with the advice and consent of the Senate, to make treaties.... The Court has described the origin and nature of the special relationship: "In the exercise of the war and treaty powers, the United States overcame the Indians and took possession of their lands, sometimes by force, leaving them an uneducated, helpless and dependent people, needing protection against the selfishness of others and their own improvidence. Of necessity, the United States assumed the duty of furnishing that protection, and with it the authority to do all that was required to perform that obligation and to prepare the Indians to take their place as independent, qualified members of the modern body politic." ...

Literally every piece of legislation dealing with Indian tribes and reservations ... single out for special treatment a constituency of tribal Indians living on or near reservations. If these laws, derived from historical relationships and explicitly designed to help only Indians, were deemed invidious racial discrimination, an entire Title of the United States Code ... would be effectively erased and the solemn commitment of the Government toward the Indians would be jeopardized....

As discussed above, Congress in 1934 determined that proper fulfillment of its trust required turning over to the Indians a greater control of their own destinies. The overly paternalistic approach of prior years had proved both exploitative and destructive of Indian interests.... [T]his preference does not constitute "racial discrimination." Indeed, it is not even a "racial" preference. Rather, it is an employment criterion reasonably designed to further the cause of Indian self-government and to make the BIA more responsive to the needs of its constituent groups. It is directed to participation by the governed in the governing agency. The preference is similar in kind to the constitutional requirement that a United States Senator, when elected, be "an Inhabitant of that State for which he shall be chosen," Art. I, §3, cl. 3, or that a member of a city council reside within the city governed by the council. Congress has sought only to enable the BIA to draw more heavily from among the constituent group in staffing its projects, all of which, either directly or indirectly, affect the lives of tribal Indians. The preference, as applied, is granted to Indians not as a discrete racial group, but, rather, as members of quasi-sovereign tribal entities whose lives and activities are governed by the BIA in a unique fashion.... Furthermore, the preference applies only to employment in the Indian service.... Here, the preference is reasonably and directly related to a legitimate, nonracially based goal....

On numerous occasions this Court specifically has upheld legislation that singles out Indians for particular and special treatment.... As long as the special treatment can be tied rationally to the fulfillment of Congress' unique obligation toward the Indians, such legislative judgments will not be disturbed. Here, where the preference is reasonable and rationally designed to further Indian self-government, we cannot say that Congress' classification violates due process. The judgment of the District Court is reversed and ... remanded.

Although the Court's explanation of the role of self-governance in decisions on who governs Native Americans seemed relatively clear after the *Mancari* ruling, the situation turned out not to be so clear for all native peoples. Thus, in 2000 the Court took a dramatically different position in a case concerning Native Hawaiians, even to the point of rejecting the idea that Native Hawaiians were to be treated like other Native Americans. That was true notwithstanding the Court's—and the Congress'—recognition of the conquest of the Hawaiian islands and toppling of its indigenous government by the U.S. government.

Rice v. Cayetano

528 U.S. 495 (2000)

INTRODUCTION: This opinion is relatively complex in part because it is another of those cases that is important not only because of its legal holding, but also because of the way it describes the authority over these native peoples taken by force and maintained in an unusual status, even for Native Americans, over such a long period. In addition, it provides a stark contrast in approach, and in substantive legal conclusions, from the *Morton v. Mancari* ruling. The facts of the case are summarized in the opinion.

Justice Kennedy wrote the opinion for the Court.

A citizen of Hawaii comes before us claiming that an explicit, race-based voting qualification has barred him from voting in a statewide election [in violation of T]he Fifteenth Amendment to the Constitution of the United States....

The Hawaiian Constitution limits the right to vote for nine trustees chosen in a statewide election. The trustees compose the governing authority of a state agency known as the Office of Hawaiian Affairs ... [which] administers programs designed for the benefit of two subclasses of the Hawaiian citizenry. The smaller class comprises those designated as "native Hawaiians," defined by statute ... as descendants of not less than one-half part of the races inhabiting the Hawaiian Islands prior to 1778.... The second, larger class of persons benefited by OHA programs is "Hawaiians," defined to be ... those persons who are descendants of people inhabiting the Hawaiian Islands in 1778.... The right to vote for trustees is limited to "Hawaiians," the second, larger class of persons, which of course includes the smaller class of "native Hawaiians." ...

Petitioner Rice, a citizen of Hawaii and thus himself a Hawaiian in a well-accepted sense of the term, does not have the requisite ancestry even for the larger class, ... so he may not vote in the trustee election. The issue presented by this case is whether Rice may be so barred.... [W]e hold Hawaii's denial of petitioner's right to vote to be a clear violation of the Fifteenth Amendment.

I. ... The [first Hawaiian people] were Polynesians who voyaged from Tahiti and began to settle the islands around A. D. 750.... When England's Captain Cook made landfall in Hawaii on his expedition in 1778, the Hawaiian people had developed ... a cultural and political structure of their own.... The society was one ... with its own identity, its own cohesive forces, its own history.... In 1810, the islands were united as one kingdom under the leadership of ... Kamehameha I....

The 1800s are a story of increasing involvement of westerners in the economic and political affairs of the Kingdom. Rights to land became a principal concern, and there was unremitting pressure to allow non-Hawaiians to use and to own land.... Beginning in 1839 ... Kamehameha III approved a series of decrees and laws designed to accommodate demands for ownership and security of title.... Arrangements were made to confer freehold title in some lands to certain chiefs and other individuals. The King retained vast lands for himself, and directed that other extensive lands be held by the government, which by 1840 had adopted the first Constitution of the islands.... In 1850, foreigners ... were given the right of land ownership....

While these developments were unfolding, the United States and European powers made constant efforts ... to influence Hawaiian political and economic affairs.... Tensions intensified between an anti-Western, pro-native bloc in the government on the one hand and Western business interests and property owners on the other. The conflicts came to the fore in 1887. Westerners forced the resignation of the Prime Minister of the Kingdom of Hawaii and the adoption of a new Constitution, which, among other things, reduced the power of the monarchy and extended the right to vote to non-Hawaiians....

Tensions continued through 1893, when they again peaked [when a] group of professionals and businessmen, with the active assistance of John Stevens, the United States Minister to Hawaii, acting with United States armed forces, replaced the monarchy with a provisional government. That government sought annexation by the United States.... President Cleveland ... denounced the role of the American forces and called for restoration of the Hawaiian monarchy.... The Queen could not resume her former place, however, and, in 1894, the provisional government established the Republic of Hawaii....

In 1898, President McKinley signed a Joint Resolution ... to annex the Hawaiian Islands as territory of the United States [under which] the Republic of Hawaii ceded all former Crown, government, and public lands to the United States.... [R]evenues from the public lands were to be "used solely for the benefit of the inhabitants of the Hawaiian Islands for educational and other public purposes." ... Two years later the Hawaiian Organic Act established the Territory of Hawaii, asserted United States control over the ceded lands, and put those lands "in the possession, use, and control of the government of the Territory of Hawaii...."

In 1993, a century after the intervention by the Committee of Safety, the Congress of the United States reviewed this history, and in particular the role of Minister Stevens. Congress passed a Joint Resolution recounting the events in some detail and offering an apology to the native Hawaiian people....

[T]wo other important matters ... affected the demographics of Hawaii.... The first is the tragedy inflicted on the early Hawaiian people by the introduction of western diseases and infectious agents. As early as ... the rule of Kamehameha I, it was becoming apparent that the native population had serious vulnerability to diseases borne to the islands by settlers. High mortality figures were experienced in infancy and adulthood, even from common illnesses such as diarrhea, colds, and measles.... In the smallpox epidemic of 1853, thousands of lives were lost. By 1878, ... the native population had been reduced to about 47,500 people....

The other important feature of Hawaiian demographics to be noted is the immigration to the islands by people of many different races and cultures. Mostly in response to the demand of the sugar industry for arduous labor in the cane fields, successive immigration waves brought Chinese, Portuguese, Japanese, and Filipinos to Hawaii. Beginning with the immigration of 293 Chinese in 1852, the plantations alone drew to Hawaii, in one estimate, something over 400,000 men, women, and children over the next century.... Each of these ethnic and national groups has had its own history in Hawaii, its own struggles with societal and official discrimination, its own successes, and its own role in creating the present society of the islands....

II. Not long after the creation of the new Territory, ... Congress enacted the Hawaiian Homes Commission Act, which set aside about 200,000 acres of the ceded public lands and created a program of loans and long-term leases for the benefit of native Hawaiians.... The Act defined "native Hawaiians" to include "any descendant of not less than one-half part of the blood of the races inhabiting the Hawaiian Islands previous to 1778."

Hawaii was admitted as the fiftieth State of the Union in 1959. With admission, the new State agreed to adopt the Hawaiian Homes Commission Act as part of its own Constitution.... In addition, the United States granted Hawaii title to all public lands and public property within the boundaries of the State, save those which the Federal Government retained for its own use.... This grant included the 200,000 acres set aside under the Hawaiian Homes Commission Act and almost 1.2 million additional acres of land....

The legislation authorizing the grant recited that these lands, and the proceeds and income they generated, were to be held "as a public trust" to be "managed and disposed of...: "[1] for the support of the public schools and other public educational institutions, [2] for the betterment of the conditions of native Hawaiians, as defined in the Hawaiian Homes Commission Act, 1920, as amended, [3] for the development of farm and home ownership on as widespread a basis as possible[,] [4] for the making of public improvements, and [5] for the provision of lands for public use." ... In 1978 Hawaii amended its Constitution to establish the Office of Hawaiian Affairs ... which has as its mission "the betterment of conditions of native Hawaiians ... [and] Hawaiians." ... OHA is overseen by a nine-member board of trustees, the members of which "shall be Hawaiians" and—presenting the precise issue in this case—shall be "elected by qualified voters who are Hawaiians, as provided by law." ... The statute defines "native Hawaiian" as ... "any descendant of not less than one-half part of the races inhabiting the Hawaiian Islands previous to 1778, as defined by the Hawaiian Homes Commission Act, 1920, as amended; provided that the term identically refers to the descendants of such blood quantum of such aboriginal peoples which exercised sovereignty and subsisted in the Hawaiian Islands in 1778 and which peoples thereafter continued to reside in Hawaii." ...

Petitioner Harold Rice is a citizen of Hawaii and ... is neither "native Hawaiian" nor "Hawaiian" as defined by the statute. Rice applied [unsuccessfully] in March 1996 to vote in the elections for OHA trustees.... Rice sued Benjamin Cayetano, the Governor of Hawaii ... on the [basis of] the Fourteenth and Fifteenth Amendments to the United States Constitution.... The District Court granted summary judgment to the State [and] Court of Appeals affirmed.... We reverse.

III. The purpose and command of the Fifteenth Amendment ... prohibits all provisions denying or abridging the voting franchise of any citizen or class of citizens on the basis of race.... [T]he voting structure now before us is neither subtle nor indirect. It is specific in granting the vote to persons of defined ancestry and to no others. The State maintains this is not a racial category at all but instead a classification limited to those whose ancestors were in Hawaii at a particular time, regardless of their race.... We reject this line of argument.

Ancestry can be a proxy for race [and is] here.... The very object of the statutory definition in question ... is to treat the early Hawaiians as a distinct people, commanding their own recognition and respect. The State, in enacting the legislation before us, has used ancestry as a racial definition and for a racial purpose....

The ancestral inquiry mandated by the State is forbidden by the Fifteenth Amendment for the ... reason that the use of racial classifications is corruptive of the whole legal order democratic elections seek to preserve.... The State's electoral restriction enacts a race-based voting qualification.

IV. The State offers three principal defenses of its voting law.... We reject each of these arguments.... The most far reaching of the State's arguments is that exclusion of non-Hawaiians from voting is permitted under our cases allowing the differential treatment of certain members of Indian tribes.... If Hawaii's restriction were to be sustained under *Mancari* we would be required to ... conclude that Congress ... has determined that native Hawaiians have a status like that of Indians in organized tribes.... It is a matter of some dispute, for instance, whether Congress may treat the native Hawaiians as it does the Indian tribes.... Even were we to take the substantial step of finding authority in Congress, delegated to the State, to treat Hawaiians or native Hawaiians as tribes, Congress may not authorize a State to create a voting scheme of this sort....

Hawaii would extend the limited exception of *Mancari* to a new and larger dimension. The State contends that "one of the very purposes of OHA ... is to afford Hawaiians a measure of self-governance," and so it fits the model of *Mancari*.... It does not follow from *Mancari*, however, that Congress may authorize a State to establish a voting scheme that limits the electorate for its public officials to a class of tribal Indians, to the exclusion of all non-Indian citizens.... [The] elections for OHA trustee are elections of the State, not of a separate quasi-sovereign, and they are elections to which the Fifteenth Amendment applies. To extend *Mancari* to this context would be to permit a State, by racial classification, to fence out whole classes of its citizens from decisionmaking in critical state affairs. The Fifteenth Amendment forbids this result.

Hawaii further contends that the limited voting franchise is sustainable under a series of cases holding that the rule of one person, one vote does not pertain to certain special purpose districts such as water or irrigation districts.... Hawaii's final argument is that the voting restriction does no more than ensure an alignment of interests between the fiduciaries and the beneficiaries of a trust. Thus, the contention goes, the restriction is based on beneficiary status rather than race.... [I]t is not clear that the voting classification is symmetric with the beneficiaries of the programs OHA administers. Although the bulk of the funds for which OHA is responsible appears to be earmarked for the benefit of "native Hawaiians," the State permits both "native Hawaiians" and "Hawaiians" to vote for the office of trustee....

Hawaii's argument fails on more essential grounds. The State's position rests, in the end, on the demeaning premise that citizens of a particular race are somehow more qualified than others to vote on certain matters. That reasoning attacks the central meaning of the Fifteenth Amendment.... Under the Fifteenth Amendment voters are treated not as members of a distinct race but as members of the whole citizenry.... The voting restriction under review is prohibited by the Fifteenth Amendment.... [R]eversed.[20]

Justice Stevens wrote a dissent, part II of which was joined by Justice Ginsburg.

The Court's holding today rests largely on the repetition of glittering generalities that have little, if any, application to the compelling history of the State of Hawaii. When that history is held up against the manifest purpose of the Fourteenth and Fifteenth Amendments, and against two centuries of this Court's federal Indian law, it is clear to me that Hawaii's election scheme should be upheld.

I. ... As explained by the senior Senator from Hawaii, Senator Inouye, who is not himself a native Hawaiian but rather (like petitioner) is a member of the majority of Hawaiian voters who supported the 1978 amendments, the amendments reflect "an honest and sincere attempt on the part of the people of Hawai'i to rectify the wrongs of the past, and to put into being the mandate of our Federal government—the betterment of the conditions of Native Hawaiians." ... The OHA election provision violates neither the Fourteenth Amendment nor the Fifteenth.

That conclusion is in keeping with three overlapping principles. First, the Federal Government [has] wide latitude in carrying out its obligations arising from the special relationship it has with the aboriginal peoples, a category that includes the native Hawaiians.... In addition, there exists in this case the State's own fiduciary responsibility—arising from its establishment of a public trust—for administering assets granted it by the Federal Government in part for the benefit of native Hawaiians. Finally, even if one were to ignore the more than two centuries of Indian law precedent and practice on which this case follows, there is simply no invidious discrimination present in this effort to see that indigenous peoples are compensated for past wrongs, and to preserve a distinct and vibrant culture that is as much a part of this Nation's heritage as any.

II. Throughout our Nation's history, this Court has recognized both the plenary power of Congress over the affairs of Native Americans and the fiduciary character of the special federal relationship with descendants of those once sovereign peoples....

Critically, neither the extent of Congress' sweeping power nor the character of the trust relationship with indigenous peoples has depended on the ancient racial origins of the people, the allotment of tribal lands, the coherence or existence of tribal self-government, or the varying definitions of "Indian" Congress has chosen to adopt. Rather, when it comes to the exercise of Congress' plenary power in Indian affairs, this Court has taken account of the "numerous occasions" on which "legislation that singles out Indians for particular and special treatment" has been upheld, and has concluded that as "long as the special treatment can be tied rationally to the fulfillment of Congress' unique obligation towards the Indians, such legislative judgments will not be disturbed." *Morton v. Mancari*....

The nature of and motivation for the special relationship between the indigenous peoples and the United States Government was articulated in explicit detail in

1993, when Congress adopted a Joint Resolution containing a formal "apology to Native Hawaiians on behalf of the United States for the overthrow of the Kingdom of Hawaii." ... In the end, however, one need not even rely on this official apology to discern a well-established federal trust relationship with the native Hawaiians. Among the many and varied laws passed by Congress in carrying out its duty to indigenous peoples, more than 150 today expressly include native Hawaiians as part of the class of Native Americans benefited. By classifying native Hawaiians as "Native Americans" for purposes of these statutes, Congress has made clear that native Hawaiians enjoy many of "the same rights and privileges accorded to American Indian, Alaska Native, Eskimo, and Aleut communities." 42 U.S.C. §11701(19). See also §11701(17)....

While splendidly acknowledging this history ... the majority fails to recognize its import. The descendants of the native Hawaiians share with the descendants of the Native Americans on the mainland or in the Aleutian Islands not only a history of subjugation at the hands of colonial forces, but also a purposefully created and specialized "guardian–ward" relationship with the Government of the United States. It follows that legislation targeting the native Hawaiians must be evaluated according to the same understanding of equal protection that this Court has long applied to the Indians on the continental United States: that "special treatment ... be tied rationally to the fulfillment of Congress' unique obligation" toward the native peoples....

Membership in a tribe, the majority suggests, rather than membership in a race or class of descendants, has been the *sine qua non* of governmental power in the realm of Indian law; *Mancari* itself, the majority contends, makes this proposition clear.... But as scholars have often pointed out, tribal membership cannot be seen as the decisive factor in this Court's opinion upholding the BIA preferences in *Mancari*; the hiring preference at issue in that case not only extended to non-tribal member Indians, it also required for eligibility that ethnic Native Americans possess a certain quantum of Indian blood. Indeed, the Federal Government simply has not been limited in its special dealings with the native peoples to laws affecting tribes or tribal Indians alone.... [W]hat matters is that the determination of indigenous status or "real group membership," ... is one to be made by Congress—not by this Court.

Of greater concern to the majority is the fact that we are confronted here with a state constitution and legislative enactment.... But ... this reality does not alter our analysis.... OHA and its trustee elections ... are the instruments for implementing the Federal Government's trust relationship with a once sovereign indigenous people. This Court has held more than once that the federal power to pass laws fulfilling its trust relationship with the Indians may be delegated to the States.... The state statutory and constitutional scheme here was without question intended to implement the express desires of the Federal Government....

The sole remaining question under *Mancari* and [*Washington v. Confederated Bands and Tribes of Yakima Nation*, 439 U.S. 463 (1979)], is thus whether the State's scheme "rationally furthers the purpose identified by the State." Under this standard, as with the BIA preferences in *Mancari*, the OHA voting requirement is certainly reasonably designed to promote "self-government" by the descendants of the indigenous Hawaiians, and to make OHA "more responsive to the needs of its constituent groups." *Mancari*.... The foregoing reasons are to me more than sufficient to justify ... trustee election provision under the Fourteenth Amendment.

III. Although the Fifteenth Amendment tests the OHA scheme by a different measure, it is equally clear to me that the trustee election provision violates neither the letter nor the spirit of that Amendment.... The OHA voter qualification speaks in terms of ancestry and current residence, not of race or color.... Ancestry surely can be a proxy for race, or a pretext for invidious racial discrimination. But it is simply neither proxy nor pretext here. All of the persons who are eligible to vote for the trustees of OHA share two qualifications that no other person old enough to vote possesses: They are beneficiaries of the public trust created by the State and administered by OHA, and they have at least one ancestor who was a resident of Hawaii in 1778. A trust whose terms provide that the trustees shall be elected by a class including beneficiaries is hardly a novel concept....

[T]he classification here is not "demeaning" at all, for it is simply not based on the "premise that citizens of a particular race are somehow more qualified than others to vote on certain matters." It is based on the permissible assumption in this context that families with "any" ancestor who lived in Hawaii in 1778, and whose ancestors thereafter continued to live in Hawaii, have a claim to compensation and self-determination that others do not.... The Court today ignores the overwhelming differences between the Fifteenth Amendment case law on which it relies and the unique history of the State of Hawaii. I respectfully dissent.[21]

The who governs question, in its broad sense, has presented unique challenges for contemporary Native Alaskans as well, but for different reasons. These differences, and a good many of the problems, stem from the Alaska Native Claims Settlement Act (ANCSA) 1971. The opinion in the *Native Village of Venetie* case discussed below explains the situation and some of the concerns that gave rise to the ANCSA, but it is also important to see the case in the larger context of the question of sovereignty and the ability to govern. Although this may not seem like what many other Americans might see as a civil rights issue, it should be clear by this point that for native peoples it is absolutely a civil rights issue of the first order.

Alaska v. Native Village of Venetie Tribal Government

522 U.S. 520 (1998)

INTRODUCTION: The facts of the case are set forth in the opinion below. It is important to note, however, that this is another of the cases that operated at two very different levels. There was the substantive legal question concerning the status of Alaskan native villages after the ANCSA and then there was the question whether those who entered into the Act thought or understood that they would be surrendering their basic rights of self-governance and their independence from control by the state government. It is also worth noting that this opinion was unanimous.

Justice Thomas wrote the opinion for the Court.

In this case, we must decide whether approximately 1.8 million acres of land in northern Alaska, owned in fee simple by the Native Village of Venetie Tribal Government pursuant to the Alaska Native Claims Settlement Act ... is "Indian country." We conclude that it is not, and we therefore reverse the judgment below.

I. The Village of Venetie, which is located in Alaska above the Arctic Circle, is home to the Neets'aii Gwich'in Indians. In 1943, the Secretary of the Interior created a reservation for the Neets'aii Gwich'in out of the land surrounding Venetie and another nearby tribal village.... This land, which is about the size of Delaware, remained a reservation until 1971, when Congress enacted the Alaska

Native Claims Settlement Act (ANCSA), a comprehensive statute designed to settle all land claims by Alaska Natives....

In enacting ANCSA, Congress sought to end the sort of federal supervision over Indian affairs that had previously marked federal Indian policy. ANCSA's text states that the settlement of the land claims was to be accomplished "without litigation, with maximum participation by Natives in decisions affecting their rights and property, without establishing any permanent racially defined institutions, rights, privileges, or obligations, [and] without creating a reservation system or lengthy wardship or trusteeship." ...

To this end, ANCSA revoked "the various reserves set aside ... for Native use" by legislative or executive action, except for the Annette Island Reserve inhabited by the Metlakatla Indians, and completely extinguished all aboriginal claims to Alaska land.... In return, Congress authorized the transfer of $962.5 million in federal funds and approximately 44 million acres of Alaska land to state-chartered private business corporations that were to be formed pursuant to the statute; all of the shareholders of these corporations were required to be Alaska Natives.... The ANCSA corporations received title to the transferred land in fee simple, and no federal restrictions applied to subsequent land transfers by them.

Pursuant to ANCSA, two Native corporations were established for the Neets'aii Gwich'in, one in Venetie, and one in Arctic Village. In 1973, those corporations elected to make use of a provision in ANCSA allowing Native corporations to take title to former reservation lands set aside for Indians prior to 1971, in return for forgoing the statute's monetary payments and transfers of nonreservation land.... The United States conveyed fee simple title to the land constituting the former Venetie Reservation to the two corporations as tenants in common; thereafter, the corporations transferred title to the land to the Native Village of Venetie Tribal Government....

In 1986, the State of Alaska entered into a joint venture agreement with a private contractor for the construction of a public school in Venetie, financed with state funds. In December 1986, the Tribe notified the contractor that it owed the Tribe approximately $161,000 in taxes for conducting business activities on the Tribe's land. When both the contractor and the State, which under the joint venture agreement was the party responsible for paying the tax, refused to pay, the Tribe attempted to collect the tax in tribal court from the State, the school district, and the contractor. The State then filed suit in Federal District Court ... to enjoin collection of the tax.... [The] District Court ... held that the Tribe's ANCSA lands were not Indian country within the meaning of 18 U.S.C. §1151(b), which provides that Indian country includes all "dependent Indian communities within the borders of the United States"; as a result, "the Tribe [did] not have the power to impose a tax upon non-members of the tribe." ... [The Court of Appeals reversed.]

II. ... The statute provides: "The term 'Indian country' ... means (a) all land within the limits of any Indian reservation under the jurisdiction of the United States Government..., (b) all dependent Indian communities within the borders of the United States whether within the original or subsequently acquired territory thereof, and whether within or without the limits of a state, and (c) all Indian allotments, the Indian titles to which have not been extinguished, including rights-of-way running through the same." ... [W]e have recognized that Indian Country ... generally applies to questions of [criminal jurisdiction and] civil jurisdiction such as the one at issue here....

Because ANCSA revoked the Venetie Reservation, and because no Indian allotments are at issue, whether the Tribe's land is Indian country depends on whether it falls within the "dependent Indian communities" prong of the statute.... We now hold that [the term "dependent Indian communities"] refers to a limited category of Indian lands that are neither reservations nor allotments, and that satisfy two requirements—first, they must have been set aside by the Federal Government for the use of the Indians as Indian land; second, they must be under federal superintendence.... [In] §1151, Congress codified these two requirements, which previously we had held necessary for a finding of "Indian country" generally....

The Tribe's ANCSA lands do not satisfy either of these requirements. After the enactment of ANCSA, the Tribe's lands are neither "validly set apart for the use of the Indians as such," nor are they under the superintendence of the Federal Government.

With respect to the federal set-aside requirement, it is significant that ANCSA ... revoked the existing Venetie Reservation, and indeed revoked all existing reservations in Alaska "set aside by legislation or by Executive or Secretarial Order for Native use," save one.... The Tribe argues ... that the ANCSA lands were set apart for the use of the Neets'aii Gwich'in, "as such," because the Neets'aii Gwich'in acquired the lands pursuant to an ANCSA provision allowing Natives to take title to former reservation lands in return for forgoing all other ANCSA transfers.... ANCSA transferred reservation lands to private, state-chartered Native corporations, without any restraints on alienation or significant use restrictions, and with the goal of avoiding "any permanent racially defined institutions, rights, privileges, or obligations." ... By ANCSA's very design, Native corporations can immediately convey former reservation lands to non-Natives, and such corporations are not restricted to using those lands for Indian purposes. Because Congress contemplated that non-Natives could own the former Venetie Reservation, and because the Tribe is free to use it for non-Indian purposes, we must conclude that the federal set-aside requirement is not met....

Equally clearly, ANCSA ended federal superintendence over the Tribe's lands.... ANCSA revoked the Venetie Reservation along with every other reservation in Alaska but one ... and Congress stated explicitly that ANCSA's settlement provisions were intended to avoid a "lengthy wardship or trusteeship." After ANCSA, federal protection of the Tribe's land is essentially limited to a statutory declaration that the land is exempt from adverse possession claims, real property taxes, and certain judgments as long as it has not been sold, leased, or developed.... These protections, if they can be called that, simply do not approach the level of superintendence over the Indians' land that existed in our prior cases. In each of those cases, the Federal Government actively controlled the lands in question, effectively acting as a guardian for the Indians.... Finally, it is worth noting that Congress conveyed ANCSA lands to state-chartered and state-regulated private business corporations, hardly a choice that comports with a desire to retain federal superintendence over the land.

The Tribe contends that the requisite federal superintendence is present because the Federal Government provides "desperately needed health, social, welfare, and economic programs" to the Tribe.... Our Indian country precedents, however, do not suggest that the mere provision of "desperately needed" social programs can support a finding of Indian country....

The Tribe's federal superintendence argument, moreover, is severely undercut by its view of ANCSA's primary purposes, namely, to effect Native self-determination and to end paternalism in federal Indian relations.... The judgment of the Court of Appeals is reversed.

Is it Possible to Take Back that which Was Unlawfully Taken in the Past?

Like other civil rights groups, many Native American advocacy organizations learned from the effective tactics of the NAACP LDF and, consequently, the late 1960s and the early 1970s saw a dramatic increase in interest group litigation. This was not limited to what are sometimes labeled as liberal groups, but extended to conservative organizations as well. Conservative groups dramatically increased their interest group litigation during the 1970s and 1980s and beyond.[22]

The late 1960s and 1970s was a period of political activism for many groups seeking civil rights and a place in the political discussion. Women, Latinos, and Native Americans not only litigated, but engaged in political action from mild forms of organizing and educational efforts to widely publicized and confrontational challenges to the political system. Since that time, many groups, including Native Americans, have worked to enhance political awareness and to actively and energetically press their causes.

For Native Americans, this political dynamism was accompanied by the official recognition of historic abuses of Native Americans, including President Nixon's message to Congress (excerpted earlier in this chapter). Efforts were launched to create Native American studies programs in universities and in their schools of law like the University of Arizona and the University of Oklahoma School of Law.

In this context, it should come as no surprise that many tribes and nations launched litigation to address historic grievances and to press for recognition of civil rights. Since tribal sovereignty was so central to civil rights for Native Americans, it is also no surprise to see that tribes sued to address longstanding disputes over tribal lands and sovereignty over those lands. One of these battles was the effort by the Oneida Nation in New York to deal with historic losses. While they pursued legal action, the Oneida devised an alternative strategy to litigating for land rights. They began to purchase parcels of real estate that were within the boundaries of their historic lands and then asserted tribal jurisdiction over those lands, including immunity from state and local government taxes. That sparked litigation that began with efforts by a local community to take the land to sell in satisfaction of outstanding taxes. The Oneida responded by removing the case to federal court, in which they asserted a counter argument, which was that the state and local governments could not tax their tribal lands and enterprises.

City of Sherrill v. Oneida Indian Nation

544 U.S. 197 (2005)

INTRODUCTION: This complex case presents a situation in which the Oneida tried to recover governance authority over lands illegally taken from them historically, not primarily by seeking a court mandate, but by purchase on the open market. Once purchased, the lands were used for business purposes. The Oneida Nation sought to reassert tribal tax immunity from the state government on grounds that these were tribal businesses on tribal land.

The details of this long battle to reassert self-governance and tribal sovereignty are presented in the opinion itself. However, it is important to note that this case marked the third time the Oneida's battle had reached the U.S. Supreme Court. It did not begin with this case, which is particularly important to remember given the argument put forth in Justice Ginsburg's opinion for the Court. As before, consider what this opinion says as much as possible from the perspective of an Oneida or, for that matter, a Native American from any other community.

Justice Ginsburg wrote the opinion for the Court.

> This case concerns properties in the city of Sherrill, New York, purchased by the Oneida Indian Nation of New York (OIN) in 1997 and 1998. The separate parcels of land in question, once contained within the Oneidas' 300,000-acre reservation, were last possessed by the Oneidas as a tribal entity in 1805. For two centuries, governance of the area in which the properties are located has been provided by the State of New York and its county and municipal units. In *County of Oneida v. Oneida Indian Nation of N. Y.*, 470 U.S. 226 (1985) (*Oneida II*), this Court held that the Oneidas stated a triable claim for damages against the County of Oneida for wrongful possession of lands they conveyed to New York State in 1795 in violation of federal law. [In the current case], OIN resists the payment of property taxes to Sherrill on the ground that OIN's acquisition of fee title to discrete parcels of historic reservation land revived the Oneidas' ancient sovereignty piecemeal over each parcel. Consequently, the Tribe maintains, regulatory authority over OIN's newly purchased properties no longer resides in Sherrill.
>
> Our 1985 decision recognized that the Oneidas could maintain a federal common-law claim for damages for ancient wrongdoing in which both national and state governments were complicit. Today, we decline to project redress for the Tribe into the present and future, thereby disrupting the governance of central New York's counties and towns. Generations have passed during which non-Indians have owned and developed the area that once composed the Tribe's historic reservation. And at least since the middle years of the 19th century, most of the Oneidas have resided elsewhere. Given the longstanding, distinctly non-Indian character of the area and its inhabitants, the regulatory authority constantly exercised by New York State and its counties and towns, and the Oneidas' long delay in seeking judicial relief against parties other than the United States, we hold that the Tribe cannot unilaterally revive its ancient sovereignty, in whole or in part, over the parcels at issue.[23] The Oneidas long ago relinquished the reins of government and cannot regain them through open-market purchases from current titleholders.
>
> I. OIN is a federally recognized Indian Tribe and a direct descendant of the Oneida Indian Nation (Oneida Nation), "one of the six nations of the Iroquois, the most powerful Indian Tribe in the Northeast at the time of the American Revolution." ... At the birth of the United States, the Oneida Nation's aboriginal homeland comprised some six million acres in what is now central New York. *Oneida Indian Nation of N. Y. v. County of Oneida*, 414 U.S. 661, 664 (1974) (*Oneida I*).
>
> In the years after the Revolutionary War, "the State of New York came under increasingly heavy pressure to open the Oneidas' land for settlement." ... Reflective of that pressure, in 1788, New York State and the Oneida Nation entered into the Treaty of Fort Schuyler. For payments in money and kind, the Oneidas ceded to New York "all their lands." ... Of the vast area conveyed, "[t]he Oneidas retained a reservation of about 300,000 acres," *Oneida II*, at 231, "for their own use and cultivation." ...
>
> The Federal Government initially pursued a policy protective of the New York Indians, undertaking to secure the Tribes' rights to reserved lands.... In 1790,

Congress passed the first Indian Trade and Intercourse Act ... of July 22, 1790.... [T]he Act bars sales of tribal land without the acquiescence of the Federal Government.[24] In 1794, in further pursuit of its protective policy, the United States entered into the Treaty of Canandaigua with the Six (Iroquois) Nations.... That treaty both "acknowledge[d]" the Oneida Reservation as established by the Treaty of Fort Schuyler and guaranteed the Oneidas' "free use and enjoyment" of the reserved territory....

New York State nonetheless continued to purchase reservation land from the Oneidas. The Washington administration objected to New York's 1795 negotiations to buy 100,000 acres of the Oneidas' Reservation without federal supervision.... Later administrations, however, "[made not] even a pretense of interfer[ing] with [the] State's attempts to negotiate treaties [with the Oneidas] for land cessions." ...[25]

The Federal Government's policy soon veered away from protection.... [T]he United States pursued a policy designed to open reservation lands to white settlers and to remove tribes westward.... As recounted by the Indian Claims Commission in 1978, early 19th-century federal Indian agents in New York State did not simply fail to check New York's land purchases, they "took an active role ... in encouraging the removal of the Oneidas ... to the west." ... Beginning in 1817, the Federal Government accelerated its efforts to remove Indian tribes from their east coast homelands....

Pressured by the removal policy to leave their ancestral lands in New York, some 150 Oneidas, by 1825, had moved to Wisconsin.... In 1838, the Oneidas and the United States entered into the Treaty of Buffalo Creek, which envisioned removal of all remaining New York Indians, including the Oneidas, to Kansas.... By this time, the Oneidas had sold all but 5,000 acres of their original reservation. Six hundred of their members resided in Wisconsin, while 620 remained in New York State....

The Oneidas who stayed on in New York after the proclamation of the Buffalo Creek Treaty continued to diminish in number and, during the 1840's, sold most of their remaining lands to the State.... A few hundred Oneidas moved to Canada in 1842, ... and "by the mid-1840s, only about 200 Oneidas remained in New York State." ... By 1843, the New York Oneidas retained less than 1,000 acres in the State.... That acreage dwindled to 350 in 1890; ultimately, by 1920, only 32 acres continued to be held by the Oneidas....

The United States eventually abandoned its efforts to remove the New York Indians to Kansas. In 1860, the Federal Government restored the Kansas lands to the public domain, and sold them thereafter....

Early litigation concerning the Oneidas' land claims trained on monetary recompense from the United States for past deprivations. In 1893, the United States agreed to be sued for disposing of the Kansas lands to settlers, and the Oneidas in New York shared in the resulting award of damages.... Seeking further compensation from the United States a half century later, the New York and Wisconsin Oneidas initiated proceedings before the Indian Claims Commission in 1951.... They sought redress for lands New York had acquired through 25 treaties of cession concluded between 1795 and 1846. The Oneidas alleged, and the Claims Commission agreed, that under the Nonintercourse Act of 1790 and successor statutes, the Federal Government had a fiduciary duty to ensure that the Oneidas received from New York "conscionable consideration" for the lands in question....

In lieu of concentrating on recovery from the United States, the Oneidas pursued suits against local governments. In 1970, the Oneidas of New York and Wisconsin ... instituted a "test case" against the New York Counties of Oneida and Madison. They alleged that the cession of 100,000 acres to New York State in 1795 ... violated the Nonintercourse Act and thus did not terminate the Oneidas' right to possession under the applicable federal treaties and statutes.... The District Court, affirmed by the Court of Appeals, dismissed the Oneidas' complaint for failure to state a claim arising under federal law. We reversed that determination, holding that federal jurisdiction was properly invoked. *Oneida I*, 414 U.S., at 675.

In the next round, the Oneidas prevailed in the lower courts. On review in *Oneida II*, we rejected various defenses the counties presented that might have barred the action for damages ... and held that the Oneidas could maintain their claim to be compensated "for violation of their possessory rights based on federal common law." ... On remand, the District Court entered a final judgment which fixed the amount of damages payable by the counties. Allowing setoffs for the counties' good-faith improvements to the land, the court ordered recoveries of $15,994 from Oneida County and $18,970 from Madison County, plus prejudgment interest.... In 2000, litigation resumed in an action held in abeyance during the pendency of the test case. In [it] the Oneidas sought damages from Oneida and Madison Counties for a period spanning over 200 years....

This brings us to the present case, which concerns parcels of land in the city of Sherrill, located in Oneida County, New York. According to the 2000 census, over 99% of the population in the area is non-Indian: American Indians represent less than 1% of the city of Sherrill's population and less than 0.5% of Oneida County's population.... OIN owns approximately 17,000 acres of land scattered throughout the Counties of Oneida and Madison, representing less than 1.5% of the counties' total area. OIN's predecessor, the Oneida Nation, had transferred the parcels at issue to one of its members in 1805, who sold the land to a non-Indian in 1807. The properties thereafter remained in non-Indian hands until OIN's acquisitions in 1997 and 1998 in open-market transactions.... OIN now operates commercial enterprises on these parcels: a gasoline station, a convenience store, and a textile facility....

Because the parcels lie within the boundaries of the reservation originally occupied by the Oneidas, OIN maintained that the properties are exempt from taxation, and accordingly refused to pay the assessed property taxes. The city of Sherrill initiated eviction proceedings in state court, and OIN sued Sherrill in federal court. In contrast to *Oneida I* and *II*, which involved demands for monetary compensation, OIN sought equitable relief prohibiting, currently and in the future, the imposition of property taxes. OIN also sued Madison County, seeking a declaration that the Tribe's properties in Madison are tax exempt.... [T]he District Court concluded that parcels of land owned by the Tribe in Sherrill and Madison are not taxable.... [T]he Second Circuit affirmed.... [We] now reverse.

II. OIN and the United States argue that because the Court in *Oneida II* recognized the Oneidas' aboriginal title to their ancient reservation land and because the Tribe has now acquired the specific parcels involved in this suit in the open market, it has unified fee and aboriginal title and may now assert sovereign dominion over the parcels.... We now reject the unification theory of OIN and the United States and hold that "standards of federal Indian law and federal equity practice" preclude the Tribe from rekindling embers of sovereignty that long ago grew cold....

The appropriateness of the relief OIN here seeks must be evaluated in light of the long history of state sovereign control over the territory. From the early 1800's into the 1970's, the United States largely accepted ... New York's governance of the land in question.... This Court has observed in the ... context of the diminishment of an Indian reservation that "[t]he longstanding assumption of jurisdiction by the State over an area that is over 90% non-Indian, both in population and in land use," may create "justifiable expectations." ... Similar justifiable expectations, grounded in two centuries of New York's exercise of regulatory jurisdiction, until recently uncontested by OIN, merit heavy weight here....

The wrongs of which OIN complains in this action occurred during the early years of the Republic. For the past two centuries, New York and its county and municipal units have continuously governed the territory. The Oneidas did not seek to regain possession of their aboriginal lands by court decree until the 1970's.... And not until the 1990's did OIN acquire the properties in question and assert its unification theory to ground its demand for exemption of the parcels from local taxation.... This long lapse of time, during which the Oneidas did not seek to revive their sovereign control through equitable relief in court, and the attendant dramatic changes in the character of the properties, preclude OIN from gaining the disruptive remedy it now seeks.

The principle that the passage of time can preclude relief has deep roots in our law, and this Court has recognized this prescription in various guises. It is well established that laches, a doctrine focused on one side's inaction and the other's legitimate reliance, may bar long-dormant claims for equitable relief....

As between States, long acquiescence may have controlling effect on the exercise of dominion and sovereignty over territory. *Ohio v. Kentucky*, 410 U.S. 641, 651 (1973).... The acquiescence doctrine does not depend on the original validity of a boundary line; rather, it attaches legal consequences to acquiescence in the observance of the boundary. *California v. Nevada*, 447 U.S. 125, 131 (1980).[26]

... When a party belatedly asserts a right to present and future sovereign control over territory, longstanding observances and settled expectations are prime considerations. There is no dispute that it has been two centuries since the Oneidas last exercised regulatory control over the properties here or held them free from local taxation. Parcel-by-parcel revival of their sovereign status, given the extraordinary passage of time, would dishonor "the historic wisdom in the value of repose." ...[27]

Finally, this Court has recognized the impracticability of returning to Indian control land that generations earlier passed into numerous private hands.... [T]he Court of Appeals concluded that the "impossibility" doctrine had no application because OIN acquired the land in the open market and does not seek to uproot current property owners.... But the unilateral reestablishment of present and future Indian sovereign control, even over land purchased at the market price, would have disruptive practical consequences similar to those that led this Court in *Yankton Sioux* to initiate the impossibility doctrine. The city of Sherrill and Oneida County are today overwhelmingly populated by non-Indians.... A checkerboard of alternating state and tribal jurisdiction in New York State ... would "seriously burde[n] the administration of state and local governments" and would adversely affect landowners neighboring the tribal patches....[28] If OIN may unilaterally reassert sovereign control and remove these parcels from the local tax rolls, little would prevent the Tribe from initiating a new generation of litigation to free the parcels from local zoning or other regulatory controls that protect all landowners in the area.

Recognizing these practical concerns, Congress has provided a mechanism for the acquisition of lands for tribal communities that takes account of the interests of others with stakes in the area's governance and well-being. Title 25 U.S.C. §465 authorizes the Secretary of the Interior to acquire land in trust for Indians and provides that the land "shall be exempt from State and local taxation." ... Section 465 provides the proper avenue for OIN to reestablish sovereign authority over territory last held by the Oneidas 200 years ago.

[T]he distance from 1805 to the present day, the Oneidas' long delay in seeking equitable relief against New York or its local units, and developments in the city of Sherrill spanning several generations, evoke the doctrines of laches, acquiescence, and impossibility, and render inequitable the piecemeal shift in governance this suit seeks unilaterally to initiate.... For the reasons stated, the judgment of the Court of Appeals for the Second Circuit is reversed, and the case is remanded for further proceedings consistent with this opinion.[29]

Justice Stevens wrote a dissenting opinion.

... Since the outset of this litigation it has been common ground that if the Tribe's properties are "Indian Country," the City has no jurisdiction to tax them without express congressional consent. For the reasons set forth at length in the opinions of the District Court and the Court of Appeals, it is abundantly clear that all of the land owned by the Tribe within the boundaries of its reservation qualifies as Indian country.... [T]he Court today nevertheless decides that the fact that most of the reservation has been occupied and governed by non-Indians for a long period of time precludes the Tribe "from rekindling embers of sovereignty that long ago grew cold." ... This is a novel holding, and in my judgment even more unwise than the Court's holding in [*Oneida II*] that the Tribe may recover damages for the alleged illegal conveyance of its lands that occurred in 1795.... In the present case, the Tribe is not attempting to collect damages or eject landowners as a remedy for a wrong that occurred centuries ago; rather, it is invoking an ancient immunity against a city's present-day attempts to tax its reservation lands.

[T]he Court has ventured into legal territory that belongs to Congress. Its decision today is at war with at least two bedrock principles of Indian law. First, only Congress has the power to diminish or disestablish a tribe's reservation. Second, as a core incident of tribal sovereignty, a tribe enjoys immunity from state and local taxation of its reservation lands, until that immunity is explicitly revoked by Congress.[30]...

[A]s a matter of equity ... the "principle that the passage of time can preclude relief" ... should be applied sensibly and with an even hand.... [T]he Tribe reacquired reservation land in a peaceful and lawful manner that fully respected the interests of innocent landowners—it purchased the land on the open market. To now deny the Tribe its right to tax immunity—at once the most fundamental of tribal rights and the least disruptive to other sovereigns—is not only inequitable, but also irreconcilable with the principle that only Congress may abrogate or extinguish tribal sovereignty. I would not decide this case on the basis of speculation about what may happen in future litigation over other regulatory issues. For the answer to the question whether the City may require the Tribe to pay taxes on its own property within its own reservation is ... clear. Under settled law, it may not. Accordingly, I respectfully dissent.

As an informational note in the edited opinion observed, it is ironic that Justice Ginsburg, who was herself an active civil rights lawyer in the 1960s and 1970s, should have referred to the doctrine of "repose," the idea that longstanding practices simply cannot be remedied because society has developed and parties have moved on over the years. Indeed, the argument is that there must be a point at which the status quo cannot be further questioned. That was the argument that was so often used by those who opposed litigation aimed at advancing civil rights against generations of discrimination.

It was in fact the argument put forth by John W. Davis in defense of segregation in the *Brown v. Board of Education* oral argument. He said: "Somewhere, sometime to every principle comes a moment of repose when it has been so often announced, so confidently relied upon, so long continued, that it passes the limits of judicial discretion and disturbance."[31] His claim was that because the *Plessy v. Ferguson* case had stood since 1896, and there had been so many cases that accepted the separate but equal doctrine, that the concept of segregation was simply beyond challenge.

Another interesting problem with the difficulty of the idea of repose is that it was the federal and state governments that continuously changed the rules over the course of the nation's history. They entered into agreements that they did not keep and then, when the mood or political pressures called for it, unilaterally redefined the agreements or imposed new legislation that sought to destroy the tribal governments directly or indirectly. Even through the twentieth century, the continual effort by the state and federal governments to decide where and when they would honor obligations to Native Americans remained in flux, as in the case of the de-recognition and relocation policies that ran until the repudiation of them by the Nixon administration and the Congress in the 1970s.

Third, it was no surprise that the Oneida and so many other groups who had recently organized and equipped themselves to fight in the courts and in the political arena to advance their interests went to court in this period rather than before. Since the late 1960s and early 1970s, Native American tribes and nations, like virtually all other groups in American society, have regularly gone to the courts to vindicate their civil rights claims. Thus, the argument that they should have come to court sooner simply ignores history, and even contemporary political and legal reality.

Conclusion

To be sure, Native Americans have experienced a deplorable history of racial and ethnic discrimination, even to the point of repeated attempts by the U.S. government to destroy them as a people. Those were not merely policies dating back to the early years of the republic, but also policies pursued through the 1950s and 1960s with de-recognition and other actions. The earlier efforts to destroy the tribal communities and break their connection to the land live on, as the Allotment Act continues to be cited in current case law as justification for denying self-government and a serious understanding of sovereignty for tribal governance.

To many Native Americans, civil rights is not only about discrimination in violation of the equal protection clause of the Fourteenth Amendment or of the Fifth Amendment due process clause, but implicates other issues as well. In particular, sovereignty, land rights, and tribal self-governance are fundamental civil rights for them.

There are other kinds of civil rights claims asserted by Native Americans as well, claims that are often not understood by others as civil rights issues properly so-called. However, for Native Americans there is no question that such matters as the behavior by government toward Native American natural resources rights and spirituality are serious civil rights concerns. Chapter 7 turns to these issues.

I. Issues for Policy and Practice

A. Consider President Nixon's speech concerning the need, given history, for a balance between ensuring Native American self-determination and also for providing sufficient resources in light of historic damages done to tribal communities. As the text indicates, it took several years to enact the Indian Self-Determination and Educational Assistance Act, but controversy continues, including a number of cases that reached the Supreme Court concerning its requirements. What policies are in place to evaluate the effectiveness of implementation of the Act and address problems found in the process?

B. *Morton v. Mancari* addressed the longstanding problem of ensuring that those in the federal government making important policy and administrative decisions about tribal communities and individual Native Americans include people from that community. What evidence is there in policy or management practice as to what the status of that effort is and whether additional steps can be taken to enhance progress in that direction?

C. There have been some indications since the Alaska Native Claims Settlement Act (ANCSA) of 1971 that some Alaska Native villages are in a worse position that they were previously, since they are, as the *Native Village of Venetie* case indicates, no longer "Indian country" under federal statute and therefore ineligible for some programs. Has there been a systematic assessment of the impact of the *Venetie* case and the ability of Alaska Native villages in the years since to access key federal programs that they need? There have been a few GAO reports on specific problems, but it is not clear that there is a more comprehensive assessment. Is there a need for legislation to address unanticipated consequences?

D. There have been longstanding difficulties with providing remedies to tribal people for lands taken illegally over time. The *City of Sherrill* case represented an innovative approach by the Oneida people to address the problem without demanding a large financial payout or dislocating people on that land presently by legal means. Instead, the idea was to purchase the land on the open market and then repatriate to tribal governance. Since the Supreme Court rejected that approach, what options are currently available to achieve justice without creating the kinds of conflict and dislocation the Oneida process was designed to avoid?

E. A number of the cases discussed in this chapter show a fundamental mismatch between the way that lands and self-governance are understood in the federal, state, and local governments and the way they are viewed in tribal communities. Is there a need for a cultural interpretation or cultural mediation capacity to assist various units of government, whether in tribal communities or in federal or state agencies or local governments? If so, is there a need for policy to develop such a capacity?

II. Discussion Questions

A. What message did the political resistance to the request to rename the mountains and the freeway in Arizona in honor of Private Piestawa send to Native Americans?

B. Do you think that Alaskan Native villagers understood when they agreed to the settlement that they were signing away their status as a sovereign community? How should they understand their community's capacity for self-governance in light of the *Native Village of Venetie* case?

C. The language suggesting that the Oneida failed for too long to take action against the state and the county even though they had for decades been in litigation with the federal government, of course, ignores the most fundamental principle of Native American law, which is that tribes or nations are not required, when it comes to tribal lands or people on them, to deal with states or their subdivisions, since the relationship is sovereign-to-sovereign between the tribal government and the U.S. government. Recall the *Kansas Indians* case and the other cases dating back to the earliest part of the nineteenth century. If that is true, why should the Oneida be criticized for not proceeding against the city and the state earlier?

D. The Court tells the Oneida that there is a statute and a Department of the Interior process for designating lands purchased by Native American tribal governments as trust lands. However, this is a case of recovering lands illegally taken from the Oneida rather than purchasing lands that were not legally theirs to begin with. Why should the Oneida be required to use a process designed for an entirely different situation?

E. Apart from the specifics of the Oneida case, how would you respond if you were Native American if you saw the Supreme Court majority using the same doctrine of repose argument (discussed in the text) that had been used by the lawyer for the Southern states in the *Brown v. Board of Education* case opposing the overturn of *Plessy v. Ferguson*?

Notes

1 Arlington National Cemetery, "John Raymond Rice," www.arlingtoncemetery.net/jrrice.htm, October 11, 2014.

2 Id.

3 Quoted in David Hendee, "More Than a Casualty of War Sting of Prejudice A Lingering Hurt," *Omaha World-Herald*, May 28, 2001, p. 1.

4 David McCullough, *Truman* (New York: Simon & Schuster, 1992), p. 860.

5 Quoted in Kate Thompson, "Memorial honors Sgt. Rice, 50 years after his burial was refused," *Sioux City Journal*, August 29, 2001, reprinted in Arlington National Cemetery, "John Raymond Rice."

6 NOTE: When the Supreme Court justices have a tied vote, the ruling of the lower court is upheld, though of course without any value as a precedent.

7 NOTE: Certiorari is the writ issued to the lower court indicating that the Supreme Court would review the case and ordering that the record be sent up for review.

8 *Associated Press State & Local Wire*, "Ariz. Governor Pushing to Rename Peak for Fallen Soldier," April 12, 2003, Saturday, BC cycle.

9 *Associated Press State & Local Wire*, "For Piestewa, Honors and a Flap Plan to Rename Peak Is Disputed," Washington Post, April 13, 2003, p. A14.

10 *Associated Press State & Local Wire*, "Ariz. Governor Pushing to Rename Peak for Fallen Soldier," April 12, 2003, Saturday, BC cycle.

11 Jacques Billeaud, "Arizona Governor Draws Criticism for Trying to Rename Peak After Servicewoman," *Associated Press*, April 14, 2003, BC cycle; Jacques Billeaud, "GOP Lawmakers Criticize Governor's Lobbying for Name Change," *Associated Press State & Local Wire*, April 21, 2003, BC Cycle.

12 P.L. 105–154, 112 Stat. 3 (1998).

13 Jacques Billeaud, "Arizona Renaming Peak After Soldier," *Deseret News* (Salt Lake City), April 19, 2003, Saturday, p. B05.

14 Nancy L. Gallagher, *Breeding Better Vermonters: The Eugenics Project in the Green Mountain State* (Hanover: University Press of New England, 1999).

15 67 Stat. B132.

16 67 Stat. 588.

17 Records of the Bureau of Indian Affairs [BIA] (Record Group 75) 1793–1989, National Archives, www.archives.gov/research/guide-fed-records/groups/075.html, January 15, 2016.

18 P.L. 93–628, 88 Stat. 2203 (1975).

19 NOTE: This means without saying so directly.

20 NOTE: Justice Breyer's concurring opinion is omitted here.

21 NOTE: Justice Ginsburg's dissent is omitted here.

22 See Karen O'Connor and Lee Epstein, "The Rise of Conservative Interest Group Litigation," *Journal of Politics* 45 (No. 2 1983), 479–489; "Amicus Curiae Participation in U.S. Supreme Court Litigation," *Law & Society Review* 16 (No. 4 1981): 311–320; Jayanth K. Krishnan and Kevin R. den Dulk, "So Help Me God: A Comparative Study of Religious Interest Group Litigation," *Georgia Journal of International & Comparative Law* 30 (No. 2 2002): 233–275; Lee Epstein, "Interest

Group Litigation During the Rehnquist Era," *Journal of Law and Politics* 9 (No. 4 1993): 639–717; John O. Heinz, "Lawyers for Conservative Causes: Clients, Ideology, and Social Distance," *Law & Society Review* 37 (2003):5–50.

23 NOTE: The language suggesting that the Oneida failed for too long to take action against the state and the county even though they had for decades been in litigation with the federal government of course ignores the most fundamental principle of Native American law, which is that tribes or nations are not required, when it comes to tribal lands or people on them, to deal with states or their subdivisions, since the relationship is sovereign-to-sovereign between the tribal government and the U.S. government. Recall the *Kansas Indians* case and the other cases dating back to the earliest part of the nineteenth century.

24 By its terms, the 1790 Nonintercourse Act governed Indian lands within the boundaries of the original thirteen States. The Act provided "[t]hat no sale of lands made by any Indians, or any nation or tribe of Indians within the United States, shall be valid to any person or persons, *or to any state, whether having the right of pre-emption to such lands or not*, unless the same shall be made and duly executed at some public treaty, held under the authority of the United States." Act of July 22, 1790, ch. 33, §4, 1 Stat. 138 (emphasis added).

25 NOTE: It is important to note that the starting point here is an admission that any so-called purchase of these lands without approval from the federal government was illegal from the outset. It is also important to recognize that the federal government's subsequent failure to protect the Oneida's rights and then to actively participate in actions in clear violation of the treaty was, in addition to everything else, a violation of its trust responsibility.

26 NOTE: These are two original jurisdiction cases that involved state boundary disputes. The majority tried to argue that they are nevertheless appropriate precedents in this case, but they are plainly very different from the current situation.

27 NOTE: There is an irony that Justice Ginsburg cites the doctrine of "repose," which holds that there must be a point at which the status quo cannot be further questioned, in light of the fact that this was precisely the argument advanced by John W. Davis in defense of segregation in the *Brown v. Board of Education* oral argument. See discussion following the opinion.

28 NOTE: It is interesting that the Court is concerned about such a blend of native and non-native land here, but has indicated no concern for the fact that this is the situation on most Native American reservations because of the sale of large amounts of that land to non-natives from the time of the Allotment Act forward. Today, tribal governments live with what the Court suggests here is an impossible situation across the nation.

29 NOTE: Justice Souter's concurring opinion is omitted here.

30 See *Montana v. Blackfeet Tribe*, 471 U.S. 759, 764–765 (1985) (citing *The Kansas Indians*, 72 U.S. 737 (1867), and *The New York Indians*, 72 U.S. 761 (1867)).

31 Quoted in Phillip B. Kurland and Gerhard Casper, eds., *Landmark Briefs and Cases of the Supreme Court of the United States: Constitutional Law* (Washington, D.C.: University Press of America, 1975), Volume 49A, p. 490, www.lib.umich.edu/exhibits/brownarchive/oral/Marshall&Moore.pdf, December 26, 2008. See also Derrick Bell, *Silent Covenants* (New York: Oxford University Press, 2004), p. 21.

References

Bell, Derrick. *Silent Covenants*. New York: Oxford University Press, 2004.

Epstein, Lee. "Interest Group Litigation During the Rehnquist Era," *Journal of Law and Politics* 9 (No. 4 1993): 639–717.

Gallagher, Nancy L. *Breeding Better Vermonters: The Eugenics Project in the Green Mountain State.* Hanover: University Press of New England, 1999.

Heinz, John O. "Lawyers for Conservative Causes: Clients, Ideology, and Social Distance," *Law & Society Review* 37 (2003): 5–50.

Krishnan, Jayanth K. and Kevin R. den Dulk, "So Help Me God: A Comparative Study of Religious Interest Group Litigation," *Georgia Journal of International & Comparative Law* 30 (No. 2 2002): 233–275.

Kurland, Phillip B. and Gerhard Casper, eds., *Landmark Briefs and Cases of the Supreme Court of the United States: Constitutional Law*. Washington, D.C.: University Press of America, 1975.

McCullough, David. *Truman*. New York: Simon & Schuster, 1992.

Nixon, Richard M. "Special Message to the Congress on Indian Affairs," July 8, 1970, in *Public Papers of the President, 1970*, pp. 565–576, Online by Gerhard Peters and John T. Woolley, The American Presidency Project, www.presidency.ucsb.edu/ws/?pid=2573, January 24, 2016.

O'Connor, Karen and Lee Epstein. "Amicus Curiae Participation in U.S. Supreme Court Litigation," *Law & Society Review* 16 (No. 4 1981): 311–320.

———. "The Rise of Conservative Interest Group Litigation," *Journal of Politics* 45 (No. 2 1983): 479–489.

7 Natural Resources and Native Spirituality
A Different Kind of Civil Rights Claim

Many legal scholars would say that natural resources are not civil rights matters, but questions of environmental law, property law, Indian law, or, perhaps, contract law. Issues of spirituality, they would say, are not matters of civil rights, but civil liberties concerns viewed as free exercise or establishment of religion problems under the First Amendment.

For many Native Americans, though, these issues present civil rights problems as well. They reject the idea that there is nothing different or special about these kinds of legal questions when raised by Native Americans. Their reaction is reminiscent of Justice Marshall's reaction to the claim that it was time to stop giving special attention to African Americans, as discussed in Chapter 1. Like Marshall, many indigenous people would say that although today perhaps many non-native peoples do not wish to acknowledge anything special about Native Americans, the government of the United States and many non-natives had no difficulty treating Native American religions and Native American control of resources as "special" in the past two centuries. Unfortunately, tribal peoples' religions were treated as something to be destroyed and their resources to be taken, often at the point of a gun. Even today, they would argue, tribes and nations are covered by special limitations that affect their use of natural resources and their ability to practice their spirituality—in particular in extremely unfair and damaging ways.

Natural Resources Cases and Tribal Sovereignty Issues

One of the areas of continuing controversy with respect to who governs in Indian Country concerns tribal policy with respect to natural resources of all types. Given the relationship of Native American tribal cultures to their physical environment, these issues take on a special significance. There are a host of complicating factors, including the fact that the federal government has long maintained a role—Native American critics would say a dominant role—in the control of natural resources on reservation land. On the other hand, and given its longstanding involvement in control over Native American resources, there are trust doctrine responsibilities related to the federal government that have too often not been honored. In the contemporary context, given the recognition of the transboundary nature of environmental and natural resource issues, there is an added international dimension to some of these problems. Here again, because tribal people around the world are so closely connected to nature, these are more than lands or property disputes for many native people; they are matters of civil rights. Consider first two contemporary Supreme Court rulings in this area, and then another case that did not get to the U.S. Supreme Court, but that presented the problem in all its contemporary complexity.

United States v. Navajo Nation

537 U.S. 488 (2003)

INTRODUCTION: This is a contemporary case that arose against a backdrop of the Allotment Act-era decision that the federal government could and would rule on the management of natural resources on reservation land. The policy was changed under the Indian Mineral Leasing Act of 1938, but even then the federal government retained a controlling role when tribal governments made decisions about whether and under what conditions to enter into mining or drilling agreements for coal, gas, or oil.

This case also came in a context in which regulated firms were receiving positive indications from some officials in the federal government that they could take political appeals directly to the administration and circumvent the legal process. In this case, that clearly led to what is termed an *ex parte* communication in the form of a meeting between the mining company lobbyist and the Secretary of the Interior that plainly shaped the department's actions, even though the secretary sought to suggest otherwise.[1]

The facts are complex and extremely troubling, even when presented by the majority that ruled against the Navajo in this case.

Justice Ginsburg wrote the opinion for the Court.

This case concerns the Indian Mineral Leasing Act of 1938 (IMLA) ... and the role it assigns to the Secretary of the Interior with respect to coal leases executed by an Indian Tribe and a private lessee. The controversy centers on 1987 amendments to a 1964 coal lease entered into by the predecessor of Peabody Coal Company and the Navajo Nation.... The Tribe seeks to recover money damages from the United States for an alleged breach of trust in connection with the Secretary's approval of coal lease amendments negotiated by the Tribe and Peabody. This Court's decisions in *United States v. Mitchell*, 445 U.S. 535 (1980) (*Mitchell I*), and *United States v. Mitchell*, 463 U.S. 206 (1983) (*Mitchell II*), control this case.... [W]e hold that the Tribe's claim for compensation from the Federal Government fails, for it does not derive from any liability-imposing provision of the IMLA or its implementing regulations.

I. The IMLA, which governs aspects of mineral leasing on Indian tribal lands, states that "unallotted lands ... may, *with the approval of the Secretary* ..., be leased for mining purposes." [Emphasis added] ... In addition "to providing Indian tribes with a profitable source of revenue," ... the IMLA aimed to foster tribal self-determination by "giving Indians a greater say in the use and disposition of the resources found on Indian lands." ... Prior to enactment of the IMLA, decisions whether to grant mineral leases on Indian land generally rested with the Government.... The IMLA, designed to advance tribal independence, empowers Tribes to negotiate mining leases themselves, and, as to coal leasing, assigns primarily an approval role to the Secretary....[2] As to coal royalties ... the [IMLA] regulations required only that the rate be "not less than 10 cents per ton." ...

Peabody mines coal on the Tribe's lands pursuant to leases covered by the IMLA. This case principally concerns Lease 8580, which took effect upon approval by the Secretary in 1964.... The Lease established a maximum royalty rate of 37.5 cents per ton of coal, ... but made that figure "*subject to reasonable adjustment by the Secretary of the Interior or his authorized representative*" [emphasis added] on the 20-year anniversary of the Lease and every ten years thereafter.... As the 20-year anniversary of Lease 8580 approached, its royalty rate of 37.5 cents per ton yielded for the Tribe only "about 2% of gross proceeds." ... This return was higher than the ten cents per ton minimum established by the then-applicable IMLA regulations.... It was substantially lower, however, than the 12½ percent of gross proceeds rate Congress established in 1977 as the minimum permissible royalty for coal mined on federal lands under the Mineral Leasing Act.... For some years starting in the 1970's ... the Tribe endeavored to renegotiate existing mineral leases with private lessees, including Peabody....

In March 1984, the Chairman of the Navajo Tribal Council wrote to the Secretary asking him to exercise his contractually conferred authority to adjust the royalty rate under Lease 8580. On June 18, 1984, the Director of the Bureau of Indian Affairs for the Navajo Area, acting pursuant to authority delegated by the Secretary, sent Peabody an opinion letter raising the rate to 20 percent of gross proceeds....

Peabody filed an administrative appeal in July 1984.... The appeal was referred to the Deputy Assistant Secretary for Indian Affairs, John Fritz.... Fritz ... appeared ready to reject Peabody's appeal.... By June 1985, both Peabody and the Tribe anticipated that an announcement favorable to the Tribe was imminent....

On July 5, 1985, a Peabody Vice President wrote to Interior Secretary Donald Hodel, asking him either to postpone decision on Peabody's appeal so the parties could seek a negotiated settlement, or to rule in Peabody's favor.... A copy of Peabody's letter was sent to the Tribe ... which then submitted its own letter urging the Secretary to reject Peabody's request and to secure the Department's prompt release of a decision in the Tribe's favor.... *Peabody representatives met privately with Secretary Hodel in July 1985...; no representative of the Tribe was present at, or received notice of, that meeting* ... [emphasis added].[3]

On July 17, 1985, Secretary Hodel sent a memorandum to Deputy Assistant Secretary Fritz.... The memorandum "suggested" that Fritz "inform the involved parties that a decision on the appeal is not imminent and urge them to continue with efforts to resolve this matter in a mutually agreeable fashion." ... "Any royalty adjustment which is imposed on those parties without their concurrence," the memorandum stated, "will almost certainly be the subject of protracted and costly appeals," and "could well impair the future of the contractual relationship" between the parties." ... Secretary Hodel added, however, that the memorandum was "not intended as a determination of the merits of the arguments of the parties with respect to the issues which are subject to the appeal." ...[4]

The Tribe was not told of the Secretary's memorandum to Fritz, but learned that " 'someone from Washington' had urged a return to the bargaining table." ... Facing "severe economic pressure," ... the Tribe resumed negotiations with Peabody in August 1985.... On September 23, 1985, the parties reached a tentative agreement on a package of amendments to Lease 8580.... They agreed to raise the royalty rate to 12½ percent of monthly gross proceeds, and to make the new rate retroactive to February 1, 1984.... The 12½ percent rate was at the time customary for leases to mine coal on federal lands and on Indian lands. The amendments acknowledged the legitimacy of tribal taxation of coal production, but stipulated that the tax rate would be capped at eight percent.... [T]he parties agreed to move jointly to vacate the Area Director's June 1984 decision, which had raised the royalty to 20 percent.... The parties signed a final agreement in November 1987 ... and Secretary Hodel approved it on December 14, 1987.... Shortly thereafter, pursuant to the parties' stipulation, the Area Director's decision was vacated....

In 1993, the Tribe brought suit against the United States in the Court of Federal Claims, alleging ... that the Secretary's approval of the amendments to the Lease constituted a breach of trust. The Tribe sought $600 million in damages.... In no uncertain terms, that court found that the Government owed general fiduciary duties to the Tribe, which ... the Secretary had flagrantly dishonored by acting in the best interests of Peabody rather than the Tribe. Nevertheless, the court concluded that the Tribe had entirely failed to link that breach of duty to any statutory or regulatory obligation which could "be fairly interpreted as mandating compensation for the government's fiduciary wrongs." ...

The Court of Appeals for the Federal Circuit reversed.... The Government's liability to the Tribe, it said, turned on whether "the United States controls the Indian resources." ... [T]he Court of Appeals determined that the measure of control the Secretary exercised over the leasing of Indian lands for mineral development sufficed to warrant a money judgment against the United States for breaches of fiduciary duties connected to coal leasing.... The appeals court agreed with the Federal Claims Court that the Secretary's actions regarding Peabody's administrative appeal violated the Government's fiduciary obligations to the Tribe, in that those actions "suppressed and concealed" the decision of the Deputy Assistant Secretary, and "thereby favored Peabody interests to the detriment of Navajo interests." ... We now reverse.

II. ... The Tribe asserts federal subject-matter jurisdiction under ... the Indian Tucker Act [which] provides: "The United States Court of Federal Claims shall have jurisdiction of any claim against the United States accruing after August 13, 1946, in favor of any tribe ... whenever such claim is one arising under the Constitution, laws or treaties of the United States, or Executive orders of the President...." Although the Indian Tucker Act confers jurisdiction upon the Court of Federal Claims, it is not itself a source of substantive rights.... To state a litigable claim, a tribal plaintiff must invoke a rights-creating source of substantive law that "can fairly be interpreted as mandating compensation by the Federal Government...."

Mitchell I and *Mitchell II* are the pathmarking precedents on the question whether a statute or regulation ... "can fairly be interpreted as mandating compensation by the Federal Government." ... In *Mitchell I*, we considered whether the Indian General Allotment Act of 1887 (GAA), ... authorized an award of money damages against the United States for alleged mismanagement of forests located on lands allotted to tribal members. The GAA authorized the President ... to allot agricultural or grazing land to individual tribal members residing on a reservation ... and provided that "the United States does and will hold the land thus allotted ... in trust for the sole use and benefit of the Indian to whom such allotment shall have been made." ... We held that the GAA did not create private rights enforceable in a suit for money damages under the Indian Tucker Act. After examining the GAA's language, history, and purpose, we concluded that it ... removed a standard element of a trust relationship by making "the Indian allottee, and not a representative of the United States, ... responsible for using the land for agricultural or grazing purposes." ...

In *Mitchell II*, we held that a network of other statutes and regulations did impose judicially enforceable fiduciary duties upon the United States in its management of forested allotted lands. "In contrast to the bare trust created by the [GAA]," we observed, "the statutes and regulations now before us clearly give the Federal Government full responsibility to manage Indian resources and land for the benefit of the Indians." ... Having determined that the statutes and regulations "established fiduciary obligations of the Government in the management and operation of Indian lands and resources," we concluded that the relevant legislative and executive prescriptions could "fairly be interpreted as mandating compensation by the Federal Government for damages sustained." ...

To state a claim cognizable under the Indian Tucker Act, ... a Tribe must identify a substantive source of law that establishes specific fiduciary or other duties, and allege that the Government has failed faithfully to perform those duties.... If that threshold is passed, the court must then determine whether the relevant source of substantive law "can fairly be interpreted as mandating compensation for damages sustained as a result of a breach of the duties [the governing law] imposes." ... Although "the undisputed existence of a general trust relationship between the United States and the Indian people" can "reinforce" the conclusion that the relevant statute or regulation imposes fiduciary duties, ... that relationship alone is insufficient to support jurisdiction under the Indian Tucker Act....

We now consider whether the IMLA and its implementing regulations can fairly be interpreted as mandating compensation for the Government's alleged breach of trust in this case. We conclude that they cannot.

The Tribe's principal contention is that the IMLA's statutory and regulatory scheme ... attaches fiduciary duties to each Government function under that scheme.... [T]he statute and regulations at issue do not provide the requisite "substantive law" that "mandates compensation by the Federal Government." ... The IMLA and its implementing regulations impose no obligations resembling the detailed fiduciary responsibilities that *Mitchell II* found adequate to support a claim for money damages. The IMLA simply requires Secretarial approval before coal mining leases negotiated between Tribes and third parties become effective ... and authorizes the Secretary ... to promulgate regulations governing mining operations.... [T]he IMLA and its regulations do not "give the Federal Government full responsibility to manage Indian resources ... for the benefit of the Indians...." Instead, the Secretary's involvement in coal leasing under the IMLA more closely resembles the role provided for the Government by the GAA regarding allotted forest lands.... [T]he GAA ... did not "authorize, much less require, the Government to manage timber resources for the benefit of Indian allottees." ... Similarly here, the IMLA and its regulations do not assign to the Secretary managerial control over coal leasing. Nor do they even establish ... *any* trust language with respect to coal leasing....

The Tribe nevertheless argues that the actions of the Secretary targeted in this case violated discrete statutory and regulatory provisions whose breach is redressable in an action for damages. [T]he Tribe relies extensively on 25 U.S.C. §399 ... [which] describes the Secretary's *leasing* authority under §399; it does not bear on the Secretary's more limited *approval* role under the IMLA.... [T]he Tribe next asserts that the Secretary violated his "duty to review and approve any proposed coal lease with care to promote IMLA's basic purpose and the [Tribe's] best interests." ... To support that assertion, the Tribe points to various Government reports identifying 20 percent as the appropriate royalty ... and to the Secretary's decision, made after receiving *ex parte* communications from Peabody, to withhold departmental action.... [T]he Tribe maintains, the Secretary's eventual approval of the 12½ percent royalty ...was "improvident," ...because it allowed the Tribe's coal "to be conveyed for what [the Secretary] knew to be about half of its value" [and] Hodel's intervention "skewed the bargaining" by depriving the Tribe of the 20 percent rate, rendering the Secretary's subsequent approval of the 12½ percent rate "unfair." ... [T]he §396a arguments fail, for they assume substantive prescriptions not found in that provision....

In sum, neither the IMLA nor any of its regulations establishes anything more than a bare minimum royalty. Hence, there is no textual basis for concluding that the Secretary's approval function includes a duty, enforceable in an action for money damages, to ensure a higher rate of return for the Tribe concerned....

The Tribe's second argument under §396a concentrates on the "skewing" effect of Secretary Hodel's 1985 intervention, *i.e.*, his direction to Deputy Assistant Secretary Fritz to withhold action on Peabody's appeal from the Area Director's decision setting a royalty rate of 20 percent.... The Secretary's actions, both in intervening in the administrative appeal process, and in approving the amended Lease, the Tribe urges, were not based upon an assessment of the merits of the royalty issue; instead, the Tribe maintains, they were attributable entirely to the undue influence Peabody exerted through *ex parte* communications with the Secretary.... Underscoring that the Tribe had no knowledge of those communications or of Secretary Hodel's direction to Fritz, ... the Tribe asserts that its bargaining position was seriously compromised when it resumed negotiations with Peabody in 1985.... The Secretary's ultimate approval of the 12½ percent royalty, the Tribe concludes, was thus an outcome fundamentally unfair to the Tribe.... Nothing in ... the IMLA's basic provision, or ... regulations proscribed the *ex parte* communications....[5]

However one might appraise the Secretary's intervention in this case, we have no warrant from any relevant statute or regulation to conclude that his conduct implicated a duty enforceable in an action for damages under the Indian Tucker Act. [Reversed and remanded.]

Justice Souter issued a dissenting opinion joined by Justices Stevens and O'Connor.

... I part from the majority because I take the Secretary's obligation to approve mineral leases under 25 U.S.C. §396a as raising a substantial fiduciary obligation to the Navajo Nation (Tribe).... I would affirm the judgment of the Federal Circuit.

IMLA requires the Secretary's approval for the effectiveness of any lease negotiated by the Tribe with a third party.... The legislative history and purposes of IMLA ... point to a fiduciary responsibility to make a more ambitious assessment of the best interest of the Tribe before signing off. The protective purpose of the Secretary's approval power has appeared in our discussions of other statutes governing Indian lands over the years. In *Tiger v. Western Investment Co.*, 221 U.S. 286 (1911), for example, we upheld the constitutionality of the Act of Apr. 26, 1906 ... which made alienation of certain allotted lands by citizen Indians "subject to the approval of the Secretary of the Interior." Although allotment and conferral of citizenship had given tribal members greater responsibility for their own interest, ... we nevertheless understood that the requirement of prior approval was supposed to satisfy the National Government's trust responsibility to the Indians.... [I]n *Anicker v. Gunsburg*, 246 U.S. 110 (1918), we held that the

Secretary's authority to approve leases of allotted lands ... was "unquestionably ... given to him for the protection of Indians against their own improvidence and the designs of those who would obtain their property for inadequate compensation." ... The Secretary's approval power was understood to be a significant component of the Government's general trust responsibility....

Congress's decision in IMLA to give the Secretary an approval authority is well understood in terms of this background, for in the enactment of IMLA, Congress devised a scheme of divided responsibility reminiscent of the old allotment legislation. While it changed the prior law by transferring negotiating authority from the Government to the tribes, it hedged that augmentation of tribal authority in leaving the Secretary with certain powers of oversight including the authority to approve or reject leases once the tribes negotiated them.... The Secretary's signature was the final step in a scheme of "uniform leasing procedures designed to protect the Indians," *Montana v. Blackfeet Tribe* ... and imposed out of a concern that existing laws were not "adequate to give the Indians the greatest return from their property," S. Rep. No. 985, 75th Cong., 1st Sess., 2 (1937); H. R. Rep. No. 1872, 75th Cong., 3d Sess., 2 (1938). The "basic purpose" of the Secretary's powers under IMLA is thus to "maximize tribal revenues from reservation lands." *Kerr-McGee Corp. v. Navajo Tribe*, 471 U.S. 195, 200 (1985).... Consistent with this aim, the Secretary's own IMLA regulations ... provide that administrative actions, including lease approvals, are to be taken "in the best interest of the Indian mineral owner." ... Thus, viewed in light of IMLA's legislative history ... §396a supports the existence of a fiduciary responsibility to review mineral leases for substance to safeguard the Indians' interest.

I do not mean to suggest that devising a specific standard of responsibility is any simple matter, for we cannot ignore the tension between IMLA's two objectives.... The Court, however, errs in the opposite direction, giving overriding weight to the interest of tribal autonomy to the point of concluding that the Secretary's approval obligation cannot be an onerous one, ... thus losing sight of the mixture of congressional objectives. The standard of responsibility simply cannot give the whole hog to the one congressional policy or the other....

[E]ven a reticent formulation of the fiduciary obligation would require the Secretary to withhold approval if he had good reason to doubt that the negotiated rate was within the range of reasonable market rates for the coal in question, or if he had reason to know that the Tribe had been placed under an unfair disadvantage at the negotiating table by his very own acts.... And those modest standards are enough to keep the present suit in court....

The record discloses serious indications that the 12½ percent royalty rate in the lease amendments was substantially less than fair market value for the Tribe's high quality coal. In the course of deciding that 20 percent would be a reasonable adjustment under the terms of the lease, the Area Director of the Board of Indian Affairs (BIA) considered several independent economic studies, each one of them recommending rates around 20 percent, and one specifically rejecting 12½ percent as "inadequate." ... These conclusions were confirmed by the expert from the BIA's Energy and Mineral Division, in a supplemental report submitted after Peabody appealed the Area Director's decision. That report not only endorsed the 20 percent rate, but expressly found that the royalty rate "should be much higher than the 12.5% that the Federal Government receives for surface-mined coal" because the Navajo coal is "extremely valuable." ... No federal study ever recommended a royalty rate under 20 percent, and yet the Secretary approved a rate little more than half that....

What is more, the Tribe has made a powerful showing that the Secretary knew perfectly well how his own intervention on behalf of Peabody had derailed the lease adjustment proceeding that would in all probability have yielded the 20 percent rate. After his *ex parte* meeting with Peabody's representatives, the Secretary put his name on the memorandum, drafted by Peabody, directing Deputy Assistant Secretary Fritz to withhold his decision affirming the 20 percent rate; directing him to mislead the Tribe by telling it that no decision on the merits of the adjustment was imminent, when in fact the affirmance had been prepared for Fritz's signature; and directing him to encourage the Tribe to shift its attention from the Area Director's appealed award of 20 percent and return to the negotiating table, where 20 percent was never even a possibility.... The purpose and predictable effect of these actions was to induce the Tribe to take a deep discount in the royalty rate in the face of what the Tribe feared would otherwise be prolonged revenue loss and uncertainty.... What these facts support is the Tribe's claim that the Secretary defaulted on his fiduciary responsibility to withhold approval of an inadequate lease accepted by the Tribe while under a disadvantage the Secretary himself had intentionally imposed.... I respectfully dissent.

Following the Supreme Court's ruling in the case, the Circuit Court of Appeals for the Federal Circuit sent the case back to the Court of Claims to determine whether there was a basis in other statutes or regulations, apart from the IMLA, for a damages suit against the government. The Court of Claims found that there was no such basis, but the Federal Circuit reversed. In the process, that Court of Appeals found:

We note at the outset that this is not a case where the government had the discretion to exercise control and did not do so. Rather, in this case, the government exerted actual and significant control over the determination of the increased royalty rate in the lease amendments because its approval was required by law.... Faced with a claim for damages for this exercise of control, the government now takes the opposite stance, asserting that it had no control ... regarding the determination of the royalty rate in lease amendments. The law does not allow the government to have it both ways. That is, the government cannot assume comprehensive control of the Nation's coal, as it did here, and disclaim liability for exercising such control.[6]

The Court found that there was indeed a network of statutory and treaty law that provided a foundation for a damage claim by the Navajo. "Accordingly, this court holds that the Nation has a cognizable money-mandating claim against the United States for the alleged breaches of trust and that the government breached its trust duties."[7]

The U.S. Supreme Court once again agreed to review the case and heard oral arguments in February 2009. This time, in addition to the parties, four former Interior secretaries of both political parties, Cecil D. Andrus, Bruce Babbitt, Manuel Lujan, Jr., and Stewart L. Udall, filed an *amicus curiae* brief in support of the Navajo and against the Department of the Interior. In so doing, their brief asserts that:

In the conduct at issue in this case, the Department ... breached its fiduciary obligations to the Navajo.... A fiduciary is required to act with care, skill, and caution, in light of the interest of his or her beneficiary. Closely coupled with the duty of care is the duty of loyalty, the duty to act solely in the interests of a beneficiary without regard to the interest of third parties. *See id.* §78. The Department plainly breached these duties. By July 1985, the Bureau of Indian Affairs had prepared and readied for signature an opinion affirming the Navajo Area Director's order to increase Lease 8580's royalty rate to 20%.... However, after an *ex parte* meeting with a lobbyist for Peabody Coal, Secretary Hodel assumed personal jurisdiction over the appeal and instructed Department officials—in a memorandum drafted by Peabody Coal—to suspend action on the appeal and wait for the parties to reach a settlement. Pet. As a result of these actions, Peabody Coal was able to reduce its royalty payments by nearly 50%.

Because the Navajo were "[f]acing severe economic pressures," ... this suspension gave Peabody Coal significant bargaining power over the Navajo, who eventually agreed to a royalty rate of 12.5%, little more than half the rate ordered by the Area Director. Moreover, the Navajo surrendered millions in unpaid royalties and back taxes, and also surrendered the Secretary's power to adjust royalties in the future.... Thus, the Navajo were deprived of hundreds of millions of dollars over the course of the lease."[8]

"This conduct," they said, "is indefensible."[9]

Even so, Justice Scalia wrote for the Court in April 2009, rejecting the Navajo claim and concluding: "Today we hold, once again, that the Tribe's claim for compensation fails. This matter should now be regarded as closed."[10] There were no dissenting opinions, although Justice Souter who had issued a strong dissent in *Navajo I* asserted that he had been right the first time, but that precedent controlled the 2009 ruling (*Navajo II*) and he was therefore forced to concur.[11]

Where Is the Trust Responsibility Now?

If the situation confronted by the Navajo in this case was not sufficient to show a breach of trust responsibility adequate to support a claim in a court of law, then tribal governments could not be blamed for asking just what the trust doctrine means in the contemporary context. The Supreme Court added fuel to that frustration in a ruling that significantly undermined the trust doctrine in a case involving the Jicarilla Apaches of New Mexico.

United States v. Jicarilla Apache Nation

131 S. Ct. 2313 (2011)

INTRODUCTION: The Jicarilla Apache Nation has a variety of natural resources, including gravel, timber, and oil and gas reserves, on its reservation in New Mexico. As is generally true of Native American natural resources, the Department of the Interior has authority over the sales of those resources under a number of federal statutes and is responsible for managing the proceeds which the federal government holds in trust for the tribe or nation under the American Indian Trust Fund Management Reform Act of 1994 and other legislation.

The Jicarilla Apache launched a suit against the federal government in 2002 alleging it had mismanaged the funds from the sale of the development and sale of the resources, and had committed a breach of trust in a number of situations during the period from the 1970s through the 1990s. The tribe brought suit before the Court of Federal Claims under the Indian Tucker Act and the Tucker Act (Federal Tort Claims Act), seeking damages in respect of the government's mismanagement.

During an alternative dispute resolution process that stretched from 2002 to 2008, the tribe sought a wide range of documents from the government. The government released the documents but withheld 226 documents that it argued were protected by the attorney–client privilege, the attorney work-product doctrine, or the deliberative-process privilege.

The tribe insisted that the government turn over the documents and pointed to the "fiduciary exception" to the attorney–client privilege in such situations. Under that doctrine a trustee cannot withhold information from the party who is the beneficiary of the trust. The idea is that a fiduciary relationship is a relationship of special trust in which the trustee must always act in the best interest of the beneficiary and cannot be in a position of conflict of interest with that beneficiary. The tribe asserted that the federal government has a specific statutory obligation to maintain the fiduciary obligation, but also the larger and long-established general trust obligation that governs the relationship between the U.S. government and Native American tribes or nations. When the negotiations failed, the tribe moved the case back into litigation and presented those arguments to the Court of Federal Claims, which ruled, in most respects, for the tribe. That decision was affirmed on appeals to the U.S. Court of Appeals for the Federal Circuit.

Justice Alito delivered the opinion of the Court, which was joined by Chief Justice Roberts, and Justices Scalia, Kennedy, and Thomas.[12]

> The attorney–client privilege ranks among the oldest and most established evidentiary privileges known to our law. The common law, however, has recognized an exception to the privilege when a trustee obtains legal advice related to the exercise of fiduciary duties. In such cases, courts have held, the trustee cannot withhold attorney–client communications from the beneficiary of the trust.

> In this case, we consider whether the fiduciary exception applies to the general trust relationship between the United States and the Indian tribes. We hold that it does not.... The trust obligations of the United States to the Indian tribes are established and governed by statute rather than the common law, and in fulfilling its statutory duties, the Government acts not as a private trustee but pursuant to its sovereign interest in the execution of federal law. The reasons for the fiduciary exception ... do not apply in this context. We granted certiorari ... and now reverse and remand for further proceedings.

> II. ... The ... aim [of the attorney–client privilege] is "to encourage full and frank communication between attorneys and their clients and thereby promote broader public interests in the observance of law and administration of justice." ... Unless applicable law provides otherwise, the Government may invoke the attorney–client privilege in civil litigation to protect confidential communications between Government officials and Government attorneys.... The Tribe argues, however, that the common law also recognizes a fiduciary exception to the attorney–client privilege and that, by virtue of the trust relationship between the Government and the Tribe, documents that would otherwise be privileged must be disclosed....

> In order to apply the fiduciary exception in this case, the Court of Appeals analogized the Government to a private trustee... The Government, of course, is not a private trustee. Though the relevant statutes denominate the relationship between the Government and the Indians a "trust," ... that trust is defined and governed by statutes rather than the common law. See ... (*Navajo I*) ... As we have recognized in prior cases, Congress may style its relations with the Indians a "trust" without assuming all the fiduciary duties of a private trustee ... at common law. *United States v. Mitchell....*

We do not question "the undisputed existence of a general trust relationship between the United States and the Indian people." ... The Government, following "a humane and self imposed policy ... has charged itself with moral obligations of the highest responsibility and trust," *Seminole Nation*, ... obligations "to the fulfillment of which the national honor has been committed." ... Congress has expressed this policy in a series of statutes that have defined and redefined the trust relationship between the United States and the Indian tribes. In some cases, Congress established only a limited trust relationship to serve a narrow purpose. See *Mitchell I* [and] *Navajo I*....

We have looked to common-law principles to inform our interpretation of statutes and to determine the scope of liability that Congress has imposed.... But the applicable statutes and regulations "establish [the] fiduciary relationship and define the contours of the United States' fiduciary responsibilities." *Mitchell II*.... When "the Tribe cannot identify a specific, applicable, trust-creating statute or regulation that the Government violated, ... neither the Government's 'control' over [Indian assets] nor common-law trust principles matter." ... The Government assumes Indian trust responsibilities only to the extent it expressly accepts those responsibilities by statute.

Over the years, we have described the federal relationship with the Indian tribes using various formulations. The Indian tribes have been called "domestic dependent nations," ... under the "tutelage" of the United States ... and subject to "the exercise of the Government's guardianship over ... their affairs." ... These concepts do not necessarily correspond to a common-law trust relationship.... That is because Congress has chosen to structure the Indian trust relationship in different ways. We will apply common-law trust principles where Congress has indicated it is appropriate to do so. For that reason, the Tribe must point to a right conferred by statute or regulation in order to obtain otherwise privileged information from the Government against its wishes.[13]

III. In this case, the Tribe's claim arises from ... provisions [that] define "the trust responsibilities of the United States" with respect to tribal funds.... The Court of Appeals concluded that the trust relationship between the United States and the Indian tribes ... is "sufficiently similar to a private trust to justify applying the fiduciary exception." We disagree.

... The two features justifying the fiduciary exception—the beneficiary's status as the "real client" and the trustee's common-law duty to disclose information about the trust—are notably absent in the trust relationship Congress has established between the United States and the Tribe.

The Court of Appeals [determined] ... that the Tribe rather than the Government was the "real client" with respect to the Government attorneys' advice.... [W]e conclude that the United States does not obtain legal advice as a "mere representative" of the Tribe; nor is the Tribe the "real client." ... In some prior cases, we have found that the Government had established the trust relationship in order to impose its own policy on Indian lands.... In this way, Congress has designed the trust relationship to serve the interests of the United States as well as to benefit the Indian tribes.

The United States has a sovereign interest in the administration of Indian trusts distinct from the private interests of those who may benefit from its administration.... The Government may need to comply with other statutory duties, such as the environmental and conservation obligations.... [W]e have recognized that the Government has "discretion to reorder its priorities from serving a subgroup of beneficiaries to serving the broader class of all Indians nationwide." ... The Government may seek the advice of counsel for guidance in balancing these competing interests....

The Court of Appeals also decided the fiduciary exception properly applied to the Government because "the fiduciary has a duty to disclose all information related to trust management to the beneficiary." ... The United States, however, does not have the same common-law disclosure obligations as a private trustee....

The fiduciary exception to the attorney–client privilege ranks among those aspects inapplicable to the Government's administration of Indian trusts.... We therefore reverse ... and remand....[14]

Justice Sotomayor issued a dissenting opinion.

Federal Indian policy, as established by a network of federal statutes, requires the United States to act strictly in a fiduciary capacity when managing Indian trust fund accounts. The interests of the Federal Government as trustee and the Jicarilla Apache Nation as beneficiary are thus entirely aligned in the context of Indian trust fund management. Where, as here, the governing statutory scheme establishes a conventional fiduciary relationship, the Government's duties include fiduciary obligations derived from common-law trust principles. Because the common-law rationales for the fiduciary exception fully support its application in this context, I would hold that the Government may not rely on the attorney–client privilege to withhold from the Nation communications between the Government and its attorneys relating to trust fund management.

The Court's decision to the contrary rests on false factual and legal premises and deprives the Nation and other Indian tribes of highly relevant evidence in scores of pending cases seeking relief for the Government's alleged mismanagement of their trust funds. But perhaps more troubling is the majority's disregard of our settled precedent that looks to common-law trust principles to define the scope of the Government's fiduciary obligations to Indian tribes. Indeed, aspects of the majority's opinion suggest that common-law principles have little or no relevance in the Indian trust context, a position this Court rejected long ago. Although today's holding pertains only to a narrow evidentiary issue, I fear the upshot of the majority's opinion may well be a further dilution of the Government's fiduciary obligations that will have broader negative repercussions for the relationship between the United States and Indian tribes.

I. ... The majority fails to appreciate the important oversight and accountability interests that underlie [the] rationale for the fiduciary exception, or explain why they operate with any less force in the Indian trust context.... Since 1831, this Court has recognized the existence of a general trust relationship between the United States and Indian tribes. See *Cherokee Nation v. Georgia*.... Our decisions over the past century have repeatedly reaffirmed this "distinctive obligation of trust incumbent upon the Government" in its dealings with Indians. *Seminole Nation v. United States* [and] (*Mitchell II*).... Congress, too, has recognized the general trust relationship between the United States and Indian tribes. Indeed, "[n]early every piece of modern legislation dealing with Indian tribes contains a statement reaffirming the trust relationship between tribes and the federal government." ...

Through [various] congressional enactments, the United States has come to manage almost $3 billion in tribal funds and collects close to $380 million per year on behalf of tribes.... [T]he Government has extensive managerial control over Indian trust funds, exercises considerable discretion with respect to their investment, and has assumed significant responsibilities to account to the tribal beneficiaries. As a result, "[a]ll of the necessary elements of a common-law trust are present: a trustee (the United States), a beneficiary (the Indian [Tribe]), and a trust corpus (Indian ...funds)." ...

II. ... I would hold as a matter of federal common law that the fiduciary exception is applicable in the Indian trust context, and thus the Government may not rely on the attorney-client privilege to withhold communications related to trust management.... [T]he twin rationales for the fiduciary exception fully support its application in this context. The majority's conclusion to the contrary rests on flawed factual and legal premises.

When the Government seeks legal advice from a government attorney on matters relating to the management of the Nation's trust funds, the "real client" of that advice for purposes of the fiduciary exception is the Nation, not the Government.... Congress has enacted an extensive network of statutes regulating the Government's management of Indian trust fund accounts [that] establishes a "conventional fiduciary relationship" in the context of Indian trust fund administration. *Navajo Nation II*....

As a conventional fiduciary, the Government's management of Indian trust funds must "be judged by the most exacting fiduciary standards." *Seminole Nation*.... Among the most fundamental fiduciary obligations of a trustee is "to administer the trust solely in the interest of the beneficiaries." ... By law, the Government cannot pursue any "independent" interest ... distinct from its responsibilities as a fiduciary.... In other words, any uniquely sovereign interest the Government may have in other contexts of its trust relationship with Indian tribes does not exist in the specific context of Indian trust fund administration....

The majority's conclusion employs a fundamentally flawed legal premise. We have never held that all of the Government's trust responsibilities to Indians must be set forth expressly in a specific statute or regulation.... [I]n *Seminole Nation*, we relied on general trust principles to conclude that the Government had a fiduciary duty to prevent misappropriation of tribal trust funds by corrupt members of a tribe, even though no specific statutory or treaty provision expressly imposed such a duty.... The majority pays lip service to these precedents, [but] the majority inexplicably rejects the application of common-law trust principles in this case....

The majority requires the Nation to "point to a right conferred by statute" to the attorney–client communications at issue ... and finding none, denies the Nation access to those communications.... I would hold that the fiduciary exception is fully applicable to the communications in this case.

III. We have described the Federal Government's fiduciary duties toward Indian tribes as consisting of "moral obligations of the highest responsibility and trust," to be fulfilled through conduct "judged by the most exacting fiduciary standards." *Seminole Nation*.... The sad and well-documented truth, however, is that the Government has failed to live up to its fiduciary obligations in managing Indian trust fund accounts. See, *e.g.*, *Cobell*, 240 F.3d at 1089 ("The General Accounting Office, Interior Department Inspector General, and Office of Management and

Budget, among others, have all condemned the mismanagement of [Indian] trust accounts over the past twenty years").... The majority's refusal to apply the fiduciary exception in this case deprives the Nation—as well as the Indian tribes in the more than 90 cases currently pending in the federal courts involving claims of tribal trust mismanagement—of highly relevant information going directly to the merits of whether the Government properly fulfilled its fiduciary duties. Its holding only further exacerbates the concerns expressed by many about the lack of adequate oversight and accountability that has marked the Government's handling of Indian trust fund accounts for decades.

But perhaps even more troubling than the majority's refusal to apply the fiduciary exception in this case is its disregard of our established precedents that affirm the central role that common-law trust principles play in defining the Government's fiduciary obligations to Indian tribes.... There is no warrant in precedent or reason for reaching that result....

If this is what it means to have a commitment of the national honor and, as Justice Sotomayor reminds us, presents according to the *Seminole* decision "moral obligations of the highest responsibility and trust," to be fulfilled through conduct "judged by the most exacting fiduciary standards," one could pardon any Native American for asking just what the trust obligation means today.

Native American Treaty Rights, National Policy, and International Agreements

There have also been important arguments by Native Americans and other indigenous people around the world that their voices, and indeed their rights, have not been adequately addressed as contemporary national governments have entered into a variety of agreements on important issues, such as environmental and wildlife treaties. Controversies under these policies have raised even more complex issues about Native American self-governance that are well explained in a case involving the Makah tribe of Washington state.

In considering the Makah case, it is important to set aside one's views on the hunting of whales and to try to understand the situation from the perspective of the Makah. Tribal communities have historically included hunting and fishing not only as a means of subsistence, but as a critically important part of the culture and, in some cases, the religion of the tribe or nation. The taking of animals or even plants is done with ritual to honor the animal or plant and the creator's role in providing the relationship between the tribe and that animal or plant. Consider the following explanation, provided by the Columbia River Inter-Tribal Fishing Commission, between the tribal people of the Pacific Northwest, the salmon, and the rivers.

From a tribal legend, we learn that when the Creator was preparing to bring forth people onto the earth, He called a grand council of all creation. From them, He asked for a gift for these new creatures—a gift to help the people survive, since they would be quite helpless and require much assistance from them all. The very first to come forward was Salmon, who offered his body to feed the people. The second to come forward was Water, who promised to be the home to the salmon.... In accordance with their sacrifice, these two receive a place of honor at traditional feasts throughout the Columbia Basin. These ceremonies always begin with a blessing on and the drinking of water, followed by a prayer of thanksgiving on and the serving of wy-kan-ush, the salmon. This ceremony reinforces the central role that salmon and water play in the health of Indian people and their culture.[15]

Anderson v. Evans

371 F.3d 475 (9th Cir. 2002)[16]

INTRODUCTION: The Makah Tribe has historically lived on the Olympic Peninsula of what is now the state of Washington. The Makah ceded the great majority of its lands to the United States in the Treaty of Neah Bay in 1855. The treaty recognized their "right of taking fish and of whaling or sealing at usual and accustomed grounds and stations." It is the only Native American treaty that specifically recognizes the importance of whale hunting to the tribe and protects its hunting rights.

The Makah stopped whale hunting in the 1920s because of concern for the decline of gray whales and under pressure from the U.S. government. However, the California gray whale was taken off the endangered species list in the 1990s. The tribe was in the midst of an effort to strengthen its culture and its community. As a part of an effort to reinvigorate commitment to its historic culture, the tribe indicated its intention to exercise its rights under the treaty and resume a limited whale hunt.

In the period since it last engaged in whale hunting, the U.S. had entered into a set of international agreements on whaling. However, the international agreements administered by the International Whaling Commission (IWC) recognize subsistence whaling by aboriginal people.[17]

The U.S. government's National Oceanic and Atmospheric Administration (NOAA) agreed to seek an international permit on the tribe's behalf. It then sought and obtained a quota from the IWC for the tribe to take not more than five whales in a year. That federal agency also undertook an Environmental Assessment (EA) under the terms of the National Environmental Policy Act (NEPA). Given the size of the hunt and the whale population, NOAA issued a "Finding of No Significant Impact" (FONSI) under NEPA and therefore did not pursue an Environmental Impact Statement (EIS), a more extensive process. It then approved the hunt.

A variety of individuals and groups sued, arguing that the government was required to prepare an EIS and further contended that the whale hunt plan was in violation of the Marine Mammal Protection Act (MMPA).[18] The district court refused to grant an injunction against the hunt, holding that the tribe had a right under the Treaty of Neah Bay to proceed and that NOAA had in fact "taken a hard look" as it was required to do under NEPA. The treaty also took precedence over the MMPA restrictions.

Judge Berzon wrote the opinion for the panel.

> ... This modern day struggle over whale hunting began when the United States granted support and approval to the Makah Tribe's ... plan to resume whaling.
>
> I. ... The California gray whales migrate annually between the North Pacific and the West Coast of Mexico.... [B]y 1994 the whale was removed from the endangered species list.... The [National Marine and Fisheries Service] NMFS has determined that the eastern North Pacific gray whale stock has now recovered to between 17,000 and 26,000 whales, a number near its carrying capacity.... Most of the migrating whales pass through the Olympic Coast National Marine Sanctuary ... adjacent to the Makah Tribe's home territory on the coast of Washington State, on their way to the Bering and Chukchi Seas, and again when heading south for the winter.
>
> Not all of the gray whales, however, make the entire journey to the Far North each summer.... Scientists ... generally support the assessment that there is a fairly small number of whales who spend some or all of the summer in the general area

of the planned Tribe hunt, and that some of these whales return to the area for more than one summer.... [T]he whales in the Tribe's proposed whaling area are a relatively small subgroup of the larger number of nonmigrating whales that forego the complete trip to the North....

[T]he United States presented a proposal for ... a quota at the annual IWC meeting in June 1996.... [H]owever, ... some members of the IWC blocked its passage. The House of Representatives Committee on Resources also passed a unanimous bipartisan resolution opposing the Tribe's hunting proposal. In the face of this opposition the United States withdrew its request....

A few months later, the NOAA and the Tribe entered into a new agreement similar to the prior one except that the new version required that the Tribe's management plan provide time and area restrictions "including ... confining hunting activities to the open waters of the Pacific Ocean outside the Tatoosh-Bonilla Line." ... This provision sought to reduce the likelihood that the Tribe would take nonmigrating whales. Four days after this agreement was reached, the NMFS issued a final EA and a finding of no significant impact (FONSI) concerning the proposed hunt.

The United States thereupon presented a joint proposal with the Russian Federation to the IWC's 1997 annual meeting.... In March 1998, the NMFS announced a quota permitting the Tribe to take five gray whales in a one-year period and allowing no more than thirty-three strikes over a five year period....

Meanwhile, ... a group of concerned citizens and animal conservation organizations filed a complaint in federal court against the federal defendants for violations of NEPA.... After the district court granted summary judgment for the defendants, the Tribe began whaling and in 1999 killed one whale.

The whale's demise did not bring this prolonged dispute to an end, for this court reversed the district court in *Metcalf*. We held that the EA was invalid because it was not produced until after the agreement with the Tribe had been consummated.... After the decision in *Metcalf*, the federal defendants dissolved the agreement with the Makah Tribe (over the Tribe's protest) and began the EA process anew. The NMFS and the NOAA published a new Draft EA in January 2001. The Draft EA, like the 1997 EA, presented as the most desirable option a whale quota targeted at migrating whales. The restriction was to be accomplished by limiting the hunt to the area west of the Tatoosh-Bonilla line and to months when northward or southward migration was underway.... Similarly, the proposed Makah Management Plan only allowed whaling in the "open waters of the Pacific Ocean which are outside the Tatoosh-Bonilla Line." ...

On July 12, 2001, the NOAA and NMFS published a Final EA, based on the amended Management Plan and once again found no significant environmental impact.... The final step in the administrative saga took place when the NOAA and the NMFS [announced] ... a quota for the "landing" of five gray whales in 2001 and 2002 and approving the latest Makah Management Plan....

II. ... If an agency decides not to prepare an EIS, the decision not to do so may be overturned only if it is "arbitrary, capricious, an abuse of discretion, or otherwise not in accordance with law." ... More specifically, this court must determine whether the agencies that prepared the EA took a "hard look at the environmental consequences" of the proposed action.... The court must defer to an agency conclusion that is "fully informed and well-considered," but need not rubber stamp a "clear error of judgment." ...

[The] NEPA ... requires ... that all federal agencies consider the environmental impact of their actions. If a federal action "significantly [affects] the quality of the human environment," then the implementing agency or agencies must prepare an EIS providing a detailed and comprehensive analysis of the potential environmental impacts of the proposed action.... Before deciding whether to complete an EIS, government agencies may prepare a less formal EA which "briefly provides sufficient evidence and analysis for determining whether to prepare an environmental impact statement or a finding of no significant impact." ... If the EA results in a finding of no significant impact—a FONSI, in NEPA lingo—then no EIS need be completed.... [T]o prevail on the claim that the federal agencies were required to prepare an EIS, the plaintiffs need not demonstrate that significant effects will occur. A showing that there are " 'substantial questions whether a project may have a significant effect' on the environment" is sufficient....

The plaintiffs first focus on the possible impact of the Tribe's whaling proposal on public safety.... The government EA analyzes these risks in some detail and finds them insignificant.... In so concluding, the EA relies in large part on a study by Kirk H. Beattie, the safety expert hired by the Tribe. Beattie made specific safety recommendations, largely adopted in the Makah Management Plan.... The agencies' finding that public safety is not endangered is neither arbitrary nor capricious....

There is no disagreement in this case concerning the EA's conclusion that the impact of the Makah Tribe's hunt on the overall California gray whale population will not be significant. What is in hot dispute is the possible impact on the whale population in the local area where the Tribe wants to hunt. In our view, the answer to this question ... is sufficiently uncertain and controversial to require the full EIS protocol. The crucial question, therefore, is whether the hunting, striking, and taking of whales from this smaller group could significantly affect the environment in the local area. The answer to this question is, we are convinced, both uncertain and controversial within the meaning of NEPA....

The EA's *only* substantive attempt to address the impact of the Tribe's whaling on the number of whales in the area of the Marine Sanctuary and the Strait of Juan de Fuca is as follows: "With the extreme movements of whales in the [PCFA] both within and between seasons ... a limit of five strikes over two years should also alleviate any potential local depletion issues." ...

In short, the record establishes that there are "substantial questions" as to the significance of the effect on the local area.... And because the EA simply does not adequately address the local impact of the Tribe's hunt, an EIS is required....

The plaintiffs argue that the approval of the Tribe's hunting quota could have such a significant precedential impact on future IWC quotas.... The quota issued jointly to Russia and the United States was limited to whaling by aboriginal groups "whose traditional aboriginal subsistence needs have been recognised." ...

[W]e cannot agree with the agencies' assessment that because the Makah Tribe is the only tribe that has an explicit treaty-based whaling right, the approval of their whaling is unlikely to lead to an increase in whaling by other domestic groups. And the agencies' failure to consider the precedential impact of our government's support for the Makah Tribe's whaling in future IWC deliberations remains a troubling vacuum. We conclude that the possible impact on the heretofore narrow aboriginal subsistence exception supports our conclusion that an EIS is necessary....

Because the agencies have not complied with NEPA, we set aside the FONSI, suspend implementation of the Agreement with the Makah Tribe, and vacate the approved whaling quota for the Tribe.

Judge Gould wrote a concurrence joined by Judges Hill and Berzon.

[P]laintiffs maintain that the federal defendants issued a gray whale quota to the Tribe in violation of the Marine Mammal Protection Act (MMPA).... Defendants maintain that the MMPA does not apply because the Tribe's whaling quota has been expressly provided for by an international treaty, or, in the alternative, because the Tribe has an Indian treaty whaling right that is not affected by the MMPA....

If the MMPA's conservation purpose were forced to yield to the Makah Tribe's treaty rights, other tribes could also claim the right to hunt marine mammals without complying with the MMPA. While defendants argue that the Makah Tribe is the only tribe in the United States with a treaty right expressly guaranteeing the right to whale, that argument ignores the fact that whale hunting could be protected under less specific treaty language.... Having concluded that the MMPA is applicable to regulate the Tribe's whaling because the MMPA's application is necessary to effectuate the conservation purpose of the statute, and because such application is consistent with the language of the Neah Bay Treaty, we conclude that the issuance by NOAA of a gray whale quota to the Tribe, absent compliance with the MMPA, violates federal law....

Of course, in holding that the MMPA applies to the Tribe, we need not and do not decide whether the Tribe's whaling rights have been abrogated by the MMPA. We simply hold that the Tribe, to pursue any treaty rights for whaling, must comply with the process prescribed in the MMPA for authorizing a "take" because it is the procedure that ensures the Tribe's whaling will not frustrate the conservation goals of the MMPA.

The Makah continued to pursue a waiver of the MMPA to permit them to exercise their treaty rights. They rejected the argument that the Congress abrogated their treaty right.

There is no evidence that Congress was even aware of our unique treaty right to take marine mammals when it enacted the MMPA, much less that it chose to abrogate those rights. On the contrary, neither the MMPA nor its legislative history even mention Indian treaty rights until Congress amended the MMPA in 1994. Far from abrogating those rights, the 1994 Amendments expressly preserved them. Section 14 of the 1994 Amendments provides: "Nothing in this Act including any amendments to the Marine Mammal Protection Act of 1972 made by this Act alters or is intended to alter any treaty between the United States and one or more Indian Tribes." Pub. L. 103–238, §14 (Apr. 30, 1994); see Historical and Statutory Notes to 16 U.S.C. §1361. Congress's stated intent in enacting this disclaimer was to "reaffirm that the MMPA does not in any way diminish or abrogate protected Indian treaty fishing or hunting rights." S. Rep. No. 220, 103rd Cong., 2nd Sess, 1994 USCCAN 514, 534. The language and legislative history of the MMPA thus evince absolutely no Congressional intent to abrogate the Tribe's Treaty right to take marine mammals.[19]

However, it turns out that the question of congressional abrogation of legal provisions has indeed affected many tribes and nations in a very different way.

Diminishing Tribal Structure and the Ability to Protect Tribal Rights

One of the important dynamics in tribal life in recent decades has been the rise of tribal gambling establishments. There is no doubt that gambling is a controversial public policy issue, and that tribal casinos have also been part of that public debate. Many tribal members will quickly point out, however, that the money that has come to various tribes because of gambling has gotten the attention of state and federal officials in a way that no amount of pleading or even political demonstrations had managed to do. However, the present discussion is not about gambling as such, but rather about a case that came out of the development of Native American gaming policy by Congress. Its importance goes well beyond gaming and to the larger problem of the ability of tribes to sue state governments for damages in cases in which states interfere with tribal self-governance.

Perhaps because it was a Native American case, and the general public unfortunately tends not to pay heed to such disputes, that there was not much attention paid to the *Seminole Tribe of Florida v. Florida* opinion when it was issued by the Supreme Court in 1996, but it has become a landmark precedent that has been used to strike down a variety of provisions of federal civil rights protections since then, including portions of the Americans with Disabilities Act of 1990[20] and the Age Discrimination in Employment Act of 1967.[21]

The larger problem for Native Americans is that civil rights issues have long relied heavily on the ability to sue for damages as a mechanism to enforce civil rights protections. That has certainly been the case since the passage of the Civil Rights Act of 1964 and includes many other civil rights statutes adopted since then. This case goes to the ability of tribal governments to vindicate their rights in court.

Seminole Tribe of Florida v. Florida

517 U.S. 44 (1996)

INTRODUCTION: As the popularity of gambling and casino construction on tribal lands grew, so did controversies within the states about the role of state governments in decisions about gambling in the state, albeit on tribal lands. Congress sought to address the problem with the passage of the Indian Gaming Regulatory Act of 1988. The statute, adopted under the so-called "Indian Commerce Clause," Art. I, §8, cl. 3 of the Constitution, required states to enter into good faith negotiations with tribes to create a compact to government gaming. It also plainly provided for suits by tribes against states that refused to negotiate. Congress specifically indicated that it was removing the immunity of states from suit to facilitate the tribal actions.

This case grew out of demands by the Seminole Tribe of Florida that the state of Florida enter into negotiations under the Indian Gaming Act. Florida rejected that demand and challenged the legitimacy of the Act and its authorization of suits against the state.

Chief Justice Rehnquist wrote the opinion for the Court.

> [W]e granted *certiorari* in order to [decide the question]: Does the Eleventh Amendment prevent Congress from authorizing suits by Indian tribes against States for prospective injunctive relief to enforce legislation enacted pursuant to the Indian Commerce Clause? ... We hold that notwithstanding Congress' clear intent to abrogate the States' sovereign immunity, the Indian Commerce Clause does not grant Congress that power, and therefore cannot grant jurisdiction over a State that does not consent to be sued.
>
> The Eleventh Amendment provides: "The Judicial power of the United States shall not be construed to extend to any suit in law or equity, commenced or

prosecuted against one of the United States by Citizens of another State, or by Citizens or Subjects of any Foreign State." Although the text of the Amendment would appear to restrict only the Article III diversity jurisdiction of the federal courts, "we have understood the Eleventh Amendment to stand not so much for what it says, but for the presupposition ... which it confirms." That presupposition, first observed over a century ago in *Hans v. Louisiana*, 134 U.S. 1 (1890), has two parts: first, that each State is a sovereign entity in our federal system; and second, that "it is inherent in the nature of sovereignty not to be amenable to the suit of an individual without its consent."

II. Petitioner argues that Congress through the Act abrogated the States' immunity from suit. In order to determine whether Congress has abrogated the States' sovereign immunity, we ask two questions: first, whether Congress has "unequivocally expressed its intent to abrogate the immunity"...; and second, whether Congress has acted "pursuant to a valid exercise of power." ...

B. [O]ur inquiry into whether Congress has the power to abrogate unilaterally the States' immunity from suit is narrowly focused on one question: Was the Act in question passed pursuant to a constitutional provision granting Congress the power to abrogate? Previously, in conducting that inquiry, we have found authority to abrogate under only two provisions of the Constitution.[22] In *Fitzpatrick v. Bitzer*, 427 U.S. 445 (1976), we recognized that the Fourteenth Amendment, by expanding federal power at the expense of state autonomy, had fundamentally altered the balance of state and federal power struck by the Constitution. We noted that §1 of the Fourteenth Amendment contained prohibitions expressly directed at the States and that §5 of the Amendment expressly provided that "The Congress shall have power to enforce, by appropriate legislation, the provisions of this article." We held that through the Fourteenth Amendment, federal power extended to intrude upon the province of the Eleventh Amendment and therefore that §5 of the Fourteenth Amendment allowed Congress to abrogate the immunity from suit guaranteed by that Amendment.

In only one other case has congressional abrogation of the States' Eleventh Amendment immunity been upheld. In *Pennsylvania v. Union Gas Co.*, 491 U.S. 1 (1989), a plurality of the Court found that the Interstate Commerce Clause, Art. I, §8, cl. 3, granted Congress the power to abrogate state sovereign immunity, stating that the power to regulate interstate commerce would be "incomplete without the authority to render States liable in damages."[23]

Both parties make their arguments from the plurality decision in *Union Gas*, and we, too, begin there.... Following the rationale of the *Union Gas* plurality, our inquiry is limited to determining whether the Indian Commerce Clause, like the Interstate Commerce Clause, is a grant of authority to the Federal Government at the expense of the States. The answer to that question is obvious. If anything, the Indian Commerce Clause accomplishes a greater transfer of power from the States to the Federal Government than does the Interstate Commerce Clause. This is clear enough from the fact that the States still exercise some authority over interstate trade but have been divested of virtually all authority over Indian commerce and Indian tribes....

We feel bound to conclude that Union Gas was wrongly decided and that it should be, and now is, overruled. In overruling *Union Gas* today, we reconfirm that the background principle of state sovereign immunity embodied in the Eleventh Amendment is not so ephemeral as to dissipate when the subject of the suit is an area, like the regulation of Indian commerce, that is under the exclusive control of the Federal Government. Even when the Constitution vests in Congress complete law-making authority over a particular area, the Eleventh Amendment prevents congressional authorization of suits by private parties against unconsenting States. The Eleventh Amendment restricts the judicial power under Article III, and Article I cannot be used to circumvent the constitutional limitations placed upon federal jurisdiction. Petitioner's suit against the State of Florida must be dismissed for a lack of jurisdiction.

Justice Stevens wrote a dissent.

This case is about power—the power of the Congress of the United States to create a private federal cause of action against a State, or its Governor, for the violation of a federal right. In *Chisholm v. Georgia*, the entire Court assumed that Congress had such power. In *Hans v. Louisiana*—a case the Court purports to follow today—the Court again assumed that Congress had such power. In *Fitzpatrick v. Bitzer* and *Pennsylvania v. Union Gas Co.*, the Court squarely held that Congress has such power. In a series of cases beginning with *Atascadero State Hospital v. Scanlon*, 473 U.S. 234, 238–239 (1985), the Court formulated a special "clear statement rule" to determine whether specific Acts of Congress contained an effective exercise of that power. Nevertheless, in a sharp break with the past, today the Court holds that with the narrow and illogical exception of statutes enacted pursuant to the Enforcement Clause of the Fourteenth Amendment, Congress has no such power.

The importance of the majority's decision to overrule the Court's holding in *Pennsylvania v. Union Gas Co.* cannot be overstated. The majority's opinion does not simply preclude Congress from establishing the rather curious statutory scheme under which Indian tribes may seek the aid of a federal court to secure a State's good-faith negotiations over gaming regulations. Rather, it prevents Congress from providing a federal forum for a broad range of actions against States, from those sounding in copyright and patent law, to those concerning bankruptcy, environmental law, and the regulation of our vast national economy.

There may be room for debate over whether, in light of the Eleventh Amendment, Congress has the power to ensure that such a cause of action may be enforced in federal court by a citizen of another State or a foreign citizen. There can be no serious debate, however, over whether Congress has the power to ensure that such a cause of action may be brought by a citizen of the State being sued.

[T]he Court's contrary conclusion is profoundly misguided. [T]he shocking character of the majority's affront to a coequal branch of our Government merits additional comment....

II. The majority appears to acknowledge that one cannot deduce from either the text of Article III or the plain terms of the Eleventh Amendment that the judicial power does not extend to a congressionally created cause of action against a State brought by one of that State's citizens. Nevertheless, the majority asserts that precedent compels that same conclusion. I disagree. The majority relies first on our decision in *Hans v. Louisiana*. *Hans* does not hold, however, that the Eleventh Amendment, or any other constitutional provision, precludes federal courts from entertaining actions brought by citizens against their own States in the face of contrary congressional direction. *Hans* instead reflects, at the most, this Court's conclusion that, as a matter of federal common law, federal courts should decline to entertain suits against unconsenting States....

III. ... In confronting the question whether a federal grant of jurisdiction is within the scope of Article III, as limited by the Eleventh Amendment, I see no reason to distinguish among statutes enacted pursuant to the power granted to Congress to regulate commerce among the several States, and with the Indian tribes, Art. I, §8, cl. 3, the power to establish uniform laws on the subject of bankruptcy, Art. I, §8, cl. 4, the power to promote the progress of science and the arts by granting exclusive rights to authors and inventors, Art. I, §8, cl. 8, the power to enforce the provisions of the Fourteenth Amendment, §5, or indeed any other provision of the Constitution. There is no language anywhere in the constitutional text that authorizes Congress to expand the borders of Article III jurisdiction or to limit the coverage of the Eleventh Amendment.

The fundamental error that continues to lead the Court astray is its failure to acknowledge that its modern embodiment of the ancient doctrine of sovereign immunity "has absolutely nothing to do with the limit on judicial power contained in the Eleventh Amendment." It rests rather on concerns of federalism and comity that merit respect but are nevertheless, in cases such as the one before us, subordinate to the plenary power of Congress.

IV. Except insofar as it has been incorporated into the text of the Eleventh Amendment, the doctrine [of sovereign immunity] is entirely the product of judge-made law. Three features of its English ancestry make it particularly unsuitable for incorporation into the law of this democratic Nation. First, the assumption that it could be supported by a belief that "the King can do no wrong" has always been absurd. Second, centuries ago the belief that the monarch served by divine right made it appropriate to assume that redress for wrongs committed by the sovereign should be the exclusive province of still higher authority. Third, in a society where noble birth can justify preferential treatment, it might have been unseemly to allow a commoner to hale the monarch into court.

In this country the sovereignty of the individual States is subordinate both to the citizenry of each State and to the supreme law of the federal sovereign....

Justice Souter wrote a dissent joined by Justices Ginsburg and Breyer.

In holding the State of Florida immune to suit under the Indian Gaming Regulatory Act, the Court today holds for the first time since the founding of the Republic that Congress has no authority to subject a State to the jurisdiction of a federal court at the behest of an individual asserting a federal right. Although the Court invokes the Eleventh Amendment as authority for this proposition, the only sense in which that amendment might be claimed as pertinent here was tolerantly phrased by Justice Stevens in his concurring opinion in *Union Gas*. There, he explained how it has come about that we have two Eleventh Amendments, the one ratified in 1795, the other invented by the Court nearly a century later in *Hans v. Louisiana*. Justice Stevens saw in that second Eleventh Amendment no bar to the exercise of congressional authority under the Commerce Clause in providing for suits on a federal question by individuals against a State, and I can only say that after my own canvass of the matter I believe he was entirely correct in that view, for reasons given below. His position, of course, was also the holding in *Union Gas*, which the Court now overrules and repudiates....

The American development of divided sovereign powers, which "shattered ... the categories of government that had dominated Western thinking for centuries" was made possible only by a recognition that the ultimate sovereignty rests in the people themselves. The people possessing this plenary bundle of specific powers were free to parcel them out to different governments and different branches of the same government as they saw fit. Chief Justice Marshall's descri[bed the situation] of the National and State Governments as [one in which] "each sovereign, with respect to the objects committed to it, and neither sovereign with respect to the objects committed to the other." *McCulloch v. Maryland*, 17 U.S. (4 Wheat.) 316 (1819).

[T]he ratification demonstrated that state governments were subject to a superior regime of law in a judicial system established, not by the State, but by the people through a specific delegation of their sovereign power to a National Government that was paramount within its delegated sphere. When individuals sued States to enforce federal rights, the Government that corresponded to the "sovereign" in the traditional common-law sense was not the State but the National Government, and any state immunity from the jurisdiction of the Nation's courts would have required a grant from the true sovereign, the people, in their Constitution, or from the Congress that the Constitution had empowered....

Given the Framers' general concern with curbing abuses by state governments, it would be amazing if the scheme of delegated powers embodied in the Constitution had left the National Government powerless to render the States judicially accountable for violations of federal rights. And of course the Framers did not understand the scheme to leave the Government powerless.

... Without citing a single source to the contrary, the Court dismisses the historical evidence regarding the Framers' vision of the relationship between national and state sovereignty. In the end, is it plausible to contend that the plan of the convention was meant to leave the National Government without any way to render individuals capable of enforcing their federal rights directly against an intransigent State?

C ... The majority today, indeed, seems to be going *Lochner v. New York*, 198 U.S. 45 (1905), one better. Today the Court is not struggling to fulfill a responsibility to reconcile two arguably conflicting and Delphic constitutional provisions, nor is it struggling with any Delphic text at all. For even the Court concedes that the Constitution's grant to Congress of plenary power over relations with Indian tribes at the expense of any state claim to the contrary is unmistakably clear....

Following these rulings and the others discussed in Chapter 6, Native Americans were rightly frustrated. It appeared that their ability to use the courts to obtain redress and protection for their sovereignty, self-governance, and protection of their resources was dramatically curtailed. It also appeared that recourse to the marketplace or even protection for fair dealings in the marketplace was being denied as well, even where the tribal government was using this in an attempt to avoid confrontational behavior. Without such protections, even where Congress had supposedly provided it by statute as in the gaming laws, it was not at all clear just how tribal communities were to protect their rights. Unfortunately, the story was far from over and there was more bad news to come, even in the twenty-first century.

Who Interprets the Law? A Core Issue of Tribal Self-Governance

The questions of civil rights in Indian country, and of self-governance and tribal sovereignty as an issue of civil rights for Native Americans, are clearly tied to the question of who decides when the law and rights have been violated. Although tribal sovereignty entails the ability of tribal courts to decide cases within their jurisdiction, there has been a long-running line of case law that tests the boundaries of tribal jurisdiction in criminal and civil matters. Consider just two cases in that field.

In the first of these cases, *United States v. Lara*, the Court addressed a claim that arose with respect to a criminal matter, but its importance lies as much in what it says about tribal sovereignty and its relationship to federal authority as in the particulars of the case. The second case, *Plains Commerce Bank v. Long Family Land & Cattle*, presented a very different kind of issue, involving whether a business law dispute on a reservation involving tribal members and a non-tribal business is to be decided by a tribal court or an outside tribunal. These cases speak to the ability of Native Americans to adjudicate claims.

United States v. Lara

541 U.S. 193 (2004)

INTRODUCTION: This case arose when a man named Billy Jo Lara, who had been ordered excluded from the Spirit Lake Sioux Reservation by the tribe, was stopped on the reservation by federal officers. He hit one of the officers and was arrested. Lara is a member of a different tribe, but married a woman who is a member of the Spirit Lake Tribe. It happens that Congress had enacted a statute in 1990 to ensure that tribal courts would have jurisdiction over criminal trials of Native Americans who were not tribal members on the reservation in which the offense occurred.

Lara was prosecuted in the tribal court and, after pleading guilty, was sentenced to 90 days in jail. However, federal authorities then charged Lara in the federal court with assaulting a law enforcement officer. Lara claimed that the federal action was double jeopardy in violation of the Fifth Amendment to the United States Constitution.

Justice Breyer wrote the opinion for the Court.

... We must decide whether Congress has the constitutional power to relax restrictions that the political branches have, over time, placed on the exercise of a tribe's inherent legal authority. We conclude that Congress does possess this power.

II. We assume, as do the parties, that Lara's double jeopardy claim turns on the answer to the "dual sovereignty" question. What is "the source of [the] power to punish" nonmember Indian offenders, "inherent *tribal* sovereignty" or delegated *federal* authority? ...

The statute says that it "recognize[s] and affirm[s]" in each tribe the "*inherent*" tribal power (not delegated federal power) to prosecute nonmember Indians for misdemeanors.... [The statute] relaxes the restrictions ... that the political branches had imposed on the tribes' exercise of inherent prosecutorial power. The question before us is whether the Constitution authorizes Congress to do so.... Congress does possess the constitutional power to lift the restrictions on the tribes' criminal jurisdiction over nonmember Indians.

First, the Constitution grants Congress broad general powers to legislate in respect to Indian tribes, powers that we have consistently described as "plenary and exclusive." ... This Court has traditionally identified the Indian Commerce Clause ...

and the Treaty Clause ... as sources of that power.... The "central function of the Indian Commerce Clause," we have said, "is to provide Congress with plenary power to legislate in the field of Indian affairs." *Cotton Petroleum Corp. v. New Mexico....*

[T]reaties made pursuant to [the treaty] power can authorize Congress to deal with "matters" with which otherwise "Congress could not deal." ... We recognize that in 1871 Congress ended the practice of entering into treaties with the Indian tribes.... But the statute saved existing treaties ... and this Court has explicitly stated that the statute "in no way affected Congress' plenary powers to legislate on problems of Indians." ...

Moreover, "at least during the first century of America's national existence ... Indian affairs were more an aspect of military and foreign policy than a subject of domestic or municipal law." ... Insofar as that is so, Congress' legislative authority would rest in part, not upon "affirmative grants of the Constitution," but upon the Constitution's adoption of preconstitutional powers necessarily inherent in any Federal Government, namely powers that this Court has described as "necessary concomitants of nationality." *Worcester v. Georgia....*

Second, ... Congress has in fact authorized at different times very different Indian policies (some with beneficial results but many with tragic consequences). Congressional policy, for example, initially favored "Indian removal," then "assimilation" and the break-up of tribal lands, then protection of the tribal land base (interrupted by a movement toward greater state involvement and "termination" of recognized tribes); and it now seeks greater tribal autonomy within the framework of a "government-to-government relationship" with federal agencies....

Such major policy changes inevitably involve major changes in the metes and bounds of tribal sovereignty. The 1871 statute, for example, changed the status of an Indian tribe from a "powe[r] ... capable of making treaties" to a "power with whom the United States may [not] contract by treaty."

One can readily find examples in congressional decisions to recognize, or to terminate, the existence of individual tribes. [See] *Menominee Tribe v. United States*, 391 U.S. 404 (1968).... Indeed, Congress has restored previously extinguished tribal status—by re-recognizing a Tribe whose tribal existence it previously had terminated. 25 U.S.C. §§ 903–903f (restoring the Menominee Tribe) ....

Third, Congress' statutory goal ... is not an unusual legislative objective. The political branches, drawing upon analogous constitutional authority, have made adjustments to the autonomous status of other such dependent entities....

Fourth, Lara points to no explicit language in the Constitution suggesting a limitation on Congress' institutional authority to relax restrictions on tribal sovereignty previously imposed by the political branches.

Fifth, the change at issue here is a limited one. It concerns a power similar in some respects to the power to prosecute a tribe's own members—a power that this Court has called "inherent." ... And the tribes' possession of this additional criminal jurisdiction is consistent with our traditional understanding of the tribes' status as "domestic dependent nations." See *Cherokee Nation v. Georgia....*

Sixth, [this] our conclusion ... is consistent with our earlier cases....

IV. For these reasons, we hold ... that the Constitution authorizes Congress to permit tribes, as an exercise of their inherent tribal authority, to prosecute nonmember Indians. We hold that Congress exercised that authority in writing this statute.... Consequently, the Double Jeopardy Clause does not prohibit the Federal Government from proceeding with the present prosecution for a discrete *federal* offense.... [The] Eighth Circuit is reversed.[24]

Justice Souter issued a dissent joined by Justice Scalia.

It is as true today as it was in 1886 that the relationship of Indian tribes to the National Government is "an anomalous one and of a complex character." *United States v. Kagama*.... Questions of tribal jurisdiction ... do not get much help from the general proposition that tribes are "domestic dependent nations," *Cherokee Nation v. Georgia* ... or "wards of the [American] nation," *Kagama*.... Our cases deciding specific questions, however, demonstrate that the tribes do retain jurisdiction necessary to protect tribal self-government or control internal tribal relations, *Montana v. United States*, 450 U.S. 544, 564 (1981), including the right to prosecute tribal members for crimes, *United States v. Wheeler*, 435 U.S. 313, 323–324 (1978) .... Furthermore, except as provided by Congress, tribes lack criminal jurisdiction over non-Indians, *Oliphant v. Suquamish Tribe*, 435 U.S. 191, 212 (1978), and over nonmember Indians, *Duro v. Reina*, 495 U.S. 676, 685, 688 (1990)....

What should also be clear, and what I would hold today, is that our previous understanding of the jurisdictional implications of dependent sovereignty was constitutional in nature.... I would therefore stand by our explanations in *Oliphant* and *Duro* and hold that Congress cannot reinvest tribal courts with inherent criminal jurisdiction over nonmember Indians....

It is interesting that the majority in *Lara* retreated to the *Worcester v. Georgia* formulation of Native American tribes as "domestic dependent nations," a phrase still laden with disrespect to Native Americans. Ironically, in his concurring opinion Justice Kennedy adds insult to injury by reminding the majority that the United States is a nation that rests for its legitimacy on the "consent of the governed."[25] For a Court that has repeatedly upheld the authority of Congress to control Native Americans with "plenary" authority, and that has continued to refer to the basis for that power as the right of conquest, such references to consent of the governed are strange indeed, at least with respect to Native Americans and other groups who were not allowed to give or withhold consent for many years after the adoption of the Constitution.

One of the continuing issues for many Native Americans goes to the question of tribal court jurisdiction over matters that arise on the reservation and involve people who are not Native American. The Court's ruling in *Plains Commerce Bank v. Long Family Land & Cattle* not only goes to that question, but touches a nerve particularly because it has to do with action by an external property owner against tribal members on the reservation. It is all the more frustrating because many of these kinds of issues arise because of the legacy of the Allotment Act, which had been adopted precisely for the purpose of undermining, and destroying if possible, the integrity of tribal governance. The wound is rendered more raw by the Chief Justice's willingness to use the Allotment Act as a foundation for rejecting tribal governance claims.

Plains Commerce Bank v. Long Family Land & Cattle

128 S. Ct. 270 (2008)

INTRODUCTION: The complex facts of this case are presented in the opinion. The sharply divided Court did not disagree as to the facts and all of the justices found a need to place a limit on the remedies provided to the Long family. That said, there was a sharp difference, at a very fundamental level, to the question of the limits of tribal sovereignty and governance with respect to transactions between tribal members and non-tribal owners of reservation land.

Chief Justice Roberts wrote the opinion for the Court.

This case concerns the sale of fee land on a tribal reservation by a non-Indian bank to non-Indian individuals. Following the sale, an Indian couple, customers of the bank who had defaulted on their loans, claimed the bank discriminated against them by offering the land to non-Indians on terms more favorable than those the bank offered to them. The couple sued on that claim in tribal court; the bank contested the court's jurisdiction. The tribal court concluded that it had jurisdiction and proceeded to hear the case. It ultimately ruled against the bank and awarded the Indian couple damages and the right to purchase a portion of the fee land. The question presented is whether the tribal court had jurisdiction to adjudicate a discrimination claim concerning the non-Indian bank's sale of fee land it owned. We hold that it did not.

I. The Long Family Land and Cattle Company, Inc., is a family-run ranching and farming operation incorporated under the laws of South Dakota. Its lands are located on the Cheyenne River Sioux Indian Reservation. Once a massive, 60-million acre affair, the reservation was appreciably diminished by Congress in the 1880s and at present consists of roughly 11 million acres located in Dewey and Ziebach Counties in north-central South Dakota. The Long Company is a respondent here, along with Ronnie and Lila Long, husband and wife, who together own at least 51 percent of the Company's shares. Ronnie and Lila Long are both enrolled members of the Cheyenne River Sioux Indian Tribe.

The Longs and their Company have been customers for many years at Plains Commerce Bank (Bank), located ... in Hoven, South Dakota. The Bank ... has no ties to the reservation other than its business dealings with tribal members. The Bank made its first commercial loan to the Long Company in 1989, and a series of agreements followed. As part of those agreements, Kenneth Long—Ronnie Long's father and a non-Indian—mortgaged to the Bank 2,230 acres of fee land he owned inside the reservation. At the time of Kenneth Long's death in the summer of 1995, Kenneth and the Long Company owed the Bank $750,000.

In the spring of 1996, Ronnie and Lila Long began negotiating a new loan contract with the Bank in an effort to shore up their Company's flagging financial fortunes and come to terms with their outstanding debts.... [T]he parties finally reached an agreement in December of that year.... The Company and the Bank signed a fresh loan contract, according to which Kenneth Long's estate deeded over the previously mortgaged fee acreage to the Bank in lieu of foreclosure.... In return, the Bank agreed to cancel some of the Company's debt and to make additional operating loans. The parties also agreed to a lease arrangement: The Company received a two-year lease on the 2,230 acres, deeded over to the Bank, with an option to purchase the land at the end of the term for $468,000.... It is at this point, the Longs claim, that the Bank began treating them badly. The Longs say the Bank initially offered more favorable purchase terms in the lease agreement, allegedly proposing to sell the land back to the Longs with a 20-year contract for deed. The Bank eventually rescinded that offer, the Longs claim, citing "possible jurisdictional problems" that might have been caused by the Bank financing an "Indian owned entity on the reservation." ...

Then came the punishing winter of 1996–1997. The Longs lost over 500 head of cattle in the blizzards that season, with the result that the Long Company was unable to exercise its option to purchase the leased acreage when the lease contract expired in 1998. Nevertheless, the Longs refused to vacate the property, prompting the Bank to initiate eviction proceedings in state court and to petition the Cheyenne River Sioux Tribal Court to serve the Longs with a notice to quit. In the meantime, the Bank sold 320 acres of the fee land it owned to a non-Indian couple. In June 1999, while the Longs continued to occupy a 960-acre parcel of the land, the Bank sold the remaining 1,910 acres to two other nonmembers.

In July 1999, the Longs and the Long Company filed suit against the Bank in the Tribal Court, seeking an injunction to prevent their eviction from the property and to reverse the sale of the land. They asserted a variety of claims, including breach of contract, bad faith, violation of tribal-law self-help remedies, and discrimination. The discrimination claim alleged that the Bank sold the land to nonmembers on terms more favorable than those offered the Company. The Bank asserted in its answer that the court lacked jurisdiction and also stated a counterclaim. The Tribal Court found that it had jurisdiction, denied the Bank's motion for summary judgment on its counterclaim, and proceeded to trial.... The jury found for the Longs on three of the four causes, including the discrimination claim, and awarded a $750,000 general verdict.... [T]he Tribal Court entered judgment awarding the Longs $750,000 plus interest ... further awarded the Longs an option to purchase the 960 acres of the land they still occupied on the terms offered in the original purchase option, effectively nullifying the Bank's previous sale of that land to non-Indians.

The Bank appealed to the Cheyenne River Sioux Tribal Court of Appeals, which affirmed.... The Bank then filed ... in the United States District Court..., seeking a declaration that the tribal judgment was null and void because ... the Tribal Court lacked jurisdiction over the Longs' discrimination claim. The District Court ... found tribal court jurisdiction proper [and the] Eighth Circuit affirmed. [We] now reverse....

III. For nearly two centuries now, we have recognized Indian tribes as "distinct, independent political communities," ... qualified to exercise many of the powers and prerogatives of self-government.... We have frequently noted, however, that the "sovereignty that the Indian tribes retain is of a unique and limited character." ... It centers on the land held by the tribe and on tribal members within the reservation.

... [T]ribes retain power to legislate and to tax activities on the reservation, including certain activities by nonmembers..., to determine tribal membership..., and to regulate domestic relations among members.... They may also exclude outsiders from entering tribal land.... But tribes do not, as a general matter, possess authority over non-Indians who come within their borders.... As we explained in *Oliphant v. Suquamish Tribe*, ... the tribes have, by virtue of their incorporation into the American republic, lost "the right of governing ... person[s] within their limits except themselves." ...

This general rule restricts tribal authority over nonmember activities taking place on the reservation, and is particularly strong when the nonmember's activity occurs on land owned in fee simple by non-Indians—what we have called "non-Indian fee land." *Strate v. A-1 Contractors*, 520 U.S. 438, 446 (1997). Thanks to the Indian General Allotment Act of 1887 ... there are millions of acres of non-Indian fee land located within the contiguous borders of Indian tribes.... [T]he effect of the Act was to convert millions of acres of formerly tribal land into ["fully alienable"][26] fee simple parcels....

[O]nce tribal land is converted into fee simple, the tribe loses plenary jurisdiction over it.... Moreover, when the tribe or tribal members convey a parcel of fee land "to non-Indians, [the tribe] loses any former right of absolute and exclusive use and occupation of the conveyed lands." *South Dakota v. Bourland*, 508 U.S. 679, 689 (1993).... This necessarily entails the "the loss of regulatory jurisdiction over the use of the land by others." ... As a general rule, then, "the tribe has no authority itself, by way of tribal ordinance or actions in the tribal courts, to regulate the use of fee land." *Brendale v. Confederated Tribes and Bands of Yakima Nation*, 492 U.S. 408, 430 (1989)....

We have recognized two exceptions to this principle.... First, "[a] tribe may regulate, through taxation, licensing, or other means, the activities of nonmembers who enter consensual relationships with the tribe or its members, through commercial dealing, contracts, leases, or other arrangements." ... Second, a tribe may exercise "civil authority over the conduct of non-Indians on fee lands within the reservation when that conduct threatens or has some direct effect on the political integrity, the economic security, or the health or welfare of the tribe." Id., at 566.... These rules have become known as the Montana exceptions, after the case that elaborated them....

[E]fforts by a tribe to regulate nonmembers, especially on non-Indian fee land, are "presumptively invalid." ... The burden rests on the tribe to establish one of the exceptions to *Montana's* general rule that would allow an extension of tribal authority to regulate nonmembers on non-Indian fee land.... These exceptions are "limited" ones ... and cannot be construed in a manner that would "swallow the rule" ... or "severely shrink" it.... The Bank contends that neither exception authorizes tribal courts to exercise jurisdiction over the Longs' discrimination claim at issue in this case. We agree. [W]e hold that the Tribal Court lacks jurisdiction to hear the Longs' discrimination claim because the Tribe lacks the civil authority to regulate the Bank's sale of its fee land.

The Longs' discrimination claim ... concerned the sale of a 2,230-acre fee parcel that the Bank had acquired from the estate of a non-Indian.... The acres at issue here were alienated from the Cheyenne River Sioux's tribal trust and converted into fee simple parcels as part of ... the 1908 Allotment Act.... In 1934, Congress passed the Indian Reorganization Act ... which "pu[t] an end to further allotment of reservation land," but did not "return allotted land to pre-General Allotment status, leaving it fully alienable." ...

Respondents and their principal *amicus*, the United States, acknowledge that the tribal tort at issue here is a form of regulation.... They argue the regulation is fully authorized by the first *Montana* exception. They are mistaken.... *Montana* does not permit Indian tribes to regulate the sale of non-Indian fee land. *Montana* and its progeny permit tribal regulation of nonmember *conduct* inside the reservation that implicates the tribe's sovereign interests. *Montana* expressly limits its first exception to the "activities of nonmembers," ... allowing these to be regulated to the extent necessary "to protect tribal self-government [and] to control internal relations." ... "*Montana* does not grant a tribe unlimited regulatory or adjudicative authority over a nonmember. Rather, *Montana* limits tribal jurisdiction under the first exception to the regulation of the *activities* of nonmembers....

[W]ith only "one minor exception, we have never upheld under *Montana* the extension of tribal civil authority over nonmembers *on non-Indian land.*" ... The exception is *Brendale v. Confederated Tribes and Bands of Yakima Nation*, 492 U.S. 408.... In that case, ... five Justices concluded that *Montana* did permit the Tribe to impose different zoning restrictions on nonmember fee land isolated in "the heart of [a] closed portion of the reservation," ... though the Court could not agree on a rationale[, but] in no case have we found that *Montana* authorized a tribe to regulate the sale of such land....

By virtue of their incorporation into the United States, the tribe's sovereign interests are now confined to managing tribal land.... [C]ertain forms of nonmember behavior, even on non-Indian fee land, may sufficiently affect the tribe as to justify tribal oversight. While tribes generally have no interest in regulating the conduct of nonmembers, then, they may regulate nonmember behavior that implicates tribal governance and internal relations....

[R]egulation of the sale of non-Indian fee land, unlike the above, cannot be justified.... This is not to suggest that the sale of the land will have no impact on the tribe. The *uses* to which the land is put may very well change from owner to owner, and those uses may well affect the tribe and its members.... [T]he tribe may quite legitimately seek to protect its members from noxious uses that threaten tribal welfare or security, or from nonmember conduct on the land that does the same. But the key point is that any threat to the tribe's sovereign interests flows from changed uses or nonmember activities, rather than from the mere fact of resale....

Not only is regulation of fee land sale beyond the tribe's sovereign powers, it runs the risk of subjecting nonmembers to tribal regulatory authority without commensurate consent. Tribal sovereignty, it should be remembered, is "a sovereignty outside the basic structure of the Constitution." *United States v. Lara* ... (Kennedy, J., concurring in judgment). The Bill of Rights does not apply to Indian tribes.... Indian courts "differ from traditional American courts in a number of significant respects." ... And nonmembers have no part in tribal government—they have no say in the laws and regulations that govern tribal territory. Consequently, those laws and regulations may be fairly imposed on nonmembers only if the nonmember has consented, either expressly or by his actions. Even then, the regulation must stem from the tribe's inherent sovereign authority to set conditions on entry, preserve tribal self-government, or control internal relations....

In commenting on the policy goals Congress adopted with the General Allotment Act, we noted that "[t]here is simply no suggestion" in the history of the Act "that Congress intended that the non-Indians who would settle upon alienated allotted lands would be subject to tribal regulatory authority." ... In fact, we said it "defies common sense to suppose" that Congress meant to subject non-Indians to tribal jurisdiction simply by virtue of the nonmember's purchase of land in fee simple.... If Congress did not anticipate tribal jurisdiction would run with the land, we see no reason why a nonmember would think so either.

The Longs point out that the Bank in this case could hardly have been surprised by the Tribe's assertion of regulatory power over the parties' business dealings. The Bank, after all, had "lengthy on-reservation commercial relationships with the Long Company." ... But as we have emphasized repeatedly in this context, when it comes to tribal regulatory authority, it is not "in for a penny, in for a Pound." ... [T]here is no reason the Bank should have anticipated that its general business dealings with respondents would permit the Tribe to regulate the Bank's sale of land it owned in fee simple....

Justice Ginsburg issued a dissenting opinion, joined by Justices Stevens, Souter, and Breyer.

> ... I dissent from the Court's decision ... to the extent that it overturns the Tribal Court's principal judgment awarding the Longs damages in the amount of $750,000 plus interest.... That judgment did not disturb the Bank's sale of fee land to non-Indians. It simply responded to the claim that the Bank, in its on-reservation commercial dealings with the Longs, treated them disadvantageously because of their tribal affiliation and racial identity. A claim of that genre, I would hold, is one the Tribal Court is competent to adjudicate. As the Court of Appeals correctly understood, the Longs' case, at heart, is not about "the sale of fee land on a tribal reservation by a non-Indian bank to non-Indian individuals." ... "Rather, this case is about the power of the Tribe to hold non-members like the bank to a minimum standard of fairness when they voluntarily deal with tribal members." ...

As the basis for their discrimination claim, the Longs essentially asserted that the Bank offered them terms and conditions on land-financing transactions less favorable than the terms and conditions offered to non-Indians. Although the Tribal Court could not reinstate the Longs as owners of the ranch lands that had been in their family for decades, that court could hold the Bank answerable in damages, the law's traditional remedy for the tortious injury the Longs experienced.

I. [Since] *Montana v. United States* [has explained] that when a tribe has authority to regulate the activity of nonmembers, tribal courts presumably have adjudicatory authority over disputes arising out of that activity.... In my view, this is a clear case for application of *Montana's* first or "consensual relationships" exception....

The history of the Bank's commercial dealings with the Long Company and the Long family is lengthy and complex.... The Bank benefitted significantly from the Long Company's status as an Indian-owned business entity, for the BIA loan guarantees "allowed [it] to greatly reduce its lending risk." ... Eventually, the Bank collected from the BIA almost $400,000, more than 80% of the net losses resulting from its loans to the Longs....

Viewing the deal they were given in comparative light, the Longs charged that the Bank offered to resell ranch land to them on terms less advantageous than those the Bank offered in similar dealings with non-Indians. Their claim, all courts prior to this one found, fit within the *Montana* exception for "activities of nonmembers who enter [into] ... commercial dealing, contracts, leases, or other arrangements" with tribal members.... I am convinced that the courts below got it right....

Hardly a stranger to the tribal court system, the Bank regularly filed suit in that forum.... The Bank enlisted tribal-court aid to serve notice to quit on the Longs in connection with state-court eviction proceedings. The Bank later filed a counterclaim for eviction and motion for summary judgment in the case the Longs commenced in the Tribal Court. In its summary judgment motion, the Bank stated, without qualification, that the Tribal Court "ha[d] jurisdiction over the subject matter of this action." ... Had the Bank wanted to avoid responding in tribal court or the application of tribal law, the means were readily at hand: The Bank could have included forum selection, choice-of-law, or arbitration clauses in its agreements with the Longs, which the Bank drafted....

II. Resolving this case on a ground neither argued nor addressed below, the Court holds that a tribe may not impose any regulation ... on a bank's dealings with tribal members regarding on-reservation fee lands.... I do not read *Montana* or any other case so to instruct....

First, I question the Court's separation of land sales tied to lending activities from other "activities of nonmembers who enter consensual relationships with the tribe or its members." ... *Montana* listed as examples of consensual relationships that tribes might have authority to regulate "commercial dealing, contracts, [and] leases." ... [W]hy would the enforcement of an antidiscrimination command be less important to tribal self-rule and dignity ... when the command relates to land sales than when it relates to other commercial relationships between nonmembers and members?

III. ... Although the Tribal Court overstepped in its supplemental judgment ordering the Bank to give the Longs an option to purchase land third parties had contracted to buy, ... it scarcely follows that the Tribal Court lacked jurisdiction to adjudicate the Longs' discrimination claim, and to order in its principal judgment ... monetary relief.... The Federal Government and every State, county, and municipality can make nondiscrimination the law governing contracts generally, and real property transactions in particular.... Why should the Tribe lack comparable authority to shield its members against discrimination by those engaging in on-reservation commercial relationships—including land-secured lending—with them? ...

For the reasons stated, I would leave undisturbed the Tribal Court's ... initial judgment, ... awarding the Longs damages, prejudgment interest, and costs as redress for the Bank's breach of contract, bad faith, and discrimination.

Chief Justice Roberts prides himself on his ability to use rhetoric carefully and to write smoothly in order to make an unpalatable conclusion go down more easily, but there was nothing smooth or careful about his opinion in this case. Read from a Native American perspective, it says everyone should have consent of the governed except Native Americans. It says that tribal people may be regulated virtually without limit and as the mood strikes the Congress and yet it has no ability to protect tribal members from bad behavior on tribal land even by a company that has repeatedly used those same tribal courts for its own purposes. It relies on the idea that the Allotment Act not only served to alienate great portions of Native American land, but continues to this day to prevent full self-governance on tribal land by tribal people. It is difficult to find a way to be more demeaning than that.

The Continuing Problem of Failure to Honor Trust Obligations: The "Indian Money" Case

No contemporary discussion of Native American civil rights claims would be complete without at least a brief consideration of what has come to be known as the "Indian money" case, commonly known as the *Cobell* case, named for Elouise Pepion Cobell, who, along with a large class of other Native American plaintiffs, challenged the federal government's maladministration of trust funds that were originally contemplated in the Allotment Act, but that were hopelessly mismanaged by any number of federal government administrations over time. The complexity of the matter is presented in cryptic, if interesting, fashion by Judge James Robertson as he began his January 2008 ruling that stemmed from the trial in the case.[27] Indeed, his summary of the facts is useful as an introduction here. He wrote:

> To say that the histories of the IIM trust and of this lawsuit have been exhaustively chronicled in district court and appellate opinions is to stretch the limits of understatement.... Appellate panels hearing *Cobell* arguments have engaged ten of our Circuit judges, some of them more than once. Upon publication, this opinion will have the shorthand title *Cobell XX* [for the 20th opinion issued in the case]. Nevertheless, those histories must be retold at least briefly in order to provide context for today's opinion.
>
> Plaintiffs are a certified class of present and former IIM account holders numbering in excess of 300,000. Some account holders have more than one IIM account. Hundreds of thousands of IIM accounts exist, managed for the United States by its trustee-delegates, the Department of Interior and the Department of Treasury. Most of these IIM accounts exist to receive income the government collects for leasing or selling Indian-owned lands and then to distribute it to account holders when account balances reach certain thresholds (usually fifteen dollars). A small percentage of the funds flowing through the IIM trust are in "Judgment" and "Per Capita" accounts, which were created to hold funds derived from litigation settlements (Judgment accounts) and tribal revenues allocable to individual Native Americans (Per Capita accounts). By far the largest amount of trust funds flow through the "land-based" IIM accounts that contain lease, royalty, and land sale payments tied to individual land allotments.
>
> Individual Indian land allotments date to a period between the late 1800's and 1934 when the federal government attempted to dismantle tribes and instill the Anglo-American concept of private ownership in Native Americans by carving reservation land into individually owned parcels of up to 160 acres (now known as "tracts" or "allotments"). See, e.g., *Yakima v. Yakima Indian Nation*, 502 U.S. 251, 254 (1992) ("The objectives of allotment were simple and clear cut: to extinguish tribal sovereignty, erase reservation boundaries, and force assimilation of Indians into the society at large.") .... The government's pursuit of the allotment policy occurred alongside its official abandonment of treaty-driven relationships with tribes in favor of "govern[ing] [tribes] by acts of Congress." *United States v. Kagama*...; see Act of March 3, 1871, ch. 120, §1, 16 Stat. 566 (1871).... This policy shift and its corollary acts—such as coercive assimilation—were carried out without so much as the pretense of tribal consent....
>
> The allotment policy was first codified in the Indian General Allotment Act (Dawes Act) ... and was reflected in several subsequent allotment acts. In the Dawes Act, Congress granted unilateral authority to the executive branch to divide reservation land west of the Mississippi into plots for individual tribal members and families. It also allowed non-Indian settlement upon and exploitation of some reservation land, resulting in the alienation of millions of acres from tribal ownership. The statute required the federal government to hold the allotted land in trust for the individual allottees and their heirs for a period of 25 years—a period subject to extension at the government's discretion—after which fee patents would issue to the allottees.... While held in trust, allotted lands were to be immune from state taxation. The expectation was that, during that time, Indians would establish self-sufficient farms and earn enough money to pay their own taxes. At the close of the 19th Century, Congress passed several acts allowing the government to lease allotments that had not been successfully cultivated.... Any income

generated from the land was to flow into IIM accounts established by the government. Native American landowners could not (and today still cannot) sell or lease allotted land without the government's consent.... The Indian Reorganization Act ... was supposed to reconsolidate Indian lands and reverse the allotment process, but the land reclamation effort prescribed by that statute was never properly funded and never materialized. Instead, the Act succeeded only in ending the creation of new allotments and, for allotted lands already held in trust, extending the trust period indefinitely.... As of 1990, some eleven million acres were held in trust for the heirs of allottees, by now several generations removed. Many trust allotments are owned in common by hundreds or even thousands of beneficiaries....

The statute that gave rise to this litigation was enacted in 1994 as the Indian Trust Fund Management Reform Act, Pub. L. No. 103–412, 108 Stat. 4239.... The 1994 Act reflected many years of congressional frustration over Interior's handling of the IIM trust. It commanded Interior, among other things, to provide an historical accounting to trust beneficiaries.... Two years after the enactment of the 1994 Act, concerned that the required accounting had been neither accomplished nor even begun, the plaintiffs filed this suit. They alleged that the defendants were in breach of their fiduciary duties, and they prayed for an accounting and various other forms of declaratory, injunctive, and other equitable relief.

Judge Lamberth [in December 1999] declared defendants to be in breach of their statutory trust obligations ... and remanded the case to the agency with an injunction to bring its actions into conformity with its fiduciary duties and to submit quarterly reports on its progress.... *Cobell v. Babbitt* ... (*Cobell V*). The Court of Appeals affirmed the declaration of breach, but vacated several of Judge Lamberth's more specific findings. *Cobell v. Norton* ... (*Cobell VI*)....

After a 44-day trial, [Lamberth] issued an historical accounting opinion, a "fixing the system" opinion, and a structural injunction. *Cobell v. Norton* ... (*Cobell X*). The historical accounting portion of the structural injunction was reversed by the D.C. Circuit on December 10, 2004, *Cobell v. Norton* ... (*Cobell XIII*); reinstated by Judge Lamberth after Congress failed to meet its self-imposed deadline for achieving the legislative settlement on which the Court of Appeals had relied in deciding *Cobell XIII*, ... (*Cobell XIV*); stayed by the Court of Appeals ... and eventually reversed ... (*Cobell XVII*). On July 11, 2006, the Court of Appeals issued its eighth and ninth published opinions in the case, and directed that the case be reassigned.... (*Cobell XVIII*); ... (*Cobell XIX*). On December 12, 2006, the case was assigned to me....

During Judge Lamberth's heroic stewardship of this case, he was beset by a host of important but ancillary issues: vulnerabilities within the Interior Department's information technology systems, civil contempt proceedings concerning several government employees, retaliatory action within the agency against agency employees testifying on plaintiffs' behalf, objections to communication between the agency and the plaintiff class, and the appointment and removal of court monitors and special masters, to name a few. The nineteen published opinions in this case have yielded no definitive, undisturbed ruling on the core question that looms over this dispute, which is: What is the scope or nature of the accounting that is required by the 1994 Act? This opinion seeks to answer that question.

Perhaps the best way to understand the view of many Native Americans, and of the judge who worked the longest to deal with this case, is to read an opinion that Judge Lamberth issued in 2002 as he struggled to get the federal government to take the proper steps forward and to explain to the federal officials in no uncertain terms that certain practices were simply not to be tolerated. It should be noted that Judge Lamberth, a conservative Reagan appointee, was the victim of dramatically unfair allegations against him by some in both Democratic and Republican administrations. A fair reading of the record by parties other than those in the midst of the political fray would clearly conclude that Lamberth's frustrations with the conduct of the Department of the Interior and its legal representatives under both the Clinton and Bush administrations was well founded. To some Native Americans, Lamberth was getting a taste of what they had so often experienced when they tried to assert their clearly established legal rights.

Cobell v. Norton

226 F. Supp. 2d 1 (D.D.C. 2002)

The opinion was written by District Judge Royce C. Lamberth.

[The court must] determine whether defendants Gale Norton, Secretary of the Interior, and Neal McCaleb, Assistant Secretary of Interior for Indian Affairs, should be held in civil contempt of court.... [T]hese defendants are in civil contempt of court....

I. INTRODUCTION—The Department of the Interior's administration of the Individual Indian Money ("IIM") trust has served as the gold standard for mismanagement by the federal government for more than a century. As the trustee-delegate of the United States, the Secretary of Interior does not know the precise number of IIM trust accounts that she is to administer and protect, how much money is or should be in the trust, or even the proper balance for each individual account. Because of the Secretary's systemic failure as a trustee-delegate, the federal government regularly issues payments to beneficiaries—of their own money—in erroneous amounts. In fact, the Interior Department cannot provide an accurate accounting to the majority of the estimated 300,000 trust beneficiaries, despite a clear statutory mandate and the century-old obligation to do so. As the Court observed more than two years ago, "it is fiscal and governmental irresponsibility in its purest form."

Equally troubling is the manner in which the Department of Interior has conducted itself during the course of this litigation.... [In 1999 T]he Court found that almost immediately after proposing a clear and unambiguous order which the Court signed, "the defendants disobeyed that order and successfully covered up their disobedience through semantics and strained, unilateral, self-serving interpretations of their own duties." The defendants' misconduct did not end there.... In short, the Department of Interior has handled this litigation the same way that it has managed the IIM trust—disgracefully.

The issue now before the Court is whether the Secretary of the Interior and the Assistant Secretary of Interior for Indian Affairs should again be held in civil contempt of court ... for: (1) failing to comply with the Court's Order of December 21, 1999, to initiate a Historical Accounting Project; (2) committing a fraud on the Court by concealing the Department's true actions regarding the Historical Accounting Project during the period from March 2000, until January 2001; (3) committing a fraud on the Court by failing to disclose the true status of the TAAMS project between September 1999 and December 21, 1999; (4) committing a fraud on the Court by filing false and misleading quarterly status reports starting in March 2000, regarding TAAMS [Trust Asset and Accounting Management System] and BIA

Data Cleanup; and (5) committing a fraud on the Court by making false and misleading representations ... regarding computer security of IIM trust data.

V. CONCLUSIONS ...

A. Failure to Initiate a Historical Accounting Project

The Court concludes that the defendants failed to initiate a historical accounting project as required by the Order of December 21, 1999. The ... Department of Interior did not take any substantive measures ... during the eighteen month period following the Court's Phase I trial decision to provide the plaintiffs with the accounting that they are legally entitled to receive. The Court is both saddened and disgusted by the Department's intransigence in the face of the Phase I trial ruling.... [M]ore than a year and a half after the ... Phase I trial ruling—the Department ... had not even taken the preliminary steps that would enable it to select a particular method to perform the historical accounting.... [T]he Court finds that ... the defendants unreasonably delayed initiating the historical accounting project that they were required to perform ... and that such delay falls within the broad category of litigation misconduct that courts have the inherent power to redress.

B ... Concealing the Department's True Actions ...

The Court concludes that the defendants committed a fraud on the Court by concealing the Department's true actions regarding the Historical Accounting Project during the period from March 2000, until January 2001. The evidence ... prove[s] just how deceitful and disingenuous the defendants can be towards both the individual Indian trust beneficiaries and this Court. The Court's factual findings further demonstrate the lengths the Department will go to avoid having to provide the 300,000 plaintiffs in this action with an accounting of their money held in trust by the United States.

C ... Failing to Disclose the True Status of the Taams Project ...

The Court concludes that the defendants committed a fraud on the Court by failing to disclose the true status of the TAAMS project between September 1999 and December 21, 1999. The Department of Interior (and its attorneys) knew, even before the Phase I trial ended, that many of the representations it had made during that trial with respect to TAAMS were inaccurate. Notwithstanding the fact that Interior was aware of these false statements and the need to correct them, the agency intentionally failed to inform the Court about the massive problems it was experiencing with the new land management system. Thus, the record upon which this Court based its Phase I trial decision was infected with numerous false statements and inaccurate documents put forth by the Interior defendants.... By intentionally failing to appraise the Court of the true status of TAAMS, the defendants plainly committed a fraud on this Court and are ... in civil contempt of court.

D ... Filing False and Misleading Quarterly Status Reports ...

The Court concludes that the defendants committed a fraud on the Court by filing false and misleading quarterly status reports starting in March 2000, regarding TAAMS and BIA Data Cleanup. The [record] clearly demonstrate[s] that the Interior defendants intentionally filed the false and misleading quarterly status reports to make this Court ... believe that significant headway had been made on these two critical sub-projects. In reality, only minimal progress—if any at all—had been made during this time period, and presently neither the TAAMS nor the BIA Data Cleanup sub-project are even remotely close to being completed.... In my fifteen years on the bench I have never seen a litigant make such a concerted effort to subvert the truth seeking function of the judicial process. I am immensely disappointed that I see such a litigant today and that the litigant is a Department of the United States government....

[T]he Department of Interior committed a fraud on the Court [and] these defendants are in civil contempt of court for doing so. There is no question that the false and misleading information contained in these reports affected the Court's ability to adjudicate this matter fairly and that it all but destroyed the plaintiffs' ability to present their case. Moreover, the implication of attorneys in the Solicitor's Office clearly make this misconduct constitute fraud on the court. It is almost unfathomable that a federal agency would engage in such a pervasive scheme aimed at defrauding the Court and preventing the plaintiffs from learning the truth....

E ... Making False and Misleading Representations ... Regarding Computer Security of IIM Trust Data

[T]he defendants committed a fraud on the Court by making false and misleading representations starting in March 2000, regarding computer security of IIM trust data.... [T]he Interior Department and its attorneys consistently represented to this Court that while there was a problem with data security, the agency was in the process of making the pertinent computer systems more physically and electronically secure. These representations were patently false, and the Department and its attorneys knew it. By deliberately making these false and misleading representations, the defendants necessarily precluded this Court from fairly and promptly adjudicating this matter and undeniably hindered the plaintiffs' ability to present its case on this critical point.

Finally, the ... Department of Interior cannot engage in the type of despicable conduct detailed in this opinion and then argue that the Court should nevertheless not hold the Secretary and Assistant Secretary in civil contempt because it may affect their prospective ability to discharge their fiduciary obligations.

VI. RELIEF. The most taxing aspect of this case has been and continues to be fashioning appropriate relief for the plaintiffs. Each time it has been confronted with this difficult issue the Court has stuck to its constitutional roots by awarding only that relief which it finds to be absolutely necessary. For example, following the first contempt trial in this action, ... the Court took the moderate steps of appointing a special master to oversee the discovery process and awarding plaintiffs reasonable expenses and attorneys' fees incurred as a result of defendants' failure to obey the orders....

Moreover, ... after the plaintiffs proved that the defendants were in breach of the fiduciary obligations that they owe to the class of 300,000 IIM trust beneficiaries, the Court granted the most mild form of relief that it could fashion. Specifically, the Court ... remanded the matter back to the administrative agency to bring itself into compliance with those duties as well as the obligations found in the 1994 Act.... So as not to interfere unduly in the inner workings of the Interior Department, the Court ... explicitly declined at that time to issue a structural injunction or even to appoint a special master to monitor the defendants' progress towards bringing themselves into compliance with their trust duties....

A ... Appointment of a Receiver over the IIM Trust.

The plaintiffs vigorously argue that the only adequate remedy to redress the defendants' egregious misconduct in this case is the appointment of a receiver over the IIM trust.... [T]he Court has determined that the more sound approach is to schedule and conduct further proceedings to determine what additional relief ... is warranted with respect to the fixing the system portion of the case [*sic*], and approve an approach to conducting a historical accounting of the IIM trust accounts....

VII. CONCLUSION. In February of 1999, at the end of the first contempt trial in this matter, I stated that "I have never seen more egregious misconduct by the federal government." Now, at the conclusion of the second contempt trial in this action, I stand corrected. The Department of Interior has truly outdone itself this time. The agency has indisputably proven to the Court, Congress, and the individual Indian beneficiaries that it is either unwilling or unable to administer competently the IIM trust. Worse yet, the Department has now undeniably shown that it can no longer be trusted to state accurately the status of its trust reform efforts....

Congress has mandated, the Court has ordered, and the beneficiaries have pleaded for meaningful reform of the IIM trust. This Court need not sit supinely by waiting, hoping that the Department of Interior complies with the orders of this Court and the fiduciary obligations mandated by Congress in the 1994 Act. To do so would be futile. I may have life tenure, but at the rate the Department of Interior is progressing that is not a long enough appointment.

Judge Lamberth's opinion employed very strong language, but, in the end, ordered relatively modest actions by the government. Even so, the administration pressed for Lamberth's removal from the case. His contempt rulings were overturned on appeal and Judge James Robertson assumed responsibility for the case after that. Ultimately, in August 2008, Robertson issued a ruling that ordered repayment of $455.6 million, far less than the $47 billion had been sought by the plaintiffs, and the battle continued.[28] The case was eventually settled by the Obama administration in the amount of $3.4 billion with the passage of the Claims Resolution of 2010 in December 2010.[29]

The Challenge of Civil Rights and Native American Spirituality

For many Native Americans, one of the serious areas of civil rights difficulty has concerned spirituality. For most constitutional scholars, the discussion of spirituality is a matter of civil liberties, rather than civil rights, and is addressed in terms of the case law that interprets the free exercise and establishment clauses of the First Amendment. However, for many Native Americans, the situation is far more complex than that and goes to issues of discrimination and other aspects of civil rights and not to narrower, though extremely important, conceptions of First Amendment civil liberties. This difference stems in part from a very important tension that is often difficult even to address. This is the fundamental connection between mind, body, and spirit in native cultures. These three elements are most often also tied to place, to the land, and to tribal tradition in its homeland. The tension also derives from fundamental differences between most Native American spiritual and religious traditions and those of Western religions.

As to the latter point, it is useful to provide a brief excerpt from a brief filed by the State of California in a case that ultimately went to the U.S. Supreme Court. It provides a useful explanation of some of the key differences between cultural approaches to religion. California argued that this different view is every bit as valid as any Western faith and just as worthy of respect and constitutional protection. The state quoted from the interagency task force report done during the debate over what was to become the American Indian Religious Freedom Act.[30]

> The mainstream religions are commemorative, that is, they trace their origins back to a specific person or event (e.g., Jesus, the Exodus, Mohammed) which their rituals commemorate. The mainstay of their beliefs is the doctrine that their particular interpretation of reality, usually revealed by the religion's founder, is the correct interpretation. Since the religious ceremonies are commemorative, where they take place is not nearly as important as the revealed truth which they honor. Major religions have established religious institutions in order to carry on the task of interpreting the "truth" for each generation and in order to protect it from heresies. Mainstream religious institutions have historically sought to impose their interpretation, as the "laws" of God, on others through laws enforced by secular penalties. It is from this commemorative tradition that most current inhabitants of the United States come, many early immigrants having come to escape attempts to force them to accept beliefs or practices which violated their own religious consciences....
>
> The tribal religions, including the American Indian tribal religions "represent the opposite pole of human experience." ... They are "continuing" religions, not traceable to a founder; their origins are lost in the mists of time. They do not have a set of doctrines or dogma. Rather, they perpetuate a set of rituals and ceremonies which must be conducted both in the same manner and in the same place. A doctrine, which would be a commentary on or interpretation of the rituals, would be inconsistent with the religious role of the rituals themselves.... "Unlike institutional religion, the tribal religions do not depend upon community participation, but upon the proper performance of the ceremony." ... Exclusion of all but those carrying out the ceremony "is central to many ceremonies."
>
> Also unlike the majority or mainstream religions, which see the world as having been created by the deity at the beginning of time, and as continuing to exist under natural laws which the deity instituted at the creation, American Indian tribal religions see creation as a continual process. This ongoing process of creation and cosmic growth brings with it the religious obligation for people to participate in that creation through World Renewal ceremonies and respect for nature.... "The primary essence of the tribal religions is to remain in a constant and consistent relationship with nature."

With those foundations in mind, there are two important rulings issued by the U.S. Supreme Court in modern history that have presented serious concerns about an attitude of disrespect and discrimination by federal law and courts to Native American culture and religion. In both cases, as has been true throughout this book, the language used and approach taken are as important to those affected and other Native Americans as are the actual rulings in the cases. Additionally, in both cases, as dissenters explain, the disparity between the treatment accorded Western religions and that affecting Native Americans is apparent.

Lyng v. Northwest Indian Cemetery Protective Association

485 U.S. 439 (1988)

INTRODUCTION: The subject of land claims has been difficult for many tribal communities because the Western concept of land ownership is a serious challenge to the natural order for many Native Americans, under which people are of nature and connected to the land rather than owners of it in "fee simple absolute," as the legal language reads.[31] All but small areas of former Native American lands that covered the western United States were in someone else's hands by the late twentieth century. Even on land that is recognized as reservation land, the Congress has adopted legislation determining the relative authority over natural resources of the Indian Nations and that of the Congress in such matters as control over mining and timber operations.[32]

For Native American tribes and nations, the connection with the land is fundamental, visceral, the very foundation of life itself.[33] And life is not merely bodily existence but a way of being that is a harmonious relationship of mind, body, and spirit.[34] This sacred relationship is not only found among native peoples of North America, but also around the world.[35]

This case can be traced back to 1972 when the U.S. Forest Service began to develop a management plan for what was known as the Blue Creek Unit of the Six Rivers National Forest in Northern California. The service published notice of its developing plan in 1974. In late 1977 the service indicated further that it was considering a number of alternatives for road construction through the area that would connect two other sections of road. The management plan was not ultimately issued until February 1981, at which time the Forest Service indicated that 733 million board feet of timber could be harvested from that area during the next 80 years. The decision on the road construction came a year after that.

In the interim, the Forest Service had commissioned a study on the impact of the proposed development on Native Americans. The study, "Cultural Resources of the Chimney Rock Section, Gasquet-Orleans Road, Six Rivers National Forest"— which became known as the Theodoratus Report—was completed in early 1979 by Dr. Dorothea Theodoratus, Dr. Joseph Chartkoff, and Ms. Kerry Chartkoff, and reviewed and approved later in the year by Dr. Joseph Winter, Forest Archeologist for the Six Rivers National Forest. It concluded:

> The completion of the G-O Road via any of the proposed Chimney Rock alternatives (Routes 1–9) will produce an irreparable impact on the spiritual and physical well-being of the adjacent Yurok, Karok and Tolowa communities. Such impact will be created through the degradation of salient environmental qualities pertinent to the power quests of medicinal and spiritual practitioners who serve these communities. It is recommended, therefore, that such an impact is, in fact, sufficient to justify the rejection of all proposed routes (Routes 1–9) of the Chimney Rock section of the G-O Road.

The Forest Service accepted the findings of the report, which concluded, among other things, that there would be significant damage and that none of the alternatives under discussion would be adequate to mitigate that damage. *Northwestern Indian Cemetery Protective Association v. Peterson*, 795 F.2d 688, 693 (9th Cir. 1985).

The Forest Service ultimately decided to build a 6-mile paved section to connect two existing sections of road from Gasquet to Orleans, which was then to be used to service the logging activity. The Yurok, Karok, and Tolowa Indian tribes objected that the road would run through their most sacred area, the very heart of their religion. The decision to build there violated the tribal people's First Amendment right to free exercise of religion under the United States Constitution.

The area to be developed was what they referred to as "the high country," the home of their religious faith and practice, as well as the dwelling place of figures central to their religion such as the "before time people" and the "thunders." This was also the place where members were trained and where they gathered the materials needed for their rituals that were key to the regular renewal of the faith. As is common for many indigenous faiths, sacred ground is often not one specific place, but an area.

Individuals hike into the high country and use "prayer seats" located at Doctor Rock, Chimney Rock, and Peak 8 to seek religious guidance or personal "power" through "engaging in emotional [and] spiritual exchange with the Creator." Such exchange is made possible by the solitude, quietness, and pristine environment found in the high country. Certain key participants in tribal religious ceremonies such as the White Deerskin and Jump Dances must visit the high country prior to the ceremony to purify themselves and to make "preparatory medicine."[36]

The tribes also indicated that medicine women go to these places to gather medicinal plants with which to treat people in their community. It was where individual members of the faith would go on individual spirit quests as well.

The tribes argued that the construction, logging, traffic, and environmental damage would effectively destroy their ability to worship in these sacred places. The Forest Service's plan to mitigate the effects of the development by creating half-mile areas known as protective zones around each of the specific sites that they identified did not resolve the problems.

Four Native Americans from the three tribes, Jimmie James, Sam Jones, Lowana Branter, and Christopher H. Peters, brought suit against the head of the U.S. Forest Service and the U.S. Secretary of Agriculture. They were joined by a number of groups, including the Northwest Indian Cemetery Protective Association, Sierra Club, the Wilderness Society, California Trout, Siskiyou Mountains Resource Council, Redwood Region Audubon Society, and Northcoast Environmental Center. At the same time, the state of California brought its own suit against the same officials and also the regional forester.

The Forest Service answered that there were overriding public interests that should prevail, even though this would result in a serious violation of the Native Americans' free exercise rights.

The district court found that the facts failed to support the Forest Service claims. There were already access areas for timber harvesting and the new road was not required for that purpose. The evidence did not show that the new development would create new jobs in the timber business. At most, it suggested that some jobs might be transferred from one area of the forest to another. There was little evidence to support claims about increased recreational use, and, even if there were proof of increases, that would hardly be important enough to raise the claims to the level of a compelling state interest—an interest so overriding that it justified knowingly abridging free exercise of religion. Similarly, there was no evidence that the road would improve administration of the forest. Neither was there any evidence that the road would increase competition for timber and result in more funds to the government. In fact, "Defendants failed to introduce any evidence whatever establishing the likely effect of the road construction on regional timber markets." ... Therefore, Judge Weigel concluded that there was no compelling interest sufficient to justify a violation of the free exercise clause. Even if there was more evidence of paramount interests, he said, the Forest Service plan was not narrowly tailored so as to be the least harmful means to accomplish those interests. He enjoined construction of the road.

The Ninth Circuit panel affirmed. However, while the case was pending, the Congress passed the California Wilderness Act of 1984, which set aside a portion of the disputed area as wilderness. Therefore, the part of the district court order requiring further environmental assessments in those areas was no longer an issue and was vacated.

However, the federal government immediately sought rehearing of the case on grounds that while the new Wilderness Act had set aside most of the land, the statute left a corridor open that would have permitted construction of the road, although the Congress did not state any intention that the road should be built. The court of appeals panel granted the Forest Service a rehearing a month later, vacated its first opinion, and substituted a second and slightly stronger argument that reached the same conclusion as it had earlier, upholding the order against the road. While the same three judges were on this panel, Judge Robert R. Beezer dissented in this second opinion, contending that the road did not infringe on the Native Americans' free exercise of religion. He based that argument in large part on the idea that the Indian perception of free exercise of religion, as explained in the Theodoratus study, was broader than the Western notion of religious practice protected by the First Amendment.

The federal government pointed to Judge Beezer's argument as the correct starting point for reexamining the case in the Supreme Court. It argued that there was no burden on the Native Americans' First Amendment protected freedom of religion, and further contended that the Court should defer to the discretion of the government in managing federal lands to the extent of creating a free exercise of religion standard in cases involving federal lands that would be far more deferential to the government than the standard that applied in every other context.

> Even if the Court concludes that the land management decisions at issue here do burden respondents' free exercise rights, those decisions should be upheld because they are supported by a sufficiently weighty government interest. The Court has stated that government action burdening an individual's free exercise rights must be justified by a compelling interest, but it has never applied that standard in the context of a challenge to government action involving the management of public land.[37]

The state of California had filed separate litigation on behalf of the state's Native American Heritage Commission and the U.S. Supreme Court consolidated the two cases to be decided together. As noted earlier, the state brief in the Supreme Court supported the Native Americans' perception of religion as different, but every bit as valid as any Western faith,[38] and in so doing quoted from the interagency task force report done during consideration of what became the American Indian Religious Freedom Act mentioned earlier. This material goes to the heart of the differences in cultural perspective between Native Americans and the majority religions in the United States.[39]

Justice O'Connor wrote the opinion for the Court.[40]

> This case requires us to consider whether the First Amendment's Free Exercise Clause forbids the Government from permitting timber harvesting in, or constructing a road through, a portion of a National Forest that has traditionally been used for religious purposes by members of three American Indian tribes in northwestern California. We conclude that it does not....
>
> III. ... The Free Exercise Clause of the First Amendment provides that "Congress shall make no law ... prohibiting the free exercise [of religion]." ... It is undisputed that the Indian respondents' beliefs are sincere and that the Government's proposed actions will have severe adverse effects on the practice of their religion. Respondents contend that the burden on their religious practices is heavy enough to violate the Free Exercise Clause unless the Government can demonstrate a

compelling need to complete the G-O road or to engage in timber harvesting in the Chimney Rock area. We disagree.

In *Bowen v. Roy*, 476 U.S. 693 (1986), we considered a challenge to a federal statute that required the States to use Social Security numbers in administering certain welfare programs. Two applicants for benefits under these programs contended that their religious beliefs prevented them from acceding to the use of a Social Security number for their two-year-old daughter because the use of a numerical identifier would " 'rob the spirit' of [their] daughter and prevent her from attaining greater spiritual power." ... Similarly, in this case, it is said that disruption of the natural environment caused by the G-O road will diminish the sacredness of the area in question and create distractions that will interfere with "training and ongoing religious experience of individuals using [sites within] the area for personal medicine and growth ... and as integrated parts of a system of religious belief and practice which correlates ascending degrees of personal power with a geographic hierarchy of power." ... The Court rejected this kind of challenge in *Roy*: "The Free Exercise Clause simply cannot be understood to require the Government to conduct its own internal affairs in ways that comport with the religious beliefs of particular citizens." ...

Respondents ... rely on several cases in which this Court has sustained free exercise challenges to government programs that interfered with individuals' ability to practice their religion. See *Wisconsin v. Yoder*, 406 U.S. 205 (1972) (compulsory school-attendance law); *Sherbert v. Verner*, 374 U.S. 398 (1963) (denial of unemployment benefits to applicant who refused to accept work requiring her to violate the Sabbath); *Thomas v. Review Board, Indiana Employment Security Div.*, 450 U.S. 707 (1981) (denial of unemployment benefits to applicant whose religion forbade him to fabricate weapons); *Hobbie [v. Unemployment Appeals Comm'n of Fla.*, 480 U.S. 136 (1987)] (denial of unemployment benefits to religious convert who resigned position that required her to work on the Sabbath).

... It is true that this Court has repeatedly held that indirect coercion or penalties on the free exercise of religion, not just outright prohibitions, are subject to scrutiny under the First Amendment.... This does not and cannot imply that incidental effects of government programs, which may make it more difficult to practice certain religions but which have no tendency to coerce individuals into acting contrary to their religious beliefs, require government to bring forward a compelling justification for its otherwise lawful actions. The crucial word in the constitutional text is "prohibit." ...

Whatever may be the exact line between unconstitutional prohibitions on the free exercise of religion and the legitimate conduct by government of its own affairs, the location of the line cannot depend on measuring the effects of a governmental action on a religious objector's spiritual development. The Government does not dispute ... that the logging and road-building projects at issue in this case could have devastating effects on traditional Indian religious practices. Those practices are intimately and inextricably bound up with the unique features of the Chimney Rock area, which is known to the Indians as the "high country." ... According to their beliefs, the[ir] rituals would not be efficacious if conducted at other sites than the ones traditionally used, and too much disturbance of the area's natural state would clearly render any meaningful continuation of traditional practices impossible....

Even if we assume that we should accept the Ninth Circuit's prediction, according to which the G-O road will "virtually destroy the Indians' ability to practice their religion," ... the Constitution simply does not provide a principle that could justify upholding respondents' legal claims. However much we might wish that it were otherwise, government simply could not operate if it were required to satisfy every citizen's religious needs and desires.... The First Amendment must apply to all citizens alike, and it can give to none of them a veto over public programs that do not prohibit the free exercise of religion....

Nothing in our opinion should be read to encourage governmental insensitivity to the religious needs of any citizen. The Government's rights to the use of its own land, for example, need not and should not discourage it from accommodating religious practices like those engaged in by the Indian respondents.... [Reversed and remanded.]

Justice Brennan wrote a dissent joined by Justices Marshall and Blackmun.

"The Free Exercise Clause," the Court explains today, "is written in terms of what the government cannot do to the individual, not in terms of what the individual can exact from the government." ... [T]he Court nevertheless concludes that even where the Government uses federal land in a manner that threatens the very existence of a Native American religion, the Government is simply not "doing" anything to the practitioners of that faith. Instead, the Court believes that Native Americans who request that the Government refrain from destroying their religion effectively seek to exact from the Government de facto beneficial ownership of federal property. These two astonishing conclusions follow naturally from the Court's determination that federal land-use decisions that render the practice of a given religion impossible do not burden that religion in a manner cognizable under the Free Exercise Clause, because such decisions neither coerce conduct inconsistent with religious belief nor penalize religious activity. The constitutional guarantee we interpret today, however, draws no such fine distinctions..., but rather is directed against any form of governmental action that frustrates or inhibits religious practice. Because the Court today refuses even to acknowledge the constitutional injury respondents will suffer, and because this refusal essentially leaves Native Americans with absolutely no constitutional protection against perhaps the gravest threat to their religious practices, I dissent.

I. For at least 200 years and probably much longer, the Yurok, Karok, and Tolowa Indians have held sacred an approximately 25 square-mile area of land situated in what is today the ... Six Rivers National Forest.... As the Government readily concedes, regular visits to this area ... have played and continue to play a "critical" role in the religious practices and rituals of these tribes....

As the Forest Service's commissioned study ... explains, for Native Americans religion is not a discrete sphere of activity separate from all others, and any attempt to isolate the religious aspects of Indian life "is in reality an exercise which forces Indian concepts into non-Indian categories." ... A pervasive feature of this lifestyle is the individual's relationship with the natural world; this relationship, which can accurately though somewhat incompletely be characterized as one of stewardship, forms the core of what might be called, for want of a better nomenclature, the Indian religious experience.... Native American faith is inextricably bound to the use of land. The site-specific nature of Indian religious practice derives from the Native American perception that land is itself a sacred, living being.... Rituals are performed in prescribed locations not merely as a matter of traditional orthodoxy, but because land, like all other living things, is unique, and specific sites possess different spiritual properties and significance. Within this belief system, therefore, land is not fungible....

For respondent Indians, the most sacred of lands is the high country where, they believe, pre-human spirits moved with the coming of humans to the earth. Because these spirits are seen as the source of religious power, or "medicine," many of the tribes' rituals and practices require frequent journeys to the area. Thus, for example, religious leaders preparing for the complex of ceremonies that underlie the tribes' World Renewal efforts must travel to specific sites in the high country in order to attain the medicine necessary for successful renewal. Similarly, individual tribe members may seek curative powers for the healing of the sick, or personal medicine for particular purposes such as good luck in singing, hunting, or love. A period of preparation generally precedes such visits, and individuals must select trails in the sacred area according to the medicine they seek and their abilities, gradually moving to increasingly more powerful sites, which are typically located at higher altitudes. Among the most powerful of sites are Chimney Rock, Doctor Rock, and Peak 8, all of which are elevated rock outcroppings.

According to the ... [USFS] Report, the qualities "of silence, the aesthetic perspective, and the physical attributes, are an extension of the sacredness of [each] particular site." ... The act of medicine making is akin to meditation: the individual must integrate physical, mental and vocal actions in order to communicate with the pre-human spirits. As a result, "successful use of the high country is dependent upon and facilitated by certain qualities of the physical environment, the most important of which are privacy, silence, and an undisturbed natural setting." ... Although few tribe members actually make medicine at the most powerful sites, the entire tribe's welfare hinges on the success of the individual practitioners....

II. The Court does not for a moment suggest that the interests served by the G-O road are in any way compelling, or that they outweigh the destructive effect construction of the road will have on respondents' religious practices. Instead, the Court embraces the Government's contention that its prerogative as landowner should always take precedence over a claim that a particular use of federal property infringes religious practices. Attempting to justify this rule, the Court argues that the First Amendment bars only outright prohibitions, indirect coercion, and penalties on the free exercise of religion.... [W]e have never suggested that the protections of the guarantee are limited to so narrow a range of governmental burdens....

A. ... [I]n *Wisconsin v. Yoder* ... we struck down a state compulsory school attendance law on free exercise grounds not so much because of the affirmative coercion the law exerted on individual religious practitioners, but because of "the impact that compulsory high school attendance could have on the continued survival of Amish communities." ... Like respondents here, the Amish view life as pervasively religious and their faith accordingly dictates their entire lifestyle....

I thus cannot accept the Court's premise that the form of the Government's restraint on religious practice, rather than its effect, controls our constitutional analysis.... Here ...respondents have claimed—and proved—that the desecration of the high country will prevent religious leaders from attaining the religious power or medicine indispensable to the success of virtually all their rituals and ceremonies.... [T]he threat posed by the desecration of sacred lands that are indisputably essential to respondents' religious practices is both more direct and more substantial than that raised by a compulsory school law that simply exposed Amish children to an alien value system. And of course respondents here do not even have the option, however unattractive it might be, of migrating to more hospitable locales; the site-specific nature of their belief system renders it non-transportable....

B. Nor can I agree with the Court's assertion that respondents' constitutional claim is foreclosed by our decision in *Bowen v. Roy* ... [in which] we repeatedly stressed the "internal" nature of the Government practice at issue.... [W]e likened the use of such recordkeeping numbers to decisions concerning the purchase of office equipment.... Federal land-use decisions, by contrast, are likely to have substantial external effects that government decisions concerning office furniture and information storage obviously will not, and they are correspondingly subject to public scrutiny and public challenge in a host of ways that office equipment purchases are not....

In the final analysis, the Court's refusal to recognize the constitutional dimension of respondents' injuries stems from its concern that acceptance of respondents' claim could potentially strip the Government of its ability to manage and use vast tracts of federal property.... These concededly legitimate concerns lie at the very heart of this case, which represents yet another stress point in the long-standing conflict between two disparate cultures—the dominant western culture, which views land in terms of ownership and use, and that of Native Americans, in which concepts of private property are not only alien, but contrary to a belief system that holds land sacred. Rather than address this conflict in any meaningful fashion, however, the Court disclaims all responsibility for balancing these competing and potentially irreconcilable interests, choosing instead to turn this difficult task over to the federal legislature. Such an abdication is more than merely indefensible as an institutional matter: by defining respondents' injury as "non-constitutional," the Court has effectively bestowed on one party to this conflict the unilateral authority to resolve all future disputes in its favor, subject only to the Court's toothless exhortation to be "sensitive" to affected religions. In my view, however, Native Americans deserve—and the Constitution demands—more than this....

III. Today, the Court holds that a federal land-use decision that promises to destroy an entire religion does not burden the practice of that faith in a manner recognized by the Free Exercise Clause. Having thus stripped respondents and all other Native Americans of any constitutional protection against perhaps the most serious threat to their age-old religious practices, and indeed to their entire way of life, the Court assures us that nothing in its decision "should be read to encourage governmental insensitivity to the religious needs of any citizen." ... I find it difficult, however, to imagine conduct more insensitive to religious needs than the Government's determination to build a marginally useful road in the face of uncontradicted evidence that the road will render the practice of respondents' religion impossible. Nor do I believe that respondents will derive any solace from the knowledge that although the practice of their religion will become "more difficult" as a result of the Government's actions, they remain free to maintain their religious beliefs. Given today's ruling, that freedom amounts to nothing more than the right to believe that their religion will be destroyed. The safeguarding of such a hollow freedom not only makes a mockery of the "policy of the United States to protect and preserve for American Indians their inherent right of freedom to believe, express, and exercise their traditional religions," ... it fails utterly to accord with the dictates of the First Amendment.

The second of the two cases in this area concerns what appears to be a very different situation, but from a Native American point of view there are important similarities. Although the *Lyng* case emphasized land use concerns, the *Smith* case focused on the use of natural substances, in this case peyote, in Native American rituals. It is important to be clear that this is not a case about recreational drug use. Again, it is important to read this opinion with careful attention to the language used.

Employment Division, Department of Human Resources of Oregon v. Smith

494 U.S. 872 (1990)

INTRODUCTION: The opinion that follows summarizes the facts of this case. It is important, though, to note the difference in tone and approach by the majority opinion written by Justice Scalia to those facts as compared to their treatment in the dissent by Justice Blackmun.

Justice Scalia wrote the opinion for the Court.

> This case requires us to decide whether the Free Exercise Clause of the First Amendment permits the State of Oregon to include religiously inspired peyote use within the reach of its general criminal prohibition on use of that drug, and thus permits the State to deny unemployment benefits to persons dismissed from their jobs because of such religiously inspired use.

> I. Oregon law prohibits the knowing or intentional possession of a "controlled substance" unless the substance has been prescribed by a medical practitioner.... Persons who violate this provision by possessing a controlled substance ... are "guilty of a Class B felony." ... Schedule I contains the drug peyote, a hallucinogen derived from the plant Lophophora williamsii Lemaire....

> Respondents Alfred Smith and Galen Black (hereinafter respondents) were fired from their jobs with a private drug rehabilitation organization because they ingested peyote for sacramental purposes at a ceremony of the Native American Church, of which both are members. When respondents applied to petitioner Employment Division for unemployment compensation, they were determined to be ineligible for benefits because they had been discharged for work-related "misconduct." The Oregon Court of Appeals reversed..., holding that the denial of benefits violated respondents' free exercise rights under the First Amendment.

> ... The Oregon Supreme Court reasoned, however, that the criminality of respondents' peyote use was irrelevant to resolution of their constitutional claim—since the purpose of the "misconduct" provision under which respondents had been disqualified was not to enforce the State's criminal laws but to preserve the financial integrity of the compensation fund, and since that purpose was inadequate to justify the burden that disqualification imposed on respondents' religious practice....

> [In 1987 we] conclud[ed] that "if a State has prohibited through its criminal laws certain kinds of religiously motivated conduct without violating the First Amendment, it certainly follows that it may impose the lesser burden of denying unemployment compensation benefits to persons who engage in that conduct." (*Smith I*). We noted, however, that the Oregon Supreme Court had not decided whether respondents' sacramental use of peyote was in fact proscribed by Oregon's controlled substance law.... Accordingly, we ... remanded for further proceedings.... On remand, the Oregon Supreme Court held that respondents' religiously inspired use of peyote fell within the prohibition of the Oregon statute,

which "makes no exception for the sacramental use" of the drug.... The court therefore reaffirmed its previous ruling that the State could not deny unemployment benefits to respondents for having engaged in that practice....

II. Respondents' claim for relief rests on our decisions in *Sherbert v. Verner*, 374 U.S. 398 (1963), *Thomas v. Review Bd. of Indiana Employment Security Div.*, 450 U.S. 707 (1981), and *Hobbie v. Unemployment Appeals Comm'n of Florida*, 480 U.S. 136 (1987), in which we held that a State could not condition the availability of unemployment insurance on an individual's willingness to forgo conduct required by his religion. As we observed in *Smith I*, however, the conduct at issue in those cases was not prohibited by law....

The Free Exercise Clause of the First Amendment, which has been made applicable to the States by incorporation into the Fourteenth Amendment, see *Cantwell v. Connecticut*, 310 U.S. 296, 303 (1940), provides that "Congress shall make no law respecting an establishment of religion, or *prohibiting the free exercise thereof....*" The free exercise of religion ... obviously excludes all "governmental regulation of religious *beliefs* as such." ... But the "exercise of religion" often involves not only belief and profession but the performance of (or abstention from) physical acts.... [A] State would be "prohibiting the free exercise [of religion]" if it sought to ban such acts or abstentions only when they are engaged in for religious reasons, or only because of the religious belief that they display.....

Respondents ... contend that their religious motivation for using peyote places them beyond the reach of a criminal law that is not specifically directed at their religious practice.... They assert, in other words, that "prohibiting the free exercise [of religion]" includes requiring any individual to observe a generally applicable law that requires (or forbids) the performance of an act that his religious belief forbids (or requires).... [W]e do not think the words must be given that meaning. It is no more necessary to regard the collection of a general tax, for example, as "prohibiting the free exercise [of religion]" by those citizens who believe support of organized government to be sinful, than it is to regard the same tax as "abridging the freedom ... of the press" of those publishing companies that must pay the tax as a condition of staying in business. It is a permissible reading of the text ... to say that if prohibiting the exercise of religion (or burdening the activity of printing) is not the object of the tax but merely the incidental effect of a generally applicable and otherwise valid provision, the First Amendment has not been offended....

We have never held that an individual's religious beliefs excuse him from compliance with an otherwise valid law prohibiting conduct that the State is free to regulate.... [Our] decisions have consistently held that the right of free exercise does not relieve an individual of the obligation to comply with a "valid and neutral law of general applicability on the ground that the law proscribes (or prescribes) conduct that his religion prescribes (or proscribes)." ... In *Prince v. Massachusetts*, 321 U.S. 158 (1944), we held that a mother could be prosecuted under the child labor laws for using her children to dispense literature in the streets, her religious motivation notwithstanding.... [See also] *Braunfeld v. Brown*, 366 U.S. 599 (1961) (plurality opinion) [and] *Gillette v. United States*, 401 U.S. 437, 461 (1971)....

Respondents argue that even though exemption from generally applicable criminal laws need not automatically be extended to religiously motivated actors, at least the claim for a religious exemption must be evaluated under the balancing test set forth in *Sherbert v. Verner*.... Under the *Sherbert* test, governmental actions that substantially burden a religious practice must be justified by a compelling governmental interest.... We have never invalidated any governmental action on the basis of the *Sherbert* test except the denial of unemployment compensation.... In recent years we have abstained from applying the *Sherbert* test (outside the unemployment compensation field) at all. [See] *Bowen v. Roy ... Lyng v. Northwest Indian Cemetery Protective Assn.,* ... *Goldman v. Weinberger*, 475 U.S. 503 (1986).... We conclude today that ... the approach in accord with the vast majority of our precedents, is to hold the [*Sherbert*] test inapplicable to such challenges. The government's ability to enforce generally applicable prohibitions of socially harmful conduct, like its ability to carry out other aspects of public policy, "cannot depend on measuring the effects of a governmental action on a religious objector's spiritual development."

Justice O'Connor issued an opinion that joined parts I and II of the opinion and concurred with the judgment. Her opinion was also joined by Justices Brennan, Marshall, and Blackmun, although they did not concur in the judgment.

Although I agree with the result the Court reaches in this case, I cannot join its opinion. In my view, today's holding dramatically departs from well-settled First Amendment jurisprudence, appears unnecessary to resolve the question presented, and is incompatible with our Nation's fundamental commitment to individual religious liberty.

I. ... The Court today ... interprets the [Free Exercise] Clause to permit the government to prohibit, without justification, conduct mandated by an individual's religious beliefs, so long as that prohibition is generally applicable.... But a law that prohibits certain conduct ... manifestly does prohibit that person's free exercise of his religion. A person who is barred from engaging in religiously motivated conduct is barred from freely exercising his religion....

The First Amendment, however, does not distinguish between laws that are generally applicable and laws that target particular religious practices.... Our free exercise cases have all concerned generally applicable laws that had the effect of significantly burdening a religious practice. If the First Amendment is to have any vitality, it ought not be construed to cover only the extreme and hypothetical situation in which a State directly targets a religious practice....

To say that a person's right to free exercise has been burdened, of course, does not mean that he has an absolute right to engage in the conduct.... [W]e have recognized that the freedom to act, unlike the freedom to believe, cannot be absolute.... Instead, we have ... requir[ed] the government to justify any substantial burden on religiously motivated conduct by a compelling state interest and by means narrowly tailored to achieve that interest....

Moreover, we have not "rejected" or "declined to apply" the compelling interest test in our recent cases.... Recent cases have instead affirmed that test as a fundamental part of our First Amendment doctrine.... The cases cited by the Court signal no retreat from our consistent adherence to the compelling interest test.... Similarly, the other cases cited by the Court for the proposition that we have rejected application of the *Sherbert* test outside the unemployment compensation field ... are distinguishable because they arose in the narrow, specialized contexts in which we have not traditionally required the government to justify a burden on religious conduct by articulating a compelling interest....

Finally, the Court today suggests that the disfavoring of minority religions is an "unavoidable consequence" under our system of government and that accommodation of such religions must be left to the political process.... In my view, however, the First Amendment was enacted precisely to protect the rights of those whose religious practices are not shared by the majority and may be viewed with hostility. The history of our free exercise doctrine amply demonstrates the harsh impact majoritarian rule has had on unpopular or emerging religious groups such as the Jehovah's Witnesses and the Amish. Indeed, the words of Justice Jackson in *West Virginia State Bd. of Ed. v. Barnette* (overruling *Minersville School Dist. v. Gobitis*, 310 U.S. 586 (1940)) are apt: "The very purpose of a Bill of Rights was to withdraw certain subjects from the vicissitudes of political controversy, to place them beyond the reach of majorities and officials and to establish them as legal principles to be applied by the courts. One's right to life, liberty, and property, to free speech, a free press, freedom of worship and assembly, and other fundamental rights may not be submitted to vote; they depend on the outcome of no elections." ...

III. The Court's holding today not only misreads settled First Amendment precedent; it appears to be unnecessary to this case. I would reach the same result applying our established free exercise jurisprudence.... [R]espondents do not seriously dispute that Oregon has a compelling interest in prohibiting the possession of peyote by its citizens.

Thus, the critical question in this case is whether exempting respondents from the State's general criminal prohibition "will unduly interfere with fulfillment of the governmental interest." ... I would conclude that uniform application of Oregon's criminal prohibition is "essential to accomplish" ... its overriding interest in preventing the physical harm caused by the use of a Schedule I controlled substance.... Under such circumstances, the Free Exercise Clause does not require the State to accommodate respondents' religiously motivated conduct.

Justice Blackmun wrote a dissenting opinion joined by Justices Brennan and Marshall.

This Court over the years painstakingly has developed a consistent and exacting standard to test the constitutionality of a state statute that burdens the free exercise of religion. Such a statute may stand only if the law in general, and the State's refusal to allow a religious exemption in particular, are justified by a compelling interest that cannot be served by less restrictive means.

Until today, I thought this was a settled and inviolate principle of this Court's First Amendment jurisprudence. The majority, however, perfunctorily dismisses it as a "constitutional anomaly." ... [T]he majority is able to arrive at this view only by mischaracterizing this Court's precedents.... In short, it effectuates a wholesale overturning of settled law concerning the Religion Clauses of our Constitution....

The State cannot plausibly assert that unbending application of a criminal prohibition is essential to fulfill any compelling interest, if it does not, in fact, attempt to enforce that prohibition. In this case, the State actually has not evinced any concrete interest in enforcing its drug laws against religious users of peyote. Oregon has never sought to prosecute respondents [or take] enforcement efforts against other religious users of peyote. The State's asserted interest thus amounts only to the symbolic preservation of an unenforced prohibition....

The State proclaims an interest in protecting the health and safety of its citizens from the dangers of unlawful drugs. It offers, however, no evidence that the religious use of peyote has ever harmed anyone.... The carefully circumscribed ritual context in which respondents used peyote is far removed from the irresponsible and unrestricted recreational use of unlawful drugs.... ("The Administrator [of the Drug Enforcement Administration (DEA)] finds that ... the Native American

Church's use of peyote is isolated to specific ceremonial occasions," and so "an accommodation can be made for a religious organization which uses peyote in circumscribed ceremonies" (quoting DEA Final Order))....

Finally, the State argues that granting an exception for religious peyote use would erode its interest in the uniform, fair, and certain enforcement of its drug laws.... This Court, however, consistently has rejected similar arguments in past free exercise cases, and it should do so here as well.... I dissent.

Of course, what Native Americans cannot forget is that their religions, and the cultures of which they are a central part, were the intentional targets of the United States government for generations that either set out to destroy the tribes and their people outright or to "kill the Indian, and leave the man." They were to be destroyed or converted to Christianity and assimilated. However, there was the problem that these tribal people were to be sovereign and their relationships were supposed to be sovereign-to-sovereign interactions. In the face of that, Justice Scalia's opinion could not be viewed as anything less than completely insensitive and disrespectful. And, ironically, Justice O'Connor was unable to see how her opinion in the *Castle Rock* case provided the foundation for the argument by Scalia that she criticized as demeaning to the foundation principles of free exercise of religion. It was a warning that Justice Brennan had provided to her in his dissent in the *Lyng* case.

Indeed, after the 2014 ruling of the Court in *Hobby Lobby v. Burwell* (see Chapter 10) that permitted a for-profit corporation to claim religious freedom as a basis to deny reproductive healthcare coverage for its women employees, it is difficult for Native Americans to read these two opinions as anything other than discriminatory against them.[41]

Conclusion

Native Americans have clearly faced a long history of cultural and racial discrimination that has undermined their ability to govern themselves and reached even to genocidal attacks on the people and their cultures. Those were not merely policies dating back to the early years of the republic, but also policies pursued through the 1950s and 1960s with de-recognition and other actions. The earlier efforts to destroy the tribal communities and break their connection to the land live on, as the Allotment Act continues to be cited in current case law as justification for denying self-government and a serious understanding of sovereignty for tribal governance.

To many Native Americans, civil rights is not only about discrimination in violation of the equal protection clause of the Fourteenth Amendment or of the Fifth Amendment due process clause, but implicates other issues as well. In particular, sovereignty, land rights, control of natural resources, and tribal self-governance are fundamental civil rights for them. Questions of spirituality are also central to civil rights concerns of Native Americans and are properly understood as different from traditional civil liberties debates in constitutional law. There are many complex issues associated with Native American spirituality and the way that it may be in conflict with non-native policy and society, but recent cases have demonstrated that the nation is far from having arrived at a serious resolution of those issues.

To this point in American history, then, there is little cause to celebrate great progress in civil rights for Native Americans. Justice Marshall's concerns that celebration of the U.S. Constitution and our claims to equal justice under law should be tempered by a recognition of the work yet to be done seems most appropriate.

I. Issues for Policy and Practice

A. The item mentioned in Chapter 6 about disconnects between the way Native Americans understand land and property and the way they are understood by federal, state, and local governments has an analog in understandings with respect to natural resources. The question for policy and practice at the end of that chapter applies here as well. It is not clear that the need for cultural interpretation and cultural mediation to address these fundamentally different understandings is being systematically addressed.

B. The two opinions in the *United States v. Navajo Nation* case did considerable damage to relationships and undermined already tenuous working relationships between tribal governments and federal authorities, who retain such important controls on the ability of the Native American communities to manage their own resources. It not only presented a serious problem concerning the technical issues in the case, but it also eroded the critically important trust doctrine and what it is supposed to mean, not only for particular obligations of federal agencies but also what it has been understood to require in statutory interpretation by federal courts. Beyond all that, it is difficult for an objective observer to read the facts of this case and not see it as a blatant example of *ex parte* communication of a sort that undermines both law and legitimacy. Given that the Court interpreted the statute that way, what legislative proposals are needed to repair what appears to be a gaping hole in basic protections for tribal governments dealing with federal authorities on natural resource negotiations? Does that require amendments to the Indian Tucker Act or other modifications in particular statutes related to specific agencies?

C. The trust doctrine was weakened by the ruling in *Navajo Nation*, but even more by the Court's opinion in *United States v. Jicarilla Apache Nation*. As the powerful dissent by Justice Sotomayor correctly indicated, this ruling not only misinterpreted and misapplied the Court's precedents on the trust doctrine, but also dramatically undermined the entire concept. Since Justice Alito and the rest of the majority has taken the position that the trust doctrine is only defined by statutory provisions in federal law, it is essential to do a comprehensive review of the status of the trust doctrine currently. Given the importance of the trust doctrine, it is then critically important to offer such legislative revisions as are needed to ensure the integrity of the concept, in practice as well as in theory.

D. Whatever the specific legal outcome of the Makah case (*Anderson v. Evans*), it left some in the Native American community wondering how meaningful their treaty rights are if the tribe is completely dependent upon representation of its interests by federal agencies, and if its relationship with the federal government is subject to intervention by so many outside parties as was the case here. It is easy to see this case as one involving support for whales as such, but the point is considerably broader than that. It is important to consider what is being done by relevant agencies to ensure the integrity of treaty commitments with tribal communities. Here again, a review may suggest a need for legislative amendment where appropriate.

E. The cases in the chapter that deal with the authority and jurisdiction of tribal courts go to a critically important subject for Native Americans, but one made infinitely more complex than it already is by virtue of the Allotment Act. That process meant that many tribal lands are checkerboards with pieces owned by non-tribal people and with businesses from outside the reservation having important decisionmaking authority over property on tribal lands. There is a need for a careful reassessment of the role and jurisdiction of tribal courts to ensure that this critically important aspect of governance on tribal lands is actually under the control of the tribal community. What policy responses may be needed to address that concern?

F. As Justice Brennan's dissent in *Lyng v. Northwest Indian Cemetery Protective Association* indicated, the problems of sacred Native American places on federal lands are complex and often involve a clash of legitimate rights, powers, and expectations. However, as he also noted, it is not adequate simply to write off the Native American perspective on those issues, particularly where, as there, the decisions made by the federal government had the effect of destroying a native religion. What options are available for working through these conflicting situations that might offer something other than a zero sum response by government?

II. Discussion Questions

A. In reading the opinion in *United States v. Navajo Nation*, take a moment to compare and contrast its treatment of the concept of the trust relationship with the Court's opinion in *Seminole Nation v. United States* presented in Chapter 5. Is this similar, different, or a dramatic departure?

B. If you were a Makah, how would you understand your treaty rights in the aftermath of *Anderson v. Evans*? This is a difficult case largely because it involves whales, but try to set that specific point aside for the moment and consider the broader question.

C. Even if we put the whale back into the center of the case, the Makah reject the idea that Western governments have room to lecture Native Americans about how to live in and with their natural environment. It is important to understand that tribal communities have historically used hunting and fishing not only as a means of subsistence, but as a critically important part of their culture, and in some cases the religion of the tribe or nation. The taking of animals or even plants is, in most instances, done with ritual to honor the animal or plant and the creator's role in providing the relationship between the tribe and that animal or plant. When we consider important controversies involving tribal communities, how do we attempt to understand their perspectives on the situation—whatever the outcome of the discussion may be?

D. As you read *Seminole Tribe of Florida v. Florida*, 517 U.S. 44 (1996), think back to the Court's statement of the scope of the power of Congress under the so-called Indian Commerce Clause in *United States v. Nice*, 241 U.S. 591 (1916). How has the Indian gaming case seemingly affected that power?

E. The *Plains Commerce Bank* case is another of those opinions that is at least as important for the way it speaks about and to tribal communities as for the specific legal issues involved. What do you think of the Chief Justice's argument that the bank is not subject to the jurisdiction of the tribal court, even though that bank regularly invokes the authority of that same tribal court to enforce its contracts and used the tribal court in an effort to remove the family from the land under dispute in this case? What do you think Native Americans think of it?

F. What is your reaction to Justice O'Connor's conclusion that in the *Lyng* case there was no sufficient injury to the free exercise of religion rights of the tribal members from the construction of the road in this case?

Notes

1 NOTE: An *ex parte* communication is an attempt by one party to a case to communicate arguments or information to a decisionmaker in a case outside the normal hearing process. See e.g., 5 U.S.C. §557(d).

2 NOTE: From a Native American perspective, however, the fact that such transactions could still only be done with U.S. government approval is discriminatory and hardly marks the arrival of full self-determination, or for that matter even full sovereignty and self-governance. It is little more than the ability of a colony to do that which its colonizer permits. And because of that continuing and pivotal role, this pattern clearly fits the justification for the trust responsibility explained in the *Seminole* case.

3 NOTE: It turns out that the Peabody representative was not just any lobbyist. As the Federal Circuit put it in a 2007 ruling in the case, "Peabody retained Stanley Hulett, who was described in a Peabody company memorandum as 'a former upper level Department of Interior employee' believed to have 'influence with the current Secretary of Interior (Don Hodel).' The government conceded in this case that Hulett was 'a former aide and friend of Secretary Hodel.'" *Navajo Nation v. United States*, 501 F.3d 1327, 1331 (Fed.Cir. 2007).

4 NOTE: It turned out that the memorandum that was sent by Hodel was drafted by attorneys for the company. See Justice Souter's dissenting opinion, 537 U.S., at 520.

5 NOTE: The opinion explains that if the tribe had transferred the case to the Board of Indian Appeals, then *ex parte* communications would have been prohibited. However, the tribe was not at that time aware that *ex parte* communications were taking place and had been given clear indications that the ruling would be in its favor. Moreover, the Court assumed without addressing the point that no general administrative law prohibitions against *ex parte* communications would apply, but such communications are clearly a violation of fundamental principles of administrative law. See the Administrative Procedures Act, 5 U.S.C. §551, et seq.

6 *Navajo Nation v. United States*, 501 F.3d 1327, 1336 (Fed.Cir. 2007).

7 Id., at 1349.

8 *United States v. Navajo Nation*, No. 07-1410, "Brief for former Secretaries of the Interior Cecil D. Andrus, Bruce Babbitt, Manuel Lujan, Jr., and Stewart L. Udall as Amici Curiae in Support of Respondent," pp. 28–29, www.americanbar.org/content/dam/aba/publishing/preview/publiced_preview_briefs_pdfs_07_08_07_1410_RespondentAmCu4FmrSecsofInterior.authcheckdam.pdf, November 6, 2015.

9 Id., at 30.

10 *United States v. Navajo Nation*, 556 U.S. 287, 289 (2009).

11 NOTE: Justice Souter's opinion was joined by Justice Stevens.

12 NOTE: Justice Kagan did not participate in this case.

13 NOTE: Notice here how Justice Alito had transformed the trust relationship from a fundamental obligation of government to something to which tribes are entitled only if they can prove that such a relationship is mandated by statute.

14 NOTE: Justice Ginsburg's brief concurring opinion joined by Justice Breyer is omitted here.

15 Columbia River Inter-Tribal Fishing Commission, "We Are All Salmon People," www.critfc.org/salmon-culture/we-are-all-salmon-people/, November 6, 2015.

16 The present opinion was amended twice and the final version as indicated here was issued on June 7, 2004.

17 As the Ninth Circuit opinion explained: "The International Convention for the Regulation of Whaling ("ICRW") was established in 1946 to restrict and regulate whaling. 62 Stat. 1716, 161 U.N.T.S. 72 (Dec. 2, 1946). The ICRW created the International Whaling Commission ("IWC"), comprised of one member from each of the ratifying countries. The IWC is empowered to set international whaling regulations and annual whaling quotas. *Id.* at arts. III, V §1. The United States signed the Convention, 62 Stat. 1716 (1946), and implemented it domestically in the Whaling Convention Act of 1949 ("WCA"), 16 U.S.C. §916 et seq. See also 50 C.F.R. §230.1 (WCA implementing regulations)." 371 F.3d, at 483, n. 6.

18 Will Anderson, Fund for Animals, Humane Society of the United States, Australians for Animals, Cetacean Society International, West Coast Anti-Whaling Society, Sandra Abels, Cindy Hansen, Patricia Ness, Robert Ness, Lisa Lamb, Margaret Owens, Charles Owens, Peninsula Citizens for the Protection of Whales, Dan Spomer, Sue Miller, and Steph Dutton.

19 Makah Tribe, "The Makah Indian Tribe and Whaling: Questions and Answers," Makah Tribal Council and Makah Whaling Commission January 2005, at www.makah.com/makahwhalingqa.pdf, as of December 29, 2008. This item is no longer live on that site, but is posted at www.lcsd.wednet.edu/cms/lib06/WA01001184/Centricity/Domain/74/Makah_Whaling_FAQ.pdf, November 6, 2015.

20 *Board of Trustees of the University of Alabama v. Garrett*, 531 U.S. 356 (2001).

21 *Kimel v. Florida Bd. of Regents*, 528 U.S. 62 (2000).

22 NOTE: Chief Justice Rehnquist is using a device he has employed in other cases but one that is fundamentally misleading—and to be even more direct, simply untrue. He sees that there are precedents that run against what he wants to rule and so he simply says these are exceptions, and only in that specific situation does the ruling apply. The cases he cites here did not say that the Congress only had the "authority to abrogate under only two provisions of the Constitution" as he says above. By doing so, he dramatically narrows the power of Congress without any real constitutional support for his claim. *Fitzpatrick* recognized authority. It did not limit it.

23 NOTE: Rehnquist could not find a way around this precedent, so he simply overturned it with no credible rationale or authority for doing so.

24 NOTE: Justice Steven's brief concurring opinion is omitted here, as are the concurring opinions of Justices Kennedy and Thomas.
25 541 U.S., p. 212, Kennedy, J., concurring.
26 NOTE: The term means that it could be sold to anyone.
27 *Cobell v. Kempthorne*, 532 F. Supp. 2d 37 (D.D.C. 2008).
28 *Cobell v. Kempthorne*, 569 F. Supp. 2d 223 (D.D.C. 2008).
29 P.L. 111–291, 124 Stat. 3064 (2010).
30 Portions of the task force report and the Theodoratus report were filed with the Court in the Joint Appendix—a document submitted by both sides in a case providing important materials from the record in the case. References below to J.A. are to the pages in the joint appendix. *Lyng v. Northwest Indian Cemetery Protective Association*, No. 86–1013, Joint Appendix. (A joint appendix is the collection of materials from the record of a case that the attorneys for the parties involved consider that appellate courts should have before them when they review a case.)
31 NOTE: The term "fee simple absolute" means full ownership without restrictions or limitations.
32 See e.g., *United States v. White Mountain Apache Tribe*, 537 U.S. 465 (2003); *United States v. Navajo Nation*, 537 U.S. 488 (2003).
33 See generally Lloyd Burton,̦ *Worship and Wilderness: Culture, Religion, and Law in Public Lands Management* (Madison, WI: University of Wisconsin Press, 2002).
34 Carol Locust, "Wounding the Spirit: Discrimination and Traditional American Indian Belief Systems," *Harvard Educational Review* 58 (No. 3 1989): 315–330; "Walking in Two Worlds: Native Americans and the VR System," *American Rehabilitation* 22 (No. 2 1996): 2–12; "The Impact of Differing Belief Systems between Native Americans and their Rehabilitation Service Providers," *Rehabilitation Education* 9 (No. 2 1995): 205–215.
35 See e.g., Colin Nicholas and Raajen Singh, eds., *Indigenous Peoples of Asia: Many People, One Struggle* (Bangkok: Asia Indigenous Peoples Pact, 1996). George Psacharopoulos and Harry Anthony Patrinos, *Indigenous People and Poverty in Latin America* (Washington, D.C.: The World Bank, 1994).
36 565 F. Supp. at 591.
37 *Lyng v. Northwest Indian Cemetery Protective Association*, No. 86-1013, Brief for the Petitioners.
38 *Lyng v. Northwest Indian Cemetery Protective Association*, No. 86-1013, Brief of State Respondent State of California.
39 Portions of the task force report and the Theodoratus report were filed with the Court in the Joint Appendix. References to J.A. in this excerpt are to the pages in the joint appendix. *Lyng v. Northwest Indian Cemetery Protective Association*, No. 86-1013, Joint Appendix.
40 Justice Kennedy did not take part in this case.
41 *Hobby Lobby v. Burwell*, 134 S. Ct. 2751 (2014). This ruling was based on the Religious Freedom Restoration Act passed following the *Smith* decision, but that does not change the fact, from a Native American perspective, that the same justices who supported the *Smith* opinion had no difficulty protecting non-native for-profit corporations as if they were citizens who had First Amendment religious freedom protections superior to the Native Americans in *Smith*.

References

Andrus, Cecil D., Bruce Babbitt, Manuel Lujan, Jr., and Stewart L. Udall. *United States v. Navajo Nation*, No. 07-1410, "Brief for former Secretaries of the Interior Cecil D. Andrus, Bruce Babbitt, Manuel Lujan, Jr., and Stewart L. Udall as Amici Curiae in Support of Respondent," www.americanbar.org/content/dam/aba/publishing/preview/publiced_preview_briefs_pdfs_07_08_07_1410_RespondentAmCu4FmrSecsofInterior.authcheckdam.pdf, November 6, 2015.
Burton, Lloyd. *Worship and Wilderness: Culture, Religion, and Law in Public Lands Management*. Madison, WI: University of Wisconsin Press, 2002.
Columbia River Inter-Tribal Fishing Commission. "We Are All Salmon People," www.critfc.org/salmon-culture/we-are-all-salmon-people/, November 6, 2015.
Locust, Carol. "The Impact of Differing Belief Systems between Native Americans and their Rehabilitation Service Providers," *Rehabilitation Education* 9 (No. 2 1995): 205–215.

———. "Walking in Two Worlds: Native Americans and the VR System," *American Rehabilitation* 22 (No. 2 1996): 2–12.

———. "Wounding the Spirit: Discrimination and Traditional American Indian Belief Systems," *Harvard Educational Review* 58 (No. 3 1989): 315–330.

Makah Tribe. "The Makah Indian Tribe and Whaling: Questions and Answers," Makah Tribal Council and Makah Whaling Commission January 2005, www.makah.com/makahwhalingqa.pdf as of December 29, 2008. This item is no longer live on that site, but is posted at www.lcsd.wednet.edu/cms/lib06/WA01001184/Centricity/Domain/74/Makah_Whaling_FAQ.pdf, November 6, 2015.

Nicholas, Colin and Raajen Singh, eds. *Indigenous Peoples of Asia: Many People, One Struggle.* Bangkok: Asia Indigenous Peoples Pact, 1996.

Psacharopoulos, George and Harry Anthony Patrinos. *Indigenous People and Poverty in Latin America.* Washington, D.C.: The World Bank, 1994.

8   Civil Rights from a Latino Perspective

According to Suffolk County, New York prosecutors, November 8, 2008 began for two students of Patchogue-Medford High School with a drive around Patchogue, Long Island, where the young men started shooting a BB gun at a Hispanic man, Mr. Marlon Garcia, whom they just happened to see in a driveway. They later allegedly went to a park with five other school friends, where they drank beer. During that episode, they decided, according to the indictment issued by a Suffolk County grand jury, to seek out and attack Latinos. The indictment stated that the young men said: "Let's go 'Beaner' hopping."[1] After driving around Medford and not finding any likely targets, the seven drove to Patchogue. There they found Marcelo Lucero, an Ecuadorean immigrant, and his friend, Angel Loja. The young men approached with racial epithets and set upon the Latinos. Loja ran away, calling the police as he escaped. The others attacked Lucero, who tried to defend himself by swinging his belt. Jeffrey Conroy, hit by the belt, allegedly pulled out a knife and stabbed Lucero to death.

Exactly one month later, two brothers from Ecuador were attacked and one later died in Brooklyn. José and Romel Sucuzhanay were reportedly attacked by two African American men, who shouted racial and anti-gay epithets as they attacked with a baseball bat. José Sucuzhanay, a local businessman, later died of his injuries. His brother was visiting the family in New York.[2] The two assailants were sentenced to 37-year prison terms.

To Latino civil rights advocates, these attacks are just some among many in a large and growing body of evidence that anti-Latino bigotry and discriminatory conduct has not been adequately addressed, and is in fact growing in the United States.[3] They point, for example, to the fact that Senator John McCain (R, AZ) during his presidential campaign in 2008 felt so pressured by anti-Latino politics in a part of his own political base that, despite the fact that he had been a champion of immigration policy reform, he ultimately rejected the very immigration policy reform that he had sponsored in the Congress with the support of the George W. Bush administration.[4] When asked directly about the change in his long-held position, McCain announced that he would indeed oppose his own proposal if it were to come to a vote.

Before that, in 2007, a federal district court struck down a set of city ordinances adopted by officials in Hazleton, Pennsylvania that were clearly a reaction to the increasing number of Latinos in the community, although the new laws were presented in the form of immigration ordinances. The city modified its ordinances while the dispute was in progress in a clear effort to avoid a discrimination finding. Nevertheless, the federal district court for the Middle District of Pennsylvania struck down the ordinances aimed at housing and jobs.[5] Other attempts at local ordinances aimed at Latinos were adopted and struck down in Escondido, California and Farmer's Branch, Texas.[6]

Beyond these examples, a Southern Poverty Law Center report concluded in 2009 that:

> The situation in Suffolk County, in fact, is a microcosm of a problem facing the entire
> United States, where FBI statistics suggest a 40% rise in anti-Latino hate crimes between

2003 and 2007, the latest numbers available. The number of hate groups in America has been rising, too, climbing more than 50% since 2000, mainly by exploiting the issue of undocumented non-white immigration.[7]

The problem is not limited to racist behavior by a few in the community or an unwillingness of some political candidates to stand up for principles, but there is often less publicized but nevertheless clear evidence of racism in the wider community. Consider the announcement by the Justice Department of the results of a civil rights investigation of the East Haven police department in 2012.

> Based on our review, we find that EHPD engages in a pattern or practice of systematically discriminating against Latinos in violation of the Fourteenth Amendment to the Constitution, Title VI, and the Safe Streets Act. In particular, we find that EHPD engages in discriminatory policing against Latinos, including but not limited to targeting Latinos for discriminatory traffic enforcement, treating Latino drivers more harshly than non-Latino drivers after a traffic stop, and intentionally and woefully failing to design and implement internal systems of control that would identify, track, and prevent such misconduct. The pattern or practice of discriminatory policing that we observed is deeply rooted in the Department's culture and substantially interferes with the ability of EHPD to deliver services to the entire East Haven community.
>
> In addition to the formal finding of discriminatory policing against Latinos, there are two additional areas [that] require additional investigation. First, we have serious concerns that EHPD's management practices and accountability systems fail to ensure that individuals are free from unlawful searches and seizures and use of excessive force. Second, we have grave concerns that Department leadership is creating a hostile and intimidating environment for anyone seeking to provide relevant information in our investigation.[8]

When asked by a Latino reporter for a New York radio station for his reaction to the Justice Department's findings, the mayor of East Haven replied, "I might have tacos when I go home; I'm not quite sure yet."[9] The Justice Department investigation resulted in an indictment of a number of East Haven officers.[10] Four officers were eventually sentenced to prison terms of various lengths.[11] After that, the city entered into a settlement agreement with the Civil Rights Division of the Department of Justice.[12] A settlement of a civil suit against East Haven was reached in mid 2014.[13] Quite apart from the criminal matters, the basis for the civil suit included such evidence as a study by Yale Law School students showing that 58% of traffic tickets were issued to Latinos in a community that has a population only 7% of which is Hispanic.[14]

Last, but by no means least, there is the long-running saga of Maricopa County, Arizona Sheriff, Joseph Arpaio, whose notorious behavior resulted in rulings against him in a 2013 civil suit for discriminatory practices against Latinos.[15] The Justice Department issued findings of discrimination against the Sheriff and his department and filed suit in 2010, a case that is still pending at the time of this writing.[16]

These are but a few exemplars of the animus so many Latinos see as directed against them, whether they are citizens, legal immigrants, or undocumented individuals. There is more than an immigration debate involved. This chapter considers civil rights with an effort to see the issues from the Latino perspective. Like the chapters on Native Americans and civil rights, many Latinos see some of the problems of discrimination that they face to be in common with those experienced by African Americans, but they also see particular concerns that present special problems for them that are different from the experience of other groups. The chapter begins with important information about civil rights and Latinos in the United States, addresses basic discrimination issues, turns to immigration-related issues, and considers linguistic discrimination.

Civil Rights and Latino/Latina Politics: Not a Racial Minority but Targeted Nonetheless

It is a matter of considerable frustration for many Latinos that so many people have used so many stereotypes of them. For example, there is the common assumption that a Latino is a Mexican, that he or she is likely a recent arrival to the United States, and, too often as well, the assumption that this person is perhaps not a legal immigrant or resident, much less a citizen. Of course, Latinos trace their ethnocultural heritage to many nations of Latin America, the Caribbean, or Europe's Iberian peninsula. These countries, in turn, are home to a wide range of diverse cultures with rich histories of great accomplishment and sophistication, including of course within Mexico. These are cultures that may be Spanish-speaking, or they may today use Portuguese, English, or any of a host of indigenous languages. Of course, the fact that a person is of Latino extraction is no assurance that he or she speaks Spanish, any more than those whose heritage is German speak that language. It is important to note at the outset that the term Hispanic is a word developed by the federal government to discuss Latinos and Latinas, although it has roots in the Spanish language as well. And like most other ethnocultural groups, many Latinos trace their heritage to a number of cultures and ethnicities, and not just one as that label implies.

Even given this complex diversity, it is true that Latinos have been treated as an identifiable ethnocultural group in the United States, and too often in a discriminatory manner. Before plunging into the court cases that have addressed civil rights issues that Latinos see as particularly important, it is important to establish some foundational understandings that often condition the civil rights concerns expressed by many Latinos.

First, it is useful to recognize that, for a long time, except in certain parts of the United States, issues faced by Latinos have largely been ignored. The discussion of civil rights has so often been focused on the serious problems of segregation and discrimination faced by African Americans, that Latino issues have not, until recently, received much attention. This concern has become obvious and significant for Latino scholars and civil rights advocates.[17] However, recent demographic information has begun to force a recognition that Latinos are a significant and growing part of the U.S. population.

The U.S. Census Bureau had projected that by 2015 Hispanics would form 17.76% of the population with Non-Hispanic Blacks 12.40%, Asians 5.12%, and Whites 61.75%. The estimates are that by 2050 the population will be 46.61% Non-Hispanic White, 27.95% Hispanic, 13% Black, 7.4% Asian, 0.72% American Indian/Native Alaskan, 0.22% Native Hawaiian/Pacific Islander.[18] The group of the population that has traditionally been thought to be the majority will, in fact, be in the minority. That is already true in some states, most notably in California.

While it is true that there have been significant numbers of Latino immigrants in recent decades—just as there have been immigrants from many other countries over time—many Latinos are not new arrivals, and neither were their parents or their parents before them. They would point out that much of what is now the western United States was Mexico until the middle of the nineteenth century. Generations of Latinos have been citizens, and distinguished citizens, of the United States, including sixty recipients of the Congressional Medal of Honor. Indeed, many like to recall that the United States is only one of the Americas and that Christopher Columbus was less the discoverer of America than a lost adventurer who was found by residents of the Americas, people who had long established complex civilizations.

Unfortunately, there is a long history of discrimination against Latinos, including the indigenous peoples who resided in what is now the United States. That even includes, in an earlier time, a form of slavery known as Mexican peonage. In part because of that discrimination, too many Latinos have not fared as well economically as other Americans. But even for those who have been successful in many aspects of life, there continues to be discrimination and a tendency not to see the particular problems that are all too apparent to Latinos and Latinas.

Foundation Issues of Discrimination

The history of civil rights with respect to African Americans traces back to slavery and its consequences, and the history of Native Americans and civil rights goes back to conquest and displacement. Latinos trace their civil rights history back to both conquest and, in some cases, to a form of slavery as well. The conquest by Spain, of course, dramatically shaped many Latin American countries and cultures. The conquistadors pushed north well into what is now the United States and east at least as far as Kansas. Much like the claims made by various European powers with respect to Native Americans, the Spanish claimed that they would civilize the natives of this hemisphere and save their souls one way or the other—even if it killed them. Mexico became independent from Spain in 1821, as did a number of other Latin American countries.

The Invasion of Mexico and the Treaty that Ended It

Later, of course, the United States invaded Mexico and effectively wrested control of what would be the western United States from that country. That conflict ended with what was known as the Treaty of Guadalupe Hidalgo of 1848. The treaty announced in its preamble that the purpose of the agreement was:

> to put an end to the calamities of the war which unhappily exists between the two Republics and to establish Upon a solid basis relations of peace and friendship, which shall confer reciprocal benefits upon the citizens of both, and assure the concord, harmony, and mutual confidence wherein the two people should live, as good neighbors.

It was fine rhetoric, but not a good prediction as to the future of the relationship.

The treaty called for the U.S. to remove its troops and return control of Mexico City and the other parts of the country then under the military control of the United States. It established the new borders that left a smaller Mexico and a much larger southwestern United States. Also important was the fact that it provided for those who were then Mexican living in the territory that had been taken by the U.S. to have freedom to choose whether to remain Mexican or to be citizens of the United States, and promised protections for their lives, freedom, and property.

> ARTICLE VIII. Mexicans now established in territories previously belonging to Mexico, and which remain for the future within the limits of the United States, as defined by the present treaty, shall be free to continue where they now reside, or to remove at any time to the Mexican Republic, retaining the property which they possess in the said territories, or disposing thereof, and removing the proceeds wherever

they please, without their being subjected, on this account, to any contribution, tax, or charge whatever.

Those who shall prefer to remain in the said territories may either retain the title and rights of Mexican citizens, or acquire those of citizens of the United States. But they shall be under the obligation to make their election within one year from the date of the exchange of ratifications of this treaty....

In the said territories, property of every kind, now belonging to Mexicans not established there, shall be inviolably respected. The present owners, the heirs of these, and all Mexicans who may hereafter acquire said property by contract, shall enjoy with respect to it guarantees equally ample as if the same belonged to citizens of the United States.

The Mexicans who, in the territories aforesaid, shall not preserve the character of citizens of the Mexican Republic ... shall be incorporated into the Union of the United States and be admitted ... to the enjoyment of all the rights of citizens of the United States, according to the principles of the Constitution.

The treaty's promise that property owned by people formerly under Mexican rule would be honored in the United States was not kept, and suits have continued even in recent decades over some of that property.[19] Many, particularly those in Mexico and Mexican Americans as well, have long considered that the United States has not maintained a relationship with its neighbor to the south that could be characterized as the treaty describes it as one of "concord, harmony, and mutual confidence." Indeed, it was not until the administration of Harry Truman that there appeared to be an effort to heal some of the wounds of the U.S. adventures under its theory of manifest destiny.

As Truman's biographer David McCullough explained it, Truman made an unscheduled visit during a trip to Mexico City in 1947 to the Chapultepec Castle.

The long motorcade pulled into the shade of an ancient grove of trees. Truman stepped out of his black Lincoln and walked to a stone monument bearing the names of Los Niños Héroes, the child heroes, six teenage cadets who had died in the Mexican–American War in 1847, when American troops stormed the castle. According to legend, five of the cadets had stabbed themselves and a sixth jumped to his death from a parapet rather than surrender. As Truman approached, a contingent of blue-uniformed Mexican cadets stood at attention. As he placed a floral wreath at the foot of the monument, several of the cadets wept silently.[20]

Peonage: Slavery of a Different Sort

The conquest of Latin America by the Spaniards and the later conquest of a portion of Mexico by the United States brought two forms of slavery not generally recognized among Americans. The first of these is what is termed in the law "peonage" and is discussed later in this section. The second was the effective enslavement of native peoples by the Spaniards and later Mexican officials during the development of the missions in California.

The effort to construct the string of missions throughout California was sanctioned by Spain, and later the Mexican government, in an arrangement under which the missions would be built as religious missionary settlements that would operate under the auspices of the church with military support, and later be converted to become the core of secular communities. One of the key leaders of the effort to build the missions was Father Junípero Serra, a Franciscan priest. Serra has been variously pictured in history as a leading figure in the development of California and as a villainous and evil man who brutalized indigenous people, who were held captive and forced to work in the building of the missions. This controversy was reinvigorated by a reinvestigation of the history of the period by Native American scholars and by the campaign for the canonization of Father Serra, who was ultimately beatified in 1988 by Pope John Paul II and elevated to sainthood by Pope Francis in 2015.[21]

Serra's defenders argued that he brought indigenous people into the missions as they were being built. Once baptized, even his defenders agree that they were subjected to harsh discipline and kept by force. Not unlike what was seen in American Indian policy, the point was supposedly to civilize the native people and integrate them into society.

> Absence, equated with apostasy, was punished swiftly and certainly. Either soldiers from the escolta, or mission guard, or soldiers from a presidial company were assigned the task of tracking and capturing runaways. The result was a whipping administered by a soldier or mission Indian, sometimes to the point of death.[22]

The argument was that the violence and subjugation visited upon the native peoples was not slavery because it was not driven by an economic motive, but it was in fact, and by any reasonable standard, enslavement.

> The missions were not agents of intentional enslavement, but rather rapid and therefore violent social and cultural change. The results were people wrenched from home, tradition and family, subjugated to an alien culture and contradictory values. Predictably these people did not submit to such treatment voluntarily and force became a necessary concomitant. The result in many cases was slavery in fact although not in intent.[23]

Peonage is another inheritance from Spain and later Mexico. It was a form of slavery in satisfaction of a debt. In theory, it was only supposed to be a labor contract, but it too often in practice turned into something far more abusive than that neutral language would suggest. It should be said that often these so-called debts were manipulations by employers to take control of individuals. Indeed, later in U.S. history the concept of peonage was used by courts to describe practices of this type not only against Latinos, but others as well. As new territories formed in the west of the growing United States, the concept of peonage came with it. A New Mexico Supreme Court opinion from 1857 provides a revealing discussion of peonage as it existed when southwestern states came into the U.S.

Jaremillo v. Jose de la Cruz Romero

1 N.M. 190 (NM 1857)

INTRODUCTION: A young woman named Mariana Jaremillo was a servant to Jose de la Cruz Romero. Her father took her away from Romero's home. The latter claimed that she owed him a debt of $51.75 and launched a suit against her in a justice of the peace court, which issued a ruling against her. A district court found that Jaremillo had defaulted on her debt and ordered her into service to Romero as a peon to work off the obligation as well as the costs of the suit. The ruling went to the New Mexico Supreme Court.

In order for the court to decide the case, it was necessary first for the court to explain the peonage system. Notice that Justice Benedict began his opinion by explaining that it was a system generally regarded as "maintaining here similar relations between masters and servants as are found to be established between the master and his slave in different states of the union." It is important to keep in mind that this ruling was issued before the adoption of the Thirteenth Amendment and, in fact, before the Civil War.

It is also worth noting that this case came to the New Mexico Supreme Court just as that Court was beginning its work in an effort to clarify and regularize the law in a context where there had been conflict and confusion before, a point emphasized by Justice Benedict at the outset of his opinion.

Benedict made no secret of his frustration with the handling of this case, including a failure to challenge the matter adequately and on procedural grounds in the court below. Indeed, he pointed out the failure to ensure proper process that "too often prevails in justices' courts in this country as to the legal rights of the unfortunate, the peon and the feeble, when contesting with the influential and more wealthy...." He denounced the proceedings as "wholly *ex parte*,[24] an outrage upon law, and a premeditated injustice."

Justice Benedict delivered the opinion of the Court.

> ... It has become our duty for the first time in this tribunal to examine and construe the laws of this territory, declaring the rights and defining the relations of masters and servants.... It includes what is commonly called the peon system of this country.... [W]e have reviewed the present condition of the laws ... in New Mexico, and called to mind a period under a former government in this country when no degree of tolerable certainty existed in judicial forms, proceedings, and decisions, and when the laws and their just benefits were so often set aside or crushed under foot by prejudice, corruption, or passion—by interest, power, and despotism. We are fully aware how naturally and easily in the minds of many then and now living, have come down from that period notions greatly rigorous as to the power of the master over his servant, and how quickly the former is alarmed as to the retention of his supposed power....

> [T]he district court ... adjudged "that the plaintiff recover of the said defendant, Mariana Jaremillo, and of Domingo Fernandez Luz Jaremillo and Juan Miguel Ortego, the securities on her appeal bond, the sum of fifty-six dollars and twenty-one cents; and also the costs of this suit to be taxed, and in default of payment hereof that she be held to serve her said master, Jose de la Cruz Romero, as a peon until said sum of money is paid." ...

> Her counsel have insisted in argument that no service of process was made upon her in the suit before the justice, and that she was not brought within his jurisdiction.... From the unscrupulous disregard which too often prevails in justices' courts in this country as to the legal rights of the unfortunate, the peon and the feeble, when contesting with the influential and more wealthy, as well as the circumstances which appear to have attended this cause before the justice, the painful but reluctant conviction is forced upon our minds that no service of process or notice was made upon Mariana; that the proceedings were wholly *ex parte*, an outrage upon law, and a premeditated injustice; and we derive gratification in marking ... with the seal of judicial condemnation, such gross violations of the rights of those who are feeble in their own defense. [However,] the record does not show that she availed herself of her first opportunity in the district court, to require its judgment upon this point....

> Upon the entry of the power of the United States within this territory in 1846 ... there was found a large class of persons commonly designated ... by the name of peons.... They appeared as servants, menials, or domestics, "bound" to some kind of "service" to their masters.... The most wealthy and powerful families were flattered in their pride in displaying their retinues of these dependants....

One fact existed universally: all were indebted to their masters.... [T]he peon could discharge himself from this service by the payment of his indebtedness to his master.... He could not abandon the service; and if he did, his master pursued, reclaimed, and reduced him to obedience and labor again; and the alcaldes[25] of the country, in the most summary manner, aided the master in bringing back his fugitive. Both male and female became peons....

Vassals and vassalage had ceased to exist under the Spanish monarchy [as of 1811], and had not been restored by the Mexican government.... [W]e have been unable to find any law creating and defining the duties and rights ... of peon[s], while the Spanish and Mexican laws and authorities are replete with rules clearly marking out the legal rights and duties of masters and servants.... In the Spanish and English dictionary by Velasquez, peon is defined [as] pedestrian, day laborer, foot soldier, pawn in chess, anything that is whirled round in play, hive of bees, servant, menial, and groom. It also says that the word ... means an Indian hired to work by the day.... [T]he condition of a peon originated in Mexico [under] the early Spanish conquerors....

Escriche, in his Diccionario Legislativo [1847] ... says "that the rights and duties attached to the condition of master and servant, depend entirely upon contract." ... [W]ithout lawful cause the servant could not leave his master during the time the contract was to endure, and if he should, he might be compelled to return, or pay the damages caused by his abandonment.... The most frequent contracts of hiring and leasing of personal labor are those made with persons in the character of servants, domestics, or dependants, who obligate themselves at day labor.... Schmidt's Civil Law of Spain and Mexico designates unlawful objects of contracts to be such as ... the sale of a man's liberty, although he may sell his services for a limited time....

These quotations are sufficient to manifest the general principles upon which the conditions of master and servant were formed where the Spanish law prevailed.... [T]hey extended to Mexico when she achieved her independence.... [T]he consent of the parties was invariably the foundation upon which a servant became bound to service....

When we turn to the legislative acts of this territory, we find that the assembly held in 1851 ... made a law ... "that all contracts celebrated between two or more persons, the one binding himself to labor in certain and determined employments ... shall be respected and enforced by the civil law according to the agreements made by their own free and voluntary will...." There is also a section in these words: "When a servant runs off, his master may present himself before any authority and take out a warrant of his debt...."

At this point we turn to an examination of the record in this cause.... [I]t has been conceded by the counsel for both parties in this court that the cause was submitted on two certain documents.... Now these documents were issued more than two years before the master and servant act of July, 1851, became a law. They are supposed to have been regarded at the time as writs carrying authority with them, but it does not seem they were ever executed. Do the writs or documents amount to proof establishing the contract binding Mariana to service, the terms and her indebtedness?

In 1846, the political relations of this country were changed from Mexico to the United States. The president of the latter, ... through General Kearny ...

proclaimed laws, established offices, prescribed their functions, and appointed officers to fill and perform the duties of the offices. Their powers and jurisdiction were defined, and he directed the manner these should be exerted. Among the grades of officers were alcaldes ... substantially justices of the peace.... The acts creating them and clothing them with authority fix and limit the bounds, beyond which an alcalde's acts are null. In the well-defined powers given him in the code, there was nothing special as to master and servant. The same course of proceeding was left a master to recover his debt from his servant or peon, as in the ordinary way from another debtor, ... when the peon had left his master's service, to compel him to return....

Appreciating this fact, it is hardly fair to conclude that it was intended that there should be left in the hands of the alcaldes the faculty of using the cast-off and summary processes of a superseded government alone against him whose fate was that of an indebted laborer and servant....

The jurisdiction given to the prefects was different. It extended to all controversies between masters and those bound to them.... The prefect of Santa Fe ... stated that Romero had presented himself before him claiming a servant, that her name was Mariana, and that her father had taken her from his service, and that there was due him the sum of fifty-one dollars and seventy-five cents.... Nothing shows that either the girl or her father was ever before the prefect to adjust the ... claims with Romero, or that any notice had been given either to appear. By what practice, then, principle or law, could Mariana be bound by the prefect's proceedings? ... She was no party to the transaction, had no opportunity to defend against the demand, and, neither expressly nor constructively, had been brought within the prefect's jurisdiction. To hold that such judgment possessed any force, that it proved anything against Mariana or her father, would be setting at open defiance the known and long-observed rules of evidence and opening the doors to irresistible and measureless wrongs and frauds.

... If the going to the prefect by Romero and making his *ex parte* representations ... proved her a debtor and bound to service, and has given a master a right to reclaim or reduce her to bondage, it is easy to perceive how any person whosoever within the territory may be made a debtor and sent into servitude, should an unscrupulous man and an ignorant and faithless prefect or probate judge devise mischief together.... So far as [the record] shows anything, it suggests strongly that the debt, if any, was due by the father, and not the girl.... The inference is patent that the girl was a minor, and, if held for a debt, it was her father's..... If it was upon her father's account, as doubtless it was, she has passed, it may be well inferred, beyond her minority, and if so, can not, against her own consent, be held bound to service by reason of her father's indebtedness.... We find here no support to that portion of the judgment of the district court which adjudged Mariana to the service of Romero as a peon, in default of her or her securities paying the money....

No debt was established against Mariana by the *ex parte* action of Romero before the alcalde. The process or certificate of the prefect of Santa Fe can not prove her bound to service, nor her indebtedness.... No notice or summons was given the girl.... She seems in no form to have been brought within the prefect's jurisdiction. All was *ex parte*. These two writs, certificates, or documents were the only evidence offered or considered in the district court. Their utter insufficiency to prove Mariana's contract of service or any indebtedness to Romero, on her part, obligates this court to reverse the judgment of the court below....

Of course, the New Mexico case was decided before the Civil War and well before the passage of the Thirteenth Amendment. However, in the first test of the meaning of the civil rights amendments to the Constitution the Supreme Court recognized that the Thirteenth Amendment did not apply only to African Americans.

> Undoubtedly while negro slavery alone was in the mind of the Congress which proposed the thirteenth article, it forbids any other kind of slavery, now or hereafter. If Mexican peonage or the Chinese coolie labor system shall develop slavery of the Mexican or Chinese race within our territory, this amendment may safely be trusted to make it void.[26]

Writing in a dissent Justice Field stressed that the concept of "involuntary servitude" prohibited by the amendment was not limited to the traditional conception of black slavery in the South.

> The words 'involuntary servitude' have not been the subject of any judicial or legislative exposition ... in this country, except that which is found in the Civil Rights Act.... It is, however, clear that they include something more than slavery in the strict sense of the term; they include also serfage, vassalage, villenage, peonage, and all other forms of compulsory service for the mere benefit or pleasure of others.... The abolition of slavery and involuntary servitude was intended to make every one born in this country a freeman, and as such to give to him the right to [enjoy] the fruits of his labor.[27]

The U.S. Supreme Court adopted this broad approach in 1911.[28]

Congress specifically outlawed peonage in 1867 and made its practice and enforcement criminal offenses.[29] The Supreme Court directly ruled peonage a violation of the Thirteenth Amendment in two cases in 1911 and 1914.[30]

Bailey v. Alabama

219 U.S. 219 (1911)

INTRODUCTION: Although the concept of peonage originated with practices in Spain and then Mexico, the use of the concept spread to other states well beyond New Mexico. Alabama adopted legislation in 1896 that made defaulting on a debt a crime and allowed the imposition of peonage to satisfy the debt and penalties associated with the violation of its terms. The original law required proof of intent to injure or defraud the lender, but amendments allowed the court to imply that criminal intent from the failure to provide the promised service. Alabama law also provided: "that the accused, for the purpose of rebutting the statutory presumption, shall not be allowed to testify 'as to his uncommunicated motives, purpose or intention.'"

Alonzo Bailey had incurred a debt of $15 in connection with a contractual obligation as a farm hand. He was convicted and "sentenced by the court to pay the fine of thirty dollars and the costs, and in default thereof to hard labor 'for twenty days in lieu of said fine and one hundred and sixteen days on account of said costs.'" While Bailey challenged the validity of the statute, it was upheld on appeal by the Alabama Supreme Court.

Justice Hughes wrote the opinion for the Court.

> We at once dismiss from consideration the fact that the plaintiff in error is a black man. While the action of a State through its officers charged with the administration of a law, fair in appearance, may be of such a character as to constitute a denial of the equal protection of the laws (*Yick Wo v. Hopkins*), such a conclusion

is here neither required nor justified. The statute, on its face, makes no racial discrimination, and the record fails to show its existence in fact. No question of a sectional character is presented, and we may view the legislation in the same manner as if it had been enacted in New York or in Idaho. Opportunities for coercion and oppression, in varying circumstances, exist in all parts of the Union, and the citizens of all the States are interested in the maintenance of the constitutional guarantees, the consideration of which is here involved....

In the present case it is urged that the statute ... violates the Thirteenth Amendment of the Constitution of the United States and the act of Congress passed for its enforcement. The Thirteenth Amendment provides: "SECTION 1. Neither slavery nor involuntary servitude, except as a punishment for crime whereof the party shall have been duly convicted, shall exist within the United States, or any place subject to their jurisdiction. SECTION 2. Congress shall have power to enforce this article by appropriate legislation."

Pursuant to the authority thus conferred, Congress passed the act of March 2, 1867, c. 187, 14 Stat. 546, the provisions of which are ... as follows: "SEC. 1990. The holding of any person to service or labor under the system known as peonage is abolished and forever prohibited in the Territory of New Mexico, or in any other Territory or State of the United States...."

The language of the Thirteenth Amendment was not new. It reproduced the historic words of the ordinance of 1787 for the government of the Northwest Territory and gave them unrestricted application within the United States and all places subject to their jurisdiction. While the immediate concern was with African slavery, the Amendment was not limited to that. It was a charter of universal civil freedom for all persons, of whatever race, color or estate, under the flag.

The words involuntary servitude have a "larger meaning than slavery." ... The plain intention was to abolish slavery of whatever name and form and all its badges and incidents; to render impossible any state of bondage; to make labor free, by prohibiting that control by which the personal service of one man is disposed of or coerced for another's benefit which is the essence of involuntary servitude.... While the Amendment was self-executing, ... Congress was authorized to secure its complete enforcement by appropriate legislation.... The act of March 2, 1867 was a valid exercise of this express authority....

Peonage is a term descriptive of a condition which has existed in Spanish America, and especially in Mexico. The essence of the thing is compulsory service in payment of a debt. A peon is one who is compelled to work for his creditor until his debt is paid. And in this explicit and comprehensive enactment, Congress was not concerned with mere names or manner of description, or with a particular place or section of the country. It was concerned with a fact, wherever it might exist; with a condition, however named and wherever it might be established, maintained, or enforced....

"What is peonage? It may be defined as a status or condition of compulsory service, based upon the indebtedness of the peon to the master. The basal fact is indebtedness. As said by Judge Benedict, delivering the opinion in *Jaremillo v. Romero* ... 'This was the cord by which they seemed bound to their masters' service.' ... But peonage, however created, is compulsory service, involuntary servitude....

The act of Congress ... necessarily embraces all legislation which seeks to compel the service or labor by making it a crime to refuse or fail to perform it.... The Thirteenth

Amendment ... does not permit [a state to] compel one man to labor for another in payment of a debt, by punishing him as a criminal if he does not perform the service or pay the debt.... [W]e conclude that §4730, as amended, of the Code of Alabama ... is in conflict with the Thirteenth Amendment and the legislation authorized by that Amendment, and is therefore invalid....

Justice Holmes wrote a dissent joined by Justice Lurton.

... The Thirteenth Amendment does not outlaw contracts for labor.... Peonage is service to a private master at which a man is kept by bodily compulsion against his will.... Breach of a legal contract without excuse is wrong conduct ... and if a State adds ... a criminal liability to fine ... it does not make the laborer a slave.

But if a fine may be imposed, imprisonment may be imposed in case of a failure to pay it.... Also the power of the States to make breach of contract a crime is not done away with by the abolition of slavery.... If the contract is one that ought not to be made, prohibit it. But if it is a perfectly fair and proper contract, I can see no reason why the State should not throw its weight on the side of performance.... [A] false representation, expressed or implied, at the time of making a contract of labor that one intends to perform it ... may be declared a case of fraud [and] may be punished like any other crime ... without in any way infringing the Thirteenth Amendment or the statutes....

The Effort to Fight Segregation of Latinos

Although peonage was formally ended both by the Constitution and implementing legislation upheld by the Supreme Court, that did not address the more general problem of discrimination against Latinos. Even as the NAACP moved forward on the march toward reversing *Plessy*, only a handful of cases presented questions of segregation of Latinos in school and elsewhere. It would not be until 1954 that the foundation of law barring discrimination against Latinos was clearly established.

The first of these rulings came in the midst of World War II in a case launched by a veteran named Ignacio Lopez against the Mayor and City Council Members of San Bernadino, California.

Lopez v. Seccombe

71 F. Supp. 769 (SDCA 1944)

INTRODUCTION: This case grew out of segregation of aquatic facilities in San Bernadino, California that barred Latino residents from the use of the public swimming pool. What follows is not a standard opinion, but a set of finding of facts and conclusions of law provided by the U.S. District Court for the Southern District of California, together with an injunction prohibiting segregation of the facilities. The manner in which the judge explains the facts makes clear just how dramatic a situation it was.

Judge Yankwich delivered the opinion and issued the injunction.

I. This court finds as true that said City of San Bernardino is a municipal corporation ... incorporated in the State of California....

II. ... W. C. Seccombe was and now is the duly qualified elected and acting Mayor of said City of San Bernardino. [Findings III–VI identify other city officials.] ...

VII. This Court finds as true that petitioners [are] citizens of the United States and residents or taxpayers of said City and County, and that each [is] of Mexican or Latin descent or extraction.

VIII. ... Petitioner Ignacio Lopez is an American citizen of Mexican descent..., a taxpayer of said County of San Bernardino, a graduate of Chaffee Jr. College and Pomona College and the University of Southern California; and recently head of the Spanish Department in the Office of Foreign Language, Division of Office of War Information, Spanish speaking director of the Office of Coordinator of Inter-American affairs at Los Angeles, California, and is editor of El Espector, a newspaper in said City and County.

[P]etitioner Rev. R. N. Nunez is an American citizen of Mexican descent, ordained Catholic Priest and presides over the San Bernardino Parish of the Guadalupe Church....

That petitioner Eugenio Nogueroa is an American citizen of Latin descent, a graduate of Cayey High School, Porto Rico, and of University of Porto Rico, a former member of the 76th Field Artillery Third Division, United States Army, and editor and publisher at San Bernardino, California....

That Virginia Prado is a student, citizen of the United States, and a resident of the City of San Bernardino, County and State as aforesaid, and of Mexican descent.

That Refael Munoz is a student, citizen of the United States, and a resident of the City of San Bernardino, County and State of aforesaid, and is a Mexican descendant.

IX. ... Petitioners herein contribute to the financial support and maintenance of said park, playground, swimming pool, plunge, and facilities mentioned and each [all] petitioners are ... beneficially interested in the privileges, management, control, use and occupation of said facilities..., and as members of the public and citizens of the United States, are entitled to admission and the use and enjoyment of said playground, swimming pool, plunge, bathhouse and facilities.

X. This Court finds as true that all ... petitioners are of clean and moral habits not suffering any disability, infectious disease, nor have they any physical or mental defect, but in all other respects are persons proper and qualified to be admitted to and enjoy the use of said bathhouse, plunge, swimming pool, park, playground, and all facilities in connection therewith. That their admission to and the use of said bathhouse, pool, plunge and facilities within said park and playground is not inimical, harmful or detrimental to the health, welfare or safety of other users thereof.

XI. This Court finds as true that for several years last past all persons of Mexican or Latin descent or extraction, though citizens of the United States of America have on repeated occasions been excluded, barred and precluded from using, enjoying or entering upon that portion of said park and playground containing said swimming pool, plunge, bath house and facilities, by respondents, their servants, agents and employees.

XII. This Court finds as true that petitioners and ... all others of Mexican or Latin descent have been denied admission to, and the use, benefit and enjoyment of said swimming pool, plunge, bath house, and facilities within said park and playground by respondents, their servants, agents and employees ... based solely upon the fact that petitioners are of Mexican or Latin descent.

XIII. This Court finds as true that petitioners and others of Mexican and Latin descent ... have sought admission to the facilities of said park as mentioned, during hours when same were open to the public at large, but said respondents … denied petitioners the right to enter and use said privileges based solely upon the fact that petitioners were of Mexican and Latin descent or extraction. That petitioners on numerous occasion [*sic*] during the year 1943 … have protested to respondents [and] have demanded admission and the use and privilege of the said facilities of said park at and during the time that such facilities are open to the public to all of which said respondents did then and there refuse and still [refuse] … solely for the reasons stated.

XIV. This Court finds as true that petitioners and other persons of Mexican and Latin descent … are denied the use and enjoyment of the facilities of said park as aforesaid notwithstanding that other persons … are allowed the use and enjoyment of said privileges…. That by reason thereof, the injury to petitioners is continuous, great and irreparable, and is calculated to affect their health and rights as citizens of the United States of America, and of the State of California.

XV. … [P]etitioners seek to redress the deprivation by respondents herein, under color of regulation, custom and usage, of petitioners' civil rights, privileges and immunities secured to them by the Laws of the United States, and as guaranteed to each of them by the Laws and Constitution of the United States of America.

XVI. This Court finds as true that respondents' conduct … is illegal and is in violation of petitioners' rights and privileges, as guaranteed by the Constitution of the United States of America, and as secured and guaranteed to them as citizens of the United States of America, as particularly provided under the Fifth and Fourteenth Amendments. That petitioners are entitled to such equal accommodations, advantages and privileges and to equal rights and treatment with other persons as citizens of the United States, in the use and enjoyment of the facilities of said park and playground and to equal treatment with other persons and to the equal protection of the laws in their use and enjoyment of said privileges as provided, and afforded to other persons at all times when the same is open and used by them….

As Conclusions of Law from the Foregoing Findings of Fact, the Court herein now concludes as follows:

I.   That respondents' conduct is illegal and is in violation of petitioners rights and privileges as guaranteed by the Constitution of the United States, and as secured and guaranteed to them as citizens of the United States, by the Constitution of the United States of America, as particularly provided under the Fifth and Fourteenth Amendments. That petitioners are entitled to such equal accommodations, advantages, and privileges and to equal rights and treatment with other persons as citizens of the United States, in the use and enjoyment of the facilities of said park and playground and to equal treatment with other persons and to equal protection of the laws in their use and enjoyment of said privileges as provided, and afforded, to other persons at all times when the same is open and used by them.

II. That said denial of the admission and usage is unconstitutional, illegal and void and is being enforced against petitioners and each of them, by such discriminatory conduct and practice by respondents, and each of them.

III. That this action is brought on behalf of petitioners and some 8,000 other persons of Mexican and Latin descent and extraction all citizens of the United States of America, residing within said district…. Therefore, these petitioners sue for the benefit of all.[31]

IV.   That this action is brought under ... 28 U.S.C.A. §41(14) to prevent the respondents from unlawfully interfering with the petitioners' equal protection of the laws and due process of law.

V.   That petitioners have no plain, speedy or adequate or any remedy at law, and that petitioners are suffering great irreparable damage.

VI.   That by this suit and proceedings, petitioners seek to redress the deprivation by respondents herein, under color of regulation, custom and usage, of petitioners' civil rights, privileges, and immunities secured to them by the laws of the United States, and as guaranteed to each of them by the laws and Constitution of the United States of America.

VII.   That petitioners are entitled to a permanent injunction against the respondents.

The second case was a challenge to school segregation in Orange County, California. It arose when the Mendez family moved to the area and rented a farm from a Japanese American family, who were sent off to a relocation center during World War II. When Ms. Mendez sought to register her children in the local school, she was informed that there was a separate school for Latino children.

There is a connection between the *Mendez* case and the previous swimming pool case. Mr. Mendez ultimately retained David C. Marcus, the lawyer in the *Lopez v. Seccombe* swimming pool case excerpted above. Marcus advised Mendez to help find plaintiffs in other neighboring school districts and ultimately filed the *Mendez* case.[32] The attorney explained that it was important to go forward with more than just a single plaintiff, a lesson that had been learned by the civil rights movement nationally, when important cases had been defeated when a problem arose with respect to the one plaintiff in that suit. Mendez did so, and Marcus brought the litigation, which resulted in a federal district court ruling, years before *Brown v. Board of Education*, that denounced segregated schools.

As California Superior Court Judge Frederick P. Aguirre later explained:

> During the trial, Garden Grove School District Superintendent James L. Kent testified that he considered Mexican American children "inferior." Court records show that Kent's testimony included opinions that Mexicans are inferior in personal hygiene, ability and in their economic outlook.... Kent also testified that "he would never allow a Latino child to attend an all-white school even if that child met all the qualifications to attend such a school."[33]

The problem of segregation of Latino children was no small matter either in terms of numbers or its significance for Latinos who suffered the discrimination. As Aguirre noted:

> In 1934, Mexican American children made up one-fourth of the total student population in Orange County. A study found that 70% of the Mexican American children attended "Mexican" segregated elementary schools. Similarly, in Texas, Arizona and all across the Southwest, "Mexican" children were forced to attend segregated public schools.[34]

Mendez v. Westminster School Dist. Of Orange County

64 F. Supp. 544 (SDCA 1946)

INTRODUCTION: This is an important decision for many Latino legal scholars who see the *Mendez* case as a part of the dynamics that led to the *Brown* ruling some years later.[35] For present purposes, it is particularly important for what it teaches about the discrimination visited upon Latino school children in southern California schools and elsewhere, a subject that is not widely known either on the West Coast or nationally.

This case was brought as a class action suit by a number of parents, led by the Mendez family, on behalf of some 5,000 children and their families, charging that the officials and schools of the Westminister, Garden Grove and El Modeno School Districts, and the Santa Ana City Schools in Orange County, California, segregated Latino children and prohibited them from attending their neighborhood schools. Two of the schools segregated students to the sixth grade and the other two to the eighth grade. All parties agreed that all of the schools were essentially equal in facilities, teachers, and curricula. They alleged that these policies and practices violated the equal protection clause of the Fourteenth Amendment and sought an injunction to stop the segregation.

Judge McCormick wrote the opinion.

> ... The ultimate question for decision may be thus stated: Does such official action of defendant district school agencies and the usages and practices pursued by the respective school authorities as shown by the evidence operate to deny or deprive the so-called non-English-speaking school children of Mexican ancestry or descent within such school districts of the equal protection of the laws [under the Fourteenth Amendment]? ... We think the pattern of public education promulgated in the Constitution of California and effectuated by provisions of the Education Code of the State prohibits segregation of the pupils of Mexican ancestry in the elementary schools from the rest of the school children.

> Section 1 of Article IX of the Constitution of California directs the legislature to "encourage by all suitable means the promotion of intellectual, scientific, moral, and agricultural improvement" of the people.... The common segregation attitudes and practices of the school authorities in the defendant school districts in Orange County pertain solely to children of Mexican ancestry and parentage. They are singled out as a class for segregation. Not only is such method of public school administration contrary to the general requirements of the school laws of the State, but we think it indicates an official school policy that is antagonistic in principle to Sections 16004 and 16005 of the Education Code of the State.

> Obviously, the children referred to in these laws are those of Mexican ancestry. And it is noteworthy that the educational advantages of their commingling with other pupils is regarded as being so important to the school system of the State that it is provided for even regardless of the citizenship of the parents. We perceive in the laws relating to the public educational system in the State of California a clear purpose to avoid and forbid distinctions among pupils based upon race or ancestry [see sections 8501–8002] except in specific situations[36] not pertinent to this action. Distinctions of that kind have recently been declared by the highest judicial authority of the United States "by their very nature odious to a free people whose institutions are founded upon the doctrine of equality" [and] "utterly inconsistent with American traditions and ideals." *Hirabayashi v. United States.*...

> Our conclusions in this action, however, do not rest solely upon what we conceive to be the utter irreconcilability of the segregation practices in the defendant school districts with the public educational system authorized and sanctioned by the laws of the State of California. We think such practices clearly and unmistakably disregard rights secured by the supreme law of the land.... "The equal

protection of the laws" pertaining to the public school system in California is not provided by furnishing in separate schools the same technical facilities, text books and courses of instruction to children of Mexican ancestry that are available to the other public school children regardless of their ancestry. A paramount requisite in the American system of public education is social equality. It must be open to all children by unified school association regardless of lineage.

We think that under the record before us the only tenable ground upon which segregation practices in the defendant school districts can be defended lies in the English language deficiencies of some of the children of Mexican ancestry as they enter elementary public school life as beginners. But even such situations do not justify the general and continuous segregation in separate schools of the children of Mexican ancestry from the rest of the elementary school population as has been shown to be the practice in the defendant school districts—in all of them to the sixth grade, and in two of them through the eighth grade.

The evidence clearly shows that Spanish-speaking children are retarded in learning English by lack of exposure to its use because of segregation, and that commingling of the entire student body instills and develops a common cultural attitude among the school children which is imperative for the perpetuation of American institutions and ideals.[37]... [T]he methods of segregation prevalent in the defendant school districts foster antagonisms in the children and suggest inferiority among them where none exists.... In the district under consideration there are two schools, the Lincoln and the Roosevelt, located approximately 120 yards apart on the same school grounds, hours of opening and closing, as well as recess periods, are not uniform. No credible language test is given to the children of Mexican ancestry upon entering the first grade in Lincoln School. This school has an enrollment of 249 so-called Spanish-speaking pupils, and no so-called English-speaking pupils; while the Roosevelt, (the other) school, has 83 so-called English-speaking pupils and 25 so-called Spanish-speaking pupils. Standardized tests as to mental ability are given to the respective classes in the two schools and the same curricula are pursued in both schools and, of course, in the English language as required by State law.... In the last school year the students in the seventh grade of the Lincoln were superior scholarly to the same grade in the Roosevelt School and to any group in the seventh grade in either of the schools in the past. It further appears that not only did the class as a group have such mental superiority but that certain pupils in the group were also outstanding in the class itself. Notwithstanding this showing, the pupils of such excellence were kept in the Lincoln School....

While the pattern or ideal of segregating the school children of Mexican ancestry from the rest of the school attendance permeates and is practiced in all of the four defendant districts, there are procedural deviations among the school administrative agencies in effectuating the general plan.... [T]he admitted practice and long established custom in [the Garden Grove] school district whereby all elementary public school children of Mexican descent are required to attend one specified school (the Hoover) until they attain the sixth grade, while all other pupils of the same grade are permitted to and do attend two other elementary schools of this district ... clearly establishes an unfair and arbitrary class distinction.... The long-standing discriminatory custom prevalent in this district is aggravated by the fact shown by the record that although there are approximately 25 children of Mexican descent living in the vicinity of the Lincoln School, none of them attend that school, but all are peremptorily assigned by the school authorities to the Hoover School, although the evidence shows that there are no school zones territorially established in the district.

The record before us shows a paradoxical situation concerning the segregation attitude of the school authorities in the Westminister School District. There are two elementary schools in this undivided area. Instruction is given pupils in each school from kindergarten to the eighth grade, inclusive. Westminister School has 642 pupils, of which 628 are so-called English-speaking children, and 14 so-called Spanish-speaking pupils. The Hoover School is attended solely by 152 children of Mexican descent. Segregation of these from the rest of the school population precipitated such vigorous protests by residents of the district that the school board in January, 1944 ... resolved to unite the two schools and thus abolish the objectionable practices which had been operative in the schools of the district for a considerable period. A bond issue was submitted to the electors to raise funds to defray the cost.... The bonds were not voted and the record before us in this action reflects no execution or carrying out of the official action of the board of trustees ... abolish[ing] the traditional segregation practices in this district....

Before considering the specific factual situation in the Santa Ana City Schools it should be noted that the omnibus segregation of children of Mexican ancestry from the rest of the student body in the elementary grades [in the Santa Ana City Schools] is not warranted by the record before us. The tests applied to the beginners are shown to have been generally hasty, superficial and not reliable. In some instances separate classification was determined largely by the Latinized or Mexican name of the child. Such methods of evaluating language knowledge are illusory and are not conducive to the inculcation and enjoyment of civil rights which are of primary importance in the public school system of education in the United States.

It has been held that public school authorities may differentiate in the exercise of their reasonable discretion as to the pedagogical methods of instruction to be pursued with different pupils.[38] And foreign language handicaps may be to such a degree in the pupils in elementary schools as to require special treatment in separate classrooms. Such separate allocations, however, can be lawfully made only after credible examination by the appropriate school authority of each child whose capacity to learn is under consideration and the determination of such segregation must be based wholly upon indiscriminate foreign language impediments in the individual child, regardless of his ethnic traits or ancestry....

[An] influx of people of Mexican ancestry in large numbers and their voluntary settlement in certain of the fourteen zones [of the Santa Ana School District] resulted in three of the zones becoming occupied almost entirely by such group of people. Two zones, that in which the Fremont School is located, and another contiguous area in which the Franklin School is situated, present the only flagrant discriminatory situation shown by the evidence in this case in the Santa Ana City Schools. The Fremont School has 325 so-called Spanish-speaking pupils and no so-called English-speaking pupils. The Franklin School has 237 pupils of which 161 are so-called English-speaking children, and 76 so-called Spanish-speaking children.

The evidence shows that approximately 26 pupils of Mexican descent who reside within the Fremont zone are permitted by the School Board to attend the Franklin

School because their families had always gone there. It also appears that there are approximately 35 other pupils not of Mexican descent who live within the Fremont zone who are not required to attend the Fremont School but who are also permitted by the Board of Education to attend the Franklin School.

Sometime in the fall of the year 1944 there arose dissatisfaction by the parents of some of the so-called Spanish-speaking pupils in the Fremont School zone who were not granted the privilege that approximately 26 children also of Mexican descent, enjoyed in attending the Franklin School. Protest was made en masse by such dissatisfied group of parents, which resulted in the Board of Education directing its secretary to send a letter to the parents of all of the so-called Spanish-speaking pupils living in the Fremont zone and attending the Franklin School that beginning September, 1945, the permit to attend Franklin School would be withdrawn and the children would be required to attend the school of the zone in which they were living....

There could have been no arbitrary discrimination claimed by plaintiffs by the action of the school authorities if the same official course had been applied to the 35 other so-called English-speaking pupils exactly situated as were the approximate 26 children of Mexican lineage, but the record is clear that the requirement of the Board of Education was intended for and directed exclusively to the specified pupils of Mexican ancestry and if carried out becomes operative solely against such group of children....

The natural operation and effect of the Board's official action manifests a clear purpose to arbitrarily discriminate against the pupils of Mexican ancestry and to deny to them the equal protection of the laws.... There are other discriminatory customs, shown by the evidence, existing in the defendant school districts as to pupils of Mexican descent and extraction, but we deem it unnecessary to discuss them in this memorandum. We conclude by holding that the allegations of the complaint (petition) have been established sufficiently to justify injunctive relief against all defendants, restraining further discriminatory practices against the pupils of Mexican descent in the public schools of defendant school districts.

The district court ruling was affirmed in the Court of Appeals for the Ninth Circuit, but on narrower grounds than those presented in the district court decision.[39] The case did not go to the U.S. Supreme Court. The question of an end to school segregation, of course, was not addressed by the Supreme Court until *Brown v. Board of Education* in 1954.

Thomas A. Saenz has provided some explanation as to why such an important case is not better known, even among civil rights specialists.[40] For one thing, he noted, most attention was focused on the battle over segregation of African American students in the Southeast and the related battle by the NAACP LDF against the *Plessy* doctrine. That said, Thurgood Marshall and his colleagues at the NAACP LDF filed a brief in support of *Mendez* when the case was appealed by the School Districts to the U.S. Court of Appeals for the Ninth Circuit. Indeed, in the late 1960s when Peter Tijerina was forming what came to be known as the Mexican American Legal Defense and Education Fund (MALDEF), he received advice and assistance in obtaining initial funding from then NAACP LDF director and chief counsel Jack Greenburg.[41]

Second, and more complex, is an explanation associated with the way in which the *Mendez* case was litigated that meant that while it was successful in California, it was unlikely to find its way to the Supreme Court or into many law school casebooks. David Marcus, the plaintiffs' attorney, sought a stipulation from all parties that the *Mendez* case was not a standard matter of race discrimination.[42] Despite that fact, as the court observed, the complaint "allege[d] a concerted policy and design of class discrimination against 'persons of Mexican or Latin descent or extraction' of elementary school age by the defendant school agencies in the conduct and operation of public schools of said districts, resulting in the denial of the equal protection of the laws to such class of persons among which are the petitioning school children,"[43] it also noted that: "It is conceded by all parties that there is no question of race discrimination in this action."[44]

There were two reasons for Marcus' effort to get the stipulation. The only basis in California law at the time for segregating school children came from a statute that called for separate schools for Asian students and for Native Americans. Since many Mexican Americans were considered to be indigenous people, a focus on a racial distinction could have allowed the district to argue that it had authority under state law for its actions. Of even greater importance, though, was the fact that if the case was presented on separate but equal grounds as racial segregation, then the controlling law at the time was the *Plessy* decision and, once again, there would have been strong arguments for the district. By avoiding these two issues, the Court of Appeals was able to affirm the district court ruling without confronting the *Plessy* line of cases, relying primarily on the argument that there was no basis in California law for the school district to establish segregated schools for Latinos. Thus, the court of appeals began by explaining that: "It is interesting to note at this juncture of the case that the parties stipulated that there is no question as to race segregation in the case."[45] That also meant, however, that this was not a case poised to go to the U.S. Supreme Court as part of the NAACP LDF effort to overturn *Plessy*.

At the same time that the Supreme Court was preparing to strike down the separate but equal doctrine, the state of Texas was arguing that the equal protection clause of the Fourteenth Amendment did not protect Latinos. In fact, the Texas Court of Criminal Appeals had held that: "[T]he equal protection clause of the Fourteenth Amendment contemplated and recognized only two classes as coming within that guarantee: the white race, comprising one class, and the Negro race, comprising the other class."[46] This case arose in the context of discrimination in selection for jury service, but the larger question was crucial, which is why the *Hernandez v. Texas* case is often regarded among Latino civil rights lawyers as the foundation case for Latino civil rights.

Hernandez v. Texas

347 U.S. 475 (1954)

INTRODUCTION: Peter Hernandez was indicted, convicted, and sentenced to life in prison for murder in Texas. His attorney unsuccessfully challenged the conviction on claims that Latinos were systematically excluded from grand juries and petit juries (trial juries) in Jackson County, Texas. This, he alleged, was clearly discrimination in violation of the equal protection clause of the Fourteenth Amendment.

Chief Justice Warren wrote the opinion for the Court.

> ... In numerous decisions, this Court has held that it is a denial of the equal protection of the laws to try a defendant of a particular race or color under an indictment issued by a grand jury, or before a petit jury, from which all persons of his race or color have, solely because of that race or color, been excluded by the State, whether acting through its legislature, its courts, or its executive or administrative officers. Although the Court has had little occasion to rule on the question directly, it has been recognized since *Strauder v. West Virginia* ... that the exclusion of a class of persons from jury service on grounds other than race or color may

also deprive a defendant who is a member of that class of the constitutional guarantee of equal protection of the laws. The State of Texas would have us hold that there are only two classes—white and Negro—within the contemplation of the Fourteenth Amendment. The decisions of this Court do not support that view.... The Fourteenth Amendment is not directed solely against discrimination due to a "two-class theory"—that is, based upon differences between "white" and Negro.

... [T]he Texas system of selecting grand and petit jurors by the use of jury commissions is fair on its face and capable of being utilized without discrimination. But ... the system is susceptible to abuse and can be employed in a discriminatory manner. The exclusion of otherwise eligible persons from jury service solely because of their ancestry or national origin is discrimination prohibited by the Fourteenth Amendment. The Texas statute makes no such discrimination, but the petitioner alleges that those administering the law do.

The petitioner's initial burden in substantiating his charge of group discrimination was to prove that persons of Mexican descent constitute a separate class in Jackson County, distinct from "whites." One method by which this may be demonstrated is by showing the attitude of the community. Here the testimony of responsible officials and citizens contained the admission that residents of the community distinguished between "white" and "Mexican." The participation of persons of Mexican descent in business and community groups was shown to be slight. Until very recent times, children of Mexican descent were required to attend a segregated school for the first four grades. At least one restaurant in town prominently displayed a sign announcing "No Mexicans Served." On the courthouse grounds at the time of the hearing, there were two men's toilets, one unmarked, and the other marked "Colored Men" and "Hombres Aqui" ("Men Here"). No substantial evidence was offered to rebut the logical inference to be drawn from these facts, and it must be concluded that petitioner succeeded in his proof.

Having established the existence of a class, petitioner was then charged with the burden of proving discrimination. To do so, he relied on the pattern of proof established by *Norris v. Alabama*, 294 U.S. 587 [1935]. In that case, proof that Negroes constituted a substantial segment of the population of the jurisdiction, that some Negroes were qualified to serve as jurors, and that none had been called for jury service over an extended period of time, was held to constitute prima facie proof of the systematic exclusion of Negroes from jury service. This holding [is] sometimes called the "rule of exclusion." ....

The petitioner established that 14% of the population of Jackson County were persons with Mexican or Latin-American surnames, and that 11% of the males over 21 bore such names. The County Tax Assessor testified that 6 or 7 percent of the freeholders on the tax rolls of the County were persons of Mexican descent. The State of Texas stipulated that "for the last twenty-five years there is no record of any person with a Mexican or Latin American name having served on a jury commission, grand jury or petit jury in Jackson County." The parties also stipulated that "there are some male persons of Mexican or Latin American descent in Jackson County who, by virtue of being citizens, householders, or freeholders, and having all other legal prerequisites to jury service, are eligible to serve as members of a jury commission, grand jury and/or petit jury."

... To rebut the strong prima facie case of the denial of the equal protection of the laws guaranteed by the Constitution thus established, the State offered the testimony of five jury commissioners that they had not discriminated against persons of Mexican or Latin-American descent in selecting jurors. They stated that their only objective had been to select those whom they thought were best qualified. This testimony is not enough to overcome the petitioner's case....

Circumstances or chance may well dictate that no persons in a certain class will serve on a particular jury or during some particular period. But it taxes our credulity to say that mere chance resulted in there being no members of this class among the over six thousand jurors called in the past 25 years. The result bespeaks discrimination, whether or not it was a conscious decision on the part of any individual jury commissioner. The judgment of conviction must be reversed.

The petitioner did not seek proportional representation, nor did he claim a right to have persons of Mexican descent sit on the particular juries which he faced. His only claim is the right to be indicted and tried by juries from which all members of his class are not systematically excluded—juries selected from among all qualified persons regardless of national origin or descent. To this much, he is entitled by the Constitution.

Civil Rights and Education Issues Continue

Given the *Hernandez* ruling, and the Supreme Court's decision that came two weeks later in *Brown v. Board of Education*, segregation of Latinos would clearly be against the law. However, that was only part of the story of civil rights issues in education for Latino children. There certainly were cases like those pursued by the NAACP LDF seeking to ensure the implementation of *Brown v. Board of Education*, but there were others as well, like those involving school finance and students with uncertain status.

School Finance: A Complex Civil Rights Problem

Many Latino families faced discrimination in the workplace and in housing as well as in education. However, the traditional system of financing public education in the United States has provided most for those who live in middle and upper middle class suburban settings, while taxing most heavily those who live in less affluent urban settings. The use of the property tax as the primary vehicle for funding education has meant that those who live in communities with significant and growing property values could obtain more funds for their schools while taxing themselves at a lower rate than those residing in less affluent areas. Since these suburban homeowners could then use their property taxes as deductions on their income tax calculations, their burden was further reduced. Those who rented in city settings, on the other hand, did not have that option. Finally, state and federal funding that was supposed to operate so as to offset some of the inequalities in the property tax system actually have often worked in the opposite way. To all of that was added the fact that wealthier families were able to provide greater opportunities for learning enrichment and educational readiness as their children prepared for school than those who had less means. Finally, educational systems that had long been segregated were not quickly and effectively transformed, such that they would provide on a fully equal basis for those who had been the disfavored groups.

These issues arose in the wake of the turmoil in the nation's cities discussed in earlier chapters. It was clear from the reports done by the Kerner Commission and other bodies that the nation's cities posed a wide range of social and economic problems that disproportionately affected Latinos and African Americans in those cities. It was equally clear that inadequate educational systems were both part of the present problem and a critical factor in whether those communities would be able to move forward in the future.

The combination of these factors led to a growing frustration with the unwillingness of state legislatures to move away from the property tax-based systems or to take other critical steps to address significant social problems in the cities. Suburban voters saw that the current system suited their interests and also viewed the city's problems as someone else's issue, notwithstanding the importance of the cities as economic engines that helped to provide the jobs that supported the suburban lifestyle. Rural voters also saw their own interests in the status quo and had little concern for the problems of the city.

That frustration at the failure to confront such glaring problems with such serious consequences prompted a variety of individuals and groups to launch lawsuits aimed at ending the property tax-based educational system. These suits were filed in both state and federal courts and argued a clear connection between the funding schemes and discrimination in violation of the federal equal protection clause or parallel provisions in state constitutions.

Those opposed responded that neither race nor ethnicity had anything to do with the situation. At root, they said, the situation was simply an economic matter that arose from the fact some people were more successful in the marketplace and were therefore able to live where they chose and educate their children in good schools, either public or private.

To many of those bringing the suits, however, the connection between race and ethnicity and the inequalities of the funding system were obvious, given the combination of employment, housing, and educational discrimination that had only so recently been outlawed. The Fair Housing Act did not pass until 1968 and communities in the North were resisting school desegregation, demands even as officials in the South continued their "massive resistance" to desegregation in that part of the country.

In the West, the tradition of discrimination against Latinos continued even as the issues were becoming more visible. From the perspective of many in the Latino community, there was nothing accidental about the current situation. One of the first cases to address this question of discriminatory financing systems came from California in *Serrano v. Priest*.

Serrano v. Priest

487 P.2d 1241 (CA 1971)

INTRODUCTION: A groups of parents brought a class action suit on behalf of themselves and their children in the Los Angeles County public school system. They sued the state Treasurer, the Superintendent of Public Instruction, and the Controller of the State of California, as well as the County Tax Collector and Treasurer, and the Superintendent of Schools.

Their suit claimed that the property tax-based system of financing public education led to disparities in the funds available to educate children, such that those in districts with a smaller tax base, generally poorer communities, were able to raise less money to support the schools, even though they often paid a higher tax rate on their property. They charged that these discrepancies violated both the state and federal constitutions. However, the trial court dismissed the suit for failure to state a cause of action and the case reached the California Supreme Court.

The opinion for the Court was presented by Justice Sullivan.

> We are called upon to determine whether the California public school financing system, with its substantial dependence on local property taxes and resultant wide disparities in school revenue, violates the equal protection clause of the Fourteenth Amendment. We have determined that this funding scheme invidiously

discriminates against the poor because it makes the quality of a child's education a function of the wealth of his parents and neighbors. Recognizing as we must that the right to an education in our public schools is a fundamental interest which cannot be conditioned on wealth, we can discern no compelling state purpose necessitating the present method of financing. We have concluded, therefore, that such a system cannot withstand constitutional challenge and must fall before the equal protection clause.... The financing scheme ... fails to meet the requirements of the equal protection clause of the Fourteenth Amendment of the United States Constitution and the California Constitution....

We begin our task by examining the California public school financing system which is the focal point of the complaint's allegations. At the threshold we find a fundamental statistic—over 90 percent of our public school funds derive from two basic sources: (a) local district taxes on real property and (b) aid from the State School Fund. By far the major source of school revenue is the local real property tax.... The amount of revenue which a district can raise in this manner thus depends largely on its tax base—i.e., the assessed valuation of real property within its borders. Tax bases vary widely throughout the state; in 1969–1970, for example, the assessed valuation per unit of average daily attendance of elementary school children ranged from a low of $103 to a peak of $952,156—a ratio of nearly 1 to 10,000.... The other factor determining local school revenue is the rate of taxation within the district.... Thus the locally raised funds which constitute the largest portion of school revenue are primarily a function of the value of the realty within a particular school district, coupled with the willingness of the district's residents to tax themselves for education.

Most of the remaining school revenue comes from the State School Fund pursuant to the "foundation program," through which the state undertakes to supplement local taxes in order to provide a "minimum amount of guaranteed support to all districts...". The state contribution is supplied in two principal forms. "Basic state aid" consists of a flat grant to each district of $125 per pupil per year, regardless of the relative wealth of the district.... "Equalization aid" is distributed in inverse proportion to the wealth of the district.... An additional state program of "supplemental aid" is available to subsidize particularly poor school districts which are willing to make an extra local tax effort....

Although equalization aid and supplemental aid temper the disparities which result from the vast variations in real property assessed valuation, wide differentials remain in the revenue available to individual districts and, consequently, in the level of educational expenditures. For example, in Los Angeles County, where plaintiff children attend school, the Baldwin Park Unified School District expended only $577.49 to educate each of its pupils in 1968–1969; during the same year the Pasadena Unified School District spent $840.19 on every student; and the Beverly Hills Unified School District paid out $1,231.72 per child.... The source of these disparities is unmistakable: in Baldwin Park the assessed valuation per child totaled only $3,706; in Pasadena, assessed valuation was $13,706; while in Beverly Hills, the corresponding figure was $50,885—a ratio of 1 to 4 to 13.... Thus, the state grants are inadequate to offset the inequalities inherent in a financing system based on widely varying local tax bases. Furthermore, basic aid, which constitutes about half of the state educational funds ... actually widens the gap between rich and poor districts....

III. ... [T]he United States Supreme Court has employed a two-level test for measuring legislative classifications against the equal protection clause [of the Fourteenth Amendment]. "In the area of economic regulation, the high court has exercised restraint, investing legislation with a presumption of constitutionality and requiring merely that distinctions drawn by a challenged statute bear some rational relationship to a conceivable legitimate state purpose."

"On the other hand, in cases involving 'suspect classifications' or touching on 'fundamental interests,' the court has adopted an attitude of active and critical analysis, subjecting the classification to strict scrutiny. Under the strict standard applied in such cases, the state bears the burden of establishing not only that it has a *compelling* interest which justifies the law but that the distinctions drawn by the law are *necessary* to further its purpose." ...

A. Wealth as a Suspect Classification. In recent years, the United States Supreme Court has demonstrated a marked antipathy toward legislative classifications which discriminate on the basis of certain "suspect" personal characteristics. One factor which has repeatedly come under the close scrutiny of the high court is wealth.... [See e.g.,] *Tate v. Short, Douglas v. California, Griffin v. Illinois*....

Plaintiffs contend that the school financing system classifies on the basis of wealth. We find this proposition irrefutable.... Although the amount of money raised locally is also a function of the rate at which the residents of a district are willing to tax themselves, as a practical matter districts with small tax bases simply cannot levy taxes at a rate sufficient to produce the revenue that more affluent districts reap with minimal tax efforts.... Baldwin Park citizens, who paid a school tax of $5.48 per $100 ... were able to spend less than half as much on education as Beverly Hills residents, who were taxed only $2.38 per $100.... Obviously, the richer district is favored when it can provide the same educational quality for its children with less tax effort. Furthermore, ... the poorer districts are financially unable to raise their taxes high enough to match the educational offerings of wealthier districts.... Thus, affluent districts can have their cake and eat it too: they can provide a high quality education for their children while paying lower taxes. Poor districts, by contrast, have no cake at all....

Defendants ... claim that no constitutional infirmity is involved because the complaint contains no allegation of purposeful or intentional discrimination... [N]one of the wealth classifications previously invalidated by the United States Supreme Court or this court has been the product of purposeful discrimination. [See *Griffin*, ... *Douglas*....]

We turn now to defendants' related contention that the instant case involves at most de facto discrimination. We disagree. Indeed, we find the case unusual in the extent to which governmental action *is* the cause of the wealth classifications.... Although private residential and commercial patterns may be partly responsible for the distribution of assessed valuation throughout the state, such patterns are shaped and hardened by zoning ordinances and other governmental land-use controls which promote economic exclusivity.... Governmental action drew the school district boundary lines, thus determining how much local wealth each district would contain....

B. Education as a Fundamental Interest. [Plaintiffs] assert that the system not only draws lines on the basis of wealth but that it ... has a direct and significant impact upon, a "fundamental interest," namely education. It is urged that these two grounds, particularly in combination, establish a demonstrable denial of equal protection of the laws.... The fundamental importance of education has been recognized ... by the United States Supreme Court ... in *Brown v. Board of Education*.... The twin themes of the importance of education to the individual and to society have recurred in numerous decisions of this court.... We are convinced that the distinctive and priceless function of education in our society warrants, indeed compels, our treating it as a "fundamental interest." ...

C. The Financing System Is not Necessary to Accomplish a Compelling State Interest ... [E]ven assuming arguendo[47] that local administrative control may be a compelling state interest, the present financial system cannot be considered necessary to further this interest. No matter how the state decides to finance its system of public education, it can still leave this decision-making power in the hands of local districts.

... We need not decide whether such decentralized financial decision-making is a compelling state interest, since under the present financing system, such fiscal free-will is a cruel illusion for the poor school districts. We cannot agree that Baldwin Park residents care less about education than those in Beverly Hills solely because Baldwin Park spends less than $600 per child while Beverly Hills spends over $1,200. As defendants themselves recognize, perhaps the most accurate reflection of a community's commitment to education is the rate at which its citizens are willing to tax themselves to support their schools. Yet by that standard, Baldwin Park should be deemed far more devoted to learning than Beverly Hills.... In summary, ... only a district with a large tax base will be truly able to decide how much it really cares about education....

We find that such financing system as presently constituted is not necessary to the attainment of any compelling state interest. Since it does not withstand the requisite "strict scrutiny," it denies to the plaintiffs and others similarly situated the equal protection of the laws. The judgment is reversed and the cause remanded to the trial court....[48]

However, the first case to find its way to the U.S. Supreme Court, *San Antonio Independent School District v. Rodriguez*, met a very different fate, as explained in Chapter 4. That was true, even though the facts of the disproportionate funding scheme presented one of the worst school funding cases to be litigated, and despite the fact that there had been a clear finding by the U.S. Commission on Civil Rights that the funding scheme was one of the key factors resulting in dramatically unequal education for Latino children in Texas.[49]

Years later, the Texas funding policy was struck down on state constitutional law grounds by the state's supreme court.[50] Indeed, a number of other state funding systems had to await rulings by state courts under state law, most of which ultimately found the educational financing system to be a violation of equal protection of the law, although the state constitutions used a variety of different language to define the constitutional principle.[51]

The sense that the society was targeting Latino children was not limited to the segregation and funding cases. These concerns have not been eased by the fact that steps taken against children have come in states with a long history of discrimination against Latinos, such as Texas and California. In particular, these states took action against undocumented children, most of whom were up to that point Latinos, and to many Latinos the sense was and is that the actions were taken because they were mostly Latino. Indeed, there has been little secret made in states such as these and others, including more recently Alabama and Georgia, that Latinos were the targets.

Texas moved to compel school districts to identify and exclude undocumented children, even where the district saw no need or advantage in doing so. This action produced an unusual alliance between the conservative Justice Lewis Powell and Justice William Brennan, generally perceived as liberal, who together found the state's action not only unjustified, but irrational.

Plyler v. Doe

457 U.S. 202 (1982)

INTRODUCTION: The facts are set forth in the opinion as edited. Justice Brennan wrote the opinion for the Court.

The question presented by these cases is whether, consistent with the Equal Protection Clause of the Fourteenth Amendment, Texas may deny to undocumented school-age children the free public education that it provides to children who are citizens of the United States or legally admitted aliens.

I. ... In May 1975, the Texas Legislature revised its education laws to withhold from local school districts any state funds for the education of children who were not "legally admitted" into the United States. The 1975 revision also authorized local school districts to deny enrollment in their public schools to [such children].

[This] is a class action, filed ... on behalf of certain school-age children of Mexican origin residing in Smith County, Tex., who could not establish that they had been legally admitted into the United States. The action complained of the exclusion of plaintiff children from the public schools of the Tyler Independent School District....

[T]he District Court ... recognized that the increases in population resulting from the immigration of Mexican nationals into the United States had created problems for the public schools of the State, and that these problems were exacerbated by the special educational needs of immigrant Mexican children. The court noted, however, that the increase in school enrollment was primarily attributable to the admission of children who were legal residents.... It also found that while the "exclusion of all undocumented children from the public schools in Texas would eventually result in economies at some level," ... funding from both the State and Federal Governments was based primarily on the number of children enrolled. In net effect then, barring undocumented children from the schools would save money, but it would "not necessarily" improve "the quality of education." ... Finally, the court noted that under current laws and practices "the illegal alien of today may well be the legal alien of tomorrow," and that without an education, these undocumented children, "[already] disadvantaged as a result of poverty, lack of English-speaking ability, and undeniable racial prejudices, ... will become permanently locked into the lowest socio-economic class." ...

II. The Fourteenth Amendment provides that "[no] State shall ... deprive any person of life, liberty, or property, without due process of law; nor deny to any person within its jurisdiction the equal protection of the laws." Appellants argue at the outset that undocumented aliens, because of their immigration status, are not "persons within the jurisdiction" of the State of Texas, and that they therefore have no right to the equal protection of Texas law. We reject this argument. Whatever his status under the immigration laws, an alien is surely a "person" in any ordinary sense of that term. Aliens, even aliens whose presence in this country is unlawful, have long been recognized as "persons" guaranteed due process of law by the Fifth and Fourteenth Amendments ... *Yick Wo v. Hopkins....* [U]ntil he leaves the jurisdiction—either voluntarily, or involuntarily in accordance with the Constitution and laws of the United States—he is entitled to the equal protection of the laws....

The more difficult question is whether the Equal Protection Clause has been violated by the refusal of the State of Texas to reimburse local school boards for the education of children who cannot demonstrate that their presence within the United States is lawful, or by the imposition by those school boards of the burden of tuition on those children....

III. The Equal Protection Clause directs that "all persons similarly circumstanced shall be treated alike."... In applying the Equal Protection Clause to most forms of state action, we ... seek only the assurance that the classification at issue bears some fair relationship to a legitimate public purpose.

But we would not be faithful to our obligations under the Fourteenth Amendment if we applied so deferential a standard to every classification. The Equal Protection Clause was intended as a restriction on state legislative action inconsistent with elemental constitutional premises. Thus we have treated as presumptively invidious those classifications that disadvantage a "suspect class," or that impinge upon the exercise of a "fundamental right." With respect to such classifications, ... the State [must] demonstrate that its classification has been precisely tailored to serve a compelling governmental interest....

A. Sheer incapability or lax enforcement of the laws barring entry into this country, coupled with the failure to establish an effective bar to the employment of undocumented aliens, has resulted in the creation of a substantial "shadow population" of illegal migrants—numbering in the millions—within our borders.[52] This situation raises the specter of a permanent caste of undocumented resident aliens, encouraged by some to remain here as a source of cheap labor, but nevertheless denied the benefits that our society makes available to citizens and lawful residents. The existence of such an underclass presents most difficult problems for a Nation that prides itself on adherence to principles of equality under law.

The children who are plaintiffs in these cases are special members of this underclass. Persuasive arguments support the view that a State may withhold its beneficence from those whose very presence within the United States is the product of their own unlawful conduct. These arguments do not apply with the same force to classifications imposing disabilities on the minor children of such illegal entrants.... Even if the State found it expedient to control the conduct of adults by acting against their children, legislation directing the onus of a parent's misconduct against his children does not comport with fundamental conceptions of justice.... [Section] 21.031 is directed against children, and imposes its discriminatory burden on the basis of a legal characteristic over which children can have little control. It is thus difficult to conceive of a rational justification for penalizing these children for their presence within the United States....

Public education is not a "right" granted to individuals by the Constitution. *San Antonio Independent School Dist. v. Rodriguez....*[53] But neither is it merely some governmental "benefit" indistinguishable from other forms of social welfare legislation. Both the importance of education in maintaining our basic institutions, and the lasting impact of its deprivation on the life of the child, mark the distinction.

The "American people have always regarded education and [the] acquisition of knowledge as matters of supreme importance." *Meyer v. Nebraska*, 262 U.S. 390, 400 (1923). We have recognized "the public schools as a most vital civic institution for the preservation of a democratic system of government," ... and as the primary vehicle for transmitting "the values on which our society rests." ... "[As] ... pointed out early in our history, ... some degree of education is necessary to prepare citizens to participate effectively and intelligently in our open political system if we are to preserve freedom and independence." ... In sum, education has a fundamental role in maintaining the fabric of our society. We cannot ignore the significant social costs borne by our Nation when select groups are denied the means to absorb the values and skills upon which our social order rests.

... The inability to read and write will handicap the individual deprived of a basic education each and every day of his life. The inestimable toll of that deprivation on the social, economic, intellectual, and psychological well-being of the individual, and the obstacle it poses to individual achievement, make it most difficult to reconcile the cost or the principle of a status-based denial of basic education with the framework of equality embodied in the Equal Protection Clause.

B. ... Undocumented aliens cannot be treated as a suspect class because their presence in this country in violation of federal law is not a "constitutional irrelevancy." Nor is education a fundamental right; a State need not justify by compelling necessity every variation in the manner in which education is provided to its population. But more is involved in these cases than the abstract question whether §21.031 discriminates against a suspect class, or whether education is a fundamental right. Section 21.031 imposes a lifetime hardship on a discrete class of children not accountable for their disabling status. The stigma of illiteracy will mark them for the rest of their lives. By denying these children a basic education, we deny them the ability to live within the structure of our civic institutions, and foreclose any realistic possibility that they will contribute in even the smallest way to the progress of our Nation. In determining the rationality of §21.031, we may appropriately take into account its costs to the Nation and to the innocent children who are its victims. In light of these countervailing costs, the discrimination contained in §21.031 can hardly be considered rational unless it furthers some substantial goal of the State.

IV. It is the State's principal argument, and apparently the view of the dissenting Justices, that the undocumented status of these children [alone] establishes a sufficient rational basis for denying them benefits that a State might choose to afford other residents.... To be sure, like all persons who have entered the United States unlawfully, these children are subject to deportation.... But there is no assurance that a child subject to deportation will ever be deported. An illegal entrant might be granted federal permission to continue to reside in this country, or even to become a citizen.... In light of the discretionary federal power to grant relief from deportation, a State cannot realistically determine that any particular undocumented child will in fact be deported until after deportation proceedings have been completed.... We are reluctant to impute to Congress the intention to withhold from these children, for so long as they are present in this country through no fault of their own, access to a basic education.

V. ... [W]e discern three colorable state interests that might support §21.031.

First, appellants appear to suggest that the State may seek to protect itself from an influx of illegal immigrants.... There is no evidence in the record suggesting that illegal entrants impose any significant burden on the State's economy. To the contrary, the available evidence suggests that illegal aliens underutilize public services, while contributing their labor to the local economy and tax money to the state fisc.... The dominant incentive for illegal entry into the State of Texas is the availability of employment; few if any illegal immigrants come to this country, or presumably to the State of Texas, in order to avail themselves of a free education. Thus, ... we think it clear that "[charging] tuition to undocumented children constitutes a ludicrously ineffectual attempt to stem the tide of illegal immigration." ...

Second, ... appellants suggest that undocumented children are appropriately singled out for exclusion because of the special burdens they impose on the State's ability to provide high-quality public education. But..., after reviewing the State's school financing mechanism, the District Court ... concluded that barring undocumented children from local schools would not necessarily improve the quality of education provided in those schools.... Of course, even if improvement in the quality of education were a likely result of barring some number of children from the schools of the State, the State must support its selection of this group as the appropriate target for exclusion. In terms of educational cost and need, however, undocumented children are "basically indistinguishable" from legally resident alien children....

Finally, appellants suggest that undocumented children are appropriately singled out because their unlawful presence within the United States renders them less likely than other children to remain within the boundaries of the State, and to put their education to productive social or political use within the State.... The State has no assurance that any child, citizen or not, will employ the education provided by the State within the confines of the State's borders. In any event, the record is clear that many of the undocumented children disabled by this classification will remain in this country indefinitely, and that some will become lawful residents or citizens of the United States. It is difficult to understand precisely what the State hopes to achieve by promoting the creation and perpetuation of a subclass of illiterates within our boundaries, surely adding to the problems and costs of unemployment, welfare, and crime. It is thus clear that whatever savings might be achieved by denying these children an education, they are wholly insubstantial in light of the costs involved to these children, the State, and the Nation.

VI. If the State is to deny a discrete group of innocent children the free public education that it offers to other children residing within its borders, that denial must be justified by a showing that it furthers some substantial state interest. No such showing was made here.... Affirmed.[54]

Justice Powell wrote a separate concurring opinion.

I join the opinion of the Court, and write separately to emphasize the unique character of the cases before us.

The classification in question severely disadvantages children who are the victims of a combination of circumstances. Access from Mexico into this country, across our 2,000-mile border, is readily available and virtually uncontrollable. Illegal aliens are attracted by our employment opportunities, and perhaps by other benefits as well. This is a problem of serious national proportions.... Perhaps because of the intractability of the problem, Congress ... has not provided effective leadership in dealing with this problem. It therefore is certain that illegal aliens will continue to enter the United States and, as the record makes clear, an unknown percentage of them will remain here. I agree with the Court that their children should not be left on the streets uneducated.

Although the analogy is not perfect, our holding today does find support in decisions of this Court with respect to the status of illegitimates. In *Weber v. Aetna Casualty & Surety Co.*, 406 U.S. 164, 175 (1972), we said: "[Visiting] ... condemnation on the head of an infant" for the misdeeds of the parents is illogical, unjust, and "contrary to the basic concept of our system that legal burdens should bear some relationship to individual responsibility or wrongdoing." ... The appellee children are innocent in this respect. They can "affect neither their parents' conduct nor their own status." *Trimble v. Gordon*, 430 U.S. 762, 770 (1977).

Our review in a case such as these [*sic*] is properly heightened.... The classification at issue deprives a group of children of the opportunity for education afforded all other children simply because they have been assigned a legal status due to a violation of law by their parents. These children thus have been singled out for a lifelong penalty and stigma. A legislative classification that threatens the creation of an underclass of future citizens and residents cannot be reconciled with one of the fundamental purposes of the Fourteenth Amendment. In these unique circumstances, the Court properly may require that the State's interests be substantial and that the means bear a "fair and substantial relation" to these interests.

In my view, the State's denial of education to these children bears no substantial relation to any substantial state interest.... The discussion by the Court ... of the State's purported interests demonstrates that they are poorly served by the educational exclusion.... The Court of Appeals and the District Courts that addressed these cases concluded that the classification could not satisfy even the bare requirements of rationality.... [I]t hardly can be argued rationally that anyone benefits from the creation within our borders of a subclass of illiterate persons many of whom will remain in the State, adding to the problems and costs of both State and National Governments attendant upon unemployment, welfare, and crime.

Chief Justice Burger wrote a dissent joined by Justices White, Rehnquist, and O'Connor.

I. ... I have no quarrel with the conclusion that the Equal Protection Clause of the Fourteenth Amendment applies to aliens.... However, as the Court concedes, this "only begins the inquiry." ... The Equal Protection Clause does not mandate identical treatment of different categories of persons....

The dispositive issue in these cases, simply put, is whether, for purposes of allocating its finite resources, a state has a legitimate reason to differentiate between persons who are lawfully within the state and those who are unlawfully there. The distinction the State of Texas has drawn—based not only upon its own legitimate interests but on classifications established by the Federal Government in its immigration laws and policies—is not unconstitutional.

A. ... The Court first suggests that these illegal alien children, although not a suspect class, are entitled to special solicitude under the Equal Protection Clause because they lack "control" over or "responsibility" for their unlawful entry into this country.... However, the Equal Protection Clause does not preclude legislators from classifying among persons on the basis of factors and characteristics over which individuals may be said to lack "control." ... [A] state legislature is not barred from considering, for example, relevant differences between the mentally healthy and the mentally ill, or between the residents of different counties, simply because these may be factors unrelated to individual choice or to any "wrongdoing." The Equal Protection Clause protects against arbitrary and irrational classifications, and against invidious discrimination stemming from prejudice and hostility; it is not an all-encompassing "equalizer" designed to eradicate every distinction for which persons are not "responsible." ...

The Court's analogy to cases involving discrimination against illegitimate children ... is grossly misleading.... [A]ppellees' status is predicated upon the circumstances of their concededly illegal presence in this country.... This Court has recognized that in allocating governmental benefits to a given class of aliens, one "may take into account the character of the relationship between the alien and this country." ... When that "relationship" is a federally prohibited one, there can, of course, be no presumption that a state has a constitutional duty to include illegal aliens among the recipients of its governmental benefits.

... The importance of education is beyond dispute. Yet we have held repeatedly that the importance of a governmental service does not elevate it to the status of a "fundamental right" for purposes of equal protection analysis.... The central question in these cases, as in every equal protection case not involving truly fundamental rights ... is whether there is some legitimate basis for a legislative distinction between different classes of persons. The fact that the distinction is drawn in legislation affecting access to public education ... cannot make a difference in the level of scrutiny applied....

[I]t simply is not "irrational" for a state to conclude that it does not have the same responsibility to provide benefits for persons whose very presence in the state and this country is illegal as it does to provide for persons lawfully present. By definition, illegal aliens have no right whatever to be here, and the state may reasonably, and constitutionally, elect not to provide them with governmental services at the expense of those who are lawfully in the state.

Sadly, even after *Plyler*'s clear ruling on the subject, California Governor Pete Wilson, and other politicians seeking to use the presence of undocumented children as a wedge issue for political advantage, pressed for passage of Proposition 187. The measure was designed not only to do what the Supreme Court had plainly forbidden, but also sought to coerce teachers and school officials into the role of informants and investigators of the children they were to educate and their parents. The measure was offered with the pretense that it was to " 'provide for cooperation between [the] agencies of state and local government with the federal government, and to establish a system of required notification by and between such agencies to prevent illegal aliens in the United States from receiving benefits or public services in the State of California.' Prop. 187, §1."[55]

However, in the run-up to the vote in November 1994 on the proposition, the state Legislative Analyst warned in the voter pamphlet that the action was clearly unconstitutional.

The exclusion of suspected illegal immigrant children from public schools would be in direct conflict with the United States Supreme Court's ruling in Plyler versus Doe that guarantees access to public education for all children in the United States. Consequently, this provision of the initiative would not be effective.[56]

If the federal courts ruled that it was a violation of law, the state could lose some $2.3 billion in federal aid. Further, the Legislative Analyst estimated that up to 300,000 students in grades K-12 could be removed from school.[57] Even so, the measure was approved by the voters.

Even the Supreme Court's findings from *Plyler* that, whether one employs a heightened standard of scrutiny or simply a rational relationship test, policies such as removal from education targeted at children are not rational and cannot stand were not enough to stop passage of the California measure. It spoke volumes that Justice Powell, of all people, had become the key vote in the *Plyler* case and that Justice Brennan had been able to work with him despite their many differences, including their sharp disagreement in the *San Antonio* case.[58]

For these and other reasons, it came as no great surprise when the challenges to Proposition 187 prevailed in federal court in *United Latin American Citizens (LULAC) v. Wilson* and the court issued an injunction against its enforcement.[59] The primary attack on several sections of the proposition was that the kind of state-level immigration policymaking and enforcement action undertaken by California was preempted by federal law. Section 7 was struck down as a denial of education under the *Plyler* precedent. The case continued and the same judge later ruled:

> After the Court's November 20, 1995 Opinion, Congress enacted the PRA [Personal Responsibility and Work Opportunity Reconciliation Act of 1996], a comprehensive statutory scheme regulating alien eligibility for public benefits.... [T]he PRA ousts state power to legislate in the area of public benefits for aliens. When President Clinton signed the PRA, he effectively ended any further debate about what the states could do in this field. As the Court pointed out in its prior Opinion, California is powerless to enact its own legislative scheme to regulate immigration. It is likewise powerless to enact its own legislative scheme to regulate alien access to public benefits.... Federal power in these areas was always exclusive and the PRA only serves to reinforce the Court's prior conclusion that substantially all of the provisions of Proposition 187 are preempted.[60]

However, as Chapter 9 explains, the targeting of Latino school children has not gone away.

Conclusion

Despite the fact that Latinos are a large and growing minority of the U.S. population and were here long before what is now the United States took over what had been Latino or Ibero-American areas, the civil rights of these Americans are often left out of discussions of contemporary civil rights issues. The fact is that Latinos were also subject to slavery in the form of peonage, endured segregation in schools and public facilities, and even confronted an argument offered by a state in the U.S. Supreme Court, made in the same year that *Brown v. Board of Education* was decided, that the Fourteenth Amendment did not even apply to Latino Americans.

Over time the courts have struck down peonage, overturned the segregation policies, and made it clear that the equal protection of the law under the Fourteenth Amendment applies to all persons in the United States. This chapter has explained this heritage and the efforts to address the history of discrimination against Latinos.

However, this story is far from over, as the discussion of the state actions aimed at school children at the end of the chapter suggests. Like African Americans and Native Americans, there are several sets of issues that still confront Latino Americans and the courts' responses to these problems are still a work in progress. It is to these issues that Chapter 9 turns.

I. Issues for Policy and Practice

A. The behavior of some political figures in the contemporary context has exacerbated existing stereotypes and even compounded some of the discriminatory attitudes directed toward Latinos. That is in addition to lack of knowledge that many Americans have about Hispanics, Latin cultures, and the history of the treatment of Latinos in this country. What opportunities are there for an educational process that can facilitate communication and cooperation within public service and in the wider community?

B. The evidence of discriminatory behavior in law enforcement directed at Latinos, like African Americans, is clear and widespread. Can an analysis of the range of cases brought and often settled by the Civil Rights Division of the Department of Justice provide a resource base for policy development aimed at curbing that kind of behavior?

C. The issues of equal educational opportunity have not really been adequately addressed, as the discussion in this chapter demonstrates. The debates regarding the No Child Left Behind Act of 2001 did not help. Neither did the economic downturn that stressed resources for education and other programs and services. It is time to take a nationwide view of the current connections between school funding and equal educational opportunity.

II. Discussion Questions

A. Why do you suppose that San Bernadino prohibited Latinos from using the swimming pool? What was it about swimming pools that was so sensitive that it became a target for segregation?

B. In considering the *Mendez* case, in reading the explanation of what was happening, it is instructive to consider the ways in which these facts are similar to but also different from the descriptions in earlier chapters of discrimination against African American children in the South and in other parts of the country as well. What was similar and what appeared to be different?

C. Many of those who learn about the Orange County school segregation are surprised or even shocked to find that this would happen in California of all places. After all, it was not a state that had legally imposed segregation at the state level and, in any case, it is a state that has long boasted of the positive attributes and history of Latino culture in the state. That raises the important question about whether and how states that were not part of the old South and never had legally imposed regimes of segregation have come to grips with a history of discrimination in their state. Even states often regarded as among the most progressive in general terms, including California, have had that history, but its residents have had difficulty confronting not only a past that involved discrimination but also a range of discriminatory behavior even today. How can communities like this begin to engage this subject and get the reality out where it can be seen and discussed?

D. As the cases presented in this chapter show, even without formal segregation, many Latinos have found discrimination in the schools and in the way that schools are assigned and resources provided. What are the connections between school funding, racial or ethnocultural discrimination, and discrimination in jobs and housing? How can that connection be addressed?

Notes

1 People of the State of New York Against Jeffrey Conroy, Jordan R. Dasch, Anthony M. Hartford, Nicholas A. Hausch, Christopher J. Overton, Jose M. Pacheco, and Kelvin P. Shea, Case No. 3032-A-B-C-D-E-F-G-08, http://graphics8.nytimes.com/packages/pdf/nyregion/20081125_CONROY_INDICTMENT.pdf, January 15, 2016, p. 3.

2 Robert D. McFadden, "Attack on Ecuadorean Brothers Investigated as Hate Crime," *New York Times*, December 9, 2008, p. A29. National Council of La Raza (NCLR), "Another Perceived Hate

Crime Murder Prompts Latino Leaders to Call for Passage of Hate Crimes Bill," Press Release, December 15, 2008.

3 See Southern Poverty Law Center, *Climate of Fear: Latino Immigrants in Suffolk County, N.Y.* (Montgomery, AL: Southern Poverty Law Center, 2009).

4 2008 Republican debate at Reagan Library in Simi Valley, California, on January 30, 2008, www.ontheissues.org/Archive/2008_GOP_Super_Tuesday_John_McCain.htm, September 5, 2015; "Countdown 2008: Front-runners Dominate GOP Debate, *Atlanta Journal-Constitution*, January 31, 2008, p. 6A.

5 *Lozono v. City of Hazleton*, 496 F. Supp. 2d 477 (MDPA 2007).

6 Information on these and other local ordinances is provided at American Civil Liberties Union, "Local Anti-Immigrant Ordinance Cases, www.aclu.org/local-anti-immigrant-ordinance-cases, April 19, 2016.

7 Southern Poverty Law Center, *Climate of Fear*, p. 5.

8 U.S. Department of Justice, Civil Rights Division, "Investigation of East Haven Police Department," December 19, 2011, www.justice.gov/crt/about/spl/documents/easthaven_findletter_12-19-11.pdf, November 20, 2014.

9 Quote in John Christoffersen Associated Press, "Conn. mayor blasted for 'taco' quip about Latinos," *ContraCosta News*, January 25, 2012, www.contracostatimes.com/ci_19821663, November 20, 2014.

10 U.S. District Court for Connecticut, Grand Jury Indictment, *United States v. Miller*, et al., www.justice.gov/archive/usao/ct/Press2012/MILLER et al indictment.pdf, April 21, 2016.

11 "Last of 4 Connecticut Officers Sentenced in Police Bias Case," *New York Times*, February 13, 2014, p. A33.

12 *United States v. Town of East Haven*, "Settlement Agreement and (Proposed) Order," 11/20/2012, www.justice.gov/crt/about/spl/documents/ehpdsettle_11-20-12.pdf, November 20, 2014.

13 *Chacón v. East Haven Police Department*, 3:10-cv-01692-AWT (D. Conn.), "Consent Motion to Approve Stipulation 07/17/2014," www.clearinghouse.net/chDocs/public/PN-CT-0002-0004.pdf, November 20, 2014.

14 Christian Nolan, "East Haven Settlement Includes Restrictions on Police," *Connecticut Law Tribune*, June 13, 2014, www.ctlawtribune.com/id=1202659313155/East-Haven-Settlement-Includes-Restrictions-On-Police#ixzz3Jd7NroVq, November 20, 2014.

15 *Melendres v. Arpaio*, No. PHX-CV-07-02513-GMS, "Findings of Fact and Conclusions of Law," 5/24/13, www.aclu.org/files/assets/arpaio_decision.pdf, November 20, 2014. This was followed by a "Supplemental Permanent Injunction/Judgment Order," www.aclu.org/sites/default/files/assets/2013.10.02.606_supplemental_permanent_injunction_judgment_order.pdf, November 20, 2014.

16 *United States v. Maricopa County*, Complaint, filed May 10, 2012, www.justice.gov/crt/about/spl/documents/mcso_complaint_5-10-12.pdf, November 20, 2014.

17 See e.g., Eduardo Luna, "How the Black/White Paradigm Renders Mexicans/Mexican Americans and Discrimination against them Invisible," *Berkeley La Raza Law Journal* 14 (No. 2 2003): 225–253; Juan F. Perea, "The Black/White Binary Paradigm of Race: The 'Normal Science' of American Racial Thought," *California Law Review* 85 (No. 5 1997): 1213–1258; Rachel F. Moran, "Neither Black Nor White," *Harvard Latino Law Review* 2 (Fall 1997): 61–99.

18 U.S. Census, 2013, "Percent Distribution of the Projected Population by Race and Hispanic Origin for the United States: 2015 to 2060," www.census.gov/population/projections/files/summary/NP2012-T6.xls, March 18, 2014.

19 NOTE: The property rights and governance provisions of the treaty continue to give rise to legal controversies to the present day. See e.g., *SWEPI v. Mora County*, 2014 U.S. Dist. LEXIS 170638 (DNM 2014). Part of the controversy is that, in addition to land grants and claims by individuals, there were community land grants, as the Government Accountability Office explained, where some grants refer to lands set aside for general communal use (*ejidos*) or for specific purposes, including hunting (*caza*), pasture (*pastos*), wood gathering (*leña*), or watering (*abrevederos*). Scholars, the land grant literature, and popular terminology commonly use the phrase "community land grants" to denote land grants that set aside common lands for the use of the entire community. U.S. Government Accountability Office, *Treaty of Guadalupe Hidalgo: Definition and List of Community Land Grants in New Mexico* (Washington, D.C.: GAO, 2001), p. 3. Many persons, including grantee heirs, scholars, and legal experts, still claim that the United States did not

protect the property of Mexican Americans and their descendants, particularly the common lands of community land grants. They charge that the common lands were lost in many ways and that this loss threatened the economic stability of small Mexican American farms and the farmers' rural lifestyle. Id. at 1–2. See also U.S. Government Accountability Office, *Treaty of Guadalupe Hidalgo: Findings and Possible Options Regarding Longstanding Community Land Grant Claims in New Mexico* (Washington, D.C.: GAO, 2004).

20 David McCullough, *Truman* (New York: Simon & Schuster, 1992), p. 542.

21 See James S. Sandos, "Junípero Serra's Canonization and the Historical Record," *American Historical Review* 93 (No. 5 1988): 1253–1269.

22 Robert Archibald, "Indian Labor at the California Missions Slavery or Salvation?" *Journal of San Diego History* 24 (No. 2 1978): 172–183.

23 Id.

24 NOTE: A term meaning one-sided and without representation of or argument by the other, and in this case weaker, party.

25 NOTE: This is a term for a local official with administrative and judicial authority.

26 *Slaughter-House Cases*, 83 U.S. 36, 72 (1873).

27 Id., at 90, Field, J., dissenting.

28 See *Bailey v. Alabama*, below.

29 Act of March 2, 1867, c. 187, 14 Stat. 546.

30 The 1914 case was *United States v. Reynolds*, 235 U.S. 133 (1914).

31 NOTE: Language required to allow a class action suit deleted.

32 Frederick P. Aguirre, "Mendez v. Westminster School District: How it Affected Brown v. Board of Education," *Orange County Lawyer* 47 (Feb. 2005): 30–31.

33 Id., at 32, quoting "Lesson Learned on School Discrimination," *Los Angeles Times*, Orange County Edition, September 9, 1996, p. 1.

34 Id., at 30. He was quoting Gary A. Greenfield and Don B. Kates, Jr., "Mexican Americans, Racial Discrimination and the Civil Rights Act of 1866," *California Law Review* 63 (No. 1 1975): 682–731.

35 See Id.; Christopher Arriola, "Knocking on the Schoolhouse Door: Mendez v. Westminster, Equal Protection, Public Education, and Mexican Americans in the 1940s," 8 *Berkeley La Raza Law Journal* 8 (No. 2 1995): 166–207.

36 "Sec. 8003.... The governing board of any school district may establish separate schools for Indian children, excepting children of Indians who are wards of the United States Government and children of all other Indians who are descendants of the original American Indians of the United States, and for children of Chinese, Japanese, or Mongolian parentage."

37 The study of American institutions and ideals in all schools located within the State of California is required by Section 10051, Education Code.

38 See *Plessy v. Ferguson*, 163 U.S. 537.

39 *Westminster School District v. Mendez*, 161 F.2d 774 (9th Cir. 1947).

40 Thomas A. Saenz, "Mendez and the Legacy of Brown: A Latino Civil Rights Lawyer's Assessment," *Berkeley La Raza Law Journal* 15 (No. 12004): 67–73. At the time of that writing, Mr. Saenz was Vice President of Litigation, Mexican American Legal Defense and Educational Fund.

41 Id., at 68.

42 Id., at 69.

43 64 F. Supp., at 545.

44 Id., at 546.

45 *Westminster School District v. Mendez*, 161 F.2d 774, 780 (9th Cir. 1947).

46 *Hernandez v. State*, 251 S.W.2d 531, 535 (TX 1952).

47 NOTE: This means "for the sake of argument."

48 Justice McComb dissented, stating only that he would affirm the judgment for the reasons expressed by Mr. Justice Dunn at the Court of Appeals level in the case.

49 U.S. Commission on Civil Rights, *Mexican American Education in Texas: A Function of Wealth* (Washington, D.C.: U.S. Civil Rights Commission, 1972).

50 *Carrollton-Farmers Branch Ind. v. Edgewood Ind. School Dist.*, 826 S.W.2d 489 (Tex. 1992); *Edgewood Ind. School Dist. v. Kirby*, 777 S.W.2d 391 (Tex. 1989) (*Edgewood I*); *Edgewood Ind. School Dist. v. Kirby*, 804 S.W.2d 491 (Tex. 1991) (*Edgewood II*).

51 See e.g., *Robinson v. Cahill*, 287 A.2d 187, 217 (Sup. Ct. NJ 1972); affm'd in part, modified in part *Robinson v. Cahill*, 303 A.2d 273, 295 (NJ 1973).

52 The Attorney General recently estimated the number of illegal aliens within the United States at between 3 and 6 million.... [He] noted that this subclass is largely composed of persons with a permanent attachment to the Nation, and that they are unlikely to be displaced from our territory.

53 NOTE: Justice Brennan had dissented in the *San Antonio* case, but it was the controlling precedent and, central to this case, he wanted very much to have the support of Justice Powell, the author of the *San Antonio* ruling, in the *Plyler* opinion. Here he was fighting a rearguard action to avoid treating education as deserving of the least protection available under the rational basis test.

54 NOTE: The concurring opinions of Justices Marshall and Blackmun are omitted.

55 Quoted in *League of United Latin American Citizens (LULAC) v. Wilson*, 908 F. Supp. 755, 763 (CDCA 1995).

56 State of California, "California Ballot Pamphlet General Election: November 9, 1994," p. 51.

57 Id., at 52.

58 This collaboration is explained in detail in Phillip J. Cooper, "Plyler at the Core: Understanding the Proposition 187 Challenge," *Chicano-Latino Law Review* 17 (Fall 1995): 64–87.

59 908 F. Supp. 755, 763 (CDCA 1995).

60 997 F. Supp. 1244, 1261 (CDCA 1997).

References

Archibald, Robert. "Indian Labor at the California Missions Slavery or Salvation?" *Journal of San Diego History* 24 (No. 2 1978): 172–183, www.sandiegohistory.org/journal/78spring/labor.htm, November 10, 2015.

Aguirre, Frederick P. "Mendez v. Westminster School District: How it Affected Brown v. Board of Education," *Orange County Lawyer* 47 (Feb. 2005): 30–31.

Arriola, Christopher. "Knocking on the Schoolhouse Door: Mendez v. Westminster, Equal Protection, Public Education, and Mexican Americans in the 1940s," *Berkeley La Raza Law Journal* 8 (No. 2 1995): 166–207.

Cooper, Phillip J. "Plyler at the Core: Understanding the Proposition 187 Challenge," *Chicano-Latino Law Review* 17 (Fall 1995): 64–87.

Greenfield, Gary A. and Don B. Kates, Jr. "Mexican Americans, Racial Discrimination and the Civil Rights Act of 1866," *California Law Review* 63 (No. 1 1975): 682–731.

Luna, Eduardo. "How the Black/White Paradigm Renders Mexicans/Mexican Americans and Discrimination against them Invisible," *Berkeley La Raza Law Journal* 14 (No. 2 2003): 225–253.

McCullough, David. *Truman*. New York: Simon & Schuster, 1992.

Moran, Rachel F. "Neither Black Nor White," *Harvard Latino Law Review* 2 (Fall 1997): 61–99.

Perea, Juan F. "The Black/White Binary Paradigm of Race: The 'Normal Science' of American Racial Thought," *California Law Review* 85 (No. 5 1997): 1213–1258.

Saenz, Thomas A. "Mendez and the Legacy of Brown: A Latino Civil Rights Lawyer's Assessment," *Berkeley La Raza Law Journal* 15 (No. 1 2004): 67–73.

Sandos, James S. "Junípero Serra's Canonization and the Historical Record," *American Historical Review* 93 (No. 5 1988): 1253–1269.

Southern Poverty Law Center. *Climate of Fear: Latino Immigrants in Suffolk County, N. Y.* Montgomery, AL: Southern Poverty Law Center, 2009.

U.S. Commission on Civil Rights. *Mexican American Education in Texas: A Function of Wealth.* Washington, D.C.: U.S. Civil Rights Commission, 1972.

U.S. Department of Justice, Civil Rights Division. "Investigation of East Haven Police Department," December 19, 2011, www.justice.gov/crt/about/spl/documents/easthaven_findletter_12-19-11.pdf, November 20, 2014.

U.S. Government Accountability Office. *Treaty of Guadalupe Hidalgo: Definition and List of Community Land Grants in New Mexico.* Washington, D.C.: GAO, 2001.

———. *Treaty of Guadalupe Hidalgo: Findings and Possible Options Regarding Longstanding Community Land Grant Claims in New Mexico.* Washington, D.C.: GAO, 2004.

9 Critical Contemporary Issues in Latino Civil Rights

Like other groups, Latinos have seen a number of issues differently from the kinds of issues that are often understood to be civil rights questions by others. As Chapter 8 explained, many Latino Americans trace their roots far into the past, well before Anglos came west in what became the United States. Even so, it is also the case that many Latinos are first- or second-generation families from a Latin American country. Some of the civil rights issues that have been and are still so important to Latinos are related to that reality. However, others that some may see only as issues about immigrants are seen by Latinos as discrimination against their culture, their heritage, and their language. It is more than just a repetition of the cycle of discrimination against immigrants that this nation of immigrants has displayed too often in the past. These issues relate to issues of language, U.S. policy related to Latin American peoples, and discrimination against legal immigrants.

Language Discrimination: It Did not Start with Spanish, but Today's Version Has Been Based on Animus

As a nation of immigrants, virtually all of those who came to what was to become the United States spoke a foreign language—unless, of course, they happened to speak the Native American languages of the tribes into whose territory they moved. Those foreign tongues included English. Over time, it became clear that policies and punitive behavior directed at those who used a language other than English were being used as a proxy for the race or ethnocultural heritage of groups of people targeted for discrimination. That problem has persisted to the present day and has prompted a range of judicial opinions with respect to the subject.

In the years following World War I, the United States slipped into an era of isolationism and xenophobia. The country had lost its innocence and learned that the Atlantic and Pacific oceans would not provide the protection against the world's problems that many Americans had happily assumed. As if the war were not enough, there followed the Bolshevik revolution in Russia that was seen as evil incarnate by a nation in the throes of the era of the gospel of wealth with an ethos of laissez faire economics. The fear and anger that emerged in the land led to what became known as the Red Scare and to the imposition of harsh immigration quotas, a considerable irony for a nation of immigrants. It also led to efforts to stamp out foreign languages and cultures, particularly those considered hostile to American interests and values.

It should have come as no surprise that the German language and culture was one of the primary targets during this period in the aftermath of World War I. A number of jurisdictions took action particularly aimed at the teaching of German in public schools, although some of the states that took such actions tried to word their policies so that they could claim that they were not in fact targeting a particular language or culture. It was these actions that brought about the first round of cases that addressed the freedom to use and teach languages other than English.

The Supreme Court soon faced two of those cases, and a third that was related by virtue of the question of the relationship between private schools and public authority.

Meyer v. Nebraska

262 U.S. 390 (1923)

INTRODUCTION: A teacher was convicted for teaching German to eighth grade students at Zion Parochial School, a Lutheran school in Hamilton County, Nebraska. It is important to recall that the United States had seen a continuing wave of immigration, particularly from European countries from the late nineteenth century until the war years. Many of the immigrant groups, like their predecessors, spread out across the nation and often settled in communities with others of similar ethnocultural backgrounds. That was true not only in the nation's growing cities in an era of growth of manufacturing and commerce, but also in rural communities. It is also well to recall that Germany was the mother country of the Lutheran faith. For these reasons and simply because of interest, there is little surprise that students in the school were enrolled in German classes. In this case, the instructor was convicted of teaching a foreign language in violation of a state statute. His conviction was upheld by the Nebraska Supreme Court.

Justice McReynolds wrote the opinion for the Court.[1]

> The problem for our determination is whether the statute as construed and applied unreasonably infringes the liberty guaranteed ... by the Fourteenth Amendment. "No State shall ... deprive any person of life, liberty, or property, without due process of law."

> While this Court has not attempted to define with exactness the liberty thus guaranteed, the term has received much consideration and some of the included things have been definitely stated. Without doubt, it denotes not merely freedom from bodily restraint but also the right of the individual to contract, to engage in any of the common occupations of life, to acquire useful knowledge, to marry, establish a home and bring up children, to worship God according to the dictates of his own conscience, and generally to enjoy those privileges long recognized at common law as essential to the orderly pursuit of happiness by free men....

> The American people have always regarded education and acquisition of knowledge as matters of supreme importance which should be diligently promoted.... Corresponding to the right of control, it is the natural duty of the parent to give his children education suitable to their station in life; and nearly all the States, including Nebraska, enforce this obligation by compulsory laws.

> Practically, education of the young is only possible in schools conducted by especially qualified persons who devote themselves thereto. The calling always has been regarded as useful and honorable, essential, indeed, to the public welfare. Mere knowledge of the German language cannot reasonabl[y] be regarded as harmful. Heretofore it has been commonly looked upon as helpful and desirable. Plaintiff ... taught this language in school as part of his occupation. His right thus to teach and the right of parents to engage him so to instruct their children, we think, are within the liberty of the Amendment.

The challenged statute forbids the teaching in school of any subject except in English; also the teaching of any other language until the pupil has attained and successfully passed the eighth grade.... The Supreme Court of the State has held that ... Latin, Greek, Hebrew are not proscribed; but German, French, Spanish, Italian and every other alien speech are within the ban. Evidently the legislature has attempted materially to interfere with the calling of modern language teachers, with the opportunities of pupils to acquire knowledge, and with the power of parents to control the education of their own.

It is said the purpose of the legislation was to promote civic development by inhibiting training and education of the immature in foreign tongues and ideals before they could learn English and acquire American ideals; and "that the English language should be and become the mother tongue of all children reared in this State." It is also affirmed that the foreign born population is very large, that certain communities commonly use foreign words, follow foreign leaders, move in a foreign atmosphere, and that the children are thereby hindered from becoming citizens of the most useful type and the public safety is imperiled.

That the State may do much, go very far, indeed, in order to improve the quality of its citizens, physically, mentally and morally, is clear; but the individual has certain fundamental rights which must be respected. The protection of the Constitution extends to all, to those who speak other languages as well as to those born with English on the tongue. Perhaps it would be highly advantageous if all had ready understanding of our ordinary speech, but this cannot be coerced by methods which conflict with the Constitution....

In order to submerge the individual and develop ideal citizens, Sparta assembled the males at seven into barracks and intrusted their subsequent education and training to official guardians. Although such measures have been deliberately approved by men of great genius, their ideas touching the relation between individual and State were wholly different from those upon which our institutions rest; and it hardly will be affirmed that any legislature could impose such restrictions upon the people of a State without doing violence to both letter and spirit of the Constitution.[2]

The desire of the legislature to foster a homogeneous people with American ideals prepared readily to understand current discussions of civic matters is easy to appreciate. Unfortunate experiences during the late war and aversion toward every characteristic of truculent adversaries were certainly enough to quicken that aspiration. But the means adopted, we think, exceed the limitations upon the power of the State and conflict with rights assured to plaintiff....

The power of the State to compel attendance at some school and to make reasonable regulations for all schools, including a requirement that they shall give instructions in English, is not questioned. Nor has challenge been made of the State's power to prescribe a curriculum for institutions which it supports. Those matters are not within the present controversy. Our concern is with the prohibition approved by the [Nebraska] Supreme Court.... No emergency has arisen which renders knowledge by a child of some language other than English so clearly harmful as to justify its inhibition with the consequent infringement of rights long freely enjoyed. We are constrained to conclude that the statute as applied is arbitrary and without reasonable relation to any end within the competency of the State.... It is well known that proficiency in a foreign language seldom comes to one not instructed at an early age, and experience shows that this is not injurious to the health, morals or understanding of the ordinary child. Reversed.[3]

At the same time the Court had a series of other cases from different parts of the country that presented the matter is a similar way. The Court's response was equally direct.

Bartels v. Iowa

262 U.S. 404 (1923)

INTRODUCTION: This is a series of cases brought at the same time as *Meyer*, involving similar state restrictions of other languages in Iowa, Ohio, and Missouri, as well as another statute in Nebraska.

Justice McReynolds wrote the opinion for the Court.

The several judgments entered in these causes by the Supreme Courts of Iowa, Ohio and Nebraska, respectively, must be reversed upon authority of *Meyer v. Nebraska*, decided today.... [In *Bartels*]. Plaintiff ... was convicted of teaching pupils in a parochial school below the eighth grade to read German.... Bohning and Pohl, of St. Johns Evangelical Congregational School, Garfield Heights, Cuyahoga County, Ohio, were severally convicted ... of violating "An act ... providing that instruction shall be in the English language," which prohibits the teaching of German to pupils below the eighth grade. [In *Nebraska District of Evangelical Lutheran Synod of Missouri, Ohio, and Other States v. McKelvie* an] injunction is sought against the Governor and Attorney General of the State and the Attorney for Platte County to prevent enforcement of "An act to declare the English language the official language of this State, and to require all official pro-ceedings, records and publications to be in such language and all school branches to be taught in said language in public, private, denominational and parochial schools," ... statute is subject to the same objections as those offered to the Act of 1919 and sustained in *Meyer v. Nebraska*, supra.... Reversed.

Justice Holmes wrote a dissent joined by Justice Sutherland.

... The part of the act with which we are concerned deals with the teaching of young children. Youth is the time when familiarity with a language is established and if there are sections in the State where a child would hear only Polish or French or German spoken at home, I am not prepared to say that it is unreason-able to provide that in his early years he shall hear and speak only English at school. But if it is reasonable it is not an undue restriction of the liberty either of teacher or scholar.... I think I appreciate the objection to the law, but it appears to me to present a question upon which men reasonably might differ, and therefore I am unable to say that the Constitution of the United States prevents the experi-ment being tried.

I agree with the Court as to the special proviso against the German language con-tained in the statute dealt with in *Bohning v. Ohio*.

These cases were followed two years later by another ruling that made it clear that parents were free to raise their children and to seek to have them educated, if they wished, in private schools, including religiously affiliated schools that were free to pass along their values to the children. That said, the state would retain the authority to establish minimum require-ments for curricula and other health and safety considerations.[4]

The question whether languages other than English could be prohibited would appear to have been resolved, but the discussion was far from finished. One of the issues was related but different and concerned the question whether public services, and particularly education, needed to be available to persons in languages other than English where the government had required participation in those education programs. Of course, it is true that education, health, and public welfare are functions under the authority of the states under the Tenth Amendment to the U.S. Constitution, rather than the authority of the federal government, but for many years the federal government has been significantly involved by virtue of the fact that it provides funds to support educational programs to the state and local governments, and those funds come with a variety of requirements under the federal law. One of these is the requirement under Title VI of the Civil Rights Act of 1964 that prohibits discrimination on the basis of race in any programs or agencies receiving federal funds. One of the questions was the degree to which language is a proxy for race, and therefore whether the government was obligated to be concerned about language barriers to federally supported public services.

Lau v. Nichols

414 U.S. 563 (1974)

INTRODUCTION: The facts of this case are presented in the opinion written by Justice Douglas for the Court.

... The District Court found that there are 2,856 students of Chinese ancestry in the [San Francisco, California] school system who do not speak English. Of those who have that language deficiency, about 1,000 are given supplemental courses in the English language. About 1,800, however, do not receive that instruction.

This class suit brought by non-English-speaking Chinese students against officials responsible for the operation of the San Francisco Unified School District seeks relief against the unequal educational opportunities, which are alleged to violate, *inter alia*, the Fourteenth Amendment. No specific remedy is urged upon us. Teaching English to the students of Chinese ancestry who do not speak the language is one choice. Giving instructions to this group in Chinese is another. There may be others. Petitioners ask only that the Board of Education be directed to apply its expertise to the problem and rectify the situation.

The District Court denied relief. The Court of Appeals affirmed, holding that there was no violation of the Equal Protection Clause of the Fourteenth Amendment or of [Title VI] of the Civil Rights Act of 1964 ... which excludes from participation in federal financial assistance, recipients of aid which discriminate against racial groups....

[Section] 71 of the California Education Code states that "English shall be the basic language of instruction in all schools." That section permits a school district to determine "when and under what circumstances instruction may be given bilingually." That section also states as "the policy of the state" to insure "the mastery of English by all pupils in the schools." And bilingual instruction is authorized "to the extent that it does not interfere with the systematic, sequential, and regular instruction of all pupils in the English language." ... Moreover, §8573 of the Education Code provides that no pupil shall receive a diploma of graduation from grade 12 who has not met the standards of proficiency in "English." ...

Under these state-imposed standards there is no equality of treatment merely by providing students with the same facilities, textbooks, teachers, and curriculum; for students who do not understand English are effectively foreclosed from any meaningful education.

Basic English skills are at the very core of what these public schools teach. Imposition of a requirement that, before a child can effectively participate in the educational program, he must already have acquired those basic skills is to make a mockery of public education. We know that those who do not understand English are certain to find their classroom experiences wholly incomprehensible and in no way meaningful.

We do not reach the Equal Protection Clause argument which has been advanced but rely solely on [Title VI] of the Civil Rights Act of 1964 ... to reverse the Court of Appeals. That section bans discrimination based "on the ground of race, color, or national origin," in "any program or activity receiving Federal financial assistance." The school district involved in this litigation receives large amounts of federal financial assistance. The Department of Health, Education, and Welfare (HEW),[5] which has authority to promulgate regulations prohibiting discrimination in federally assisted school systems ... in 1968 issued one guideline that "school systems are responsible for assuring that students of a particular race, color, or national origin are not denied the opportunity to obtain the education generally obtained by other students in the system." ... In 1970 HEW made the guidelines more specific, requiring school districts that were federally funded "to rectify the language deficiency in order to open" the instruction to students who had "linguistic deficiencies." ...

By §602 of the Act, HEW is authorized to issue rules, regulations, and orders to make sure that recipients of federal aid under its jurisdiction conduct any federally financed projects consistently with §601. HEW's regulations ... specify that the recipients may not "(ii) Provide any service, financial aid, or other benefit to an individual which is different, or is provided in a different manner, from that provided to others under the program; ... (iv) Restrict an individual in any way in the enjoyment of any advantage or privilege enjoyed by others receiving any service, financial aid, or other benefit under the program."

Discrimination among students on account of race or national origin that is prohibited includes "discrimination ... in the availability or use of any academic ... or other facilities of the grantee or other recipient." Id., §80.5 (b).

Discrimination is barred which has that effect even though no purposeful design is present: a recipient "may not ... utilize criteria or methods of administration which have the effect of subjecting individuals to discrimination" or have "the effect of defeating or substantially impairing accomplishment of the objectives of the program as respect individuals of a particular race, color, or national origin." ...

It seems obvious that the Chinese-speaking minority receive fewer benefits than the English-speaking majority from respondents' school system which denies them a meaningful opportunity to participate in the educational program—all earmarks of the discrimination banned by the regulations. In 1970 HEW issued clarifying guidelines ... which include the following:

"Where inability to speak and understand the English language excludes national origin-minority group children from effective participation in the educational program offered by a school district, the district must take affirmative steps to rectify the language deficiency in order to open its instructional program to these students." "Any ability grouping or tracking system employed by the school system to deal with the special language skill needs of national origin-minority group children must be designed to meet such language skill needs as soon as possible and must not operate as an educational dead end or permanent track."

Respondent school district contractually agreed to "comply with Title VI of the Civil Rights Act of 1964 ... and all requirements imposed by or pursuant to the Regulation" of HEW ... which are "issued pursuant to that title..." and also immediately to "take any measures necessary to effectuate this agreement." ... Simple justice requires that public funds, to which all taxpayers of all races contribute, not be spent in any fashion which encourages, entrenches, subsidizes, or results in racial discrimination.... Reversed and remanded.[6]

Justice Stewart wrote a concurring opinion joined by Chief Justice Burger and Justice Blackmun.

[T]he petitioners do not contend, however, that the respondents have affirmatively or intentionally contributed to this inadequacy, but only that they have failed to act in the face of changing social and linguistic patterns. Because of this laissez-faire attitude on the part of the school administrators, it is not entirely clear that [Title VI] standing alone, would render illegal the expenditure of federal funds on these schools.... On the other hand, the interpretive guidelines published by the Office for Civil Rights of the Department of Health, Education, and Welfare in 1970 ... clearly indicate that affirmative efforts to give special training for non-English-speaking pupils are required by Tit. VI as a condition to receipt of federal aid to public schools.... I concur in the result reached by the Court.[7]

The U.S. Justice Department later issued a formal opinion indicating that a failure to provide federally funded public services to persons with limited English proficiency in forms they could access was a violation of Title VI.[8] At that time, President Clinton issued an executive order grounded in that Justice Department (DOJ) interpretation, requiring administrative agencies to generate regulations on the manner in which they would guarantee access to persons with limited English proficiency.[9] After that DOJ issued a revised guidance document on the requirements entitled "Guidance to Federal Financial Assistance Recipients Regarding Title VI Prohibition against National Origin Discrimination Affecting Limited English Proficient Persons" in 2002.[10] Later still, DOJ established a website to assist those receiving federal funds to better comply with these requirements and avoid a Title VI violation.[11] Once again, it seemed, the law and the courts had taken considerable steps toward ensuring that one's language would not be the basis for discrimination. However, the discussion was far from over.

At various points in American history, and particularly during periods of economic downturn, animus against immigrants, and particularly against Latinos, has emerged. That was certainly the case beginning with the recession of the early 1980s and after, and continued to be the case through the 1990s and the recessions of the early years of the twenty-first century. And, as they have in the past, politicians have learned that they could ride the wave of anger, suspicion, and prejudice to victory. Indeed there have been political figures who made their campaigns against Latinos key issues. Although they sometimes claimed that they were only targeting illegal immigrants, it became obvious, particularly in light of their support for English-only laws and other policies aimed at Latinos, that there was more at issue here than immigration. This behavior produced a host of troubling situations, some of which seem downright perverse. One such case arose from the criminal justice system in New York state.

It was one thing when some reacted critically to mandates, without accompanying funding, that federal agencies and state and local governments receiving federal funds take action to ensure access to persons with limited English proficiency, but pressures to prohibit the use of languages other than English flew in the face of the Supreme Court's clear rejection of such actions as far back as the *Meyer* case. The discussion of the New York case below shows that some officials were willing to use the mere fact that one was bilingual as a reason to disqualify a citizen from serving on a jury. In understanding the efforts to block the use of languages other than English by service providers or those who dealt with government agencies, it is important to understand that interpretation services are sometimes not readily available, and those that are provided are sometimes not carefully regulated to ensure that those translating have the necessary knowledge and skills. Inaccuracies in translation have led to serious difficulties in the areas such as healthcare and in the criminal justice system. And in the criminal justice system there have long been assumptions that minority jurors would be likely to favor minority defendants and, as the *Hernandez v. Texas* case indicated, local officials have long sought to exclude Hispanics from jury service in the same way as they had African Americans.[12]

Hernandez v. New York

500 U.S. 352 (1991)

INTRODUCTION: This case came about as a result of a prosecutor's removal of potential jurors from a case because they were bilingual. That action was all the more difficult to understand in any positive way in light of the fact that the parties were Latino and spoke Spanish and that the alleged crime had occurred in New York City's Spanish Harlem.

Justice Kennedy announced the plurality opinion and announced the judgment of the Court.

> Petitioner Dionisio Hernandez asks us to review the New York state courts' rejection of his claim that the prosecutor in his criminal trial exercised peremptory challenges to exclude Latinos from the jury by reason of their ethnicity. If true, the prosecutor's discriminatory use of peremptory strikes would violate the Equal Protection Clause as interpreted by our decision *in Batson v. Kentucky*.... We must determine whether the prosecutor offered a race-neutral basis for challenging Latino potential jurors and, if so, whether the state courts' decision to accept the prosecutor's explanation should be sustained.
>
> I. ... After 63 potential jurors had been questioned and 9 had been empaneled, defense counsel objected that the prosecutor had used four peremptory challenges to exclude Latino potential jurors.... [W]e concentrate on ... two [of the] excluded individuals.
>
> [T]he prosecutor volunteered his reasons for striking the jurors in question. He explained: "Your honor, my reason for rejecting these two jurors ... is I feel very uncertain that they would be able to listen and follow the interpreter." ... I believe that in their heart they will try to follow it, but I felt there was a great deal of uncertainty as to whether they could accept the interpreter as the final arbiter of what was said by each of the witnesses, especially where there were going to be Spanish-speaking witnesses, and I didn't feel, when I asked them whether or not they could accept the interpreter's translation of it, I didn't feel that they could. They each looked away from me and said with some hesitancy that they would try...."
>
> II. In *Batson*, we outlined a three-step process for evaluating claims that a prosecutor has used peremptory challenges in a manner violating the Equal Protection Clause.... First, the defendant must make a prima facie showing that the prosecutor has exercised peremptory challenges on the basis of race.... Second, if the

requisite showing has been made, the burden shifts to the prosecutor to articulate a race-neutral explanation for striking the jurors in question.... Finally, the trial court must determine whether the defendant has carried his burden of proving purposeful discrimination....

B. Petitioner contends that the reasons given by the prosecutor for challenging the two bilingual jurors were not race-neutral.... A neutral explanation in the context of our analysis here means an explanation based on something other than the race of the juror.... Unless a discriminatory intent is inherent in the prosecutor's explanation, the reason offered will be deemed race-neutral.

Petitioner argues that Spanish-language ability bears a close relation to ethnicity, and that, as a consequence, it violates the Equal Protection Clause to exercise a peremptory challenge on the ground that a Latino potential juror speaks Spanish. He points to the high correlation between Spanish language ability and ethnicity in New York, where the case was tried. We need not address that argument here, for the prosecutor did not rely on language ability without more, but explained that the specific responses and the demeanor of the two individuals during *voir dire*[13] caused him to doubt their ability to defer to the official translation of Spanish-language testimony.[14]

The prosecutor here offered a race-neutral basis for these peremptory strikes. As explained by the prosecutor, the challenges rested neither on the intention to exclude Latino or bilingual jurors, nor on stereotypical assumptions about Latinos or bilinguals. The prosecutor's articulated basis for these challenges divided potential jurors into two classes: those whose conduct during *voir dire* would persuade him they might have difficulty in accepting the translator's rendition of Spanish-language testimony and those potential jurors who gave no such reason for doubt. Each category would include both Latinos and non-Latinos. While the prosecutor's criterion might well result in the disproportionate removal of prospective Latino jurors, that disproportionate impact does not turn the prosecutor's actions into a per se violation of the Equal Protection Clause.

Petitioner contends that despite the prosecutor's focus on the individual responses of these jurors, his reason for the peremptory strikes has the effect of a pure, language-based reason because "any honest bilingual juror would have answered the prosecutor in the exact same way." ...

But even if we knew that a high percentage of bilingual jurors would hesitate in answering questions like these and, as a consequence, would be excluded under the prosecutor's criterion, that fact alone would not cause the criterion to fail the race-neutrality test.... Equal protection analysis turns on the intended consequences of government classifications. Unless the government actor adopted a criterion with the intent of causing the impact asserted, that impact itself does not violate the principle of race neutrality. Nothing in the prosecutor's explanation shows that he chose to exclude jurors who hesitated in answering questions about following the interpreter because he wanted to prevent bilingual Latinos from serving on the jury.[15]...

C. Once the prosecutor offers a race-neutral basis for his exercise of peremptory challenges, "the trial court then [has] the duty to determine if the defendant has established purposeful discrimination." ... If a prosecutor articulates a basis for a peremptory challenge that results in the disproportionate exclusion of members of a certain race, the trial judge may consider that fact as evidence that the prosecutor's stated reason constitutes a pretext for racial discrimination.[16]

In the context of this trial, the prosecutor's frank admission that his ground for excusing these jurors related to their ability to speak and understand Spanish raised a plausible, though not a necessary, inference that language might be a pretext for what in fact were race-based peremptory challenges. This was not a case where by some rare coincidence a juror happened to speak the same language as a key witness, in a community where few others spoke that tongue. If it were, the explanation that the juror could have undue influence on jury deliberations might be accepted without concern that a racial generalization had come into play. But this trial took place in a community with a substantial Latino population, and petitioner and other interested parties were members of that ethnic group. It would be common knowledge in the locality that a significant percentage of the Latino population speaks fluent Spanish, and that many consider it their preferred language, the one chosen for personal communication, the one selected for speaking with the most precision and power, the one used to define the self.

The trial judge can consider these and other factors when deciding whether a prosecutor intended to discriminate. For example, though petitioner did not suggest the alternative to the trial court here, Spanish-speaking jurors could be permitted to advise the judge in a discreet way of any concerns with the translation during the course of trial. A prosecutor's persistence in the desire to exclude Spanish-speaking jurors despite this measure could be taken into account in determining whether to accept a race-neutral explanation for the challenge.

The trial judge in this case chose to believe the prosecutor's race-neutral explanation for striking the two jurors in question, rejecting petitioner's assertion that the reasons were pretextual.[17]... We discern no clear error in the state trial court's determination that the prosecutor did not discriminate on the basis of the ethnicity of Latino jurors....

D. Language permits an individual to express both a personal identity and membership in a community, and those who share a common language may interact in ways more intimate than those without this bond. Bilinguals, in a sense, inhabit two communities, and serve to bring them closer. Indeed, some scholarly comment suggests that people proficient in two languages may not at times think in one language to the exclusion of the other. The analogy is that of a high hurdler, who combines the ability to sprint and to jump to accomplish a third feat with characteristics of its own, rather than two separate functions.... This is not to say that the cognitive processes and reactions of those who speak two languages are susceptible of easy generalization, for even the term "bilingual" does not describe a uniform category. It is a simple word for a more complex phenomenon with many distinct categories and subdivisions.[18]...

Our decision today does not imply that exclusion of bilinguals from jury service is wise, or even that it is constitutional in all cases. It is a harsh paradox that one may become proficient enough in English to participate in trial ... only to encounter disqualification because he knows a second language as well.[19]...

Just as shared language can serve to foster community, language differences can be a source of division. Language elicits a response from others, ranging from admiration and respect, to distance and alienation, to ridicule and scorn. Reactions of the latter type all too often result from or initiate racial hostility. In holding that a race-neutral reason for a peremptory challenge means a reason other than race, we do not resolve the more difficult question of the breadth with which the concept of race should be defined for equal protection purposes. We would face a quite different case if the prosecutor had justified his peremptory challenges with the explanation that he did not want Spanish-speaking jurors.[20] It may well be, for certain ethnic groups and in some communities, that proficiency in a particular language, like skin color, should be treated as a surrogate for race under an equal protection analysis.... And, as we make clear, a policy of striking all who speak a given language, without regard to the particular circumstances of the trial or the individual responses of the jurors, may be found by the trial judge to be a pretext for racial discrimination. But that case is not before us. Affirmed.

Justice O'Connor wrote an opinion joined by Justice Scalia concurring in the judgment.

Consistent with our established equal protection jurisprudence, a peremptory strike will constitute a *Batson* violation only if the prosecutor struck a juror because of the juror's race.... In this case, the prosecutor's asserted justification for striking certain Hispanic jurors was his uncertainty about the jurors' ability to accept the official translation of trial testimony.... If this truly was the purpose of the strikes, they were not strikes because of race, and therefore did not violate the Equal Protection Clause under *Batson*. They may have acted like strikes based on race, but they were not based on race. No matter how closely tied or significantly correlated to race the explanation for a peremptory strike may be, the strike does not implicate the Equal Protection Clause unless it is based on race....

Justice Stevens dissented, joined by Justice Marshall and in part by Justice Blackmun.

A violation of the Equal Protection Clause requires what our cases characterize as proof of "discriminatory purpose." By definition, however, a prima facie case is one that is established by the requisite proof of invidious intent. Unless the prosecutor comes forward with an explanation for his peremptories that is sufficient to rebut that prima facie case, no additional evidence of racial animus is required to establish an equal protection violation. In my opinion, the Court therefore errs when it concludes that a defendant's *Batson* challenge fails whenever the prosecutor advances a nonpretextual justification that is not facially discriminatory.

I. ... If any explanation, no matter how insubstantial and no matter how great its disparate impact, could rebut a prima facie inference of discrimination provided only that the explanation itself was not facially discriminatory, "the Equal Protection Clause 'would be but a vain and illusory requirement.'" ... By requiring that the prosecutor's explanation itself provide additional, direct evidence of discriminatory motive, the Court has imposed on the defendant the added requirement that he generate evidence of the prosecutor's actual subjective intent to discriminate. Neither *Batson* nor our other equal protection holdings demand such a heightened quantum of proof.

II. Applying the principles outlined above to the facts of this case, I would reject the prosecutor's explanation without reaching the question whether the explanation was pretextual....

The prosecutor's explanation was insufficient for three reasons. First, the justification would inevitably result in a disproportionate disqualification of Spanish-speaking venire persons. An explanation that is "race neutral" on its face is nonetheless unacceptable if it is merely a proxy for a discriminatory practice. Second, the prosecutor's concern could easily have been accommodated by less drastic means. As is the practice in many jurisdictions, the jury could have been instructed that the official translation alone is evidence; bilingual jurors could have been instructed to bring to the attention of the judge any disagreements they might have with the translation so that any disputes could be resolved by the court.... Third, if the prosecutor's concern was valid and substantiated by the record, it would have supported a challenge for cause. The fact that the prosecutor did not make any such challenge ... should disqualify him from advancing the concern as a justification for a peremptory challenge.

Each of these reasons considered alone might not render insufficient the prosecutor's facially neutral explanation. In combination, however, they persuade me that his explanation should have been rejected as a matter of law.

Sadly, the evidence has become increasingly clear over time that prosecutors were indeed discriminating in an effort to avoid Latinos and African Americans on juries. The U.S. Supreme Court is hearing a case at the time of this writing concerning removal of minorities from juries that elicited a highly unusual *amicus curiae* brief from well-known federal and state prosecutors opposing the behavior of other prosecutors. These prosecutors began their brief as follows:

Amici are former prosecutors who recognize, and refuse to condone, the blatant illegality of the prosecutorial misconduct at issue in this case: specifically, the racially discriminatory use of strikes during jury selection to ensure that a black defendant accused of a crime against a white victim would face an all-white jury.[21]

Indeed, they said: "Some prosecutors have even provided trainings that encourage racial discrimination and explain how to conceal improper motivation from the courts."[22] They went on:

Prosecutorial race discrimination is sometimes frighteningly overt. In 1986, Jack McMahon, an assistant district attorney in Philadelphia, created a training film teaching prosecutors to exclude young blacks from juries. He explains in the video that "blacks from the low-income areas are less likely to convict"; "you don't want those people on your jury"; "it may appear as if you're being racist, but again, you're just being realistic"; "young black women are very bad" because "they're downtrodden in two respects," namely "[t]hey are women and they're black" and "they somehow want to take it out on somebody and you don't want it to be you."[23]

This particular case concerned an African American, but these well-known former prosecutors make clear that it is about racial selection generally.

By the 1990s there were major political efforts in various states to adopt English-only legislation or even state constitutional amendments to that effect. To many Latinos, it was abundantly clear that the purposes were discriminatory, particularly in light of the fact that these policies often had perverse effects. It was equally clear to many Latinos that the target was Spanish-speakers and not the myriad of other persons with different language backgrounds. The connections in the debates over these measures were often thinly veiled statements of animus toward Latinos. One example of such a situation arose in Alabama, where a constitutional amendment forced state agencies to halt multilingual or bilingual programs in a variety of areas. In the case of Alabama, the specific matter that precipitated litigation was the decision to force the state's Department of Motor Vehicles to stop its multilingual licensing program.

The *Sandoval v. Hagan* case came about after the Alabama English-only amendment forced an end to a program to provide driver's testing and materials in various languages that had been in place for more than two decades.[24] By far the largest number of persons served by the program were Spanish-speakers. The program was operated by volunteer translators and therefore was not a financial burden on the state. State DMV officials saw this as a way to reduce the number of persons driving without a license, obtain identification information for drivers in the event of a motor vehicle infraction or accident, and obtain evidence of insurance. There had been no problem with the program and no reason given as to why it should not continue. Marha Sandoval challenged the Alabama action on grounds that it violated both Title VI of the Civil Rights Act of 1964 and the equal protection clause of the Fourteenth Amendment. Witnesses from the Hispanic Ministry of the Catholic Diocese of Birmingham and the Hispanic Ministry of the Catholic Diocese of Mobile testified that the English-only requirement would not only affect a great many people and their ability to complete the licensing process, but by prohibiting them from driving it would also affect their employment and other important activities of daily life. In any case, it was also shown at trial that:

> the hearing-impaired, illiterate, deaf, and disabled residents receive substantial accommodation on the written exam and road skills test.... Illiterate English speakers may take the test orally from a state examiner.... For those hearing-impaired applicants, who cannot adequately read and write English, a video exam is offered.... Additionally, the Department also grants driver's licenses to applicants of foreign descent who possess valid driver's licenses from other states or countries.[25]

A former head of the Driver's License Division testified that there had been no difficulties with the program and that it was helpful to the agency and the mission of improving driver safety. The trial court issued an injunction against the state requirement.[26]

In affirming the district court, the Eleventh Circuit saw such a clear violation of Title VI that it did not rule on the equal protection question. In so doing, the panel observed:

> Both Supreme Court precedent and longstanding congressional provisions and federal agency regulations have repeatedly instructed state entities for decades that a nexus exists between language and national origin. In *Lau v. Nichols* ... a school district, that received federal funds, was adjudged liable under Title VI disparate impact regulations for an English language policy that adversely affected non-English-speaking Chinese students.... [T]he Supreme Court explicitly struck down the policy as unlawful national origin discrimination under Title VI.[27]

It came as a shock to many when the Eleventh Circuit ruling was overturned by the United States Supreme Court in *Alexander v. Sandoval*.[28] The Court did not find that the lower court had been incorrect on the merits, but rather that Title VI did not allow an individual to bring an implied private right of action to enforce its provisions. That is, private individuals could not bring suit themselves to address discrimination they encountered in a federally funded program, but would have to rely on the federal government to take enforcement action against the state or local government involved to do that. This was a dramatic departure by the Court from prior precedents rendered by a 5–4 majority in an opinion by Justice Scalia. Justice Stevens, writing for the dissenters concluded: "Today, in a decision unfounded in our precedent and hostile to decades of settled expectations, a majority of this Court carves out an important exception to the right of private action long recognized under Title VI."[29] In fact, he pointed specifically to *Lau v. Nichols* as one of those precedents.

> In separate lawsuits spanning several decades, we have endorsed an action identical in substance to the one brought in this case, see *Lau v. Nichols*...; demonstrated that Congress intended a private right of action to protect the rights guaranteed by Title VI, see *Cannon v. University of Chicago*, 441 U.S. 677 (1979); and concluded that private individuals may seek declaratory and injunctive relief against state officials for violations of regulations promulgated pursuant to Title VI, see *Guardians Assn. v. Civil Serv. Comm'n of New York City*, 463 U.S. 582 (1983).[30]

The dissenters clearly saw that the *Sandoval* ruling would be used as a tool to undermine the effectiveness of Title VI. In fact, after that ruling challenges were brought to policy guidance provided by federal agencies with respect to requirements for access to federally funded programs for persons with limited English proficiency, to the point that the Department of Health and Human Services had to explain that:

> the Supreme Court, in the *Sandoval* decision, did not strike down Title VI itself or Title VI's disparate impact regulations (at HUD, that would be its civil rights-related program requirements or "CRRPRs"), but only ruled that individuals could not enforce these Title VI regulations through the courts and could only bring such court action under the statute itself.[31]

One of the states that had adopted an English-only constitutional amendment was Arizona, which did so in 1988. States such as Arizona, Texas, and California, which were part of Mexico, seem to have been particularly prone to such actions even though they have a large Latino population. Interestingly, Arizona's ballot measure only passed in November 1988 with a vote of 50.5%.[32] It resulted in a strong statement by the Arizona Supreme Court that the measure was unconstitutional for more than one reason.

Ruiz v. Hull

957 P.2d 984 (AZ 1997)

INTRODUCTION: Unlike the previous cases, the focus of this litigation was on the First Amendment freedom of expression. The claims were not only that the English-only restriction interfered with the First Amendment expression rights of public officials, but also that it interfered with the free flow of information so as to present barriers to access to public services by the primary Spanish speakers. The case also presented challenges based on the equal protection clause of the Fourteenth Amendment.

Arizonans for Official English ("AOE") used the petition process to get the amendment making English the official language of the state and prohibiting any officials at any level from doing business in any language except English.

Immediately after the English-only amendment to the Arizona Constitution was adopted, Maria-Kelley F. Yñiguez, a bilingual state employee who regularly did business in both Spanish and English and particularly with clients with limited English proficiency, sued in federal court, charging that the measure violated her First

Amendment free speech protections. She prevailed in the federal district court and court of appeals,[33] but by the time the case reached the U.S. Supreme Court in 1997, she had left her job with the state. The Supreme Court vacated the lower court rulings on grounds that the case was moot.[34]

However, even as *Yñiguez* was in progress, four elected officials, five state employees, and one school teacher launched a challenge in state court, claiming violations of the First, Ninth, and Fourteenth Amendments of the U.S. Constitution. The superior court rejected the challenge and the appeals court reversed in part and affirmed in part. The state supreme court halted proceedings until the U.S. Supreme Court ruled in the *Yñiguez* case. The suit resumed once the Supreme Court ruled her case was moot.

The opinion was written by Justice James Moeller.

> This opinion addresses the constitutionality of Article XXVIII of the Arizona Constitution, which was adopted in 1988 and which provides, *inter alia*, that English is the official language of the State of Arizona and that the state and its political subdivisions—including all government officials and employees performing government business—must "act" only in English.

> We hold that the Amendment violates the First Amendment to the United States Constitution because it adversely impacts the constitutional rights of non-English-speaking persons with regard to their obtaining access to their government and limits the political speech of elected officials and public employees. We also hold that the Amendment violates the Equal Protection Clause of the Fourteenth Amendment to the United States Constitution because it unduly burdens core First Amendment rights of a specific class without materially advancing a legitimate state interest....

> At the outset, we note that this case concerns the tension between the constitutional status of language rights and the state's power to restrict such rights. On the one hand, in our diverse society, the importance of establishing common bonds and a common language between citizens is clear.... We recognize that the acquisition of English language skills is important in our society. For instance, as a condition to Arizona's admission to the Union, Congress required Arizona to create a public school system and provided that "said schools shall always be conducted in English." ... That same Act requires all state officers and members of the Legislature to have the "ability to read, write, speak and understand the English language...." Congress has recognized ... the need for the education of non-English-speaking students, Equal Educational Opportunity Act of 1974....

> However, the American tradition of tolerance "recognizes a critical difference between encouraging the use of English and repressing the use of other languages." ... We agree with the Ninth Circuit's statement that Arizona's rejection of that tradition by enacting the Amendment has severe consequences not only for Arizona's public officials and employees, but also for the many thousands of persons who would be precluded from receiving essential information from government employees and elected officials in Arizona's governments.[35] If the wide-ranging language of the prohibitions contained in the Amendment were to be implemented as written, the First Amendment rights of all those persons would be violated, a fact now conceded by the proponents of the Amendment, who, instead, urge a restrictive interpretation in accordance with the Attorney General's narrow construction [of its terms]....

> Every duly enacted state and federal law is entitled to a presumption of constitutionality.... However, ... where the regulation in question impinges on core

constitutional rights, the standards of strict scrutiny apply and the burden of showing constitutionality is shifted to the proponent of the regulation....

Although English-only provisions have recently become quite common, Arizona's is unique.... Twenty-one states[36] and forty municipalities[37] have official English statutes. However, most of those provisions are substantially less encompassing and certainly less proscriptive than the Amendment.... Unlike other English-only provisions, the [Arizona] Amendment explicitly and broadly prohibits government employees from using non-English languages even when communicating with persons who have limited or no English skills....

"Whatever differences may exist about interpretations of the First Amendment, there is practically universal agreement that a major purpose of that Amendment was to protect the free discussion of governmental affairs." *Landmark Communications v. Virginia* (1978).... [W]e find that the Amendment unconstitutionally inhibits "the free discussion of governmental affairs" in two ways. First, it deprives limited- and non-English-speaking persons of access to information about the government when multilingual access may be available and may be necessary to ensure fair and effective delivery of governmental services to non-English-speaking persons.... The United States Supreme Court has held that First Amendment protection is afforded to the communication, its source, and its recipient. *Virginia State Board of Pharmacy v. Virginia Citizens Consumer Council* (1976).

... The Amendment contravenes core principles and values undergirding the First Amendment—the right of the people to seek redress from their government—by directly banning pure speech on its face. By denying persons who are limited in English proficiency, or entirely lacking in it, the right to participate equally in the political process, the Amendment violates the constitutional right to participate in and have access to government, a right which is one of the "fundamental principle[s] of representative government in this country." ...

The Amendment violates the First Amendment by depriving elected officials and public employees of the ability to communicate with their constituents and with the public. We hold that the Amendment goes too far because it effectively cuts off governmental communication with thousands of limited-English-proficient and non-English-speaking persons in Arizona, even when the officials and employees have the ability and desire to communicate in a language understandable to them.... Under such circumstances, prohibiting an elected or appointed governmental official or an employee from communicating with the public violates the employee's and the official's rights.... As the Ninth Circuit noted, the Amendment could "hardly be more inclusive"; it "prohibit[s] the use in all oral and written communications by persons connected with the government of all words and phrases in any language other than English." *Yniguez v. AOE*....

Citizens of limited English proficiency, such as many of the named legislator's constituents, often face obstacles in petitioning their government for redress and in accessing the political system. Legislators and other elected officials attempting to serve limited-English-proficient constituents face a difficult task in helping provide those constituents with government services and in assisting those constituents in both understanding and accessing government.... In Arizona, English is not the primary language of many citizens. A substantial number of Arizona's Native Americans, Spanish-speaking citizens, and other citizens for whom English is not a primary language, either do not speak English at all or do not speak English well enough to be able to express their political beliefs, opinions, or needs to their elected officials. Under the Amendment, with few exceptions, no elected official can speak with his or her constituents except in English, even though such a requirement renders the speaking useless. While certainly not dispositive, it is also worth noting that in everyday experience, even among persons fluent in English as a second language, it is often more effective to communicate complex ideas in a person's primary language because some words, such as idioms and colloquialisms, do not translate well, if at all. In many cases, though, it is clear that the Amendment jeopardizes or prevents meaningful communication between constituents and their elected representatives, and thus contravenes core principles and values undergirding the First Amendment.... By requiring that government officials communicate only in a language which is incomprehensible to non-English speaking persons, the Amendment effectively bars communication itself. Therefore, its effect cannot be characterized as merely a time, place, or manner restriction because such restrictions, by definition, assume and require the availability of alternative means of communication....

In *National Treasury Employees Union*, the Court recognized that a ban on speech ... constitutes a "wholesale deterrent to a broad category of expression by a massive number of potential speakers" and thus "chills potential speech before it happens." ... The chilling effect of the Amendment's broad applications is reinforced by Section 4 which provides that elected officials and state employees can be sued for violating the Amendment's prohibitions.... We conclude that the Amendment violates the First Amendment.

Section One of the Fourteenth Amendment provides, in pertinent part, that "no state shall ... deny to any person within its jurisdiction the equal protection of the laws." The right to petition for redress of grievances is one of the fundamental rights guaranteed by the First Amendment.... A corollary to the right to petition for redress of grievances is the right to participate equally in the political process.... The Amendment is subject to strict scrutiny because it impinges upon the fundamental First Amendment right to petition the government for redress of grievances.... Because the Amendment curtails First Amendment rights, however, it is presumed unconstitutional and must survive this court's strict scrutiny.... AOE and the state defendants bear the burden of ... demonstrating that it is drawn with narrow specificity to meet a compelling state interest.

[T]he United States Supreme Court has not addressed the constitutionality of official English statutes since the 1920s. In *Meyer* [*v. Nebraska*] the Court ... noted: "The individual has certain fundamental rights which must be respected. The protection of the Constitution extends to all, to those who speak other languages as well as to those born with English on the tongue. Perhaps it would be highly advantageous if all had ready understanding of our ordinary speech, but this cannot be coerced by methods which conflict with the Constitution—a desirable end cannot be promoted by prohibited means." ... In *Meyer*, the Court held that the statute violated Fourteenth Amendment due process and equal protection rights.... We believe the Amendment suffers from the same constitutional infirmity.

... Even assuming arguendo that AOE and the state defendants could establish a compelling state interest for the Amendment..., they cannot satisfy the narrow specificity requirement. [T]he Amendment ... is a general prohibition of the use of non-English languages by all state personnel during the performance of government business and by all persons seeking to interact with all levels of government in Arizona. The Amendment's goal to promote English as a common language does not require a general prohibition on non-English usage. English can be promoted without prohibiting the use of other languages by state and local governments. Therefore, the Amendment does not meet the compelling state interest test and thus does not survive First Amendment strict scrutiny analysis.... The opinion of the court of appeals is vacated and the trial court's judgment is reversed.[38]

Although outright bans on languages other than English, and the obvious targeting of Spanish in those actions, has been the focus of much attention, Latinos are very aware that this is only one part of the picture. There have been a variety of other actions, some matters of policy and others actions by particular officials or private employers, that have not only targeted those who speak Spanish but in which the language is clearly a proxy for race and ethnicity. A few examples are sufficient to demonstrate the range and continuity of the problem.

In 1995 a Texas judge in Amarillo ordered a mother not to speak Spanish to her 5-year-old daughter at home in a matter that arose during a custody battle between the parents.[39] In April 1999 in Houston Judge Lisa Millard ordered Natalia Gonzalez not to speak Spanish to her daughter, a mandate that she later expanded to include anyone in the family, including the girl's father, Ramon Gonzalez.[40] This again arose in the context of a custody fight. In 2003 a Nebraska judge ordered Mr. Eloy Amador to avoid speaking Spanish to his daughter. News reports indicated that at the hearing:

> [Judge] Reagan told Amador that he doesn't have a problem with instruction of the language, but the main form of communication 'better be in a language' the girl understands. "That's English, OK?" he said. "Are you telling me I can teach it to her, but I can't speak it to her?" Amador asked, referring to Spanish. "That's right," Reagan said.[41]

An aide at a Winatchee, Washington senior care facility was fired in 2002 for speaking Spanish while at work.[42] A situation in northern Georgia was even more dramatic. A regional state healthcare supervisor issued Policy 164 in 2002 that prohibited employees from speaking anything other than English and warned that: "Failure to abide by this policy will result in disciplinary action up to and including termination from employment."[43] The irony of this policy was particularly clear in a region of the state where some 20% of the population was Latino and that had experienced a 500% increase in Hispanics during the 1990s.[44] State officials responded when the American Civil Liberties Union (ACLU) wrote to them of the many complaints received from employees. They rescinded the policy amidst statewide condemnation, but not before the damage had been done and a very clear message had been sent by the physician who was the state's regional supervisor to the residents of the community and the state.[45]

One battle over language, of a different sort, arose in Arizona. The case found its way to the U.S. Supreme Court. It is a complex class action suit that alleged violations by the state of the federal requirements for instruction of English Language Learners (ELL) under the provisions of the Equal Education Act of 1974 (EEOA)[46] and Title VI of the Civil Rights Act of 1964 as interpreted by the Supreme Court in *Lau v. Nichols*.[47] State and local officials in Arizona were divided on the matter and actually participated on opposite sides of the case. The Arizona Superintendent of Public Instruction, the Speaker of the Arizona House of Representatives, and the President of the Arizona Senate challenged the federal district court and Ninth Circuit rulings requiring improvements by the state. However, the State of Arizona and the Arizona Board of Public Education supported the federal court rulings, which had ruled in favor of the families' call for better instructional services. The United States Department of Justice filed as a friend of the court also in support of the lower court rulings.

Originally entitled *Flores v. Arizona*,[48] the case arose because of complaints that began in 1992 in the schools in the border city of Nogales, Arizona, a community with many ELL students. In addition to the EEOA and Title VI challenges, the district court explained that the parents:

> challenge[d] the Defendants' funding, administration and oversight of the public school system in districts enrolling predominantly low-income minority children because Defendants allow these schools to provide less educational benefits and opportunities than those available to students who attend predominantly anglo-schools.[49]

The trial court found that the school district was in violation of the EEOA because the state's financing was not adequate to implement the plan that had been put forward to address the ELL inadequacies. The state, the court said, "failed to follow through with practices, resources and personnel necessary to transform theory into reality."[50] The court ordered the state to correct the deficiencies.

The case returned to the court in 2006, when the Superintendent of Public Instruction and legislative leaders insisted that they had done what was needed and it was time for the federal court to terminate its remedial order and end the case. However, the district court in 2007 concluded that "More than 7 years later, circumstances … remain the same."[51]

A sharply divided U.S. Supreme Court ruled in favor of the state officials who demanded termination of the order.[52] The four dissenters pointed out that the state of Arizona, the Arizona Board of Public Instruction, and the U.S. Department of Justice supported the claims of the family, together with the findings of the lower courts that the state had not remedied the problems that had started the case all those years before, and that in several respects the trend was moving in the wrong direction.

While that case was pending, something else happened that raised serious questions among Latinos with respect to ELL instruction. The enactment of the No Child Left Behind Act of 2001 required testing in districts throughout the nation. It also was a period that saw a rise in Charter Schools—schools that receive public funding but are not part of the regular public school system. There has been continuing concern about whether ELL students are being excluded or just not counted in records and reporting documents in order to avoid issues under testing programs. Although it did not investigate any issue of intentional failure to include ELL students in records and reports, the Government Accountability Office (GAO) issued a report confirming that there is a significant problem in terms of a lack of record-keeping and reporting of ELL students in charter schools.[53] The GAO report explained that "for over one-third of charter schools, the field for reporting the counts of ELLs enrolled in ELL programs was left blank."[54]

And, notwithstanding the issues with ESL (English as a second language) and ELL programs in various places, others have had the experience of having schools mandate ESL/ELL assessments for their children who were born, raised, and educated in the United States when they moved to a new school district or a different state, simply because the child had a Hispanic surname or appeared to be Latino.

Some of the more recent actions discussed above designed to block or discourage the speaking of Spanish now find their way into the newspapers, but the problems persist. These situations today bring back memories for many Latino parents, who remember that, as children, they were punished in school for speaking Spanish. It would be comforting to think that those days had ended, but the evidence is clear that the problem continues. In March 2014 the contract of the principal of a Hempstead, Texas middle school was not renewed by the district after she warned students over the school intercom not to speak Spanish in class. This was in a district that is over 50% Hispanic.[55] Augustin Pinedo, Regional Director of the League of United Latin American Citizens, was quoted in the media with respect to the events in Hempstead: "When you start banning aspects of ethnicity or cultural identity, it sends the message that the child is not wanted: 'We don't want your color. We don't want your kind.' They then tend to drop out early."[56] If this were one incident in one state, it would be troubling enough; but sadly there have been others in other places as well.[57] To those in the Hispanic community who see this continuing train of attacks on the speaking of Spanish over decades that shows little sign of ending, and who do not see similar targeting of speakers of other languages, it is ludicrous to conclude that these actions are really about language as opposed to clear and continuing evidence of racism.

U.S. Attitudes and Actions against Latin America and its People: Harkening Back to the Conquest

The United States has a long history of malign neglect toward Latin American nations and their people. That history conveys in strong terms to many Latinos the message that the U.S. does not recognize those countries or the people who trace their ethnocultural heritage to them as deserving of equal stature or respect. They see this country consistently behaving toward those in Latin America in ways it does not and would not demonstrate toward others. And that pattern of behavior has not been directed only at one or two countries, but regionally in a way that makes it difficult to interpret it in a manner other than one of disrespect and discrimination. It is a pattern that conveys an attitude toward Latinos not only in terms of their countries or ethnicities of origin, but that also carries over in important ways into the United States and provides strong evidence of ingrained, systemic, and institutionalized racism. In order to understand this issue and its importance among Latinos, it is necessary to delve into the matter in some depth.

The Monroe Doctrine, the Roosevelt Corollary, and Manifest Destiny: U.S. Claims to Primacy

Consider first the historic foundations of that pattern of behavior that reach back to the early nineteenth century in the Monroe Doctrine and the concept of manifest destiny, and then some of the examples of that pattern of U.S. behavior over the decades since then. The discussion turns next to a modest selection of opinions that speak to this situation in U.S. courts.

In his annual address to Congress in 1823, President James Monroe presented what has come to be known as the Monroe Doctrine, warning Europeans not to try to intervene in or control Latin American countries and asserting U.S. authority to set boundaries on Latin American policy. He said in part:

> We owe it, therefore, to candor and to the amicable relations existing between the United States and those [European] powers to declare that we should consider any attempt on their part to extend their system to any portion of this hemisphere as dangerous to our peace and safety. With the existing colonies or dependencies of any European power we have not interfered and shall not interfere. But with the Governments who have declared their independence and maintain it, and whose independence we have, on great consideration and on just principles, acknowledged, we could not view any interposition for the purpose of oppressing them, or controlling in any other manner their destiny, by any European power in any other light than as the manifestation of an unfriendly disposition toward the United States. In the war between those new Governments and

Spain we declared our neutrality at the time of their recognition, and to this we have adhered, and shall continue to adhere, provided no change shall occur which, in the judgement of the competent authorities of this Government, shall make a corresponding change on the part of the United States indispensable to their security.

It is impossible that the allied powers should extend their political system to any portion of either continent without endangering our peace and happiness; nor can anyone believe that our southern brethren, if left to themselves, would adopt it of their own accord. It is equally impossible, therefore, that we should behold such interposition in any form with indifference. If we look to the comparative strength and resources of Spain and those new Governments, and their distance from each other, it must be obvious that she can never subdue them.[58]

At the time, the president's warnings appeared primarily designed for European powers that might be contemplating an intrusion into Latin American affairs. However, President Theodore Roosevelt extended and sharpened the Monroe Doctrine in what has come to be known as the Roosevelt Corollary, so as to claim U.S. authority to intervene in Latin American countries when the U.S. considered it necessary.

It is not true that the United States feels any land hunger or entertains any projects as regards the other nations of the Western Hemisphere save such as are for their welfare. All that this country desires is to see the neighboring countries stable, orderly, and prosperous. Any country whose people conduct themselves well can count upon our hearty friendship. If a nation shows that it knows how to act with reasonable efficiency and decency in social and political matters, if it keeps order and pays its obligations, it need fear no interference from the United States. Chronic wrongdoing, or an impotence which results in a general loosening of the ties of civilized society, may in America, as elsewhere, ultimately require intervention by some civilized nation, and in the Western Hemisphere the adherence of the United States to the Monroe Doctrine may force the United States, however reluctantly, in flagrant cases of such wrongdoing or impotence, to the exercise of an international police power. If every country washed by the Caribbean Sea would show the progress in stable and just civilization which with the aid of the Platt Amendment Cuba has shown since our troops left the island, and which so many of the republics in both Americas are constantly and brilliantly showing, all question of interference by this Nation with their affairs would be at an end. Our interests and those of our southern neighbors are in reality identical.... While they thus obey the primary laws of civilized society they may rest assured that they will be treated by us in a spirit of cordial and helpful sympathy. We would interfere with them only in the last resort, and then only if it became evident that their inability or unwillingness to do justice at home and abroad had violated the rights of the United States or had invited foreign aggression to the detriment of the entire body of American nations....

In asserting the Monroe Doctrine, in taking such steps as we have taken in regard to Cuba, Venezuela, and Panama ... we have acted in our own interest as well as in the interest of humanity at large. There are, however, cases in which, while our own interests are not greatly involved, strong appeal is made to our sympathies. Ordinarily it is very much wiser and more useful for us to concern ourselves with striving for our own moral and material betterment here at home than to concern ourselves with trying to better the condition of things in other nations.... Nevertheless there are occasional crimes committed on so vast a scale and of such peculiar horror as to make us doubt whether it is not our manifest duty to endeavor at least to show our disapproval of the deed and our sympathy with those who have suffered by it. The cases must be extreme in which such a course is justifiable. There must be no effort made to remove the mote from our brother's eye if we refuse to remove the beam from our own. But in extreme cases action may be justifiable and proper. What form the action shall take must depend upon the circumstances of the case; that is, upon the degree of the atrocity and upon our power to remedy it.[59]

The Monroe Doctrine and the Roosevelt Corollary would be repeatedly cited as authority for U.S. intervention throughout Latin America in the decades that followed. This unilateral claim to hegemony over the hemisphere has not been recognized or accepted by other nations in the region. Even so, read in their most favorable light, these declarations may appear only to offer support and assistance; but when coupled with the U.S. claims to manifest destiny, other nations in the Americas see them differently and as far from benign.

The term manifest destiny refers to a concept that asserts a right to dominion over the entire continent and, when understood alongside the Monroe Doctrine, has been extended to encompass the hemisphere. The term manifest destiny goes back to the writings of a newspaper editor, John L. O'Sullivan, who first used it in 1839 as he argued in support of the annexation of Texas, but it had its greatest effect after he used it in an 1845 editorial about the U.S. claim to the Oregon territory.[60] It was then employed in the congressional debate on the subject as such "a convenient summing up of the self-confident nationalist and expansionist sentiment of the time that it passed into the permanent national vocabulary."[61] In that debate, Representative Robert C. Winthrop of Massachusetts said that the U.S. claim over Oregon was most fundamentally justified by:

> that new revelation of right which has been designated as the right of our manifest destiny to spread over this whole continent. It has been openly avowed in a leading Administration journal that this, after all, is our best and strongest title—one so clear, so pre-eminent, and so indisputable, that if Great Britain had all our other titles in addition to her own, they would weigh nothing against it. The right of our manifest destiny![62]

This claim could be and has been read as an assertion of cultural and political superiority to others who are indigenous people of what is now the United States, as well as the people of Latin American countries; and it has indeed been used repeatedly in exactly that manner.

The Pattern of U.S. Intervention in Latin America: Repeated Assertions of Superiority

One of the first demonstrations of the impact of manifest destiny was the U.S. war against Mexico in 1846. President Polk had sent troops into disputed territory in order to provoke a clash and create a pretext for the invasion of Mexico that would permit the U.S. to seize large portions of Mexican territory. That war ended with the Treaty of Guadalupe Hidalgo (discussed earlier), by which the U.S. acquired major parts of what is today the southwestern U.S. The U.S. would have grabbed more land except for the fact that Nicholas Trist, who had been sent by Polk to negotiate a resolution, ignored additional instructions from the president and reached agreement on the Guadalupe Hidalgo treaty.[63]

Expansionist efforts were not limited to official U.S. foreign policy. William Walker, a San Francisco doctor, lawyer, and journalist, led a small group of men into Baja California, where he took over the capital of the region and promptly renamed it the Republic of Lower California, set himself up as president, and declared slavery legal. He tried to take Sonora but failed, and returned to the U.S. He later went to Nicaragua, took control of the country, and declared himself president in 1855—a government that was quickly recognized by then President Franklin Pierce. However, Costa Rica and other countries saw Walker as a threat to all of Central America and sent a group to drive him out, an effort that was supported by Cornelius Vanderbilt and others who wanted Walker out of the way of their business enterprises. Walker was expelled, but returned later, only to be turned over to the Nicaraguan military, who executed him in 1860.

After the Civil War, as westward movement continued and industrialization drove change in the nation, the U.S. began again to watch events abroad, including the clash between Cuban revolutionaries and Spain. The U.S. asserted the Monroe Doctrine and events led to war with Spain in 1898. Following that war, the U.S. found itself with the previous Spanish possessions of Puerto Rico, Guam, and the Philippines. The peace also promised independence for Cuba and a commitment by the U.S. not to annex the island, but it also meant that the U.S. would be the dominant power in the Caribbean region.

Just three years later, the Theodore Roosevelt administration concluded the Hay–Pauncefote Treaty with Great Britain under which the U.S. would build and operate what came to be known as the Panama Canal. When U.S. efforts to negotiate an agreement with Colombia broke down, the U.S. backed an independence movement in that part of the country that was to become Panama. Roosevelt sent warships to both the Atlantic and Pacific sides of the country, giving rise to the term "gun-boat diplomacy" during the Roosevelt years and after.[64] The U.S. quickly concluded the Hay–Bunau–Varilla Treaty of 1903, which gave the U.S. control over the canal zone and provided a U.S. guarantee for Panamanian independence.[65] These actions and the treaty also meant nearly a century of U.S. presence in Central America until the Carter administration returned control of the canal zone to Panama.

These events coupled with the Roosevelt Corollary to the Monroe Doctrine also led, during the Roosevelt, Wilson, and later administrations, to interventions in Haiti, the Dominican Republic, Cuba, Nicaragua, and Mexico. The U.S. involvement in the region was in no sense limited to Panama.[66]

The coming of the Cold War after World War II shaped decades of U.S. action in the region. Shortly after taking office, President Eisenhower issued a national security directive (NSC 144/1) that established a Cold War policy for Latin America based on concerns about a trend "toward radical and nationalistic regimes" that saw Latin America in Cold War terms.[67] One of the first targets of the new administration's policy was Guatemala, and in August 1953 the president, through the National Security Council, authorized covert action there.[68] A month later the Central Intelligence Agency (CIA) produced a "General Plan of Action" to remove the democratically elected government of Jacobo Arbenz Guzmán that went forward as Operation PB Success.[69]

Actually, the coup was the result of a campaign by the United Fruit Company and its lobbyists, with John Foster Dulles and Allen Dulles as key advocates in the Department of State and the CIA. As CIA historian Nick Cullather explained in his 1994 report for the agency, the Arbenz government came to office after a free and fair election and neither he nor his government was communist.[70] In fact, at the time one of Eisenhower's friends noted that there were more communists in San Francisco than in Guatemala.[71] Arbenz was committed to a variety of reforms to address serious economic problems and growing social tensions that stemmed from a dramatic and widening gap between the rich and the poor in Guatemala. For example, his government adopted a new labor code that permitted unions and collective bargaining. He also launched a program of land reforms, under which uncultivated land would be taken with compensation for redistribution. The United Fruit Company, a U.S. firm, complained about virtually all of these reforms to the U.S. embassy and the State Department. It particularly attacked the land reform, under which some of the company's uncultivated land was taken with compensation at the value that the company itself had placed on the land for tax purposes. The firm engaged a public relations and lobbying campaign in Washington to prompt intervention by the U.S. government.[72]

The Eisenhower administration decided to replace Arbenz and the coup went forward in mid-1954. In the aftermath, the U.S. supported numerous right-wing dictatorships that had been deadly violators of human rights. These actions also ensured that those in Central America and other parts of Latin America would have a solid set of reasons for resentment and distrust of the United States, and a clear sense that they were seen as pawns to be manipulated and ignored when they were not useful to the U.S. Indeed, the CIA's Chief Historian J. Kenneth McDonald wrote: "In light of Guatemala's unstable and often violent history since the fall of Jacobo Arbenz Guzmán in 1954, we are perhaps less certain today than Americans were at the time that this operation was a Cold War victory."[73]

McDonald went on to point out that "Allan Dulles' CIA concluded that the apparent triumph in Guatemala, in spite of a long series of blunders in both planning and execution, made PBSUCCESS a sound model for future operations." It was a model "that failed so disastrously as a guide for an ambitious attempt to overthrow Fidel Castro at the Bay of Pigs in 1961."[74] Ironically, as McDonald indicated, many in the CIA and elsewhere consider the Guatemala coup a success. Indeed, Cullather quoted then CIA case officer E. Howard Hunt: "If the Agency had not had Guatemala, … it probably would not have had Cuba."[75] Unfortunately, just over two months after taking office President John F. Kennedy approved the Bay of Pigs operation, Operation JMATE.[76]

The Bay of Pigs disaster only marked the beginning of a lengthy covert effort, Operation Mongoose, to overthrow Castro.[77] Although Mongoose was supposedly suspended in 1962, a long-running covert campaign designed to topple the Castro regime continued long after that and included a wide range of tactics, including economic warfare.[78] Ironically, the U.S. covert efforts over the next several decades helped Castro make the case that Cuba was a country under siege, and helped him justify even harsher constraints on the liberty of its citizens while attracting engagement from those who were rivals of the U.S. for power and influence. Those actions, in turn, fed a toxic political dynamic that persisted for years, as anti-Castro groups in the U.S. used them to support continued assistance for their cause. At the same time other Latinos in the U.S. and elsewhere asked why the U.S. continued its isolation of Cuba when it was perfectly prepared to engage with the People's Republic of China and other countries with human rights records at least as deplorable as that of Cuba.

As part of its post-Bay of Pigs political charm offensive, the Kennedy administration launched the Alliance for Progress, but as the State Department historian explains, the promise of Latin American development assistance did not last long, and in fact most U.S. assistance took the form of military assistance. It became another phase of Cold War operations aimed more at discouraging the political left rather than a serious commitment to address the social and economic disparities and poverty of the region.[79]

Cold War tendencies to see any politics left of center as communist or likely to lead to communism, along with protection of U.S. companies and economic interests, were very much at the heart of the Nixon administration's actions in Chile, Argentina, and Uruguay.

In Chile, even before Nixon came to office, the U.S. provided money to support the campaign of Eduardo Frei and his Christian Democratic Party in 1964.[80] In the 1970 election the U.S. worked first to block the election of Salvador Allende and his Popular Unity (Unidad Popular or UP), a coalition of groups from the political left. When the Nixon administration could not prevent the election, there were efforts to prevent Allende from taking office. Once in office, Allende launched a series of economic and social policies that included nationalization of copper businesses owned by two U.S. companies and the telephone system that had been an ITT enterprise.

The Nixon administration, with the particular advocacy of then National Security Adviser Henry Kissinger (a month later he would also be appointed Secretary of State), was hopeful that the Allende regime would be removed. On September 11, 1973 a military coup did just that and placed in power General Augusto Pinochet, a brutal dictator who ended elections and ruled ruthlessly. Although CIA officials continue to deny direct involvement in the coup itself, there is no question that there was a careful effort by the CIA and by Kissinger in both the Nixon and Ford administrations to support Pinochet and his dictatorship, even in the face of evidence of massive arrests, disappearances, and executions. Just two days after the coup the State Department sent a cable to the U.S. embassy in Chile, stating in part: "The USG wishes to make clear its desire to cooperate with the military junta and to cooperate in an appropriate way."[81] Just over a month after the coup the CIA reported that an estimated 1,600 civilians had been killed by the regime and some 13,500 people had been taken prisoner by the military.[82] Despite the fact that reports indicated ongoing human rights violations, the U.S. continued support for the regime, with the Secretary of State telling General Pinochet in 1976 that: "You did a great service to the world in overthrowing Allende."[83] He explained to Pinochet that for domestic U.S. political reasons he was going to have to give a speech calling on the junta to address reports of human rights violations, but made it clear to Pinochet that he was strongly supportive and that it was necessary to make such public statements or face serious constraints by the Congress on the Ford administration's ability to provide assistance to Chile. "My evaluation is that you are a victim of all left-wing groups around the world, and your greatest sin was that you overthrew a government that was going Communist."[84]

In Argentina there were intense internal tensions among political forces and particularly between the conservative elites and those demanding reform. By the mid-1970s the situation was deteriorating rapidly and the military launched a coup in March 1976 that removed the civilian government of Isabel Perón, and put in place a military junta who took the Chilean coup as a model, including dramatic actions that were intended to terrorize and break the back of any political opposition. As part of those efforts, which became known as the "dirty war," there were massive arrests, extra-judicial killings, and large numbers of people labeled as the "disappeared." Three months into the junta's rule Secretary Kissinger met with Admiral Guzzetti, the Chilean foreign minister in Santiago. Guzzetti told Kissinger that:

> Our main problem in Argentina is terrorism.... There are two aspects to the solution. The first is to ensure the internal security of the country; the second is to solve the most urgent economic problems over the next 6 to 12 months. Argentina needs United States understanding and support to overcome problems in these two areas."[85]

Kissinger replied: "We wish the new government well. We wish it will succeed. We will do what we can to help it succeed. We are aware you are in a difficult period.... We understand you must establish authority." Guzzetti complained that there appeared to be an international press conspiracy against the junta, to which Kissinger commented: "The worst crime as far as the press is concerned is to have replaced a government of the left."[86]

After a discussion of the problem of international perceptions of the regime, Kissinger warned that they should do what they needed to do to deal with people they considered terrorists and criminals, but they needed to get it over with quickly. He said: "If there are things that have to be done, you should do them quickly. But you must get back quickly to normal procedures."[87] Guzzetti reported this conversation to President Videla and his colleagues as U.S. approval of their actions and encouragement to deal with those who were considered problematic quickly. In fact, when U.S. Ambassador Robert Hill asked Admiral Guzzetti what the government was going to do to address violations of human rights and specifically the murder of priests and the mass murder at Pilar, the ambassador indicated in his report to Kissinger that Guzzetti expressed surprise that there was such concern about these events. The Ambassador said:

> When he had seen SCY of State Kissinger in Santiago, the latter had said "He hoped the Argentine Govt would get the terrorist problem under control as quickly as possible." Guzzetti said that he had reported this to President Videla and to the Cabinet, and that their impression had been that USG's overriding concern was not human rights but rather that GOA "get it over quickly."[88]

Ambassador Hill was particularly frustrated when Guzzetti returned from a visit to Washington in October 1976, ecstatic with the reception he received and the reinforcement of the message to just get it over with quickly. He could not see how he could try to address the violations while Washington was giving conflicting messages. Hill wrote:

> Guzzetti's remarks both to me and to the Argentine press since his return are not those of a man who has been impressed with the gravity of the human rights problem as seen from the U.S. both personally and professionally and in [the press] account of his trip. Guzzetti's reaction indicates little reason for concern over the human rights issue. Guzzetti went to the US fully expecting to hear some strong, firm, direct warning of his govt's human rights practices. Rather than that, he has returned, in a state of jubilation, convinced that there is no real problem with the USG over this issue. Based on what Guzzetti is doubtless reporting to the GOA, it must now believe that if it has any problems with the US over human rights, they are confined to certain elements of Congress and what it regards as biased and/or uninformed minor segments of public opinion. While that conviction lasts it will be unrealistic and unbelievable for this embassy to press representations to the GOA over human rights violations.[89]

By 1978 an Argentine military intelligence report indicated that some 22,000 persons had been killed or disappeared in the period from 1975 to 1978.[90] That number is far more than the 9,089 figure used by the National Commission on the Disappeared (CONADEP) or the 15,000 reported by U.S. embassy official F. Allen "Tex" Harris.[91]

While the events in Chile and Argentina and the U.S. involvement with them captured international press attention and congressional criticism, there were other operations in progress. The U.S. joined efforts by Great Britain to influence the outcome of the elections in Uruguay in 1970. Even more expansive was U.S. support and encouragement for Operation Condor, a joint operation of the intelligence services of Argentina, Bolivia, Brazil, Chile, Uruguay, and Paraguay to locate, capture, and return those targeted as terrorists or dissidents in one of the member countries to the country of origin, where they were often executed. As CIA documents show, Operation Condor also provided a vehicle for psychological warfare cooperation.[92] An example was an agreement to plant a news story provided by one country's government in the media of another country to make it appear that the story was unbiased reporting about those targeted. The U.S. was supportive of the efforts of Operation Condor, although it denied having played a role in its creation. Latin American military personnel, however, indicated that Operation Condor had strong ties to officers trained at the School of the Americas, a base that trained large numbers of military personnel from a variety of Latin American countries, then operated by the U.S. in Panama and later moved to Georgia.[93]

Then attention turned once again to Central America, but that attention led to another sad chapter in U.S. policy toward Latin America. President Carter repeatedly asserted his intentions to be sensitive to human rights and to avoid interventions in Latin America, but his administration clearly was not ready to deal with the reality of a region where repression at the hands of authoritarian juntas was rampant and there was dramatic intensification of the gap between the rich and the poor. Like their predecessors, Carter administration officials were ready to see any serious effort at reform or change in Latin America as communist-inspired. U.S. policy continued to emphasize stability and control as compared to an acceptance of an inevitably complex and difficult process of change in a more positive direction for the countries of the region.

With the collapse in Nicaragua of Somosa's rule, another corrupt and brutal regime, and the success of the Sandanistas who came to power, U.S. fear of communism or leftist governments (which were simply assumed to be communist or communist-inspired) only intensified. The Carter administration maintained what can charitably be described as false hope that any of the ruling governments were going to be moderate or reformist, as Secretary of State Cyrus Vance described the junta in El Salvador in March 1980, even though massive bloodshed and assassinations were already well known to have taken place.[94] Indeed, El Salvador saw dramatic abuses both from the Duarte government and from right-wing death squads. The Carter administration thought it was supporting Duarte to avoid an even worse right-wing junta or a communist takeover, so it continued military assistance to El Salvador in 1979 and 1980, which intensified military operations against civilians and the hunt for anyone regarded as leftist.

The assassination of Archbishop Oscar Romero marked a dramatic low. Romero had been conservative and was hardly regarded as a threat to anyone. In fact, his appointment as bishop was supported by the Salvadoran establishment.[95] However, the parish priest of El Paisnal village, Father Rutillo Grande, as well as a boy and an old man who went with him to mass, were killed in March 1977, their bodies riddled with bullets. Romero regarded Rutillo as a committed priest and a close friend. His death moved Romero and others to press for an end to the violence and repression of the regime, and demand protection from others outside government who were allowed to wage an illegal and bloody campaign against anyone they regarded as a threat or a reformer. Indeed, just before his assassination Grande had warned that everything was being labeled subversive and that soon only the covers of the Bible would be permitted, since everything inside was obviously considered subversive and that Jesus himself would be prevented from entering the country as a foreign troublemaker. Romero demanded answers from the government about Grande's assassination and instead simply found himself criticized, not only by the government and the right-wing groups, but also by other bishops who did not want him to ask uncomfortable questions.

Romero was extremely troubled that the Carter administration was continuing to provide military assistance to the government and urged that the aid stop. His position and willingness to tell the truth about what was happening also attracted many Salvadorans to him, which only made him more of a target. In a 1978 visit with Pope John Paul II he explained the situation in El Salvador and came away with a sense of support. However, a year later when Romero met with the Pope, he left dejected because the Pope had made it clear that he was not listening to Romero but to Romero's critics. Meanwhile, the U.S. government was pressuring Romero to step back. Romero met with the Pope for the last time in January 1980 and it was clear that he was both on his own and in trouble in the Vatican.

Romero published an open letter to President Carter, warning that the previous military assistance to the government had only led to stepped-up violence and repression and calling on him to stop the aid. Secretary of State Vance wrote back to him to let him know that would not happen, and indeed that the Carter administration considered the government of El Salvador to be "moderate and reformist." Romero gave a homily directed to soldiers and others, asking them to stop the violence and refuse to kill innocent people. He was assassinated soon afterwards on March 24, 1980 while saying mass in a chapel of the hospital where he lived.

Later John Paul II would open a cause for sainthood for him, but that effort was suspended. A month after stepping into the papacy, Pope Francis unblocked the process for sainthood for Romero and made a point of saying so very directly in a news conference on board his return flight from a trip to Korea. Part of expediting that process depended upon whether Romero was considered a martyr, a decision which was forthcoming in January 2015. At the time he announced the action on Romero, Pope Francis also made it known that once that matter was cleared up, Father Grande's case would be a priority.

If the Carter administration's actions were considered naive or at least based upon a completely inadequate understanding of the situation in Central America, the Reagan administration's approach was direct, purposeful, and disastrous, leaving thousands dead in its wake as it actively supported ruthless regimes in several nations in the region, none more so than those in Nicaragua, El Salvador, and Guatemala. It was Cold War power politics and ideological action at its most intense level. Stability and control were the watchwords and anything left of that was regarded as a threat, if not a direct result of action by the Soviet Union and its clients.

Less than two months after taking office in early 1981, the Reagan administration launched its covert operations, first with the establishment of the CIA Central American Task Force and later in the year with the issuance by the president of a presidential finding that provided authorization for covert CIA action with $19 million in support for those opposing the Sandinista government.[96] The president also immediately authorized money and military advisers to support the government of El Salvador. Even after Congress tried in 1982 to block the Reagan actions with the Boland Amendment,[97] the White House moved through what became known as the Iran/Contra affairs to create a vehicle for exchanging missiles with Iran for money that could be laundered and funneled back to the Contras in Nicaragua seeking to bring down the Sandinista regime.[98]

Support for the right-wing dictatorship in El Salvador intensified and efforts by refugees to come to the U.S. to escape the carnage were singled out for rejection. The civil war in El Salvador in which the U.S was supporting repressive regimes left some 75,000 civilians dead and another 8,000 missing, or as the term is used in Latin America, disappeared and presumed dead.[99] Over time, and despite continued refusal of the government to provide information to the United Nations Truth Commission created as part of the peace agreement in 1991, evidence emerged that provided some of the gruesome details of the disappearances, tortures, and murders committed by the governments, including the so-called *Libro Amarillo* (Yellow Book), which contains names, pictures, biographies, and target information.[100] Ironically, the actions of the military and civilian right-wing death squads sparked the rise and development of the Farabundo Martí National Liberation Front (FMLN), which attracted support from Cuba and elsewhere. The UN Truth Commission found that the FMLN's tactics in turn led to a dramatic expansion in the indiscriminate air and ground attacks on civilians. Indeed, the Commission found that in addition to the deaths and disappearances during the period, there were half a million displaced persons within El Salvador and another 245,500 refugees outside the country.[101] Through all of this, the U.S. provided money, weapons, and military training, a fact not lost on Latinos. Indeed, the U.S. violated the neutrality of friendly countries like Costa Rica and engaged in a range of covert activities to support the Contras that violated U.S. law. Lawrence E. Walsh, the Iran-Contra Independent Counsel, found, among other things, that:

- the sale of arms to Iran contravened United States Government policy and may have violated the Arms Export Control Act;
- the provision and coordination of support to the Contras violated the Boland Amendment ban on aid to military activities in Nicaragua;

- the policies behind both the Iran and Contra operations were fully reviewed and developed at the highest levels of the Reagan Administration;
- although there was little evidence of National Security Council (NSC) level knowledge of most of the actual Contra-support operations, there was no evidence that any NSC member dissented from the underlying policy—keeping the Contras alive despite congressional limitations on Contra support;
- the Iran operations were carried out with the knowledge of, among others, President Ronald Reagan, Vice President George Bush, Secretary of Defense Casper W. Weinberger, Director of Central Intelligence William J. Casey, and national security advisers Robert C. McFarlane and John M. Poindexter. Of these officials, only Weinberger and [Secretary of State George P.] Shultz dissented from the policy decision, and Weinberger eventually acquiesced by ordering the Department of Defense to provide the necessary arms;
- large volumes of highly relevant, contemporaneously created documents were systematically and willfully withheld from investigation by several Reagan administration officials; and
- following the revelation of these operations in October and November 1986, Reagan administration officials deliberately deceived the Congress and the public about the level and extent of official knowledge of and support for these operations.[102]

Eleven of those involved in the Iran/Contra affair were convicted or pleaded guilty as a result of the matter, but the convictions of the president's National Security Advisor John M. Poindexter and National Security Council staff member Lt. Col. Oliver North were overturned, largely because the congressional committee investigating the matter had granted wide-ranging immunity in return for testimony and prosecutors could not prove that none of that information was used in the later prosecution.[103] Other cases were pending at the end of the George Herbert Walker Bush administration, but he granted an eleventh-hour pardon in the form of Proclamation 6518 to those involved, including defense secretary Casper Weinberger, Elliott Abrams, Duane Clarridge, Alan Fiers, Clair George, and Robert McFarlane. This pardon was issued just before President Bush was to leave office and the trial of former Secretary of Defense Weinberger was to begin that would likely have included calls for evidence from Bush. The fact that those deeply implicated in the deaths and destruction in El Salvador and neighboring countries escaped accountability for their actions was not lost on anyone in Latin America. It was also not lost on anyone that some of those figures, including Eliot Abrams, resurfaced in significant roles in the George W. Bush administration.

In Guatemala, the years following the U.S.-sponsored coup saw one repressive regime after another, which only intensified with a civil conflict lasting more than three decades and formally ending with the Oslo Peace Accords in 1994. The Commission for Historical Clarifications (CEH), sometimes referred to as the Guatemalan Truth Commission, created by the Oslo accords, began its report by explaining that:

> Guatemala has seen periods marked by beauty and dignity from the beginning of the ancient Mayan culture to the present day.... However, in Guatemala, pages have also been written of shame and infamy, disgrace and terror, pain and grief, all as a product of the armed confrontation among brothers and sisters. For more than 34 years, Guatemalans lived under the shadow of fear, death and disappearance as daily threats in the lives of ordinary citizens.[104]

During that time the Commission found a total of 200,000 people had been killed or disappeared during that time. Not only was this a period of violent repression, but it was also a genocidal attack on the Maya. Of the specific cases that the CEH documented, some "eighty-three percent of fully identified victims were Mayan."[105] It further concluded that:

> state forces and related paramilitary groups were responsible for 93% of the violations documented by the CEH, including 92% of the arbitrary executions and 91% of forced disappearances. Victims included men, women and children of all social strata: workers, professionals, church members, politicians, peasants, students and academics; in ethnic terms, the vast majority were Mayans.[106]

The Commission found that these casualties among the Maya were intentional.

> In consequence, the CEH concludes that agents of the State of Guatemala, within the framework of counterinsurgency operations carried out between 1981 and 1983, committed acts of genocide [within the meaning of Article II of UN Convention on Prevention and Punishment of the Crime of Genocide] against groups of Mayan people.[107]

And as the Commission found, the U.S. was implicated throughout in its support for the Guatemalan military, and especially during the 1980s. The report also estimated somewhere between half a million and a million and a half persons were internally displaced or forced to leave the country as refugees in fear for their lives.[108]

For many Latinos the question was why the lives of children, women, and men in Latin American countries have counted for so little, even as the U.S. denounced countries like Cuba and the Soviet Union for human rights violations and a lack of freedom and democracy. It was a continuation and intensification of a long, brutal history that conveyed the message that these people somehow do not seem to matter to U.S. officials. The actions suggested that Latinos were not to be seen as equal, and certainly not to be afforded equal protection under the law or the principles of democracy that the U.S. so often proclaimed. They were dramatic evidence of systemic and institutionalized racism at its worst.

As the recent history demonstrates, U.S. actions in Central America had a great deal to do with the fact that so many people became refugees and a significant number sought asylum in the United States. When they arrived in the U.S., they found that what was then the Immigration and Naturalization Service (INS) was quick to grant asylum seekers from Cuba or Nicaragua refugee status, but rejected applicants from El Salvador and Guatemala.[109] A Senate Judiciary Committee report in 1987 found that: "an estimated 62,000 innocent civilians have been killed since the start of the current civil war in El Salvador."[110] In spite of that situation, "In the first half of FY 1987, the Immigration and Naturalization Service granted asylum to 3 percent of those Salvadoran asylum applications adjudicated and 88 percent of those by Nicaraguans."[111] It became clear that asylum seekers from other places were being treated very differently. In fact, during the same period of time the U.S. government granted refugee status to 49 percent of those coming from Poland and 66 percent of applicants from Iran receiving asylum in the same period of time. That was true despite the fact that in these countries there was not the kind of large-scale systematic violence against civilians that was clearly the case in El Salvador and Guatemala.[112]

The persistent pattern of political discrimination against Salvadorans and Guatemalans was too clear to ignore. Although it refused to formally admit the discrimination, the U.S. government settled the *American Baptist Churches v. Thornburgh* case by consent decree, which was, as a practical matter if not in technical legal terms, an admission of discrimination.[113] It the process, the government recognized that:

> foreign policy and border enforcement considerations are not relevant to the determination of whether an applicant for asylum has a well-founded fear of prosecution; the

fact than an individual is from a country whose government the United States supports or with which it has favorable relations is not relevant to the determination of whether an application for asylum has a well-founded fear of persecution; whether or not the United States Government agrees with the political or ideological beliefs of the individual is not relevant to the determination of whether an applicant for asylum has a well-founded fear of persecution."[114]

The U.S. agreed to reexamine all of the Salvadoran and Guatemalan refugee claimants. However, the INS was not staffed adequately to handle all of those cases in a timely fashion and the government showed virtually no interest in taking the steps necessary to meet its obligations under the settlement. Beyond that, those who had clearly been discriminated against so badly before were asked to come forward for what many of them had good reason to believe was likely to be bad treatment again. Given these factors, the government tacitly accepted the fact that there would be thousands of refugees left completely adrift in the U.S. as undocumented persons, with no access to assistance and in legal limbo, who would continue to bear the burden for what the ABC settlement clearly established had been discriminatory and illegal treatment in the first place.

The fact is that the discriminatory treatment continued after the settlement, as the following opinion from the U.S. Circuit Court of Appeals for the Second Circuit makes clear.[115] Consider this one case as an example of the kind of situation that asylum seekers from Guatemala and El Salvador faced.

Osorio v. Immigration and Naturalization Service

18 F.3d 1017 (2nd Cir. 1994)

Judge Oakes wrote the opinion for the panel.

> On March 15, 1989, Vicente Osorio, a Guatemalan union leader, and his wife, Maria Aracely Morales, entered the United States in violation of [The Immigration] Act.... They sought asylum or, in the alternative, withholding of deportation.... Instead, on August 22, 1990, Immigration Judge John K. Speer (the "IJ") denied Osorio's application for asylum, or withholding of deportation.... On April 22, 1993, the Board of Immigration Appeals (the "BIA") affirmed. We now reverse the BIA's denial of Osorio's eligibility for asylum and order that withholding of deportation be granted to Osorio.
>
> ... [I]n effect, the BIA held that, as a matter of law, a Guatemalan union leader, who is persecuted on account of his or her membership in or leadership of a union and the activities that flow therefrom, is not eligible for asylum on any basis.... We now hold that the BIA's interpretation of "political asylum" was incorrect as a matter of law because it contradicts the plain language of the statute, and ignores the interpretation of "political asylum" as set forth by the Supreme Court.... We further hold that Osorio has ... demonstrat[ed] his eligibility for political asylum and withholding of deportation.
>
> ... Osorio, is a former Guatemalan sanitation worker, who began working for the City of Guatemala in 1971. In 1984, Osorio became a member of the union, Sindicato Central de Trabajadores Municipales (Central Municipal Workers Union) (the "SCTM"). On February 7, 1984, he was elected to the SCTM's Executive Committee for a two-year term. In February 1986, Osorio's co-workers re-elected him to a second term. Of the 6,000 municipal workers in Guatemala City at that time, 3,500 were members of the SCTM. As a member of the SCTM

Executive Committee, Osorio was in charge of 500 employees at his work site. Furthermore, as a union leader, Osorio negotiated with the municipal government, and organized demonstrations and strikes—including a strike in April 1986 in which the Guatemalan central government sent police into a municipal building overtaken by the strikers; the police beat and attacked the workers with tear gas.

On November 12, 1986, the SCTM held a general strike of more than 3,000 workers because, as Osorio testified, the "rights of the workers were being trampled upon." The strike lasted only eleven days because, as Osorio testified, union members were being killed. The SCTM Executive Committee went to the Guatemalan Labor Minister for help. Although the Minister declared the strike illegal, he agreed to act as a mediator between the SCTM and the Mayor. In November or December of 1986, the Mayor of Guatemala City selectively fired Osorio and 75 other union members for engaging in the illegal strike.

Several acts of violence against members of the SCTM punctuated the time leading to the November 1986 strike. First, on January 17, 1986, several unidentified armed men shot and killed SCTM member Efrain Cotzal Sisimit in Guatemala City. Then, in February of that year, three heavily-armed men kidnapped SCTM Finance Secretary Jose Mercedes Sotz Cate, who was beaten before escaping from his abductors. Three months later, Sotz Cate witnessed the shooting of his three-year-old son, an attack undoubtedly meant for Sotz Cate himself, leaving the boy paralyzed from the waist down.... Then, on July 23, 1986, SCTM Secretary Justo Rufino Reyes was stabbed to death near the municipal building.... The IJ characterized these acts of violence surrounding the SCTM as "unfortunate incidents." Incredibly, the BIA makes no reference to these incidents in its decision, although it does discuss in detail the "illegal" November strike.... After the November strike, Osorio unsuccessfully sought reinstatement for the terminated workers. Osorio also testified that he could never again obtain employment in Guatemala City because of his SCTM activities.

Osorio also organized a mass media campaign. During his media appearances, Osorio accused the government of human rights violations, including charging the government with responsibility for the escalated killings and abductions of union members.... At this time, violence against the union and its members continued. For example, in 1987, SCTM member Carlos Oscal was kidnapped for three days. Furthermore, despite the election of a civilian government in 1986 to replace the former military dictatorship, violence against organized labor in general continued throughout the period between 1986 and 1989 when Osorio fled Guatemala....

In December 1988, Osorio received an anonymous note at his home warning him "to abandon the struggle, to stop with the outspokenness, because if I continue with the struggle and my outspokenness, something more serious would happen to me." ... In January 1989, Angel Melgar, a former rebel, suggested in a publicly-televised interview that certain unidentified Guatemalan unions had been infiltrated by subversive, communist guerrillas. Although Osorio denied that he or his union had been affiliated with the guerrillas, he feared that Melgar's charges left him open to government reprisal.... In February 1989, Osorio received a second note containing a death threat against him and his family. Fearing for their lives, Osorio and his wife fled Guatemala in March 1989.

... On March 15, 1989, officials in Texas arrested him and his wife, Maria Aracely Morales de Osorio, also a citizen of Guatemala, upon entering the United States without inspection in violation of the Act.... The Osorios have left in Guatemala three children, ages 8 to 15, currently cared for by their maternal grandmother. The only family tie of the Osorios in the United States is the aunt of Maria Aracely Morales, who is a legal permanent resident of the United States living in New York.... Although the Osorios are legally entitled to return to Guatemala, and although the Osorios wish to return to their homeland, Osorio stated that they cannot return to Guatemala at this time because "[he] believes [he] will be killed because of the death threat [he] received ... [He] would return to [his] country if the circumstances changed so that [he was] no longer in danger." ...

... According to the expert testimony of Frank Howard, an attorney with Americas Watch, which is a non-profit organization that monitors human rights abuses in Central America, there are two types of labor unions in Guatemala: independent and government-controlled. SCTM is an independent labor union. The independent labor unions of Guatemala historically have been at the forefront of democratic opposition to the military governments which ruled from 1954 through 1986. During this time, labor organizers and union members have suffered severe political repression as a result of their opposition activities....

After the election of the first civilian government in over thirty years, experts and commentators in the field speculated that the election of a civilian government would reduce, if not eliminate, the violence against union members and other individuals or groups considered by authorities to be subversive or leftist sympathizers.... This prediction never materialized.

"In several respects, the human rights situation has grown appreciably worse following each of two coup attempts in May 1988 and May 1989. In recent months political killings and other attacks have been targeted against prominent labor leaders, human rights activists, student leaders and others who are now or have been involved in political activities." ... Osorio presented substantial evidence that the Guatemalan civilian government also viewed the demands of the independent unions as a challenge to its authority rather than solely an economic matter of bargaining over the terms and conditions of employment....

... On March 23, 1990, the Osorios had a combined deportation and asylum hearing before the IJ.... At the hearing, Osorio testified about the abuses committed against several union colleagues for their union activities, including the abduction of Sotz Cate, the shooting of his son, and the stabbing death of Reyes. Taken in its entirety, Osorio's testimony establishes a pattern of government abuse against members of his union consistent with outside accounts of the political abuses against members of Guatemalan unions in general. On August 2, 1990 ... the IJ denied asylum and withholding of deportation to both Osorio and his wife....

Osorio immediately filed a notice of appeal with the BIA. Osorio asked the BIA to expedite consideration of his case because the Guatemalan authorities have been known to harm family members of union leaders (such as the son of Sotz Cate), and the Osorios had left their three small children in Guatemala.... Despite these repeated requests for expedition, the BIA's decision did not come down until April 22, 1993, over two and one-half years after the decision of the IJ. During the long delay, Amnesty International reported that Guatemalan authorities again threatened the life of Osorio's union colleague, Sotz Cate, forcing him to leave the country. The threatening letter read in part: "We are aware of the denunciations you made against the Government while you were abroad, and that you are back in Guatemala working in the trade union movement ... We are giving you a limited time to leave the country or else be physically eliminated." ...

An alien who enters the United States without inspection is subject to deportation proceedings.... Under such circumstances, the alien may apply for asylum in the United States or request withholding of deportation to a specific country if the "alien expresses fear of persecution or harm upon return to his country of origin or to a country to which he may be deported after exclusion from the United States."

... The government will grant Osorio's request for asylum if he can prove that (1) he is eligible for asylum, and (2) there are no significant reasons for denying asylum.... Osorio is eligible for asylum if he shows that he is a refugee within the meaning of section 101(a)(42)(A) of the Act... "The term 'refugee' means (A) any person who is outside any country of such person's nationality ... and who is unable or unwilling to return to, and is unable or unwilling to avail himself or herself of the protection of, that country because of persecution or a well-founded fear of persecution on account of race, religion, nationality, membership in a particular social group, or political opinion ... Moreover, the government may grant asylum to the children or spouse of Osorio if the government grants asylum to Osorio.... Osorio may establish his refugee status on one of two bases: (1) actual past persecution on account of Osorio's political opinions or his membership in a particular social group, or (2) well-founded fear of future persecution on account of Osorio's political opinions or his membership in a particular social group....

Congress has set forth five grounds of persecution: (1) race, (2) religion, (3) nationality, (4) membership in a particular social group, and (5) political opinion.... The key issue on appeal is whether Osorio's fear of future persecution is on account of two specific grounds for asylum: his political opinion or his membership in a social group. Assuming Osorio was persecuted because of his membership in or leadership of SCTM, discussed infra, we must determine whether such persecution constitutes persecution because of (1) political opinion or (2) membership in a social group. The first question, persecution because of political opinion, turns on the answer to the question whether the BIA's characterization of the dispute between Osorio and the City of Guatemala as "economic" precludes a finding that the persecution resulting therefrom may also be properly characterized as political....

The BIA dismissed Osorio's plea for asylum in one paragraph.... Distilled to its basic form, the BIA argues as follows: The dispute between Osorio and Guatemala is fundamentally "economic"; therefore, Osorio is ineligible for asylum.... At oral argument, counsel for Osorio made this point well when she likened the BIA's view to the opinion that Aleksandr Solzhenitsyn[116] would not have been eligible for political asylum because his dispute with the former Soviet Union is properly characterized as a literary, rather than a political, dispute. Regardless of whether their dispute might have been characterized as a literary dispute, it might also have been properly characterized as a political dispute....

Any attempt to unravel economic from political motives is untenable in this case. No substantial evidence supports the view that Osorio's dispute with the Guatemalan governmental officials was solely economic. Rather, substantial evidence ... compels the view that Guatemalan authorities persecuted Osorio because he and his union posed a political threat to their authority via their organized opposition activities. Although several conflicts between Osorio and his government were in the context of economic disputes, the death threats to him and others were independent of these disputes. Osorio and his union colleagues presented grievances to the government often, but not solely in the form of strikes. And after Osorio's termination, such grievances manifested themselves into an organized media campaign led by Osorio who "became well-known in Guatemala because of the continuous demands that I spoke out...."

While acknowledging government persecution of a union leader on account of his union activities, the BIA summarily dismissed the underlying political motives of Osorio's persecutors as irrelevant and argued that Osorio "has not demonstrated that his fear of persecution is premised upon political opinion or any of the other enumerated grounds." ... In so concluding, the BIA examined neither the political dimension of this dispute nor its political context. The BIA neglected what the Act made critical—political motive....

Thus, by drawing the conclusion that the dispute between Osorio and Guatemala was economic and not political, the BIA ignored the political context of the dispute. In particular, in a country where the standard of living is low, and where the government suppresses civil liberties and commits widespread human rights violations, unions (and student organizations) are often the only vehicles for political expression.... Thus, Guatemalan government persecution of Osorio and other union members on account of their union activities is not political solely because the government views union activities as subversive although such views are some evidence of the persecutor's motives and therefore of the appropriate characterization of the dispute for purposes of asylum. And the persecution is not political solely because of the nature of Osorio's actions, his media campaigning, for instance. Osorio's non-government-controlled union activities, which manifested themselves as opposition to government policies, coupled with his actions after his termination, represented a political threat to the government's authority....

Osorio's union activities imply a political opinion. The Government argues that he has not established what his political opinion is, but the Government's view of what constitutes a political opinion is too narrow. The Government complains that Osorio has never stated "which political party he belongs to, which political philosophy he espouses or which political leaders he supports. He never placed himself, SCTM or the city government at any point along the political spectrum." ... We agree with Osorio that the Government's argument betrays an impoverished view of what political opinions are, especially in a country like Guatemala where certain democratic rights have only a tenuous hold.... Osorio is not a politician in the tradition of those who run for office in the twentieth-century United States. Rather, like Aleksandr Solzhenitsyn, Osorio is a dissident, and accordingly marked by the authorities for persecution. Refugee law does not require that Osorio be a politician, only that he is persecuted in his home country for his political beliefs. We believe that Osorio's activities clearly evince the political opinion that strikes by municipal workers should be legal and that workers should be given more rights. Guatemala's persecution of Osorio was motivated in large part because it wanted to silence the expression of these political beliefs. Consequently, the BIA decision incorrectly stands for the proposition that if a government persecutes a national or resident on account of such person's political beliefs, but the individual is a union organizer whose fame and mode of communication comes through the organization of a labor movement, the individual is not eligible for political asylum because such activity is predominantly economic, not political.... This interpretation of the Act contradicts the plain meaning of the Act.... In short, we hold that the BIA's interpretation of political asylum contradicts the plain language and congressional intent of the Act. We further hold that Osorio suffered persecution on account of his political beliefs and that the BIA's characterization of

Osorio's persecution as solely on account of his economic activities is not reasonably supported by substantial evidence on the record. [H]aving determined that Osorio feared persecution on account of his political beliefs, we now examine the question whether Osorio was eligible for political asylum.

... Osorio may establish his eligibility for asylum on one of two bases: (1) actual past persecution, or (2) well-founded fear of future persecution on account of his political opinions.... We find that substantial evidence on the record compels the conclusion that Osorio is eligible for asylum because he has a well-founded fear of persecution on account of his political beliefs.... To establish a well-founded fear of persecution, Osorio must establish that (1) "he has a fear of persecution in [Guatemala] on account of ... political opinion," (2) "there is a reasonable possibility of actually suffering such persecution if he were to return to [Guatemala]," and (3) "he is unable or unwilling to return to or avail himself of the protection of [Guatemala] because of such fear." ... We have established that Osorio fears persecution because of his political opinion and that he is unwilling to return to Guatemala because of a well-founded fear of persecution. Therefore, we focus on whether there is a reasonable possibility that Osorio would actually suffer such persecution if he were to return to Guatemala.

... Osorio's testimony coupled with the background facts of this case establish an overwhelming "pattern ... in [Guatemala] of persecution of groups of persons similarly situated to [Osorio] on account of ... [his] political opinion." ... The tragic events preceding the November 1986 general strike themselves compel us to conclude that union leaders like Osorio are at grave risk of persecution by Guatemalan authorities. The IJ incorrectly dismissed these events as "unfortunate incidents," and the BIA, by failing to re-open the hearing to hear evidence that Guatemalan authorities again threatened the life of Osorio's union colleague, Sotz Cate, because of his denunciations of the Guatemalan government while abroad, failed to give "due consideration to evidence that the [Guatemalan government] persecutes its nationals or residents if they leave the country without authorization or seek asylum in another country." ...

The overall picture reveals a pattern of persecution that is horrific, and rivalled in this hemisphere perhaps only by the pattern of persecution in El Salvador.... There is no doubt that Osorio identifies with the group of individuals who are commonly persecuted in Guatemala. It is his identification with this group of individuals, union leaders, that makes his fear of future persecution credible, and well-founded. In short, we hold that, as a matter of law, Osorio was eligible for political asylum, and that the IJ and the BIA were incorrect in holding otherwise.

Although Osorio was eligible for asylum, the Attorney General, in her discretion, may deny asylum to eligible applicants like Osorio. Because of the strength of Osorio's fear of persecution if he were to return to Guatemala, we believe it would be an abuse of discretion not to grant him asylum.... Substantial evidence on the record compels us to conclude that it is more likely than not that his life or freedom would be threatened in Guatemala on account of his political opinion. Many of Osorio's close colleagues have already perished at the hands of the Guatemalan government. In 1986 alone, immediately prior to the November general strike, Osorio's fellow union member, Efrian Cotzal Sisimit, was shot and killed in Guatemala City; his fellow SCTM leader, Sotz Cate, was kidnapped and beaten; Sotz Cate's three-year-old son was shot and paralyzed; and SCTM secretary, Justo Rufino Reyes, was stabbed to death near the municipal building in

Guatemala City. Further, all outside accounts of events in Guatemala confirm that union leaders are among those targeted for life-threatening political persecution. Osorio himself was the subject of several death threats. Thus, we hold that the IJ and BIA were incorrect in denying Osorio's application for withholding of deportation. In conclusion, we reverse the order of the BIA. We hold that Osorio is eligible for asylum and order that withholding of deportation be granted to him.

Of course the long history of U.S. behavior toward Latin Americans early on involved its attitude and behavior towards Mexico. It has been an ongoing source of frustration for Latinos, and particularly for those of Mexican ancestry, that these behaviors persist even in an era when the U.S. proclaims itself as a friend and ally of Mexico. At the same time, the U.S. has focused on building walls along its southern border with discussions of homeland security, even though there is no evidence that that border has been the means of access for terrorists or would-be terrorists. Latinos point out that the 9/11 attackers came to the U.S. with valid papers. They also point out that those who have been apprehended trying to cross from a neighboring country have come through Canada and not Mexico. Then there is the continuing claim that Mexico has not done enough to stem the flow of drugs into the U.S. from the south. However, Mexico is quick to point out that if the United States did not supply the world's most lucrative market for illegal drugs, many Latin American countries would not have to deal with the death and destruction of narco-traffickers, violence that is exacerbated by their easy access to cash and weapons from the United States. And the memory of the invasion of Mexico by the U.S. in the nineteenth century remains. That memory was rekindled not so long ago when U.S. officials decided they could ignore a recently renegotiated extradition treaty and simply use kidnappers to nab a suspect they wanted to bring to the U.S. for trial. Worse yet, despite its recognition of the blatant violation of the territorial integrity of Mexico under international law, the U.S. Supreme Court nevertheless allowed the suspect to be tried in U.S. courts, notwithstanding the patently illegal manner in which he had been obtained.

United States v. Alvarez-Machain

504 U.S. 655 (1992)

INTRODUCTION: U.S. Drug Enforcement (DEA) Agent Enrique Camarena and a Mexican colleague, Alfredo Zavala-Avelar, were murdered in Mexico. The Mexican government undertook investigations and, later, prosecutions of suspects, with a number convicted and sentenced to lengthy prison terms. The U.S. government sought to bring suspects to this country for trial, but the Mexican government refused and made clear its intentions to deal with criminals itself, as was its right under the recently revised extradition treaty between the two countries.[117] Agents of the DEA caused others in Mexico to kidnap Dr. Alvarez-Machain and others and deliver them to an airport in Guadalajara. Alvarez-Machain was flown from there to El Paso, Texas, where he was arrested by the DEA and transported to California for trial.

He was initially convicted, but the district court later changed position, after receiving additional information in a related case. The judge concluded that the defendant could not lawfully be tried in a U.S. court because he had been illegally seized and brought to the U.S. in violation of the U.S.–Mexico extradition treaty. The government appealed, but lost in the U.S. Circuit Court of Appeals.

Chief Justice Rehnquist wrote the opinion for the Court.

The issue in this case is whether a criminal defendant, abducted to the United States from a nation with which it has an extradition treaty, thereby acquires a defense to the jurisdiction of this country's courts. We hold that he does not, and that he may be tried in federal district court for violations of the criminal law of the United States.....

In *Ker v. Illinois*, 119 U.S. 436 (1886), ... we addressed the issue of a defendant brought before the court by way of a forcible abduction. Frederick Ker had been tried and convicted in an Illinois court for larceny; his presence before the court was procured by means of forcible abduction from Peru. A messenger was sent to Lima with the proper warrant to demand Ker by virtue of the extradition treaty between Peru and the United States.[118] The messenger, however, ... forcibly kidnaped Ker and brought him to the United States. We distinguished Ker's case from *Rauscher*, on the basis that Ker was not brought into the United States by virtue of the extradition treaty.... We rejected Ker's due process argument more broadly, holding in line with "the highest authorities" that "such forcible abduction is no sufficient reason why the party should not answer when brought within the jurisdiction of the court ... and presents no valid objection to his trial."

The only differences between *Ker* and the present case are that *Ker* was decided on the premise that there was no governmental involvement in the abduction...; and Peru ... did not object to his prosecution.... [O]ur first inquiry must be whether the abduction of respondent from Mexico violated the Extradition Treaty between the United States and Mexico. If we conclude that the Treaty does not prohibit respondent's abduction, the rule in *Ker* applies, and the court need not inquire as to how respondent came before it.

... The Treaty says nothing about the obligations of the United States and Mexico to refrain from forcible abductions of people from the territory of the other nation, or the consequences under the Treaty if such an abduction occurs.... According to respondent, Article 9 embodies the terms of the bargain which the United States struck: If the United States wishes to prosecute a Mexican national, it may request that individual's extradition. Upon a request from the United States, Mexico may either extradite the individual or submit the case to the proper authorities for prosecution in Mexico. In this way, respondent reasons, each nation preserved its right to choose whether its nationals would be tried in its own courts or by the courts of the other nation. This preservation of rights would be frustrated if either nation were free to abduct nationals of the other nation for the purposes of prosecution. More broadly, respondent reasons, as did the Court of Appeals, that all the processes and restrictions on the obligation to extradite established by the Treaty would make no sense if either nation were free to resort to forcible kidnaping to gain the presence of an individual for prosecution in a manner not contemplated by the Treaty....

We do not read the Treaty in such a fashion. Article 9 does not purport to specify the only way in which one country may gain custody of a national of the other country for the purposes of prosecution. In the absence of an extradition treaty, nations are under no obligation to surrender those in their country to foreign authorities for prosecution.... The Treaty thus provides a mechanism which would not otherwise exist, requiring, under certain circumstances, the United States and Mexico to extradite individuals to the other country, and establishing the procedures to be followed when the Treaty is invoked.... The remaining question, therefore, is whether the Treaty should be interpreted so as to include an implied term prohibiting prosecution where the defendant's presence is obtained by means other than those established by the Treaty....

Respondent contends that the Treaty must be interpreted against the backdrop of customary international law, and that international abductions are "so clearly prohibited in international law" that there was no reason to include such a clause in the Treaty itself.... Respondent would have us find that the Treaty acts as a prohibition against a violation of the general principle of international law that one government may not "exercise its police power in the territory of another state." ... There are many actions which could be taken by a nation that would violate this principle ... but it cannot seriously be contended that an invasion of the United States by Mexico would violate the terms of the Extradition Treaty between the two nations. In sum, ... [t]he general principles cited by respondent simply fail to persuade us that we should imply in the United States–Mexico Extradition Treaty a term prohibiting international abductions.

Respondent and his amici may be correct that respondent's abduction was "shocking," ... and that it may be in violation of general international law principles. Mexico has protested the abduction of respondent through diplomatic notes ... and the decision of whether respondent should be returned to Mexico, as a matter outside of the Treaty, is a matter for the Executive Branch. We conclude, however, that respondent's abduction was not in violation of the Extradition Treaty between the United States and Mexico.... The fact of respondent's forcible abduction does not therefore prohibit his trial in a court in the United States for violations of the criminal laws of the United States. The judgment of the Court of Appeals is therefore reversed, and the case is remanded....

Justice Stevens wrote a dissent joined by Justices Blackmun and O'Connor.

[This case] does not involve an ordinary abduction by a private kidnaper, or bounty hunter, as in *Ker*.... Rather, it involves this country's abduction of another country's citizen; it also involves a violation of the territorial integrity of that other country, with which this country has signed an extradition treaty.

A Mexican citizen was kidnaped in Mexico and charged with a crime committed in Mexico; his offense allegedly violated both Mexican and American law.[119] Mexico has formally demanded on at least two separate occasions that he be returned to Mexico and has represented that he will be prosecuted ... for his offense.[120] It is clear that Mexico's demand must be honored if this official abduction violated the 1978 Extradition Treaty.... [A] fair reading of the treaty in light of our decision in *United States v. Rauscher*, 119 U.S. 407 (1886) and applicable principles of international law, leads inexorably to the conclusion that the District Court and ... the Ninth Circuit ... correctly construed that instrument.

... From the preamble, through the description of the parties' obligations ... the Treaty appears to have been designed to cover the entire subject of extradition.... Moreover, ... Article 9 expressly provides that neither contracting party is bound to deliver up its own nationals, ... but if it does not do so, it "shall submit the case to its competent authorities for purposes of prosecution."

The Government's claim that the Treaty is not exclusive, but permits forcible governmental kidnaping, would transform [this], and other, provisions into little more than verbiage. For example, provisions requiring "sufficient" evidence to grant extradition (Art. 3), withholding extradition for political or military offenses (Art. 5), withholding extradition when the person sought has already been tried (Art. 6), withholding extradition when the statute of limitations for the crime has lapsed (Art. 7), and granting the requested country discretion to refuse to extradite an individual who would face the death penalty in the requesting country (Art. 8), would serve little purpose if the requesting country could simply kidnap the person. [A]ll of these provisions "only make sense if they are understood as requiring each treaty signatory to comply with those procedures whenever it wishes to obtain jurisdiction over an individual who is located in another treaty nation."

It is true ... that there is no express promise by either party to refrain from forcible abductions.... Relying on that omission, the Court, in effect, concludes that the Treaty merely creates an optional method of obtaining jurisdiction over alleged offenders, and that the parties silently reserved the right to resort to self-help whenever they deem force more expeditious than legal process. If the United States, for example, thought it more expedient to torture or simply to execute a person rather than to attempt extradition, these options would be equally available because they, too, were not explicitly prohibited by the Treaty. That, however, is a highly improbable interpretation of a consensual agreement, which on its face appears to have been intended to set forth comprehensive and exclusive rules concerning the subject of extradition. In my opinion, "the manifest scope and object of the treaty itself," ... plainly imply a mutual undertaking to respect the territorial integrity of the other contracting party. That opinion is confirmed by a consideration of the "legal context" in which the Treaty was negotiated....

In *Rauscher*, the Court construed an extradition treaty that was far less comprehensive than the 1978 Treaty with Mexico.... Although the treaty did not purport to place any limit on the jurisdiction of the demanding state after acquiring custody of the fugitive, this Court held that he could not be tried for any offense other than murder. Thus, the treaty constituted the exclusive means by which the United States could obtain jurisdiction over a defendant within the territorial jurisdiction of Great Britain....

Rejecting an argument that the sole purpose of Article X was to provide a procedure for the transfer of an individual from the jurisdiction of one sovereign to another, the Court stated: "No such view of solemn public treaties between the great nations of the earth can be sustained by a tribunal called upon to give judicial construction to them.... The opposite view has been attempted to be maintained in this country upon the ground that there is no express limitation in the treaty.... Although the Court's conclusion in *Rauscher* was supported by a number of judicial precedents, the holdings in these cases were not nearly as uniform as the consensus of international opinion that condemns one nation's violation of the territorial integrity of a friendly neighbor. It is shocking that a party to an extradition treaty might believe that it has secretly reserved the right to make seizures of citizens in the other party's territory."[121] Justice Story found it shocking enough that the United States would attempt to justify an American seizure of a foreign vessel in a Spanish port." ... *The Apollon*, 22 U.S. 362, 370–371 (1824).

The law of nations, as understood by Justice Story in 1824, has not changed.... Commenting on the precise issue raised by this case, the chief reporter for the American Law Institute's Restatement of Foreign Relations used language reminiscent of Justice Story's characterization of an official seizure in a foreign jurisdiction as "monstrous": "When done without consent of the foreign government, abducting a person from a foreign country is a gross violation of international law and gross disrespect for a norm high in the opinion of mankind. It is a blatant violation of the territorial integrity of another state; it eviscerates the extradition system (established by a comprehensive network of treaties involving virtually all states)." ...

A critical flaw pervades the Court's entire opinion. It fails to differentiate between the conduct of private citizens, which does not violate any treaty obligation, and conduct expressly authorized by the Executive Branch of the Government, which unquestionably constitutes a flagrant violation of international law, and in my opinion, also constitutes a breach of our treaty obligations.... The Court's admittedly "shocking" disdain for customary and conventional international law principles ... is thus entirely unsupported by case law and commentary.

[T]here is reason to believe that respondent participated in an especially brutal murder of an American ... agent. That fact, if true, may explain the Executive's intense interest in punishing respondent in our courts. Such an explanation, however, provides no justification for disregarding the Rule of Law that this Court has a duty to uphold.... [W]e should remember and be guided by our duty "to render judgment evenly and dispassionately according to law, as each is given understanding to ascertain and apply it." ... The way that we perform that duty in a case of this kind sets an example that other tribunals in other countries are sure to emulate.

The significance of this Court's precedents is illustrated by a recent decision of the Court of Appeal of the Republic of South Africa. Based largely on its understanding of the import of this Court's cases ... that court held that the prosecution of a defendant kidnaped by agents of South Africa in another country must be dismissed. *S v. Ebrahim*, S. Afr. L. Rep. (Apr.–June 1991).[122] The Court of Appeal of South Africa—indeed, I suspect most courts throughout the civilized world—will be deeply disturbed by the "monstrous" decision the Court announces today.

It is difficult to understand how Mexicans are to accept that the U.S. is not engaged in blatant discrimination when it invades the territory of a sovereign state and treats that country's nationals in clear violation of international law in a set of behaviors that even the majority of the Court that upheld those actions acknowledges as "shocking," and this just after the U.S. had concluded a revised extradition treaty with Mexico. Unfortunately, there was more to come; and the events that followed with respect to treatment of Mexican nationals by the U.S., and found by the International Court of Justice (ICJ) to be clearly illegal, once again met with a Supreme Court majority ready to demonstrate to the satisfaction of many Latinos that the historical attitudes and practices of discrimination against Hispanics is alive and well in the U.S. in the twenty-first century.

The Vienna Convention requires that foreign nationals arrested for a crime have access to officials from their home country's consulate or embassy. Mexico brought suit against the United States in the International Court of Justice after fifty-two Mexican nationals were convicted and given death sentences in several states, including Texas, despite the fact that they were not told of their right to consular assistance and none was provided to them.[123] President George W. Bush attempted to deal with the order by issuing a presidential memorandum intended to stop states from executing these prisoners or taking any further action against them until the U.S. had determined how it would respond to the ICJ ruling.[124] The state of Texas informed the U.S. Justice Department that it had no intention of complying with the president's directive and that it was not obligated to respond to the treaty or the ICJ ruling. That case went to the U.S. Supreme Court, which issued a decision that again shocked the international community, and many in the U.S., when it ruled in favor of Texas.[125]

The case was shocking because the U.S. is a signatory to the Vienna Convention as well as to the Optional Protocol under that treaty in which the United States agreed to "comply with the decision of the [ICJ] in any case to which it is a party."

Chief Justice Roberts wrote for the five-person majority, finding that "neither Avena nor the President's Memorandum constitutes directly enforceable federal law that pre-empts state limitations on the filing of successive habeas petitions."[126] Justice Breyer dissented and reminded the Court that the Supremacy Clause of Article VI of the Constitution, which states "all Treaties ... which shall be made ... under the Authority of the United States, shall be the supreme Law of the Land; and the Judges in every State shall be bound thereby" and reminding the Court that, since at least 1829, the Court had maintained that: "The Clause means that the 'courts' must regard 'a treaty ... as equivalent to an act of the legislature, whenever it operates of itself without the aid of any legislative provision.'"[127] He also reminded the Court that the Optional Protocol to the Vienna Convention made the countries who signed it subject to "compulsory jurisdiction" for the purpose of "compulsory settlement" and was therefore binding on the United States, as were the rulings of the ICJ. Breyer also pointed out that the U.S. was party to some seventy other treaties that had similar language[128] and added to his opinion a list of twenty-nine cases, including twelve that had ruled that state law or policy was invalid, in which the Supreme Court had "held or assumed that particular treaty provisions are self-executing, automatically binding the States without more."[129]

So much for the enduring friendship for Mexico. Given this ruling and the history of U.S. policy and attitudes toward the people and nations of Latin America that preceded it, it is difficult to conclude that there is not and has not been a pervasive and longstanding attitude and practice of discrimination.

Immigration, Scapegoating, and the Question of How Much Protection: Taxes and Obligations but not Necessarily Equal Protection

Even for Latinos and others who have come to the U.S. as lawful permanent residents, there has been a longstanding pattern of discriminatory and exclusionary behavior. That has been true even though permanent residents face all of the responsibilities of U.S. citizens, from the payment of taxes to availability for compulsory military service in the event of a draft. The U.S. Supreme Court has helped to address those problems, but at other times in recent history it has seemed to be part of the problem rather than the solution. This problem certainly did not start only with Latinos, but also persons who came to the U.S. from many countries. However, in the recent past the fact that significant numbers of Hispanics have come to the U.S. as refugees or immigrants has blended with the historic racial animus, which is all too evident in the politics and society of this country, to produce exclusionary policies and practices.

Graham v. Richardson

403 U.S. 365 (1971)

INTRODUCTION: Most social service programs that provide assistance to persons in need, including both federal and state funded programs, have required that recipients of the assistance be citizens of the U.S. Where they have provided assistance to lawful permanent residents, they often gave a lower level of assistance. It bears repeating that persons who are lawful permanent residents of the United States have all of the legal responsibilities of citizens, including tax obligations and availability for a military draft if the nation's leaders choose to activate that program.

This case is a consolidated appeal involving three parties. Ms. Carmen Richardson came to the United States in 1956 from Mexico. At the time this case began, she was 64 and had become totally disabled. She applied for a program that combines federal and state resources, including Social Security. However, she was denied assistance since the program required, among other things, that a recipient be a citizen or have lived in the state for 15 years. She met all of the requirements except for those two. She brought a class action suit against the Commissioner of the Arizona Department of Public Welfare seeking an injunction and also the assistance she would have received but for these two requirements.[130] She contended that the requirements violated the equal protection clause of the Fourteenth Amendment and the constitutional right to travel, as well as the provisions of the federal Social Security Act that preempt state requirements under the Supremacy Clause of Article VI of the Constitution. A three-judge federal district court ruled in her favor on the equal protection claim and the Commission appealed to the Supreme Court.[131]

Ms. Elsie Mary Jane Leger, who came to the U.S. from Scotland in 1957, lived in Pennsylvania and was denied assistance because citizenship was required in addition to other federal program requirements. She had worked and paid taxes all the years she was in the U.S. until illness made it impossible for her to continue to work. She also brought a class action suit in the federal district court against the state and local government officials and obtained a temporary injunction against the citizenship requirements.

Beryl Jervis, originally from Panama, was added to this case as an additional plaintiff. She also worked until illness made that impossible. Again, the three-judge district court found a violation of the equal protection clause. The officials appealed.

Justice Blackmun delivered the opinion of the Court.

> The issue here is whether the Equal Protection Clause of the Fourteenth Amendment prevents a State from conditioning welfare benefits either (a) upon the beneficiary's possession of United States citizenship, or (b) if the beneficiary is an alien, upon his having resided in this country for a specified number of years....

> The Fourteenth Amendment provides, "Nor shall any State deprive any person of life, liberty, or property, without due process of law; nor deny to any person within its jurisdiction the equal protection of the laws." It has long been settled ... that the term "person" in this context encompasses lawfully admitted resident aliens as well as citizens of the United States and entitles both citizens and aliens to the equal protection of the laws of the State in which they reside. *Yick Wo v. Hopkins*, 118 U.S. 356, 369 (1886); *Truax v. Raich*, 239 U.S. 33, 39 (1915); *Takahashi v. Fish & Game Comm'n*, 334 U.S. [410, 420 (1948)]. Nor is it disputed that the Arizona and Pennsylvania statutes in question create two classes of needy persons, indistinguishable except with respect to whether they are or are not citizens of this country....

> Under traditional equal protection principles, a State retains broad discretion to classify as long as its classification has a reasonable basis.... But the Court's decisions have established that classifications based on alienage, like those based on nationality[132] or race,[133] are inherently suspect and subject to close judicial scrutiny. Aliens as a class are a prime example of a "discrete and insular" minority ... for whom such heightened judicial solicitude is appropriate. Accordingly,

"the power of a state to apply its laws exclusively to its alien inhabitants as a class is confined within narrow limits."

Arizona and Pennsylvania seek to justify their restrictions on the eligibility of aliens for public assistance solely on the basis of a State's "special public interest" in favoring its own citizens over aliens in the distribution of limited resources such as welfare benefits.... [Following] *Takahashi v. Fish & Game Comm'n*, 334 U.S. 410 (1948), we conclude that a State's desire to preserve limited welfare benefits for its own citizens is inadequate to justify Pennsylvania's making noncitizens ineligible for public assistance, and Arizona's restricting benefits to citizens and longtime resident aliens. First, the special public interest doctrine was heavily grounded on the notion that "whatever is a privilege, rather than a right, may be made dependent upon citizenship." But this Court now has rejected the concept that constitutional rights turn upon whether a governmental benefit is characterized as a "right" or as a "privilege." *Sherbert v. Verner*, 374 U.S. 398, 404 (1963); *Shapiro v. Thompson*, 394 U.S., at 627 n. 6; *Goldberg v. Kelly*, 397 U.S. 254, 262 (1970); *Bell v. Burson*, 402 U.S. 535, 539 (1971). Second, as the Court recognized in *Shapiro*: "[A] State has a valid interest in preserving the fiscal integrity of its programs. It may legitimately attempt to limit its expenditures, whether for public assistance, public education, or any other program. But a State may not accomplish such a purpose by invidious distinctions between classes of its citizens...." Since an alien as well as a citizen is a "person" for equal protection purposes, a concern for fiscal integrity is no more compelling a justification for the questioned classification in these cases than it was in *Shapiro*. The classifications involved in the instant cases ... are inherently suspect and are therefore subject to strict judicial scrutiny whether or not a fundamental right is impaired.

We agree with the three-judge court in the Pennsylvania case that the "justification of limiting expenses is particularly inappropriate and unreasonable when the discriminated class consists of aliens. Aliens like citizens pay taxes and may be called into the armed forces.... [A]liens may live within a state for many years, work in the state and contribute to the economic growth of the state." There can be no "special public interest" in tax revenues to which aliens have contributed on an equal basis with the residents of the State. Accordingly, we hold that a state statute that denies welfare benefits to resident aliens and one that denies them to aliens who have not resided in the United States for a specified number of years violate the Equal Protection Clause.

Just two years after its ruling in *Graham*, the Supreme Court issued two more opinions reaffirming that policies and actions by government that single out people for denial of public benefits or positions on grounds of alienage are inherently suspect and will not be permitted, unless the government can meet the rigorous requirements of strict judicial scrutiny. In the first of these, Fre Le Poole Griffiths, a woman from the Netherlands married to an American citizen, was denied admission to the bar to practice law in Connecticut. In rejecting the state's restriction, the Court explained further that including lawful aliens is not only required by the equal protection clause, but is also consistent with the forces that had made the United States the great nation it had become. The fact that she was seeking a very responsible professional credential that would make her, as an attorney, an officer of the court did not change the ban on discrimination and was not a special interest of the state sufficient to block her effort to be admitted to the bar.

In re Griffiths

413 U.S. 717 (1973)

Justice Powell wrote the opinion for the Court.

We ... hold that the rule unconstitutionally discriminates against resident aliens.

I ... From its inception, our Nation welcomed and drew strength from the immigration of aliens. Their contributions to the social and economic life of the country were self-evident, especially during the periods when the demand for human resources greatly exceeded the native supply. This demand was by no means limited to the unskilled or the uneducated. In 1873, this Court noted that admission to the practice of law in the courts of a State "in no sense depends on citizenship of the United States." ...

In ... 1886 [the Court held] that a lawfully admitted resident alien is a "person" within the meaning of the Fourteenth Amendment's directive that a State must not "deny to any person within its jurisdiction the equal protection of the laws." *Yick Wo v. Hopkins*, 118 U.S. 356, 369.... Some years later, the Court struck down an Arizona statute requiring employers of more than five persons to employ at least 80% "qualified electors or native-born citizens of the United States or some subdivision thereof." *Truax v. Raich*, 239 U.S. 33, 35 (1915).... [I]n *Takahashi v. Fish & Game Comm'n*, 334 U.S. 410 (1948) ... ruling unconstitutional a California statute barring issuance of fishing licenses to persons "ineligible to citizenship," the Court stated that "the power of a state to apply its laws exclusively to its alien inhabitants as a class is confined within narrow limits." ...

Indeed, with the issue squarely before it in *Graham v. Richardson*, ... the Court concluded: "Classifications based on alienage, like those based on nationality or race, are inherently suspect and subject to close judicial scrutiny." ... The Court has consistently emphasized that a State which adopts a suspect classification "bears a heavy burden of justification." ... Resident aliens, like citizens, pay taxes, support the economy, serve in the Armed Forces, and contribute in myriad other ways to our society. It is appropriate that a State bear a heavy burden when it deprives them of employment opportunities.

We hold that the Committee, acting on behalf of the State, has not carried its burden.... We hold that §8(1) violates the Equal Protection Clause.

On the same day, the Court issued an opinion in another case on alienage, *Sugarman v. Dougall*.[134] In this case, Patrick Dougall, Esperanza Jorge, Teresa Vargas, and Sylvia Castro, who held civil service positions with the city of New York, had their employment terminated. Justice Blackmun explained that: "The Court is faced only with the question whether New York's flat statutory prohibition against the employment of aliens in the competitive classified civil service is constitutionally valid." The Court concluded that it was not. Blackmun started from what was by then the clear foundation that alienage is a suspect classification.

It is established, of course, that an alien is entitled to the shelter of the Equal Protection Clause. *Graham v. Richardson*.... This protection extends, specifically, in the words of Mr. Justice Hughes, to aliens who "work for a living in the common occupations of the community." ... In *Graham v. Richardson*, we observed that aliens as a class "are a prime example of a 'discrete and insular minority' and that classifications based on alienage are 'subject to close judicial scrutiny.'"

In the case of the New York prohibition, he wrote:

> The citizenship restriction sweeps indiscriminately. Viewing the entire constitutional and statutory framework in the light of the State's asserted interest, the great breadth of the requirement is even more evident.... In view of the breadth and imprecision of §53 in the context of the State's interest, we conclude that the statute does not withstand close judicial scrutiny.

Chief Justice Burger wrote a dissent joined by Justice Rehnquist in the *Griffiths* case, and Rehnquist wrote a dissent in *Sugarman*. Burger asserted that the states reserve power to regulate professions and the special nature of attorneys as officers of the court adds to the reason for deference to the state. Rehnquist anchored his dissent in the adamant argument that the Fourteenth Amendment only made classifications based on race suspect, rejecting the entire premise of the alienage cases.

Other state constraints faced similar difficulties in the Supreme Court, which made it clear that alienage is a suspect class and strict judicial scrutiny would be used to test any such restriction. In one such case, two permanent residents challenged restrictions on New York university tuition assistance programs. The state argued that under *Sugarman* there should be an exception for the state to the usual application of strict scrutiny. In *Nyquist v. Mauclet* Justice Blackmun, the author of the *Sugarman* ruling, admonished the state that it should not try to make a narrow possible exception mentioned in *Sugarman* into a major area of exception to the normal protections against discrimination against lawful residents, and rejected the state's case. In so doing he warned:

> In *Sugarman* ... the Court recognized that the State's interest "in establishing its own form of government, and in limiting participation in that government to those who are within 'the basic conception of a political community'" might justify some consideration of alienage. But as *Sugarman* makes quite clear, the Court had in mind a State's historical and constitutional powers to define the qualifications of voters, or of "elective or important nonelective" officials "who participate directly in the formulation, execution, or review of broad public policy." *In re Griffiths*, decided the same day, reflects the narrowness of the exception. In that case, despite a recognition of the vital public and political role of attorneys, the Court found invalid a state-court rule limiting the practice of law to citizens....
>
> Certainly, the justifications for §661(3) offered by appellants sweep far beyond the confines of the exception defined in *Sugarman*. If the encouragement of naturalization through these programs were seen as adequate, then every discrimination against aliens could be similarly justified. The exception would swallow the rule. *Sugarman* clearly does not tolerate that result. Nor does the claimed interest in educating the electorate provide a justification; although such education is a laudable objective, it hardly would be frustrated by including resident aliens, as well as citizens, in the State's assistance programs.[135]

However, led by Chief Justice Burger and Justice Rehnquist, a badly divided Court began to significantly expand that possible exception to which Blackmun had referred in *Sugarman*. In a case involving an applicant as a New York State Trooper, Burger took the exception language from *Sugarman* out of context to develop what came to be known as the political function exception to the requirement for strict scrutiny. He wrote: "The essence of our holdings to date is that although we extend to aliens the right to education and public welfare, along with the ability to earn a livelihood and engage in licensed professions, the right to govern is reserved to citizens."[136] From that he proceeded to start the development of a list of positions that were involved in essential government functions, including law enforcement officers. The dissenters vigorously attacked what was clearly the kind of language that would allow the exception to swallow the rule. Just how far some members of the Court were willing to push that exception became clear in a 1982 case.

Cabell v. Chavez-Salido

454 U.S. 432 (1982)

INTRODUCTION: As the Court explained, California statutes required "'public officers or employees declared by law to be peace officers' to be citizens of the United States [and] provides that probation officers and deputy probation officers are 'peace officers.'" Three lawful permanent residents applied for Los Angeles County Deputy Probation Officers positions and were rejected, two clearly because they were not citizens.

A three-judge federal district court concluded that the state statute was discriminatory and violated the equal protection clause of the Fourteenth Amendment both on its face and also as applied.

Justice White wrote the opinion for the Court.

Over the years, this Court has many times considered state classifications dealing with aliens.... Since *Graham*, the Court has confronted claims distinguishing between the economic and sovereign functions of government. This distinction has been supported by the argument that although citizenship is not a relevant ground for the distribution of economic benefits, it is a relevant ground for determining membership in the political community.... While not retreating from the position that restrictions on lawfully resident aliens that primarily affect economic interests are subject to heightened judicial scrutiny, ... we have concluded that strict scrutiny is out of place when the restriction primarily serves a political function.... We have thus "not abandoned the general principle that some state functions are so bound up with the operation of the State as a governmental entity as to permit the exclusion from those functions of all persons who have not become part of the process of self-government." ... And in those areas the State's exclusion of aliens need not "clear the high hurdle of 'strict scrutiny,' because [that] would 'obliterate all the distinctions between citizens and aliens, and thus depreciate the historic value of citizenship.'" *Foley v. Connelie*....

The limits on this category within which citizenship is relevant to the political community are not easily defined, but our cases since *Sugarman*—*Foley v. Connelie* ... and *Ambach v. Norwick*...—suggest that this Court will not look to the breadth of policy judgments required of a particular employee. Rather, the Court will look to the importance of the function as a factor giving substance to the concept of democratic self-government.

Sugarman advised that a claim that a particular restriction on legally resident aliens serves political and not economic goals is to be evaluated in a two-step process. First, the specificity of the classification will be examined: a classification that is substantially overinclusive or underinclusive tends to undercut the governmental claim that the classification serves legitimate political ends.... Second, even if the classification is sufficiently tailored, it may be applied in the particular case only to "persons holding state elective or important nonelective executive, legislative, and judicial positions," those officers who "participate directly in the formulation, execution, or review of broad public policy" and hence "perform functions that go to the heart of representative government." ... We must therefore inquire whether the "position in question ... involves discretionary decisionmaking, or execution of policy, which substantially affects members of the political community." *Foley v. Connelie*.... The restriction at issue in this case passes both of the *Sugarman* tests.

The District Court assumed that if the statute was overinclusive at all, it could not stand. This is not the proper standard. Rather, the inquiry is whether the restriction reaches so far and is so broad and haphazard as to belie the State's claim that it is only attempting to ensure that an important function of government be in the hands of those having the "fundamental legal bond of citizenship." ... Under this standard, the classifications used need not be precise; there need only be a substantial fit. Our examination of the California scheme convinces us that it is sufficiently tailored to withstand a facial challenge.

... The general law enforcement character of all California "peace officers" is underscored by the fact that all have the power to make arrests ... and all receive a course of training in the exercise of their respective arrest powers and in the use of firearms.... *Foley* made clear that a State may limit the exercise of the sovereign's[137] coercive police powers over the members of the community to citizens. The California statutes at issue here are an attempt to do just that. They are sufficiently tailored in light of that aim to pass the lower level of scrutiny we articulated as the appropriate equal protection standard for such an exercise of sovereign power in *Sugarman*.

IV. The District Court also held that the citizenship requirement was invalid as applied to the positions at issue here—deputy probation officers. In reaching this conclusion, it focused too narrowly on a comparison of the characteristics and functions of probation officers with those of the state troopers at issue in *Foley* and the teachers in *Ambach*. *Foley* and *Ambach* did not describe the outer limits of permissible citizenship requirements.... Definition of the important sovereign functions of the political community is necessarily the primary responsibility of the representative branches of government, subject to limited judicial review.... [W]e conclude that [probation officers], like the state troopers involved in *Foley*, sufficiently partake of the sovereign's power to exercise coercive force over the individual that they may be limited to citizens.... The judgment of the District Court is reversed.

Justice Blackmun (who had been the author of the *Sugarman* opinion) wrote the dissent joined by Justices Brennan, Marshall, and Stevens.

Appellees Jose Chavez-Salido, Pedro Luis Ybarra, and Ricardo Bohorquez are American-educated Spanish-speaking lawful residents of Los Angeles County, California. Seven years ago, each had a modest aspiration—to become a Los Angeles County "Deputy Probation Officer, Spanish-speaking." Each was willing to swear loyalty to the State and Federal Governments; indeed, appellee Chavez-Salido declared his intent to become a citizen. By competitive examination, two of the appellees, and possibly the third, demonstrated their fitness for the jobs they desired. Appellants denied them those jobs solely because they were not citizens.

The Court today concludes that appellees' exclusion from their chosen profession is "a necessary consequence of the community's process of political self-definition." ... The Court reaches this conclusion by misstating the standard of review it has long applied to alienage classifications. It then asserts that a lawfully admitted permanent resident alien is disabled from serving as a deputy probation officer because that job "[goes] to the heart of representative government." ... In my view, today's decision rewrites the Court's precedents, ignores history, defies common sense, and reinstates the deadening mantle of state parochialism in public employment. I must dissent.

I. The Court properly acknowledges that our decisions regarding state discrimination against permanent resident aliens have formed a pattern.... Since *Yick Wo v. Hopkins* ... this Court has recognized and honored the right of a lawfully admitted permanent resident alien to work for a living in the common occupations of the community. In *Truax v. Raich* ... the Court declared that right to be "the very essence of the personal freedom and opportunity that it was the purpose of the [Fourteenth] Amendment to secure.... If this could be refused solely upon the ground of race or nationality, the prohibition of the denial to any person of the equal protection of the laws would be a barren form of words."

In *Sugarman v. Dougall* ... we expressly refused to exempt public employment positions from this general rule. *Sugarman*, an 8–1 decision, struck down as facially inconsistent with the Equal Protection Clause a New York statute that excluded lawfully admitted aliens from all state civil service jobs offered on the basis of competitive examinations. *Sugarman* directed that permanent resident aliens may not be barred as a class from the common public occupations of the community. There, as here, the State had asserted its substantial interest in ensuring "that sovereign functions must be performed by members of the State." ... Without denying the weight of that interest, the Court concluded that, "judged in the context of the State's broad statutory framework and the justifications the State [presented]," ... the State's chosen means were insufficiently precise to uphold its broad exclusion of aliens from public employment.

Since *Sugarman*, the Court consistently has held that in each case where the State chooses to discriminate against permanent resident aliens, "the governmental interest claimed to justify the discrimination is to be carefully examined in order to determine whether that interest is legitimate and substantial, and inquiry must be made whether the means adopted to achieve the goal are necessary and precisely drawn." *Examining Board v. Flores de Otero*, 426 U.S. 572, 605 (1976). See also *Nyquist v. Mauclet*...; *In re Griffiths*...; *Graham v. Richardson*....

Applying this stringent standard here, I would hold that, on its face, [the California statute] violates the Equal Protection Clause.... When appellees first sought their jobs, the "peace officer" category encompassed more than 70 public occupations, including such apparently unrelated positions as toll takers, cemetery sextons, fish and game wardens, furniture and bedding inspectors, voluntary fire wardens, racetrack investigators, county coroners, State Supreme Court and Courts of Appeal bailiffs, messengers at the State Treasurer's office, and inspectors for the Board of Dental Examiners.... To this day, the legislature has offered no reason why such divergent classes of public jobs were gathered under the "peace officer" umbrella.... In 1961, without stating any rationale, "in one fell swoop, the legislature passed Government Code Section 1031 which applied the mandatory citizenship requirement to all of the positions on the list." ... Nine years after [that] California's own Attorney General stated: "It is our opinion that ... this citizenship requirement can no longer validly be imposed...."

Without even a glance at [the state statute's] history, the Court today reverses, reasoning that the District Court improperly "applied a standard of review far stricter than that approved in *Sugarman* and later cases." ... The Court's analysis fundamentally distorts *Sugarman*. That decision did not condone a looser

standard for review of classifications barring aliens from "political" jobs....
Under the *Sugarman* standard, a state statute that bars aliens from political positions lying squarely within the political community nevertheless violates the Equal
Protection Clause if it excludes aliens from other public jobs in an unthinking or
haphazard manner....

Thus, exactly like the statute struck down in *Sugarman*, California's statutory
exclusion of aliens is fatally overinclusive and underinclusive. It bars aliens from
employment in numerous public positions where the State's proffered justification
has little, if any, relevance. At the same time, it allows aliens to fill other positions
that would seem naturally to fall within the State's asserted purpose....

II. While *Sugarman* unambiguously proscribed blanket exclusion of aliens from
state jobs, its dictum acknowledged a State's power to bar noncitizens as a class
from a narrowly circumscribed range of important nonelective posts involving
direct participation "in the formulation, execution, or review of broad public
policy." ...

As originally understood, the *Sugarman* exception was exceedingly narrow. Less
demanding scrutiny was deemed appropriate only for statutes deriving from "a
State's historical power to exclude aliens from participation in its democratic
political institutions" or its "constitutional responsibility for the establishment
and operation of its own government." ...

I only can conclude that California's exclusion of these appellees from the position of deputy probation officer stems solely from state parochialism and hostility
toward foreigners who have come to this country lawfully. I find it ironic that the
Court invokes the principle of democratic self-government to exclude from the
law enforcement process individuals who have not only resided here lawfully, but
who now desire merely to help the State enforce its laws. Section 1031(a) violates
appellees' rights to equal treatment and an individualized determination of fitness.

Justice Blackmun was, of course, the author of the *Sugarman* opinion, and he was upset first
by such an obvious effort by a slim majority of the Court to reread that case in a manner
that dramatically undermined the very protections *Sugarman* had sought to ensure. Second,
he was clearly worried that the majority was taking dictum (language not essential to the
holding in the case) and turning it into the controlling standard to be used to assess restrictions on resident aliens. And he was just as concerned that the breadth of the Court's language would be seen to dramatically undermine the protection against discrimination that
Sugarman, and its 8–1 majority opinion, was written to protect. His fears were born out,
as various jurisdictions used broad prohibitions to keep lawful permanent residents out of
public positions. In a case in which Texas went so far as to bar permanent residents from
positions as "notary public," the Court was called upon to put a stop to the wide-ranging
discrimination. Reacting to this situation, eight members of the Court, in an opinion by
Justice Marshall, insisted that the Court would not permit the political function exception
to swallow the proposition that classifications based on alienage are inherently suspect.

Bernal v. Fainter

467 U.S. 216 (1984)

INTRODUCTION: The facts of the case are provided within the opinion below.
   Justice Marshall wrote the opinion for the Court, which was joined by Justices
Burger, Brennan, White, Blackmun, Powell, Stevens, and O'Connor.

The question posed by this case is whether a statute of the State of Texas violates the equal protection clause of the Fourteenth Amendment of the United States Constitution by denying aliens the opportunity to become notaries public. The Court of Appeals for the Fifth Circuit held that the statute does not offend the Equal Protection Clause. We ... reverse.

I. Petitioner, a native of Mexico, is a resident alien who has lived in the United States since 1961. He works as a paralegal for Texas Rural Legal Aid, Inc., helping migrant farmworkers on employment and civil rights matters. In order to administer oaths to these workers and to notarize their statements for use in civil litigation, petitioner applied in 1978 to become a notary public. Under Texas law, notaries public authenticate written instruments, administer oaths, and take out-of-court depositions. The Texas Secretary of State denied petitioner's application because he failed to satisfy the statutory requirement that a notary public be a citizen of the United States....

The District Court ... reviewed the State's citizenship requirement under a strict-scrutiny standard and concluded that the requirement violated the Equal Protection Clause. [It] also suggested that even under a rational-relationship standard, the state statute would fail to pass constitutional muster.... [The] Fifth Circuit reversed....

As a general matter, a state law that discriminates on the basis of alienage can be sustained only if it can withstand strict judicial scrutiny. In order to withstand strict scrutiny, the law must advance a compelling state interest by the least restrictive means available. Applying this principle, we have invalidated an array of state statutes that denied aliens the right to pursue various occupations. In *Sugarman v. Dougall*, ... we struck down a state statute barring aliens from employment in permanent positions in the competitive class of the state civil service. In *In re Griffiths*, ... we nullified a state law excluding aliens from eligibility for membership in the State Bar. And in *Examining Board v. Flores de Otero*, ... we voided a state law that excluded aliens from the practice of civil engineering.

We have, however, developed a narrow exception to the rule that discrimination based on alienage triggers strict scrutiny. This exception has been labeled the "political function" exception and applies to laws that exclude aliens from positions intimately related to the process of democratic self-government.... The rationale behind the political-function exception is that within broad boundaries a State may establish its own form of government and limit the right to govern to those who are full-fledged members of the political community. Some public positions are so closely bound up with the formulation and implementation of self-government that the State is permitted to exclude from those positions persons outside the political community, hence persons who have not become part of the process of democratic self-determination.... We have therefore lowered our standard of review when evaluating the validity of exclusions that entrust only to citizens important elective and nonelective positions whose operations "go to the heart of representative government." *Sugarman*....

To determine whether a restriction based on alienage fits within the narrow political-function exception, we devised in *Cabell* a two-part test.... "First, the specificity of the classification will be examined: a classification that is substantially overinclusive or underinclusive tends to undercut the governmental claim that the classification serves legitimate political ends.... Second, even if the classification is sufficiently tailored, it may be applied in the particular case only to 'persons holding state elective or important nonelective executive, legislative, and judicial positions,' those officers who 'participate directly in the formulation, execution, or review of broad public policy' and hence 'perform functions that go to the heart of representative government.' ... (quoting *Sugarman*).[138]

[This] ... statute is not overinclusive; it applies narrowly to only one category of persons: those wishing to obtain appointments as notaries. Less clear is whether Article 5949(2) is fatally underinclusive. Texas does not require court reporters to be United States citizens even though they perform some of the same services as notaries. Nor does Texas require that its Secretary of State be a citizen, even though he holds the highest appointive position in the State and performs many important functions, including supervision of the licensing of all notaries public. We need not decide this issue, however, because of our decision with respect to the second prong of the *Cabell* test.

In support of the proposition that notaries public fall within that category of officials who perform functions that "go to the heart of representative government," the State emphasizes that notaries are designated as public officers by the Texas Constitution. Texas maintains that this designation indicates that the State views notaries as important officials occupying posts central to the State's definition of itself as a political community. This Court, however, has never deemed the *source* of a position ... as the dispositive factor in determining whether a State may entrust the position only to citizens. Rather, this Court has always looked to the actual *function* of the position as the dispositive factor. The focus of our inquiry has been whether a position was such that the officeholder would necessarily exercise broad discretionary power over the formulation or execution of public policies importantly affecting the citizen population—power of the sort that a self-governing community could properly entrust only to full-fledged members of that community. As the Court noted in *Cabell*, in determining whether the function of a particular position brings the position within the narrow ambit of the exception, "the Court will look to the importance of the function as a factor giving substance to the concept of democratic self-government." ...

The State maintains that, even if the actual function of a post is the touchstone of a proper analysis, Texas notaries public should still be classified among those positions from which aliens can properly be excluded because the duties of Texas notaries entail the performance of functions sufficiently consequential to be deemed "political." ... [A] notary's duties, important as they are, hardly implicate responsibilities that go to the heart of representative government. Rather, these duties are essentially clerical and ministerial. In contrast to state troopers, *Foley* ... notaries do not routinely exercise the State's monopoly of legitimate coercive force. Nor do notaries routinely exercise the wide discretion typically enjoyed by public school teachers when they present materials that educate youth respecting the information and values necessary for the maintenance of a democratic political system. See *Ambach*.... To be sure, considerable damage could result from the negligent or dishonest performance of a notary's duties. But the same could be said for the duties performed by cashiers, building inspectors, the janitors who clean up the offices of public officials, and numerous other categories of personnel upon whom we depend for careful, honest service. What distinguishes such personnel from those to whom the political-function exception is properly applied is that the latter are invested either with policymaking responsibility or broad discretion in the execution of public policy that requires the routine exercise of authority over individuals. Neither of these characteristics pertains to the functions performed by Texas notaries.

The inappropriateness of applying the political-function exception to Texas notaries is further underlined by our decision in *In re Griffiths* ... in which we subjected to strict scrutiny a Connecticut statute that prohibited noncitizens from becoming members of the State Bar. Along with the usual powers and privileges accorded to members of the bar, Connecticut gave to members of its Bar additional authority that encompasses the very duties performed by Texas notaries.... In striking down Connecticut's citizenship requirement, we concluded that "[i]t in no way denigrates a lawyer's high responsibilities to observe that [these duties] hardly involve matters of state policy or acts of such unique responsibility as to entrust them only to citizens." ... If it is improper to apply the political-function exception to a citizenship requirement governing eligibility for membership in a state bar, it would be anomalous to apply the exception to the citizenship requirement that governs eligibility to become a Texas notary. We conclude, then, that the "political function" exception is inapplicable to Article 5949(2) and that the statute is therefore subject to strict judicial scrutiny.

IV. To satisfy strict scrutiny, the State must show that Article 5949(2) furthers a compelling state interest by the least restrictive means practically available.... There is nothing in the record that indicates that resident aliens, as a class, are so incapable of familiarizing themselves with Texas law as to justify the State's absolute and classwide exclusion. The possibility that some resident aliens are unsuitable for the position cannot justify a wholesale ban against all resident aliens. Furthermore, if the State's concern with ensuring a notary's familiarity with state law were truly "compelling," one would expect the State to give some sort of test actually measuring a person's familiarity with the law. The State, however, administers no such test. To become a notary public in Texas, one is merely required to fill out an application that lists one's name and address and that answers four questions pertaining to one's age, citizenship, residency, and criminal record—nothing that reflects the State's asserted interest in ensuring that notaries are familiar with Texas law. Similarly inadequate is the State's purported interest in ensuring the later availability of notaries' testimony. This justification fails because the State fails to advance a factual showing that the unavailability of notaries' testimony presents a real, as opposed to a merely speculative, problem to the State. Without a factual underpinning, the State's asserted interest lacks the weight we have required of interests properly denominated as compelling.

V. We conclude that Article 5949(2) violates the Fourteenth Amendment of the United States Constitution.... The judgment of the Court of Appeals is reversed [and remanded].[139]

Despite the fact that the Court sought to draw a line under how far such restrictions could go, it left standing a number of decisions about, for example, teachers. It is difficult for those excluded, including those who have applied for citizenship but who face a lengthy process of waiting years for approval (particularly in the years after 2001), to see how positions like teaching fit the Court's statement in *Bernal* as being positions to which "the political-function exception is properly applied" because "the latter are invested either with policymaking responsibility or broad discretion in the execution of public policy."

Conclusion

For many Latinos, the longstanding pattern of discrimination is clear and continuing. The stereotypes that are regularly applied to Latinos and the continuing pattern of discrimination by state governments and local law enforcement agencies and schools, as well as by others in the community, are ongoing. The reaction against Spanish-speakers as compared to those speaking other languages is difficult to understand as anything other than discrimination on the basis of race or ethnicity. The Supreme Court's self-contradictory opinion in the New York jury case that allowed exclusion because those involved were Latino and bilingual—and it is difficult to read that case in any other way given the facts—flies in the face of great pronouncements about equal protection of the law. The fact that so many state and local officials have continued even to the present to take what are patently offensive actions to block the use of Spanish only serves as a reminder that this discrimination is alive and well.

These problems do not stand alone. They continue alongside a clear and consistent history of malign neglect toward the countries of origin of many Latino families or their forebears that is difficult to interpret in any positive manner. It conveys a clear pattern that suggests that the leaders and people of the United States have a long held belief that somehow those nations and the people from them are less worthy of respect and proper treatment under international law, and that the disastrous impact of U.S. policy over time, measured in some places by the deaths of hundreds of thousands, is somehow less terrible than a similar loss would be in this country. Whether it is Argentina, Chile, Panama, Nicaragua, Costa Rica, El Salvador, Guatemala, or Mexico, to name only some of the countries adversely affected, the record is clear and the damage continues to the present day.

Similarly, it is difficult for many to understand why Latinos who are in the U.S. as lawful permanent residents have been the target of exclusion from public programs and positions that are not related to policymaking and do not carry broad discretion, even though those lawful residents are subject to all of the responsibilities of any citizen of the U.S. Restrictions on voting or holding elective office are one thing; prohibition on teaching one's native language in school or serving as a deputy probation officer are quite another. Ironically, the applicant for state trooper in the *Foley* case had applied for citizenship but was caught between the delays in the processing of his application (even after his five years of lawful residency in the U.S.) and New York State's age limitation on new state troopers.

It is clear that there remains an unfinished agenda for civil rights among Latinos and a continuing and intense set of serious cases in a wide range of settings of overt and obvious discrimination, as well as those behaviors that are more subtle. It is interesting that what appears to promise likely action to address some of these problems is coming not from a change of heart, but from the realities of a demographic chart that show Hispanics as a rapidly rising segment of the U.S. population that will be able to command attention at the polls and in public office in the years ahead.

I. Issues for Policy and Practice

A. As this chapter demonstrates, language discrimination as a proxy for race and ethnicity has been a serious and continuing problem for Latinos. Although it was not the first example of such discrimination, as the discussion of *Meyer* and related cases shows, it has been persistent and there is a clear and obvious connection to race and ethnicity in many instances. Even so, there has not been a serious effort to address this problem as a matter of policy. What policies might be implemented to address this ongoing problem?

B. The *amicus curiae* brief filed by Messrs. Joseph DiGenova, Gil Garcetti, Glenn F. Ivey, Robert M. A. Johnson, Harry L. Shorstein, Larry D. Thompson, Scott Turow, and John Van de Kamp in November 2015 in the *Foster v. Chapman* case pending before the U.S. Supreme Court makes a solid argument that prosecutors are deliberately removing jurors because of their race, ethnicity, and stereotype assumptions about their expected behavior. What policy options are available to address this problem that is now, after years in the shadows, being dragged out into the light?

C. Justice Scalia's opinion for a 5–4 majority in the *Alexander v. Sandoval* case was, as the dissenters explained, contrary to a number of clear precedents and plainly contrary to the intent and design of Title VI of the Civil Rights Act of 1964. That ruling and some that have followed have rendered Title VI nearly meaningless in practical terms and in any broad sense of effective enforcement. (See also the discussion in Chapter 13.) It requires action to make it the effective tool it was intended to be for the enforcement of civil rights, with the ability of those injured to take action where government cannot or will not. What policy options are available to address that problem?

D. U.S. attitudes toward and treatment of Latin American countries is one of those subjects that is rarely discussed publicly, but is frequently a subject of conversation among Latinos in private settings. On the other hand, there is little evidence that Anglos are even aware that there is a long pattern of troublesome behavior that suggests a negative attitude toward Latin American countries and Latinos. There is need for education about this history and continuing pattern of behavior, both to correct it in the future but also to understand why it is so offensive and problematic in the attitude it conveys.

E. The need for education extends to helping everyone in the workplace and in the community understand that Latin America is not one culture or one country any more than Asia is. Even though that is obvious, it is common in discussions of Latino issues to assume that everything concerns Mexico and to stereotype even that country and its people.

II. Discussion Questions

A. Think about the Court's opinion in *Hernandez v. New York*. What was the logic in eliminating a juror because they were bilingual from a case in which the victim was a Spanish speaker, the defendant a Spanish speaker, and the witnesses Spanish speakers? Is it likely that the real reason for this was the possibility that the juror might not be diligent in listening to the translator? What if the translator made an error, as happens too often in many settings? Should that juror not be allowed to at least raise a question for the judge to consider?

B. Given the *amicus curiae* brief filed in the October term 2015 case before the Court that shows evidence of prosecutors practicing and teaching others to use facially neutral explanations for eliminating prospective jurors because of their race or ethnicity, as discussed in the chapter, how are members of minority groups to take seriously the pledge of equal justice under law? What can be done to address this problem?

C. In the *Chavez-Salido* opinion Justice White says: "Definition of the important sovereign functions of the political community is necessarily the primary responsibility of the representative branches of government, subject to limited judicial review." If that is to be the case, then how would a person be able to challenge an exclusion established by the legislature or an elected executive? Is this a circular argument?

D. It is possible to gain some sense of the reaction to U.S. attitudes and policy by asking how Americans and other countries are reacting in the contemporary era to assertions by the People's Republic of China to rights to control areas that have traditionally been regarded as international waters or, in some cases, the territory of other countries? One can go back in time to the colonial era dominated by the European colonial powers of England, France, and Spain, among others. How would Americans view it if some other country were to assert that it has the right to operate in and control areas in and around the U.S. or U.S. territories in the Pacific on a claim like manifest destiny?

E. How would Americans respond if there were the kind of clear evidence of covert operations by other countries in the United States that resulted in thousands of deaths, operations of the kind in which the U.S. has engaged in Latin American countries? What would it say about the attitudes of that other country and its people toward Americans?

F. What would be the American reaction if Mexico chose to kidnap Americans to take back to Mexico for trial, even though the two countries have an extradition treaty? That is, of course, what the U.S. did to Mexico in the *Alvarez-Machain* case. What would such an action say about Mexican attitudes toward the United States and its people? What did the U.S. action in *Alvarez-Machain* say about U.S. attitudes toward Mexico and its people?

G. What is the message sent to Latinos when the state of Texas, and other states, refused to comply with the requirements for consular access for those accused of capital crimes in violation of the Vienna Convention, and then refused the U.S. Justice Department call to stop executions pending a review of how to comply with the international court ruling on the case? What does the fact that the U.S. upheld the action by Texas say? How would Americans respond if the same thing happened to an American arrested in another country?

H. What does it say to Latinos that the U.S. has taken a very different approach to facilitating special visas or immigration with regard to people coming from India or other parts of the world, but has treated those coming from most Latin American countries very differently?

Notes

1 NOTE: Another case, *Bartels v. Iowa*, 262 U.S. 404 (1923), which involved similar restrictions in Iowa and Ohio as well as Nebraska, was decided on the basis of *Meyer*.

2 NOTE: Native Americans who were taken off to the Indian boarding schools would perhaps welcome this statement but find it ironic in light of their experience. See David Wallace Adams, *Education for Extinction: American Indians and the Boarding School Experience 1875–1928* (Lawrence, KS: University Press of Kansas, 1995) and the discussion of the boarding schools in Chapter 5.

3 NOTE: Justice Holmes wrote a dissent joined by Justice Sutherland and published in *Bartels v. Iowa*.

4 *Pierce v. Society of Sisters*, 268 U.S. 510 (1925).

5 NOTE: In the years after this case, what was the U.S. Department of Health, Education, and Welfare was divided into the Department of Education and the Department of Health and Human Services.

6 NOTE: Justice White concurred in the result.

7 NOTE: The concurring opinion of Justice Blackmun joined by Chief Justice Burger is omitted here.

8 U.S. Department of Justice, "Enforcement of Title VI of the Civil Rights Act of 1964—National Origin Discrimination Against Persons with Limited English Proficiency." 65 Fed. Reg. 50123 (2000).

9 Executive Order 13166, "Improving Access to Services for Persons With Limited English Proficiency," 65 Fed. Reg. 50121 (2000).

10 67 Fed. Reg. 41455 (2002).

11 U.S. Department of Justice, "Limited English Proficiency," www.lep.gov/, January 2, 2015.

12 See *Batson v. Kentucky*, 476 U.S. 79 (1986); *Swain v. Alabama*, 380 U.S. 202 (1965); and *Strauder v. West Virginia*, 100 U.S. 303 (1880).

13 NOTE: *Voir dire* is the process by which attorneys question potential jurors to determine whether to object to their participation on the jury.

14 NOTE: Justice Kennedy does not explain why someone should be required to defer to a translator, when no English-speaking juror would ever be required to defer to the interpretation of testimony given by a third party if English were the language used by participants in the case. The Court also

never addresses the question why a Spanish-speaking juror should not be able to be a better juror by virtue of understanding the witnesses directly and being capable of pointing out to the court, or at least to raise questions about, errors in the interpreter's translation.

15 NOTE: Of course, this does not consider just how a judge is supposed to address the actions of a prosecutor who actually is seeking to pack the jury with persons who are not Latino, so long as the prosecutor offers some kind of explanation other than ethnicity.

16 NOTE: The Court does not address the fact that four Latino prospective jurors were eliminated, nor does the opinion indicate how many potential jurors drawn for this jury pool were Latino.

17 NOTE: There is no indication in this opinion as to how an appeals court is to determine that a judge's choice to allow exclusion is to be assessed.

18 NOTE: Is it clear what this paragraph means? Does it have a meaning if one is not prepared to use stereotypes? Even if true, how does one get from these vague generalizations to a basis for excluding persons of a particular ethnocultural group from a jury?

19 NOTE: The Court does not explain why a "harsh paradox" of this kind is not the clear example of discrimination that it appears to be.

20 NOTE: The examples here would require a prosecutor to effectively declare openly the intention to discriminate in order to satisfy the court's requirement. How likely is that to happen in even the worst case scenario?

21 *Foster v. Chapman*, No. 14–8249, Brief of Joseph DiGenova, Gil Garcetti, Glenn F. Ivey, Robert M. A. Johnson, Harry L. Shorstein, Larry D. Thompson, Scott Turow, and John Van de Kamp, as Amici Curiae in Support of Petitioner, www.scotusblog.com/wp-content/uploads/2015/08/14-8349_20tsac_20Joseph_20diGenova.pdf, November 12, 2015, p. 1.

22 Id., at 3.

23 Id., at 6.

24 197 F.3d 484 (11th Cir. 1999).

25 Id., at 490.

26 *Sandoval v. Hagan*, 7 F. Supp. 2d 1234 (MDAL1998).

27 197 F.3d, at 510.

28 532 U.S. 235 (2001).

29 Id., at 294 (Stevens, J., dissenting).

30 Id., at 534.

31 U.S. Department of Health and Human Services, "Final Guidance to Federal Financial Assistance Recipients Regarding Title VI Prohibition Against National Origin Discrimination Affecting Limited English Proficient Persons," 75 Fed. Reg. 2732, 2733 (2007).

32 See *Yñiguez v. Arizonans for Official English* ("AOE"), 69 F.3d 920, 924 (9th Cir. 1995) (en banc).

33 Id.

34 *Arizonans for Official English v. Arizona*, 520 U.S. 43 (1997).

35 NOTE: The Arizona Supreme Court explained its frequent references to the Ninth Circuit ruling in the previous *Yñiguez v. AOE* case: "[T]he Ninth Circuit's opinion in *Yñiguez v. AOE* was vacated by the United States Supreme Court because Yniguez lacked standing. *AOE v. Arizona*, 520 U.S. 43 (1997).... On the merits of the case, however, we agree with the result and with much of the reasoning of the Ninth Circuit opinion. Thus, we refer to the Ninth Circuit opinion throughout this opinion, recognizing that it has been vacated on grounds unrelated to the merits of the issues with which we are presented."

36 NOTE: In addition to the Arizona provision, the state laws cited by the court come from Alabama, Arkansas, California, Colorado, Florida, Georgia, Illinois, Indiana, Kentucky, Nebraska, Mississippi, Montana, New Hampshire, North Carolina, North Dakota, South Carolina, South Dakota, Tennessee, and Wyoming.

37 See Cecilia Wong, "Language Is Speech: The Illegitimacy of Official English after *Yñiguez v. Arizonans for Official English*," *U.C. Davis Law Review* 30 (Fall 1996): 278.

38 NOTE: Justice Martone's concurring opinion is omitted here.

39 Patty Reinert, "Amarillo judge does about-face," *Houston Chronicle*, September 19, 1995, p. a11.

40 Juan A. Lozano, "Hispanic leaders angry at decree that parents not speak Spanish to daughter," *Associated Press*, August 21, 2000, Monday, BC cycle.

41 Rick Ruggles, "Chambers calls for discipline of judge," *Omaha World Herald*, October 15, 2003, Pg. 3b.

42 Marsha King, "Care facilities walk fine line enforcing language policies. Workers', residents' rights clash over communication," *Seattle Times*, September 8, 2002, Pg. B1.

43 Mark Bixler, "State Leaps to Reverse Hall's English-only Policy," *Atlanta Journal and Constitution*, June 12, 2002, p. 1A.

44 Id.

45 Editorial, "English-only work rule is dumb in any language," *Atlanta Journal and Constitution*, June 13, 2002, Pg. 17A; Mark Bixler, "State Leaps to Reverse Hall's English-only Policy," *Atlanta Journal and Constitution*, June 12, 2002, p. 1A.

46 Title 20 U.S.C. § 1703(f). The language reads: "No state shall deny equal educational opportunity to an individual on account of his or her race, color, sex, or national origin, by … (f) the failure by an educational agency to take appropriate action to overcome language barriers that impede equal participation by its students in its instructional programs."

47 42 U.S.C. § 2000d. See *Lau v. Nichols* excerpted earlier in this chapter.

48 172 F. Supp. 2d 1225 (DAZ 2000).

49 *Flores v. Arizona*, 48 F. Supp. 2d 937, 939 (DAZ 1999).

50 171 F. Supp. 2d, at 1239.

51 *Flores v. Arizona*, 480 F. Supp. 2d 1157, 1167 (DAZ 2007).

52 *Horne v. Flores*, 557 U.S. 433 (2009).

53 U.S. Government Accountability Office, *Education Needs to Further Examine Data Collection on English Language Learners in Charter Schools, GAO-13-655R* (Washington, D.C.: GAO, 2013). This report came a year after the GAO had completed a report on issues related to students with disabilities in charter schools. U.S. Government Accountability Office, *Charter Schools: Additional Federal Attention Needed to Help Protect Access for Students with Disabilities, GAO-12-543* (Washington, D.C.: GAO, 2012).

54 GAO, *Education Needs to Further Examine Data Collection on English Language Learners in Charter Schools*, at 2.

55 Lisa Gray, "Principal who told kids not to speak Spanish will lose job," *Houston Chronicle*, March 18, 2014, www.chron.com/news/education/article/Principal-who-told-kids-not-to-speak-Spanish-will-5327528.php, January 10, 2015.

56 Quoted in Id.

57 See Scott J. Bent, "If You Want to Speak Spanish, Go Back to Mexico"?: A First Amendment Analysis of English-Only Rules in Public Schools," *Ohio State Law Journal* 73 (No. 2 2012): 343–394.

58 The Avalon Project, "President Monroe's seventh annual message to Congress," December 2, 1823, Yale Law School, Avalon Project, http://avalon.law.yale.edu/19th_century/monroe.asp, January 15, 2015.

59 U.S. National Archives & Records Administration, "Transcript of Theodore Roosevelt's Corollary to the Monroe Doctrine (1905) (Excerpted from Theodore Roosevelt's Annual Message to Congress, December 6, 1904)," www.ourdocuments.gov/doc.php?doc=56&page=transcript, January 18, 2015.

60 See Julius W. Pratt, "The Origin of 'Manifest Destiny'" *American Historical Review*, 32 (Jul. 1927): 795–798.

61 Id., 798.

62 Quoted in Id., 795.

63 U.S. Department of State, Office of the Historian, "The Annexation of Texas, the Mexican–American War, and the Treaty of Guadalupe-Hidalgo, 1845–1848," https://history.state.gov/milestones/1830-1860/texas-annexation, January 15, 2015. NOTE: The author has deliberately chosen to use the Department of State Historian for a number of references here as compared to other sources to indicate that these are not disputed points, but accepted even as part of official U.S. history.

64 U.S. Department of State, Office of the Historian, Building the Panama Canal, 1903–1914, https://history.state.gov/milestones/1899-1913/panama-canal, January 15, 2015.

65 Id.

66 U.S. National Archives & Records Administration, "Transcript of Theodore Roosevelt's Corollary to the Monroe Doctrine (1905) (Excerpted from Theodore Roosevelt's Annual Message to Congress, December 6, 1904)," www.ourdocuments.gov/doc.php?doc=56&page=transcript, January 18, 2015.

67 Chester J. Pach, Jr. and Elmo Richardson, *The Presidency of Dwight D. Eisenhower* (Lawrence, KS: University Press of Kansas, 1991), pp. 89–90.

68 Nick Cullather, *Secret History: The CIA's Classified Account of its Operations in Guatemala, 1952–1954* (Stanford, CA: Stanford University Press, 1999), 38. Cullather was a CIA historian and this book was actually a publicly published form of an official analysis of the PBSuccess, written for the CIA by Cullather, which he produced for the agency as a classified report in 1994 entitled *Operation PBSuccess: The United States and Guatemala, 1952–1954*, www.foia.cia.gov/sites/default/files/document_conversions/89801/DOC_0000134974.pdf, January 22, 2015.

69 Memorandum for the Director of Central Intelligence, "Guatemala—General Plan of Action," September, 11 1953. CIA, Electronic Document Release Center, www.foia.cia.gov/sites/default/files/document_conversions/89801/DOC_0000135872.pdf, January 22, 2015.

70 Cullather explained that although four of the sixty-one votes in Arbenz's coalition were communist, none of the ministers of his government were (p. 21), and in fact communists were barred from positions in a number of ministries (p. 90).

71 Id., 90.

72 Id., 15–17.

73 J. Kenneth McDonald, "Preface," in Cullather, *Operation PB Success*, p. ix.

74 Id.

75 Cullather, *Secret History*, p. 110.

76 Bromley K. Smith, *Organizational History of the National Security Council during the Kennedy and Johnson Administrations* (Washington, D.C.: National Security Council, 1988), p. 35.

77 U.S. Department of State, Office of the Historian, "The Bay of Pigs Invasion and its Aftermath, April 1961–October 1962," https://history.state.gov/milestones/1961-1968/bay-of-pigs, January 22, 2015.

78 Central Intelligence Agency, Memorandum, "Current US Policy With Respect to Cuba," December 12, 1963, www.foia.cia.gov/sites/default/files/document_conversions/89801/DOC_0000237505.pdf, January 22, 2015.

79 U.S. Department of State, Office of the Historian, "Alliance for Progress and Peace Corps, 1961–1969," https://history.state.gov/milestones/1961-1968/alliance-for-progress, January 16, 2015.

80 U.S. Department of State, Office of the Historian, "The Allende Years and the Pinochet Coup, 1969–1973," https://history.state.gov/milestones/1969-1976/allende, January 16, 2015.

81 Secretary of State to U.S. Embassy Chile, September 13, 1973, www2.gwu.edu/~nsarchiv/NSAEBB/NSAEBB212/19730913%20Attitude%20toward%20Junta.pdf, January 27, 2015.

82 CIA Intelligence Report, October 27, 1973, www2.gwu.edu/~nsarchiv/NSAEBB/NSAEBB212/19731027%20Intelligence%20Report.pdf, January 27, 2015.

83 Department of State, Memorandum of Conversation, June 8, 1976, www2.gwu.edu/~nsarchiv/NSAEBB/NSAEBB437/docs/Doc%2010%20-%20Kissinger-Pinochet%20memcon%20Jun%208%201976.pdf, January 27, 2015, p. 10.

84 Id., p. 3.

85 U.S. Department of State, Memorandum of Conversation, Santiago, Chile, June 6 [*sic*—The actual date was June 10], 1976, www2.gwu.edu/~nsarchiv/NSAEBB/NSAEBB133/19760610%20Memorandum%20of%20Conversation%20clean.pdf, January 27, 2015, p. 3.

86 Id., p. 4.

87 Id., p. 9.

88 Ambassador Robert Hill to Secretary of State, September 20, 1976, www2.gwu.edu/~nsarchiv/NSAEBB/NSAEBB73/760920.pdf, January 27, 2015, p. 2.

89 Ambassador Robert Hill to Secretary of State, October 19, 1976, www2.gwu.edu/~nsarchiv/NSAEBB/NSAEBB73/761019.pdf, January 27, 2015, p. 3.

90 Report from Enrique Arancibia Clavel (alias "Luis Felipe Alemparte Diaz") to DINA (Chilean Military Intelligence), estimates based on Argentine Army Intelligence Battalion 601 records, July 1978, www2.gwu.edu/~nsarchiv/NSAEBB/NSAEBB185/19780715%20%5BReport%20on%20Argentina%27s%20dissappeared%5D%20A0000514c.pdf, January 27, 2015.

91 F. Allen "Tex" Harris, Memorandum to File, "Disappearance Numbers," December 27, 1978, www2.gwu.edu/~nsarchiv/NSAEBB/NSAEBB185/19781227%20Disappearance%20Numbers%20 0000A8B1.pdf, January 27, 2015.

92 CIA Cable on Meeting 13–16 December 1976, www.foia.cia.gov/sites/default/files/document_ conversions/89801/DOC_0001000972.pdf, January 24, 2015; CIA Memorandum, April 18, 1977, www.foia.cia.gov/sites/default/files/document_conversions/89801/DOC_0000345186.pdf, January 24, 2015.

93 Congressional Research Service, *U.S. Army School of the Americas: Background and Congressional Concerns*, April 16, 2001, www.au.af.mil/au/awc/awcgate/crs/rl30532.pdf, November 13, 2015.

94 Secretary of State Cyrus Vance to Archbishop Oscar Arnulfo Romero, March 1, 1980, www2.gwu.edu/~nsarchiv/NSAEBB/NSAEBB339/doc05.pdf, January 29, 2015. This letter was in response to Romero's open letter to President Carter pleading with him not to continue aid to the junta. American Embassy San Salvado to Secretary of State, "Text of Archbishop's Letter to President Carter," www2.gwu.edu/~nsarchiv/NSAEBB/NSAEBB339/doc04.pdf, January 29, 2015.

95 Charles Plock, "A Prophet for All Ages," *St. Johns University Humanities Review* 4 (No. 2 Fall 2006), http://facpub.stjohns.edu/~ganterg/sjureview/vol4-2/05Plock.htm, January 29, 2015.

96 Transactions with Iran and the Senate Select Committee on Secret Military Assistance to Iran and the Nicaraguan Opposition, *Iran-Contra Investigation*, 100th Cong., 1st sess. (1987), Testimony of John M. Poindexter, 503. (Hereafter cited as *Iran-Contra Hearings*), pp. 31–32.

97 Defense Appropriations Act for Fiscal Year 1983, Pub. L. No. 97–377, §793, 96 Stat. 1833, 1865 (1982).

98 See *Iran-Contra Hearings*. See also President's Special Review Board, *The Tower Commission Report* (New York: Bantam Books, 1987).

99 National Security Archives, Electronic Briefing Book No. 485, "The Yellow Book: Secret Salvadoran military document from the civil war era catalogued "enemies," many killed or disappeared," Posted September 28, 2014, http://nsarchive.gwu.edu/NSAEBB/NSAEBB486/, January 13, 2015.

100 Id. As the National Security Archives explanation of the Yellow Book indicated, it was produced in 1987, well before the violence ended, and was created by the "Intelligence Department (C-II) of the Estado Mayor Conjunto de la Fuerza Armada Salvadoreña (EMCFA, Joint Staff of the Armed Forces)." Id.

101 United Nations, Commission on the Truth for El Salvador, *From Madness to Hope: The 12-Year War in El Salvador: The Report of the Commission on Truth for El Salvador*, www.un.org/en/ga/search/view_doc.asp?symbol=S/25500, January 31, 2015, p. 32.

102 Lawrence E. Walsh, *Iran-Contra: The Final Report of the Independent Counsel* (New York: Random House, 1993), pp. xiii–xiv.

103 *U.S. v. Poindexter*, 951 F.2d 369 (D.C. Cir. 1991); *U.S. v. North*, 910 F.2d 843 (D.C. Cir. 1990).

104 Commission for Historical Clarification (CEH), *Guatemala Memory of Silence: Report of the Commission for Historical Clarification*, 1999, p. 11, www.aaas.org/sites/default/files/migrate/uploads/mos_en.pdf, February 3, 2015.

105 Id., 17.

106 Id., 20.

107 Id., 41.

108 Id., 30.

109 See e.g., U.S. Senate, Hearing Before the Subcommittee on Immigration and Refugee Affairs of the Committee on the Judiciary, *Central American Migration to the United States*, 101st Cong., 1st Sess. (1989); U.S. House of Representatives, Hearing before the Subcommittee on Immigration, Refugees, and International Law of the Committee on the Judiciary, *Central American Asylum-Seekers*, 101st Cong., 1st Sess. (1989).

110 U.S. Senate, Report of the Committee on the Judiciary to Accompany S. 332 as Amended, *Providing for a GAO Study on Conditions of Displaced Salvadorans and Nicaraguans, and for Other Purposes*, 100th Cong., 1st Sess. (1987), p. 3.

111 Id., 4.

112 U.S. Senate, Hearing Before the Committee on the Judiciary, *Consultation on Refugee Admissions for Fiscal Year 1989*, 100th Cong., 2nd Sess. (1989), p. 18.

113 760 F. Supp. 796 (NDCA 1991).

114 Id., at 799.

115 NOTE: The United States Circuit Court of Appeals is the level of federal courts below the U.S. Supreme Court and is divided geographically across the nation, with the Second Circuit being the court sitting in New York.

116 NOTE: Solzhenitsyn was a prominent Soviet dissident, perhaps best known for his book *The Gulag Archipelago*. He was granted asylum in the U.S.

117 NOTE: An extradition treaty is an agreement between nations under which those accused of violating the law will be surrendered to the nation making the charge. Such treaties often permit the surrendering nation to refuse extradition if the country requesting extradition intends to take criminal action against the defendant, as was the case in this instance.

118 NOTE: What the Court does not make clear here is that the individual sent to retrieve Ker was not a government officer but a private investigator, who simply decided to take the law into his own hands.

119 Mexico requested an official report on the role of the United States in the abduction, and on May 16, 1990, and July 19, 1990, it sent diplomatic notes of protest from the Embassy of Mexico to the United States Department of State. In the May 16 note, Mexico said that it believed that the abduction was "carried out with the knowledge of persons working for the U.S. government, in violation of the procedure established in the extradition treaty in force between the two countries," and in the July 19 note, it requested the provisional arrest and extradition of the law enforcement agents allegedly involved in the abduction.

120 Mexico has already tried a number of members involved in the conspiracy that resulted in the murder of the Drug Enforcement Administration agent. For example, Rafael Caro-Quintero, a co-conspirator of Alvarez-Machain in this case, has already been imprisoned in Mexico on a 40-year sentence.

121 When Abraham Sofaer, Legal Adviser of the State Department, was questioned at a congressional hearing, he resisted the notion that such seizures were acceptable: "Can you imagine us going into Paris and seizing some person we regard as a terrorist...? How would we feel if some foreign nation—let us take the United Kingdom—came over here and seized some terrorist suspect in New York City, or Boston, or Philadelphia, ... because we refused through the normal channels of international, legal communications, to extradite that individual?" Hearing before the Subcommittee on Security and Terrorism of the Senate Committee on the Judiciary, 99th Cong., 1st Sess., 63 (1985).

122 NOTE: This case involved a kidnapping of a member of the African National Congress, who was returned to South Africa for trial by the Apartheid government of the day. His conviction was overturned on the basis of international law and, specifically, U.S. precedent.

123 *Case Concerning Avena and Other Mexican Nationals* (Mex. v. U.S.), 2004 I.C.J. 12, 26 (Judgment of Mar. 31) (Avena). This is a ruling of the International Court of Justice, sometimes known as the World Court.

124 The president's memorandum to the Attorney General issued in February 2005 said in part: "I have determined, pursuant to the authority vested in me as President by the Constitution and the laws of the United States of America, that the United States will discharge its international obligations under the decision of the International Court of Justice in the Case Concerning Avena and Other Mexican Nationals (Mexico v. United States of America) (Avena), 2004 ICJ 128 (Mar. 31), by having State courts give effect to the decision in accordance with general principles of comity in cases filed by the 51 Mexican nationals addressed in that decision." Memorandum for the Attorney General, "Compliance with the Decision of the International Court of Justice in Avena," February 28, 2005, http://georgewbush-whitehouse.archives.gov/news/releases/2005/02/20050228-18.html, April 30, 2013.

125 *Medillin v. Texas*, 552 U.S. 491 (2008).

126 Id., at 498–499.

127 Id., at 538 (Breyer, dissenting), citing *Foster v. Neilson*, 27 U.S. 253 (1829).

128 Id., at 541.

129 Id., at 545.

130 NOTE: A class action is a suit in which one or more people bring suit on behalf of a large number of persons in similar circumstances with the same legal problem.

131 NOTE: When the law allows a suit before a three-judge federal district court, any appeal goes directly to the U.S. Supreme Court rather than to a U.S. Circuit Court of Appeals.

132 See *Oyama v. California*, 332 U.S. 633, 644–646 (1948); *Korematsu v. United States*, 323 U.S. 214, 216 (1944); *Hirabayashi v. United States*, 320 U.S. 81, 100 (1943).

133 *McLaughlin v. Florida*, 379 U.S. 184, 191–192 (1964); *Loving v. Virginia*, 388 U.S. 1, 9 (1967); *Bolling v. Sharpe*, 347 U.S. 497, 499 (1954).

134 413 U.S. 634 (1973).
135 *Nyquist v. Mauclet*, 432 U.S. 1, 11 (1977).
136 *Foley v. Connelie*, 435 U.S. 291, 297 (1978).
137 NOTE: In this situation the Court is referring to the political community's authority.
138 We emphasize, as we have in the past, that the political-function exception must be narrowly construed; otherwise the exception will swallow the rule....
139 NOTE: Only Justice Rehnquist dissented and only by saying that he stood by his dissent in the *Sugarman* case.

References

Adams, David Wallace. *Education for Extinction: American Indians and the Boarding School Experience 1875–1928*. Lawrence, KS: Kansas University Press, 1995.

Bent, Scott J. "If You Want to Speak Spanish, Go Back to Mexico?": A First Amendment Analysis of English-Only Rules in Public Schools," *Ohio State Law Journal* 73 (No. 2 2012): 343–394.

Commission for Historical Clarification (CEH), *Guatemala Memory of Silence: Report of the Commission for Historical Clarification*, 1999, www.aaas.org/sites/default/files/migrate/uploads/mos_en.pdf, February 3, 2015.

Congressional Research Service, *U.S. Army School of the Americas: Background and Congressional Concerns*, April 16, 2001, www.au.af.mil/au/awc/awcgate/crs/rl30532.pdf, November 13, 2015.

Cullather, Nick. *Operation PBSuccess: The United States and Guatemala, 1952–1954*, Washington, D.C.: Central Intelligence Agency, 1994, www.foia.cia.gov/sites/default/files/document_conversions/89801/DOC_0000134974.pdf, January 22, 2015.

———. *Secret History: The CIA's Classified Account of its Operations in Guatemala, 1952–1954*. Stanford, CA: Stanford University Press, 1999.

DiGenova, Joseph, Gil Garcetti, Glenn F. Ivey, Robert M. A. Johnson, Harry L. Shorstein, Larry D. Thompson, Scott Turow, and John Van de Kamp. *"Foster v. Chapman*, No. 14–8249, Brief of Joseph DiGenova, Gil Garcetti, Glenn F. Ivey, Robert M. A. Johnson, Harry L. Shorstein, Larry D. Thompson, Scott Turow, and John Van de Kamp, as Amici Curiae in Support of Petitioner," www.scotusblog.com/wp-content/uploads/2015/08/14-8349_20tsac_20Joseph_20diGenova.pdf, November 12, 2015.

Government Accountability Office, *Education Needs to Further Examine Data Collection on English Language Learners in Charter Schools, GAO-13-655R* (Washington, D.C.: GAO, 2013).

Pach, Chester J. Jr. and Elmo Richardson. *The Presidency of Dwight D. Eisenhower*. Lawrence, KS: University Press of Kansas, 1991.

Plock, Charles, "A Prophet for All Ages," *St. Johns University Humanities Review* 4 (No. 2 Fall 2006), http://facpub.stjohns.edu/~ganterg/sjureview/vol4-2/05Plock.htm, January 29, 2015.

Pratt, Julius W. "The Origin of 'Manifest Destiny,'" *American Historical Review* 32 (Jul. 1927): 795–798.

President's Special Review Board. *The Tower Commission Report*. New York: Bantam Books, 1987.

Smith, Bromley K. *Organizational History of the National Security Council during the Kennedy and Johnson Administrations*. Washington, D.C.: National Security Council, 1988.

United Nations, Commission on the Truth for El Salvador. *From Madness to Hope: The 12-Year War in El Salvador: The Report of the Commission on Truth for El Salvador*, www.un.org/en/ga/search/view_doc.asp?symbol=S/25500, January 31, 2015.

U.S. Congress, Joint Hearings Before the House Select Committee to Investigate Covert Arms Transactions with Iran and the Senate Select Committee on Secret Military Assistance to Iran and the Nicaraguan Opposition, *Iran-Contra Investigation*, 100th Cong., 1st sess. (1987).

U.S. Government Accountability Office. *Charter Schools: Additional Federal Attention Needed to Help Protect Access for Students with Disabilities, GAO-12-543*. Washington, D.C.: GAO, 2012.

———. *Education Needs to Further Examine Data Collection on English Language Learners in Charter Schools, GAO-13-655R*. Washington, D.C.: GAO, 2013.

U.S. House of Representatives, Hearing before the Subcommittee on Immigration, Refugees, and International Law of the Committee on the Judiciary, *Central American Asylum-Seekers*, 101st Cong., 1st Sess. (1989).

U.S. Senate. Hearing Before the Committee on the Judiciary, *Consultation on Refugee Admissions for Fiscal Year 1989*, 100th Cong., 2nd Sess. (1989).

———. Hearing Before the Subcommittee on Immigration and Refugee Affairs of the Committee on the Judiciary, *Central American Migration to the United States*, 101st Cong., 1st Sess. (1989).

———. Select Committee on Secret Military Assistance to Iran and the Nicaraguan Opposition, *Iran-Contra Investigation*, 100th Cong., 1st Sess. (1987).

———. Report of the Committee on the Judiciary to Accompany S. 332 as Amended, *Providing for a GAO Study on Conditions of Displaced Salvadorans and Nicaraguans, and for Other Purposes*, 100th Cong., 1st Sess. (1987).

Walsh, Lawrence E. *Iran-Contra: The Final Report of the Independent Counsel*. New York: Random House, 1993.

Wong, Cecilia. "Language Is Speech: The Illegitimacy of Official English after Yñiguez v. Arizonans for Official English," *U.C. Davis Law Review* 30 (Fall 1996): 277–310.

10   Gender Discrimination

The Rise of the So-Called Middle Standard

Lilly Ledbetter had been working at a Goodyear Tire plant for years and was a supervisor. She learned from an anonymous note that men working in the same position as hers were being paid a good deal more than she received. She sued under Title VII of the Civil Rights Act and received a $3.3 million judgment. However, that decision was overturned on appeal on the grounds that she had failed to file her claim within 180 days of the first paycheck in which she was paid less than her male counterparts. Of course, she could not have known at that time of the existence of the pay discrepancy, since the company was not about to admit it was engaged in pay discrimination. Even so, the U.S. Supreme Court found that she could not proceed against the company because of the time limits for filing.[1] Sadly, it took an act of Congress to overturn the Supreme Court's interpretation of the statute for the future, but that did not help Ms. Ledbetter. The Lilly Ledbetter Act was the first bill that President Obama signed into law in 2009.[2]

In addition to the fact that the discrimination she endured was not remedied, the Supreme Court majority ignored the obvious catch-22 in which their ruling placed women. If employers were sufficiently devious in their discrimination against women, they were rewarded and the women who suffered the loss were left with no recourse. If there was a positive side to Ms. Ledbetter's case, it was that it made indisputably clear to many legislators and the general public what had been happening to women in the workplace. Regardless of the specific legal rules that applied or the particular facts of this case, the opinion demonstrated that sexism was alive and well in the twenty-first century, more than four decades after the passage of the Civil Rights Act of 1964 made discrimination on the basis of sex illegal.

Although efforts to address discrimination against women reach far back into our history—after all the Seneca Falls Convention was held in 1848[3]—the fact is that modern law and policy designed to address civil rights for women date primarily from 1971.[4] Although the Civil Rights Act of 1964 included prohibition of discrimination on the basis of sex,[5] the statute was primarily designed to address race, and it was not until the 1970s that Supreme Court rulings and legislation made gender equality an important focus.[6]

In addition to the fact that the law and policy is so recent, it is important to be aware that, despite the tendency of the entertainment and news media to emphasize what is often termed the "war between the sexes," gender equality concerns both men and women. Indeed, a number of the cases that have been important to the development of gender-related civil rights have been brought by men. And well before Justices Sandra Day O'Connor, Ruth Bader Ginsburg, Elena Kagan, and Sonia Sotomayor[7] joined the Court, justices like William Brennan were crafting important rulings in pursuit of gender equality and attacking stereotypes that, as he put it, represented "an attitude of 'romantic paternalism' which ... put women, not on a pedestal, but in a cage."[8] Indeed, he led the effort in the Supreme Court to address sex discrimination throughout the 1970s and 1980s.

There was another sense of commonality, which was that women have experienced, along with men, the many difficulties encountered by each of the groups discussed to this point in the book, including slavery. Recall that the discussion of the Fugitive Slave Law began with the *Prigg* case, in which a Maryland woman sent slave catchers to drag another woman and her children back from the freedom of Pennsylvania into her service. Remember as well the discussion of Mariana Jaremillo, who was held in peonage in New Mexico until the State Supreme Court denounced the practice. Today the form is different, often taking the form of human trafficking for sexual exploitation or effective enslavement of domestic workers by those who take women's documents and force them into what is, by any reasonable definition, slavery. These forms of enslavement are well known and obviously illegal, but are difficult to combat.[9] As the Federal Bureau of Investigation puts it: "It's sad but true: here in this country, people are being bought, sold, and smuggled like modern-day slaves."[10]

Thus, in a number of respects, gender issues pervade the full range of civil rights problems and developments over time. Even so, as noted above, the body of Supreme Court decisions that actually have sought to recognize and engage our history of sex discrimination is very recent.

Historic Challenges and the Rise of Gender Issues in Civil Rights

In the area of gender discrimination, there is, as there has been in the other aspects of civil rights, a history of opinions that are hard to read because it is difficult to accept that the nation's highest court could say such things. But, as Justice Thurgood Marshall said of race, it is essential to read and understand that history to understand what has shaped the experiences of women and the policies that affect them.

Early Interpretations of the Fourteenth Amendment Rejected Women's Rights

Two cases in particular mark a low point in Supreme Court discussion of gender discrimination, and both reach back in time to the era just after the Fourteenth Amendment to the Constitution came into effect. The women in both cases thought that the provision of that amendment that said "No State shall make or enforce any law which shall abridge the privileges or immunities of citizens of the United States" meant what it said, and that those privileges and immunities must surely include at least the right to pursue a lawful occupation and a right to vote. However, as the discussion of race in Chapter 2 explained, the Supreme Court in those years reversed by interpretation that which the framers of the Civil War amendments sought to protect.[11] Sadly, the two gender cases that are discussed below were further examples of the Court's destructive efforts.

Bradwell v. State

83 U.S. 130 (1873)

INTRODUCTION: Myra Bradwell was born in Manchester, Vermont. She lived in several states. She and her husband ultimately moved to Chicago, where her husband developed a successful legal career, became a judge, and later was elected a state legislator. Ms. Bradwell apprenticed in his firm, a common route to legal practice in those days. She began publishing a newspaper on legal matters, the *Chicago Legal News*, in 1868, which quickly became an authoritative journal recognized in Illinois law.[12] She passed the Illinois bar examination and applied for admission to the Illinois bar, but was rejected on that grounds that she "as a married woman would be bound neither by her express contracts nor by those implied contracts which it is the policy of the law to create between attorney and client." This conclusion that she could not contract stemmed from the doctrine of coverture, under which the legal identity of the woman was not independent but rested with the husband in the marriage. That doctrine was not fully eliminated until the 1960s.[13] Bradwell rejected the idea that the fact that she was a married woman had anything at all to do with her fitness to practice law in the state and appealed. The Illinois Supreme Court rejected that appeal and she took her case to the U.S. Supreme Court.

Even as the U.S. Supreme Court was considering her case, the Illinois legislature passed a law in 1872 providing that "No person shall be precluded or debarred from any occupation, profession or employment (except military) on account of sex."[14] Another woman, Alta M. Hulett, was able to be admitted as a result of that law in 1873. Ms. Bradwell did not think she should have to reapply, and in 1890 the Illinois Supreme Court admitted her to the bar without an additional filing and backdated that admission to the date of her original application in 1868. The U.S. Supreme Court did the same in 1892. Because of the date of admission, Bradwell is often recognized as the first licensed woman attorney in the United States.[15]

The U.S. Supreme Court provided portions of the Illinois Supreme Court opinion with its opinion in the *Bradwell* case. These excerpts indicate just how extreme the position of the state was and are worthy of attention both for what they say of attitudes toward women, and also in setting the context within which the U.S. Supreme Court ruled. The state court said, in part:

> Whether, in the existing social relations between men and women, it would promote the proper administration of justice, and the general well-being of society, to permit women to engage in the trial of cases at the bar, is a question opening a wide field of discussion, upon which it is not necessary for us to enter. It is sufficient to say that ... [i]f we were to admit them, we should be exercising the authority conferred upon us in a manner which ... was never contemplated by the legislature.

> It is to be remembered that at the time this statute was enacted we had, by express provision, adopted the common law of England.... [F]emale attorneys at law were unknown in England, and a proposition that a woman should enter the courts of Westminster Hall in that capacity, or as a barrister, would have created hardly less astonishment than one that she should ascend the bench of bishops, or be elected to a seat in the House of Commons.

> It is to be further remembered, that when our act was passed, that school of reform which claims for women participation in the making and administering of the laws had not then arisen, or, if here and there a writer had advanced such theories, they were regarded rather as abstract speculations than as an actual basis for action.

> That God designed the sexes to occupy different spheres of action, and that it belonged to men to make, apply, and execute the laws, was regarded as an almost axiomatic truth.

> In view of these facts, we are certainly warranted in saying that when the legislature gave to this court the power of granting licenses to practice law, it was with not the slightest expectation that this privilege would be extended to women.

Justice Miller wrote the opinion for the U.S. Supreme Court.

> [T]he plaintiff asserted her right to a license on the grounds, among others, that she was a citizen of the United States, and that having been a citizen of Vermont at one time, she was, in the State of Illinois, entitled to any right granted to citizens of the latter State.... [T]he plaintiff ... has stated very clearly a case to which [the privileges and immunities clause of the Fourteenth Amendment] is inapplicable.
>
> ... [C]ounsel for the plaintiff in this court truly says that there are certain privileges and immunities which belong to a citizen of the United States as such; otherwise it would be nonsense for the Fourteenth Amendment to prohibit a State from abridging them, and he proceeds to argue that admission to the bar of a State of a person who possesses the requisite learning and character is one of those which a State may not deny.
>
> In this latter proposition we are not able to concur.... We agree with him that there are privileges and immunities belonging to citizens of the United States ... and that it is these and these alone which a State is forbidden to abridge. But the right to admission to practice in the courts of a State is not one of them. This right in no sense depends on citizenship of the United States. It has not, as far as we know, ever been made in any State, or in any case, to depend on citizenship at all. Certainly many prominent and distinguished lawyers have been admitted to practice, both in the State and Federal courts, who were not citizens of the United States or of any State. But, on whatever basis this right may be placed, ... as to the courts of a State, it would relate to citizenship of the State, and as to Federal courts, it would relate to citizenship of the United States.
>
> The opinion just delivered in the *Slaughter-House Cases* renders elaborate argument in the present case unnecessary.... [T]he right to control and regulate the granting of license to practice law in the courts of a State is one of those powers which are not transferred for its protection to the Federal government, and its exercise is in no manner governed or controlled by citizenship of the United States in the party seeking such license.... Judgment affirmed.

Justice Bradley wrote a concurring opinion joined by Justices Swayne and Field.

> ... The claim ... assumes that it is one of the privileges and immunities of women as citizens to engage in any and every profession, occupation, or employment in civil life.... It certainly cannot be affirmed, as an historical fact, that this has ever been established as one of the fundamental privileges and immunities of the sex. On the contrary, the civil law, as well as nature herself, has always recognized a wide difference in the respective spheres and destinies of man and woman. Man is, or should be, woman's protector and defender. The natural and proper timidity and delicacy which belongs to the female sex evidently unfits it for many of the occupations of civil life. The constitution of the family organization, which is founded in the divine ordinance, as well as in the nature of things, indicates the domestic sphere as that which properly belongs to the domain and functions of womanhood. The harmony, not to say identity, of interests and views which belong, or should belong, to the family institution is repugnant to the idea of a woman adopting a distinct and independent career from that of her husband. So firmly fixed was this sentiment in the founders of the common law that it became a maxim of that system of jurisprudence that a woman had no legal existence separate from her husband, who was regarded as her head and representative in the

social state; and, notwithstanding some recent modifications of this civil status, many of the special rules of law flowing from and dependent upon this cardinal principle still exist in full force in most States. One of these is, that a married woman is incapable, without her husband's consent, of making contracts which shall be binding on her or him.[16] This very incapacity was one circumstance which the Supreme Court of Illinois deemed important in rendering a married woman incompetent fully to perform the duties and trusts that belong to the office of an attorney and counsellor.

It is true that many women are unmarried and not affected by any of the duties, complications, and incapacities arising out of the married state, but these are exceptions to the general rule. The paramount destiny and mission of woman are to fulfil the noble and benign offices of wife and mother. This is the law of the Creator. And the rules of civil society must be adapted to the general constitution of things, and cannot be based upon exceptional cases.

The humane movements of modern society, which have for their object the multiplication of avenues for woman's advancement, and of occupations adapted to her condition and sex, have my heartiest concurrence. But I am not prepared to say that it is one of her fundamental rights and privileges to be admitted into every office and position, including those which require highly special qualifications and demanding special responsibilities. In the nature of things it is not every citizen of every age, sex, and condition that is qualified for every calling and position. It is the prerogative of the legislator to prescribe regulations founded on nature, reason, and experience for the due admission of qualified persons to professions and callings demanding special skill and confidence. This fairly belongs to the police power of the State; and, in my opinion, in view of the peculiar characteristics, destiny, and mission of woman, it is within the province of the legislature to ordain what offices, positions, and callings shall be filled and discharged by men, and shall receive the benefit of those energies and responsibilities, and that decision and firmness which are presumed to predominate in the sterner sex. For these reasons ... the laws of Illinois ... [do not abridge] the privileges and immunities of citizens of the United States.

The Chief Justice dissented without opinion.

The other case that came almost at the same time as *Bradwell* concerned a claim to a right to vote by a woman who had been born in a state where women had that right. Once again the U.S. Supreme Court rejected the attempt to bury the legacy of the *Dred Scott* case through passage of the Fourteenth Amendment. It is ironic, after all, that the Fourteenth Amendment was specifically designed to compel states and their local governments to ensure the protections of rights that should be enjoyed by all Americans. It is perhaps particularly ironic that this case came from Missouri, the state in which Dred Scott originated.

Minor v. Happersett

88 U.S. 162 (1874)

INTRODUCTION: The facts of this case are explained in the opinion. However, they should be placed in the context of the discussion above regarding the language and purposes of the amendment, as well as the ideological approach of the then Supreme Court majority.

Chief Justice Waite wrote the opinion for the Court.

... It is contended that the provisions of the constitution and laws of the State of Missouri which confine the right of suffrage and registration therefor to men are in violation of the Constitution of the United States, and therefore void. The argument is, that as a woman [who] is a citizen of the United States and of the State in which she resides, she has the right of suffrage as one of the privileges and immunities of her citizenship, which the State cannot by its laws or constitution abridge.

There is no doubt that women may be citizens. They are persons, and by the Fourteenth Amendment "all persons born or naturalized in the United States and subject to the jurisdiction thereof" are expressly declared to be "citizens of the United States and of the State wherein they reside." ... [C]ertainly more cannot be necessary to establish the fact that sex has never been made one of the elements of citizenship in the United States.... The Fourteenth Amendment did not affect the citizenship of women any more than it did of men.... The amendment prohibited the State, of which [Minor] is a citizen, from abridging any of her privileges and immunities as a citizen of the United States.... If the right of suffrage is one of the necessary privileges of a citizen of the United States, then the constitution and laws of Missouri confining it to men are in violation of the Constitution of the United States, as amended, and consequently void....

The Constitution does not define the privileges and immunities of citizens.... In this case we need not determine what they are, but only whether suffrage is necessarily one of them. It certainly is nowhere made so in express terms....

The amendment did not add to the privileges and immunities of a citizen. It simply furnished an additional guaranty for the protection of such as he already had. No new voters were necessarily made by it. Indirectly it may have had that effect, because it may have increased the number of citizens entitled to suffrage under the constitution and laws of the States, but it operates for this purpose, if at all, through the States and the State laws, and not directly upon the citizen.

It is clear, therefore, we think, that the Constitution has not added the right of suffrage to the privileges and immunities of citizenship as they existed at the time it was adopted. This makes it proper to inquire whether suffrage was coextensive with the citizenship of the States at the time of its adoption.... When the Federal Constitution was adopted, all the States, with the exception of Rhode Island and Connecticut, had constitutions of their own.... Upon an examination of those constitutions we find that in no State were all citizens permitted to vote....

In this condition of the law in respect to suffrage in the several States it cannot for a moment be doubted that if it had been intended to make all citizens of the United States voters, the framers of the Constitution would not have left it to implication. So important a change in the condition of citizenship as it actually existed, if intended, would have been expressly declared.

... [A]fter the adoption of the Fourteenth Amendment, it was deemed necessary to adopt a fifteenth.... If suffrage was one of these privileges or immunities, why amend the Constitution to prevent its being denied on account of race, &c.? ...

It is true that the United States guarantees to every State a republican form of government [Article 4, §4] ... The guaranty [of a republican form of government] necessarily implies a duty on the part of the States themselves to provide such a government.... As has been seen, all the citizens of the States were not invested with the right of suffrage. In all, save perhaps New Jersey, this right was only bestowed upon men and not upon all of them. Under these circumstances it is certainly now too late to contend that a government is not republican ... because women are not made voters.... The right of suffrage, when granted, will be protected. He who has it can only be deprived of it by due process of law, but in order to claim protection he must first show that he has the right....

The Constitution was ... ratified by nine States in 1788, and finally by the thirteen original States in 1790. Vermont was the first new State admitted to the Union, and it came in [1791] under a constitution which conferred the right of suffrage only upon men of the full age of twenty-one years.... Kentucky followed with a constitution confining the right of suffrage to free male citizens of the age of twenty-one years.... Then followed Tennessee, in 1796, with voters of freemen of the age of twenty-one years and upwards.... No new State has ever been admitted to the Union which has conferred the right of suffrage upon women, and this has never been considered a valid objection to her admission. On the contrary, as is claimed in the argument, the right of suffrage was withdrawn from women as early as 1807 in the State of New Jersey, without any attempt to obtain the interference of the United States to prevent it....

If the law is wrong, it ought to be changed; but the power for that is not with us.... No argument as to woman's need of suffrage can be considered. We can only act upon her rights as they exist. It is not for us to look at the hardship of withholding. Our duty is at an end if we find it is within the power of a State to withhold. Being unanimously of the opinion that the Constitution of the United States does not confer the right of suffrage upon any one, and that the constitutions and laws of the several States which commit that important trust to men alone are not necessarily void, we affirm the judgement.

Although the Fifteenth Amendment, ratified in 1870, prohibited efforts to block access to the ballot on the basis of race, that protection was not accorded to women until the passage of the Nineteenth Amendment in 1920.

The Post-War Period and the Back and Forth of Gender Equality

World War II demanded the full attention of the nation and the engagement of its men and women. Women's contributions were many, and the iconic image of "Rosie the Riveter" is only one symbol of the broad and deep engagement of women in the effort. And yet, soon after the war ended, things changed quickly and moved back in quite a conservative direction in many important respects, including the role of women in the society. The focus on the millions of families that came together to makes lives for themselves as the war ended and veterans returned home was on finding homes, many of which were in the burgeoning suburban areas where relatively inexpensive housing was available and which promised to be communities where these families would be happy to raise their children. In addition, the marketplace once again became extremely competitive, with post-war recession and the need of millions of veterans to find work as they returned home. There was also a search for security and stability in the years following the war and the Great Depression that had preceded it.

There was also a new force of television, that came of age in the 1950s and 1960s, as a forum in which discussions of families and the men, women, and children who comprise them took place. Such extremely popular programs as the "Adventures of Ozzie and Harriett," "Father Knows Best," "Leave it to Beaver," and "I Love Lucy" became images of what many Americans thought life should be like. It was an era when families gathered around the television after dinner. They laughed at the foibles of the characters in these programs and responded to the idealized sense of family and belonging that they presented. Although they often left the viewers warm and feeling a sense of calm, order, and a predictable orderly way of life, they also created some stereotypes and reinforced others.

They not only portrayed the expected roles for men, women, and children in the family and in society, but they also projected an assumption that Americans lived a middle-class lifestyle. Their casts were white and obviously enjoyed a substantial income with few really serious problems. The programs were carefully watched by their production companies and the networks to ensure that they did not take on controversial or challenging characters or subject matter.[17] These presentations of life were mirrored in magazines and newspaper advertisements of the time, an era when both of these means of communication were far more prevalent and influential than they are today.

Ironically, this development of lifestyle and role expectations was happening as the battle for civil rights was heating up, with the NAACP/LDF regularly taking cases to the courts to challenge segregation in universities, housing, and then in elementary and secondary schools. Even so, as earlier chapters have indicated, President Eisenhower focused more on maintaining and encouraging those expectations about stability, order, predictability, and economic prosperity and avoiding engaging the civil rights struggle until he was forced to do so in the Little Rock schools crisis. Instead of addressing serious and growing issues at home, official attention was primarily focused on the Cold War abroad and the hunt for those thought to be communists or pro-left at home.

Even as the U.S. Supreme Court was issuing important rulings in the area of race and civil rights, it appeared that they were not ready to move on gender issues in the same way. In one case the Court rejected a challenge by a female tavern owner and her daughter to a Michigan law denying bartender licenses to females—except for wives and daughters of male tavern owners. Justice Frankfurter was dismissive of the very idea of the challenge, writing "Beguiling as the subject is, it need not detain us long," and just as clear about rejecting out of hand the idea that the changes in society with respect to women so important during the war years were of constitutional significance.

Goesaert v. Cleary

335 U.S. 464 (1948)

The claim, denied below ... and renewed here, is that Michigan cannot forbid females generally from being barmaids and at the same time make an exception in favor of the wives and daughters of the owners of liquor establishments. Beguiling as the subject is, it need not detain us long. To ask whether or not the Equal Protection of the Laws Clause of the Fourteenth Amendment barred Michigan from making the classification the State has made between wives and daughters of owners of liquor places and wives and daughters of non-owners, is one of those rare instances where to state the question is in effect to answer it.

We are, to be sure, dealing with a historic calling. We meet the alewife, sprightly and ribald, in Shakespeare, but centuries before him she played a role in the social life of England.... The Fourteenth Amendment did not tear history up by the roots, and the regulation of the liquor traffic is one of the oldest and most untrammeled of legislative powers. Michigan could, beyond question, forbid all women from working behind a bar. This is so despite the vast changes in the social and legal position of women. The fact that women may now have achieved the virtues that men have long claimed as their prerogatives and now indulge in vices that men have long practiced, does not preclude the States from drawing a sharp line between the sexes, certainly in such matters as the regulation of the liquor traffic.... The Constitution does not require legislatures to reflect socio-logical insight, or shifting social standards, any more than it requires them to keep abreast of the latest scientific standards.

While Michigan may deny to all women opportunities for bartending, Michigan cannot play favorites among women without rhyme or reason. The Constitution in enjoining the equal protection of the laws upon States precludes irrational dis-crimination as between persons or groups of persons in the incidence of a law. But the Constitution does not require situations "which are different in fact or opinion to be treated in law as though they were the same." ... Since bartending by women may, in the allowable legislative judgment, give rise to moral and social problems against which it may devise preventive measures, the legislature need not go to the full length of prohibition if it believes that as to a defined group of females other factors are operating which either eliminate or reduce the moral and social problems otherwise calling for prohibition. Michigan evidently believes that the oversight assured through ownership of a bar by a barmaid's husband or father minimizes hazards that may confront a barmaid without such protect-ing oversight. This Court is certainly not in a position to gainsay such belief by the Michigan legislature. If it is entertainable, as we think it is, Michigan has not violated its duty to afford equal protection of its laws. We cannot cross-examine either actually or argumentatively the mind of Michigan legislators nor question their motives. Since the line they have drawn is not without a basis in reason, we cannot give ear to the suggestion that the real impulse behind this legislation was an unchivalrous desire of male bartenders to try to monopolize the calling....

Nor is it unconstitutional for Michigan to withdraw from women the occupa-tion of bartending because it allows women to serve as waitresses where liquor is dispensed. The District Court has sufficiently indicated the reasons that may have influenced the legislature in allowing women to be waitresses in a liquor establish-ment over which a man's ownership provides control.... Judgment affirmed.

Justice Rutledge wrote a dissent joined by Justices Douglas and Murphy.

While the equal protection clause does not require a legislature to achieve "abstract symmetry" or to classify with "mathematical nicety," that clause does require lawmakers to refrain from invidious distinctions of the sort drawn by the statute challenged in this case.[18]

The statute arbitrarily discriminates between male and female owners of liquor establishments. A male owner, although he himself is always absent from his bar, may employ his wife and daughter as barmaids. A female owner may neither work as a barmaid herself nor employ her daughter in that position, even if a man is always present in the establishment to keep order. This inevitable result of the classification belies the assumption that the statute was motivated by a legislative solicitude for the moral and physical well-being of women who, but for the law, would be employed as barmaids. Since there could be no other conceivable justi-fication for such discrimination against women owners of liquor establishments, the statute should be held invalid as a denial of equal protection.

The 1960s, Civil Rights Energy, and the Reinvigoration of the Women's Movement

From the perspective of those coming of age in the twenty-first century, it is easy to assume that the major change in civil rights protections related to discrimination on the basis of gender have been in place for a long time. However, in the scheme of American national history, the rise of the contemporary women's movement and the development of important legislation and judicial opinions addressing key issues, these protections are really quite recent.

It is true that the 1960s marked an era of considerable ferment in the U.S. as well as in other countries. There were many dynamics shaping those years, including of course the effort to make the promise of *Brown v. Board of Education* real in the face of massive resistance to desegregation. The environmental movement, Native American civil rights efforts, and Latino civil rights work, including the leadership by Caesar Chavez of the United Farmworkers, was intensifying, particularly in the second half of the decade. The Latino civil rights work in the courts was informed by the work of the NAACP/LDF and other African American leaders, as were the Native American efforts, evolving environmental advocacy, and the contemporary women's movement. It was also an era of anti-war protests.

In some ways, the context supported the rise of new civil rights efforts, but there was also competition for energy, involvement, and public attention. Although there were leaders seeking to build the new women's movement and events that did bring attention, like the publication of Betty Friedan's book *The Feminine Mystique* in 1963,[19] the National Organization for Women was not founded until 1966.

Efforts would intensify, in part centered on the attempt to enact an Equal Rights Amendment to the Constitution. Interestingly, those efforts engendered a backlash from conservative women in such groups as the Eagle Forum. Ultimately the amendment was not ratified, even though the time for ratification was extended.

The Civil Rights Act of 1964 contained only one section that addressed sex discrimination, which was Title VII dealing with employment discrimination. There continues to be argument over just why and how that provision was added, but what was clear, and became increasingly obvious over time, was that the 1964 civil rights legislation was designed and enacted primarily with a focus on racial discrimination. It would take eight more years before the Equal Opportunity Amendments of 1972 were adopted, which really were designed with concern for gender.

The Family, Parenting, Birth Control, and the Growing Role of the Courts

Perhaps it should not come as a surprise that the momentum in the courts with respect to cases addressing civil rights issues related to gender grew out of assumptions about the family, parenting, and birth control, although only some of these cases came as claims of sex discrimination under the equal protection clause of the Fourteenth Amendment (or the equal protection element of the due process clause of the Fifth Amendment in the case of federal government matters). It does, however, come as a considerable surprise to many students new to civil rights issues that some of these cases came so late in American history. It was only in 1965 that the high court established a constitutional right to privacy in *Griswold v. Connecticut* and struck down a Connecticut law making it a crime to counsel married couples on the use of contraceptives.[20] It was not until 1967 that the Supreme Court struck down bans on interracial marriage.[21] Even later, in 1972, the U.S. Supreme Court struck down laws making birth control counseling or providing contraceptives to single persons a criminal offense.[22] It seems strange to many in an era in which it is not at all unusual to have children born out of wedlock, but even in the late 1960s and into the 1970s there were serious burdens imposed on those who either chose to have children when not married or who unexpectedly found themselves pregnant.[23] Recall as well that it was not until 1973 that prohibitions on abortion were struck down by the Supreme Court, so that pregnancy most often meant childbirth and all that comes with it.[24] Not only did pregnancies out of wedlock, or unplanned or sometimes unwanted pregnancies, present challenges for women, they also meant legal burdens for the children born under what was historically termed the "bar sinister." Old laws that assumed one could deter sexual activity out of marriage by threatening to impose legal burdens on the children remained in force until the Supreme Court began to address those issues in the 1970s. Then there were issues about fathers of children born out of wedlock, who nevertheless lived with the mother and were fathers to their children in every other respect.[25]

Quite apart from these issues about marriage and childbirth, there were, as there have been throughout history, laws that dealt with other aspects of family life, provisions based upon sets of gender expectations and biases. It was one of these, *Reed v. Reed*, that is generally seen as the start of the development in the Supreme Court of protections for civil rights associated with gender. The case is interesting, among other reasons, because one of the advocates in that litigation, Ruth Bader Ginsburg, would herself later become a justice of the Court.

Reed v. Reed

404 U.S. 71 (1971)

INTRODUCTION: The opinion provides the facts of the case. This case presented what is called an irrebuttable presumption, which is an assumption made in a statute that cannot be challenged. And there have been any number of such presumptions based on gender, as will become clearer in the *Frontiero v. Richardson* case presented later in this chapter.

Chief Justice Burger wrote the opinion for the Court.

Richard Lynn Reed, a minor, died intestate[26] in Ada County, Idaho, on March 29, 1967. His adoptive parents, who had separated sometime prior to his death, are the parties to this appeal. Approximately seven months after Richard's death, his mother, appellant Sally Reed, filed a petition in the Probate Court of Ada County, seeking appointment as administratrix[27] of her son's estate.... Cecil Reed, [Richard's] father..., filed a competing petition seeking to have himself appointed administrator.... The probate court ... treated §§15–312 and 15–314 of the Idaho Code as ... compelling a preference for Cecil Reed because he was a male.

Section 15–312 ... lists 11 classes of persons who are ... entitled [to administer the estate of one who dies intestate, including] "the father or mother" of the person dying intestate. Under this section, then, appellant and appellee ... would seem to have been equally entitled to administer their son's estate. Section 15–314 provides, however, that "of several persons claiming and equally entitled [under §15–312] to administer, males must be preferred to females, and relatives of the whole to those of the half blood."

In issuing its order, the probate court ... ruled ... that appellee, being a male, was to be preferred to the female appellant "by reason of Section 15–314 of the Idaho Code." In stating this conclusion, the probate judge gave no indication that he had attempted to determine the relative capabilities of the competing applicants to perform the functions incident to the administration of an estate. It seems clear the probate judge considered himself bound by statute to give preference to the male candidate over the female, each being otherwise "equally entitled."

Sally Reed appealed.... [T]he District Court of the Fourth Judicial District of Idaho ... held that the challenged section violated the Equal Protection Clause of the Fourteenth Amendment.... [T]he Idaho Supreme Court ... reversed.... [W]e have concluded that the arbitrary preference established in favor of males by §15–314 of the Idaho Code cannot stand in the face of the Fourteenth Amendment's command that no State deny the equal protection of the laws to any person within its jurisdiction....

Section 15–314 ... establishes a classification subject to scrutiny under the Equal Protection Clause.... The question presented by this case, then, is whether a difference in the sex of competing applicants for letters of administration bears a rational relationship to a state objective that is sought to be advanced by the operation of §§15–312 and 15–314.

In upholding the latter section, the Idaho Supreme Court concluded that its objective was to eliminate one area of controversy when two or more persons ... seek letters of administration.... Clearly the objective of reducing the workload on probate courts by eliminating one class of contests is not without some legitimacy. The crucial question, however, is whether §15–314 advances that objective in a manner consistent with the command of the Equal Protection Clause. We hold that it does not. To give a mandatory preference to members of either sex over members of the other, merely to accomplish the elimination of hearings on the merits, is to make the very kind of arbitrary legislative choice forbidden by the Equal Protection Clause of the Fourteenth Amendment; and whatever may be said as to the positive values of avoiding intrafamily controversy, the choice in this context may not lawfully be mandated solely on the basis of sex.... Reversed and remanded.

Of course, gender-related presumptions have been made about men as well as women and, as noted earlier, some of the most important cases on sex discrimination were brought by men. The law explained in those cases applies to both men and women. A case about how states treat parents of children born out of wedlock provided the setting for an important statement about the need to avoid gender-based stereotypes, whoever might be the subject of that prejudice.

Stanley v. Illinois

405 U.S. 645 (1972)

INTRODUCTION: Under Illinois law at the time, a father of children born outside of marriage was presumed to be an unfit parent. Even if he wanted to adopt his children, he was placed last in line behind any others, related or not, who wanted to adopt the children and were considered qualified, and there was no opportunity for a hearing at which to argue against the presumption.

Peter Stanley and Joan Stanley had three children and had been together for some 18 years, though they were not married. He had acknowledged paternity and was providing support and care. When she died, the children were taken by the state on the basis of the Illinois presumption, even though there was no evidence and had been no finding that he was an unfit parent. He challenged the Illinois presumption.

Justice White delivered the opinion of the Court.[28]

The State's right—indeed, duty—to protect minor children through a judicial determination of their interests in a neglect proceeding is not challenged here. Rather, we are faced with a dependency statute that empowers state officials to circumvent neglect proceedings on the theory that an unwed father is not a "parent" whose existing relationship with his children must be considered.

Under Illinois law, therefore, while the children of all parents can be taken from them in neglect proceedings, that is only after notice, hearing, and proof of such unfitness as a parent as amounts to neglect, an unwed father is uniquely subject to the more simplistic dependency proceeding. By use of this proceeding, the State, on showing that the father was not married to the mother, need not prove unfitness in fact, because it is presumed at law. Thus, the unwed father's claim of parental qualification is avoided as "irrelevant."

In considering this procedure under the Due Process Clause, we recognize ... that "what procedures due process may require under any given set of circumstances must begin with a determination of the precise nature of the government function involved as well as of the private interest that has been affected by governmental action." *Goldberg v. Kelly*, 397 U.S. 254, 263 (1970). The private interest here, that of a man in the children he has sired and raised, undeniably warrants deference and, absent a powerful countervailing interest, protection. It is plain that the interest of a parent in the companionship, care, custody, and management of his or her children "come[s] to this Court with a momentum for respect...." The Court has frequently emphasized the importance of the family. The rights to conceive and to raise one's children have been deemed "essential," *Meyer v. Nebraska*, 262 U.S. 390, 399 (1923), "basic civil rights of man," *Skinner v. Oklahoma*, 316 U.S. 535, 541 (1942), and "rights far more precious ... than property rights," *May v. Anderson*, 345 U.S. 528, 533 (1953). "It is cardinal with us that the custody, care and nurture of the child reside first in the parents, whose primary function and freedom include preparation for obligations the state can neither supply nor hinder." *Prince v. Massachusetts*, 321 U.S. 158, 166 (1944). The integrity of the family unit has found protection in the Due Process Clause of the Fourteenth Amendment, ... the Equal Protection Clause of the Fourteenth Amendment..., and the Ninth Amendment....

Nor has the law refused to recognize those family relationships unlegitimized by a marriage ceremony. The Court has declared unconstitutional a state statute denying natural, but illegitimate, children a wrongful-death action for the death of their mother, emphasizing that such children cannot be denied the right of other children because familial bonds in such cases were often as warm, enduring, and important as those arising within a more formally organized family unit. *Levy v. Louisiana*, 391 U.S. 68, 71–72 (1968). "To say that the test of equal protection should be the 'legal' rather than the biological relationship is to avoid the issue. For the Equal Protection Clause necessarily limits the authority of a State to draw such 'legal' lines as it chooses." *Glona v. American Guarantee Co.*, 391 U.S. 73, 75–76 (1968). These authorities make it clear that, at the least, Stanley's interest in retaining custody of his children is cognizable and substantial.

[W]e are here not asked to evaluate the legitimacy of the state ends, rather, to determine whether the means used to achieve these ends are constitutionally defensible. What is the state interest in separating children from fathers without a hearing designed to determine whether the father is unfit in a particular disputed case? We observe that the State registers no gain towards its declared goals when it separates children from the custody of fit parents. Indeed, if Stanley is a fit father, the State spites its own articulated goals when it needlessly separates him from his family....

It may be, as the State insists, that most unmarried fathers are unsuitable and neglectful parents. It may also be that Stanley is such a parent and that his children should be placed in other hands. But all unmarried fathers are not in this category; some are wholly suited to have custody of their children. This much the State readily concedes, and nothing in this record indicates that Stanley is or has been a neglectful father who has not cared for his children. Given the opportunity to make his case, Stanley may have been seen to be deserving of custody of his offspring. Had this been so, the State's statutory policy would have been furthered by leaving custody in him....

[I]t may be argued that unmarried fathers are so seldom fit that Illinois need not undergo the administrative inconvenience of inquiry in any case, including Stanley's. The establishment of prompt efficacious procedures to achieve legitimate state ends is a proper state interest worthy of cognizance in constitutional adjudication. But the Constitution recognizes higher values than speed and efficiency. Indeed, one might fairly say of the Bill of Rights in general, and the Due Process Clause in particular, that they were designed to protect the fragile values of a vulnerable citizenry from the overbearing concern for efficiency and efficacy that may characterize praiseworthy government officials no less, and perhaps more, than mediocre ones.

Procedure by presumption is always cheaper and easier than individualized determination. But when, as here, the procedure forecloses the determinative issues of competence and care, when it explicitly disdains present realities in deference to past formalities, it needlessly risks running roughshod over the important interests of both parent and child. It therefore cannot stand.

[The state] insists on presuming rather than proving Stanley's unfitness solely because it is more convenient to presume than to prove. Under the Due Process Clause that advantage is insufficient to justify refusing a father a hearing when the issue at stake is the dismemberment of his family.

The State of Illinois assumes custody of the children of married parents, divorced parents, and unmarried mothers only after a hearing and proof of neglect. The children of unmarried fathers, however, are declared dependent children without a hearing on parental fitness and without proof of neglect. Stanley's claim in the state courts and here is that failure to afford him a hearing on his parental qualifications while extending it to other parents denied him equal protection of the laws. We have concluded that all Illinois parents are constitutionally entitled to a hearing on their fitness before their children are removed from their custody. It follows that denying such a hearing to Stanley and those like him while granting it to other Illinois parents is inescapably contrary to the Equal Protection Clause. The judgment of the Supreme Court of Illinois is reversed and the case is remanded to that court for proceedings not inconsistent with this opinion.

Chief Justice Burger wrote a dissenting opinion, joined by Justice Blackmun.

The only constitutional issue raised and decided in the courts of Illinois in this case was whether the Illinois statute that omits unwed fathers from the definition of "parents" violates the Equal Protection Clause.... I agree with the State's argument that the Equal Protection Clause is not violated when Illinois gives full recognition only to those father–child relationships that arise in the context of family units bound together by legal obligations arising from marriage or from adoption proceedings. Quite apart from the religious or quasi-religious connotations that marriage has ... for a large proportion of this Nation's citizens, it is in law an essentially contractual relationship, the parties to which have legally enforceable rights and duties, with respect both to each other and to any children born to them. Stanley and the mother of these children never entered such a relationship.... Where there is a valid contract of marriage, the law of Illinois presumes that the husband is the father of any child born to the wife during the marriage; as the father, he has legally enforceable rights and duties with respect to that child. When a child is born to an unmarried woman, Illinois recognizes the readily identifiable mother, but makes no presumption as to the identity of the biological father....

The Illinois Supreme Court correctly held that the State may constitutionally distinguish between unwed fathers and unwed mothers. Here, Illinois' different treatment of the two is part of that State's statutory scheme for protecting the welfare of illegitimate children. In almost all cases, the unwed mother is readily identifiable, generally from hospital records, and alternatively by physicians or others attending the child's birth. Unwed fathers, as a class, are not traditionally quite so easy to identify and locate. Many of them either deny all responsibility or exhibit no interest in the child or its welfare; and, of course, many unwed fathers are simply not aware of their parenthood.

Furthermore, I believe that a State is fully justified in concluding, on the basis of common human experience, that the biological role of the mother in carrying and nursing an infant creates stronger bonds between her and the child than the bonds resulting from the male's often casual encounter. This view is reinforced by the observable fact that most unwed mothers exhibit a concern for their offspring either permanently or at least until they are safely placed for adoption, while unwed fathers rarely burden either the mother or the child with their attentions or loyalties. Centuries of human experience buttress this view of the realities of human conditions and suggest that unwed mothers of illegitimate children are generally more dependable protectors of their children than are unwed fathers. While these, like most generalizations, are not without exceptions, they nevertheless provide a sufficient basis to sustain a statutory classification whose objective is not to penalize unwed parents but to further the welfare of illegitimate children in fulfillment of the State's obligations as *parens patriae.*

As this case shows, some members of the Court have argued in favor of longstanding social presumptions and against change, even where there was no constitutional case law that supported that position. This idea that gender roles and stereotypes are justified because they have been held historically by significant portions of society has been important to a number of courts and judges from the earliest time, as the earlier discussion of the post-Civil War cases make clear, and this attitude continued long after *Stanley*, as will become clear in the dissents filed in the case involving the exclusion of women from admission to the Virginia Military Institute decided by the Court in 1996,[29] and in the dissents in cases involving protections of gay rights in 2003.[30]

Of course, these stereotypes and prejudices have most often been visited upon women, and courts have been called upon to address them, particularly since the 1970s. More than a decade after the *Griswold v. Connecticut* case and a year after *Roe v. Wade*, the Supreme Court still found itself reviewing school board rules that required women teachers to take leave months before they were due to deliver a baby. Although the districts tried to justify the rules on other grounds, as Justice Powell pointed out, the evidence was clear that they just did not want obviously pregnant teachers in the classroom for reasons that had nothing to do with the teachers' fitness to teach or their desire to do so. The Court took this case because there were conflicting opinions in the lower courts about this matter, which serves to demonstrate that even in the mid-1970s, Victorian attitudes about pregnancy were alive and well.

Cleveland Board of Education v. LaFleur

414 U.S. 632 (1974)

INTRODUCTION: The Cleveland Board of Education required school teachers who became pregnant to take an unpaid leave five months before they were due to deliver and not to return until the next term after their children reached three months old. If a woman failed to obey the policy, her employment was subject to termination. To return, a woman had to provide a physician's certificate stating that she was in good health, and even then the district court could require additional medical examinations. Even with all of that, the woman had no assurance that she would be rehired or reemployed at the same school. She only had a priority for a position.

The school districts justified the policies on grounds of the need for the district to manage and plan for teaching needs, on the one hand, and to protect the health and welfare of the woman and the unborn child, on the other. However, the Court noted in its opinion that:

> The records in these cases suggest that the maternity leave regulations may have originally been inspired by other, less weighty, considerations. For example, Dr. Mark C. Schinnerer, who served as Superintendent of Schools in Cleveland at the time the leave rule was adopted, testified in the District Court that the rule had been adopted in part to save pregnant teachers from embarrassment at the hands of giggling schoolchildren; the cutoff date at the end of the fourth month was chosen because this was when the teacher "began to show." Similarly, at least several members of the Chesterfield County School Board thought a mandatory leave rule was justified in order to insulate schoolchildren from the sight of conspicuously pregnant women. One member of the school board thought that it was "not good for the school system" for students to view pregnant teachers, "because some of the kids say, my teacher swallowed a water melon, things like that."

In his concurring opinion, Justice Powell went so far as to say: "The records before us abound with proof that a principal purpose behind the adoption of the regulations was to keep visibly pregnant teachers out of the sight of school-children."

This case also consolidated challenges to a similar Chesterfield County, Virginia policy, which required a four-month pre-delivery leave, but it required that notice be given at least six months before the expected due date. That district also required a physician's certification before return and the woman could not resume work until the next school year after her delivery.

Jo Carol LaFleur and Ann Elizabeth Nelson intended to take the leave, but each wanted to teach the full academic year before they were due. They had to start leave in March. They challenged the policy, but lost in the district court. That decision was reversed by the Circuit Court of Appeals.

In the Virginia case, Ms. Susan Cohen notified the district of her pregnancy in November 1970 and was required to begin leave in December rather than in April, which was what she had requested. The Chesterfield County rule allowed the superintendent to grant a later leave than the four months. The federal district court ruled in her favor, but the Fourth Circuit ultimately reversed.

Justice Stewart wrote the opinion for the Court.

> This Court has long recognized that freedom of personal choice in matters of marriage and family life is one of the liberties protected by the Due Process Clause of the Fourteenth Amendment. *Roe v. Wade,* ... *Loving v. Virginia,* ... *Griswold v. Connecticut,* ... *Pierce v. Society of Sisters,* ... *Meyer v. Nebraska,* ... See also *Prince v. Massachusetts,* ... *Skinner v. Oklahoma*... As we noted in *Eisenstadt v. Baird,* ... there is a right "to be free from unwarranted governmental intrusion into matters so fundamentally affecting a person as the decision whether to bear or beget a child."

> By acting to penalize the pregnant teacher for deciding to bear a child, overly restrictive maternity leave regulations can constitute a heavy burden on the exercise of these protected freedoms. Because public school maternity leave rules directly affect "one of the basic civil rights of man," *Skinner v. Oklahoma,* ... the Due Process Clause of the Fourteenth Amendment requires that such rules must not needlessly, arbitrarily, or capriciously impinge upon this vital area of a teacher's constitutional liberty. The question before us in these cases is whether the interests advanced in support of the rules of the Cleveland and Chesterfield County School Boards can justify the particular procedures they have adopted.

> The school boards ... contend that the firm cutoff dates are necessary to maintain continuity of classroom instruction [and to] protect the health of the teacher and her unborn child.... [After stating the other reasons noted above but not argued in the case, the Court added:] The school boards have not contended in this Court that these considerations can serve as a legitimate basis for a rule requiring pregnant women to leave work; we thus note the comments only to illustrate the possible role of outmoded taboos in the adoption of the rules. [Citing a Second Circuit case, the Court said:] "Whatever may have been the reaction in Queen Victoria's time, pregnancy is no longer a dirty word".[31] ... It cannot be denied that continuity of instruction is a significant and legitimate educational goal.... But, as the Court of Appeals for the Second Circuit noted ... "Where a pregnant teacher provides the Board with a date certain for commencement of leave ... that value [continuity] is preserved...."

> Thus, while the advance-notice provisions in the Cleveland and Chesterfield County rules are wholly rational and may well be necessary to serve the objective of continuity of instruction, the absolute requirements of termination at the end of the fourth or fifth month of pregnancy are not. Were continuity the only goal, cut-off dates much later during pregnancy would serve as well as or better than the challenged rules, providing that ample advance notice requirements were retained. Indeed, continuity would seem just as well attained if the teacher herself were allowed to choose the date upon which to commence her leave, at least so long as the decision were required to be made and notice given of it well in advance of the date selected. In fact, since the fifth or sixth month of pregnancy will obviously begin at different times in the school year for different teachers, the present Cleveland and Chesterfield County rules may serve to hinder attainment of the very continuity objectives that they are purportedly designed to promote.

We thus conclude that the arbitrary cutoff dates embodied in the mandatory leave rules before us have no rational relationship to the valid state interest of preserving continuity of instruction. As long as the teachers are required to give substantial advance notice of their condition, the choice of firm dates later in pregnancy would serve the boards' objectives just as well, while imposing a far lesser burden on the women's exercise of constitutionally protected freedom.

The question remains as to whether the cutoff dates at the beginning of the fifth and sixth months can be justified on the other ground advanced by the school boards—the necessity of keeping physically unfit teachers out of the classroom. There can be no doubt that such an objective is perfectly legitimate, both on educational and safety grounds. And, despite the plethora of conflicting medical testimony in these cases, we can assume, *arguendo*,[32] that at least some teachers become physically disabled from effectively performing their duties during the latter stages of pregnancy.

The mandatory termination provisions of the Cleveland and Chesterfield County rules surely operate to insulate the classroom from the presence of potentially incapacitated pregnant teachers. But the question is whether the rules sweep too broadly.... That question must be answered in the affirmative, for the provisions amount to a conclusive presumption that every pregnant teacher who reaches the fifth or sixth month of pregnancy is physically incapable of continuing. There is no individualized determination by [a doctor] as to any particular teacher's ability to continue at her job. The rules contain an irrebuttable presumption of physical incompetency, and that presumption applies even when the medical evidence as to an individual woman's physical status might be wholly to the contrary.

As the Court noted last Term in *Vlandis v. Kline*, ... "permanent irrebuttable presumptions have long been disfavored under the Due Process Clauses of the Fifth and Fourteenth Amendments.... [See also] *Stanley v. Illinois* .... These principles control our decision in the cases before us.... [T]he medical experts in these cases [agreed that] the ability of any particular pregnant woman to continue at work past any fixed time in her pregnancy is very much an individual matter. The school boards have argued that the mandatory termination dates serve the interest of administrative convenience, since there are many instances of teacher pregnancy, and the rules obviate the necessity for case-by-case determinations.... But, as the Court stated in *Stanley* ... "The Constitution recognizes higher values than speed and efficiency...." While it might be easier for the school boards to conclusively presume that all pregnant women are unfit to teach past the fourth or fifth month or even the first month, of pregnancy, administrative convenience alone is insufficient to make valid what otherwise is a violation of due process of law. The Fourteenth Amendment requires the school boards to employ alternative administrative means, which do not so broadly infringe upon basic constitutional liberty, in support of their legitimate goals.... While the regulations no doubt represent a good-faith attempt to achieve a laudable goal, they cannot pass muster under the Due Process Clause of the Fourteenth Amendment, because they employ irrebuttable presumptions that unduly penalize a female teacher for deciding to bear a child.

In addition to the mandatory termination provisions, both the Cleveland and Chesterfield County rules contain limitations upon a teacher's eligibility to return to work after giving birth.... [T]he question is not whether the school board's goals are legitimate, but rather whether the particular means chosen to achieve those objectives unduly infringe upon the teacher's constitutional liberty.

The respondents ... do not seriously challenge either the medical requirements of the Cleveland rule or the policy of limiting eligibility to return to the next semester following birth.... The Cleveland rule, however, [also] requires the mother to wait until her child reaches the age of three months before the return rules begin to operate. The school board has offered no reasonable justification for this supplemental limitation, and we can perceive none. To the extent that the three-month provision reflects the school board's thinking that no mother is fit to return until that point in time, it suffers from the same constitutional deficiencies that plague the irrebuttable presumption in the termination rules. The presumption, moreover, is patently unnecessary, since the requirement of a physician's certificate or a medical examination fully protects the school's interests in this regard.... Thus, we conclude that the Cleveland return rule, insofar as it embodies the three-month age provision, is wholly arbitrary and irrational, and hence violates the Due Process Clause of the Fourteenth Amendment.... We perceive no such constitutional infirmities in the Chesterfield County rule. In that school system, the teacher becomes eligible for re-employment upon submission of a medical certificate from her physician; return to work is guaranteed no later than the beginning of the next school year following the eligibility determination....

[W]e hold that the mandatory termination provisions of the Cleveland and Chesterfield County maternity regulations [as well as the three-month provision of the Cleveland return rule] violate the Due Process Clause of the Fourteenth Amendment.

Justice Powell issued a concurring opinion.

I concur in the Court's result, but I am unable to join its opinion. In my view these cases should not be decided on the ground that the mandatory maternity leave regulations impair any right to bear children or create an "irrebuttable presumption." It seems to me that equal protection analysis is the appropriate frame of reference.

... [N]ot every government policy that burdens childbearing violates the Constitution. Limitations on the welfare benefits a family may receive that do not take into account the size of the family illustrate this point.... Undoubtedly Congress could, as another example, constitutionally seek to discourage excessive population growth by limiting tax deductions for dependents. That would represent an intentional governmental effort to "penalize" childbearing.... The regulations here do not have that purpose. Their deterrent impact is wholly incidental....

I am also troubled by the Court's return to the "irrebuttable presumption" line of analysis.... [The] Court should approach that doctrine with extreme care ... [and focus instead on] the Equal Protection Clause. These cases present precisely the kind of problem susceptible of treatment by classification.... The constitutional difficulty is not that the boards attempted to deal with this problem by classification. Rather, it is that the boards chose irrational classifications.

... The records before us abound with proof that a principal purpose behind the adoption of the regulations was to keep visibly pregnant teachers out of the sight of school-children. The boards do not advance this today as a legitimate objective, yet its initial primacy casts a shadow over these cases. Moreover, most of the after-the-fact rationalizations proposed by these boards are unsupported in the records.... [T]he classifications chosen by these boards ... are either counterproductive or irrationally overinclusive.... Accordingly, in my opinion these regulations are invalid under rational-basis standards of equal protection review.

... It is particularly appropriate to avoid teacher turnover in the middle of a semester.... That aspect of the Cleveland regulation limiting a teacher's eligibility to return to the classroom to the semester following delivery ... rationally serves this legitimate state interest. But the four- and five-month prebirth leave periods of the two regulations and the three-month post-birth provision of the Cleveland regulation do not. As the Court points out, ... such cutoff points are more likely to prevent continuity of teaching than to preserve it.... The boards' reference to continuity of teaching also encompasses their need to assure constant classroom coverage by teachers who are up to the task. This interest is obviously legitimate.... But the objectionable portions of these regulations appear to be bottomed on factually unsupported assumptions about the ability of pregnant teachers to perform their jobs.... [B]y forcing all pregnant teachers undergoing a normal pregnancy from the classroom so far in advance of term, the regulations compel large numbers of able-bodied teachers to quit work....

Justice Rehnquist issued a dissent joined by Chief Justice Burger.

The Court rests its invalidation of the school regulations involved in these cases on the Due Process Clause of the Fourteenth Amendment, rather than on any claim of sexual discrimination under the Equal Protection Clause of that Amendment. My Brother Stewart thereby enlists the Court in another quixotic engagement in his apparently unending war on irrebuttable presumptions....

All legislation involves the drawing of lines, and the drawing of lines necessarily results in particular individuals who are disadvantaged by the line drawn being virtually indistinguishable for many purposes from those individuals who benefit from the legislative classification. The Court's disenchantment with "irrebuttable presumptions," and its preference for "individualized determination," is in the last analysis nothing less than an attack upon the very notion of lawmaking itself.

The lines drawn by the school boards in the city of Cleveland and Chesterfield County in these cases require pregnant teachers to take forced leave at a stage of their pregnancy when medical evidence seems to suggest that a majority of them might well be able to continue teaching without any significant possibility of physical impairment. But, so far as I am aware, the medical evidence also suggests that in some cases there may be physical impairment at the stage of pregnancy fastened on by the regulations in question, and that the probability of physical impairment increases as the pregnancy advances. If legislative bodies are to be permitted to draw a general line anywhere short of the delivery room, I can find no judicial standard of measurement which says the ones drawn here were invalid. I therefore dissent.

Toward an Equal Protection Standard to Address Gender Discrimination

Many of these cases were not decided on equal protection grounds, but on due process grounds under the Fourteenth Amendment. They were partly matters of procedural due process that concerned the opportunity to have a hearing to contest assumptions based on gender and partly on substantive due process grounds. The latter concerned the Court's conclusion that the term "liberty" within the meaning of the due process clause included a substantive protection for fundamental choices, such as decisions about marriage and childbearing. Although the question of discrimination in violation of the equal protection clause had been raised in some of these cases, it was not the primary focus as it was in *Reed v. Reed.* However, the *Reed* opinion had not stated clearly what test should be applied in cases of alleged gender discrimination—at least there was later disagreement within the Court as to what that standard was. That was a task for the Supreme Court during the 1970s and beyond.

As earlier chapters explained, by 1973 the Court had developed what has come to be known as the two-tier test for equal protection.[33] Under this standard, when someone challenges a policy or practice as discriminatory, the burden of proof is normally on the challenger and the government need only show that its actions are rationally related to a legitimate state purpose. However, if the policy or practice treats people differently on the basis of a suspect classification, like race, or if it treats them differently with respect to the ability to exercise a fundamental right, like the freedom to marry and have children, then the Court shifts to a different level of review known as strict judicial scrutiny. At that point, the burden shifts to the government to show that its actions were needed to address a compelling state interest and, even if there is a compelling interest, the government must show that it used narrowly tailored means to meet that compelling interest. The Court had long since established that race was a suspect classification because it is a group into which one is born that has traditionally been the subject of invidious discrimination and, largely because of that discrimination, the group has been unable to obtain redress for the situation from the majoritarian political process. To many Americans, women were in exactly that position and policies or practices that treated people differently on the basis of gender should also be considered suspect. Therefore, the Court should impose strict judicial scrutiny on any such policies or practices. The question whether gender is a suspect class came before the Court in a case decided in 1973.

Frontiero v. Richardson

411 U.S. 677 (1973)

INTRODUCTION: Justice Brennan explained the facts of this case succinctly in his opinion. It is important to note at the outset that this was a plurality opinion of four justices (Brennan, Douglas, White, and Marshall). Only Justice Rehnquist dissented, but the others concurred rather than joining Brennan's opinion. It was not a majority opinion, and that fact meant that the effort would necessarily continue to develop a standard that would be supported by a majority of the justices. Even so, the *Frontiero* case marked an important turning point in civil rights protections for women, not only because of the substantive ruling, but also for the language used to address the problem of sex discrimination and the need to move to a modern response to it.

Justice Brennan wrote the opinion for the plurality.

> ... Under statute, a serviceman may claim his wife as a "dependent" without regard to whether she is in fact dependent upon him for any part of her support.... A servicewoman, on the other hand, may not claim her husband as a "dependent" under these programs unless he is in fact dependent upon her for over one-half of his support.... Thus, the question for decision is whether this difference in treatment constitutes an unconstitutional discrimination against servicewomen in violation of the Due Process Clause of the Fifth Amendment. A three-judge District Court for the Middle District of Alabama ... sustained the constitutionality of the provisions of the statutes making this distinction.... We reverse.

> ... [A] member of the uniformed services with dependents is entitled to an increased "basic allowance for quarters" and ... a member's dependents are provided comprehensive medical and dental care.... Sharron Frontiero, a lieutenant

in the United States Air Force, sought increased quarters allowances, and housing and medical benefits for her husband on the ground that he was her "dependent." Although such benefits would automatically have been granted with respect to the wife of a male member of the uniformed services, appellant's application was denied because she failed to demonstrate that her husband was dependent on her for more than one-half of his support. Appellants then commenced this suit, contending that, by making this distinction, the statutes unreasonably discriminate on the basis of sex in violation of the Due Process Clause of the Fifth Amendment....

[A] majority of the three-judge District Court surmised that Congress might reasonably have concluded that, since the husband in our society is generally the "breadwinner" in the family—and the wife typically the "dependent" partner—"it would be more economical to require married female members claiming husbands to prove actual dependency than to extend the presumption of dependency to such members." ... Indeed, given the fact that approximately 99% of all members of the uniformed services are male, the District Court speculated that such differential treatment might conceivably lead to a "considerable saving of administrative expense and manpower."

At the outset, appellants contend that classifications based upon sex, like classifications based upon race, alienage, and national origin, are inherently suspect and must therefore be subjected to close judicial scrutiny. We agree and, indeed, find at least implicit support for such an approach in our unanimous decision only last Term in *Reed v. Reed....*

In *Reed*, the Court considered the constitutionality of an Idaho statute providing that, when two individuals are otherwise equally entitled to appointment as administrator of an estate, the male applicant must be preferred to the female.... The Court noted that the Idaho statute "provides that different treatment be accorded to the applicants on the basis of their sex; it thus establishes a classification subject to scrutiny under the Equal Protection Clause." ... Under "traditional" equal protection analysis, a legislative classification must be sustained unless it is "patently arbitrary" and bears no rational relationship to a legitimate governmental interest.... [T]he Court held the statutory preference for male applicants unconstitutional. In reaching this result, the Court implicitly rejected appellee's apparently rational explanation of the statutory scheme, and concluded that, ... even though the State's interest in achieving administrative efficiency "is not without some legitimacy," [it] make[s] the very kind of arbitrary legislative choice forbidden by the [Constitution] ...." This departure from "traditional" rational-basis analysis with respect to sex-based classifications is clearly justified.

There can be no doubt that our Nation has had a long and unfortunate history of sex discrimination. Traditionally, such discrimination was rationalized by an attitude of "romantic paternalism" which, in practical effect, put women, not on a pedestal, but in a cage. Indeed, this paternalistic attitude became so firmly rooted in our national consciousness that, 100 years ago, a distinguished Member of this Court was able to proclaim: "... The natural and proper timidity and delicacy which belongs to the female sex evidently unfits it for many of the occupations of civil life.... The harmony ... of interests and views which belong, or should belong, to the family institution is repugnant to the idea of a woman adopting a distinct and independent career from that of her husband.... The paramount destiny and mission of woman are to fulfil the noble and benign offices of wife and mother. This is the law of the Creator." *Bradwell v. State* ... (Bradley, J., concurring).

As a result of notions such as these, our statute books gradually became laden with gross, stereotyped distinctions between the sexes and, indeed, throughout much of the 19th century the position of women in our society was, in many respects, comparable to that of blacks under the pre-Civil War slave codes. Neither slaves nor women could hold office, serve on juries, or bring suit in their own names, and married women traditionally were denied the legal capacity to hold or convey property or to serve as legal guardians of their own children.... And although blacks were guaranteed the right to vote in 1870, women were denied even that right ... until adoption of the Nineteenth Amendment half a century later.

It is true, of course, that the position of women in America has improved markedly in recent decades. Nevertheless, it can hardly be doubted that, in part because of the high visibility of the sex characteristic, women still face pervasive, although at times more subtle, discrimination in our educational institutions, in the job market and, perhaps most conspicuously, in the political arena.[34]...

Moreover, since sex, like race and national origin, is an immutable characteristic determined solely by the accident of birth, the imposition of special disabilities upon the members of a particular sex because of their sex would seem to violate "the basic concept of our system that legal burdens should bear some relationship to individual responsibility...." And what differentiates sex from such nonsuspect statuses as intelligence or physical disability, and aligns it with the recognized suspect criteria, is that the sex characteristic frequently bears no relation to ability to perform or contribute to society. As a result, statutory distinctions between the sexes often have the effect of invidiously relegating the entire class of females to inferior legal status without regard to the actual capabilities of its individual members....

With these considerations in mind, we can only conclude that classifications based upon sex, like classifications based upon race, alienage, or national origin, are inherently suspect, and must therefore be subjected to strict judicial scrutiny. Applying the analysis mandated by that stricter standard of review, it is clear that the statutory scheme now before us is constitutionally invalid.

The sole basis of the classification established in the challenged statutes is the sex of the individuals involved.... [A] female member of the uniformed services seeking to obtain housing and medical benefits for her spouse must prove his dependency in fact, whereas no such burden is imposed upon male members. In addition, the statutes operate so as to deny benefits to a female member ... who provides less than one-half of her spouse's support, while at the same time granting such benefits to a male member who likewise provides less than one-half of his spouse's support. Thus, to this extent at least, it may fairly be said that these statutes command "dissimilar treatment for men and women who are ... similarly situated." *Reed v. Reed.*

Moreover, the Government concedes that the differential treatment accorded men and women under these statutes serves no purpose other than mere "administrative convenience." In essence, the Government maintains that, as an empirical matter, wives in our society frequently are dependent upon their husbands, while husbands rarely are dependent upon their wives. Thus, the Government argues that Congress might reasonably have concluded that it would be both cheaper and easier simply conclusively to presume that wives of male members are financially dependent upon their husbands, while burdening female members with the task of establishing dependency in fact.[35]

The Government offers no concrete evidence, however, tending to support its view that such differential treatment in fact saves the Government any money. In order to satisfy the demands of strict judicial scrutiny, the Government must demonstrate, for example, that it is actually cheaper to grant increased benefits with respect to all male members, than it is to determine which male members are in fact entitled to such benefits and to grant increased benefits only to those members whose wives actually meet the dependency requirement. Here, however, there is substantial evidence that, if put to the test, many of the wives of male members would fail to qualify for benefits.[36] And in light of the fact that the dependency determination with respect to the husbands of female members is presently made solely on the basis of affidavits, rather than through the more costly hearing process, the Government's explanation of the statutory scheme is, to say the least, questionable.

[A]lthough efficacious administration of governmental programs is not without some importance, "the Constitution recognizes higher values than speed and efficiency." *Stanley v. Illinois*…. And when we enter the realm of "strict judicial scrutiny," there can be no doubt that "administrative convenience" is not a shibboleth, the mere recitation of which dictates constitutionality…. On the contrary, any statutory scheme which draws a sharp line between the sexes, solely for the purpose of achieving administrative convenience, necessarily commands "dissimilar treatment for men and women who are … similarly situated," and therefore involves the "very kind of arbitrary legislative choice forbidden by the [Constitution] …." We therefore conclude that, by according differential treatment to male and female members of the uniformed services for the sole purpose of achieving administrative convenience, the challenged statutes violate the Due Process Clause of the Fifth Amendment insofar as they require a female member to prove the dependency of her husband.

Justice Stewart "concurs in the judgment, agreeing that the statutes before us work an invidious discrimination in violation of the Constitution. *Reed v. Reed*."

Justice Powell wrote a concurring opinion joined by Chief Justice Burger and Justice Blackmun.

I agree that the challenged statutes constitute an unconstitutional discrimination against servicewomen in violation of the Due Process Clause of the Fifth Amendment, but I cannot join the opinion of Mr. Justice Brennan which would hold that all classifications based upon sex … are "inherently suspect and must therefore be subjected to close judicial scrutiny." … It is unnecessary for the Court in this case to characterize sex as a suspect classification, with all of the far-reaching implications of such a holding. *Reed v. Reed* … which abundantly supports our decision today, did not add sex to the narrowly limited group of classifications which are inherently suspect. In my view, we can and should decide this case on the authority of *Reed* and reserve for the future any expansion of its rationale.

Justice Rehnquist wrote a dissent, merely citing the dissenting opinion of the district court.

Since Justice Brennan's opinion was not able to get a majority of the Court to accept that gender is an inherently suspect classification, the discussion of the proper standard by which to judge gender classifications continued. Brennan, and others on the Court who agreed with him, were not about to give up so easily and simply relegate gender classifications to the lowest standard of review, the rational basis test. Instead, Brennan was able in a later case to muster a majority for a new heightened level of scrutiny (sometimes referred to as a middle tier or intermediate scrutiny), less rigorous than strict scrutiny but more probing than the minimum rational basis test. It was a case brought by a young man about, of all things, different age requirements in the state of Utah for the ability to buy so-called 3–2 beer that provided the context for the new standard.

Craig v. Boren

429 U.S. 190 (1976)

INTRODUCTION: As noted above, Justice Brennan was able to attract a majority Court for this opinion, which set forth a new intermediate level of scrutiny for gender-based classifications. This time Justice Powell joined the opinion. He added a very interesting footnote to his own concurring opinion that shows that although he had concerns about the standard announced by Brennan, he was not prepared to relegate the review of gender-based classifications to a mere rational basis test.

Justice Brennan wrote the opinion for the Court.

[T]wo sections of an Oklahoma statute [§§241 and 245] [prohibits] the sale of "non-intoxicating" 3.2% beer to males under the age of 21 and to females under the age of 18. The question ... is whether such a gender-based differential constitutes a denial ... of the equal protection of the laws in violation of the Fourteenth Amendment.

This action was brought by ... a male then between 18 and 21 years of age, and ... a licensed vendor of 3.2% beer ... against enforcement of the gender-based differential on the ground that it constituted invidious discrimination against males.... A three-judge court ... sustained the constitutionality of the statut[es]. We reverse.

... Oklahoma defined the commencement of civil majority at age 18 for females and age 21 for males.... In contrast, females were held criminally responsible as adults at age 18 and males at age 16.... After the Court of Appeals for the Tenth Circuit held in 1972, on the authority of *Reed v. Reed* ... that the age distinction was unconstitutional, ... the Oklahoma Legislature fixed age 18 as applicable to both males and females.... In 1972, 18 also was established as the age of majority for males and females in civil matters, ... except that §§241 and 245 of the 3.2% beer statute were simultaneously codified to create an exception to the gender-free rule.

... *Reed* emphasized that statutory classifications that distinguish between males and females are "subject to scrutiny under the Equal Protection Clause." ... To withstand constitutional challenge, previous cases establish that classifications by gender must serve important governmental objectives and must be substantially related to achievement of those objectives.... Decisions following *Reed* similarly have rejected administrative ease and convenience as sufficiently important objectives to justify gender-based classifications. See, e.g., *Stanley v. Illinois ... Frontiero v. Richardson....* And only two Terms ago, *Stanton v. Stanton* ... held that *Reed* required invalidation of a Utah differential age-of-majority statute....

Reed has also provided the underpinning for decisions that have invalidated statutes employing gender as an inaccurate proxy for other, more germane bases of classification. Hence, "archaic and overbroad" generalizations ... concerning the financial position of servicewomen, *Frontiero v. Richardson...*, and working women, *Weinberger v. Wiesenfeld*, 420 U.S. 636, 643 (1975), could not justify use of a gender line in determining eligibility for certain governmental entitlements. Similarly, increasingly outdated misconceptions concerning the role of females in the home rather than in the "marketplace and world of ideas" were rejected as loose-fitting characterizations incapable of supporting state statutory schemes that were premised upon their accuracy. *Stanton v. Stanton*....

We turn then to the question whether, under *Reed*, the difference between males and females with respect to the purchase of 3.2% beer warrants the differential in age drawn by the Oklahoma statute. We conclude that it does not....

C ... [T]he objective underlying §§241 and 245 [was supposed to be] the enhancement of traffic safety[,] ... an important function of state and local governments. However, appellees' statistics in our view cannot support the conclusion that the gender-based distinction closely serves to achieve that objective and therefore the distinction cannot under *Reed* withstand equal protection challenge....

Even were this statistical evidence accepted as accurate, it nevertheless offers only a weak answer to the equal protection question presented here. The most focused and relevant of the statistical surveys, arrests of 18–20-year-olds for alcohol-related driving offenses, exemplifies the ultimate unpersuasiveness of this evidentiary record. Viewed in terms of the correlation between sex and the actual activity that Oklahoma seeks to regulate—driving while under the influence of alcohol—the statistics broadly establish that .18% of females and 2% of males in that age group were arrested for that offense. While such a disparity is not trivial in a statistical sense, it hardly can form the basis for employment of a gender line as a classifying device. Certainly if maleness is to serve as a proxy for drinking and driving, a correlation of 2% must be considered an unduly tenuous "fit." Indeed, prior cases have consistently rejected the use of sex as a decisionmaking factor even though the statutes in question certainly rested on far more predictive empirical relationships than this....

Suffice to say that the showing offered by the appellees does not satisfy us that sex represents a legitimate, accurate proxy for the regulation of drinking and driving. In fact, when it is further recognized that Oklahoma's statute prohibits only the selling of 3.2% beer to young males and not their drinking the beverage once acquired (even after purchase by their 18–20-year-old female companions), the relationship between gender and traffic safety becomes far too tenuous to satisfy *Reed*'s requirement that the gender-based difference be substantially related to achievement of the statutory objective. We hold, therefore, that ... Oklahoma's 3.2% beer statute invidiously discriminates against males....

Justice Powell wrote a concurring opinion.

I join the opinion of the Court.... I do have reservations as to some of the discussion concerning the appropriate standard for equal protection analysis.... *Reed* and subsequent cases involving gender-based classifications make clear that the Court subjects such classifications to a more critical examination than is normally applied when "fundamental" constitutional rights and "suspect classes" are not present.[37]

... No one questions the legitimacy or importance of ... the promotion of highway safety. The decision of the case turns on whether the state legislature, by the classification it has chosen, has adopted a means that bears a "fair and substantial relation" to this objective.... I am not persuaded that these facts and the inferences fairly drawn from them justify this classification based on a three-year age differential between the sexes, and especially one that is so easily circumvented as to be virtually meaningless. Putting it differently, this gender-based classification does not bear a fair and substantial relation to the object of the legislation.[38]

Justice Rehnquist wrote a dissenting opinion joined by Chief Justice Burger.[39]

> The Court's disposition of this case is objectionable on two grounds. First is its conclusion that men challenging a gender-based statute which treats them less favorably than women may invoke a more stringent standard of judicial review than pertains to most other types of classifications. Second is the Court's enunciation of this standard ... "classifications by gender must serve important governmental objectives and must be substantially related to achievement of those objectives." ... The only redeeming feature of the Court's opinion, to my mind, is that it apparently signals a retreat by those who joined the plurality opinion in *Frontiero v. Richardson*, ... from their view that sex is a "suspect" classification.... I think the Oklahoma statute challenged here need pass only the "rational basis" [test] and I believe that it is constitutional under that analysis....
>
> [T]he Court's application here of an elevated or "intermediate" level scrutiny ... raises the question of why the statute here should be treated any differently from countless legislative classifications unrelated to sex which have been upheld under a minimum rationality standard.... The applicable rational-basis test is one which: "permits the States a wide scope of discretion in enacting laws which affect some groups of citizens differently than others. The constitutional safeguard is offended only if the classification rests on grounds wholly irrelevant to the achievement of the State's objective.... A statutory discrimination will not be set aside if any state of facts reasonably may be conceived to justify it." ...
>
> The Oklahoma Legislature could have believed that 18–20-year-old males drive substantially more, and tend more often to be intoxicated than their female counterparts; that they prefer beer and admit to drinking and driving at a higher rate than females; and that they suffer traffic injuries out of proportion to the part they make up of the population. Under the appropriate rational-basis test for equal protection, it is neither irrational nor arbitrary to bar them from making purchases of 3.2% beer, which purchases might in many cases be made by a young man who immediately returns to his vehicle with the beverage in his possession.... There being no violation of either equal protection or due process, the statute should accordingly be upheld.

A series of cases followed, but one case came at a particularly interesting moment in history—the arrival of the first woman on the Supreme Court. Justice Sandra Day O'Connor joined the Court in 1981. President Ronald Reagan had promised to name a woman to the Court during his campaign, and that opportunity came soon after he took office.

Justice O'Connor came from a ranching family in Arizona. She graduated third in her class at Stanford Law School and was a member of the law review editorial board along with her later Supreme Court colleague, William Rehnquist. But while Rehnquist was able to move from law school to a Supreme Court clerkship with Justice Robert Jackson, Ms. O'Connor found herself unable to obtain employment as an attorney in a major firm because of blatant sex discrimination. When she interviewed with the Gibson-Dunn firm in California, she was told by then partner William French Smith that she could be hired as a legal secretary but certainly not as an attorney.[40] She took a job as a deputy county counsel in San Mateo County. Later, when she and her husband moved to Arizona, she was again unable to find a job at a firm and entered private practice. She later became an assistant attorney general. She served in the state legislature and after that was appointed by Democratic Governor Bruce Babbitt to the Arizona Court of Appeals. She was serving on that Court when she was appointed by President Reagan to the U.S. Supreme Court.

In one of the interesting and ironic moments in history, William French Smith was then Reagan's Attorney General, responsible for supporting her Supreme Court nomination through the confirmation process in the Senate. One of her earliest opinions for the Court came in a case that raised a clear case of gender discrimination, involving a refusal to admit a man to a nursing program at a state university.

Mississippi University for Women v. Hogan

458 U.S. 718 (1982)

INTRODUCTION: The Mississippi University for Women (MUW) was originally chartered in 1884 as the Mississippi Industrial Institute and College for the Education of White Girls of the State of Mississippi. As Justice O'Connor explained, that made it "the oldest state-supported all-female college in the United States." She also noted the MUW "has from its inception limited its enrollment to women." Even in the 1980s, at the time of this case, the university's charter stated that:

> The purpose and aim of the Mississippi State College for Women is the moral and intellectual advancement of the girls of the state by the maintenance of a first-class institution for their education in the arts and sciences, for their training in normal school methods and kindergarten, for their instruction in bookkeeping, photography, stenography, telegraphy, and typewriting, and in designing, drawing, engraving, and painting, and their industrial application, and for their instruction in fancy, general and practical needlework, and in such other industrial branches as experience, from time to time, shall suggest as necessary or proper to fit them for the practical affairs of life. Miss. Code Ann. §37-117-3 (1972).

Whatever one might think of such language at a modern university, the fact is that the "W," as the school is affectionately known by many in the state, developed a very strong reputation for the quality of its educational programs. The MUW launched a school of nursing in the 1970s, which developed an associates degree, a four-year undergraduate baccalaureate program, and a graduate program. Not surprisingly, these programs quickly developed a strong reputation befitting the University's general stature in the state.

As the attorneys for Mr. Hogan noted in their brief:

> Although MUW strictly adheres to its all-female enrollment policy for students receiving academic credit, it does permit men to audit courses. In the past 10 years, at least 138 such courses were taken by men. Auditing students at MUW participate fully in classes and in many other campus activities, although they receive no academic credit for their work.[41]

The respondent, Joe Hogan, lived in Columbus, Mississippi, which is the home of the MUW. He was a registered nurse and a nursing supervisor, but he did not have a four-year degree. He contacted the MUW in 1976 to learn how he could apply for admission, saying that he was a registered nurse but did not hold a baccalaureate degree in nursing. He was informed that his application would be summarily rejected because he was a man.

In an attempt to further his education, Hogan began taking courses at Itawamba Junior College, a 62-mile commute each way. He was a married man with a full-time job and owned a home in Columbus, so he could not simply go away to school. He took as many credits as he could at the community college, but still wanted a four-year degree and instruction beyond what that school could offer.

He then applied to the MUW nursing program in 1979, but was rejected because of his gender. He was told that he was free to take courses at MUW, but could not receive college credit for them. There were programs at the University of Southern Mississippi in Hattiesburg, but that was 178 miles from Columbus, and the University of Mississippi in Jackson, 147 miles away.

He sued in the federal district court, charging that the discrimination in admissions on the basis of gender violated the equal protection clause of the Fourteenth Amendment. Although the district court rejected his claims and upheld the MUW policy, the Court of Appeals for the Fifth Circuit reversed.

Justice O'Connor wrote the opinion for the Court.

> This case presents the narrow issue of whether a state statute that excludes males from enrolling in a state-supported professional nursing school violates the Equal Protection Clause of the Fourteenth Amendment.
>
> ... Because the challenged policy expressly discriminates among applicants on the basis of gender, it is subject to scrutiny under the Equal Protection Clause of the Fourteenth Amendment. *Reed v. Reed*.... That this statutory policy discriminates against males rather than against females does not exempt it from scrutiny or reduce the standard of review. *Caban v. Mohammed* .... Our decisions also establish that the party seeking to uphold a statute that classifies individuals on the basis of their gender must carry the burden of showing an "exceedingly persuasive justification" for the classification.... The burden is met only by showing at least that the classification serves "important governmental objectives and that the discriminatory means employed" are "substantially related to the achievement of those objectives." ...[42]
>
> If the State's objective is legitimate and important, we next determine whether the requisite direct, substantial relationship between objective and means is present. The purpose of requiring that close relationship is to assure that the validity of a classification is determined through reasoned analysis rather than through the mechanical application of traditional, often inaccurate, assumptions about the proper roles of men and women. The need for the requirement is amply revealed by reference to the broad range of statutes already invalidated by this Court, statutes that relied upon the simplistic, outdated assumption that gender could be used as a "proxy for other, more germane bases of classification," *Craig v. Boren* ... to establish a link between objective and classification....
>
> The State's primary justification for maintaining the single-sex admissions policy of MUW's School of Nursing is that it compensates for discrimination against women and, therefore, constitutes educational affirmative action.... As applied to the School of Nursing, we find the State's argument unpersuasive.
>
> In limited circumstances, a gender-based classification favoring one sex can be justified if it intentionally and directly assists members of the sex that is disproportionately burdened. See *Schlesinger v. Ballard*, 419 U.S. 498 (1975). However, we consistently have emphasized that "the mere recitation of a benign, compensatory purpose is not an automatic shield which protects against any inquiry into the actual purposes underlying a statutory scheme." ... The same searching analysis must be made, regardless of whether the State's objective is to eliminate family controversy, ... to achieve administrative efficiency..., or to balance the burdens borne by males and females.

It is readily apparent that a State can evoke a compensatory purpose to justify an otherwise discriminatory classification only if members of the gender benefitted by the classification actually suffer a disadvantage related to the classification.... In sharp contrast, Mississippi has made no showing that women lacked opportunities to obtain training in the field of nursing or to attain positions of leadership in that field when the MUW School of Nursing opened its door or that women currently are deprived of such opportunities. In fact, in 1970, the year before the School of Nursing's first class enrolled, women earned 94 percent of the nursing baccalaureate degrees conferred in Mississippi and 98.6 percent of the degrees earned nationwide.... As one would expect, the labor force reflects the same predominance of women in nursing. When MUW's School of Nursing began operation, nearly 98 percent of all employed registered nurses were female....

Rather than compensate for discriminatory barriers faced by women, MUW's policy of excluding males from admission to the School of Nursing tends to perpetuate the stereotyped view of nursing as an exclusively woman's job. By assuring that Mississippi allots more openings in its state-supported nursing schools to women than it does to men, MUW's admissions policy lends credibility to the old view that women, not men, should become nurses, and makes the assumption that nursing is a field for women a self-fulfilling prophecy.... Thus, we conclude that, although the State recited a "benign, compensatory purpose," it failed to establish that the alleged objective is the actual purpose underlying the discriminatory classification.

The policy is invalid also because it fails the second part of the equal protection test, for the State has made no showing that the gender-based classification is substantially and directly related to its proposed compensatory objective. To the contrary, MUW's policy of permitting men to attend classes as auditors fatally undermines its claim that women, at least those in the School of Nursing, are adversely affected by the presence of men.

MUW permits men who audit to participate fully in classes. Additionally, both men and women take part in continuing education courses offered by the School of Nursing, in which regular nursing students also can enroll.... In sum, the record in this case is flatly inconsistent with the claim that excluding men from the School of Nursing is necessary to reach any of MUW's educational goals.

Thus, considering both the asserted interest and the relationship between the interest and the methods used by the State, we conclude that the State has fallen far short of establishing the "exceedingly persuasive justification" needed to sustain the gender-based classification. Accordingly, we hold that MUW's policy of denying males the right to enroll for credit in its School of Nursing violates the Equal Protection Clause of the Fourteenth Amendment.

Justice Blackmun wrote a dissent.

... I have come to suspect that it is easy to go too far with rigid rules in this area of claimed sex discrimination, and to lose—indeed destroy—values that mean much to some people by forbidding the State to offer them a choice while not depriving others of an alternative choice.... While the Court purports to write narrowly, declaring that it does not decide the same issue with respect to "separate but equal" undergraduate institutions for females and males ... or with respect to units of MUW other than its School of Nursing, ... there is inevitable spillover from the Court's ruling today. That ruling, it seems to me, places in constitutional jeopardy any state-supported educational institution that confines its student body in any area to members of one sex, even though the State elsewhere provides an equivalent program to the complaining applicant. The Court's reasoning does not stop with the School of Nursing of the Mississippi University for Women.

Justice Powell wrote a dissent joined by Justice Rehnquist.[43]

The Court's opinion bows deeply to conformity. Left without honor—indeed, held unconstitutional—is an element of diversity that has characterized much of American education and enriched much of American life. The Court in effect holds today that no State now may provide even a single institution of higher learning open only to women students. It gives no heed to the efforts of the State of Mississippi to provide abundant opportunities for young men and young women to attend coeducational institutions, and none to the preferences of the more than 40,000 young women who over the years have evidenced their approval of an all-women's college by choosing Mississippi University for Women (MUW) over seven coeducational universities within the State. The Court decides today that the Equal Protection Clause makes it unlawful for the State to provide women with a traditionally popular and respected choice of educational environment. It does so in a case instituted by one man, who represents no class, and whose primary concern is personal convenience.

Coeducation, historically, is a novel educational theory.... [M]uch of the Nation's population during much of our history has been educated in sexually segregated classrooms. At the college level, for instance, until recently some of the most prestigious colleges and universities ... had long histories of single-sex education. As Harvard, Yale, and Princeton remained all-male colleges well into the second half of this century, the "Seven Sister" institutions established a parallel standard of excellence for women's colleges....

Despite the continuing expressions that single-sex institutions may offer singular advantages to their students, there is no doubt that coeducational institutions are far more numerous. But their numerical predominance does not establish ... that individual preferences for single-sex education are misguided or illegitimate, or that a State may not provide its citizens with a choice....

By applying heightened equal protection analysis to this case, the Court frustrates the liberating spirit of the Equal Protection Clause. It prohibits the States from providing women with an opportunity to choose the type of university they prefer. And yet it is these women whom the Court regards as the victims of an illegal, stereotyped perception of the role of women in our society. The Court reasons this way in a case in which no woman has complained, and the only complainant is a man who advances no claims on behalf of anyone else. His claim, it should be recalled, is not that he is being denied a substantive educational opportunity, or even the right to attend an all-male or a coeducational college. It is only that the colleges open to him are located at inconvenient distances.

The Court views this case as presenting a serious equal protection claim of sex discrimination. I do not, and I would sustain Mississippi's right to continue MUW on a rational-basis analysis. But I need not apply this "lowest tier" of scrutiny. I can accept for present purposes the standard applied by the Court: that there is a gender-based distinction that must serve an important governmental objective by means that are substantially related to its achievement.... The record in this case reflects that MUW has a historic position in the State's educational system.... More than 2,000 women presently evidence their preference for MUW by having enrolled there. The choice is one that discriminates invidiously against no one. And the State's purpose in preserving that choice is legitimate and substantial.

However, the question of exactly what the standard is for gender-based classifications was not over yet. By this point, after all of the decisions that used the *Craig v. Boren* heightened scrutiny standard, it appeared that the question of the proper test for sex discrimination was settled. But then came a significant twist in an opinion by Justice Ginsburg in a highly publicized case from Virginia, involving admissions to the Virginia Military Institute (VMI).

United States v. Virginia

518 U.S. 515 (1996)

INTRODUCTION: The Virginia Military Institute (VMI) is a state higher education institution, founded in 1839, with a proud tradition of producing military officers, but also civilians who are prepared for leadership in whatever walk of life they choose. As the opinion points out, only about 15 percent of graduates actually go on to serve in the military after graduation. VMI is the only single-sex school in the state system. Although women had indicated an interest in admission, VMI maintained its male-only policy.

A young woman who sought admission to VMI filed a complaint in 1990 with the Attorney General. That led to a suit brought by the United States against the Commonwealth of Virginia and VMI, asserting violations of the equal protection clause of the Fourteenth Amendment. There had been inquiries from 347 women in the two years before that suit, so that there could have been a critical mass for a training group with the corps of cadets, and the presence of women would, in turn, have led to an education process that would more closely resemble the military for which students were being trained.

The District Court rejected the challenge to the VMI policy, but the Court of Appeals for the Fourth Circuit disagreed. Following that ruling, the state offered a program separate from, but, they claimed, in parallel with the men's program to be known as the Virginia Women's Institute for Leadership (VWIL). That program would be provided through a private liberal arts college for women, Mary Baldwin College.

Justice Ginsburg explained that:

> The average combined SAT score of entrants at Mary Baldwin is about 100 points lower than the score for VMI freshmen.... Mary Baldwin's faculty holds "significantly fewer Ph. D.'s than the faculty at VMI," ... and receives significantly lower salaries.... While VMI offers degrees in liberal arts, the sciences, and engineering, Mary Baldwin, at the time of trial, offered only bachelor of arts degrees.

Those who designed the program, Ginsburg wrote, "determined that a military model would be 'wholly inappropriate' for VWIL...." The students in that program would be enrolled in the Reserve Officer Training Corps (ROTC) program. They would have leadership courses, do an externship, do community service projects, and have a speaker series. The district court found the plan acceptable, a decision affirmed by the Court of Appeals.

Justice Ginsburg wrote the opinion for the Court.[44]

> The United States maintains that the Constitution's equal protection guarantee precludes Virginia from reserving exclusively to men the unique educational opportunities VMI affords. We agree. The cross-petitions in this case present two

ultimate issues. First, does Virginia's exclusion of women from the educational opportunities provided by VMI ... deny to women ... the equal protection of the laws guaranteed by the Fourteenth Amendment? Second, if VMI's ... single-sex public institution of higher education offends the Constitution's equal protection principle, what is the remedial requirement?

We note, once again, ... parties who seek to defend gender-based government action must demonstrate an "exceedingly persuasive justification" for that action.

Today's skeptical scrutiny of official action denying rights or opportunities based on sex responds to volumes of history.... In 1971, for the first time in our Nation's history, this Court ruled in favor of a woman who complained that her State had denied her the equal protection of its laws. *Reed v. Reed....* Since *Reed*, the Court has repeatedly recognized that neither federal nor state government acts compatibly with the equal protection principle when a law or official policy denies to women, simply because they are women, full citizenship stature—equal opportunity to aspire, achieve, participate in and contribute to society based on their individual talents and capacities....

Without equating gender classifications ... to classifications based on race or national origin, the Court, in post-*Reed* decisions, has carefully inspected official action that closes a door or denies opportunity to women (or to men).... [T]he reviewing court must determine whether the proffered justification is "exceedingly persuasive." The burden of justification is demanding and it rests entirely on the State. See *Mississippi Univ. for Women....* The State must show "at least that the [challenged] classification serves 'important governmental objectives and that the discriminatory means employed' are 'substantially related to the achievement of those objectives.' " ... The justification must be genuine, not hypothesized or invented post hoc in response to litigation. And it must not rely on overbroad generalizations about the different talents, capacities, or preferences of males and females....

The heightened review standard our precedent establishes does not make sex a proscribed classification. Supposed "inherent differences" are no longer accepted as a ground for race or national origin classifications.... Physical differences between men and women, however, are enduring: "The two sexes are not fungible; a community made up exclusively of one [sex] is different from a community composed of both." ... "Inherent differences" between men and women, we have come to appreciate, remain cause for celebration, but not for denigration of the members of either sex or for artificial constraints on an individual's opportunity.... But such classifications may not be used, as they once were ... to create or perpetuate the legal, social, and economic inferiority of women.

Measuring the record in this case against the review standard just described, we conclude that Virginia has shown no "exceedingly persuasive justification" for excluding all women from the citizen-soldier training afforded by VMI. We therefore affirm the Fourth Circuit's initial judgment, which held that Virginia had violated the Fourteenth Amendment's Equal Protection Clause. Because the remedy proffered by Virginia—the Mary Baldwin VWIL program—does not cure the constitutional violation, i.e., it does not provide equal opportunity, we reverse the Fourth Circuit's final judgment in this case.

In cases of this genre, our precedent instructs [that] ... a tenable justification must describe actual state purposes, not rationalizations for actions in fact differently grounded.... *Mississippi Univ. for Women* is immediately in point. There the State asserted, in justification of its exclusion of men from a nursing school, that it was engaging in "educational affirmative action" by "compensating for discrimination against women." ... [T]he Court [there] found no close resemblance between "the alleged objective" and "the actual purpose underlying the discriminatory classification." ... Pursuing a similar inquiry here, we reach the same conclusion.

Neither recent nor distant history bears out Virginia's alleged pursuit of diversity through single-sex educational options.... [T]he historical record indicates action more deliberate than anomalous: First, protection of women against higher education; next, schools for women far from equal in resources and stature to schools for men; finally, conversion of the separate schools to coeducation....

Our 1982 decision in *Mississippi Univ. for Women* prompted VMI to reexamine its male-only admission policy.... A Mission Study Committee, appointed by the VMI Board of Visitors, studied the problem from October 1983 until May 1986, and ... counseled against "change of VMI status as a single-sex college." [W]e can hardly extract from that effort any commonwealth policy evenhandedly to advance diverse educational options....

In sum, we find no persuasive evidence in this record that VMI's male-only admission policy "is in furtherance of a state policy of 'diversity.'" ... A purpose genuinely to advance an array of educational options ... is not served by VMI's historic ... plan to "afford a unique educational benefit only to males." ... That is not equal protection.

Virginia next argues that VMI's adversative method of training provides educational benefits that cannot be made available, unmodified, to women. Alterations to accommodate women would necessarily be "radical," so "drastic," Virginia asserts, as to transform, indeed "destroy," VMI's program....

The United States ... emphasizes that time and again since this Court's turning point decision in *Reed v. Reed*, we have cautioned reviewing courts to take a "hard look" at generalizations or "tendencies" of the kind pressed by Virginia.... State actors controlling gates to opportunity, we have instructed, may not exclude qualified individuals based on "fixed notions concerning the roles and abilities of males and females." ...

Education, to be sure, is not a "one size fits all" business. The issue, however, is not whether "women—or men—should be forced to attend VMI"; rather, the question is whether the Commonwealth can constitutionally deny to women who have the will and capacity, the training and attendant opportunities that VMI uniquely affords....

The notion that admission of women would downgrade VMI's stature, destroy the adversative system and, with it, even the school, is a judgment hardly proved, a prediction hardly different from other "self-fulfilling prophec[ies]" ... once routinely used to deny rights or opportunities. When women first sought admission to the bar and access to legal education, concerns of the same order were expressed....

Medical faculties similarly resisted men and women as partners in the study of medicine.... More recently, women seeking careers in policing encountered resistance based on fears that their presence would "undermine male solidarity," ... deprive male partners of adequate assistance, ... and lead to sexual misconduct. Field studies did not confirm these fears....

Women's successful entry into the federal military academies, and their participation in the Nation's military forces, indicate that Virginia's fears for the future of

VMI may not be solidly grounded. The Commonwealth's justification for excluding all women from "citizen-soldier" training for which some are qualified, in any event, cannot rank as "exceedingly persuasive," as we have explained and applied that standard....

A remedial decree, this Court has said, must closely fit the constitutional violation; it must be shaped to place persons unconstitutionally denied an opportunity or advantage in "the position they would have occupied in the absence of [discrimination]." See *Milliken v. Bradley*, 433 U.S. 267, 280 (1977).... The constitutional violation in this case is the categorical exclusion of women from an extraordinary educational opportunity afforded men. A proper remedy for an unconstitutional exclusion, we have explained, aims to "eliminate [so far as possible] the discriminatory effects of the past" and to "bar like discrimination in the future." ...

Virginia chose not to eliminate, but to leave untouched, VMI's exclusionary policy. For women only, however, Virginia proposed a separate program, different in kind from VMI and unequal in tangible and intangible facilities. Having violated the Constitution's equal protection requirement, Virginia was obliged to show that its remedial proposal "directly addressed and related to" the violation, the equal protection denied to women ready, willing, and able to benefit from educational opportunities of the kind VMI offers. Virginia described VWIL as a "parallel program," and asserted that VWIL shares VMI's mission of producing "citizen-soldiers" and VMI's goals of providing "education, military training, mental and physical discipline, character ... and leadership development."

VWIL affords women no opportunity to experience the rigorous military training for which VMI is famed.... VWIL students participate in ROTC and a "largely ceremonial" Virginia Corps of Cadets, ... but Virginia deliberately did not make VWIL a military institute. The VWIL House is not a military-style residence and VWIL students need not live together throughout the 4-year program, eat meals together, or wear uniforms during the school day.... VWIL students thus do not experience the "barracks" life "crucial to the VMI experience.".…

VWIL students receive their "leadership training" in seminars, externships, and speaker series, ... episodes and encounters lacking the "physical rigor, mental stress, ... minute regulation of behavior, and indoctrination in desirable values" made hallmarks of VMI's citizen-soldier training.... Kept away from the pressures, hazards, and psychological bonding characteristic of VMI's adversative training ... VWIL students will not know the "feeling of tremendous accomplishment" commonly experienced by VMI's successful cadets....

In myriad respects other than military training, VWIL does not qualify as VMI's equal. VWIL's student body, faculty, course offerings, and facilities hardly match VMI's. Nor can the VWIL graduate anticipate the benefits associated with VMI's 157-year history, the school's prestige, and its influential alumni network.... Virginia, in sum, while maintaining VMI for men only, has ... created a VWIL program fairly appraised as a "pale shadow" of VMI in terms of the range of curricular choices and faculty stature, funding, prestige, alumni support and influence....

Virginia's VWIL solution is reminiscent of the remedy Texas proposed 50 years ago, in response to a state trial court's 1946 ruling that, given the equal protection guarantee, African Americans could not be denied a legal education at a state facility. See *Sweatt v. Painter*....

[In *Sweatt* t]his Court contrasted resources at the new school with those at the school from which Sweatt had been excluded.... More important than the tangible features, the Court emphasized, are "those qualities which are incapable of objective measurement but which make for greatness" in a school, including "reputation of the faculty, experience of the administration, position and influence of the alumni, standing in the community, traditions and prestige."... Facing the marked differences reported in the *Sweatt* opinion, the Court unanimously ruled that Texas had not shown "substantial equality in the [separate] educational opportunities" the State offered.... Accordingly, the Court held, the Equal Protection Clause required Texas to admit African Americans to the University of Texas Law School.... In line with *Sweatt*, we rule here that Virginia has not shown substantial equality in the separate educational opportunities the Commonwealth supports at VWIL and VMI.... [The] Court of Appeals ... is reversed, and the case is remanded for further proceedings consistent with this opinion.

Chief Justice Rehnquist wrote a concurring opinion.

While I agree with [the majority's] conclusions, I disagree with the Court's analysis....

Two decades ago in *Craig v. Boren*, ... we announced that "to withstand constitutional challenge, ... classifications by gender must serve important governmental objectives and must be substantially related to achievement of those objectives." We have adhered to that standard of scrutiny ever since.... While the majority adheres to this test today, ... it also says that the Commonwealth must demonstrate an "exceedingly persuasive justification" to support a gender-based classification.... It is unfortunate that the Court thereby introduces an element of uncertainty respecting the appropriate test.

While terms like "important governmental objective" and "substantially related" are hardly models of precision, they have more content and specificity than does the phrase "exceedingly persuasive justification." That phrase is best confined, as it was first used, as an observation on the difficulty of meeting the applicable test, not as a formulation of the test itself.... To avoid introducing potential confusion, I would have adhered more closely to our traditional, "firmly established" ... standard that a gender-based classification "must bear a close and substantial relationship ... to important governmental objectives." ...

While I ultimately agree that the Commonwealth has not carried the day with this justification, I disagree with the Court's method of analyzing the issue.... Long after the adoption of the Fourteenth Amendment, and well into this century, legal distinctions between men and women were thought to raise no question under the Equal Protection Clause.... Then, in 1971, we decided *Reed v. Reed*, ... which the Court correctly refers to as a seminal case. But its facts have nothing to do with admissions to any sort of educational institution.... In *Mississippi Univ. for Women v. Hogan*, ... a case actually involving a single-sex admissions policy in higher education, the Court held that the exclusion of men from a nursing program violated the Equal Protection Clause. This holding did place Virginia on notice that VMI's men-only admissions policy was open to serious question.... The reasons given ... for not changing the policy were the changes that admission of women to VMI would require, and the likely effect of those changes on the institution. That VMI would have to change is simply not helpful in addressing the constitutionality of the status after *Hogan*.

Before this Court, Virginia has sought to justify VMI's single-sex admissions policy primarily on the basis that diversity in education is desirable, and that while most of the public institutions of higher learning in the Commonwealth are coeducational, there should also be room for single-sex institutions. I agree with the Court that there is scant evidence in the record that this was the real reason that Virginia decided to maintain VMI as men only.... Even if diversity in educational opportunity were the Commonwealth's actual objective, the Commonwealth's position would still be problematic. The difficulty with its position is that the diversity benefitted only one sex; there was single-sex public education available for men at VMI, but no corresponding single-sex public education available for women....

Virginia offers a second justification for the single-sex admissions policy: maintenance of the adversative method. I agree with the Court that this justification does not serve an important governmental objective. A State does not have substantial interest in the adversative methodology unless it is pedagogically beneficial....

The Court defines the constitutional violation in these cases as "the categorical exclusion of women from an extraordinary educational opportunity afforded to men." ... By defining the violation in this way, and by emphasizing that a remedy for a constitutional violation must place the victims of discrimination in "the position they would have occupied in the absence of [discrimination]," the Court necessarily implies that the only adequate remedy would be the admission of women to the all-male institution. As the foregoing discussion suggests, I would not define the violation in this way; it is not the "exclusion of women" that violates the Equal Protection Clause, but the maintenance of an all-men school without providing any—much less a comparable—institution for women.

Accordingly, the remedy should not necessarily require either the admission of women to VMI or the creation of a VMI clone for women. An adequate remedy in my opinion might be a demonstration by Virginia that its interest in educating men in a single-sex environment is matched by its interest in educating women in a single-sex institution.

Justice Scalia wrote a dissenting opinion.

Today the Court shuts down an institution that has served the people of the Commonwealth of Virginia with pride and distinction for over a century and a half. To achieve that desired result, it rejects ... the factual findings of two courts below, sweeps aside the precedents of this Court, and ignores the history of our people. As to facts: It explicitly rejects the finding that there exist "gender-based developmental differences" supporting Virginia's restriction of the "adversative" method to only a men's institution, and the finding that the all-male composition of the Virginia Military Institute (VMI) is essential to that institution's character. As to precedent: It drastically revises our established standards for reviewing sex-based classifications. And as to history: It counts for nothing the long tradition, enduring down to the present, of men's military colleges supported by both States and the Federal Government.

Much of the Court's opinion is devoted to deprecating the closed-mindedness of our forebears with regard to women's education, and even with regard to the treatment of women in areas that have nothing to do with education. Closed-minded they were—as every age is, including our own, with regard to matters it cannot guess, because it simply does not consider them debatable. The virtue of a democratic system with a First Amendment is that it readily enables the people, over time, to be persuaded that what they took for granted is not so, and to change their laws accordingly. That system is destroyed if the smug assurances of each age are removed from the democratic process and written into the Constitution. [O]ur ancestors ... left us free to change. The same cannot be said of this most illiberal Court, which has embarked on a course of inscribing one after another of the current preferences of the society ... into our Basic Law. Today it enshrines the notion that no substantial educational value is to be served by an all-men's military academy.... Since it is entirely clear that the Constitution of the United States ... takes no sides in this educational debate, I dissent.

... I have no problem with a system of abstract tests such as rational basis, intermediate, and strict scrutiny.... Such formulas are essential to evaluating whether the new restrictions that a changing society constantly imposes upon private conduct comport with that "equal protection" our society has always accorded in the past. But in my view the function of this Court is to preserve our society's values regarding ... equal protection, not to revise them; to prevent backsliding from the degree of restriction the Constitution imposed upon democratic government, not to prescribe, on our own authority, progressively higher degrees. For that reason it is my view that, whatever abstract tests we may choose to devise, they cannot supersede ... those constant and unbroken national traditions that embody the people's understanding of ambiguous constitutional texts. More specifically, it is my view that "when a practice not expressly prohibited by the text of the Bill of Rights bears the endorsement of a long tradition of open, widespread, and unchallenged use that dates back to the beginning of the Republic, we have no proper basis for striking it down."[45]... The same applies ... to a practice asserted to be in violation of the post-Civil War Fourteenth Amendment....

The all-male constitution of VMI comes squarely within such a governing tradition.... [T]he tradition of having government-funded military schools for men is as well rooted in the traditions of this country as the tradition of sending only men into military combat. The people may decide to change the one tradition, like the other, through democratic processes; but the assertion that either tradition has been unconstitutional through the centuries is not law, but politics-smuggled-into-law.

And the same applies, more broadly, to single-sex education in general, which, as I shall discuss, is threatened by today's decision with the cutoff of all state and federal support. Government-run nonmilitary educational institutions for the two sexes have until very recently also been part of our national tradition. "[It is] coeducation, historically, [that] is a novel educational theory." ... Today, however, change is forced upon Virginia, and reversion to single-sex education is prohibited nationwide, not by democratic processes but by order of this Court.... This is not the interpretation of a Constitution, but the creation of one.

Although the Court in two places recites the test as stated in *Hogan* which asks whether the State has demonstrated "that the classification serves important governmental objectives and that the discriminatory means employed are substantially related to the achievement of those objectives," the Court never answers the question presented in anything resembling that form. When it engages in analysis, the Court instead prefers the phrase "exceedingly persuasive justification" from

Hogan. The Court … proceeds to interpret "exceedingly persuasive justification" in a fashion that contradicts the reasoning of *Hogan* and our other precedents.

Only the amorphous "exceedingly persuasive justification" phrase, and not the standard elaboration of intermediate scrutiny, can be made to yield this conclusion that VMI's single-sex composition is unconstitutional because there exist several women … willing and able to undertake VMI's program. Intermediate scrutiny has never required a least-restrictive-means analysis, but only a "substantial relation" between the classification and the state interests that it serves.… There is simply no support in our cases for the notion that a sex-based classification is invalid unless it relates to characteristics that hold true in every instance.…

It is beyond question that Virginia has an important state interest in providing effective college education for its citizens. That single-sex instruction is an approach substantially related to that interest should be evident enough from the long and continuing history in this country of men's and women's colleges.…

The Court's analysis at least has the benefit of producing foreseeable results. Applied generally, it means that whenever a State's ultimate objective is "great enough to accommodate women" (as it always will be), then the State will be held to have violated the Equal Protection Clause if it restricts to men even one means by which it pursues that objective—no matter how few women are interested in pursuing the objective by that means, no matter how much the single-sex program will have to be changed if both sexes are admitted, and no matter how beneficial that program has theretofore been to its participants.

The fact that the Court found that Virginia failed heightened scrutiny was not a surprise. What did cause discussion was the way that Justice Ginsburg presented and applied that standard. Up to and through *Mississippi University for Women v. Hogan* there were two parts to that test. What was required to provide an exceedingly persuasive justification was to show that there was an important governmental objective and that what the state had done was substantially related to achieving that objective. That phrase was not a separate element of the standard for assessing gender-based classifications. In the *VMI* case, however, although Justice Ginsburg stated the two parts of the standard, her rejection of the state's actions repeatedly emphasized the failure to provide an exceedingly persuasive justification as if it were a third piece of the standard. The concurring and dissenting opinions argued that this was meant to be a new third element in the standard, or even that this requirement was a new standard in its own right. It remains to be seen how the Court will explain and present its heightened scrutiny standard in the future.

One of the reasons that the Court did not quickly explain in another case just what the standard meant for the future is that relatively few gender discrimination cases come to the Court in the contemporary context raising constitutional questions. Instead, most have been brought on the basis of statutes like Title VII of the Civil Rights Act of 1964. One of the reasons for that lies in the Supreme Court's increasingly challenging demand for proof that alleged discrimination was intentional. Chapter 4 explained the Court's development of that standard for proving intent, concluding with a 1979 case involving gender discrimination that mandated that: "Discriminatory purpose, however, implies more than intent as volition or intent as awareness of consequences.… It implies that the decisionmaker, in this case a state legislature, selected or reaffirmed a particular course of action at least in part 'because of,' not merely 'in spite of,' its adverse effects upon an identifiable group."[46] It is an important case not only because of that standard, but also for what it shows about discrimination against women even at that relatively late date.

Personnel Administrator of Massachusetts v. Feeney

442 U.S. 256 (1979)

INTRODUCTION: The Court explains the facts in the opinion. One of the most interesting facts was reduced to a footnote in the Court's opinion. It read:

The Women's Armed Services Integration Act of 1948 ... established the women's services on a permanent basis. Under the Act, women were given regular military status. However, quotas were placed on the numbers who could enlist, 62 Stat. 357, 360–361 (no more than 2% of total enlisted strength), eligibility requirements were more stringent than those for men, and career opportunities were limited.

Thus, the fact is that women who wanted to serve were in many cases unable to do so because of legal restrictions on the number of women who could serve. In addition to the legal limit on the number of women, Justice Marshall pointed out in a footnote that:

[E]nlistment and appointment requirements have been more stringent for females than males with respect to age, mental and physical aptitude, parental consent, and educational attainment.... Until the 1970's, the Armed Forces precluded enlistment and appointment of women, but not men, who were married or had dependent children.... Sex-based restrictions on advancement and training opportunities also diminished the incentives for qualified women to enlist.

It was interesting to many observers that only Justices Marshall and Brennan dissented. Justice Stewart wrote the opinion for the Court.

This case presents a challenge to the constitutionality of the Massachusetts veterans' preference statute ... on the ground that it discriminates against women in violation of the Equal Protection Clause of the Fourteenth Amendment. Under [that statute] all veterans who qualify for state civil service positions must be considered for appointment ahead of any qualifying nonveterans. The preference operates overwhelmingly to the advantage of males.

The appellee Helen B. Feeney is not a veteran. She brought this action pursuant to 42 U.S.C. §1983, alleging that the absolute-preference formula ... inevitably operates to exclude women from consideration for the best Massachusetts civil service jobs and thus unconstitutionally denies them the equal protection of the laws.

The District Court found that the absolute preference afforded by Massachusetts to veterans has a devastating impact upon the employment opportunities of women. Although it found that the goals of the preference were worthy and legitimate and that the legislation had not been enacted for the purpose of discriminating against women, the court reasoned that its exclusionary impact upon women was nonetheless so severe as to require the State to further its goals through a more limited form of preference ... and enjoined its operation.... [T]his Court vacated the judgment and remanded the case for further consideration in light of our intervening decision in *Washington v. Davis* [which] held that a neutral law does not violate the Equal Protection Clause [unless it can] be traced to a purpose to discriminate....

Upon remand, the District Court ... concluded that a veterans' hiring preference is inherently nonneutral because it favors a class from which women have traditionally been excluded, and that the consequences of the Massachusetts absolute-preference formula for the employment opportunities of women were too inevitable to have been "unintended." ...

[A]ll applicants for employment must take competitive examinations. Grades are based on a formula that gives weight both to objective test results and to training and experience.... [H]owever, [the policy requires] that disabled veterans, veterans, and surviving spouses and surviving parents of veterans be ranked ... above all other candidates....

[Feeney] ... first entered the state civil service system in 1963, having competed successfully for a position as Senior Clerk Stenographer in the Massachusetts Civil Defense Agency. There she worked for four years. In 1967, she was promoted to the position of Federal Funds and Personnel Coordinator in the same agency. The agency, and with it her job, was eliminated in 1975.

During her 12-year tenure as a public employee, Ms. Feeney took and passed a number of open competitive civil service examinations.... [I]n 1971 [she earned] the second highest score on an examination for a job with the Board of Dental Examiners, and in 1973 the third highest on a test for an Administrative Assistant position with a mental health center.... Because of the veterans' preference, she was ranked sixth behind five male veterans on the Dental Examiner list ... and a lower scoring veteran was eventually appointed. On the 1973 examination, she was placed in a position on the list behind 12 male veterans, 11 of whom had lower scores.... In 1975, shortly after her civil defense job was abolished, she commenced this litigation.

The veterans' hiring preference in Massachusetts ... has traditionally been justified as a measure designed to reward veterans for the sacrifice of military service, to ease the transition from military to civilian life, to encourage patriotic service, and to attract loyal and well-disciplined people to civil service occupations....

The first Massachusetts veterans' preference statute defined the term "veterans" in gender-neutral language.... Women who have served in official United States military units during wartime, then, have always been entitled to the benefit of the preference....

When this litigation was commenced, then, over 98% of the veterans in Massachusetts were male; only 1.8% were female.... On each of 50 sample eligible lists that are part of the record in this case, one or more women who would have been certified as eligible for appointment on the basis of test results were displaced by veterans whose test scores were lower.... The impact of the veterans' preference law upon the public employment opportunities of women has thus been severe....

The sole question for decision on this appeal is whether Massachusetts, in granting an absolute lifetime preference to veterans, has discriminated against women in violation of the Equal Protection Clause of the Fourteenth Amendment.

Classifications based upon gender ... have traditionally been the touchstone for pervasive and often subtle discrimination.... This Court's recent cases teach that such classifications must bear a close and substantial relationship to important governmental objectives, *Craig v. Boren* ... and are in many settings unconstitutional.... When a statute gender-neutral on its face is challenged on the ground that its effects upon women are disproportionably adverse, a twofold inquiry is thus appropriate. The first question is whether the statutory classification is indeed neutral in the sense that it is not gender-based. If the classification itself, covert or overt, is not based upon gender, the second question is whether the adverse effect reflects invidious gender-based discrimination.... In this second inquiry, ... purposeful discrimination is "the condition that offends the Constitution." ...

Apart from the facts that the definition of "veterans" in the statute has always been neutral as to gender and that Massachusetts has consistently defined veteran status in a way that has been inclusive of women who have served in the military, this is not a law that can plausibly be explained only as a gender-based classification....

The dispositive question, then, is whether the appellee has shown ... a gender-based discriminatory purpose.... The contention that this veterans' preference is "inherently nonneutral" or "gender-biased" presumes that the State, by favoring veterans, intentionally incorporated into its public employment policies the panoply of sex-based and assertedly discriminatory federal laws that have prevented all but a handful of women from becoming veterans.... To the extent that the status of veteran is one that few women have been enabled to achieve, every hiring preference for veterans, however modest or extreme, is inherently gender-biased.... The District Court's conclusion that the absolute veterans' preference was not originally enacted or subsequently reaffirmed for the purpose of giving an advantage to males as such necessarily compels the conclusion that the State intended nothing more than to prefer "veterans." ... The enlistment policies of the Armed Services may well have discriminated on the basis of sex.... But the history of discrimination against women in the military is not on trial in this case.

... [I]t cannot seriously be argued that the Legislature of Massachusetts could have been unaware that most veterans are men. It would thus be disingenuous to say that the adverse consequences of this legislation for women were unintended, in the sense that they were not volitional or in the sense that they were not foreseeable.... "Discriminatory purpose," however, implies more than intent as volition or intent as awareness of consequences.... It implies that the decisionmaker, in this case a state legislature, selected or reaffirmed a particular course of action at least in part "because of," not merely "in spite of," its adverse effects upon an identifiable group. Yet nothing in the record demonstrates that this preference for veterans was originally devised or subsequently re-enacted because it would accomplish the collateral goal of keeping women in a stereotypic and predefined place in the Massachusetts Civil Service.... The judgment is reversed, and the case is remanded....[47]

Justice Marshall wrote a dissent joined by Justice Brennan.

... In my judgment, Massachusetts' choice of an absolute veterans' preference system evinces purposeful gender-based discrimination. And because the statutory scheme bears no substantial relationship to a legitimate governmental objective, it cannot withstand scrutiny under the Equal Protection Clause.

[T]he critical constitutional inquiry is not whether an illicit consideration was the primary or but-for cause of a decision, but rather whether it had an appreciable role in shaping a given legislative enactment. Where there is "proof that a discriminatory purpose has been a motivating factor in the decision, ... judicial deference is no longer justified." *Arlington Heights*.... To discern the purposes underlying facially neutral policies, this Court has therefore considered the degree, inevitability, and foreseeability of any disproportionate impact....

In the instant case, the impact of the Massachusetts statute on women is undisputed. Because less than 2% of the women in Massachusetts are veterans, the absolute-preference formula has rendered desirable state civil service employment an almost exclusively male prerogative.... [T]his consequence follows ... inexorably, from the long history of policies severely limiting women's participation in the military.... Where the foreseeable impact of a facially neutral policy is so disproportionate, the burden should rest on the State to establish that sex-based considerations played no part in the choice of the particular legislative scheme.

Clearly, that burden was not sustained here. The legislative history of the statute reflects the Commonwealth's patent appreciation of the impact the preference system would have on women, and an equally evident desire to mitigate that impact only with respect to certain traditionally female occupations. Until 1971, the statute and implementing civil service regulations exempted from operation of the preference any job requisitions "especially calling for women." ... In practice, this exemption, coupled with the absolute preference for veterans, has created a gender-based civil service hierarchy, with women occupying low-grade clerical and secretarial jobs and men holding more responsible and remunerative positions.... The Court's conclusion to the contrary ... displays a singularly myopic view of the facts established below.

To survive challenge under the Equal Protection Clause, statutes reflecting gender-based discrimination must be substantially related to the achievement of important governmental objectives.... And in this case, the Commonwealth has failed to establish a sufficient relationship between its objectives and the means chosen to effectuate them....

In its present unqualified form, the veterans' preference statute precludes all but a small fraction of Massachusetts women from obtaining any civil service position also of interest to men.... Given the range of alternatives available, this degree of preference is not constitutionally permissible.

It was interesting that Justice Stevens wrote a very brief concurring opinion joined by Justice White. He simply concluded that because many men were disadvantaged by the policy as well as women, it was clear that this was not sex discrimination.[48] However, he did not come to grips with the core claim by the woman in the case, which was that the men had a choice as to whether to serve or not that was not subject to the legally imposed quota and other requirements that blocked Feeney and other women from serving in the military, and therefore qualifying for a veteran's preference.

The critically important ruling was the requirement that intent meant that the policymakers had to have gone beyond knowing that their actions would have a clear and disproportionate adverse effect on women, and instead to have acted precisely because that would happen. If that burden is not met, then the person charging sex discrimination cannot even get to the point of determining whether the policy served an "important government objective and was substantially related to achieving that objective." This is a key reason that most cases involving sex discrimination are now being presented under one statute or another rather than the Constitution.

Workplace Discrimination: A Complex Conversation a Long Way from Being Resolved

Workplace discrimination has been a continuing theme in gender cases. In addition to outright bans on women in certain fields in earlier days, there have been a variety of other issues, some of which may seem obvious, while others have not drawn as much attention.

For reasons noted above, although some of those cases have been focused on the Fourteenth or Fifth Amendments, many others have been brought on the basis of statutory protections against discrimination, such as Title VII of the Civil Rights Act of 1964.[49] The purpose of the statute was also to provide more protections than had been understood to be mandated by the Constitution alone. Thus, women brought claims of discrimination in the workplace on the basis of pregnancy under Title VII after the Court rejected similar claims under the Constitution.[50]

General Electric v. Gilbert

429 U.S. 125 (1976)

INTRODUCTION: Title VII of the Civil Rights Act of 1964 outlawed discrimination by an employer "against any individual with respect to his compensation, terms, conditions, or privileges of employment, because of such individual's race, color, religion, sex, or national origin."[51] In 1972, the Equal Employment Opportunity Commission (EEOC) issued guidelines holding that Title VII mandated that employment programs not exclude pregnancy-related matters.

General Electric provided a disability program that excluded pregnancy as a disability in its leave, sickness, and accident benefits rules. As the dissenters explained, it is important here to understand the behavior of the company. They showed that when the company policy is viewed in light of its history and development, it was anything but neutral and clearly was based on archaic and overbroad generalizations about women. Thus, Justice Brennan explained that:

> General Electric's disability program was developed in an earlier era when women openly were presumed to play only a minor and temporary role in the labor force. As originally conceived in 1926, General Electric offered no benefit plan to its female employees because "women did not recognize the responsibilities of life, for they probably were hoping to get married soon and leave the company." ... It was not until the 1930's and 1940's that the company made female employees eligible to participate in the disability program. In common with general business practice, however, General Electric continued to pursue a policy of taking pregnancy and other factors into account in order to scale women's wages at two-thirds the level of men's.... More recent company policies reflect common stereotypes concerning the potentialities of pregnant women, ... and have coupled forced maternity leave with the nonpayment of disability payments.... In February 1973, approximately coinciding with commencement of this suit, the company abandoned its forced-maternity-leave policy by formal directive.

In 1974, the Court ruled in *Geduldig v. Aiello* that the exclusion of insurance coverage for pregnancy was discrimination in violation of the Constitution.[52] However, there were cases, including the *General Electric* case, moving up through appeals that found that exclusion of pregnancy was sex discrimination in violation of Title VII. The district court found that it violated that statute and the court of appeals affirmed. That ruling was consistent with decisions of the other circuits that had addressed the issue.

Justice Rehnquist wrote the opinion for the Court.

> ... [By] the time this case was decided by the Court of Appeals, we decided *Geduldig v. Aiello* ... where we rejected a claim that a very similar disability program ... violated the Equal Protection Clause of the Fourteenth Amendment

because that plan's exclusion of pregnancy disabilities represented sex discrimination. The majority of the Court of Appeals felt that *Geduldig* was not controlling because it arose under the Equal Protection Clause of the Fourteenth Amendment, and not under Title VII....

[I]n the case of defining the term "discrimination," which Congress has nowhere in Title VII defined, [decisions construing the Equal Protection Clause of the Fourteenth Amendment] afford an existing body of law analyzing ... that term in a legal context not wholly dissimilar to the concerns which Congress manifested in enacting Title VII. We think, therefore, that our decision in *Geduldig v. Aiello* ... is quite relevant in determining whether or not the pregnancy exclusion did discriminate on the basis of sex.... [In that] opinion we noted: "[T]his case is thus a far cry from cases like *Reed* ... and *Frontiero* ... involving discrimination based upon gender as such. The California insurance program does not exclude anyone from benefit eligibility because of gender but merely removes one physical condition—pregnancy—from the list of compensable disabilities. While it is true that only women can become pregnant, it does not follow that every legislative classification concerning pregnancy is a sex-based classification like those considered in *Reed* and *Frontiero*. Normal pregnancy is an objectively identifiable physical condition with unique characteristics. Absent a showing that distinctions involving pregnancy are mere pretexts designed to effect an invidious discrimination against the members of one sex or the other, lawmakers are constitutionally free to include or exclude pregnancy from the coverage of legislation such as this on any reasonable basis, just as with respect to any other physical condition...." [O]ur reason for rejecting appellee's equal protection claim in that case was that the exclusion of pregnancy from coverage ... was not in itself discrimination based on sex.... The Court of Appeals was therefore wrong in concluding that the reasoning of *Geduldig* was not applicable to an action under Title VII....

Pregnancy is, of course, confined to women, but it is in other ways significantly different from the typical covered disease or disability. The District Court found that it is not a "disease" at all, and is often a voluntarily undertaken and desired condition.... We do not therefore infer that the exclusion of pregnancy disability benefits from petitioner's plan is a simple pretext for discriminating against women. The contrary arguments adopted by the lower courts and expounded by our dissenting Brethren were largely rejected in *Geduldig*....

The instant suit was grounded on Title VII rather than the Equal Protection Clause, and our cases recognize that a prima facie violation of Title VII can be established in some circumstances upon proof that the effect of an otherwise facially neutral plan or classification is to discriminate against members of one class or another.... For example, in the context of a challenge ... to a facially neutral employment test, this Court held that a prima facie case of discrimination would be established if, even absent proof of intent, the consequences of the test were "invidiously to discriminate on the basis of racial or other impermissible classification." ... Even assuming that it is not necessary in this case to prove intent to establish a prima facie violation ... the respondents have not made the requisite showing of gender-based effects.

... The Plan ... is nothing more than an insurance package, which covers some risks, but excludes others.... The "package" ... covers exactly the same categories of risk, and is facially nondiscriminatory in the sense that "[t]here is no risk from which men are protected and women are not. Likewise, there is no risk from which women are protected and men are not." ... As there is no proof that the package is in fact worth more to men than to women, it is impossible to find any gender-based discriminatory effect in this scheme simply because women disabled as a result of pregnancy do not receive benefits; that is to say, gender-based discrimination does not result simply because an employer's disability-benefits plan is less than all-inclusive. For all that appears, pregnancy-related disabilities constitute an additional risk, unique to women, and the failure to compensate them for this risk does not destroy the presumed parity of the benefits, accruing to men and women alike, which results from the facially evenhanded inclusion of risks.

We are told, however, that this analysis ... is inconsistent with the guidelines of the EEOC, which, it is asserted, are entitled to "great deference" in the construction of the Act.... The guideline upon which respondents rely most heavily was promulgated in 1972, and states in pertinent part: "Disabilities caused or contributed to by pregnancy, miscarriage, abortion, childbirth, and recovery therefrom are, for all job-related purposes, temporary disabilities and should be treated as such under any health or temporary disability insurance or sick leave plan available in connection with employment.... [Benefits] shall be applied to disability due to pregnancy or childbirth on the same terms and conditions as they are applied to other temporary disabilities."

In evaluating this contention it should first be noted that Congress, in enacting Title VII, did not confer upon the EEOC authority to promulgate rules or regulations pursuant to that Title.... [Thus,] courts properly may accord less weight to such guidelines than to administrative regulations which Congress has declared shall have the force of law.... The EEOC guideline ... is not a contemporaneous interpretation of Title VII, since it was first promulgated eight years after the enactment of that Title. More importantly, the 1972 guideline flatly contradicts the position which the agency had enunciated at an earlier date, closer to the enactment of the governing statute.... There are also persuasive indications that the more recent EEOC guideline sharply conflicts with ... the proper interpretation of the sex-discrimination provisions of Title VII.... The EEOC guideline of 1972, conflicting as it does with earlier pronouncements of that agency, and containing no suggestion that some new source of legislative history had been discovered in the intervening eight years, stands virtually alone.... We therefore agree with petitioner that its disability-benefits plan does not violate Title VII because of its failure to cover pregnancy-related disabilities. Reversed.[53]

Justice Brennan dissented, joined by Justice Marshall.

The Court holds today that without violating Title VII ... a private employer may adopt a disability plan that compensates employees for all temporary disabilities except one affecting exclusively women, pregnancy.... [T]he soundness of the Court's underlying assumption that the plan is the untainted product of a gender-neutral risk-assignment process can be examined against the historical backdrop of General Electric's employment practices and the existence or nonexistence of gender-free policies governing the inclusion of compensable risks. Secondly, the resulting pattern of risks insured by General Electric can then be evaluated in terms of the broad social objectives promoted by Title VII. I believe that the first inquiry compels the conclusion that the Court's assumption that General Electric engaged in a gender-neutral risk-assignment process is purely fanciful. The second demonstrates that the EEOC's interpretation that the exclusion of pregnancy from a disability insurance plan is incompatible with the overall objectives of Title VII has been unjustifiably rejected.

[In] *Geduldig v. Aiello* ... a state-operated disability insurance system containing a pregnancy exclusion was held not to violate the Equal Protection Clause.... *Geduldig* itself obliges the Court to determine whether the exclusion of a sex-linked disability ... was actually the product of neutral, persuasive actuarial considerations, or rather stemmed from a policy that purposefully downgraded women's role in the labor force. In *Geduldig*, that inquiry coupled with the normal presumption favoring legislative action satisfied the Court that the pregnancy exclusion in fact was prompted by California's legitimate fiscal concerns, and therefore that California did not deny equal protection.... But the record in this case makes such deference impossible here. Instead, in reaching its conclusion that a showing of purposeful discrimination has not been made ... the Court simply disregards a history of General Electric practices that have served to undercut the employment opportunities of women who become pregnant while employed. Moreover, the Court studiously ignores the undisturbed conclusion of the District Court that General Electric's "discriminatory attitude" toward women was "a motivating factor in its policy," ... and that the pregnancy exclusion was "neutral [neither] on its face" nor "in its intent." ...

Plainly then, the Court's appraisal of General Electric's policy as a neutral process of sorting risks and "not a gender-based discrimination at all," ... cannot easily be squared with the historical record in this case. The Court, therefore, proceeds to a discussion of purported neutral criteria that suffice to explain the lone exclusion of pregnancy from the program. The Court argues that pregnancy is not "comparable" to other disabilities since it is a "voluntary" condition rather than a "disease." ... The fallacy of this argument is that even if "non-voluntariness" and "disease" are to be construed as the operational criteria for inclusion of a disability in General Electric's program, application of these criteria is inconsistent with the Court's gender-neutral interpretation of the company's policy.

For example, the characterization of pregnancy as "voluntary" is not a persuasive factor, for as the Court of Appeals correctly noted, "other than for childbirth disability, [General Electric] had never construed its plan as eliminating all so-called 'voluntary' disabilities," including sport injuries, attempted suicides, venereal disease, disabilities incurred in the commission of a crime or during a fight, and elective cosmetic surgery.... Similarly, the label "disease" rather than "disability" cannot be deemed determinative since General Electric's pregnancy disqualification also excludes the 10% of pregnancies that end in debilitating miscarriages ... the 10% of cases where pregnancies are complicated by "diseases" in the intuitive sense of the word, and cases where women recovering from childbirth are stricken by severe diseases unrelated to pregnancy."

Moreover, even the Court's principal argument for the plan's supposed gender neutrality cannot withstand analysis. The central analytical framework relied upon to demonstrate the absence of discrimination is the principle described in *Geduldig*: "There is no risk from which men are protected and women are not ... [and] no risk from which women are protected and men are not." ... For although all mutually contractible risks are covered irrespective of gender, ... the plan also insures risks such as prostatectomies, vasectomies, and circumcisions that are specific to the reproductive system of men and for which there exist no female counterparts covered by the plan. Again, pregnancy affords the only disability, sex-specific or otherwise, that is excluded from coverage.

Accordingly, the District Court appropriately remarked: "[The] concern of defendants in reference to pregnancy risks, coupled with the apparent lack of concern regarding the balancing of other statistically sex-linked disabilities, buttresses the Court's conclusion that the discriminatory attitude characterized elsewhere in the Court's findings was in fact a motivating factor in its policy."

... [T]he history of General Electric's employment practices and the absence of definable gender-neutral sorting criteria under the plan warrant rejection of the Court's view in deference to the plaintiffs'. Indeed, the fact that the Court's frame of reference lends itself to such intentional, sex-laden decisionmaking makes clear the wisdom and propriety of the EEOC's contrary approach to employment disability programs.

Of course, the demonstration of purposeful discrimination is not the only ground for recovery under Title VII.... [T]his Court, see *Washington v. Davis*, 426 U.S. 229, 238–239 (1976); *Albemarle Paper Co. v. Moody*, 422 U.S. 405, 422 (1975); *McDonnell Douglas Corp. v. Green*, 411 U.S. 792, 802 (1973); *Griggs v. Duke Power Co.*, 401 U.S. 424, 432 (1971), [has] firmly settled that a prima facie violation of Title VII, whether under §703(a)(1) or §703(a)(2), also is established by demonstrating that a facially neutral classification has the effect of discriminating against members of a defined class.

General Electric's disability program has three divisible sets of effects. First, the plan covers all disabilities that mutually afflict both sexes.... Second, the plan insures against all disabilities that are male-specific or have a predominant impact on males. Finally, all female-specific and female-impacted disabilities are covered, except for the most prevalent, pregnancy. The Court focuses on the first factor ... and therefore understandably can identify no discriminatory effect arising from the plan. In contrast, the EEOC and plaintiffs rely upon the unequal exclusion manifested in effects two and three to pinpoint an adverse impact on women.... [T]he determinative question must be whether the social policies and aims to be furthered by Title VII ... forbid an ultimate pattern of coverage that insures all risks except a commonplace one that is applicable to women but not to men.

As a matter of law and policy, this is a paradigm example of the type of complex economic and social inquiry that Congress wisely left to resolution by the EEOC pursuant to its Title VII mandate.... [A]ccordingly, prior Title VII decisions have consistently acknowledged the unique persuasiveness of EEOC interpretations in this area. These prior decisions ... hold that the EEOC's interpretations should receive "great deference." *Albemarle Paper*...; *Griggs*.... Nonetheless, the Court today abandons this standard in order squarely to repudiate the 1972 Commission guideline....

It is true ... that only brief mention of sex discrimination appears in the early legislative history of Title VII. It should not be surprising, therefore, that the EEOC, charged with a fresh and uncharted mandate, candidly acknowledged that further study was required before the contours of sex discrimination as proscribed by Congress could be defined.... Although proceeding cautiously, the Commission from the outset acknowledged the relationship between sex discrimination and pregnancy, announcing that "policies would have to be devised which afforded female employees reasonable job protection during periods of pregnancy." ... During the succeeding seven years, the EEOC worked to develop a coherent policy toward pregnancy-oriented employment practices both through the pursuit of its normal adjudicatory functions and by engaging in comprehensive studies with such organizations as the President's Citizens' Advisory Council on the Status of Women.... These investigations on the role of pregnancy in the labor market coupled with the Commission's "review ... [of] its case decisions on maternity preparatory to issuing formal guidelines," ... culminated in the 1972 guideline, the agency's first formalized, systematic statement on "employment policies relating to pregnancy and childbirth." ... It is bitter irony that the care that preceded promulgation of the 1972 guideline is today condemned by the Court as tardy indecisiveness, its unwillingness irresponsibly to challenge employers' practices during the formative period is labeled as evidence of inconsistency, and this indecisiveness and inconsistency are bootstrapped into reasons for denying the Commission's interpretation its due deference.

For me, the 1972 guideline represents a particularly conscientious and reasonable product of EEOC deliberations and, therefore, merits our "great deference." ... [Moreover,] Congress enacted just such a pregnancy-inclusive rule to govern the distribution of benefits for "sickness" under the Railroad Unemployment Insurance Act.... [S]hortly following the announcement of the EEOC's rule, Congress approved and the President signed an essentially identical promulgation by the Department of Health, Education, and Welfare under Title IX of the Education Amendments of 1972.... [F]ederal workers [under] the Civil Service Commission now are eligible for maternity and pregnancy coverage under their sick leave program....

These policy formulations are reasonable responses to the uniform testimony of governmental investigations which show that pregnancy exclusions built into disability programs both financially burden women workers and act to break down the continuity of the employment relationship, thereby exacerbating women's comparatively transient role in the labor force.... In dictating pregnancy coverage under Title VII, the EEOC's guideline merely settled upon a solution now accepted by every other Western industrial country....

A realistic understanding of conditions found in today's labor environment warrants taking pregnancy into account in fashioning disability policies.... [C]ontemporary disability programs are not creatures of a social or cultural vacuum devoid of stereotypes and signals concerning the pregnant woman employee. Indeed, no one seriously contends that General Electric or other companies actually conceptualized or developed their comprehensive insurance programs disability-by-disability in a strictly sex-neutral fashion. Instead, the company has devised a policy that, but for pregnancy, offers protection for all risks, even those that are "unique to" men or heavily male dominated. In light of this social experience, the history of General Electric's employment practices, the otherwise all-inclusive design of its disability program, and the burdened role of the contemporary working woman, the EEOC's construction of sex discrimination under §703(a)(1) is fully consonant with the ultimate objective of Title VII, "to assure equality of employment opportunities and to eliminate those discriminatory practices and devices which have fostered [sexually] stratified job environments to the disadvantage of [women]." ... I would affirm the judgment of the Court of Appeals.

Justice Stevens also issued a dissent.

The word "discriminate" does not appear in the Equal Protection Clause. Since the plaintiffs' burden of proving a prima facie violation of that constitutional provision is significantly heavier than the burden of proving a prima facie violation of a statutory prohibition against discrimination, the constitutional holding in *Geduldig v. Aiello* … does not control the question of statutory interpretation presented by this case. And, of course, when it enacted Title VII of the Civil Rights Act of 1964, Congress could not possibly have relied on language which this Court was to use a decade later in the *Geduldig* opinion.[54] We are, therefore, presented with a fresh, and rather simple, question of statutory construction: Does a contract between a company and its employees which treats the risk of absenteeism caused by pregnancy differently from any other kind of absence discriminate against certain individuals because of their sex? …

By definition, such a rule discriminates on account of sex; for it is the capacity to become pregnant which primarily differentiates the female from the male. The analysis is the same whether the rule relates to hiring, promotion, the acceptability of an excuse for absence, or an exclusion from a disability insurance plan. Accordingly, without reaching the questions of motive, administrative expertise, and policy, … I conclude that the language of the statute plainly requires the result which the Courts of Appeals have reached unanimously.

The Court's ruling in the *Geduldig* and *Gilbert* cases prompted Congress to pass the Pregnancy Discrimination Act of 1978, which amended Title VII as follows:

That section 701 of the Civil Rights Act of 1964 is amended by adding at the end thereof the following new subsection:

(k) The terms 'because of sex' or 'on the basis of sex' include, but are not limited to, because of or on the basis of pregnancy, childbirth, or related medical conditions; and women affected by pregnancy, childbirth, or related medical conditions shall be treated the same for all employment-related purposes, including receipt of benefits under fringe benefit programs, as other persons not so affected but similar in their ability or inability to work, and nothing in section 703(h) of this title shall be interpreted to permit otherwise. This subsection shall not require an employer to pay for health insurance benefits for abortion, except where the life of the mother would be endangered if the fetus were carried to term, or except where medical complications have arisen from an abortion: Provided, That nothing herein shall preclude an employer from providing abortion benefits or otherwise affect bargaining agreements in regard to abortion.[55]

But there were other kinds of benefits questions that affected women differently from men, some imposed by employers and some by public policy. The public policy matters can be traced back to the assumptions rejected in the *Frontiero* case that men were presumed to support their families but women were not. This question arose when men applied for survivor's benefits on the death of their wives. The tone of reaction against the men was that these men should be ashamed of themselves for claiming those benefits, but the Court's response was different. The question was not about the widower's right to the benefits, but the wife's right to expect that her family would be protected on her death in the same way that a man's would be. In 1975 the Court struck down a ban on widowers receiving survivor's benefits that would have been available to a widow.[56] The following year, a slightly different case raising a similar issue came before the Court and the justices made clear that the Constitution protected the woman worker as well as the man.

Califano v. Goldfarb

430 U.S. 199 (1977)

INTRODUCTION: The Social Security program known as the Old-Age, Survivors, and Disability Insurance Benefits paid benefits to the widow of a husband who had been covered by social security benefits. However, widowers were only eligible to receive benefits if they could prove that they received at least half of their support from their wife's income.

Mrs. Hannah Goldfarb had been a secretary in New York City public schools for nearly 25 years when she died. Her husband, who was 72 at the time, had retired from the federal civil service. His application to receive social security survivor's benefits after her death was denied.

Justice Brennan wrote the opinion for the plurality.

> The question in this case is whether this gender-based distinction violates the Due Process Clause of the Fifth Amendment. A three-judge District Court ... held that the different treatment of men and women ... constituted invidious discrimination against female wage earners by affording them less protection for their surviving spouses than is provided to male employees.... We affirm.

> ... *Frontiero* concluded that, by according ... differential treatment to male and female members of the uniformed services for the sole purpose of achieving administrative convenience, the challenged statute violated the Fifth Amendment.... *Weinberger v. Wiesenfeld* ... held unconstitutional a provision that denied ... insurance benefits to surviving widowers with children in their care, while authorizing ... benefits to similarly situated widows.... The Court reversed, holding that the gender-based distinction made by [the statute] was "indistinguishable from that invalidated in *Frontiero*." ...

> Precisely the same reasoning condemns the gender-based distinction ... in this case. For that distinction, too, operates "to deprive women of protection for their families which men receive as a result of their employment": social security taxes were deducted from Hannah Goldfarb's salary during the quarter century she worked as a secretary, yet ... she also "not only failed to receive for her [spouse] the same protection which a similarly situated male worker would have received [for his spouse] but she also was deprived of a portion of her own earnings in order to contribute to the fund out of which benefits would be paid to others." ...

> Appellant, however, would focus equal protection analysis, not upon the discrimination against the covered wage earning female, but rather upon whether her surviving widower was unconstitutionally discriminated against by burdening him but not a surviving widow with proof of dependency. The gist of the argument is that, analyzed from the perspective of the widower, "the denial of benefits reflected the congressional judgment that aged widowers as a class were sufficiently likely not to be dependent upon their wives that it was appropriate to deny them benefits unless they were in fact dependent." ...

> But *Weinberger v. Wiesenfeld* rejected the virtually identical argument.... The Court ... analyzed the classification from the perspective of the wage earner and concluded that the classification was unconstitutional because "benefits must be distributed according to classifications which do not without sufficient justification differentiate among covered employees solely on the basis of sex." ...

"To withstand constitutional challenge ... classifications by gender must serve important governmental objectives and must be substantially related to the achievement of those objectives." *Craig v. Boren*.... Such classifications, however, have frequently been revealed on analysis to rest only upon "old notions" and "archaic and overbroad" generalizations ... and so have been found to offend the prohibitions against denial of equal protection of the law....

Therefore, *Wiesenfeld* ... expressly rejected the argument ... that the "noncontractual" interest of a covered employee in future social security benefits precluded any claim of denial of equal protection. Rather, *Wiesenfeld* held that ... benefits "directly related to years worked and amount earned by a covered employee, and not to the need of the beneficiaries directly," like the employment-related benefits in *Frontiero*, "must be distributed according to classifications which do not without sufficient justification differentiate among covered employees solely on the basis of sex." ...[57]

Justice Rehnquist wrote a dissenting opinion joined by Chief Justice Burger and Justices Stewart and Blackmun.

In light of this Court's recent decisions ... one cannot say that there is no support in our cases for the result reached by the Court.... Indeed, it seems to me that there are two largely separate principles which may be deduced from these cases which indicate that the Court has reached the wrong result. The first of these principles is that cases requiring heightened levels of scrutiny for particular classifications under the Equal Protection Clause, which have originated in areas of the law outside of the field of social insurance legislation, will not be uncritically carried over into that field....

The second principle upon which I believe this legislative classification should be sustained is that ... [t]he effect of the statutory scheme is to make it easier for widows to obtain benefits than it is for widowers, since the former qualify automatically while the latter must show proof of need. Such a requirement in no way perpetuates or exacerbates the economic disadvantage which has led the Court to conclude that gender-based discrimination must meet a different test from other types of classifications. It is, like the property tax exemption to widows in *Kahn v. Shevin* [1974], a differing treatment which "[rests] upon some ground of difference having a fair and substantial relation to the object of the legislation." ...

I agree with the plurality's statement that "[t]here is no indication whatever in any of the legislative history that Congress gave any attention to the specific case of nondependent widows, and found that they were in need of benefits despite their lack of dependency...." But neither is there any reason to doubt that it singled out the group of aged widows for especially favorable treatment ... because it saw prevalent throughout that group a characteristically high level of need....

The second legislative judgment ... is that widows, as a practical matter, are much more likely to be without adequate means of support than are widowers.

... The very most that can be squeezed out of the facts of this case in the way of cognizable "discrimination" is a classification which favors aged widows. Quite apart from any considerations of legislative purpose and "administrative convenience" which may be advanced to support the classification, this is scarcely an invidious discrimination. Two of our recent cases have rejected efforts by men to challenge similar classifications. We have held that it is not improper for the military to formulate "up-or-out" rules taking into account sex-based differences in employment opportunities in a way working to the benefit of women, *Schlesinger v. Ballard* ...

(1975), or to grant solely to widows a property tax exemption in recognition of their depressed plight. *Kahn v. Shevin....* The classification challenged here ... in no way perpetuates the economic discrimination which has been the basis for heightened scrutiny of gender-based classifications, and is, in fact, explainable as a measure to ameliorate the characteristically depressed condition of aged widows.

It bears repeating that the Court's point was that archaic and overbroad generalizations about men and women cannot be used to deny women's employment equal status with that of men, including their expectation of benefits. There were other challenges that concerned benefits, specifically retirement. One of these arose from the way that women paid into their retirement program.

The Los Angeles Department of Water & Power operated a retirement program that, like other plans, was based on actuarial statistics to calculate what the payout would likely be for retirees as a way to calculate how much money needed to be contributed to the plan by employees and the employer to ensure that the retirement fund was adequate.[58] Employers argued that because those statistics indicated that most women lived longer than men and would therefore collect more retirement checks than their male counterparts, women employees would be required to pay roughly 15 percent more from their paychecks into the retirement program, which meant that their pay was reduced relative to men in the department. Women sued on grounds that this differential was sex discrimination in violation of Title VII. While the case was pending, the state legislature enacted a law that prohibited municipal governments from charging women more and the city and the department changed their policy accordingly to eliminate the differential. But the case continued and the women who had paid the increased contributions sought a recovery of that money.

Writing for the Court, Justice Stevens said:

> Women, as a class, do live longer than men.... It is equally true, however, that all individuals in the respective classes do not share the characteristic that differentiates the average class representatives. Many women do not live as long as the average man and many men outlive the average woman. The question, therefore, is whether the existence or nonexistence of "discrimination" is to be determined by comparison of class characteristics or individual characteristics.[59]

The Court began with the language of the statute that addressed that question.

> The statute makes it unlawful "to discriminate against any *individual* with respect to his compensation, terms, conditions, or privileges of employment, because of such *individual's* race, color, religion, sex, or national origin." 42 U.S.C. §2000e-2 (a)(1) (emphasis added). The statute's focus on the individual is unambiguous. It precludes treatment of individuals as simply components of a racial, religious, sexual, or national class. If height is required for a job, a tall woman may not be refused employment merely because, on the average, women are too short. Even a true generalization about the class is an insufficient reason for disqualifying an individual to whom the generalization does not apply.[60]

The Court added:

> Even if the statutory language were less clear, the basic policy of the statute requires that we focus on fairness to individuals rather than fairness to classes. Practices that classify employees in terms of religion, race, or sex tend to preserve traditional assumptions about groups rather than thoughtful scrutiny of individuals.[61]

Employers argued that the Bennet Amendment had been added, which said that a differential was not a violation if it was permitted by the Equal Pay Act, and one of the four criteria under that act that allowed a differential was a "differential based on any other factor other than sex." The argument was that the factor was longevity, not sex, citing the *General Electric* and *Geduldig* cases. However, the Court said, the only factor considered by the employer here was sex and not other factors that could affect longevity. Even as it ruled that this kind of differential violated Title VII, the Court recognized that "the prohibition against sex-differentiated employee contributions represents a marked departure from past practice"[62] and retroactive damages could be "devastating" to pension plans nationally. Even so, the law was clear and now firmly established that such differentials were unacceptable under Title VII.

The *Manhart* Court was correct about the likely reaction to its ruling. The pension industry and employers saw a dramatic impact on the whole foundation of the way that contributions and premiums were calculated. Some employers tried a different way of addressing that situation.[63] A number gave employees the choice of different annuity companies, but all of those annuity plans paid less per month to women than they did to men, again on actuarial grounds. In a one-paragraph *per curiam* opinion, the Court concluded: "[T]his practice does constitute discrimination on the basis of sex in violation of Title VII, and that all retirement benefits derived from contributions made after the decision today must be calculated without regard to the sex of the beneficiary."[64] However, the Court did not make the ruling retroactive.

Sexual Harassment: A Dark and Difficult Problem to Resolve

One of the other serious and longstanding problems is sexual harassment. Part of the difficulty in providing protections against it is that when the Civil Rights Act of 1964 was enacted, the new statute said nothing about this subject, and only one point in Title VII addressed sex discrimination at all. As part of the effort to raise consciousness and advocate for women's rights, the subject of sexual harassment on the job began to surface slowly in the national discussion. One of the important questions was just what legal protections could be cited to stop the behavior and to seek recompense for those injured by it. It became quickly apparent that there was no specific federal statute that addressed the subject.

The Equal Employment Opportunity Commission (EEOC) was created as a weak agency, without even the authority to issue rules having the force of law or to bring litigation to enforce civil rights statutes. However, the EEOC could issue guidelines, and it used that as a vehicle to influence both employers and the courts by defining sexual harassment as sex discrimination under Title VII. This action came in guidelines issued by the EEOC in 1980.[65]

Equal Employment Opportunity Commission Sexual Harassment[66]

(a) Harassment on the basis of sex is a violation of section 703 of title VII. Unwelcome sexual advances, requests for sexual favors, and other verbal or physical conduct of a sexual nature constitute sexual harassment when (1) submission to such conduct is made either explicitly or implicitly a term or condition of an individual's employment, (2) submission to or rejection of such conduct by an individual is used as the basis for employment decisions affecting such individual, or (3) such conduct has the purpose or effect of unreasonably interfering with an individual's work performance or creating an intimidating, hostile, or offensive working environment.

(b) In determining whether alleged conduct constitutes sexual harassment, the Commission will look at the record as a whole and at the totality of the circumstances, such as the nature of the sexual advances and the context in which the alleged incidents occurred. The determination of the legality of a particular action will be made from the facts, on a case by case basis.

(c) [Reserved][67]

(d) With respect to conduct between fellow employees, an employer is responsible for acts of sexual harassment in the workplace where the employer (or its agents or supervisory employees) knows or should have known of the conduct, unless it can show that it took immediate and appropriate corrective action.

(e) An employer may also be responsible for the acts of non-employees, with respect to sexual harassment of employees in the workplace, where the employer (or its agents or supervisory employees) knows or should have known of the conduct and fails to take immediate and appropriate corrective action. In reviewing these cases the Commission will consider the extent of the employer's control and any other legal responsibility which the employer may have with respect to the conduct of such non-employees.

(f) Prevention is the best tool for the elimination of sexual harassment. An employer should take all steps necessary to prevent sexual harassment from occurring, such as affirmatively raising the subject, expressing strong disapproval, developing appropriate sanctions, informing employees of their right to raise and how to raise the issue of harassment under title VII, and developing methods to sensitize all concerned.

(g) Other related practices: Where employment opportunities or benefits are granted because of an individual's submission to the employer's sexual advances or requests for sexual favors, the employer may be held liable for unlawful sex discrimination against other persons who were qualified for but denied that employment opportunity or benefit.

Some governors moved to address harassment in the state workforce. For example, former New York Governor Mario Cuomo took steps to stop sexual harassment in the state civil service with Executive Order 19 in May 1983, a directive that continues in force as state policy at the time of this writing.[68]

Interpreting the Scope and Character of Sexual Harassment in the Courts

It was actually the U.S. Supreme Court that put the pieces together and provided the authoritative statement that sexual harassment is sex discrimination within the meaning of Title VII.

Meritor Savings Bank v. Vinson

477 U.S. 57 (1986)

INTRODUCTION: The facts of the case are presented in the opinion below. Justice Rehnquist wrote the opinion for the Court.

This case presents important questions concerning claims of workplace "sexual harassment" brought under Title VII of the Civil Rights Act of 1964 ... 42 U.S.C. §2000e *et seq.*

In 1974, respondent Mechelle Vinson met Sidney Taylor, a vice president of what is now petitioner Meritor Savings Bank ... and manager of one of its branch offices.... With Taylor as her supervisor, respondent started [work] as a teller-trainee, and thereafter was promoted to teller, head teller, and assistant branch manager. She worked at the same branch for four years, and it is undisputed that her advancement there was based on merit alone. In September 1978, respondent notified Taylor that she was taking sick leave for an indefinite period. On November 1, 1978, the bank discharged her for excessive use of that leave.

Respondent brought this action against Taylor and the bank, claiming that during her four years at the bank she had "constantly been subjected to sexual harassment" by Taylor in violation of Title VII. She sought injunctive relief, compensatory and punitive damages against Taylor and the bank, and attorney's fees.

At ... trial, ... respondent testified that during her probationary period as a teller-trainee, Taylor treated her in a fatherly way and made no sexual advances. Shortly thereafter, however, he invited her out to dinner and, during the course of the meal, suggested that they go to a motel to have sexual relations. At first she refused, but out of what she described as fear of losing her job she eventually agreed. According to respondent, Taylor thereafter made repeated demands upon her for sexual favors, usually at the branch, both during and after business hours; she estimated that over the next several years she had intercourse with him some 40 or 50 times. In addition, respondent testified that Taylor fondled her in front of other employees, followed her into the women's restroom when she went there alone, exposed himself to her, and even forcibly raped her on several occasions. These activities ceased after 1977, respondent stated, when she started going with a steady boyfriend.

Respondent also testified that Taylor touched and fondled other women employees of the bank, and she attempted to call witnesses to support this charge. But while some supporting testimony apparently was admitted without objection, the District Court did not allow her "to present wholesale evidence of a pattern and practice relating to sexual advances to other female employees in her case in chief." ... Finally, respondent testified that because she was afraid of Taylor she never reported his harassment to any of his supervisors and never attempted to use the bank's complaint procedure.

Taylor denied respondent's allegations of sexual activity.... He contended instead that respondent made her accusations in response to a business-related dispute. The bank also denied respondent's allegations and asserted that any sexual harassment by Taylor was unknown to the bank and engaged in without its consent or approval.

The District Court ... ultimately found that respondent "was not the victim of sexual harassment and was not the victim of sexual discrimination" while employed at the bank.... The Court of Appeals for the District of Columbia Circuit reversed. [We] affirm....

Title VII of the Civil Rights Act of 1964 makes it "an unlawful employment practice for an employer ... to discriminate against any individual with respect to his compensation, terms, conditions, or privileges of employment, because of such individual's race, color, religion, sex, or national origin." ... The prohibition against discrimination based on sex was added to Title VII at the last minute on the floor of the House of Representatives.... [T]he bill quickly passed as amended, and we are left with little legislative history to guide us in interpreting the Act's prohibition against discrimination based on "sex."

... Without question, when a supervisor sexually harasses a subordinate because of the subordinate's sex, that supervisor "discriminate[s]" on the basis of sex.

Petitioner ... contends ... that in prohibiting discrimination with respect to "compensation, terms, conditions, or privileges" of employment, Congress was concerned with what petitioner describes as "tangible loss" of "an economic character," not "purely psychological aspects of the workplace environment." ...

We reject petitioner's view. First, the language of Title VII is not limited to "economic" or "tangible" discrimination. The phrase "terms, conditions, or privileges of employment" evinces a congressional intent "to strike at the entire spectrum of disparate treatment of men and women" in employment....

Second, in 1980 the EEOC issued Guidelines specifying that "sexual harassment," as there defined, is a form of sex discrimination prohibited by Title VII. As an "administrative interpretation of the Act by the enforcing agency," ... these Guidelines, "while not controlling upon the courts by reason of their authority, do constitute a body of experience and informed judgment to which courts and litigants may properly resort for guidance," .... The EEOC Guidelines fully support the view that harassment leading to noneconomic injury can violate Title VII.

In defining "sexual harassment," the Guidelines first describe the kinds of workplace conduct that may be actionable under Title VII. These include "[unwelcome] sexual advances, requests for sexual favors, and other verbal or physical conduct of a sexual nature." ... Relevant to the charges at issue in this case, the Guidelines provide that such sexual misconduct constitutes prohibited "sexual harassment," whether or not it is directly linked to the grant or denial of an economic quid pro quo, where "such conduct has the purpose or effect of unreasonably interfering with an individual's work performance or creating an intimidating, hostile, or offensive working environment." ...

In concluding that so-called "hostile environment" (i.e., non *quid pro quo*) harassment violates Title VII, the EEOC drew upon a substantial body of judicial decisions and EEOC precedent holding that Title VII affords employees the right to work in an environment free from discriminatory intimidation, ridicule, and insult.... *Rogers v. EEOC*, 454 F.2d 234 (5th Cir. 1971) ... was apparently the first case to recognize a cause of action based upon a discriminatory work environment. In *Rogers*, the Court of Appeals for the Fifth Circuit held that a Hispanic complainant could establish a Title VII violation by demonstrating that her employer created an offensive work environment for employees by giving discriminatory service to its Hispanic clientele. The court explained that an employee's protections under Title VII extend beyond the economic aspects of employment.... Courts applied this principle to harassment based on race..., religion..., and national origin....

Since the Guidelines were issued, courts have uniformly held, and we agree, that a plaintiff may establish a violation of Title VII by proving that discrimination based on sex has created a hostile or abusive work environment.... Of course ... not all workplace conduct that may be described as "harassment" affects a "term, condition, or privilege" of employment within the meaning of Title VII.... For sexual harassment to be actionable, it must be sufficiently severe or pervasive "to alter the conditions of [the victim's] employment and create an abusive working environment." ... Respondent's allegations in this case—which include not only pervasive harassment but also criminal conduct of the most serious nature—are plainly sufficient to state a claim for "hostile environment" sexual harassment.

The question remains, however, whether the District Court's ultimate finding that respondent "was not the victim of sexual harassment," ... effectively disposed of respondent's claim. The Court of Appeals recognized, we think correctly, that this ultimate finding was likely based on one or both of two erroneous views of the law.... Since it appears that the District Court made its findings without ever considering the "hostile environment" theory of sexual harassment, the Court of Appeals' decision to remand was correct.

Second, the District Court's conclusion that no actionable harassment occurred might have rested on its earlier "finding" that "[if] [respondent] and Taylor did engage in an intimate or sexual relationship..., that relationship was a voluntary one." ... But the fact that sex-related conduct was "voluntary," in the sense that the complainant was not forced to participate against her will, is not a defense to a sexual harassment suit brought under Title VII. The gravamen of any sexual harassment claim is that the alleged sexual advances were "unwelcome." ... While the question whether particular conduct was indeed unwelcome presents difficult problems of proof and turns largely on credibility determinations committed to the trier of fact, the District Court in this case erroneously focused on the "voluntariness" of respondent's participation in the claimed sexual episodes. The correct inquiry is whether respondent by her conduct indicated that the alleged sexual advances were unwelcome, not whether her actual participation in sexual intercourse was voluntary.

Petitioner contends that ... the Court of Appeals erred in one of the terms of its remand. Specifically, the Court of Appeals stated that testimony about respondent's "dress and personal fantasies," ... which the District Court apparently admitted into evidence, "had no place in this litigation." ... The apparent ground for this conclusion was that respondent's voluntariness ... in submitting to Taylor's advances was immaterial to her sexual harassment claim. While "voluntariness" in the sense of consent is not a defense to such a claim, it does not follow that a complainant's sexually provocative speech or dress is irrelevant as a matter of law in determining whether he or she found particular sexual advances unwelcome. To the contrary, such evidence is obviously relevant. The EEOC Guidelines emphasize that the trier of fact must determine the existence of sexual harassment in light of "the record as a whole" and "the totality of circumstances, such as the nature of the sexual advances and the context in which the alleged incidents occurred." ... Respondent's claim that any marginal relevance of the evidence in question was outweighed by the potential for unfair prejudice is the sort of argument properly addressed to the District Court. In this case the District Court concluded that the evidence should be admitted, and the Court of Appeals' contrary conclusion was based upon the erroneous, categorical view that testimony about provocative dress and publicly expressed sexual fantasies "had no place in this litigation." ...

Although the District Court concluded that respondent had not proved a violation of Title VII, it nevertheless went on to consider the question of the bank's liability. Finding that "the bank was without notice" of Taylor's alleged conduct, and that notice to Taylor was not the equivalent of notice to the bank, the court concluded that the bank therefore could not be held liable for Taylor's alleged actions. The Court of Appeals took the opposite view, holding that an employer is strictly liable for a hostile environment created by a supervisor's sexual advances, even though the employer neither knew nor reasonably could have known of the alleged misconduct. The court held that a supervisor, whether or not he possesses the authority to hire, fire, or promote, is necessarily an "agent" of his employer for all Title VII purposes, since "even the appearance" of such authority may enable him to impose himself on his subordinates.... This debate over the appropriate standard for employer liability has a rather abstract quality about it given the state of the record in this case. We do not know at this stage whether Taylor made any sexual advances toward respondent at all, let alone whether those advances were unwelcome, whether they were sufficiently pervasive to constitute a condition of employment, or whether they were "so pervasive and so long continuing ... that the employer must have become conscious of [them]." ...

We therefore decline the parties' invitation to issue a definitive rule on employer liability, but we do agree with the EEOC that Congress wanted courts to look to agency principles for guidance in this area.... [W]e hold that the Court of Appeals erred in concluding that employers are always automatically liable for sexual harassment by their supervisors.... For the same reason, absence of notice to an employer does not necessarily insulate that employer from liability....

Finally, we reject petitioner's view that the mere existence of a grievance procedure and a policy against discrimination, coupled with respondent's failure to invoke that procedure, must insulate petitioner from liability. While those facts are plainly relevant, the situation before us demonstrates why they are not necessarily dispositive. Petitioner's general nondiscrimination policy did not address sexual harassment in particular, and thus did not alert employees to their employer's interest in correcting that form of discrimination.... Moreover, the bank's grievance procedure apparently required an employee to complain first to her supervisor, in this case Taylor.... Petitioner's contention that respondent's failure should insulate it from liability might be substantially stronger if its procedures were better calculated to encourage victims of harassment to come forward.

In sum, we hold that a claim of "hostile environment" sex discrimination is actionable under Title VII, that the District Court's findings were insufficient to dispose of respondent's hostile environment claim, and that the District Court did not err in admitting testimony about respondent's sexually provocative speech and dress. As to employer liability, we conclude that the Court of Appeals was wrong to entirely disregard agency principles and impose absolute liability on employers for the acts of their supervisors, regardless of the circumstances of a particular case.... Remanded.

Justice Marshall wrote a concurring opinion joined by Justices Brennan, Blackmun, and Stevens.[69]

I fully agree with the Court's conclusion that workplace sexual harassment is illegal, and violates Title VII. Part III of the Court's opinion, however, leaves open the circumstances in which an employer is responsible under Title VII for such conduct. Because I believe that question to be properly before us, I write separately.

The issue the Court declines to resolve is addressed in the EEOC Guidelines on Discrimination Because of Sex, which are entitled to great deference.... The Commission, in issuing the Guidelines, explained that its rule was "in keeping with the general standard of employer liability with respect to agents and supervisory employees.... [The] Commission and the courts have held for years that an employer is liable if a supervisor or an agent violates the Title VII, regardless of knowledge or any other mitigating factor." ... I would adopt the standard set out by the Commission.

I would apply in this case the same rules we apply in all other Title VII cases, and hold that sexual harassment by a supervisor of an employee under his supervision, leading to a discriminatory work environment, should be imputed to the employer for Title VII purposes regardless of whether the employee gave "notice" of the offense.

With the Court's ruling that sexual harassment is sex discrimination in violation of Title VII, the discussion turned to the problem of identifying just what circumstances fit that part of the definition of harassment known as hostile environment harassment. Lower courts were divided about whether, in order to be serious enough to violate Title VII, the victim had to suffer the equivalent of serious psychological injury. The Supreme Court took the case in order to deal with these differing rulings below. It concluded that Title VII did not require the extreme showing of serious psychological injury. "When the workplace is permeated with discriminatory intimidation, ridicule, and insult, ... that is sufficiently severe or pervasive to alter the conditions of the victim's employment and create an abusive working environment, ... Title VII is violated."[70] The Court added:

> [W]hether an environment is "hostile" or "abusive" can be determined only by looking at all the circumstances. These may include the frequency of the discriminatory conduct; its severity; whether it is physically threatening or humiliating, or a mere offensive utterance and whether it unreasonably interferes with an employee's work performance.[71]

The discussion about just what behavior met that hostile environment standard was far from over. For one thing, it was clear that women and men did not always understand the concept of sexual harassment in the same way. It was also the case, as is true in other areas, that harassment is often about a power differential and control as much as, or perhaps even more than, sexual conduct itself. The effort by the courts and, for that matter, society to sort out these dynamics is likely to continue for some time. But before that discussion would receive further consideration in the U.S. Supreme Court, there remained the unresolved question of the liability of higher officials in the public or private sector for the conduct of lower level supervisors. The Court issued an important ruling in a case from Boca Raton, Florida. It was significant in part because it sought to clarify the obligations of employers, and at the same time to make clear that employees had some responsibilities as well in terms of making superiors aware of inappropriate behavior to allow the employer to take action to remedy the situation.

Faragher v. City of Boca Raton

524 U.S. 775 (1998)

INTRODUCTION: Beth Ann Faragher took a job as a lifeguard for the City of Boca Raton. Faragher alleged that her supervisors maintained a "sexually hostile atmosphere" and subjected women lifeguards to "uninvited and offensive touching," lewd language, and sexist comments. Although the lifeguards worked for the city parks and recreation department, they had virtually no contact with officials of that department or other city units. They were in many respects isolated from the other city offices. In fact, when in 1990 the city revised its sexual harassment policy, the lifeguards and their unit were not informed of it.

Although the behavior of her two immediate supervisors was allegedly extremely vulgar and demeaning, Faragher did not complain to superiors about their actions. At one point she spoke informally to the unit director, but made no formal complaint and took the matter no further. The unit director did nothing and did not report the information Faragher had related to him.

In spring 1990 another lifeguard wrote to the city personnel director complaining about the harassment. The city found the complaints valid, but the two men were given the choice of taking a leave without pay or forfeiting some of their accumulated leave time. Faragher quit shortly thereafter. She sued for violations of Title VII of the Civil Rights Act of 1964 and sought damages from the city for the behavior of her supervisors.

Justice Souter wrote the opinion for the Court.

This case calls for identification of the circumstances under which an employer may be held liable under Title VII of the Civil Rights Act of 1964 ... for the acts of a supervisory employee whose sexual harassment of subordinates has created a hostile work environment amounting to employment discrimination. We hold that an employer is vicariously liable[72] for actionable discrimination caused by a supervisor, but subject to an affirmative defense looking to the reasonableness of the employer's conduct as well as that of a plaintiff victim.

Since our decision in *Meritor*, Courts of Appeals have struggled to derive manageable standards to govern employer liability for hostile environment harassment perpetrated by supervisory employees. We now reverse the judgment of the Eleventh Circuit and remand for entry of judgment in Faragher's favor.

... We have repeatedly made clear that although [Title VII] mentions specific employment decisions with immediate consequences, the scope of the prohibition "is not limited to 'economic' or 'tangible' discrimination," *Harris v. Forklift Systems* ... and that it covers more than "'terms' and 'conditions' in the narrow contractual sense." Thus, in *Meritor* we held that sexual harassment so "severe or pervasive" as to "alter the conditions of [the victim's] employment and create an abusive working environment" violates Title VII.

[We have] explained that in order to be actionable under the statute, a sexually objectionable environment must be both objectively and subjectively offensive, one that a reasonable person would find hostile or abusive, and one that the victim in fact did perceive to be so. We directed courts to determine whether an environment is sufficiently hostile or abusive by "looking at all the circumstances," including the "frequency of the discriminatory conduct; its severity; whether it is physically threatening or humiliating, or a mere offensive utterance; and whether it unreasonably interferes with an employee's work performance." ... Most recently, we explained that Title VII does not prohibit "genuine but innocuous differences in the ways men and women routinely interact with members of the same sex and of the opposite sex." ... A recurring point in these opinions is that "simple teasing," offhand comments, and isolated incidents (unless extremely serious) will not amount to discriminatory changes in the "terms and conditions of employment."

... These standards for judging hostility are sufficiently demanding to ensure that Title VII does not become a "general civility code." ... Properly applied, they will filter out complaints attacking "the ordinary tribulations of the workplace, such as the sporadic use of abusive language, gender-related jokes, and occasional teasing." We have made it clear that conduct must be extreme to amount to a change in the terms and conditions of employment, and the Courts of Appeals have heeded this view.

Meritor's statement of the law is the foundation on which we build today. Neither party before us has urged us to depart from our customary adherence to *stare decisis*[73] in statutory interpretation....

We agree with Faragher that in implementing Title VII it makes sense to hold an employer vicariously liable for some tortious conduct[74] of a supervisor made possible by abuse of his supervisory authority.... When a person with supervisory authority discriminates in the terms and conditions of subordinates' employment, his actions necessarily draw upon his superior position over the people who report to him, or those under them, whereas an employee generally cannot check a supervisor's abusive conduct the same way that she might deal with abuse from a co-worker. When a fellow employee harasses, the victim can walk away or tell the offender where to go, but it may be difficult to offer such responses to a supervisor. Recognition of employer liability when discriminatory misuse of supervisory authority alters the terms and conditions of a victim's employment is underscored by the fact that the employer has a greater opportunity to guard against misconduct by supervisors than by common workers; employers have greater opportunity and incentive to screen them, train them, and monitor their performance.

In sum, there are good reasons for vicarious liability for misuse of supervisory authority. That rationale must, however, satisfy one more condition. We are not entitled to recognize this theory under Title VII unless we can square it with *Meritor*'s holding that an employer is not "automatically" liable for harassment by a supervisor who creates the requisite degree of discrimination....

As long ago as 1980, the Equal Employment Opportunity Commission (EEOC) ... adopted regulations advising employers to "take all steps necessary to prevent sexual harassment from occurring, such as ... informing employees of their right to raise and how to raise the issue of harassment" and in 1990 the Commission issued a policy statement enjoining employers to establish a complaint procedure designed to encourage victims of harassment to come forward [without requiring] a victim to complain first to the offending supervisor." It would therefore implement clear statutory policy and complement the Government's Title VII enforcement efforts to recognize the employer's affirmative obligation to prevent violations and give credit here to employers who make reasonable efforts to discharge their duty. Indeed, a theory of vicarious liability for misuse of supervisory power would be at odds with the statutory policy if it failed to provide employers with some such incentive.

The requirement to show that the employee has failed in a coordinate duty to avoid or mitigate harm reflects an equally obvious policy imported from the general theory of damages.... An employer may, for example, have provided a proven, effective mechanism for reporting and resolving complaints of sexual harassment, available to the employee without undue risk or expense. If the plaintiff unreasonably failed to avail herself of the employer's preventive or remedial apparatus, she should not recover damages that could have been avoided if she had done so....

[W]e adopt the following holding in this case and in *Burlington Industries, Inc. v. Ellerth* also decided today. An employer is subject to vicarious liability to a victimized employee for an actionable hostile environment created by a supervisor with immediate (or successively higher) authority over the employee. When no tangible employment action is taken, a defending employer may raise an affirmative defense to liability or damages, subject to proof by a preponderance of the evidence. The defense comprises two necessary elements: (a) that the employer exercised reasonable care to prevent and correct promptly any sexually harassing behavior, and (b) that the plaintiff employee unreasonably failed to take advantage of any preventive or corrective opportunities provided by the employer or to avoid harm otherwise. While proof that an employer had promulgated an anti-harassment policy with complaint procedure is not necessary in every instance as a matter of law, the need for a stated policy suitable to the employment circumstances may appropriately be addressed in any case when litigating the first element of the defense. And while proof that an employee failed to fulfill the corresponding obligation of reasonable care to avoid harm is not limited to showing an unreasonable failure to use any complaint procedure provided by the employer, a demonstration of such failure will normally suffice to satisfy the employer's burden under the second element of the defense. No affirmative defense is available, however, when the supervisor's harassment culminates in a tangible employment action, such as discharge, demotion, or undesirable reassignment.

Applying these rules here, we believe that the judgment of the Court of Appeals must be reversed. The District Court found that the degree of hostility in the work environment rose to the actionable level and was attributable to Silverman and Terry. It is undisputed that these supervisors "were granted virtually unchecked authority" over their subordinates, "directly controlling and supervising all aspects of [Faragher's] day-to-day activities." It is also clear that Faragher and her colleagues were "completely isolated from the City's higher management." The City did not seek review of these findings.

While the City would have an opportunity to raise an affirmative defense if there were any serious prospect of its presenting one, it appears from the record that any such avenue is closed. The District Court found that the City had entirely failed to disseminate its policy against sexual harassment among the beach employees and that its officials made no attempt to keep track of the conduct of supervisors like Terry and Silverman. The record also makes clear that the City's policy did not include any assurance that the harassing supervisors could be bypassed in registering complaints.... Under such circumstances, we hold as a matter of law that the City could not be found to have exercised reasonable care to prevent the supervisors' harassing conduct.... [The] Eleventh Circuit is reversed, and the case is remanded for reinstatement of the judgment of the District Court.

Justice Thomas wrote a dissent.

For the reasons given in my dissenting opinion in *Burlington Industries v. Ellerth*, absent an adverse employment consequence, an employer cannot be held vicariously liable if a supervisor creates a hostile work environment. Petitioner suffered no adverse employment consequence; thus the Court of Appeals was correct to hold that the City is not vicariously liable for the conduct of Chief Terry and Lieutenant Silverman....

I disagree with the Court's conclusion that merely because the City did not disseminate its sexual harassment policy, it should be liable as a matter of law. The City should be allowed to show either that: (1) there was a reasonably available avenue through which petitioner could have complained to a City official who supervised both Chief Terry and Lieutenant Silverman or (2) it would not have learned of the harassment even if the policy had been distributed. Petitioner, as the plaintiff, would of course bear the burden of proving the City's negligence.

The Court's ruling in *Faragher* makes clear the importance of having an effective policy and a process to address sexual harassment issues in an organization, and that it is just as important to communicate that policy and information about that process effectively throughout the organization. If employers do not do so, they may encourage or at least not discourage behavior that is damaging not only to individuals but also to the organization as a whole, and, in the end, find themselves facing liability not only for their own behavior but for that of their subordinates. At the same time, if employees do not understand or take seriously the available policies and processes, they may be left with little meaningful recourse in the event of a problem.

One aspect of the problem that had yet to be addressed in *Meritor* was same-sex harassment. Because of the clear history of harassment of women by men, there had been little attention given to same-sex harassment, whether that was male-on-male or female-on-female. In 1998, the Court held that same-sex harassment is also sex discrimination in violation of Title VII.

Oncale v. Sundowner Offshore Services

523 U.S. 75 (1998)

INTRODUCTION: The opinion provides a brief summary of the facts. In reading the opinion, note that Justice Scalia, writing for the Court, took the opportunity to shape the language about just how one is to know when the threshold had been reached at which courts would find a hostile environment. He did so in a way that is troubling to many advocates of women's rights, and to those of men as well. He suggests that it is not difficult to determine when there is a hostile environment because "common sense" tells us. However, what he regards as normal "horse-play" or "flirtation" is exactly the behavior that women, in particular, and many men as well have complained has been accepted for too long, and does indeed create a hostile environment that employees are required to endure despite the fact that it is disrespectful and offensive to them.

Justice Scalia wrote the opinion for the Court.

This case presents the question whether workplace harassment can violate Title VII ... when the harasser and the harassed employee are of the same sex.

In late October 1991, [Joseph] Oncale was working for respondent Sundowner Offshore Services on a Chevron ... oil platform in the Gulf of Mexico. He was employed as a roustabout on an eight-man crew which included respondents John Lyons, Danny Pippen, and Brandon Johnson. Lyons, the crane operator, and Pippen, the driller, had supervisory authority.... On several occasions, Oncale was forcibly subjected to sex-related, humiliating actions against him by Lyons, Pippen and Johnson in the presence of the rest of the crew. Pippen and Lyons also physically assaulted Oncale in a sexual manner, and Lyons threatened him with rape.

Oncale's complaints to supervisory personnel produced no remedial action; in fact, the company's Safety Compliance Clerk, Valent Hohen, told Oncale that Lyons and Pippen "picked [on] him all the time too," and called him a name suggesting homosexuality.... Oncale eventually quit—asking that his pink slip reflect that he "voluntarily left due to sexual harassment and verbal abuse." ... When asked at his deposition why he left Sundowner, Oncale stated "I felt that if I didn't leave my job, that I would be raped or forced to have sex." ...

Oncale filed a complaint against Sundowner in the United States District Court for the Eastern District of Louisiana, alleging that he was discriminated against in his employment because of his sex. [T]he district court held that [he had] "no cause of action under Title VII for harassment by male co-workers." ... [T]he Fifth Circuit ... affirmed....

Title VII's prohibition of discrimination "because of ... sex" protects men as well as women ... and in the related context of racial discrimination in the workplace we have rejected any conclusive presumption that an employer will not discriminate against members of his own race. "Because of the many facets of human motivation, it would be unwise to presume as a matter of law that human beings of one definable group will not discriminate against other members of that group."
... If our precedents leave any doubt on the question, we hold today that nothing in Title VII necessarily bars a claim of discrimination "because of ... sex" merely because the plaintiff and the defendant (or the person charged with acting on behalf of the defendant) are of the same sex.

Courts have had little trouble with that principle in cases like *Johnson v. Transportation Agency, Santa Clara Cty.*, 480 U.S. 616 (1987), where an employee claims to have been passed over for a job or promotion. But when the issue arises in the context of a "hostile environment" sexual harassment claim, the state and federal courts have taken a bewildering variety of stances. Some, like the Fifth Circuit in this case, have held that same-sex sexual harassment claims are never cognizable under Title VII.... Other decisions say that such claims are actionable only if the plaintiff can prove that the harasser is homosexual (and thus presumably motivated by sexual desire).... Still others suggest that workplace harassment that is sexual in content is always actionable, regardless of the harasser's sex, sexual orientation, or motivations....

We see no justification in the statutory language or our precedents for a categorical rule excluding same-sex harassment claims from the coverage of Title VII.... [M]ale-on-male sexual harassment in the workplace was assuredly not the principal evil Congress was concerned with when it enacted Title VII. But statutory prohibitions often go beyond the principal evil to cover reasonably comparable evils.... Title VII prohibits "discrimination ... because of ... sex" in the "terms" or "conditions" of employment. Our holding that this includes sexual harassment must extend to sexual harassment of any kind that meets the statutory requirements.

Respondents and their amici contend that recognizing liability for same-sex harassment will transform Title VII into a general civility code for the American workplace. But that risk is no greater for same-sex than for opposite-sex harassment, and is adequately met by careful attention to the requirements of the statute. Title VII does not prohibit all verbal or physical harassment in the workplace; it is directed only at "discrimination ... because of ... sex." We have never held that workplace harassment, even harassment between men and women, is automatically discrimination because of sex merely because the words used have sexual content or connotations....

Courts and juries have found the inference of discrimination easy to draw in most male–female sexual harassment situations, because the challenged conduct typically involves explicit or implicit proposals of sexual activity.... But harassing conduct need not be motivated by sexual desire to support an inference of discrimination on the basis of sex. A trier of fact might reasonably find such discrimination, for example, if a female victim is harassed in such sex-specific and derogatory terms by another woman as to make it clear that the harasser is motivated by general hostility to the presence of women in the workplace. A same-sex harassment plaintiff may also, of course, offer direct comparative evidence about how the alleged harasser treated members of both sexes in a mixed-sex workplace. Whatever evidentiary route the plaintiff chooses to follow, he or she must always prove that the conduct at issue was not merely tinged with offensive sexual connotations, but actually constituted "discrimination ... because of ... sex."

And there is another requirement that prevents Title VII from expanding into a general civility code: As we emphasized in *Meritor* and *Harris*, the statute does not reach genuine but innocuous differences in the ways men and women routinely interact with members of the same sex and of the opposite sex. The prohibition of harassment on the basis of sex requires neither asexuality nor androgyny in the workplace; it forbids only behavior so objectively offensive as to alter the "conditions" of the victim's employment. "Conduct that is not severe or pervasive enough to create an objectively hostile or abusive work environment—an environment that a reasonable person would find hostile or abusive—is beyond Title VII's purview." ... We have always regarded that requirement as crucial, and as sufficient to ensure that courts and juries do not mistake ordinary socializing in the workplace—such as male-on-male horseplay or intersexual flirtation—for discriminatory "conditions of employment."

We have emphasized, moreover, that the objective severity of harassment should be judged from the perspective of a reasonable person in the plaintiff's position, considering "all the circumstances." ... In same-sex (as in all) harassment cases, that inquiry requires careful consideration of the social context in which particular behavior occurs and is experienced by its target. A professional football player's working environment is not severely or pervasively abusive, for example, if the coach smacks him on the buttocks as he heads onto the field—even if the same behavior would reasonably be experienced as abusive by the coach's secretary (male or female) back at the office.... Common sense, and an appropriate sensitivity to social context, will enable courts and juries to distinguish between simple teasing or roughhousing among members of the same sex, and conduct which a reasonable person in the plaintiff's position would find severely hostile or abusive. Reversed.[75]

Harassment Outside the Employment Context: The Challenges in Schools and Colleges

As the Supreme Court was busy responding to calls for the development of protections against sexual harassment in the workplace, it began to receive cases seeking similar protections in the academic context. Schools and colleges were both places of employment and also institutions in which there was a concern about power differentials between teachers or administrators and students. To the degree that these concerns focus on relationships between teachers or professors and their superiors, it was clearly an employment relationship like the others raised in the cases decided by the Court under Title VII of the Civil Rights Act of 1964. However, apart from the employment relationship, the situation was different, since Title VII focused specifically on behavior that altered the terms of conditions of someone's employment. Thus, those seeking protection relied on Title IX of the Education Amendments of 1972.[76]

Title IX barred discrimination on the basis of sex or blindness in educational institutions and programs receiving federal funds.[77] What was then the U.S. Department of Health, Education, and Welfare, now the Department of Education, was given responsibility to administer the legislation.[78]

This legislation came at an important time in the efforts to ensure civil rights protections for women and to address sex discrimination broadly. In 1972 Congress passed Title IX, enacted the Equal Opportunity Amendments of 1972, which sought to strengthen the Civil Rights Act of 1964 to deal more effectively with sex discrimination, and sent the Equal Rights Amendment to the states for ratification. However, neither of the two statutes addressed sexual harassment.

The Supreme Court dealt with sexual harassment in the education context twenty years later in 1992 in a case concerning an extremely bad situation in a Georgia school in an Atlanta suburb. The case involved alleged harassment of a high school student by a teacher and sports coach at North Gwinnett High School. The Court said:

> Unquestionably, Title IX placed on the Gwinnett County Public Schools the duty not to discriminate on the basis of sex, and "when a supervisor sexually harasses a subordinate because of the subordinate's sex, that supervisor 'discriminate[s]' on the basis of sex." *Meritor Sav. Bank v. Vinson....* We believe the same rule should apply when a teacher sexually harasses and abuses a student.[79]

The Court also held that the school district and administrators could be held liable for harassment committed by their subordinates, but only if:

> an official who at a minimum has authority to address the alleged discrimination and to institute corrective measures on the recipient's behalf has actual knowledge of discrimination in the recipient's programs and fails adequately to respond. We think, moreover, that the response must amount to deliberate indifference to discrimination.[80]

Four justices dissented and would have held the district to a higher standard.

Once the basic principles of protection were established, parents began to bring suits that involved harassment by other students, either in school or on school buses.[81] Arguments ensued about how teachers and administrators could and should prevent or respond to student-on-student harassment, not only in the high school years but also with respect to younger students. Part of the difficulty in this area has been that these facts are a long way from the employment relationship that gave rise to sexual harassment law and policy, but there remained a lack of legislation specifically designed to address these types of problems, serious as they are.

Despite everything that has happened, whether in the employment context or in schools, Congress has not clearly and directly responded to the need for legislation that is updated to take into account the lessons learned about harassment and what needs to be done to guard against it, on the one hand, or deal with those involved if it does occur, on the other. This might be termed a work in progress, except that there has been relatively little progress, at least on the legislative front.

Private Organizations and Exclusion of Women

As the discussion to this point has indicated, exclusion has been an important theme and problem with respect to sex discrimination. Some of these situations have been paradoxical in nature as well as unacceptable in effect. In the modern context, for example, the military has both been at the leading edge in some areas of civil rights, in part because the president could directly order policy change, and in part because of the experience and needs of the military over time. At the same time, the military has long been an inherently conservative institution and one that has often resisted change, including and sometimes particularly in the area of civil rights. One need only recall the dramatic resistance by many top military commanders to President Truman's order desegregating the armed forces.

In some cases, such as the exclusion of women from some kinds of leadership positions and the line command experiences needed to attain those ranks, this discrimination was imposed politically, as was true in the case of the firm cap on the percentage of women who could serve in the uniformed services that existed for many years and the related inability to obtain veterans' benefits, which was considered in the *Feeney* case (discussed above). The Supreme Court upheld some of these policies, such as a modification of the up-or-out policy for promotion of officers in light of the exclusion of women from combat command positions.[82] It also rejected claims that the draft registration that is limited to men was sex-discriminatory on grounds that women were excluded from combat positions and therefore could reasonably be excluded from the draft registration requirement.[83] While some advocates might have seen these decisions as good for women, for those involved in those cases, and at that moment in time, what the rulings did was to reinforce the exclusion from various key aspects of a military career for those women who wanted to serve and build a career in the military.

There is a complex history leading to the end of the exclusion from combat positions, which came in a January 2013 memorandum from Secretary of Defense Leon Panetta and Chief of the Joint Chiefs of Staff Martin Dempsey, to the secretaries of the services, but it left open an opportunity until January 1, 2016 for the services to request exceptions based on evaluation of their position.[84] On December 3, 2015 Secretary of Defense Ash Carter issued a memorandum to all service secretaries that read in part:

> I have now determined that no exceptions are warranted to full implementation of the rescission of the "1994 Ground Combat Definition and Assignment Rule." Anyone, who can meet the operationally relevant and gender neutral standards, regardless of gender, should have the opportunity to serve in any position.[85]

However, there have been other kinds of exclusion that have persisted over time, one of which was exclusion from social and fraternal organization. In these situations, organizations claimed a right to freedom of association under the First Amendment, which implies a right not to associate. Various states have, however, enacted human rights statutes that barred such exclusions. This kind of situation came to the Supreme Court in a case involving one such state, Minnesota, and a well-known organization, the Jaycees.

Roberts v. Jaycees

468 U.S. 609 (1984)

INTRODUCTION: Justice Brennan explains the facts in the opinion. It is important to read his explanation of the importance of gender inclusion as a governmental interest. Indeed, the Court finds that "eradicating discrimination against its female citizens" is a compelling state interest. His treatment of the limits of the right not to associate is also important, since it comes up again in a later case involving the Boy Scouts, a case that received a very different response in an opinion by Chief Justice Rehnquist (see Chapter 11).

Justice Brennan wrote the opinion for the Court.

> This case requires us to address a conflict between a State's efforts to eliminate gender-based discrimination against its citizens and the constitutional freedom of association asserted by members of a private organization. In the decision under review, the Court of Appeals for the Eighth Circuit concluded that, by requiring the United States Jaycees to admit women as full voting members, the Minnesota

Human Rights Act violates the First and Fourteenth Amendment rights of the organization's members. We ... reverse.

The United States Jaycees [Junior Chamber of Commerce] is a nonprofit membership corporation.... The organization's bylaws establish seven classes of membership, including individual or regular members, associate individual members, and local chapters. Regular membership is limited to young men between the ages of 18 and 35, while associate membership is available to individuals or groups ineligible for regular membership, principally women and older men. An associate member ... may not vote, hold local or national office, or participate in certain leadership training and awards programs.... At the time of trial in August 1981, the Jaycees had approximately 295,000 members in 7,400 local chapters affiliated with 51 state organizations.... The national organization's executive vice president estimated at trial that women associate members make up about two percent of the Jaycees' total membership....

In 1974 and 1975, respectively, the Minneapolis and St. Paul chapters of the Jaycees began admitting women as regular members.... In December 1978, the president of the national organization advised both chapters that a motion to revoke their charters would be considered at a forthcoming meeting of the national board of directors.... [M]embers of both chapters filed charges of discrimination with the Minnesota Department of Human Rights, alleg[ing] that the exclusion of women from full membership ... violated the Minnesota Human Rights Act (Act), which provides in part: "It is an unfair discriminatory practice: To deny any person the full and equal enjoyment of the goods, services, facilities, privileges, advantages, and accommodations of a place of public accommodation because of race, color, creed, religion, disability, national origin or sex." ... The term "place of public accommodation" is defined in the Act as "a business, accommodation, refreshment, entertainment, recreation, or transportation facility of any kind, whether licensed or not, whose goods, services, facilities, privileges, advantages or accommodations are extended, offered, sold, or otherwise made available to the public." ...

Before th[e] hearing took place, however, the national organization brought suit against various state officials ... to prevent enforcement of the Act. The complaint alleged that ... requiring the organization to accept women as regular members ... would violate the male members' constitutional rights of free speech and association.... [T]he District Court entered judgment in favor of the state officials.... [The] Court of Appeals reversed....

Our decisions have referred to constitutionally protected "freedom of association" in two distinct senses. [T]he Court has concluded that choices to enter into and maintain certain intimate human relationships must be secured against undue intrusion by the State because of the role of such relationships in safeguarding the individual freedom that is central to our constitutional scheme. In this respect, freedom of association receives protection as a fundamental element of personal liberty. In another set of decisions, the Court has recognized a right to associate for the purpose of engaging in those activities protected by the First Amendment—speech, assembly, petition for the redress of grievances, and the exercise of religion. The Constitution guarantees freedom of association of this kind as an indispensable means of preserving other individual liberties.

The ... nature and degree of constitutional protection afforded freedom of association may vary depending on the extent to which one or the other aspect of the constitutionally protected liberty is at stake in a given case. We therefore find it useful to consider separately the effect of applying the Minnesota statute to the Jaycees on what could be called its members' freedom of intimate association and their freedom of expressive association.

The Court has long recognized that, because the Bill of Rights is designed to secure individual liberty, it must afford the formation and preservation of certain kinds of highly personal relationships a substantial measure of sanctuary from unjustified interference by the State....

The personal affiliations that exemplify these considerations ... are those that attend the creation and sustenance of a family—marriage...; childbirth...; the raising and education of children...; and cohabitation with one's relatives.... Family relationships, by their nature, involve deep attachments and commitments to the necessarily few other individuals with whom one shares not only a special community of thoughts, experiences, and beliefs but also distinctively personal aspects of one's life.... [T]hey are distinguished by such attributes as relative smallness, a high degree of selectivity in decisions to begin and maintain the affiliation, and seclusion from others in critical aspects of the relationship. As a general matter, only relationships with these sorts of qualities are likely to reflect the considerations that have led to an understanding of freedom of association as an intrinsic element of personal liberty....

[S]everal features of the Jaycees clearly place the organization outside of the category of relationships worthy of this kind of constitutional protection. The undisputed facts reveal that the local chapters of the Jaycees are large and basically unselective groups.... Apart from age and sex, neither the national organization nor the local chapters employ any criteria for judging applicants for membership, and new members are routinely recruited and admitted with no inquiry into their backgrounds.... Indeed, numerous nonmembers of both genders regularly participate in a substantial portion of activities..., including ... community programs, awards ceremonies, and recruitment meetings.... Accordingly, we conclude that the Jaycees chapters lack the distinctive characteristics that might afford constitutional protection to the decision of its members to exclude women.

We turn therefore to consider the extent to which application of the Minnesota statute to compel the Jaycees to accept women infringes the group's freedom of expressive association.... [P]rotection [of] collective effort on behalf of shared goals is especially important in preserving political and cultural diversity and in shielding dissident expression from suppression by the majority.... *NAACP v. Alabama ex rel. Patterson*, 357 U.S. 449 (1958). Consequently, we have long understood as implicit in the right to engage in activities protected by the First Amendment a corresponding right to associate with others in pursuit of a wide variety of political, social, economic, educational, religious, and cultural ends. In view of the various protected activities in which the Jaycees engages ... that right is plainly implicated in this case.

Government actions that may unconstitutionally infringe upon this freedom can take a number of forms [such as] interfer[ing] with the internal organization or affairs of the group.... By requiring the Jaycees to admit women as full voting members, the Minnesota Act works an infringement of [this] type. There can be no clearer example of an intrusion into the internal structure or affairs of an association than a regulation that forces the group to accept members it does not desire.... Freedom of association therefore plainly presupposes a freedom not to associate.

The right to associate for expressive purposes is not, however, absolute. Infringements on that right may be justified by regulations adopted to serve compelling state interests, unrelated to the suppression of ideas, that cannot be achieved through means significantly less restrictive of associational freedoms. We are persuaded that Minnesota's compelling interest in eradicating discrimination against its female citizens justifies the impact that application of the statute to the Jaycees may have on the male members' associational freedoms. On its face, the Minnesota Act does not aim at the suppression of speech, does not distinguish between prohibited and permitted activity on the basis of viewpoint, and does not license enforcement authorities to administer the statute on the basis of such constitutionally impermissible criteria.... Instead, ... the Act reflects the State's strong historical commitment to eliminating discrimination and assuring its citizens equal access to publicly available goods and services.... That goal, which is unrelated to the suppression of expression, plainly serves compelling state interests of the highest order....

By prohibiting gender discrimination in places of public accommodation, the Minnesota Act protects the State's citizenry from a number of serious social and personal harms.... [T]his Court has frequently noted that discrimination based on archaic and overbroad assumptions about the relative needs and capacities of the sexes forces individuals to labor under stereotypical notions that often bear no relationship to their actual abilities. It thereby both deprives persons of their individual dignity and denies society the benefits of wide participation in political, economic, and cultural life. See, e.g., *Mississippi University for Women* ... *Frontiero*....

In applying the Act to the Jaycees, the State has advanced those interests through the least restrictive means of achieving its ends. Indeed, the Jaycees has failed to demonstrate that the Act imposes any serious burdens on the male members' freedom of expressive association.... Moreover, the Jaycees already invites women to share the group's views and philosophy and to participate in much of its training and community activities....

[E]ven if enforcement of the Act causes some incidental abridgment of the Jaycees' protected speech, that effect is no greater than is necessary to accomplish the State's legitimate purposes.... [A]cts of invidious discrimination in the distribution of publicly available goods, services, and other advantages cause unique evils that government has a compelling interest to prevent.... [S]uch practices are entitled to no constitutional protection.... In prohibiting such practices, the Minnesota Act ... "abridges no more speech or associational freedom than is necessary to accomplish that purpose." ... The judgment of the Court of Appeals is reversed.[86]

Justice O'Connor wrote an opinion concurring in part and concurring in the judgment.[87]

... I agree with the Court that application of the Minnesota law to the Jaycees does not contravene the First Amendment, but I reach that conclusion for reasons distinct from those offered by the Court....

The Court analyzes Minnesota's attempt to regulate the Jaycees' membership using a test that I find both overprotective of activities undeserving of constitutional shelter and underprotective of important First Amendment concerns. The Court declares that the Jaycees' right of association depends on the organization's making a "substantial" showing that the admission of unwelcome members "will change the message communicated by the group's speech." ... I am not sure what showing the Court thinks would satisfy its requirement of proof of a membership–message connection, but whatever it means, the focus on such a connection is objectionable.... Whether an association is or is not constitutionally protected in the selection of its membership should not depend on what the association says or why its members say it....

Many associations cannot readily be described as purely expressive or purely commercial.... In my view, an association should be characterized as commercial, and therefore subject to rationally related state regulation of its membership and other associational activities, when, and only when, the association's activities are not predominantly of the type protected by the First Amendment.... Once it enters the marketplace of commerce in any substantial degree, it loses the complete control over its membership that it would otherwise enjoy if it confined its affairs to the marketplace of ideas....

Minnesota's attempt to regulate the membership of the Jaycees chapters operating in that State presents a relatively easy case for application of the expressive–commercial dichotomy.... Notwithstanding its protected expressive activities, the Jaycees ... is, first and foremost, an organization that, at both the national and local levels, promotes and practices the art of solicitation and management.... The Jaycees itself refers to its members as customers and membership as a product it is selling....

Recruitment and selling are commercial activities, even when conducted for training rather than for profit. The State of Minnesota has a legitimate interest in ensuring nondiscriminatory access to the commercial opportunity presented by membership in the Jaycees. The members of the Jaycees may not claim constitutional immunity from Minnesota's antidiscrimination law by seeking to exercise their First Amendment rights through this commercial organization.

Notice that Justice O'Connor would have taken a narrower approach to deciding the case, focusing only on the fact that it was a commercial organization. That, of course, would leave open the question what would happen if the organization was not commercial in character and still excluded women.

Conclusion

As this chapter shows, the discussion of civil rights issues concerned with gender, and in particular sex discrimination, is complex and diverse, but the case law and legislation providing protections against that kind of discrimination are relatively recent in American history. And despite the numerous Supreme Court rulings and legislative actions, it is still very much a work in progress. That is perhaps in part because this aspect of civil rights is one that the society in general has only been engaging directly, at least in terms of the modern discussion, in relatively recent years. Although it might seem as if a great deal has been accomplished, the evidence and the case law suggest that there is a long way to go.

Although there is often an assumption that younger generations will adapt and grow so that some of the challenges will naturally disappear, there is also the risk that some of those young people are not fully informed about the complexity involved or the policy and law issues that have not really been resolved, much less eliminated.

I. Issues for Policy and Practice

A. Given that the legal momentum for change to eliminate gender discrimination, in the Supreme Court at least, only dates from 1971, how can we assess the state of relationships across policy domains today? There are certainly individual issues that arise, but is there any effort to make a comprehensive assessment of the state of policy in terms of sex discrimination?

B. There are certainly a variety of policies that have been put in place by statute, regulation, or even ordinances in some places over the past four decades to address gender-based discrimination. What evaluations have been done of those policies to determine their effectiveness? Gross measures like income disparity suggest that there is much that has not been resolved, but how systematic is the knowledge broadly or in one's own organization?

C. From a management perspective, does one's organization have job categories that are assumed to be held by women as compared to men? Are they compensated at a fair rate or based on stereotyped assumptions about women's needs?

D. What has been the record of promotions within the organization in terms of gender equality? Are there career tracks that have historically been dominated by one group or the other?

E. As the case law emphasizes, it is extremely important for organizations to have a clear policy against sexual harassment and an effective and accessible process for handling complaints. However, is it clear to employees what sexual harassment includes? Do the women and the men in the organization have a common understanding of what is included in the concept? Some organizations do anonymous surveys to ask questions, not only about understanding of the concept, but also the experience people in the organization have had, including their view of whether the process for complaints is accessible and effective.

II. Discussion Questions

A. There is a tendency today to assume that, with all that has happened since the 1970s, surely we have changed society to address sex discrimination and to create more appropriate and positive ways to ensure effective working and social relationships between men and women and among women or men. Is that optimistic assessment even anywhere close to being true? If not, where are we in the process of moving away from the "archaic and overbroad generalizations" of the past and toward a future of gender equality?

B. There is discussion in the chapter and in the *VMI* case itself about whether the Court applied the same standard as in the previous cases to determine whether there was gender discrimination, or was the language about "exceedingly persuasive justification" treated so as to make it a new requirement, apart from the intermediate standard that requires that the state show that the classification at least serves "important governmental objectives and that the discriminatory means employed" are "substantially related to the achievement of those objectives?"

C. Justice Scalia suggests that "common sense" is sufficient to understand what constitutes a hostile environment in the workplace in terms of sexual harassment, and it does not include "horseplay", "flirtation", or off-color language unless this rises to an unacceptable level. However, is it really true that men and women, in particular, agree on how much and what kind of language or behavior is too much and creates a hostile environment?

D. What are the differences between the way men often understand sexual harassment and what women regard as harassment?

E. As the case law discussed in this chapter indicates, there have been any number of important cases in which policies and practices based on stereotypes about men have actually resulted in discrimination with regard to both men and women. Are there stereotypes about men that survive even this far into the twenty-first century? If so, do those stereotypes imply stereotypes about women?

Notes

1 *Ledbetter v. Goodyear Tire & Rubber*, 550 U.S. 618 (2007).
2 Lilly Ledbetter Fair Pay Act of 2009, P.L. 111–2, 123 Stat. 5.
3 National Park Service, The First Women's Rights Convention, www.nps.gov/wori/learn/history culture/the-first-womens-rights-convention.htm, March 6, 2015.
4 *Reed v. Reed*, 404 U.S. 71 (1971).
5 42 U.S.C. §2000e.
6 The Equal Pay Act, P.L. 88–38, was passed before that in 1963 as an amendment to the Fair Labor Standards Act, but it was difficult for those who faced the discrimination to know that they were being paid less.
7 It was not until 1982 that the first women came to the Court. Justice Sandra Day O'Connor retired in 2006. Justice Ruth Bader Ginsburg took her seat in 1993, Justice Sonia Sotomayor in 2009, and Justice Elena Kagan in 2010.
8 *Frontiero v. Richardson*, 411 U.S. 677, 684 (1973).
9 See Newsweek's cover story on the subject. Max Kutner, "Sex Slaves on the Farm," *Newsweek*, February 13, 2015, p. 1.
10 Federal Bureau of Investigation, "Human Trafficking," www.fbi.gov/about-us/investigate/civil-rights/human_trafficking, March 7, 2015.
11 Recall the discussions of the *Slaughter-House Cases*, 83 U.S. 36 (1873), the *Civil Rights Cases*, 109 U.S. 3 (1883), and, of course, *Plessy v. Ferguson*, 163 U.S. 537 (1896).
12 James Martin of the Library of Congress notes that: "This paper was launched in the same year and quickly became noted for its authoritative reporting on legal developments and commentary. In 1869, the State of Illinois enacted a law providing that the state's courts could take judicial notice of the statutes of Illinois and the decisions of the state's Supreme Court that were published in the paper." See http://blogs.loc.gov/law/2012/05/the-chicago-legal-news-myra-bradwell-and-susan-b-anthony-pic-of-the-week/, March 27, 2015. He also provided a PDF of the inscription to the first edition of the paper provided by Susan B. Anthony when she donated it to the library, http://blogs.loc.gov/law/files/2012/05/Anthony-Inscription5.jpg, March 27, 2015.
13 See *United States v. Yazell*, 382 U.S. 341, 343 (1966); *United States v. Dege et Vir.*, 364 U.S. 51, 54 (1960).
14 The Revised Statutes of the State of Illinois, 1903, Chapter 48, §3.
15 The Law Dictionary, http://thelawdictionary.org/article/who-was-myra-bradwell-americas-first-woman-lawyer/, March 27, 2015.
16 NOTE: This is a reference to the common law doctrine of coverture, as explained in the introduction to this case.
17 There were exceptions, of course. This was also an era of journalists like Edward R. Morrow. And there were drama specials that addressed challenges and problems, but these were indeed exceptions to the nightly fare regularly watched by American families.
18 NOTE: At this point, Justice Rutledge sought to draw the attention of the Court to the inconsistency of its ruling with other precedents, including among others *Missouri ex rel. Gaines v. Canada* and *Yick Wo v. Hopkins*.
19 New York: W. W. Norton, 1963.
20 381 U.S. 479 (1965).
21 *Loving v. Virginia*, 388 U.S. 1 (1967).
22 *Eisenstadt v. Baird*, 405 U.S. 438 (1972).
23 See *Levy v. Louisiana*, 391 U.S. 68 (1968); *Weber v. Aetna Casualty & Security*, 406 U.S. 164 (1968); *Glona v. American Guaranty & Liability*, 391 U.S. 73 (1968); and *Gomez v. Perez*, 409 U.S. 535 (1973). And even after this round of cases finding such treatment inherently suspect, the Court issued a series of problematic rulings on legitimacy. See *Labine v. Vincent*, 401 U.S. 532 (1971); *Mathews v. Lucas*, 427 U.S. 495 (1976); *Fiallo v. Bell*, 430 U.S. 787 (1968).
24 *Roe v. Wade*, 410 U.S. 113 (1973).
25 *Stanley v. Illinois*, 405 U.S. 645 (1972).

26 NOTE: The term simply means without a will.
27 NOTE: The "administratrix" is simply a feminine version of administrator. This gender-specific language is found in various parts of the law, even though we try to avoid such usages in today's parlance.
28 NOTE: Justices Powell and Rehnquist did not participate in this case.
29 *United States v. Virginia*, 518 U.S. 515 (1996).
30 *Lawrence v. Texas*, 539 U.S. 558 (2003).
31 *Green v. Waterford Board of Education*, 473 F.2d 629, 635 (2nd Cir 1973).
32 NOTE: The term means "for the sake of argument."
33 See *San Antonio Independent School District v. Rodriguez*, 411 U.S. 1 (1973).
34 "It is true, of course, that when viewed in the abstract, women do not constitute a small and powerless minority. Nevertheless, in part because of past discrimination, women are vastly under-represented in this Nation's decisionmaking councils. There has never been a female President, nor a female member of this Court. Not a single woman presently sits in the United States Senate, and only 14 women hold seats in the House of Representatives. And, as appellants point out, this underrepresentation is present throughout all levels of our State and Federal Government."
35 "It should be noted that these statutes are not in any sense designed to rectify the effects of past discrimination against women.... On the contrary, these statutes seize upon a group—women—who have historically suffered discrimination in employment, and rely on the effects of this past discrimination as a justification for heaping on additional economic disadvantages."
36 "In 1971, 43% of all women over the age of 16 were in the labor force, and 18% of all women worked full time 12 months per year.... Moreover, 41.5% of all married women are employed. See U.S. Bureau of Labor Statistics, Dept. of Labor, Work Experience of the Population in 1971, p. 4 (Summary Special Labor Force Report, Aug. 1972). It is also noteworthy that, while the median income of a male member of the armed forces is approximately $3,686, ... the median income for all women over the age of 14, including those who are not employed, is approximately $2,237.... Applying the statutory definition of 'dependency' to these statistics, it appears that, in the 'median' family, the wife of a male member must have personal expenses of approximately $4,474, or about 75% of the total family income, in order to qualify as a 'dependent.'"
37 "As is evident from our opinions, the Court has had difficulty in agreeing upon a standard of equal protection analysis that can be applied consistently to the wide variety of legislative classifications. There are valid reasons for dissatisfaction with the 'two-tier' approach that has been prominent in the Court's decisions in the past decade. Although viewed by many as a result-oriented substitute for more critical analysis, that approach—with its narrowly limited 'upper-tier'—now has substantial precedential support. As has been true of Reed and its progeny, our decision today will be viewed by some as a 'middle-tier' approach. While I would not endorse that characterization and would not welcome a further subdividing of equal protection analysis, candor compels the recognition that the relatively deferential 'rational basis' standard of review normally applied takes on a sharper focus when we address a gender-based classification."
38 NOTE: Justice Stevens's concurring opinion is omitted here.
39 NOTE: Justice Burger added his own brief dissent, but that is omitted here.
40 Robert Marquand, "Conversations with Outstanding Americans: Sandra Day O'Connor," *Christian Science Monitor*, January 28, 1997, p. 10.
41 *Mississippi University for Women v. Hogan*, No. 81–406, Brief for Respondent, 1981 U.S. Briefs 406, p. 8.
42 NOTE: Here Justice O'Connor uses the phrase "exceedingly persuasive justification" and explains that to be such a justification, such that any discrimination on the basis of gender must show that "the classification serves 'important governmental objectives and that the discriminatory means employed' are 'substantially related to the achievement of those objectives.'" That is, it is necessary to satisfy the standard announced by the Court in *Craig v. Boren* and used in all the cases following that. She then goes on in the paragraphs that follow to address the two parts of the *Craig* standard. The phrase "exceedingly persuasive justification" was not part of that standard but was descriptive language used in two cases, both of which actually relied on the *Craig* standard. This was Justice Marshall's opinion in *Kirchberg v. Feenstra*, 450 U.S. 455, 461 (1981) and Justice Stewart's opinion

in *Personnel Administrator of Massachusetts v. Feeney*, 442 U.S. 256, 273 (1979). This twist of language becomes important later, as Justice Ginsburg used it quite differently in the later Virginia Military Institute case discussed below.

43 NOTE: Chief Justice Burger also joined Powell, but issued his own brief dissent that has been omitted here.

44 NOTE: Justice Thomas did not participate in this case.

45 NOTE: He is not citing a precedent here, but his own dissenting opinion in an earlier case. *Rutan v. Republican Party of Ill.*, 497 U.S. 62, 95 (1990) (Scalia, J., dissenting). He made that assertion in a case that had nothing to do with either equal protection of the law or gender, but rather concerned patronage hiring, and even then cited no precedent to support his dramatic assertion. What he was really asserting, as his colleagues correctly charged at that time, was the doctrine of repose, discussed earlier in Chapter 6—the argument that had been employed by the opponents of desegregation in *Brown v. Board of Education*. In his *Rutan* opinion, Scalia had to add a footnote attempting to differentiate himself from that doctrine, but it was a failed effort to avoid what Justice Stevens pointed out in his concurring opinion in that case was a clear reference to that discredited use of an incorrect doctrine to sustained violations of constitutional rights and liberties. Id., n. 1 (Scalia, J., dissenting).

46 *Personnel Administrator of Massachusetts v. Feeney*, 442 U.S. 256, 279 (1979).

47 NOTE: The concurring opinion by Justice Stevens is omitted.

48 442 U.S., at 281, Stevens, J., concurring.

49 42 U.S.C. §2000e *et seq.*

50 *Geduldig v. Aiello*, 417 U.S. 484 (1974).

51 42 U.S.C. § 2000e-2(a)(1).

52 417 U.S. 484 (1974).

53 NOTE: The brief concurring opinions of Justices Stewart and Blackmun are omitted here.

54 Quite clearly Congress could not have intended to adopt this Court's analysis of sex discrimination, because it was seven years after the statute was passed that the Court first intimated that the concept of sex discrimination might have some relevance to equal protection analysis. See *Reed v. Reed*, 404 U.S. 71 (1971).

55 P.L. 95–555, 92 Stat. 2076 (1978).

56 *Weinberger v. Wiesenfeld*, 420 U.S. 636 (1975).

57 NOTE: Justice Stevens's concurring opinion omitted here.

58 *Los Angeles Department of Water & Power v. Manhart*, 435 U.S. 702 (1978).

59 Id., at 707–708.

60 Id., at 708.

61 Id., at 709.

62 Id., at 722.

63 *Arizona Governing Committee for Tax Deferred Annuity and Deferred Compensation Plans v. Norris*, 463 U.S. 1073 (1983).

64 Id., at 1074.

65 U.S. Equal Employment Opportunity Commission (EEOC) 45 Fed. Reg. 74676 (November 10, 1980).

66 29 C.F.R. 1604.11 (2013). The C.F.R. is the *Code of Federal Regulations*, which is where the rules issued by federal administrative agencies are published.

67 NOTE: A previous section (c) was rescinded following rulings by the U.S. Supreme Court that defined the liability of employers for harassment committed by supervisors in their organizations. See *Burlington Industries v. Ellerth*, 524 U.S. 742 (1998); *Faragher v. City of Boca Raton*, 524 U.S. 775 (1998). After those rulings, the EEOC issued a policy document about their implications that provided guidance with respect to vicarious liability for harassment by supervisors. "Enforcement Guidance: Vicarious Employer Liability for Unlawful Harassment by Supervisors," www.eeoc.gov/policy/docs/harassment.html, May 29, 2015. Vicarious liability means that someone can be held responsible for the misdeeds of people under their supervision, which in this case refers to the responsibility of senior management for harassment by line supervisors.

68 Executive Order No. 19, May 31, 1983 which was reaffirmed by Governor Andrew Cuomo in Executive Order No. 2, January 1, 2011, www.governor.ny.gov/executiveorder/2, May 21, 2015.

69 NOTE: Justice Stevens joined both the majority opinion and the concurring opinion prepared by Justice Marshall.

70 *Harris v. Forklift Systems, Inc.*, 510 U.S. 17, 21 (1993).

71 Id., at 23.

72 NOTE: Vicarious liability is responsibility for injury caused by the conduct of another person. In this case, it refers to a claim that the City of Boca Raton should be responsible as the employer for the conduct of its managers toward subordinate city employees.

73 NOTE: *Stare decisis* is the technical term for the rule of precedent.

74 NOTE: Tortious conduct is the commission of a tort, a civil violation of law, for which one may collect damages from the tortfeasor (the person who commits the tort).

75 NOTE: Brief concurrence of Justice Thomas omitted here.

76 P.L. 92–318, Title IX, Sec. 901, June 23, 1972, 86 Stat. 373.

77 Codified at 20 U.S.C. §1681, *et seq.*

78 Those regulations are found at 34 C.F.R. Part 106.

79 *Franklin v. Gwinnett County Public Schools*, 503 U.S. 60, 75 (1972).

80 *Gebser v. Lago Vista Ind. School Dist.*, 524 U.S. 274, 290 (1998).

81 *Fitzgerald v. Barnstable School Committee*, 555 U.S. 246 (2009).

82 See *Schlesinger v. Ballard*, 419 U.S. 498 (1975).

83 *Rostker v. Goldberg*, 453 U.S. 57 (1981).

84 Leon Panetta, Memorandum for Secretaries of the Military Departments, Acting Under Secretary of Defense for Personnel and Readiness, Chiefs of the Military Services, "Elimination of the 1994 Direct Ground Combat Definition and Assignment Rule," January 24, 2013, www.defense.gov/news/WISRJointMemo.pdf, December 2, 2015. See generally, National Women's Law Center, Restrictions on Assignments of Military Women: A Brief History, www.nwlc.org/resource/restrictions-assignments-military-women-brief-history, June 2, 2015.

85 Ash Carter, Memorandum for Secretaries of the Military Departments, Acting Under Secretary of Defense for Personnel and Readiness, Chiefs of the Military Services, Commander, U.S. Special Operations Command, "Implementation Guidance for the Full Integration of Women in the Armed Forces," December 3, 2015, www.defense.gov/Portals/1/Documents/pubs/OSD014303-15.pdf, December 12, 2015.

86 NOTE: Chief Justice Burger and Justice Blackmun did not participate in the case. Both were from the twin cities.

87 NOTE: Justice Rehnquist concurred in the judgment, but issued no opinion.

References

Carter, Ash. Memorandum for Secretaries of the Military Departments, Acting Under Secretary of Defense for Personnel and Readiness, Chiefs of the Military Services, Commander, U.S. Special Operations Command, "Implementation Guidance for the Full Integration of Women in the Armed Forces," December 3, 2015, www.defense.gov/Portals/1/Documents/pubs/OSD014303-15.pdf, December 12, 2015.

Equal Employment Opportunity Commission, "Enforcement Guidance: Vicarious Employer Liability for Unlawful Harassment by Supervisors," www.eeoc.gov/policy/docs/harassment.html, May 29, 2015.

Federal Bureau of Investigation. "Human Trafficking," www.fbi.gov/about-us/investigate/civilrights/human_trafficking, March 7, 2015.

Friedan, Betty. *The Feminine Mystique*. New York, W. W. Norton, 1963.

National Women's Law Center. Restrictions on Assignments of Military Women: A Brief History, www.nwlc.org/resource/restrictions-assignments-military-women-brief-history, June 2, 2015.

Panetta, Leon. Memorandum for Secretaries of the Military Departments, Acting Under Secretary of Defense for Personnel and Readiness, Chiefs of the Military Services, "Elimination of the 1994 Direct Ground Combat Definition and Assignment Rule," January 24, 2013, www.defense.gov/news/WISRJointMemo.pdf, December 12, 2015.

11 Civil Rights and Sexual Orientation and Identity

Ms. Judy Shepard told the Senate Judiciary Committee that on October 8, 1998, "my husband and I were awakened in the middle of the night ... by a telephone call no parent should ever have to receive. What we heard changed our lives forever. Our son, we were told, was in a coma after having been brutally attacked, in part because he was gay."[1] She continued:

> On October 12, Matt was pronounced dead.... Matt is no longer with us today because the men who killed him learned to hate. Somehow and somewhere, they received the message that the lives of gay people are not as worthy of respect, dignity and honor as the lives of other people. They were given the impression that society condoned, or at least was indifferent to violence against gay and lesbian Americans.[2]

She was describing a terrible crime that shocked the nation, committed by two men who tied Matthew Shepard to a fence outside Laramie, Wyoming, brutally pistol-whipped him, and left him for dead. He was discovered by a bicyclist some hours later.

As if this brutal crime were not enough, it came on the heels of another horrific murder: this one in Jasper, Texas in June of that same year, where two men tied James Byrd, Jr., an African American man, to the back of a pickup truck and dragged him until he was dead and his body mutilated. Three men were convicted and two were sentenced to death for the crime. As his execution neared, one of the men told a Houston television station reporter: "As far as any regrets, no, I have no regrets, Brewer says. No, I'd do it all over again, to tell you the truth."[3]

These savage murders shocked the nation and brought demands for some kind of action against hate crimes.[4] The death of Matthew Shepard also forced the nation to pay attention to what had been a long-running, sordid history of discrimination and even violence against people because of their sexual orientation or identity. His mother's comments came in testimony before the Senate Judiciary Committee in 1999 about a proposed hate crimes bill, legislation that was not finally passed and signed into law until ten years later as the "Matthew Shepard and James Byrd, Jr., Hate Crimes Prevention Act of 2009."[5]

There has been what can only be termed a dramatic change in public opinion with respect to sexual orientation in American society since the time of Shepard's death. Public opinion polls suggest that attitudes toward gays are changing rapidly, compared to attitudes toward race and ethnicity in our history. The Pew Research Center noted in 2015 that: "In 2001, Americans opposed same-sex marriage by a 57% to 35% margin. Since then, support for same-sex marriage has steadily grown. Today, the numbers are reversed. A majority of Americans (57%) support same-sex marriage, compared with 39% who oppose it."[6] The Gallup polling organization explained that 60 percent of those asked in May 2015 whether gay marriage should be regarded as valid said yes, 37 percent said no, and 3 percent had no opinion. That compares to results from 1996 that showed that only 27 percent said yes, 68 percent said no, and 5 percent had no opinion.[7]

A number of state attorneys refused to defend state bans on gay marriage, even in traditionally conservative states. An example was the dramatic announcement by the newly elected Attorney General of Virginia that he intended to switch positions in the pending case concerning the state ban on same-sex marriage.

> After thorough legal review, I have now concluded that Virginia's ban on marriage between same sex couples violates the Fourteenth Amendment of the U.S. Constitution on two grounds: marriage is a fundamental right being denied to some Virginians, and the ban unlawfully discriminates on the basis of both sexual orientation and gender.... Virginia has argued on the wrong side of some of our nation's landmark cases—in school desegregation in 1954, on interracial marriage with the 1967 Loving decision, and in 1996 on state-supported single-gender education at VMI. It's time for the Commonwealth to be on the right side of history and the right side of the law.[8]

The change is dramatic for many reasons, but particularly because of just how extreme discrimination against people because of sexual orientation has been, and how recently the change has taken place. Even with such a general shift, however, that does not mean an end to discrimination—or even to violence. The FBI reported that there were 1,402 hate crimes based on sexual orientation in 2013, some 20.8 percent of the total number of reported hate crimes.[9] That is actually higher than the 14 percent number from the FBI reports of 1997 that Ms. Shepard cited in her Senate testimony shortly after Matthew Shepard's death.[10] The FBI numbers were reported for the first time in 1991 because the bureau only began reporting hate crimes after the passage of the Hate Crimes Statistics Act, which was enacted in 1990.[11]

One of the most dramatic statements of change came in June 2015, when the Supreme Court announced in *Obergefell v. Hodges* (excerpted later in this chapter) that both the due process and equal protection clauses of the Fourteenth Amendment protect the right of same-sex couples to marry and to have those marriages recognized in other states. It was a momentous change in civil rights law. However, notwithstanding this ruling and the significant shift in public opinion polls, the discussion of civil rights related to sexual orientation or identity is, by historical standards, relatively recent in the United States. As is true of other areas of civil rights law and policy, it is very much a work in progress. This chapter considers what has happened thus far and some of the many issues and challenges that remain to be addressed.

From No Protection to a Recognition of Due Process and Equal Protection Guarantees

It was not long ago that the U.S. Supreme Court rejected the idea that discrimination on the basis of sexual orientation or identity triggered any constitutional or statutory protection. The Court stated that conclusion in no uncertain terms in 1986 and in language, as the dissenters made clear, far broader and more dramatic than necessary to address that case from the state of Georgia. On the other hand, the *Bowers v. Hardwick* case (discussed below) provided a forum that displayed publicly the emerging debate on sexual orientation within the Supreme Court.

This was in stark contrast to the Court's actions a decade earlier, when it took the unusual step of affirming without opinion—or even the basic process of briefing on the merits and oral argument—a ruling by a three-judge federal district court for the Eastern District of Virginia that upheld a Virginia sodomy statute as applied to two adult men involved in a consensual relationship.[12] Justices Brennan, Marshall, and Stevens announced that they would have noted probable jurisdiction and set case for oral argument. That ruling in the Virginia case was important because it carried force as precedent, even though it was rendered summarily and without opinion. Indeed, the Virginia decision was central to a district court ruling that brought the *Bowers* case from Georgia to the Supreme Court in 1985.

Bowers v. Hardwick

478 U.S. 186 (1986)

INTRODUCTION: The opinion presents the facts of the case. The two Georgia men in this case were initially arrested and charged with a violation of the Georgia sodomy statutes for engaging in sexual conduct, even though this was consensual and at home. The prosecutor decided not to press the case and dismissed the charges. However, the men sued, arguing that they had been arrested, charged, and remained under threat of arrest and prosecution in the future if the authorities decided to enforce the Georgia law against them. They challenged the statute on several constitutional grounds in the district court. The district court, citing the Supreme Court's ruling in the earlier Virginia case, dismissed the case and rejected the idea that they enjoyed any protections under the Constitution.[13] The court of appeals reversed.[14]

Justice White wrote the opinion for the Court.

> In August 1982, respondent Hardwick was charged with violating the Georgia statute criminalizing sodomy by committing that act with another adult male in the bedroom of respondent's home. Respondent ... asserted that he was a practicing homosexual, that the Georgia sodomy statute, as administered by the defendants, placed him in imminent danger of arrest, and that the statute for several reasons violates the Federal Constitution. The District Court granted the defendants' motion to dismiss for failure to state a claim, relying on *Doe v. Commonwealth's Attorney....* We agree with petitioner that the Court of Appeals erred, and hence reverse its judgment.
>
> ... The issue presented is whether the Federal Constitution confers a fundamental right upon homosexuals to engage in sodomy and hence invalidates the laws of the many States that still make such conduct illegal and have done so for a very long time.... We first register our disagreement with the Court of Appeals ... that the Court's prior cases have construed the Constitution to confer a right of privacy that extends to homosexual sodomy and for all intents and purposes have decided this case.... [*Pierce v. Society of Sisters*; *Meyer v. Nebraska*; *Prince v. Massachusetts*; *Skinner v. Oklahoma ex rel. Williamson*; *Loving v. Virginia*; *Griswold v. Connecticut*; *Eisenstadt v. Baird*; and *Roe v. Wade*.] ... [N]one of the rights announced in those cases bears any resemblance to the claimed constitutional right of homosexuals to engage in acts of sodomy....
>
> [R]espondent would have us announce ... a fundamental right to engage in homosexual sodomy. This we are quite unwilling to do. It is true that ... the cases are legion in which those [Due Process Clauses of the Fifth and Fourteenth Amendments] Clauses have been interpreted to have substantive content, subsuming rights that to a great extent are immune from federal or state regulation or proscription....

... [T]he Court has sought to identify the nature of the rights qualifying for heightened judicial protection. In *Palko v. Connecticut*, 302 U.S. 319 (1937), it was said that this category includes those fundamental liberties that are "implicit in the concept of ordered liberty," such that "neither liberty nor justice would exist if [they] were sacrificed." A different description ... appeared in *Moore v. East Cleveland*, 431 U.S. 494, 503 (1977) where they are characterized as those liberties that are "deeply rooted in this Nation's history and tradition." ...

It is obvious to us that neither of these formulations would extend a fundamental right to homosexuals to engage in acts of consensual sodomy. Proscriptions against that conduct have ancient roots.... Sodomy was a criminal offense at common law and was forbidden by the laws of the original 13 States.... In 1868, when the Fourteenth Amendment was ratified, all but 5 of the 37 States in the Union had criminal sodomy laws. In fact, until 1961 all 50 States outlawed sodomy, and today, 24 States and the District of Columbia continue to provide criminal penalties for sodomy performed in private and between consenting adults.... Against this background, to claim that a right to engage in such conduct is "deeply rooted in this Nation's history and tradition" or "implicit in the concept of ordered liberty" is, at best, facetious.

Nor are we inclined to take a more expansive view of our authority to discover new fundamental rights imbedded in the Due Process Clause.... There should be ... great resistance to expand[ing] the category of rights deemed to be fundamental. Otherwise, the Judiciary necessarily takes to itself further authority to govern the country without express constitutional authority. The claimed right pressed on us today falls far short of overcoming this resistance.

Respondent, however, asserts that the result should be different where the homosexual conduct occurs in the privacy of the home. He relies on *Stanley v. Georgia* [1969], where the Court held that the First Amendment prevents conviction for possessing and reading obscene material in the privacy of one's home.... *Stanley* ... was firmly grounded in the First Amendment. The right pressed upon us here has no similar support in the text of the Constitution, and it does not qualify for recognition under the prevailing principles for construing the Fourteenth Amendment....

Even if the conduct at issue here is not a fundamental right, respondent asserts that there must be a rational basis for the law and that there is none in this case other than the presumed belief of a majority of the electorate in Georgia that homosexual sodomy is immoral and unacceptable.... The law, however, is constantly based on notions of morality, and if all laws representing essentially moral choices are to be invalidated under the Due Process Clause, the courts will be very busy indeed.... We do not agree.

Chief Justice Burger issued a concurring opinion.

I join the Court's opinion, but I write separately to underscore my view that in constitutional terms there is no such thing as a fundamental right to commit homosexual sodomy.

[P]roscriptions against sodomy have very "ancient roots." Decisions of individuals relating to homosexual conduct have been subject to state intervention throughout the history of Western civilization. Condemnation of those practices is firmly rooted in Judeo-Christian moral and ethical standards. Homosexual sodomy was a capital crime under Roman law.... During the English Reformation ... the first

English statute criminalizing sodomy was passed.... Blackstone described "the infamous crime against nature" as an offense of "deeper malignity" than rape, a heinous act "the very mention of which is a disgrace to human nature," and a "crime not fit to be named."[15] The common law of England, including its prohibition of sodomy, became the received law of Georgia and the other Colonies. In 1816 the Georgia Legislature passed the statute at issue here, and that statute has been continuously in force in one form or another since that time. To hold that the act of homosexual sodomy is somehow protected as a fundamental right would be to cast aside millennia of moral teaching.

This is essentially not a question of personal "preferences" but rather of the legislative authority of the State. I find nothing in the Constitution depriving a State of the power to enact the statute challenged here.

Justice Powell wrote a concurring opinion.

I join the opinion of the Court. I agree with the Court that there is no fundamental right ... such as that claimed by respondent.... This is not to suggest, however, that respondent may not be protected by the Eighth Amendment of the Constitution. The Georgia statute at issue in this case ... authorizes a court to imprison a person for up to 20 years for a single private, consensual act of sodomy. In my view, a prison sentence for such conduct ... would create a serious Eighth Amendment issue....

In this case, however, respondent has not been tried, much less convicted and sentenced. Moreover, respondent has not raised the Eighth Amendment issue below. For these reasons this constitutional argument is not before us.

Justice Blackmun issued a dissenting opinion joined by Justices Brennan, Marshall, and Stevens.

This case is no more about "a fundamental right to engage in homosexual sodomy," ... than *Stanley v. Georgia* ... was about a fundamental right to watch obscene movies.... Rather, this case is about "the most comprehensive of rights and the right most valued by civilized men," namely, "the right to be let alone." *Olmstead v. United States*, 277 U.S. 438, 478 (1928) (Brandeis, J., dissenting).

The statute at issue ... denies individuals the right to decide for themselves whether to engage in particular forms of private, consensual sexual activity. The Court concludes that ... it is valid essentially because "the laws of ... many States ... still make such conduct illegal and have done so for a very long time." ... But the fact that the moral judgments expressed by statutes ... may be "natural and familiar ... ought not to conclude our judgment upon the question whether statutes embodying them conflict with the Constitution of the United States." *Roe v. Wade*, 410 U.S. 113, 117 (1973).... Like Justice Holmes, I believe that "[it] is revolting to have no better reason for a rule of law than that so it was laid down in the time of Henry IV. It is still more revolting if the grounds upon which it was laid down have vanished long since, and the rule simply persists from blind imitation of the past." Holmes, "The Path of the Law," 10 *Harv. L. Rev.* 457, 469 (1897). I believe we must analyze respondent Hardwick's claim in the light of the values that underlie the constitutional right to privacy. If that right means anything, it means that, before Georgia can prosecute its citizens for making choices about the most intimate aspects of their lives, it must do more than assert that the choice they have made is an "abominable crime not fit to be named among Christians." ...

... I disagree with the Court's refusal to consider whether §16-6-2 runs afoul of the Eighth or Ninth Amendments or the Equal Protection Clause of the Fourteenth Amendment.... Respondent's complaint expressly invoked the Ninth Amendment ... and he relied heavily before this Court on *Griswold v. Connecticut,* ... which identifies that Amendment as one of the specific constitutional provisions giving "life and substance" to our understanding of privacy.... More importantly, the procedural posture of the case requires that we affirm the Court of Appeals' judgment if there is *any* ground on which respondent may be entitled to relief. This case is before us on petitioner's motion to dismiss for failure to state a claim.... I need not reach either the Eighth Amendment or the Equal Protection Clause issues because I believe that Hardwick has stated a cognizable claim that §16-6-2 interferes with constitutionally protected interests in privacy and freedom of intimate association. But neither the Eighth Amendment nor the Equal Protection Clause is so clearly irrelevant that a claim resting on either provision should be peremptorily dismissed.[16]...

"Our cases long have recognized that the Constitution embodies a promise that a certain private sphere of individual liberty will be kept largely beyond the reach of government." *Thornburgh v. American College of Obstetricians & Gynecologists,* 476 U.S. 747, 772 (1986). In construing the right to privacy, the Court has proceeded along two somewhat distinct, albeit complementary, lines. First, it has recognized a privacy interest with reference to certain *decisions* that are properly for the individual to make. E. g., *Roe v. Wade...*; *Pierce v. Society of Sisters....* Second, it has recognized a privacy interest with reference to certain *places* without regard for the particular activities in which the individuals who occupy them are engaged. E. g., *United States v. Karo,* 468 U.S. 705 (1984).... The case before us implicates both the decisional and the spatial aspects of the right to privacy.

The Court concludes today that none of our prior cases dealing with various decisions that individuals are entitled to make free of governmental interference "bears any resemblance to the claimed constitutional right of homosexuals to engage in acts of sodomy that is asserted in this case." ... While it is true that these cases may be characterized by their connection to protection of the family, ... the Court's conclusion that they extend no further than this boundary ignores the warning in *Moore v. East Cleveland* [that w]e protect those rights [under the Fourteenth Amendment's Due Process Clause] not because they contribute, in some direct and material way, to the general public welfare, but because they form so central a part of an individual's life.... And so we protect the decision whether to marry precisely because marriage "is an association that promotes a way of life, not causes; a harmony in living, not political faiths; a bilateral loyalty, not commercial or social projects." *Griswold v. Connecticut....* We protect the decision whether to have a child because parenthood alters so dramatically an individual's self-definition, not because of demographic considerations or the Bible's command to be fruitful and multiply.... And we protect the family because it contributes so powerfully to the happiness of individuals, not because of a preference for stereotypical households....

Only the most willful blindness could obscure the fact that sexual intimacy is "a sensitive, key relationship of human existence, central to family life, community welfare, and the development of human personality." ... The fact that individuals define themselves in a significant way through their intimate sexual relationships with others suggests, in a Nation as diverse as ours, that there may be many "right" ways of conducting those relationships, and that much of the richness of a relationship will come from the freedom an individual has to *choose* the form and nature of these intensely personal bonds....

In a variety of circumstances we have recognized that a necessary corollary of giving individuals freedom to choose how to conduct their lives is acceptance of the fact that different individuals will make different choices.... The Court claims that its decision today merely refuses to recognize a fundamental right to engage in homosexual sodomy; what the Court really has refused to recognize is the fundamental interest all individuals have in controlling the nature of their intimate associations with others.

The behavior for which Hardwick faces prosecution occurred in his own home, a place to which the Fourth Amendment attaches special significance. The Court's treatment of this aspect of the case is symptomatic of its overall refusal to consider the broad principles that have informed our treatment of privacy in specific cases. Just as the right to privacy is more than the mere aggregation of a number of entitlements to engage in specific behavior, so too, protecting the physical integrity of the home is more than merely a means of protecting specific activities that often take place there. Even when our understanding of the contours of the right to privacy depends on "reference to a 'place'," ... "the essence of a Fourth Amendment violation is 'not the breaking of [a person's] doors, and the rummaging of his drawers,' but rather is 'the invasion of his indefeasible right of personal security, personal liberty and private property.'" ...

The Court's interpretation of the pivotal case of *Stanley v. Georgia* ... is entirely unconvincing. *Stanley* held that Georgia's undoubted power to punish the public distribution of constitutionally unprotected, obscene material did not permit the State to punish the private possession of such material. According to the majority here, *Stanley* relied entirely on the First Amendment, and thus, it is claimed, sheds no light on cases not involving printed materials.... But that is not what *Stanley* said. Rather, the *Stanley* Court anchored its holding in the Fourth Amendment's special protection for the individual in his home....

The central place that *Stanley* gives Justice Brandeis' dissent in *Olmstead*, a case raising *no* First Amendment claim, shows that *Stanley* rested as much on the Court's understanding of the Fourth Amendment as it did on the First.... Indeed, the right of an individual to conduct intimate relationships in the intimacy of his or her own home seems to me to be the heart of the Constitution's protection of privacy....

[P]etitioner asserts that the acts made criminal by the statute may have serious adverse consequences for "the general public health and welfare," such as spreading communicable diseases or fostering other criminal activity.... I see no justification for the Court's attempt to equate the private, consensual sexual activity at issue here with the "possession in the home of drugs, firearms, or stolen goods" ... to which *Stanley* refused to extend its protection.... Nothing in the record before the Court provides any justification for finding the activity forbidden by §16-6-2 to be physically dangerous, either to the persons engaged in it or to others.

The core of petitioner's defense of §16-6-2, however, is that respondent and others who engage in the conduct ... interfere with Georgia's exercise of the "right of the Nation and of the States to maintain a decent society," *Paris Adult Theatre I v. Slaton*, 413 U.S. 49 (1973).... Essentially, ... the Court agrees [with petitioner] that the fact that the acts described in §16-6-2 "for hundreds of years, if not thousands, have been uniformly condemned as immoral" is a sufficient reason to permit a State to ban them today....

I cannot agree that either the length of time a majority has held its convictions or the passions with which it defends them can withdraw legislation from this Court's scrutiny. See, e. g., *Roe v. Wade*...; *Loving v. Virginia*...; *Brown v. Board of Education*....[17] As Justice Jackson wrote ... in *West Virginia Board of Education v. Barnette*, 319 U.S. 624, 641–642 (1943), "we apply the limitations of the Constitution with no fear that freedom to be intellectually and spiritually diverse or even contrary will disintegrate the social organization.... [Freedom] to differ is not limited to things that do not matter much. That would be a mere shadow of freedom. The test of its substance is the right to differ as to things that touch the heart of the existing order." ... It is precisely because the issue raised by this case touches the heart of what makes individuals what they are that we should be especially sensitive to the rights of those whose choices upset the majority.

The assertion that "traditional Judeo-Christian values proscribe" the conduct involved ... cannot provide an adequate justification for §16-6-2. That certain, but by no means all, religious groups condemn the behavior at issue gives the State no license to impose their judgments on the entire citizenry. The legitimacy of secular legislation depends instead on whether the State can advance some justification for its law beyond its conformity to religious doctrine.... [P]etitioner's invocation of Leviticus, Romans, St. Thomas Aquinas, and sodomy's heretical status during the Middle Ages undermines his suggestion that §16-6-2 represents a legitimate use of secular coercive power. A State can no more punish private behavior because of religious intolerance than it can punish such behavior because of racial animus....

Nor can §16-6-2 be justified as a "morally neutral" exercise of Georgia's power to "protect the public environment." ... Certainly, some private behavior can affect the fabric of society as a whole. Reasonable people may differ about whether particular sexual acts are moral or immoral, but "we have ample evidence for believing that people will not abandon morality ... merely because some private sexual practice which they abominate is not punished by the law." ... [T]he mere fact that intimate behavior may be punished when it takes place in public cannot dictate how States can regulate intimate behavior that occurs in intimate places....

It took but three years for the Court to see the error in its analysis in *Minersville School District v. Gobitis*, 310 U.S. 586 (1940), and to recognize that the threat to national cohesion posed by a refusal to salute the flag was vastly outweighed by the threat to those same values posed by compelling such a salute. See *West Virginia Board of Education v. Barnette*. I can only hope that here, too, the Court soon will reconsider its analysis and conclude that depriving individuals of the right to choose for themselves how to conduct their intimate relationships poses a far greater threat to the values most deeply rooted in our Nation's history than tolerance of nonconformity could ever do. Because I think the Court today betrays those values, I dissent.

Justice Stevens dissented, joined by Justices Brennan and Marshall.

... Because the Georgia statute expresses the traditional view that sodomy is an immoral kind of conduct regardless of the identity of the persons who engage in it, I believe that a proper analysis of its constitutionality requires consideration of two questions: First, may a State totally prohibit the described conduct by means of a neutral law applying without exception to all persons subject to its jurisdiction? If not, may the State save the statute by announcing that it will only enforce the law against homosexuals? The two questions merit separate discussion.

Our prior cases make two propositions abundantly clear. First, the fact that the governing majority in a State has traditionally viewed a particular practice as immoral is not a sufficient reason for upholding a law prohibiting the practice; neither history nor tradition could save a law prohibiting miscegenation from constitutional attack.[18] Second, individual decisions by married persons, concerning the intimacies of their physical relationship, even when not intended to produce offspring, are a form of "liberty" protected by the Due Process Clause of the Fourteenth Amendment. Griswold v. Connecticut.... Moreover, this protection extends to intimate choices by unmarried as well as married persons. *Carey v. Population Services International*, 431 U.S. 678 (1977); *Eisenstadt v. Baird*, 405 U.S. 438 (1972).

In consideration of claims of this kind, the Court has emphasized the individual interest in privacy, but its decisions have actually been animated by an even more fundamental concern. As I wrote some years ago: "These cases do not deal with the individual's interest in protection from unwarranted public attention, comment, or exploitation. They deal, rather, with the individual's right to make certain unusually important decisions that will affect his own, or his family's, destiny. The Court has referred to such decisions as implicating 'basic values,' as being 'fundamental,' and as being dignified by history and tradition...."

[W]hen individual married couples are isolated from observation by others, the way in which they voluntarily choose to conduct their intimate relations is a matter for them—not the State—to decide. The essential "liberty" that animated the development of the law in cases like *Griswold, Eisenstadt*, and *Carey* surely embraces the right to engage in nonreproductive, sexual conduct that others may consider offensive or immoral.... Paradoxical as it may seem, our prior cases thus establish that a State may not prohibit sodomy within "the sacred precincts of marital bedrooms," *Griswold* ... or, indeed, between unmarried heterosexual adults. *Eisenstadt*.... [I]t is perfectly clear that the State of Georgia may not totally prohibit the conduct proscribed by §16-6-2 of the Georgia Criminal Code.

If the Georgia statute cannot be enforced as it is written ... the State must assume the burden of justifying a selective application of its law. Either the persons to whom Georgia seeks to apply its statute do not have the same interest in "liberty" that others have, or there must be a reason why the State may be permitted to apply a generally applicable law to certain persons that it does not apply to others.

The first possibility is plainly unacceptable.... [E]very free citizen has the same interest in "liberty" that the members of the majority share. From the standpoint of the individual, the homosexual and the heterosexual have the same interest in deciding how he will live his own life, and, more narrowly, how he will conduct himself in his personal and voluntary associations with his companions....

The second possibility is similarly unacceptable. A policy of selective application must be supported by a neutral and legitimate interest—something more substantial than a habitual dislike for, or ignorance about, the disfavored group. Neither the State nor the Court has identified any such interest in this case....

Nor, indeed, does the Georgia prosecutor even believe that all homosexuals who violate this statute should be punished.... The record of nonenforcement, in this case and in the last several decades, belies the Attorney General's representations about the importance of the State's selective application of its generally applicable law. Both the Georgia statute and the Georgia prosecutor thus completely fail to justif[y that] a selective application of the generally applicable law has been met.... I respectfully dissent.

Justice Lewis Powell's concurring opinion in the *Bowers* case was both critical to the ruling upholding the Georgia restrictions, given the five to four vote, and rather ironic. It was ironic because Powell said at the time that he had never met anyone who was homosexual, but C. Cabell Chinnis, who was one of his clerks at the time, was openly gay.[19] In fact, Powell was found in one study to be the justice most likely to have gay law clerks, having hired at least one gay person in each of six terms during the 1980s.[20] Another irony is the fact that the person who was ultimately confirmed to take Powell's seat following his retirement was Justice Anthony Kennedy, the author of all of the Court's transformative opinions on sexual orientation, including the 2015 *Obergefell v. Hodges* ruling.

Following the *Bowers* ruling and a national political picture that was turning more conservative, many advocates for gay rights decided to target state legislatures and state courts, emphasizing state law as venues for change in their efforts to achieve civil rights protections. They began to achieve successes, including a 1999 Vermont Supreme Court ruling in *Baker v. State* and the decision by the Supreme Judicial Court of Massachusetts in 2003 in *Goodridge v. State Department of Health*, which provided the first clear rulings that a state ban on same-sex marriage was unconstitutional under the state's Constitution.[21] Following the judicial action, Vermont adopted legislation in 2000, creating what were then known as "civil unions."[22] Vermont went on to legalize same-sex marriage in 2009.

Even with this focus on the states, advocates had not given up on the federal courts. They brought a variety of cases, in some cases sparked by legislation or constitutional amendments adopted as a backlash against increasing recognition of a need for civil rights protection with respect to sexual orientation. One such case came from Colorado and concerned a voter-approved constitutional amendment that barred any action by the state or its local governments that would provide such protections. That case, *Romer v. Evans*, reached the U.S. Supreme Court and, in the first ruling in this field by Justice Kennedy, was found in violation of the equal protection clause of the Fourteenth Amendment.[23] An even more eventful opinion was rendered by the Court in an opinion by Justice Kennedy in 2003, a ruling that reversed the *Bowers v. Hardwick* precedent.

Lawrence v. Texas

539 U.S. 558 (2003)

INTRODUCTION: The facts are provided in the opinion. Justice Kennedy wrote the opinion for the Court.

Liberty protects the person from unwarranted government intrusions into a dwelling or other private places.... Liberty presumes an autonomy of self that includes freedom of thought, belief, expression, and certain intimate conduct.... The question before the Court is the validity of a Texas statute making it a crime for two persons of the same sex to engage in certain intimate sexual conduct.

In Houston, Texas, officers of the Harris County Police Department were dispatched to a private residence in response to a reported weapons disturbance. They entered an apartment where one of the petitioners, John Geddes Lawrence, resided. The right of the police to enter does not seem to have been questioned.

The officers observed Lawrence and another man, Tyron Garner, engaging in a sexual act.... The complaints described their crime as "deviate sexual intercourse, namely anal sex, with a member of the same sex (man)." ...

The petitioners ... challenged the statute as a violation of the Equal Protection Clause of the Fourteenth Amendment and of a like provision of the Texas Constitution.... Those contentions were rejected. The petitioners, having entered a plea of nolo contendere,[24] were each fined $200 and assessed court costs of $141.25.... The Court of Appeals ... affirmed the convictions....

We granted certiorari[25] ... to consider three questions:

1. Whether Petitioners' criminal convictions under the Texas "Homosexual Conduct" law—which criminalizes sexual intimacy by same-sex couples, but not identical behavior by different-sex couples—violate the Fourteenth Amendment guarantee of equal protection of laws?

2. Whether Petitioners' criminal convictions for adult consensual sexual intimacy in the home violate their vital interests in liberty and privacy protected by the Due Process Clause of the Fourteenth Amendment?

3. Whether *Bowers v. Hardwick* ... should be overruled? ...

The petitioners were adults at the time of the alleged offense. Their conduct was in private and consensual.

We conclude the case should be resolved by determining whether the petitioners were free as adults to engage in the private conduct in the exercise of their liberty under the Due Process Clause of the Fourteenth Amendment to the Constitution. For this inquiry we deem it necessary to reconsider the Court's holding in *Bowers*.

There are broad statements of the substantive reach of liberty under the Due Process Clause in earlier cases, ... but the most pertinent beginning point is our decision in *Griswold v. Connecticut* [in which] the Court invalidated a state law prohibiting the use of drugs or devices of contraception and counseling or aiding and abetting the use of contraceptives. The Court described the protected interest as a right to privacy and placed emphasis on the marriage relation and the protected space of the marital bedroom....

After *Griswold* it was established that the right to make certain decisions regarding sexual conduct extends beyond the marital relationship. In *Eisenstadt v. Baird*, ... the Court invalidated a law prohibiting the distribution of contraceptives to unmarried persons. The case was decided under the Equal Protection Clause, ... but with respect to unmarried persons, the Court went on to state the fundamental proposition that the law impaired the exercise of their personal rights....

The opinions in *Griswold* and *Eisenstadt* were part of the background for the decision in *Roe v. Wade*.... Although the Court held the woman's rights were not absolute, her right to elect an abortion did have real and substantial protection as an exercise of her liberty under the Due Process Clause.... *Roe* recognized the right of a woman to make certain fundamental decisions affecting her destiny and confirmed once more that the protection of liberty under the Due Process Clause has a substantive dimension of fundamental significance in defining the rights of the person.

In *Carey v. Population Services Int'l*, ... the Court confronted a New York law forbidding sale or distribution of contraceptive devices to persons under 16 years of age.... Both *Eisenstadt* and *Carey*, as well as the holding and rationale in *Roe*, confirmed that the reasoning of *Griswold* could not be confined to the protection of rights of married adults. This was the state of the law ... when the Court considered *Bowers v. Hardwick*.... The Court ... sustained the Georgia law [in *Bowers*].... Four Justices dissented [Blackmun, Brennan, Marshall, and Stevens].

... To say that the issue in *Bowers* was simply the right to engage in certain sexual conduct demeans the claim the individual put forward, just as it would demean a married couple were it to be said marriage is simply about the right to have sexual intercourse. The laws involved in *Bowers* and here are, to be sure, statutes that purport to do no more than prohibit a particular sexual act. Their penalties and purposes, though, have more far-reaching consequences, touching upon the most private human conduct, sexual behavior, and in the most private of places, the home. The[y] ... seek to control a personal relationship that, whether or not entitled to formal recognition in the law, is within the liberty of persons to choose without being punished as criminals....

It suffices for us to acknowledge that adults may choose to enter upon this relationship in the confines of their homes and their own private lives and still retain their dignity as free persons. When sexuality finds overt expression in intimate conduct with another person, the conduct can be but one element in a personal bond that is more enduring. The liberty protected by the Constitution allows homosexual persons the right to make this choice.

Having misapprehended the claim of liberty there presented to it, and thus stating the claim to be whether there is a fundamental right to engage in consensual sodomy, the *Bowers* Court said: "Proscriptions against that conduct have ancient roots." ... In academic writings, and in many of the scholarly amicus briefs filed to assist the Court in this case, there are fundamental criticisms of th[ose] historical premises.... [T]he following considerations counsel against adopting the definitive conclusions upon which *Bowers* placed such reliance.

At the outset it should be noted that there is no longstanding history in this country of laws directed at homosexual conduct as a distinct matter.... The English prohibition was understood to include relations between men and women as well as relations between men and men.... Thus early American sodomy laws were not directed at homosexuals as such but instead sought to prohibit nonprocreative sexual activity more generally....

Laws prohibiting sodomy do not seem to have been enforced against consenting adults acting in private. A substantial number of sodomy prosecutions and convictions for which there are surviving records were for predatory acts against those who could not or did not consent, as in the case of a minor or the victim of an assault....

The reported decisions concerning the prosecution of consensual, homosexual sodomy between adults for the years 1880–1995 [often] involved conduct in a public place.... It was not until the 1970's that any State singled out same-sex relations for criminal prosecution, and only nine States have done so.... Over the course of the last decades, States with same-sex prohibitions have moved toward abolishing them. [Cites to cases from Arkansas, Montana, Tennessee, Kentucky, and Nevada.] In summary, the historical grounds relied upon in *Bowers* are more complex than th[at case] indicate[d]. Their historical premises are not without doubt and, at the very least, are overstated.

... [T]he Court in *Bowers* was making the broader point that ... there have been powerful voices to condemn homosexual conduct as immoral. The condemnation has been shaped by religious beliefs, conceptions of right and acceptable behavior, and respect for the traditional family.... The issue is whether the majority may use the power of the State to enforce these views on the whole society through operation of the criminal law....

[W]e think that our laws and traditions in the past half century ... show an emerging awareness that liberty gives substantial protection to adult persons in deciding how to conduct their private lives in matters pertaining to sex.... This emerging recognition should have been apparent when *Bowers* was decided. In 1955 the American Law Institute promulgated the Model Penal Code and made clear that it did not recommend or provide for "criminal penalties for consensual sexual relations conducted in private." ... It justified its decision on three grounds: (1) The prohibitions undermined respect for the law by penalizing conduct many people engaged in; (2) the statutes regulated private conduct not harmful to others; and (3) the laws were arbitrarily enforced and thus invited the danger of blackmail.... In 1961 Illinois changed its laws to conform to the Model Penal Code. Other States soon followed....

The sweeping references by Chief Justice Burger [in *Bowers*] to the history of Western civilization and to Judeo-Christian moral and ethical standards did not take account of other authorities pointing in an opposite direction. A committee advising the British Parliament recommended in 1957 repeal of laws punishing homosexual conduct.... Parliament enacted the substance of those recommendations 10 years later....

Of even more importance, almost five years before *Bowers* was decided the European Court of Human Rights considered a case with parallels to *Bowers* and to today's case.... The court held that the [Northern Ireland] laws proscribing the conduct were invalid under the European Convention on Human Rights. *Dudgeon v. United Kingdom*, 45 Eur. Ct. H. R. (1981) P52. Authoritative in all countries that are members of the Council of Europe (21 nations then, 45 nations now), the decision is at odds with the premise in *Bowers* that the claim put forward was insubstantial in our Western civilization.

In our own constitutional system the deficiencies in *Bowers* became even more apparent in the years following its announcement. The 25 States with laws prohibiting the relevant conduct referenced in the *Bowers* decision are reduced now to 13, of which 4 enforce their laws only against homosexual conduct.... The State of Texas admitted in 1994 that as of that date it had not prosecuted anyone under those circumstances....

Two principal cases decided after *Bowers* cast its holding into even more doubt. In *Planned Parenthood of Southeastern Pa. v. Casey*, 505 U.S. 833 (1992), the Court reaffirmed the substantive force of the liberty protected by the Due Process Clause. The *Casey* decision again confirmed that our laws and tradition afford constitutional protection to ... "matters, involving the most intimate and personal choices a person may make in a lifetime, choices central to personal dignity and autonomy, [and] are central to the liberty protected by the Fourteenth Amendment. At the heart of liberty is the right to define one's own concept of existence, of meaning, of the universe, and of the mystery of human life. Beliefs about these matters could not define the attributes of personhood were they formed under compulsion of the State." Persons in a homosexual relationship may seek autonomy for these purposes, just as heterosexual persons do. The decision in *Bowers* would deny them this right.

The second post-*Bowers* case of principal relevance is *Romer v. Evans* ... (1996). There the Court struck down class-based legislation directed at homosexuals as a violation of the Equal Protection Clause. *Romer* invalidated an amendment to Colorado's constitution which named as a solitary class persons who were homosexuals, lesbians, or bisexual either by "orientation, conduct, practices or relationships," ... and deprived them of protection under state antidiscrimination laws. We concluded that the provision was "born of animosity toward the class of persons affected" and further that it had no rational relation to a legitimate governmental purpose....

As an alternative argument in this case, counsel for the petitioners and some amici contend that *Romer* provides the basis for declaring the Texas statute invalid under the Equal Protection Clause. That is a tenable argument, but we conclude the instant case requires us to address whether *Bowers* itself has continuing validity. Were we to hold the statute invalid under the Equal Protection Clause some might question whether a prohibition would be valid if drawn differently, say, to prohibit the conduct both between same-sex and different-sex participants.

Equality of treatment and the due process right to demand respect for conduct protected by the substantive guarantee of liberty are linked in important respects, and a decision on the latter point advances both interests. If protected conduct is made criminal and the law which does so remains unexamined for its substantive validity, its stigma might remain even if it were not enforceable as drawn for equal protection reasons. When homosexual conduct is made criminal by the law of the State, that declaration in and of itself is an invitation to subject homosexual persons to discrimination both in the public and in the private spheres. The central holding of *Bowers* has been brought in question by this case, and it should be addressed. Its continuance as precedent demeans the lives of homosexual persons.

The stigma this criminal statute imposes, moreover, is not trivial. The offense, to be sure, is but a class C misdemeanor, a minor offense in the Texas legal system. Still, it remains a criminal offense with all that imports for the dignity of the persons charged. The petitioners will bear on their record the history of their criminal convictions.... We are advised ... the convicted person would come within the registration laws of at least four States were he or she to be subject to their jurisdiction....

The foundations of *Bowers* have sustained serious erosion from our recent decisions in *Casey* and *Romer*.... The doctrine of *stare decisis* is essential to the respect accorded to the judgments of the Court and to the stability of the law. It is not, however, an inexorable command.... The rationale of *Bowers* does not withstand careful analysis. In his dissenting opinion in *Bowers* Justice Stevens came to these conclusions: "Our prior cases make two propositions abundantly clear. First, the fact that the governing majority in a State has traditionally viewed a particular practice as immoral is not a sufficient reason for upholding a law prohibiting the practice; neither history nor tradition could save a law prohibiting miscegenation from constitutional attack. Second, individual decisions by married persons, concerning the intimacies of their physical relationship, even when not intended to produce offspring, are a form of "liberty" protected by the Due Process Clause of the Fourteenth Amendment. Moreover, this protection extends to intimate choices by unmarried as well as married persons." ...

Justice Stevens' analysis, in our view, should have been controlling in *Bowers* and should control here. *Bowers* was not correct when it was decided, and it is not correct today. It ought not to remain binding precedent. *Bowers v. Hardwick* should be and now is overruled.

... The petitioners are entitled to respect for their private lives. The State cannot demean their existence or control their destiny by making their private sexual conduct a crime. Their right to liberty under the Due Process Clause gives them the full right to engage in their conduct without intervention of the government.... The Texas statute furthers no legitimate state interest which can justify its intrusion into the personal and private life of the individual.

Justice O'Connor wrote a concurring opinion.

The Court today overrules *Bowers v. Hardwick*.... I joined *Bowers*, and do not join the Court in overruling it. Nevertheless, I agree with the Court that Texas' statute banning same-sex sodomy is unconstitutional.... Rather than relying on the substantive component of the Fourteenth Amendment's Due Process Clause, as the Court does, I base my conclusion on the Fourteenth Amendment's Equal Protection Clause.

The Equal Protection Clause of the Fourteenth Amendment "is essentially a direction that all persons similarly situated should be treated alike." *Cleburne v. Cleburne Living Center*.... Under our rational basis standard of review, "legislation is presumed to be valid and will be sustained if the classification drawn by the statute is rationally related to a legitimate state interest." *Cleburne*....

Laws such as economic or tax legislation that are scrutinized under rational basis review normally pass constitutional muster.... We have consistently held, however, that some objectives, such as "a bare ... desire to harm a politically unpopular group," are not legitimate state interests.... When a law exhibits such a desire to harm a politically unpopular group, we have applied a more searching form of rational basis review to strike down such laws under the Equal Protection Clause.

We have been most likely to apply rational basis review to hold a law unconstitutional under the Equal Protection Clause where, as here, the challenged legislation inhibits personal relationships.... In *Eisenstadt v. Baird*, ... we refused to sanction a law that discriminated between married and unmarried persons by prohibiting the distribution of contraceptives to single persons.... And in *Romer v. Evans*, we disallowed a state statute that "imposed a broad and undifferentiated disability on a single named group"—specifically, homosexuals.... Texas' sodomy law would not pass scrutiny under the Equal Protection Clause, regardless of the type of rational basis review that we apply....

The statute at issue here makes sodomy a crime only if a person "engages in deviate sexual intercourse with another individual of the same sex." ... Sodomy between opposite-sex partners, however, is not a crime in Texas. That is, Texas treats the same conduct differently based solely on the participants.... Indeed, Texas itself has previously acknowledged the collateral effects of the law, stipulating in a prior challenge to this action that the law "legally sanctions discrimination against [homosexuals] in a variety of ways unrelated to the criminal law," including in the areas of "employment, family issues, and housing." *State v. Morales*....

This case raises a different issue than *Bowers*: whether, under the Equal Protection Clause, moral disapproval is a legitimate state interest to justify by itself a statute that bans homosexual sodomy, but not heterosexual sodomy. It is not. Moral disapproval of this group, like a bare desire to harm the group, is an interest that is insufficient to satisfy rational basis review under the Equal Protection Clause....

Texas argues, however, that the sodomy law does not discriminate against homosexual persons. Instead, the State maintains that the law discriminates only against homosexual conduct.... When a State makes homosexual conduct criminal, and not "deviate sexual intercourse" committed by persons of different sexes, "that declaration in and of itself is an invitation to subject homosexual persons to discrimination both in the public and in the private spheres." ...

The State has admitted that because of the sodomy law, being homosexual carries the presumption of being a criminal.... Texas' sodomy law therefore results in discrimination against homosexuals as a class in an array of areas outside the criminal law.... In *Romer v. Evans*, we refused to sanction a law that singled out homosexuals "for disfavored legal status." ... The same is true here....

That this law as applied to private, consensual conduct is unconstitutional under the Equal Protection Clause does not mean that other laws distinguishing between heterosexuals and homosexuals would similarly fail under rational basis review. Texas cannot assert any legitimate state interest here, such as national security or preserving the traditional institution of marriage. Unlike the moral disapproval of same-sex relations ... other reasons exist to promote the institution of marriage beyond mere moral disapproval of an excluded group.

Justice Scalia wrote a dissenting opinion joined by Chief Justice Rehnquist and Justice Thomas.[26]

... I begin with the Court's surprising readiness to reconsider a decision rendered a mere 17 years ago in *Bowers v. Hardwick*. I do not myself believe in rigid adherence to *stare decisis* in constitutional cases; but I do believe that we should be consistent rather than manipulative in invoking the doctrine....

I do not quarrel with the Court's claim that *Romer v. Evans* ... "eroded" the "foundations" of *Bowers'* rational-basis holding.... But *Roe* and *Casey* have been equally "eroded" by *Washington v. Glucksberg*, 521 U.S. 702, 721 (1997), which held that only fundamental rights which are "deeply rooted in this Nation's history and tradition" qualify for anything other than rational basis scrutiny under the doctrine of "substantive due process." ...

Bowers, the Court says, has been subject to "substantial and continuing [criticism], disapproving of its reasoning in all respects, not just as to its historical assumptions." ... Of course, *Roe* too (and by extension *Casey*) had been (and still is) subject to unrelenting criticism....

"There has been," the Court says, "no individual or societal reliance on *Bowers* of the sort that could counsel against overturning its holding...." Countless judicial decisions and legislative enactments have relied on the ancient proposition that a governing majority's belief that certain sexual behavior is "immoral and unacceptable" constitutes a rational basis for regulation.... We ourselves relied extensively on *Bowers* when we concluded, in *Barnes v. Glen Theatre, Inc.*, 501 U.S. 560, 569 (1991), that Indiana's public indecency statute furthered "a substantial government interest in protecting order and morality." ... State laws against bigamy, same-sex marriage, adult incest, prostitution, masturbation, adultery, fornication, bestiality, and obscenity are likewise sustainable only in light of *Bowers'* validation of laws based on moral choices. Every single one of these laws is called into question by today's decision; the Court makes no effort to cabin the scope of its decision to exclude them from its holding....

Having decided that it need not adhere to *stare decisis*, the Court still must establish that *Bowers* was wrongly decided and that the Texas statute, as applied to petitioners, is unconstitutional. [This Texas law] undoubtedly imposes constraints on liberty. So do laws prohibiting prostitution, recreational use of heroin, and, for that matter, working more than 60 hours per week in a bakery....

Our opinions applying the doctrine known as "substantive due process" hold that the Due Process Clause prohibits States from infringing fundamental liberty interests, unless the infringement is narrowly tailored to serve a compelling state interest.... We have held repeatedly, in cases the Court today does not overrule, that only fundamental rights qualify for this so-called "heightened scrutiny" protection—that is, rights which are "deeply rooted in this Nation's history and tradition." ... All other liberty interests may be abridged or abrogated pursuant to a validly enacted state law if that law is rationally related to a legitimate state interest.... *Bowers* concluded that a right to engage in homosexual sodomy was not "deeply rooted in this Nation's history and tradition." ... [H]aving failed to establish that the right to homosexual sodomy is "deeply rooted in this Nation's history and tradition," the Court concludes that the application of Texas's statute to petitioners' conduct fails the rational-basis test, and overrules *Bowers'* holding to the contrary....

The Court's description of "the state of the law" at the time of *Bowers* only confirms that *Bowers* was right.... The Court points to *Griswold v. Connecticut*.... But that case expressly disclaimed any reliance on the doctrine of "substantive due process," and grounded the so-called "right to privacy" in penumbras of constitutional provisions other than the Due Process Clause. *Eisenstadt v. Baird* ... likewise had nothing to do with "substantive due process"; it invalidated a Massachusetts law prohibiting the distribution of contraceptives to unmarried persons solely on the basis of the Equal Protection Clause....

... [The Court refers to] "an emerging awareness that liberty gives substantial protection to adult persons in deciding how to conduct their private lives in matters pertaining to sex." ... Apart from the fact that such an "emerging awareness" does not establish a "fundamental right," the statement is factually false. States continue to prosecute all sorts of crimes by adults "in matters pertaining to sex": prostitution, adult incest, adultery, obscenity, and child pornography. Sodomy laws, too, have been enforced "in the past half century," in which there have been 134 reported cases involving prosecutions for consensual, adult, homosexual sodomy....

The Texas statute undeniably seeks to further the belief of its citizens that certain forms of sexual behavior are "immoral and unacceptable," *Bowers* ... the same interest furthered by criminal laws against fornication, bigamy, adultery, adult incest, bestiality, and obscenity. *Bowers* held that this was a legitimate state interest. The Court today ... embraces instead Justice Stevens' declaration in his *Bowers* dissent, that "the fact that the governing majority in a State has traditionally viewed a particular practice as immoral is not a sufficient reason for upholding a law prohibiting the practice." ... This effectively decrees the end of all morals legislation. If, as the Court asserts, the promotion of majoritarian sexual morality is not even a legitimate state interest, none of the above-mentioned laws can survive rational-basis review.

Finally, I turn to petitioners' equal-protection challenge, which no Member of the Court save Justice O'Connor ... embraces. On its face §21.06(a) applies equally to all persons. Men and women, heterosexuals and homosexuals, are all subject to its prohibition of deviate sexual intercourse with someone of the same sex.... The objection is made, however, that the antimiscegenation laws invalidated in *Loving v. Virginia*, 388 U.S. 1, 8 (1967), similarly were applicable to whites and blacks alike, and only distinguished between the races insofar as the partner was concerned. In *Loving*, however, we correctly applied heightened scrutiny, rather than the usual rational-basis review, because the Virginia statute was "designed to maintain White Supremacy." ... A racially discriminatory purpose is always sufficient to subject a law to strict scrutiny.... No purpose to discriminate against men or women as a class can be gleaned from the Texas law, so rational-basis review applies. That review is readily satisfied here by the same rational basis that satisfied it in *Bowers*—society's belief that certain forms of sexual behavior are "immoral and unacceptable." ... This is the same justification that supports many other laws regulating sexual behavior that make a distinction based upon the identity of the partner—for example, laws against adultery, fornication, and adult incest, and laws refusing to recognize homosexual marriage.

Today's opinion is the product of a Court, which is the product of a law-profession culture, that has largely signed on to the so-called homosexual agenda, by which I mean the agenda promoted by some homosexual activists directed at eliminating the moral opprobrium that has traditionally attached to homosexual conduct. I noted in an earlier opinion the fact that the American Association of Law Schools ... excludes from membership any school that refuses to ban from its job-interview facilities a law firm (no matter how small) that does not wish to hire as a prospective partner a person who openly engages in homosexual conduct....

[T]he Court has taken sides in the culture war, departing from its role of assuring, as neutral observer, that the democratic rules of engagement are observed. Many Americans do not want persons who openly engage in homosexual conduct as partners in their business, as scoutmasters for their children, as teachers in their children's schools, or as boarders in their home. They view this as protecting themselves and their families from a lifestyle that they believe to be immoral and destructive. The Court views it as "discrimination" which it is the function of our judgments to deter. So imbued is the Court with the law profession's anti-anti-homosexual culture, that it is seemingly unaware that the attitudes of that culture are not obviously "mainstream"; that in most States what the Court calls "discrimination" against those who engage in homosexual acts is perfectly legal; that proposals to ban such "discrimination" under Title VII have repeatedly been rejected by Congress...; that in some cases such "discrimination" is mandated by federal statute, see 10 U.S.C. §654(b)(1) (mandating discharge from the armed forces of any service member who engages in or intends to engage in homosexual acts); and that in some cases such "discrimination" is a constitutional right, see *Boy Scouts of America v. Dale*, 530 U.S. 640 (2000).

Let me be clear that I have nothing against homosexuals, or any other group, promoting their agenda through normal democratic means.... That homosexuals have achieved some success in that enterprise is attested to by the fact that Texas is one of the few remaining States that criminalize private, consensual homosexual acts. But persuading one's fellow citizens is one thing, and imposing one's views in absence of democratic majority will is something else.... What Texas has chosen to do is well within the range of traditional democratic action, and its hand should not be stayed through the invention of a brand-new "constitutional right" by a Court that is impatient of democratic change.

Notice the sharp language in the dissent not only with respect to the majority opinion of Justice Kennedy, but also directed at the concurring opinion by Justice O'Connor. Gay and lesbian readers would, not surprisingly, suggest that Justice Scalia's attempt to say that "I have nothing against homosexuals, but...," sounds exactly like the language used by those engaged in discrimination on race or other grounds throughout modern history, particularly if one reads it in light of the paragraph that preceded it. Justice Scalia not only starkly reiterated support for the *Bowers* ruling and condemned the overturning of that precedent by the majority, but, if one reads carefully, also accused Justice O'Connor of attempting to have it both ways by voting to overturn the Texas statute and yet trying to preserve limits on same-sex marriage, a gambit, he argued, that was doomed to fail.

As some state laws began to fall and public opinion changed, it was only a matter of time before the Court would be asked to address barriers to same-sex marriage. At the same time, there was a backlash against these efforts and moves to block recognition of gay and lesbian relationships. One of the most significant of these moves was the passage of the Defense of Marriage Act (DOMA) in 1996.[27] The measure was passed at the height of a congressional election and a presidential reelection campaign. Voting on the measure was strongly partisan. That said, the measure, introduced by Representative Bob Barr (R-GA), who was himself running for reelection, passed the House of Representatives with a vote of 342–67 and the Senate 85–14 (with no Republican votes against in the Senate and 1 in the House). President Clinton signed the bill on September 21, just over a month before the election.

DOMA was a very brief piece of legislation with only two key sections. Section 2 of the act stated that:

> No State, territory, or possession of the United States, or Indian tribe, shall be required to give effect to any public act, record, or judicial proceeding of any other State, territory, possession, or tribe respecting a relationship between persons of the same sex that is treated as a marriage under the laws of such other State, territory, possession, or tribe, or a right or claim arising from such relationship.

Section 3 provided:

> In determining the meaning of any Act of Congress, or of any ruling, regulation, or interpretation of the various administrative bureaus and agencies of the United States, the word "marriage" means only a legal union between one man and one woman as husband and wife, and the word "spouse" refers only to a person of the opposite sex who is a husband or a wife.

In announcing that the president would sign the bill, Clinton press secretary Michael McCurry called it "gay baiting, pure and simple ... a classic use of wedge politics designed to provoke anxieties and fears."[28] However, the president announced just before signing the bill that although he opposed discrimination against anyone, "I have long opposed governmental recognition of same-gender marriages and this legislation is consistent with that position."[29]

Under DOMA the federal government found itself in the position of being at once the nation's defender of constitutional and statutory civil rights and yet refusing recognition of gay relationships, even in situations in which the states had authorized same-sex marriage. In another irony, the administration of President Barack Obama found itself in this same position notwithstanding the president's assertions of a need to end discrimination where and when it existed. The federal government—and ultimately the Supreme Court—would be put to the test as more states recognized same-sex marriage and others moved to block it. Cases from California and New York led to that day of reckoning.

The California case was *Hollingsworth v. Perry* and was decided by the Supreme Court in 2013.[30] The case traces back to a 2008 ruling by the California Supreme Court finding that the state's restriction against same-sex marriage violated the equal protection clause of the state Constitution.[31] In reaction, voters approved Proposition 8 as an amendment to the state Constitution that banned same-sex marriage. That amendment was challenged as a violation of the due process and equal protection clauses of the Fourteenth Amendment. The state supported Proposition 8 at the trial court level, but decided not to appeal the ruling by the district court that the measure violated equal protection under the U.S. Constitution.[32] The original backers of Proposition 8 sought authorization to take the case on appeal and the court of appeals permitted that. However, the Ninth Circuit ultimately ruled against Proposition 8 as well. The Supreme Court took the case, but only addressed the question whether the advocates had standing to defend the proposition if the state government would not. It concluded that they lacked standing to do so.

The New York case was not based on a state ban on same-sex marriage, but rather was a challenge to DOMA, concerning whether there was a violation of the U.S. Constitution if the federal government refused to recognize a marriage deemed valid under state law. While the case was pending, the Obama administration decided to change position and not to defend §3 of DOMA. A group of U.S. House of Representative members known as the Bipartisan Legal Advisory Group (BLAG) chose to do so, but the lower courts refused to allow BLAG to intervene in the case. This case eventually reached the U.S. Supreme Court.

United States v. Windsor

133 S. Ct. 2675 (2013)

INTRODUCTION: Advocates continued their efforts in state courts and legislatures to gain recognition for same-sex marriage. However, the Defense of Marriage Act had been passed in 1996 so that federal recognition was denied.[33] The State of New York did not authorize same-sex marriage, but Edith Windsor and Thea Spyer traveled to nearby Ontario, Canada in 2007 to be married. However, Ms. Spyer died two years later, having bequeathed her estate to Ms. Windsor. Under DOMA, Windsor was not recognized as Spyer's spouse and was therefore not eligible for the exemption from estate taxes that would have been available to a heterosexual couple.

Windsor paid the tax but then sued, claiming that DOMA discriminated against her in violation of the Constitution. While the case was pending, New York changed its laws to allow same-sex marriage and to recognize marriages lawful in other jurisdictions.[34] The district court found this restriction unconstitutional and the court of appeals affirmed.

The federal government appealed the ruling to the U.S. Supreme Court and Ms. Windsor was not provided with a refund while the case was pending. BLAG also sought an appeal to allow it to defend DOMA in the Supreme Court. The Court asked the parties to determine the standing questions and whether it should decide the merits of the case given the change of the federal government on defending DOMA.

The Court allowed the case to move forward on grounds that the executive was continuing to enforce DOMA pending the outcome of the case and had not paid Windsor the claimed refund. Therefore, the case was live and the federal government had standing. The Court concluded that it "need not decide whether BLAG would have standing to challenge the District Court's ruling and its affirmance in the Court of Appeals on BLAG's own authority" and allowed the case to move forward to the merits with the arguments of the parties. "And," the Court added, "the capable defense of the law by BLAG ensures that these prudential issues do not cloud the merits question, which is one of immediate importance to the Federal Government and to hundreds of thousands of persons." The edited version of the opinion below omits the arguments on these aspects of the case and focuses only on the merits of the challenge to DOMA.

Justice Kennedy wrote the opinion for the Court.

This Court ... now affirms the judgment in Windsor's favor.

When at first Windsor and Spyer longed to marry, neither New York nor any other State granted them that right.... It seems fair to conclude that, until recent years, many citizens had not even considered the possibility that two persons of the same sex might aspire to occupy the same status and dignity as that of a man and woman in lawful marriage. For marriage between a man and a woman no doubt had been thought of by most people as essential to the very definition of that term and to its role and function throughout the history of civilization. That belief, for many who long have held it, became even more urgent, more cherished when challenged. For others, however, came the beginnings of a new perspective, a new insight. Accordingly some States concluded that same-sex marriage ought to be given recognition and validity in the law for those same-sex couples who wish to define themselves by their commitment to each other. The limitation of lawful marriage to heterosexual couples, which for centuries had been deemed both necessary and fundamental, came to be seen in New York and certain other States as an unjust exclusion.

... New York came to acknowledge the urgency of this issue for same-sex couples who wanted to affirm their commitment to one another before their children, their family, their friends, and their community. And so New York recognized same-sex marriages performed elsewhere; and then it later amended its own marriage laws to permit same-sex marriage. New York, in common with, as of this writing, 11 other States and the District of Columbia, decided that same-sex couples should have the right to marry and so live with pride in themselves and their union and in a status of equality with all other married persons....

Against this background of lawful same-sex marriage in some States, the design, purpose, and effect of DOMA should be considered as the beginning point in deciding whether it is valid under the Constitution. By history and tradition the definition and regulation of marriage ... has been treated as being within the authority and realm of the separate States. Yet it is further established that Congress, in enacting discrete statutes, can make determinations that bear on marital rights and privileges.... [The] DOMA ... enacts a directive applicable to over 1,000 federal statutes and the whole realm of federal regulations [and applies] to a class of persons that the laws of New York, and of 11 other States, have sought to protect.

In order to assess the validity of that intervention it is necessary to discuss the extent of the state power and authority over marriage as a matter of history and tradition. State laws defining and regulating marriage, of course, must respect the constitutional rights of persons, see, *e.g.*, *Loving v. Virginia*...; but, subject to those guarantees, "regulation of domestic relations" is "an area that has long been regarded as a virtually exclusive province of the States." *Sosna v. Iowa*, 419 U.S. 393, 404 (1975).... The definition of marriage is the foundation of the State's broader authority to regulate the subject of domestic relations with respect to the "[p]rotection of offspring, property interests, and the enforcement of marital responsibilities." … Consistent with this allocation of authority, the Federal Government, through our history, has deferred to state-law policy decisions with respect to domestic relations.…

Here the State's decision to give this class of persons the right to marry conferred upon them a dignity and status of immense import. When the State used its historic and essential authority to define the marital relation in this way, its role and its power in making the decision enhanced the recognition, dignity, and protection of the class in their own community. DOMA, because of its reach and extent, departs from this history and tradition of reliance on state law to define marriage.…

The Federal Government uses this state-defined class … to impose restrictions and disabilities. That result requires this Court now to address whether the resulting injury and indignity is a deprivation of an essential part of the liberty protected by the Fifth Amendment. What the State of New York treats as alike the federal law deems unlike by a law designed to injure the same class the State seeks to protect.

The States' interest in defining and regulating the marital relation, subject to constitutional guarantees, stems from the understanding that marriage is more than a routine classification for purposes of certain statutory benefits. Private, consensual sexual intimacy between two adult persons of the same sex may not be punished by the State, and it can form "but one element in a personal bond that is more enduring." *Lawrence v. Texas.*… By its recognition of the validity of same-sex marriages performed in other jurisdictions and then by authorizing same-sex unions and same-sex marriages, New York sought to give further protection and dignity to that bond. For same-sex couples who wished to be married, the State acted to give their lawful conduct a lawful status. This status is a far-reaching legal acknowledgment of the intimate relationship between two people, a relationship deemed by the State worthy of dignity in the community equal with all other marriages. It reflects both the community's considered perspective on the historical roots of the institution of marriage and its evolving understanding of the meaning of equality.

DOMA seeks to injure the very class New York seeks to protect. By doing so it violates basic due process and equal protection principles applicable to the Federal Government.… The Constitution's guarantee of equality "must at the very least mean that a bare congressional desire to harm a politically unpopular group cannot" justify disparate treatment of that group. *Department of Agriculture v. Moreno*, 413 U.S. 528, 534–535 (1973). In determining whether a law is motived by an improper animus or purpose, "[d]iscriminations of an unusual character" especially require careful consideration.… DOMA cannot survive under these principles.… DOMA's unusual deviation from the usual tradition of recognizing and accepting state definitions of marriage here operates to deprive same-sex couples of the benefits and responsibilities that come with the federal recognition of their marriages.… The avowed purpose and practical effect of the law here in question are to impose a disadvantage, a separate status, and so a stigma upon all who enter into same-sex marriages made lawful by the unquestioned authority of the States.

The history of DOMA's enactment and its own text demonstrate that interference with the equal dignity of same-sex marriages, a dignity conferred by the States in the exercise of their sovereign power, was more than an incidental effect of the federal statute. It was its essence.… The stated purpose of the law was to promote an "interest in protecting the traditional moral teachings reflected in heterosexual-only marriage laws." … Were there any doubt of this far-reaching purpose, the title of the Act confirms it: The Defense of Marriage.... The Act's demonstrated purpose is to ensure that if any State decides to recognize same-sex marriages, those unions will be treated as second-class marriages for purposes of federal law. This raises a most serious question under the Constitution's Fifth Amendment.

DOMA's operation in practice confirms this purpose.... DOMA writes inequality into the entire United States Code. The particular case at hand concerns the estate tax, but DOMA is more than a simple determination of what should or should not be allowed as an estate tax refund. Among the over 1,000 statutes and numerous federal regulations that DOMA controls are laws pertaining to Social Security, housing, taxes, criminal sanctions, copyright, and veterans' benefits.

DOMA's principal effect is to identify a subset of state-sanctioned marriages and make them unequal. The principal purpose is to impose inequality, not for other reasons like governmental efficiency. Responsibilities, as well as rights, enhance the dignity and integrity of the person. And DOMA contrives to deprive some couples married under the laws of their State, but not other couples, of both rights and responsibilities. By creating two contradictory marriage regimes within the same State, DOMA forces same-sex couples to live as married for the purpose of state law but unmarried for the purpose of federal law, thus diminishing the stability and predictability of basic personal relations the State has found it proper to acknowledge and protect. By this dynamic DOMA undermines both the public and private significance of state-sanctioned same-sex marriages; for it tells those couples, and all the world, that their otherwise valid marriages are unworthy of federal recognition. This places same-sex couples in an unstable position of being in a second-tier marriage. The differentiation demeans the couple, whose moral and sexual choices the Constitution protects, see *Lawrence*..., and whose relationship the State has sought to dignify. And it humiliates tens of thousands of children now being raised by same-sex couples. The law in question makes it even more difficult for the children to understand the integrity and closeness of their own family and its concord with other families in their community and in their daily lives.

Under DOMA, same-sex married couples have their lives burdened, by reason of government decree, in visible and public ways. By its great reach, DOMA touches many aspects of married and family life, from the mundane to the profound. It prevents same-sex married couples from obtaining government healthcare benefits they would otherwise receive.... It deprives them of the Bankruptcy Code's special protections for domestic-support obligations.... It forces them to follow a complicated procedure to file their state and federal taxes jointly.... It prohibits them from being buried together in veterans' cemeteries.... DOMA also brings financial harm to children of same-sex couples. It raises the cost of health care for families by taxing health benefits provided by employers to their workers' same-sex spouses.... And it denies or reduces benefits allowed to families upon the loss of a spouse and parent, benefits that are an integral part of family security.... DOMA divests married same-sex couples of the duties and responsibilities that are an essential part of married life and that they in most cases would be honored to accept were DOMA not in force.

... What has been explained to this point should more than suffice to establish that the principal purpose and the necessary effect of this law are to demean those persons who are in a lawful same-sex marriage. This requires the Court to hold, as it now does, that DOMA is unconstitutional as a deprivation of the liberty of the person protected by the Fifth Amendment of the Constitution.

The liberty protected by the Fifth Amendment's Due Process Clause contains within it the prohibition against denying to any person the equal protection of the laws.... While the Fifth Amendment itself withdraws from Government the power to degrade or demean in the way this law does, the equal protection guarantee of the Fourteenth Amendment makes that Fifth Amendment right all the more specific and all the better understood and preserved.

... DOMA instructs all federal officials, and indeed all persons with whom same-sex couples interact, including their own children, that their marriage is less worthy than the marriages of others. The federal statute is invalid, for no legitimate purpose overcomes the purpose and effect to disparage and to injure those whom the State, by its marriage laws, sought to protect in personhood and dignity. By seeking to displace this protection and treating those persons as living in marriages less respected than others, the federal statute is in violation of the Fifth Amendment.... [A]ffirmed.

Chief Justice Roberts issued a dissenting opinion.

I agree with Justice Scalia that this Court lacks jurisdiction to review the decisions of the courts below.... I also agree with Justice Scalia that Congress acted constitutionally in passing the Defense of Marriage Act (DOMA). Interests in uniformity and stability amply justified Congress's decision to retain the definition of marriage that, at that point, had been adopted by every State in our Nation, and every nation in the world....

The majority sees a more sinister motive.... At least without some more convincing evidence that the Act's principal purpose was to codify malice, and that it furthered *no* legitimate government interests, I would not tar the political branches with the brush of bigotry.

But while I disagree with the result to which the majority's analysis leads it in this case, I think it more important to point out that its analysis leads no further. The Court does not have before it, and the logic of its opinion does not decide, the distinct question whether the States ... may continue to utilize the traditional definition of marriage.

Justice Scalia issued a dissenting opinion joined by Justice Thomas, and as to the discussion of standing by Chief Justice Roberts.

... We have no power to decide this case. And even if we did, we have no power under the Constitution to invalidate this democratically adopted legislation....

I. The Court is eager—hungry—to tell everyone its view of the legal question at the heart of this case. Standing in the way is an obstacle, a technicality of little interest to anyone but the people of We the People, who created it as a barrier against judges' intrusion into their lives. They gave judges, in Article III ... a power to decide not abstract questions but real, concrete "Cases" and "Controversies." Yet the plaintiff and the Government agree entirely on what should happen in this lawsuit. They agree that the court below got it right; and they agreed in the court below that the court below that one got it right as well. What, then, are we *doing* here?

... Windsor won below, and so *cured* her injury, and the President was glad to see it. True, says the majority, but judicial review must march on regardless, lest we "undermine the clear dictate of the separation-of-powers principle that when an Act of Congress is alleged to conflict with the Constitution, it is emphatically the province and duty of the judicial department to say what the law is." ...

That is jaw-dropping. It is an assertion of judicial supremacy over the people's Representatives in Congress and the Executive. It envisions a Supreme Court standing (or rather enthroned) at the apex of government, empowered to decide all constitutional questions, always and everywhere "primary" in its role.... The judicial power as Americans have understood it ... is the power to adjudicate, with conclusive effect, disputed government claims (civil or criminal) against private persons, and disputed claims by private persons against the government or other private persons. Sometimes ... the parties before the court disagree not with regard to the facts of their case ... but with regard to the applicable law—in which event ... it becomes the "province and duty of the judicial department to say what the law is." ... That is completely absent here. Windsor's injury was cured by the judgment in her favor....

II. ... Given that the majority has volunteered its view of the merits, however, I proceed to discuss that as well.... There are many remarkable things about the majority's merits holding. The first is how rootless and shifting its justifications are. For example, the opinion starts with seven full pages about the traditional power of States to define domestic relations.... But no one questions the power of the States to define marriage..., so what is the point of devoting seven pages to describing how long and well established that power is? ...

Equally perplexing are the opinion's references to "the Constitution's guarantee of equality." ... [T]he Equal Protection Clause as incorporated in the Due Process Clause, is not the basis for today's holding. But the portion of the majority opinion that explains why DOMA is unconstitutional (Part IV) begins by citing *Bolling v. Sharpe*, ... *Department of Agriculture v. Moreno*..., and *Romer v. Evans* ...—all of which are equal-protection cases. And those three cases are the *only* authorities that the Court cites in Part IV about the Constitution's meaning, except for its citation of *Lawrence v. Texas* ... (not an equal-protection case) to support its passing assertion that the Constitution protects the "moral and sexual choices" of same-sex couples.... I would review this classification only for its rationality.... But the Court certainly does not *apply* anything that resembles that deferential framework....

As I have observed before, the Constitution does not forbid the government to enforce traditional moral and sexual norms.... It is enough to say that the Constitution neither requires nor forbids our society to approve of same-sex marriage, much as it neither requires nor forbids us to approve of no-fault divorce, polygamy, or the consumption of alcohol....

It is one thing for a society to elect change; it is another for a court of law to impose change by adjudging those who oppose it *hostes humani generis*, enemies of the human race.... It takes real cheek for today's majority to assure us, as it is going out the door, that a constitutional requirement to give formal recognition to same-sex marriage is not at issue here—when what has preceded that assurance is a lecture on how superior the majority's moral judgment in favor of same-sex marriage is to the Congress's hateful moral judgment against it. I promise you this: The only thing that will "confine" the Court's holding is its sense of what it can get away with....

By formally declaring anyone opposed to same-sex marriage an enemy of human decency, the majority arms well every challenger to a state law restricting marriage to its traditional definition. Henceforth those challengers will lead with this Court's declaration that there is "no legitimate purpose" served by such a law, and will claim that the traditional definition has "the purpose and effect to disparage and to injure" the "personhood and dignity" of same-sex couples.... The majority's limiting assurance will be meaningless in the face of language like that, as the majority well knows. That is why the language is there. The result will be a judicial distortion of our society's debate over marriage—a debate that can seem in need of our clumsy "help" only to a member of this institution....

In the majority's telling, this story is black-and-white: Hate your neighbor or come along with us. The truth is more complicated. It is hard to admit that one's political opponents are not monsters, especially in a struggle like this one, and the challenge in the end proves more than today's Court can handle. Too bad....We might have let the People decide.

Justice Alito issued a dissent joined by Justice Thomas.

Our Nation is engaged in a heated debate about same-sex marriage.... The Constitution ... leaves the choice to the people, acting through their elected representatives at both the federal and state levels. I would therefore hold that Congress did not violate Windsor's constitutional rights by enacting §3 of the Defense of Marriage Act (DOMA)....[35]

Windsor and the United States argue that §3 of DOMA violates the equal protection principles.... Same-sex marriage presents a highly emotional and important question of public policy—but not a difficult question of constitutional law. The Constitution does not guarantee the right to enter into a same-sex marriage. Indeed, no provision of the Constitution speaks to the issue.

The Court has sometimes found the Due Process Clauses to have a substantive component that guarantees liberties beyond the absence of physical restraint. And the Court's holding that "DOMA is unconstitutional as a deprivation of the liberty of the person protected by the Fifth Amendment of the Constitution," ... suggests that substantive due process may partially underlie the Court's decision today. But it is well established that any "substantive" component to the Due Process Clause protects only "those fundamental rights and liberties which are, objectively, 'deeply rooted in this Nation's history and tradition.'" ... It is beyond dispute that the right to same-sex marriage is not deeply rooted in this Nation's history and tradition.... What Windsor and the United States seek, therefore, is not the protection of a deeply rooted right but the recognition of a very new right, and they seek this innovation not from a legislative body elected by the people, but from unelected judges. Faced with such a request, judges have cause for both caution and humility....

At present, no one ... can predict with any certainty what the long-term ramifications of widespread acceptance of same-sex marriage will be. And judges are certainly not equipped to make such an assessment.... [I]f the Constitution contained a provision guaranteeing the right to marry a person of the same sex, it would be our duty to enforce that right. But the Constitution simply does not speak to the issue of same-sex marriage....

Perhaps because they cannot show that same-sex marriage is a fundamental right under our Constitution, Windsor and the United States couch their arguments in equal protection terms.... In my view, the approach that Windsor's and the United States advocate is misguided.... By asking the Court to strike down DOMA as not satisfying some form of heightened scrutiny, Windsor and the United States are really seeking to have the Court resolve a debate between two competing views of marriage. The first and older view, which I will call the "traditional" or "conjugal" view, sees marriage as an intrinsically opposite-sex institution.... [V]irtually every culture, including many not influenced by the Abrahamic religions, has limited marriage to people of the opposite sex.... While modern cultural changes have weakened the link between marriage and procreation in the popular mind, there is no doubt that, throughout human history and across many cultures, marriage has been viewed as an exclusively opposite-sex institution and as one inextricably linked to procreation and biological kinship.

The other, newer view is what I will call the "consent-based" vision of marriage, a vision that primarily defines marriage as the solemnization of mutual commitment ... between two persons.... Proponents of same-sex marriage argue that because gender differentiation is not relevant to this vision, the exclusion of same-sex couples from the institution of marriage is rank discrimination.

The Constitution does not codify either of these views of marriage.... Yet, Windsor and the United States implicitly ask us to endorse the consent-based view of marriage and to reject the traditional view.... Because our constitutional order assigns the resolution of questions of this nature to the people, I would not presume to enshrine either vision of marriage in our constitutional jurisprudence.... Accordingly, both Congress and the States are entitled to enact laws recognizing either of the two understandings of marriage....

... [T]he Court strikes down §3 of DOMA ... in part because it believes that §3 encroaches upon the States' sovereign prerogative to define marriage.... To the extent that the Court takes the position that the question of same-sex marriage should be resolved primarily at the state level, I wholeheartedly agree. I hope that the Court will ultimately permit the people of each State to decide this question for themselves....

All that §3 does is to define a class of persons to whom federal law extends certain special benefits and upon whom federal law imposes certain special burdens.... Congress used marital status as a way of defining this class.... Assuming that Congress has the power under the Constitution to enact the laws affected by §3, Congress has the power to define the category of persons to whom those laws apply [and therefore §3] does not violate the Fifth Amendment.

Notice that Justice Kennedy took a dramatic step forward toward recognition of protections for gays and lesbians in the language of the opinion, but he also limited this ruling in terms of the situation presented by state recognition of the marital relationship and federal discrimination against it. In fact, the dissents clearly attacked the fact that the majority was making a broad argument but attempting to portray it as something far more limited.

As one lower court after another struck down state bans on gay marriage, citing the language of the *Windsor* and *Lawrence* opinions, it was clear that it was only a matter of time before the Supreme Court would be faced with the direct question whether same-sex marriage was constitutionally protected. When the Court of Appeals for the Sixth Circuit upheld the bans imposed by four states, that set up a conflict among the circuits, virtually ensuring a Supreme Court review. That long-awaited ruling came in 2015.

Obergefell v. Hodges

135 S. Ct. 2584 (2015)

INTRODUCTION: A number of states adopted statutes or constitutional amendments that banned same-sex marriage, and gay and lesbian couples sought the elimination of these bans. Where they could not obtain legislative relief, they launched litigation in the federal district courts, which produced a variety of rulings against barriers to same-sex marriage that were affirmed by courts of appeals.

Michigan, Kentucky, Ohio, and Tennessee were among the states that had bans on same-sex marriage that were challenged, and the district courts rulings against the states were consolidated on appeal to the U.S. Court of Appeals for the Sixth Circuit. As the Supreme Court explained, the petitioners were 14 same-sex couples and two men whose same-sex partners were deceased. The Court's opinion added more detail about these plaintiffs. The Court of Appeals reversed, holding that there was no constitutional requirement for the states to allow same-sex marriage or to recognize such marriages from other states where they were permitted.[36]

The other circuits had ruled against state bans, and this decision of the Sixth Circuit created a conflict among the states that led to a grant of certiorari by the Supreme Court. However, in taking the case, the Court ordered that the parties were to address two issues. As the Court explained, "The first, presented by the cases from Michigan and Kentucky, is whether the Fourteenth Amendment requires a State to license a marriage between two people of the same sex. The second, presented by the cases from Ohio, Tennessee, and, again, Kentucky, is whether the Fourteenth Amendment requires a State to recognize a same-sex marriage licensed and performed in a State which does grant that right."

Justice Kennedy wrote the opinion for the Court.

> The Constitution promises liberty to all within its reach, a liberty that includes certain specific rights that allow persons, within a lawful realm, to define and express their identity. The petitioners in these cases seek to find that liberty by marrying someone of the same sex and having their marriages deemed lawful on the same terms and conditions as marriages between persons of the opposite sex.
>
> ... [T]he annals of human history reveal the transcendent importance of marriage. The lifelong union of a man and a woman always has promised nobility and dignity to all persons, without regard to their station in life. Marriage is sacred to those who live by their religions and offers unique fulfillment to those who find meaning in the secular realm. Its dynamic allows two people to find a life that could not be found alone, for a marriage becomes greater than just the two persons. Rising from the most basic human needs, marriage is essential to our most profound hopes and aspirations.
>
> ... Since the dawn of history, marriage has transformed strangers into relatives, binding families and societies together....There are untold references to the beauty of marriage in religious and philosophical texts spanning time, cultures, and faiths, as well as in art and literature in all their forms. It is fair and necessary to say these references were based on the understanding that marriage is a union between two persons of the opposite sex.
>
> That history is the beginning of these cases. The respondents say it should be the end as well. To them, it would demean a timeless institution if the concept and lawful status of marriage were extended to two persons of the same sex. Marriage, in their view, is by its nature a gender-differentiated union of man and woman. This view long has been held—and continues to be held—in good faith by reasonable and sincere people here and throughout the world.
>
> The petitioners acknowledge this history but contend that these cases cannot end there. Were their intent to demean the revered idea and reality of marriage, the petitioners' claims would be of a different order. But that is neither their purpose nor their submission. To the contrary, it is the enduring importance of marriage that underlies the petitioners' contentions. This, they say, is their whole

point. Far from seeking to devalue marriage, the petitioners seek it for themselves because of their respect—and need—for its privileges and responsibilities. And their immutable nature dictates that same-sex marriage is their only real path to this profound commitment.

Recounting the circumstances of three of these cases illustrates the urgency of the petitioners' cause from their perspective. Petitioner James Obergefell, a plaintiff in the Ohio case, met John Arthur over two decades ago. They fell in love and started a life together, establishing a lasting, committed relation. In 2011, however, Arthur was diagnosed with amyotrophic lateral sclerosis, or ALS. This debilitating disease is progressive, with no known cure. Two years ago, Obergefell and Arthur decided to commit to one another, resolving to marry before Arthur died. To fulfill their mutual promise, they traveled from Ohio to Maryland, where same-sex marriage was legal. It was difficult for Arthur to move, and so the couple were wed inside a medical transport plane as it remained on the tarmac in Baltimore. Three months later, Arthur died. Ohio law does not permit Obergefell to be listed as the surviving spouse on Arthur's death certificate. By statute, they must remain strangers even in death, a state-imposed separation Obergefell deems "hurtful for the rest of time." ... He brought suit to be shown as the surviving spouse on Arthur's death certificate.

April DeBoer and Jayne Rowse are co-plaintiffs in the case from Michigan. They celebrated a commitment ceremony to honor their permanent relation in 2007.... In 2009, DeBoer and Rowse fostered and then adopted a baby boy. Later that same year, they welcomed another son into their family. The new baby, born prematurely and abandoned by his biological mother, required around-the-clock care. The next year, a baby girl with special needs joined their family. Michigan, however, permits only opposite-sex married couples or single individuals to adopt, so each child can have only one woman as his or her legal parent. If an emergency were to arise, schools and hospitals may treat the three children as if they had only one parent. And, were tragedy to befall either DeBoer or Rowse, the other would have no legal rights over the children she had not been permitted to adopt. This couple seeks relief from the continuing uncertainty their unmarried status creates in their lives.

Army Reserve Sergeant First Class Ijpe DeKoe and his partner Thomas Kostura, co-plaintiffs in the Tennessee case, fell in love. In 2011, DeKoe received orders to deploy to Afghanistan. Before leaving, he and Kostura married in New York. A week later, DeKoe began his deployment, which lasted for almost a year. When he returned, the two settled in Tennessee, where DeKoe works full-time for the Army Reserve. Their lawful marriage is stripped from them whenever they reside in Tennessee, returning and disappearing as they travel across state lines. DeKoe, who served this Nation to preserve the freedom the Constitution protects, must endure a substantial burden.

The cases now before the Court involve other petitioners as well, each with their own experiences. Their stories reveal that they seek not to denigrate marriage but rather to live their lives, or honor their spouses' memory, joined by its bond.

... The history of marriage is one of both continuity and change. That institution ... has evolved over time. For example, marriage was once viewed as an arrangement by the couple's parents based on political, religious, and financial concerns; but by the time of the Nation's founding it was understood to be a voluntary contract between a man and a woman.... As the role and status of women changed, the institution further evolved. Under the centuries-old doctrine of coverture, a married man and woman were treated by the State as a single, male-dominated legal entity.... As women gained legal, political, and property rights, and as society began to understand that women have their own equal dignity, the law of coverture was abandoned.... These and other developments in the institution of marriage over the past centuries were not mere superficial changes. Rather, they worked deep transformations in its structure, affecting aspects of marriage long viewed by many as essential....

These new insights have strengthened, not weakened, the institution of marriage. Indeed, changed understandings of marriage are characteristic of a Nation where new dimensions of freedom become apparent to new generations, often through perspectives that begin in pleas or protests and then are considered in the political sphere and the judicial process.

This dynamic can be seen in the Nation's experiences with the rights of gays and lesbians. Until the mid-20th century, same-sex intimacy long had been condemned as immoral by the state itself in most Western nations, a belief often embodied in the criminal law. Even ... after World War II ... same-sex intimacy remained a crime in many States. Gays and lesbians were prohibited from most government employment, barred from military service, excluded under immigration laws, targeted by police, and burdened in their rights to associate.

For much of the 20th century, moreover, homosexuality was treated as an illness. When the American Psychiatric Association published the first Diagnostic and Statistical Manual of Mental Disorders in 1952, homosexuality was classified as a mental disorder, a position adhered to until 1973.... Only in more recent years have psychiatrists and others recognized that sexual orientation is both a normal expression of human sexuality and immutable. See Brief for American Psychological Association et al. as Amici Curiae 7–17....

In 1993, the Hawaii Supreme Court held Hawaii's law restricting marriage to opposite-sex couples constituted a classification on the basis of sex and was therefore subject to strict scrutiny under the Hawaii Constitution.... Although this decision did not mandate that same-sex marriage be allowed, some States were concerned by its implications and reaffirmed in their laws that marriage is defined as a union between opposite-sex partners. So too in 1996, Congress passed the Defense of Marriage Act ... defining marriage for all federal-law purposes as "only a legal union between one man and one woman as husband and wife." ...

The new and widespread discussion of the subject led other States to a different conclusion. In 2003, the Supreme Judicial Court of Massachusetts held the States Constitution guaranteed same-sex couples the right to marry.... After that ruling, some additional States granted marriage rights to same-sex couples, either through judicial or legislative processes.... Two Terms ago, in *United States v. Windsor* ... this Court invalidated DOMA to the extent it barred the Federal Government from treating same-sex marriages as valid even when they were lawful in the State where they were licensed....

Under the Due Process Clause of the Fourteenth Amendment, no State shall "deprive any person of life, liberty, or property, without due process of law." The fundamental liberties protected by this Clause include most of the rights enumerated in the Bill of Rights.... In addition these liberties extend to certain personal choices central to individual dignity and autonomy, including intimate choices that define personal identity and beliefs. See, *e.g.*, *Eisenstadt v. Baird*...; *Griswold v. Connecticut*.... The identification and protection of fundamental rights is an enduring part of the judicial duty to interpret the Constitution.... [I]t requires courts to exercise reasoned judgment in identifying interests of the person so fundamental that the State must accord them its respect.... History and tradition guide and discipline this inquiry but do not set its outer boundaries.... When new insight reveals discord between the Constitution's central protections and a received legal stricture, a claim to liberty must be addressed.

Applying these established tenets, the Court has long held the right to marry is protected by the Constitution. In *Loving v. Virginia*..., which invalidated bans on interracial unions, a unanimous Court held marriage is "one of the vital personal rights essential to the orderly pursuit of happiness by free men." The Court reaffirmed that holding in *Zablocki v. Redhail*, 434 U. S. 374, 384 (1978), which held the right to marry was burdened by a law prohibiting fathers who were behind on child support from marrying....

In defining the right to marry these cases have identified essential attributes of that right based in history, tradition, and other constitutional liberties inherent in this intimate bond.... And in assessing whether the force and rationale of its cases apply to same-sex couples, the Court must respect the basic reasons why the right to marry has been long protected.... This analysis compels the conclusion that same-sex couples may exercise the right to marry....

A first premise of the Court's relevant precedents is that the right to personal choice regarding marriage is inherent in the concept of individual autonomy. This abiding connection between marriage and liberty is why *Loving* invalidated interracial marriage bans under the Due Process Clause.... Like choices concerning contraception, family relationships, procreation, and child rearing, all of which are protected by the Constitution, decisions concerning marriage are among the most intimate that an individual can make. See *Lawrence*.... The nature of marriage is that, through its enduring bond, two persons together can find other freedoms, such as expression, intimacy, and spirituality. This is true for all persons, whatever their sexual orientation. See *Windsor*.... There is dignity in the bond between two men or two women who seek to marry and in their autonomy to make such profound choices.

A second principle in this Court's jurisprudence is that the right to marry is fundamental because it supports a two-person union unlike any other in its importance to the committed individuals. This point was central to *Griswold v. Connecticut*, which held the Constitution protects the right of married couples to use contraception.... *Griswold* described marriage this way: "Marriage is a coming together for better or for worse, hopefully enduring, and intimate to the degree of being sacred. It is an association that promotes a way of life, not causes; a harmony in living, not political faiths; a bilateral loyalty, not commercial or social projects. Yet it is an association for as noble a purpose as any involved in our prior decisions." ... The right to marry thus dignifies couples who "wish to define themselves by their commitment to each other." *Windsor*....

As this Court held in *Lawrence*, same-sex couples have the same right as opposite-sex couples to enjoy intimate association.... [I]t acknowledged that "[w]hen sexuality finds overt expression in intimate conduct with another person, the conduct can be but one element in a personal bond that is more enduring." ... But while *Lawrence* confirmed a dimension of freedom that allows individuals to engage in intimate association without criminal liability, it does not follow that freedom stops there. Outlaw to outcast may be a step forward, but it does not achieve the full promise of liberty.

A third basis for protecting the right to marry is that it safeguards children and families and thus draws meaning from related rights of child rearing, procreation, and education. See *Pierce v. Society of Sisters*.... The Court has recognized these connections by describing the varied rights as a unified whole: "[T]he right to 'marry, establish a home and bring up children' is a central part of the liberty protected by the Due Process Clause." *Zablocki*.... By giving recognition and legal structure to their parents' relationship, marriage allows children "to understand the integrity and closeness of their own family and its concord with other families in their community and in their daily lives." *Windsor*.... Marriage also affords the permanency and stability important to children's best interests....

As all parties agree, many same-sex couples provide loving and nurturing homes to their children, whether biological or adopted. And hundreds of thousands of children are presently being raised by such couples.... Most States have allowed gays and lesbians to adopt, either as individuals or as couples, and many adopted and foster children have same-sex parents.... This provides powerful confirmation from the law itself that gays and lesbians can create loving, supportive families.

Excluding same-sex couples from marriage thus conflicts with a central premise of the right to marry. Without the recognition, stability, and predictability marriage offers, their children suffer the stigma of knowing their families are somehow lesser. They also suffer the significant material costs of being raised by unmarried parents.... The marriage laws at issue here thus harm and humiliate the children of same-sex couples.... That is not to say the right to marry is less meaningful for those who do not or cannot have children. An ability, desire, or promise to procreate is not and has not been a prerequisite for a valid marriage in any State....

Fourth and finally, this Court's cases and the Nation's traditions make clear that marriage is a keystone of our social order. Alexis de Tocqueville recognized this truth on his travels through the United States almost two centuries ago.... In *Maynard v. Hill*, 125 U. S. 190, 211 (1888), the Court echoed de Tocqueville, explaining that marriage is "the foundation of the family and of society, without which there would be neither civilization nor progress." Marriage, the *Maynard* Court said, has long been "a great public institution, giving character to our whole civil polity." ...

For that reason, just as a couple vows to support each other, so does society pledge to support the couple, offering symbolic recognition and material benefits to protect and nourish the union.... These aspects of marital status include: taxation; inheritance and property rights; rules of intestate succession; spousal privilege in the law of evidence; hospital access; medical decisionmaking authority; adoption rights; the rights and benefits of survivors; birth and death certificates; professional ethics rules; campaign finance restrictions; workers' compensation benefits; health insurance; and child custody, support, and visitation rules.... Valid marriage under state law is also a significant status for over a thousand provisions of federal law....

[B]y virtue of their exclusion from that institution, same-sex couples are denied the constellation of benefits that the States have linked to marriage. This harm results in more than just material burdens. Same-sex couples are consigned to an instability many opposite-sex couples would deem intolerable in their own lives. As the State itself makes marriage all the more precious by the significance it attaches to it, exclusion from that status has the effect of teaching that gays and lesbians are unequal in important respects. It demeans gays and lesbians for the State to lock them out of a central institution of the Nation's society....

The limitation of marriage to opposite-sex couples may long have seemed natural and just, but its inconsistency with the central meaning of the fundamental right to marry is now manifest. With that knowledge must come the recognition that laws excluding same-sex couples from the marriage right impose stigma and injury of the kind prohibited by our basic charter.

... [R]espondents refer to *Washington v. Glucksberg*, 521 U. S. 702, 721 (1997), ... [which] insist[ed] that liberty under the Due Process Clause must be defined in a most circumscribed manner.... Yet while that approach may have been appropriate for the asserted right there involved (physician-assisted suicide), it is inconsistent with the approach this Court has used in discussing other fundamental rights, including marriage and intimacy. *Loving* did not ask about a "right to interracial marriage" ... and *Zablocki* did not ask about a "right of fathers with unpaid child support duties to marry." Rather, each case inquired about the right to marry in its comprehensive sense, asking if there was a sufficient justification for excluding the relevant class from the right.... That principle applies here. If rights were defined by who exercised them in the past, then received practices could serve as their own continued justification and new groups could not invoke rights once denied. This Court has rejected that approach, both with respect to the right to marry and the rights of gays and lesbians. See *Loving*..., *Lawrence*....

The right to marry is fundamental as a matter of history and tradition, but rights come not from ancient sources alone. They rise, too, from a better informed understanding of how constitutional imperatives define a liberty that remains urgent in our own era. Many who deem same-sex marriage to be wrong reach that conclusion based on decent and honorable religious or philosophical premises, and neither they nor their beliefs are disparaged here. But when that sincere, personal opposition becomes enacted law and public policy, the necessary consequence is to put the imprimatur of the State itself on an exclusion that soon demeans or stigmatizes those whose own liberty is then denied. Under the Constitution, same-sex couples seek in marriage the same legal treatment as opposite-sex couples, and it would disparage their choices and diminish their personhood to deny them this right.

The right of same-sex couples to marry that is part of the liberty promised by the Fourteenth Amendment is derived, too, from that Amendment's guarantee of the equal protection of the laws. The Due Process Clause and the Equal Protection Clause are connected in a profound way, though they set forth independent principles.... This interrelation of the two principles furthers our understanding of what freedom is and must become.

The Court's cases touching upon the right to marry reflect this dynamic. In *Loving* the Court invalidated a prohibition on interracial marriage under both the Equal Protection Clause and the Due Process Clause. The Court first declared the prohibition invalid because of its unequal treatment of interracial couples. It stated: "There can be no doubt that restricting the freedom to marry solely because of racial classifications violates the central meaning of the Equal Protection Clause." ... With this link to equal protection the Court proceeded to hold the prohibition offended central precepts of liberty: "To deny this fundamental freedom on so unsupportable a basis as the racial classifications embodied in these statutes, classifications so directly subversive of the principle of equality at the heart of the Fourteenth Amendment, is surely to deprive all the State's citizens of liberty without due process of law." ...

Indeed, in interpreting the Equal Protection Clause, the Court has recognized that new insights and societal understandings can reveal unjustified inequality within our most fundamental institutions that once passed unnoticed and unchallenged. To take but one period, this occurred with respect to marriage in the 1970's and 1980's. Notwithstanding the gradual erosion of the doctrine of coverture ... invidious sex-based classifications in marriage remained common through the mid-20th century.... These classifications denied the equal dignity of men and women.... Responding to a new awareness, the Court invoked equal protection principles to invalidate laws imposing sex-based inequality on marriage. See, e.g., *Kirchberg v. Feenstra*, 450 U. S. 455 (1981); ... *Califano v. Goldfarb*...; *Frontiero v. Richardson*....

In Lawrence the Court acknowledged the interlocking nature of these constitutional safeguards in the context of the legal treatment of gays and lesbians.... Although Lawrence elaborated its holding under the Due Process Clause, it acknowledged, and sought to remedy, the continuing inequality that resulted from laws making intimacy in the lives of gays and lesbians a crime against the State.... Lawrence therefore drew upon principles of liberty and equality to define and protect the rights of gays and lesbians....

This dynamic also applies to same-sex marriage. It is now clear that the challenged laws burden the liberty of same-sex couples, and it must be further acknowledged that they abridge central precepts of equality.... [T]his denial to same-sex couples of the right to marry works a grave and continuing harm. The imposition of this disability on gays and lesbians serves to disrespect and subordinate them. And the Equal Protection Clause, like the Due Process Clause, prohibits this unjustified infringement of the fundamental right to marry....

These considerations lead to the conclusion that the right to marry is a fundamental right inherent in the liberty of the person, and under the Due Process and Equal Protection Clauses of the Fourteenth Amendment couples of the same-sex may not be deprived of that right and that liberty. The Court now holds that same-sex couples may exercise the fundamental right to marry. No longer may this liberty be denied to them ... and the State laws challenged by Petitioners in these cases are now held invalid to the extent they exclude same-sex couples from civil marriage on the same terms and conditions as opposite-sex couples.[37]

There may be an initial inclination in these cases to proceed with caution—to await further legislation, litigation, and debate. The respondents warn there has been insufficient democratic discourse before deciding an issue so basic as the definition of marriage.... Yet there has been far more deliberation than this argument acknowledges. There have been referenda, legislative debates, and grassroots campaigns, as well as countless studies, papers, books, and other popular and scholarly writings. There has been extensive litigation in state and federal courts. See Appendix A....[38] Judicial opinions addressing the issue have been informed by the contentions of parties and counsel, which, in turn, reflect the more general, societal discussion of same-sex marriage and its meaning that has occurred over the past decades. As more than 100 *amici* make clear in their filings, many of the central institutions in American life ... have devoted substantial attention to the question. This has led to an enhanced understanding of the issue....

Of course, the Constitution contemplates that democracy is the appropriate process for change, so long as that process does not abridge fundamental rights.... But ... [a]n individual can invoke a right to constitutional protection when he or she is harmed, even if the broader public disagrees and even if the legislature refuses to act. The idea of the Constitution "was to withdraw certain subjects from the vicissitudes of political controversy, to place them beyond the reach of majorities and officials and to establish them as legal principles to be applied by the courts." *West Virginia Bd. of Ed. v. Barnette*.... This is why "fundamental rights may not be submitted to a vote; they depend on the outcome of no elections." ... The issue before the Court here is the legal question whether the Constitution protects the right of same-sex couples to marry.... Properly presented with the petitioners' cases, the Court has a duty to address these claims and answer these questions....

The respondents also argue allowing same-sex couples to wed will harm marriage as an institution by leading to fewer opposite-sex marriages. This may occur, the respondents contend, because licensing same-sex marriage severs the connection between natural procreation and marriage.... The respondents have not shown a foundation for the conclusion that allowing same-sex marriage will cause the harmful outcomes they describe....

Finally, it must be emphasized that religions, and those who adhere to religious doctrines, may continue to advocate with utmost, sincere conviction that, by divine precepts, same-sex marriage should not be condoned. The First Amendment ensures that religious organizations and persons are given proper protection as they seek to teach the principles that are so fulfilling and so central to their lives and faiths, and to their own deep aspirations to continue the family structure they have long revered. The same is true of those who oppose same-sex marriage for other reasons. In turn, those who believe allowing same-sex marriage is proper or indeed essential, whether as a matter of religious conviction or secular belief, may engage those who disagree with their view in an open and searching debate. The Constitution, however, does not permit the State to bar same-sex couples from marriage on the same terms as accorded to couples of the opposite sex.

These cases also present the question whether the Constitution requires States to recognize same-sex marriages validly performed out of State.... Being married in one State but having that valid marriage denied in another is one of "the most perplexing and distressing complication[s]" in the law of domestic relations.... Leaving the current state of affairs in place would maintain and promote instability and uncertainty. For some couples, even an ordinary drive into a neighboring State to visit family or friends risks causing severe hardship in the event of a spouse's hospitalization while across state lines. In light of the fact that many States already allow same-sex marriage—and hundreds of thousands of these marriages already have occurred—the disruption caused by the recognition bans is significant and ever-growing.

As counsel for the respondents acknowledged at argument, if States are required by the Constitution to issue marriage licenses to same-sex couples, the justifications for refusing to recognize those marriages performed elsewhere are undermined.... The Court, in this decision, holds same-sex couples may exercise the fundamental right to marry in all States. It follows that the Court also must hold—and it now does hold—that there is no lawful basis for a State to refuse to recognize a lawful same-sex marriage performed in another State on the ground of its same-sex character.

No union is more profound than marriage, for it embodies the highest ideals of love, fidelity, devotion, sacrifice, and family. In forming a marital union, two people become something greater than once they were. As some of the petitioners in these cases demonstrate, marriage embodies a love that may endure even past death. It would misunderstand these men and women to say they disrespect the idea of marriage. Their plea is that they do respect it, respect it so deeply that they seek to find its fulfillment for themselves. Their hope is not to be condemned to live in loneliness, excluded from one of civilization's oldest institutions. They ask for equal dignity in the eyes of the law. The Constitution grants them that right. The judgment of the Court of Appeals for the Sixth Circuit is reversed.

Chief Justice Roberts issued a dissent, joined by Justices Scalia and Thomas.

Petitioners' ... position has undeniable appeal.... But this Court is not a legislature.... Under the Constitution, judges have power to say what the law is, not what it should be.... Although the policy arguments for extending marriage to same-sex couples may be compelling, the legal arguments for requiring such an extension are not. The fundamental right to marry does not include a right to make a State change its definition of marriage. And a State's decision to maintain the meaning of marriage that has persisted in every culture throughout human history can hardly be called irrational. In short, our Constitution does not enact any one theory of marriage. The people of a State are free to expand marriage to include same-sex couples, or to retain the historic definition.... The majority's decision is an act of will, not legal judgment. The right it announces has no basis in the Constitution or this Court's precedent....

There is no serious dispute that, under our precedents, the Constitution protects a right to marry and requires States to apply their marriage laws equally. The real question in these cases is what constitutes "marriage," or—more precisely—*who decides* what constitutes "marriage"? ...

[For] millennia, across all those civilizations, "marriage" referred to only one relationship: the union of a man and a woman.... Marriage did not come about as a result of a political movement, discovery, disease, war, religious doctrine, or any other moving force of world history—and certainly not as a result of a prehistoric decision to exclude gays and lesbians. It arose in the nature of things to meet a vital need: ensuring that children are conceived by a mother and father committed to raising them in the stable conditions of a lifelong relationship....

... The human race must procreate to survive. Procreation occurs through sexual relations between a man and a woman. When sexual relations result in the conception of a child, that child's prospects are generally better if the mother and father stay together rather than going their separate ways. Therefore, for the good of children and society, sexual relations that can lead to procreation should occur only between a man and a woman committed to a lasting bond. Society has recognized that bond as marriage. And by bestowing a respected status and material benefits on married couples, society encourages men and women to conduct sexual relations within marriage rather than without.... This singular understanding of marriage has prevailed in the United States throughout our history....

The Constitution itself says nothing about marriage, and the Framers thereby entrusted the States with "[t]he whole subject of the domestic relations of husband and wife." *Windsor*.... There is no dispute that every State ... until a dozen years ago ... defined marriage in the traditional, biologically rooted way.... This

Court's precedents have repeatedly described marriage in ways that are consistent only with its traditional meaning.... The majority may be right that the "history of marriage is one of both continuity and change," but the core meaning of marriage has endured....

Shortly after this Court struck down racial restrictions on marriage in *Loving*, a gay couple in Minnesota sought a marriage license.... The Minnesota Supreme Court rejected their analogy to *Loving*, and this Court summarily dismissed an appeal. *Baker v. Nelson*.... In the decades after *Baker*, greater numbers of gays and lesbians began living openly, and many expressed a desire to have their relationships recognized as marriages. Over time, more people came to see marriage in a way that could be extended to such couples....

Over the last few years, public opinion on marriage has shifted rapidly.... In all, voters and legislators in eleven States and the District of Columbia have changed their definitions of marriage to include same-sex couples. The highest courts of five States have decreed that same result under their own Constitutions. The remainder of the States retain the traditional definition of marriage....

[T]he majority's approach has no basis in principle or tradition, except for the unprincipled tradition of judicial policymaking that characterized discredited decisions such as *Lochner v. New York*.... Stripped of its shiny rhetorical gloss, the majority's argument is that the Due Process Clause gives same-sex couples a fundamental right to marry because it will be good for them and for society. If I were a legislator, I would certainly consider that view as a matter of social policy. But as a judge, I find the majority's position indefensible as a matter of constitutional law.

Petitioners do not contend that their States' marriage laws violate an *enumerated* constitutional right, such as the freedom of speech protected by the First Amendment....[39] They argue instead that the laws violate a right *implied* by the Fourteenth Amendment's requirement that "liberty" may not be deprived without "due process of law".... Allowing unelected federal judges to select which unenumerated rights rank as "fundamental" ... raises obvious concerns about the judicial role. Our precedents have accordingly insisted that judges "exercise the utmost care" in identifying implied fundamental rights, "lest the liberty protected by the Due Process Clause be subtly transformed into the policy preferences of the Members of this Court." *Washington v. Glucksberg*....

The need for restraint in administering the strong medicine of substantive due process is a lesson this Court has learned the hard way. The Court first applied substantive due process to strike down a statute in *Dred Scott v. Sandford*....[40] In a series of early 20th-century cases, most prominently *Lochner v. New York*, this Court invalidated state statutes that presented "meddlesome interferences with the rights of the individual," and "undue interference with liberty of person and freedom of contract." ... Eventually, the Court recognized its error and vowed not to repeat it.... Rejecting *Lochner* does not require disavowing the doctrine of implied fundamental rights, and this Court has not done so. But ... [o]ur precedents have required that implied fundamental rights be "objectively, deeply rooted in this Nation's history and tradition," and "implicit in the concept of ordered liberty, such that neither liberty nor justice would exist if they were sacrificed." ...

The majority ... relies primarily on precedents discussing the fundamental "right to marry." ... These cases do not hold, of course, that anyone who wants to get married has a constitutional right to do so.... [T]he "right to marry" cases stand for the important but limited proposition that particular restrictions on access to marriage *as traditionally defined* violate due process.... Neither petitioners nor the majority cites a single case or other legal source providing any basis for such a constitutional right. None exists, and that is enough to foreclose their claim....

It is striking how much of the majority's reasoning would apply with equal force to the claim of a fundamental right to plural marriage. If "[t]here is dignity in the bond between two men or two women who seek to marry and in their autonomy to make such profound choices," ... why would there be any less dignity in the bond between three people who, in exercising their autonomy, seek to make the profound choice to marry? If a same-sex couple has the constitutional right to marry because their children would otherwise "suffer the stigma of knowing their families are somehow lesser," ... why wouldn't the same reasoning apply to a family of three or more persons raising children? ... I do not mean to equate marriage between same-sex couples with plural marriages in all respects. There may well be relevant differences that compel different legal analysis. But if there are, petitioners have not pointed to any....

In addition to their due process argument, petitioners contend that the Equal Protection Clause requires their States to license and recognize same-sex marriages.... [T]he marriage laws at issue here do not violate the Equal Protection Clause, because distinguishing between opposite-sex and same-sex couples is rationally related to the States' "legitimate state interest" in "preserving the traditional institution of marriage."[41]...

The legitimacy of this Court ultimately rests "upon the respect accorded to its judgments." ... That respect flows from the perception—and reality—that we exercise humility and restraint in deciding cases according to the Constitution and law. The role of the Court envisioned by the majority today, however, is anything but humble or restrained....

When decisions are reached through democratic means, some people will inevitably be disappointed with the results. But those whose views do not prevail at least know that they have had their say, and accordingly are—in the tradition of our political culture—reconciled to the result of a fair and honest debate.... But today the Court puts a stop to all that. By deciding this question under the Constitution, the Court removes it from the realm of democratic decision. There will be consequences to shutting down the political process on an issue of such profound public significance. Closing debate tends to close minds.... Indeed, however heartened the proponents of same-sex marriage might be on this day, it is worth acknowledging what they have lost, and lost forever: the opportunity to win the true acceptance that comes from persuading their fellow citizens of the justice of their cause. And they lose this just when the winds of change were freshening at their backs.

... Today's decision, for example, creates serious questions about religious liberty. Many good and decent people oppose same-sex marriage as a tenet of faith, and their freedom to exercise religion [under] the Constitution.... Respect for sincere religious conviction has led voters and legislators in every State that has adopted same-sex marriage democratically to include accommodations for religious practice.... Hard questions arise when people of faith exercise religion in ways that may be seen to conflict with the new right to same-sex marriage—when, for example, a religious college provides married student housing only to opposite-sex married couples, or a religious adoption agency declines to place children with same-sex married couples. Indeed, the Solicitor General candidly acknowledged that the tax exemptions of some religious institutions would be in question if they opposed same-sex marriage.... There is little doubt that these and similar questions will soon be before this Court. Unfortunately, people of faith can take no comfort in the treatment they receive from the majority today.

Perhaps the most discouraging aspect of today's decision is the extent to which the majority feels compelled to sully those on the other side of the debate.... It is one thing for the majority to conclude that the Constitution protects a right to same-sex marriage; it is something else to portray everyone who does not share the majority's "better informed understanding" as bigoted....

If you are among the many Americans ... who favor expanding same-sex marriage, by all means celebrate today's decision. Celebrate the achievement of a desired goal. Celebrate the opportunity for a new expression of commitment to a partner. Celebrate the availability of new benefits. But do not celebrate the Constitution. It had nothing to do with it. I respectfully dissent.

Justice Scalia issued a dissent joined by Justice Thomas.

I join the Chief Justice's opinion in full. I write separately to call attention to this Court's threat to American democracy.

The substance of today's decree is not of immense personal importance to me.... It is of overwhelming importance, however, who it is that rules me. Today's decree says that my Ruler, and the Ruler of 320 million Americans coast-to-coast, is a majority of the nine lawyers on the Supreme Court. The opinion in these cases is the furthest extension in fact ... of the Court's claimed power to create "liberties" that the Constitution and its Amendments neglect to mention. This practice of constitutional revision by an unelected committee of nine, always accompanied (as it is today) by extravagant praise of liberty, robs the People of the most important liberty they asserted in the Declaration of Independence and won in the Revolution of 1776: the freedom to govern themselves.

Until the courts put a stop to it, public debate over same-sex marriage displayed American democracy at its best. Individuals on both sides of the issue passionately, but respectfully, attempted to persuade their fellow citizens to accept their views. Americans considered the arguments and put the question to a vote.... Win or lose, advocates for both sides continued pressing their cases, secure in the knowledge that an electoral loss can be negated by a later electoral win. That is exactly how our system of government is supposed to work.

The Constitution places some constraints on self-rule—constraints adopted *by the People themselves* when they ratified the Constitution and its Amendments.... Aside from these limitations, those powers "reserved to the States respectively, or to the people" can be exercised as the States or the People desire. These cases ask us to decide whether the Fourteenth Amendment contains a limitation that requires the States to license and recognize marriages between two people of the same sex....

When the Fourteenth Amendment was ratified in 1868, every State limited marriage to one man and one woman, and no one doubted the constitutionality of doing so. That resolves these cases.... We have no basis for striking down a practice that is not expressly prohibited by the Fourteenth Amendment's text,[42] and that bears the endorsement of a long tradition of open, widespread, and unchallenged use dating back to the Amendment's ratification....

Buried beneath the mummeries and straining-to-be-memorable passages of the opinion is a candid and startling assertion: No matter *what* it was the People ratified, the Fourteenth Amendment protects those rights that the Judiciary, in its "reasoned judgment," thinks the Fourteenth Amendment ought to protect.... This is a naked judicial claim to legislative—indeed, *super*-legislative—power; a claim fundamentally at odds with our system of government.... A system of government that makes the People subordinate to a committee of nine unelected lawyers does not deserve to be called a democracy....

[T]he Federal Judiciary is hardly a cross-section of America.... The predominant attitude of tall-building lawyers with respect to the questions presented in these cases is suggested by the fact that the American Bar Association deemed it in accord with the wishes of its members to file a brief in support of the petitioners....

But what really astounds is the hubris reflected in today's judicial Putsch. The five Justices who compose today's majority are entirely comfortable concluding that every State violated the Constitution for all of the 135 years between the Fourteenth Amendment's ratification and Massachusetts' permitting of same-sex marriages in 2003.... And they are willing to say that any citizen who does not agree with that, who adheres to what was, until 15 years ago, the unanimous judgment of all generations and all societies, stands against the Constitution.

The opinion is couched in a style that is as pretentious as its content is egotistic. It is one thing for separate concurring or dissenting opinions to contain extravagances, even silly extravagances, of thought and expression; it is something else for the official opinion of the Court to do so. Of course the opinion's showy profundities are often profoundly incoherent.... The world does not expect logic and precision in poetry or inspirational pop-philosophy; it demands them in the law. The stuff contained in today's opinion has to diminish this Court's reputation for clear thinking and sober analysis. If, even as the price to be paid for a fifth vote, I ever joined an opinion for the Court that began: "The Constitution promises liberty to all within its reach, a liberty that includes certain specific rights that allow persons, within a lawful realm, to define and express their identity," I would hide my head in a bag. The Supreme Court of the United States has descended from the disciplined legal reasoning of John Marshall and Joseph Story to the mystical aphorisms of the fortune cookie.

Hubris is sometimes defined as o'erweening pride; and pride, we know, goeth before a fall.... With each decision of ours that takes from the People a question properly left to them—with each decision that is unabashedly based not on law, but on the "reasoned judgment" of a bare majority of this Court—we move one step closer to being reminded of our impotence.

Justice Thomas issued a dissent joined by Justice Scalia.

The Court's decision today is at odds not only with the Constitution, but with the principles upon which our Nation was built. Since well before 1787, liberty has been understood as freedom from government action, not entitlement to government benefits. The Framers created our Constitution to preserve that understanding of liberty. Yet the majority invokes our Constitution in the name of a "liberty" that the Framers would not have recognized, to the detriment of the liberty they sought to protect. Along the way, it rejects the idea—captured in our Declaration of Independence—that human dignity is innate and suggests instead that it comes from the Government. This distortion of our Constitution not only ignores the text, it inverts the relationship between the individual and the state in our Republic. I cannot agree with it.

... I have elsewhere explained the dangerous fiction of treating the Due Process Clause as a font of substantive rights.... It distorts the constitutional text, which guarantees only whatever "process" is "due" before a person is deprived of life, liberty, and property.... Worse, it invites judges to do exactly what the majority has done here—"'roa[m] at large in the constitutional field' guided only by their personal views" as to the "fundamental rights" protected by that document....

By straying from the text of the Constitution, substantive due process exalts judges at the expense of the People from whom they derive their authority.... [Petitioners] ask nine judges on this Court to enshrine their definition of marriage in the Federal Constitution and thus put it beyond the reach of the normal democratic process for the entire Nation. That a "bare majority" of this Court ... is able to grant this wish, wiping out with a stroke of the keyboard the results of the political process in over 30 States....

Even if the doctrine of substantive due process were somehow defensible ... petitioners still would not have a claim. To invoke the protection of the Due Process Clause ... a party must first identify a deprivation of "life, liberty, or property." ... Even assuming that the "liberty" in those Clauses encompasses something more than freedom from physical restraint, it would not include the types of rights claimed by the majority. In the American legal tradition, liberty has long been understood as individual freedom *from* governmental action, not as a right *to* a particular governmental entitlement....

Petitioners claim that as a matter of "liberty," they are entitled to access privileges and benefits that exist solely *because of* the government. They want, for example, to receive the State's *imprimatur* on their marriages—on state issued marriage licenses, death certificates, or other official forms. And they want to receive various monetary benefits, including reduced inheritance taxes upon the death of a spouse, compensation if a spouse dies as a result of a work-related injury, or loss of consortium damages in tort suits. But receiving governmental recognition and benefits has nothing to do with any understanding of "liberty" that the Framers would have recognized....

Aside from undermining the political processes that protect our liberty, the majority's decision threatens the religious liberty our Nation has long sought to protect.... In our society, marriage is not simply a governmental institution; it is a religious institution as well.... Today's decision might change the former, but it cannot change the latter. It appears all but inevitable that the two will come into conflict, particularly as individuals and churches are confronted with demands to participate in and endorse civil marriages between same-sex couples. The majority appears unmoved by that inevitability.... I respectfully dissent.

Justice Alito issued a dissent joined by Justices Scalia and Thomas.

... The question in these cases, however, is not what States *should* do about same-sex marriage but whether the Constitution answers that question for them. It does not. The Constitution leaves that question to be decided by the people of each State.

The Constitution says nothing about a right to same-sex marriage, but the Court holds that the term "liberty" in the Due Process Clause of the Fourteenth

Amendment encompasses this right.... For today's majority, it does not matter that the right to same-sex marriage lacks deep roots or even that it is contrary to long-established tradition. The Justices in the majority claim the authority to confer constitutional protection upon that right simply because they believe that it is fundamental.

Although the Court expresses the point in loftier terms, its argument is that the fundamental purpose of marriage is to promote the well-being of those who choose to marry.... And by benefitting persons who choose to wed, marriage indirectly benefits society because persons who live in stable, fulfilling, and supportive relationships make better citizens. It is for these reasons, the argument goes, that States encourage and formalize marriage, confer special benefits on married persons, and also impose some special obligations. This understanding of the States' reasons for recognizing marriage enables the majority to argue that same-sex marriage serves the States' objectives in the same way as opposite-sex marriage.

This understanding of marriage, which focuses almost entirely on the happiness of persons who choose to marry, is shared by many people today, but it is not the traditional one. For millennia, marriage was inextricably linked to the one thing that only an opposite-sex couple can do: procreate....

Today's decision usurps the constitutional right of the people to decide whether to keep or alter the traditional understanding of marriage.... It will be used to vilify Americans who are unwilling to assent to the new orthodoxy.... By imposing its own views on the entire country, the majority facilitates the marginalization of the many Americans who have traditional ideas.... [I]f that sentiment prevails, the Nation will experience bitter and lasting wounds.

... I do not doubt that my colleagues in the majority sincerely see in the Constitution a vision of liberty that happens to coincide with their own. But this sincerity is cause for concern, not comfort. What it evidences is the deep and perhaps irremediable corruption of our legal culture's conception of constitutional interpretation.

Dramatic as it was both in substance and tone, the *Obergefell* ruling did not deal with the much wider array of challenges that current laws and practices engender with respect to sexual orientation or identity. In this respect, it is comparable to *Brown v. Board of Education* in that *Brown* was an extremely important substantive and symbolic victory for civil rights aimed especially at that point at African Americans, but it focused on only one aspect of civil rights challenges with respect to race, and much more would be needed to address that wider picture. The same is true of the situation following the *Obergefell* opinion.

Social Exclusion and the Law

As was true of discrimination against women, Americans have been excluded from certain activities or groups by virtue of their sexual orientation or identity. Indeed, as Chapter 10 explained, the Supreme Court decided *Roberts v. Jaycees*, an important case about such gender-based exclusions, in 1984.[43] With that in mind, LGBT groups pressed to be included in various activities and groups to break the exclusion, to express their pride in their identity, and to join in community activity and social groups that are attractive to any other person in the community.

The City of Boston, Massachusetts has a variety of ethnic groups who regularly celebrate their heritage with parades and other activities, one of which is the annual celebration in

South Boston of Evacuation Day (the departure of British troops in 1776), along with a celebration of St. Patrick, the patron saint of Ireland. In 1947 Mayor James Michael Curley handed over the authority for the St. Patrick's Day–Evacuation Day Parade to a group known as the South Boston Allied War Veterans Council.[44] A group of gay, lesbian, and bisexual Irish residents of Boston formed a group and applied to participate in the parade. They were rejected, but obtained a court order allowing them to march. They participated and the event went forward without incident. They applied again the following year and were again rejected. Again, they sued, and the trial court found that it was not a private event but a public one and rejected the exclusion, citing the *Roberts v. Jaycees* ruling by the U.S. Supreme Court. That ruling was affirmed by the Supreme Judicial Court of Massachusetts.[45]

The U.S. Supreme Court unanimously reversed the Massachusetts court. Justice Souter, writing for the unanimous Court, stated: "The issue in this case is whether Massachusetts may require private citizens who organize a parade to include among the marchers a group imparting a message the organizers do not wish to convey. We hold that such a mandate violates the First Amendment."[46] Justice Souter then went to what he saw as the core of the matter:

> Rather like a composer, the Council selects the expressive units of the parade from potential participants, and though the score may not produce a particularized message, each contingent's expression in the Council's eyes comports with what merits celebration on that day. Even if this view gives the Council credit for a more considered judgment than it actively made, the Council clearly decided to exclude a message it did not like from the communication it chose to make, and that is enough to invoke its right as a private speaker to shape its expression by speaking on one subject while remaining silent on another. The message it disfavored is not difficult to identify. Although GLIB's point (like the Council's) is not wholly articulate, a contingent marching behind the organization's banner would at least bear witness to the fact that some Irish are gay, lesbian, or bisexual, and the presence of the organized marchers would suggest their view that people of their sexual orientations have as much claim to unqualified social acceptance as heterosexuals and indeed as members of parade units organized around other identifying characteristics. The parade's organizers may not believe these facts about Irish sexuality to be so, or they may object to unqualified social acceptance of gays and lesbians or have some other reason for wishing to keep GLIB's message out of the parade. But whatever the reason, it boils down to the choice of a speaker not to propound a particular point of view, and that choice is presumed to lie beyond the government's power to control.[47]

This ruling dealt a dramatic blow to groups who had been working diligently to advance civil rights with respect to sexual orientation and identity. Media reports made clear the frustration those advocates experienced in the wake of the Boston ruling. The Atlanta Journal and Constitution observed:

> Gay rights organizations have been on the losing end of a string of court decisions, seemingly confirming a rightward tilt against them: The Virginia Supreme Court last month took custody of a 3-year-old boy away from his lesbian mother, ruling that she would bring "social condemnation" on him. A federal court threw out the case of a gay sailor being forced out of the Navy and upheld the constitutionality of the "don't ask, don't tell" policy. Last week, a federal appeals court ruled in connection with a Cincinnati case that gays and lesbians are not entitled to protection from discrimination under the Constitution, leaving cities and states free to repeal gay and lesbian

rights ordinances, or ban them from ever being passed. This week, the Supreme Court ruled that organizers of a St. Patrick's Day parade in Boston could bar gay and lesbian groups from marching.[48]

However, there was more to come from the U.S. Supreme Court, including a very important ruling concerning the Boy Scouts. It was important not only because of the merits of that particular exclusion, but also because of the manner in which the Court appeared to move significantly away from its *Jaycees* opinion. It was not only the reinterpretation of the *Jaycees* case that so angered gay rights advocates, but also its tone. This time Justice Souter was on the other side of the case, and the Court was anything but unanimous.

Boy Scouts of America v. Dale

530 U.S. 640 (2000)

INTRODUCTION: The majority opinion provides a very brief statement of facts, but notice how different this case looks when the reader sees the facts presented in the dissents that were not mentioned by the majority. The reason the facts are so important in this case is because it becomes clear that the organization was attempting to construct a policy and definition of message that did not actually exist in the organization's core materials when the action against Mr. Dale started.

Another factor that was not clear from the case itself is the fact that so many scout units are sponsored by churches. The organization found itself—and continues to find itself—in the middle of its reliance on these groups, which regard the Boy Scouts as helping with socialization into a set of values with which they agree and that fits the church teachings, on the one hand, and the movement of the society in general and the law in particular toward recognition of civil rights related to sexual identity and orientation, on the other.[49]

Chief Justice Rehnquist wrote the opinion for the Court.

... The Boy Scouts is a private, not-for-profit organization engaged in instilling its system of values in young people. The Boy Scouts asserts that homosexual conduct is inconsistent with the values it seeks to instill. Respondent is James Dale, a former Eagle Scout whose adult membership in the Boy Scouts was revoked when the Boy Scouts learned that he is an avowed homosexual and gay rights activist. The New Jersey Supreme Court held that New Jersey's public accommodations law requires that the Boy Scouts admit Dale. This case presents the question whether applying New Jersey's public accommodations law in this way violates the Boy Scouts' First Amendment right of expressive association. We hold that it does....

Dale applied for adult membership in the Boy Scouts in 1989. The Boy Scouts approved his application for the position of assistant scoutmaster of Troop 73.... After arriving at Rutgers [University], Dale first acknowledged to himself and others that he is gay. He quickly became involved with, and eventually became the co-president of the Rutgers University Lesbian/Gay Alliance. In 1990, Dale attended a seminar addressing the psychological and health needs of lesbian and gay teenagers. A newspaper covering the event interviewed Dale about his advocacy of homosexual teenagers' need for gay role models. In early July 1990, the newspaper published the interview and Dale's photograph over a caption identifying him as the co-president of the Lesbian/Gay Alliance.

Later that month, Dale received a letter from Monmouth Council Executive James Kay revoking his adult membership. Dale wrote to Kay requesting the reason for Monmouth Council's decision. Kay responded by letter that the Boy Scouts "specifically forbid membership to homosexuals." ... In 1992, Dale filed a complaint against the Boy Scouts in the New Jersey Superior Court. The complaint alleged that the Boy Scouts had violated New Jersey's public accommodations statute and its common law by revoking Dale's membership based solely on his sexual orientation.... Ultimately, The New Jersey Supreme Court ... held that the Boy Scouts was a place of public accommodation subject to the public accommodations law, that the organization was not exempt from the law under any of its express exceptions, and that the Boy Scouts violated the law by revoking Dale's membership based on his avowed homosexuality....

In *Roberts v. United States Jaycees* ... we [affirmed the] "right to associate with others in pursuit of a wide variety of political, social, economic, educational, religious, and cultural ends." This right is crucial in preventing the majority from imposing its views on groups that would rather express other, perhaps unpopular, ideas.... Forcing a group to accept certain members may impair the ability of the group to express those views ... that it intends to express. Thus, "[f]reedom of association ... plainly presupposes a freedom not to associate." ...

The forced inclusion of an unwanted person in a group infringes the group's freedom of expressive association if the presence of that person affects in a significant way the group's ability to advocate public or private viewpoints.... But the freedom of expressive association ... is not absolute. We have held that the freedom could be overridden "by regulations adopted to serve compelling state interests, unrelated to the suppression of ideas, that cannot be achieved through means significantly less restrictive of associational freedoms." ... To determine whether a group is protected by the First Amendment's expressive associational right, we must determine whether the group engages in "expressive association." ... [T]o come within its ambit, a group must engage in some form of expression, whether it be public or private.

... The Boy Scouts seeks to instill [a particular set of] values by having its adult leaders spend time with the youth members, instructing and engaging them in activities like camping, archery, and fishing. During the time spent with the youth members, the scoutmasters and assistant scoutmasters inculcate them with the Boy Scouts' values—both expressly and by example. It seems indisputable that an association that seeks to transmit such a system of values engages in expressive activity....

Given that the Boy Scouts engages in expressive activity, we must determine whether the forced inclusion of Dale as an assistant scoutmaster would significantly affect the Boy Scouts' ability to advocate public or private viewpoints.... The Boy Scouts asserts that homosexual conduct is inconsistent with the values embodied in the Scout Oath and Law, particularly with the values represented by the terms "morally straight" and "clean." Obviously, the Scout Oath and Law do not expressly mention sexuality or sexual orientation.... And the terms "morally straight" and "clean" are by no means self-defining. Different people would attribute to those terms very different meanings.... The Boy Scouts asserts that it "teaches that homosexual conduct is not morally straight" ... and that it does "not want to promote homosexual conduct as a legitimate form of behavior." ...

We must then determine whether Dale's presence as an assistant scoutmaster would significantly burden the Boy Scouts' desire to not "promote homosexual conduct as a legitimate form of behavior." ... As we give deference to an association's assertions regarding the nature of its expression, we must also give deference to an association's view of what would impair its expression.... That is not to say that an expressive association can erect a shield against anti-discrimination laws simply by asserting that mere acceptance of a member from a particular group would impair its message. But here Dale, by his own admission, is one of a group of gay Scouts who have "become leaders in their community and are open and honest about their sexual orientation." ... Dale's presence in the Boy Scouts would, at the very least, force the organization to send a message, both to the youth members and the world, that the Boy Scouts accepts homosexual conduct as a legitimate form of behavior....

As the presence of GLIB in Boston's St. Patrick's Day parade would have interfered with the parade organizers' choice not to propound a particular point of view [*Hurley v. Irish-American Gay, Lesbian and Bisexual Group of Boston*], the presence of Dale as an assistant scoutmaster would just as surely interfere with the Boy Scout's choice not to propound a point of view contrary to its beliefs.... First, associations do not have to associate for the "purpose" of disseminating a certain message in order to be entitled to the protections of the First Amendment. An association must merely engage in expressive activity that could be impaired in order to be entitled to protection....

Second, even if the Boy Scouts discourages Scout leaders from disseminating views on sexual issues ... the First Amendment protects the Boy Scouts' method of expression. If the Boy Scouts wishes Scout leaders to avoid questions of sexuality and teach only by example, this fact does not negate the sincerity of its belief discussed above.

Third, the First Amendment simply does not require that every member of a group agree on every issue in order for the group's policy to be "expressive association." The Boy Scouts takes an official position with respect to homosexual conduct, and that is sufficient for First Amendment purposes.... The presence of an avowed homosexual and gay rights activist in an assistant scoutmaster's uniform sends a distinctly different message from the presence of a heterosexual assistant scoutmaster who is on record as disagreeing with Boy Scouts policy. The Boy Scouts has a First Amendment right to choose to send one message but not the other....

Having determined that the Boy Scouts is an expressive association and that the forced inclusion of Dale would significantly affect its expression, we inquire whether the application of New Jersey's public accommodations law to require that the Boy Scouts accept Dale as an assistant scoutmaster runs afoul of the Scouts' freedom of expressive association. We conclude that it does.

State public accommodations laws were originally enacted to prevent discrimination in traditional places of public accommodation—like inns and trains.... Over time, [as] the public accommodations laws have expanded to cover more places ... such as restaurants, bars, and hotels, to membership organizations such as the Boy Scouts, the potential for conflict between state public accommodations laws and the First Amendment rights of organizations has increased. We recognized in cases such as *Roberts* and *Duarte* [*Board of Directors of Rotary Int'l v. Rotary Club of Duarte*, 481 U.S. 537 (1987)] that States have a compelling interest in eliminating discrimination against women in public accommodations. But in each of these cases we went on to conclude that the enforcement of these statutes would not materially interfere with the ideas that the organization sought to express.... We thereupon concluded in each of these cases that the organizations' First Amendment rights were not violated by the application of the States' public accommodations laws....

In *Hurley*, we applied traditional First Amendment analysis to hold that the application of the Massachusetts public accommodations law to a parade violated the First Amendment rights of the parade organizers.... We have already concluded that a state requirement that the Boy Scouts retain Dale as an assistant scoutmaster would significantly burden the organization's right to oppose or disfavor homosexual conduct. The state interests embodied in New Jersey's public accommodations law do not justify such a severe intrusion on the Boy Scouts' rights to freedom of expressive association. That being the case, we hold that the First Amendment prohibits the State from imposing such a requirement through the application of its public accommodations law....

Justice Stevens wrote a dissenting opinion joined by Justices Souter, Ginsburg, and Breyer.

... The majority holds that New Jersey's law violates BSA's right to associate and its right to free speech. But that law does not "impose any serious burdens" on BSA's "collective effort on behalf of [its] shared goals," *Jaycees*, ... nor does it force BSA to communicate any message that it does not wish to endorse. New Jersey's law, therefore, abridges no constitutional right of the Boy Scouts.

... To bolster its claim that its shared goals include teaching that homosexuality is wrong, BSA directs our attention to two terms appearing in the Scout Oath and Law. The first is the phrase "morally straight," which appears in the Oath...; the second term is the word "clean," which appears in a list of 12 characteristics together comprising the Scout Law.... The Boy Scout Handbook defines "morally straight," as such: "To be a person of strong character, guide your life with honesty, purity, and justice. Respect and defend the rights of all people. Your relationships with others should be honest and open. Be clean in your speech and actions, and faithful in your religious beliefs. The values you follow as a Scout will help you become virtuous and self-reliant." ...

As for the term "clean," the Boy Scout Handbook offers the following: "A Scout is CLEAN. A Scout keeps his body and mind fit and clean. He chooses the company of those who live by these same ideals.... There's another kind of dirt that won't come off by washing. It is the kind that shows up in foul language and harmful thoughts. Swear words, profanity, and dirty stories are weapons that ridicule other people and hurt their feelings. The same is true of racial slurs and jokes making fun of ethnic groups or people with physical or mental limitations. A Scout knows there is no kindness or honor in such mean-spirited behavior. He avoids it in his own words and deeds. He defends those who are targets of insults." ...

It is plain as the light of day that neither one of these principles—"morally straight" and "clean"—says the slightest thing about homosexuality. Indeed, neither term in the Boy Scouts' Law and Oath expresses any position whatsoever on sexual matters. BSA's published guidance on that topic underscores this point. Scouts, for example, are directed to receive their sex education at home or in school, but not from the organization: "Your parents or guardian or a sex education teacher should give you the facts about sex that you must know." *Boy Scout Handbook*.... To be sure, Scouts are not forbidden from asking their Scoutmaster about issues of a sexual nature, but Scoutmasters are, literally, the last person Scouts are encouraged to ask.... Moreover, Scoutmasters are specifically directed to steer curious adolescents to other sources of information....

The Court seeks to fill the void by pointing to a statement of "policies and procedures relating to homosexuality and Scouting" signed by BSA's President and

Chief Scout Executive in 1978 and addressed to the members of the Executive Committee of the national organization.... But when the entire 1978 letter is read, BSA's position is far more equivocal [than the majority suggests] ....

First, at most this letter simply adopts an exclusionary membership policy. But simply adopting such a policy has never been considered sufficient, by itself, to prevail on a right to associate claim.... Second, the 1978 policy was never publicly expressed—unlike, for example, the Scout's duty to be "obedient." It was an internal memorandum, never circulated beyond the few members of BSA's Executive Committee.... Third, it is apparent that the draftsmen of the policy statement foresaw the possibility that laws against discrimination might one day be amended to protect homosexuals from employment discrimination.... Fourth, the 1978 statement simply says that homosexuality is not "appropriate." It makes no effort to connect that statement to a shared goal or expressive activity of the Boy Scouts....

It is clear, then, that nothing in these policy statements [issued before Dale was terminated] supports BSA's claim. The only policy written before the revocation of Dale's membership was an equivocal, undisclosed statement that evidences no connection between the group's discriminatory intentions and its expressive interests....

BSA's claim finds no support in our cases.... For example, we have routinely and easily rejected assertions of this right by expressive organizations with discriminatory membership policies, such as private schools, law firms, and labor organizations. In fact, until today, we have never once found a claimed right to associate in the selection of members to prevail in the face of a State's anti-discrimination law....

In *Roberts* ... we addressed just such a conflict.... [W]e held that "infringements on that right may be justified by regulations adopted to serve compelling state interests, unrelated to the suppression of ideas, that cannot be achieved through means significantly less restrictive of associational freedoms." ... We found the State's purpose of eliminating discrimination is a compelling state interest that is unrelated to the suppression of ideas.... We also held that Minnesota's law is the least restrictive means of achieving that interest....

We took a similar approach in *Rotary Int'l v. Rotary Club of Duarte*, 481 U.S. 537 (1987) ..., holding that "the evidence fails to demonstrate that admitting women to Rotary Clubs will affect in any significant way the existing members' ability to carry out their various purposes." ...

Several principles are made perfectly clear by *Jaycees* and *Rotary Club*. First, to prevail on a claim of expressive association in the face of a State's anti-discrimination law, it is not enough simply to engage in some kind of expressive activity.... Second, it is not enough to adopt an openly avowed exclusionary membership policy.... Third, it is not sufficient merely to articulate some connection between the group's expressive activities and its exclusionary policy.... As in *Jaycees*, there is "no basis in the record for concluding that admission of [homosexuals] will impede the [Boy Scouts'] ability to engage in [its] protected activities or to disseminate its preferred views" and New Jersey's law "requires no change in [BSA's] creed." ... [L]ike Rotary Club, New Jersey's law "does not require [BSA] to abandon or alter any of" its activities....

BSA has not contended, nor does the record support, that Dale had ever advocated a view on homosexuality to his troop before his membership was revoked.... The majority ... contends that Dale's mere presence among the Boy Scouts will itself force the group to convey a message about homosexuality.... Unlike GLIB,

Dale did not carry a banner or a sign; he did not distribute any fact sheet; and he expressed no intent to send any message....

The only apparent explanation for the majority's holding, then, is that homosexuals are simply so different from the rest of society that their presence alone ... should be singled out for special First Amendment treatment. Under the majority's reasoning, an openly gay male is irreversibly affixed with the label "homosexual." That label, even though unseen, communicates a message that permits his exclusion wherever he goes. His openness is the sole and sufficient justification for his ostracism. Though unintended, reliance on such a justification is tantamount to a constitutionally prescribed symbol of inferiority....

The State of New Jersey has decided that people who are open and frank about their sexual orientation are entitled to equal access to employment as school teachers, police officers, librarians, athletic coaches, and a host of other jobs filled by citizens who serve as role models for children and adults alike. Dozens of Scout units throughout the State are sponsored by public agencies, such as schools and fire departments, that employ such role models. BSA's affiliation with numerous public agencies that comply with New Jersey's law against discrimination cannot be understood to convey any particular message endorsing or condoning the activities of all these people.

Unfavorable opinions about homosexuals "have ancient roots." ... Over the years, however, interaction with real people, rather than mere adherence to traditional ways of thinking about members of unfamiliar classes, have modified those opinions. A few examples: The American Psychiatric Association's and the American Psychological Association's removal of "homosexuality" from their lists of mental disorders; a move toward greater understanding within some religious communities; ... Georgia's invalidation of the statute upheld in *Bowers*; and New Jersey's enactment of the provision at issue in this case....

That such prejudices are still prevalent and that they have caused serious and tangible harm to countless members of the class New Jersey seeks to protect are established matters of fact that neither the Boy Scouts nor the Court disputes. That harm can only be aggravated by the creation of a constitutional shield for a policy that is itself the product of a habitual way of thinking about strangers. As Justice Brandeis so wisely advised, "we must be ever on our guard, lest we erect our prejudices into legal principles." ...

Justice Souter wrote a dissenting opinion joined by Justices Ginsburg and Breyer.

... The right of expressive association does not, of course, turn on the popularity of the views advanced by a group that claims protection. Whether the group appears to this Court to be in the vanguard or rearguard of social thinking is irrelevant to the group's rights. I conclude that BSA has not made out an expressive association claim, therefore, not because of what BSA may espouse, but because of its failure to make sexual orientation the subject of any unequivocal advocacy, using the channels it customarily employs to state its message. As Justice Stevens explains, no group can claim a right of expressive association without identifying a clear position to be advocated over time in an unequivocal way. To require less, and to allow exemption from a public accommodations statute based on any individual's difference from an alleged group ideal, however expressed and however inconsistently claimed, would convert the right of expressive association into an easy trump of any anti-discrimination law.

It was perhaps an ironic twist on the exclusion problem when in 2006 the Supreme Court ruled against law schools that sought to bar military recruiters from campus because of the military ban on gays in the armed services. When law schools began to apply their nondiscrimination policies to military recruiters, Congress countered by adopting the so-called Solomon amendment that imposed penalties in the form of cuts in federal funds to schools that would not permit the military efforts on their campuses. A unanimous Supreme Court with an opinion by Chief Justice Roberts upheld the Solomon amendment and made it clear to law schools that they would have to deal with the congressional penalties.[50] The message that went forward was that the military could discriminate against gays and lesbians, but civil rights advocates in various institutions could not penalize the military for that behavior. The military and the White House may have won that particular battle, but, as gay rights advocates saw it, this ruling helped them to dramatize the fundamental absurdity of the "Don't Ask, Don't Tell" policy, and a number of leading media outlets recognized their point.[51] The *Washington Post* editorialized: "A combination of bigotry and inertia keeps the gay ban in place. Now that the military has proved it can constitutionally exempt itself from university nondiscrimination rules, Congress should decide whether it really wants a military that requires such an exemption."[52]

In 2010, however, the Court ruled in favor of a Hastings College of Law "all comers" policy, under which student groups seeking university recognition and support had to allow all students to join. The school rejected the application of the Christian Legal Society for recognition and the society complained, unsuccessfully, that the university was compelling the group to accept members who did not accept its views on sexual orientation.[53]

It was bad enough, to many gay rights advocates, that there was even a need for discussion of exclusion of people based on sexual orientation or identity at such a late date in the nation's history, but it was even worse that the Supreme Court would render some of the opinions that it did.

The Workplace–Employment Discrimination

It was one thing for the nation to have what appeared to be rather general discussions about making progress against social exclusion but, to some at least, it was even more pressing to deal with an ongoing history of discrimination in the workplace. It may have taken nearly a decade to see the enactment of the hate crimes legislation, but the Employment Non-Discrimination Act (ENDA) that would add to the existing Civil Rights Act protection against discrimination on the basis of sexual orientation or identity has never been passed. That is true even though it was first introduced in 1994 and has been in every Congress since then.[54] Ironically, polling suggests that Americans think discrimination against LGBT persons in the workplace is already prohibited by law, but 29 states have no such protections and no federal statute has been enacted to provide that protection. That is not to say that there have not been important actions, both positive and negative during these years.

Evolving Case Law on Employment and Sexual Identity and Orientation but not Supreme Court Support

Although the Supreme Court has not ruled in favor of workplace protections, there have been many cases decided in lower courts, both before and after the *Lawrence* decision, that are continuing a discussion of what, if any, rights are available. There have been presidential actions as well that have led to administrative rulemaking at the federal level. There have also been steps taken at the state level. However, there have also been reactions against gay rights protections. Even so, there is little resolution and great uncertainty with respect to civil rights protections in the workplace concerning sexual orientation and identity.

As the Congressional Research Service explained to Congress in a 2013 study, "Although some have argued that sex discrimination encompasses sexual orientation discrimination, the courts have generally rejected that theory, reasoning that the prohibition against sex discrimination refers only to the traditional definition of biological sex."[55]

Even though there are numerous cases denying protections in the workplace, what many who have been subject to this kind of discrimination know is not so much the legal argument as the kinds of stories and personal experiences that brought about the litigation in the first place, and that are so often repeated because of the lack of protections. In a case involving a woman who applied for a job with the Federal Bureau of Investigation,[56] the court noted that:

> Eight years ago, the Bureau formally represented to this court that it "has always had an absolute policy of dismissing proven or admitted homosexuals from its employ." *Ashton v. Civiletti*, 613 F.2d 923, 926 (D.C. Cir. 1979). Two months later, FBI Director Webster issued a somewhat different formulation of the Bureau's position toward homosexuality: "Now we treat it as a factor, and I must say in candor, it's a significant factor. It's a troublesome thing; I hope that the particular case will be handled with fairness and justice and I hope that at some point we will have a better understanding of the problem and the policy that should be addressed to it."[57]

However, the court said:

> John Mintz, an Assistant Director of the FBI and the FBI's Legal Counsel, answered inquiries from law schools and after promising that there was no illegal discrimination "conceded that: in fairness ... based upon experience, I can offer no specific encouragement that a homosexual applicant will be found who satisfies all of the requirements."[58]

The court concluded that the FBI decision was nonreviewable.

In a case involving the CIA that went to the Supreme Court, a man who had successfully served first as a clerk-typist and later as an electronics technician was fired after he had stated that he was homosexual. He passed a polygraph test, indicating that he had not had any "sexual relations with any foreign nationals and maintained that he had not disclosed classified information to any of his sexual partners." He was nevertheless fired from his position. He sued on both statutory and constitutional grounds, but the Supreme Court found the claims based on statute to be unreviewable. However, it found that this idea of nonreviewability did not apply to his claims that the firing violated the due process clause and denied him the equal protection of the law.[59] When the case was sent back to the district court to consider the constitutional argument, that court concluded that the government action was rationally related to the legitimate interest of protecting national security and that the court should defer to the government's judgment on that point.[60] On the other hand, the Court concluded that there was a due process problem and ruled in favor of the challenger. On appeal, the D.C. Circuit Court of Appeals reversed the district court due process ruling as well, leaving Mr. Doe with no recourse.[61]

The difficulty from the employee's perspective was that, as the quotes from the FBI officials above indicated, the bases for these actions were simply homophobic stereotypes. Even what the courts generally saw as a rational basis—the fear of blackmail by foreign security agents—was circular. The argument ran that because society viewed homosexuality as such a terrible thing, anyone who was gay would have to hide their sexual orientation and that secret would make them subject to blackmail. But obviously if a gay person publicly acknowledged their sexual orientation to their employer as well as their family and friends, there would be no way to blackmail them. Therefore, the blackmail opportunity came principally from the discriminatory behavior of the employer. It was maddening that none of the decisionmakers involved or the courts reviewing them would call that circular logic what it was. In addition to the fundamental flaw in the logic, it was also a case of blaming the victim.

If the treatment of these applicants and employees in the federal agencies was bad, the stories that emerged in some state and local governments and in private firms was in some situations even more insidious and vicious. One case arose in a Utah case brought by Wendy Weaver. She had been a high school teacher for nineteen years and an extremely successful women's soccer coach, having led the Spanish Fork High School in the Nebo School District to four state championships. She took a leave from the role as a coach while she completed a graduate degree, but planned to return to coaching 1997. U.S. District Judge Bruce Jenkins explained what happened.

> In the late spring and early summer of 1997, Ms. Weaver began preparing for the upcoming school volleyball season—as she did in the past—by organizing two summer volleyball camps for prospective team players. As usual, these camps were to be held at Spanish Fork High School in June and July of 1997. Ms. Weaver telephoned prospective volleyball team members to inform them of the camp schedules. One of the calls went to a senior team member. During the conversation, the team member asked Ms. Weaver. "Are you gay"? Ms. Weaver truthfully responded, "Yes." The team member then told Ms. Weaver that she would not play on the volleyball team in the fall. On July 14, 1997, the team member and her parents met with defendants Almon Mosher, Director of Human Resources for the Nebo School District, and Larry Kimball, Director of Secondary Education for the Nebo School District, and told them that Ms. Weaver told them that she is gay and that the team member decided she would not play volleyball.
>
> In April of 1997, Gary Weaver, Ms. Weaver's ex-husband and a school psychologist for the Nebo School District, spoke with Principal Wadley about Ms. Weaver's sexual orientation. In May of 1997, Nedra Call, the Curriculum Coordinator for the School District, received two calls concerning Ms. Weaver's "lifestyle and her actions." She related the substance of these calls to defendant Mosher. Defendant Dennis Poulsen, Superintendent of the Nebo School District, also received calls about Ms. Weaver. In addition, several adults affiliated or formerly affiliated with the school contacted Principal Wadley with comments or questions about Ms. Weaver's sexual orientation. Principal Wadley held a meeting with his two assistant principals to discuss Ms. Weaver's sexual orientation. On May 22, 1997, before the phone conversation with Ms. Weaver, the team member and her mother telephoned Principal Wadley to let him know that the team member would not be playing volleyball because she was uncomfortable playing on the team knowing that Ms. Weaver is gay. On May 22nd, Principal Wadley discussed Ms. Weaver's sexual orientation with defendant Larry Kimball. Even the School Advisory Council wanted to discuss Ms. Weaver's sexual orientation.
>
> In response to these reports, and after meeting again with the team member's family on July 14, 1997, defendants Mosher and Kimball discussed taking some action against Ms. Weaver because they felt Ms. Weaver's comments about her sexual orientation were in "violation of district policy." Several days later, on July 21, 1997, Ms. Weaver met with Principal Wadley, who informed her that she

would not be assigned to coach volleyball for the 1997–98 school year. This discussion was memorialized in a letter to Ms. Weaver dated the same day but sent subsequently.

The following day, Ms. Weaver was called to a meeting at the School District office and presented a letter, printed on the School District letterhead, which reads in part: "The District has received reports that you have made public and expressed to students your homosexual orientation and lifestyle. If these reports are true, we are concerned about the potential disruption in the school community and advise you of the following:

You are not to make any comments, announcements or statements to students, staff members, or parents of students regarding your homosexual orientation or lifestyle.

If students, staff members, or parents of students ask about your sexual orientation or anything concerning the subject, you shall tell them that the subject is private and personal and inappropriate to discuss with them.

This memo is to place you on notice of the expectations the school district has for you concerning this matter. A violation of these requirements may jeopardize your job and be cause for termination.

The letter was drafted by defendant Mosher, signed by him and Larry Kimball, was reviewed by defendant Dennis Poulsen, delivered to Ms. Weaver, and placed in her personnel file.

On August 8, 1997, a similar letter was issued to Gary Weaver. It reads in part: The District has received reports that you have made remarks within the school setting about your ex-wife's sexual orientation. If these reports are true we ... advise you of the following:

You are not to make comments, announcements or statements to students, staff members, or parents regarding your ex-wife's sexual orientation.

If students, staff members or parents of students ask about your ex-wife's sexual orientation, you shall tell them the subject is private and personal and inappropriate to discuss with them.

This memo is to place you on notice of the expectations the school district has for you concerning this matter. A violation of these requirements may jeopardize your job and be cause for termination.[62]

Jenkins began his analysis of the legal questions by stating the situation in clear terms:

Despite mounting evidence that gay males and lesbians suffer from employment discrimination and, as recent events in Wyoming remind us, other more life-threatening expressions of bias,[63] courts, including the Supreme Court, have not yet recognized a person's sexual orientation as a status that deserves heightened protection. To date, Congress has expressly prohibited employment discrimination on the basis of race, religion, national origin, gender, age, and disability, but not sexual orientation. As of this year, eleven states and the District of Columbia offer statutory protection against discrimination on the basis of sexual orientation; thirty-nine states, including Utah, do not.

Nevertheless, the Fourteenth Amendment of the United States Constitution entitles all persons to equal protection under the law.... It appears that the plain language of the Fourteenth Amendment's Equal Protection Clause prohibits a state government or agency from engaging in intentional discrimination—even on the basis of sexual orientation—absent some rational basis for so doing. The Supreme Court has recognized that an "irrational prejudice" cannot provide the rational basis to support a state action against an equal protection challenge.

He quoted the Supreme Court's opinion in *City of Cleburne v. Cleburne Living Center* for the point that even under the rational basis standard:

> "'a bare ... desire to harm a politically unpopular group' is not a legitimate state interest.... Indeed, the Court noted that 'mere negative attitudes, or fear, unsubstantiated by factors which are properly cognizable in [the circumstances], are not permissible bases' for differential treatment by the government...."[64]

Jenkins also cited cases concluding that simple "animus directed at a defined minority ... cannot be supported under the Equal Protection Clause." See, e.g., *Harris v. McRae*, 448 U.S. 297, 322 (1980) and specifically the *Romer v. Evans* case, discussed earlier in this chapter, on the same point. In the end, he concluded that the school district's action violated both the equal protection clause and Ms. Weaver's First Amendment rights.

Even so, her difficulties were not over. After winning her case in federal court, some students, parents, and even taxpayers who had no students in the system tried to get officials to fire Weaver. Ultimately, they sued in state court. The ACLU of Utah represented Weaver and argued that the case was nothing more than a continuation of attacks against her because she was a lesbian and that there was no foundation for a case against her. The district court issued a lengthy opinion dismissing claimed causes of action and denying standing to some of the plaintiffs. The court indicated what the defects were in the complaint and allowed time to file an amended complaint, but the plaintiffs appealed to the Utah Supreme Court. The state supreme court affirmed the lower court ruling and awarded legal fees for the appeal to Weaver.[65]

A Williamsburg, Ohio teacher who is a gay man found himself a target in another case that demonstrates the nature of actions taken to fire people because of their sexual orientation, and the discriminatory attitude and harsh behavior of the community and officials. His contract was not renewed. Again, the best way to convey the mood and character of the situation is to let the judge explain it.

> The lowest mark received by Glover in his first semester evaluation was in the category of conformity to professional standards. On the evaluation form, McEvoy [the person responsible for his teaching evaluations] added a comment to explain the low score: "Mr. Glover has used some indiscretions which may have had a detrimental effect on the respect he receives from students. He was warned at the beginning of the school year not to repeat such behavior." In fact, Glover had never received any warning and he had committed no indiscretion whatsoever. The low score was based on a false rumor which had been relayed to McEvoy. The rumor involved Glover and his partner, John Wright, allegedly holding hands at school during a holiday party.
>
> Superintendent Campbell testified that he first heard the rumor when a woman phoned him in early January, 1996. The woman was concerned because she had heard that Glover and Wright were holding hands at school during the sixth grade Christmas party. There had in fact been a Christmas party in December, and Glover had invited several adults, including Wright, to help out with the party. Other teachers at Williamsburg had also invited friends and spouses to help out at

holiday parties and other school events. Wright attended the party briefly to help with festivities and then left. At no time did Glover and Wright hold hands.

After receiving the phone call, Campbell reported the rumor to McEvoy. The testimony of Campbell and McEvoy conflicted over exactly how the information was presented to McEvoy. According to McEvoy, Campbell was upset when he reported the complaint to McEvoy, and Campbell presented it as the truth, not as a rumor. McEvoy then incorporated the alleged indiscretion into Glover's evaluation, giving him a rating of "poor" for conformity with professional standards. Neither Campbell nor McEvoy checked out the rumor or asked Glover about it.

On January 10, 1996, Glover met with McEvoy to review his first semester evaluation. Upon seeing the low mark for unidentified "indiscretions," Glover was understandably concerned and he asked McEvoy to explain. McEvoy told Glover that the low mark was due to his holding hands with Mr. Wright during the holiday party. Although Glover asked where McEvoy had heard the rumor, McEvoy would not reveal the source of the information. McEvoy told Glover that Mr. Wright was not to come to the school again. Glover protested that the hand-holding did not occur, and he urged McEvoy to speak with other adults who had attended the party.

Later, Glover asked for a meeting with McEvoy to further discuss the rumor and the low mark on his evaluation. A couple of weeks later, this meeting occurred with McEvoy, Campbell, Glover, and Kurt Blimline, a representative of the teachers union. In the interim, McEvoy had contacted certain parents who had attended the party, and he discovered that the rumor was false. Thus, McEvoy and Campbell informed Glover at the meeting that his evaluation would be revised. Glover asked Campbell for the name of the person who had reported the rumor, but Campbell refused to give the name. McEvoy ultimately revised Glover's teaching evaluation, giving Glover a "4" for conformity with professional standards. McEvoy removed the earlier comment about Glover's "indiscretions" and the fact the Glover had been warned not to repeat such behavior.

At the meeting, however, Campbell and McEvoy did not merely revise the evaluation to correct their earlier mistake. They also made efforts to warn Glover about his behavior. McEvoy and Campbell cautioned Glover about how easily rumors can start in a small, conservative community like Williamsburg. Although the hand-holding rumor was untrue, Campbell and McEvoy warned Glover to be careful not to do anything which might fuel rumors and upset the community.

McEvoy was not the only person to whom Campbell reported the alleged indiscretion. Sometime in early January, Campbell reported the incident to School Board, which was meeting in executive session. The exact date is unclear, but the meeting occurred after Campbell received the complaint about Glover and before the rumor was found to be untrue. Jan Humphries, a Board member, testified that Campbell told the Board he had received a complaint about Mr. Wright being in Glover's classroom during the holiday party. Other Board members had also heard of the rumor about Wright visiting the classroom, and people were "stirred up" about the incident. Campbell told the Board he had received some complaints and would check it out. Despite subsequently learning that the rumor was false, Campbell never reported back to the Board about the incident.

In the second semester, McEvoy increased his observations of Glover's teaching. Instead of conducting the required two observations per semester (as was done in the first semester), McEvoy made six observations. It appears that McEvoy's increased observations were motivated at least in part by a complaint he received from Board Member Jan Humphries. Humphries had a son in Glover's class who reported to her that the class was unruly. At some point early in the second semester, Humphries complained about this to McEvoy. The master contract for the Williamsburg School District provides that the Principal, upon hearing a concern from someone in the community, will notify the teacher of the nature of the concern and the identity of the concerned party. The teacher can then request a meeting with the Principal and the complainant to resolve the conflict. However, as when McEvoy heard the rumor regarding Glover's alleged indiscretion, McEvoy failed to follow this procedure and notify Glover. McEvoy failed to inform Glover of the complaint despite the fact that the complaining parent was also a member of the School Board.

After completing his observations, McEvoy produced a teaching evaluation for Glover for the second semester. Glover's scores dropped from the first semester evaluation.[66]

The district court ultimately found that the board had fired Glover because of his sexual orientation in violation of the equal protection clause.[67]

These cases show just how vicious and patently discriminatory some of the behaviors of those involved in targeting people because of their sexual orientation have been and, in some cases, continue to be. There was some success for the plaintiffs in these cases because they could seek redress under the Constitution, even though they could not obtain help under Title VII. However, as some of the cases mentioned to this point show, it is not common for courts to find that government failed the very low level rational basis test in absence of obviously egregious conduct as in the *Weaver* and *Glover* cases. Beyond that, the constitutional arguments are not even available when dealing with private employers.

The same kind of extreme behavior seen in these two cases is also present in many gender identity cases in which transgender employees or applicants are targeted. One example is a Salem, Ohio case in which an officer of the fire department was targeted based on the claim that his appearance and demeanor did not match the expectations for gender and were not "masculine enough." The facts as alleged indicated that the officer's superiors met with other city officials to determine how to fire Lt. Smith. Smith sued, the district court dismissed the case for failure to state a claim, but the Court of Appeals for the Sixth Circuit reversed and concluded that there was a claim under Title VII.[68] Indeed, the U.S. Department of Justice has taken the position in a number of cases that, whatever may be the limits of Title VII with respect to sexual orientation, where there is a case of sexual identity in which an individual is subjected to sexual stereotyping, the Supreme Court's ruling in *Price Waterhouse* means that this is a case of sex discrimination within the meaning of Title VII.[69] The Supreme Court has yet to rule on that argument with respect to gender identity.

A Lack of Congressional Support for Equality against a History of Discrimination in the Federal Government and Elsewhere

The battle on the congressional front has continued. In 2014 the Senate had passed the ENDA and there was pressure for House members to do so, despite opposition from the Speaker and other party leaders on the Republican side of the aisle. However, some gay rights groups withdrew their support for the legislation because of language in the bill that would allow what they considered broad exemptions that could be claimed for asserted religious reasons. Although there have for some time been exemptions from some protections under Title VII for religious employers, the ability to claim a religious exemption took on a whole new meaning after the Supreme Court's decision in the *Hobby Lobby* case in 2014.[70] *Hobby Lobby* was a case about the scope and nature of exemptions that could be claimed by a for-profit corporation under the Religious Freedom Restoration Act (RFRA).[71] This particular case involved claims to exemption from some requirements of the Patient Protection and Affordable Care Act (ACA) with respect to women's reproductive health care coverage by employers.[72] As the four dissenters in that case pointed out, the majority's reading of the scope of the coverage and scope of the exemption by virtue of RFRA was sweeping and would allow many organizations not previously regarded as religious to claim exceptions to a range of broad-based federal statutes. And for those that are more traditional religiously affiliated groups, it seemed more likely that they would be able claim more exceptions for more generally applicable policies in more circumstances than before. Hence media reports showed gay rights groups withdrawing their support for the NDRA shortly after the *Hobby Lobby* ruling largely because of those concerns.[73]

Of course, the contemporary discussion of employment discrimination based on sexual orientation and identity, like the other aspects of civil rights, takes place within a historical context that matters. In this case, even as public officials are attempting to address public sector problems and leverage private sector organizations to move forward, that history, largely unknown by the public and rarely discussed outside the LGBT community, is stark. As was true in other areas of civil rights, the language is ugly and hurtful, but it must be seen and engaged in all its ugliness to understand the situation and the challenges.

In terms of employment and the government, the modern history reaches back to 1950, the beginnings of the so-called Second Red Scare and the rise of what is now known as McCarthyism. In June of that year the Senate passed Senate Resolution 280, which provided in pertinent part:

> Resolved, That the Committee on Expenditures in the Executive Departments, or any duly authorized subcommittee thereof, is authorized and directed to make a thorough and comprehensive study and investigation of (a) the employment by the departments and agencies of the Government of homosexuals and other moral perverts, and (b) the preparedness and diligence of authorities of the District of Columbia, as well as the appropriate authorities of the Federal Government, for the protection of life and property against the threat to security, inherent in the employment of such perverts by such departments and agencies.[74]

This resolution came about as a result of the report of a two-person subcommittee that investigated the District of Columbia government in a closed process.[75] The report in response to S. Res 280, provided in December 1950, fed efforts to drive gays from government. The report noted at the outset that this was the first "government-wide" investigation of this subject. "The primary objective of the subcommittee in this inquiry was to determine the extent of the employment of homosexuals and other sex perverts in Government: to consider reasons why their employment by the Government is undesirable; and to examine into the efficacy of the methods used in dealing with the problem."[76] The report states the committee's conclusions at the outset. "In the opinion of this subcommittee homosexuals and other sex perverts are not proper persons to be employed in Government for two reasons; first, they are generally unsuitable, and second, they constitute security risks."[77]

Ironically, the report asserted that one of the reasons why their employment was such a problem was the severe "social stigma" attached to homosexuality.[78] "Aside from the criminality and immorality involved in sex perversion such behavior is so contrary to the normal accepted standards of social behavior that persons who engaged in such activity are looked upon as outcasts by society generally."[79] Using just about every possible homophobic stereotype, the report alleged that such employees posed a danger to others:

> Most of the authorities agree and our investigation has shown that the presence of a sex pervert in a Government agency has a corrosive influence upon his fellow employees. These perverts will frequently attempt to entice normal individuals to engage in perverted practices. This is particularly true in the case of young and impressionable people who might come under the influence of a pervert.[80]

As to security, the report asserts: "The lack of emotional stability which is found in most sex perverts and the weakness of their moral fiber, makes them susceptible to the blandishments of the foreign espionage agent."[81]

These assertions, exacerbated by the declaration by the psychiatric community in the authoritative Diagnostic and Statistical Manual of Mental Disorders (DSM-1) in 1952 that homosexuality was a personality disorder, fueled Senator McCarthy and others involved in his campaign of terror to demand action from the Chief Executive.[82] President Truman, much to his later regret, responded to the anti-communist hysteria and the political campaign that pressed it with creation of the Loyalty-Security program.[83] That program became a useful device for those attacking gays in government as well.

When he came to office, President Eisenhower acceded to the homophobia by issuing Executive Order 10450.[84] The order set out requirements to ensure that employees in sensitive positions be cleared as reliable and trustworthy. However, it quickly became clear that the order would be used to seek out and remove from employment or prevent hiring on the basis of sexual orientation or identity. Section 8(a)(1) of E.O. 10450 stated some of the factors to be investigated to determine unfitness for public service. They included in part:

(iii)   Any criminal, infamous, dishonest, immoral, or notoriously disgraceful conduct, habitual use of intoxicants to excess, drug addiction, sexual perversion.

(iv)   Any illness, including any mental condition, of a nature which in the opinion of competent medical authority may cause significant defect in the judgment or reliability of the employee, with due regard to the transient or continuing effect of the illness and the medical findings in such case.

(v)   Any facts which furnish reason to believe that the individual may be subjected to coercion, influence, or pressure which may cause him to act contrary to the best interests of the national security.

Federal officials understood these terms and provisions to apply to gays and lesbians.

In fact, media sources discovered that as late as 1964 the Eisenhower order, as well as guidance developed within agencies under it, was still being cited for action against employees or applicants on grounds that they were unsuitable for employment and represented security risks.[85] In a memorandum for O. Glenn Stahl, then Director, United States Civil Service Commission (CSC) Bureau of Policies and Standards, CSC Chief of Program Systems and Instructions Division John W. Steele cited these same provisions from the Eisenhower order, as well as the Federal Personnel Manual, and, taken together, these were used to remove or disqualify from employment applicants for various positions.[86] "In cases of homosexuality, we automatically find the individual not suitable for federal employment unless there is *evidence of rehabilitation*. This is our stated policy."[87] Steele concluded his memo:

> Our tendency to "lean over backwards" to rule against a homosexual is simply a manifestation of the revulsion which homosexuality inspires in the normal person. What it

boils down to is that most men look upon homosexuality as something uniquely nasty, not just as a form of immorality. It is problematic whether any study of the subject could result in overcoming an attitude this ingrained.[88]

Just how many people lost their jobs or were barred from employment from the early post-World War II years to 1998 will never be known, but it was clearly in the thousands by any estimate.

In 1998 President Clinton issued Executive Order 13087, which amended equal opportunity in government hiring orders issued by Presidents Johnson in 1965[89] and Nixon in 1969[90] to include protection for sexual orientation. Of course, the Clinton administration did not apply that requirement to the military and instituted the "Don't Ask, Don't Tell" policy that was not ended until the Obama years. President Obama went on to issue Executive Order 13672 in 2014 to include sexual identity as well as sexual orientation.[91] He also issued Proclamation 9136 on Lesbian, Gay, Bisexual, and Transgender Pride Month, in which he called for passage of the ENDA, but that has not happened as at the time of this writing.[92]

A number of states moved forward through executive orders or legislation to provide protections against employment discrimination. A 2012 study found that thirty-two states had some kind of policy in place, sixteen and the District of Columbia that had passed legislation that banned discrimination on the basis of sexual orientation or gender identity, while another five had laws on orientation but not identity.[93] Some of them provide broad protections, whereas others are limited to state employment or provide only some protection. Indeed, the same study found that "49 percent of gay and transgender workers live in states that do not provide any protections on the basis of sexual orientation or gender identity."[94]

State and Local Backlash against Efforts to Stop Discrimination on Sexual Orientation and Identity

At the same time, there have been strong reactions against the movement to ensure full civil rights protections for LGBT citizens. Not unlike the situation with respect to race, at each point where there were court rulings or policies adopted to end discrimination, there have been cases in which there has been a backlash or outright resistance to compliance. Colorado voters adopted a referendum in 1992 that read:

> No Protected Status Based on Homosexual, Lesbian or Bisexual Orientation.
>
> Neither the State of Colorado, through any of its branches or departments, nor any of its agencies, political subdivisions, municipalities or school districts, shall enact, adopt or enforce any statute, regulation, ordinance or policy whereby homosexual, lesbian or bisexual orientation, conduct, practices or relationships shall constitute or otherwise be the basis of or entitle any person or class of persons to have or claim any minority status, quota preferences, protected status or claim of discrimination. This Section of the Constitution shall be in all respects self-executing.[95]

As Justice Kennedy pointed out when the Supreme Court overturned this measure, the supporters of the referendum were reacting against ordinances adopted by the cities of Aspen, Boulder, and Denver prohibiting discrimination on the basis of sexual orientation in such areas as housing, employment, education, public accommodations, and health and welfare services.[96] California's Proposition 8, discussed earlier, banning same-sex marriage is one of many examples of states that reacted against state court rulings and state legislation providing protections for gay rights.

As the Colorado example shows, these actions have been aimed not only at state policies but also at blocking local actions in cities and counties intended to end discrimination. In 1993 voters approved, by a vote of 62 per cent to 38 per cent, an amendment to the City Charter of Cincinnati designed to overturn an Equal Employment Opportunity Ordinance adopted in 1991 and a Human Rights Ordinance adopted in 1992.[97] A challenge to that measure was successful in the federal district court,[98] but that ruling was reversed by the Court of Appeals for the Sixth Circuit and the Supreme Court refused to hear an appeal.[99]

Even where federal courts have ruled in favor of same-sex marriage, some state officials have refused to honor the clear meaning and requirements of the rulings and have avoided compliance. In the case of Alabama, the Chief Justice went so far as to issue his own ruling, telling officials at the county level not to issue marriage licenses and purporting, on his own, to effectively overturn the merits of the opinion by the federal court.[100] Following the Supreme Court's ruling in *Obergefell*, that behavior has spread to other states where officials have refused, in some jurisdictions, to issue any marriage licenses at all. This is eerily reminiscent of the resistance seen in the years after *Brown v. Board of Education*.

In addition to these actions, some politicians have been determined to roll back policies previously adopted to provide civil rights protection. In one notable example, Kansas Governor Sam Brownback issued an executive order in February 2015, Executive Order 15–01,[101] repealing an equal opportunity order, E.O. 7–24, issued by Governor Kathleen Sebelius in 2007.[102] In so doing, he rejected the idea that Sebelius could add "sexual orientation, gender identity" to the list of other categories protected by equal opportunity. Media sources quoted Sebelius as responding thus:

> "I was totally surprised and really incredibly unhappy with him taking this action eight years after the executive order was issued," Sebelius said, adding it sends a "terrible message" to state employees and lesbian, gay, bisexual and transgender people throughout the state. "I have no idea why the governor would do this."[103]

Sexual Orientation and Identity in Schools

In the period following rulings by the lower federal courts and eventually the Supreme Court in sexual harassment cases brought under Title VII, parents sought similar protections in the educational setting under Title IX of the Education Amendments of 1972. Indeed, the Supreme Court agreed that these protections are available under that legislation. Similarly, students and parents have sought protections against discrimination and harassment on the basis of sexual orientation or identity under Title IX. To this point, however, there is no Supreme Court ruling on that subject, and limited and mixed results in the lower courts. Students have also challenged the actions of school officials and sometimes their failure to act in the face of serious abuse by other students as violations of the equal protection and due process clauses of the Fourteenth Amendment.

Again, it is important to understand the situations in which students sometimes find themselves. As before, one way to understand this is to employ a judge's presentation of the facts. Consider the case of a student in Wisconsin. The Court of Appeals for the Seventh Circuit was asked to review a summary ruling by the lower court dismissing the student's complaint against school officials and the district. (Since there had not been a trial, the appeals court was required to accept the facts as stated by the plaintiff.) In this instance, Judge Eschbach made clear that this student's case presented "wrenching facts."[104]

> Jamie Nabozny was a student in the Ashland Public School District ... in Ashland, Wisconsin throughout his middle school and high school years. During

that time, Nabozny was continually harassed and physically abused by fellow students because he is homosexual. Both in middle school and high school Nabozny reported the harassment to school administrators. Nabozny asked the school officials to protect him and to punish his assailants. Despite the fact that the school administrators had a policy of investigating and punishing student-on-student battery and sexual harassment, they allegedly turned a deaf ear to Nabozny's requests. Indeed, there is evidence to suggest that some of the administrators themselves mocked Nabozny's predicament....

When Nabozny graduated to the Ashland Middle School in 1988, his life changed. Around the time that Nabozny entered the seventh grade, Nabozny realized that he is gay. Many of Nabozny's fellow classmates soon realized it too. Nabozny decided not to "closet" his sexuality, and considerable harassment from his fellow students ensued. Nabozny's classmates regularly referred to him as "faggot," and subjected him to various forms of physical abuse, including striking and spitting on him. Nabozny spoke to the school's guidance counselor, Ms. Peterson, about the abuse, informing Peterson that he is gay. Peterson took action, ordering the offending students to stop the harassment and placing two of them in detention. However, the students' abusive behavior toward Nabozny stopped only briefly. Meanwhile, Peterson was replaced as guidance counselor by Mr. Nowakowski. Nabozny similarly informed Nowakowski that he is gay, and asked for protection from the student harassment. Nowakowski, in turn, referred the matter to school Principal Mary Podlesny; Podlesny was responsible for school discipline.

Just before the 1988 Winter holiday, Nabozny met with Nowakowski and Podlesny to discuss the harassment. During the meeting, Nabozny explained the nature of the harassment and again revealed his homosexuality. Podlesny promised to protect Nabozny, but took no action. Following the holiday season, student harassment of Nabozny worsened, especially at the hands of [two students].... Nabozny complained to Nowakowski, and school administrators spoke to the students. The harassment, however, only intensified. A short time later, in a science classroom, [one of these students] grabbed Nabozny and pushed him to the floor. [The two of them] held Nabozny down and performed a mock rape on Nabozny, exclaiming that Nabozny should enjoy it. The boys carried out the mock rape as twenty other students looked on and laughed. Nabozny escaped and fled to Podlesny's office. Podlesny's alleged response is somewhat astonishing; she said that "boys will be boys" and told Nabozny that if he was "going to be so openly gay," he should "expect" such behavior from his fellow students. In the wake of Podlesny's comments, Nabozny ran home. The next day Nabozny was forced to speak with a counselor, not because he was subjected to a mock rape in a classroom, but because he left the school without obtaining the proper permission. No action was taken against the students involved. Nabozny was forced to return to his regular schedule. Understandably, Nabozny was "petrified" to attend school; he was subjected to abuse throughout the duration of the school year.

The situation hardly improved when Nabozny entered the eighth grade. Shortly after the school year began, several boys attacked Nabozny in a school bathroom, hitting him and pushing his books from his hands. This time Nabozny's parents met with Podlesny and the alleged perpetrators. The offending boys denied that the incident occurred, and no action was taken. Podlesny told both Nabozny and his parents that Nabozny should expect such incidents because he is "openly" gay. Several similar meetings between Nabozny's parents and Podlesny followed subsequent incidents involving Nabozny. Each time perpetrators were identified to Podlesny. Each time Podlesny pledged to take action. And, each time nothing was done. Toward the end of the school year, the harassment against Nabozny intensified to the point that a district attorney purportedly advised Nabozny to take time off from school. Nabozny took one and a half weeks off from school. When he returned, the harassment resumed, driving Nabozny to attempt suicide. After a stint in a hospital, Nabozny finished his eighth grade year in a Catholic school.

The Catholic school attended by Nabozny did not offer classes beyond the eighth grade. Therefore, to attend the ninth grade, Nabozny enrolled in Ashland High School. Almost immediately Nabozny's fellow students sang an all too familiar tune. Early in the year, while Nabozny was using a urinal in the restroom, Nabozny was assaulted. [One] Student struck Nabozny in the back of the knee, forcing him to fall into the urinal. [Another student] then urinated on Nabozny. Nabozny immediately reported the incident to the principal's office. Nabozny recounted the incident to the office secretary, who in turn relayed the story to Principal William Davis. Davis ordered Nabozny to go home and change clothes. Nabozny's parents scheduled a meeting with Davis and Assistant Principal Thomas Blauert. At the meeting, the parties discussed numerous instances of harassment against Nabozny, including the restroom incident.

Rather than taking action against the perpetrators, Davis and Blauert referred Nabozny to Mr. Reeder, a school guidance counselor. Reeder was supposed to change Nabozny's schedule so as to minimize Nabozny's exposure to the offending students. Eventually the school placed Nabozny in a special education class; [the two students who assaulted him] were [also] special education students. Nabozny's parents continued to insist that the school take action, repeatedly meeting with Davis and Blauert among others. Nabozny's parents' efforts were futile; no action was taken. In the middle of his ninth grade year, Nabozny again attempted suicide. Following another hospital stay and a period living with relatives, Nabozny ran away to Minneapolis. His parents convinced him to return to Ashland by promising that Nabozny would not have to attend Ashland High. Because Nabozny's parents were unable to afford private schooling, however, the Department of Social Services ordered Nabozny to return to Ashland High.

In tenth grade, Nabozny fared no better. Nabozny's parents moved, forcing Nabozny to rely on the school bus to take him to school. Students on the bus regularly used epithets, such as "fag" and "queer," to refer to Nabozny. Some students even pelted Nabozny with dangerous objects such as steel nuts and bolts. When Nabozny's parents complained to the school, school officials changed Nabozny's assigned seat and moved him to the front of the bus. The harassment continued. Ms. Hanson, a school guidance counselor, lobbied the school's administration to take more aggressive action to no avail. The worst was yet to come, however. One morning when Nabozny arrived early to school, he went to the library to study. The library was not yet open, so Nabozny sat down in the hallway. Minutes later he was met by a group of eight boys led by [one of the students who had assaulted him previously]. [He] began kicking Nabozny in the stomach, and continued to do so for five to ten minutes while the other students looked on laughing. Nabozny reported the incident to Hanson, who referred him to the school's "police liaison" Dan Crawford. Nabozny told Crawford that he wanted to press charges, but Crawford dissuaded him. Crawford promised to speak to the offending boys instead. Meanwhile, at Crawford's behest, Nabozny reported the incident to Blauert. Blauert, the school official supposedly in charge of disciplining, laughed and told Nabozny that Nabozny deserved such treatment because he is gay. Weeks later Nabozny collapsed from internal bleeding that resulted from Huntley's beating. Nabozny's parents and counselor Hanson repeatedly urged Davis and Blauert to take action to protect Nabozny. Each time aggressive action was promised. And, each time nothing was done.

Finally, in his eleventh grade year, Nabozny withdrew from Ashland High School. Hanson told Nabozny and his parents that school administrators were unwilling to help him and that he should seek educational opportunities elsewhere. Nabozny left Ashland and moved to Minneapolis where he was diagnosed with Post Traumatic Stress Disorder. In addition to seeking medical help, Nabozny sought legal advice.[105]

The student sued on grounds that both the actions taken by school officials and the actions they failed to take discriminated on the basis of gender and also sexual orientation. He also asserted that their actions failed to protect him and also encouraged students to injure him by virtue of their failure to act in violation of his rights under the due process clause of the Fourteenth Amendment. The appeals court agreed with the lower court that due process did not require officials to protect him. However, they said:

> We conclude that, based on the record as a whole, a reasonable fact-finder could find that the District and defendants Podlesny, Davis, and Blauert violated Nabozny's Fourteenth Amendment right to equal protection by discriminating against him based on his gender or sexual orientation. Further, the law establishing the defendants' liability was sufficiently clear to inform the defendants at the time that their conduct was unconstitutional. Nabozny's equal protection claims against the District, Podlesny, Davis, and Blauert are reinstated in toto.[106]

In a California case the students claimed that school officials had violated Title IX as well as provisions of the California and United States constitutions. Again the students alleged that school officials ignored repeated harassment by other students or provided only minor and ineffective responses, even in the face of serious incidents.[107] In this case, the Ninth Circuit Court of Appeals concluded: "The record contains sufficient evidence for a jury to conclude that the defendants intentionally discriminated against the plaintiffs in violation of the Equal Protection Clause. At the time of the harassment, the plaintiffs' right to be free from intentional discrimination on the basis of sexual orientation was clearly established."[108]

At this time, the protections available in the educational context are evolving and it is a long way from clear just what those protections are and how they will be applied. There is no Supreme Court case law that clarifies the situation and the discussion of the way that Title IX applies is a work in progress.

Judges, Juries, Parental Rights, Sexual Orientation Change Programs and a host of Additional Issues

This lack of clarity and certainty in protections for civil rights related to sexual orientation and sexual identity extends to many other fields as well, from parental rights, to courts and juries, to clinical efforts to change the sexual orientation of minors, and a host of others. Several sets of issues have arisen in these areas that will require attention, but consider just a few examples.

For instance, there are cases in which trial courts permitted prospective jurors to be removed by attorneys because they were gay. In one such case, involving a civil suit between

Smithkline Beecham and Abbott Laboratories, a district court allowed an attorney to use a peremptory challenge to remove the only "self-identified gay person" in the jury pool. The Ninth Circuit reversed, concluding that:

> This appeal's central question is whether equal protection prohibits discrimination based on sexual orientation in jury selection. We must first decide whether classifications based on sexual orientation are subject to a standard higher than rational basis review. We hold that such classifications are subject to heightened scrutiny. We also hold that equal protection prohibits peremptory strikes based on sexual orientation and remand for a new trial.[109]

In the very high profile case contesting California's ban on same-sex marriage, supporters of Proposition 8 even attempted to have the ruling vacated by the district judge who took over the case on the grounds that Chief District Judge Vaughn R. Walker, who first held the proposition unconstitutional, should be disqualified since he was gay and in a same-sex relationship at the time. Judge James Ware, who took over the case after Walker retired, rejected that attempt.[110] Issues related to parental rights as well as to divorce and custody are also evolving.

Another area that has engendered both legislative and judicial response are efforts by parents to force children into so-called therapy designed to turn them away from a gay sexual orientation or identity. For example, in 2013, the Governor of New Jersey signed into law Assembly Bill A 3371, which provided that:

a. A person who is licensed to provide professional counseling ... shall not engage in sexual orientation change efforts with a person under 18 years of age.
b. As used in this section, "sexual orientation change efforts" means the practice of seeking to change a person's sexual orientation, including, but not limited to, efforts to change behaviors, gender identity, or gender expressions, or to reduce or eliminate sexual or romantic attractions or feelings toward a person of the same gender; except that sexual orientation change efforts shall not include counseling for a person seeking to transition from one gender to another, or counseling that:
    (1) provides acceptance, support, and understanding of a person or facilitates a person's coping, social support, and identity exploration and development, including orientation-neutral interventions to prevent or address unlawful conduct or unsafe sexual practices; and
    (2) does not seek to change sexual orientation.[111]

The Third Circuit upheld the New Jersey statute against claims that it violated free speech and free exercise of religion protections under the First Amendment.[112] Similarly, the Ninth Circuit upheld California's Senate Bill 1172, which also prohibited these practices with respect to minors.[113] More states are taking such actions, but the case law is still developing.

Conclusion

Although there is a long history of discrimination on the basis of sexual orientation and identity, the United States has only recently begun to take serious steps to ensure civil rights in this field. To be sure, there have been important rulings by the Supreme Court with respect to same-sex marriage and some other aspects of these relationships, but there are many other issues remaining. There is rapid change at the state level as well as in the position of the U.S. Department of Justice in several areas, but this is very much a work in progress.

I. Issues for Policy and Practice

A. The Supreme Court's rulings in *Windsor* and *Obergefell* suggest the need for a careful reexamination of human resource policies in virtually all areas of government.

B. As this chapter indicates, there are dramatic differences across states and even within states in terms of policies that impact people within government or in the community because of sexual orientation or identity. Federal legislation has not been forthcoming, despite the many times the Employment Non-Discrimination Act (ENDA) has been introduced in Congress. That situation adds to the difficulty and complexity of the picture.

C. Given the differences across jurisdiction and the lack of federal law, there is a need for careful studies of existing policies to identify areas that have significant impacts related to sexual orientation or identity.

D. Many organizations have diversity programs that seek to address race and gender, but it is not clear how many consider sexual orientation and identity.

E. Since the law and public opinion have been evolving rapidly in this field of civil rights, it is not clear what resources are available to assist policymakers and managers in moving forward. The U.S. Department of Justice has established an LGBTI Working Group, but more is needed. It is important to develop inventories of available resources for policy and management change as well as for educational programs.

F. As this chapter indicates, courts have generally refused to apply Title VII prohibitions on sex discrimination to sexual orientation. However, the Justice Department is consistently arguing that Title VII does apply in cases of sexual identity where people gender stereotypes are used to discriminate against employees, as in the fire fighter who was not perceived to be masculine enough to suit his superiors. In the absence of congressional action to address the gap in Title VII protection, what can you do in your organization to ensure against discrimination?

G. The dissenters in the *Obergefell* case striking down bans on same-sex marriage virtually invited individuals with religious objections to challenge changed policies or practices that they perceive affect them. What does that mean for your organization?

H. Given that so many agencies or local governments have ongoing relationships with nongovernmental organizations for service delivery or other purposes, is there a policy or management practice in place for dealing with those organizations that excludes people based on sexual orientation or identity?

II. Discussion Questions

A. In his dissent in *Hardwick*, Justice Blackmun focused on the right to privacy and intimate association, but concluded that other claims including equal protection and the Eighth Amendment's prohibition on cruel and unusual punishment also provided bases for overturning the Georgia law. He added a footnote that would seem old news today, but was hotly debated even as late as the 1980s when *Bowers* was decided. "Despite historical views of homosexuality, it is no longer viewed by mental health professionals as a 'disease' or disorder. See Brief for American Psychological Association and American Public Health Association as *Amici Curiae* 8–11. But, obviously, neither is it simply a matter of deliberate personal election. Homosexual orientation may well form part of the very fiber of an individual's personality." Blackmun dissenting, Fn. 1. What should the importance that these leading professional associations had made these changes and viewed homosexual behavior as a part of one's personhood have been to the case?

B. As you read the *Lawrence v. Texas* opinion by Justice Kennedy, are you clear about whether he was relying primarily on equal protection of the law or due process? See what the concurring and dissenting opinions said about that.

C. In his dissent in *Lawrence*, Justice Scalia accuses the majority of having "signed on to the so-called homosexual agenda" and says that the majority has "taken sides in the culture war." What does the rhetoric in his dissent and the other dissents in *Lawrence, Windsor,* and *Obergefell* communicate to the LGBT community?

D. If you were in a management position tomorrow, where would you look for resources to help you assess the treatment of people related to sexual orientation or identity and address any problems that you find?

E. As this chapter has indicated, in the aftermath of the *Obergefell* and *Windsor* rulings various state or local officials tried to block implementation in ways reminiscent of the reaction against Supreme Court rulings against racial discrimination. How would you respond to those efforts to block civil rights protections?

F. The *Jaycees* opinion and the *Boy Scouts* case create serious confusion over when states may outlaw exclusion. How should government deal with organizations that exclude people based upon such distinctions as gender or sexual orientation or identity?

Notes

1 U.S. Senate, Hearing before the Committee on the Judiciary, *Combating Hate Crimes: Promoting a Responsive and Responsible Role for the Federal Government,* 106 Cong., 1st Sess. (1999) pp. 27–28.
2 Id.
3 James Byrd's killer: 'I'd do it all over again', KHOU.com, www.khou.com/story/news/2014/07/17/ 11531380/, June 25, 2015.
4 The term "hate crime" was defined by Congress as "a crime in which the defendant intentionally selects a victim, or in the case of a property crime, the property that is the object of the crime, because of the actual or perceived race, color, religion, national origin, ethnicity, gender, gender identity, disability, or sexual orientation of any person." Defined in Section 280003(a) of the Violent Crime Control and Law Enforcement Act of 1994 (Public Law 103–322; 108 Stat. 2096) amended by Section 4703 of the "Matthew Shepard and James Byrd, Jr. Hate Crimes Prevention Act" P.L. 111–84, 123 Stat. 2835 (2009).
5 P.L. 111–84, 123 Stat. 2835 (2009), codified at 18 U.S.C. §249. The act was passed as Division E of the National Defense Authorization Act for Fiscal Year 2010.
6 Pew Research Center, "Changing Attitudes on Gay Marriage," www.pewforum.org/2015/06/08/ graphics-slideshow-changing-attitudes-on-gay-marriage/, June 11, 2015.
7 Gallup, Marriage, www.gallup.com/poll/117328/marriage.aspx, June 11, 2015.
8 Office of the Attorney General, Commonwealth of Virginia, Press Release, Attorney General Herring Changes Virginia's Legal Position in Marriage Equality Case, www.oag.state.va.us/ index.php/media-center/news-releases/96-attorney-general-herring-changes-virginia-s-legal-position-in-marriage-equality-case, June 26, 2015. He immediately filed a "Notice of Change in Legal Position of Defendant Janet M. Rainey," *Bostic v. Rainey,* Civil Action No. 2:13-cv-00395, U.S. District Court for the Eastern District of Virginia, January 23, 2014, www.ag.virginia.gov/ images/NewsReleases/Notice_of_Change_in_Position_by_Rainey_and_Memorandum_in_ Support_%28Bostic_v_Rainey_1-23-2014%29.pdf, June 26, 2015.
9 Federal Bureau of Investigation, "Latest Hate Crime Statistics Report Released," www.fbi.gov/ news/stories/2014/december/latest-hate-crime-statistics-report-released, June 18, 2015.
10 Shepard in U.S. Senate, *Combating Hate Crimes,* at 29. The precise number was 13.7% as reported in FBI, Hate Crime Statistics 1997, p. 5, www.fbi.gov/about-us/cjis/ucr/hate-crime/1997/hatecrime97. pdf, June 28, 2015.
11 P.L. 101–275, 104 Stat. 140 (1990).
12 *Doe v. Commonwealth's Attorney for the City of Richmond,* 403 F. Supp. 1199 (EDVA 1975). The Supreme Court affirmed the lower court ruling without opinion. 425 U.S. 901 (1976).
13 *Bowers v. Hardwick,* 478 U.S. 186, 188 (1986).
14 *Bowers v. Hardwick,* 760 F.2d 1202 (11th Cir. 1985).
15 NOTE: Burger here cites 4 W. Blackstone, Commentaries 215. Blackstone's commentaries have often been cited because so much of British common law was borrowed by the United States,

primarily because of its private law heritage of dispute resolution. However, one of the fundamental flaws in the reference to Blackstone is that when it comes to public law, the United States moved dramatically away from the British common law tradition and to a written Constitution, and in general a positive law system very different from that of England. Indeed, James Madison warned against analogizing from that British tradition when it comes to constitutional understanding of the American system. He wrote: "Writers such as Locke, and Montesquieu, who have discussed more the principles of liberty and the structure of government, lie under the same disadvantage of having written before these subjects were illuminated by the events and discussions which distinguish a very recent period. Both of them, too, are evidently warped by a regard to the particular government of England, to which one of them owed allegiance; and the other professed an admiration bordering on idolatry.... The chapter on prerogative shows how much the reason of the philosopher was clouded by the Royalism of the Englishman." James Madison, *The Writings of James Madison*, ed. Gaillard Hunt, 9 vols. (New York: G. P. Putnam's Sons, 1906), Vol. 6, p. 144.

16 "In *Robinson v. California*, 370 U.S. 660 (1962), the Court held that the Eighth Amendment barred convicting a defendant due to his 'status' as a narcotics addict, since that condition was 'apparently an illness which may be contracted innocently or involuntarily.' ... Despite historical views of homosexuality, it is no longer viewed by mental health professionals as a 'disease' or disorder. See Brief for American Psychological Association and American Public Health Association as *Amici Curiae* 8–11. But, obviously, neither is it simply a matter of deliberate personal election. Homosexual orientation may well form part of the very fiber of an individual's personality. Consequently, the Eighth Amendment may pose a constitutional barrier to sending an individual to prison for acting on that attraction regardless of the circumstances. An individual's ability to make constitutionally protected 'decisions concerning sexual relations,' *Carey* v. *Population Services International*, 431 U.S. 678, 711 (1977) (POWELL, J., concurring in part), is rendered empty indeed if he or she is given no real choice but a life without any physical intimacy."

17 "The parallel between *Loving* and this case is almost uncanny. There, too, the State relied on a religious justification for its law.... There, too, defenders of the challenged statute relied heavily on the fact that when the Fourteenth Amendment was ratified, most of the States had similar prohibitions.... There, too, at the time the case came before the Court, many of the States still had criminal statutes concerning the conduct at issue.... Yet the Court held, not only that the invidious racism of Virginia's law violated the Equal Protection Clause, ... but also that the law deprived the Lovings of due process by denying them the 'freedom of choice to marry' that had 'long been recognized as one of the vital personal rights essential to the orderly pursuit of happiness by free men.'"

18 "See *Loving v. Virginia*, 388 U.S. 1 (1967). Interestingly, miscegenation was once treated as a crime similar to sodomy. See Hawley & McGregor, The Criminal Law, at 287 (discussing crime of sodomy); *id.*, at 288 (discussing crime of miscegenation)."

19 See Debra Cassens Weiss, "Justice Who Said He Never Met a Homosexual Actually Had Several Gay Law Clerks," *ABA Journal*, Posted Jun 10, 2013, www.abajournal.com/news/article/justice_who_said_he_never_met_a_homosexual_actually_had_several_gay_law_cle/, July 4, 2015.

20 Id.

21 *Baker v. State*, 170 Vt. 194, 744 A. 2d 864 (VT 1999); *Goodridge v. State Department of Health*, 440 Mass. 309; 798 N.E.2d 941 (MA 2003).

22 H. 847, codified as 15 V.S.A. Chapter 23.

23 *Romer v. Evans*, 517 U.S. 620 (1996).

24 NOTE: Loosely translated as "no contest."

25 NOTE: An order issued to a lower court to send the record in a case up to be reviewed by a higher court such as the U.S. Supreme Court.

26 NOTE: Justice Thomas joined Justice Scalia's dissent, but added a brief dissent noting that while he thought the Texas law was, quoting Justice Stewart's dissent in *Griswold*, "an uncommonly silly" law, he did not think he had the authority to strike it down.

27 P.L. 104–199, 110 Stat. 2419 (1996), 28 U.S.C. §1738C.

28 See John E. Yang, "House Votes to Curb Gay Marriages; Bitter Debate Precedes Lopsided Outcome; Clinton Would Sign Bill," *Washington Post*, July 13, 1996, p. A1.

29 William Clinton, "Statement on Same-Gender Marriage," September 20, 1996, 32 *Weekly Compilation of Presidential Documents*, 1829–30 (1996).

30 133 S. Ct. 2652 (2013).

31 *In re Marriage Cases*, 43 Cal. 4th 757, 76 Cal. Rptr. 3d 683, 183 P. 3d 384 (2008).

32 *Perry v. Schwarzenegger*, 704 F. Supp. 2d 921 (NDCA 2010); *Perry v. Brown*, 671 F.3d 1052, 1070 (9th Cir. 2012).

33 P.L. 104–199, 110 Stat. 2419 (1996), 28 U.S.C. §1738C.

34 NOTE: The Court noted that: "After a statewide deliberative process that enabled its citizens to discuss and weigh arguments for and against same-sex marriage, New York acted to enlarge the definition of marriage to correct what its citizens and elected representatives perceived to be an injustice that they had not earlier known or understood. See Marriage Equality Act, 2011 N.Y. Laws 749 (codified at N.Y. Dom. Rel. Law Ann. §§10-a, 10-b, 13 (West 2013))."

35 NOTE: Justice Alito would also deny standing.

36 *DeBoer v. Snyder*, 772 F. 3d 388 (6th Cir. 2014).

37 NOTE: At this point, the Court said that "*Baker v. Nelson*[, 409 U.S. 810 (1972)] must be and now is overruled." This was a 1972 case that declined to find a substantial federal question to review in a same-sex marriage case. The reason to overrule here is that such a decision has some force as precedent and is inconsistent with the Court's ruling in the *Obergefell* case.

38 NOTE: The appendix not included here.

39 NOTE: The Chief Justice is attempting here to treat the bill of rights as if were a closed list of enumerated rights, and if anyone wishes to find other protections they bear a heavy burden to justify that assertion, since the enumerated list is what should matter.

The Chief Justice has worked hard to say in other cases that the idea of enumerated powers means that is if something is "not specifically granted," the matter is left to the states. *Shelby County v. Holder*, 133 S. Ct. 2612, 2623 (2013). In that case, he was trying to take the Constitution back to the days of the Articles of Confederation, before the U.S. Constitution was written. Article II of the Articles of Confederation had indicated that the states retained all powers not "expressly delegated" to the national government.

The Constitution was written in significant part because of the failure of the Articles of Confederation. The framers of the Constitution rejected that "expressly delegated" language used in the Articles of Confederation when they drafted the Constitution and again when the first ten amendments were added. They wrote to avoid that kind of exclusivity, and indeed included the necessary and proper clause of Article I, section 8 to make clear that the powers were not limited only to those specifically listed.

Indeed, the framers indicated that one of the reasons they did not include a bill of enumerated rights in the Constitution was the fear that this kind of narrow exclusionary approach might be taken in the future. James Madison, among others, made clear the framers' concern that they had originally avoided a listing of rights for fear that they might not be able to list all important rights, and that someone would assume that only those rights specifically listed were protected. See e.g. Lance Banning, *Jefferson and Madison: Three Conversations from the Founding* (Lanham, MD: Roman & Littlefield, 1995), 7–8. When they were forced to add a bill of rights because of commitments during the constitutional ratification debates, they added the Ninth Amendment to protect against a narrow, specifically enumerated approach, writing "The enumeration in the Constitution, of certain rights, shall not be construed to deny or disparage others retained by the people."

40 NOTE: The Chief Justice here cites *Dred Scott* as a substantive due process case, which is a dramatic misstatement of that case for the deliberate purpose of attempting to tie the decision in the same-sex marriage case to the most reviled ruling in the history of the U.S. Supreme Court. As the *Dred Scott* opinion, presented in Chapter 2, clearly shows, substantive due process was not the basis of the Court's ruling in that terrible decision.

41 NOTE: The Chief Justice here quotes a line from a concurring opinion in the *Lawrence* case by Justice Sandra Day O'Connor and not the majority opinion. Notice that he is applying here the lowest possible equal protection standard, which assumes that there is no difference in treatment with respect to a fundamental right. Justice O'Connor's opinion in the *Lawrence* case concluded that it was not even necessary to examine which standard should apply because the Texas law in question

could not satisfy even a rationale basis test. It is also interesting that the Chief Justice here is using a classic circular argument, saying, in effect, that the challenged restriction is justified because the states say it is. His arguments are usually more careful and logically presented than this one.

42 NOTE: Notice here Justice Scalia's echo of the *Roberts* argument about enumerated rights, only in even more stark terms.

43 468 U.S. 609 (1984). See also *Board of Directors of Rotary Int'l v. Rotary Club of Duarte*, 481 U.S. 537 (1987).

44 *Hurley v. Irish-American Gay, Lesbian and Bisexual Group of Boston*, 515 U.S. 557, 560 (1995).

45 *Irish-American Gay, Lesbian and Bisexual Group of Boston v. Boston*, 418 Mass. 238, 636 N.E.2d 1293 (1994).

46 *Hurley v. Irish-American Gay, Lesbian and Bisexual Group of Boston*, 515 U.S., at 559.

47 Id., at 574–575.

48 Tom Baxter, Gay Rights in '95: A Troubling Crossroad; Court Setbacks: From Boston to Cincinnati, Cases HAVE BEEN LOST," *Atlanta Journal and Constitution*, June 22, 1995, p. 4A.

49 See e.g. Erik Eckholm, Boy Scouts Are Poised to End Ban on Gay Leaders, *New York Times*, July 27, 2015, p. A10; Erik Eckholm, Scouts' Head Calls for End to Ban on Gay Leaders, *New York Times*, May 22, 2015, p. A1.

50 *Rumsfeld v. Forum for Academic and Institutional Rights (FAIR)*, 547 U.S. 47 (2006).

51 See John Files, "Advocates Hope Supreme Court Ruling Can Renew Attention to 'Don't Ask, Don't Tell'," *New York Times*, March 13, 2006, p. 16. See also Editorial, "Time to Repeal 'Don't Ask, Don't Tell,'" *USA Today*, March 8, 2006, p. 10A.

52 Editorial, "Now Repeal the Ban," *Washington Post*, March 7, 2006, p. A16.

53 *Christian Legal Society Chapter of the University of California, Hastings College of Law v. Martinez*, 561 U.S. 661 (2010).

54 It has not been introduced in the 114th Congress as of the time of this writing.

55 Jody Feder and Cynthia Brougher, "Sexual Orientation and Gender Identity Discrimination in Employment: A Legal Analysis of the Employment Non-Discrimination Act (ENDA)," Congressional Research Service, July 15, 2013, www.fas.org/sgp/crs/misc/R40934.pdf, January 14, 2016, p. 3. Supporting references from the original are: "See, e.g., *Spearman v. Ford Motor Co.*, 231 F.3d 1080 (7th Cir. 2000); *Higgins v. New Balance Ath. Shoe, Inc.*, 194 F.3d 252 (1st Cir. 1999); *Williamson v. A.G. Edwards & Sons, Inc.*, 876 F.2d 69 (8th Cir. 1989); *DeSantis v. Pacific Tel. and Tel. Co.*, 608 F.2d 327 (9th Cir. 1979); *Smith v. Liberty Mut. Ins. Co.*, 569 F.2d 325 (5th Cir. 1978)."

56 *Pedula v. Webster*, 822 F.2d 97 (D.C. Cir. 1987).

57 Id. at 927 n. 5.

58 Id. at 99.

59 *Webster v. Doe*, 486 U.S. 592 (1988).

60 *Doe v. Webster*, 769 F. Supp. 1 (D.D.C. 1991).

61 *Doe v. Gates*, 981 F.2d 1316 (D.C. Cir. 1993).

62 *Weaver v. Nebo School District*, 29 F. Supp. 2d 1279, 1281–82 (DUT 1998).

63 NOTE: Jenkins added in a footnote at this point: "The deep-seated prejudice on the part of some persons against the gay and lesbian community can be summed up in a single quote from ardent anti-gay activist and former entertainer Anita Bryant: 'I'd rather my child be dead than be a homosexual.' See Millie Ball, 'I'd Rather My Child be Dead Than Homo,' *The Times-Picayune*, June 19, 1977, at 3 (quoting Ms. Bryant)." Id. at 1287, n. 5.

64 Id., at 1287.

65 *Miller v. Weaver*, 66 P.3d 592 (2003).

66 *Glover v. Williamsburg School Dist. Bd. Of Ed.*, 20 F. Supp. 2d 1160, 1164–1166 (SDOH 1998).

67 Id., at 1174.

68 *Smith v. City of Salem, Ohio*, 378 F.3d 566, 578 (6th Cir. 2004). The court also concluded that he stated a claim under 42 U.S.C. §1983.

69 *Price Waterhouse v. Hopkins*, 490 U.S. 228 (1989). See the DOJ statements of interest in, among others, *Burnett v. City of Philadelphia-Free Library*, Civil Action 09-4378 (EDPA 2014) and *Jamal v. SAKS & Co.*, Civil Action 14–2782 (SDTX 2015), as well as the complaint in *U.S. v. Southeastern Oklahoma University*, Civil Action 15-324-C (WDOK 2015). For these and

other filings, see the "Documents" tab on the Department of Justice LGBT Working Group website at www.justice.gov/crt/about/wg/lgbti/, April 24, 2016.

70 *Burwell v. Hobby Lobby Stores*, 134 S. Ct. 2751 (2014).

71 P.L. 103–141, 107 Stat. 1488 (1993).

72 P.L. 110–148, 124 Stat. 119 (2010).

73 See Ed O'Keefe, "Gay Rights Groups Pull Support for Anti-Bias Bill," *Washington Post*, July 9, 2014, p. A03.

74 Senate Resolution 280, 81st Cong., 2d Sess., June 7, 1950, in Subcommittee on Investigations, Committee on Expenditures in the Executive Departments, *Employment of Homosexuals and Other Sex Perverts in Government: Interim Report Pursuant to S. Res. 280*, 81st Cong., 2nd Sess. (1950), Appendix I.

75 Id., at p. 1. On Wherry and his homophobic behavior, see Randolph W. Baxter, "'Homo-Hunting' in the Early Cold War: Senator Kenneth Wherry and the Homophobic Side of McCarthyism," *Nebraska History* 84 (2003): 119–132, www.nebraskahistory.org/publish/publicat/history/fulltext/2003-Homo_Hunting.pdf, January 26, 2016.

76 Id.

77 Id., at 3.

78 Id., at 3–5.

79 Id., at 3.

80 Id., at 4.

81 Id., at 5.

82 See e.g., U.S. Senate, Committee on Government Operations. *Executive Sessions of the Senate Permanent Subcommittee on Investigations of the Committee on Government Operations*, 83rd Cong. 1st Sess. (1953), Vol. I (Committee Print, 2003).

83 E.O. 9835, 12 Fed. Reg. 133 (January 9, 1947). He later admitted that he issued this order "under the climate of opinion that then existed," but later admitted that "it was terrible." David McCullough, *Truman* (New York: Simon & Schuster, 1992), p. 553.

84 18 Fed. Reg. 2489 (1953).

85 Matt Apuzzo, "Uncovered Papers Show Past Government Efforts to Drive Gays From Jobs," *New York Times*, May 21, 2014, p. 13.

86 John W. Steele to O. Glenn Stahl, "Homosexuality and Government Employment," November 17, 1964, https://s3.amazonaws.com/s3.documentcloud.org/documents/1164936/original-memo-from-1964.pdf, July 17, 2015. The reference to the FPM is the rating standard for "Homosexuality and sexual perversion," in the "FPM Supplement (Internal) 731–31, Suitability Rating Installment 6 dated December 1964." See Federal Personnel Manual System, Letter (Internal), from Warren B. Irons, Executive Director, March 8, 1965, www.mwe.com/info/mattachineamicus/document38.pdf, July 18, 2015.

87 Id., at 2 (emphasis in original).

88 Id., at 3.

89 E.O. 11246, 30 Fed. Reg. 12319 (September 28, 1965).

90 E.O. 11478, 34 Fed. Reg. 12985 (August 12, 1969).

91 79 Fed. Reg. 42971 (July 23, 2014).

92 79 Fed. Reg. 32427 (June 4, 2014).

93 Jerome Hunt, "A State-by-State Examination of Nondiscrimination Laws and Policies: State Nondiscrimination Policies Fill the Void but Federal Protections Are Still Needed," Center for American Progress Action Fund, June 2012, www.americanprogress.org/wp-content/uploads/issues/2012/06/pdf/state_nondiscrimination.pdf, July 18, 2015, pp. 1–2.

94 Id., at 5.

95 "Amendment 2," Colo. Const., Art. II, §30b.

96 *Romer v. Evans*, 517 U.S. 620, 623–624 (1996).

97 *Equality Foundation of Greater Cincinnati v. City of Cincinnati*, 54 F.3d 261, 263–264 (6th Cit. 1995), Cert. Denied, 525 U.S. 943 (1998).

98 *Equality Found. v. City of Cincinnati*, 860 F. Supp. 417 (S.D. Ohio, 1994).

99 *Equality Found. v. City of Cincinnati*, Cert. Denied, 525 U.S. 943 (1998).

100 Administrative Order of the Chief Justice of Alabama, February 8, 2015, http://web.pdx. edu/~pcooper/AlaChiefJusticeOrdertoBlockGayMarriage02082015.pdf, July 18, 2015. See also his letter to the governor telling him of his duty to resist the federal court decision, http://web. pdx.edu/~pcooper/CJMooreltrGovBentleyMarriage.1.27.15.pdf, July 18, 2015, Chief Justice Roy S. Moore to Governor Robert Bentley, January 27, 2015, http://web.pdx.edu/~pcooper/ CJMooreltrGovBentleyMarriage.1.27.15.pdf, July 18, 2015.
101 Executive Order No. 15–01, February 10, 2015, "Rescinding Certain Executive Orders," https:// kslib.info/DocumentCenter/View/4171, July 18, 2015.
102 Executive Order, 7–24, August 21, 2007, https://kslib.info/DocumentCenter/View/547, July 18, 2015.
103 Jan Biles, "Sebelius: Brownback's rescindment of executive order 'terribly troubling,'" *Topeka Capital-Journal*, February 13, 2015 Friday, http://cjonline.com/news/2015-02-12/sebelius-totally-surprised-brownbacks-terribly-troubling-move-strip-protection-gay, July 18, 2015.
104 *Nabozny v. Podlesny*, 92 F.3d 446, 460 (7th Cir. 1996).
105 Id., at 449–453.
106 Id., at 460–461.
107 See *Flores v. Morgan Hill Unified School District*, 324 F.3d 1130 (9th Cir. 2003).
108 Id., at 1138.
109 *Smithkline Beecham v. Abbott Laboratories*, 740 F.3d 471, 474 (9th Cir. 2014).
110 *Perry v. Schwarzenegger*, 790 F. Supp. 2d 1119 (NDCA 2011).
111 N.J. Stat. Ann. §45:1–55.
112 *King v. Governor of the State of New Jersey*, 767 F.3d 216 (3rd Cir. 2014) and *Doe v. Governor of the State of New Jersey*, 783 F.3d 150 (3rd Cir. 2015).
113 *Pickup v. Brown*, 740 F.3d 1208 (9th Cir. 2014).

References

Baxter, Randolph W. "'Homo-Hunting' in the Early Cold War: Senator Kenneth Wherry and the Homophobic Side of McCarthyism," *Nebraska History* 84 (2003): 119–132, www.nebraskahistory. org/publish/publicat/history/full-text/2003-Homo_Hunting.pdf, January 26, 2016.

Feder, Jody and Cynthia Brougher. "Sexual Orientation and Gender Identity Discrimination in Employment: A Legal Analysis of the Employment Non-Discrimination Act (ENDA)," Congressional Research Service, July 15, 2013, www.fas.org/sgp/crs/misc/R40934.pdf, January 14, 2016.

Hunt, Jerome. "A State-by-State Examination of Nondiscrimination Laws and Policies: State Nondiscrimination Policies Fill the Void but Federal Protections Are Still Needed," Center for American Progress Action Fund, June 2012, www.americanprogress.org/wp-content/uploads/ issues/2012/06/pdf/state_nondiscrimination.pdf, July 18, 2015.

Madison, James. *The Writings of James Madison*, ed. Gaillard Hunt, 9 vols. New York: G. P. Putnam's Sons, 1906.

McCullough, David. *Truman*. New York: Simon & Schuster, 1992.

U.S. Senate. Committee on Government Operations. *Executive Sessions of the Senate Permanent Subcommittee on Investigations of the Committee on Government Operations*, 83rd Cong., 1st Sess. (1953), Vol. I (Committee Print, 2003).

———. Hearing before the Committee on the Judiciary, *Combating Hate Crimes: Promoting a Responsive and Responsible Role for the Federal Government*, 106 Cong., 1st Sess. (1999).

———. Subcommittee on Investigations, Committee on Expenditures in the Executive Departments, *Employment of Homosexuals and Other Sex Perverts in Government: Interim Report Pursuant to S. Res. 280*, 81st Cong., 2nd Sess. (1950).

12 Civil Rights and Disabilities in America
Paternalism, Discrimination, or Equality?

Unless they die in a sudden and unexpected way, virtually everyone will, at some point in their lives, deal with a disability. Of course, when many Americans think of someone with a disability they imagine a person who was born with a physical or cognitive condition that presents challenges to their daily life, or someone who acquired such a condition as a result of an accident, injury, or perhaps in the military. On the other hand, many of those who are often considered persons with disabilities are quick to point out that the challenges most often arise from the environment and the society that creates and alters it, rather than just from a physical or developmental condition. From that perspective, disability is as much a social construct as a physical matter. People who experience disabilities, however defined, have historically faced segregation, isolation, sterilization, and more. This was not just the efforts by Hitler's regime to eliminate people considered somehow less than perfect. Many of these things happened in the United States under the banner of eugenics.

The effort to ensure civil rights for persons with disabilities is among the most recent of the civil rights struggles in America and is, as is true in other fields, clearly a work in progress, with much remaining to be done before anyone can claim that there is equal protection of the law. This chapter considers that ongoing drive for full civil rights protection for persons with disabilities that protects self-determination and supports independent living. The discussion examines first the sad history that has characterized much of the nation's life, the disability rights movement, the search for constitutional protections, and the statutory framework for civil rights in this field.

A Sad and Infuriating Legacy: A History of Segregation and Discrimination

As has been the case in other areas of civil rights history, the Supreme Court and other courts have often been part of the problem and not always part of the solution. Perhaps the lowest point in the nation's judicial history when it comes to civil rights and disabilities was the Court's ruling in the infamous *Buck v. Bell* case. It may have been a brief opinion, but its message, tone, and implications were devastating.

Buck v. Bell

274 U.S. 200 (1927)

INTRODUCTION: Like each of the areas of civil rights, there is a history concerning persons with disabilities in America that is, from today's perspective, difficult to imagine, let alone to read. This is such a case. It is all the more dramatic in its impact because it was authored by the famous Justice Oliver Wendell Holmes, Jr. The opinion is brief and is only lightly edited.

This was a period in which the eugenics movement, about which more will be said later in the chapter, was strong not only in the U.S., but also internationally. In addition to the issue of mandatory sterilization, the other obvious question not raised in this case, and indeed until many years later, was the matter of institutionalization. Additionally, there was the question of what the supposed disabilities of persons who were institutionalized actually were and on what evidence such disabilities were diagnosed. In this case, the diagnosis was "feeble-mindedness." Obviously, those who are in an institution and under the control of those who administer that institution face a variety of fundamental issues with respect to constitutional rights and liberties. Those who actually do have significant intellectual disabilities or mental health issues face much more difficulty in respect of ways in which their civil rights can be assured.

Justice Holmes presented the facts as they were understood in the case, but there were additional facts that were clearly not considered during the litigation that have been published by Joan Echtenkamp Klein, Alvin V. and Nancy Baird Curator for Historical Collections, of the Claude Moore Health Sciences Library of the University of Virginia Health System.[1] They explained that Carrie Buck was 17 at the time these events unfolded and in the care of foster parents. She was raped by a relative of the foster parents and gave birth to a child as a result.[2] This critically important fact was not addressed in the case. Her foster parents then had her committed to the Virginia Colony for Epileptics and Feeble Minded, later known as the Lynchburg Colony.

The Superintendent of the Colony, Albert Priddy, began lobbying the legislature in 1914 for a sterilization law. The Commonwealth of Virginia adopted the statute in 1924 that allowed sterilization of those committed to institutions and the Superintendent of the Virginia Colony then sought a case to affirm the validity of the new legislation. He selected Carrie Buck for the procedure.[3]

The case for applying the sterilization law to her was built around the assertion that she had inherited mental health or developmental issues, and that she had been born to a mother who had herself been committed and was unmarried. However, as her marriage license shows, Emma Harlow had married Frank Buck in September 1896.[4] As the history explains, the attorney who represented Carrie Buck introduced no witnesses to counter the witnesses who testified for the institution that she was feeble-minded, without anything that would today be regarded as evidence of an intellectual disability.[5] Justice Holmes recited the process requirements and concluded that there could be no problem of procedural due process, but the facts noted above show that although the form was in place, there was no serious substance to the proceeding.

Justice Holmes wrote the opinion for the Court.

> This is ... a review of a judgment of the Supreme Court of Virginia, affirming a judgment of the Circuit Court of Amherst County, by which ... the superintendent of the State Colony for Epileptics and Feeble Minded was ordered to perform the operation of salpingectomy upon Carrie Buck ... for the purpose of making her sterile.[6] The case comes here upon the contention that the statute authorizing the judgment is void under the Fourteenth Amendment as denying to [Ms. Buck] the due process of law and the equal protection of the laws.
>
> Carrie Buck is a feeble minded white woman who was committed to the State Colony.... She is the daughter of a feeble minded mother in the same institution, and the mother of an illegitimate feeble minded child. She was eighteen years old at the time of the trial of her case in the Circuit Court, in the latter part of

1924. An Act of Virginia, approved March 20, 1924, recites that the health of the patient and the welfare of society may be promoted in certain cases by the sterilization of mental defectives, under careful safeguard, &c.; that the sterilization may be effected in males by vasectomy and in females by salpingectomy, without serious pain or substantial danger to life; that the Commonwealth is supporting in various institutions many defective persons who if now discharged would become a menace but if incapable of procreating might be discharged with safety and become self-supporting with benefit to themselves and to society; and that experience has shown that heredity plays an important part in the transmission of insanity, imbecility, &c. The statute then enacts that whenever the superintendent of certain institutions ... shall be of opinion that it is for the best interests of the patients and of society that an inmate under his care should be sexually sterilized, he may have the operation performed upon any patient afflicted with hereditary forms of insanity, imbecility, &c., on complying with the very careful provisions by which the act protects the patients from possible abuse.... There can be no doubt that so far as procedure is concerned the rights of the patient are most carefully considered, and as every step in this case was taken in scrupulous compliance with the statute and after months of observation, there is no doubt that in that respect the plaintiff in error has had due process of law.

The attack is not upon the procedure but upon the substantive law. It seems to be contended that in no circumstances could such an order be justified. It certainly is contended that the order cannot be justified upon the existing grounds. The judgment finds the facts that have been recited and that Carrie Buck "is the probable potential parent of socially inadequate offspring, likewise afflicted, that she may be sexually sterilized without detriment to her general health and that her welfare and that of society will be promoted by her sterilization," and thereupon makes the order. In view of the general declarations of the legislature and the specific findings of the Court, obviously we cannot say as matter of law that the grounds do not exist, and if they exist they justify the result. We have seen more than once that the public welfare may call upon the best citizens for their lives. It would be strange if it could not call upon those who already sap the strength of the State for these lesser sacrifices, often not felt to be such by those concerned, in order to prevent our being swamped with incompetence. It is better for all the world, if instead of waiting to execute degenerate offspring for crime, or to let them starve for their imbecility, society can prevent those who are manifestly unfit from continuing their kind. The principle that sustains compulsory vaccination is broad enough to cover cutting the Fallopian tubes. *Jacobson v. Massachusetts*, 197 U.S. 11 [1905]. Three generations of imbeciles are enough.

But, it is said, however it might be if this reasoning were applied generally, it fails when it is confined to the small number who are in the institutions named and is not applied to the multitudes outside.... Of course so far as the operations enable those who otherwise must be kept confined to be returned to the world, and thus open the asylum to others, the equality aimed at will be more nearly reached. Judgement affirmed.[7]

This opinion was used by defendants at the Nuremberg War Crimes trials in their defense.[8]

The Commonwealth of Virginia did not repeal that sterilization law until 1974. In 2002 the governor apologized on behalf of the state to Carrie Buck and others who were victims of the state's actions.[9] However, the apology came too late. Ms. Buck had died in 1983.

Although this opinion marked a low point in U.S. history with respect to disability issues, it was neither the beginning nor the end of the problem. In an opinion rejecting a damage claim under the Americans with Disabilities Act in 2001, excerpted later in this chapter, Chief Justice Rehnquist was dismissive of the heritage of extreme discrimination against people with disabilities, sounding as if it was ancient history.

> The record does show that some States, adopting the tenets of the eugenics movement of the early part of this century, required extreme measures such as sterilization of persons suffering from hereditary mental disease. These laws were upheld against constitutional attack 70 years ago in *Buck v. Bell....* But there is no indication that any State had persisted in requiring such harsh measures as of 1990 when the ADA was adopted.[10]

He neglected to mention that a number of states did not fully remove their legislation or repudiate their actions until the 1970s and 1980s. He also neglected to mention that the Supreme Court has never reversed *Buck v. Bell.* Indeed, as Justice Souter said concurring in a later decision, "the statutes and their judicial vindications sat on the books long after eugenics lapsed into discredit."[11] Even as progressive a state as Oregon did not eliminate its state eugenics board, known as the Board of Social Protection, until 1983. Governor Kitzhaber's apology on behalf of the state explains how long and dark the history of this behavior has been and is similar to apologies issued in the period by other governors.

Governor John Kitzhaber

Proclamation of Human Rights Day, and Apology for Oregon's Forced Sterilization of Institutionalized Patients

Salem, Oregon December 2, 2002[12]

Today, I am here to acknowledge a great wrong done to more than 2,600 Oregonians over a period of about 60 years—forced sterilization in accordance with a doctrine called eugenics. Most of these Oregonians were patients in state-run institutions. The majority of them suffered from mental disorders and disabilities. Others were criminal offenders, sufferers of epilepsy or other conditions that required institutional care. Many were children. Virtually all of them were vulnerable, helpless citizens entrusted to the care of the State of Oregon by their families or by courts....

1. Background

During the early decades of the last century, the doctrine of eugenics gained widespread support in scientific circles, philosophy and government.... [T]he doctrine sought to improve the human condition by simply breeding better human beings. The method was to encourage reproduction by people with "good" genes, while discouraging reproduction by those with "bad" genes. At various times, supporters of eugenics urged passage of laws to keep ethnic groups separate from one another, to restrict immigration to America by people from eastern and southern Europe, and to impose sterilization on those considered "unfit."

Between 1900 and 1925, Oregon was one of 33 states that enacted laws to provide forced sterilization. The Oregon law established a state Board of Eugenics, later to become the Board of Social Protection, which included the superintendents of the state institutions. The Board's job was to decide which people should undergo involuntary sterilization in the interest of promoting a higher quality of human beings in succeeding generations.

2. Abolishment of the Board of Social Protection and Other Reforms

In 1983, I was a young state senator from Roseburg. I served on the subcommittee that gained the abolishment of the Board of Social Protection.... Since the late 1970's, Oregon has undergone a steady sea-change in policies that affect care, therapy and protection of rights for people who have such conditions. These changes reflect the growing awareness of the need to safeguard human dignity and to ensure that the state relegates no one to second-class citizenship because of illness or affliction. They include:

Compensation of residents in institutions. Before the late 1970's, peonage was a common practice in our institutions—a practice that denied compensation to patients and residents for their work. We've ended that practice....

Physical restraints, drugs and isolation. Until the mid-1980's, staff in the institutions commonly used inhumane devices to restrain and control patients—devices such as leather cuffs, helmets, straightjackets, and inappropriately high dosage of sedatives and psychotropic medications. Isolation for long periods was also common. Advances in professional knowledge and new legal requirements have dramatically reduced or eliminated such practices in Oregon.

Patients' privacy. Oregon has discontinued the practice of housing institutional residents in large, open dormitories, in favor of smaller, more personal quarters that protect individual privacy. The state also ensures protection of their personal mail, their personal possessions, and access to telephones on a regular basis.

Transition to community care. Like the rest of the nation, Oregon has sought to maximize the benefits of integrating vulnerable Oregonians into the community and the family, rather than warehouse them in institutions. In the past ten years, the state has progressed to a point at which we actually devote more resources to community care than to institutions—which illustrates how far we've come. We have replaced the traditional old rambling institutions with smaller facilities and a vast array of options for community housing and employment for those who suffer mental disorders and disabilities....

Conclusion. Oregon has made remarkable progress in treating citizens who suffer mental illness or disabilities. But even as we celebrate the progress we've made, we must also acknowledge the realities that darken the history of our state institutions. The time has come to apologize for misdeeds that resulted from widespread misconceptions, ignorance and bigotry. It's the right thing to do, the just thing to do. The time has come to apologize for public policies that labeled people as "defective" simply because they were ill, and declared them unworthy to have children of their own.

To those who suffered, I say, The people of Oregon are sorry. Our hearts are heavy for the pain you endured.

In the nineteenth century and before that persons with disabilities were hidden by families or locked away in institutions or even jails. This was the case for people with many different kinds of disabilities, but particularly so for those with intellectual disabilities or mental health issues. Society did not want to see them and families thought others might see their families as cursed or in some way subject to divine punishment for something in the past. Tragically today, a century later, there are still people who think that a disability is a punishment for misdeeds or sinfulness in the family, mothers who are blamed by their husbands for giving birth to a child with disabilities, and mothers who question whether they did something wrong somewhere in their pregnancy or in early child-rearing that led to disabilities.[13]

Many of these superstitions and social taboos were legitimized by what purported to be science in the form of the eugenics movement. Ironically, many of those who supported this movement saw themselves as progressives, only interested in improving society. As Paul Gray wrote, "They had imbibed their Darwin and decided that the process of natural selection would improve if it were guided by human intelligence. They did not know they were shaping a rationale for atrocities."[14] The movement was very much like that of those progressives of that era who supported creation of the Indian Boarding Schools discussed in Chapter 5.[15]

Sir Francis Galton is credited with having coined the term eugenics and as the founder of what came to be regarded as an important field of science in his day. Galton wrote of "cultivation of race, or, as we might call it with 'eugenic' questions" and defined it as concerning "questions bearing on what is termed in Greek, *eugenes*, namely, good in stock, hereditarily endowed with noble qualities."[16] He promoted the concept and the theory behind it during a period when society in England and, as it turned out, other countries were ready to accept that they could breed better people and, in so doing, eliminate social problems. Social Darwinism then spread in various forms.

The first International Eugenics Congress was held in London in 1912 with some 400 delegates from various countries.[17] A variety of papers were presented at the Congress, including a report, presented by Bleeker Van Wagenen, from the Eugenics Section of the American Breeders' Association, entitled "Preliminary Report of the Committee of the Eugenic Section of the American Breeders' Association to Study and to Report on the Best Practical Means for Cutting Off the Defective Germ-Plasm in the Human Population."[18] The second international conference was held in 1916, but this time in New York in the somewhat ironic venue of the Museum of Natural History's Hall of Man.[19] From that time through the mid-1920s numerous states enacted sterilization statutes that particularly targeted persons who were regarded as having disabilities and therefore considered—to use the terrible though common language of that day—defective.[20] It was this set of policies that led to the *Buck v. Bell* ruling. They were in place for decades to come, even in some of the states that might seem likely to have repudiated them years earlier, as the Oregon governor's remarks above indicate.

"Nothing about Us, without Us": Strengths, Culture, and Self-Determination

Even in the face of all that, however, there was born what has come to be known as a disability rights movement, and, with it, advocacy for some critically important perspectives and actions. It included groups that would grow and demand self-determination and independent living, an insistence on a shift from a deficits perspective to a strengths perspective in discussions of persons with disabilities, de-institutionalization and a right to treatment or habilitation, and the emergence of cultural perspectives within the communities of persons with disabilities. Over time, the effort was to ensure not only fair and appropriate treatment and a lack of discrimination but also policies that ensured that persons with a disability would not simply be acted upon, but would have a strong voice in what the policies did and how they did it. The term that became popular is "nothing about us, without us."[21]

World Wars I and II marked a critical period for the rise of disability rights, which is ironic because the eugenics movement was flourishing before and after World War I. However, the attitude was that disabled veterans were different in that they had incurred their disabilities in the service of the country, and therefore were not subject to the same level of social opprobrium as other people who were born with disabilities or dealt with disabilities as a result of accidents or illness. Notwithstanding the absurdity of the distinctions society was attempting to draw, the large number of veterans with disabilities fueled an emergence of rehabilitation as a field and an area of medical practice with the leadership of people like Dr. Howard A. Rusk.

One of those who supported that effort was President Franklin Delano Roosevelt who, in 1944, directed that "No overseas casualty is discharged from the armed forces until he has received the maximum benefit of hospitalization and convalescent facilities, which must include physical and psychological rehabilitation, vocational guidance, prevocational training, and resocialization."[22] Among the many sad ironies in this history is the fact that this president, who suffered from the ravages of polio, felt the need to hide his disabilities from general public view. In a day without television cameras and a more cooperative press corps, many Americans had no idea of the challenges to his mobility and health that resulted from the polio. The fact of his many accomplishments and great leadership should have dispelled any myths about the limitations of people with disabilities, but it was not a subject that was discussed.

Of course, the fact that there was some attention to veterans did not mean an end to the challenges of obtaining policy and financial support to address even the needs of that part of the population with disabilities. Each conflict since then has resulted in further political battles needed to get adequate and appropriate care and support. As battlefield medical practice improved, a larger percentage of wounded veterans survived and came home with needs for support and assistance ranging from prostheses to counseling for Post-Traumatic Stress Disorder, a condition not even recognized until after the war in Vietnam.

The post-war period also saw others organizing to obtain needed services and to battle against efforts to segregate and isolate persons with various disabilities, including intellectual disabilities—then referred to as mental retardation. In 1950 parents and other advocates joined together to form what was in earlier days called the National Association for Retarded Children, National Association for Retarded Citizens, Association for Retarded Citizens of the United States (ARC) and, now, The Arc of the United States.[23] As time moved on and other advocacy groups emerged, the discrimination, isolation, and demeaning treatment afforded persons with disabilities was not going away, even with their many efforts to move society forward. Part of the problem was based in policy and concerned such problems as the tendency to institutionalize—in reality to warehouse—people with disability, often without treatment or habilitation. In other cases, the issues concerned attitudes and social behavior that conveyed a derogatory view of a person with a disability.

The movement intensified during the 1960s and 1970s, as was the case with other aspects of civil rights development. One of the challenges for those seeking to ensure that there was a framework of civil rights protections that covered persons with disabilities along with other groups in society was that there are so many different types of disabilities and those who live with them have different needs and concerns. There were many areas, however, where there was common ground and it was possible, even in the midst of so many competing policy demands, to make progress in those areas. They included employment discrimination and the need to ensure equal educational opportunity.

One of the major steps forward with respect to employment, as well as in other areas, was the passage of the Rehabilitation Act of 1973.[24] The legislation was designed to replace existing federal rehabilitation statutes and to expand services, but it took an additional important step with respect to employment. Sections 501–504 required actions to increase federal hiring of persons with disabilities, required federal contractors and subcontractors to do the same, and added: "SEC. 504. No otherwise qualified handicapped individual in the United States, as defined in section 7(6), shall, solely by reason of his handicap, be excluded from the participation in, be denied the benefits of, or be subjected to discrimination under any program or activity receiving Federal financial assistance." This is often viewed as a shift to a civil rights perspective on addressing disabilities as compared to a very different earlier approach of attempting to fix or cure someone with a disability to make them productive for the society. "With the passage of the final version of the Rehabilitation Act of 1973, Congress explicitly recognized the pervasive discrimination against people with disabilities yet still did not view them as equal citizens."[25]

Although the 1973 act was a major step forward, it had very definite limits, most notably that it applied these employment requirements to the federal government, federal contractors, and programs receiving federal funds. It did not address private employment outside the context of government grants and contracts. Additionally, there was criticism that implementing regulations and interpretations of the legislation rendered the policy more limited in operation than many of its proponents had wished.[26]

Another significant victory was passage of the Education for All Handicapped Children Act in 1975.[27] (The legislation was later renamed the Individuals with Disabilities Education Act (IDEA) in part to remove unacceptable language.) The effort to ensure a "free and appropriate public education in the least restrictive environment" (FAPE) was not only about efforts to end the practice of segregating young people out of the public schools and into institutions, but also to ensure that they would receive a quality education. However, since no two children with disabilities are exactly alike, that meant a need to ensure an education appropriate to their needs and conditions. The legislation aimed to meet that need through a process that would produce an Individualized Education Plan (IEP) for which the local education authority (usually a school district) was responsible, not only in terms of ensuring that the procedural requirements were met, but also for ensuring that the IEP was properly implemented. If those responsibilities were not met, families could seek administrative and then judicial review if necessary.

The legislation was based on grants to the states with the FAPE and IEP as conditions of the grant. There is no doubt that what is now known as IDEA was a dramatic leap forward from what had existed before and actually provided children and their parents with rights that were judicially enforceable. However, there were and are many shortcomings, a number of which will be discussed later in the chapter. One of these is that what was supposed to be the amount of federal money available was never actually fully funded; and even if it had been, it would only have represented 40 percent of the cost incurred by state and local governments to implement the statute and ensure a FAPE to all students. Additionally, as a practical matter, the statute relies heavily upon parents to serve as effective advocates for their children in a process that is legally, educationally, and medically complex. Although parents do their best and are, as one would expect, determined advocates, they are often no match for school districts and the legal and expert resources they can bring to bear. And as the costs of developing and implementing IEPs have escalated over the years, some of those districts experience pressure from the community and their governing bodies to limit or even reduce costs. As will become clear later in this chapter, that has led districts to take an adversarial attitude toward parents, and in some instances to use the legal process to constrain the FAPE rather than to ensure its implementation.

There were three other critically important elements that evolved over time as the disability rights movement grew. They included a demand for a strengths-based approach, a recognition of the right to independent living and self-determination, and an awareness of cultural perspectives within the communities of persons with disabilities.

It is common to hear people who have disabilities say "I'm not broken. I don't need you to try to fix me." As Drimmer points out in his study of the history of legislation that addresses disabilities, there is a long tradition of treating anyone with a disability as if he or she were somehow defective or broken, and therefore the attitude has often been to blame or pity these men and women and to suggest that society needs to mend them medically or in some other way.[28] Another common reaction is to say "I am not a diagnosis." Someone may have been diagnosed with a particular disability or related illness, but he or she is a person and not just a set of symptoms. And when even well-meaning professionals or colleagues respond that way, they are working from a language of deficits rather than from the strengths a person has. The term strengths-based perspective is generally attributed to social work literature, but the idea of rejecting the deficit approach reaches far back in time to a rejection of the eugenics orientation and attitude.[29]

There are those who are concerned that even the concept of a strengths-based approach suggests some kind of problem, but the key point is that it would be difficult to find anyone who would appreciate it if those with whom they work, live, or do business approached them with the idea that this relationship is about problems rather than simply taking a person as they are. At some point, the deficit approach lends itself to discrimination or exclusion, neither of which is acceptable.

Related to this concern is what should be the obvious fact that everyone is entitled to self-determination and independence in how they live their lives. The disability rights movement has made clear that society has historically not recognized that fact, sometimes from a compassionate intent and sometimes from the less positive lens of deficits. That is also true of policies put in place over time, policies that do not recognize that fundamental rights are inherently discriminatory. Alternatively, policies and practices that place barriers in the way of one's ability to live a fully independent life are the real disabilities for many and should be subject to legal challenge. That is one of the many reasons why the passage of the Americans with Disabilities Act in 1990 was seen as so important and necessary.

Finally, and related to some of these points, is that fact that the disability rights movement prompted discussions about disability cultures. This is a difficult term to discuss because it can easily lend itself to abuse or discrimination. Indeed, Steven E. Brown began his discussion of the subject by noting that this involves two concepts, both of which touch a variety of sensitivities—culture and disability.[30] Brown and his cofounder, of the Institute of Disability Culture, explain what they mean by disability culture:

> People with disabilities have forged a group identity. We share a common history of oppression and a common bond of resilience. We generate art, music, literature, and other expressions of our lives and our culture, infused from our experience of disability. Most importantly, we are proud of ourselves as people with disabilities. We claim our disabilities with pride as part of our identity. We are who we are: we are people with disabilities.[31]

However, as Brown explains, there are groups of people who share life experience with particular disabilities who see themselves as having a particular culture, one of the most widely known of which is termed deaf culture. The Laurent Clerc Center of Galludet University explains deaf culture and provides a discussion of core values, starting with the idea that "American Deaf culture centers on the use of ASL and identification and unity with other people who are Deaf."[32]

All of these elements are central to the experience that people with disabilities have shared in their efforts to live the kind of life that any other person in society expects and indeed demands the right to enjoy. That said, there is a clear awareness that much remains to be done in law and public policy, not to mention social attitudes, to reach that point.

In Search of Constitutional Protection: Only the Lowest Level Standard Applies

One major strand of civil rights efforts for those with disabilities has been the effort to achieve the kinds of constitutional protections that other groups in society who have suffered a history of discrimination now enjoy. As is true of each of those other groups, however, there are unique experiences that have presented challenges for those with disabilities that are different from others. One of these is the question of constitutional protection from segregation and deprivation of liberty in the form of institutionalization and lack of treatment or habilitation where people have been committed to institutions. Consider first the general question of equal protection of the law.

What Kind of Equal Protection? The Lowest Level of Review, the Supreme Court, and Persons with Disabilities

As earlier chapters have explained, the Supreme Court has found that some ways that law and policy classify people are inherently suspect, the classic example of which is race. In other cases, such as gender, the Court has not found a suspect class but has determined that something higher than simply a rational basis test should apply—sometimes commonly referred to as heightened or intermediate scrutiny.[33] Some justices have argued vigorously about which groups should or should not be seen as subject to suspect classifications. Justice Powell explained in the *San Antonio* case that suspect classes involve people who constitute an identifiable group that has suffered a long history of invidious discrimination, often having membership in that group by birth or for other reasons not involving their own choice, and who have lacked a meaningful opportunity to cause the majoritarian political process to change policy to end discrimination and provide protection.[34] Justice Brennan argued that, if those are the criteria, then certainly classifications by gender should be seen as suspect, given the discrimination against and exclusion of women over the nation's history, but he could only attract a plurality of the Court to support that view and not a majority.[35] If the classification is not considered suspect on these grounds and there is not what the Court sees as a fundamental right at issue, then judges are to apply the lowest level of scrutiny of public policies. Under that standard, as the *San Antonio* opinion explained, they look only to see if the action is rationally related to some legitimate state purpose, a standard that rarely results in a finding of discrimination.

Given history, one might think that classifications based on disability would surely be inherently suspect, but the Court has rejected that argument and, indeed, has gone to the other end of the spectrum. The case that made that clear came from Texas and involved what was plainly an extreme example of discrimination in housing based on disability. However, what is particularly interesting about the opinion written by Justice Byron White for the Court is not just its reasoning in general, but also the way it speaks of persons with disabilities and their relationship to the larger society. It is all the more interesting and troublesome to read this material in light of the fact that it was written in 1985.

City of Cleburne, Texas v. Cleburne Living Center

473 U.S. 432 (1985)

INTRODUCTION: The City of Cleburne, Texas had an ordinance that required anyone seeking to open a group home for developmentally disabled residents to apply for a special permit. In order to obtain the permit the owners would have "to obtain the signatures of the property owners within two hundred (200) feet of the property to be used," and the permit would have to be renewed each year. These requirements would not be applied to apartment buildings, fraternity or sorority houses, senior citizen residences, or hospitals.

A home was purchased at 201 Featherston Street and leased to the Cleburne Living Center, which planned to open a fully staffed group home for 13 developmentally disabled adults, both men and women. It was in all relevant respects physically adequate and fire-safe. Even so, the City refused the permit. Cleburne Living sued, alleging discrimination under the Fourteenth Amendment.

Justice White wrote the opinion for the Court.

> The general rule is that legislation is presumed to be valid and will be sustained if the classification drawn by the statute is rationally related to a legitimate state interest.... The general rule gives way, however, when a statute classifies by race,

alienage, or national origin.... [T]hese laws are subjected to strict scrutiny and will be sustained only if they are suitably tailored to serve a compelling state interest.... Similar oversight by the courts is due when state laws impinge on personal rights protected by the Constitution....

[W]e conclude ... that the Court of Appeals erred in holding mental retardation a quasi-suspect classification calling for a more exacting standard of judicial review than is normally accorded economic and social legislation. First, it is undeniable ... that those who are mentally retarded have a reduced ability to cope with and function in the everyday world....[36] They are thus different, immutably so, in relevant respects, and the States' interest in dealing with and providing for them is plainly a legitimate one....

[T]he distinctive legislative response, both national and state, to the plight of those who are mentally retarded demonstrates not only that they have unique problems, but also that the lawmakers have been addressing their difficulties in a manner that belies a continuing antipathy or prejudice and a corresponding need for more intrusive oversight by the judiciary. [Cites to §504 of the Rehabilitation Act of 1973, 29 U. S. C., §794, Developmental Disabilities Assistance and Bill of Rights Act of 1975, and the Education of the Handicapped Act, discussed later in this chapter.] The State of Texas has similarly enacted legislation that acknowledges the special status of the mentally retarded by conferring certain rights upon them, such as "the right to live in the least restrictive setting appropriate to [their] individual needs and abilities," including "the right to live ... in a group home."

Such legislation thus singling out the retarded for special treatment reflects the real and undeniable differences between the retarded and others. That a civilized and decent society expects and approves such legislation indicates that governmental consideration of those differences in the vast majority of situations is not only legitimate but also desirable.... Even assuming that many of these laws could be shown to be substantially related to an important governmental purpose, merely requiring the legislature to justify its efforts in these terms may lead it to refrain from acting at all. Much recent legislation intended to benefit the retarded also assumes the need for measures that might be perceived to disadvantage them. The Education of the Handicapped Act, for example, requires an "appropriate" education, not one that is equal in all respects to the education of nonretarded children; clearly, admission to a class that exceeded the abilities of a retarded child would not be appropriate. Similarly, the Developmental Disabilities Assistance Act and the Texas Act give the retarded the right to live only in the "least restrictive setting" appropriate to their abilities, implicitly assuming the need for at least some restrictions that would not be imposed on others. Especially given the wide variation in the abilities and needs of the retarded themselves, governmental bodies must have a certain amount of flexibility and freedom from judicial oversight in shaping and limiting their remedial efforts.

Third, the legislative response, which could hardly have occurred and survived without public support, negates any claim that the mentally retarded are politically powerless in the sense that they have no ability to attract the attention of the lawmakers. Any minority can be said to be powerless to assert direct control over the legislature, but if that were a criterion for higher level scrutiny by the courts, much economic and social legislation would now be suspect.[37]

Our refusal to recognize the retarded as a quasi-suspect class does not leave them entirely unprotected from invidious discrimination. To withstand equal protection review, legislation that distinguishes between the mentally retarded and others must be rationally related to a legitimate governmental purpose....

We turn to the issue of the validity of the zoning ordinance insofar as it requires a special use permit for homes for the mentally retarded. We inquire first whether requiring a special use permit for the Featherston home in the circumstances here deprives respondents of the equal protection of the laws.... The city does not require a special use permit in an R-3 zone for apartment houses, multiple dwellings, boarding and lodging houses, fraternity or sorority houses, dormitories, apartment hotels, hospitals, sanitariums, nursing homes for convalescents or the aged (other than for the insane or feebleminded or alcoholics or drug addicts), private clubs or fraternal orders, and other specified uses.... May the city require the permit for this facility when other care and multiple-dwelling facilities are freely permitted?

It is true ... that the mentally retarded as a group are indeed different from others not sharing their misfortune, and in this respect they may be different from those who would occupy other facilities that would be permitted in an R-3 zone without a special permit. But this difference is largely irrelevant unless the Featherston home and those who would occupy it would threaten legitimate interests of the city in a way that other permitted uses such as boarding houses and hospitals would not. Because in our view the record does not reveal any rational basis for believing that the Featherston home would pose any special threat to the city's legitimate interests, we affirm the judgment below insofar as it holds the ordinance invalid as applied in this case.

The District Court found that the City Council's insistence on the permit rested on several factors. First, the Council was concerned with the negative attitude of the majority of property owners located within 200 feet of the Featherston facility, as well as with the fears of elderly residents of the neighborhood. But mere negative attitudes, or fear, unsubstantiated by factors which are properly cognizable in a zoning proceeding, are not permissible bases for treating a home for the mentally retarded differently from apartment houses, multiple dwellings, and the like.... [T]he city may not avoid the strictures of [the Equal Protection] Clause by deferring to the wishes or objections of some fraction of the body politic....

Second, the Council had two objections to the location of the facility. It was concerned that the facility was across the street from a junior high school, and it feared that the students might harass the occupants of the Featherston home. But the school itself is attended by about 30 mentally retarded students, and denying a permit based on such vague, undifferentiated fears is again permitting some portion of the community to validate what would otherwise be an equal protection violation. The other objection to the home's location was that it was located on "a five hundred year flood plain." This concern with the possibility of a flood, however, can hardly be based on a distinction between the Featherston home and, for example, nursing homes, homes for convalescents or the aged, or sanitariums or hospitals, any of which could be located on the Featherston site without obtaining a special use permit. The same may be said of another concern of the Council—doubts about the legal responsibility for actions which the mentally retarded might take. If there is no concern about legal responsibility with respect to other uses that would be permitted in the area, such as boarding and fraternity houses, it is difficult to believe that the groups of mildly or moderately mentally retarded individuals who would live at 201 Featherston would present any different or special hazard.

... [T]he Council was concerned with the size of the home and the number of people that would occupy it. The District Court found, and the Court of Appeals repeated, that "[if] the potential residents of the Featherston Street home were not mentally retarded, but the home was the same in all other respects, its use would be permitted under the city's zoning ordinance." ... Given this finding, there would be no restrictions on the number of people who could occupy this home as a boarding house, nursing home, family dwelling, fraternity house, or dormitory. The question is whether it is rational to treat the mentally retarded differently....

In the courts below the city also urged that the ordinance is aimed at avoiding concentration of population and at lessening congestion of the streets. These concerns obviously fail to explain why apartment houses, fraternity and sorority houses, hospitals and the like, may freely locate in the area without a permit. So, too, the expressed worry about fire hazards, the serenity of the neighborhood, and the avoidance of danger to other residents fail rationally to justify singling out a home such as 201 Featherston for the special use permit, yet imposing no such restrictions on the many other uses freely permitted in the neighborhood.

The short of it is that requiring the permit in this case appears to us to rest on an irrational prejudice against the mentally retarded, including those who would occupy the Featherston facility and who would live under the closely supervised and highly regulated conditions expressly provided for by state and federal law.[38]

Justice Marshall dissented in part, joined by Justices Brennan and Blackmun.

The Court holds that all retarded individuals cannot be grouped together as the "feebleminded" and deemed presumptively unfit to live in a community. Underlying this holding is the principle that mental retardation per se cannot be a proxy for depriving retarded people of their rights and interests without regard to variations in individual ability. With this holding and principle I agree. The Equal Protection Clause requires attention to the capacities and needs of retarded people as individuals. I cannot agree, however, with the way in which the Court reaches its result or with the narrow, as-applied remedy it provides for the city of Cleburne's equal protection violation....

I have long believed the level of scrutiny employed in an equal protection case should vary with "the constitutional and societal importance of the interest adversely affected and the recognized invidiousness of the basis upon which the particular classification is drawn." ... When a zoning ordinance works to exclude the retarded from all residential districts in a community, these two considerations require that the ordinance be convincingly justified as substantially furthering legitimate and important purposes....

First, the interest of the retarded in establishing group homes is substantial. The right to "establish a home" has long been cherished as one of the fundamental liberties embraced by the Due Process Clause.... For retarded adults, this right means living together in group homes, for as deinstitutionalization has progressed, group homes have become the primary means by which retarded adults can enter life in the community....

Second, the mentally retarded have been subject to a "lengthy and tragic history," ... of segregation and discrimination that can only be called grotesque. During much of the 19th century, mental retardation was viewed as neither curable nor dangerous and the retarded were largely left to their own devices. By the latter part of the century and during the first decades of the new one, however, social views of the retarded underwent a radical transformation. Fueled by the rising tide of Social Darwinism, the "science" of eugenics, and the extreme xenophobia of those years, leading medical authorities and others began to portray the "feebleminded" as a "menace to society and civilization ... responsible in a large degree for many, if not all, of our social problems." A regime of state-mandated segregation and degradation soon emerged that in its virulence and bigotry rivaled, and indeed paralleled, the worst excesses of Jim Crow. Massive custodial institutions were built to warehouse the retarded for life; the aim was to halt reproduction of the retarded and "nearly extinguish their race." Retarded children were categorically excluded from public schools, based on the false stereotype that all were ineducable and on the purported need to protect nonretarded children from them. State laws deemed the retarded "unfit for citizenship."

Segregation was accompanied by eugenic marriage and sterilization laws that extinguished for the retarded one of the "basic civil rights of man"—the right to marry and procreate.... Marriages of the retarded were made, and in some States continue to be, not only voidable but also often a criminal offense. The purpose of such limitations, which frequently applied only to women of child-bearing age, was unabashedly eugenic: to prevent the retarded from propagating. To assure this end, 29 States enacted compulsory eugenic sterilization laws between 1907 and 1931.... See *Buck v. Bell*....

Not until Congress enacted the Education of the Handicapped Act ... were "the [doors] of public education" opened wide to handicapped children. But most important, lengthy and continuing isolation of the retarded has perpetuated the ignorance, irrational fears, and stereotyping that long have plagued them.

In light of the importance of the interest at stake and the history of discrimination the retarded have suffered, the Equal Protection Clause requires us to do more than review the distinctions drawn by Cleburne's zoning ordinance as if they appeared in a taxing statute or in economic or commercial legislation....

The Court downplays the lengthy "history of purposeful unequal treatment" of the retarded ... by pointing to recent legislative action that is said to "[belie] a continuing antipathy or prejudice." ... It is natural that evolving standards of equality come to be embodied in legislation.... [However], even when judicial action has catalyzed legislative change, that change certainly does not eviscerate the underlying constitutional principle. The Court, for example, has never suggested that race-based classifications became any less suspect once extensive legislation had been enacted on the subject....

For the retarded, just as for Negroes and women, much has changed in recent years, but much remains the same; outdated statutes are still on the books, and irrational fears or ignorance, traceable to the prolonged social and cultural isolation of the retarded, continue to stymie recognition of the dignity and individuality of retarded people. Heightened judicial scrutiny of action appearing to impose unnecessary barriers to the retarded is required in light of increasing recognition that such barriers are inconsistent with evolving principles of equality embedded in the Fourteenth Amendment....

As the history of discrimination against the retarded and its continuing legacy amply attest, the mentally retarded have been, and in some areas may still be, the targets of action the Equal Protection Clause condemns. With respect to a liberty so valued as the right to establish a home in the community, and so likely to be denied on the basis of irrational fears and outright hostility, heightened scrutiny is surely appropriate....

The fact that the Court struck down the ordinance in this particular case was hardly a consolation for the disability rights movement. The attempt by Justice White to paint such a benign picture of the current state of treatment, in law as well as in fact, of persons with intellectual disabilities seemed at best incredibly uninformed and naive. In the end, the Court held flatly that classifications based on disabilities are not inherently suspect and the state need only provide a rational basis for its actions—the most deferential equal protection standard that exists.

Institutions and Rights: Institutionalization and Right to Treatment or Habilitation

The practice of hiding people with disabilities away or segregating them in institutions has a long history. This has been a particular danger for those with intellectual disabilities, other kinds of developmental disabilities, or mental health issues. Even today, there appears to be little awareness that many people with such conditions can and do—and indeed have every right to—live their own lives without interference from others. There are many people with a diagnosis on the autism spectrum who are highly educated and accomplished. Many who have intellectual disabilities live independently and work every day. A great many people have one or another form of mental health issues, but manage them very effectively through therapy or medication, or both. Even so, society continues to stereotype anyone with these kinds of disabilities and often behaves as if the community would rather not recognize that they exist.

At its worst, this ignorance and the fears that often accompany it have resulted in a common practice of depriving people of their liberty and institutionalizing those who plainly did not need to be in residential care. And just as society did not want to deal openly and positively with these disabilities, neither did the taxpayers want to provide financial support for those institutions adequate to ensure that they were safe and supportive places that would provide treatment where needed or education and developmental support. In case after case, investigations revealed conditions that horrified the public once they were known, but even then it often took protracted battles to shut them down, or to reform them to operate in a safe and supportive manner in situations where closing the facilities was not approved, or in those rare cases where alternatives to hospitalization were not available for those in extreme circumstances.

These tendencies across society brought the courts into the picture. The cases raised three types of questions. The first had to do with the protections available to adults and children who appeared to be placed into institutions, not because of a specific need to be there, but because families or the state did not know what else to do with them. Second, if one is committed to an institution, is there a right to treatment for those who have an illness that requires it or for habilitation for those who, like persons with intellectual disabilities, are not ill but who have support needs? Third, whatever the reason for the institutionalization, is there any guarantee of a safe and adequate environment?

The Supreme Court during the 1960s made it clear that the due process clause of the Fourteenth Amendment requires protections for a person committed to an institution. Even if there are emergency circumstances that require immediate hospitalization to ensure the safety of the patient or the safety of others, the opportunity for due process is required thereafter. The Supreme Court has said that institutionalization involves a "massive curtailment of liberty"[39] and that "civil commitment for any purpose constitutes a significant deprivation of liberty that requires due process protection."[40] Apart from the procedural protections, however, there are limits as to the reasons for which a person can be institutionalized. As the Court explained:

> A finding of "mental illness" alone cannot justify a State's locking a person up against his will and keeping him indefinitely in simple custodial confinement. Assuming that

that term can be given a reasonably precise content and that the "mentally ill" can be identified with reasonable accuracy, there is still no constitutional basis for confining such persons involuntarily if they are dangerous to no one and can live safely in freedom.... In short, a State cannot constitutionally confine without more a nondangerous individual who is capable of surviving safely in freedom by himself or with the help of willing and responsible family members or friends.[41]

This clear statement that mental illness alone is not a sufficient reason to commit someone to an institution against his or her will marked a major step forward in constitutional protections, given a long national history of doing precisely that. Put in less polite language, there has been a long history of dumping people into institutions for all kinds of reasons even if they could, with reasonable support, function well in society.

This problem has been a particularly painful issue where children are concerned. The problem is made more difficult because there are at least four sets of participants in the decision process with legal authority or rights. They include the parents, who may or may not be together and may disagree on whether a child needs to be hospitalized, the child, and the state. The state may elect to assert its authority and obligation to protect the child even against the asserted rights of the parents, or in some instances to protect the challenge against abuse or neglect. Also, the state has authority for children who are wards of the state, for whom the state makes the kinds of decisions parents might make *in loco parentis*.[42]

A federal district court in Georgia found that there were serious problems in the state mental health system, noting that a state commission report on mental health services had found: "It is the observation of both hospital personnel and the Commission that more than half of the hospitalized children would not need hospitalization if other forms of care were available in the community."[43] As the district judge concluded, these are children whose conditions do not require that they be in an institution and are there only because the state, even knowing of the situation, refused to address the need. Moreover, the district judges quoted the Director of Child and Adolescent Mental Health Services as making clear that: "While parents generally make such applications with the best of intentions and with the sincere desire to seek help for their child, the defendants nevertheless recognize what society knows but had rather not admit—'there are a lot of people who still treat [mental hospitals] as dumping grounds.'"[44] The three-judge federal district court concluded:

It is thus apparent that this statute supplies not the flexible due process that the situation of the plaintiff children demands but, instead, absolutely no due process. It is also apparent that it affords to parents, guardians, the Department of Human Resources as Custodian, and superintendents the "unchecked and unbalanced power over [the] essential liberties..." of these children that is universally mistrusted by our "whole scheme of American government." The double-check that is needed is that which is guaranteed by the Fourteenth Amendment—due process of law. There being none the statute in question violates the Due Process Clause of the Fourteenth Amendment and is unconstitutional."

However, the U.S. Supreme Court reversed in an opinion by Chief Justice Burger. Burger explained that the presumption is that parents will do what is best for the children and, so long as there is an independent third party like an admitting physician involved, there is no due process requirement for a hearing or other protections.[45] He also did not find a difficulty where the child is a ward of the state, because it is to be assumed that the state will act in the best interest of the child. Justice Brennan, writing for the three dissenters, responded: "With equal logic, it could be argued that criminal trials are unnecessary since prosecutors are not supposed to prosecute innocent persons."[46]

It was becoming apparent from studies and litigation through the 1960s and 1970s that there were significant numbers of adults and children who were institutionalized without any legitimate, medical, or public safety justification. It was just as obvious that there were others in those facilities who were receiving virtually no treatment, and that the conditions in many of the facilities were so bad that they were in fact dangerous to the life and health of the patients or residents. In light of these conditions questions were posed as to whether there were rights to treatment and to safe conditions.

It is important to stress what should be well understood but has too often been ignored, which is that children and adults with intellectual disabilities do not have a mental illness. The distinction in the development of civil rights law is that they have not sought a right to treatment but rather a right to habilitation. Habilitation services are defined by the Department of Health and Human Services as:

> health care services and devices that help a person keep, learn, or improve skills and functioning for daily living (habilitative services). Examples include therapy for a child who is not walking or talking at the expected age. These services may include physical and occupational therapy, speech-language pathology and other services for people with disabilities in a variety of inpatient and/or outpatient settings.[47]

The right to treatment or habilitation discussion in modern civil rights traces back to the early 1960s. In 1960 Morton Birnbaum, a physician and lawyer, published a seminal article in the *American Bar Association Journal* entitled "The Right to Treatment," in which he asserted that a person who was committed to hospital for mental illness has a "legal right ... to adequate medical treatment for his mental illness" grounded in the due process clause of the Fourteenth Amendment.[48] The *American Bar Association Journal* in which that article was published took an editorial position in support of Birnbaum's argument.[49] The American Bar Foundation sponsored a major study to inform next steps in the field, which was published in 1961.[50] Also in 1961 and again in 1963, the Senate Judiciary's Subcommittee on Constitutional Rights held hearings on the subject, which resulted in a new mental health statute for the District of Columbia.[51] These activities also influenced a number of states to rewrite their laws in this area over the course of the next several years.

With these activities in progress, and with the disability rights movement growing, a series of legal challenges were brought by individuals, families, and groups concerning both the right to treatment or habilitation and also conditions in state facilities. In a 1966 case, Judge David L. Bazelon of the U.S. Court of Appeals for the D.C. Circuit wrote that there was a right to treatment for persons committed to the mental health facility in the District of Columbia based on the reformed D.C. legislation recently passed by Congress, but the opinion also suggested a broader right to treatment.[52] In 1971 Judge Frank Johnson issued his ruling in *Wyatt v. Stickney*, firmly asserting that the due process clause of the Fourteenth Amendment did indeed provide a right to treatment for those committed to a mental institution.[53]

What emerged from these and other cases during the period, and what they also demonstrated in striking terms, was not only that persons who had been committed to state institutions were largely being warehoused without any meaningful treatment or habilitation, but also that the conditions of many of the institutions were, without exaggeration, horrific. That was true not only of facilities for adults, but also of institutions for children.

The situation in Alabama was one of the many locations in the country where the conditions and lack of treatment or habilitation were particularly dreadful.[54] The state that ranked last in expenditures for those in state facilities made yet another round of cuts to staff at the state's largest facility, Bryce State Hospital. That precipitated a legal challenge that quickly evolved into one of the most important legal cases on right to treatment or habilitation and institutional conditions. The state had two large facilities that were principally intended for those with mental health issues (Bryce and Searcy) and one that was supposed to address the needs of children with intellectual disabilities (Partlow State School and Hospital). The Court of Appeals later explained:

> First, it is clear that the environment at the hospitals was a far cry from the "humane psychological and physical environment" the district court envisioned as *sine qua non* of rehabilitative treatment. Bryce Hospital was built in the 1850's; it had 5,000 inmates of whom 1,500 to 1,600 were geriatrics, 1,000 were mental retardates, and there were allegedly other non-mentally ill persons. Patients in the hospitals were afforded virtually no privacy: the wards were overcrowded; there was no furniture where patients could keep clothing; there were no partitions between commodes in the bathrooms. There were severe health and safety problems: patients with open wounds and inadequately treated skin diseases were in imminent danger of infection because of the unsanitary conditions existing in the wards, such as permitting urine and feces to remain on the floor; there was evidence of insect infestation in the kitchen and dining areas. Malnutrition was a problem: the United States described the food as "com[ing] closer to 'punishment' by starvation" than nutrition. At Bryce, the food distribution and preparation systems were unsanitary, and less than 50 cents per day per patient was spent on food. Dr. Donald L. Clopper, Associate Commissioner for Mental Retardation for the Alabama Department of Mental Health, testified that Partlow was a "stepchild" in the State of Alabama; that the physical environment was inadequate for treating inmates; that "we don't have the staff, we don't have the facilities, nor do we have the financial resources." According to Dr. Clopper, at least 300 Partlow inmates could be discharged immediately, and about 70 percent of the inmates should never have been committed; yet it was 60 percent over-crowded. Patients at Partlow were forced to perform uncompensated labor. Aides frequently put patients in seclusion or under physical restraints, including straitjackets, without physicians' orders. One resident had been regularly confined in a straitjacket for more than nine years. The Evaluation Report on Partlow by the American Association on Mental Deficiency stated that nine working residents would feed 54 young boys ground food from one very large bowl with nine plates and nine spoons; "since there were no accommodations to even sit down to eat," it was impossible to tell which residents had been fed and which had not been fed with this system. Seclusion rooms were large enough for one bed and a coffee can, which served as a toilet. The patients suffered brutality, both at the hands of the aides and at the hands of their fellow patients; testimony established that four Partlow residents died due to understaffing, lack of supervision, and brutality.

> [The court added a footnote at this point, explaining that: "One of the four died after a garden hose had been inserted into his rectum for five minutes by a working patient who was cleaning him; one died when a fellow patient hosed him with scalding water; another died when soapy water was forced into his mouth; and a fourth died from a self-administered overdose of drugs which had been inadequately secured."]

> The hospitals failed to meet the second condition, adequate staffing. The defendants' chief witness on standards maintained that treatment could be delivered with the ratio of one psychiatrist, one graduate level psychologist, and one masters level social worker for every 125 patients, and the district court ultimately adopted this

recommendation. The organizations appearing as amici had recommended higher ratios—one psychiatrist, one psychologist, and one social worker for every 30–50 patients. But at the time this suit was instituted there were ratios of only one medical doctor with some psychiatric training for 5,000 patients, one Ph.D. psychologist for every 1,670 patients, and one masters level social worker for every 2,500 patients at Bryce. The parties and amici agreed completely on the minimums necessary for treatment of the mentally retarded. They agreed that adequate treatment could be delivered at Partlow with ratios of one masters level psychologist and one masters level social worker for every sixty patients, and one physician for every two hundred patients. Yet at Partlow there were only one psychologist with masters level training or above for every 1,200 patients; one masters level social worker for every 730 patients; and one physician for every 550 patients. Of the four physicians at Partlow, two were not licensed to practice in Alabama.

A severe shortage of nonprofessional staff paralleled the inadequacies of professional staff. After a tour of Bryce, defendants' own consultants noted that: "Aide staff is spread very thin, creating extreme stresses for individual aides, who at times must cover one or two or three wards, housing as many as 100 or 200 patients." Obviously, it is impossible under such circumstances to provide anything more than a cursory observation and the hope of avoiding disturbing incidents. An aide under these circumstances is hard pressed to meet even minimum patient needs.

The institutional staff was inadequate not only in sheer numbers but also in training; there was no effective "in-service training" program for, or even any regular supervision over, the non-professionals.[55]

Given this situation and the financial shortages facing the institutions, the health, sanitation, nutrition and safety conditions were, by any measure, horrendous. There was also a dramatic lack of facilities maintenance. All of that was quite apart from what was essentially a total breakdown in any serious program of treatment.

The situation at Partlow was not uncovered until after Judge Johnson had issued his initial rulings on Bryce and Searcy, announcing that there was a right to treatment and safe and healthful conditions.[56] As the parties went through months of negotiations on what became extensive consent decrees to correct the situation, the state resisted attempts by the plaintiffs and amicus curiae to inspect the facility. Those inspections were ordered in January 1972 and the state was rocked by the revelation of the terrible conditions in which the children were being warehoused. In addition to the conditions set forth in the opinion above, the reports of those who inspected the facilities were so wrenching that Judge Johnson issued an emergency order after the hearing on the conditions to protect the lives and safety of the children there.

One of those who reported was Dr. Philip Roos, then Executive Director of the National Association of Retarded Children. He found children who had been kept in isolation or in physical restraints for years—without even a review of their situation—and the same was true of prescriptions that had not been reviewed for years at a time. He found children with wounds that obviously had gone untreated for some time. Consider just two of his observations regarding a ward for girls.

> I noticed one of the residents was in a camisole tied to a bench. A camisole is a restraining device in which the hands and arms are held roughly in this position (gestures). I asked the charge attendant about this, why it was necessary; and she explained that this was necessary because the girl sucked her hands and her fingers. And I asked the attendant how long this girl had been in a camisole; the attendant indicated as long as she, the attendant, had been on that unit, which I ascertained was the last nine years....[57]

I found one girl squatting on the floor in a sort of wooden case-like contrivance. And I asked about this, and I was told that she spent her waking hours in this wooden cage. And I asked what happened when she is released from this thing, and I was told that she would then scoot along the floor. I was also told that she could stand. And I asked the attendant what happened if this girl was given a walker, and I was told this had never been done; it had never been tried. I noticed one of the other young girls who was tied in bed by a waist restraint jumped out of bed and stood next to the bed and was promptly put back in the bed. Asked why she was tied; I was told that the doctors had mandated that she be tied in bed, because when she assumed an upright position, she tended to vomit.[58]

It would have been bad enough if this situation had only existed in one state, but it became increasingly clear throughout the decade of the 1970s and into the 1980s that terrible conditions and a lack of treatment or habilitation was a problem in many places around the nation. In addition to the litigation that was drawing the attention of the disability rights movement and the federal government, extreme examples of the problem surfaced in the media, such as in the case of the Willowbrook facility in New York State, where a hidden camera brought into the facility provided the media with graphic video of the situation and resulted in litigation and efforts to enforce agreements that lasted well into the 1980s.[59]

The U.S. Supreme Court did not reach the conditions issue in these facilities until 1982, when another notorious institution, Pennsylvania's Pennhurst State School and Hospital, prompted *Youngberg v. Romeo*.[60] The lower court in that case had concluded that persons in such facilities had rights under the "Due Process Clause of the Fourteenth Amendment to (i) safe conditions of confinement; (ii) freedom from bodily restraints; and (iii) training or 'habilitation.'"[61] In an opinion by Justice Powell, the Court agreed that there were rights to the first two of these.

> The mere fact that Romeo has been committed under proper procedures does not deprive him of all substantive liberty interests under the Fourteenth Amendment.... Indeed, the State concedes that respondent has a right to adequate food, shelter, clothing, and medical care. We must decide whether liberty interests also exist in safety, freedom of movement, and training. If such interests do exist, we must further decide whether they have been infringed in this case:
>
> Respondent's first two claims involve liberty interests recognized by prior decisions of this Court, interests that involuntary commitment proceedings do not extinguish. The first is a claim to safe conditions. In the past, this Court has noted that the right to personal security constitutes a "historic liberty interest" protected substantively by the Due Process Clause. *Ingraham v. Wright*, 430 U.S. 651, 673 (1977). And that right is not extinguished by lawful confinement, even for penal purposes. See *Hutto v. Finney*, 437 U.S. 678 (1978). If it is cruel and unusual punishment to hold convicted criminals in unsafe conditions, it must be unconstitutional to confine the involuntarily committed—who may not be punished at all—in unsafe conditions.
>
> Next, respondent claims a right to freedom from bodily restraint. In other contexts, the existence of such an interest is clear in the prior decisions of this Court. Indeed, "[liberty] from bodily restraint always has been recognized as the core of the liberty protected by the Due Process Clause from arbitrary governmental action." ... This interest survives criminal conviction and incarceration. Similarly, it must also survive involuntary commitment.[62]

The Court went to recognize only a limited right to some kind of training or habilitation. Indeed, the opinion warns other courts that they should exercise great deference to the professionals at the institution about this and other elements of the case:

> Moreover, we agree that respondent is entitled to minimally adequate training. In this case, the minimally adequate training required by the Constitution is such training as may be reasonable in light of respondent's liberty interests in safety and freedom from unreasonable restraints. In determining what is "reasonable"— in this and in any case presenting a claim for training by a State—we emphasize that courts must show deference to the judgment exercised by a qualified professional. By so limiting judicial review of challenges to conditions in state institutions, interference by the federal judiciary with the internal operations of these institutions should be minimized. Moreover, there certainly is no reason to think judges or juries are better qualified than appropriate professionals in making such decisions.... For these reasons, the decision, if made by a professional, is presumptively valid; liability may be imposed only when the decision by the professional is such a substantial departure from accepted professional judgment, practice, or standards as to demonstrate that the person responsible actually did not base the decision on such a judgment. In an action for damages against a professional in his individual capacity, however, the professional will not be liable if he was unable to satisfy his normal professional standards because of budgetary constraints; in such a situation, good-faith immunity would bar liability.[63]

Unfortunately, the lack of resources had been one of the key factors that put professionals in the difficult ethical and clinical situation of using and tolerating practices that few of them would ever want to have to defend. And the situation only got worse, as the economy of the nation was in difficulty through the late 1970s and well into the 1980s.

Once it became clear that institutions were not meeting their obligations and were in fact causing injury to those placed within their walls, the deinstitutionalization movement gained momentum. The prevailing argument was that hospitalization should only happen in those extreme situations in which someone was a danger to themselves or others and those conditions could not be addressed in a less restrictive environment.

Even in many of the most challenging situations, the assumption was that a combination of medication and outpatient community-based treatment was the preferred method of action. Of course, the problem was that budget-cutting under both Democrats and Republicans meant that many of the community-based programs that provided these services either did not receive funding or were provided with so little money that they were unlikely to address more than a fraction of the need. In addition, other federally funded programs that provided support for community-based social service agencies meant that the network of support overall was being weakened year after year across a wide range of services. It is important to note that flat-funding (no increases year-on-year) of these programs for extended periods in reality mean dramatic cuts as the costs of providing services increases.

The sad irony of these factors is that, nearly a century and a half after Dorothea Dix exposed the dumping of persons with illnesses or disabilities into local jails that were never designed to provide for such inmates and certainly not to provide them with services, the same situation has reemerged nationwide in the United States. There are certainly more community-based treatment options than there were when the deinstitutionalization movement was getting underway. And many of the institutions that were the focus of that effort have closed. However, it has become abundantly clear across the nation that too many people who need some assistance are not able to access the programs and support they should have. In an economy that has dramatically increased the gap between the rich and the poor, eliminating living wage jobs that might be available, persons with disabilities have suffered disproportionately with unemployment rates that far exceed the rest of the population.

There has also been less willingness than promised during the reform debates to provide tax support for community-based programs. For these and other reasons, significant numbers of people with mental health issues have found themselves homeless and without the treatment they need. Too often some of these men and women find themselves in county jails. That situation has continued, even though one county sheriff after another has complained to the media about the problem.[64] They end up there after an encounter with law enforcement officers and that has, in itself, resulted in serious difficulties, since those officers do not have the training or support that are necessary to deal with these encounters.[65]

Quite apart from these issues related to mental health, the unemployment and underemployment rates of men and women with other types of disabilities, from mobility issues to deafness to visual impairments, have also contributed, together with housing discrimination, to significant rates of homelessness.[66] In many cases the programs that are supposed to assist them are too often overwhelmed and underfunded.

The Emphasis on Legislative Protection: The ADA, IDEA, and Others

As this discussion shows, although there are some constitutional protections for people with disabilities, these fall woefully short of the kinds of civil rights guarantees needed by them and available to other groups who have such a long history of exclusion and discrimination. It has been in part the lack of such constitutional protections that has led to the enactment of a framework of legislation that has developed over time. Such statutes as the Rehabilitation Act of 1973, the IDEA, the Americans with Disabilities Act of 1990, and the Developmental Disabilities Assistance and Bill of Rights Act of 1975 have helped to build a body of civil rights protections, but it is a limited fabric of guarantees that has many weaknesses that in practice leave efforts to ensure civil rights for those with disabilities a work in progress that is far from complete.

No **Brown v. Board of Education** *for Children with Disabilities, but an IDEA*

Contrary to what some people think, there was no *Brown v. Board of Education* for students with disabilities. Disability rights advocates thought there should be, but the Supreme Court never spoke to that question. What did draw national attention was a set of two opinions that came from the U.S. District Court for the District of Columbia and Eastern District of Pennsylvania in 1971 and 1972, known popularly as the *PARC* and *Mills* cases.

The fact is that these were only two district court decisions. One was merely an action to compel compliance with a consent agreement submitted by the parties in a case.[67] The other did address a right to equal educational opportunity for children with disabilities.[68] However, this is a long way from the kinds of claims that are sometimes made about the importance of these two cases. They were not appellate court rulings and never went to the Supreme Court. Their significance really came from their influence on the legislative debates taking place at the time that led to the statute to come.

These two rulings came at a time when members of Congress were responding to disability rights advocates, and holding hearings on the fact that so many children with disabilities were either excluded from educational opportunity, or put in a position of second-class status as students that too often led them to drop out of school. It was this advocacy and the legal and political arguments that led to passage of the Education for All Handicapped Children Act (EAHA) in 1975.

It was one thing to mandate a free and appropriate public education in the least restrictive environment, but quite another to define what "appropriate" meant for the thousands of children covered by the legislation, each of whom had particular needs and challenges. Defining what appropriate meant for each of these children also implied that resources would have to be found to implement the IEPs that explained what was needed for each child.

For parents and disability rights advocates, an education would not be appropriate if it provided only enough support to allow a student to make minimal progress through school, as compared to providing what was needed to ensure that each student could reach his or her true potential. The very first case to reach the Supreme Court concerning the EAHA asked what the legislation required.

Bd. of Ed. of the Hendrick Hudson Central School Dist. v. Rowley

458 U.S. 176 (1982)

INTRODUCTION: The Education for All Handicapped Children Act was enacted in 1975.[69] It required a free and appropriate public education in the least restrictive environment (FAPE) for children with disabilities. New York received the federal grant under the act and was therefore covered by its requirements.

Amy Rowley was a student at Furnace Woods School in the Hendrick Hudson Central School District in Peekskill. She was deaf and had only minimal residual hearing. She had strong lipreading skills. Her parents, who were also deaf, met with school officials to determine what kinds of support she would need in the regular kindergarten class. Before she came to the school, some of the district's people took a sign-language course and put in a teletype machine to facilitate communication with her parents.

School personnel did an assessment after a trial period. They agreed that she should stay in the regular class in which she was placed, but also decided to provide her with an FM hearing aid and to install the FM equipment for the teacher and classroom to make that system operational. She performed adequately in the kindergarten year.

In compliance with the EAHA, the school carried out a process to produce an Individualized Education Plan (IEP) for Amy for first grade. Again, she was to be in the regular class, would again have the FM system, and would receive an hour per day of tutoring from someone qualified to work with deaf students. Her parents accepted the IEP, except that they insisted that she have a sign language interpreter in all her academic classes.

An interpreter was in her kindergarten class for two weeks, but the interpreter indicated that Amy did not need those services at that point. The school personnel decided she would not need an interpreter in first grade either, following a finding by the district Committee on the Handicapped, which had taken evidence from her parents and her teacher and had visited a class for deaf students.

Amy's parents demanded an administrative hearing to contest the IEP, but the examiner upheld the school decision on grounds that "'Amy was achieving educationally, academically, and socially' without such assistance." That decision was upheld by the state Commissioner of Education. The Rowleys sought judicial review.

The District Court agreed that Amy needed the sign language interpreter. She was "'advancing easily from grade to grade,' ... but ... 'she understands considerably less of what goes on in class than she could if she were not deaf' and thus 'is not learning as much, or performing as well academically, as she would without her handicap.'" Since she was not learning at the level of her potential, she was not receiving a FAPE. The Second Circuit affirmed.

Justice Rehnquist wrote the opinion for the Court.

Petitioners contend that the Court of Appeals and the District Court misconstrued the requirements imposed by Congress upon States which receive federal funds under the Education of the Handicapped Act. We agree and reverse the judgment of the Court of Appeals.

... In order to qualify for federal financial assistance under the Act, a State must demonstrate that it "has in effect a policy that assures all handicapped children the right to a free appropriate public education." ... States receiving money under the Act ... "to the maximum extent appropriate" must educate handicapped children "with children who are not handicapped." ... The Act broadly defines "handicapped children" to include "mentally retarded, hard of hearing, deaf, speech impaired, visually handicapped, seriously emotionally disturbed, orthopedically impaired, [and] other health impaired children, [and] children with specific learning disabilities." ...

The "free appropriate public education" required by the Act is tailored to the unique needs of the handicapped child by means of an "individualized educational program" (IEP).... The IEP ... is prepared at a meeting between a qualified representative of the local educational agency, the child's teacher, the child's parents or guardian, and, where appropriate, the child.... We granted certiorari to ... consider ... What is meant by the Act's requirement of a "free appropriate public education"?

This is the first case in which this Court has been called upon to interpret any provision of the Act.... The United States, appearing as *amicus curiae* on behalf of respondents, states that "[although] the Act includes definitions of a 'free appropriate public education' and other related terms, the statutory definitions do not adequately explain what is meant by 'appropriate.'" ...

According to the definitions contained in the Act, a "free appropriate public education" consists of educational instruction specially designed to meet the unique needs of the handicapped child, supported by such services as are necessary to permit the child "to benefit" from the instruction. Almost as a checklist for adequacy under the Act, the definition also requires that such instruction and services be provided at public expense and under public supervision, meet the State's educational standards, approximate the grade levels used in the State's regular education, and comport with the child's IEP. Thus, if personalized instruction is being provided with sufficient supportive services to permit the child to benefit from the instruction, and the other items on the definitional checklist are satisfied, the child is receiving a "free appropriate public education" as defined by the Act.

When [the] express statutory findings and priorities are read together with the Act's extensive procedural requirements and its definition of "free appropriate public education," the face of the statute evinces a congressional intent to bring previously excluded handicapped children into the public education systems of the States and to require the States to adopt *procedures* which would result in individualized consideration of and instruction for each child.

Noticeably absent from the language of the statute is any substantive standard prescribing the level of education to be accorded handicapped children. Certainly the language of the statute contains no requirement like the one imposed by the lower courts—that States maximize the potential of handicapped children "commensurate with the opportunity provided to other children." ... Thus, the intent of the Act was more to open the door of public education to handicapped children on appropriate terms than to guarantee any particular level of education once inside....

Respondents contend that "the goal of the Act is to provide each handicapped child with an equal educational opportunity." ... We think, however, that the requirement that a State provide specialized educational services to handicapped children generates no additional requirement that the services so provided be sufficient to maximize each child's potential "commensurate with the opportunity provided other children." ... [W]e do not think that such statements imply a congressional intent to achieve strict equality of opportunity or services.

The educational opportunities provided by our public school systems undoubtedly differ from student to student, depending upon a myriad of factors that might affect a particular student's ability to assimilate information presented in the classroom. The requirement that States provide "equal" educational opportunities would thus seem to present an entirely unworkable standard requiring impossible measurements and comparisons. Similarly, furnishing handicapped children with only such services as are available to nonhandicapped children would in all probability fall short of the statutory requirement of "free appropriate public education"; to require, on the other hand, the furnishing of every special service necessary to maximize each handicapped child's potential is, we think, further than Congress intended to go. Thus to speak in terms of "equal" services in one instance gives less than what is required by the Act and in another instance more. The theme of the Act is "free appropriate public education," a phrase which is too complex to be captured by the word "equal" whether one is speaking of opportunities or services....

The District Court and the Court of Appeals thus erred when they held that the Act requires New York to maximize the potential of each handicapped child commensurate with the opportunity provided nonhandicapped children. Desirable though that goal might be, it is not the standard that Congress imposed upon States which receive funding under the Act. Rather, Congress sought primarily to identify and evaluate handicapped children, and to provide them with access to a free public education.

Implicit in the congressional purpose of providing access to a "free appropriate public education" is the requirement that the education to which access is provided be sufficient to confer some educational benefit upon the handicapped child.... The statutory definition of "free appropriate public education," in addition to requiring that States provide each child with "specially designed instruction," expressly requires the provision of "such ... supportive services ... as may be required to assist a handicapped child *to benefit* from special education." §1401(17) (emphasis added). We therefore conclude that the "basic floor of opportunity" provided by the Act consists of access to specialized instruction and related services which are individually designed to provide educational benefit to the handicapped child....

The determination of when handicapped children are receiving sufficient educational benefits to satisfy the requirements of the Act presents a more difficult problem. The Act requires participating States to educate a wide spectrum of handicapped children, from the marginally hearing-impaired to the profoundly retarded and palsied. It is clear that the benefits obtainable by children at one end of the spectrum will differ dramatically from those obtainable by children at the other end, with infinite variations in between. One child may have little difficulty competing successfully in an academic setting with nonhandicapped children while another child may encounter great difficulty in acquiring even the most basic of self-maintenance skills. We do not attempt today to establish any one test for determining the adequacy of educational benefits conferred upon all children covered by the Act. Because in this case we are presented with a handicapped child who is receiving substantial specialized instruction and related services, and who is performing above average in the regular classrooms of a public school system, we confine our analysis to that situation.

... When the language of the Act and its legislative history are considered together, the requirements imposed by Congress become tolerably clear. Insofar as a State is required to provide a handicapped child with a "free appropriate public education," we hold that it satisfies this requirement by providing personalized instruction with sufficient support services to permit the child to benefit educationally from that instruction. Such instruction and services must be provided at public expense, must meet the State's educational standards, must approximate the grade levels used in the State's regular education, and must comport with the child's IEP. In addition, the IEP, and therefore the personalized instruction, should be formulated in accordance with the requirements of the Act and, if the child is being educated in the regular classrooms of the public education system, should be reasonably calculated to enable the child to achieve passing marks and advance from grade to grade.[70]

Justice White wrote a dissent joined by Justices Brennan and Marshall.

In order to reach its result in this case, the majority opinion contradicts itself, the language of the statute, and the legislative history. Both the majority's standard for a "free appropriate education" and its standard for judicial review disregard congressional intent.

... I agree that the language of the Act does not contain a substantive standard beyond requiring that the education offered must be "appropriate." However, if there are limits not evident from the face of the statute on what may be considered an "appropriate education," they must be found in the purpose of the statute or its legislative history. The Act itself announces it will provide a *"full* educational opportunity to all handicapped children." ... These statements elucidate the meaning of "appropriate." According to the Senate Report, for example, the Act does "guarantee that handicapped children are provided *equal* educational opportunity." ... Indeed, at times the purpose of the Act was described as tailoring each handicapped child's educational plan to enable the child "to achieve his or her maximum potential." H. R. Rep. No. 94–332, pp. 13, 19 (1975); see 121 Cong. Rec. 23709 (1975)....

The majority opinion announces a different substantive standard, that "Congress did not impose upon the States any greater substantive educational standard than would be necessary to make such access meaningful." ... While "meaningful" is no more enlightening than "appropriate," the Court purports to clarify itself. Because Amy was provided with *some* specialized instruction from which she obtained *some* benefit and because she passed from grade to grade, she was receiving a meaningful and therefore appropriate education....

This falls far short of what the Act intended. The Act details as specifically as possible the kind of specialized education each handicapped child must receive. It would apparently satisfy the Court's standard ... for a deaf child such as Amy to be given a teacher with a loud voice, for she would benefit from that service. The

Act requires more. It defines "special education" to mean "specifically designed instruction, at no cost to parents or guardians, to *meet the unique needs* of a handicapped child ...." Providing a teacher with a loud voice would not meet Amy's needs and would not satisfy the Act. The basic floor of opportunity is instead, as the courts below recognized, intended to eliminate the effects of the handicap, at least to the extent that the child will be given an equal opportunity to learn if that is reasonably possible. Amy Rowley, without a sign-language interpreter, comprehends less than half of what is said in the classroom—less than half of what normal children comprehend. This is hardly an equal opportunity to learn, even if Amy makes passing grades....

The issue before us is what standard the word "appropriate" incorporates when it is used to modify "education." The answer given by the Court is not a satisfactory one.... Because the standard of the courts below seems to me to reflect the congressional purpose and because their factual findings are not clearly erroneous, I respectfully dissent.

The language and tone of Justice Rehnquist's opinion as well as the attitude it conveyed was not lost on disability rights advocates. The goal was not to be maximizing a child's potential or anything even close to that. The act was, according to the Court, little more than an assurance of a process and that all that was needed in the end was the ability of the child to move from grade to grade.

The opinion also signaled that parents had to be prepared for a long-running fight with school officials if they wanted to get what they considered was a free and appropriate education for their child. And over time it became increasingly clear that the Supreme Court, at least, was not hearing the arguments of the parents and the advocates.

The challenges for parents and children are many and complex. On the one hand, parents are with their children all the time and know their capabilities and limitations intimately, whereas school officials have limited amounts of time to spend with individual children. Families may have a family physician, and they often deal with a variety of health care providers from speech pathologists to physical therapists to occupational therapists to psychologists and beyond. However, they often have limited time and limited resources because of all that they need to do for their children. They also have pressing financial needs and other obligations to address. School districts, on the other hand, have staff in-house and access to experts. Families need to find ways to pay for that assistance if they seek it.

These factors often make it difficult for parents to get the attention of the key people at the school district in order to ensure that the IEP is adequate and current for the child's needs. It also means that districts have incentives and pressures (whether they are conscious of them or not) to seek to limit the scope and nature of IEPs. Indeed, when President George W. Bush created his commission on special education by executive order, he made it abundantly clear that a major part of policy change in this area would be concern with costs.[71] For school districts, there is also the fear of the slippery slope. If the district agrees to something for one child, then, the theory goes, other parents will demand that and more. Finally, because it is so difficult for parents to bring attention to difficulties, by the time there is an exchange, it can be less positive and more confrontational than either side would hope to see. These factors have led some districts to retain law firms that make clear their intention to protect the district against the demands of parents and to aggressively litigate cases to deter parental pressures.

Parents are almost always at a distinct disadvantage in a situation in which the district chooses to take a hard position. They frequently do not have the resources to hire attorneys and would not know how to retain counsel with the appropriate knowledge and experience in this highly technical arena. Such attorneys are in short supply, even in states that have generally had a reputation for disability rights advocacy. Then there is often a need for experts who can provide additional evidence and informed opinion to support the child and family. The Supreme Court has held that even where parents eventually win their case and may obtain legal fees, they cannot recover the costs of the experts.[72] The Court has also held that where the dispute appears evenly balanced between the family and the district, the burden is on the family to persuade the court of the need for a change or enhancement of the IEP, not the district to prove that the IEP is adequate.[73]

For these and other reasons, it is clear that although the IDEA is a dramatic improvement over the situation before 1975, it is a challenging policy to administer and one which places heavy burdens on families in their efforts to ensure that their child is in fact receiving a free and appropriate public education in the least restrictive environment.

The Developmental Disabilities Assistance and Bill of Rights Act

Even before the IDEA developed, the foundations were laid for what would later become the Developmental Disabilities Assistance and Bill of Rights Act.[74] Early in the 1960s President Kennedy took a number of steps to address the calls of the emerging disability rights movement, and in particular focused on children with intellectual disabilities, starting with his appointment of the President's Panel on Mental Retardation. That group reported a year later in a document entitled "A Proposed Program for National Action to Combat Mental Retardation." The administration used that report to rally support for a number of bills in 1962 and 1963. Indeed, the Developmental Disabilities Services and Facilities Construction Amendments of 1970 moved beyond speaking of mental retardation to emphasize developmental disabilities, which included not only intellectual disabilities but also a variety of other issues such as cerebral palsy, epilepsy, and certain other neurological conditions.[75] These pieces of legislation provided support for a variety of programs and related federal government operations.

In 1975 the act was again amended to become the Developmental Disabilities Assistance and Bill of Rights Act. In addition to adding to the programs established in the previous legislation noted above, the new statute added a bill of rights for those with developmental disabilities that provided:

(1) Persons with developmental disabilities have a right to appropriate treatment, services, and habilitation for such disabilities.

(2) The treatment, services, and habilitation for a person with developmental disabilities should be designed to maximize the developmental potential of the person and should be provided in the setting that is least restrictive of the person's personal liberty.

(3) The Federal Government and the States both have an obligation to assure that public funds are not provided to any institutional or other residential program for persons with developmental disabilities that—

    (A) does not provide treatment, services, and habilitation which is appropriate to the needs of such persons; or

    (B) does not meet the following minimum standards:

        (i) Provision of a nourishing, well-balanced daily diet to the persons with developmental disabilities being served by the program.

        (ii) Provision to such persons of appropriate and sufficient medical and dental services.

        (iii) Prohibition of the use of physical restraint on such persons unless absolutely necessary and prohibition of the use of such restraint as a punishment or as a substitute for a habilitation program.

(iv)   Prohibition on the excessive use of chemical restraints on such persons and the use of such restraints as punishment or as a substitute for a habilitation program or in quantities that interfere with services, treatment, or habilitation for such persons.

(v)   Permission for close relatives of such persons to visit them at reasonable hours without prior notice.

(vi)   Compliance with adequate fire and safety standards as may be promulgated by the Secretary.

(4)   All programs for persons with developmental disabilities should meet standards which are designed to assure the most favorable possible outcome for those served, and—

(A)   in the case of residential programs serving persons in need of comprehensive health-related, habilitative, or rehabilitative services, which are at least equivalent to those standards applicable to intermediate care facilities for the mentally retarded promulgated in regulations of the Secretary on January 17, 1974 (39 Fed. Reg. pt. II), as appropriate when taking into account the size of the institutions and the service delivery arrangements of the facilities of the programs;

(B)   in the case of other residential programs for persons with developmental disabilities, which assure that care is appropriate to the needs of the persons being served by such programs, assure that the persons admitted to facilities of such programs are persons whose needs can be met through services provided by such facilities, and assure that the facilities under such programs provide for the humane care of the residents of the facilities, are sanitary, and protect their rights; and

(C)   in the case of nonresidential programs, which assure the care provided by such programs is appropriate to the persons served by the programs.[76]

This came as a number of the right to treatment/habilitation and institutional conditions cases were pending in federal courts. One of the major cases was brought by a young man who was institutionalized in the Pennhurst State School and Hospital in Pennsylvania. It was a class action suit joined by a variety of other families and nongovernmental organizations. The U.S. government intervened in the case in support of those challenges to the practices and conditions at Pennhurst. The federal district court found a variety of problems at Pennhurst and that litigation found its way to the United States Supreme Court.

In particular, the case called upon the Supreme Court to rule for the first time on the provisions of the Developmental Disabilities Assistance and Bill of Rights Act. However, the Court refused to read the act as an actual bill of rights that had teeth. Justice Rehnquist, writing for the majority, said:

> The Court of Appeals for the Third Circuit held that the Act created substantive rights in favor of the mentally retarded, that those rights were judicially enforceable, and that conditions at the Pennhurst State School and Hospital (Pennhurst), a facility for the care and treatment of the mentally retarded, violated those rights. For the reasons stated below, we reverse the decision of the Court of Appeals and remand the cases for further proceedings.[77]...
>
> [W]e find nothing in the Act or its legislative history to suggest that Congress intended to require the States to assume the high cost of providing "appropriate treatment" in the "least restrictive environment" to their mentally retarded citizens.... We are persuaded that §6010, when read in the context of other more specific provisions of the Act, does no more than express a congressional preference for certain kinds of treatment. It is simply a general statement of "findings" and, as such, is too thin a reed to support the rights and obligations read into it by the court below.[78]

Justice White wrote the dissent joined by Justices Brennan and Marshall. Citing the plain language of the statute and on the basis of a careful analysis of the legislative history, the dissenters concluded:

As clearly as words can, §6010(1) declares that the developmentally disabled have the right to appropriate treatment, services, and habilitation. The ensuing parts of §6010 implement this basic declaration. Section 6010(3), for example, *obligates* the Federal and State Governments not to spend the public funds on programs that do not carry out the basic requirement of §6010(1) and, more specifically, do not meet minimum standards with respect to certain aspects of treatment and custody....

Standing on its own bottom, therefore, §6010 cannot be treated as only wishful thinking on the part of Congress or as playing some fanciful role in the implementation of the Act. The section clearly states rights which the developmentally disabled are to be provided as against a participating State.[79]

Since that time, the legislation has been amended several times, most notably in the Developmental Disabilities Assistance and Bill of Rights Act of 2000.[80] Congress sought to strengthen the programs and organizations created over the history of the legislation and sets out the following statement of goals.

[T]he goals of the Nation properly include a goal of providing individuals with developmental disabilities with the information, skills, opportunities, and support to—

(A) make informed choices and decisions about their lives;
(B) live in homes and communities in which such individuals can exercise their full rights and responsibilities as citizens;
(C) pursue meaningful and productive lives;
(D) contribute to their families, communities, and States, and the Nation;
(E) have interdependent friendships and relationships with other persons;
(F) live free of abuse, neglect, financial and sexual exploitation, and violations of their legal and human rights; and
(G) achieve full integration and inclusion in society, in an individualized manner, consistent with the unique strengths, resources, priorities, concerns, abilities, and capabilities of each individual;....[81]

Although these are certainly important goals, they remain part of the congressional findings section of the legislation which the *Pennhurst* Court said does not represent an enforceable bill of rights. The funding requirements both procedural and substantive for those seeking funding from the programs provided by the act have certainly increased, but it has not become what many people in the disability rights movement hoped and expected that it would be.

The Americans With Disabilities Act—Promise and Problems

Given the limitations of IDEA and of the Rehabilitation Act of 1973, and the manner in which the Supreme Court has responded to the Developmental Disabilities Assistance and Bill of Rights Act, it became apparent that more was needed in order to provide anything like a civil rights statute adequate to ensure protections for persons with disabilities and their families. There were needs and gaps with respect to transportation, places of public accommodation, private sector employment, education, and more. It was also clear that reliance on grant programs with conditions attached was not working in the way Congress intended, and was not adequate, given Supreme Court interpretations, to ensure the civil rights that legislators thought they had protected or that citizens thought were available to them. Those gaps and needs gave rise to the Americans with Disabilities Act (ADA), enacted in 1990. This time Congress enacted a civil rights law that was grounded in the Fourteenth Amendment and its authority under the commerce clause of Article I, and which does not depend upon a federal funding connection.

Like other civil rights legislation before it, the ADA did not come with a federal administrative agency established for and charged with ensuring implementation and compliance. Instead, different agencies were given pieces of the policy to consider, such as the Department of Transportation and the Department of Justice. Indeed, one of things that President George Herbert Walker Bush and others who supported the law liked about it was that it allowed them to repeat the political mantra—no new bureaucracy. Instead, the statute relied principally on voluntary cooperation by everyone in society with the requirements of the statute and on the ability and willingness of persons with disabilities who thought their rights under the legislation had been violated to bring suit for enforcement.

However, ensuring reasonable accommodations and other aspects of the law required interpretation and explanation. That would mean many lawsuits filed in a host of different courts around the country, with delays in getting clear answers to some of the important questions under the act. Additionally, although some jurisdictions and private organizations tried hard to comply, there would inevitably be others who saw how unlikely it was that they would face serious costs if they did not comply, just because of the difficulty of obtaining enforcement.

One of the important expectations in that respect was that those injured by violations of the statute would be able to sue for damages, which should encourage compliance and deter others who were less inclined to cooperate. To ensure that their intent on this point was clear, Congress stated its intent to abrogate any immunity that states might have to protect themselves against damage claims. It was this provision that led to an important Supreme Court ruling that rejected that provision of the statute. Quite apart from the specific technical ruling, the language of the opinion for the Court by Chief Justice Rehnquist could hardly be seen as anything but a clear hostility toward the ADA and what it represented—and it was indeed seen in just that way. In reading the opinion, pay particular attention to the way in which Rehnquist discusses persons with disabilities and the state's authority to discriminate against them.

Board of Trustees of the University of Alabama v. Garrett

531 U.S. 356 (2001)

INTRODUCTION: This is a case concerned with the doctrine of immunity of states from damage claims following the dramatic change in the law that came with the Court's 1996 opinion in *Seminole Tribe of Florida v. Florida*. The facts of this case are provided in the opinion. Notice that Chief Justice Rehnquist tries to make it appear that the immunity is a long-settled doctrine, but be aware that the cases only go back to the *Seminole* case in 1996. Then there is reference to an 1890 case, which in fact was an entirely different kind of case in which there had been no congressional authorization to sue and was therefore completely unlike the current line of cases. Additionally, the opinion suggests that it was also clearly established that Congress could only abrogate the immunity of a state (make it subject to suit) if the legislature was using section 5 of the Fourteenth Amendment to the Constitution. Again, that was, as the dissenters stated clearly, made up in *Seminole*. There is no literal or historical reason that supports that claim. There is more, but the point is that this is not an opinion to be taken at face value.

The facts of this case reach back to the adoption in 1990 of the ADA and particularly to Title I of that statute, which prohibits discrimination in employment against persons with disabilities. Patricia Garrett was the Director of Nursing, OB/Gyn/Neonatal Services, for the University of Alabama in Birmingham Hospital. She was diagnosed with breast cancer in 1994 and took a leave from her job to receive treatment. After she completed that treatment, she indicated that she would return to her job in July 1995. However, her supervisor indicated that although she could return as a nurse, she would no longer have her position as Director of the unit.[82]

Garrett sued for damages under the ADA in the federal district court. The employer asked the court for a summary judgment on the claim that Congress did not have the authority to abrogate the state's immunity under the Eleventh Amendment. The district court agreed with that argument, but the court of appeals reversed, upholding the congressional action.

Chief Justice Rehnquist wrote the opinion for the Court.

> We decide here whether employees of the State of Alabama may recover money damages by reason of the State's failure to comply with the provisions of Title I of the Americans with Disabilities Act of 1990 (ADA or Act).... We hold that such suits are barred by the Eleventh Amendment.
>
> The ADA prohibits certain employers, including the States, from "discriminating against a qualified individual with a disability because of the disability of such individual in regard to job application procedures, the hiring, advancement, or discharge of employees, employee compensation, job training, and other terms, conditions, and privileges of employment." ... To this end, the Act requires employers to "make reasonable accommodations to the known physical or mental limitations of an otherwise qualified individual with a disability who is an applicant or employee, unless [the employer] can demonstrate that the accommodation would impose an undue hardship on the operation of the [employer's] business." ... The Act also prohibits employers from "utilizing standards, criteria, or methods of administration ... that have the effect of discrimination on the basis of disability." ...
>
> The Act defines "disability" to include "(A) a physical or mental impairment that substantially limits one or more of the major life activities of such individual; (B) a record of such an impairment; or (C) being regarded as having such an impairment." ... A disabled individual is otherwise "qualified" if he or she, "with or without reasonable accommodation, can perform the essential functions of the employment position that such individual holds or desires." ...
>
> The Eleventh Amendment provides: "The Judicial power of the United States shall not be construed to extend to any suit in law or equity, commenced or prosecuted against one of the United States by Citizens of another State, or by Citizens or Subjects of any Foreign State." ... Although by its terms the Amendment applies only to suits against a State by citizens of another State, our cases have extended the Amendment's applicability to suits by citizens against their own States. See *Kimel v. Florida Bd. of Regents*, 528 U.S. 62, 72–73 (2000); *College Savings Bank v. Florida Prepaid Postsecondary Ed. Expense Bd.*, 527 U.S. 627, 669–670 (1999); *Seminole Tribe of Fla. v. Florida*, 517 U.S. 44, 54 (1996); *Hans v. Louisiana*, 134 U.S. 1, 15 (1890). The ultimate guarantee of the Eleventh Amendment is that nonconsenting States may not be sued by private individuals in federal court....
>
> We have recognized, however, that Congress may abrogate the States' Eleventh Amendment immunity when it both unequivocally intends to do so and "acts pursuant to a valid grant of constitutional authority." ... The first of these requirements is not in dispute here.... The question, then, is whether Congress acted within its constitutional authority by subjecting the States to suits in federal court for money damages under the ADA.

Congress may not, of course, base its abrogation of the States' Eleventh Amendment immunity upon the powers enumerated in Article I. See *Kimel* ...; *Seminole Tribe*.... As a result, we concluded, Congress may subject nonconsenting States to suit in federal court when it does so pursuant to a valid exercise of its §5 power.... Accordingly, the ADA can apply to the States only to the extent that the statute is appropriate §5 legislation.

Section 1 of the Fourteenth Amendment provides, in relevant part: "No State shall make or enforce any law which shall abridge the privileges or immunities of citizens of the United States; nor shall any State deprive any person of life, liberty, or property, without due process of law; nor deny to any person within its jurisdiction the equal protection of the laws." ... Section 5 of the Fourteenth Amendment grants Congress the power to enforce the substantive guarantees contained in §1 by enacting "appropriate legislation." ... Congress is not limited to mere legislative repetition of this Court's constitutional jurisprudence. "Rather, Congress' power 'to enforce' the Amendment includes the authority both to remedy and to deter violation of rights guaranteed thereunder by prohibiting a somewhat broader swath of conduct, including that which is not itself forbidden by the Amendment's text." ...

City of Boerne [*v. Flores*, 521 U.S. 507 (1997)] also confirmed, however, the long-settled principle that it is the responsibility of this Court, not Congress, to define the substance of constitutional guarantees.... Accordingly, §5 legislation reaching beyond the scope of §1's actual guarantees must exhibit "congruence and proportionality between the injury to be prevented or remedied and the means adopted to that end." ...

The first step in applying these now familiar principles is to identify with some precision the scope of the constitutional right at issue. Here, that inquiry requires us to examine the limitations §1 of the Fourteenth Amendment places upon States' treatment of the disabled....

In *Cleburne* ... we [held that classifications like mental retardation] incurs only the minimum "rational-basis" review applicable to general social and economic legislation.... Under rational-basis review, ... "Such a classification cannot run afoul of the Equal Protection Clause if there is a rational relationship between the disparity of treatment and some legitimate governmental purpose." ... Moreover, the State need not articulate its reasoning at the moment a particular decision is made. Rather, the burden is upon the challenging party to negative "any reasonably conceivable state of facts that could provide a rational basis for the classification." ...

Justice Breyer suggests that *Cleburne* stands for the broad proposition that state decisionmaking reflecting "negative attitudes" or "fear" necessarily runs afoul of the Fourteenth Amendment.... Although such biases may often accompany irrational (and therefore unconstitutional) discrimination, their presence alone does not a constitutional violation make. As we noted in *Cleburne*: "Mere negative attitudes, or fear, *unsubstantiated by factors which are properly cognizable* in a zoning proceeding, are not permissible bases for treating a home for the mentally retarded differently...." This language, read in context, simply states the unremarkable and widely acknowledged tenet of this Court's equal protection jurisprudence that state action subject to rational-basis scrutiny does not violate the Fourteenth Amendment when it "rationally furthers the purpose identified by the State." ...

Thus, the result of *Cleburne* is that States are not required by the Fourteenth Amendment to make special accommodations for the disabled, so long as their actions towards such individuals are rational. They could quite hardheadedly—and perhaps hardheartedly—hold to job-qualification requirements which do not make allowance for the disabled. If special accommodations for the disabled are to be required, they have to come from positive law and not through the Equal Protection Clause.

Just as §1 of the Fourteenth Amendment applies only to actions committed "under color of state law," Congress' §5 authority is appropriately exercised only in response to state transgressions.... The legislative record of the ADA, however, simply fails to show that Congress did in fact identify a pattern of irrational state discrimination in employment against the disabled....

Congress made a general finding in the ADA that "historically, society has tended to isolate and segregate individuals with disabilities, and, despite some improvements, such forms of discrimination against individuals with disabilities continue to be a serious and pervasive social problem." ... The record assembled by Congress includes many instances to support such a finding. But the great majority of these incidents do not deal with the activities of States....

Several of these incidents undoubtedly evidence an unwillingness on the part of state officials to make the sort of accommodations for the disabled required by the ADA. Whether they were irrational under our decision in *Cleburne* is more debatable, particularly when the incident is described out of context. But even if it were to be determined that each incident upon fuller examination showed unconstitutional action on the part of the State, these incidents taken together fall far short of even suggesting the pattern of unconstitutional discrimination on which §5 legislation must be based....

Justice Breyer maintains that Congress applied Title I of the ADA to the States in response to a host of incidents representing unconstitutional state discrimination in employment against persons with disabilities. A close review of the relevant materials, however, undercuts that conclusion. Justice Breyer's Appendix C consists not of legislative findings, but of unexamined, anecdotal accounts of "adverse, disparate treatment by state officials." ... [N]ot only is the inference Justice Breyer draws unwarranted, but there is also strong evidence that Congress' failure to mention States in its legislative findings addressing discrimination in employment reflects that body's judgment that no pattern of unconstitutional state action had been documented.[83]...

The ADA's constitutional shortcomings are apparent when the Act is compared to Congress' efforts in the Voting Rights Act of 1965 to respond to a serious pattern of constitutional violations.... Concluding that it was a valid exercise of Congress' enforcement power under §2 of the Fifteenth Amendment,[84] we noted that "before enacting the measure, Congress explored with great care the problem of racial discrimination in voting."[85]...

The contrast between this kind of evidence, and the evidence that Congress considered in the present case, is stark.[86] Congressional enactment of the ADA represents its judgment that there should be a "comprehensive national mandate for the elimination of discrimination against individuals with disabilities." ... Congress is the final authority as to desirable public policy, but in order to authorize private individuals to recover money damages against the States, there must be a pattern of discrimination by the States which violates the Fourteenth Amendment, and the remedy imposed by Congress must be congruent and proportional to the targeted violation. Those requirements are not met here, and to uphold the Act's application to the States would allow Congress to rewrite the Fourteenth

Amendment law laid down by this Court in *Cleburne*. Section 5 does not so broadly enlarge congressional authority. The judgment of the Court of Appeals is therefore reversed....[87]

Justice Breyer wrote a dissent joined by Justices Stevens, Souter, and Ginsburg.

Reviewing the congressional record as if it were an administrative agency record, the Court holds the statutory provision before us ... unconstitutional. The Court concludes that Congress assembled insufficient evidence of unconstitutional discrimination ... that Congress improperly attempted to "re-write" the law we established in *Cleburne*..., and that the law is not sufficiently tailored to address unconstitutional discrimination....

Section 5, however, grants Congress the "power to enforce, by appropriate legislation" the Fourteenth Amendment's equal protection guarantee.... As the Court recognizes, state discrimination in employment against persons with disabilities might "run afoul of the Equal Protection Clause" where there is no "rational relationship between the disparity of treatment and some legitimate governmental purpose." ... In my view, Congress reasonably could have concluded that the remedy before us constitutes an "appropriate" way to enforce this basic equal protection requirement. And that is all the Constitution requires.

The Court says ... that "Congress assembled only ... minimal evidence of unconstitutional state discrimination in employment." ... In fact, Congress compiled a vast legislative record documenting "massive, society-wide discrimination" against persons with disabilities. S. Rep. No. 101–116, pp. 8–9 (1989) (quoting testimony of Justin Dart, chairperson of the Task Force on the Rights and Empowerment of Americans with Disabilities). In addition to the information presented at 13 congressional hearings ... and its own prior experience gathered over 40 years during which it contemplated and enacted considerable similar legislation ... Congress created a special task force to assess the need for comprehensive legislation. That task force held hearings in every State, attended by more than 30,000 people, including thousands who had experienced discrimination first hand.... The task force hearings, Congress' own hearings, and an analysis of "census data, national polls, and other studies" led Congress to conclude that "people with disabilities, as a group, occupy an inferior status in our society, and are severely disadvantaged socially, vocationally, economically, and educationally." ... As to employment, Congress found that "two-thirds of all disabled Americans between the age of 16 and 64 [were] not working at all," even though a large majority wanted to, and were able to, work productively.... And Congress found that this discrimination flowed in significant part from "stereotypic assumptions" as well as "purposeful unequal treatment." ...

The powerful evidence of discriminatory treatment throughout society in general, including discrimination by private persons and local governments, implicates state governments as well, for state agencies form part of that same larger society. There is no particular reason to believe that they are immune from the "stereotypic assumptions" and pattern of "purposeful unequal treatment" that Congress found prevalent. The Court claims that it "makes no sense" to take into consideration constitutional violations committed by local governments.... But the substantive obligation that the Equal Protection Clause creates applies to state and local governmental entities alike....

In any event, there is no need to rest solely upon evidence of discrimination by local governments or general societal discrimination. There are roughly 300 examples of discrimination by state governments themselves in the legislative record. See, *e.g.*, Appendix C, *infra*. I fail to see how this evidence "falls far short of even suggesting the pattern of unconstitutional discrimination on which §5 legislation must be based." ...

The congressionally appointed task force collected numerous specific examples, provided by persons with disabilities themselves, of adverse, disparate treatment by state officials. They reveal, not what the Court describes as "half a dozen" instances of discrimination ... but hundreds of instances of adverse treatment at the hands of state officials—instances in which a person with a disability found it impossible to obtain a state job, to retain state employment, to use the public transportation that was readily available to others in order to get to work, or to obtain a public education, which is often a prerequisite to obtaining employment....

As the Court notes, those who presented instances of discrimination rarely provided additional, independent evidence sufficient to prove in court that, in each instance, the discrimination they suffered lacked justification from a judicial standpoint.... But a legislature is not a court of law. And Congress, unlike courts, must, and does, routinely draw general conclusions ... from anecdotal and opinion-based evidence of this kind, particularly when the evidence lacks strong refutation.... In reviewing §5 legislation, we have never required the sort of extensive investigation of each piece of evidence that the Court appears to contemplate.... Nor has the Court traditionally required Congress to make findings as to state discrimination, or to break down the record evidence, category by category....

Regardless, Congress expressly found substantial unjustified discrimination against persons with disabilities.... Moreover, it found that such discrimination typically reflects "stereotypic assumptions" or "purposeful unequal treatment." ... Adverse treatment that rests upon such motives is unjustified discrimination in *Cleburne's* terms.

The evidence in the legislative record bears out Congress' finding that the adverse treatment of persons with disabilities was often arbitrary or invidious in this sense, and thus unjustified. For example, one study that was before Congress revealed that "most ... governmental agencies in [one State] discriminated in hiring against job applicants for an average period of five years after treatment for cancer," based in part on coworkers' misguided belief that "cancer is contagious." ... A school inexplicably refused to exempt a deaf teacher, who taught at a school for the deaf, from a "listening skills" requirement.... A State refused to hire a blind employee as director of an agency for the blind—even though he was the most qualified applicant.... A complete listing of the hundreds of examples of discrimination by state and local governments that were submitted to the task force is set forth in Appendix C, *infra*. Congress could have reasonably believed that these examples represented signs of a widespread problem of unconstitutional discrimination.

The Court's failure to find sufficient evidentiary support may well rest upon its decision to hold Congress to a strict, judicially created evidentiary standard, particularly in respect to lack of justification.... Imposing this special "burden" upon Congress, the Court fails to find in the legislative record sufficient indication that Congress has "negatived" the presumption that state action is rationally related to a legitimate objective....

The problem with the Court's approach is that neither the "burden of proof" that favors States nor any other rule of restraint applicable to *judges* applies to *Congress* when it exercises its § 5 power.... And the Congress of the United States is not a lower court.... Unlike courts, Congress can readily gather facts from across the Nation, assess the magnitude of a problem, and more easily find an appropriate remedy.... Unlike courts, Congress directly reflects public attitudes and beliefs, enabling Congress better to understand where, and to what extent, refusals to accommodate a disability amount to behavior that is callous or unreasonable to the point of lacking constitutional justification. Unlike judges, Members of Congress can directly obtain information from constituents who have first-hand experience with discrimination and related issues.

Moreover, unlike judges, Members of Congress are elected. When the Court has applied the majority's burden of proof rule, it has explained that we, *i.e.*, the courts, do not "sit as a superlegislature to judge the wisdom or desirability of legislative policy determinations." ... To apply a rule designed to restrict courts as if it restricted Congress' legislative power is to stand the underlying principle—a principle of judicial restraint—on its head....

The Court argues in the alternative that the statute's damage remedy is not "congruent" with and "proportional" to the equal protection problem that Congress found.... The Court suggests that the Act's "reasonable accommodation" requirement ... and disparate impact standard ... "far exceed what is constitutionally required." ... And what is wrong with a remedy that, in response to unreasonable employer behavior, requires an employer to make accommodations that are reasonable? Of course, what is "reasonable" in the statutory sense and what is "unreasonable" in the constitutional sense might differ. In other words, the requirement may exceed what is necessary to avoid a constitutional violation. But it is just that power—the power to require more than the minimum—that §5 grants to Congress, as this Court has repeatedly confirmed. As long ago as 1880, the Court wrote that §5 "brought within the domain of congressional power" whatever "tends to enforce submission" to its "prohibitions" and "to secure to all persons ... the equal protection of the laws." *Ex parte Virginia*, 100 U.S. 339, 346 (1880)....

I recognize nonetheless that this statute imposes a burden upon States in that it removes their Eleventh Amendment protection from suit, thereby subjecting them to potential monetary liability. Rules for interpreting §5 that would provide States with special protection, however, run counter to the very object of the Fourteenth Amendment. By its terms, that Amendment prohibits *States* from denying their citizens equal protection of the laws.... Hence "principles of federalism that might otherwise be an obstacle to congressional authority are necessarily overridden by the power to enforce the Civil War Amendments 'by appropriate legislation.' Those Amendments were specifically designed as an expansion of federal power and an intrusion on state sovereignty." ... For these reasons, I doubt that today's decision serves any constitutionally based federalism interest.

The Court, through its evidentiary demands, its non-deferential review, and its failure to distinguish between judicial and legislative constitutional competencies, improperly invades a power that the Constitution assigns to Congress.... Its decision saps §5 of independent force, effectively "confining the legislative power ... to the insignificant role of abrogating only those state laws that the judicial branch [is] prepared to adjudge unconstitutional." ... Whether the Commerce Clause does or does not enable Congress to enact this provision, in my view, §5 gives Congress the necessary authority.

The *Garrett* case was soon followed by others that sought to constrain and minimize the ADA, and even to have other parts declared unconstitutional. One of those cases came from Tennessee as a challenge to Title II of the act, and involved a set of facts that made it abundantly clear why the ADA was needed, and just as obvious why a vigorous approach to its enforcement was needed.

Tennessee v. Lane

541 U.S 509 (2004)

INTRODUCTION: This case arose against a backdrop of the *Garrett* ruling striking down Title I of the ADA insofar as it authorized money damage suits against the states.[88] This case tested Title II of the ADA, concerning access to public programs, activities, and facilities, in light of those developments.

In 1996 the Commission on the Future of the Tennessee Judicial System reported that "for persons with significant physical or mental impairment, the system can be quite literally inaccessible."[89] And when this case was filed in 1998, at least 23 counties in the state had courthouses that were not accessible to persons with mobility-related disabilities.[90]

In that same year, George Lane had to appear for an arraignment in the Benton County, Tennessee court. He had been in an automobile accident and had a crushed hip and pelvis. Both legs were in casts and he was in a wheelchair. There was no elevator in the building and he was told that he had better get himself upstairs to the courtroom. He had to crawl up the two flights of stairs to get to that courtroom. He reported that the judge and other people who worked in there "stood at the top of the stairs and laughed at me."[91] He then had to return for a hearing. He refused to crawl back up the stairs again. He charged that the people who had previously laughed at him when he crawled up the stairs offered to carry him this time, but he feared that they would drop him, deliberately or otherwise. He was arrested and jailed for failing to appear in the court. At future proceedings, he had to wait at the bottom of the stairs while his attorney came back and forth from the courtroom to speak with him.[92] When another misdemeanor charge was brought against him, his attorney asked that the court stay the proceedings until arrangements were made to hold them in a place that would be accessible. The judge denied the motion and told him that Lane could bring a civil suit, but that he was not going to delay or move the other matter.[93] At the end of the process Lane plead guilty to driving with a revoked driver's license.

Beverly Jones has paraplegia and requires a wheelchair. She was a court reporter who asked for accessibility accommodations in four different counties, but her requests were rejected.[94] In the Wilson County, Tennessee courthouse she had to have a local judge carry her to and from the women's bathroom. Years later, Ms. Jones testified before the Senate Judiciary Committee and explained what had brought her to sue Tennessee:

> I lost my ability to walk due to a traffic accident in 1984, and have used a wheelchair ever since. At the time I became disabled, I decided that I would not allow what I wanted in life to be denied because of my physical limitations. At the time of my accident, I was a wife and mother, but had little education and limited job skills. A local judge encouraged me to look into becoming a court reporter and from there my ambitions began.

> I completed court reporting school the year that the ADA was passed. But, to my surprise, when I began my first assignments, I found that I could not get into many of Tennessee's courtrooms and courthouses because they were inaccessible

to people who use wheelchairs. I was forced to turn down jobs, or face humiliating experiences.

Approximately seven out of ten courthouses in Tennessee were inaccessible when I filed my suit. In some cases, I could not even get in the door. In the years following the passage of the ADA, some courthouses became more accessible. But even in 1998, when my lawsuit was filed, a number of the courthouses I worked in remained inaccessible to me. Courtrooms were located only on upper floors, and reachable only by climbing stairs. I was often forced to ask complete strangers to carry me up the stairs or into rooms, including non accessible restrooms.

This experience was humiliating and frightening. But as a single mom supporting myself and two kids, I could not afford to quit my job or strictly limit my work to accessible courthouses. After the passage of the ADA, I worked tirelessly to bring the law to the attention of public officials throughout Tennessee, and to encourage them to follow the law's requirements to make public buildings, including courthouses, accessible. I spoke to local, state, and federal officials. Almost all of my inquiries were met with polite ambivalence; a shrug of a shoulder; a pat on the back; a comment about keeping it up. I just could not seem to get any action. I filed a complaint with the Justice Department, however I never heard anything back. The door that I thought had been opened was still closed and my freedom to live my dream was still a dream, and turning into a nightmare. Nobody took either me or the law seriously until I and others brought a lawsuit.[95]

In August 1998 respondents George Lane and Beverly Jones filed this action based on Title II of the ADA against the State of Tennessee and a number of Tennessee counties. The District Court denied a motion to dismiss and the U.S. Court of Appeals for the Sixth Circuit affirmed the lower court. The United States intervened in the case in the Sixth Circuit in order to defend Title II of the ADA against the claim by the state that its abrogation of state immunity from damages violated the Eleventh Amendment.

After the case was filed, four other plaintiffs who had similarly experienced an inability to access courtrooms in Tennessee entered the case. Ann Marie Zappola had a spinal cord injury that made it all but impossible to climb stairs. She was a defendant in a civil case and later a complainant in a juvenile matter. She had to climb stairs to get to a third-floor courtroom at the Houston County Courthouse. Ralph E. Ramsey had a circulatory problem that again meant he could not climb stairs. However, when he explained to officials at the Cocke County Courthouse that he could not get up the stairs to the courtroom, the trial judge found against him in the case because he failed to appear. Dennis Cantrel who had paraplegia, in order to attend a County Commission meeting, had to crawl up the stairs of the Fayette County Courthouse. A. Russell Larson was an attorney who also had a disability that made it extremely difficult to climb stairs. He faced limitations in courthouses that made it impossible for him to effectively represent his clients.[96]

This case was clearly seen as extremely important and it attracted a range of friends of the court briefs. The American Bar Association filed an *amicus curiae* brief in support of Lane and Jones, which asserted at the outset that this case was about far more than just individual access to a building.

That courts be barrier free—and thus open to all—is vital to the legitimacy of and public confidence in the administration of justice. A lack of equal access to the courts harms not only those persons who are excluded, but also the system itself, which is deprived of the benefits of their inclusion. In addition, the exclusion from the justice system of any segment of society undermines public confidence in the system. It therefore is imperative that the courts ensure that individuals with disabilities are not excluded from participation in any capacity—as litigants, witnesses, attorneys, judges, jurors, courthouse staff, or observers.[97]

Justice Stevens wrote the opinion for the Court.

Title II of the Americans with Disabilities Act of 1990 (ADA or Act) ... provides that "no qualified individual with a disability shall, by reason of such disability, be excluded from participation in or be denied the benefits of the services, programs or activities of a public entity, or be subjected to discrimination by any such entity." The question presented in this case is whether Title II exceeds Congress' power under §5 of the Fourteenth Amendment. In *Garrett* ... we concluded that the Eleventh Amendment bars private suits seeking money damages for state violations of Title I of the ADA. We left open, however, the question whether the Eleventh Amendment permits suits for money damages under Title II....

The ADA was passed by large majorities in both Houses of Congress after decades of deliberation and investigation into the need for comprehensive legislation to address discrimination against persons with disabilities. In the years immediately preceding the ADA's enactment, Congress held 13 hearings and created a special task force that gathered evidence from every State in the Union. [Congress found] ... that "individuals with disabilities are a discrete and insular minority who have been faced with restrictions and limitations, subjected to a history of purposeful unequal treatment, and relegated to a position of political powerlessness in our society, based on characteristics that are beyond the control of such individuals and resulting from stereotypic assumptions not truly indicative of the individual ability of such individuals to participate in, and contribute to, society."[98]...

Invoking "the sweep of congressional authority, including the power to enforce the fourteenth amendment and to regulate commerce," the ADA is designed "to provide a clear and comprehensive national mandate for the elimination of discrimination against individuals with disabilities." ... It forbids discrimination against persons with disabilities in three major areas of public life: employment, which is covered by Title I of the statute; public services, programs, and activities, which are the subject of Title II; and public accommodations, which are covered by Title III.

Title II ... prohibits any public entity from discriminating against "qualified" persons with disabilities in the provision or operation of public services, programs, or activities. The Act defines the term "public entity" to include state and local governments, as well as their agencies and instrumentalities.... Persons with disabilities are "qualified" if they, "with or without reasonable modifications to rules, policies, or practices, the removal of architectural, communication, or transportation barriers, or the provision of auxiliary aids and services, mee[t] the essential eligibility requirements for the receipt of services or the participation in programs or activities provided by a public entity." ...

Our cases have ... held that Congress may abrogate the State's Eleventh Amendment immunity. To determine whether it has done so in any given case, we "must resolve two predicate questions: first, whether Congress unequivocally expressed its intent to abrogate that immunity; and second, if it did, whether Congress acted pursuant to a valid grant of constitutional authority." ...

The first question is easily answered in this case. The Act specifically provides: "A State shall not be immune under the eleventh amendment to the Constitution of the United States from an action in Federal or State court of competent jurisdiction for a violation of this chapter." ... The question, then, is whether Congress had the power to give effect to its intent.

In *Fitzpatrick v. Bitzer*, 427 U.S. 445 (1976), we held that Congress can abrogate a State's sovereign immunity when it does so pursuant to a valid exercise of its power under §5 of the Fourteenth Amendment to enforce the substantive guarantees of that Amendment.... This enforcement power, as we have often acknowledged, is a "broad power indeed." ... It includes "the authority both to remedy and to deter violation of rights guaranteed [by the Fourteenth Amendment] by prohibiting a somewhat broader swath of conduct, including that which is not itself forbidden by the Amendment's text." ... We have thus repeatedly affirmed that "Congress may enact so-called prophylactic legislation that proscribes facially constitutional conduct, in order to prevent and deter unconstitutional conduct." *Nev. Dep't of Human Res. v. Hibbs*, 538 U.S. 721, 727–728 (2003).... The most recent affirmation of the breadth of Congress' §5 power came in *Hibbs*, in which we ... upheld the [Family and Medical Leave Act of 1993] FMLA as a valid exercise of Congress' §5 power to combat unconstitutional sex discrimination, even though there was no suggestion that the State's leave policy was adopted or applied with a discriminatory purpose that would render it unconstitutional under the rule of *Personnel Adm'r of Massachusetts v. Feeney*.... When Congress seeks to remedy or prevent unconstitutional discrimination, §5 authorizes it to enact prophylactic legislation proscribing practices that are discriminatory in effect, if not in intent, to carry out the basic objectives of the Equal Protection Clause.

Congress' §5 power is not, however, unlimited. In *City of Boerne v. Flores*, ... we recognized that ... Section 5 legislation is valid if it exhibits "a congruence and proportionality between the injury to be prevented or remedied and the means adopted to that end." ... In view of the significant differences between Titles I and II, however, *Garrett* left open the question whether Title II is a valid exercise of Congress' §5 enforcement power. It is to that question that we now turn.

The first step ... requires us to identify the constitutional ... rights that Congress sought to enforce when it enacted Title II.... In *Garrett* we ... observed, classifications based on disability violate that constitutional command if they lack a rational relationship to a legitimate governmental purpose.... Title II, like Title I, seeks to enforce this prohibition on irrational disability discrimination. But it also seeks to enforce a variety of other basic constitutional guarantees, infringements of which are subject to more searching judicial review.... These rights include some, like the right of access to the courts at issue in this case, that are protected by the Due Process Clause of the Fourteenth Amendment. The Due Process Clause and the Confrontation Clause of the Sixth Amendment, as applied to the States via the Fourteenth Amendment, both guarantee to a criminal defendant such as respondent Lane the "right to be present at all stages of the trial where his absence might frustrate the fairness of the proceedings." ... The Due Process Clause also requires the States to afford certain civil litigants a "meaningful opportunity to be heard" by removing obstacles to their full participation in judicial proceedings.... And, finally, we have recognized that members of the public have a right of access to criminal proceedings secured by the First Amendment....

While §5 authorizes Congress to enact reasonably prophylactic remedial legislation, the appropriateness of the remedy depends on the gravity of the harm it seeks to prevent.... It is not difficult to perceive the harm that Title II is designed to address. Congress enacted Title II against a backdrop of pervasive unequal treatment in the administration of state services and programs, including systematic deprivations of fundamental rights. For example, "[a]s of 1979, most States ... categorically disqualified 'idiots' from voting, without regard to individual capacity." The majority of these laws remain on the books, and have been the subject of legal challenge as recently as 2001. Similarly, a number of States have prohibited and continue to prohibit persons with disabilities from engaging in activities such as marrying and serving as jurors. The historical experience that Title II reflects is also documented in this Court's cases, which have identified unconstitutional treatment of disabled persons by state agencies in a variety of settings....

This pattern of disability discrimination persisted despite several federal and state legislative efforts to address it. In the deliberations that led up to the enactment of the ADA, Congress identified important shortcomings in existing laws that rendered them "inadequate to address the pervasive problems of discrimination that people with disabilities are facing." ... It also uncovered further evidence of those shortcomings, in the form of hundreds of examples of unequal treatment of persons with disabilities by States and their political subdivisions.... [T]he "overwhelming majority" of these examples concerned discrimination in the administration of public programs and services....

With respect to the particular services at issue in this case, Congress learned that many individuals, in many States across the country, were being excluded from courthouses and court proceedings by reason of their disabilities. A report before Congress showed that some 76% of public services and programs housed in state-owned buildings were inaccessible to and unusable by persons with disabilities, even taking into account the possibility that the services and programs might be restructured or relocated to other parts of the buildings. U.S. Civil Rights Commission, Accommodating the Spectrum of Individual Abilities 39 (1983). Congress itself heard testimony from persons with disabilities who described the physical inaccessibility of local courthouses.... And its appointed task force heard numerous examples of the exclusion of persons with disabilities from state judicial services and programs, including exclusion of persons with visual impairments and hearing impairments from jury service, failure of state and local governments to provide interpretive services for the hearing impaired, failure to permit the testimony of adults with developmental disabilities in abuse cases, and failure to make courtrooms accessible to witnesses with physical disabilities....

The conclusion that Congress drew from this body of evidence is set forth in the text of the ADA itself: "[D]iscrimination against individuals with disabilities persists in such critical areas as ... education, transportation, communication, recreation, institutionalization, health services, voting, and *access to public services.*" ... This finding, together with the extensive record of disability discrimination that underlies it, makes clear beyond peradventure that inadequate provision of public services and access to public facilities was an appropriate subject for prophylactic legislation.

The only question that remains is whether Title II is an appropriate response to this history and pattern of unequal treatment.... Congress' chosen remedy for the pattern of exclusion and discrimination described above, Title II's requirement of program accessibility, is congruent and proportional to its object of enforcing the right of access to the courts. The unequal treatment of disabled persons in the administration of judicial services has a long history, and has persisted despite several legislative efforts to remedy the problem of disability discrimination. Faced with considerable evidence of the shortcomings of previous legislative responses, Congress was justified in concluding that this "difficult and intractable proble[m]" warranted "added prophylactic measures in response." ...

The remedy Congress chose is nevertheless a limited one. Recognizing that failure to accommodate persons with disabilities will often have the same practical effect as outright exclusion, Congress required the States to take reasonable measures to remove architectural and other barriers to accessibility.... But Title II does not require States to employ any and all means to make judicial services accessible to persons with disabilities, and it does not require States to compromise their essential eligibility criteria for public programs. It requires only "reasonable modifications" that would not fundamentally alter the nature of the service provided, and only when the individual seeking modification is otherwise eligible for the service.... As Title II's implementing regulations make clear, the reasonable modification requirement can be satisfied in a number of ways. In the case of facilities built or altered after 1992, the regulations require compliance with specific architectural accessibility standards.... But in the case of older facilities, for which structural change is likely to be more difficult, a public entity may comply with Title II by adopting a variety of less costly measures, including relocating services to alternative, accessible sites and assigning aides to assist persons with disabilities in accessing services.... Only if these measures are ineffective in achieving accessibility is the public entity required to make reasonable structural changes.... And in no event is the entity required to undertake measures that would impose an undue financial or administrative burden, threaten historic preservation interests, or effect a fundamental alteration in the nature of the service....

Judged against this backdrop, Title II's affirmative obligation to accommodate persons with disabilities in the administration of justice cannot be said to be "so out of proportion to a supposed remedial or preventive object that it cannot be understood as responsive to, or designed to prevent, unconstitutional behavior." ... It is, rather, a reasonable prophylactic measure, reasonably targeted to a legitimate end.... For these reasons, we conclude that Title II, as it applies to the class of cases implicating the fundamental right of access to the courts, constitutes a valid exercise of Congress' §5 authority to enforce the guarantees of the Fourteenth Amendment.

Justice Souter wrote a concurring opinion joined by Justice Ginsburg.

... Although I concur in the Court's approach..., I note that if the Court engaged in a more expansive enquiry as the Chief Justice suggests, ... the evidence to be considered would underscore the appropriateness of action under §5 to address the situation of disabled individuals before the courts, for that evidence would show that the judiciary itself has endorsed the basis for some of the very discrimination subject to congressional remedy under §5. *Buck v. Bell* ... was not grudging in sustaining the constitutionality of the once-pervasive practice of involuntarily sterilizing those with mental disabilities.... Laws compelling sterilization were often accompanied by others indiscriminately requiring institutionalization, and prohibiting certain individuals with disabilities from marrying, from voting, from attending public schools, and even from appearing in public. One administrative action along these lines was judicially sustained in part as a justified precaution against the very sight of a child with cerebral palsy, lest he "produc[e] a depressing and nauseating effect" upon others. *State ex rel. Beattie v. Board of Ed. of Antigo*, 169 Wis. 231, 232, 172 N.W. 153 (1919) (approving his exclusion from public school).... In sustaining the application of Title II today, the Court takes a welcome step away from the judiciary's prior endorsement of blunt instruments imposing legal handicaps.

Justice Ginsburg wrote a concurring opinion joined by Justices Souter and Breyer.

... Legislation calling upon all government actors to respect the dignity of individuals with disabilities is entirely compatible with our Constitution's commitment to federalism, properly conceived. It seems to me not conducive to a harmonious federal system to require Congress, before it exercises authority under §5 of the Fourteenth Amendment, essentially to indict each State for disregarding the equal-citizenship stature of persons with disabilities.... Members of Congress are understandably reluctant to condemn their own States as constitutional violators, complicit in maintaining the isolated and unequal status of persons with disabilities. I would not disarm a National Legislature for resisting an adversarial approach to lawmaking better suited to the courtroom.

... Congress considered a body of evidence showing that in diverse parts of our Nation, and at various levels of government, persons with disabilities encounter access barriers to public facilities and services. That record, the Court rightly holds, at least as it bears on access to courts, sufficed to warrant the barrier-lowering, dignity-respecting national solution the People's representatives in Congress elected to order.

Chief Justice Rehnquist dissented, joined by Justices Kennedy and Thomas.

... I disagree with [the] conclusion that Title II is valid §5 enforcement legislation.... In *Garrett*, we conducted the three-step inquiry ... to determine whether Title I of the ADA satisfied the congruence-and-proportionality test.... The first step is to "identify with some precision the scope of the constitutional right at issue." ... In this case, the task of identifying the scope of the relevant constitutional protection is ... difficult because Title II purports to enforce a panoply of constitutional rights of disabled persons: not only the equal protection right against irrational discrimination, but also certain rights protected by the Due Process Clause.... Having traced the "metes and bounds" of the constitutional rights at issue, the next step in the congruence-and-proportionality inquiry requires us to examine whether Congress "identified a history and pattern" of violations of these constitutional rights by the States with respect to the disabled.... "Congress' §5 power is appropriately exercised *only* in response to state transgressions." ... But the majority identifies nothing in the legislative record that shows Congress was responding to widespread violations of the due process rights of disabled persons.

Rather than limiting its discussion of constitutional violations to the due process rights on which it ultimately relies, the majority sets out on a wide-ranging account of societal discrimination against the disabled.... This digression recounts historical discrimination against the disabled through institutionalization laws, restrictions on marriage, voting, and public education, conditions in mental hospitals, and various other forms of unequal treatment in the administration of public programs and services.... We discounted much the same type of outdated, generalized evidence in *Garrett* as unsupportive of Title I's ban on employment discrimination....

Even if it were proper to consider this broader category of evidence, much of it does not concern *unconstitutional* action by the *States*.... Most of the brief anecdotes do not involve States at all, and those that do are not sufficiently detailed to determine whether the instances of "unequal treatment" were irrational, and thus unconstitutional under our decision in *Cleburne*.... With respect to the due process "access to the courts" rights on which the Court ultimately relies, Congress' failure to identify a pattern of actual constitutional violations by the States is even more striking. Indeed, there is *nothing* in the legislative record or statutory findings to indicate that disabled persons were systematically denied the right to be present at criminal trials, denied the meaningful opportunity to be heard in civil cases, unconstitutionally excluded from jury service, or denied the right to attend criminal trials....

Even if the anecdotal evidence and conclusory statements relied on by the majority could be properly considered, the mere existence of an architecturally "inaccessible" courthouse—*i.e.*, one a disabled person cannot utilize without assistance—does not state a constitutional violation.... Nor does an "inaccessible" courthouse violate the Equal Protection Clause, unless it is irrational for the State not to alter the courthouse to make it "accessible." But financial considerations almost always furnish a rational basis for a State to decline to make those alterations.... Thus, evidence regarding inaccessible courthouses, because it is not evidence of constitutional violations, provides no basis to abrogate States' sovereign immunity....

The third step of our congruence-and-proportionality inquiry removes any doubt as to whether Title II is valid §5 legislation. At this stage, we ask whether the rights and remedies created by Title II are congruent and proportional to the constitutional rights it purports to enforce and the record of constitutional violations adduced by Congress.... The ADA's findings make clear that Congress believed it was attacking "discrimination" in all areas of public services, as well as the "discriminatory effect" of "architectural, transportation, and communication barriers." In sum, Title II requires, on pain of money damages, special accommodations for disabled persons in virtually every interaction they have with the State....

The majority, however, claims that Title II also vindicates fundamental rights protected by the Due Process Clause ... that are subject to heightened Fourteenth Amendment scrutiny.... But Title II is not tailored to provide prophylactic protection of these rights; instead, it applies to any service, program, or activity provided by any entity.... Thus, as with Title I in *Garrett*, ... it is unlikely "that many of the [state actions] affected by [Title II] ha[ve] any likelihood of being unconstitutional." ... Viewed as a whole, then, there is little doubt that Title II of the ADA does not validly abrogate state sovereign immunity.

Justice Scalia wrote a dissenting opinion.

... Requiring access for disabled persons to all public buildings cannot remotely be considered a means of "enforcing" the Fourteenth Amendment. The considerations of long accepted practice and of policy that sanctioned such distortion of language where state racial discrimination is at issue do not apply in this field of social policy far removed from the principal object of the Civil War Amendments.... It is past time to draw a line limiting the uncontrolled spread of a well-intentioned textual distortion. For these reasons, I respectfully dissent from the judgment of the Court.[99]

Again, it is extraordinarily difficult to read the dissents in this case and not to find complete insensitivity and indeed a hostility to the idea of protection for persons with disabilities. As the majority opinion in this case and the dissenting opinion in *Garrett* make clear, Chief Justice Rehnquist makes an extreme attempt to deny what is overwhelmingly documented not only in the facts of the pending cases themselves, but in countless other examples set forth in the legislative history and other congressional hearings and studies. It strains credulity to read the facts of this case and then accept as a reasonable reaction the dissenters' blithe dismissal of such extreme and humiliating treatment at the hands of state and local officials. The idea that a woman court reporter would have to depend upon a male judge to place her on the toilet, or that a defendant in a case would be forced to crawl up courthouse stairs with people laughing at him, would be utterly dismissed by three justices of the U.S. Supreme Court is evidence in itself of why Congress found legislative action necessary.

It also did not escape notice that some of the members of the Court, particularly Rehnquist, Scalia, and Thomas, who have often loudly denounced others for attempting to substitute their own judgment for that of the Congress, did that to an extent that simply strained credulity.

But the diatribe was far from over. Another round came in what seemed like a relatively innocuous case, and yet it was an occasion for Justice Scalia to make it abundantly clear that although the twenty-first century may have arrived, the attitudes of a previous day concerning persons with disabilities were alive and well.

PGA Tour, Inc. v. Martin

532 U.S. 661 (2001)

INTRODUCTION: The facts of the case are provided in the opinion. Indeed, it is interesting to see how carefully the majority explained those facts in order to address the questions of just what constitutes a reasonable accommodation.
Justice Stevens wrote the opinion for the majority.

> This case raises two questions concerning the application of the Americans with Disabilities Act of 1990 ... to a gifted athlete: first, whether the Act protects access to professional golf tournaments by a qualified entrant with a disability; and second, whether a disabled contestant may be denied the use of a golf cart because it would "fundamentally alter the nature" of the tournaments ... to allow him to ride when all other contestants must walk.

> Petitioner PGA TOUR, Inc. ... sponsors and cosponsors professional golf tournaments conducted on three annual tours. About 200 golfers participate.... The entire field usually competes in two 18-hole rounds played on Thursday and Friday; those who survive the "cut" play on Saturday and Sunday and receive prize money in amounts determined by their aggregate scores for all four rounds. The revenues generated by television, admissions, concessions, and contributions from cosponsors amount to about $300 million a year, much of which is distributed in prize money.

> There are various ways of gaining entry into particular tours.... [A] player who wins three NIKE TOUR events in the same year, or is among the top-15 money winners on that tour, earns the right to play in the PGA TOUR. Additionally, a golfer may obtain a spot in an official tournament through successfully competing in "open" qualifying rounds, which are conducted the week before each tournament. Most participants, however, earn playing privileges in the PGA TOUR

or NIKE TOUR by way of a three-stage qualifying tournament known as the "Q-School."

Any member of the public may enter the Q-School [qualifying school] by paying a $3,000 entry fee and submitting two letters of reference from [tour] members. The $3,000 entry fee covers the players' greens fees and the cost of golf carts, which are permitted during the first two stages, but which have been prohibited during the third stage since 1997....

Three sets of rules govern competition in tour events. First, the "Rules of Golf" ... apply to the game as it is played ... throughout the United States and worldwide [and] also by the professionals in the tournaments.... Those rules do not prohibit the use of golf carts at any time. Second, the "Conditions of Competition and Local Rules," often described as the "hard card," apply specifically to petitioner's professional tours. The hard cards for the [tour] require players to walk the golf course during tournaments, but not during open qualifying rounds.... Third, "Notices to Competitors" are issued for particular tournaments and cover conditions for that specific event....

The basic Rules of Golf, the hard cards, and the weekly notices apply equally to all players in tour competitions. As one of petitioner's witnesses explained with reference to "the Masters Tournament ... the key is to have everyone tee off on the first hole under exactly the same conditions and all of them be tested over that 72-hole event under the conditions that exist during those four days of the event." ...

Casey Martin is a talented golfer. As an amateur, he won 17 Oregon Golf Association junior events before he was 15, and won the state championship as a high school senior. He played on the Stanford University golf team that won the 1994 National Collegiate Athletic Association (NCAA) championship. As a professional, Martin qualified for ... the PGA TOUR in 2000. In the 1999 season, he entered 24 events, made the cut 13 times, and had 6 top-10 finishes, coming in second twice and third once.

Martin is also an individual with a disability as defined in the Americans with Disabilities Act of 1990. Since birth he has been afflicted with Klippel-Trenaunay-Weber Syndrome, a degenerative circulatory disorder that obstructs the flow of blood from his right leg back to his heart. The disease is progressive; it causes severe pain and has atrophied his right leg. During the latter part of his college career, because of the progress of the disease, Martin could no longer walk an 18-hole golf course. Walking not only caused him pain, fatigue, and anxiety, but also created a significant risk of hemorrhaging, developing blood clots, and fracturing his tibia so badly that an amputation might be required. For these reasons, Stanford made written requests to the Pacific 10 Conference and the NCAA to waive for Martin their rules requiring players to walk and carry their own clubs. The requests were granted.

When Martin turned pro and entered petitioner's Q-School, the hard card permitted him to use a cart during his successful progress through the first two stages. He made a request, supported by detailed medical records, for permission to use a golf cart during the third stage. Petitioner refused to review those records or to waive its walking rule for the third stage. Martin therefore filed this action. A preliminary injunction entered by the District Court made it possible for him to use a cart in the final stage of the Q-School and as a competitor in the NIKE TOUR and PGA TOUR. Although not bound by the injunction, and despite its support for petitioner's position in this litigation, the USGA voluntarily granted Martin a similar waiver in events that it sponsors, including the U.S. Open.

In the District Court, petitioner moved for summary judgment on the ground that it is exempt from coverage under Title III of the ADA as a "private club or establishment," or alternatively, that the play areas of its tour competitions do not constitute places of "public accommodation" within the scope of that Title. The Magistrate Judge concluded that petitioner should be viewed as a commercial enterprise operating in the entertainment industry for the economic benefit of its members rather than as a private club. Furthermore, after noting that the statutory definition of public accommodation included a "golf course," he rejected petitioner's argument that its competitions are only places of public accommodation in the areas open to spectators.... Accordingly, he denied petitioner's motion for summary judgment.

At trial, petitioner ... asserted that the condition of walking is a substantive rule of competition, and that waiving it as to any individual for any reason would fundamentally alter the nature of the competition. Petitioner's evidence included the testimony of a number of experts, among them some of the greatest golfers in history. Arnold Palmer, Jack Nicklaus, and Ken Venturi explained that fatigue can be a critical factor in a tournament, particularly on the last day when psychological pressure is at a maximum. Their testimony makes it clear that, in their view, permission to use a cart might well give some players a competitive advantage over other players who must walk. They did not, however, express any opinion on whether a cart would give Martin such an advantage.

Rejecting petitioner's argument that an individualized inquiry into the necessity of the walking rule in Martin's case would be inappropriate, the District Court stated that it had "the independent duty to inquire into the purpose of the rule at issue, and to ascertain whether there can be a reasonable modification made to accommodate plaintiff without frustrating the purpose of the rule" and thereby fundamentally altering the nature of petitioner's tournaments.... The judge found that the purpose of the rule was to inject fatigue into the skill of shot-making, but that the fatigue injected "by walking the course cannot be deemed significant under normal circumstances." ... Furthermore, Martin presented evidence, and the judge found, that even with the use of a cart, Martin must walk over a mile during an 18-hole round, and that the fatigue he suffers from coping with his disability is "undeniably greater" than the fatigue his able-bodied competitors endure from walking the course.... As the judge observed: "Plaintiff is in significant pain when he walks, and even when he is getting in and out of the cart. With each step, he is at risk of fracturing his tibia and hemorrhaging. The other golfers have to endure the psychological stress of competition as part of their fatigue; Martin has the same stress plus the added stress of pain and risk of serious injury. As he put it, he would gladly trade the cart for a good leg. To perceive that the cart puts him—with his condition—at a competitive advantage is a gross distortion of reality." ...

As a result, the judge concluded that it would "not fundamentally alter the nature of the PGA Tour's game to accommodate him with a cart." ... The judge accordingly entered a permanent injunction requiring petitioner to permit Martin to use a cart in tour and qualifying events. [The Ninth Circuit affirmed the ruling in Martin's favor.] ...

Congress enacted the ADA in 1990 to remedy widespread discrimination against disabled individuals.... After thoroughly investigating the problem, Congress concluded that there was a "compelling need" for a "clear and comprehensive national mandate" to eliminate discrimination against disabled individuals, and to integrate them "into the economic and social mainstream of American life." ...

In the ADA, Congress provided that broad mandate.... To effectuate its sweeping purpose, the ADA forbids discrimination against disabled individuals in major areas of public life, among them employment (Title I of the Act), public services (Title II), and public accommodations (Title III). At issue now ... is the applicability of Title III to petitioner's golf tours and qualifying rounds, in particular to petitioner's treatment of a qualified disabled golfer wishing to compete in those events.

Title III of the ADA prescribes, as a "general rule": "No individual shall be discriminated against on the basis of disability in the full and equal enjoyment of the goods, services, facilities, privileges, advantages, or accommodations of any place of public accommodation by any person who owns, leases (or leases to), or operates a place of public accommodation." 42 U.S.C. §12182(a). The phrase "public accommodation" is defined in terms of 12 extensive categories, which the legislative history indicates "should be construed liberally" to afford people with disabilities "equal access" to the wide variety of establishments available to the nondisabled.

It seems apparent, from ... the comprehensive definition of "public accommodation," that petitioner's golf tours and their qualifying rounds fit comfortably within the coverage of Title III, and Martin within its protection. The events occur on "golf courses," a type of place specifically identified by the Act as a public accommodation. §12181(7)(L).... As a lessor and operator of golf courses, then, petitioner must not discriminate against any "individual" in the "full and equal enjoyment of the goods, services, facilities, privileges, advantages, or accommodations" of those courses.... Certainly, among the "privileges" offered by petitioner on the courses are those of competing in the Q-School and playing in the tours; indeed, the former is a privilege for which thousands of individuals from the general public pay, and the latter is one for which they vie. Martin, of course, is one of those individuals. It would therefore appear that Title III of the ADA, by its plain terms, prohibits petitioner from denying Martin equal access to its tours on the basis of his disability....

To be clear about its position, ... petitioner admits that its tournaments are conducted at places of public accommodation.... Rather, petitioner reframes the coverage issue by arguing that the competing golfers are not members of the class protected by Title III of the ADA....

[P]etitioner's argument falters even on its own terms. If Title III's protected class were limited to "clients or customers," it would be entirely appropriate to classify the golfers who pay petitioner $3,000 for the chance to compete in the Q-School and, if successful, in the subsequent tour events, as petitioner's clients or customers. In our view, petitioner's tournaments ... simultaneously offer at least two "privileges" to the public—that of watching the golf competition and that of competing in it. Although the latter is more difficult and more expensive to obtain than the former, it is nonetheless a privilege that petitioner makes available to members of the general public. In consideration of the entry fee, any golfer with the requisite letters of recommendation acquires the opportunity to qualify for and compete in petitioner's tours. Additionally, any golfer who succeeds in the open qualifying rounds for a tournament may play in the event.... In *Daniel v. Paul*, 395 U.S. 298, 306 (1969), applying Title II to the Lake Nixon Club in Little Rock, Arkansas, we held that the definition of a "place of exhibition or entertainment," as a public accommodation, covered participants "in some sport or activity" as well as "spectators or listeners." ... [A]s a public accommodation during its tours and qualifying rounds, petitioner may not discriminate against either spectators or competitors on the basis of disability.

The question whether petitioner has violated ["Title III's general rule prohibiting public accommodations from discriminating against individuals because of their disabilities"] depends on a proper construction of the term "discrimination," which is defined by Title III to include: "a failure to make reasonable modifications in policies, practices, or procedures, when such modifications are necessary to afford such goods, services, facilities, privileges, advantages, or accommodations to individuals with disabilities, *unless the entity can demonstrate that making such modifications would fundamentally alter the nature* of such goods, services, facilities, privileges, advantages, or accommodations." ... (Emphasis added by the Court.)

Petitioner does not contest that a golf cart is a reasonable modification that is necessary if Martin is to play in its tournaments. Martin's claim thus differs from one that might be asserted by players with less serious afflictions that make walking the course uncomfortable or difficult, but not beyond their capacity. In such cases, an accommodation might be reasonable but not necessary. In this case, however, the narrow dispute is whether allowing Martin to use a golf cart, despite the walking requirement that applies to the PGA TOUR, the NIKE TOUR, and the third stage of the Q-School, is a modification that would "fundamentally alter the nature" of those events.

... We are not persuaded that a waiver of the walking rule for Martin would work a fundamental alteration.... [T]he use of carts is not itself inconsistent with the fundamental character of the game of golf. From early on, the essence of the game has been shot-making—using clubs to cause a ball to progress from the teeing ground to a hole some distance away with as few strokes as possible.... There is nothing in the Rules of Golf that either forbids the use of carts, or penalizes a player for using a cart.... The walking rule that is contained in petitioner's hard cards, based on an optional condition buried in an appendix to the Rules of Golf, is not an essential attribute of the game itself.

Indeed, the walking rule is not an indispensable feature of tournament golf either. As already mentioned, petitioner permits golf carts to be used in the SENIOR PGA TOUR, the open qualifying events for petitioner's tournaments, the first two stages of the Q-School, and, until 1997, the third stage of the Q-School as well.... Moreover, petitioner allows the use of carts during certain tournament rounds in both the PGA TOUR and the NIKE TOUR....

Petitioner, however, distinguishes the game of golf as it is generally played from the game that it sponsors in the PGA TOUR, NIKE TOUR [as] golf at the "highest level." According to petitioner, "the goal ... is to assess and compare the performance of different competitors, a task that is meaningful only if the competitors are subject to identical substantive rules." ... As a consequence, the reasonable modification Martin seeks would fundamentally alter the nature of petitioner's highest level tournaments even if he were the only person in the world who has both the talent to compete in those elite events and a disability sufficiently serious that he cannot do so without using a cart....

Even if we accept the ... argument—that the walking rule is "outcome affecting" because fatigue may adversely affect performance—its legal position is fatally flawed. Petitioner's refusal to consider Martin's personal circumstances in deciding whether to accommodate his disability runs counter to the clear language and purpose of the ADA. As previously stated, the ADA was enacted to eliminate discrimination against "individuals" with disabilities, ... and to that end Title III of the Act requires without exception that any "policies, practices, or procedures" of a public accommodation be reasonably modified for disabled "individuals" as necessary to afford access unless doing so would fundamentally alter what is offered.... To comply with this command, an individualized inquiry must be made to determine whether a specific modification for a particular person's disability would be reasonable under the circumstances as well as necessary for that person, and yet at the same time not work a fundamental alteration....

Under the ADA's basic requirement that the need of a disabled person be evaluated on an individual basis, we have no doubt that allowing Martin to use a golf cart would not fundamentally alter the nature of petitioner's tournaments. As we have discussed, the purpose of the walking rule is to subject players to fatigue, which in turn may influence the outcome of tournaments. Even if the rule does serve that purpose, it is an uncontested finding of the District Court that Martin "easily endures greater fatigue even with a cart than his able-bodied competitors do by walking." ... The purpose of the walking rule is therefore not compromised in the slightest by allowing Martin to use a cart. A modification that provides an exception to a peripheral tournament rule without impairing its purpose cannot be said to "fundamentally alter" the tournament. What it can be said to do, on the other hand, is to allow Martin the chance to qualify for and compete in the athletic events petitioner offers to those members of the public who have the skill and desire to enter. That is exactly what the ADA requires. As a result, Martin's request for a waiver of the walking rule should have been granted....

Justice Scalia wrote a dissent joined by Justice Thomas.

In my view today's opinion exercises a benevolent compassion that the law does not place it within our power to impose. The judgment distorts the text of Title III, the structure of the ADA, and common sense. I respectfully dissent.

... The provision of Title III at issue here ... is a public-accommodation law, and it is the traditional understanding of public-accommodation laws that they provide rights for *customers*.... The professional golfers on the tour are no more "enjoying" ... the entertainment that the tour provides, or the facilities of the golf courses on which it is held, than professional baseball players "enjoy" the baseball games in which they play or the facilities of Yankee Stadium. To be sure, professional ballplayers *participate* in the games, and *use* the ballfields, but no one in his right mind would think that they are *customers* of the American League or of Yankee Stadium.... And professional golfers are no different....

[T]he Court then erroneously answers ... a second question. The ADA requires covered businesses to make such reasonable modifications of "policies, practices, or procedures" as are necessary to "afford" goods, services, and privileges to individuals with disabilities; but it explicitly does not require "modifications [that] would fundamentally alter the nature" of the goods, services, and privileges....

[E]ven if respondent here is a consumer of the "privilege" of the PGA TOUR competition ... I see no basis for considering whether the rules of that competition must be altered. It is as irrelevant to the PGA TOUR's compliance with the statute whether walking is essential to the game of golf as it is to the shoe store's compliance whether "pairness" is essential to the nature of shoes. If a shoe store wishes to sell shoes only in pairs it may; and if a golf tour (or a golf course) wishes to provide only walk-around golf, it may. The PGA TOUR cannot deny respondent *access* to that game because of his disability, but it need not provide him a game different (whether in its essentials or in its details) from that offered to everyone else.

... [T]he Court must then confront the question whether respondent's requested modification ... would "fundamentally alter the nature" of the PGA TOUR game.... Nowhere is it writ that PGA TOUR golf must be classic "essential" golf. Why cannot the PGA TOUR, if it wishes, promote a new game, with distinctive rules.... If members of the public do not like the new rules ... they can withdraw their patronage. But the rules are the rules. They are ... entirely arbitrary, and there is no basis on which anyone ... can pronounce one or another of them to be "nonessential" if the rulemaker (here the PGA TOUR) deems it to be essential.

If one assumes, however, that the PGA TOUR has some legal obligation to play classic, Platonic golf ... then we Justices must confront what is indeed an awesome responsibility. It has been rendered the solemn duty of the Supreme Court of the United States, laid upon it by Congress ... to decide What Is Golf. I am sure that the Framers of the Constitution, aware of the 1457 edict of King James II of Scotland prohibiting golf because it interfered with the practice of archery, fully expected that sooner or later the paths of golf and government, the law and the links, would once again cross, and that the judges of this August Court would some day have to wrestle with that age-old jurisprudential question, for which their years of study in the law have so well prepared them: Is someone riding around a golf course from shot to shot *really* a golfer? The answer, we learn, is yes. The Court ultimately concludes, and it will henceforth be the Law of the Land, that walking is not a "fundamental" aspect of golf.

Either out of humility or out of self-respect ... the Court should decline to answer this incredibly difficult and incredibly silly question. To say that something is "essential" is ordinarily to say that it is necessary to the achievement of a certain object. But since it is the very nature of a game to have no object except amusement..., it is quite impossible to say that any of a game's arbitrary rules is "essential." ... I suppose there is some point at which the rules of a well-known game are changed to such a degree that no reasonable person would call it the same game. If the PGA TOUR competitors were required to dribble a large, inflated ball and put it through a round hoop, the game could no longer reasonably be called golf. But this criterion ... is surely not the test of "essentialness" or "fundamentalness" that the Court applies, since it apparently thinks that merely changing the diameter of the *cup* might "fundamentally alter" the game of golf....

Having concluded that dispensing with the walking rule would not violate federal-Platonic "golf" ... the Court moves on to the second part of its test: the competitive effects of waiving this nonessential rule.... [T]he Court relies upon the District Court's finding that even with a cart, respondent will be at least as fatigued as everyone else.... This, the Court says, *proves* that competition will not be affected. Far from thinking that reliance on this finding cabins the effect of today's opinion, I think it will prove to be its most expansive and destructive feature.... One can envision the parents of a Little League player with attention deficit disorder trying to convince a judge that their son's disability makes it at least 25% more difficult to hit a pitched ball. (If they are successful, the only thing that could prevent a court order giving the kid four strikes would be a judicial determination that, in baseball, three strikes are metaphysically necessary, which is quite absurd.)

The statute, of course, provides no basis for this individualized analysis that is the Court's last step on a long and misguided journey. The statute seeks to assure that a disabled person's disability will not deny him *equal access* to (among other things) competitive sporting events—not that his disability will not deny him an *equal chance to win* competitive sporting events. The latter is quite impossible, since the very *nature* of competitive sport is the measurement, by uniform rules, of unevenly distributed excellence. This unequal distribution is precisely what determines the winners and losers—and artificially to "even out" that distribution, by giving one or another player exemption from a rule that emphasizes his particular weakness, is to destroy the game.... In the Court's world, there is one set of rules that is "fair with respect to the able-bodied" but "individualized" rules, mandated by the ADA, for "talented but disabled athletes." ... The ADA mandates no such ridiculous thing. Agility, strength, speed, balance, quickness of mind, steadiness of nerves, intensity of concentration—these talents are not evenly distributed. No wild-eyed dreamer has ever suggested that the managing bodies of the competitive sports that test precisely these qualities should try to take account of the uneven distribution of God-given gifts when writing and enforcing the rules of competition. And I have no doubt Congress did not authorize misty-eyed judicial supervision of such a revolution....

Complaints about this case are not "properly directed to Congress." ... They are properly directed to this Court's Kafkaesque determination that professional sports organizations, and the fields they rent for their exhibitions, are "places of public accommodation" to the competing athletes, and the athletes themselves "customers" of the organization that pays them; its Alice in Wonderland determination that there are such things as judicially determinable "essential" and "nonessential" rules of a made-up game; and its Animal Farm determination that fairness and the ADA mean that everyone gets to play by individualized rules which will assure that no one's lack of ability ... will be a handicap. The year was 2001, and "everybody was finally equal." K. Vonnegut, Harrison Bergeron, in Animal Farm and Related Readings 129 (1997).

That Justice Scalia developed a well-earned reputation for intemperate and cynical rhetoric about his colleagues' opinions is well known; and that behavior only intensified over time.[100] However, Justice Thurgood Marshall long ago made clear that whatever a person might say as an individual takes on a different character and has a different impact when it comes from a high official of the United States, and especially so for members of the U.S. Supreme Court, given the nature of their role and the institution in which they serve. That Justice Scalia would decide to target the parents of a hypothetical Little League baseball player with attention deficit disorder as part of his diatribe is the kind of dismissive and insensitive, not to say deliberately provocative, rhetoric that could only be seen as a gratuitous and needlessly vicious comment about persons with disabilities. It was also just as clearly an attempt to trivialize the situation of a professional golfer with a serious disability who plays through intense pain and seeks only to compete with a minimal degree of accommodation.

It should be clear by this point that interpretations of virtually all of these statutory protections are still developing, and that is particularly true for the ADA. There are cases in which it is clear that a majority of the Court has worked hard to understand the legislation and the situation and to consider carefully how to deal with the widely varying fact patterns that arise in different cases. The Court has also tried to understand the intended scope and substantive range of protection of the ADA. For example, members of the Court have even considered that it is a basis for ordering deinstitutionalization.

In *Olmstead v. L.C.*, 527 U.S. 581 (1999), Justice Ginsburg wrote for the Court:

> This case concerns the proper construction of the anti-discrimination provision contained in the public services portion (Title II) of the Americans with Disabilities Act of 1990.... Specifically, we confront the question whether the proscription of discrimination may require placement of persons with mental disabilities in community settings rather than in institutions. The answer, we hold, is a qualified yes. Such action is in order when the State's treatment professionals have determined that community placement is appropriate, the transfer from institutional care to a less restrictive setting is not opposed by the affected individual, and the placement can be reasonably accommodated, taking into account the resources available to the State and the needs of others with mental disabilities."[101]

However, her opinion was for the Court on Parts I, II, and III-A of the opinion, but only for a plurality for Part III-B.[102]

On the other hand, the Court has issued other opinions, some of which have been discussed above, that have clearly constrained the effectiveness of the ADA and narrowed its application. In fact, two of those rulings were central in the passage by Congress of the ADA Amendments Act of 2008.[103] In its statement of findings, Congress said:

> (4) the holdings of the Supreme Court in *Sutton v. United Air Lines, Inc.*, 527 U.S. 471 (1999) and its companion cases have narrowed the broad scope of protection intended to be afforded by the ADA, thus eliminating protection for many individuals whom Congress intended to protect; (5) the holding of the Supreme Court in *Toyota Motor Manufacturing, Kentucky, Inc. v. Williams*, 534 U.S. 184 (2002) further narrowed the broad scope of protection intended to be afforded by the ADA; (6) as a result of these Supreme Court cases, lower courts have incorrectly found in individual cases that people with a range of substantially limiting impairments are not people with disabilities.[104]

It seems likely that the effort to develop the ADA and the rest of the statutory framework of protections for the rights of persons with disabilities will be continuing for the foreseeable future.

Conclusion

Issues faced by those with disabilities of various kinds in our society may no longer be relegated only to the shadows, with those persons hidden away from view by their families or in public institutions, but the challenge of ensuring their civil rights is very much an emerging enterprise. Although lower courts have been willing in some circumstances to provide constitutional protections, the U.S. Supreme Court has been willing only to apply very limited readings to the equal protection and due process clauses in extreme situations. Unlike the lower courts, the Supreme Court has been unwilling to support the broad claim for a right to treatment or habilitation under the Fourteenth Amendment.

Even when Congress has responded by statute, the Court has often tended to read the statutory protections in a relatively limited manner, in some cases in ways that dramatically constrained what many Americans with disabilities clearly thought the legislation meant. Even where the Court has supported a solid reading of the statute as in the *PGA v. Martin* case, there have been members of the Court, like Justice Scalia, willing even at this late date in the civil rights history of the nation to use derogatory and demeaning language. The same could be said of opinions by other members of the Court in modern history, particularly Chief Justice Rehnquist. It seems clear that the road forward for development of civil rights for persons with disabilities in the United States lies with enactment of serious national and state legislation that has the institutional capacity and resources to ensure implementation and the teeth to respond to those who will not respect those policies.

I. Issues for Policy and Practice

A.   Given that there is a collection of legislation at the federal level and in the states on disabilities, has your organization or jurisdiction organized its requirements into a comprehensive and comprehensible form?

B.   Are issues of disability included in discussions of diversity within your organization? Are employees trained in how to meet the needs of those in the organization or in the community beyond what the law specifically requires?

C.   In connection with the former, what is the record of the organization in terms of hiring and promotion of people with disabilities?

D.   Given the fact that many people will become disabled during their working years, let alone at other points in their lives, are there management policies or practices in place that would help to retain those valuable people in their jobs once they face a disability?

E.   Have the families of persons with disabilities been consulted when policies are being considered that are likely to have an impact on those with physical or cognitive disabilities? Too often the answer to that question is no. There is also a tendency not to consider the wide range of programs and services that do have significant disability issues associated with them, whether they are in public works, emergency services, human service delivery, education or other fields.

F.   Has there been an assessment to ensure that in fact public facilities and programs actually are accessible?

G.   Does the organization have a strengths-based perspective on dealing with people within the organization or those in the service community, or do those in the organization tend to operate from a deficit approach?

H.   Years after the de-institutionalization movement succeeded in shutting down terrible institutions that were doing little more than warehousing people, the promised support for community treatment has fallen woefully short of the need. That, as this chapter has noted, has left many people in the streets and meant that county jails have become among the largest mental health facilities in the nation. Has each state assessed the state of services for those with mental health disabilities? Has meeting those needs been a funding priority where a federal investigation or lawsuit filed by advocates has not forced the issue?

II. Discussion Questions

A.   Justice Holmes in the *Buck v. Bell* case said that it was obvious that there was no violation of procedural due process in the way that patients, including Carrie Buck, were set for sterilization, after which he lays out the process. Although there was notice and a hearing, from the facts of this case can it be said that the process was meaningful, or was it really pro forma? If the patient really did have a mental illness or a severe intellectual disability, was it adequate as described to protect the patient against arbitrariness?

B.   Thinking back over your education and life experience, have you learned to consider disability as part of a conversation about civil rights or have those with disabilities been treated as somehow separate and apart from others?

C. There is a tendency to look back on the days of eugenics with horror and to assume that nothing similar could happen today. However, to what degree do people avert their eyes when they see someone with an obvious physical disability or when they encounter someone they think has a cognitive or developmental disability?

D. People with disabilities and their families often go through a difficult process when they interact with government, or with private organizations as well for that matter. They begin by going to those organizations to deal with issues or obtain services with a positive attitude. However, over time and after meeting with barrier after barrier, it is easy to become extraordinarily frustrated and even angry. When they come to your agency, people with disabilities have often had to educate people in various offices about their needs and their rights. How can we better prepare to meet those needs and deal with the understandable frustration that those coming to us for services often feel?

E. There is a difference in civil rights between exclusion or segregation, on the one hand, and full inclusion on the other. One assumes a legal minimum while the other starts from the premise that everyone has something to offer and therefore should be engaged and included. How do you suppose your community has considered persons with disabilities in this regard?

F. What kind of message would you receive if you were a person with a disability from the decision by the Supreme Court in *Pennhurst State School and Hospital v. Halderman* that the bill of rights provided in the Developmental Disabilities Assistance and Bill of Rights Act was not really a binding set of rights and obligations?

G. Similarly, what is the message you receive from Chief Justice Rehnquist's language in the *Garrett* case concerning the lack of any obligation on the part of states to consider the needs of those with disabilities?

H. Again, read the dissents in the *Tennessee v. Lane* and *PGA v. Martin* cases. What messages does the language in these two dissents convey to people who have disabilities? It is true that the language is in dissent in both cases, unlike in the *Garrett* case, but the message is clear and the language is harsh. Whether it is in dissent or in the majority, it comes from justices of the United States Supreme Court.

Notes

1 Joan Klein, "Buck v. Bell: The Test Case for Virginia's Eugenical Sterilization Act," http://exhibits.hsl.virginia.edu/eugenics/3-buckvbell/, April 24, 2016.

2 Id.

3 Id.

4 Id. The marriage license is published on the website.

5 Id. The evidence and witnesses as well as the performance of her attorney are discussed in the history.

6 NOTE: This is an operation to remove fallopian tubes.

7 NOTE: Justice Butler dissented without opinion.

8 Georgia State University College of Law Reading Room, "Nuremberg Documents," in *Buck v. Bell Documents*, http://readingroom.law.gsu.edu/cgi/viewcontent.cgi?article=1044&context=buckvbell, August 12, 2015.

9 Brendan Wolfe, "Buck v. Bell," in Virginia Foundation for the Humanities with the Library of Virginia, *Virginia Encyclopedia*, www.encyclopediavirginia.org/buck_v_bell_1927#start_entry, August 12, 2015.

10 *Board of Trustees of the University of Alabama v. Garrett*, 531 U.S. 356, 369, n. 6 (2001).

11 *Tennessee v. Lane*, 541 U.S. 509, 535 (2004), Souter, J., concurring.

12 Governor John Kitzhaber, Proclamation of Human Rights Day, and Apology for Oregon's Forced Sterilization of Institutionalized Patients, Salem, Oregon, December 2, 2002, http://archivedwebsites.sos.state.or.us/Governor_Kitzhaber_2003/governor/speeches/s021202.htm, August 12, 2015.

13 Thus in the 1940s Leo Kanner's articles identifying autism spectrum disorders and his later pieces on the disorders gave rise to the theory of "refrigerator mothers," which suggested that autism was the result of frigid parents who did not provide emotional nurture. See Leo Kanner, "Autistic Disturbances of Affective Contact," *Nervous Child* 2 (1943): 217–250; "Problems of Nosology and Psychodynamics of Early Infantile Autism," *American Journal of Orthopsychiatry* 19 (1949): 416–426. See generally Sean Cohmer, "Early Infantile Autism and the Refrigerator Mother Theory" (1943–1970), Arizona State University, Embryo Project Encyclopedia, https://embryo.asu.edu/pages/early-infantile-autism-and-refrigerator-mother-theory-1943-1970#sthash.hm0dW4jz.dpuf, December 22, 2015.

14 Quoted in Nicholas W. Gillham, "Sir Francis Galton and the Birth of Eugenics," *Annual Review of Genetics 2001* 35 (2001): 83–101, p. 84.

15 David Wallace Adams, *Education for Extinction: American Indians and the Boarding School Experience 1875–1928* (Lawrence, KS: Kansas University Press, 1995), p. 53.

16 Galton, Francis, *Inquiries into Human Faculty and its Development* (London: Macmillan, 1883), p. 23, quoted in Gillham, "Sir Francis Galton and the Birth of Eugenics," p. 98.

17 First Eugenics Congress: Four Hundred Delegates in London—Americans to Read Papers, *New York Times*, July 25, 1912, p. 5.

18 Bleeker Van Wagenen, "Preliminary Report of the Committee of the Eugenic Section of the American Breeders' Association to Study and to Report on the Best Practical Means for Cutting Off the Defective Germ-Plasm in the Human Population," *Buck v Bell Documents*, Paper 74, http://readingroom.law.gsu.edu/buckvbell/74, August 13, 2015.

19 "Eugenics Congress Here: Second International Conference to Be Opened Tomorrow," *New York Times*, September 21, 1921, p. 8.

20 See the *Buck v. Bell* decision above.

21 The origins of this expression are unclear and the phrase has been used in many different kinds of contexts quite apart from discussions of persons with disabilities. However, it has very often been used within the disability rights community both domestically and internationally. See e.g., James I. Charlton, *Nothing About Us Without Us: Disability Oppression and Empowerment* (Berkeley, CA: University of California Press, 2000); United Nations Enable, "International Day of Disabled Persons, 2004—Nothing about Us, Without Us," www.un.org/esa/socdev/enable/iddp2004.htm, April 24, 2016 (United Nations Enable is the official website of the Secretariat for the Convention on the Rights of Persons with Disabilities (SCRPD)).

22 Franklin D. Roosevelt to Secretary of War, December 4, 1944, reproduced in Norman Q. Brill, "Station and Regional Hospitals," in Robert J. Bernucci and Albert J. Glass, eds., Office of Medical History, U.S. Army Medical Department. *Neuropsychiatry in World War II*, http://history.amedd.army.mil/booksdocs/wwii/NeuropsychiatryinWWIIVolI/chapter10.htm, December 22, 2015, Vol. I, Chapter X.

23 History of the Arc, The Arc, www.thearc.org/who-we-are/history/name-change, August 13, 2015.

24 P.L. 93–112, 87 Stat. 355 (1973).

25 Jonathan C. Drimmer, "Cripples, Overcomers, and Civil Rights: Tracing the Evolution of Federal Legislation and Social Policy for People with Disabilities," *UCLA Law Review* 40 (June 1993): 1385–1410.

26 Id., at 1387.

27 P.L. 94–142, 89 Stat. 773 (1975).

28 Drimmer, "Cripples, Overcomers, and Civil Rights."

29 See e.g., Dennis Saleebey, "The Strengths Perspective in Social Work Practice: Extensions and Cautions," *Social Work* 41 (No. 3 1996): 296–305.

30 Steven E. Brown, "What Is Disability Culture," *Disability Studies Quarterly* 22 (No. 2 2002): 34–50.

31 Institute on Disability Culture, "What We Mean by Disability Culture," www.instituteondisabilityculture.org/what-we-mean-by-disability-culture.html, August 14, 2015.

32 Laurent Clerc National Deaf Education Center, Gallaudet University, "About American Deaf Culture," www.gallaudet.edu/clerc-center/info-to-go/deaf-culture/american-deaf-culture.html, December 21, 2015

33 *Craig v. Boren*, 429 U.S. 190 (1976); *Mississippi University for Women v. Hogan*, 458 U.S. 718 (1982); *United States v. Virginia*, 518 U.S. 515 (1996).

34 See the excerpt of the *San Antonio Independent School District v. Rodriguez* case in Chapter 4.

35 See the excerpt of the *Frontiero v. Richardson* case in Chapter 10.

36 NOTE: Justice White was operating with extremely limited and simplistic information that was outdated even as he wrote the opinion. Today, the term used to describe the condition is "intellectual disability," which is far less negative in character than the term "retarded." Persons who were not long ago labeled in this way, institutionalized, and declared unable to "cope with and function in the everyday world," now generally live in community contexts, and often in the kind of group-living residences under consideration in this case. Indeed, the change was only formally made to the *Diagnostic and Statistical Manual (DSM)* 5 in 2013. In issuing the change, The American Psychiatric Association explained that "Intellectual disability (intellectual development disorder) as a DSM-5 diagnostic term places 'mental retardation' used in previous editions of the manuals.... [T]hese revisions bring DSM into alignment with terminology used by the World Health Organization's International Classification of Diseases, other professional disciplines and organizations, such as the American Association on Intellectual and Developmental Disabilities, and the U.S. Department of Education." *American Psychiatric Association, DSM-5 Development*, www. dsm5.org/Pages/Default.aspx, August 27, 2015.

37 NOTE: As Justice Marshall's dissent makes clear, the fact that the federal government began in the 1970s to provide some legislative protections in no way addresses the long history of discrimination of this group of Americans. And it bears repeating that these laws did not change the fact that many states still had blatantly discriminatory statutes in places, including the fact that their sterilization laws remained in effect, and additionally that the horrific conditions and lack of habilitation in state facilities for those with intellectual disabilities were only beginning to be addressed by multiple lawsuits and not by legislative action, as explained later in this chapter.

38 NOTE: Justice Stevens's concurring opinion is omitted.

39 *Humphrey v. Cady*, 405 U.S. 504, 509 (1972).

40 *Addington v. Texas*, 441 U.S. 418, 425 (1979).

41 *O'Connor v. Donaldson*, 422 U.S. 563, 575–576 (1975).

42 NOTE: The term simply means in place of the parents.

43 Report of the Study Commission on Mental Health Services for Children and Youth, November 9, 1973, p. 24, quoted in *J.L. v. Parham*, 412 F. Supp. 112, 122 (MDGA 1976).

44 *J.L. v. Parham*, 412 F. Supp., at 133, in part quoting Deposition of Dr. John P. Filley, Director, Child and Adolescent Mental Health Services.

45 *Parham v. J.R.*, 442 U.S. 584 (1979).

46 Id., at 637, Brennan, J., dissenting.

47 U.S. Department of Health and Human Services, Patient Protection and Affordable Care Act; HHS Notice of Benefit and Payment Parameters for 2016, Final Rule, 80 Fed. Reg. 10750, 10871 (2015).

48 Morton Birnbaum, "The Right to Treatment," *American Bar Association Journal* 46 (May 1960): 499–504.

49 "Editorial: A New Right," *American Bar Association Journal* 46 (May 1960): 516.

50 Frank R. Lindman and Fr. Donald McIntyre, eds., *The Mentally Disabled and the Law: Report of the American Bar Foundation on the Rights of the Mentally Ill* (Chicago: University of Chicago Press, 1961).

51 U.S. Senate, Hearings Before the Subcommittee on Constitutional Rights of the Committee on the Judiciary, *Constitutional Rights of the Mentally Ill*, 87th Cong., 1st Sess. (1961); U.S. Senate, Hearings Before the Subcommittee on Constitutional Rights of the Committee on the Judiciary, *To Protect the Constitutional Rights of the Mentally Ill*, 88th Cong., 1st Sess. (1963).

52 *Rouse v. Cameron*, 373 F.2d 451 (D.C. Cir. 1966).

53 *Wyatt v. Stickney*, 325 F. Supp. 781 (MDAL 1971).

54 The author has analyzed in depth the situation in Alabama leading up to the *Wyatt v. Stickney* litigation in "Wyatt v. Stickney: Judge Frank Johnson and Mental Health in Alabama," in Phillip J. Cooper, *Hard Judicial Choices: Federal District Court Judges and State and Local Officials* (New York: Oxford University Press, 1988).

55 *Wyatt v. Aderholt*, 503 F.2d 1305, 1311 (5th Cir. 1974).

56 *Wyatt v. Stickney*, 325 F. Supp. 781 (MDAL 1971).

57 *Wyatt v. Stickney*, Civ. No. 3195-N, "Hearing Before the Honorable Frank M. Johnson, at Montgomery, Alabama, February 28–29 and March 1, 1972," at 291.

58 Id., at 285.

59 This involved the story of the Willingboro state facility for children with intellectual disabilities. See *New York State Ass'n for Retarded Children v. Carey*, 393 F. Supp. 715 (EDNY 1975). This is the decision approving the consent decree to remedy the situation. There followed a series of rulings by the district court and court of appeals well into the 1980s. See generally David J. Rothman and Sheila M. Rothman, *The Willowbrook Wars* (New York: Harper & Row, 1984).

60 457 U.S. 307 (1982).

61 Id., at 309. The lower court opinion was rendered by the Court of Appeals for the Third Circuit, 644 F.2d 147 (3rd Cir. 1980).

62 Id., at 315–316.

63 Id., at 322–323.

64 For example, "On any given day, between 25–30 percent of the inmates at Cook County Jail suffer from mental illnesses. The majority of these inmates are in jail for nonviolent offences closely associated with their mental health issues and would be far better served by treatment rather than incarceration." Office of Mental Health Policy & Advocacy, Office of the Cook County Sheriff, www.cookcountysheriff.com/MentalHealth/MentalHealth_main.html, December 22, 2015; Matt Ford, America's Largest Mental Hospital Is a Jail, Atlantic Monthly, Jun 8, 2015, www.theatlantic.com/politics/archive/2015/06/americas-largest-mental-hospital-is-a-jail/395012/, December 22, 2015.

65 See the consent decree between the U.S. Department of Justice and the Portland, Oregon Police Bureau with respect to law enforcement and persons with mental illness, *United States v. City of Portland*, Case No. 3:12-cv-02265-SI, Settlement Agreement Pursuant to Fed. R. Civ. Pr. 41(a)(2), www.portlandoregon.gov/police/article/506328, December 22, 2015. The findings letter from the Civil Rights Division of the Department of Justice that led to the negotiated agreement is Thomas Perez to Sam Adams, September 12, 2012, Investigation of the Portland Police Bureau, www.justice.gov/sites/default/files/crt/legacy/2012/09/17/ppb_findings_9-12-12.pdf, December 22, 2015.

66 U.S. Department of Labor, Bureau of Labor Statistics, "Highlights from the 2014 Data," "In 2014, 17.1 percent of persons with a disability were employed, the U.S. Bureau of Labor Statistics reported today. In contrast, the employment-population ratio for those without a disability was 64.6 percent." The report added, "For all age groups, the employment-population ratio was much lower for persons with a disability than for those with no disability. Unemployment rates were higher for persons with a disability than for those with no disability among all educational attainment groups. In 2014, 33 percent of workers with a disability were employed part time, compared with 18 percent for those with no disability." See www.bls.gov/news.release/disabl.nr0.htm, August 28, 2015. A July 2015 report from the U.S. Department of Labor, Office of Disability Employment Policy, indicated a slightly higher workforce participation ratio, but still showed unemployment for those seeking employ almost double that of persons without disabilities. "Labor Force Participation—People with Disabilities: 19.8% People without Disabilities: 69.0% Unemployment Rate—People with Disabilities: 10.4% People without Disabilities: 5.4%. "Current Disability Employment Statistics," www.dol.gov/odep/, August 28, 2015.

67 *Mills v. Bd. of Ed. of the District of Columbia*, 348 F. Supp. 866 (DDC 1972).

68 *Pennsylvania Association for Retarded Children (PARC) v. Pennsylvania*, 334 F. Supp. 1257 (EDPA 1971).

69 P.L. 94–142.

70 NOTE: Justice Blackmun's brief concurring opinion is omitted here.

71 Executive Order 13227, President's Commission on Excellence in Special Education, 66 Fed. Reg. 51287 (2001).

72 *Arlington Central School District v. Murphy*, 548 U.S. 291 (2006).

73 *Schaffer v. Weast*, 546 U.S. 49 (2005).

74 P.L. 94–103, 89 Stat. 486 (1975).

75 Administration on Intellectual and Developmental Disabilities (AIDD), U.S. Department of Health and Human Services, "History of the DD Act," www.acl.gov/Programs/AIDD/DD_History/index.aspx, August 25, 2015.

76 42 U.S.C. §6010.

77 *Pennhurst State School and Hospital v. Halderman*, 451 U.S. 1, 5 (1981).

78 Id., at 18–19.

79 Id., at 39–40, White, J., dissenting.

80 P.L. 106–402, 114 Stat. 1677 (2000).

81 Section 101(a)(16).

82 NOTE: This case also consolidated an action brought by Milton Ash, who was employed by the Alabama Department of Youth Services. He brought an ADA Title I suit against his employer for failing to provide reasonable accommodations related to his asthma and sleep apnea, and indeed alleged that his employer took action to downgrade his performance appraisals.

83 Only a small fraction of the anecdotes Justice Breyer identifies in his Appendix C relate to state discrimination against the disabled in employment. At most, somewhere around 50 of these allegations describe conduct that could conceivably amount to constitutional violations by the States, and most of them are so general and brief that no firm conclusion can be drawn. The overwhelming majority of these accounts pertain to alleged discrimination by the States in the provision of public services and public accommodations, which areas are addressed in Titles II and III of the ADA.

84 Section 2 of the Fifteenth Amendment is virtually identical to §5 of the Fourteenth Amendment.

85 NOTE: It is interesting that the Chief Justice points out that the enforcement clause language of the Fifteenth Amendment is identical to that in the Fourteenth Amendment, but his opinion makes it clear that only the Fourteenth Amendment enforcement clause could be used as a valid basis to abrogate immunity.

86 NOTE: It must be noted that the Supreme Court had made up the new immunity doctrine in 1996 in *Seminole Tribe of Fla. v. Florida*, 517 U.S. 44, 54 (1996). There was no expectation when the ADA was passed in 1990 that the Supreme Court would later take it upon itself to decide that Congress needed to prove discrimination at some particular level to justify legislation designed to end any existing problem and prevent future discrimination. The authority to enact legislation to prevent or end discrimination was clearly authorized by section 5 of the Fourteenth Amendment. This was coupled in 2000 by a new approach to the commerce clause, which had not been employed since before 1937, that also put Congress under a burden of proof to satisfy the judiciary as to the adequacy of its justification for legislation, such that the Court would examine for itself the evidence—as if the legislature had to try its legislative proposal before the Court and satisfy a burden of proof to win a judgment. See *United States v. Morrison*, 529 U.S. 598 (2000).

87 NOTE: Justice Kennedy's concurring opinion joined by Justice O'Connor is omitted.

88 Previously, the *Kimel v. Florida Bd. of Regents*, 528 U.S. 62 (2000) case also came to a similar conclusion regarding the Age Discrimination in Employment Act (ADEA). Of the statutes challenged in this way, only the damages claim provisions of the Family Medical Leave Act had survived review.

89 Commission on the Future of the Tennessee Judicial System, Final Report, p. 31, www.tsc.state. tn.us/sites/default/files/docs/report_of_future_of_tn_judicial_system.pdf, September 2, 2015.

90 *Tennessee v. Lane*, Brief for Private Respondents, p. 4.

91 Quoted in Adam Cohen, Editorial Observer, "Can Disabled People Be Forced to Crawl Up the Courthouse Steps?" *New York Times*, January 11, 2004, Section 4, p. 14.

92 *Tennessee v. Lane*, U.S. Supreme Court, No. 02-1667, Brief for Private Respondents, p. 5.

93 Id.

94 Id., at 5–6.

95 Testimony of Beverly Jones, in U.S. Senate, Committee on the Judiciary, *Confirmation Hearing on the Nomination of John G. Roberts to Be Chief Justice of the United States*, 109th Cong., 1st Sess. (2005), pp. 921–922.

96 *Tennessee v. Lane*, U.S. Supreme Court, No. 02-1667, Brief for Private Respondents, p. 6.

97 *Tennessee v. Lane*, U.S. Supreme Court, No. 02-1667, Brief for American Bar Association as Amicus Curiae in Support of Respondents, p. 4.

98 NOTE: Here Congress was obviously telling the Court that persons with disabilities clearly meet the criteria required to show that disability should be a suspect class. And, in so doing, the Congress was reacting against the Court's ruling in *Cleburne*.

99 NOTE: Justice Thomas's dissent omitted.

100 See his dissenting opinion in the *Obergefell* case in Chapter 11.
101 527 U.S., at 587.
102 Justices O'Connor, Souter, and Breyer joined her on that part.
103 P.L. 110–325, 122 Stat. 3553 (2008).
104 Id., at Sec. 2(a)(4)–(6).

References

Adams, David Wallace. *Education for Extinction: American Indians and the Boarding School Experience 1875–1928*. Lawrence, KS: Kansas University Press, 1995.

American Bar Association Journal. "Editorial: A New Right," *American Bar Association Journal* 46 (May 1960): 516.

Birnbaum, Morton. "The Right to Treatment," *American Bar Association Journal* 46 (May 1960): 499–504.

Brown, Steven E. "What Is Disability Culture," *Disability Studies Quarterly* 22 (No. 2 2002): 34–50.

Charlton, James I. *Nothing About Us Without Us: Disability Oppression and Empowerment*. Berkeley, CA: University of California Press, 2000.

Cohmer, Sean. "Early Infantile Autism and the Refrigerator Mother Theory" (1943–1970), Arizona State University, Embryo Project Encyclopedia, https://embryo.asu.edu/pages/early-infantile-autism-and-refrigerator-mother-theory-1943–1970#sthash.hm0dW4jz.dpuf, December 22, 2015.

Cooper, Phillip J. *Hard Judicial Choices: Federal District Court Judges and State and Local Officials*. New York: Oxford University Press, 1988.

Drimmer, Jonathan C. "Cripples, Overcomers, and Civil Rights: Tracing the Evolution of Federal Legislation and Social Policy for People with Disabilities," *UCLA Law Review* 40 (June 1993): 1385–1410.

Galton, Francis. *Inquiries into Human Faculty and its Development*. London: Macmillan, 1883.

Gillham, Nicholas W. "Sir Francis Galton and the Birth of Eugenics," *Annual Review of Genetics 2001* 35 (2001): 83–101.

Kanner, Leo. "Autistic Disturbances of Affective Contact," *Nervous Child* 2 (1943): 217–250.

———. "Problems of Nosology and Psychodynamics of Early Infantile Autism," *American Journal of Orthopsychiatry* 19 (1949): 416–426.

Klein, Joan Echtenkamp. "Eugenics: Carrie Buck, Virginia's Test Case," www.hsl.virginia.edu/historical/eugenics/3-buckvbell.cfm, August 7, 2012.

Lindman, Frank R. and Donald McIntyre, Fr., eds. *The Mentally Disabled and the Law: Report of the American Bar Foundation on the Rights of the Mentally Ill*. Chicago: University of Chicago Press, 1961.

Rothman, David J. and Sheila M. Rothman. *The Willowbrook Wars*. New York: Harper & Row, 1984.

Saleebey, Dennis. "The Strengths Perspective in Social Work Practice: Extensions and Cautions," *Social Work* 41 (No. 3 1996): 296–305.

United Nations Enable. "International Day of Disabled Persons, 2004—Nothing about Us, Without Us," www.un.org/disabilities/default.asp?id=114, August 26, 2015.

U.S. Senate, Beverly Jones, Committee on the Judiciary, *Confirmation Hearing on the Nomination of John G. Roberts to be Chief Justice of the United States*, 109th Cong., 1st Sess. (2005).

———. Hearings before the Subcommittee on Constitutional Rights of the Committee on the Judiciary, *Constitutional Rights of the Mentally Ill*, 87th Cong., 1st Sess. (1961).

———. Hearings Before the Subcommittee on Constitutional Rights of the Committee on the Judiciary, *To Protect the Constitutional Rights of the Mentally Ill*, 88th Cong., 1st Sess. (1963).

Van Wagenen, Bleeker. "Preliminary Report of the Committee of the Eugenic Section of the American Breeders' Association to Study and to Report on the Best Practical Means for Cutting Off the Defective Germ-Plasm in the Human Population," *Buck v Bell Documents*, Paper 74, http://readingroom.law.gsu.edu/buckvbell/74, August 13, 2015.

13 Now the Work Begins

The Agenda for Policy and Practice Going Forward

On election night in 2008, President-Elect Barack Obama said: "It's been a long time coming, but tonight, because of what we did on this date in this election at this defining moment change has come to America."[1] A *New York Times* article announcing the victory began: "Barack Hussein Obama was elected the 44th president of the United States on Tuesday, sweeping away the last racial barrier in American politics with ease as the country chose him as its first black chief executive."[2] The *Washington Post* story entitled "America's History Gives Way to Its Future," declared a new day in America: "From its founding, the United States has seen itself as a special place, an example to other nations, 'a city on the hill.' With the election of its first black president, it can now begin to erase one of the stains on that reputation, one that repeatedly shamed us in front of other countries."[3] President Obama went on to announce that, as important as breaking this racial barrier was, "I'm not the president of black America. I'm the president of the United States of America."[4] The election, and reactions to it, led many to speak of a new post-civil rights era or post-racial era in America. Those dynamics came along with the fact that there had been a variety of civil rights laws adopted and some evidence that some progress was being made for some women and some minority group members. National civil rights organizations feared for the future because of difficulty in attracting young people to move into the leadership of those organizations, given the impression that these were problems of their parents' generation. That fear was felt particularly by those who had been involved in civil rights work long enough to know that the country was a long way from realizing its professed principles.

Even if it were true that the needed civil rights protections were in place, achieving the promise of those laws and judicial opinions would remain a serious and ongoing challenge. And, as Justice Marshall explained (see Chapter 1), the harsh sides of our history, including extremely destructive opinions by the U.S. Supreme Court and actions by legislatures and chief executives at all levels of government, have filtered through the society. Their effects have been so pervasive and insidious that many people in the workplace today or who come to a city or county, or to a state or federal agency for service do not understand all of the heritage they have absorbed, but they feel it nonetheless. These stresses in public service are likely to remain for as long as one can see into the future.

As if this fundamental set of issues were not enough, as recent history has demonstrated, America is in anything but a post-racial era, and it certainly is not ready to declare a post-civil rights era either. With that same President Obama entering the last years of his second term, racial tensions that had always been present came to national prominence in a most dramatic way that has since come to be known by the single place name—Ferguson. In August 2014 Michael Brown, an unarmed young African American, was shot by a white police officer in that Missouri city. It became clear once the U.S. Department of Justice investigation was released that this was not a one-off incident involving a particular individual, but a community in which there was a well-established record of racial profiling and discriminatory behavior. In its findings letter issued to city officials, the Civil Rights Division of the Department of Justice wrote:

> We have concluded that we have reasonable cause to believe that the Ferguson Police Department engages in a pattern or practice of unlawful conduct that violates the United States Constitution and federal statutory law. Specifically, our investigation found that: (1) FPD conducts stops without reasonable suspicion and arrests without probable cause in violation of the Fourth Amendment; (2) FPD infringes on free expression and retaliates for protected expression in violation of the First Amendment; (3) FPD engages in a pattern of excessive force in violation of the Fourth Amendment; (4) the Ferguson Municipal Court engages in a pattern or practice of conduct that violates due process requirements of the Fourteenth Amendment; and (5) Ferguson's law enforcement exerts a disparate impact on African Americans that is not necessary to any legitimate goal and thus violates the Safe Streets Act and Title VI, and that is motivated, at least in part, by a discriminatory purpose in violation of the Equal Protection Clause of the Fourteenth Amendment.[5]

Indeed, the Missouri Supreme Court considered the situation so serious that it issued an order transferring a court of appeals judge to Ferguson to take over the municipal court, "including the authority to revise court policies and procedures to ensure the rights of defendants and to help restore the integrity of the system."[6]

The Brown case was followed by the choking death of Eric Garner in a widely viewed video of a takedown and choke-hold in New York in which Garner was heard to say that he could not breathe. Then there was the death of 25-year-old Freddie Gray in Baltimore that led to charges against a number of police officers. In relatively quick succession there were cases in Charleston, South Carolina, Pasco, Washington, Texas, and California, involving the deaths of African Americans or Latinos. Tragically, a few individuals acted out by shooting police officers in a number of cities around the nation, although it is not yet clear what prompted a number of unprovoked attacks on these officers. Some law enforcement leaders have seen these attacks as related to wide-ranging criticisms of police officers in the wake of the earlier incidents.

Then there were officials, including some state court judges, who attempted to block implementation of the U.S. Supreme Court's ruling in the *Obergefell* case, recognizing the right to same-sex marriage. Even before the Supreme Court issued its ruling, the Chief Justice of Alabama took it upon himself to order county officials not to comply with the order of the U.S. District Court to issue marriage licenses to same-sex couples.[7] After the federal court renewed its order, the Alabama Supreme Court issued a ruling claiming that it could decide for itself what the law was in this field and rejecting the district court's opinion.[8]

In Kentucky, Rowan County Clerk Kim Davis not only refused to issue marriage licenses to same-sex couples in compliance with the *Obergefell* ruling, but to any couples. When Federal District Judge David L. Bunning issued a preliminary injunction requiring her to issue the licenses, she persisted.[9] Judge Bunning allowed her time to seek a stay from a higher court, but, when both the Sixth Circuit and the U.S. Supreme Court refused to stay his order, she simply declared that she would refuse to obey the court mandate. She was held in contempt and jailed. Not only would she not issue the licenses herself, but she also refused to avoid interfering with the deputy clerks in the office complying with the order.

In Hamilton County Tennessee, Judge Jeffrey M. Atherton, a Chancery Court judge, refused to grant a divorce to a heterosexual couple who wanted one and used his opinion dismissing the case to launch a diatribe against the U.S. Supreme Court's ruling in *Obergefell*.[10]

As these and many other events indicate, and as the previous chapters have shown, the U.S. is a long way from achieving civil rights guarantees for all its citizens. Indeed, it is not clear how much is being done to address the legacy of discrimination and exclusion that has characterized the nation's past, including its recent history. Each chapter has identified areas of progress, but each has also shown that there are many issues that have not yet been addressed. This chapter brings those pieces together to provide an agenda for discussion and action, bearing in mind both the need to address particular changes in law and policy, and also the importance of the messages sent by those in public service to all Americans, including those with whom they work. It considers constitutional challenges, statutory problems, administrative issues, problems of law and legitimacy in public institutions, and the impacts on civil rights in public service from the contemporary social context.

Constitutional Challenges: Broad Problems and More Focused Issues

The book began from the Miles' Law perspective that "where one stands depends on where one sits." The chapters that followed demonstrated that, although there are certain common elements of civil rights that flow through them, different groups within society have experienced different kinds of civil rights issues over time and have an accumulated history of action and inaction that continues to have effects. Each chapter considered the particular kinds of issues and concerns the different groups have experienced and, in many cases, continue to face. In addition to these more specific unfinished agendas, there are three broad areas of constitutional difficulty. They include the confusing set of standards used to address constitutional claims by different groups of people in varied situations, the problem of proving intent to discriminate, and the continuing difficulties posed by an 1883 precedent that has never been overturned.

Equal Protection of the Law: When Is a Two-Part Standard not a Two-Part Standard?

In its 1973 ruling in *San Antonio Independent School District v. Rodriguez* (see Chapter 4) the Supreme Court synthesized a wide range of rulings on equal protection of the law into what has come to be known as the two-tier test. Even so, the situation is far from clear, or at least consistent, in terms of just what the standard is to determine whether there has been discrimination in violation of the equal protection clause of the Fourteenth Amendment (or the Fifth Amendment in the case of federal policies or practices). Indeed, some justices of the Supreme Court, such as Brennan and Blackmun, have indicated that this is partly due to the Court's own inconsistency in how it has attempted to use that two-part standard, while for others, most notably Justice Marshall, the test itself is flawed and predestined to produce the inconsistencies and injustices that have been evident over time.

The two-tier test is relatively easy to state. The starting assumption is that the government acts lawfully, and therefore anyone alleging discrimination has the burden to demonstrate it, with the government required only to show that its actions are rationally related to a legitimate state interest. If, on the other hand, the government actions are based on a suspect class, or if they affect a fundamental right, the Court invokes what is known as strict judicial scrutiny. That approach shifts the burden to the government to show a compelling state interest to justify its policy or practice, and it must also demonstrate that it has employed narrowly tailored means to achieve that interest.[11] As Chapter 4 explained, it is rare for the Court to strike down a government action under the rational basis tier of the test, but also rare for the Court to uphold a policy or practice if it applies strict judicial scrutiny.

The Court has found a suspect class in cases involving, for example, race, legitimacy, and alienage. As it explained in *San Antonio*, these are situations in which there is an identifiable group (often referred to as a discrete and insular minority) that shares a common characteristic (often gained at birth), and in which the group has suffered a long history of invidious discrimination. Finally, these groups have generally been unable to utilize the majoritarian political process to correct the situation.

Justice Brennan has argued that if those are the criteria, then certainly classifications by gender should qualify as suspect. In *Frontiero v. Richardson* (see excerpt in Chapter 10) Brennan wrote that gender fitted all of these requirements and was comparable to racial classifications.

> [O]ur statute books gradually became laden with gross, stereotyped distinctions between the sexes and, indeed, throughout much of the 19th century the position of women in our society was, in many respects, comparable to that of blacks under the pre-Civil War slave codes. Neither slaves nor women could hold office, serve on juries, or bring suit in their own names, and married women traditionally were denied the legal capacity to hold or convey property or to serve as legal guardians of their own children.[12]

Notwithstanding the fact that women seemed not only to fit all of the so-called "indicia of suspectness" (the criteria for a suspect classification), Brennan could only manage a plurality and not a majority to support his position.

Justice Marshall thought the whole idea of a two-tier test vastly oversimplified the concept of equal protection and was difficult to apply. He insisted in his concurring opinion in the *Cleburne* case (see excerpt in Chapter 12) that even by the measure of the *San Antonio* test, decisions based on the fact that people have intellectual disabilities meet the test for a suspect class. He wrote:

> [T]he mentally retarded have been subject to a "lengthy and tragic history" of segregation and discrimination that can only be called grotesque.... Fueled by the rising tide of Social Darwinism, the "science" of eugenics, and the extreme xenophobia of those years, leading medical authorities and others began to portray the "feebleminded" as a "menace to society and civilization ... responsible in a large degree for many, if not all, of our social problems." A regime of state-mandated segregation and degradation soon emerged that in its virulence and bigotry rivaled, and indeed paralleled, the worst excesses of Jim Crow.... Retarded children were categorically excluded from public schools, based on the false stereotype that all were ineducable and on the purported need to protect nonretarded children from them. State laws deemed the retarded "unfit for citizenship."[13]
>
> Segregation was accompanied by eugenic marriage and sterilization laws that extinguished for the retarded one of the "basic civil rights of man"—the right to marry and procreate.... Marriages of the retarded were made, and in some States continue to be, not only voidable but also often a criminal offense.[14] The purpose of such limitations, which frequently applied only to women of child-bearing age, was unabashedly eugenic: to prevent the retarded from propagating. To assure this end, 29 States enacted compulsory eugenic sterilization laws between 1907 and 1931....
>
> Prejudice, once let loose, is not easily cabined.... As of 1979, most States still categorically disqualified "idiots" from voting, without regard to individual capacity and with discretion to exclude left in the hands of low-level election officials. Not until Congress enacted the Education of the Handicapped Act ... were "the [doors] of public education" opened wide to handicapped children.... But most important, lengthy and continuing isolation of the retarded has perpetuated the ignorance, irrational fears, and stereotyping that long have plagued them.[15]

He rejected the idea that persons with intellectual disabilities are not "politically powerless" because some legislation has been adopted that addresses some protections. If that were true, then there should be no heightened scrutiny for race-based or gender classifications, at least since the Civil Rights Act of 1964. However, he explained, the evidence was abundantly clear that, even as of the mid-1980s when this opinion was written, the legal protections were limited and inadequate, and many forms of discrimination and exclusion of those with intellectual disabilities continued.[16]

Marshall was also frustrated by the Court's unwillingness to recognize that the right of the residents of the Cleburne Living Center to have a home free from discriminatory exclusion was sufficiently fundamental to require careful scrutiny by the Court.[17] Just as upsetting to him was Justice Powell's claim that: "Education, of course, is not among the rights afforded explicit protection under our Federal Constitution. Nor do we find any basis for saying it is implicitly so protected."[18] However, Justice Marshall stressed the key passage from *Brown v. Board of Education* that: "[T]he opportunity of education, 'where the state has undertaken to provide it, is a right which must be made available to all on equal terms.'"[19] In sum, the way that the Court was treating what qualified as a fundamentally protected right that would trigger strict scrutiny was, to say the least, contradictory and arbitrary.

Justice Blackmun also spoke to this problem in a case concerning discrimination against lawful permanent residents in the United States. In this case, he said, the problem was not whether strict scrutiny should apply, but arbitrariness in how it was applied. In a case concerning exclusion of permanent residents for jobs as probation officers, he dissented on behalf of four members of the Court.[20] The majority purported to rely on the standard as he had explained in an earlier case,[21] but Blackmun said, "The Court reaches this conclusion by misstating the standard of review it has long applied to alienage classifications.... In my view, today's decision rewrites the Court's precedents, ignores history, defies common sense, and reinstates the deadening mantle of state parochialism in public employment."[22]

Over time, the Court has addressed this gap between strict scrutiny and a mere rational basis test by applying intermediate or heightened scrutiny in areas such as gender. Thus, since the mid-1970s the Court has applied the *Craig* standard that requires that: "To withstand constitutional challenge, previous cases establish that classifications by gender must serve important governmental objectives and must be substantially related to achievement of those objectives."[23] However, even here there are some uncertainties. Thus, Justice Ginsburg's opinion in *United States v. Virginia* (see Chapter 10) was unclear about whether she intended to add a third piece to that test—the need to show an "exceedingly persuasive justification"—or whether she was using that phrase as Justice O'Connor used it in *Mississippi University for Women v. Hogan*. O'Connor wrote in that opinion that government meets that exceedingly persuasive justification by showing that its actions "serve important governmental objectives and must be substantially related to achievement of those objectives."[24]

In the Supreme Court's rulings from the *Lawrence v. Texas* case through the *Obergefell* decision, Justice Kennedy had taken considerable criticism from within the Court for not being clear enough as to precisely what standard he was using. He sharpened the focus in response. By the time of the *Obergefell* cases he made plain his reliance on both due process of law and equal protection as the basis for the ruling, but his colleagues continued to raise concerns about the standard that he was using and how he was using it.

For all these reasons, one of the important challenges in the years ahead at the constitutional level is the need for clarity and consistency in the explanation and application of the legal standard for ensuring equal protection of the law under the Fourteenth or the Fifth Amendment.

The Overwhelming Requirement for Proof of Intentional Discrimination

Even before discrimination cases reach the point at which the Court applies a standard to the situation, there is the problem of demonstrating that there was an intent to discriminate. Before the Supreme Court's ruling in the *Washington v. Davis* case in 1976 (see Chapter 4), the Court had rejected the idea that those who experienced discrimination had to prove both the effect of discrimination and the intent to discriminate.[25] As Justice Marshall explained at length in later cases, given the fact that those with discriminatory intent had long since learned to avoid using language or providing evidence of their intention, even as they took what they knew and intended to be discriminatory action, made it so extremely difficult to prove intent, many egregious situations were left standing.[26] He had endured long and bitter experience before he came to the Court with language that avoided outright discriminatory assertions, but "[t]oo often in our Nation's history, statements such as these have been little more than code phrases for racial discrimination."[27]

The Court took the next large leap in requirements for proving intent in the 1979 *Feeney* case, which involved gender discrimination and veterans' preferences:

> Discriminatory purpose, however, implies more than intent as volition or intent as awareness of consequences.... It implies that the decisionmaker, in this case a state legislature, selected or reaffirmed a particular course of action at least in part "because of," not merely "in spite of," its adverse effects upon an identifiable group.[28]

In doing so, the Court made it nearly impossible in all but the most dramatic cases to mount a constitutional challenge. Unless a university admissions policy banned women[29] or a state statute or constitutional amendment plainly stated an intention to treat people differently on the basis of sexual orientation,[30] it would be extraordinarily difficult to meet the intent requirement. Given that there are relatively few such policies or people who will provide such dramatic evidence of their intent to discriminate, it is unclear just how meaningful recourse to what are supposed to be equal protection of the law guarantees from the Constitution will be.

The proof-of-intent requirement has meant that those who face discrimination must, in the vast majority of cases, rely upon statutory civil rights protections, but, as the preceding chapters have shown (and as will be discussed further in this chapter), the statutory protections have their own difficulties, and it is not clear when or if Congress will be prepared to address them.

Indeed, the Supreme Court has come to apply a version of draconian proof of intent test in a different way, this time applied to the Congress and a requirement that it demonstrate intentional discrimination in order to act. Thus, the Court struck down part of the Violence Against Women Act on grounds that Congress had not proven to the majority's satisfaction that the problem was serious enough in terms of its effects on commerce and other factors to justify their legislation.[31] Similarly, in the cases posing Eleventh Amendment immunity to suits for money damages, which had long been a standard remedy for civil rights violations, the majority repeatedly treated the Congress as if it had not adequately proven intent to discriminate—using the judicially imposed requirement that remedies meet the Court's requirements for "congruence and proportionality between the injury to be prevented or remedied and the means adopted to that end."[32] The majority in these cases has refused to concede that Congress provided enough proof of discrimination in cases where the evidence was overwhelmingly clear, not to mention the fact that Congress is an elected body and generally not constitutionally required to prove to judges that it had a reason to act. In effect, the Court has, in these cases, treated Congress as if it were a prosecutor who had to prove its case, practically beyond a reasonable doubt, in order to demonstrate that very real discrimination was a good enough reason for it to use its enforcement power in Section 5 of the Fourteenth Amendment as well as its Article I powers.

A Ghost of the Segregation Era Lives to Bar Civil Rights Progress

The Rehnquist Court was aided in this tour de force by the failure of the Supreme Court to reverse the 1883 ruling in the *Civil Rights Cases*.[33] The fact that it has been left intact has meant that Congress has had to use its commerce clause powers to do the work for which the enforcement clause of the Fourteenth Amendment was clearly designed as a basis. It is telling that in its opinion in *United States v. Morrison* concerning the Violence Against Women Act, as in other recent rulings constraining congressional ability to act, the majority has been willing to cite the 1883 case. As long as that case remains undisturbed, that ruling will continue to pose a serious potential barrier to action.

The strongest modern voice for eliminating this barrier so that Congress could do with section 5 what needed to be done was Justice Douglas, but he was by no means the first. In fact, it is important to go back to the early round of cases in the immediate aftermath of the enactment of the Civil War Amendments, when one of the most extreme Courts in history issued a series of decisions from the *Slaughter-House Cases* through *Plessy v. Ferguson* that were clearly designed to neutralize much of the effect of these amendments, particularly the Fourteenth Amendment. The decision in the *Civil Rights Cases* was one of these. Just as Justice Harlan's lone voice rang out in dissent in *Plessy*, so too did he write a powerful solo dissent in that case (see excerpt in Chapter 2).

Harlan explained patiently, and at length, what the conditions were at the time of the adoption of those amendments, including many of the problems created or at least sanctioned by opinions of the U.S. Supreme Court, tracing back to the days of the fugitive slave cases. He explained that these amendments were not narrow, either in terms or in meaning, but a set of constitutional changes designed to ensure that those who had no rights before had full rights forever after. Those rights included all of the elements of citizenship, including those private relationships facilitated and enforced by the laws of the states. Beyond that, he explained, the kinds of public accommodations and infrastructure enterprises may have been privately owned, but they were recognized as having a public function and were therefore operating under licenses and regulatory systems imposed by government. Long before those constitutional amendments, public accommodations from transportation to inns had been covered by common law rules imposing limitations on the private owners of those businesses to ensure that their services were available to all. Thus, when the Thirteenth, Fourteenth, and Fifteenth Amendments conveyed to Congress the authority to enforce by appropriate regulations those parts of the Constitution, they had a broad task to ensure the rights of any other citizen of the United States to those who had formerly been slaves or treated as of that social caste. It is a powerful and carefully supported case that the restriction by the Court of congressional enforcement under the Fourteenth Amendment to "state action" was not only contrary to the purpose and design of the Civil War Amendments, but also to existing law as to the role that government played in what that Court was calling purely private action.

In his 1964 opinion for the Court in *Heart of Atlanta Motel v. United States* (Chapter 4), Justice Clark noted that after the 1883 ruling in the *Civil Rights Cases*, "No major legislation in this field had been enacted by Congress for 82 years when the Civil Rights Act of 1957 became law."[34] Of course, the great step forward came with enactment of the Civil Rights Act of 1964 and the Court sidestepped the 1883 ruling to uphold the new law principally on the power of Congress to regulate interstate commerce.

Justice Douglas's concurring opinion in *Heart of Atlanta* stated flatly:

> I repeat what I said earlier, that our decision should be based on the Fourteenth Amendment, thereby putting an end to all obstructionist strategies and allowing every person—whatever his race, creed, or color—to patronize all places of public accommodation without discrimination whether he travels interstate or intrastate.[35]

He was not content with sidestepping the problem.

> Though I join the Court's opinions, I am somewhat reluctant here, as I was in *Edwards v. California* [1941] to rest solely on the Commerce Clause. My reluctance is not due to any conviction that Congress lacks power to regulate commerce in the interests of human rights. It is rather my belief that the right of people to be free of state action that discriminates against them because of race, like the "right of persons to move freely from State to State" ... "occupies a more protected position in our constitutional system than does the movement of cattle, fruit, steel and coal across state lines." ... I would prefer to rest on the assertion of legislative power contained in §5 of the Fourteenth Amendment which states: "The Congress shall have power to enforce, by appropriate legislation, the provisions of this article"—a power which the Court concedes was exercised at least in part in this Act.
>
> A decision based on the Fourteenth Amendment would have a more settling effect, making unnecessary litigation over whether a particular restaurant or inn is within the commerce definitions of the Act or whether a particular customer is an interstate traveler. Under my construction, the Act would apply to all customers in all the enumerated places of public accommodation. And that construction would put an end to all obstructionist strategies and finally close one door on a bitter chapter in American history.[36]

This was not the first time Douglas had made this argument, repeating many of the key points that Harlan had made nearly a century earlier, and adding a good many more based on the history of civil rights in the ensuing period as well as the Court's rulings over that time.[37] But the Court did not choose then or later to overturn the *Civil Right Cases*, either directly or by reinterpretation of Section 5 of the Fourteenth Amendment. That is why, to this day, Congress is required in many cases to rely on the commerce clause and the taxing and spending clause to do, as Justice Harlan wrote in 1883, what the Civil War Amendments were designed to do at the time of their adoption. As the ruling in *United States v. Morrison* indicated,[38] it remained a series problem as the nation entered the twenty-first century.

Statutory Problems: The Weaknesses of What Appears to Be a Strong Framework of Protection

Given what the Court has done with the requirements for proof of intent to discriminate as well as other interpretations of constitutional civil rights protections, most people today turn for protection not to the United States Constitution but to a variety of statutes adopted by Congress, all of which have been discussed at various points in this text. However, it turns out that the need to rely on these statutes and the problems associated with these particular pieces of legislation, as well as the way the Supreme Court has interpreted them, mean that there are many difficulties to be overcome and vigilance to be maintained if the fabric of modern civil rights law is to be developed as a complete tapestry and one that can withstand the continued challenges to its integrity. That kind of overall perspective and ongoing assessment is generally not done for a variety of reasons, given that the individual pieces are particularly important to certain groups of Americans. Even those groups often do not focus on the need to see the entire tapestry in order to understand both its overall character and strengths and also its weak spots and challenges.

On the positive side of the ledger, Congress, some state legislatures, and some local governing bodies, both cities and counties, have taken steps to address gaps in civil rights protection in a number of areas, including responding to judicial opinions that have undermined existing statutory protections.

Even so, there are important weaknesses in the fabric that include: the problems of the civil rights policy model; ineffectiveness of the grant threat, eleventh amendment immunity, and lack of private rights of action or checks on enforcement discretion; cobbled-together laws; religious exemptions from civil rights laws; voter initiatives; and dysfunctional Congress and state and local legislatures.

Legislatures, Laws, and Courts

There have been times when the courts have led the legislatures in the protection of civil rights, but legislatures have also sometimes led—or even countered—the courts in order to ensure civil rights protections. The Supreme Court had certainly delivered a variety of important rulings before Congress enacted the Civil Rights Act of 1964, but there is no question that the act was a dramatic step forward and far more comprehensive than the previous judicial actions. The 1964 act and the Voting Rights Act that followed in 1965 required hard fought political battles to achieve their enactment and the willingness of President Johnson to use his political clout and famed personal arm-twisting to move those fights forward. The Fair Housing Act that came in 1968 was another key element in the developing fabric of legislation that was woven piece by piece over time. The Equal Opportunity Amendments and the Education Amendments of 1972 sought to expand on and enhance the effectiveness of the earlier legislation, as well as to ensure its application to education policy and practice. And in that policy space, the Congress acted in the face of little case law and no Supreme Court action to address the needs of students with disabilities in Public Law 94–142, which evolved into the Individuals with Disabilities Education Act. With the Supreme Court not responding to calls for effective protections for those with disabilities, Congress enacted Section 503 of the Rehabilitation Act of 1973 and the Developmental Disabilities and Bill of Rights Act of 1975. When the Supreme Court would not protect women with pregnancy-related disabilities, Congress enacted the Pregnancy Disability Amendments. When the Supreme Court refused to provide meaningful constitutional protection against discrimination on the basis of age,[39] the Congress amended the Age Discrimination in Employment Act of 1967.[40] With the Supreme Court being far from supportive of protections for Native Americans, Congress enacted the Indian Self-Determination Act of 1975. Later, in 1978, as overwhelming evidence established a pattern of removal of Native American children from their homes with placement in non-native families, the Congress adopted the Indian Child Welfare Act.[41]

In addition, the Congress has, in a number of cases, overturned interpretations of civil rights statutes by the Supreme Court when the legislature found that the rulings had undermined the purposes and protections of the legislation. Thus, the 1991 Civil Rights Act specifically announced the Congress's intention of overturning rulings on Title VII that Congress and President George Herbert Walker Bush agreed had inappropriately narrowed access to the protections of the law.[42] Similarly, in adopting the Americans with Disabilities Act Amendments Act of 2008, the Court announced its intention to "reject the requirement enunciated by the Supreme Court in *Sutton v. United Air Lines, Inc.*, 527 U.S. 471 (1999) and its companion cases that whether an impairment substantially limits a major life activity is to be determined with reference to the ameliorative effects of mitigating measures" and "to reject the standards enunciated by the Supreme Court in *Toyota Motor Manufacturing, Kentucky, Inc. v. Williams*, 534 U.S. 184 (2002), that the terms 'substantially' and 'major' in the definition of disability under the ADA 'need to be interpreted strictly to create a demanding standard for qualifying as disabled,' and that to be substantially limited in performing a major life activity under the ADA 'an individual must have an impairment that prevents or severely restricts the individual from doing activities that are of central importance to most people's daily lives.'"[43] In other words, the Court's interpretations were far too restrictive.

Those legislative efforts have happened not only at the national level, but in states and in local governments as well. State legislatures sometimes responded to state courts, but in other cases led with legislation prohibiting discrimination against persons on the basis of sexual orientation and identity. Some local governments have fought discrimination against Latinos by enacting ordinances creating welcome programs that sought to show not only a refusal to discriminate but also an affirmative desire to attract diverse groups to the state.[44] Similarly, some communities have adopted ordinances that include protections for employees against discrimination on the basis of sexual orientation (Chapter 11).

All that having been said, there have been and continue to be significant difficulties with legislation and some legislatures with respect to the fabric of civil rights that apply not only to particular segments of civil rights law, but more generally. One of the most important starting points for that discussion is the fact that legislatures have throughout history often been the sources of discriminatory laws, and that is true at all levels of government as the previous chapters have clearly indicated. Moreover, what one legislature gives at one time, it may weaken or remove at another. Indeed, the chapter on sexual orientation and identity made clear that state actions as well as some local government actions have reduced protections that were previously available. In addition, since many statutes have sunset provisions that require reauthorization on a regular basis, a simple failure to act or to act in a manner that will reduce protections is often a problem. Indeed, key portions of something so fundamental as the Voting Rights Act have faced stiff opposition on reauthorization more than once.

Second, it is important to remember that the voters act as a legislative body through the initiative and referendum processes available in a number of states. Those processes have been the source of efforts to reverse progress in civil rights protections or to block efforts to move forward in a variety of areas, from restrictive housing provisions aimed at African Americans, to English-only amendments and statutes aimed very clearly at Latinos, to anti-gay legislation in other cases.

James Madison made clear long ago that the framers of the U.S. Constitution feared that local majorities could be as big a danger as any political figure, and perhaps more so. He wrote to Jefferson warning that:

> Wherever the real power in government lies, there is the danger of oppression. In our governments, the real power of government lies in the majority of the community, and the invasion of private rights is chiefly to be apprehended, not from acts of Government contrary to the sense of its constituents, but from acts in which the Government is the mere instrument of the majority number of the constituents.[45]

These are among the reasons why the founders were so concerned about fashioning a republic as a representative government that was supposed to filter passions, and then provide both a separation of powers and checks and balances to protect that separation. These elements were all part of what they said was the "the necessity of auxiliary precautions" against abuses.[46]

Apart from these broad concerns, there are several lessons learned from the previous chapters concerning problems that require attention by legislatures, but which also provide cautions about the next steps to be taken.

The Civil Rights Policy Model: A Useful Tool but with Significant Limits

As the discussions throughout the text show, the use of litigation to force action on civil rights goes well back in American history, but was particularly important as Charles Hamilton Houston and later his student Thurgood Marshall worked on behalf of the

NAACP to move the Supreme Court through a series of cases and on to the direct challenge to *Plessy v. Ferguson* that came in the *Brown v. Board of Education* ruling. The NAACP and then the NAACP Legal Defense and Education Fund litigated in a variety of areas from fair housing to transportation to voting rights. Other groups learned from those efforts, and in fact, as Chapter 8 explained, the Mexican American Legal Defense and Education Fund was formed with the assistance of the NAACP LDF. Cases brought by women's advocacy groups, LGBT organizations, and disability rights advocates also used this approach to force attention to and change in longstanding discriminatory policies and practices. Although this approach worked when used for targeted policy change efforts, it has proven insufficient by itself to ensure ongoing implementation and enforcement of civil rights. Consider first the attractiveness and pervasive use of what is appropriately termed the civil rights policy model and then the limitations it presents for day-to-day efforts to ensure civil rights.

When the Civil Rights Act of 1964 was enacted, the NAACP litigation model for civil rights protection was well known. The statute provided an avenue for individuals to bring suit to enforce the rights against discrimination whether in places of public accommodation or employment. Title VI made organizations receiving federal funds responsible for ensuring that those programs did not discriminate in violation of the act. In fact, although the act provided authority for the U.S. Department of Justice to bring suits to enforce the act, and even though it created the Equal Employment Opportunity Commission and authorized it to refer matters to the Justice Department, it should have been clear that this would not be sufficient to ensure implementation. Indeed, it was clear that individuals would bring actions to force compliance. Thus, Title VII process meant that once a complaint was filed and investigated, the commission would issue what has come to be known as a "right to sue" letter, permitting that person to bring suit for enforcement. However, the resources and authority of the EEOC were limited and fell far short of rendering it adequate to enforce even the employment portion of the act, let alone the other provisions. Even after the Equal Employment Opportunity Act of 1972 expanded its authority, there was still no likelihood that the commission would be adequate to do more than lead on policy development through its guidelines, process complaints (in cooperation with state human rights commissions) for private litigation, and bring a very limited number of suits itself in order to attempt to shape policy and practice. At the end of the day, this model assumed that private individuals who thought their civil rights had been violated would be the ones to implement the act through the mechanisms of lawsuits brought in courts around the nation.

This civil rights policy model was attractive in part because it did not mandate the development of a major new federal agency. It required only very limited financial resources, largely for investigative and policy development processes. It was attractive to many in the civil rights community in part because it allowed groups and individuals the autonomy to take enforcement action without waiting for the federal government to do so on their behalf. Given a long history over which there had been at best lethargy and at most discriminatory policy and practice in government, this freedom to act appeared particularly important.

For these and other reasons, the civil rights policy model became a virtual template for a body of civil rights statutes that followed. These laws came both as amendments to the 1964 act, such as the Pregnancy Disability Amendments, and also as individual statutes that used the same basic model of enforcement by individual lawsuit with no primary federal implementing agency. Examples include the Family Medical Leave Act, the Age Discrimination in Employment Act, the Individuals with Disabilities Education Act, and the Americans with Disabilities Act, to name only some of the statutes. Although the Department of Justice would issue rules for implementation of the ADA and could bring enforcement actions, it was once again clear that no federal agency was going to be created to ensure implementation and that private lawsuits across the nation would be the primary vehicle to ensure compliance. The Department of Education would issue regulations for the implementation of the Individuals with Disabilities Education Act, but the real compliance and enforcement actions would take place at the school district and individual family level. The statute provided procedural protections for parents who were not satisfied with the individualized education plan (IEP) developed by the district or who found that the schools were not implementing that IEP. It then allowed parents who disagreed with the schools to seek judicial review of the school district actions.

However, most people do not understand the complex requirements they need to meet if they wish to seek enforcement of these civil rights statutes. Even parents who are accustomed to advocating for their children rarely understand the legal dimensions, including what rights and responsibilities they have in the administrative or judicial processes. Even if they do, few have the resources to retain counsel who are trained in that area of the law. As noted in Chapter 12, there are relatively few attorneys who are trained and experienced in these fields in any given community. If they do not have an attorney, there is a good chance that families will not understand the procedural requirements and the deadlines they must meet if they wish to move the matter forward. If they do have an attorney, there is a still a question whether families will have the resources and the time to ensure adequate case preparation and witnesses to see the matter through. Indeed, there are reasons to be concerned that those who most need the protections of these laws are often people who are least able to call forth the resources to ensure the protections of the rights they are supposed to ensure.

All that having been said, the civil rights model does produce significant numbers of lawsuits in various courts around the country. In order to ensure coherence among these various rulings, it is necessary to move cases through the appellate process to obtain consistency across jurisdictions. It took years for the Supreme Court to rule on ADA cases, for example. The Court has produced 25 opinions that address the ADA in the quarter century since its passage, but that is a relatively small number given that the model relies ultimately on clarification from that Court for understanding and enforcement. Indeed, some of those rulings were reversed by the ADA amendments as too restrictive, as explained in Chapter 12.

In sum, the civil rights policy model provides necessary but not sufficient means to ensure that the civil rights supposedly protected by statute are in fact ensured in practice. A relatively small number of cases brought annually by the Department of Justice and even the very few brought by the EEOC do not begin to meet the need. There has not been an effort to determine what is needed institutionally and administratively at the national level to address the full fabric of civil rights statutes in practice.

Problems of Access to Courts and Meaningful Remedies: Immunity from Damages, Unchecked Enforcement Discretion, and Limited Private Rights of Action

These concerns about the day-to-day implementation of and compliance with the civil rights statutes is made more complex by changes in some rather technical, but important, aspects of the law. It is useful to begin with the recognition that the enforcement discretion of federal agencies that have some responsibility for enforcement under civil rights statutes is presumptively unreviewable. In an era of severe federal budget constraints, that means that, on a regular basis, federal agencies take action in fewer situations, which in turn means that many other problems that are worthy of action will go unaddressed. It also means that once the decision is made not to act, there will be no review by a court unless the statute involved mandates enforcement in a particular situation.[47]

Until relatively recently, one way that such limitations could be addressed was through what are known as implied private rights of action. Translated into ordinary language, these are often called private attorney general suits: cases in which a private individual brings an enforcement action where government cannot or will not do so. Until the 1980s, the Supreme Court had directed courts to give a fairly generous interpretation to when such private rights of action could be brought, even in situations where the legislation involved did not say that there was a private cause of action available.[48] However, starting in 1981 the Court asserted a strong presumption against any such private suit unless the statute actually said there could be such an action, or clearly implied it by its terms or the basic design of the legislation.[49] The Court has taken a consistently tight approach since that time.

Even so, most observers did not think that limiting approach would apply to civil rights statutes. For one thing, it was abundantly clear that the civil rights policy model, which was the design used by Congress for so many of these statutes, plainly assumed that private individuals would be the ones to carry the load for enforcement through particular cases, with the Justice Department or other agencies bringing only a few important cases, largely to establish important policy points or clarify specific interpretations. Second, the Court had delivered a number of rulings making clear that civil rights statutes authorized implied rights of action, one example of which was Title VI of the Civil Rights Act of 1964, which concerns programs receiving federal funds. However, as Chapter 9 explained, that changed dramatically in 2001 when a 5–4 Court in an opinion by Justice Scalia rejected the claims that Title VI provided such a private right of action.[50] The four dissenters were outraged.

> In separate lawsuits spanning several decades, we have endorsed an action identical in substance to the one brought in this case, see *Lau v. Nichols*, 414 U.S. 563 (1974); demonstrated that Congress intended a private right of action to protect the rights guaranteed by Title VI, see *Cannon v. University of Chicago*, 441 U.S. 677 (1979); and concluded that private individuals may seek declaratory and injunctive relief against state officials for violations of regulations promulgated pursuant to Title VI, see *Guardians Assn. v. Civil Serv. Commission of New York City*, 463 U.S. 582 (1983).[51]

One of the critically important foundations of the civil rights policy model has been dramatically eroded.

A third critical problem is the Supreme Court's dramatic development of a body of law since 1996 that created broad immunity for state governments from claims for money damages under civil rights and other federal statutes that were clearly designed to ensure that state governments would be answerable in damages for violations. The *Garrett* opinion that struck down the congressional effort to make states answerable in money damages for violations of Title I of the ADA, demonstrated the problem (see Chapter 12). Again, this was only one of a number of such rulings in which the Court blocked congressional efforts to ensure that there was a strong incentive for states to ensure compliance. It had been clear early on that damage awards were to be important enforcement tools for virtually all of the civil rights legislation. It also left the ironic situation that local governments and private firms were subject to damage claims, but state governments or their agencies were not.

These limitations are weaknesses in the fabric of civil rights legislation. If they are to be meaningful, those laws must be readily enforceable in ways that will not only provide remedies for those injured, but also give clear incentives for various organizations to bring themselves into compliance. That will require attention by the Congress in particular, but state legislatures as well, to the means by which implementation and enforcement will be done and meaningful remedies that can be effectively pursued in the event of noncompliance.

The Threat of Loss of Federal Funds Matters in Theory but is Rarely Meaningful in Practice

In some instances, of course, Congress provided civil rights protection not in the form of direct action, but indirectly through federal grant programs. In some cases the particular grants carry specific requirements, as in the case of the Individuals with Disabilities Education Act, while in other situations the assumption is that Title VI prohibitions of discrimination in programs receiving federal funds will ensure compliance. In theory, and given the importance of federal funds to state and local governments, that should provide a strong incentive for compliance.

However, the Supreme Court has also issued a series of rulings in which it has concluded that affected individuals are not able to force compliance and that only the federal granting agency can do that. As a practical matter, federal agencies have rarely been willing to remove a state's federal funding because a particular person or group or people suffered injuries for failure to comply. Justice Scalia made it clear that the majority in *Sandoval* saw the remedy for a Title VI violation to be an action by the relevant federal funding agency to remove funding as the way to enforce that statute. It made a similar finding with regard to other provisions as well.[52]

In various reports over time, the Government Accountability Office (GAO) has cited the need for more effective Title VI enforcement both in terms of capacity and action. The U.S. Department of Justice Office of Civil Rights reported that from 2008 to 2013 it conducted compliance audits of 107 state agencies in the 50 states and territories. It has included allegations of Title VI violations in a number of "findings letters" and reference to it in some litigation, but the report does not document any cases in which federal funds were actually withdrawn as a result.[53] There are many guidance documents issued by federal agencies, but little evidence that, at the end of the day, state or local agencies or a meaningful number of others receiving federal funds are actually having their funding terminated. Just over one hundred compliance audits for the entire country over a four-year period is not a credible deterrent to discrimination. Additionally, unless there really is evidence to think that funds will indeed be cut to major programs or large organizations, it is difficult to see Title VI as accomplishing the purpose for which it was designed. There was a threat when individuals could bring private rights of action to enforce it, but the ruling in *Alexander v. Sandoval* dealt a devastating blow to that mechanism unless and until Congress changes the law to provide for a private attorney general action. There is little evidence that the Congress is interested in doing that, and indeed there are few incentives for members of Congress to take firm action that may result in a loss of federal dollars to their districts and their states.

This problem has been exacerbated by the Supreme Court's opinion in the first case concerning the Affordable Care Act of 2010, which concluded that the Medicaid extension was a new program rather than an amendment to the existing Medicaid program (a position that Congress specifically considered and rejected during passage), and therefore states could refuse to implement the Medicaid extension without losing any of their existing Medicaid funds.[54] That ruling not only dramatically weakened the federal authority with respect to Medicaid in terms of present and future changes to the program, but also opened the door to future challenges to the use of the taxing and spending power to enforce policy through grants and contracts. The idea that adding requirements to grants with the warning that violations mean loss of funding will be more subject to legal challenge because of that ruling.

Cobbled-Together Law in Place of Carefully Crafted Legislation

As the previous chapters have demonstrated, civil rights law and policy are continually developing. Over time, elements of that law and policy come from judicial rulings, legislation, executive orders, administrative rules, voter initiatives, and other means. To the degree that the fabric of civil rights protections has become increasingly dependent upon legislative and administrative policymaking as compared to constitutional foundations, that suggests a need to update legislation within reasonable periods of time to ensure that the law and policy are clear, both so that governments and individual citizens can comply with it and also to make clear how those who suffer violations can obtain relief.

Thus, protections against sexual harassment arose by individual claims in some lower courts that such behavior was sex discrimination, but the principal route was the issuance by the EEOC in 1980 of guidelines that defined harassment and asserted that it was a violation of Title VII of the Civil Rights Act of 1964. The Supreme Court deferred to that interpretation in its 1986 ruling that firmly established that sexual harassment was indeed a violation of Title VII.[55] In later decisions, the Supreme Court extended that interpretation to same-sex harassment and also to schools under Title IX of the Education Amendments of 1972 (see the discussion in Chapter 10). However, Congress has not enacted legislation that specifically addresses sexual harassment in the civil rights statutes. It has done so largely with respect to the military and military academies, and principally because of scandals that have arisen. This is a complex area and it is important to make the law as clear as possible, as well as to integrate it with the other elements of civil rights law. That has not been accomplished in legislation in all the years since the 1986 ruling. Also, the case law was largely fashioned on the employer/employee relationship, but then extended to the educational context. Although few people would debate the importance of ensuring protection against sexual harassment in educational institutions, it is different from the employment relationship and therefore legislative clarification and explanation are important. These difficulties have been highlighted by, for example, cases brought by parents because other elementary school children harassed their child. This is an important problem to address, but it is a long way from the employment context and it requires appropriately drawn legislation.

A second example is the development of law under Title VI related to provision of public services to persons with limited English proficiency. As Chapter 9 explained, the Justice Department issued a policy guidance document based on long standing case law, making clear that denying persons with limited English proficiency access to federally funded programs was a violation of Title VI of the Civil Rights Act of 1964, and announcing "general principles for agencies to apply in developing guidelines for services to individuals with limited English proficiency."[56] President Clinton issued an executive order which, among other things, requires executive branch agencies to "draft title VI guidance specifically tailored to its recipients that is consistent with the LEP Guidance issued by the Department of Justice."[57] Two years after that, the Department of Justice issued its "Guidance to Federal Financial Assistance Recipients Regarding Title VI Prohibition Against National Origin Discrimination Affecting Limited English Proficient Persons."[58] Federal agencies in turn began issuing their requirements for those receiving grants or contracts from that institution. To date, however, this body of civil rights requirements has not been incorporated into statute.

Another example arises from a situation in which the Supreme Court has issued rulings on constitutional grounds, that of sexual orientation. Given the Court's decisions (see Chapter 11), state and federal laws are needed to bring existing practices into compliance with the constitutional requirements. Although these rulings specifically addressed same-sex marriage, the language of the Court and its statements about discrimination based on sexual orientation should make clear that a much wider look at existing statutes, administrative rules, and local government ordinances is needed. Even if one were to look only at the marriage issue, that still requires attention to legislation that affects status, property rights, and employment practices to include fringe benefits.

There is one final example, and it is an area in which the Supreme Court has created a serious problem for existing legislation. In 2013 the Court struck the existing Section 4 of the Voting Rights Act of 1965 that provided the mandatory coverage of the law for purposes of preclearance of voting requirements under Section 5 of that statute.[59] This had been included in the law to ensure that states with a history of voting discrimination and others that developed problematic voting requirements over time would have any changes for the future reviewed before they could take effect. The four dissenters objected that the Congress in a "voluminous record" had made clear that the reasons that originally compelled the Section 4 coverage and the Section 5 preclearance mandates still existed, despite progress in some areas.

The majority said that Congress might still be able to save these provisions if it could provide some acceptable formula that would justify which jurisdictions should remain within the mandatory coverage requirement. There has been no serious attempt to address that problem, notwithstanding a range of efforts in a number of the states previously under Section 4 coverage to add burdens to registration and voting in recent years. It is still possible for the Justice Department to bring individual enforcement actions, and then Attorney General Holder declared that the Justice Department would do exactly that. Even so, it was clear from the time of the Supreme Court ruling that unless Congress does act to address the problem, the design and function of the Voting Rights Act has been dramatically altered.

Thus, there is an ongoing need to update and address in legislation at all levels of government the changes in civil rights law and policy, so as to ensure the integrity of the fabric of civil rights policy. That is not to suggest that this process is easy or that there is ready agreement on what needs to be done. However, it is necessary if the fabric of civil rights policy is to be coherent and strong.

Dysfunctional Legislatures: What Happens when Reasonable Behavior Disappears

This last point raises a problem for which there is no simple answer, but that requires attention nevertheless. Critics with affiliations with both major political parties have joined in a common chorus of criticism directed at the United States Congress not so much because of specific legislation that it has enacted but for its profound condition of institutional dysfunction.[60] Some state and local legislative bodies have been in danger of slipping into a similar breakdown.

The point is not that anyone is about to end partisanship or the importance of ideological differences among legislators—or for that matter the constituencies that elect them. Indeed, the legislatures that enacted the Civil Rights Act of 1964, the Voting Rights Act of 1965, the Fair Housing Act of 1968, and the Civil Rights Act of 1991 all had partisan and ideological divides, and there were strong debates in a variety of fields. However, there was some sense of boundaries, of the importance of the institution, and of the need to get the people's business done. Compromise was not considered a dirty word and personal attacks were most often avoided as damaging to all of those essential legislative goals, and of the ability of policymakers to work together to do what the nation required.

However, dysfunctional legislatures with some members willing to do great damage to the institutions in order to get their way without regard to how it affected the community, state, or nation have been a problem for some time. An ends-justifies-the-means mentality has been a dangerous attitude and, even when it is present only among a limited number of members, can disable the entire body.

Political analysts will debate the causes and consequences of this situation in the years to come, but from the perspective of a nation and communities in need of a strong and effective fabric of civil rights law and policy, it represents the denial of important needs at a critical time. Those needs are all the more important in light of some of the problematic rulings of the U.S. Supreme Court in a variety of areas that, as the previous chapters have explained, make reliance on the legislature extremely important. For much of civil rights history in the United States, attention has been on the courts for reasons explained throughout this text. However, it is clearly important to remain vigilant with respect to legislatures as well as to courts in the years ahead.

Administrative Issues: "It Sounds Good, But ..."

In light of the many challenges considered above, and indeed throughout the text, it is somewhat surprising that there has been relatively little attention to the administrative problems involved in dealing with civil rights matters. As a starting point, it is useful to consider at least three dimensions of the challenge, including capacity, focus, and approach.

Inadequate Capacity Based in Part on the Civil Rights Policy Model

If one looks to advocacy organizations or individual legal actions to drive enforcement of civil rights using the civil rights policy model, then it is perhaps not surprising that there has been so little attention to the nature of administrative challenges involved in implementing civil rights law and policy, or building the institutional capacity to address them. There are certainly offices and agencies that have various responsibilities for pieces of civil rights policy, but there is little evidence that they have the capacity to do what even the officials of those agencies would regard as minimally necessary to meet the need.

First, there is a broad question to which there does not appear to be a clear answer at the present time. What is the administrative structure and process for implementing, advancing, and improving civil rights law and policy in the United States? The United States Civil Rights Commission was created by the Civil Rights Act of 1957. However, as an independent commission, its work is principally to study and report on "alleged deprivations of voting rights and alleged discrimination based on race, color, religion, sex, age, disability, or national origin, or in the administration of justice."[61] It is supposed to provide information and analysis, but it is not a body that administers civil rights law and policy.

The other organization that was created by the 1957 legislation, and the one to which most observers point as the lead agency of the federal government on civil rights, is the Civil Rights Division of the Department of Justice. There is no question that the Civil Rights Division is an important unit of the Department of Justice and brings experience and expertise to the cases it enters. However, its capacity is far more limited than is generally understood, as indicated by a recent statement: "To continue its service to this country in FY 2016, the Civil Rights Division requests a total of $175,015,000, 893 positions, 697 direct FTE, and 478 attorneys to protect, defend, and advance civil rights in our nation."[62] From that, it must staff 10 sections, including the Appellate, Disability Rights, Educational Opportunities, Employment Litigation, Federal Coordination and Compliance, Housing and Civil Enforcement, Office of Special Counsel for Immigration-Related Unfair Employment Practices, Policy, Special Litigation, and Voting units. One of those, the Federal Coordination and Compliance section, is supposed to "ensur[e] that all federal agencies consistently and effectively enforce civil rights statutes and Executive Orders that prohibit discrimination in federally conducted and assisted programs and activities."[63] Its scope of responsibility is extremely broad, including coordination with some thirty different federal agencies on Title VI and a variety of other programs. There is simply no way that an organization the size of the Civil Rights Division, and with the scope of responsibilities it carries, can take more than a limited, if extremely important, role in the administration of civil rights law and policy. It must pick and choose its cases and its other work with care from among a broad and complex array of needs. It is supposed to have a coordinating role as noted above, but it must deal with other agencies, each of which has its own budget and its own statutory authority.

The other federal agency that many professionals think of when the idea of national civil rights administration comes to mind is the Equal Employment Opportunity Commission (EEOC). Here again, it is a small agency, by any measure, and particularly when judged against the scope of work it faces on a national scale. It has only 2,200 staff and has faced many years of budget cuts. As the Chair of the Commission explained even as late as the 2014 Performance Report, the commission had taken serious budget cuts and hiring freezes in the previous two years that had affected the agency's capacity.

> Following two years of significant budget reductions and hiring freezes, these chal-
> lenges have endangered the hard won, but fragile, progress reported in recent PARs
> and threatened the agency's ability to meet the demand for the EEOC's services. As an
> example, the significant reductions in our private sector inventory gained in FY 2011
> and FY 2012 could not be sustained due to the decline in staffing and resources.[64]

The limitations on its resources has meant, for example, that "The agency filed 133 merits lawsuits during FY 2014 through its field legal units. These included 105 individual suits, 11 non-systemic class suits, and 17 systemic suits."[65] In a nation of 322,000,000 people and more than 20 million firms, it is clear that there are severe limits to what the EEOC can do.[66]

The situation state-by-state varies dramatically and in some cases, as the earlier chapters explained, changes with political transitions—not always in a positive direction. Unfortunately, there have also been times when the national agencies have been affected by political winds that have not supported active civil rights implementation. Thus, civil rights groups mark the period during the 1980s when William Bradford Reynolds was Assistant Attorney General for Civil Rights as a low point in the modern history of the agency, while the work of Assistant Attorney General Thomas Perez from 2009 until his nomination as Secretary of Labor in 2013 was an extremely active period in which the division was a visible national leader in the field.[67] However, those characteristics made Perez a target of political criticism when he faced confirmation for a cabinet position.

Each of the cabinet departments has an office of civil rights and each is supposed to take responsibility for civil rights policy and law for its department. Here again, though, these are units that have generally limited capacity relative to the scope of the task they face. And they are, after all, designed to work within the policy domain occupied by their department, as compared to a broad national perspective across policy domains.

None of these statements is meant to underestimate the outstanding work that has been and is being done by organizations like the Civil Rights Division. The EEOC is certainly an important agency, but, however significant its work, its capacity is plainly limited. There are some civil rights units within certain cabinet departments that have been particularly active in their policy domain, but the limits are clear.

It would seem, then, that it is important to ask how to develop the capacity needed to ensure that civil rights law and policy do not, in the end, fall to individuals to enforce through lawsuits that too many people cannot afford and would not know how to undertake in any case. Even though there is a Civil Rights Attorneys Fees Act for those who prevail in those suits, they take years and cost a great deal before the point at which the resources can be obtained. Thus the question remains: what is the structure and process for the administration of civil rights, and how will it be provided with sufficient capacity at a time when the needs are greater than ever before because the task is so much larger and more complex than before? There does not appear at this time to be a serious effort to answer that question.

Focus: How Do We Understand the Challenge?

Given that scope and complexity, it is an ongoing challenge to find a focus from which to assess what is happening, what is not, and act to address both. That challenge appears, given history and contemporary discussions and advocacy, to have two principal components. They include the need for attention to the whole fabric of civil rights law and policy, and the importance of continuing discussion on the level and perspective from which to approach the work.

This text has provided a broad perspective on civil rights challenges in public service, but that is a perspective that is relatively unusual. Most often, civil rights today is approached either in terms of a particular problem that arises at a moment in time, such as police use of deadly force, or with respect to a particular policy issue, as in the example of the Lily Ledbetter law responding to narrow interpretation of Title VII or treatment of same-sex couples. These are, of course, natural reactions to problems in policy and society at any point.

The difficulty is that as this kind of focus dominates debate, policymaking, and administration in civil rights over time, it tends to keep attention on the particular and to ignore the broad fabric of civil rights law and policy, and the way it is or is not being administered. It also tends to keep the focus on the present rather than encouraging a clear perspective on how what seems most urgent at any particular moment in time fits into a larger understanding. As the preceding chapters have made clear, although particular issues have dominated attention at different points in time, they are part of a much larger progression, including periods of backsliding, in civil rights.

A lack of attention to the full fabric, which includes all of the law and policy understood in context, including its development, current challenges, and likely future movement, is problematic. Piecemeal developments that are done without a focus on the overall context are likely to have limited impacts and, at best, often only affect small pieces of the broader reality of what is needed to strengthen and even to maintain the fabric of civil rights. It also leads to the question of just who is paying attention to the overall context and how they can be effective in that broad work. As hard as they may work, the staff of the coordination section of the Civil Rights Division cannot do more than a part of that work. Although the Civil Rights Commission has played important roles in encouraging debate and action in some aspects of the field, such as its work on policing in the nation's cities in the 1960s and 1970s and its work on environmental justice, it has not been able to provide more than a limited role in maintaining that broad perspective and ensuring action where and when needed from a policymaking, law, and administration perspective.

Perhaps most problematic of all is the fact that there has been relatively little national discussion that the broad focus on the fabric is needed and who will provide the leadership in doing it, as well as how that work should be accomplished in terms of providing not only assessments but also follow-on work to repair or strengthen the fabric where policy change is needed, and to support and encourage effective administration on an ongoing basis.

The other major aspect of the focus problem is the levels problem. Perhaps because of the widespread use of the civil rights policy model, there is a tendency to focus discussion on individuals with a particular case or issue. Alternatively, there is often emphasis on a particular group, which may arise because of a civil rights challenge that is currently in the news or that arose because of an especially egregious situation. Also, as the text shows, different groups within society experience different civil rights challenges and they each have had to advocate for the changes that they need in policy or for enforcement of what already exists in an effort to address those problems. Again, this is an understandable perspective, in significant part because different groups of people have had to work so diligently and sacrifice so much over such a long period of time to obtain what they justifiably argue they should have had all along.

The challenge is to think about how, by recognizing the importance of each person and each group and how they see the situation from where they sit, we can find ways to bring the conversation together into a whole that will address the entire fabric as well as the contemporary challenges to it. There have been some efforts to deal with aspects of this very larger concern, like the work of the Leadership Conference for Civil Rights. However, it is not so clear where this is happening in government. Occasionally, the White House will convene a conference on civil rights issues, but that really is not an ongoing mechanism to deal with the levels problem and how to think about it and work within it. Neither is it clear how state or local governments are addressing these issues. As the preceding chapters show, there has historically been a wide range of concern for and protection of civil rights across the different states and even among cities. This is true in states and communities that have traditionally had a limited range of diversity among their residents, and also in those situations in which there have been many residents of color. Of course, issues of gender flow across all of these, and yet here too there is considerable variation.

To recap, the problem of focus presents the challenge of maintaining a broader and integrative sense of the state of civil rights, while the problem of perspective reminds us to consider just whose perspective is central to the discussion at any given time.

Varied Approaches to Administration of Civil Rights in Public Service

There is one more aspect to the administrative challenges of civil rights in public service, which is the need to understand the general approach that an agency, group, or individual is taking at any given time. These vary from policymaking to enforcement to managerial efforts to education.

When Charles Hamilton Houston, and later Thurgood Marshall, led NAACP and NAACP LDF efforts, they were using litigation to achieve their goals, but those goals were to change policy and law. That is a quite different enterprise than the work of ensuring enforcement of established civil rights policy on a day-to-day basis. The use of the courts was necessary, not only because they were seeking to overturn prior precedents that supported segregation and discrimination, but also because African-Americans and other minorities had little realistic access to change through the majoritarian political process. Americans of color demanding change were met with voting discrimination, and also faced political parties and legislatures that were primarily dominated by white males. In some places there were legislatures that were bound and determined to maintain the status quo. That is one reason why Marshall was so convinced—and Lyndon Johnson made the same assertion—that things would change once all Americans could vote freely in fair elections.

There are times, such as when the effort is to establish that there is a constitutional protection for a group, that litigation is a necessary approach. However, all other things being equal and because of the nature of the differences between legal opinions and legislation, it is more useful to have a legislature enact a statute to establish policy. But, as Thurgood Marshall has pointed out on more than one occasion, all other things are not equal where legislatures have historically been unwilling to adopt important civil rights policies without pressure from the courts.[68]

For reasons explained earlier, the policies that emerged frequently employed the civil rights policy model that relied heavily on individual lawsuits to implement and enforce those policies. Additionally, because of the dramatic resistance to civil rights policy, whether it came from courts or as legislation, an enforcement approach has been used for much of the civil rights work required over time. Given history and contemporary problems, there is little reason to think that any civil rights policy will be effective without the existence of meaningful and believable enforcement capabilities. On the other hand, litigation is an adversarial process, and when there is a likelihood—or for some people even a chance—of litigation, behavior can become very defensive, communications may be dramatically reduced, and, as a result, problem solving can suffer. If the only—or even the first—option for civil rights administration is enforcement, the many possible difficulties are obvious. Most people experienced in civil rights law and policy would likely agree that enforcement is a necessary but not sufficient approach for implementing and administering civil rights law and policy.

These realities and the lack of capacity in the civil rights agencies have encouraged the use of an educational approach as compared to over-reliance on enforcement. The reality is that litigation alone cannot ensure that individuals and organizations will honor the civil rights of others, although it certainly can deter some people and provide some recompense for individuals who have suffered particularly grievous violations. As the information about the capacity of the EEOC and the Civil Rights Division plainly showed, there is only a limited capacity in the federal government to litigate compared to the size of the population and scope of challenges. Besides, if education can lead people and organizations to change their behavior and their policies so that litigation becomes unnecessary, there are a great many benefits to be had.

However, education is a broad term and in practice education for civil rights falls along a wide continuum, at one end of which is the narrow sort of training provided to help organizations comply with the law and at the other is an educational process designed to make fundamental changes, not only in the way individuals behave and organizations operate, but also in the communities in which those people and organizations function. Even the narrowest conception offers benefits, since if people come into compliance with the law, they are presumably treating those around them more equally than might otherwise be the case. On the other hand, training for compliance goes to a kind of lowest common denominator and may produce little real change. Education at the other end of the spectrum takes time, resources, and a commitment to that level of engagement that seeks to achieve fundamental change. It is not clear that many organizations are ready to make that level of commitment, and there is also little evidence that government agencies can support something on that scale.

In the middle is what is often termed diversity training. It is a compromise and one that is increasingly common in both public and private organizations, usually provided by outside consultants. Its aims are broader and more substantive than mere compliance training. Unfortunately, perhaps because of the way it has been done or because of the attitudes of those in the organizations, there are tendencies to stereotype these kinds of efforts and to approach them with a kind of grudging engagement. It can also happen that those who do the training find themselves being stereotyped and treated as someone to be endured. As one experienced national consultant who happened to be African American indicated at a recent International City/County Management Association conference, she often gets someone who raises their hand at such sessions and says "Hey diversity lady, ..." That attitude has been a problem for decades.

What is clear is that one-time sessions or educational programs that are not clearly supported by all levels of management, demonstrated in part by their participation in those sessions, are unlikely to engender fundamental change. In fact, signals from above that all of this is required but not important send a very loud and seriously problematic message, whatever the official line may be. It is important, even where there is a real commitment, to recognize that there will be difficulties from time to time and a serious program requires the capacity to address these difficulties, learn from them, and move on in a positive way.

There are two continuing challenges in all of this. The first is that there can often be a great deal of fear and anger among people who must work or interact with each other. This text has shown just how and why people often come to work or to a public agency's service desk carrying a lifetime of bad experiences and a legacy of a society with a long history of discrimination. By the same token, others have come to be afraid of engaging issues of civil rights for fear that they will embarrass themselves, antagonize someone else, or even trigger a lawsuit. Related to this problem is the fact that it is often those most in need of a constructive dialogue on civil rights who are least willing to engage in it and most likely to do or say exactly what they are required to say to satisfy the boss—and nothing more.

The other challenge, and one that is perhaps somewhat more tractable, is the effort to move from addressing civil rights primarily by reacting to specific problems as compared to doing so by a search for opportunities to build positive foundations for the future. This is perhaps among the most important and yet most difficult challenges for public service professionals in the foreseeable future, but one worthy of the effort.

Conclusion: Civil Rights Leadership in Public Service

This last challenge suggests that there is a need for public service professionals to commit to leadership in civil rights law, policy, and administration. The preceding chapters have indicated some of the many remaining challenges across a range of domains. They also provide an understanding that any thought that civil rights is settled and was a problem for previous generations is simply wrong. They show that civil rights in public service is very much a work in progress, with some areas of relatively positive development and others far from it.

Public service professionals engage civil rights regularly, whether they do it intentionally and with a commitment toward progress or not. The organizations in which they work and the communities they serve are more diverse than ever. Those who have suffered from the history of denial of civil rights in the past are no longer prepared to accept that fate. They demand what everyone has a right to expect—dignity and equality. In such a context, the responsible public service professional is obligated to assume a responsibility toward coworkers and the community he or she serves, and to participate in an effort to lead toward a future in which civil rights are the reality and not merely a promise.

Notes

1 CNN, Transcript: "'This Is Your Victory,' Says Obama," November 4, 2008, http://edition.cnn.com/2008/POLITICS/11/04/obama.transcript/, September 7, 2015.
2 Adam Nagourney, "Obama: Racial Barrier Falls in Decisive Victory," *New York Times*, November 5, 2008, p. 1.
3 Kevin Merida, "America's History Gives Way to Its Future," *Washington Post*, November 5, 2008, p. A1.
4 Byron Tau, "Obama: 'I'm Not the President of Black America'," *Politico.com*, www.politico.com/blogs/politico44/2012/08/obama-im-not-the-president-of-black-america-131351, September 8, 2015.
5 Vanita Gupta, Acting Assistant Attorney General Civil Rights Division, United States Department of Justice, to City Manager John Shaw, City of Ferguson and Chief Thomas Jackson, Investigation of the Ferguson Police Department, March 3, 2015, www.justice.gov/sites/default/files/crt/legacy/2015/03/04/ferguson_cover_3-4-15.pdf, September 8, 2015, p. 1.
6 In the Supreme Court of Missouri (en banc), March 9, 2015, www.courts.mo.gov/pressrel.nsf/fa1bcbaea6d7c117862567670079a321/7f70e2b78919dca486257e030077b4ec/$FILE/transfer%20order%2003-09-15.pdf, September 8, 2015.
7 Administrative Order of the Chief Justice of Alabama, February 8, 2015, http://media.al.com/news_impact/other/CJ%20Moore%20Order%20to%20Ala.%20Probate%20Judges.pdf, September 8, 2015.
8 *Ex parte State of Alabama ex rel. Alabama Policy Institute*, 1140460, 2015 Ala. LEXIS 33 (AL 2015).
9 *Miller v. Davis*, 2015 U.S. Dist. LEXIS 105822 (EDKY 2015).

10 *Bumgardner v. Bumgardner*, Case No. 14-0626, Hamilton County Chancery Court, August 31, 2015, http://chattanoogan.com/Breaking-news/BUMGARDNERorder.pdf, September 8, 2015.

11 *San Antonio Independent School District v. Rodriguez*, 411 U.S. 1, 17 (1973).

12 Id., at 685.

13 Act of Apr. 3, 1920, ch. 210, §17, 1920 Miss. Laws 288, 294.

14 See, e.g., Act of Mar. 19, 1928, ch. 156, 1928 Ky. Acts 534, *remains in effect*, Ky. Rev. Stat. §402.990(2) (1984); Act of May 25, 1905, No. 136, §1, 1905 Mich. Pub. Acts 185, 186, *remains in effect*, Mich. Comp. Laws §551.6 (1979); Act of Apr. 3, 1920, ch. 210, §29, 1920 Miss. Gen. Laws 288, 300, *remains in effect* with minor changes, Miss. Code Ann. §41-21-45 (1972).

15 *City of Cleburne, Texas v. Cleburne Living Center*, 473 U.S. 432, 461-464 (1985) at 461–464.

16 Id., at 466–467.

17 Id., at 461.

18 *San Antonio Independent School District v. Rodriguez*, 411 U.S. 1, 35 (1973).

19 Id., at 116, Marshall, J., dissenting.

20 *Cabell v. Chavez-Salido*, 454 U.S. 432 (1982) (see excerpt Chapter 9).

21 *Sugarman v. Dougall*, 413 U.S. 634, 647 (1973).

22 *Cabell v. Chavez-Salido*, 454 U.S. 432, 448-449 (1982), Blackmun, J., dissenting.

23 *Craig v. Boren*, 429 U.S. 190, 197 (1976).

24 Her language in Hogan was "Our decisions also establish that the party seeking to uphold a statute that classifies individuals on the basis of their gender must carry the burden of showing an 'exceedingly persuasive justification' for the classification.... The burden is met only by showing at least that the classification serves 'important governmental objectives and that the discriminatory means employed' are 'substantially related to the achievement of those objectives.'" *Wengler v. Druggists Mutual Ins. Co.*, 446 U.S. 142, 150 (1980).

25 See e.g., *Palmer v. Thompson*, 403 U.S. 217 (1971); *Wright v. Council of City of Emporia*, 407 U.S. 451 (1972).

26 See Justice Marshall's dissent in *Memphis v. Greene*, 451 U.S. 100 (1981), excerpted in Chapter 4.

27 Id., at 136.

28 *Personnel Administrator of Massachusetts v. Feeney*, 442 U.S. 256, 279 (1979).

29 See *United States v. Virginia*, 518 U.S. 515 (1996) (see Chapter 10).

30 *Obergefell v. Hodges*, 135 S. Ct. 2584 (2015) (see Chapter 11).

31 *United States v. Morrison*, 529 U.S. 598 (2000).

32 *Board of Trustees of the University of Alabama v. Garrett*, 531 U.S. 356 (2001) (see excerpt in Chapter 12).

33 109 U.S. 3 (1883) (see excerpt in Chapter 2).

34 *Heart of Atlanta Motel v. United States*, 379 U.S. 241, 246 (1964).

35 Id., at 286, Douglas, J., dissenting.

36 Id., at 279–280.

37 See *Bell v. Maryland*, 378 U.S. 226, 242 (1964), Douglas, J., concurring in part; *Lombard v. Louisiana*, 373 U.S. 267 (1963), Douglas, J., concurring.

38 *United States v. Morrison*, 529 U.S. 598 (2000).

39 *Massachusetts v. Murgia*, 427 U.S. 307 (1976).

40 See the Age Discrimination in Employment Act Amendments of 1986, P.L. 99–592, 100 Stat. 3342 (1986) and the "Older Workers Benefit Protection Act," P.L. 101–433, 104 Stat. 978 (1990).

41 P.L. 95–608, 92 Stat. 3069 (1978).

42 Civil Rights Act of 1991, P.L. 102–166, 105 Stat. 1071 (1991), Sec. 1–2.

43 ADA Amendments Act of 2008, P.L. 110–325,122 Stat. 3553 (2008), Sec. 2(b)(2–5).

44 Office of the Mayor of Chicago, Press Release, "Mayor Emanuel Introduces Welcoming City Ordinance, Ensure Trust And Good Relationships Between Chicago's Immigrant Communities, Regardless Of Immigration Status," July 10, 2012, www.cityofchicago.org/dam/city/depts/mayor/Press%20Room/Press%20Releases/2012/July/7.10.12Welcoming.pdf, October 3, 2015. See also Detroit's initiative entitled "Global Detroit: Mobilizing Detroit's Immigrant Potential," www.globaldetroit.com/, October 3, 2015; Office of the Mayor of Baltimore, "Mayor Rawlings-Blake Signs Executive Order to Protect New Americans from Discrimination," Press Release, March 2,

2012, http://archive.baltimorecity.gov/OfficeoftheMayor/NewsMedia/tabid/66/ID/2561/Mayor_ Rawlings-Blake_Signs_Executive_Order_to_Protect_New_Americans_from_Discrimination. aspx, October 3, 2015; City of Dayton, Ohio, "Welcome Dayton—Immigrant Friendly City," www.welcomedayton.org/, October 3, 2015.

45 James Madison to Thomas Jefferson, October 17, 1788, in Ralph Ketcham, *Selected Writings of James Madison* (Indianapolis, IN: Hackett Publishing Co., 2006), p. 160.

46 See Alexander Hamilton, James Madison, and John Jay, *The Federalist Papers* (New York: Mentor Books, 1961), p. 322.

47 *Heckler v. Chaney*, 470 U.S. 821 (1985).

48 See e.g., *Cort v. Ash*, 422 U.S. 66 (1975).

49 *Middlesex County Sewerage Authority v. National Sea Clammers Association*, 453 U.S. 1 (1981).

50 *Alexander v. Sandoval*, 532 U.S. 235 (2001).

51 Id., at 534.

52 See e.g., *Gonzaga University v. Doe*, 536 U.S. 273 (2002).

53 U.S. Department of Justice, Office for Civil Rights, Office of Justice Programs, Title VI of the Civil Rights Act of 1964, http://ojp.gov/about/ocr/pdfs/OCR_TitleVI.pdf, October 8, 2015. See also U.S. Department of Justice, "Protecting Against Race, Color, and National Origin Discrimination by Recipients of Federal Funds," www.lep.gov/4_YEAR_OUTRACH_.pdf, October 8, 2015.

54 *National Federal of Independent Business v. Sebelius*, 132 S. Ct. 2566 (2012).

55 *Meritor Savings Bank v. Vinson*, 477 U.S. 57 (1986) (see the excerpt in Chapter 10).

56 U.S. Department of Justice, "Enforcement of Title VI of the Civil Rights Act of 1964—National Origin Discrimination Against Persons with Limited English Proficiency," 65 Fed. Reg. 50123 (2000).

57 Executive Order 13166, "Improving Access to Services for Persons With Limited English Proficiency," 65 Fed. Reg. 50121 (2000).

58 67 Fed. Reg. 41455 (2002).

59 *Shelby County v. Holder*, 133 S. Ct. 2612 (2013).

60 See Thomas E. Mann and Norman Ornstein, *The Broken Branch: How Congress Is Failing America and How to Get it Back on Track* (New York: Oxford University Press, 2006), and Mann and Ornstein, *It's Even Worse than it Looks: How the American Constitutional System Collided with the New Politics of Extremism* (New York: Basic Books, 2012).

61 U.S. Commission on Civil Rights, "Mission," www.usccr.gov/about/index.php, October 13, 2015.

62 U.S. Department of Justice, Civil Rights Division, "FY2016 Performance Budget, Congressional Submission, www.justice.gov/sites/default/files/jmd/pages/attachments/2015/02/01/14._civil_rights_ division_crt.pdf, October 10, 2015, p. 2.

63 U.S. Department of Justice, Civil Rights Division, Federal Coordination and Compliance Section, www.justice.gov/crt/fcs, April 26, 2016.

64 EEOC FY 2014 Performance and Accountability Report, Message from the Chair, p. vi.

65 Id., at p. 3.

66 On the number and nature of firms, see U.S. Census Bureau, "Number of Firms, Number of Establishments, Employment, Annual Payroll, and Estimated Receipts by Enterprise Employment Size for the United States and States, Totals: 2012," www2.census.gov/econ/susb/data/2012/us_ state_totals_2012.xls, October 13, 2015.

67 On the Reynolds era, see "Why Reynolds Lost," Civil Rights Monitor, Leadership Conference for Civil Rights, Vol. 1, No. 1, August 1985, www.civilrights.org/monitor/august1985/art2p1.html, October 13, 2015.

68 A unanimous Supreme Court made exactly that point, addressing continued and massive resistance to compliance with school desegregation cases, and saying that: "All things being equal, with no history of discrimination, it might well be desirable to assign pupils to schools nearest their homes. But all things are not equal in a system that has been deliberately constructed and maintained to enforce racial segregation." *Swann v. Charlotte-Mechlenburg Bd. of Ed.*, 402 U.S. 1, 28 (1971).

References

Hamilton, Alexander, James Madison, and John Jay. *The Federalist Papers.* New York: Mentor, 1961.

Ketcham, Ralph. *Selected Writings of James Madison.* Indianapolis, IN: Hackett Publishing Co., 2006.

Mann, Thomas E. and Norman Ornstein. *The Broken Branch: How Congress Is Failing America and How to Get it Back on Track.* New York: Oxford University Press, 2006.

———. *It's Even Worse than it Looks: How the American Constitutional System Collided with the New Politics of Extremism.* New York: Basic Books, 2012.

U.S. Department of Justice. "Enforcement of Title VI of the Civil Rights Act of 1964—National Origin Discrimination Against Persons with Limited English Proficiency," 65 Fed. Reg. 50123 (August 16, 2000).

———. "Protecting Against Race, Color, and National Origin Discrimination by Recipients of Federal Funds," www.lep.gov/4_YEAR_OUTRACH_.pdf, October 8, 2015.

Glossary

Amicus Curiae—The term means friend of the court. It refers to individuals or groups who are not parties in a legal case who present arguments to the court, most often in the form of written legal briefs, that seek to provide additional information to the court in an effort to influence the decision in the case.

Arguendo—A term that means "for the sake of argument", often used in judicial opinions.

Brief—The term is used in two senses: (1) The formal written arguments submitted to the court by the parties in the case setting forth the issues, the argument, the legal authorities that support it, and the relief requested from the court; (2) A note-taking process used by students of the law for systematically summarizing a judicial opinion.

Cases of first impression—A legal case or issue for which there is no clear precedent and that must be addressed for the first time by the court.

Certiorari—An order issued to a lower court to send the record in a case up to be reviewed by a higher court such as the U.S. Supreme Court.

Class action suit—A legal action brought by a small number of named people representing a large group of people experiencing the same legal problem because of the actions of officials or organizations (either public or private).

Concurring opinion—An opinion announced by a member of a multi-judge court that agrees with the ruling in a case but disagrees with the reasoning used by the majority to reach and explain that conclusion.

Coram nobis—A writ issued by a court to correct a manifest injustice (see the discussion of the *Korematsu* and *Hirabayashi* cases in Chapter 3).

Coverture—A legal doctrine according to which the legal identity of a married woman was not independent but rested with the husband in the marriage.

Dicta (or *Obiter Dictum*)—Language in a legal opinion that is not essential to the holding or reasoning of the court.

Disposition—A statement by a court of what is to happen to a case going forward. Will the lower court's decision be affirmed (upheld), reversed (overturned), remanded (sent back to the lower court for further action), or vacated (where the entire record in a case is thrown out and the lower court is told to start over)?

Dissenting opinion—An opinion announced by a member of a multi-judge court that disagrees with the ruling by the majority of that court.

Ex parte communication—A term meaning a one-sided intervention in a proceeding without representation, argument, or often even knowledge of the communication by the other party.

Executive order—A legally binding directive issued by the president (or in the states by the governor) to officials within the executive branch to take or refrain from taking a certain action.

Facial challenge—A legal challenge to a statute, administrative rule, ordinance, or some other policy, based on the policy as written, as compared to a challenge to a policy based upon the way it is applied in practice.

Federal district court—The trial court in the federal judicial system. There is at least one federal district court in every state.

Fee simple absolute—Ownership of land that is complete and unconditional.

Fiduciary relationship—A fiduciary obligation is a relationship of special trust that imposes extraordinary responsibilities on the one who is the fiduciary.

Genocide—"genocide means any of the following acts committed with intent to destroy, in whole or in part, a national, ethnical, racial or religious group, as such:

(a) Killing members of the group;
(b) Causing serious bodily or mental harm to members of the group;
(c) Deliberately inflicting on the group conditions of life calculated to bring about its physical destruction in whole or in part;
(d) Imposing measures intended to prevent births within the group;
(e) Forcibly transferring children of the group to another group."

Convention on the Prevention of the Crime of Genocide, Adopted by the General Assembly of the United Nations, 9 December 1948, 78 UNTS 278, 280 (1951).

habeas corpus—A legal doctrine that requires officials to produce a person in court and demonstrate a legitimate legal reason for holding that person in custody.

Hate crimes—Defined by Congress as "a crime in which the defendant intentionally selects a victim, or in the case of a property crime, the property that is the object of the crime, because of the actual or perceived race, color, religion, national origin, ethnicity, gender, gender identity, disability, or sexual orientation of any person." Section 280003(a) of the Violent Crime Control and Law Enforcement Act of 1994 (Public Law 103–322; 108 Stat. 2096) amended by Section 4703 of the "Matthew Shepard and James Byrd, Jr. Hate Crimes Prevention Act" P.L. 111–84, 123 Stat. 2835 (2009).

Holding—An announcement by the Court of the principle on which a legal question was decided.

Implied private rights of action—The ability of a private party injured by conduct that he or she claims violated federal law to bring suit where the government will not or cannot do so, whether the federal legislation specifically said that there was such a right or not.

Injunction—A court order prohibiting illegal action or mandating action to enforce legal rights.

in loco parentis—A term that literally means in the place of the parents, referring to actions taken by government when it steps in to protect a child and act in the child's best interest where the parents cannot or will not do so, or where there are no parents present.

inter alia—A term that means "among other things," which is often used in judicial opinions.

Intermediate (or heightened) scrutiny—A standard by which judges assess claims of discrimination that is in between the rational basis test and strict judicial scrutiny, which requires that the government's action serves important governmental objectives and the means chosen are substantially related to the achievement of those interests.

Intestate—This term refers to one who dies without making a will.

Issue—A legal issue is the question of law presented to a court for decision.

Jim Crow segregation—A series of laws enacted in the South during the reconstruction era to ensure segregation and inequality among African Americans after they had been freed from slavery.

Jurisdiction—The area, people, or organizations over whom a court or other governmental body can assert its authority.

Legal standards—Tests applied by a court to determine whether a provision of law has been violated.

Manifest destiny—A concept that asserts a U.S. right to dominion over the entire continent and, when understood alongside the Monroe Doctrine, has been extended to encompass the hemisphere.

per curiam—A term that literally means "for the court" and which is used to indicate an opinion issued in the name of the court, as opposed to one that is signed by a specific justice as author. These are open brief opinions.

Peremptory challenge—A process by which attorneys can reject possible jurors without presenting a specific reason.

Petit jury—A term that refers to a trial court jury (as compared to a grand jury, which performs investigations or considers whether to formally accuse someone of a crime with an indictment).

Plurality opinion—An opinion from a multi-judge court agreed to by the largest number of justices, but not an actual majority of that Court (for example, by four members of the U.S. Supreme Court, which has nine justices).

Rational basis test—The lowest standard by which judges assess claims of discrimination, in which the burden is on the challenger and the state need only show that its actions were rationally related to a legitimate state purpose.

Rationale—The legal reasoning by which a court explains how it reached its ruling on the meaning of the law and explaining that interpretation.

Remand—The action of an appellate court that sends a case back down to a lower court or administrative agency for further consideration in light of the appeals court opinion.

Restrictive covenant—An agreement attached to the deed to property in which the owner agrees not to sell the property to persons from various racial or religious groups under threat of lawsuits from others in that neighborhood.

sine qua non—A Latin term meaning "without which nothing."

Standard—The legal criteria or test for deciding a case.

Strict judicial scrutiny—The highest standard by which judges assess claims of discrimination, in which the burden is on the state to show that its actions were required by a compelling state interest and that the means used to attain those ends were narrowly tailored.

sub silentio—A term that means literally "under silence," which is used in judicial opinions to refer to something that is implied or assumed but not stated.

Substantive due process—The idea that the word liberty in the due process clauses of the Fourteenth and Fifth Amendments has substantive meaning and the clauses are not just statements of the procedures that must be used in a legal matter.

sui juris—A person with will full legal rights and obligations.

U.S. Court of Appeals—The United States Circuit Court of Appeals is the level of federal courts below the U.S. Supreme Court and is divided geographically across the nation into circuits.

Vacate—A decision by an appellate court to nullify a lower court ruling and eliminate the record or decision, so that the lower court will start the case over again. This comes when there is a fundamental problem in a case that simply cannot be correct, so that all previous records are invalid.

Venire—A group of possible jurors from whom the actual jury is chosen.

Voir dire—The process by which attorneys question potential jurors to determine whether to object to their participation on the jury.

Opinions Cited

Index